DATE DUE

DEMCO 38-296

INTERNATIONAL ENCYCLOPEDIA OF PUBLIC POLICY AND ADMINISTRATION

INTERNATIONAL ENCYCLOPEDIA OF PUBLIC POLICY AND ADMINISTRATION

Jay M. Shafritz

EDITOR IN CHIEF

Volume 3: L-Q

Westview Press

A Member of the Perseus Books Group

Copyright © 1998 by Westview Press, A Member of the Perseus Books Group

Published in 1998 in the United States of America by Westview Press, 5500 Central Avenue, Boulder, Colorado 80301-2877, and in the United Kingdom by Westview Press, 12 Hid's Copse Road, Cumnor Hill, Oxford OX2 9JJ

Library of Congress Cataloging-in-Publication Data

The international encyclopedia of public policy and administration /
  Jay M. Shafritz, editor in chief.
      p.   cm.
    Includes bibliographical references (p.   ) and index.
    Contents: v. 1. A-C – v. 2. D-K – v. 3. L-Q – v. 4. R-Z, index.
    ISBN 0-8133-9973-4 (vol. 1 : hardcover : alk. paper). – ISBN
  0-8133-9974-2 (vol. 2 : hardcover : alk. paper). – ISBN
  0-8133-9975-0 (vol. 3 : hardcover : alk. paper). – ISBN
  0-8133-9976-9 (vol. 4 : hardcover : alk. paper)
    1. Public policy–Encyclopedias.   2. Public administration–
  Encyclopedias.   I. Shafritz, Jay M.
  H97.I574   1998
  351'.03–dc21   97-34169
                                                        CIP

The paper used in this publication meets the requirements of the American National Standard for Permanence of Paper for Printed Library Materials Z39.48-1984.

10   9   8   7   6   5   4   3

L

LABOR LAW. The law as set forth in statute, constitutional provision, court decisions, and practice that deals with the protection or improvement of conditions of workers and with the rights of unions, employees, employers, and the public. In the United States, labor law is found in federal and state legislation and local ordinances, as well as in federal and state court decisions and attorney general opinions. It is highly variable by jurisdiction and level of government.

Private-sector labor law is coherent and concise as it applies to unionization and collective bargaining. The National Labor Relations Act (NLRA) of 1935, also known as the Wagner Act, is the primary piece of legislation, as amended by the Labor Management Relations Act of 1947 (the Taft-Hartley Act) and the Labor Management Reporting and Disclosure Act of 1959 (the Landrum-Griffin Act).

These statues apply to all workers in the private and nonprofit sectors throughout the country. Under this legal framework, labor policy is administered by the National Labor Relations Board, which investigates and adjudicates allegations of unfair labor practices and administers questions concerning the composition of the employee bargaining unit and selection of the union representative. National policy, at least in a formal sense, is to encourage private sector workers to form unions and engage in collective bargaining with their employers. Taft-Hartley imposes certain restrictions on union procedures and conduct (e.g., it prohibits compulsory union membership). Landrum-Griffin requires unions to meet various internal operating standards, such as guaranteeing their members' right to free association and speech, maintaining certain financial records, and accounting for expenditures.

Public sector labor law in the United States is much more variable in its provisions, and it is found in a plethora of state and local statutory and other actions. It typically addresses the following issues:

1. Establishment of the collective bargaining relationship. This includes qualifications for and certification of the bargaining unit, determining the appropriate bargaining unit, unit status of employees (e.g., supervisors), selecting collective bargaining representatives through elections or other means, and judicial review of representational proceedings.
2. Obligation and duty to bargain. This includes the scope of bargaining, elements of good-faith bargaining, and the public's role and right to know.
3. Union security, including constitutional, statutory, and policy considerations that support establishment of various union security provisions including union shop, agency shop, maintenance of membership, fair share, and dues checkoff.
4. The right to strike, picket, and protest.
5. Impasse resolution, including mediation, factfinding, and arbitration. Strikes are usually, but not always, prohibited in government employment (see **strike**).
6. Enforcement of the collective bargaining relationship. This entails the legal status of the contract, grievance procedures, individual rights under the collective bargaining agreement, union and employer rights, and unfair labor practices. Unfair labor practices apply to either or to both employee organization and employer and consist of prohibited practices such as interfering with employees attempting to form a union or refusing to meet and bargain in good faith.
7. Political and civil rights of public employees, including due process, regulations of partisan political activities, and employment discrimination issues.
8. Establishment of the administrative agency to administer the labor law and collective negotiations. Whether they are called Public Employee Relations Boards or some other label, they are all dedicated to managing labor relations in state and local government employment.

During the early labor history of the United States, public employees were denied the right to form and join unions and the right to bargain collectively. The sovereignty doctrine, which declared that the sovereign, or state, should not abrogate its authority to set the terms and conditions of employment for government workers, acted as a bar to unionization and collective bargaining in most public jurisdictions. The arguments that public services are "essential" and monopolistic also suppressed unionization. Public employees were not covered by the Wagner Act (NLRA) of 1935 or the Taft-Hartley Act its (amendments), although a provision of the Taft-Hartley Act prohibits federal employee strike activity, and a 1955 law (Public Law 330) makes federal employee strike activity a felony.

For many years, the federal courts resisted recognizing the right of public employees to join unions and to bargain collectively. In the case of *McAuliffe v. City of New Bedford* (1892), for example, Justice Holmes asserted that although a former police officer "may have a constitutional right to talk politics, . . . he has no constitutional right to be a policeman." In 1967, however, the federal courts began to favor the right to form and join unions in the cases of *Keyshian v. Board of Regents* and *McLaughlin v. Tilendis*, followed two years later by *Atkins v. City of Charlotte* and *Letter Carriers v. Blount.* Thus, today the constitutional right of public employees to organize and join unions is protected by the courts under the First and Fourteenth Amendments. However, in the absence of legislation mandating collective bargaining, the courts have not granted public employees and their unions the right to force their employers to recognize and bargain collectively with them.

Federal labor policy for public employees is usually traced back to the Pendleton Act of 1883, which granted Congress the sole authority to establish and regulate wages, hours, and terms and conditions of employment. In executive orders in 1902 and 1906, President Theodore Roosevelt banned federal employee lobbying for improved wages, working conditions, or other benefits, either individually or through employee associations. This presidential "gag order" was overturned by Congress in the 1912 Lloyd-LaFollette Act, which had the related effect of establishing the right of federal workers to join unions. Federal employee bargaining received encouragement from construction of the Alaskan railroad in the early 1900s, as previously organized construction workers negotiated contracts with the federal government. Finally, the Classification Act of 1949 provided for a system of setting the wages of wage board, or blue collar, employees of the national government.

The first comprehensive legislation for federal workers was the Postal Reorganization Act of 1970, which granted postal employees collective bargaining rights very similar to those of private sector employees. Most other federal workers today are covered by Title VII of the Civil Service Reform Act of 1978. The CSRA evolved from a series of executive orders issued by presidents Kennedy, Nixon, and Ford, the most important being President Kennedy's Executive Order 10988, which is considered the Magna Carta of public sector labor law. The Kennedy order established for the first time that federal employees have the right to form and join unions and bargain collectively (see **collective bargaining**). It proved to be an important stimulant for organization and bargaining at all levels of government, and it established certain principles that continue to be important to federal sector labor relations under Title VII of the CSRA.

Under the CSRA, federal employee labor rights were placed into statute for the first time. The Federal Labor Relations Authority (FLRA) was created to administer the labor relations program. The Office of Labor-Management Relations was established within the Office of Personnel Management to provide technical advice on labor policies, leadership, and contract administration to federal agencies. Title VII covers all federal workers except for supervisory personnel, members of the armed forces, foreign service employees, and workers in the Government Accounting Office, FBI, CIA, TVA, National Security Agency, and the Postal Service.

Under the labor law provisions of the CSRA, covered federal employees are guaranteed the rights to form or join unions or to "refrain from any such activity, freely and without fear of reprisal." They are further granted the right to engage in collective bargaining over the conditions of employment, defined as "personnel policies, practices, and matters . . . affecting working conditions." Excluded from the scope of bargaining are wages and benefits, prohibited political activities, and position classification, along with certain management rights. Negotiated grievance procedures are extended to federal employees, with binding arbitration as the final step to resolve grievance impasses. Federal workers are granted the right to engage in informational picketing, given limited protections during reductions-in-force, and permitted to exercise the dues check-off for union membership payments.

The FLRA is a three-member, bipartisan board that administers labor relations under the CSRA. It serves as the final authority in labor relations questions, including bargaining unit determination, supervising and conducting elections, resolving unfair labor practices, resolving exceptions to arbitrators' awards, and determining issues to be excluded from the scope of bargaining. The FLRA has been heavily criticized by all relevant parties for its inconsistencies and inadequacies.

In the mid-1990s, the federal labor relations regime under the CSRA was undergoing review and various recommendations for change were put forward. One suggestion was to expand the scope of bargaining to wages and benefits. Another was to mandate union security under the fair share arrangement so that unions could avoid the serious free rider problem, where members of the federal bargaining units enjoy the benefits of union representation without paying dues (see **union security provisions**).

The labor law for state and local government employees is highly fragmented. Each state and many local jurisdictions have in place their own statutes and ordinances. Although there has been congressional debate on a national law for regulating state and local labor relations, the chances for such a law appeared very limited in the mid-1990s. However, there are several federal laws that regulate certain aspects of state and local employee relations. These include the Civil Rights Act of 1964 (employment discrimination), the Fair Labor Standards Act of 1938 (minimum wages and hours), the Equal Pay Act of 1963 (pay discrimination by gender), the Occupational Safety and Health Act of 1970 (hazards in the workplace), the Vocational Rehabilitation Act of 1973, the Americans with Disabilities Act of 1991 (discrimination against the disabled), and the Civil Rights Act of 1990 (employment discrimination).

Today, more than 100 separate and diverse statutes regulate public employee labor relations. Labor policies range from a single, comprehensive state statute that provides collective bargaining rights and processes for virtually all state and local employees to total prohibition of collective bargaining. The earliest state labor laws were intended to abolish strikes and other work stoppages. Eight states enacted antistrike legislation following World War II. Wisconsin became the first state to establish statutory collective bargaining rights for local employees in 1959. Today,

bargaining laws covering at least one category of employees are in effect in 42 states, and all states except Arkansas, Arizona, and Mississippi regulate some aspect of employer-employee relations.

The great majority of state laws establish collective bargaining relationships. Some, however, set up a meet-and-confer approach, which differs from collective bargaining in that the employer in a meet-and-confer situation retains final decisionmaking authority on matters concerning wages, benefits, and conditions of work; there is no legal obligation to sign a contract with the union. In practice, meet-and-confer tends to evolve into de facto bargaining not unsimiliar to that permitted in the private sector under the National Labor Relations Act.

Most of the state bargaining laws were adopted over a ten-year period from the mid-1960s to the mid-1970s. They vary greatly in scope, administrative provisions, principles, and specific policies. Twenty-eight states and the District of Columbia provide for collective bargaining for all major employee functions, either through a comprehensive law or through a series of laws applying to specific functions such as police or education. Fourteen states provide for collective bargaining in one to four occupational categories. Nine states do not specifically permit bargaining for any category of public employees. There is a correlation between extent of bargaining coverage and geography, with the strongest bargaining laws in the northeast and midwest. The weakest laws are in sunbelt states. Public sector bargaining laws are also strongest in urbanized states with a history of private sector unionism.

Six southern states (Arkansas, Louisiana, Mississippi, North Carolina, South Carolina, and Virginia) and three western states (Arizona, Colorado, Utah) do not formally provide for bargaining by public employees. North Carolina and Virginia specifically prohibit collective bargaining, the former by statute and the latter by court decision. In the remaining states without specific bargaining legislation, various forms of bilateral relations prevail, from meet-and-confer arrangements to informal bargaining.

Policies permitting some form of bilateral relations for one or more groups of organized employees are in effect in 14 states, most commonly for police and firefighters (examples include Tennessee, Nevada, Georgia, and Idaho). In some cases states have achieved comprehensive bargaining laws through a piecemeal approach that incrementally incorporates various employee functions into a collective bargaining system. For these remaining 14 states, however, the negative political and economic climates for unions makes it unlikely that full coverage for all major state and local groups will be won. Several of these states, like all of those states with legal environments not conducive to collective bargaining noted above, are "right-to-work" states. This means that they have taken advantage of a provision of the Taft-Hartley Act to prohibit union security arrangements (see **union security**) such as the union shop, agency shop, and fair share. Right-to-work states are generally considered to be unfriendly to organized labor.

The comprehensive bargaining states generally consist of those states above the Mason-Dixon line as extended across the nation to the Pacific Coast. Only California, Florida, and Hawaii are exceptions to this geographical tendency. Florida is truly an anomaly as the only southern state with comprehensive collective bargaining. Florida's bargaining law was essentially initiated and implemented by the state supreme court in a 1968 case (*Dade County Classroom Teachers Association v. Ryan*) in a controversial interpretation of the state constitutional language concerning public employee rights. The remaining comprehensive bargaining states are mostly strong, two-party, competitive political systems with active and influential organized labor in private employment.

Labor law in the state and local sector has been stable during the 1990s, as most of the labor-management conflicts have either been statutorily resolved or have reached a condition of stalemate. If there is a trend, however, it is in favor of management and against the unions. State and local financial problems, worsened by taxpayer resistance to paying for public services, have resulted in downsizing of public workforces and an overall atmosphere that must be considered hostile to the interests of public employee unions. Union growth is very slow or nonexistent in many jurisdictions; in others, unions are actually losing membership from downsizing and reductions-in-force.

United States labor law evolved at a different time and in a very different direction from labor law in Europe. The first labor law of significance was the 1791 Le Chapelier Law in France, which prohibited coalitions of craft workers from seeking changes (improvements) in the conditions of work through withholding labor or offering labor at a predetermined rate. Violations could lead to imprisonment for six days to one month. This law became the foundation in France and other countries of Europe for more than a half century of police action against trade unions.

The British Combination Acts of 1799–1800 made illegal any "combination" to change labor laws but, unlike the Le Chapelier law, was not actively enforced. The Combination Acts were repealed near the end of the Napoleonic Wars, as labor peace began to prevail in Britain. During the 1860s, the British version of collective bargaining developed and was followed by various countries of Europe, including France, Germany, Spain, and Austria.

During the liberal period of the 1860s, a wave of labor legislation was enacted to protect children and women from the abuses of the Industrial Revolution. Such laws included bans on child labor, age limits for labor (ranging from 9 to 12 years), prohibitions on underground mine work for children and women, and a reduction in the length of the work week.

In one legal conflict of the times that strikes a familiar chord today, the protection of women produced a conflict between socialists and feminists. Feminists, particularly those of middle-class status, opposed legal protections as a violation of the principle of equality that would, in the long run, only worsen the position of women by reducing job opportunities and reinforcing the stereotype of woman as housewife. Feminists desired no less than full equality and opportunity under the law, including equal pay and admission into trades historically dominated by men. Women in the Socialist Movement argued to the contrary, pointing out that many working-class women labored under a double burden of a job in the workforce plus running the household and caring for children. They argued that certain legal protections could ease the burden of women and improve the conditions of the working class as a whole.

A second wave of labor legislation was strongly influenced by socialism in Germany. It resulted in laws covering worker illness, work accidents, and old age through payments from employees and employers. Various other social welfare schemes for workers were adopted in Germany, Austria, and Denmark, as well as in Australia and New Zealand. Such legislation was very slow to extend to countries of Eastern Europe.

After the turn of the century, labor law in Europe addressed similar issues as well as old age pensions and unemployment insurance. Gradually, the regulation of union contracts was more closely regulated by national governments. Disciplinary and dismissal procedures were codified and restricted, and the length of the work was reduced to the eight-hour day. Eventually, collective bargaining procedures and impasse and grievance procedures were placed into law. France became the first country to create a Ministry of Labor and to place social legislation into a single code of labor in 1910.

Today, in comparison to the United States, the labor laws of industrialized countries are more conducive to unionization and collective bargaining in both the public and private sectors. This is reflected in the much higher percentages of organized public and private sector employees outside the United States. Unions in Europe have close ties to political parties, which tends to increase their legislative influence, especially in the public sector.

RICHARD C. KEARNEY

BIBLIOGRAPHY

Kearney, Richard C., 1992. *Labor Relations in the Public Sector.* New York: Marcel Dekker, chapter 2.
Schneider, B. V. H., 1979. "Public Sector Labor Legislation–An Evolutionary Analysis." In B. J. Aaron, J. R. Grodin and J. L. Stern, eds., *Public Sector Bargaining.* Washington, DC: Bureau of National Affairs.

LABOR MOVEMENT.
An inclusive term that encompasses a variety of actions by organized groups of workers over time. Such actions include economic and political activities and collective bargaining by labor unions and worker collectives. The broader labor movement involves the mass actions of a working population that are usually aimed at improving the overall lot of working people through political, economic, and social action in a community or nation. In countries of Europe and Latin America, the labor movement has ideological foundations, with a relatively coherent concern for working conditions as well as for social welfare. In the United States, the labor movement with few exceptions has been concerned with immediate workplace conditions and increasing the power of workers to determine or influence those conditions, that have included job opportunities, hours of work, safety and health of workers, pay, and benefits. However, particularly during the early history of the American labor movement, unions have also sought to improve the general conditions for all workers through political action.

The first laborers in the early American experience were itinerant workers who moved from farmhouse to farmhouse applying their tools and skills. Some eventually built homes with workshops, selling their labor and products from there. As urbanization expanded markets, workshop proprietors employed journeymen to increase production, thereby producing America's first industrial class. Other early colonial enterprises with employer-employee relationships were commerce, especially that associated with land and sea transportation, and fishing. Colonial labor was categorizable into three areas: indentured servants, who were immigrants contracted to masters for a period of years; free laborers, who worked as farm help, artisans, mill hands, or longshoremen; and seagoing labor, including fishermen, whalers, and sailors. For all of these workers, conditions were rough and sometimes abusive.

Various combinations of workers developed in the trades, mechanical arts, and among journeymen, but the first true workingmen's organizations emerged after the Revolution among cordwainers, printers, and shoemakers in New York and Philadelphia. In the early 1800s, associations and societies were formed among carpenters, cabinetmakers, coopers, masons, tailors, and other occupations in the cities. The basic concern of such organizations was an adequate wage scale; failure to win their demands peacefully often resulted in a strike against the employer. Soon, employer associations appeared to counteract the labor organizations and to hold down wages through concerted actions and through the courts.

During the first 150 years of the American labor movement, the fortunes of labor were highly dependent on economic conditions. Recessions and depressions severely damaged organized labor and its causes through mass unemployment. Alternatively, when markets expanded during periods of prosperity, strong demand for labor resulted in favorable conditions for growth and development of organized labor. Among the items sought by labor organizations in the "Workingmen's Platform" during the early

1800s, and eventually won during many decades of labor strife and employer opposition, were the ten-hour day, universal male suffrage, abolition of debtor prisons, and equal and universal education. Progress of the labor movement was slow, however, because of periodic economic crises and other circumstances unique to the United States, such as the Western frontier, slavery, Protestant work ethic, and the widespread acceptance of a capitalistic economic system.

Employer opposition was another important factor in taking the wind out of the sails of the labor movement. For instance, following the rapid rise in unionization between 1897 and 1904, employer groups such as the National Association of Manufacturers promoted the "open shop" as part of the "American Plan" for combating unions. (In practice, this approach closed the door to jobs for union members.) Strike funds were created to assist firms battling unions who called their members off the job, and union organizers were "blacklisted" so they would not be hired elsewhere. Employer violence was not uncommon in the mining industry, where company guards, Pinkertons and "goon squads" were called out and armed to break strikes. In the coal mines of West Virginia and Colorado, for example, bloody battles occurred, including the infamous "Ludlow Massacre" in 1914 in Colorado, in which 50 people were killed in ten days of fighting.

Looking back, one is hard-pressed to find any sort of coherence in the American labor movement; rather, it can best be characterized as a series of unconnected efforts and actions involving a wide cast of organizations and individuals with varied goals and ideologies. Communists, Marxists, and some socialists have sought to overthrow the capitalistic system and American democracy in their entirety, but the great majority of labor organizations and activists have been willing to work for change within the basic economic and political systems.

Unlike their counterparts in many European countries, American workers and their organizations have accepted as final the loss of ownership of the tools and means of production that occurred during the Industrial Revolution and sought to improve their lot by bargaining with employers on the terms and conditions of employment. Although American workers and their employers live in two very different worlds, there is little sense of "class consciousness." Rather, the "bread and butter" unionism espoused by Samuel Gompers has triumphed in the twentieth century at the expense of communism, socialism, and other "foreign" dogmas.

Despite the near-imminent demise of the labor movement at various times, it has survived. A major factor in sustaining the labor movement and nudging it into its contemporary character was federal legislation. Beginning with the Norris-LaGuardia Act of 1932, the National Industrial Recovery Act of 1933, and the Wagner Act of 1935, federal laws protected and encouraged unionization and collective bargaining (see **labor law**). Aiding a new and expanding national interest in, and acceptance of, unions was the organizational rivalry between the American Federation of Labor and the Congress of Industrial Organization in the 1930s, which was accompanied by strong organizing drives that drove up union membership (see **AFL-CIO**). Eventually, of course, the two rivals merged into the AFL-CIO.

If one uses total union membership as a measure of the health of the labor movement, then the movement peaked during the mid-1950s at about 27 percent of the civilian labor force. Since then, union membership has declined in the private sector until in 1990 only about 12 percent of the civilian labor force belonged to unions (see **unions**). Many factors appear to be at work in reducing the appeal and organizing success of private-sector unions, including a shift in the structure of employment from manufacturing to services; federal and state legislation that abrogates some of the traditional issues of unions such as worker health and safety; a downturn in favorable public opinion toward unions; increasingly effective, peaceful, and mostly legal employer resistance to unions (which may be distinguished from violent opposition in the early years); and, according to some critics, an increasingly ineffective union leadership that has been unable to exploit changes in the workplace and workforce that have challenged the labor movement during the past three decades.

Unions continue to offer certain advantages to workers, however. The economic benefits are obvious to most workers, as is the advantage of having a collective voice to speak for them on conditions of work. Unions effectively represent employees in grievance processes and ensure due process for aggrieved or accused employees. And, in the present environment of labor-management participation experiments, unions provide a ready-made point of contact for employers wanting to change important workplace structures, processes, and behaviors.

The healthiest element in the American labor movement today is public employment, where organization of state and local employees approaches 40 percent nationwide and where unions remain politically and economically strong in spite of the many problems that have plagued government since the 1970s. The federal, state, and local governments differ greatly, of course, in union organization and collective bargaining outcomes. The labor movement is practically nonexistent in nonunion states such as North Carolina and South Carolina, whereas it thrives in states of the northeast and midwest. The single most important factor with respect to the fortunes of the labor movement in the public sector is the legal environment for collective bargaining.

Yet, even in the public sector the labor movement is confronting a crisis of sorts. The period of government retrenchment that has defined the 1980s and 1990s has damaged public employee unions and has slowly begun to disempower them. Cuts in services and operating budgets, privatization, and contracting out of services, relatively low wage and benefit increases, and related actions have undermined public employee unions. Public opinion has also turned against public sector unions to some extent, and as a consequence the general public tends to be less sympathetic to union demands and the occasional job action. And as unwilling pawns in political chess games between elected officials, administrators, and hostile taxpayers, public employees have learned that job security—once a guarantee in government employment—is now negotiable. Layoffs and hiring freezes, attrition policies and wages freezes, givebacks and copayments—all pose threats to the pocketbooks of union members and to the membership rolls of their organizations. Retrenchment has meant stable or declining membership rolls and a resultant loss of dues income and thus economic stability for unions. Reinventing government initiatives in the federal, state, and local sectors promises to shift public service provision and jobs to the nonprofit and private sectors, where organized labor is weaker. These trends portend hard times for unions in government and call for unions in the public sector to redefine themselves in order to remain relevant beyond the turn of the century.

In other countries, conditions have also become less favorable. Here, too, unions have been stressed by broad changes in their social, political, and economic environments. Labor market situations are rapidly evolving with high unemployment rates in many countries of Europe, Asia, and Latin America, the decline of manufacturing employment because of automation and other factors, the increasing internationalization of labor markets and the flood of cheap labor from and within developing countries, and the decline nearly everywhere of socialist and statist ideologies that have served as strong historical supports for the labor movement.

Yet, unions have not been beating a rapid retreat in Europe, Latin America, and elsewhere. Available data on union membership indicate only a moderate decline in Japan, the United Kingdom, and France, and relative stability and even increases in countries such as Denmark, Sweden, Germany, Canada, and Australia. Labor parties in these countries help defend the interests of the labor movement and express its viewpoints, and the continuing consciousness of class interests tends to support its relative prosperity.

RICHARD C. KEARNEY

BIBLIOGRAPHY

Freeman, Richard B. and James L. Medoff, 1984. *What Do Unions Do?* New York: Basic Books.
Greenstone, David J., 1977. *Labor in American Politics.* Chicago: University of Chicago Press.
Rayback, Joseph G., 1966. *A History of American Labor.* New York: Free Press.
Rosenbloom, David H. and Jay M. Shafritz, 1985. *Essentials of Labor Relations.* Reston, VA: Reston Publishing.

LABOR ORGANIZATION.

A group of workers in an association who combine for the common purpose of protecting and advancing their compensation, hours of employment, working conditions, and job security. Labor organizations may be union or nonunion organizations, or those created for social, political, or mutual benefit purposes. Some have the primary purpose of engaging in collective bargaining with employers; others engage in politics as political parties.

The origins of labor organizations are usually traced to worker guilds, which were joint associations of employers and craftsmen seeking to restrict outside competition and promote mutual benefits. Examples include shoemakers and haberdashers. Labor organizations later developed in skilled trades, such as plumbing and steelmaking, and eventually expanded to industrial concerns and the factory floor, as well as to government at all levels.

According to political philosopher Karl Marx, labor organizations arise from worker alienation, which results inevitably from industrialization. Workers realize their common plight, develop a class consciousness, and eventually overthrow the capitalist system. Left-wing organizations were strong in Europe during the late 1800s and early 1900s, and in the United States there was some spillover from the European experience in organizations such as the Industrial Workers of the World (the Wobblies). But Marx's analysis never really applied to the United States, where, as labor scholar Selig Perlman observed, labor organizations were more concerned with job security and economic issues.

Labor organizations are ensconced in government at local, state, and national levels. Some engage in lobbying for improved compensation and working conditions but do not participate in collective bargaining; examples include state employee associations and labor unions in nonbargaining states such as Virginia or North Carolina. Others are collective bargaining organizations that sometimes engage in broader political activities through lobbying and electoral activities, such as the American Federation of Teachers or the American Federation of State, County, and Municipal Employees. Government employees from virtually all functions belong to such organizations, although some, such as confidential employees or those in policy-making positions, may be prohibited from participating in collective bargaining and related activities. In some jurisdictions, supervisory employees belong to labor organizations, usually separate from rank-and-file organizations.

In the United States, labor organizations reached the height of their political and economic power following enactment of the National Labor Relations Act of 1935. Union membership rose in private employment until the 1950s, when it began a long decline that has continued to the present time. In government, President John F. Kennedy's Executive Order 10988 in 1964 served as a strong impetus for unionization. Approximately 40 percent of state and local employees belong to labor organizations today. The proportion is lower for federal employees, with the exception of the U.S. Postal Service. Labor organizations have achieved much in terms of improvements in wages, benefits, employee rights, and the conditions of work in the United States and in other countries.

Labor organizations differ greatly in internal organization and processes. Some use democratic rule with majority membership voting procedures. Others function with tight hierarchies and limited membership participation. Dues are normally required for members in exchange for collective representation and other services rendered.

RICHARD C. KEARNEY

BIBLIOGRAPHY

Auerbach, Jerold S., ed., 1969. *American Labor in the 20th Century.* Indianapolis, IN: Bobbs-Merrill.
Rayback, Joseph G., 1966. *A History of American Labor.* New York: Free Press.
Taft, Philip, 1964. *Organized Labor in American History.* New York: Harper and Row.

LABOR ORGANIZER.

An employee of a labor union whose job is to identify potential organizational targets for unionization and, through various strategies, convince workers in those organizations to join the union. The union organizer tries to convince workers that they have legitimate complaints about the terms and conditions of their employment and that the union will help them gain improvements. The organizer may emphasize broad ideological goals such as nondiscrimination or narrower, immediate objectives such as a wage increase in persuading employees of a firm or a public or nonprofit jurisdiction to join.

Common strategies for a union organizer include identifying specific sources of employees' dissatisfaction with their jobs or with the employer and pointing out inadequacies in wages, benefits, or working conditions in relation to workers in similar occupations or organizations. Inequities, unfair management decisions, and management favoritism often receive special emphasis.

After determining the target for unionization, the organizer gathers data on wages, benefits, and conditions of work; develops an organizing plan including a platform or statement of principles; finds and enlists the support of prounion employees in the target organization to provide

access to the place of work; and assembles an organizing committee and trains its members. If unionization efforts are successful, committee members may later serve as leadership for the local. To expand support for the union among workers, the organizer makes personal visits to homes, distributes pamphlets and other literature, makes telephone calls, and holds large and small group organizational and informational meetings for members of the potential bargaining unit. The mass media may be brought into play in an effort to influence popular opinion in favor of the union and to bring to the attention of a larger public the struggle for recognition.

A very important goal is to convince employees to sign cards supporting the union as their representative in collective bargaining and other interactions with management or to comply with other specific requirements of collective bargaining-enabling legislation. In some settings, including most industrialized countries of Europe, a designated percentage of authorizing cards signed by members of the prospective bargaining unit is sufficient for management recognition of the union as bargaining agent. In other settings, such as the United States' private sector under the National Labor Relations Act of 1935 and in the public sector in most state government legislation, an election is held to certify which union, if any, will represent the bargaining unit.

Union organizers are usually full-time employees of the national union, trained to develop and direct organizational campaigns. The task of the organizer is both delicate and complex. The organizer must be able to cope with extended time away from home, repeated rejection, threats, arrests, and even violence. Resourcefulness, strong interpersonal skills, and persistence are among the traits of the successful union organizer.

Union organizers are becoming increasingly sophisticated to combat the virulent antiunion efforts of certain employers and their consultants. They are also developing strategies to organize women, people of color, and other groups who have not been predisposed to unions.

RICHARD C. KEARNEY

BIBLIOGRAPHY

Gagala, Ken, 1983. *Union Organizing and Staying Organized.* Reston, VA: Reston Publishing.
Reed, Thomas F., 1989. "Do Union Organizers Matter? Individual Differences, Campaign Practices, and Representative Election Outcomes." *Industrial and Labor Relations Review* (October) 103–119.

LABOR RELATIONS.

The connections and dealings between members and representatives of labor organizations and management. Before unions and collective bargaining, labor-management relations were dominated by employers. In the Middle Ages, serfs were provided by their employers with food, water, shelter, and other things in exchange for their labor. Conditions and the exchange relationship varied greatly across employers and geography. Slavery, abolished by the middle of the nineteenth century in most of the world, essentially placed workers at the mercy and good will of their owners.

Later, in France, a livret system developed between servants and masters, in which employers recorded in a notebook the servant's discharge of work obligations, as provided for by an 1803 law. When all obligations were completed, the livret was returned to the worker, who was then free to find another employer. Indentured servitude similarly bound workers to a period of service in the early United States and in European countries. Indeed, a large proportion of the early immigrants to the United States (as much as 50 percent before the American Revolution) arrived as indentured servants, eventually becoming free laborers.

Industrialization revolutionized labor-management relations as it spread across Europe to Japan and to the United States. From a dominant model of independent craftsmen and farmers, self-sufficient in their labor, developed an industrial model of specialization and division of labor in factories operated with wage laborers dependent on large organizations for their livelihood. Industrialization separated workers from the finished product and emphasized repetitive work and coordination and routine instead of individual worker ability and creativity.

Those events were precursors to the rise of the bureaucratic organization described in Max Weber's "ideal-type bureaucracy," with hierarchy, specialization of labor, and impersonal rules, policies, and procedures, among other traits. Labor markets grew in geographic scope within and across nations, as did labor market competition. The factory system created new management functions such as recruitment, selection, and performance appraisal, as well as the rise of a new managerial class with very different interests from the laboring class.

Labor-management relations were rather unidirectional before the rise of unions. Employee discipline and discharge were enforced arbitrarily and in the absence of published rules. Employees were subject to fines for tardiness, swearing, and even speaking on the shop floor. Workers were considered to be essentially irresponsible and treated accordingly but held personally responsible for such events as machine breakdowns and work accidents. In many factories, especially in the textile industry, payment-in-kind systems were used, with workers paid primarily with food, shelter, and "chits" to be used at the company store. In sum, workers—except for the highly skilled—were highly dependent on their employers.

Toward the end of the eighteenth century, labor organizations began to emerge, beginning with craftsmen and workers in the skilled trades such as shoemakers and tailors. Eventually, labor organization spread to the factories and to federal government, and these organizations engaged in political action and reform activities.

In Europe, socialism was an important doctrine in the labor movement; its success in the United States was quite modest. In Europe, labor-management relations were defined by class conflict and labor parties, with clearly delimited economic and social boundaries between workers and the owners of the means of production. In the United States, little class consciousness developed with respect to the working class. Social class and occupational mobility and the heterogeneity of American society mitigated the rise of class consciousness, as did the strategies of early union leaders such as Samuel Gompers, who pursued "bread and butter" unionism instead of ideology (see **labor movement**).

In the United States, labor organizations first emerged as mutual benefit organizations to protect and promote the economic and social welfare of their members. As organizing activities moved from the skilled trades to the shop floor, unions sought higher wages, shorter hours, job security, improved conditions of work, and collective bargaining as the means for structuring labor-management relations into bilateral decisionmaking.

Early on, collective bargaining was looked upon by the courts and other political institutions as criminal conspiracy in restraint of trade and generally held to be illegal. Employer resistance to unions and collective bargaining was vehement and sometimes violent (see **strike**). The courts assumed a highly important role in the development of labor-management relations in the United States in both the public and private sectors that continues today by enjoining strikes, overturning reforms, and creating labor law.

Labor-relations systems are divided by labor scholar John Dunlop into four components: actors, rules, ideology, and environmental context. These variables may be applied across levels of government, across sectors, and across nations to guide comparative analysis. Actors in labor-management relations include labor and management officials, employees, third-party neutrals, and the government. Rules are the legal procedures, including collective bargaining, that comprise the framework for determining the scope of bargaining, means for resolving impasses, union security arrangements, and for setting wages and benefits. Ideology refers to the public policy objectives of the labor-management relationship. Found within the environmental context are broader economic, social, and technological variables, as well as international forces.

Labor-management relations vary across nations according to Dunlop's categories. In Latin American countries, there is a strong ideological and political base for labor-management relations, along with voluminous labor laws and government rules and regulations. Labor parties run candidates for elections. Mexico, Argentina, and Chile generally have more advanced systems than other Latin American countries. In Europe, negotiations and relationships tend to be more centralized than in the United States, and in several countries, worker participation in decisionmaking is mandatory. Union membership is much higher in European countries than it is in the United States. Japanese labor-management relations are characterized by consensual decisionmaking and modest union goals. Throughout most of the democracies of the world today, collective bargaining now defines most labor-management relationships.

RICHARD C. KEARNEY

BIBLIOGRAPHY

Dunlop, John, 1958. *Industrial Relations Systems.* New York: Henry Holt.

Jones, William A., 1983. "Historical Context." In Jack Rabin et al., eds. *Handbook on Public Personnel: Administration and Labor Relations.* New York: Marcel Dekker.

LABOR-MANAGEMENT COOPERATION.

Worker representation in the governance of an organization or industry.

At the turn of the century, industrial capitalism gave rise to employer-worker conflict, which resulted in numerous attempts to maintain a balance of economic and social power between management and workers. At one extreme, the theories of laissez-faire by Adam Smith advocated total management control over workers, who were considered commodities subject to the laws of supply and demand. At the other extreme, Marxist-influenced activists preached total worker control of the means of production. However, most labor union movements in Europe and the United States, in particular, eventually were regulated by government to compromise in balancing economic and social power between management and workers.

Historically, labor unions cooperated with management in the development of participatory reforms during periods of wartime political crises and tight labor markets. After World War I, in Great Britain, labor-management Whitley councils engaged in joint consultation. Sweden, Austria, Holland, and Japan, among other industrialized nations, codified worker-manager cooperation through legislation in the 1920s. Post–World War II Germany spurred the development of worker-control movements and the institutionalization of labor union representation in the governance of industry, while in the 1960s, tight labor markets in Sweden and Japan provided a conducive environment to experiment with small-group participatory reforms on a broad scale. These small-group reforms eventually led to the development of management-controlled "quality circles" and other employee involvement programs in Japan, while the small-group innovations under the workers' control in Sweden were more characteristic of the industrial democracy movements prevalent in Western Europe.

Likewise, the development and implementation of Quality of Work Life (QWL) programs, an integral part of the labor-management cooperative efforts in Western Europe, have differed from those in Japan and the United States. These differences are primarily due to, and are reflective of, the relatively unfavorable balance of power between unions and management in Japan and the United States when compared to Western Europe, which has a longer history of structured and institutionalized worker involvement in industry and a longer history in the development of various theories of industrial democracy.

In Western Europe, labor union and management cooperative reforms range from the development of codetermination, which requires by law that union representatives participate in decisions affecting the general working environment at the highest level in the organization, to joint union-management committees, which involve collaboration on specific work-related issues.

Cooperation in the form of labor-management committees is not new. In 1917, Great Britain created the Whitley labor-management committees in response to tight labor market conditions. These committees focused on the wartime need for increased production. By the 1980s, particularly in the Scandinavian countries of Sweden, Norway, Denmark, and Finland, labor-management committees had progressed to a point where worker and union representatives participated in various stages of the design process of new products. These efforts at cooperation have taken the form of local study circles and joint union-management technology committees.

In the 1980s in the United States, some municipal and state governments experimented with the QWL approach to management that is based on various forms of employee participation. Like the private sector, quality of work life in the public sector seeks to create a more participatory, team-oriented, open-surfacing-of-problems approach in place of a rigid, bureaucratic civil service management system. However, unlike the private sector, the literature suggests that one of the primary obstacles to municipal public sector QWL programs of joint labor-management cooperation is undue political influence from public sector managers, public sector union leaders, and the media.

The new hazards associated with major technology industries caused QWL programs to converge and focus on health and safety issues. The rapid changes in the work environment due to the technological advances and the resulting new health and safety hazards created increased worker participation in labor-management health and safety committees.

In Italy, worker participation in health and safety matters is established through contractual agreement. In

France, Belgium, and Great Britain there are statutory provisions for the establishment of health and safety committees, while in Germany, the Netherlands, and Luxembourg safety committees are subordinate to the labor-management work councils. In some cases, workers can exercise the veto power over managerial decisions affecting health and safety, and exercise codetermination over the choice of company health and safety staff.

In Norway and Sweden, labor-management cooperative systems on health and safety have been in existence longer than in many other countries. In those countries, health and safety have been part of a larger program of industrial democracy, which combines a unified approach to upgrading the work environment and enhancing worker involvement. Worker participation in Norway and Sweden is secured through national legislation. This European model of cooperation and participation is characterized by workers actively involved in developing study circles using materials written by unions, instead of listening to lectures by company engineers and experts. In striking contrast, the United States responded to pressure to increase the health and safety of the work environment by changing from a self-regulated industry and management-controlled volunteer system to a highly bureaucratic, professionally administered, rule-based, and punishment-centered system under the Occupational Safety and Health Administration (OSHA) established in 1970. The European model is much more flexible than the American system. With lower transaction costs and a more effective inspection process, there are greater opportunities for collaboration and cooperation among inspectors, managers, and workers, and less emphasis on rules, fines, and adversarial procedures. Workers in the European system have been granted effective rights through national legislation to participate actively in regulation at the local level.

Other issues, such as self-management of time, have been affected by worker participation in the context of labor-management cooperation. Changing the standard work week has become an increasingly legitimate concern of a growing number of women in the workforce who attempt to balance work and family life. Changing work values among younger workers as well as greater longevity of older workers also have led to a variety of recent work-time innovations, which include job sharing, permanent part-time work, voluntarily reduced work time, flexitime and flexi-year schedules, compressed workshifts, innovative workshifts, innovative shift systems, and sabbaticals in nonacademic settings.

As in the case of safety and health, where division of labor and control issues emerge out of concern with the work environment, so it is with time flexibility. Management has prevailed on the labor scene, especially in the United States, with regard to who has the authority to set time schedules for workers. However, most innovative work options have been initiated by workers—not management—and these have been most successful where workers participate in the self-management of time. In some cases, these innovative work options have become formalized arrangements through the cooperative interaction of labor-management committees.

In Japan, the time autonomy achieved through flexible scheduling has stimulated other needs for autonomy and participation at work. Participative self-management has led workers to raise issues having to do with control in other areas that directly affect their jobs.

In the 1990s, drawing on the Japanese experience, which has become a paragon of contemporary management culture, advocates representing all segments of the labor economy have called for greater employer-employee cooperation. Studies in the 1990s have examined the trend in participative decisionmaking (PDM) to determine if it can help government agencies cope with intense political, economic, and social pressures on their service delivery and regulatory functions. Evidence indicates that PDM provides personal benefits to employees, as well as human resource management-related and task-related benefits to organizations, although the effects of PDM on the quality and quantity of outputs are not certain.

In some private sector organizations, PDM has converged with various quality management programs, creating a conducive environment for successful labor-management partnerships. In the private sector, quality management programs are intended to improve organizational effectiveness and the working life of employees. Similar programs are on the rise in government. Despite increased attention given to such programs, less notice has been given to the role of modern unions in these ventures. One case study reports successful labor-management partnerships improving agency operations and the work experiences of employees throughout the more than 800 regional and field locations of the U.S. Department of Labor. The Department of Labor's Employee Involvement and Quality Improvement project was inspired by successful joint ventures in the private sector, in particular Saturn and Xerox, and was based entirely on labor-management cooperation and the idea of equal partnership. In this case, labor-management cooperation supplemented, rather than substituted for, collective bargaining. Cooperation strategies reduced the "we-they" mentality that can pervade employee-management relations systems to the detriment of both parties.

Recent trends in the United States to further reduce the "we-they" mentality in both public and private sectors have been in the form of employee involvement (EI) programs, or "labor-management jointness." These EI programs may be industry's best hope for success in the worldwide economic competition. Although many union officers in the United States are still opposed to employee participation, workers and laborers are increasingly willing to participate in employee involvement programs in hopes of making their employers more competitive and their jobs more secure.

Since the mid-1980s, participatory methods have advanced far beyond mere problem-solving techniques copied from the Japanese. In American-style teamwork, workers not only gain a more direct voice in shop floor operations but also in managerial duties. The team idea is spreading throughout manufacturing and also is gaining ground among financial services companies. U.S. companies are discovering that people are the keys to success in global competition. Some unionists fear, however, that participation may bring the demise of their organizations.

In the last analysis, all forms of labor-management cooperative experiments in the United States, including the most popular of the employee involvement programs, will remain techniques of limited effectiveness unless management, labor, and government join forces. Rapid technological changes and competitive pressures sweeping across Western economies are breathing new life into efforts to establish partnerships between workers and management. Such arrangements are hindered to a greater extent in the United States than in Europe because of lower union membership, less government regulation, and outmoded labor legislation. However, it is the belief of many in business, government, academia, and organized labor that worker-employer cooperation is the key to future economic survival.

Ross Prizzia

BIBLIOGRAPHY

Armshaw, Jim, David Carnevale, and Bruce Waltuck, 1993. "Union-Management Partnership in the U.S. Department of Labor." *Review of Public Personnel Administration*, vol. 13 (Summer) 14.

Guzda, Henry P., 1993. "Workplace Partnerships in the United States and Europe." *Monthly Labor Review*, vol. 116 (Oct) 67–72.

Hoerr, John, 1989. "The Payoff from Teamwork." *Business Week*, vol. 3114 (July) 56–62.

Kearney, Richard, and Steven W. Hays, 1994. "Labor-Management Relations and Participative Decision Making: Toward a New Paradigm." *Public Administration Review*, vol. 54 (Jan.-Feb.) 44–51.

Krim, Robert M. and Michael B. Arthur, 1989. "Quality of Work Life in City Hall: Toward an Integration of Political and Organizational Realities." *Public Administration Quarterly*, vol. 13 (Spring) 14–30.

Prasnikar, Janez, 1991. *Workers' Participation and Self-Management in Developing Countries*. Boulder, CO: Westview Press.

Sirianni, Carmen, ed., 1987. *Worker Participation and the Politics of Reform*. Philadelphia: Temple University Press.

Tsiganou, Helen A., 1991. *Workers' Participative Schemes—The Experience of Capitalist and Plan-based Societies*. New York: Greenwood Press.

Turner, Lowell, 1991. *Democracy at Work—Changing World Markets and the Future of Labor Unions*. Ithaca, NY: Cornell University Press.

LABORATORY TRAINING AND T (TRAINING)-GROUPS.

Related concepts referring to basic techniques as well as the setting for a kind of learning that seeks to improve human sensitivities and skills in interpersonal relations and groups. The "T-Group" is a value-guided technique or tool—a small number of persons, often strangers who have no past or future together and who learn from one another about their impact on one another. This for many persons constitutes a neglected way of "learning how to learn" and takes place in the context of a "laboratory" for training or education. Such laboratories typically involve many other elements in addition to the T-Group—lecturettes, simulations, role plays, large group exercises, and so on—all in combination that facilitate testing human reactions. This is analogous to learning about reactions between elements and compounds in a chemistry laboratory.

"Laboratory training" is a relatively new learning technology in the behavioral sciences and at one time was a very high flyer. Introduced in 1947, the rate of diffusion of the innovation peaked in the late 1970s, although various spinoffs of laboratory training continue to appear. Many consider laboratory training, now as well as then, a premier advance in learning (e.g., Bradford, Gibb, and Benne 1964).

What accounts for this great initial impact, as well as the substantial staying power? Four emphases provide a working answer. These emphases involve a brief set of orienting cues, a discussion of laboratory training values and how they are energized, a description of "learning how to learn," and some factors that motivate having a laboratory training experience.

A Brief Overview

Laboratory training is often linked with the terms "T-Groups" or "sensitivity training groups." Here, the latter terms are different labels for the basic learning unit in laboratory training. Typically, each lab contains a number of T-Groups, which meet separately for periods totaling up to 40 hours or more. Participants in laboratory training typically also convene in "community sessions" for lecturettes, skill-building exercises, and so on.

Succeeding emphases will provide details about what goes on in the typical laboratory and why. An early overview will help orient this discussion. Overall, laboratory training:

■ provides an experience in creating a miniature society for learning purposes;

- highlights working with processes that emphasize inquiry, exploration, and experimentation with attitudes and behavior;
- emphasizes learning how to learn;
- values the development of a psychologically safe environment that facilitates learning and is usually successful in inducing that environment; and
- acts on an agenda for learning largely determined by participants, although a professional "trainer" or "facilitator" is usually available to provide guidance and to help serve as a gatekeeper for laboratory values (Golembiewski and Blumberg 1970, pp. 5–6).

Guiding Values and a Typical Start-Up

The description above highlights values because laboratory training may seem to some like an unguided missile—perhaps powerful, but lacking in direction. Some may put that interpretation on these more or less typical words by a T-Group trainer or facilitator at an opening session:

This group will meet for many hours and will serve as a kind of laboratory where each individual can increase his [or her] understanding of the forces which influence individual behavior and the performance of groups and reactions. We begin with no definite structure or organization, no agreed-upon procedures, and no specific agenda. It will be up to us to fill the vacuum created by the lack of these familiar elements and to study our group as we evolve.

My role will be to help the group to learn from its own experience, but not to act as a traditional chairman nor to suggest how we should organize, what our procedure should be, or exactly what our agenda will be.

With these few comments, I think we are ready to begin in whatever way you feel will be most helpful (Golembiewski and Blumberg 1970, p. 15).

Such start-ups trigger unusual learning opportunities within a specific normative context. Without that supportive context, risk would be high and barriers to revelation and discovery might well inhibit learning.

What are some of these normative supports? Concerns about psychological safety dominate, and they are operationalized by insistence on learner-pacing. The major emphasis in T-Groups is not on change, for example, but rather on informed choice-making by individual T-Group members about when they want learning and when they "have had enough." Relatedly, T-Groups focus on the here-and-now—on the ideas and feelings generated in the learning setting about which members are the experts. In contrast, "encounter groups" and therapy are often there-and-then oriented, as in searching for the causes of problems in early developmental experiences.

Given such a supporting normative environment, people can reveal aspects of themselves as well as examine reactions to such revelations. In various ways, the T-Group can take on aspects of a laboratory for testing and hence for learning. One way in which this testing can take place is to experiment with one's behavior—to do and say things differently—and to get feedback from other group members concerning its impact on them. For example, a person whose customary style is to be very active and talk a lot may choose to be quiet for a while. One can observe the effects of silence on oneself and others, get feedback from them concerning how the behavior affects them, and reflect on personal feelings about being quiet as well as on choice-making about future expressions of self.

Learning How to Learn

Viewed broadly, laboratory training is about "learning how to learn"—a way to learn about oneself and others that extends beyond "normal education," and especially beyond higher education. This is true in three major senses to illustrate the broader implications.

First, T-Groups have an inductive and experiential orientation, thus differing from educational experiences that emphasize rationality and transmission of knowledge by authority figures. Most T-Group participants have to learn that they can also really learn in a setting where most of the real answers are provided by themselves.

Second, although some participants may come with specific agendas involving career or life changes, learning objectives for most T-Group members may be general, at least at the outset. Not infrequently, participants will be amazed at how they are seen by others, in particulars or overall. Satisfying agendas will develop in most cases but learning how to learn in a T-Group typically involves the development of a relatively high tolerance for ambiguity. If participants do not allow themselves to be open to unfolding experiences, they will cut off opportunities to learn.

A third component of "learning how to learn" involves the relationship of one's peers to one's own learning. In a T-Group, the teacher is any member of the group who can provide data for learning, which radically expands the resources available to the learner.

Some Motivators to Experience a Laboratory

Multiple motivations can encourage people to engage in laboratory training. Thus, organizations have sponsored such efforts to gain knowledge and skills relevant to building more effective relationships between people and groups, often as a prelude to cultural change at work. Individuals may attend because they have questions about how others see them, especially if they lack trustworthy sources back home to provide the necessary feedback. Individuals who are undergoing some change—in career, in job, or various other transitions—also may be attracted to a T-Group experience as a kind of basic training.

Of course, not everyone can learn in a T-Group (Lieberman, Yalom, and Miles 1973). Experience seems to indicate that those people whose needs for structure and authority are very high and rigid may not find the experience of much worth. The T-Group is simply too ambiguous for them and too much at odds with their needs. People who are forced to go to a laboratory by their organization also can be expected, in general, to have a less productive experience.

ROBERT T. GOLEMBIEWSKI

BIBLIOGRAPHY

Bradford, Leland P., Jack R. Gibb and Kenneth D. Benne, eds., 1964. *T-Group Theory and Laboratory Method*. New York: John Wiley and Sons.
Golembiewski, Robert T. and Arthur Blumberg, eds., 1977 3rd ed.. *Sensitivity Training and the Laboratory Approach*. Itasca, IL: F. E. Peacock.
Lieberman, Morton A., Irwin D. Yalom, and Matthew B. Miles, 1973. *Encounter Groups*. New York: Basic Books.

LAMBERT COMMISSION.

The Canadian Royal Commission on Financial Management And Accountability appointed by the Canadian government in 1976 and chaired by Allen T. Lambert.

The Royal Commission on Financial Management and Accountability and its counterpart, the Special Committee on Personnel Management and the Merit Principle (chair: Guy D'Avignon), were important endeavors of Canadian federal government in the late 1970s to regain control of the direction and course of administrative development.

The modern public service of Canada derives from a series of reviews in the early and mid-1960s of which the most prominent was the Royal Commission on Government Organisation (chair: J. Grant Glassco). Also significant was the Preparatory Committee on Collective Bargaining headed by A.D.P. Heeney. These reviews provided the foundations for new legislation in 1967 for public service governance in Canada, the Financial Administration Act, the Public Service Employment Act, and the Public Service Staff Relations Act.

Under the 1967 framework, the Treasury Board, a statutory committee of ministers, assumed a general responsibility for management of government embracing expenditure budgeting, management improvement, public sector staff relations (the employer function for collective bargaining purposes), and administrative policy. The staffing ("merit") system was the responsibility of the Public Service Commission, a three-member body reporting to Parliament. A Public Service Staff Relations Board was established to oversee the newly established public sector collective bargaining system.

Other changes in this period, one of prosperity and optimism, included adoption of the program method of budgeting and a new Auditor General Act partly designed to address problems that had arisen during the 1960s in the performance of the audit function. As early as 1971, a senior official was writing of "saturation psychosis" in relation to administrative reform. By the mid-1970s, the high hopes of the 1960s were clearly giving way to pessimism. In 1975, inflation compelled the Trudeau government to adopt restrictive measures on wages on an economywide basis.

Within government itself, the auditor general signalled in dramatic language that all was not well. In a much-quoted passage in his 1976 report he wrote: "I am deeply concerned that Parliament—and indeed the Government—has lost or is close to losing effective control of the public purse" (Report of the Auditor General of Canada to the House of Commons for the Fiscal Year ended March 31, 1976, para. 2.1, p. 9). He successfully proposed appointment of an officer of chief executive rank reporting to the Treasury Board to promote better financial management. It was in these unpromising circumstances that the Lambert Royal Commission was appointed in late 1976, followed early in 1978 by the Special Committee.

The Royal Commission was headed by a prominent banker from Toronto (Lambert), a Montreal accountant (Robert Despres), an academic expert on Canadian government (J. E. Hodgetts), and an official of chief executive (deputy minister) rank (O. G. Stoner).

Like the Glassco Royal Commission before it, the Lambert Royal Commission essentially conducted its inquiry privately; even some submissions were confidential. It was entirely Ottawa-based, although a number of consultants were hired from elsewhere in Canada. Individual members of the commission held meetings in provincial capitals as well as in Washington, London, and Paris.

The report was presented in March 1979. Its main recommendations essentially took the form of refining and heightening the program-based expenditure management system that had been developing in Canada in the post-Glassco era. The centerpiece was a five-year expenditure plan (the Fiscal Plan) for the effective management of which departmental and agency heads were to be responsible in a framework overseen by central agencies.

The report sought a reorganization of central agencies. It proposed abolition of the Treasury Board and its replacement by a ministerial Board of Management, which would have the responsibilities of the Treasury Board combined with the executive responsibilities of the Public

Service Commission. The commission itself was to continue its appeal and review functions.

The new Board of Management under the Lambert framework was to be served by two chief executives, the comptroller general heading a Financial Management Secretariat responsible for expenditure and financial management matters, and the secretary for Personnel Management heading a Personnel Management Secretariat responsible for personnel and resource management.

Other recommendations sought to encourage Parliament to take a stronger role in its scrutiny functions.

Early arrangements made by the Trudeau government to oversee implementation of the Lambert recommendations were attacked almost immediately by the auditor general as a case of inviting the fox to look after security in the henhouse.

The minority Clark Progressive Conservative government elected shortly afterwards accordingly appointed a senior official from the provincial government of Ontario to oversee implementation. Implementation largely centered on refinement of the post-Glassco management system, but the organization proposals were ignored not least in the face of strong resistance by the Public Service Commission. Complementary changes in personnel management were secured through creation of the Senior Management Senior Executive category at the highest levels below deputy ministers.

The D'Avignon Special Committee, which endorsed Lambert's organization proposals, recommended a governmentwide form of collective bargaining to oversee the workings of the merit system. These recommendations were not adopted.

The Lambert and D'Avignon inquiries essentially marked the end of attempts to reform Canadian national administration by qualitative systematic means. In the early 1980s, pay matters became the focus for public administration. Shortly after the election of the Mulroney Conservative government in 1984, it embarked on a fairly conventional cost-cutting exercise under a minister (the Nielson Task Force).

The late 1980s did witness, in cautious form, an endeavor to resurrect public service reform through a series of investigations under the rubric of Public Service 2000, one result of which were the first amendments to the public service legislation in a generation.

JOHN R. NETHERCOTE

BIBLIOGRAPHY

Report of the Royal Commission on Financial Management and Accountability, 1979. Chair: Allen T. Lambert, Ottawa.
Report of the Special Committee on Personnel Management and the Merit Principle, 1979. Chair: Guy D'Avignon, Ottawa.

LATIN AMERICAN ADMINISTRATIVE TRADITION.

The administrative traditions and practices of Latin America, the 19 Spanish-speaking countries of North, Central, and South America.

In order to understand current Latin American public administration, it is necessary to look at the formation and development of society, the state and public administration in the region. The first part of this section does that. The second part adopts a more static approach and describes the basic nature of the Latin American state and public administration in the twentieth century. In trying to draw a panoramic view, some generalizations will be made; obviously, they do not apply equally to all Latin American nations. Finally, in order to better illustrate some of the general features of Latin American public administration, brief descriptions of public administration in Brazil and Peru are presented.

Latin American Public Administration: An Historic View

Several historical facts have strongly influenced the evolution of public administration and the state in Latin America.

To begin with, Latin America was to a great extent a conquered rather than a colonized region. It was only after bloody battles that the Spanish Crown was able to dominate the main Indian kingdoms in Mexico and the Andes in the sixteenth century. Then, the Spanish focused on overexploiting the human and natural resources of the new provinces, which led to frequent Indian rebellions. The Portuguese did not have to fight numerous Indian kingdoms in Brazil. Nevertheless, they ended up establishing a regime very similar to the Spanish one (in part because from 1581 to 1640 both areas were under the same reign).

The conquest of Latin America was a political and religious enterprise as much as an economic one. It was legitimized by highly centralist medieval Thomist principles. Through them, the Crown was presented as the soldier of the Catholic faith and the architect of an organic (i.e., corporatist) community.

To extract resources, the Spanish and Portuguese empires had to establish a highly hierarchical, bureaucratic, and patrimonialist system (just as the Spanish had done before, first by organizing Castile and later by reconquering Spain from the Arabs). The Crown offered land as a prize for conquering the Americas, but then it had to establish a way of curbing the feudalistic power of the settlers. This was done through three mechanisms: a strong hierarchy, punctilious administrative regulations, and a public administration with multiple and overlapping spheres of influence. We could say that the main features of this system were a personalized and radial administrative structure around the king and a distributive policy orientation. The king distributed benefits, appointed all important officials, and many people could appeal to him.

Given the impracticality of this highly regulatory system, the attitude of many colonial administrators was that of "obey but do not comply" (which was actually a common saying then). In those times, as in more recent ones, the state allowed such practices but kept overregulation in order to apply it in a discretionary way. As it can be expected, the system caused widespread corruption. Latin America has been a region with strict rules that are flexibly applied, contrary to other regions or countries where there are fewer rules that are strictly applied.

Under this colonial regime, which lasted from the early sixteenth century to the early nineteenth century, it was difficult if not impossible for local entrepreneurship and social groups to develop. Furthermore, the conquest would soon lead to the emergence of highly divided nations in social, economic, and even regional terms, a feature we could call structural heterogeneity (Méndez 1986).

These features and consequences of the conquest in turn led to the development of conflicts and a profound distrust among social groups. Since people do not trust each other and do not trust politicians either, the bureaucracy soon emerged as the strongest actor in Latin American societies (Peters 1984).

In short, during the colonial times the bases for the emergence of a corporatist, legalistic, centralized, distributive, and highly regulatory state were laid down. Later on, underdevelopment, divisionism, and dependency pushed toward keeping the same system. From that very moment, the region became trapped in a vicious circle, where its political, economic, and social problems fed each other.

The lack of trust led to social relations based on informal, personalized links rather than on a more formal system of rules. The personalization of power, in turn, favored the development of strongmen at the local or sectorial level as well as a tendency to look after the interests of the primary group—kinship, friendship, or patron-clientelism—rather than any abstract concept of the common good. This pattern of social relations blocked the expansion of power at both vertical (bureaucratic) and horizontal (national) levels as well as the development of an effective public administration. Instead of emerging from a political credo and system of abstract rules, the Latin American nation-state needed to emerge from the military and political strength of central governments. The problem is that once having conquered the central state, national leaders resisted transferring power. Instability then grew again, often promoted by local strongmen, until such leaders were overthrown. Politics have been seen then as a zero-sum game, in part because public administration has been under the spoils system. In this way, Latin America's political and administrative evolution could be characterized by cycles of chaos and authoritarianism.

In the colonial regime, social groups were basically linked by the centralized state. Therefore, when in the early nineteenth century Latin American nations won their independence, they found themselves highly divided, underdeveloped, and lacking political and administrative experience. Governments were weak, both because they tended to import foreign models and because they were rarely able to implement an effective fiscal system. In addition to that, foreign companies or governments, at this time especially English or French ones, were constantly using and deepening this weakness. Most countries (e.g., Mexico, Peru, Bolivia, Colombia, Ecuador) took several decades to establish their first stable and hegemonic regime, the so-called oligarchic state (based on the big landowners). In this way, it was not until the end of the nineteenth century that many states were able to develop a stable army and a more organized—though rather small—public administration (with some exceptions, such as Brazil).

In most cases, these new regimes were highly authoritarian. At the beginning of this century, several of them were overthrown by the poorest social sectors and/or the new middle classes. A new regime type emerged, the so-called populist state (e.g., 1934–1945 in Mexico, 1937–1945 in Brazil, and 1946–1955 in Argentina). These regimes established an interventionist and welfare-oriented state. As a result, public administration grew considerably in several cases. The government was the sole agent available for dealing with crises such as the Great Depression, World War II, and the unrest of the Cold War period.

The populist project, however, was contradictory. It attacked but did not aim at eliminating the old oligarchic class of landowners. It induced popular masses to mobilize against the rich, but it was scared of mobilizing them too much.

In the 1950s and 1960s, the personalized populist governments were substituted by more liberal-democratic regimes (e.g., the radical governments of the 1964–1966 period in Argentina, the Eduardo Frei [1964–1970] and Fernando Belaúnde Terry [1963–1968] administrations in Chile and Peru, etc.). As Oszlak (1986) has shown, these regimes established a more poliarchic decisionmaking structure, where the legislature, political parties, and pressure groups played an important role. Bureaucracy was more fragmented, taxation and budgeting more dispersed, and public policy more politicized. This type of regime involved a redistributive policy style, where funding one program involves taking from another.

These regimes became soon highly clientelistic and fragmented, and strong fights within the bureaucracy and between Congress and the executive often led to stalemates. This, together with the politicization of the Latin

American armies and the emergence of guerilla movements, led to a new type of regime: the bureaucratic-military regime (e.g., in Argentina from 1966 to 1972 and from 1977 to 1984; in Brazil from 1964 to 1985; in Chile from 1973 to 1989). These regimes aimed at "remaking" and "stabilizing" their nations. They dissolved Congress and strongly controlled social organizations. A pyramidal administrative structure was set and military personnel named for the different positions. At the same time, however, military delegates were appointed to supervise each organization. Therefore, decisions were processed through parallel channels. These regimes tried to depoliticize social relations by assuming a more techno-bureaucratic approach. Since they saw the state's role as "subsidiary," debureaucratization, privatization, and deconcentration, together with the reduction of the public deficit, became central goals (Oszlak 1986; Hughes and Mijeski 1984).

In the 1980s, the military regimes were not able to resist the increasing popular opposition. Then, Latin America began to live a new redemocratization and reform wave, in this case in the context of a world trend toward market-oriented models. Most Latin American states have been attempting to implement comprehensive institutional reforms. Some have drafted new constitutions (e.g., Colombia in 1991, Brazil in 1988, Peru in 1979 and in 1993). Some have attempted or implemented "reforms of the state" (e.g., Mexico, Venezuela, and Argentina). Privatization processes have been important in many nations. Mexico, Bolivia, Chile, Peru, and to some extent Argentina have significantly changed the size and nature of their public enterprises. Several states have carried out important public administration reforms, especially Bolivia, Chile, Peru, and Argentina (the latter one established in 1991 one of the most developed Latin American civil service and training systems). Furthermore, Mexico, Argentina, Chile, and Peru carried out significant fiscal, financial, and labor reforms, among others. Decentralization has been high on the agenda of countries such as Mexico, Colombia, Brazil, or Peru (although only in the first two has there been progress in this regard). In fact, decentralization claims have been increasing in most countries despite the fact that regional identities are not as strong as in other parts of the world (probably with the exception of Brazil, Colombia, and Ecuador). Redemocratization has brought about more decentralized and participatory decisionmaking systems but sometimes also problems of governability or administrative efficiency (e.g., Brazil). In short, there has been change, but there still remains a profound "management deficit." Many reforms have aimed at the size of the state and organizational charts rather than at administrative capacity; often they have not constituted continuous public policies (Kliksberg 1989).

Latin American State and Public Administration: A Static View

As I said, the colonial system first and structural heterogeneity, dependency, and underdevelopment later made of the state the central actor of Latin American societies. The state has had to push economic development and at the same time be a mediator of social conflicts, mainly between workers and businessmen. However, playing those roles has been a difficult task because it has not been easy to find models on which all actors agree. In addition to that, the state has also had to be a mediator among foreign and local actors.

In this way, the Latin American state has been "strong" and "weak" at the same time (Méndez 1986). It is a sort of hollow state. From outside it can look as an imposing fortress, but when we get inside we can see its thin buttresses and feel its fragile floor. This is true for at least three reasons.

1. If the state has often had foreign support that further backs it, such support has also weakened it because then it appears as the representative of foreign capital, imperialism, or the like. The usually difficult socioeconomic conditions and the strong political, economic, and social differences justify the leading role of the state. However, while the former limits the possibilities for growth, the latter can hardly be resolved in the short term. In short, dependency, underdevelopment, and structural heterogeneity both strengthen and weaken the state.
2. Due to the legitimacy deficit, the state often has to use force and tends to be more authoritarian and centralized. This makes it seem strong, but in reality it makes it lose touch with social processes. Therefore, it often promotes illegal opposition.
3. While the state has been highly interventionist and rather big, this makes it a clear target for the opposition and pushes toward administrative disorganization and inefficiency.

As a result of all this, political regimes in Latin America have often been looking for a political compromise, which is always fragile (Lechner 1977, p. 412).

Just as in the case of the state, it could be argued that in Latin America public administration may seem strong but that in reality it has had low capacity. In fact, this low capacity is at the same time an effect and a cause of the weakness of the state.

One the one hand, the bureaucracy often has been able to act in a more unified fashion, since the executive branch tends to dominate Congress and the judicial branch as well as the regions. Given its central role, Latin American bureaucracy can intervene in a wider range of areas (e.g., what in other countries are considered private personal matters).

It also has a wider range of policy options and instruments (Sloan 1984). Policy formulation usually takes place in closed "bureaucratic rings" within the federal executive (Cardoso 1979). The adoption of civil (codified) law since colonial times has greatly facilitated these patterns.

On the other hand, as I said, public administration's real capacity is low. This is true for various reasons:

Political legitimacy has been fragile. Therefore, the state constantly has to be striking deals with local strongmen or corporatist leaders. It may be true that at the formulation stage they tend to agree with policies. However, they often wait until the implementation phase to boycott the policies with which they disagree. Therefore, participation and bargaining may be low at first, but then it increases as the policy process unfolds, especially in the bigger countries (Grindle 1980).

Schmitter (in Sloan 1984) has argued that Latin America has a "structural overbureaucratization" and a "behavioral underbureaucratization." In other words, it has often had a presidential, bureaucratized, and regulatory decisionmaking system and, at the same time, a heterogeneous and inconsistent administrative behavior. As mentioned previously, the region has had strict rules that are flexibly applied. In Latin America, it may be easier to formulate a policy or pass a regulation, but often it has been difficult to get them effectively implemented.

Due to the weak division of powers and federalism, presidents have been more powerful. However, here we should introduce two caveats.

First, political fights are transferred to the executive bureaucracy, which therefore became bulky and fragmented. Since cutting or reorganizing public agencies may alienate political support, governments have tended to create new agencies besides the already existing ones. Actually, the need to get political support has led to overstaffing. Given all these factors, plus higher interventionism, Latin American presidents tend to be stronger and hold high regulatory powers but face fragmented bureaucracies and low implementation capacity.

Second, despite the long-standing centralism, most Latin American countries are middle sized or big. Some central ministries have numerous field offices. Intergovernmental systems have gone through cycles of de- and recentralization, but in general they are more complex than it is usually thought (Graham 1990). Several nations have somewhat decentralized economic systems, either in federal republics such as Brazil or in traditionally unitary governments such as Colombia. Even in those that do not, some regions have often opposed centralized policies (e.g., Arequipa in unitarian Peru or Mendoza in Argentina).

In short, behind the apparently strong facades, in Latin America we find a "politicized" (Chalmers 1977) or "fluid" (Graham 1990) state (the Mexican system has been an exception to this pattern, although only to some extent) (Méndez 1994). Institutions respond more to the political needs of the moment than to general ideological principles. Rhetoric is rather high since changing institutions calls for the reconstruction of basic meanings. Therefore, the policy process is more "spectacular." However, such a process is not one of continual radical change. Chalmers called it politicized because it involves neither orderly bargaining nor violent confrontation.

Political survival is a daily concern of state officers (Ames 1987). The lower level of legitimacy of the state has led governments to favor symbolic, highly visible, or short-term public policies. It is the so-called *plazismo,* that is, the tendency of public officers to focus on public works (sometimes useful ones, but on other occasions just the rebuilding of squares and parks).

The public policy environment is more uncertain. Governments and institutions have been more fragile. Usually, inflation and demographic rates are higher as well as dependency on foreign markets and capitals. Resources, well-trained personnel, and information have been limited while demands have been greater.

The degree of professionalism of the bureaucracy is lower than in more developed nations. The regulatory, discretionary, and personalized nature of public administration, together with lower wages, have led to comparatively higher levels of corruption. Although several countries have been trying to develop a public ethos and civil service systems since the 1930s—most notably Colombia, Uruguay, and Brazil—or the 1950s and 1960s—such as Argentina, Venezuela, and Peru—progress in this regard has been subject to cycles. Professionalism is rather uneven. Civil service systems have been maintained basically in those countries where two equally powerful parties have been rotating in power (Geddes 1991). In addition, the civil service systems are often circumvented in many ways. Several countries have more developed training systems (for instance, Colombia, Brazil, Argentina, and Peru) but most do not. Given the above-mentioned trend to create new organizations besides the old ones, we often find so-called islands of efficiency (especially in areas more related to economic development). The shifts of officers and personnel along vertical and horizontal lines are more frequent (although the bureaucratic class tends to be somewhat more stable, in part due to the limited access to education).

In conclusion, hierarchical and overbureaucratized decisionmaking structures, at one level, and clientelistic and fragmented practices, at another, have both been enduring patterns of Latin American public administration. Therefore, political and administrative practices have been more complex and even—in their own ways—pluralist than is usually thought. In this sense, they also may have been more similar to more developed countries like the United States than we are used to thinking. Even more so when we could argue that the United States is more integrated than its fragmented formal structure would lead us to believe (although this would be a separate matter of investigation, programs seem to get implemented more effectively than in Latin America, thanks to the existence of intergovernmental and policy networks as well as a more professionalized administrative culture). Of course the United States and Latin America are different. The point is that we really do not know how different they are because we have seldom compared them. It seems that differences are more a matter of degree than essence (Peters 1996).

Public Administration and the State in Brazil

Political Background

Brazil is the largest Latin American country and the fifth largest in the world. It is almost as large as the United States. In the early 1990s, it had 150 million inhabitants.

It was colonized by the Portuguese in the sixteenth century and achieved its independence in 1822. It was a more or less stable monarchy until 1888. In 1889, a federal republic was proclaimed. It lasted until 1930, when a revolutionary movement headed by Getulio Vargas deposed the republican president. Vargas became the new president, and in 1937 he inaugurated the *estado novo,* a nationalist, reformist, and corporatist dictatorship that lasted until 1945. Vargas came back to power in 1950, this time as constitutional president, but committed suicide in 1954. Juscelino Kubitschek (1956–1961) promoted industrialization. After the seven-month government of Janio Quadros, a more social-oriented leader, Joao Goulart, became president. In the context of the implementation of various social reforms and a political stalemate, the military deposed Goulart in 1964. They stayed in power until the mid-1980s, when a redemocratization process took place. José Sarney became president after the death of Tancredo Neves, indirectly elected for the 1985–1990 period. In 1988, a new republican constitution was signed, which involved a federal state with division of powers. In 1990, Fernando Collor de Mello became the first directly elected president in 26 years. However, after a corruption scandal, he was impeached in 1992 and substituted by the vice president, Itamar Franco. In 1994, the candidate of the political center, Fernando Henrique Cardoso, won the presidential elections.

The Evolution of Public Administration

The contemporary political-administrative history of Brazil can be divided into four periods. The first one goes from the proclamation of the first republic in 1889 until the Vargas revolution of 1930. During this time, the state was small and had basically regulatory functions. For instance, for some time it only had seven ministries (war, navy, foreign affairs, justice, finance, public works, and agriculture). Although there was some modernization of public administration, it was limited to a few aspects, such as uniformizing public accounts. Public administration was under the spoils system. It aimed at providing jobs and business opportunities, especially for the then main dominant groups, the coffee growers, sugar plantation owners, and cattle ranchers. In this period, subnational states and political groups had a considerable autonomy (it must be noted that although in general terms very similar to its neighbors, Brazil has had a more decentralized system even from colonial times.)

The second period begins with the revolution headed by Vargas in 1930 against the oligarchic state and ends with the military coup of 1964. During this time, there was a trend toward increasing public intervention, regulation, and, to some extent, professionalization of civil servants.

In the early 1930s, Vargas tried to establish a merit system. However, it was blocked by the old political class. Only after setting up the *estado novo,* was he able to establish in 1938 the Civil Service Administrative Department (DASP), a powerful and highly independent agency aimed at developing a civil service and a system of government procurement. Vargas also inaugurated what came to be called "indirect administration." By 1945, he created 32 semi-independent agencies. He also added two ministries to the "direct" administration, the most important of which was the labor one. He centralized the intergovernmental system.

Vargas' successors, Jose Linhares and Eurico Gaspar Dutra, weakened DASP, eliminated civil service exams, and gave back to members of Congress the power to distribute jobs. Perhaps with the exception of the short comeback of Vargas (1951–1954), DASP would never again have the power it initially had. Due to their weak political base, all the following presidents favored the spoils system. President Juscelino Kubitschek introduced civil service in the various social security institutes. However, he did it because they were a stronghold of the political opposition. He filled many positions in several ministries with his supporters. Although a subsequent president, Joao Goulart, created a Ministry for Planning and elaborated a National Plan, he increased political appointments, also due to his very weak political base. The national plan was born dead and the politicization of the bureaucracy led to administrative chaos (Geddes 1991). During the 1946–1964 period, Brazil went back to a more decentralized pattern of intergovernmental relations.

As mentioned before, given the need to have a minimally efficient public apparatus but due to the problems to reform existing agencies, a parallel bureaucracy developed throughout the years, the so-called islands of efficiency, as for instance the National Bank for Economic Development, the Foreign Affairs Ministry, or the oil company (Geddes 1991; Martins 1985).

The third period of Brazilian public administration begins with the military coup in 1964 and ends in the mid-1980s with the redemocratization process. This stage was characterized by an even greater expansion of indirect administration, especially public utilities (571 by 1976). In Brazil, indirect administration showed to be more flexible and dynamic than the direct one (that is, the central ministries). In 1967, decree-law 200 initiated a process of deregulation, debureaucratization, and administrative deconcentration. At the same time, the military tried to make the labor statute more flexible and to better control indirect administration. They created a Planning Ministry similar to that of Goulart. They recentralized a number of the attributions of the states; in fact, centralization reached its peak during this period. In general, the military centralized decisionmaking in the military cabinet and the National Security Council. As political competition increased, they increasingly distributed jobs to political supporters.

The fourth period begins in 1986 with the presidency of Sarney. He formulated an administrative reform, especially of the central administration, aimed at the rationalization and reduction of public spending and agencies, the reinforcement of the merit and the training systems, the better regulation of public procurement and public utilities, and the promotion of participation in some indirect agencies. DASP disappeared and was substituted by the new Ministry for Public Administration. He offered incentives so that employees would find jobs in the private sector.

In general, the 1988 constitution fragmented power. First, it enhanced the power of the legislative branch, although presidents were still able to closely control some policies through executive decrees. Second, it deconcentrated functions and resources to the states and municipalities.

In 1990, Collor de Mello implemented a major administrative reorganization, which reduced ministries from 20 to 12. He merged the economic promotion, treasury, and planning functions into one ministry (Franco, however, would later reverse this measure).

The 1988 constitution and the new "organic" law of 1990 set general legal parameters for all public employees, from the lowest (e.g., secretaries) to the highest levels. Still there is a variety of specific legal statutes; in addition, each state has its own statute. Theoretically, entry depends on exams and qualifications, but often the process is far from impersonal. Roughly one third of public employees are part of the more formal civil service. In fact, most employees can feel secure in their jobs. Foreign relations, finance, higher education, and the judiciary have the most developed civil service systems and the most professionalized staffs. At any rate, it is common that the third and even the second highest position in each ministry is occupied by a member of the civil service. After the Collor scandal, the Audit Court, already highly professional, was further strengthened.

In the first months of his administration, Cardoso was trying to make more flexible the statutes for public employees and to make further changes to the Constitution to be able to implement a variety of reforms (both social and economic).

The State and Public Administration in Peru

Political Background

Peru is the third largest South American country; it is over twice the size of France. In the early 1990s, it had a population of 22 million inhabitants. It achieved independence from Spain in 1824. The nineteenth century saw internal fights between conservative and liberal groups and wars with neighboring countries. The Peruvian regimes of these times were also based on the traditional oligarchical order.

The crisis of this social order began in the 1920s, when the leftist party Alianza Popular Revolucionaria Americana (APRA) promoted the popular mobilization against it. Although it won several elections, several military coups kept it from taking power. In 1956, APRA was coopted through a sort of cogovernment deal and reduced its radicalism. With the election in 1963 of President Fernando Belaúnde, there were new hopes of reform. However, Belaúnde's reform efforts were slow, in part because his government was obstructed by Congress and an APRA-conservative coalition. In 1968, there was a leftist military coup, led by Juan Velazco Alvarado. The military regime lasted until 1980, when the country was redemocratized. A new constitution was signed in 1979 and Belaúnde was again elected president for the 1980–1985 period. He was followed by Alán García, who implemented a rather populist program and faced a strong guerrilla movement (Sendero Luminoso). Alberto Fujimori was elected for the 1990–1995 period. In 1992, he dissolved Parliament and a battle between the two powers developed. From the end of 1992 to the end of 1993, a new congress worked on a new constitution, which, after a referendum, was promulgated in December 1993. It confirmed the unitary and presidential system established by the previous one. Although in a complex way, the new constitution strengthened the president's power, it favored a more market-oriented economy and allowed for the president's reelection. In 1995, Fujimori was reelected for another five years.

The Evolution of Public Administration

The more recent history of Peruvian public administration can be divided into three periods.

The first one goes from the first decades of the twentieth century to the military coup of 1968. During these years, public administration was smaller and less differentiated than those of the other major Latin American nations. However, it was characterized by severe fragmentation. The system of tax collection and expenditures was highly fragmented. Successive governments used tax contracts to reward allies and coopt or punish their enemies. Although there were fights over the tax collection system, they concerned the division of spoils not the system itself. By the 1950s, several entities collected taxes and paid out obligations, each with its own accounting system. At the beginning of the 1960s, only one-fifth of investment funds were allocated through the regular budgetary system and some 30,000 separate regulations ruled the fiscal system. The basic sources of funds for public investment were special accounts which earmarked funds for specific purposes. Surpluses in these accounts were in most cases carried over to the next year. With the partial exception of the foreign ministry, there was no career system for upper-echelon bureaucrats. Neither the president nor the cabinet had a professional staff to coordinate programs. Ministerial functions overlapped and ministries had no clear legal authority over autonomous agencies. In 1966, the Bank of the Nation was formed. The treasury became an independent bureau within the increasingly powerful Ministry of Finance. However, other agencies kept collecting taxes and disbursing funds. In the mid-1960s, special purpose taxes accounted for 40 to 50 percent of all revenues (Schmidt 1984). Furthermore, favoritism and corruption were common in the Finance Ministry.

The second period of Peruvian public administration starts in 1968 with the military coup of general Velazco and ends in 1990. It was characterized by the expansion (especially from 1968 to 1975), centralization, and sectoralization of the public apparatus. The military diversified and reorganized the ministerial structure. All autonomous agencies were grouped into well-defined sectors. A strong cabinet secretariat, the COAP, became the power base of the military. Ministers were given clear responsibility for sectoral policy. The country's finances were centralized in the Ministry of Economics. The public finance and budgetary systems were consolidated. Almost all earmarked taxes were eliminated. All income and expenditures were channelled through a General Bureau of the Treasury within Finance. This facilitated having a more effective accounting system. As a result, the planning system was also reinforced and the National Institute of Planning (INP, created in the 1960s) was more able to induce compliance with the plans (Giesecke 1987; Cleaves and Scurrah 1980; Schmidt 1984). By 1975, Peru's bureaucracy and state had become much more professional (this, however, would be somewhat reversed in the late 1970s, when many highly professional civil servants were dismissed due to the debt crisis). Despite the crucial effort at state-building of the

military, they clearly failed in attaining other objectives (e.g., regionalization) (Hamergreen 1983).

In 1980, Peru inaugurated a new democratic regime under the 1979 constitution, which greatly strengthened the executive while weakening Congress. It did not change the major administrative reforms undertaken by the military. Belaúnde did not make major changes to the administrative structure developed by the military. He carried on, however, an administrative decentralization within several sectors and significantly improved wages in the upper levels of the public sector. Public utilities were put under private law, and an austerity program was implemented (especially after 1983). As this unfolded, the development planning functions of the INP decreased and the Ministry of Finance started to centralize decisionmaking power.

With García, the more centralized system remained largely unchanged. However, he tried to revitalize the planning system and attract more top-level technocrats back to the INP, as well as to transfer budgeting authority from the Finance Ministry back to the Institute (more attuned to his ideology) (Schmidt, 1984). García started a political and administrative decentralization program. According to it, several autonomous "regions" were created. However, since public administration is rather politicized, García pushed this program for political reasons (Méndez 1990).

Confirming such a politicization, President Fujimori has blocked it to a great extent and tended to work with the previous administrative "departments." With his government, the third period of Peruvian public administration began. It was characterized by even further centralization, but this time together with the reduction of the state to less than half of its previous size and attempts at more flexible personnel regimes. According to Fujimori, fighting the guerillas, solving the economic crisis, and governing was impossible with the set of institutions he inherited. Although Belaúnde and García ruled to some extent by decree, based on small, insulated teams of advisers, Fujimori's government culminated in the marginalization of state agencies (not to speak of Congress), including those with a significant number of well-trained professionals. He implemented an extremely rigorous (and up to early 1995, successful) program of economic stabilization. It included a better control of public spending and a more professional and efficient revenue system.

In 1950, the first law regulating the civil service was promulgated. It had been further developed and complemented by the constitution of 1979 and 1993, as well as by more specific laws, such as those of 1984 and 1994. Entry and promotion throughout the different categories theoretically depend on exams and qualifications. However, often officers have found ways of going around the law to decide based on the contacts of the applicant (Cleaves and Scurrah 1980; Giesecke 1987). In short, a civil service and a training system have been gradually developed, but it still is subject to political influence (although less in some areas than others, as for instance, finance). Traditionally wages have been rather low (Giesecke 1987), which has pushed people toward holding down two or more jobs. Fujimori implemented an important privatization program and cut several agencies, among them the INP. Through privatization, dismissals, and incentives to leave the civil service, he reduced the number of public employees from around 700,000 to around 325,000. The greater insulation and reduction of the state have probably weakened rather than strengthened the capacity of the Peruvian state.

JOSÉ LUIS MÉNDEZ

BIBLIOGRAPHY

Ames, Barry, 1987. *Political Survival; Politicians and Public Policy in Latin America.* Berkeley: University of California.

Cardoso, Fernando H., 1979. "On the Characterization of the Authoritarian Regimes in Latin America." In David Collier, ed., *The New Authoritarianism in Latin America.* Princeton, NJ: Princeton University Press, 33–57.

Chalmers, Douglas A., 1977. "The Politicized State in Latin America." In James Malloy, ed., *Authoritarianism and Corporativism in Latin America.* Pittsburgh, PA: University of Pittsburgh Press, 23–45.

Cleaves, Peter S., and Martin J. Scurrah, 1980. *Agriculture, Bureaucracy, and the Military Government in Peru.* Ithaca, NY: Cornell University Press.

Geddes, Barbara, 1990. "Building 'State' Autonomy in Brazil, 1930–1964." *Comparative Politics,* vol. 22 (January) 217–235.

———, 1991. "A Game Theoretical Model of Reform in Latin American Democracies." *American Political Science Review,* vol. 85 (June) 371–389.

Giesecke, Alberto, 1987. *Cómo Funciona La Administración Pública Peruana?* Lima: Fundación Ebert.

Graham, Lawrence, 1990. *The State and Policy Outcomes in Latin America.* New York: Praeger.

Grindle, Merilee S., 1980. *Politics and Policy Implementation in the Third World.* Princeton, NJ: Princeton University Press.

Hamergreen, A. L., 1983. *Development and the Politics of Administrative Reform; Lessons from Latin America.* Boulder, CO: Westview.

Hughes, Steven W., and Kenneth J. Mijeski, 1984. *Politics and Public Policy in Latin America.* Boulder, CO: Westview.

Kliksberg, Bernardo, 1989. *Cómo transformar el Estado?* Mexico, DF: Fondo de Cultura Económica.

Lechner, Norbert, 1977. "La Crisis Del Estado En América Latina." *Revista Mexicana de Sociología,* vol. 39 (April-June) 389-426.

Martins, L., 1985. *Estado Capitalista E Burocracia No Brazil Pos-1964.* Rio de Janeiro: Pac e Terra.

Méndez, José Luis, 1986. *Modelos De Desarrollo Economico Y Social En América Latina.* Mexico, DF: Universidad Iberoamericana.

———, 1990. "La Reforma De Descentralización En El Perú, 1978–1989." *Foro Internacional,* vol. 31 (July-September) 88–119.

———, 1994. "Mexico under Salinas: Towards a New Record for One Party's Domination?" *Governance,* vol. 7 (April) 182–207.

Oszlak, Oscar, 1986. *Políticas Públicas Y Regímenes Políticos; Reflexiones A Partir De Algunas Experiencias Latinoamericanas,* vol. 3,

no. 2. Buenos Aires: CEDES. English shorter version in *International Social Science Journal,* vol. 38, No. 2: 219–235.

Peters, B. Guy, 1984. *The Politics of the Bureaucracy.* New York: Longman.

———, 1996. "The Policy Process in Developed and Less Developed Political Systems." *International Journal of Public Administration.* vol. 19, no. 9: 1639.

Schmidt, Gregory D., 1984. "State, Society, and the Public Process: Planning, Decentralization, and Public Investment in Peru, 1956–1980." Ph.D. thesis, Cornell.

Sloan, John W., 1984. *Public Policy in Latin America. A Comparative Survey.* Pittsburgh PA: Pittsburgh University Press.

LAYOFFS.

The involuntary dismissal of workers, typically as a response to financial difficulty or business necessity. Layoffs can be either temporary or permanent, depending upon the circumstances that trigger the employer's action. When prompted by financial exigencies, layoffs are putatively temporary in that workers may be reassured that when the budget situation improves, they will be recalled. Layoffs arising from organizational restructuring ("downsizing" or the lowering of personnel ceilings), by contrast, are almost always intended to be permanent.

Whether temporary or permanent, government agencies generally use the term "Reduction in Force" (RIF) when trimming their workforces. The term "furlough" also appears frequently in public management. Furloughs are layoffs that are strictly temporary and occur on a regularized basis. Under typical furlough plans, for instance, employees may be required to stay home one day every two weeks, or one week every month, until the budgetary crisis has passed. This enables the employing agency to save salary money and thus possibly to avoid permanent layoffs.

Historical Background

Historically, employers have encountered few impediments to laying workers off to accommodate short- or long-term contingencies. The discretion of managers was virtually absolute in that decisions regarding both the number and identity of the targeted workers were managerial prerogatives.

Although managers continue to exercise considerable discretion concerning the necessity for layoffs, their influence over which specific workers will be laid off has ebbed over time. Worker demands for equitable treatment prompted many public jurisdictions to adopt statutes and/or civil service regulations that regularize relevant procedures and govern the layoff sequence (i.e., who gets laid off in what order). Meanwhile, unemployment compensation systems were created in many industrial countries to soften the blow for workers who lose their jobs under layoff conditions.

Within the United States and many other industrialized countries, such procedures have not had a great deal of relevance to civil servants because layoffs traditionally occurred so infrequently. Public employees once enjoyed a much higher level of job security than their counterparts in the private sector. Even during the Great Depression of the 1930s, the unemployment rate of civil servants was about one-third of that in business and industry. The quid pro quo was that public sector salaries were not as competitive as those in the nongovernmental sector; public employees were "paid" in part by job security.

Beginning in earnest with the tax revolts of the 1970s, this envied job perquisite eroded in the face of recessions, taxpayer resentment, decreased federal aid for state and local government, and a worldwide effort to "reinvent" a smaller and more efficient government apparatus. Consequently, layoffs have now become common fixtures in civil service systems throughout the world. During the first major recession of the 1980s (1981–1983), for example, about 200,000 public workers in the United States were laid off. In subsequent years, even larger numbers of public employees were involuntarily severed from employment to meet budgetary goals. Proportionate numbers of civil servants in Australia, Brazil, Canada, England, and many other countries met the same fate as conservative governments sought to reduce their administrative overheads.

As the twentieth century draws to a close, layoffs appear to be one of the true constants in international public administration. The public-policy agendas in most countries are dominated by efforts to privatize, downsize, deregulate, and "debureaucratize." The desire to trim government expenditures—and, notably, public payrolls—is pervasive. As a consequence, civil servants increasingly cast a nervous eye in the direction of their jurisdictions' layoff policy, quietly assessing their chances for retention during times of increased fiscal stress.

Layoff Procedures

Layoff procedures follow a highly consistent pattern across fully articulated civil service systems. Once it is determined that a layoff is necessary, the affected agency must target programs and employees for termination. This involves the identification of both competitive areas (the organizational units that will be affected, such as a specific program or department) and competitive groups (the specific job classes or categories from which layoffs will be made).

In general, decisionmakers exercise a great deal of discretion in making these difficult choices. Civil service procedures may simply state that decisions be made "according to critical needs," or they may require attention to such issues as the impact that layoffs will have on the racial or gender composition of the labor force.

Public managers often use layoffs as an opportunity to implement changes that were being considered in a different context. If a particular program had earlier been a candidate for reorganization or downsizing, for instance, it will almost certainly become the prime target for layoffs when a financial emergency is declared. Similarly, a RIF can provide public managers with a convenient tool (or "excuse") for eliminating ineffective workers who otherwise enjoy job security. For this reason, administrators try to define the narrowest possible competitive groups. At the extreme, a competitive group may contain only one person (a practice that is frowned upon by many courts and grievance bodies). Employee groups, conversely, always try to keep competitive groups as broad as possible.

For employees unfortunate enough to find themselves in a targeted competitive group, the question of central concern becomes the order of layoff. In determining how each employee measures up in the RIF pecking order, almost all public agencies calculate retention points. Although a variety of criteria are potentially available, most state and local governments in the United States use seniority exclusively or a combination of seniority and performance. If collective bargaining agreements are in force, seniority is usually the sole criterion. Jurisdictions that lack strong employee unions are much more likely to include performance criteria or other considerations in the computation of retention points.

Seniority is measured simply by "continuous service," with one retention point credited for every year of service. Where performance is considered, the results of employee performance evaluations are assigned retention points according to a diverse set of decision rules. An "excellent" performance score may be rewarded with five retention points, while a "poor" rating may earn the recipient zero points. Additional retention points are sometimes granted to veterans (another form of "veterans' preference"), to workers in protected categories (a legally troublesome practice), or to workers deemed to be highly promotable. Courts in some states have rejected the use of performance evaluations as a basis for layoff decisions because they are regarded as being unreliable and even prejudicial (they are thought to disadvantage women and minorities). The practice of granting additional retention points to veterans—followed by a handful of states and the federal government—has also been attacked as potentially detrimental to the interests of women.

Once each employee's retention credits are calculated, "bumping" is set into motion. Bumping refers to the process by which employees with more retention points displace (take the jobs of) workers with fewer points who occupy positions in the same competitive area. In order to lend a measure of rationality to this potentially chaotic process, certain ground rules apply. Employees cannot bump "up"–that is, take the position of a worker in a higher classification. Also, they are not necessarily guaranteed their old salaries after bumping workers in lower classifications. Some agencies, such as the federal government, usually allow workers to retain their previous salaries for a specified period (e.g., two years), while others immediately assign salaries commensurate with the new (lower) position.

Two additional facets of the layoff process are contained in most RIF procedures, "outplacement" and "recall." Outplacement refers to the job-placement services that the agency provides laidoff workers. These may consist merely of assistance with unemployment compensation paperwork, or they may call for the agency to provide a wide array of placement services (résumé writing, job counseling, and the like). Recall provisions detail the employees' rights in the event that the agency's situation improves sufficiently to reemploy some or all of the laid off workers. Employees typically are given a one-year right to recall, after which they possess no more claim on an agency's jobs than any member of the general public. Should a recall take place, workers are almost always recalled in inverse order of termination; the last person terminated is the first person called back.

The Costs and Consequences of Layoffs

Although layoffs offer politicians a seductive means of lowering public expenditures, they are not as cost-free as they initially appear. Both direct and indirect costs are incurred during any layoff.

Evidence of the direct costs can be found in a federal study revealing that each layoff typically requires an expenditure of about two-thirds of the employee's annual salary. This figure includes severance pay, unused vacation allowance, and refunds from retirement contributions. An additional direct expense is incurred in providing outplacement assistance. And, once unemployed, the worker moves from the taxpayer roll to the tax-free unemployment roll, thereby multiplying the direct and indirect costs to government. Analyses of layoffs in other governmental settings have demonstrated that due to direct outlays associated with RIFs, most public agencies underestimate the number of layoffs that are required to make up a given revenue shortfall. Once the layoffs commence, additional terminations become necessary due to the unanticipated costs.

The indirect costs of layoffs are reflected in two major ways. First, layoffs have a profoundly negative effect on the employees who are lucky enough to retain their positions. Many recent studies, most notably the Volcker Commission Report, lament the fact that the civil service is being decimated by the departures of talented workers who are demoralized by past layoffs, furloughs, and similar treatment. Bureaucracy is suffering a "brain drain" that is partly attributable to lessened job security; similarly, it has be-

come increasingly difficult to recruit talented individuals to government employment. Worker morale and productivity have also been shown to decline in many settings in which layoffs have occurred.

The second indirect cost of layoffs is the threat that they represent to equal employment goals. Minority groups routinely bear the brunt of public layoffs. Despite efforts on the part of many public jurisdictions to reduce the adverse impact of layoffs on minorities, a hugely disproportionate number of blacks and females have been victimized by past RIFs. During recent layoffs in state governments, for example, more than 50 percent of all terminations affected protected categories of workers. This phenomenon is attributable to the old adage, "last hired, first fired." Additionally, women and minorities are concentrated in labor-intensive departments that are required to absorb the lion's share of terminations.

Alternatives to Layoffs

When searching for ways to reduce their budgets, public jurisdictions ordinarily begin to RIF employees only after they have implemented less painful measures. The first cutback strategies involve reductions in operating expenditures, after which hiring freezes are usually instituted. By allowing normal attrition and/or early retirement schemes to whittle down the workforce, involuntary separations can often be avoided. One significant disadvantage of this approach is that attrition cannot be planned; it "just happens" and may therefore affect agencies in arbitrary and inequitable ways. Thus, systematic planning is thwarted and productivity suffers.

In order to upgrade their arsenal of weapons for dealing with fiscal stress, some jurisdictions have experimented with a number of innovative strategies that can be employed as alternatives to layoffs. Short-time compensation, for example, places employees on a four-day work week and pays pro-rated unemployment compensation for the fifth day. This effectively reduces personnel costs by about 10 to 12 percent. Another approach is to institute a system of layoff rotation. The basic idea here is to spread the burden of budget cutbacks by laying off workers in rotating shifts. Participating employees may be laid off one week during each four month period, for example. As with short-time compensation, employees participating in layoff rotation would qualify for unemployment compensation during their nonworking weeks. Both of these strategies closely resemble furloughs. The primary difference is that furloughs make no formal provision to permit employees to receive unemployment compensation during their layoff periods.

Other strategies that have been used to avoid or reduce the number of layoffs are payless holidays and job sharing. Agencies with high workloads may ask their employees to sacrifice holidays without pay in order to meet job demands. Job sharing, in contrast, entails assigning two workers to one job. Thus, instead of terminating employees, the agency offers selected employees the option of sharing a position with a coworker. This strategy often appeals to working parents who wish to protect their evening or morning hours to be with their children. The benefits to the organization can be quite high, since employees in a job-sharing arrangement are not normally eligible to receive fringe benefits. Also, they may be "fresher" and more highly motivated than a full-time worker spending eight or more hours a day in the organization.

In sum, layoffs will almost certainly be a fixture within civil service systems for the foreseeable future. These alternatives do not provide a full answer to the problem but are likely to become more prevalent as organizations struggle to meet the pressing demands of contemporary public administration.

STEVEN W. HAYS

BIBLIOGRAPHY

Bureau of National Affairs, 1982. *BNA Special Survey: RIFS, Layoffs, and EEO in State Government.* Washington, DC: Bureau of National Affairs.
Federal Government Task Force on Alternatives to RIFS, 1990. *Alternatives to RIFS.* Washington, DC: General Counsel, Federal Government Task Force, U.S. House of Representatives.
Feldman, Les, 1989. "Duracell's First Aid for Downsizing Survivors." *Personnel Journal,* vol. 59 (August) 91–104.
Hays, Steven W., 1991. "Cutting Back: Reductions in Force as a Management Tool." *The Policy Forum,* vol. 2 (October-December) 16–23.
Hom, Peter, Rodger Griffeth, and Paula P. Carson, 1995. "Turnover of Personnel." In Jack Rabin, Thomas Vocino, W. B. Hildreth, and Gerald Miller, eds., *Handbook of Public Personnel Administration.* New York: Marcel Dekker, 531–582.
Hood, Christopher, 1990. *Beyond the Bureaucratic State: Public Administration in the 1990s.* London: School of Economics.
Morin, William, and Lyle York, 1982. *Outplacement Techniques.* New York: AMACOM.
Rudary, Robert, and J. Garrett Ralls, 1988. "Manpower Planning for Reductions-in-Force." *University of Michigan Business Review,* vol. 33: 1–7.
United States Office of Personnel Management, 1988. *Reductions in Force in Federal Agencies.* Washington, DC: Office of Personnel Management.

LEADERSHIP. The actions of a person who, whether elected, appointed, or emerging by group consensus, directs, coordinates, and supervises the work of others for the purpose of accomplishing a given task. This excludes, for example, fashion or opinion leaders, and leaders of groups designed to enhance the growth or adjustment of their members, or to provide for the members' enjoyment. It has been said that there are as many definitions of leadership as people who write about it. Although this may be poetic license, there is no doubt that the number of definitions is considerable.

Leadership has fascinated humanity for at least as long as the existence of written records. Plato's *Republic* (about 500 B.C.E.) is an early example, but there are even earlier references to leadership in ancient Egyptian documents. The popular concern with leadership is perhaps best seen by the more than 7,500 empirical leadership studies that have been reported in the literature (Bass 1990). The reasons for the popularity of this topic are not difficult to find. Leadership is an ever-present social phenomenon in all cultures. Furthermore, the quality of leadership frequently determines the fate of a group or an organization. In addition, a leader is almost always required whenever a job cannot be done by one person alone. Leadership has been a peculiarly American concern, in large part because in most other countries, the question of who should be a leader was academic since higher management positions in government, business, and the military were automatically preempted by the aristocracy. Also, according to Meindl and Ehrlich (1987), Americans have a strong belief in the importance of leadership as a major force in the development and success of organizations.

Whether this belief is warranted is another question. Pfeffer (1977) has argued, for example, that so many factors influence organizational performance that leadership makes little or no additional contribution. He cites a study by Salancik and Pfeffer (1977), which showed that city mayors account for "only" about 10 percent of the city's performance. However, Pfeffer's interpretation cannot be supported. First, 10 percent is a rather sizable amount of the variance when we consider all the other extraneous factors that a criterion of this nature involves (Fiedler and House 1988). More to the point, a review by Hogan, Curphy, and Hogan (1994) cites evidence that leaders make a difference in samples as diverse as flight crews, United States presidents, and Methodist ministers. Most telling is a study by Thorlindsson (in Fiedler and House 1988) on over 100 trawlers in the Icelandic herring fishing fleet. These ships, usually staffed by a crew of 10 or 11, are highly comparable and fish under highly competitive conditions at times set by the Ministry of Fisheries. Thorlindsson found that the captains of these ships accounted for 35 to 49 percent of the variation in the yearly catch. These findings leave no doubt that the leader does affect performance.

What makes some leaders effective and others ineffective? One problem in answering this question is that studies often define leadership effectiveness quite differently. A leader may be effective on the basis of one criterion (profitability) but ineffective when we measure performance on a different criterion (e.g., satisfaction of followers). Compounding this complexity is that the current week's profits may be unrelated to the company's profitability over the

next three years. Unfortunately, the more delayed the outcome, the more it is contaminated by extraneous events. One strategy is to use multiple criteria in order to assess the pattern of outcomes that result from leader actions. While this may sound good, such criteria as performance, job satisfactions, development of subordinates, and the like usually are not related and cannot, therefore, be combined into one single measure of performance. We shall here focus primarily on performance.

Major Approaches to the Study of Leadership

Leadership theories can be categorized roughly into two types. One type is based primarily on personal attributes and abilities. This includes the charismatic and transformational leaders and influence based on such attributes as intellectual abilities, expertise, and experience. The other type includes the so-called transactional theories of leadership, where influence is based on an explicit social contract, for example, an employment agreement with stated wages, salaries, and working conditions, or a labor contract. Needless to say, these two types of leadership frequently occur together, and there are few pure types. We begin with a brief historical overview and then discuss several transactional theories, followed by a discussion of the charismatic and transformational theories of leadership that more recently came to prominence. Given the limitations of space, we believe the reader will gain more if we discuss one or two examples of each class of theories in some detail rather than try to cover all the theories and empirical studies.

The "Great Man" Theories and Leadership Traits

In the minds of most people, the ability to lead is associated with personality. The view of trait theorists is that "great men" rise to leadership positions because of their superior abilities and attributes. The underlying basis of the "great man" theory is probably the oldest conception of leadership (Hollander 1985) and probably arose as a result of two converging forces. One was the physical, intellectual, and educational superiority of the aristocracy, who were able to enjoy better nutrition as well as educational advantages. The other was the close tie between religion and the ruling classes. Kings and nobles held their place by the grace of God, and every person was expected to be satisfied with the place in the social order to which one had been born. Attempts to rise above one's station were viewed with disfavor and generally discouraged and often regarded as treason. Early research focused on identifying the traits that differentiated leaders from nonleaders or effective from ineffective leaders. Hook, a prominent spokesman for this view, wrote that "all factors in history, save men, are inconsequential" (1955, p. 14).

The trait approach was the dominant research model until Stogdill (1948) reviewed 43 years of research and failed to find one single trait that identified a person as a leader regardless of the situation. While Stogdill's conclusion was interpreted too literally, it spelled the decline of research on leadership traits. Leadership research instead turned from personality variables to looking at the specific behaviors that would differentiate effective from ineffective leaders. The feeling was that if one could identify behaviors that resulted in effective leadership performance, one could then train leaders to use these effective behaviors.

Leader Behaviors

The most influential work on leader behaviors was conducted at Ohio State University. Researchers asked followers to rate their leaders on nine categories by rating the frequency with which the leader exhibited each type of behavior. An analysis of thousands of questionnaires identified two major factors in leader behavior (Stogdill and Coons 1957). These were labeled (1) "consideration" and included behaviors concerned with the well-being and esteem of followers, such as listening for followers' opinions and being friendly and approachable; and (2) "initiation of structure," which included behaviors designed to assign tasks and roles to group members and to focus the group on performing the task.

Unfortunately, the way in which leaders behaved had little to do with how they performed (Korman 1966). One result of these findings was the development of increasingly more complex category systems of leader behavior. For example, Yukl's (1994) Integrating Taxonomy of Managerial Behavior consists of 14 behavioral categories. This and similar taxonomies offer promising new insights of how leaders behave, but they have not radically affected leadership theory (Landy 1989).

Several prominent training programs were based on behavioral theories. One of the most popular was, and still is, the Managerial Grid (Blake and Mouton 1964), which categorizes leaders on concern for people and concern for production. Despite its acceptance by many business and industrial organizations there is little evidence in support of this model or of its effectiveness as a training device.

The Situational (Structural) Approach

The situation approach grew out of dissatisfaction with and the perceived limitations of the trait and behavioral approaches. The view of this school is that leaders are successful (or unsuccessful) because they happened upon the right (or wrong) circumstances at the right time.

Theorists here focused on the task as the primary relevant characteristic of leadership performance. Because the task is generally the most important element in leadership activities, early research focused on differences between tasks as a basis for determining who emerged as the leader (Carter and Nixon 1949). Structuralists saw performance as dependent on characteristics of the organization rather than those of the leader. The best-known researchers in this area include Woodward (1958) and Simon (1947).

The situational school served as a needed counterpoint to the overemphasis on traits and brought attention to another class of variables important in the leadership equation. However, by assuming that the individual is unimportant, it also failed to consider the effects of multiple factors as they interacted in effecting leadership. This final shift in thought was accomplished by the contingency approach.

Transactional Theories of Leadership

Transactional theories of leadership had early beginnings in the 1930s but did not emerge as the dominant theories of leadership until the 1950s. Two primary forces were behind the ascendancy: frustration and disappointment with the trait theories and dramatic post-World War II advances in the applied behavioral sciences.

Contingency Theories

Contingency theories assert that the effects of a leader's personality or behavioral style on performance depend on (are contingent on) the nature of the leadership situation. These theories therefore attempt to integrate the role of personality and situational factors in their predictions of leadership performance. The first theory to do so was the Contingency Model of Leadership Effectiveness (Fiedler 1967).

The Contingency Model of Leadership Effectiveness. This theory holds that the effectiveness of a group depends upon two interacting elements: (1) the leader's personality and (2) the degree to which the situation gives the leader control and influence over the group process and outcomes. The relevant personality component is the leader's motivational structure (the hierarchy of goals the leader seeks to satisfy at work). This variable is measured by the "least-preferred coworker" scale (LPC), which is obtained by asking leaders to think of all the people with whom they ever worked and to describe the one person with whom it was most difficult to get the job done. Low-LPC persons describe their least-preferred coworkers in highly negative terms. These leaders are primarily task-motivated and react emotionally to those who keep them from getting the job done. To these leaders, getting the job done is so important that poorly performing coworkers are seen not only as incompetent but as having generally undesirable personalities. On the other hand, high-LPC leaders describe their least-preferred coworkers in more positive terms. These leaders are relatively more concerned with interpersonal re-

lationships than task accomplishment, so they can view their least-preferred coworkers more objectively, describing them as lazy but honest or incompetent but pleasant.

As we mentioned, LPC measures a motivational hierarchy—whether the leader sets a higher value on getting the job done or on interpersonal relations. The high-LPC leader places a higher value on relationships, while the low-LPC leader values the task more highly. However, leaders do not always behave in accordance with their primary goals. So, low-LPC leaders behave in a task-oriented way only as long as they feel there will be difficulty getting the task accomplished. Once they feel certain the task will be completed, they turn to their secondary goal of maintaining good relations. High-LPC leaders strive for good interpersonal relationships only as long as the situation makes them feel uncertain that good interpersonal relations can be reached. Once good relations with group members seem assured, these leaders turn their attention to the task.

A second major aspect of the contingency model is situational control, which indicates the perceived probability on the part of the leader that the task will get done. It consists of (1) leader-member relations, the degree to which the leader feels accepted by followers and the degree to which followers get along, (2) task structure, the degree to which the task is clear cut, programmed, and structured, and (3) position power, the degree to which the leader's position provides power to reward and punish to obtain compliance. Basically, low-LPC leaders perform best when their situational control is either high or relatively low. High-LPC leaders perform best when their situational control is moderate.

The contingency model views leadership as a dynamic process. As situational control changes, so will the match between leadership style and situational control. It is therefore possible to predict the changes in leadership performance that are likely to occur as a result of changes in the leader's situational control. For example, training should increase the structure of the task and hence the leader's situational control. An experiment by Chemers, Rice, Sundstrom, and Butler (1975) found that training improved the situational control of teams from low to moderate, but training did not improve overall performance. Rather, training improved the performance of high-LPC leaders, but the same training was detrimental to the performance of groups with low-LPC leaders.

The contingency model is arguably the most tested leadership theory and the majority of studies support the model as well as Fiedler's interpretation of LPC. The theory is complex and does not provide easy answers. We shall discuss the training applications of this model in a later section of this entry.

Path-Goal Theory. This theory is an extension of expectancy theory, which states that individuals' actions or effort levels are based on their perceived probabilities that

their efforts (or actions) will lead to outcomes they desire. According to House and Mitchell (1974), then, the leader's basic functions (in order to maximize follower performance) are to ensure that the outcomes followers desire (the goal) are available to them and to help subordinates reach that goal (the path). By doing these things, the effective leader strengthens the followers' beliefs that their efforts will accomplish the task and that task accomplishment will lead to valued outcomes. Effective leadership may lead to increased follower motivation, and also satisfaction, to the extent followers see the leader's behavior as an immediate source of goal attainment or a source of future goal attainment.

According to this theory, the most effective leadership style depends on follower and task characteristics. Essentially, the leader should provide whatever the situation (followers or task) does not. Conversely, leader behaviors seen as redundant are generally met with follower dissatisfaction and/or low motivation. In general, leader behavior should match the level of follower confidence; the lower the confidence, the more directive the leader should be. Mitchell, Smyser, and Weed (1975) found that followers with low confidence were most satisfied with directive leaders, and followers with high confidence were most satisfied with participative leaders. When the task is structured, follower confidence in accomplishing such a task is high. Under these conditions, the leader's directiveness seems redundant, or like an attempt to exert excessive control, and therefore results in subordinate dissatisfaction. When task structure is low, subordinates look to the leader for direction to clarify the path to the goal. Although path-goal theory has been more effective in predicting job satisfaction than performance, it has shed some light on potentially critical situational variables (Yukl 1994).

The Normative Decision Model. Vroom and Yetton (1973) proposed that leader effectiveness is a function of knowing when and how much to allow followers to participate in decisionmaking. Their model defines five levels of participation, from autocratic (leader solves the problem or makes the decision alone using information available) through consultative to joint (leader shares the problem with the group, and together they generate alternatives and attempt to reach a decision). The critical leader behavior consists of the level of participation the leader grants to followers. The key to effective leadership is to decide which behavior to exhibit and when; again, the answer depends on situational factors.

Before a recommendation is made on participation level, seven facets of the situation are considered, from the amount of information available to the likelihood that conflict among followers over the preferred solution will result. The situational factors are listed in the form of questions. Answering the questions leads to a set of alternatives regarding participation level. Once the set of alternatives is

reached, the model supplies considerations for choosing among them. The predictions of this model have not yet been fully tested. Most studies examined only whether decisions made by leaders matched the prescriptions of the model; few attempts have been made to tie these decisions to organizational performance.

Life-Cycle Theory (Situational Leadership Theory, or SLT). Hersey and Blanchard (1982) relate the maturity of the group to prescribed leader behaviors. As in path-goal, SLT's leader behaviors are borrowed from the Ohio State dimensions. Unlike the Managerial Grid, however, which emphasized 9, 9 leadership (high concern for both the task and interpersonal relationships) as the most effective style, SLT asserts that no one behavior is appropriate for all circumstances; leaders must adjust their behavior to the maturity of the followers. Follower maturity consists of job maturity—the task-relevant knowledge, experience, and ability possessed by followers—and psychological maturity—the self-confidence and motivation relative to the task. Note that followers are described by their confidence (perceived ability to get the job done), much like path-goal theory and the contingency model's situational control. This confidence notion seems to be a common thread in many contingency models.

SLT predicts that with an immature work group, the appropriate leader behavior is to be directive with little concern for relationships. Again, note the similarity of this prescription to that of path-goal theory and the contingency model. As the group matures, the leader must maintain concern with the task but also increase considerate behaviors. As maturity increases further, the need for both structure and consideration decreases until, when the group is fully mature, the need for both subsides completely. Personnel turnover, reorganization, or change of mission may reduce group maturity, again requiring leader-specific action.

While SLT provides simplicity and a commonsense approach, there is little support for the model. Group maturity is left to the leader's judgment to determine. Further, the model provides little rationale for how or why follower maturity and leader behavior interact to effect performance. Finally, leadership effectiveness is defined as simply those behaviors that match the prescriptions of SLT; it is not linked to outside criteria of organizational performance. As a result, virtually no reported research supports the theory.

Multiple Linkage Model (MLM). Contingency theories have been criticized for being too simplistic, since they describe leader behaviors or the situation, for example, in terms of only one or two characteristics. The Multiple Linkage Model (Yukl 1989) is an example of a leadership theory that responds to such criticisms. The theory starts by detailing 14 behaviors that define possible ways for leaders to act, including supporting, delegating, rewarding, developing, clarifying, monitoring, representing, and networking. MLM states that such leader behaviors effect group processes, which in turn effect unit performance. In other words, according to MLM, group processes intervene between leader behaviors and unit outcomes. The use of such intervening variables in a leadership model helps explain why the effects of leader behaviors on performance are often delayed; leader actions must first affect the intervening variables before these can in turn affect group outcomes.

MLM consists of two basic propositions. First, in the short term, the leader best improves unit effectiveness by correcting deficiencies in intervening variables (the group processes). Leaders usually have a choice as to which variable to improve and which corrective behavior to use. This choice notion is a substantial departure from other models, which assumed that there was a best style of leadership for a given type of situation. Second, in the long term, effective leaders best increase unit effectiveness by improving the situation. In so doing, they indirectly influence the intervening variable.

The Multiple Linkage Model treats leaders and situations more comprehensively than other models. It also treats intervening variables explicitly, clarifying how leader behaviors affect unit performance. MLM also makes a valuable distinction between short- and long-term strategies for improving leadership effectiveness. Success in the long and short run is often brought about by different mechanisms, and the MLM provides prescriptions for addressing both concerns. However, the model does suffer some shortcomings. It ignores characteristics of followers that might effect their reactions to leader actions. For example, experienced followers may resent leaders who unnecessarily structure the work. Second, there is little explanation of the mechanisms that tie leader behaviors to the intervening group process variables. Third, given its complexity, the model may be difficult for practitioners and trainers to use. Nevertheless, the model must be viewed as an advance over previous contingency models.

Personality, Charismatic and Transformational Leadership

In recent years, a significant number of leadership theorists have moved beyond the transactional approaches to focus on leadership from a variety of perspectives most notably: personalities, charismatic, and transformational leadership.

Leader Personality Revisited

In the past, leadership trait research was often hard to interpret because studies used different terminology. For example, conscientiousness has been called conformity, constraint, and will to achieve, among other labels. Research tying together these and other such studies was therefore never properly integrated because of label confusion. Recently, these personality descriptors have been mapped onto the "big-five" model of personality (Hogan and Hogan 1992), which holds that personality can be described in terms of five broad dimensions: surgency (dominance), agreeableness, conscientiousness, emotional stability, and intellect. The model provides a common vocabulary for interpreting the results of personality research as it relates to leadership (Hogan, Curphy, and Hogan 1994).

Research using the model has been encouraging. Gough (1990), for example, found the dominance, capacity for status, sociability, and social presence (surgency), self-acceptance and achievement via independence (emotional stability), and empathy (agreeableness) scales of the California Psychological Inventory were correlated with ratings for leader emergence. Hogan, Curphy, and Hogan (1994) summed up the recent evidence by stating, "The big-five model provides a convenient way to summarize both leaderless group discussion and assessment center research. The results also suggest that measures of surgency, agreeableness, conscientiousness, and emotional stability can be used to predict . . . leadership potential" (p. 497). More supporting evidence for the role of leader personality should emerge in the future.

Charisma

Although the charismatic leader has long dominated the popular imagination, empirical study of charismatic leadership is relatively recent. The term charisma, coined by Weber (1946), is derived from the Greek word for gift and suggests that certain leaders have a divine gift that enables them to engender such loyalty and devotion that followers will not only obey unquestioningly but sacrifice their possessions and even their lives at the leader's command. Such recent events as the 1978 Jonestown murder/suicide of over 800 people and the similar 1993 tragedy in Waco, Texas, dramatically attest to the charismatic leader's power. Thus, charismatic leadership is an important topic for study.

What makes leaders charismatic? First, charismatic leaders are able to articulate a clear vision of the future, often a reaction to perceived fundamental discrepancies between the way things are and the way they ought to be. In so doing, they offer to help a group move from their present circumstances to a "promised land." Second, charismatic leaders possess a gift for rhetoric—they are skilled communicators who heighten the emotions of followers and inspire them to embrace the vision. They have a strong and unshakable belief in their vision and the eventual achievement of their goals. Moreover, they are skilled image-builders and communicators who can give themselves the appearance of infallibility.

Leaders with these and similar characteristics will not necessarily be charismatic, however. As always, the followers and situation must be taken into account. Charismatic leadership is as much a function of follower reactions as it is the leader's traits. It might even be said that charismatic leadership is defined by these reactions: strong affection for the leader, heightened emotional levels, willing subordination to the leader and trust in the correctness of the leader's beliefs, and feelings of empowerment. Situational factors are equally important in determining whether leaders are seen as charismatic. Probably the most important is the presence or absence of a crisis. Followers who perceive crises are more willing to follow a leader who promises change and a vision to resolve the crisis. Sensing this, some leaders purposely create or accentuate the perceptions of crisis for their own ends. Apart from the power leaders enjoy, followers of charismatic leaders tend to be more satisfied and motivated with their participation, and the groups are more cohesive. However, there is not much evidence that charismatic leaders are necessarily more successful.

Transformational Leadership
Burns (1978) has postulated that some charismatic leaders are also "transformational," that is, able to raise the moral and ethical standards of their followers and to enlist them in actions that go beyond their own self-interest. Bass (1985) and others have supported Burns's theory and shown that transformational leaders also stimulate their group members to greater intellectual accomplishments and unselfish deeds. This is a relatively new development in the area of leadership and will, no doubt, become more developed and systematized in the years to come. Bass and his coworkers recently developed promising methods designed to help leaders become more transformational.

Cognitive Resource Theory
Although it is generally assumed that effective leadership requires a high level of intelligence, technical abilities, and experience, empirical research shows rather conclusively that these "cognitive resources" do not, by themselves, contribute to organizational performance. This conclusion is difficult to accept because many leadership functions involve intellectual abilities (e.g., planning, decisionmaking, and problemsolving). In light of our experience with other leadership factors, and in light of the lessons of the contingency models, it seems likely that the effective contribution of cognitive abilities and experience also depends, or is contingent, on certain situational factors.

Cognitive Resource Theory, or CRT (Fiedler and Garcia 1987), attempts to discover the conditions under which leaders make effective use of their own, and their follow-

ers', intellectual abilities and job-relevant knowledge. CRT identified two major situational factors that effect how the leader's cognitive resources contribute to leadership and organizational performance. First, the leader has to be willing and able to direct and supervise the group. For example, Blades and Fiedler (1964) showed that the leader's intelligence and task-relevant knowledge correlated highly with group performance only if the leader was directive as well as supported by the group. Second, stress, especially caused by conflict with the immediate superior, strongly inhibits the leader's ability to make effective use of intellectual abilities and creativity. In somewhat oversimplified terms, leaders in stress-free situations use their intelligence and creativity but not their experience. Leaders in stressful situations use their experience but not their intellectual abilities. In fact, under high stress, leader intelligence correlates negatively with performance; under low stress, leader experience tends to correlate negatively with performance.

To explain these findings, CRT has advanced the hypothesis that experience represents overlearned behavior and that this type of behavior becomes dominant under stress and in emergency conditions (Gibson 1992). So, under stress the leader falls back on that previously overlearned behavior. Gibson, Fiedler, and Barrett (1993) showed that the language of comparatively more intelligent leaders became less intelligible and that they "babbled" more (more words—less content) in stressful than nonstressful conditions.

These finding are explained by noting that leaders who have experience tend to discourage thoughtful consideration of problems for which they think they already know the answer; hence, the more experienced they are, the less their intellectual abilities will be used. Intelligent or creative leaders are less likely to rely on their own and their group members' intuition and hunch (i.e., experience). This tendency (wanting to consider all options before making a decision) serves them well under low stress, but it seriously inhibits appropriate response under high stress.

Improving Leadership

One reason for the popularity of leadership study is its perceived impact on the bottom line. We also indicated factors associated with leadership effectiveness. Here these lines of discussion are integrated; one can use knowledge gained from research to improve leadership and in turn organizational effectiveness. This section reviews some approaches and major techniques.

Selection and Placement
Sometimes the best way to improve leadership is to match leader and job by hiring individuals to fill a position (selection) or assigning someone to a position (placement).

For this approach to succeed, one must know the requirements of the job; this is accomplished through job analysis. Following a job analysis, the organization should assess the characteristics of prospective leaders. Some characteristics might derive from the big-five model, which indicates traits that predispose leaders to succeed across a range of positions. Specific skills and knowledge required are determined from the job analysis.

Often, organizations assess leaders through résumés and job interviews. A more comprehensive approach is the assessment center, the primary purpose of which is to provide in-depth descriptions of leaders or candidates using interviews, tests, role playing, and work samples. The measurements in most centers provide fairly accurate information about leadership motivation, personality traits, and skills. When this is combined with information about a candidate's prior experience and performance, assessment centers make reasonably good predictions about leadership potential in specific positions (Howard and Bray 1988).

Situational Engineering

One alternative to matching leaders and positions is changing the situation to make it more favorable for the leader, or to conduct situational engineering. The only formal program for doing so is Leader Match. Based on Fiedler's model, Fiedler and Chemers (1984) developed a self-paced training manual assuming it is difficult for leaders to change their leadership style every time their situation changes. It is easier to diagnose situations in which leaders are likely to perform best and to modify situations so they match the leader's style. The training first asks the individual to complete an LPC scale. The trainee is then taught how to measure situational control. The final sections provide instruction on modifying the situation so it matches one's leadership style.

Leader Match has been tested in several studies that concluded the program improved leader performance. A review of leadership training research (Burke and Day 1986) also concluded Leader Match increased leader effectiveness and recommended its use, based on its effectiveness and low cost.

Leadership Training

Another alternative is to change the leader to fit the requirements of the position—to train the leader. Given the perception that leadership effects bottom lines, billions of dollars are spent each year on leadership training and scores of programs are available. Leadership training programs most often develop knowledge and skills relevant for effectiveness in the short term, but newer programs train in areas from self-insight to visioning (Conger 1992). These skills are difficult to develop formally, so specialized techniques like case analyses and role playing are often used.

Although research on the effectiveness of these techniques is sparse, initial results indicate promise, with the most supported techniques being role modeling and simulations. Future research will provide more definitive conclusions regarding which programs develop which skills and under which conditions.

To summarize, leadership is a vibrant and steadily growing area of research, with considerable potential for improving organizational performance. At this point, the most important need for the future is the development of sound theoretically based programs for selecting and developing leaders and managers.

FREDERICK W. GIBSON AND FRED E. FIEDLER

BIBLIOGRAPHY

Bass, Bernard M., 1985. *Leadership and Performance Beyond Expectations.* New York: Free Press.
———, 1990. *Handbook of Leadership.* New York: Free Press.
Blades, Jon W., and Fred E. Fiedler, 1973. "The Influence of Intelligence, Task Ability and Motivation on Group Performance." *Organizational Research Technical Report,* 76–78. Seattle: University of Washington.
Blake, Robert R., and Jane S. Mouton, 1964. *The Managerial Grid.* Houston: Gulf Publishing.
Burke, Michael J., and Russell R. Day, 1986. "A Cumulative Study of the Effectiveness of Managerial Training." *Journal of Applied Psychology,* vol. 71: 232–246.
Burns, James M., 1978. *Leadership.* New York: Harper & Row.
Carter, J., and M. Nixon, 1949. "Ability, Perceptual, Personality and Interest Factors Associated with Different Criteria of Leadership." *Journal of Psychology,* vol. 27: 377–388.
Chemers, Martin M., Robert W. Rice, Eric Sundstrom, and William M. Butler, 1975. "Leader Esteem for the Least Preferred Co-worker Scale, Training, and Effectiveness: An Experimental Investigation." *Journal of Personality and Social Psychology,* vol. 31: 401–408.
Conger, Jay A., 1992. *Learning to Lead: The Art of Transforming Managers into Leaders.* San Francisco: Jossey-Bass.
Fiedler, Fred E., 1967. *A Theory of Leadership Effectiveness.* New York: McGraw-Hill.
———, and Martin M. Chemers, 1984. *Improving Leadership Effectiveness: The Leader Match Concept,* 2nd ed. New York: Wiley.
———, and Joseph E. Garcia, 1987. *New Approaches to Effective Leadership: Cognitive Resources and Organizational Performance.* New York: Wiley.
———, and Robert J. House, 1988. "Leadership Theory and Research: A Report of Progress." In Cary L. Cooper and Ivan Robertson, eds., *International Review of Applied Psychology.* New York: Wiley, 73–92.
Gibson, Frederick W., 1992. "Leader Abilities and Group Performance as a Function of Stress." In Kenneth E. Clark, Miriam B. Clark, and David P. Campbell, eds., *Impact of Leadership.* Greensboro, NC: Center for Creative Leadership, 333–343.
———, Frederick W., Fred E. Fiedler, and Kelley M. Barrett, 1993. "Stress, Babble, and the Utilization of the Leader's Intellectual Abilities." *The Leadership Quarterly,* vol. 4:189–208.
Gough, Harrison G., 1990. "Testing for Leadership with the California Psychological Inventory." In Kenneth E. Clark and

Miriam B. Clark, eds., *Measures of Leadership.* West Orange, NJ: Leadership Library of America, 355–379.

Hersey, Paul, and Kenneth H. Blanchard, 1982. *Management of Organizational Behavior: Utilizing Human Resources,* 4th ed. Englewood Cliffs, NJ: Prentice-Hall.

Hogan, Robert, Gordon J. Curphy, and Joyce Hogan, 1994. "What We Know About Leadership." *American Psychologist,* vol. 49: 493–504.

———, Robert, and Joyce Hogan, 1992. *Hogan Personality Inventory Manual.* Tulsa, OK: Hogan Assessment Systems.

Hollander, Edwin P., 1985. "Leadership and Power." In Gardner Lindzey and Elliot Aronson, eds., *Handbook of Social Psychology,* 3d ed. New York: Random House.

Hook, Sidney, 1955. *The Hero in History.* Boston: Beacon Press.

House, Robert J., and Terrence R. Mitchell, 1974. "Path-Goal Theory of Leadership." *Journal of Comtemporary Business,* vol. 3: 81–97.

Howard, Ann, and Douglas W. Bray, 1988. *Managerial Lives in Transition: Advancing Age and Changing Times.* New York: Guilford Press.

Korman, Abraham K., 1966. "'Consideration,' 'Initiating Structure,' and Organizational Criteria—A Review." *Personnel Psychology,* vol. 10: 349–361.

Landy, Frank J., 1989. *Psychology of Work Behavior,* 4th ed. Pacific Grove, CA: Brooks/Cole.

Meindl, James R., and Sanford B. Ehrlich, 1987. "The Romance of Leadership and the Evaluation of Organizational Performance." *Academy of Management Journal,* vol. 30: 91–109.

Mitchell, Terence R., Charles M. Smyser, and Stanley E. Weed, 1975. "Locus of Control: Supervision and Work Satisfaction." *Academy of Management Journal,* vol. 18: 623–630.

Pfeffer, Jeffrey, 1977. "The Ambiguity of Leadership." *Academy of Management Review,* vol. 2: 104–112.

Salancik, Gerald R., and Jeffrey Pfeffer, 1977. "Constraints on Administrative Discretion: The Limited Influence of Mayors on City Budgets." *Urban Affairs Quarterly,* vol. 12: 447–498.

Simon, Herbert A., 1947. *Administrative Behavior: A Study of Decision-Making Process in Administrative Organizations.* New York: Macmillan.

Stogdill, Ralph M., 1948. "Personal Factors Associated with Leadership: A Survey of the Literature." *Journal of Psychology,* vol. 25: 35–71.

———, Ralph M., and A. E. Coons, 1957. *Leader Behavior: Its Description and Measurement.* Columbus: Ohio State University, Bureau of Business Research.

Vroom, Victor H., and Philip W. Yetton, 1973. *Leadership and Decision-Making.* Pittsburgh, PA: University of Pittsburgh Press.

Weber, Max, 1946. "The Sociology of Charismatic Authority." In H. H. Mills and C. W. Mills, eds. and trans., *Essays in Sociology.* New York: Oxford University Press.

Woodword, Joan, 1958. *Management and Technology.* London: Her Majesty's Stationery Office.

Yukl, Gary, 1989. *Leadership in Organizations,* 2d ed. Englewood Cliffs, NJ: Prentice-Hall.

———, 1994. *Leadership in Organizations,* 3d ed. Englewood Cliffs, NJ: Prentice-Hall.

LEADERSHIP, AGENTIAL.

A principal component of the agency perspective, first elaborated in the *Blacksburg Manifesto* and later expanded in *Refounding Public Administration* (see **Blacksburg Manifesto**). In this normative concept, the agency is viewed both as a social construct of intended rationality and of intended community—a center of social learning, technical expertise, and phronesis (practical wisdom) dedicated to the pursuit of the public interest and ever-mindful of acting for and with other citizens. Viewed this way, the agency constitutes a potentially valuable social resource due to the collective experience of its members in dealing with particular policy areas and with the interest groups and other actors associated with these policy areas.

The public agency is an institution whose members are citizens set apart by the responsibilities inherent in their role as agents for "the rest of us," who are called upon to apply their skills, their experience, and their practical wisdom to the problems citizens bring to government for solution. The public administrator acts as an agent or steward—as a responsible constitutional officer "who acts for or in place of another (the principal) by authority from him" (Wamsley, et al. 1990, p. 117). Later writings by Wamsley have shifted the emphasis from agential leaders acting on behalf of citizens to their acting with citizens as well as for them (Wamsley and Wolf 1996). This concept of public administrators acting as citizens with other citizens in the context of the public agency was first developed by Camilla Stivers in *Refounding Public Administration* in an article (1990) and later expanded in her work *Gender Images in Public Administration* (1993).

Agential leadership does not aim principally at efficiency or instrumental rationality but rather at the fostering and nurturance of legitimate authority in the agency and the evocation of citizen development. This is best accomplished through involving citizens in the search for the broadest possible definition of the public interest derivable from statutory mandates, maintaining fiscal integrity and acting in a manner consistent with constitutional requirements and intent. Agential leadership sincerely searches for consensus on what constitutes the common good within the particular policy area for which the agency is responsible. And the relationship among citizens around a shared conception of the common good, fostered by the agential leader, brings to the agency that sense of community that distinguishes governance from management.

The autonomous, but subordinate, agential role described here is based on unique claims by public administration to participate in the governance process. Those claims include "(1) expertise in operationalizing policy in the form of specific programs; (2) expertise in creating and sustaining processes and dialogue that results in the broadest possible definition of the public interest; (3) skills in community-building politics and the fostering of active citizenship; and (4) guardianship (along with other constitutional officers) of the Constitution and other constitutional processes" (Wamsley et al. 1990, pp. 115–116).

Agential leadership, then, builds upon and goes beyond a traditional understanding of leadership. It does not ignore concerns for effectiveness in the administration of public policy or neglect the well-being of the public organizations and institutions of which it is a part. What sets agential leadership apart from mere management is the primacy it accords to service—acting with and for fellow citizens—and its instrumental role in the development of citizens in the community. These are elements in what the authors of *Refounding Public Administration* have called the "soul" of governance.

KAREN G. EVANS AND GARY L. WAMSLEY

BIBLIOGRAPHY

Stivers, Camilla, 1993. *Gender Images in Public Administration.* Newbury Park, CA: Sage.
Wamsley, Gary L. et al., 1990. *Refounding Public Administration.* Newbury Park, CA: Sage.
Wamsley, Gary L., and James F. Wolf, eds., 1996, *Refounding Democratic Public Administration.* Newbury Park, CA: Sage.

LEAVE POLICY. Provisions for permitting employees time off from work for various reasons. Leave may be paid or unpaid. Governmental jurisdictions in the United States generally are generous in granting employees holidays, vacations, sick leave, and leave for jury duty and military service. Some employers also provide personal leave days with no explanation needed for taking it.

Most government employers in the United States give employees time off for Christmas, New Year's, Martin Luther King Day, Veterans' Day, Thanksgiving, Memorial Day, Independence Day, and Labor Day. Additionally, some give a day off for President's Day and for Columbus Day. In some states, there are also state holidays, which might be given to employees. Individual employees often also are eligible to take their religious holidays as paid leave. In 1993, federal legislation required employers to provide for family leave (see **family leave**). Most of these leave policies have been common in European countries. Holiday leave, as many Europeans refer to vacation, often is more generous in Western Europe as well.

Vacation leave is common with the length of paid vacation time dependent upon length of time employed by the organization. Most governments require six months to a year employment before an individual becomes eligible for vacation. It is common for employers to give one week of paid vacation after one year of employment and then two weeks after three or five years of employment. Increasingly common is an accrual on the basis of months of work. Thus, employees may qualify for a half a day, one day, or one and a half days vacation for each month worked. There usually are rules concerning when the vacation can be taken, how much vacation leave can be accrued before it is lost, and whether individuals can be paid in

cash for unused vacation time when they leave employment with the organization.

Sick leave is common to most organizations in the United States as well. Sick leave is to be used by the employee who is too ill to work or who is likely to contaminate other employees by coming to work. Abuse of sick leave occurs when employees claim sick leave when they are not ill. As with vacation leave, policies generally stipulate when an employee becomes eligible for sick leave and how much each employee is entitled to. Policies similar to those for vacation also govern what happens to unused sick leave.

Employers are required to provide leave for such events as voting, jury duty, and military service. Voting leave is relevant only for employees who work hours which encompass those during which the polls are open. Since polls generally are open at least 12 hours, voting leave is usually not necessary. Jury duty takes people away from their jobs and they usually have no option but to serve. Thus national and state laws protect the jobs of employees in most cases. Although the job must be protected, employers are under no obligation to pay for the time off although most do so or provide payment minus whatever the employee receives for jury duty by the court system. Military duty including national guard duty also takes people away from their jobs. Again, the time must be provided but payment of the employee during that time is not required and rarely is granted.

Many jurisdictions in the United States now provide personal leave days. They are particularly common in school districts and in unionized organizations. Personal leave days, usually one, two, or three a year, can be used by the employee at any time. There may be requirements for planning it ahead of time. Personal leave days have been instituted, in part, to help alleviate abuse of sick leave by granting time without requiring an explanation of what it is for. In some instances individuals are given their birthday off as a form of personal leave.

The Family and Medical Leave Act of 1993 requires employers to permit employees to take up to 12 weeks of unpaid leave during any 12-month period. The purpose is to permit employees to care for family members who require attention as well as to allow ill employees unpaid leave in addition to their paid sick leave.

Leave policies are considered part of the benefits employees receive from employers. They are an added cost to employers but pay off in terms of retention and productivity of employees.

N. JOSEPH CAYER

BIBLIOGRAPHY

Harvey, Barron H., Jerome F. Rogers, and Judy A. Schultze, 1983. "Sick Pay v. Well Pay: An Analysis of the Impact of

Rewarding Employees for Being on the Job." *Public Personnel Management,* vol. 12 (Summer) 218–214.

Romzek, Barbara S., 1985. "Balancing Work and Nonwork Obligations." In Carolyn Ban and Norma M. Riccucci, eds., *Public Personnel Management: Current Concerns, Future Challenges.* New York: Longman, 227–239.

Winkler, D. R., 1980. "The Effects of Sick-Leave Policy on Teacher Absenteeism." *Industrial and Labor Relations Review,* vol. 33 (January) 232–240.

LEGAL SERVICES.

Government subsidized legal representation in industrialized countries, also referred to as legal aid. In the United States, as well as in Western Europe and in some parts of Africa and Asia, provision of legal services entails an economic needs test. The programs are designed to enable the poor to access the legal system by removing the financial barriers.

Historical Background

Modern versions of legal services for the poor have their roots in Roman law. Initially, the poor were able to seek out a patron to assist them in legal difficulties in exchange for services (the *clientela* system). By the Middle Ages in Europe, the feudal structure and the influence of the Catholic Church dictated a different solution. Where the poor could not rely on the lord, the church urged charity. Charity, or *charitas,* meant both individual good works and the more organized forms, created in canon law, that had spread to secular forums, such as representation of the poor by an employee (of the church or the court) and the waiving of court fees (and, occasionally, the assignment of free counsel).

Based on mercy rather than on a notion of justice, this charitable model left the actual provision of legal services to the poor uncertain. In 1215, the Magna Carta promised every man in England the right to justice. From that evolved a right to counsel codified in 1495, with the *In Forma Pauperis* Act.

The emphasis had shifted from mercy, and a reliance on the individual's need or desire to be charitable, to justice with the development of nation-states. By the eighteenth century, with the American and French Revolutions, a belief had taken hold that the natural rights of man, including a right to justice, belonged equally to all.

In the second half of the nineteenth century, following the American Civil War and the reform movements in Western Europe, the basis for the provision of legal services changed. Statutes enacted in civil as well as common law countries created systems for accessing justice that prescribed the appointment of free lawyers and the waiver of court costs for those entitled to assistance. Government subsidy became essential to implement the new laws.

The amount of government subsidy varied from country to country as did the form of the legal services program.

Eventually, four principal models emerged. A modified version of the charitable model, discussed earlier continues today in Italy. The second is a compensated private attorney model, of which Britain's is a good example. Canada and the Netherlands combine the compensated private attorney system with the hired staff model used in the United States. Some determination of economic need is required in each delivery model. Sweden also uses a sliding fee scale to extend legal services to the middle income person. The issues for each in the 1990s are quality, cost effectiveness, and distribution of services. Lack of adequate resources is the primary obstacle facing the African countries with legal services programs, regardless of the model followed, as it is with some Asian countries. The programs in Latin America are distinguishable from the others by virtue of their overtly political agendas.

Practice in the United States

The provision of legal services for the poor developed somewhat differently in the United States than it did in Western Europe. The American colonists, while sharing a belief in a right to justice, did not see a need for counsel to protect that right and created a judicial system that was to function in fairness for all without lawyers. Although the U.S. Constitution promises the right to justice for all, it limits the right to counsel. Legal representation in federal criminal proceedings was not guaranteed until the 1938 Supreme Court decision in *Johnson v. Zerbst.* It was another 25 years before the Court, in *Gideon v. Wainright,* extended the same guarantee to criminal defendants in state courts. There is no right to representation in civil cases on either the federal or state levels.

The first organized legal aid programs in the United States were established in New York (the German Society's *Der Deutsche Rechtsschutz Verein* in 1876 to protect the legal rights of German immigrants, followed by the Legal Aid Society of New York City in 1890) and Chicago (the Protective Agency for Women and Children in 1885, which merged with the Bureau of Justice, established in 1888, to form the Legal Aid Society of Chicago in 1905). They were formed by local business people, civic leaders, and representatives of the newly arriving immigrant populations for the urban working poor. Privately funded, these organizations would pay private attorneys to represent those who met the financial standard set by the societies. Because the caseloads usually involved wage claims, fraudulent installment sales, and usurious loans, in addition to a high volume of family matters, much of the legal work took on a mantle of reform. In the early years, legal aid societies were engaged in a mixture of individual client service and reform activity. By World War I, several large cities in the United States had programs—each operating independently of the other and without the support of the American Bar Association (ABA).

In 1919, Reginald Heber Smith's *Justice and the Poor* was published. In it, he described the unevenness of the administration of justice in America. He blamed the inequality on lack of resources—not enough money to pay court costs or litigation fees; not enough money to afford a lawyer. To address the problem, Smith recommended a national framework for legal services. Eventually, his recommendation was endorsed by the ABA. In 1923, the National Association of Legal Aid Organizations (now the National Legal Aid and Defender Association [NLADA]) was established. The relationship that developed between the bar associations and the legal aid societies resulted in increased funding support nationally for legal services and enabled new legal services groups to start up.

The Great Depression of the 1930s, followed by World War II, halted any further growth in the United States until 1949 when Britain enacted the Legal Aid and Advice Scheme. The act provided for a comprehensive national program of legal aid, centrally funded but administered by the Law Society. To stave off what the various state and local bar associations in the United States feared would be government control, they renewed their support for legal services programs. But it was not until President Lyndon Johnson's War on Poverty in the 1960s that these programs were firmly established.

Through the Office of Economic Opportunity (OEO), local programs were federally funded to provide free legal assistance to the indigent in non criminal matters. The programs hired attorneys to provide both individual assistance and to advocate for systems change. The model reflected the compromise struck between those who stressed community control of the assault on poverty (the Community Action Agencies [CAA]) and the ABA, which emphasized lawyer-driven traditional legal services delivery.

Under its second director, Earl Johnson, Jr., OEO-funded legal services programs emphasized law reform over direct client service because of the greater impact reform could have on the entire class of poor people.

In 1974, the emphasis shifted to individual client service with the creation of the Legal Services Corporation (LSC) under President Richard M. Nixon. That emphasis continues, reinforced by a variety of federal regulations governing the daily operations of the field programs.

Funding constraints imposed by President Ronald Reagan in the early 1980s and continued by President George Bush forced most local programs to reduce services to advice, counsel, and representation in only the most critical areas, such as housing evictions, utility shutoffs, denial or termination of government benefits, and selected family matters. In 1996, Congress passed P.L. 104–134, severely restricting legal services programs funded by LSC. Despite early political support from President Bill Clinton, federal funding for legal services remains under attack.

Despite its weaknesses, the uncertain funding, and the ongoing tension between direct service and reform activity,

the American version of a government-funded, staff-driven legal services program for the poor is looked to as the model for cost-effective, comprehensive service by most Western European countries.

MICHELE T. COLE

BIBLIOGRAPHY

Cahn, Edgar, and Jean Cahn, 1964. "The War on Poverty: A Civilian Perspective." *Yale Law Journal*, vol. 73: 1317–1352.

Cappelletti, Mauro, James Gordley, and Earl Johnson, Jr., 1975. *Toward Equal Justice: A Comparative Study of Legal Aid in Modern Societies.* Dobbs Ferry, NY: Oceana Publications.

Johnson, Earl, Jr., 1978. *Justice and Reform: The Formative Years of the American Legal Services Program.* New Brunswick, NJ: Transaction Books.

Kilwein, John C., 1992. "Local Determinants of Legal Assistance Providers' Litigation Styles: A Tale of Two Cities." Ph.D. diss., Ohio State University.

Rowley, Charles K., 1991. *The Right to Justice: The Political Economy of Legal Services in the United States.* Brookfield, VT: Edward Elgar.

Smith, Reginald Heber, 1919. *Justice and the Poor.* New York: Carnegie Foundation.

LEVEL PLAYING FIELD.

A regulatory framework which does not discriminate between the activities or persons to which it applies.

The notion of the "level playing field" has a wide currency in semipopular and even official debates about public policy. Freely used from the mid-1980s in discussions about international trade, the term is now applied in a variety of contexts, most often to describe a hoped-for situation in which competition between producers will be fair to all sides.

Like all such phrases, the "level playing field" has become popular because it represents an abstract concept in a way that is understandable to most people. It is easy to imagine competition as a game being played between contending teams. It is also easy to accept that in order to be fair, the game should be played on a level surface.

Interests believing themselves to be disadvantaged have been quick to turn this perception to good account. Manufacturers complain that the governments of other countries discriminate against them and urge retaliatory action to "level the playing field." Banks argue that separate regulation for credit unions creates an uneven playing field that advantages credit unions in their competition for customers. Private-sector firms contend that subsidies for state-owned firms competing in the same marketplace should be abolished, and so on.

While the levelness of the playing field is often in the eye of the team captain, the idea has proved a useful way of organizing debate about public policy because of its provenance in economic theory. The concept of the level playing field, if not the terminology, derives from standard neoclassical economic theory. The sporting analogy gives a recognizable form to the economist's view that where there are no externalities, choices between alternatives are best presented and most efficiently made in a competitive marketplace. Governments, according to this view, should not attempt to "tilt the playing field" one way or the other but should aim to ensure that competition operates freely and fairly.

The application of the level playing field idea does not imply that governments should not intervene in private decisionmaking. In some cases, levelling the playing field may involve government in extensive action, for example, where structural barriers or irrational beliefs prevent particular groups from being treated on their merits. Measures to promote equal employment opportunity are justified by their proponents on the grounds that women and minority groups will be discriminated against in the competition for jobs unless action is taken to overcome practices that put them at a disadvantage.

The operation of the General Agreement on Tariffs and Trade (GATT) is another example of the application of the level playing field idea. The GATT provides a framework of rules for trade relations between nations, the most fundamental of which is that trade must be conducted in a nondiscriminatory way. Thus, all contracting parties to the GATT compete on equal terms in each other's markets. Advocates of free trade go further, arguing that there should be no discrimination between producers in the home market and those seeking to export to it—in other words, that there should be zero protection.

The formation of regional trading blocs such as the European Economic Community and the North American Free Trade Area (NAFTA) has brought the level playing field problem to the forefront of the policy agenda in the nations concerned. This is because, if trade between countries within the bloc is to be truly free, businesses based in each country must be able to compete on equal terms in each other's markets. Regulatory policies in one country may give some of its firms a competitive edge in the markets of other bloc members (and where investment is allowed to flow freely, may cause firms to relocate into that country.) Conversely, policies may disadvantage domestic firms, causing them to consider leaving their original location. If countries are not to engage in self-destructive competition or, alternatively, slide into a limbo of lowest common denominator regulation, agreement is required to "level the playing field" in a way that is acceptable to the contracting parties.

Academic critics of the level playing field have taken a number of approaches. The first is that, however desirable the concept might be in theory, in practice, political pressures inevitably push governments into favoring some groups at the expense of others. Indeed, the standard cri-

tique of policymaking in democratic states, Downs' *An Economic Theory of Democracy* (1957), proposes that information asymmetries between groups of producers and groups of consumers will inevitably lead to policies that favor the former at the expense of the latter. According to this view, attempts to level the playing field in one respect—for example, by reducing tariff barriers on a multilateral basis—will simply lead to nations creating other, less visible, barriers to trade as pressure from producers takes its toll.

The second critique is normative in character. It is argued that the role of government is not solely or even primarily to create a framework for decisionmaking that favors no one course of action over any other. Governments are elected in order to make political choices, whose nature is precisely to discriminate in favor of one course of action over another.

Thus, if a government determines that industrial development should be a national goal and decides to favor domestic production over imports as a means of achieving that goal, such tilting of the playing field would be considered a proper use of public power rather than a misapplication of it.

The third view takes issue with those who argue that the way to level playing fields is to fight subsidies with subsidies, rather than attempting to reduce those that already exist. These critics, who are usually economists, point out that imposing countervailing duties on products that receive subsidies in their countries of origin simply increases prices to consumers without necessarily affecting government policy in the offending country.

As competition—for markets, jobs, and customers—intensifies, the rules that govern competition, both within and between nations, will come under increasing scrutiny. Proponents of the level playing field propose that there should be one rule for all. In an unequal world, it is doubtful whether the concept could, or should, prevail. But circumstances dictate that the debate, and the phrase, will continue to flourish in business, academic, and official circles for some time to come.

JENNY STEWART

BIBLIOGRAPHY

Brittan, Leon, 1992. *European Competition Policy: Keeping the Playing Field Level.* London: Brassey's for CEPS.

Downs, Anthony, 1957. *An Economic Theory of Democracy.* New York: Harper.

Spizizen, Gary, 1992. "The ISO 9000 Standards: Creating a Level Playing Field for International Quality." *National Productivity Review* (Summer) 331–346.

Stewart, Jenny, 1994. *The Lie of the Level Playing Field: Industry Policy and Australia's Future.* Melbourne: Text Publishing.

Weimer, David L., and Aidan R. Vining, 1992. *Policy Analysis: Concepts and Practice,* 2nd ed. Englewood Cliffs, NJ: Prentice-Hall.

LEWIN, KURT (1890–1947).

The experimental psychologist who originated the concepts of group dynamics, action research, field theory, and sensitivity theory.

Because he so firmly believed that knowledge for its own sake was not useful to society unless it could be applied, Lewin has been called the "practical theorist." Indeed his most famous statement is that "there is nothing so practical as a good theory" (Marrow 1969, p. viii). The importance of Lewin's place in applied psychology was summed up by Edward C. Tolman (in Marrow 1969): "Freud the clinician and Lewin the experimentalist—these are the two men whose names will stand out before all others in the history of our psychological era. For it is their contrasting but complementary insights which first made psychology a science applicable to real human beings and real human society" (p. ix).

Early Beginnings

Lewin was born on September 9, 1890, in the small Polish village of Mogilno to a middle-class Jewish family. After receiving his doctorate from the University of Berlin in 1919, he began to be interested in gestalt psychology and soon became a "hot gestaltist" (Patnoe 1988, p. 5). The gestalt perception of phenomena as organized "wholes" that are more than the sum of their parts fascinated Lewin.

While a student, and then later as a postdoctorate researcher, Lewin had been drawing attention to himself via his scholarly writings. A cadre of followers, among them American students, began to surround Lewin in Germany. When the Nazis came to power, Lewin emigrated to the United States in 1933 and joined the faculty at Cornell University. In 1935, he left to take an appointment at the University of Iowa, where his interest in social theory and social problems led to a number of significant studies aimed to bridge the gap between theory and action (Lewin 1948, 1951). At the same time, Lewin was becoming dismayed to discover anti-Semitism on American university campuses similar to what he had experienced in Germany. Perhaps because of this, he produced several articles during this time on Jewish themes (Lewin 1939, 1941, 1948). While at Iowa, Lewin began to be courted by both the University of California at Berkeley and the Massachusetts Institute of Technology to develop a center for the study of group dynamics on those campuses. The MIT offer came first, and hence in 1944, he left Iowa to establish his Center for Group Dynamics there. This endeavor also launched a new Ph.D. program in group psychology and attracted talented students who had encountered Lewin's ideas, or the charismatic Lewin himself, and were eager to learn what he had to offer. After Lewin's death, the entire Research Center was moved to the University of Michigan and was joined with Rensis Likert's Survey Research Center to form the Institute for Social Research.

Lewin has come to be regarded as a giant in the field of organizational behavior, because he contributed widely to all aspects of it. His most important contribution to organization theory was to move the focus of behavioral theory and research from individuals to groups (Ott 1989, p. 145). Many of Lewin's students, postdoctoral fellows, and associates—Ronald Lippitt, Leon Festinger, Erik Wright, John P. R. French, John Thibaut, Dorwin Cartwright, among many others—went on to their own distinguished careers in the field. Such authorities as Chris Argyris, Warren Bennis, Douglas McGregor, and Rensis Likert have built their theories upon Lewin's work (Marrow 1969, p. xiv). Lewin died in 1947 at the age of 57.

Lewin's Legacy

Lewin's deep interest in the psychology of groups and group dynamics was stimulated in part by his experience in Nazi Germany. His efforts to rescue friends, Jewish scientists, colleagues, and others from Hitler's death machines raised in Lewin many questions about human motivation and behavior. He recognized the need to explore these questions at the level of the collective.

Through concepts derived from his motivational theory called "field theory," Lewin described social organization as "resting in a state of stable quasi-stationary equilibrium" (Ott 1989, p. 516). It was within this state of equilibrium that Lewin discovered his mechanism to create social change. His famous "force field" analysis described two basic approaches for achieving transformation—adding forces in the desired direction and reducing forces in the opposite direction (Ott 1989, pp. 516–517). Lewin favored the first approach as being more constructive. He viewed these two mechanisms as being able to create permanent organizational and individual change only when used in a three-step process that involved unfreezing, change, and refreezing.

Lewin described his research as being the kind that seeks truth by successive approximations. Instead of trying to produce generalizations of the logical-positive mode, $X = f(y)$, he sought to use metaphor and non-quantitative methodology to produce holistic representations of behavior in organizations. To understand and explain his concepts of the field and its forces, Lewin used the geometrical discipline of topology—a nonqualitative geometry, which he thought more suitable for solving problems of a social and psychological nature (Marrow 1969, p. 36). By this methodology, he was able to graphically represent his key motivational concepts: need, tension, valence, force, and energy.

Many of Lewin's theories are commonplace in the organization theory and public administration literature today; group dynamics, T-Groups (see **laboratory training and T-Groups**), feedback, action research, force field analysis, life space, life value, gatekeeper, space of free movement, and group atmosphere, to name just a few. Through these and other related concepts Lewin provided knowledge of group behavior, the laws of their development, the interrelations between groups, and interactions between groups and individuals. His theories explained things such as resistance to change and the effects of leadership on group behavior.

His career was also shaped by his boundless enthusiasm for collaboration with present and former students, and cooperative enterprises with scholars from diverse disciplines. The result is an impressive array of 100 scholarly documents in English, German, and French.

Yet another contributing factor that molded Kurt Lewin's career was his belief that the scientist must integrate knowledge with responsibilities as a citizen in a democratic society. "He showed that the experimental mode could be placed in the service of change" and that he "was concerned about placing social science in the service of democracy" (Argyris 1993, p. 10). Thus, abstract hypotheses that did not interconnect with problems of the every day life of citizens were of little value to Lewin.

Also notable about Lewin was the way he viewed the subjects in his research. He thought of them as clients, who could help him achieve understanding, as much as he could help them through his production of actionable knowledge.

Throughout his academic career, Lewin displayed a keen interest and direct approach to the dynamics of human minds. Psychology was in its infancy and was not considered a true scientific discipline in those times. Lewin took it upon himself to break through the taboos by treating psychology as a science that could be verified by scientific principles.

Summary

Although he remained at the periphery of the psychology establishment, the Lewinian tradition has "influenced modern life as fully as John Dewey, Marx, Darwin, or Freud" (Stivers and Wheelan 1986, preface). Indeed Warren Bennis, one of the pioneers of organizational development, observed, "Now I have come to believe that we have so carefully disguised our identification that we forget that we are all Lewinians" (Marrow 1969, p. 234).

BREENA E. COATES

BIBLIOGRAPHY

Argyris, Chris, 1993. *Knowledge for Action*. San Francisco, CA: Jossey-Bass.
Lewin, Kurt, 1935. "Experiments on Autocratic and Democratic Atmospheres." *The Social Frontier*, vol. 4, no. 37: 316–319.
———, 1936. *Principles of Topological Psychology*. New York: McGraw Hill.
———, 1939. "When Facing Dangers." *Jewish Frontier*.
———, 1940. "Jewish Education and Reality." *Jewish Education*, vol 15, no. 3.
———, 1941. "Personal Adjustment and Group Belongingness." *Jewish Social Service Quarterly*, vol. 17, no. 64: 362–366.
———, 1948. *Resolving Social Conflicts: Selected Papers on Group Dynamics*. New York: Harper and Row.
———, 1951. *Field Theory in Social Science*. New York: Harper and Row.
Marrow, Alfred J., 1969. *The Practical Theorist*. New York: Basic Books.
Ott, J. Steven, 1989. *Classic Readings in Organizational Behavior*. Belmont, CA: Wadsworth.
Patnoe, Shelley, 1988. *A Narrative History of Experimental Social Psychology: The Lewin Tradition*. New York: Springer-Verlag.
Stivers, Eugene, and Susan Wheelan, 1986. *The Lewin Legacy: Field Theory in Current Practice*. Berlin: Springer-Verlag.

LINDBLOM, CHARLES E. (1917–).

Sterling Professor Emeritus of Economics and Political Science at Yale University; one of the most influential scholars in public administration and public policy of the post–World War II period—best known for his introduction of the model of incrementalism to the subfield of decision-making in public organizations.

Charles E. Lindblom was born in Turlock, California, in 1917 and graduated from Turlock High School in 1933. He received his bachelor of arts in economics and political science from Stanford University in 1937 and his doctorate in economics from the University of Chicago in 1945. He served as an instructor in economics at the University of Minnesota from 1939 until 1946. In 1946, he joined the Yale University Economics Department as an assistant professor. During his distinguished career at Yale, he served as director of social science, chairperson of the Political Science Department, and director of the Institution for Social and Policy Studies. He has been president of the American Political Science Association and the Association for Comparative Economic Studies.

He has been a consultant to the governor of Connecticut, economic advisor to the director of the U.S. Aid Mission to India, and a consultant to the National Academy of Sciences.

He was twice awarded a Guggenheim Fellowship and held fellowships from the German Marshall Fund, the Ford Foundation, and the Center for Advanced Studies in the Behavioral Sciences. He won the Woodrow Wilson Award of the American Political Science Association and the Brownlow Award of the National Academy of Public Administration. He holds an honorary degree from the University of Chicago. He is the husband of Rose W. Lindblom and the father of three children.

Although originally trained as an economist, his contributions have been especially noteworthy as a scholar in political science and public administration. The integration of his insights and training from both disciplines is evident in his teaching and scholarship during his distinguished career at Yale University from 1946 onward.

Professor Lindblom's scholarship has had a major influence on the fields of public administration and in political science in the areas of policy studies, political theory, and political economy. In public administration his most significant scholarly contributions have been in the subfields of decisionmaking in public organizations and in public budgeting and financial management.

Other than Herbert Simon, no scholar in decisionmaking in public organizations has had a greater influence in the post–World War II period than Charles Lindblom. Both his normative and descriptive approach, called various names by Lindblom himself, "successive limited comparisons," "the branch method," "disjointed incrementalism," or simply "incrementalism," have been the dominant explanatory themes in the subfield for over three decades. Even though there have been attempts by critics to dislodge the incremental approach from the mainstream of thought on the subject, today it remains predominant in public administration and policy. Indeed, Lindblom's themes have become such a part of the study of public administration and policy that it is hard to encounter any study on decisionmaking in the public sector that does not devote a section to incrementalism and what Lindblom calls the politics of "muddling through."

Although much of the background to understanding the incremental model can be discovered in Lindblom's book *Politics, Economics, and Welfare* (1953), coauthored with fellow political scientist Robert Dahl, the essential components of the model are found in Lindblom's 1959 article "The Science of 'Muddling Through,'" which appeared in the *Public Administration Review*. This path-breaking article has been reproduced in over 40 anthologies.

Lindblom's model of incrementalism was clarified and broadened further in *The Strategy of Decision: Policy Evaluation and Social Process* (1963), coauthored with political philosopher David Braybrooke, and in his own study *The Intelligence of Democracy* (1965). In 1979, Lindblom wrote an updated version of his original 1959 article, "Still Muddling, Not Yet Through," which was published in the *Public Administration Review*. The study attempted to answer his critics and to revise and expand on his original model.

Prior to the scholarly contributions of Charles Lindblom and Herbert Simon, the subfield of public decisionmaking was dominated by the classical approach, the rational comprehensive model. According to this model, a policymaker in arriving at a decision had to first identify and clarify all of the relevant values, prioritize them, select a series of goals and objectives, develop a list of policies that best fit the ideal goals, and then select a policy that would maximize the value chosen.

Charles Lindblom in the background explanation of his model criticized the rational comprehensive theory as unrealistic in the real world because it assumed decisionmakers had the cognitive ability, complete information, and the time to carry through the rational decisionmaking process without interference from their organizations and from political restraints. The incremental model is preferable according to Lindblom both descriptively and prescriptively because it takes into account the human and environmental limits involved in decisionmaking, and it is a process that is both efficient and consensual.

According to Lindblom, the incremental model is a more appropriate one for explanation of and prescription for the decisionmaking process because it makes the assumption that policymakers are limited by past policy decision and by their inabilities to identify all values and goals because of conflicts among values and individual differences over their rankings in the hierarchy. Values cannot be prioritized in reality because decisionmakers may have difficulty ranking their own values and because citizens may disagree among themselves about the priority of values. To a policymaker, the choice among values is always a trade-off between better and best. Value choices are always marginal at best.

Therefore, goals have to be selected on the basis of limited objectives which are feasible. Desired outcomes cannot be determined without considering the feasibility of the means to attain them. Some means and outcomes have to be ruled out because they are unobtainable. The test of a good policy is not how close it comes to the ideal choice using the rational model approach, but whether the policy achieves consensual political support even when there are disagreements on values.

Implicit in Lindblom's incremental model is an assumption that the democratic pluralistic system provides sufficient political stability and flexibility so as to stimulate efficient and beneficial policy outcomes. In essence, according to Lindblom, policy decisions are gradual, step by step, and marginal when compared to the present status.

Lindblom's scholarship has not only had a significant impact on public sector decisionmaking theory but also on the subfield of public budgeting and financial management. The use of the incremental model to explain and analyze the public budgeting process served to replace the prevailing rational model approach and to emphasize the importance of politics in explaining the process. In effect, it brought the study of political science back into the study of public budgeting.

Although Lindblom provided the incremental model, it is Aaron Wildavsky, one of Lindblom's graduate students at Yale, who applied the model to budgeting in his numerous publications, including the 1964 book *The Politics of the Budgetary Process*.

Wildavsky in his many studies argues that policymakers find it difficult to look at an entire budget comprehensively because of the limitations cited by Lindblom in his model. Instead, decisionmakers generally use the existing budget as a base, examine only small portions of the total, and arrive at their decisions by making minor adjustments in the entire existing budget.

Gloria A. Grizzle (1989) in her article "Five Great Issues in Budgeting and Financial Management," in the *Handbook of Public Administration*, credits Charles Lindblom with another contribution to the understanding of the public budgeting process, the theory of "partisan mutual adjustment," which Lindblom describes as a bargaining and negotiation process.

Decisionmakers who make decisions based on their own goals, and not those shared by others who are linked to them in the budgetmaking process, are referred to by Lindblom as "partisan decisionmakers." In making decisions, all partisans have to limit themselves to only those policy alternatives that are politically possible. Analysis of options is confined to those limited alternatives and choices that most likely will differ only marginally from each other. Policy decisions are made one by one but in the end are viewed by the partisan decisionmaker as a series of decisions linked together. Values in the budgetmaking process are only examined in relation to feasible policy choices not to the ideal.

Policy differences among partisans may arise because of the intensity with which each partisan holds strong views that are attached to the alternatives. If there are differences among partisans as to the best policy choice, these are usually resolved through negotiation, bargaining, and logrolling to achieve consensus.

In the process of bargaining, key consequences of policy choices may be neglected by individual partisans. This problem is resolved by the process of mutual adjustment since key interests will likely be represented in the process, and therefore all consequences eventually will be considered. In the end, the budgeting process itself will ensure the best budgetary choices.

Charles Lindblom's third major contribution to the field of public administration and policy has been in the subfield of public policy. Political Scientist Yehezkel Dror, a major critic of Lindblom's incremental model, credits Charles Lindblom with being the first scholar to accurately use and apply the term "policy analysis."

Just as the incremental model was applied to decision- and budgetmaking, so too has it been used frequently by political scientists to explain the policymaking process. Lindblom was among the first contemporary political scientists to distinguish among the study of policies as descriptive, prescriptive, and as analysis.

Louis Gawthrop (1970) describes Charles Lindblom as being one of the first policy analysts to distinguish between policy goals and policy statements (pp. 242–250). In his early works, Lindblom concretely described public policies as representing broad statements of goals with explicit value statements behind them. The statements, he said, were normative justifications for public action. Specific policy programs, according to Lindblom, were the actual public policy decisions that were tied to the specific objective policy statements.

Although all of Lindblom's scholarship has some application to policy studies, probably the most relevant is *Usable Knowledge: Social Science and Social Problem Solving* coauthored with David Cohen, Professor of Education and Social Policy in the Harvard University Graduate School of Education (1979). In this study, the two authors explain some of the inadequacies of social science and social problem solving such as insufficient integration of knowledge from other fields, misunderstanding of the problemsolving process, and the "mistaken pursuit of authoritativeness," which occurs because of social scientists' failure to realize that their contributions are never complete.

Lindblom and Cohen in their study recommend that social science methods of inquiry be applied to the social sciences themselves, that the criteria for identifying topics for research be altered to expressive, more practical concerns, that social scientists adapt research strategies similar to those used by decisionmakers, and that social science researchers attempt to identify and solve real social problems rather than theoretical ones.

Similar themes to those contained in *Usable Knowledge* are treated by Lindblom in *Inquiry and Change* (1990). Again, Lindblom critiques contemporary methods of inquiry in the social sciences. He devotes a considerable portion of the study to an attack on powerful economic and political elites who, he says, successfully manipulate the public through their political influences.

In 1980, Lindblom published a textbook for the students and teachers of the growing subfield of public policy. *The Policy-Making Process* was one of a number of small texts in the Prentice-Hall Foundations of Modern Political Science Series. In it, Lindblom incorporates most of his previously explained ideas in the policy context. In section one, he provides an overview of policymaking, defines policy analysis and its limitations, explains partisan analysis, and describes scientific and strategic policymaking.

In part two of the text, Lindblom discusses the types of use of political power and authority by policymakers, democratic rules on the use of power, policy implementation, and interest group roles in policymaking. He singles out the privileged position of business in policymaking and the inequality its exaggerated role creates in the system. In the final section of the text, Lindblom analyzes the role of voting in the policy process and the role of citizens in agenda setting.

In political science, Lindblom had made substantial contributions in the subfield of political theory, specifically democratic theory. In his incremental model, his measure of a "good" policy decision is the degree to which a majority of citizens agree by consensus. His acceptance of majority rule as a given clearly places him in the classical pluralism analysis school.

His assumptions are that in a democratic open society, there are many competing elites operating in different policy arenas, and while political and economic power are not evenly distributed, most citizens have some potential power to participate in the decisionmaking process if they feel strongly enough about an issue. No single elite will dominate, all outcomes will be fair and beneficial to all. Bargaining and consensus among groups to reach decisions promote "polyarchy," as Lindblom describes it.

It is no coincidence that Lindblom's early works so strongly endorsed democratic pluralism. At the time he worked closely with Robert Dahl, one of the best-known advocates of democratic pluralism. Critics of the democratic pluralism school argue that it does not fit reality because the powerful elites are often overrepresented, and the poor and politically unorganized are not.

In his later works, Lindblom modified his beliefs in democratic pluralism, perhaps in response to his critics or to the events of the times, the Vietnam War, Watergate, inflation and unemployment, and greater economic inequities between the wealthy and the poor in the United States. He began to question his original view of democratic pluralism, called for major reforms in the political system, greater redistribution of wealth, and criticized the domination of economic elites in American society.

In the 1976 edition of *Politics, Economics, and Welfare,* Lindblom and Dahl argue that Americans are so committed to private ownership and economic control that they cannot reason clearly about any economic relationships. Economic control has been a serious problem in the United States because governments have become more responsive to the wealthy. Governments promote policies that encourage inequality, and business interests are much more influential than any other group in American society. This situation creates an imbalance in interest group competition. Major structural reforms are needed along with major redistribution of wealth, Lindblom and Dahl conclude.

Similar arguments are made by Lindblom in his presidential address to the American Political Science Association in 1982 and in his book *Politics and Markets: The World's Political-Economic Systems* (1977). In this comparative study of the political and economic systems of the United States, Britain, and France compared to the Soviet Union, China, and Cuba, he states that the communist system has provided more equality than the Western societies because Western societies are overdominated by corporate elites.

Charles Lindblom has provided valuable contributions in another subfield of political science, political economy. Even during the many years when the subfield was neglected by American political scientists Lindblom was always linking economics and politics together in interesting and provocative ways. Charles W. Anderson (1978) argues that Lindblom's concept of the definition of political economy is a traditional one, that is, an analysis of the interconnection of political and economic institutions and processes. To Lindblom, the study of economics and politics are not complete unless studied together. Although all of his works involve economics and politics, clearly the studies which emphasize the two are *Unions and Capitalism* (1949), *The Intelligence of Democracy* (1965), *Politics, Economics, and Welfare* (1953), and *Politics and Markets* (1977).

While Lindblom's ideas in public administration, policy, and political science and economics have withstood over 30 years of analysis to emerge relatively unchanged, his scholarship has not been accepted totally without criticism. References have already been made to some criticisms of his view of democratic pluralism. Other critics have attacked his ideas on political economy.

Perhaps the most relevant attacks have been on his explanations and justifications of his incremental model. One of the most common criticisms of Lindblom's model is that it provides no place for the rational model and that it does not totally describe what takes place in the real world. For example, Rune Premfor's review article of Charles Lindblom's and Aaron Wildavsky's scholarship (1981) contends that the incremental model is of more limited utility than Lindblom acknowledges and that in the model there is a conservative bias toward support of the status quo.

Perhaps the two most prominent critics of Lindblom's model are Amitai Etzioni and Yehezkel Dror. Etzioni (1967) argues that Lindblom has provided too simplistic a view of decisionmaking. He says there are actually two levels of decisionmaking: a high level, big picture approach, which addresses fundamental questions and establishes basic parameters; and a lower level process, which aids the decisionmaker in preparing for major decisionmaking. The rational model can be used at the higher level, author Etzioni argues, and the incremental model at the lower level. In a 1967 article Etzioni proposes his own alternative model, "the mixed scanning strategy," which he argues is a combination of both the rational and incremental models.

Etzioni also criticizes Lindblom's model for accepting classical pluralism as given. He contends that in real society the powerful are always overrepresented, and the politically unrepresented and economically disadvantaged are not involved in decisionmaking.

Yehezkel Dror's criticism of incrementalism (1968) is similar to Etzioni's. Like Etzioni, he presents an alternative model, the "normative optimum model," in which he suggests ways and means to clarify values, consider alternatives, and calculate costs and benefits using some aspects of the rational model.

John R. Gist (1989) points out that other critics of Lindblom's model argue that incrementalism is an appropriate model for some areas of policymaking but not others. For instance, incrementalism does not seem to apply in policy areas where there are threshold effects. Policies, he notes, that are primarily affected by thresholds include space, environmental protection, and medical research policies.

Other critics have criticized Lindblom's model for being nontheoretical and for not distinguishing between normative and empirical theory.

Lindblom, while basically defending his theory in his 1979 update in the *Public Administration Review*, does not totally reject the arguments of his critics. He agrees that the incremental model has its limitations and emphasizes that he covers this problem in his 1963 coauthored study *A Strategy of Decision* (Braybrooke and Lindblom). He also says that the incremental model meets Yehezkel Dror's criteria as specified in Dror's "normative-optimum" model.

To the critics' charge that his model is noninnovative and status quo biased, Lindblom argues that societal changes can and do occur step by step and that in the end, abrupt societal changes and step by step changes can have the same long-range effect. Most societies and political systems, he points out, prefer marginal, step by step changes over abrupt drastic one-time changes.

In his 1979 article, Lindblom's answer to all his critics is that decisionmakers should not abandon incrementalism as a strategy but use it more skillfully and carefully. He acknowledges that in his earlier explanations of the model he did not clearly distinguish between incrementalism used as a description of the policymaking process and as a tool of analysis of decisionmakers. Also he admits that in the beginning he did not clearly differentiate among three separate meanings of incrementalism: simple incremental analysis, that is, analysis limited to only those policies marginally different from the status quo; disjointed incrementalism, a prescriptive method of analysis involving all of the steps spelled out in his earlier works: and incrementalism as a tool of strategic analysis for the decisionmaker, that is, a carefully crafted set of logical steps, which can be practically used to solve real policy problems.

Despite the minor criticisms aimed at particular studies and at the incremental model, Charles E. Lindblom's contributions to public administration and policy in the subfields of public decisionmaking, the public budgetary process, and in policy studies have remained significant for over 30 years. His impact in political science in the areas of policy studies and analysis, democratic theory, and political economy have been equally important. Charles E. Lindblom and his ideas will no doubt remain influential well into the twenty-first century.

ROGER ANDERSON

BIBLIOGRAPHY

Works by Charles E. Lindblom:

Braybrooke, David, and Charles E. Lindblom, 1963. *A Strategy of Decision: Policy Evaluation as a Social Process.* New York: Free Press.

Cohen David K., and Charles E. Lindblom, 1979. "Solving Problems of Bureaucracy. Limits on Social Science." *American Behavioral Scientist,* vol. 22 (May) 547–560.

Dahl, Robert, and Charles E. Lindblom, 1953 (2nd ed. 1976). *Politics, Economics, and Welfare: Planning and Politico-Economic Systems Resolved into Basic Social Processes.* New York: Harper.

Lindblom, Charles E., 1949. *Unions and Capitalism.* New Haven, CT: Yale University Press.

———, 1958. "Policy Analysis." *American Economic Review.* vol. 48, (June) 298–312.

———, 1959. "The Science of 'Muddling Through.'" *Public Administration Review,* vol. 19 (Spring) 79–88.

———, 1961. "Decision Making in Taxation and Expenditure." In Bureau of Economic Research, *Public Finance's Needs, Sources, Utilization.* Princeton, NJ: Princeton University Press, 236–295.

———, 1965. *The Intelligence of Democracy: Decision Making Through Mutual Adjustment.* New York: Free Press.

———, 1968. *The Policy-Making Process.* Englewood Cliffs, NJ: Prentice-Hall.

———, 1977. *Politics and Markets: The World's Political-Economic Systems.* New York: Basic Books.

———, 1979. "Still Muddling, Not Yet Through." *Public Administration Review,* vol. 39 (November/December) 517–526.

———, 1980. *The Policy-Making Process,* 2d ed. Englewood Cliffs, NJ: Prentice Hall.

———, 1982. "Another State of Mind." *American Political Science Review,* vol. 76: 9–21.

———, 1990. *Inquiry and Change: The Troubled Attempt to Understand and Shape Society.* New Haven, CT: Yale University Press; Russell Sage Foundation.

Lindblom, Charles E., and David K. Cohen, 1979. *Usable Knowledge. Social Science and Social Problem Solving.* New Haven, CT: Yale University Press.

Works on Charles E. Lindblom:

Adams, Bruce, 1979. "The Limits of Muddling Through: Does Anyone in Washington Really Think Anymore?" *Public Administration Review,* vol. 39 (November/December) 545–552.

Anderson, Charles W., 1978. "The Political Economy of Charles E. Lindblom," *American Political Science Review,* vol. 72 (September) 1012–1016.

Bailey, John J., and Robert J. O'Connor, 1975. "Operationalizing Incrementalism: Measuring the Muddles," *Public Administration Review,* vol. 35 (January/February) 60–66.

Balzer, Anthony J., 1979. "Reflections on Muddling Through," *Public Administration Review,* vol. 39 (November/December) 537–544.

Denhardt, Robert B., 1993. *Theories of Public Organization,* 2d ed. Belmont, CA: Wadsworth, 95–97.

Dror, Yehezkel, 1964. "Muddling Through–'Science' or Inertia." *Public Administration Review,* vol. 24 (September) 153–157.

———, 1968. *Public Policymaking Reexamined.* Scranton, NJ: Chandler.

Etzioni, Amitai, 1967. "Mixed Scanning. A 'Third' Approach to Decision Making." *Public Administration Review,* vol. 27 (December) 385–392.

Etzioni, Amitai, 1968. *The Active Society: A Theory of Societal and Political Processes.* New York: Free Press.

Gawthrop, Louis C., 1970. *The Administrative Process and Democratic Theory.* Boston: Houghton Mifflin.

Gist, John R., 1989. "Decision Making in Public Administration." In Jack Rabin, W. Bartley Hidreth and Gerald J. Miller, eds., *Handbook of Public Administration.* New York: Dekker, pp. 225–251.

Grizzle, Gloria A., 1989. "Five Great Issues in Budgeting and Financial Management." In Jack Rabin, W. Bartley Hidreth, and Gerald J. Miller, eds., *Handbook of Public Administration.* New York: Marcel Dekker, 193–223.

Lewis, Carol, 1989. "The Field of Public Budgeting and Financial Management, 1789–1985." In Jack Rabin, W. Bartley Hidreth and Gerald J. Miller, eds., *Handbook of Public Administration.* New York: Marcel Dekker, 129–192.

Manley, John F., 1983. "Neo-Pluralism: A Class Analysis of Pluralism I and Pluralism II." *The American Political Science Review,* vol. 77 (June) 368–383.

Premfors, Rune, 1981. "Review Article: Charles Lindblom and Aaron Wildavsky." *British Journal of Political Science,* vol. 11 (April) 201–225.

Wildavsky, Aaron B., 1964. *The Politics of the Budgetary Process.* Boston: Little, Brown.

LINE-ITEM BUDGET.

A traditional budget format that presents proposed expenditures according to the object-of-expenditure classification system. Line-item budgets are especially useful for purposes of financial control and are the easiest budget format to link to governmental accounting systems.

The line-item budget is probably the most easily recognized format for government and nonprofit organization budgets in the United States. Nearly 80 percent of U.S. local governments use a line-item format either to present their budgets to elected officials and the public or as a supporting document or supplement to a primary budget presentation in another format. Many state governments also use line-item budgets as either the sole budget format or as a back-up document, as do most nonprofit organizations. Although other types of budgets present more information about the functions, efficiency, outputs, and results of government activities, the line-item budget provides the most detailed information on expenditures for the inputs required to operate government organizations.

Before the twentieth century, budgets in the United States and most European countries focused on the overall expenditure and revenue levels of government agencies rather than the spending details. The U.S. Department of the Treasury compiled the annual expenditure and revenue estimates for each department of the federal government and submitted them to Congress as the proposed budget, without altering, coordinating, or integrating them. Except during wartime, for most of the history of the United States until the end of the nineteenth century, the federal government enjoyed budget surpluses because the government was small and revenue from tariffs exceeded total expenditures. As a result, there was little incentive to limit agency spending or create elaborate budget systems to achieve financial control or enhance political decision-making. Budgets were presented as requests for lump sum appropriations for agencies or functions, without details of either input expenditure categories or expected outcomes.

By the end of the nineteenth century, the fiscal situation in the U.S. federal government and in state and local governments had tightened considerably. At the same time, there was a strong reform movement led by "muckrakers" like Lincoln Steffens and Ida M. Tarbell aimed at cleaning up the municipal corruption that resulted from boss rule in many large cities. As a result of the "good government" movement that was a response both to muckrakers and to government corruption and scandals. There was also pressure from the business community for government at all levels to operate in a more businesslike manner. These pressures began to result in calls for specific reforms because the federal government and many state and local governments were experiencing fiscal deficits as a result of increasing demands for services, reduced income from conventional revenue sources, and lax financial management practices. Rather than pay higher taxes, business leaders wanted government to increase fiscal responsibility and reduce expenses. One way to achieve this was through budgetary reform and increased financial control.

All of these factors converged at the beginning of the twentieth century to create a climate ready for more responsible budgeting methods at all levels of U.S. governments. For example, when the National Municipal League proposed a model municipal corporation act in 1899, it included an executive budget system. The first report of the newly created New York Bureau of Municipal Research in 1907 was entitled "Making a Municipal Budget," which recommended a new budget system for New York City. Similarly, the Commission on Economy and Efficiency, appointed by President Taft in 1910 and charged with improving the way the public's business was conducted, made its first report in 1912, entitled "The Need for a National Budget." As a result of these reform movements, by the end of the 1920s budget reform had been implemented in most cities, states, and the national government. The focus of the reform efforts at all levels of government was on financial control, and the budget reform proposed was the line-item budget.

After being eclipsed by other budget formats during the post–World War II years, line-item budgets enjoyed a resurgence in use in the 1970s, because they are easy to prepare from computerized accounting systems. The compatibility of the object-of-expenditure classifications used in both accounting and line-item budgets simplified preparation of the latter, and many governments took advantage of this as an efficiency move. By the mid-1980s, most government agencies and many nonprofit organizations had access to and used either mainframe or desktop microcomputers for administrative purposes. The prevalence of commercial spreadsheet programs that operated on microcomputers made line-item budgeting even more attractive because preparing a budget with a spreadsheet that could be programmed to perform all of the calculations quickly and easily was so much simpler than many alternative methods. Eventually, as both customized and commercial accounting and budgeting programs became more plentiful and sophisticated, line-item budgets were not the only format that could be produced easily on a mainframe or microcomputer. Nonetheless, the continued popularity of line-item budgets for small organizations is at least in part attributable to their ease of preparation using readily available computer spreadsheet programs.

Technically, a line-item budget is a financial plan developed according to governmental accounting based object-of-expenditure classifications. Objects of expenditure are detailed categories of goods and services purchased by governments, such as personal services, supplies, contrac-

tual services, travel, and equipment. The uniform object-of-expenditure classifications are used in governmental accounting and line-item budgeting systems to identify the exact category of each expenditure of public funds and to establish controls to limit spending to the appropriated amounts for each expenditure category. Table I illustrates a hypothetical line-item budget for a city police department using object-of-expenditure categories.

As Table I shows, line-item budgets are very detailed financial plans for expenditures during the budget year. They provide the highest level of financial control over spending of any budget format and are easiest to connect to a government's accounting system. Most governmental accounting systems also use the same object-of-expenditure classifications as line-item budgets, so once the budget has passed, it is very easy for the accounting staff to establish accounts for every expenditure category. Since a line-item budget is usually divided by agency or organizational division within the government, the object-of-expenditure amounts in the

TABLE I. CITY POLICE DEPARTMENT LINE-ITEM BUDGET

Expenditures and Appropriations	Actual Expenditures 1992–93	Estimated Expenditures 1993–94	Budget Appropriation 1994–95
Personal Services			
Civilian employee salaries	13,166,797	13,264,350	14,706,194
Police officer salaries	62,331,171	61,695,000	65,881,354
Marksmanship bonus	56,182	99,000	99,105
Overtime: civilian	249,802	141,300	21,057
Overtime: police officers	5,557,629	4,449,600	10,790,240
Employee benefits	18,119,505	17,990,250	19,341,010
Subtotal personal services	99,481,086	97,639,500	110,838,960
Operating Expenditures			
Printing and binding	102,721	146,400	161,785
Travel and transportation	108,275	110,850	107,730
Ammunition	107,460	103,050	133,630
Contractual services	889,625	906,600	931,890
Field equipment	740,114	736,050	736,185
Institutional supplies	189,340	210,450	210,465
Petroleum products	702,015	657,150	657,275
Traffic and signal operations	28,013	46,050	46,110
Uniforms	108,486	151,650	226,475
Office supplies and equipment	256,990	315,600	316,345
Operating supplies	159,438	179,400	195,335
Subtotal operating expenditures	3,392,477	3,563,250	3,723,225
Equipment			
Office and technical equipment	10,506	3,150	45,955
Transportation equipment	26,367	825,150	32,500
Other operating equipment	24,561	99,900	57,345
Subtotal equipment	61,434	928,200	135,800
Total Police Department	102,934,997	102,930,950	114,697,985

budget can serve as controls within the accounting system to limit spending to the appropriated levels for each agency. In addition, the line-item budget categories for each agency can be aggregated to show the government's total budgeted expenditures in each object-of-expenditure category. These totals can be useful for year-end comparisons of actual expenditures with the budgeted amounts for planning and analysis purposes.

Object-of-expenditure classifications in line-item budgets provide the most detailed information about the operating costs of government organizations of any budgeting system. As Table I illustrates, a line-item budget includes specific expenditure amounts for each type of product or service a government plans to use in the budget year, from salaries to travel. Within the personal services category in Table I, for example, the budget separates salaries by type of employee, either civilian employees or police officers, and by type of expenditure, including the marksmanship bonus, overtime, which is budgeted in the same categories as regular salaries, and nonsalary compensation in the form of employee benefits. In the same way, budgeted operating costs are shown in detail in the operating expenditures section, and equipment is shown by categories in that section. Some line-item budgets include object-of-expenditure items in more extensive categories than the ones shown in Table I in order to provide even greater detail for planning and expenditure control.

The primary purpose of a line-item budget and its strongest advantage is expenditure control. This is also a major reason that line-item budgets continue to be used in many local governments, nonprofit agencies, and some states, even though other more sophisticated budget formats such as performance, program, zero-based, and entrepreneurial budgets have been developed and gained popularity in the latter half of the twentieth century. Taxpayers and the legislators they elect usually want to keep taxes as low as possible, and one way to do that is to exercise control over spending by government agencies. While alternative budget formats provide many other types of information to assist in budgetary decisionmaking, none of them is as effective for expenditure control as a line-item budget. When used in conjunction with a detailed accounting system, the line-item object-of-expenditure amounts in the budget become absolute expenditure limits by category, precluding expenditures in excess of the budgeted amount in any category without explicit legislative or executive approval and modification of the appropriations.

Line-item budgets have drawbacks as well as advantages, however. Line-item object-of-expenditure amounts tell the decisionmaker or citizen reading the budget only how much the government plans to spend on each item to be purchased or consumed by the agency. They do not provide information about the activities performed by the government agency or the results of those activities. A line-item budget makes it easy for a legislator to know how much a government department plans to spend on travel expenses, for example, but does not provide information on the purpose of the travel, nor on its relation to the mission of the department. If the mission of the department in question is to inspect nursing homes throughout a state to assure their compliance with health and safety regulations, travel to and from the facilities is an essential part of the department's activities. By contrast, some agencies may use travel funds for purposes that are more optional, such as regional meetings that could also be accomplished by conference telephone calls if funds were limited. In that case, however, reductions in travel might require increases in expenditures for long distance telephone charges. Line-item budgets show only the objects of expenditure, such as travel or telephone charges; they do not explain the specific purposes for which the expenditures are needed. This could lead to problems if decisionmakers do not understand the nature of the agency's activities or make decisions solely on the basis of input costs presented in a line-item budget without allowing agency officials to provide additional administrative or programmatic information in hearings or supplemental documents.

Line-item budgets do not include performance, outcome, or results measures that show what is expected to be accomplished by the agency during the budget year, and they do not provide incentives for creative activity. Alternative budget formats tend to focus the attention of decisionmakers on particular criteria for budget allocation other than financial control. As a result, when decisionmakers are concerned about outcomes or efficiency but also want to exercise control over spending, a combination of formats is often used. In these cases, the other format provides programmatic or efficiency information and the line-item budget serves as a back-up document for fiscal control, accountability, and linkages to the accounting system.

Most nonprofit, nongovernmental organizations (NGOs) use line-item budgets. Although some NGOs present their budgets to their boards of directors, members, or the public in a programmatic format, nearly all of the them prepare line-item budget documents for both decisionmaking and financial control. The annual reports of nonprofit organizations tend to include information about their activities and accomplishments as well as their financial statements, but budgets usually contain only line-item object-of-expenditure information. The main reason for line-item budgeting in nonprofit organizations is an emphasis on financial control. Except for a few wealthy foundations or extremely well endowed organizations, nonprofits tend to have limited budgets and may have to account for their use of funds to a number of financial supporters and granting agencies, all of which usually require detailed expenditure accounting. Line-item budgets with their natural linkages to accounting systems are more amenable to this type of expenditure control and reporting than are other formats.

In addition, many nonprofit organizations receive most of their funding from government or foundation grants. Granting agencies usually require line-item budgets as part of their grant proposals. It is easier for those non-profits to use the same type of budget for both the grant proposals and for their own decisionmaking, especially if more than one grant is received. Aggregation of several grant budgets for overall NGO budgeting purposes and subsequent disaggregation for grant reporting to the donor agencies is easiest to accomplish with a line-item budget. Similarly, some membership nonprofit organizations that need to report the use of membership contributions or dues find that line-item budgets are often the format with which the members feel most comfortable. In some cases, nonprofit organizations with multiple programs or purposes use an alternative budget format to show fund allocation by program and a supplemental line-item budget for financial control and accountability to donors or members.

The traditional line-item budget is a versatile tool for financial accountability and expenditure control, but provides limited information beyond the cost of specific object-of-expenditure inputs. It is most often used as a supplemental or back-up document in large governments, including large cities, counties, and states, but is used as the main or only budget document more often in smaller governments and nonprofit organizations. It is likely that line-item budgets, with their advantages of financial control, accountability for every penny, and ease of preparation on computers, will continue to be used in some form as long as budget scarcity and the need for accountability and efficiency prevail in the public sector. Legislators, city council members, county supervisors, nonprofit boards of directors, and other elected and appointed officials responsible for the use of public funds will continue to value the strengths of line-item budgets, even while they use other budget formats or additional sources of information to compensate for their deficiencies.

GLEN HAHN COPE

BIBLIOGRAPHY

Aronson, J. Richard, and Eli Schwartz, eds., 1981. *Management Policies in Local Government Finance.* Washington, DC: International City/County Management Association.

Burkhead, Jesse, 1956. *Government Budgeting.* New York: John Wiley & Sons.

Cope, Glen Hahn, 1995, "Budgeting for Performance in Local Government." In *Municipal Year Book 1995.* Washington, DC: International City/County Management Association, 42–52.

Mikesell, John L., 1995. *Fiscal Administration: Analysis and Applications for the Public Sector,* 4th ed. Belmont, CA: Wadsworth.

LINE-ITEM VETO.

The power of chief executives to veto lines or items of an appropriations bill without having to negate the entire bill. The line-item veto, possessed by 43 governors, developed in part because the executive veto, possessed by 49 governors, was ineffective when dealing with wasteful and pork-barrel spending in appropriations bills. Unlike other bills, appropriations bills are not constitutionally limited to one subject, represent a wide variety of compromises on state policy and typically contain many items favored by the governor as well as a few objectional items added to the executive budget by the legislature. Vetoing such a bill is always extremely difficult and usually unthinkable for governors. The line-item veto was intended to restore the governor's ability to protect the executive budget by being able to veto objectional elements of appropriations bills. It first appeared in the Constitution of the Confederate States of America (1861). Article I, Section 7 of that document states, "The President may approve any appropriation and disapprove any other appropriation in the same bill." Georgia (1865) was the first state to adopt the line-item veto. Today, only Indiana, Maine, New Hampshire, Nevada, Rhode Island, and Vermont do not have the line-item veto, and North Carolina has neither the line-item veto nor the executive veto.

Defining the Items

A common misperception about the line-item veto is that it is only used to eliminate appropriation (dollar) items. However, item vetoes commonly are directed against narratives that impose conditions or limitations on items of expenditure or against narratives that constitute substantive legislation. For example, in Georgia between 1962 and 1992 only 26 percent of line-item vetoes were used to eliminate specific appropriations of money. There has been a substantial amount of litigation regarding the prerogative of legislatures to include narrative provisions in appropriations bills and of governors' authority to veto them. Unfortunately, court decisions have resulted in numerous inconsistencies on these matters among the states.

Item Reduction Veto

The item reduction veto is a special form of the line-item veto possessed by governors in approximately one-fourth of the item veto states. Emergence of the reduction veto resulted from failure of the ordinary item veto to achieve its objectives. Legislaturses began to bundle objects of expenditure into broad appropriation categories so as to make the negation of particular projects or items difficult, if not impossible. Even if the legislature used detailed line-items in appropriations bills, governors found the ordinary item veto wanting if they wished to reduce appropriations rather than entirely negate them. The item reduction veto was an attempt to revitalize the ordinary line-item veto by including power to reduce, just as years earlier the ordinary line-item veto was an attempt to restore the ability of governors to protect their executive budgets by being able to remove selected items from appropriations bills. Ten state constitutions provide for the power of item reduction: Alaska, California, Hawaii, Illinois, Massachusetts, Missouri, Nebraska, New Jersey, Tennessee, and West Virginia. The Pennsylvania Supreme Court interpreted the line-item veto provision so as to include a reduction feature.

Amendatory Veto

The amendatory veto is another form of gubernatorial veto authority, which is related to the line-item veto. In seven states, governors may make changes in an enacted bill and return it to the legislature with approval contingent upon legislative acceptance of the changes. If the legislature does not accept the governor's changes, the bill is vetoed. Like the item reduction veto, the amendatory veto gives governors more flexibility than does the ordinary line-item veto. The amendatory veto often is used to make technical corrections in enacted bills, but when it is used to change legislative intent, it tends to strain the executive-legislative relationship.

Legislative Overrides

Of the states with gubernatorial line-item vetoes, five allow a simple majority of the legislature to override such a veto, 32 required a two-thirds vote, and five require a three-fifths vote. However, irrespective of the majority requirement, overrides in many states are not feasible because appropriations bills typically are passed near the end of the legislative session and if legislatures are restricted in the number of days per year they are permitted to meet they may not be in session to respond to the governor's vetoes. Further, legislative overrides may not occur because some items are inserted in appropriations bills to satisfy the constituency and district needs of individual legislators with the expectation that governors will protect the fiscal interests of the state (and absorb political blame) by vetoing such items.

Presidential Line-Item Veto

In 1996, Congress enacted legislation that gives the president the equivalent of the line-item veto in the form of enhanced rescission authority. The new authority, which took effect on January 1, 1997, ends the requirement that the president must approve or reject an appropriations bill in its entirety. A true line-item veto probably would require

the amendment of Article I, Section 7 of the U.S. Constitution, which requires the president to approve or disapprove all bills in their entirety.

Within five days of signing an appropriations bill, the president can transmit to Congress a message listing items to be rescinded. This feature differs from state line-item vetoes, which permit governors to strike lines and items from appropriations bills only at the time such bills are considered for signature. Rescissions may include items in lump-sum categories that are more fully described in committee reports, but may not extend to policy provisions attached to appropriations bills or to limitations or restrictions on how funds are to be spent. The lump-sum category in an appropriations bill that included the rescinded items then would be reduced by the amount designated for the rescinded items. Line-item rescissions must go to deficit reduction—the so-called lockbox provision of the act. Budget caps in the discretionary portion of the budget would be reduced by the amounts vetoed. Rescissions would take effect unless Congress passed a disapproval bill within a period of 30 days in which both houses of Congress are in session. Enhanced rescission is a variation of the rescission authority found in the Congressional Budget and Impoundment Control Act (1974). However, in contrast to that act the new line-item veto legislation places the burden on Congress to disapprove rescissions in order to prevent them from becoming law. The president could veto a disapproval bill. Congress could override a presidential veto by a two-thirds veto. The new law allows the president to rescind, in addition to spending items, special interest tax breaks (defined as benefiting 100 or fewer beneficiaries), and new entitlement legislation in nonappropriations bills.

The new enchanced rescission/item veto was attained through legislative enactment rather than the more difficult process of constitutional amendment. The constitutionality of this action may be questionable because Article I, Section 7 of the U.S. Constitution gives the president only three options when considering acts of Congress: to sign them, veto them, or permit them to become law without signature. Enhanced rescission gives the president authority to make substantive changes in a law after it has been enacted and signed. This delegation of authority to the president is the most important aspect of the new legislation because unlike state appropriation acts, federal appropriations typically contain lump-sums, not line-items. Vetoing an entire appropriations act would almost always be unthinkable for a president. Whether or not enhanced rescission is a permissible delegation to the president of authority granted to Congress in Article I remains to be determined. In anticipation of this question, the new legislation provided for expedited appeal to the Supreme Court of suits challenging its constitutionality.

Item Reduction Veto and Enhanced Rescission: The Similarity

In the states, the item reduction veto has been more effective than the ordinary line-item veto in controlling wasteful and pork-barrel spending. The president's new enhanced rescission authority is similar to the item reduction veto available to some governors. Although a provision of the enhanced rescission law, which permits only entire items to be rescinded, seems to preclude the reduction of items, in effect, enhanced rescission will be a reduction veto. Federal appropriations bills typically contain lump-sum categories, not line-items. Dollar amounts in lump-sum appropriation categories are identifiable as items only when they are linked to item descriptions in committee reports. When lump-sum categories are reduced by the dollar amounts associated with rescinded items described in committee reports, the rescission may be of an entire item, but it also will be a reduction of the lump-sum category.

Fiscal and Institutional Expectations

The line-item veto usually is characterized as an instrument for eliminating wasteful and pork-barrel spending and controlling total government spending. However, it probably has been more effective in eliminating selected pork-barrel items than in controlling overall spending. At the federal level, the line-item veto in the form of enhanced rescission may be effective in eliminating some wasteful expenditures and pork-barrel items, but probably it will be ineffective in dealing with deficits and debt.

Originators of the item veto also viewed it as enhancing the role of the governor in the appropriations process and strengthening the executive budget. They sought to establish an appropriations process where the budget that was prepared by the chief executive could be defended by the line-item veto from legislative tendencies to add constituency and district-oriented spending items. Opponents of the new presidential item veto argue that the president's budget preparation and execution powers already are so strong that the addition of the item veto will contribute to an imbalance in the separation of power between Congress and the president. That possibility can only be assessed in the future.

GLENN ABNEY AND THOMAS P. LAUTH

BIBLIOGRAPHY

Abney, Glenn and Thomas P. Lauth, 1985. "The Line-Item Veto in the States: An Instrument for Fiscal Restraint or an Instrument for Partisanship?" *Public Administration Review,* vol. 45 (May/June) 372–377.

Bellamy, Calvin, 1988. "Item Veto: Shield Against Deficits or Weapon of Presidential Power?" *Valparaiso University Law Review,* vol. 22: 557–591.
———, 1989. "Item Veto: Dangerous Constitutional Tinkering." *Public Administration Review,* vol. 49 (January/February) 46–51.
Cronin, Thomas E. and Jeffrey J. Weill, 1985. "An Item Veto for the President?" *Congress and the Presidency,* Vol. 12 (Autumn) 127–151.
Fisher, Louis, and Neal Devins, 1986. "How Successfully Can the States' Item Veto Be Transferred to the President?" *Georgetown Law Review,* vol. 75: 159–157.
Gosling, James J.,1986. "Wisconsin Item Veto Lessons." *Public Administration Review,* vol. 46 (July/August) 292–300.
Lauth, Thomas P., 1996. "The Line-Item Veto in Government Budgeting." *Public Budgeting and Finance,* vol. 16 (Summer) 97–110.
Moe, Ron C., 1985. "Prospects for the Item Veto at the Federal Level: Lessons from the States," National Academy of Public Administration Occasional Paper, Washington, DC, 1–34.
Nice, David N., 1988. "The Item Veto and Expenditure Restraint. " *Journal of Politics,* vol. 50 (May) 487–499.
Reischauer, Robert D., 1995. "Statement on the Statutory Item Veto Proposals," Congressional Budget Office Testimony before the Committee on Governmental Affairs, United States Senate, and Committee on Government Reform and Oversight, U.S. House of Representatives, Washington, DC (January 12), 1–18.
Thompson, Pat, and Steven R. Boyd, 1994. "Use of the Item Veto in Texas, 1940–90." *State and Local Government Review,* vol. 26 (Winter) 38–45.
Wells, Roger, 1924. "The Item Veto and State Budget Reform." *American Political Science Review,* vol. 18 (November) 782–791.

LINE AND STAFF CONFLICT.

The inherent organizational conflict between command oriented line managers and the more bureaucratically focused managers of staff supplied goods and services.

From the literature on organization, the two concepts of line and staff are found. The first centers around the type of functions performed; the second emphasizes the nature of authority relationships existing within and between line and staff.

The functional concept of line and staff perceives an organization as an entity built around those functions that contribute directly and substantially to the accomplishment of the organization's goals and those that contribute indirectly and nonsubstantially to the organization's goals. The former is identified as line; the latter as staff. The line function is concerned with the activities associated with primary organizational objectives; whereas the staff function is concerned with activities auxiliary to and supportive of the line.

The authority concept recognizes that line and staff are distinguished by their authority relationships rather than their functions. Line authority is characterized by an unbroken chain of command authority within the "kernel" of organizational activities and policy; staff has no direct command authority over any part of organization except the immediate subordinates within a staff department. Staff advises, assists, and counsels the line organization.

From the viewpoint of public administration, the line is involved in executing public policy and implementing programs of a government agency and also holds accountability and responsibility for the outcome of its performance. Line is embodied by the structure of organization as a hierarchy of authority, ranging from the chief executive all the way down to the rank of a clerk, police officer, and foot soldier. Staff is devised to support the most efficient and effective way in which the line works to carry out public policy.

King, president, prime minister, governor, and mayor are all line officers in government. In the case of the United States of America at the federal level, the secretary of cabinet departments and its unbroken direct chain of subordinates constitute line authority under the direct command of the president. For example, the Executive Office of the President of the United States (commonly abbreviated as EOP) is widely known as a hallmark symbol of the most powerful staff office in the U.S. government, comprising the Office of Management and Budget (OMB), the National Security Council (NSC), the Domestic Policy Staff, and the White House Office (WHO). The EOP is designed to serve as advisory staff assisting only the president but has no direct command authority over the members of cabinet departments and their subordinates.

The line authority of a state government oversees primary programs directly associated with major policies of the state government, including administration of criminal justice, education, and highways. At the county and municipal levels of a government, the major responsibilities of the line include the recording of property, administration of police, fire, recreation, zoning, and the removal of garbage and sewage. Staff in the state and local governments is designed to relieve extraneous burdens laid on governors, mayors, and city managers with respect to planning, legal process, and research.

Staff evolves in response to the need for assistants or advisors as "eyes, ears, and brains" for the line, who normally has neither time nor special skills and professional knowledge in dealing with sophisticated and diverse management problems. In view of the rapid pace of technological change, an unpredictable and competitive environment, and unprecedented fiscal constraints, the line is expected to require more professional advice and technical assistance from staff in dealing with these problems.

To avoid unnecessary confusion and conflicts between line and staff, it is important that the organization is built on a structure that clearly draws the boundary between line and staff. The distinction between line and staff can only be made by formal authority, not by person, and should explicitly be illustrated in the organizational chart. The staff's functional authority should be clearly defined in terms of its scope and relationships with the line authority.

From a theoretical view of organizational structure, the authority relationships between line and staff are discerned so decisively that there may be neither confusion nor conflict, but only order and harmony in their relationships. In reality, however, it is almost impossible to draw a precise boundary delineating which organizational authorities belong exclusively to line and which functional activities are confined only to staff. From a managerial viewpoint, the distinction between line and staff in an organization is often obscure.

The obscure relationship between line and staff tends to result in conflicts in management practice contrary to the harmonious relationship between line and staff envisioned by management theorists. This conflict produces one of the most serious management problems, dichotomizing separate sources of authority within an organization, thereby undercutting the organization's effectiveness.

A careful review of the historical development of line-staff concepts is necessary for an understanding of causes of, and possible remedies for, the "menacing" line and staff conflict. This review process entails critical examination of the conceptual foundation of line and staff, the tracing of the origins of modern line and staff practice, and investigations of the authority relationships between the line and staff in organizations.

Historical Development

A historical development of line and staff concepts can be traced back to the ancient political and military systems. James Mooney (1947) found applications of staff concepts in the ancient Greek senate, in the early Roman senate, and in the central administration of Catholic church organizations consisting of the College of Cardinals and the different divisions of Curia.

The modern concept of line and staff was originated from military antecedents in Europe and the United States. It was recorded as early as the seventeenth century, when Gustavus Adolphus of Sweden began to use a general staff in the military. In the early nineteenth century, General Gerhard von Scharnhorst instituted a general staff in the Prussian army designed to help army field commanders carry out a variety of auxiliary functions. The army general staff was not established to affect in any way the formal army line command authority but only to act as an auxiliary function to the army command following the strict chain of command.

For the U.S. Army, the general staff was instituted during the War of 1812, only to be confined to the area of auxiliary service functions such as furnishing supplies. The limited functions continued in the army until 1904 when Mr. Elihu Root, the secretary of war, made an effort to adopt a plan for a modern general staff that performed overall planning. According to John M. Pfiffner and Robert Presthus (1967), for many years thereafter the general staff mixed administrative and planning functions; not until after World War I did the general staff's functions as a planning agency become finally established. Staff activities were regarded as very different from those of line.

In the private sector, the modern concept of staff function was widely developed at a rapid pace after the Great Depression, as business organizations grew in size, resulting in greater complexities of management problems such as labor, legal, technical, and government regulations.

Staff was widely adopted as a functional necessity, as observed in the development of organizations in the private as well as public sectors. It increased an organization's ability to deal with problems through professional assistance, not only in relieving the burden of line's work loads but also in helping line concentrate on policy and administrative matters.

Public administration learned a principal lesson on the concept of staff from the general staff practices of the army as well as civilian management. Since the establishment of the Executive Office of the President of the United States, including the White House Office by the Reorganization Act of 1939, as advisory staff to the president of the United States, the White House staff increased its size in number and expanded the scope of its influence as well.

Academic research studies on line and staff were very active during the 1950s and 1960s. Both empirical research and theoretical discussions were found in the literature, notably beginning with the empirical studies by Melvin Dalton (1950, 1959), Robert Golembiewski (1966, 1967), Harold Koontz and Cyril O'Donnell (1972), and James Belasco and Joseph Alutto (1969). However, during the 1970s and 1990s the level of academic enthusiasm in this subject declined only to find a few studies including Philip Browne and Robert Golembiewski (1974), and Hillel Schmid (1990) even though the importance of the relationships between the line and staff remains unchanged. Only a brief introduction to the key concept of line and staff is sketched in the most basic introductory textbooks of business management and public administration.

Conceptual Framework

Organization structure is classified into line command and functional authority depending on the nature of authority and type of activities involved. The authority of command is line authority, where power is located to make final decisions affecting the primary goal of an organization. The concept of the line authority is synonymous with the unity of command and scalar principle as Henri Fayol (1949), James Mooney and Allan Reiley (1931), and Luther Gulick and Lyndall Urwick (1937) advocated in *Principles of Management.* Line is viewed as having relatively unlimited and ultimate authority to supervise and give orders to subordinates, including the staff under its command.

On the other hand, functional authority of staff is the authority of ideas over particular policies, processes, and practices, of which the scope of authority is limited to the extent the line delegates its authority to staff functions depending upon what functional activities are needed in an organization. However, it should be noted that these staff functions are not directly aligned with the scalar process but serve only an auxiliary and supplementary function, adhering to the line sideways along the main primary course of the organization.

Staff is categorized into three types according to its roles: personal staff, general staff, and specialized staff.

Personal Staff

A special position is created for a person to perform the role as a personal aide assigned to a particular individual rather than to an entire organization and to serve only in the limited and fixed portion of authority that the line delegates to the staff; often a personal aide represents the superior in various function. Standard performance involves administrative details, routine management practices, and daily normal operations. The "assistant-to" is designated as an organizational title (substituting for "personal staff") where frequent personnel turnovers or mobility of high-ranking officials require that there be relatively stable and permanent staff sufficiently familiar with organizational activities, programs, and procedures in organizations of considerable size such as government, big corporations, and the military. The personal staff is considered as the traditional pure concept of staff role of advice and assistant to line. Staff has no authority to force the line to accept or implement what it advises. If the line accepts staff's advice, it becomes line's idea and line's responsibility.

General Staff

The top management level of an organization often needs general staffs who are required to support line based on their special knowledge and skills in accomplishing the primary goal, such as planning, disseminating, and evaluating information, reviewing and summarizing reports, analyzing problems, and recommending solutions. They are usually considered as immediately related to the chief executive, but they have their own hierarchical structure within the general staff.

The army has adopted the general staff concept by having general officers in charge of the separate functions of G-1 for personnel staff, G-2 for intelligence staff, G-3 for operation staff, and G-4 for supply staff. Each staff has its own hierarchical authority, confined to its staff's substructure in the organization.

The advice of general staff is often compulsory, sought and consulted but not necessarily followed, by the line manager depending on the purpose, nature, and timing of advice. In general, it should be spelled out but should not limit the discretion of the line executive.

Specialized Staff

Equipped with unique professional, technical, personal knowledge or skills of a scientific, technical, health, or legal nature, the specialized staff serves as adviser or consultant to a certain portion of the organization (or the entire organization), just like line officers.

Specialized staff is similar to the general staff concept in the army in that it can assist or advise other managers above or below it but cannot order other managers to take particular actions, even if those managers are of a lower rank in the hierarchy. The general and specialized staffs, however, may exert line authority by issuing orders not only to their own subordinates but also to other departments upon authorization obtained from the chief executive.

The use of specialized staffs is commonly found in all types of organizations in environmental, health, labor, and legal fields, in which staff services are often legally mandated by the law or necessitated by internal needs for specialized functions. In these organizations, the staff's special advice and opinions are required to be concurrently consulted and agreed upon by the line executive before a final decision is reached. In this respect, the line manager's discretion is limited.

The line executive and the specialized staff share harmoniously and concurrently the authority of making final decisions and of implementing programs on matters legally mandated and technically required. The specialized staff is a part of the line executive's decision and implementation processes.

When staff is authorized by the line executive to give an order to a line manager, staff acts on behalf of the line executive and the action carries the same weight as an order from a line superior. It imposes the greatest limitation on the line manager's discretion. An order may be rescinded by a superior executive, but until an order is rescinded, it stands. This type of staff authority is usually limited to specific functions of a job about which a staff person has a particular expertise. But the staff cannot order other line managers of a lower rank to take particular action, except those under the staff's immediate supervision.

The Conflict Between Line and Staff

Contrary to the principles of unity of command, which recognizes no conflict between line and staff, the line-staff conflict is imbedded in organizational practice, undercutting the organization's ability to achieve its goals. This conflict discards harmonious relationships of cooperation and coordination between line and staff. The conflict tends to perpetuate, causing increasing resentment, frustration, and frictions, thereby demoralizing and hampering the organization's human resources.

Major sources of the conflict between line and staff are generally related to the blurring line and staff distinctions, the separate responsibilities and priorities, the different behavioral patterns of line and staff, and the dispute over authority relationships.

The Blurring of Line-Staff Authority Distinctions

The modern environment, characterized by an unprecedent and rapid pace of technological change, fierce competition, and scarcity of resources, forces organizations to quickly change their internal structure to adapt to their changing external factors. This change often involves corresponding changes in the authority relationships between line and staff.

Management practice relies more on professionals, making extensive use of staff functions bypassing the traditional concepts of the principles of management. Management decreases its recognition of the traditional concept of authority, while it increases its dependence on professionals in management practices. This results in the blurring of the line and staff distinction, creating the appearance of inconsistent observance of the principle of unity of command authority in reality.

The staff plays the role of a de facto line authority expanding over the limited scope of functional authority defined in the chart, thus broadening its advisory role, crossing the line authority to the extent that staff exerts its influence on the executive in the determination of the final course of management action. Staff often becomes central to the attribution of either success or failure.

For example, the perennial conflict between the U.S. president's Executive Office staff (the White House staff) and the cabinet departments becomes a classic example of the conflict between line and staff. The conflict between presidential staff and departmental officials has often escalated to a full-fledged power struggle over policymaking authority.

Line managers may feel deprived of their rightful authority over particular activities by staffs' functional activities. It is not unusual to find line executives delegating authority to the staff to act on their behalf, as is the case in transmitting a certain piece of information, proposal, or order descending to the line command through a staff person. It is rather common for chief executives to bring their own staff with surrogate authority to reduce the chief executive's time and effort. However, this practice eventually leads to a flare-up of conflict between line and staff. The fact that line is compelled to receive orders from staff is not only a violation of the principles of command authority but also deprivation of line authority.

Separate Responsibilities and Different Priorities

Line activities are those involved primarily with substantive operations of an organization, dealing with daily implementation of programs or policies making a direct impact on outside clienteles. Staff activities are those involved with supportive functions to the line, concerning planning, research, and advisory activities that are essential to the long-term well-being of the organization.

One most obvious point of line-staff conflict is in their different time perspectives and order of priorities. Line personnel tend to concentrate on immediate, practical, substantive, and "here-and-now" issues and problems, while staff personnel pay attention to the organization's long-range goals and futuristic ideals.

The top management must bring the activities of line and staff together under an overarching framework to interrelate and integrate them, so that they may be able to work together toward the achievement of the organization's short- and long-term goals.

Different Behavior Patterns Between Line and Staff

Staff persons, on the whole, are younger, better educated, more professionally trained, more mobile in their careers, and tend to occupy better strategic positions in the organization so as to have easier access to the chief executive than line personnel.

Also, staff persons tend to be more articulate, persuasive, and confident than line personnel when interacting with their supervisors, peers, and subordinates. These discrepant behavior patterns of the staff persons can intimidate line persons, causing them feelings of inferiority, frustration, resentment, and isolation.

Rolf Rogers (1975) noted that the line felt resentful, frustrated, inferior, isolated, and threatened by the staff over management practices. The line sees its authority as increasingly restricted as the scope of activities by the staff expands and the recognition of the importance of staff functions increases within organizations. The line tends to guard its authority too carefully, resenting the staff advice and counsel it needs or is required to seek.

Competition over Authority and Influence

Line executives' unique supervisory talents and longevity of managerial experience can be made less vital to the organi-

zation's existence and success as the staff's dominant command status grows in an organization. However, erosion of authority and influence can be more perception than reality on the part of the line personnel. In a highly competitive organizational setting, staff persons may feel frustrated as well because they have no authority to implement their proposals; they can only recommend and advise. Line will take all the credit and glory, while staff is charged with the responsibility and gets blamed if its proposal fails.

A staff adviser can override line authority through manipulation. If a line executive does not agree with the staff proposal, the staff adviser can persuade the line executive to accept it. The staff proposal that was once rejected by the line superior may be overridden by the staff's exploiting its strategic position of being close to the chief executive. The staff manipulates persistently and aggressively to have its advice and suggestions accepted by the superior line executive. These types of staff practices are resented by line colleagues.

Conflict Resolutions

To help prevent the drifting apart of line and staff, which often results in inefficiency, organizations may consider implementing the following preventive measures and/or remedies:

1. Ideally the best but not the easiest way to avoid some of the line-staff conflicts is to make their distinctions as clear as possible. In order to achieve such clarity, it is imperative that a statement of authority relationships between line and staff be spelled out in the organization chart.

2. Despite the desirability of authority distinctions between line and staff, in most organizations some delegation of functional authority to staff departments is unavoidable and necessary. When this happens, the reasons for delegated authority must be clearly communicated to both line and staff departments involved so that the need for assistance from staff experts is known.

3. The duration of time for delegation of authority should be clarified, especially when the need for the use of staff is temporary and on an ad hoc committee basis. The ad hoc committee consisting of line and staff should facilitate the close coordination between line and staff functions and help resolve line-staff conflict if and when it occurs.

4. Staff assistance must be needed and appreciated by the line to justify its existence in the organization. If staff advice and recommendations are found to be useless, unrealistic, or unimplementable by the line managers time after time, it would be prudent to abolish them altogether or help them shape up. The best way to im-

prove the quality of staff help is to keep the staff department continuously informed of the relevant and important aspects of line functions and their ever-changing problems.

5. Staff proposals and recommendations should be made concrete, complete, and applicable to the intended line department. Toward this end, preconsultation meetings should be conducted prior to a particular proposal being drafted by the staff department, with the line personnel who will be charged with the responsibility of implementing it. This practice will help foster the spirit of coordination and cooperation between line and staff.

6. Line should be encouraged to make full use of staff service and assistance. One way to ease tension between overly defensive line managers and overly zealous staff persons over important policy matters is to force line managers to consult staff advisers before submitting a major program or policy to the top executive. This arrangement will provide line managers with the opportunity to find that doing so can improve their chances of getting their proposals approved or adopted by top management.

7. It must be recognized that most managerial jobs have elements of both line and staff. Line managers and their subordinates should clearly understand whether they operate in a line or in a staff position at a given situation and time. Line authority means making decisions and acting on them, whereas staff authority means the right to advise and consult.

8. Possible rotation of jobs across line and staff will provide the involved personnel with the opportunity to familiarize themselves with the nature, complexity, and key phases of each job, which they might not have been able to fully appreciate before. This may help diminish or narrow the disparity of misconception and mistrust existing between line and staff.

9. Functional authority should be sparingly used only when and where needed. If there is uncertainty about authority relationships between line and staff, top management should step in and limit the area of functional authority, clarify the ambiguity of the relationships, and create new standards and procedures that can be applied for future similar occurrences.

10. Policies on upgrading education of line personnel to help them keep up with rapidly advancing knowledge and skills should be considered. This can be accomplished by encouraging them to enter degree programs or to take special professional courses. In addition, "recruitment-within" and "in-service training" with line and staff may be instituted to allow easier job mobility within the organization, thereby easing conflicts and tension between line and staff.

JAE TAIK KIM

BIBLIOGRAPHY

Belasco, James A., and Joseph A. Alutto, 1969. "Line Staff Conflicts: Some Empirical Insights." *Academy of Management Journal,* vol. 12 (Dec.) 469–477.

Browne, Philip J., and Robert T. Golembiewski, 1974. "The Line-Staff Concept Revisited: An Empirical Study of Organizational Images." *Academy of Management Journal,* vol. 17 (Sept.) 406–417.

Dalton, Melvin, 1950. "Conflicts Between Staff and Line Managerial Officers." *American Sociological Review,* Vol. 15 (June) 342–351.

————,1959. *Men Who Manage.* New York: Wiley.

Fayol, Henri, 1949. *General and Industrial Management.* New York: Pitman.

Golembiewski, Robert T., 1967. *Organizing Men and Power: Patterns of Behavior and Line-Staff Models.* Chicago: Rand McNally.

Golembiewski, Robert T., Clinton Brown, and John Lanzano, 1966. "Personality and Organization Structure: Staff Models and Behavioral Patterns." *Academy of Management Journal,* vol. 9 (September) 217–232.

Gordon, George J., 1992. *Public Administration in America,* 4th ed. New York: St. Martin's.

Gulick, Luther H., and Lyndall F. Urwick, 1937. *Papers on the Science of Administration.* New York: Columbia University, Institute of Public Administration.

Koontz, Harold, and Cyril O'Donnell, 1972. *Principles of Management: An Analysis of Managerial Functions,* 5th ed. New York: McGraw-Hill.

Mooney, James D., 1947. *Principles of Organization.* New York: Harper & Row.

Mooney, James D., and Allan C. Reiley, 1931. *Onward Industry.* New York: Harper and Brothers.

Pfiffner, John M., and Robert Presthus, 1967. *Public Administration,* 5th ed. New York: Ronald Press.

Pursley, Robert D., and Neil Snortland, 1980. *Managing Government Organizations.* North Scituate, MA: Duxbury Press.

Rogers, Rolf E., 1975. *Organizational Theory.* Boston, MA: Allyn and Bacon.

Schmid, Hillel, 1990. "Staff and Line Relationships Revisited: The Case of Community Service Agencies." *Public Personnel Management,* vol. 19 (Spring) 71–83.

LOAN GUARANTEES. As currently used in the budget process of the United States government, this term refers to any guarantee, insurance, or other pledge by the federal (national) government to pay in part or in full the interest and/or principal on any debt obligation of a nonfederal borrower to a nonfederal lender. The term is defined in law Sec. 502 (3) and (4) of the Federal Credit Reform Act of 1990. The term excludes insurance or guarantees of deposits, shares, or other withdrawable accounts in financial institutions (i.e., it excludes insurance of deposits in banks, savings and loan associations, and similar institutions). (For further information, see **credit reform.**)

THOMAS J. CUNY

LOBBYING.

LOBBYING. The effort by representatives of various groups to influence the outcome of legislative and administrative decisions of government. Lester Milbrath (1963) in his book *The Washington Lobbyists* defined lobbying as "the stimulation and transmission of a communication, by someone other than a citizen acting on his behalf, directed at a governmental decision-maker with the hope of influencing his decision" (p. 8).

Background

The term "lobbying" is derived from the name of a waiting room or a hall adjacent to the legislative chambers called a "lobby." Traditionally, representatives of interest groups met legislators at the corridors of such legislative chambers to influence the outcome of legislation. Today, lobbying can take place in different personal and informal settings in places such as the office of a legislator, at a luncheon or dinner party, at a vacation or a resort place, and other special functions routinely sponsored and paid for by lobbyists.

The goals of lobbying organizations are to promote or secure the passage of legislative, administrative and judicial decisions that are in the interest of their members and to defeat those that are not in their interest. Furthermore, interest groups engage in lobbying to cajole or pressure government officials to either support or oppose a particular policy measure based on how the policy affects their interests. Interest groups focus their lobbying efforts on government institutions because only government has the constitutional authority to formulate policy and institute change.

Although the practice of lobbying dates back to seventeenth-century England, it is now used more openly and widely in the United States than elsewhere in the world. Today, lobbying of public officials exists in virtually all countries regardless of the system of government, although at varying degrees of openness. However, as a recognized political activity, it flourishes better in democratic than autocratic systems of government. Democratic systems are more open and accord groups the freedom to lobby their governments without severe restrictions. When lobbying efforts are suppressed, affected groups are usually forced to resort to other means of persuasion, including violence, to get their viewpoint to the public. For instance, until recently the Irish Republican Army (IRA) and the African National Congress (ANC) used violence as a result of their ban by the British and the South African governments, respectively. In the United States, the freedom of organized groups to lobby and reshape public and government policy is considered one of the greatest strengths of the American system of government (Mack 1989).

Lobbying is not confined to interest groups alone; levels and branches of government, foreign governments, and agencies at the federal, state, and local levels routinely lobby each other. In the United States, current laws prohibit federal officials from using taxpayers' money for lobbying purposes. The limited scope of the existing laws means that public officials can still find ways to engage in lobbying. The following examples show some variants of lobbying activities among branches and levels of government: White House officials lobby members of Congress when a bill critical to the success of the president's political agenda is at stake; the Department of Defense staff routinely lobbies the president and Congress to bolster continuous funding of research of new weapon systems or to prevent drastic cuts of existing programs; state and local governments lobby the federal government for increase in intergovernmental grants and relaxation of restrictions governing spending of federal funds; foreign private interests and governments also spend large sums of money lobbying the U.S. government on various issues ranging from gaining easier trade terms under the "most-favored" principle to increased U.S. foreign assistance.

The bulk of lobbying efforts is undertaken by various economic and noneconomic private interest groups. The most prominent are businesses, labor unions, farm groups, church groups, professional organizations, public organizations, ethnic and racial groups, and ideologically based groups. Business and other economically based special interest lobbyists play a greater role in influencing elected officials largely through contribution of funds to support political campaigns. Economic interest groups use Political Action Committees (PACs) as the legal instruments to channel financial support to prospective public officials seeking election or reelection to a public office. By supporting candidates through PAC money, lobbyists hope to enhance their access as well as influence on key decision-makers in Washington and state capitols across the country. Moreover, lobbyists working for business interests perform several important tasks. Archie Carroll (1993) in his book *Business and Society* listed the following as the services business lobbyists provide their clients:

> get access to key legislators; monitor legislation; establish communication channels with regulatory bodies; protect firms against surprise legislation; draft legislation; slick ad campaigns; provide issue papers on anticipated effects of legislative activity; communicate sentiments of association or company on key issues; influence of legislation; assist companies in coalition building around issues that various groups may have in common; and help legislators get reelected (p. 229).

Lobbyists working for nonbusiness groups perform similar tasks.

Depending on the issue at hand, interest groups usually direct their lobbying activities at either the judicial, legislative, or executive branches of government or some combination of them. Groups or individuals lobby the judicial branch in an attempt to "influence the climate of judicial opinion to ensure that their issue receives a more friendly hearing than it might otherwise receive if the preliminary work had not been performed" (Hrebrenar and Scott 1990, pp. 194–195). Moreover, the publication of articles, books, and law review studies covering a specific problem is another lobbying approach employed by interest groups to influence the legal system. The appointment and selection of judges is also an example of an area where groups often exert their lobbying efforts. Interest groups realize that the ideological and political (liberal or conservative) background of future judges can have long-term implications on how they will rule on key issues that affect their interests. The filing of amicus curiae, or "friend of the court" briefs, is a direct method of judicial lobbying used by some groups during litigation with the intention of influencing court decisions in favor of the group's position.

Recognizing the role the executive branch or the bureaucracy play in policy formation and implementation, interest groups spend a considerable amount of time and money through contributions by PACs attempting to influence public officials in the executive branch of government. It is important to note that during the twentieth century, the power and responsibilities of the executive branch increased rapidly as a result of the federal government's increased involvement in setting and directing the social and economic affairs of the nation. As a result, federal agencies increasingly became the target of interest group lobbying. When dealing with bureaucrats, lobbyists try to make known the position and views of the groups they represent and if necessary provide information that agencies find useful. In the event of disagreement with bureaucrats on regulatory matters or program implementation, lobbyists may question the technical competence of agency decisions and challenge the standard of enforcement of agency regulations (Sinclair 1976).

Legislative lobbying involves attempts by groups to get legislators to vote in favor of or against a particular measure of concern to them. Generally, organized groups use the services of paid lobbyists to influence the U.S. Congress or state legislatures. Such lobbyists are usually professionals who run their own private consulting firms and have experience in how the government operates. They include lawyers, public relations consultants, or former public officials such as legislators, cabinet members, bureaucrats, and former presidential, gubernatorial, and legislative staffers who have previously served in the government for several years. Groups hire lobbyists because of their knowledge, expertise, and communication skills. Lobbyists can articulate effectively the reasons for a group's support or opposition to a particular piece of legislation.

Lobbying Techniques

Organized groups use several lobbying techniques to defeat or gain the attention and support of public officials on particular public policy measures that affect their interests. The key lobbying techniques can be classified into two groups, notably, "direct" and "indirect" techniques. "Direct lobbying" involves interaction of interest group representatives with public officials on a face-to-face basis. The major techniques used in direct lobbying are characterized by direct communication between lobbyists and public officials and include creation of access channels to facilitate the communication process, set appointments to visit legislators and administrators, personal presentation of the group's views before agency bureaucrats, testifying of group representatives at legislative or congressional committee hearings, and presentation intervention in litigation processes. Thus, direct lobbying enables lobbyists to keep their constituencies abreast about developments in Washington and state capitols that may affect their interests.

"Indirect lobbying," commonly referred to as "grassroots lobbying," involves the use of the group's constituency to lobby government officials. Rather than employ the services and efforts of paid lobbyists directly, grassroots lobbying involves mobilization of group members at the constituent level to communicate with legislators. The "grassroots" include individuals and citizens who are most likely to be affected by governmental decisions and actions. Grassroots lobbying enables legislators to know where their constituencies stand on a particular issue.

The techniques used by interest groups to impact and influence the legislative process include asking individuals at the grassroots level to flood the offices of their legislators or administrators with letter-writing campaigns, telephone calls, fax messages, telegrams, electronic messages, and other ways of communication. Other indirect lobbying techniques include persuasion of the local media to publicize the group's concerns; mobilization of local groups such as churches, unions, neighborhood associations to voice their concerns; organization of press conferences and public meetings; and mobilization of individuals at the grassroots level to stage demonstrations. Moreover, groups may attempt to change public policy by influencing the outcome of elections by contributing funds to support or defeat candidates, publishing voting records of legislators, releasing research results, and mounting public relations campaigns (Berry 1970, p. 214).

Regulation of Lobbying

The right of individuals and groups to lobby the U.S. Congress has long been recognized as a central component of the American system of government. It stemmed from the First Amendment to the U.S. Constitution, which guarantees free speech and the right of the people to petition the government for a redress of grievances (*Congressional Quarterly Service* 1965, p. 2). Although it was recognized that the process of lobbying provided useful information and original research to legislators and administrators as well as enlightened specific groups on how proposed legislation or regulations work in practice, critics charged that lobbying only benefited interest groups and did not necessarily serve the general public interest. According to the critics, lobbying can corrupt the political system and lead to undue influence of public officials. In response to pressure for lobbying reforms, Congress started to conduct a string of investigations beginning in 1913, which later led to deliberation of registration-reporting bills in 1928, 1935, and 1936. These bills, however, failed to clear both chambers of Congress and were never enacted into law. Congress finally passed a general lobbyist registration law called the Federal Regulation of Lobbying Act in 1946. The 1946 act mandated paid lobbyists to register and file financial reports on a quarterly basis with the clerk of the U.S. House of Representatives. The act, however, fell short of severely limiting the influence of lobbyists on congressional voting. In a 1954 ruling (*U.S. v. Harriss*), the U.S. Supreme Court upheld the constitutionality of the Lobbying Act of 1946 but restricted its scope by overturning provisions found in violation of the First Amendment of the U.S. Constitution. Donald Hall (1970) summarized the interpretation of the Court's ruling as follows:

(1) persons or groups spending their own funds were not covered by the Act; (2) organizations whose principal purpose was not the influencing of legislation were not covered by the Act; and (3) unless the organization carried on or contemplated direct contact with members of Congress, for the purpose of influencing legislation, the legislation was not covered by the Act (p. 301).

The *Harriss* decision somewhat weakened the position of individuals who sought stringent regulation of lobbying activities. In its ruling, the Supreme Court intended to maintain a balance between the need to curb the use of dishonest lobbying practices and the protection of constitutional rights of free speech and petition. Although the U.S. Congress has from time to time attempted to institute further reforms in congressional lobbying practices, the initiatives always get defeated largely due to special interest "lobbying" and concerns about crossing constitutional boundaries.

It is important to mention that early initiatives to regulate lobbying in the United States came from individual states. After the end of the Civil War, Alabama, Georgia, and California enacted constitutional provisions prohibiting corrupt lobbying practices. Massachusetts was the first state to pass a law requiring registration of lobbyists in 1890 followed by Wisconsin in 1905. Although not uniform in terms of the requirements needed to engage in lobbying, most states require lobbyists to register with a state official as well as to file periodic financial and activity reports.

The most recent law directed at curbing the influence of lobbyists and at promoting ethical behavior in government is the Ethics Reform Act of 1989, which banned all federal officers and employees from accepting honoraria. The Ethics in Government Reform Act further addressed other issues such as acceptance of gifts, outside earned income, financial disclosure, ethics committee procedures, and the use of official resources (Golden 1991). Another recent law formulated by the Internal Revenue Service (IRS), IRC Section 162(e) governing lobbying, prohibits deductions of lobbying expenses of businesses, trade associations, and other groups that lobby the government (Repass et al. 1994).

The number of registered lobbyists in Washington, D.C., increased from 3,420 to 8,800 between 1976 and 1986. The total number of lobbyists including unregistered ones is estimated to exceed 20,000. Lack of specific regulations governing lobbying in the executive branch makes it harder to know the actual number of lobbyists operating in the nation's capital. Similarly, the total amount spent by lobbyists annually is unknown, although estimates run in excess of US $1.5 billion. In 1987, registered lobbyists reported expenditures of about US $63.5 million, up by 4.5 percent from a year ago (Buchholz 1992, p. 134). Like previous administrations, the Clinton administration proposed major lobbying reforms that currently seem to head nowhere.

ALEX SEKWAT

BIBLIOGRAPHY

Berry, Jeffrey M., 1971. *Lobbying for the People.* Princeton, NJ: Princeton University Press.
Buchholz, Rogene, 1992. *Business Environment and Public Policy.* Englewood Cliffs, NJ: Prentice-Hall.
Carroll, Archie B., 1993. *Business and Society.* Cincinatti: South-Western Publishing Co.
Golden, David A., 1991. "The Tax Reform Act of 1989: Why the Taxman Can't Be a Paperback Writer." *Brigham Young University Law Review,* vol. 1991, no. 2: 1025–1051.
Hall, Donald R., 1970. *Cooperative Lobbying–The Power of Pressure.* Tucson: University of Arizona Press.
Hrebrenar, Ronald J., and Ruth K. Scott, 1990. *Interest Group Politics in America.* Englewood Cliffs, NJ: Prentice-Hall.
Mack, Charles S., 1989. *Lobbying and Government Relations: A Guide for Executives.* New York: Quorum Books.
Milbrath, Lester W., 1963. *The Washington Lobbyists.* Chicago: Rand McNally.
Repass, David M., Jeffrey R. Levey, and James F. Carlisle, Jr., 1994. "Coping with the Lobbying Deduction Disallowance." *Journal of Accountancy,* vol. 177, no. 5: 70–73.
Rich, Spencer, 1965. *Legislators and the Lobbyists.* Washington, DC: Congressional Quarterly Service.
Sinclair, John E., 1976. *Interest Groups in America.* Morristown, NJ: General Learning Press.

LOCAL GOVERNMENTS.

Numerous, lower-tier, electorally accountable political units with limited autonomy, providing choices and participation to citizens and influencing the physical and social character of a geographical area.

Evolution and Functions

Central governments have often delegated powers to self-governing cities and towns to organize defenses, provide services, and raise taxes. Local government first emerged in the semiautonomous Greek city-states, and the Roman empire granted cities self-government. Largely autonomous cities flourished in Europe from the tenth century. Early municipal "corporations" were not democratic in the modern sense and were dominated by self-serving business interests.

According to the American political scientist Hardy Wickwar (1970) in his book *The Political Theory of Local Government,* the term "local government" was first used by the English Philosopher Jeremy Bentham in 1832. Lord John Russell used the term in introducing the Municipal Corporations Bill in the House of Commons in 1835. The foundations of the modern democratic local government system were in place in most Western countries by the end of the nineteenth century. Local self-government was most important then because higher tiers lacked the administrative capabilities to service growing cities or to control local units.

The American colonies developed more democratic local government forms by adapting English models. Mercantile communities established boroughs and some groups established cohesive participative communities devoted to social control and civic betterment. Agricultural areas developed a more democratic form of the English county. These early innovators emphasized contracts between the state and communities, important for future definitions of local autonomy. Local autonomy is defined as the capacity of local governments to act without fear of having their every decision scrutinized, reviewed, or reversed by higher tiers of government. American local authorities continue to emphasize local rights and have resisted integration into state or federal government administrative and political systems. The French writer Alexis de Tocqueville (1835) first observed the unusual strength of local governments in the United States in his book *Democracy in America.* The pluralistic American federal system still fosters local diversity and provides more freedom for local units than is possible in most European states.

Local governments are an important part of the modern state. In 1992, local governments in the United States accounted for 29 percent of all public spending, only slightly less than the 31 percent spent by the states. Local governments are large employers because they deliver labor-intensive services. In 1991, local government employees comprised 59 percent of all civilian government employees in the United States, more than three times as many as the federal government and more than twice as many as state governments. Local government is even more important in most parts of Europe, spending around two-thirds of all public outlays in Denmark and Finland.

Local authorities are not autonomous mini-states but govern a limited area within a complex intergovernmental system. Each nation delivers a different but restricted range of physical and social services locally, often as administrative agents of higher-tier authorities. In the past, local governments emphasized physical infrastructure such as roads, refuse collection, parks, and land use control but are now increasingly involved in social services such as education, health, and welfare. The growth of the complex modern state creates an advantage for local government, which has more information about local needs and preferences than centralized administrations.

The division of functions between levels of government is rarely a neat, layered hierarchy, with each government responsible for a particular service. In a chapter on federalism, the American political scientist Morton Grodzins (1960) popularized the intergovernmental pattern as resembling an uneven and complex "marble cake." Former Governor Terry Sanford (1967) suggested that the intergovernmental pattern may be best understood by the "picket fence" metaphor. The levels of government are the horizontal supports, while each specialized function represents the vertical slats of the picket fence. Administrators, politicians, and pressure groups in each functional area develop strong intergovernmental coordinating links that can diminish the potential chaos of fragmented government in a region.

Numbers

Local authorities in the world differ greatly in areas and populations, but most local governments are small. The United States leads the world in having the largest number of local governments with significant functions. In 1987, there were 83,186 governments in the United States. By 1992, numbers had increased to 86,743 governments: 3,043 counties; 35,962 cities and townships; 14,556 school districts; 33,131 special districts and 50 states and the federal government. In 1992, there were over 500,000 elected local officials in the United States. There were also 502 regional coordinating councils and over 150,000 residential community associations, increasingly numerous "private" local governments providing municipal-type services.

Most American governments are small: 72 percent of general purpose local governments in the United States have fewer than 3,000 residents, and more than half have populations of fewer than 1,000. Apart from the United Kingdom, most local governments in other countries are also small in population. Americans often demand less government but, more than any other country, create more new governmental units rather than expand existing ones. European governments have routinely dismissed local objections against their large-scale reductions in the numbers of local units. Fragmented local government systems in the United States, France, and Italy have been most resistant to centrally imposed restructuring. The average populations of local authorities in 1990 is shown in Table I.

Fragmentation and Effective Government

With modern technology, the survival of local government is threatened. The writings of sociologist Max Weber on the decline of local institutions were published in *Economy and Society* (1922). To Weber, local government could have only minimal power in a world of expertise and centralized and uniform bureaucratic systems. Higher tiers of government may now have the information capability to deliver many local services and may gain from economies of scale. Australia is an example of a large area with a weak local government system and a powerful central government with centralized revenue raising and a wide range of decentralized service delivery arrangements.

Critics claim the survival of so many small local units is merely a sign of political inertia, demonstrating the power of vested local interests to resist scale enlargement and modernization. Fragmented local government systems have difficulty coping with modern social and economic problems. Economic decline, residential segregation of the poor, and infrastructure inadequacies in growing suburban areas all require regional approaches.

Numerous small local units, say supporters, provide an opportunity for widespread political participation that is difficult in larger areas. Local communities provide a sense of identity and attachment to place. Local government often provides the one level of government where the average citizen can understand most issues, influence decisionmaking, and learn about democratic processes. Public meetings, citizen initiative, and referendums allow direct democracy. Small governments allow for less government because citizens—not representatives or bureaucracies—have more opportunity to control spending and taxing levels. Small governments compete to provide sensitive solutions to diverse local needs.

The United States has developed the only modern economic argument for a highly fragmented local government system. In an influential article published in the *Journal of Political Economy* in 1956, the American public choice economist Charles Tiebout argued that people need multiple local governments to choose a location that satisfies diverse demands for public services and lifestyles. Shopping for a local government and its services is much like shopping for other goods. Multiple local governments mean competition between units for increasingly mobile businesses and residents; they encourage experimentation, responsiveness, and higher levels of efficiency. American cities follow the Tiebout model, with a high level of resi-

TABLE I. Lowest Tier Local Authorities: Average Populations and Numbers of Units, c1993

Country	Average Population per Unit	Number of Units
Australia	26,317	678
Austria	3,284	2,374
Belgium	17,093	589
Canada	6,467	4,238
Denmark	18,976	273
Finland	10,989	460
France	1,565	36,664
Germany	4,977	16,127
Greece	1,710	6,022
Ireland	38,554	92
Italy	7,054	8,074
Japan	38,351	3,245
Luxembourg	3,136	126
Netherlands	19,122	800
New Zealand	47,100	74
Norway	9,596	448
Poland	16,007	2,400
Portugal	35,853	275
Spain	4,842	8,027
Sweden	30,805	284
Switzerland	2,100	3,000
United Kingdom	119,831	484
United States	7,100	35,962

SOURCE: National Year Books.

Note: The United Kingdom was in the process of reducing the number of local units in 1993. The figures for the United States refer to cities and townships. The figures for Australia included major amalgamations implemented in 1994.

dential concentration by income and lifestyle. Groups of people with similar demands for local services have a strong advantage in locating in the same jurisdiction.

The American public seems to support small local governments and has a higher regard for local government than for state or federal government. An Advisory Commission on Intergovernmental Relations survey, *Changing Public Attitudes on Governments and Taxes* (1993) showed that 35 percent of the population thought local government spent taxpayers' money most wisely, compared to 14 percent for state governments, and only 7 percent for the federal government. Local communities resist consolidation into larger units, suggesting satisfaction with small governments.

The public choice model accepts the federalism values of bargaining, competition, conflict, and marketlike relationships between large numbers of governments. Critics of the fragmentation model emphasize bureaucratic values of hierarchy, coordination, scale economies, and consistency. To them, the pluralistic local government system in the United States leads to "ungovernable" cities. Local governments are blamed for low-density suburbanization and racial segregation in financially troubled, declining central cities. Numerous local governments are also blamed for high administrative costs, excessive duplication, and for creating complex intergovernmental management problems. To critics, "local autonomy" is an excuse for inaction, selfishness, low taxes, and poor quality public services.

Regional Government

There is a strong movement worldwide to strengthen regional or county governments. Over the past 20 years, entirely new systems of regional elected governments have been created in France, Italy, Spain, Belgium, and Portugal, and county governments have been strengthened in Norway, Sweden, Denmark, the United Kingdom, and parts of Germany. These governments are not amalgamations of smaller local units, but a new middle area of decisionmaking and administration, operating at a level between small participative units and the central government.

Special districts that deal with regional functions are the most rapidly increasing type of local government in the United States, increasing from 12,340 in 1952 to 23,885 in 1972, and from 29,532 in 1987 to 33,131 in 1992. Most special districts perform a single function such as water and sewerage, fire services, housing, transport, hospitals, and environmental control. Special districts are favored because they can have a regional focus, overlap municipal boundaries, and usually have their own funding sources. Traditional municipal government may be weakened as more technical functions are managed by separate districts often insulated from local political pressures.

Britain has also created about 5,500 special districts, referred to as "quangos," which now rival municipal spending as they manage local services formerly managed by multipurpose local governments. Health, housing, training, education, police, waste disposal, and planning are now often managed by authorities with centrally appointed rather than elected boards.

County governments are increasing in importance in the United States, especially in delivering public welfare, education, hospitals, police, correction, and highway services. Counties are also expanding their roles in regional functions such as transportation, air quality, conservation, landfill, and toxic waste, growth management and economic development. State governments may find it easier to deal with a far smaller number of counties. Their larger area may enable them to deliver regional services more effectively than numerous small municipalities. Smaller communities, such as in Los Angeles, often contract services from counties, enabling production efficiency to be combined with small democratic units.

Many of the 3,042 counties in the United States are small in population. Their boundaries are a product of history rather than rational administrative criteria. A common county size is between 10,000 and 25,000 residents and ranges from a population of 164 in Loving County, Texas, to 8 million in Los Angeles County. Changing county boundaries is as difficult as changing township and city borders.

Resources

Local governments throughout the world face financial problems, as they lack the financial resources to pay for expanded roles or unfunded "mandates" forced on them by higher levels of government or by community demands. A mandate is a legal requirement—constitutional, statutory, or administrative—on local government that commands a specific local activity or service fulfilling state or federal centrally determined requirements. Mandates are enforced by the courts. Federal and state directives to local governments in the United States and other parts of the world are likely to deal with environmental protection, programs to combat race, sex, and age discrimination, open government, handicapped access, bilingual education, health planning, and other areas of the welfare state. The emphasis is now on aid to specific groups of people rather than to places in general.

Local government is not mentioned in the United States Constitution and the courts have little consistent respect for local autonomy. Legally, local government is a creation of higher tier governments. The meaning of local autonomy is the subject of complex legal debate in Western countries. Ninety percent of American state governments allow cities "home rule," but autonomy is increasingly curtailed. Through aggressive lobbying, American local authorities have gained some success in slowing the number of unfunded mandates from state and federal governments. Their historic claims to local autonomy have moral and political, if not legal, value.

German local governments have strong constitutional protection, but judicial interpretation still allows large-scale, centrally imposed reorganization of boundaries against local opinion. Many European localities have powers of general competence, in contrast to the "ultra vires" restriction in British-derived systems, which limits local actions to specific devolved powers. In practice, however, all local governments are constrained by higher tiers. By 1989, 25 European countries had signed or ratified the European Charter of Self-Government that gives widespread—if vague—rights to local governments and their communities. Britain refused to sign the charter, claiming it was alien to British traditions.

Centrally directed public sector deregulation and privatization weaken local autonomy. Improvements in public sector performance require changes to local service delivery systems in which most public servants are employed.

In the United States, for example, 354 federal statutes directing state and local government actions have been enacted between 1789 and 1990. Of these, 190 have been introduced since 1969, 95 during the Reagan "New Federalism" era, mostly to implement federal deregulation policies. Britain, Australia, New Zealand, Sweden, and many other countries are enforcing compulsory competitive tendering, enlarged scale, and other detailed controls on local government as part of national microeconomic reform programs and overall restrictions on public spending.

Higher-level governments devolve functions to local governments, who then pay the political costs of raising taxes, reducing outlays, or improving efficiency in service delivery. By devolving austerity, financially stressed central or state governments can reduce citizen demands for more public services by applying benefit-based "user pays" taxes and charges to local communities. Small-scale local units provide the opportunity for people to see the link between taxes and service levels.

Local governments in the United States, Canada, Australia, Ireland, and the United Kingdom are heavily reliant on the problematic local property tax. The property tax is criticized because of its visibility, its lack of relation to capacity to pay, its volatility due to fluctuating property values, and its susceptibility to popular tax revolts. Households and businesses have a strong incentive to move to low tax communities. Local governments in Denmark, Germany, Japan, and Switzerland are heavily reliant on local income taxes for revenue, making them less prone to fiscal stress because income taxes are related to capacity to pay, not property values. All local governments are diversifying revenue sources, and favoring benefit-based taxation such as user charges. The fiscal pressures in American and European local governments have produced many innovations in service delivery, such as the use of outside contractors and public-private partnerships.

Despite tax revolts, American local governments increased property taxes by 128 percent between 1980 and 1990. Politically, tax increases at the local level may be more feasible than for central governments. Central governments can borrow, while local borrowing is restricted and units are required to have balanced budgets. Local governments are forced to face financial realities. Higher-tier governments must tax to finance often unpopular redistributive welfare services, while local government in most countries controls functions with clear middle-class benefits. Many local politicians in America and other countries have been able to convince the middle class that tax increases are vital to maintain local facilities such as education, police and fire protection, land use control, physical infrastructure, and regional and local amenities such as libraries, parks, and museums. The middle classes benefit from these services, which underpin local property values.

Intergovernmental Relations

Local governments in the United States raise nearly two-thirds of revenue locally, while European units generally only raise between 35 and 50 percent of revenue from local sources. Local financial self-reliance creates problems. Low income areas with many needs have the lowest capacity to pay local taxes. Intergovernmental grants are vital to local financial capability but inevitably reduce local autonomy. Higher levels of government demand accountability for local grants and need to control local spending as part of broad economic management.

In the United Kingdom, local governments depend on central government for a high proportion of revenue. This dependency has weakened British local government, which is now highly regulated from the center. Central government controls rate and spending levels and has removed many functions from local control. Local authority boundaries are routinely changed by central government, with little regard for local opinion. Councils are increasingly regarded as service delivery agencies of central government.

Well-designed intergovernmental transfer systems can overcome different revenue-raising capacities and ensure minimum service standards are maintained. Each county has developed its own particular systems for intergovernmental assistance, all of them imperfect. Central government has great difficulty in developing accurate equalization systems because it suffers from informational problems about local needs, the reason for local government's existence in the first place. There is little political support for similar equalization in the United States, where the large number of small and diverse local authorities makes it difficult to develop accurate technical methods for distributing aid. Many social and economic problems are national or regional and can only be solved by complex reforms in intergovernmental management.

Financial problems in higher tiers reduce the real level of grant resources available to local governments. Federal grants to local government in the United States have declined from 9 percent of local revenue in 1980 to only 3.6 percent in 1990. Central governments want local governments to undertake more functions but fail to provide the funding. In the United States, for example, "cooperative" federalism has been replaced by "coercive," "compulsory," "shift and shaft," and "combat" federalism.

Donor governments like to maintain control and to direct spending toward current priorities. All Western governments are increasing controls over local government operations. From 1978 to 1990, American states enacted an average of 16 new laws on local government issues, most commonly on financial management and personnel matters. Many American states now impose limits on local property taxes and borrowing levels and dictate budgeting procedures.

Efficiency and Participation

Limited financial resources force local government to become more professionalized. Reform movements in the United States late last century led to the creation of the "City Manager" plan in 1908, and the application of business management methods to local administration has become increasingly widespread. There is now more emphasis on customer service, marketing, strategic planning, efficiency, and performance measurement. Terms such as community, citizen, democracy, participation, and liberty are heard less commonly in local government. There is a danger that local government could become dominated by professional managers, who may not have much sympathy with participative democratic values. Professionalized local authorities then become indistinguishable from state and central government management cultures. Local governments lose their diversity and strong local political cultures and become part of the general state apparatus. These trends are already apparent in the United States, Britain, Sweden, and Australia. Local government can lose the capacity for local choices and become merely local administration. Many larger local authorities are experimenting with administrative and political decentralization to reconcile rising managerial professionalism with demands for more control and influence by councillors and community groups.

Local governments are particularly susceptible to business influence because each unit normally wants to increase its tax base by attracting industry and residents. Fiscal pressure and economic change make the local economic base increasingly important in local politics. Growth can provide the additional revenue to balance budgets and avoid service reductions or tax increases. Local politics are often dominated by clashes between pro- and anti-growth interests. Local autonomy over land use decisions is likely to be eroded by pro-growth higher-tier governments unless local units become more skilled at managing growth conflicts.

In the future, local units are likely to gain power and influence through superior local capacities in service delivery and the ability to link taxes and charges with specific spending programs. Their small democratic structures provide the main opportunities for political participation in large complex societies. Local government remains the only tier that governs particular small areas, provides democratic participation, and can duplicate the competitive incentives of the private market.

MICHAEL JONES

BIBLIOGRAPHY

Advisory Commission on Intergovernmental Relations, 1992. *Metropolitan Organization: The Allegheny County Case*. Report M181, Washington, DC.

Clark, Gordon L., 1985. *Judges and the Cities: Interpreting Local Autonomy*. Chicago: University of Chicago Press.

Dente, Bruno, and Francesco Kjellberg, eds., 1988. *The Dynamics of Institutional Change: Local Government Reorganisation in Western Democracies*. London: Sage.

Gottdiener, M., 1987. *The Decline of Urban Politics: Political Theory and the Crisis of the Local State*. Newbury Park, CA: Sage.

Grodzins, Morton, 1960. "The Federal System." *Goals for Americans*, ed. The Committee on National Goals. New York: The American Assembly.

Jones, Michael, 1993. *Transforming Australian Local Government: Making It Work*. Sydney: Allen and Unwin.

Lyons, W. E., David Lowery, and Ruth Hoogland De Hoog, 1992. *The Politics of Dissatisfaction: Citizens, Services, and Urban Institutions*. New York: M E Sharpe.

Norton, Alan, 1994. *International Handbook of Local and Regional Government: A Comparative Analysis of Advanced Democracies*. Aldershot: Edward Elgar.

Page, Edward C., 1991. *Localism and Centralism in Europe: The Political and Legal Bases of Local Self-Government*. Oxford: Oxford University Press.

Peterson, Paul, E., 1981. *City Limits*. Chicago: University of Chicago Press.

Sanford, Terry, 1967. *Storm Over the States*. New York: McGraw-Hill.

Sharpe, L. J., 1993. *The Rise of Meso Government in Europe*. London: Sage.

Svara, James H., 1990. *Official Leadership in the City: Patterns of Conflict and Cooperation*. New York: Oxford University Press.

Tiebout, Charles, 1956. "A Pure Theory of Local Expenditure." *Journal of Political Economy*, vol. 64: 416-24.

Tocqueville, Alexis de ([1835] 1945). *Democracy in America*. New York: Vintage.

Weber, Max, ([1922] 1968). *Economy and Society*. New York: Bedminster.

Wickwar, W. Hardy, 1970. *The Political Theory of Local Government*. Columbia: University of South Carolina Press.

Wright, Deil S., 1988. *Understanding Intergovernmental Relations*, 3d ed. Pacific Grove, CA: Brooks/Cole.

LOCAL GOVERNMENT BUDGETING.

The process and documents pertaining to the financial plans of towns, cities, counties, school districts, and special districts.

General

The subject of local government budgeting is a broad topic, and attempts at generalizations are fraught with errors. In the United States alone, there are over 80,000 local governments, including school districts. When discussing local government budgeting, then, it is important to specify which of the four types of local government is being considered: cities, counties, school districts, or special districts. Furthermore, the budget process and the budget itself are affected by the different organizational and legal structures of local governments.

The who, when, what, and how questions of budgeting apply to local governments in different ways, depending upon the type of government in question and its structure. Who budgets in local governments and how the budgeting is done is largely a function of the structure of the government. What is budgeted and for what purposes is more a function of the type of local government. When budgeting is done is rather arbitrary, dependent largely on the laws of the individual states, which create and define the local budgeting process. An annual budget cycle is common to all local governments in the United States largely due to their heavy revenue reliance on the property tax base, which is assessed annually to allow property tax levies to be adjusted according to current needs by the local governments.

This raises a fundamental point about local government budgeting that pervades all types of local polities: U.S. local governments are creatures of the states, and they have no independent standing in the U.S. Constitution. The wide variety of local government budgeting is based first on the 50 different states that create them. Each of the major local government types is described below with the caveat that even these generalizations are difficult to assert and that the specifics of who budgets, when, for what, and how is particular to the city and state at least as much as to the type of government and its internal organization and structure. The same can be said for local governments in developing nations and the newly independent states of Central and Eastern Europe and the former Soviet Union.

A second generalization about local governments around the world is that they are usually dependent to some degree on intergovernmental grants for part of their revenue base. In some cases, they receive grants for specific services they agree to provide for a higher level of government (regional or national). In other cases, they receive block grants for a general function (e.g., public safety), within which they have some allocative discretion (e.g., more squad cars versus community policing programs). In some countries, and formerly in the United States, local governments receive general revenue grants (usually on a per capita basis), which they are free to spend without restrictions from higher levels of government. In still other countries, such as in Poland, local governments have access to shared taxes levied by the central government. The intergovernmental financing of local governments is both a blessing and a curse. On the one hand, it is helpful to have supplements to a revenue base; on the other hand, most local governments operate under strict revenue limitations from the creator governments and find it very difficult to shift revenue dependencies when the upper-level government arbitrarily reduces grant transfers or eliminates them entirely.

Cities

Local government budgeting is often equated with city budgeting. This is the type of local government unit common to many nations around the world. Yet, cities come in all shapes and sizes, and the budget process and budget documents vary to meet the needs and conditions of the different cities.

One factor in the variation of cities is the internal legal structure of the government. There are basically two models of executive governance for U.S. cities. The traditional council-mayor model has a strong, independently elected mayor and a city council. The mayor appoints department heads and reviews their budget requests, crafts and presents an executive budget to the city council, and implements the budget, which is ultimately passed by the council after its review and modification. The council-manager model has a city manager (or city administrator), who is hired by the city council and who in turn hires department heads. The manager may review department requests and only prepare preliminary budget estimates for the council, which then assembles and approves the city budget. Or the manager may analyze department requests, craft and present an executive budget to the city council, and implement the budget as modified and approved by the council. In either model, the city executive may have one or more budget assistants to help with budget preparation, analysis, and implementation. In large cities, there is usually a separate budget office with a complement of budget officers who have year-round responsibility for budget development and execution. The budget cycle for cities is usually stipulated in state laws.

Cities can be grouped into small, medium, and large communities, with the small cities category including towns and villages. As the first generalization, it is fair to say that the complexity of local government functions is greater for larger cities than smaller ones and, consequently, that budgeting for larger cities tends to be more complex than for smaller cities. Small cities tend to provide only basic city services, such as public safety (police and fire services), streets, water and sewer, regulation (health inspections, building inspections, zoning), and recreation (parks). Larger cities recently have been given more responsibilities and provide even more comprehensive basic services than in earlier days (e.g., hazardous materials units in fire protection services). What services the city provides and how they are provided impact the budget process and the budget document, as is evident in discussions about each size of city.

Small Communities—Cities, Towns, and Villages

Budgeting in small cities, towns, and villages is often a legislative function. Local budgeting is traditionally the project of the department heads and the city council. Even where there is city manager, department heads often present their budget requests to the legislative body, with comments by the manager. The local "budget staff" has largely been the chief administrator and an assistant (who also has other duties beyond the budget).

Smaller communities tend to provide the same basic set of public services every year. The level of budget complexity is relatively low and easily comprehensible to citizen legislators, who can review the budget requests of the departments.

Often they are familiar with a specific budget area because it is related to their "real" lives in the private sector. There is little to debate about the proportional budget allocations that have remained relatively stable over the previous years. Debates focus on whether to raise taxes to fund employee pay raises or new capital equipment or to lower taxes to give neighbors more pocket money. Budgeting in small communities is intimate because citizens are friends and neighbors and the budget choices are relatively simple.

The principal function of the small local budget is accountability, providing citizens and elected officials with a reckoning of how the money is spent, and ensuring that expenditures do not exceed levels authorized by the city council. Small city councils commonly insist on involvement in the details of the budget: How much sand will be purchased, what are the salaries of each employee, what kind of fire truck can be purchased? The desire for intimate knowledge of the process is fulfilled by line-item, object code budgeting.

Finally, the simple structure and process of local budgeting has been reinforced by the heavy reliance of local governments on the property tax for revenues. The property tax base increases (or decreases) incrementally and is relatively stable overall. It has been well matched to services provided by local governments to property owners: police, fire, garbage, sewer, and water. The revenue is relatively elastic with respect to basic expenditure demands; as new property is added to the local property rolls and requires property services, the property is also added to the tax rolls and contributes to the funding for the services.

The traditional function of local governments, to provide the same basic and important services in a consistent, efficient, and effective manner every year gives small city budgeting a distinctive incrementalist flavor, using a simple line-item format. The principal expenditure categories of a typical city budget and the proportional allocation among the major categories changes little over the years. Large proportional swings from fire protection to streets, or from streets to police services, are unlikely because these services are basic to our lives at the local level. Thus, budget decisionmakers have generally focused on the marginal changes to the budgets of each department, such as the number of police officers or squad cars to be added (or subtracted) to the police budget. In this setting, there is little "policy analysis" associated with local budgeting because basic polices do not change. These cities continue to do what they have always done.

Large Cities

Large cities in the United States not only provide basic local services on a grander scale than smaller communities, they tend to provide more comprehensive services and a broader array of them. Large cities have ports and airports as well as public transportation and streets. Recreation services have outgrown simple parks to include organized activities and a comprehensive array of facilities. Garbage services now commonly include recycling services. Fire services now include hazardous waste teams to meet chemical emergencies and to protect the environment and citizens from potential disasters. Libraries have multiple branches and bookmobiles.

Administrative and fiscal decentralization have also added new responsibilities to local governments, such as providing comprehensive welfare and judicial services. The War on Poverty in the 1960s provided substantial federal funding for urban renewal programs, including public housing projects and economic development grants. The withdrawal of the grants in the 1980s and continued urban property base decay have increased the complexity of governing large local governments. Fortunately, many states have also granted local governments a broader array of revenue sources, supplementing the staid property tax with sales taxes and even income taxes. Cities also increasingly rely on user fees to pay for new services. As a result, the choices inherent in their budgets have increased dramatically.

Budgeting in large cities has changed significantly in recent years. The simple, line-item budgets that changed incrementally every year have been reformed into amalgams of program and performance budgets that reflect the increasingly complex array of services provided by local governments. Varieties of zero-based budgeting and target-based budgeting are adapted to the political and economic circumstances of individual cities.

Common to the change from incremental, line-item budgeting to performance and program budgeting is an increased emphasis on analyzing the outputs and outcomes of city activities funded by the budget. Although performance measures in budgets may themselves change only incrementally over the years, the programmatic structure and array of performance measures indicates to the city executive and the city council what can be expected by funding program A at level X and program B at level Y.

Large cities tend to use the strong mayor governance model. However, there are many exceptions, including Kansas City, Missouri, and Dayton, Ohio. Large cities do tend to have a corps of budgeteers who perform budget analysis and budget implementation functions year-round in a central budget office. The central budget office is a key management tool of the mayor or city manager, and the budget officers are expected to be intimately familiar with the operational details of their assigned departments.

The budget process in large cities tends to follow an executive budget model, with the department heads submitting budget requests to the city budget office for review. The budgeteers then analyze the request and recommend funding levels to the city executive. The comprehensive package of recommendations approved by the city executive is then submitted to the city council for review, modification, and approval. The central budget office staff is then responsible for implementing the adopted budget, even as it begins analyzing potential department requests for the next budget cycle (see **budget analyst**).

Large cities also tend to have large and distinct capital budgets. Infrastructure maintenance lays significant claim to city revenues as urban sewer and water systems, road and bridge systems, and municipal buildings decay and require repairs and replacement. The capital budget process requires more extensive planning and analysis than operating budget items. It is often on a separate cycle that precedes the operating budget cycle so that priority capital projects can be fused with operating budget priorities and funded from the total revenue base of the city.

Medium Cities

Recent decades have heralded increased responsibilities for medium-sized city governments. Increasing suburbanization has required sophisticated and costly infrastructure systems. Many cities of this size must try to match growing demands for services with revenue sources that may not grow as fast as the demands for services. Budgeting becomes increasingly complex as the array of choices and alternatives expands with demands for new and more comprehensive services.

Budgeting for medium cities is more difficult to describe than for the smaller or larger cities. Budgeting may be done by a small budget staff of one or two individuals or may be the part-time responsibility of accountants or assistant city managers. The budget process is likely an amalgam of program budget organization, with extensive line-item detail, and perhaps a growing number of performance indicators to help guide council analyses and decisions. As the services provided by the city grow more complex, less reliance is placed on line-item details because the decisions move to larger issues of whether the city should venture into a new service area (e.g., new class of airport) or into a new revenue source (e.g., levy a state-authorized sales tax option). These types of choices are not supported well by line-item detail, and decisionmakers often find performance goals and other outcome-oriented budgeting techniques more helpful.

Counties

County budgeting in the United States is among the least-studied topics. In part, this stems from the rather low profile counties have played in U.S. governance. The primary duties of counties have been roads, jails, property regulation, and elections. The staid routine of county service provisions has been supported by the traditional line-item budget model, with annual budgeting decisions focusing on the incremental changes (increases and decreases) to de-

partment budgets to reflect more sheriff's deputies, squad car and dump truck replacements, and salary increases for county personnel. Traditional county governance uses a commission model, in which the county department heads are elected officials, such as the sheriff, treasurer, assessor, and registrar of deeds.

Urban Counties

In recent decades, counties have received increasing responsibilities from two directions. First, some states have tried to relieve urban cities of difficult fiscal responsibilities such as general welfare by shifting service provision to the county level with its broader tax base (which includes the suburban communities with a healthier sales and property tax base). States have also decentralized other responsibilities to counties, such as environmental protection, which might formerly have gone directly to communities.

The increasing responsibilities of counties, especially urban counties, has had two effects. First, there has been movement to "reform" the county governance model toward a professional manager model. The county board hires a professional county executive (or the county executive is elected at large) and the county executive then hires many of the department heads. Although the sheriff, treasurer, and registrar of deeds are still elected officials, the assessor, as well as the public works and jail administrators, may become appointed officials.

Second, the county budget has become much more complex, both in terms of revenue sources and expenditure choices. The line-item budget that was well suited to the routine adjustments to basic county services provided in former years is often found to be inadequate by professional county executives. Program budget structures and performance indicators, laced with decision unit aspects of zero-based and target budgeting, are adapted to local tastes and preferences to provide county board members with information about the allocation choices they must make. Urban counties also have growing capital budget demands, especially for transportation, and the sophistication of capital budgeting has increased as well.

County budgeting has traditionally been a legislative activity, with department heads presenting their line-item budgets directly to the county board. When counties are reformed to the county executive model, one of the principal changes is also transforming the budget process into an executive budget model, where the department heads submit budget requests to the county executive, who reviews them and submits an executive budget to the county board for its modification and approval. Many large counties (such as Hennepin County, Minnesota, and Johnson County, Kansas) also have a separate budget office, with professional budgeteers who develop, analyze, and implement the county budget year-round.

Rural Counties

The pace of governance and budget reform is much slower in rural counties in the United States. Growth in responsibilities outside urban areas is much slower. The unperturbed duties of the county are little changed, and so too the line-item budgeting process. County department heads are often commissioners and—even if not—submit their incrementally changed budget requests directly to the county board. There is little need for sophisticated budgeting techniques because the choices are well known and focus on marginal allocations to the settled proportional allocation of funds between roads, jails, and elections.

School Districts

School districts are usually separate local governments in the United States, governed by an independently elected board. This is not the custom in the rest of the world, where schools are often a national responsibility administered at the local level. School budgeting is even less studied than county budgeting, which is rather surprising when you consider that schools usually consume the lion's share of the property tax levy in many communities. In fact, much more attention is paid to school financing than to the expenditure aspects. The recently heightened debate over school effectiveness may increase the attention budgeting scholars pay to school budgeting. To date, there is a dearth of studies about performance budgeting or other budget reforms that might apply to school budgeting.

At root, school budgeting is rather simple, because teacher and administrator salaries are almost the entire district budget. The most important budget decision is therefore whether and to what degree teachers will receive salary increases. Many states allow teachers to collectively bargain salaries with school boards, and mediation-arbitration provisions to prevent strikes are important legislative debates, but also important factors that determine the extent to which school budgets can rise in any given year.

School budgeting is complicated in three ways. First, intergovernmental grants play an extraordinary role in school financing, and with the grants come expenditure requirements and constraints that limit the flexibility of the local school board to tailor programs to local preferences. Second, increased attention to the rights of disabled children (physically and developmentally) has increased the requirements on school districts to provide special programs to educate these groups. Third, social problems such as crime and illiteracy are increasingly attacked by state legislatures with solutions that place intervention programs in the schools. The burden of increasing social responsibilities beyond traditional education programs (e.g., breakfast and lunch programs, after-school childcare programs, social worker and psychologist offices) places increased demands on limited school revenue bases, especially when the mandates are only partially funded by state legislatures.

School budgeting is the primary responsibility of the school superintendent, who is hired by the board to be a professional manager of the district's business. The school principals submit individual budget requests to the superintendent, who is often aided in budget development and implementation work by an assistant superintendent who has overall district financial responsibility. The board modifies and approves the budget submitted by the superintendent.

Capital budgeting in school districts is a highly visible process and often controversial. Constructing new schools, major renovations of old schools, and general maintenance of buildings with high safety requirements often require school districts to fund capital projects through bond issues, which must be approved in public referenda. Bonds are usually repaid through property tax levies and the unpopularity of the property tax often casts unfavorable sentiments toward capital bond issues for the school budget. Capital bond issues are viewed by some as important opportunities for local democracy and are widely researched.

Special Districts

Partly in response to the growing service mandates from state and local governments, partly in response to the regional nature of certain problems (such as public transportation), and partly in an effort to overcome taxpayer resistance to increases in general taxes, cities and counties have increasingly opted to create special purpose tax districts to provide services that would otherwise be a responsibility of a general local government. Examples of special districts include Chicago's Regional Transportation Authority (RTA), the Port Authority of New York and New Jersey, Nevada's Reno-Sparks Tourism and Convention Authority, and Milwaukee's Metropolitan Sewage District. These special districts are often governed by a board of directors appointed by the legislative bodies of member jurisdictions. The board hires an executive director, who develops and implements the budget that funds the district. Depending upon the complexity of the district's operations, budgeting may follow the line-item or more program- and performance-oriented models.

Newly Independent Local Governments

The newly independent local governments of the former Soviet Union and Central and Eastern Europe (CEE) have the opportunity to develop local government models that draw on the examples found in the United States, Western Europe, and developing nations around the world. Local governments in Western Europe often provide a wider range of public services than is typical of U.S. local governments (such as health care), but that is changing as U.S. counties increasingly provide health care and other social services and increasingly are asked to administer state programs for more effective service delivery. Local governments in developing nations often lack independent and viable revenue sources that can sustain the level of service provision desired at the local level. A repeated lesson of decentralization efforts in developing nations has been that administrative decentralization without fiscal decentralization impairs the sustainability of the reform from the outset.

In CEE nations such as Poland, administrative decentralization had been supported with fiscal decentralization. Local governments have been given responsibilities for primary education, transportation, social services, and community development on top of responsibilities for primary services such as public transportation, housing, planning, and public works. Governance structures in CEE nations vary; elected city councils in Poland hire a city manager and assistant city managers who form an executive board that provides daily governance. In Ukraine, a mayor is elected at large and works with an elected city council.

Budgeting in CEE local governments is evolving to meet the changing circumstances wrought by newly gained independence and decentralized fiscal and administrative responsibilities. As in many local governments in developing nations, the budget has been merely an accounting tool to inform the central government of compliance with expenditure mandates. Increased independence means increased choices that are better supported with program budget structures and performance indicators that highlight the effectiveness of local expenditures to city councils. The evolution in local government budgeting that has taken 50 years in the United States is taking less than a decade in the new local governments, which can learn important lessons from sister cities around the world.

KURT THURMAIER

BIBLIOGRAPHY

Lehan, Edward A., 1981. *Simplified Government Budgeting.* Chicago: Municipal Finance Officers Association of the United States and Canada (now GFOA).

Moak, Lennox L., and Kathryn Killian Gordon, 1965. *Budgeting for Smaller Governmental Units.* Chicago: Municipal Finance Officers Association of the United States and Canada.

Petersen, John E., and Dennis R. Strachota, eds., 1991. *Local Government Finance: Concepts and Practices.* Chicago: Government Finance Officers Association (GFOA).

Schneider, Mark, and Kee Ok Park, 1989. "Metropolitan Counties as Service Delivery Agents: The Still Forgotten Governments." *Public Administration Review,* vol. 49 (July-August) 345–352.

Sokolow, Alvin D., and Beth Walter Honadle, 1984. "How Rural Local Governments Budget: The Alternatives to Executive Preparation." *Public Administration Review,* vol. 44 (September-October) 373–383.

Thurmaier, Kurt, 1994. "The Evolution of Local Government Budgeting in Poland: From Accounting to Policy in a Leap and a Bound." *Public Budgeting and Finance* (Winter) 83–96.

———, 1995. "Execution Phase Budgeting in Local Governments: It's Not Just for Control Anymore!" *State and Local Government Review* (Spring) 102–117.

LOCAL GOVERNMENT LEADERSHIP.
The capacity to effect change in the structure, purposes, performance, and/or operation of local government.

The manifestation of leadership can be substantive, as reflected in innovation in legal arrangements, policies, programs, or practices. It can also be process-oriented, as reflected by the ability to secure support, mobilize action, and move followers to act.

Local government leadership is a complex and multifaceted topic. Leadership can be exercised by elected officials, administrators, or officials in the private sector. Leaders can operate from inside or outside government, and the focus can either be government itself or the community and its citizens. The nature and methods of leadership will differ to some extent depending on who is providing it and the focus of the leadership. Leadership may also vary in the ends toward which it is directed, whether the object is maintenance and effective handling of recurring tasks or fundamental reordering of the local government agenda and political process.

Familiarity with the variations in local government leadership is important to officials who need to understand the kinds of leadership they themselves practice and the kinds offered (at least potentially) by others. There are no "wrong" ways to approach the subject among those considered. Rather the question is how many "right" aspects of leadership one should try to encompass in one's own behavior and how to balance them. Furthermore, activists and citizens need to understand variations in leadership in order to work more effectively with officials and to identify who gets things done in their community.

The first part of the discussion examines variation in the ways that leadership is conceptualized. These approaches are considered: leadership through use of power; leadership through fostering positive relationships; leadership as innovation; and the purpose and scope of leadership. Each of the approaches is discussed briefly along with consideration of the methods and resources associated with each. The next section briefly examines a critical contextual factor that affects the approach to leadership—the degree of conflict or cooperation in the interactions among officials. In the final section, the approaches will be used to examine leadership among elected officials, administrators, and private sector leaders and to examine leadership in intergovernmental settings.

Alternate Conceptual Approaches

The major approaches are presented as alternatives, but certain of the approaches may be combined in the actual behavior of leaders.

Leadership Through Use of Power

In this approach to leadership, leaders and followers have unequal positions. Leadership is achieved by gaining leverage over other actors or, as stated in a classic question about the nature of power, "How does A get B to do something B would not do otherwise?" A variant is, "How does A prevent B from accomplishing something B wants?" The former represents a positive action as the leader induces the follower through incentives or sanctions to support the leader's intention. The latter is a "nondecision" in which the failure to act prevents change from occurring. Formal and informal resources are instrumental to the exercise of leadership in this approach because it is presumed that there is a "cost" in getting other actors to do something they would not have chosen to do on their own or in blocking their efforts. In organizations, differences in power and authority are institutionalized in superior/subordinate relationships.

Resources are involved in "exchanges" between actors, for example exchanging support of the leader for a benefit to the follower. A key attribute of leaders, according to the power-oriented approach, is their ability to pyramid resources by investing their assets to get more power than they started with.

An example of leadership based on power would be a mayor who assembles an electoral coalition and wins the support of important voter groups in the election by trading support with candidates for other offices and promising jobs and appointments to key leaders, wins support for her policy agenda by including her budget projects in the districts of a majority of council members, and secures successful implementation of her programs by threatening to dismiss department heads who oppose her. It is important to note that, in this example, it is presumed that individuals and groups will be opposed to the leader (or at best indifferent) if their support is not secured.

Leadership Through Fostering Positive Relationships

This approach to leadership emphasizes the interaction among actors rather than the differences in power between them. The key question in this approach is, "How does A get B to recognize they have a common goal and can both be better off if they work together?" The leader accomplishes this not by offering or threatening to do something but rather by building trust and inviting the follower to share in setting goals. In this approach, the leader shapes relationships and sets the tone, particularly through the example of the leader's own behavior. This approach stresses facilitation, an approach to leadership which has the following characteristics:

- *Attitude toward other officials:* The leader empowers others by drawing out their contributions and helping them accomplish their goals; the leader also values and maintains mutual respect and trust.
- *Kind of interactions fostered:* The leader promotes open and honest communication among officials, seeks to manage conflict and to resolve differences in a way that advances the mutual interests of all officials,

shares leadership, forms partnerships, and fosters understanding of distinct roles and coordinated effort among officials.

- *Approach to goal setting:* The leader fosters the creation of a shared vision incorporating personal goals and the goals of others, promotes commitment to the shared vision, and focuses the attention and efforts of officials on accomplishing the shared vision.

An example of leadership through fostering positive relationships is a mayor who works with the city council to determine a common set of goals. The mayor helps to ensure that administrators have the opportunity to offer their expertise to help elected officials define the goals clearly. The mayor monitors how the goals are being accomplished and ensures that administrators provide extensive feedback to the council on progress. When council members consider new initiatives that would divert resources from established goals, the mayor helps them "rediscover" the bases for their earlier decisions and persuades them to maintain their commitments. It is important to note that in this example, it is presumed that officials are inclined to cooperate and/or willing to take part in an effort to identify common ground among them.

Leadership as Innovation and Adaptation

This approach stresses the nature of ideas. Leadership is associated with creativity, invention, the introduction of new methods or approaches, and developing strategies to secure opportunities or minimize threats. Creativity and risk taking are elements that have been associated with entrepreneurial leaders. For example, leaders can accomplish change and/or win followers' support because of the appeal of a development project that revitalizes a city's central business district, an innovative goal solving process that engages the whole community, or a customer-oriented operating system to replace bureaucratic methods in a city agency. Often the leaders of movements inspire followers to action because of the attractiveness of the program they advocate as a response to a widely perceived problem. Examples include the use of nonviolent protest to combat discrimination, property tax rollbacks to reduce perceived tax burdens, or recycling as a solution to solid waste problems.

Related to this approach is the view of leadership as developing approaches that are appropriate to a particular context. The leader recognizes the situation the organization faces and brings it into alignment with its context. This may be accomplished by activating latent support for a new policy in the city rather than overriding opposition. According to this approach, it is the nature of the ideas presented by the leader that is essential for success.

Scope and Purpose of Leadership

This approach stresses the ends toward which leadership is directed. The question here is whether leadership is "transactional" or "transformational." Transactional leaders focus on how things are done and engage in exchanges of resources to secure an immediate end. Each party in the relationship has interests to be satisfied, and a form of leadership occurs when the leader initiates the interaction and is successful in securing agreement that advances the goal the leader wishes to accomplish. As James MacGregor Burns (1978) observes, such actions do not bind the "leader and follower together in a mutual and continuing pursuit of a higher purpose" (p. 20). Examples are a power-oriented leader who uses benefits to assemble a short-term coalition or a facilitative leader who secures superficial consensus support for a collection of individual preferences without identifying underlying shared goals.

Transformational leaders seek to identify and express a higher purpose toward which all strive—a vision for their organizations or communities. As a consequence, such leadership alters attitudes and behaviors. Within an organization, the transformational leader causes followers to become aware of issues of consequence and influences them to transcend self-interest for the good of the group as a whole. In community leadership, it refers to reaching higher levels of motivation and morality in which the leader and follower are bound together in the pursuit of higher purpose. Burns has equated transforming leadership with "elevating, mobilizing, inspiring, exalting, uplifting, preaching, exhorting, evangelizing" (p. 20).

An example of the alternate ends to which leadership is put is found in the response of a police chief to the concerns of residents of a high crime neighborhood. Transactional leadership could be expressed by efforts to get resident input about the types and location of crime that concern them most and redeploying patrols to reduce these crimes. Transformational leadership would be manifested in establishing a new relationship between residents and the police who, in close cooperation with other city departments, establish a "community policing" approach, which is committed to identifying and removing the causes of crime and fostering a continuing partnership between residents and the police.

Patterns of Interaction Among Actors

The patterns of interaction among officials in local government and between private sector leaders and government may be characterized by varying levels of conflict and cooperation. The former is a situation in which actors see their goals as incompatible and use blocking behaviors to prevent others from achieving their goals as well as seeking to advance the accomplishment of their own goals. The actors in a conflict situation view rewards as being "zero-sum" in character, that is, the gains of one actor come at the expense of another. They have a "win-lose" view that turns competition into conflict. In a situation with a high level of cooperation, actors work toward common goals, they coordinate their activities, and they share rewards. Organizations with a legitimate authority structure are likely to have extensive cooperation, even if the larger political context is conflictual. The actors in a cooperative situation view rewards as "positive-sum," that is, all can gain and a "win-win" orientation is possible. Competition and differences in preferences can be accommodated without conflict if there is a commitment to find common ground and share the benefits of action.

The conflictual pattern tends to be associated with power-oriented approaches to leadership since opposing individuals or groups are seeking to secure dominance over each other. The cooperative pattern, on the other hand, permits greater emphasis on leadership through promoting positive relationships. Innovation is potentially important in either situation and may be essential to identifying new relationships or shifting the ways that actors define their interests. Transactional or transformational leadership may also be found in either setting, although the conditions of the conflictual pattern tend to keep actors focused on the short-run realities of securing advantages or arranging compromises and, therefore, keep the participants focused on transactional rather than transformational ends.

Leadership by Chief Elected Officers

Much of the writing on leadership in local government has centered on the contributions of the mayor in city government and, more specifically, the executive mayor in mayor-council governments. In recent years, increasing attention has been given to the roles of the mayor in council-manager cities, in which the mayor does not have executive powers. These two kinds of mayors differ in their formal power and typically operate within contrasting political processes. Mayor-council cities with separation of powers between the executive and legislature are commonly characterized by conflict, whereas council-manager cities based on the unitary model are likely to manifest cooperative relationships among officials. The approach to leadership and the resources on which it is based are likely to differ as well.

Mayors in Mayor-Council Cities

The prototypical mayor in mayor-council cities is an entrepreneur or innovator who provides creative solutions to problems and pyramids resources to gain leverage over other actors and to support coalition building. The approach to leadership is essentially power oriented; ideal leaders are also creative. This mayor is effective at both initiation and also implementation of policies and programs, as was the case with the previous example of the effective leader who uses the power as the basis for leadership.

Formal and informal resources are critical to the mayor's effectiveness, but the mayor's political skill in using these resources will determine success. Formal resources include powers of the office over appointments, budget formulation and execution, and veto. Informal resources include support of a party organization and other key organizations in the city. Personal resources include, in addition to political skill, creativity, clarity of purpose, energy, and effectiveness in media relations.

Effective leadership by the mayor is critical in the mayor-council city. Without it, the offsetting powers of the mayor and council can produce stalemate. If the mayor is a caretaker with no goals, the city will drift and be reactive when problems occur. If the mayor is a reformer or policy initiator but poor at getting things done or a broker who can arrange compromise but has a weak policy agenda, city government will lack a key element of leadership. This form functions best when the mayor is an innovator who can help provide a clear direction for city government and ensure that city departments are focused on accomplishing the goals of elected officials.

Mayors in Council-Manager Cities

The prototypical mayor in council-manager cities is a facilitator who promotes positive interaction and a high level of communication among officials in city government and with the public and who also provides guidance in goal setting and policymaking. This type of leadership is well suited to the conditions of the council-manager city, in which cooperative relationships among officials are common, and the city manager provides support to the elected officials to whom the manager is accountable. Effective leadership by this kind of mayor improves the working relationships among officials, makes the form of government function more smoothly, and increases the involvement of elected officials in setting policy. This mayor must understand how to use the traditional roles of the office—ceremonial leader, presiding officer, link to the public, and representative and promoter of the city—along with the roles of team builder, communicator, and liaison with the manager as the foundation for goal setting, organizing, and policy initiation.

Although these mayors lack formal powers over other officials; they occupy a strategic location in the communication channels with the council, the manager, and the public. Other resources that are derived from the position are access to information and support of and interaction with the city manager. The informal resources are support of key groups in the community and contact with an extensive network of citizens and community leaders. The personal resources include a clear conception of the office, creativity, clarity of purpose, time to devote to office, energy, and effectiveness in media relations. In addition, the facilitator must manifest a commitment to full involvement of members of the governing board through inclusiveness, sharing of information, supporting expression of divergent views, and accepting the initiative of other members, as well as having respect for the authority of the city manager.

The moderately effective mayor goes beyond ceremonial leadership to provide effective coordination and communication. The highly effective mayor also helps to develop a common set of goals with wide council support.

Leadership by Council Members

In addition to the efforts of mayors, council members can also effect change in local government through their activities. Council members, like legislators at other levels of government who generally react to the initiatives of the executive, may be viewed as simply the endorsers of change and, therefore, not as leaders in their own right. The roles filled by council members, however, allow for leadership if filled appropriately. This is particularly true in council-manager cities and counties in which the council can effect change by setting the policy framework within which the city manager operates, by its choice of the manager, and, based on continuing assessment of the manager's performance, by determining whether the executive will remain or will be replaced.

All council members, however, fill three broad roles that provide the opportunity for leadership. The first is the representational role through which council members link their constituents to government and can affect the pattern of service allocation and the level of staff responsiveness to citizens. The second is the governing role through which council members not only sanction policy decisions but may also initiate consideration of issues and shape the content of policies. The third is the oversight role through which council members can assess the effectiveness of programs and the efficiency of resource use by government. If the council is cohesive and guided by a clear sense of purpose—qualities that are easier to achieve in the council-manager form but neither guaranteed nor found exclusively in that form—it can have impact on the direction and operation of local government.

Leadership by Administrators

The first question that must be addressed regarding leadership by administrators is what kinds of leadership they are expected to provide. The well-established tendency to think of decisionmaking in local government as being divided into policy and administrative realms has supported the contention that administrators are to confine themselves to administrative, that is internal organizational, leadership. Since this "dichotomy model" is commonly attributed to the scholars and activists who created the council-manager form of government in the early twentieth century, it is important to note that the founders of this form intended for the city managers to be leaders in policy formation as well as innovative directors of the administrative organization. The commentary published in 1919 that explained the endorsement of the council-manager form by the National Municipal League in its second Model City Charter was explicit on this matter: The manager was to be a leader who formulated policies and urged their adoption by the council. The reformers did not intend to simply add an administrative technician who would take charge of implementation of policies. Only in the late twenties and thirties did the simple dichotomy model emerge, and empirical studies of city managers' roles have consistently shown that city managers can influence policy choice and be community leaders as well as leaders within city government. With variations, the same can be true of administrators in the mayor-council form and of department directors in all local governments.

Thus, administrators potentially provide leadership in three areas: within the organization, in the community, and in support of elected officials.

- *Organizational:* Administrators have the choice of using power-based or facilitative approaches to internal leadership. The former stresses hierarchy, control, and task orientation. The later stresses developing commitment to a shared vision, empowering employees, and flattening the organization. Most of the current studies of public and private-sector leadership stress the superiority of the facilitative approach to leadership. Administrators are also challenged to be innovative and to concentrate on clarifying the ends toward which they work rather than focusing exclusively on the means of accomplishing tasks.
- *Community:* Administrators vary in the extent to which they are involved in community affairs and seek to strengthen the linkages between local government and individuals and groups in the community. Leadership by administrators in the community realm is typically facilitative in nature, since administrators do not legitimately use the resources of governments on their own initiative to secure control over community groups. Rather, leadership consists of strengthening communication with the community, maintaining support from key groups, and involving segments of the community that do not normally participate extensively in community affairs. Administrators have taken the initiative in many local governments to (1) establish citizen participation councils for policy input and/or program evaluation, (2) create coproduction arrangements by which citizens share in the production of a public service, for instance, separation of garbage by citizens to support recycling programs, and (3) utilize citizen surveys to assess the quality of service delivery.
- *Elected officials:* Administrators support elected officials—and thus provide facilitative leadership—and provide information and recommendations that can lead to innovation in goals and policies pursued by local government. When administrators are providing innovative leadership, they raise the awareness of elected officials regarding conditions that require attention and offer creative solutions to community problems. Administrators also support the exercise of leadership by helping elected officials accomplish their goals. Leadership can be more negative and power oriented when administrators use their internal resources to obstruct policy change through ineffective implementation or active resistance. City government employees can also use the weight of their numbers to determine who is elected to the city council or the mayor's office in order to influence policy choices.

Other Community Leaders

This aspect of leadership entails looking for influential persons in the social, economic, service, and political spheres of the community. To some, community leadership is found in a stratified community power structure drawn from the economic elite. To others, the persons with greatest influence are those who are active in government and service agencies. These activists originate ideas, get them accepted, and work on their implementation. These divergent views represent the well-established "elitist" and "pluralist" models of community power. The views may also reveal distinct facets of "influence," all of which are important.

Various sources of community leadership can have differing amounts of influence at distinct stages in the process of community action. Contributors to the origination of ideas can be citizen activists as well as economic elites. An interest group can demonstrate in order to draw attention to a problem, and a developer's plan for a large project can prompt city government action. A second stage in issue formation is legitimization and approval or opposition. Typically, the opinionmakers—who can support or veto new ideas—are part of the community's elite, including key figures in the media. Approval of an idea, by contrast, may require broad-based citizen support. When an idea or project needs resources beyond those that government can generate, those who control wealth and other resources obviously exert great influence over whether that project is accomplished. Finally, new ideas need to be accomplished. The activists who will play the key roles in implementation are likely to come from government, a wide range of civic organizations and agencies, and interest groups. Although these actors are not typically thought of as being power holders, they are usually crucial to the actual success of a new project or program.

There is also evidence that networks of economic and political influence (including elected officials) represent a "regime" that originates action and secures support for certain kinds of activities, usually related to economic development. This governing coalition can also block actions that interfere with or divert resources from its agenda.

The range of participants–those who have more or less influence over affairs in the community–are varied in their background and prominence. It is the rare community in which an economic power elite exerts comprehensive control, and this occurrence is becoming less common. Officials and activists in a given community should carefully assess all those whose support and contributions are necessary for specific projects. It is a mistake to either ignore the major economic interests in the community or to assume that they control all decisions.

Leadership in the Intergovernmental Setting

This discussion has focused on leadership within a single city or county. Another setting in which leadership may be exercised is the loosely defined collection of governments in a metropolitan area. Leaders–usually operating in a facilitative way–may be creative at identifying new relationships and networks, new ways of looking at sharing of resources and costs, and new structures or processes to promote coordinated action among governments, businesses, and other private organizations in the urban region.

JAMES H. SVARA

BIBLIOGRAPHY

Abney, Glenn, and Thomas P. Lauth, 1986. *The Politics of State and City Administration.* Albany: State University of New York Press.

Banfield, Edward C., 1965. *Political Influence.* New York: Free Press.

Browning, Rufus P., Dale Rogers Marshall, and David H. Tabb, 1984. *Protest Is Not Enough.* Berkeley: University of California Press.

Burns, James MacGregor, 1978. *Leadership.* New York: Harper & Row.

Dahl, Robert, 1961. *Who Governs?* New Haven, CT: Yale University Press.

Ehrenhalt, Alan, 1992. *The United States of Ambition.* New York: Times Books.

Ferman, Barbara, 1985. *Governing the Ungovernable City: Political Skill, Leadership, and the Modern Mayor.* Philadelphia: Temple University Press.

Jones, Bryan D., 1989. *Leadership and Politics: New Perspectives in Political Science.* Lawrence: University Press of Kansas.

Prewitt, Kenneth, 1970. *The Recruitment of Political Leaders.* Indianapolis: Bobbs-Merrill.

Stone, Clarence N., 1989. *Regime Politics: Governing Atlanta 1946–1988.* Lawrence: University Press of Kansas.

Svara, James H., 1990. *Official Leadership in the City.* New York: Oxford University Press.

———, 1994. *Facilitative Leadership in Local Government.* San Francisco: Jossey-Bass.

Trounstine, Phillip J., and Terry Christensen, 1982. *Movers and Shakers.* New York: St. Martin's Press.

Welch, Susan, and Timothy Bledsoe, 1988. *Urban Reform and Its Consequences.* Chicago: University of Chicago Press.

LOGISTICS. The techniques and capacities by which organizations store, move, and supply goods, essentially supporting the purposes for which those organizations exist. The most common meaning of the term is the art or science of supplying military forces and delivering them to the field of battle. However, through commercial practices and the changing relationship between marketing methods and wholesale warehousing, the term is now often used loosely to refer to the whole range of requirements regarding the implementation of any activity involving the supply of goods to a delivery point. In the military context, logistics concerns itself with both the movement of men and machines to the battle arena and the provision of the materiel that armed forces require to sustain operations and actual combat. This involves the provision of ammunition, food, water, spares, battlefield building materials, medical supplies, and petrol, oil, and other lubricants. In a wider sense, logistic support also includes all of the supply, transport, administrative, communications, medical, and industrial support required to sustain modern forces in combat.

Success in the logistics field demands not only the physical availability of material but also the staff skills involved in ensuring that the right equipment and supplies are in the right place at the right time. The logistician, as a result, must be an expert not only on narrow stores issues but also with the dynamic problems involved moving these resources around a battlefield where the fog of war and enemy action create yet further problems. Logistical skills in trade and industry are now comparable in that the prevailing need to cut overhead costs in warehouse storage has led to the widespread adoption of the doctrine of "just enough, just in time." Of necessity, this creates conditions that give added value to the role of logistics, somewhat replicating the dynamics of war by the "fog" of commercial rivalry being conducted in the context of a national or regional transport infrastructure.

The importance of logistics has long been noted by the great strategic writers and practitioners. Some have focused on the sheer difficulties caused by logistical demands. Sun Tsu believed that the problem was so intractable that the only solution was to rely on those supplies that could be found locally or taken from the enemy. Antoine H. Jomini, writing from the other side of the industrial and scientific revolution, was more optimistic and gave logistics a similarly high priority while noting its heavy demands on effort and skill. The line between what is accomplishable with great effort and what is too difficult to try remains one that we explore today. Similarly, while some generals are seen as logisticians and others as warfighters dependent upon them, it is the case that few succeeded without some real understanding of the subject. Indeed, the great commanders have tended, like Napoleon and Wellington, to be successful precisely because they mastered logistics problems that defeated others. Armies do indeed march on their stomachs, but they also ride on the success of their support arms in satiating the other requirements of a hungry war machine.

The impact of logistical factors can also be clearly seen in the history of warfare. Logistics has influenced, and often decided, the conduct and outcomes of wars and peacetime strategic choices. Inability to sustain forces at a distance from home has proved fatal to many leaders with overreaching ambition. Russia particularly has survived successive invaders by adopting scorched earth tactics to deny invaders access to local supplies, leaving the invader exposed at the end of long supply lines. Conversely, those armies that have managed to master the logistic constraints that limited other armies of their day have tended to do well. The success of the Mongols and Huns flowed in part from their use of livestock for both mobility and reuseable food supplies. The eventual failure of the Mongols, conversely, owed something to the fact that their horse armies could not find adequate fodder when they ventured too far off the steppes into the forests of Europe. The U.S. Civil War showed the need to master the techniques of supplying forces: The Confederacy failed in mastering the problems of taking the war decisively to the enemy before Northern industrial power could prevail. The United States in World War II showed what sheer logistic capability could support on the battlefield. Arguably, one of the most important innovations of that war was the advent of the first fully motorized fighting force as the United States solved many of the problems that had faced previous commanders with sheer truck power.

Logistics can also determine the pattern of war: Campaigns in World War I and the Soviet advance into Germany in World War II were timetabled in effect by the need to build up stocks for each offensive and then to recover and rebuild for the next attempt to move forward. Allied amphibious operations were also constrained by the limited amount of available sealift, with the result that the strategic timetables of the war were set by the need to recover from one operation and redeploy ships to the next. Logistics has also determined the onset of war and the shape of the subsequent peace. The inherent complexity of mobilization planning for mass armies was certainly a factor in 1914. As preplanning became essential, options were reduced and timescales shortened—perhaps to the point that statesmen were forced to set in motion mobilization schedules that contained their own inflexible momentum into war. Equally, in 1945, even in the unlikely event that U.S. statesmen had decided to advance more quickly into Germany to

secure it from Russian invasion, there were logistic limitations on the U.S. Army that precluded that. In a war with massive industrial and societal support for the Armed Services, the sheer difficulty of moving large forces across oceans and continents imposes its own logic on strategy.

Despite its historic importance, logistics remains an underappreciated art. The complexities of the subject have deterred many analysts. Political leaders are usually only confronted with the consequence of logistical factors—in the form of recommendations on options—rather than reaching a full understanding of logistical implications, requirements, and limitations. The reality of the cold war for the West—and, possibly, on different timescales, for the Soviet bloc too—was that conventional war simply could not be sustained beyond 10 to 14 days. The requirement for everything from spares to ammunition to gas masks—even to fight a 30-day war—proved simply unaffordable for NATO. And there was not much hope of maintaining a working logistics infrastructure in the midst of what would have been the most destructive engagement in history. For much of the period from 1952 to 1989, therefore, the working, professional assumption was that major war was not sustainable. Even in the post–cold war era, the scale of the problem is simply too immense for easy comprehension—the Gulf War in 1990–1991 required, for the United States alone, the movement of 503,000 men, around 3.7 million tons of equipment, and 6.1 million tons of fuel using 13,610 flights and 460 shiploads. All of this then had to be moved from the ports and airports to the frontline using a massive infrastructure of intermediate supply depots, trucks, and specially laid roads. This was more than had been moved across the English Channel, a far shorter distance, in seven months in 1944–1945 and more than four times what was moved during the 1948 Berlin airlift.

It is arguable that the Gulf War may represent the limit of what is physically achievable in sustaining modern, potentially high intensity, combat. Given less time to deploy and organize, an aggressive enemy, less available support from the host nation, and fewer ports and airheads to deploy into, it is very questionable whether Desert Shield and Desert Storm could have proved the logistical triumphs they in fact became. Indeed, it is possible that the very success of Western logistics in the Gulf War may have produced the wrong conclusions about the logistical needs of the post–cold war era. The reality of future military operations is that they are likely to be conducted at short notice in distant lands. Opponents are likely to run the spectrum from those only capable of offering guerrilla-type resistance to medium powers with large quantities of obsolete equipment augmented by some long-range striking power, potentially increasingly in the form of ballistic missiles. In such circumstances, the difficulties of getting viable forces to a region where the indigenous infrastructure is deficient in most respects may be exacerbated by the fact that the logisticians themselves may be under attack from the start of the operation as the distinction between the frontline and, supposedly, safe rear areas is exposed as false. If the operation then turns out to be protracted, and it has to be fought using equipment, spares, and manpower designed and procured only for use over the short periods anticipated for cold war scenarios, there is a danger that logistic requirements could quite easily exceed capability. Although computerization has aided the logistician, equipment has become more reliable, and modern munitions have reduced the need for sheer numbers of rounds, the reality is that much of this has been offset by the increase in the cost of mobility, the sheer range of equipment and skills needed, the fragility of some modern technology and the vulnerability of the whole to an enemy with offensive reach. Mankind, in short, has not yet solved the problem of supplying war.

This is an important conclusion, because the ease of the Gulf operation may have produced a feeling of unwarranted complacency—even a perception that cold war levels of support may now safely be cut. Far from being a less demanding world where logistics infrastructure can be sacrificed in favor of maintaining the frontline, or even one where support tasks can be civilianized, it appears that the future environment for armed forces is one that will require a continuation of the trend toward relatively larger combat support forces supporting a declining frontline. Deploying forces actually to fight, rather than just deter, as in the cold war, will bring increased demands to sustain potentially protracted conflicts. Fighting, or peacemaking, in the underdeveloped world will require the movement of the developed world's infrastructure around the globe. The logistician's skills will still be in demand in the future. The logistician's costs will be high. The cost of not providing logistical support—thereby creating a hollow window-dressing force—will, as always, be higher. For countries whose military establishments have adopted the commercial doctrine of "just enough, just in time," this could be especially challenging.

D. JOHN PAY

BIBLIOGRAPHY

Creveld, Martin van, 1977. *Supplying War: Logistics from Wallenstien to Patton.* London: Cambridge University Press.
Jomini, Antoine-Henri, 1862. *The Art of War.* Philadelphia: Lippincott.
Keegan, John, 1993. *A History of Warfare.* New York: Knopf.

LOTTERIES. A form of gambling in which players selected by chance win cash prizes.

Public, private, and charitable lotteries have been popular in America since colonial times. These lotteries helped fund major universities and public buildings and services. Lotteries in the early period were corrupt and involved unethical and immoral practices (e.g., fraud, delaying draw-ings, and defaulting on awarding prizes) that contributed to their scandalous reputation. Outrage at these abuses gained momentum among those who already opposed lotteries on moral grounds. Congress, spurred by antilottery sentiments, passed a series of increasingly effective restrictions on the use of the mail system to conduct lotteries. The last legal mail lottery was shut down in the United States in 1894, when federal regulations prohibited interstate lottery transactions (Clotfelter and Cook 1989).

Government lotteries did not exist again until 1964 when the New Hampshire legislature authorized a state lottery in an effort to avoid increasing the general sales and individual income taxes. The proceeds from this and the 1967 New York lottery did not meet expectations. State lotteries were considered a fiscal dud until 1971 when the New Jersey lottery began marketing its games as entertainment. This technique proved to be successful because the proceeds that were generated exceeded expectations. The success of the New Jersey lottery contributed to the adoption of lotteries in other states. Within a four-year time frame, 13 states sponsored lotteries. States adopt lotteries by initiatives and referenda, and through legislation.

Lottery revenues are often earmarked for certain functions such as education, programs for the elderly, economic development, infrastructure and transportation, agricultural projects, parks and recreation, and the arts. Interest groups in 14 states have succeeded in earmarking lottery revenues for their own use, for example, education and the elderly. Earmarking is important because it guarantees financial support for certain services even during difficult budgetary periods.

Lotteries as an Alternative Source of Revenue

During the late 1970s, many states experienced a tax revolt spurred by California's Proposition 13, which reduced property tax revenues by 57 percent and limited future increases to no more than 2 percent annually. From 1978 until 1980, other states responded to the California message with tax and spending limitation measures, which meant that fewer revenues went into the states' coffers. States responded by increasing sales and income taxes, adding a few pennies to gasoline taxes, extending user fees for services, and creating state sponsored lotteries. In the aftermath of taxpayer revolts and reductions in intergovernmental aid, then, lotteries gained popularity as an alternative source of revenue.

In fiscal year 1992–1993 the total generated from state lotteries exceeded US $19 billion (U.S. Department of Commerce 1994). Despite this seemingly high return rate, lotteries do not become productive revenue sources overnight. The greatest lottery revenues per capita are in states that implemented lotteries before 1975. Successful lotteries are a relatively minor feature of state fiscal policy and are not ready solutions to short-term deficits or long-term revenue needs, however. This is due, in part, to high administrative costs and cash prizes, which together amount to more than half the proceeds. In terms of administrative cost rates, lotteries compare unfavorably and are a less efficient source of revenue generation than more traditional options. However, lotteries are able to cover their operating costs, making them better than most user fees for funding state services. States cannot rely on the lottery as a stable or reliable source of net revenue because lotteries are affected by changing consumer preferences, the introduction of new games, state marketing efforts, competitor lotteries, illegal gambling, and other factors beyond a state's control (Mikesell and Zorn 1986, pp. 311–320).

Opposition to State Lotteries

One criticism of a lottery deals with its fairness as a method for distributing the cost of government. Opponents note that state lotteries place a greater relative burden on low income groups than on high income groups. Studies show that low income individuals spend a substantially greater share of their income on lotteries than do those with higher incomes. By some measures, the lottery is twice as regressive as a state sales tax. Proponents counter that the lottery is nearly ideal because participation is voluntary and broad (Mikesell and Zorn 1986, pp. 311–320).

Some opponents criticize state sponsorship of an activity that creates social problems, such as economic distress or gambling addiction. States are also criticized for involvement in a business that does not clearly advertise the odds of winning and misquotes the present value of cash prizes. This is a critical issue because private firms are not permitted to utilize these deceptive marketing strategies. As a result, a state's role in operating an enterprise at this level is questioned. Despite these problems, proponents argue that state-operated lotteries provide an alternative to illegal gambling. In addition, modern lotteries are free from the scandals of their predecessors (Mikesell and Zorn 1986, pp. 311–320).

Some argue that lottery administrators make claims about the use of lottery funds to enhance certain earmarked programs and services despite difficulties in linking expenditure patterns to lottery revenues. Despite claims of a lack of state accountability, 32 states now have lotteries (U.S. Department of Commerce 1994).

BERNADETTE T. MUSCAT

BIBLIOGRAPHY

Clotfelter, Charles T., and Philip J. Cook, 1989. *Selling Hope: State Lotteries in America.* Cambridge, MA: Harvard University Press.
Mikesell, John L., and C. Kurt Zorn, 1986. "State Lotteries as Fiscal Savior or Fiscal Fraud: A Look at the Evidence." *Public Administration Review,* vol. 46, no. 4 (July–August) 311–320.

U.S. Department of Commerce, 1994. "Table No. 482, Gross Revenue from Parimutuel and Amusement Taxes and Lotteries–Selected States: 1992." *The National Data Book: State Abstract of the United States,* 114th ed., 311.

LUHMANNIAN PERSPECTIVES ON PUBLIC ADMINISTRATION AND POLICY.

The writings and teachings of the scholar Niklas Luhmann considers social systems—particularly governmental and political systems—as complexity reducing mechanisms. His intellectual inspirations on the general theory of social systems and their environments derive both from his personal experience in administration and from his education and professorial background in the areas of public administration, decisionmaking, and bureaucracy.

Introduction

Niklas Luhmann's oeuvre represents today one of the very few grand post-Parsonian theory designs in sociology. This observation makes it all the more striking that he started his work with publications on the theory and practice of public administration and public policy. Luhmann, who had studied law in Freiburg, Germany, from 1946 to 1949, worked as a civil servant at the Oberverwaltungsgericht at Lüneburg and the parliament of Niedersachsen before he received a fellowship from the Graduate School of Public Administration at Harvard University. He then moved on to the Hochschule für Verwaltungswissenschaften at Speyer, the Sozialforschungsstelle Dortmund, and finally, as a Professor of Sociology, to Bielefeld. His intellectual trajectory indicates that important aspects of his general theory of social systems were inspired by the insights and concerns of theories of public administration, decisionmaking, bureaucracy, as well as by his personal experience in administration.

In the following, we will reconstruct aspects of Luhmann's early writings on public administration, especially his critiques of Max Weber's understanding of bureaucracy. We will then show how this early work informed Luhmann's approach to social systems in general and politics and government in particular. In a last section, we will deal with the "autopoiesis" of the welfare state and its consequences for bureaucratic adaptiveness and governmental steering.

The Theory and Practice of Public Administration: The Departure from Classical Theory

It is instructive to present Luhmann's (1982b, pp. 20–46) views on a theory of administration and bureaucracy as a departure from Weber's classical discussion. Weber (1947), as is well known, understood bureaucratic administration as the typical manifestation of rational or legal authority (pp. 329–336).

Luhmann challenges the classical model on empirical grounds. His two main targets of critique are Weber's "means/ends schema" and "command and control model." Because much of the means/ends critique has become a commonplace, we do not need to go into details. Ends do not necessarily precede means; and they are not always "instructive" in the sense that they always prescribe a "correct," much less the only "correct," means of obtaining them. Moreover, organizations can have contradictory goals. Stipulated ends in organized systems are not the motive for the actions of the members. They can be modified, reinterpreted, or altered. The identity of a system need not change with a modification of ends, even with a modification of "highest" or "ultimate" ends. In addition, the attainment of the system's ends does not imply survival. In other words, success defined by internal criteria does not necessarily represent a successful response to changes occurring in the system's environment (1982b, pp. 26–29).

The second target of Luhmann's critique is the "command and control model," which is implicit in Weber's analysis. According to Luhmann, there are at least four instances in which the model does not correspond to empirical reality. First, the command model can only see the process of rationalization from the point of view of a single participant. In modern organizations, there is simply no single controller. Second, the model neglects that subordinates are often more knowledgeable than their superiors and excludes possibilities of learning as well as of functional differentiation along the vertical axis. Hence, the command model underestimates the relevance of the flow of information from bottom to top. Third, it neglects that consensus, which is all the more needed when goals are unclear and uninstructive, cannot be commanded. Finally, whereas the actual power structure of an organization is reflected in the decisionmaking process, the command model inaccurately emphasizes the mere implementation of decisions (1982b, pp. 31–36).

According to Luhmann, the crucial discovery in empirical organization research that made it necessary to depart from Weber was made by Elton Mayo and his colleagues in the famous experiments in the Hawthorne factory of the Western Electric Company. To be sure, it had long been generally acknowledged that people do not always obey officially proclaimed goals. People can be lazy. They may not perform to their highest ability, and they may make mistakes and break rules. The new insight, however, was that deviations from norms are part of the social order of an organization. They are expected and sometimes obligatory. Deviations from norms, often discredited as "mistakes," actually contribute to the maintenance and preservation of the system. Luhmann (1982b) observes that this empirical finding cannot properly be understood in Weber's methodology of ideal types (p. 46).

Luhmann's early critique of Weber's model of bureaucracy summarized a number of theoretical trends in public administration theory that were prominent in the 1950s and 1960s. All these trends were directed against the "science of administration" school, which had thought of rationalization only in terms of an optimal use of people and resources in order to arrive at stipulated ends. Herbert Simon (1947, 1957) responded to the limitations of this school with his concepts of "bounded rationality" and "satisficing routine behaviour". Political scientists like David Easton (1953), Robert Dahl (1947), and Gabriel Almond and James Coleman (1960) emphasized the relation between system and environment. The incorporation of the environment of the system into organization studies is also at the heart of contingency theory. The critique of the "myth of the unitary decisionmaker" is a recurrent theme in the field up to today (Majone 1986). Finally, bottom-up approaches to bureaucratic organization attracted much attention in the 1970s and 1980s precisely because they seemed to depart from the classical model of unidirectional top-bottom hierarchies.

The Theory and Practice of Public Administration: Administration and Systems

Luhmann's early work on public administration and organization theory provided the basis for his theory of social systems. Because the significance of system building rests not only in an "internal ordering of parts into a whole" but in a system's negotiations with its environment, any theory of organizations, bureaucracy, or even social systems in general would have to start with the distinction between system and environment. Luhmann's (1970) "systems theory," at that time still to be written, has always been a "system/environment theory" (pp. 39–40).

Bureaucratic systems also show how bureaucracy frees systems from a concern with the "motivational structure" and personal conditions of its members. People come and go, but the organization remains. From this observation, Luhmann concludes that, in general, rationality at the level of individual action is not the same as rationality at the level of social systems. Hence, the thoughts of individual persons are to be conceptualized as systems of their own. "Persons" always belong to the environment of a social system. Even the "members" of an organization belong to the environment of that organization. The meaning an action has for an organization differs from the meaning it has to its individual members. In fact, most organizations will be indifferent toward the personal concerns of its members (1964, pp. 25–26). This distinction between personal (conscious) and social (communicative) systems later evolved into one of the pillars of Luhmann's theory (1981b, p. 16). Luhmann gives Parsons the credit for having been the last theorist to think of the relations between personal and social systems as intrasystemic relations (1981b, p. 154).

At this early stage of his work, Luhmann describes the relationship between system and environment as a slope of complexity. The world is excessively complex in that it always contains more possibilities than the system can respond or adapt to (1968, p. 5). In other words, the environment is always more complex than the system. The difference between the system and environment is the difference between the indeterminate, undeterminable, unmanipulatable complexity of the world and the concrete, determinate, manipulatable complexity a system represents to itself (Habermas and Luhmann 1971, pp. 11, 15–16, 19). The function of a system is precisely to make complexity accessible by "reducing" it. By being selective, the system selectively transforms problems it finds in its environment into internal–"systemic"–problems. The problems are not solved but reformulated, simplified, limited, distributed so that the system can deal with them. The system builds up defensive internal complexity against the causal pressure of an environment that is always too complex. Complexity is here the ultimate reference point for functional analysis.

Again, public bureaucracy, or call it "government," serves as the prototypical example. The governmental system is "rational" to the extent that it is able to stabilize its relationship to its environment (Luhmann 1966, pp. 9–25; Van der Eyden 1980, pp. 147–160). Hence, rationalization means system differentiation. The formation of the system is manifested in the possibility of regulating action, the normative adherence to expectations, and in the existence of criteria evaluating the rationality of "solutions" (Luhmann 1966, pp. 112–113).

For government, the slope of complexity differentiating it from its environment is visible in the multitude of demands and problems to be dealt with. The system cannot deal with all problems, and those it selects to consider cannot always be dealt with simultaneously. Proposals of solutions depend on the previous selection of problems. Neglected problems are likely to crop up at a later stage, confronting the system with the contingency of its proposed solutions. Decisionmaking and problem solving become permanent necessities. There is no final, ultimate answer to the complexity of the environment. The system, therefore, continues to exist.

System differentiation is essentially a process of stabilization of expectations. It occurs along three dimensions: temporal, material, and social. The notion of "time" is used by systems whenever they interpret reality in terms of the distinction between past and future. Systems constitute their own time horizons. For government to be autonomous, it needs time. It cannot deal with all problems and demands simultaneously. It breaks up its dealings with the environment in input and output instances. For the legal system, whether or not a case belongs to the "past" depends on whether it has been decided in the court of last instance. For a political party organization, the future may not

begin tomorrow but only (perhaps) after the next election. In the material dimension (Sachdimension), the system divides reality into what it deems relevant and "everything else," into what it considers significant for its own operation and all other aspects of the world toward which it remains indifferent. In government, this allows for a differential treatment of issues and demands. In the social dimension, the system defines its boundaries by defining its "alter ego," that is, by defining other systems in its environment to which it can relate (Luhmann 1964, p. 68; 1981b, p. 119). By defining itself as an "organization," a social system makes itself comparable to other organizations. It even adopts legal frameworks applicable to all organizations.

A "program" is a pattern the system uses in selectively processing information picked up from its environment. Luhmann (1968) distinguishes two different types of programs depending on whether they are oriented toward input or output. "Goal programs" are those which take a particular systemic response as invariant and accordingly select "causes" that bring it about. Conditional programs hold constant particular "causes" that, whenever they occur, trigger a particular type of action (pp. 98, 201, 231). Goal programs may be justified ideologically. Conditional programs are typical in a legal context. They lower the discretionary power of officeholders and offer objective criteria for deciding. The weight given to one or the other type of program determines the government's ideological or legal orientation in problem solving (1982b, pp. 110–113).

Luhmann considers conditional programming to be more elastic than goal programming. Heavy reliance on goal programs usually reflects a belief in rational planning, in optimal modelling, and in fact in many of the assumptions characteristic of the "science of administration school." It is characteristic for central planning and multi-annual planning, which typically assume that all alternatives can be compared and consistently integrated. Governments seem most able to cope with complexity when they combine both types of programming (Luhmann 1971). Defined in rather broad terms, goals may incorporate conditional programming. A first step of conditional openness to the environment may provide decisional premises upon which goal programs operate. In this way, goal programming resembles "steering." A mixture of conditional and goal programs often corresponds to a mixture of centralized (goal) and decentralized (conditional) decisionmaking. In decentralized systems, goal programs are executed at lower levels of complexity and interdependency. Decentralization thus prevents that problems of complexity are channelled up to a level where they can no longer be adequately dealt with. In an empirical study in urban and spatial planning, Miryam Beck (1986) was able to trace the obsoleteness and inefficiency of planning models back to a missing linkage between conditional and goal programming. For Beck, the absence of this linkage is in turn caused by an insufficient implementation of reflexivity.

Reflexivity is an important tool in the differentiation of a system and hence in the reduction of complexity. Processes become reflexive when they are applied to themselves. By deciding how to make decisions, one decision eventually represents a multitude of decisions. By learning how to learn, one insight allows and predetermines a multitude of further insights (Luhmann 1970, pp. 92–112). "Planning," as a decision on what decisions need to be made in the future, is a reflexive process almost by definition (Luhmann 1971, p. 67). Reflexivity divides the reductions of complexity into two or more sequential stages. In fact, reflexivity is a response to complexity in that it increases the selectivity of actions. Highly complex environments thus call for a complex, reflexive organization of decisionmaking precisely because decisions will be made at various parts of the system.

Politics, Government, and the Welfare State: The Function of the Political System

The political system is a functional subsystem of society just like science, economics, or religion. Society is as the totality of communication the all-encompassing social system (Habermas and Luhmann 1971, pp. 16–19. Luhmann's most elaborate account of the political system is *Political Theory in the Welfare State* (1981a; 1990a). Although he does not yet use the word "autopoiesis" to describe the systemic nature of politics, it is evident that Luhmann is close to making a commitment to Maturana's and Varela's terminology. Systems are defined as "self-referential." In other words, a system produces and reproduces the elements out of which it is composed. In the case of the political system, these elements are "political decisions" (Luhmann 1990a, p. 40). Even openness is now produced by the system. On the basis of its self-referential closure, the system continuously mediates between openness and closure. We do not consider the introduction of the concept "autopoiesis" (1982a) as a departure from Luhmann's earlier writings. Instead, it radicalizes and clarifies Luhmann's earlier use of the concept "system." In a sense, *Political Theory in the Welfare State* reflects the continuity behind Luhmann's writings. Although the concept "autopoiesis" is not used in the book, it is nevertheless clear that its later introduction is merely an introduction of a label to what has always been at the center of Luhmann's concerns.

The function of the political system in society is to "integrate" society (Luhmann 1982b, p. 144). In other words, its function is to supply the capacity to enforce collectively binding decisions (Luhmann 1990a, p. 73). A decision is binding when it effectively restructures the expectations of those affected and thus becomes the premise for their future behavior (Luhmann 1982b, p. 145). This function already entails several consequences for the "architecture" of politics as a system. For example, the internal differentiation of the political system must not correspond to the external

differentiation of its environment. For if internal and external differentiation did correspond, cross-boundary alliances would be likely to dissolve the system (Luhmann 1982b, p. 144). Another precondition for the operation and indeed emergence of the political system is the absence of one solid power in its environment (e.g., a church or a big stockholder). The functional differentiation of society means precisely that systems condense around particular functions. If the political system saw itself faced with one solid power, the very need for "integration" would not exist. The differentiation of a political system is thus a historical phenomenon (Luhmann 1989, pp. 65–148).

Whereas these requirements are both located in the social dimension of the system's "autonomy," equally important conditions of the existence of the political system need to be secured in the temporal and material dimension. The system must develop its own time horizons so that it cannot always be forced to react immediately to outside impulses (Luhmann 1982b, p. 143). In the material dimension, the political system must be able to presuppose that it is more or less generally accepted in its environment. This level of acceptance must be abstract enough so that breakdowns, disappointments, failures at the level of daily transactions, do not question the existence and necessity of politics.

The advanced democratized political system of today is internally differentiated into a "politically relevant public," "government" (including legislation, jurisdiction, and public bureaucracy) and "(party) politics." Democratization implies that a politically relevant public affects the meaning of all political operations. The qualification "politically relevant" is necessary to distinguish the "political" public from the population at large. The political system assigns meaning to people only to the extent that they are, say, taxpayers or voters, that is, to the extent that they fulfill certain roles. These roles are creations of the political system and, taken together, form a subsystem of their own. Government and legislation, in some translations referred to as "public bureaucracy" or "bureaucratic administration," comprise the totality of "institutions that create binding decisions pursuant to political viewpoints and political mandate" (Luhmann 1990a, p. 48). Political parties as permanent organizations transformed the dichotomy between "state" and "public" into a more complex arrangement. With the disappearance of traditional and religious forms of domination, the political premises for decisions have become variable. Law has become "positive" and the public "politically relevant." The result is the differentiation of a "genuine" sphere of politics within the political system. Political parties arose under these new circumstances precisely because political support now needs to be continually cultivated.

The internal dynamics of the political system are largely determined by the intersystem relations between its subsystems. As the three subsystems of the political system are all self-referentially closed, they need to break up the

"I'll do what you want if you do what I want" circle in their relationships. In order to do this, the systems must make their respective environments relevant. For the relation between the political public and (party) politics, the main environmental reference is "public opinion." (Party) politics and government coordinate their operations mainly in their orientation toward persons who hold offices or who can be considered for holding them. Finally, for government and the public, law functions as the main external reference point. It is through these reference points—public opinion, law, and persons—that information about the environment is gathered and political relevance assessed. The necessity to externalize internal indeterminacies in inter-subsystem relations is the ultimate guarantee for the "openness" of the political system.

On the Differentiation Between Government and Politics

In Luhmann's view, "politics" and "government" are functionally and analytically differentiated. "Politics," in the narrow sense of "party politics," deals with the articulation and generalization of interests (Luhmann 1971, pp. 74–75). By gathering consensus and by transforming preferences into demands, "politics" is responsible for the legitimation of power. Hence, political parties appear instrumental and opportunistic. The primary goal in the political struggle is to acquire and to hold power. Political programs as means are subordinate to the end of reelection. Values appear as variable and functional and hence become instrumentalized. However, Luhmann emphasized (1982b, p. 97, referring to Braybrooke and Lindblom 1963) that the instrumental use of values is an immediate consequence of the absence of stable criteria for the evaluation of values. Under these circumstances, the political power struggle is not a sign of decadence, but an organizational mechanism for the consideration (and selection) of particular values in relation to other values.

Hence, by stabilizing the decisional premises, political processes reduce complexity into a form that is manageable for the government (Luhmann 1971, pp. 66–83). The government can implement programs only to the extent that it is understood that the "political" aspects of decisions, the generalization of consensus and the provision of legitimacy, are taken care of elsewhere. The differentiation of politics and government as separate mechanisms serves to de-burden administrative processes (Luhmann 1971, pp. 74–75).

The government, in turn, processes information and issues decisions according to its "programmatic structure." The programmatic structure is a set of decisional premises, a preselection of possible options. The legitimacy of those structures is based on the fact that they can be changed in a nonarbitrary way via procedures designed for that purpose. The procedural changeability of the programmatic structure is the basis of its legitimacy (Luhmann 1969; 1971, pp. 81–89; Van der Eyden 1980, pp. 153–155). In this framework, we can say that the relations between politics and government are located at the level of the programmation of decisions. The government obtains its programmatic structure through its "structural coupling" with politics. In contrast, it is not the programmatic structure as a whole but individual programmed decisions that are at stake in the relations between government and public.

Many of the dichotomies that are prominent in classical public administration theory lose their familiarity, if not their meaning, once we switch to Luhmann's framework. There is no simple distinction between civil servants and politicians, between "up" and "under," between "goals" and "means," or between decisionmaking and implementation. None of these distinctions describes adequately the complex relationship between "politics" and what we called "government." Moreover, the relationship between the two is not easily translatable into a particular institutional boundary. The difference between "politics" and "government" as subsystems of the political system is simply the difference between two rationalities (Luhmann 1971, pp. 80–82).

Politics, Government, and the Welfare State: Politics in the Welfare State

The defining characteristic of welfare states is the realization of "political inclusion" (Luhmann 1990a, p. 35). "Political inclusion" means the encompassing of the entire population in the performances of the political system, that is, the "encompassing of ever broader aspects of modes of living within the domain of political guarantees" (p. 35). Moreover, inclusion implies that both access to and dependence on the political system become universal.

Politics in the welfare state tends to promote those systems whose functions translate quickly and convincingly into gains for persons or groups, such as economy, education, health care (Luhmann 1990a, p. 77). It is in those domains where "inclusion" has the most concrete effects. Because the idea of "inclusion" only determines that everyone deserves political inclusion but not how, the process is essentially open-ended. As "welfare" is also potentially unlimited, the modern welfare state is at a loss to provide any objective indicators for the boundaries of state activity. As a consequence, the political system is often the creator of the complexity it faces in its ongoing operation.

The political system uses money and law as symbolically generalized media of communication (Luhmann 1990a, p. 82). Such communicative media do not just transmit communication. They also condition responses to the communication they transmit. They entail motivational structures (Luhmann 1990a, p. 82; 1975b, pp. 170–192; 1975a). Law and money provide external reasons for adjusting one's behavior to specific conditions. As they provide premises for decisions and are able to transfer their binding effects, both media make centralized decisions possible.

As its activities do not know "limits," the welfare state will tend to overestimate the power of law and money to realize "inclusion." The result is frequently an overloading of these means. The welfare state is too expensive and the expansion of the legal domain–"Verrechtlichung"–leads to overregulation. The side effect of this is also that rules are not applied anymore. Noncompliance, tax evasion, civil disobedience, corruption, and black market phenomena are all parts of the welfare state. Moreover, their abstractness and modes of functioning make law and money into a catalyst for the establishment of large organizational systems and hence of bureaucracies. In the absence of criteria for limits of growth, bureaucratic organizations often measure "success" in terms of self-satisfaction. The bureaucracy operates "successfully" if the situation of its own personnel is improved. Similarly, the success of welfare state policies is measured in terms of the proliferation of bureaucratic offices dealing with welfare issues. Public health conditions are considered to be improving with an increase in the number of hospitals. Public education seems to flourish with the number of schools and teachers. The result of this self-referential measurement is a "dynamic conservatism" in which the preservation of the bureaucratic system is valued higher than performance (Kickert 1993).

In the practice of self-satisfaction, failure is attributed to a lack of cooperation and organization, hence to a lack of more bureaucracy and less often to the unsuitability of money and law as media for the attainment of desired goals. In their pioneering study on implementation, Pressmann and Wildavsky (1973) explained the failure of large-scale community projects by referring to the very complexity of joint action. Fritz Scharpf's (Sharpf et al. 1976) study on "Politikverflechtung" pursues similar lines. However, both take for granted what Luhmann questions at a much deeper level: the very efficiency of money and law as means of communication. Law and money, Luhmann (1990a) says, "cannot change the people themselves. 'People processing' cannot be steered causally and technically by means of law and money" (pp. 83–84).

Luhmann's systems theory presents the openness of systems toward their environments as an achievement. The system's (selective) openness is not given but needs to be maintained in the operation of the system. Luhmann's work is thus well suited to remind public administration theorists as well as practitioners of the dangers of "systemic blindness." At the level of theory, the self-perpetuation of bureaucracy received a great deal of attention in "population ecology," a branch in organization theory that studies the "births" and "deaths" of organizations. In practice bureaucratic excrescence is often countered with "sunset laws" (Kickert 1993). Sunset laws introduce time limits for policies and hence provide decisional premises for terminating decisionmaking. In the end, however, the only way to break bureaucratic self-perpetuation is to force the system to perpetually rethink the relationship to its environment.

The alleged crisis of the welfare state is, of course, a popular theme. Scholars point to a paradox of overregulation and underimplementation in this context (Majone 1995). Michel Crozier's distinction between a "decisional," a "financial," and a "confidence" crisis of the welfare state highlights that the problems occur in all three dimensions of the autonomy of the political system: temporal, material, and social (Crozier 1991).

However, Luhmann's design emphasizes that what appear to be pathological symptoms of "crises" are in fact deeply rooted in the very self-understanding of the welfare state itself. By raising the levels of abstraction in his theoretical work and pointing to the complexity of modern society, Luhmann tries to discipline criticisms of society. A political critique of bureaucracy criticizes, after all, a "self-created, self-desired, self-affirmed phenomenon" (Luhmann 1990a, p. 89; 1991).

Autopoiesis and the Possibility of Steering

If systems are self-referentially closed–"autopoietic"–and if they respond to the environment only to the extent that it is internally represented in such systems (Teubner 1993, p. 74), then the very possibility of purposeful access and "steering" is questioned. If a system always follows its own rationality, how can its operation be influenced from outside (Willke 1985)? Hence, Luhmann's work became a focal point for debates about a "regulatory crisis" and a "Steuerungspessimismus" (Scharpf 1989).

This controversy on the possibility of societal guidance fits nicely into a number of recent developments in modern public administration theory. First, the move from a monocentric state approach, to a polycentric approach, which articulates the importance and multiplicity of relatively autonomous actors, is discussed in Vincent Ostrom and Elinor Ostrom (1965), Vincent Ostrom (1972), Kenneth Hanf and Fritz Scharpf (1987), Fritz Scharpf (1989), and Helmut Willke (1992), among others. The classical monocentric approach is driven by the assumption of a single guidance center capable of improving policymaking and implementation through reorganization, coordination through purposeful planning and regulation, and the employment of better control mechanisms. For the polycentric approach, policy is not the outcome of one central decision, but the sum, if not more than the sum, of several decisions made by a multiplicity of actors and organizations (Klijn and Teisman 1991). We find similar ideas in network analysis. However, the network analysis literature is still based on what is sometimes called "methodological individualism," whereby human beings, either on their own or as members of groups and organizations, are the units linked by the network (Klijn and Teisman 1991, pp. 110–111). The central units of network analysis thus are actors whose behavior is patterned by resource dependence and bargaining structures. We need not repeat here that Luhmann refers to individuals in a very different way.

Recent ideas about de-regulative privatization and "steering from a distance" (Kickert 1995) also emphasize a combination of regulation and self-organization. It is not accidental that this approach has been used in research on policymaking and implementation in the European Union. More generally, the mismatching of policy instruments and the "policed" field has provoked a renewed interest in the instruments of government (Mayntz 1983, 1993; In't Veld et al. 1991; de Bruijn and ten Heuvelhof 1991; Majone 1990). Hood's (1983) *Tools of Government* reflects this trend in the United Kingdom. The new literature distinguishes between regulation (legal instruments or "the stick"), subsidization (economic instruments or "the carrot"), and political rhetoric (communicative instruments or "the sermon").

Finally, two more recent developments in public administration theory need to be addressed, one far remote from the spirit of Luhmann's work and the other surprisingly close. The first phenomenon is the return of beliefs in economic rationality and optimal modelling in the form of managerialism and of what Christopher Hood (1995) calls the "economicization of policy." As Andrew Gray and Bill Jenkins (1995) note, much of the public management agenda represents a return to the classical dichotomy between politics and administration in which "public management is offered as neutral and transferable technology to improve the public sector without offending traditional values" and in which "administrative structures are simply 'providers' of services and activities determined in the political sphere" (p. 81). Hence, Luhmann's critique of the classical model applies as well to the optimism of the new public management. In addition, his concept of autopoiesis underscrores the limits of adopting the internal logic of the economic subsystem in the public sector.

Among the recent trends, new institutionalism seems to come closest to Luhmann's perspective. We understand as new institutionalism the renewed interest in the study of institutions, values, and norms in political science and public administration (see Thelen and Steinmo 1992 for definitions). The main representatives of this approach, James March and Johan Olsen (1984, 1989), "de-emphasize the simple primacy of micro-processes," question the existence of "optimal solutions," and emphasize the centrality of meaning and symbolic action over metaphors of choice and allocative outcomes (1984, p. 738). In short, they criticize reductionism, functionalism, utilitarianism, and instrumentalism (1984, p. 735). According to March and Olsen, "institutional thinking emphasizes the part played by institutional structures in imposing elements of order on a potentially inchoate world" (p. 743). They confirm that "processes of politics may be more important than their outcomes" (p. 724) and share Luhmann's constructivist outlook by stating that "politics creates and confirms interpretations of life" (p. 741). Their overall assessment of the possibilities of societal steering via politics is more optimistic, however, than Luhmann's. It is striking that references to

Luhmann's work are absent in March's and Olsen's new institutionalism. Much of the similarities in their discourse and arguments, however, may be explained by the fact that all three authors' early works on public administration and policy shared Herbert Simon's influence. We expect that an exploration of both differences and similarities in their works could be a fruitful enterprise.

Conclusions

Niklas Luhmann's theory is a modest theory. It does not boast of its practical relevance. Indeed, the general advice he gives—that responsivity could be more important than efficiency and that indeterminacy (in certain limits) is an achievement—can be translated into practice in many ways. At a more concrete level, Niklas Luhmann does not tell us what to do.

It is important to understand that his refusal to prescribe "solutions" is not a shortcoming of the theory. On the contrary, Luhmann's modesty is prescribed by the contents of his theory. The conditions of modern society are such that science (knowledge) cannot replace the political option. A sociological theory that would have to produce laws of societal development would be overburdened scientifically and politically. Luhmann's theory presents structured options among which a choice can be made (1990a, p. 100), but the choice remains with the reader. The role of "science" is therapeutic rather than prescriptive (1990b, p. 648).

The great advantage of Luhmann's theory for the study of public administration is its openness. The theory's unity does not lie in a particular topic, substance, or content but in a network of interrelated concepts. These concepts are rendered precise by being related to other concepts of the same network. The flexibility of this construct, or of this "system," enables it to handle (reduce) extreme degrees of complexity.

MARLEEN BRANS AND STEFAN ROSSBACH

BIBLIOGRAPHY

Almond, Gabriel A., and James S. Coleman, 1960. *The Politics of the Developing Areas.* New York: Princeton University Press.

Beck, Miryam, 1986. *Ruimte voor Bestuur, Bestuur foor de Ruimte: de sociale Systeemtheorie van Niklas Luhmann toegepast op de Nederlandse Bestuurssituatie en de Ruimtelijk Ordening.* Utrecht: Rijksuniversiteit Utrecht.

Braybrooke, David, and Charles E. Lindblom, 1963. *A Strategy of Decision: Policy Evaluation as a Social Process.* New York: Free Press.

Crozier, Michel, 1991. "Le Changement dans les Organisations." *Revue Francaise d'Administration Publique,* vol. 59: 185–196.

Dahl, Robert A., 1947. "The Science of Administration: Three Problems." *Public Administration Review* 7, 1–11.

de Bruijn, Johan A., and Ernst S. ten Heuvelhof, 1991. "Policy Instruments for Steering Autopoietic Actors." In Roel J. In 't Veld et al., eds., *Autopoiesis and Configuration Theory: New*

Approaches to Societal Steering. Dordrecht: Kluwer Academic Publishers, 161–170.

Easton, David, 1953. *The Political System.* New York: Knopf.

Gray, Andrew, and Bill Jenkins, 1995. "From Public Administration to Public Management: Reassessing a Revolution?" *Public Administration,* vol. 73, no. 1: 75–99.

Hanf, Kenneth, and Fritz W. Scharpf, eds., 1978. *Inter-organizational Policy-making: Limits to Central Organization and Control.* London: Sage.

Hood, Christopher C., 1983. *The Tools of Government.* London: Macmillan.

———, 1995. "Emerging Issues in Public Administration" *Public Administration,* vol. 72, no. 1: 165–183.

In 't Veld, Roel J., et al., eds., 1991. *Autopoiesis and Configuration Theory: New Approaches to Societal Steering.* Dordrecht: Kluwer Academic Publishers.

Kickert, Walter J. M., 1993. "Autopoiesis and the Science of (Public) Administration: Essence, Sense and Nonsense." *Organization Studies,* vol. 14, no. 2: 261–278.

———, 1995. "Steering at a Distance: A New Paradigm of Governance in Dutch Higher Education." *Governance,* vol. 8, no. 1: 135–157.

Klijn, Eric H., and Geert R. Teisman, 1991. "Effective Policy-Making in a Multi-Actor Setting: Networks and Steering." In Roel J. In 't Veld et al., eds., *Autopoiesis and Configuration Theory: New Approaches to Societal Steering.* Dordrecht: Kluwer Academic Publishers, 99–111.

Majone, Giandomenico, 1986. "Analyzing the Public Sector: Shortcomings of Current Approaches. Part A: Policy Science." In Frans-Xavier Kaufman, Giandomenico Majone, and Vincent Ostrom, eds., *Guidance, Control, and Evaluation in the Public Sector.* Berlin/New York: de Gruyter, 61–70.

———, 1990. *Deregulation or Re-regulation? Regulatory Reform in Europe and the United States.* London: Pinter.

———, 1995. *Mutual Trust, Credible Commitments, and the Evolution of Rules for a Single European Market.* Florence: European University Institute Working Paper RSC 95/1.

March, James G., and Johan P. Olsen, 1984. "The New Institutionalism: Organizational Factors in Political Life." *American Political Science Review,* vol. 78 (September) 734–49.

———, 1989. *Rediscovering Institutions: The Organizational Basis of Politics.* New York: Free Press.

Mayntz, Renate, 1983. "The Conditions for Effective Public Policy: A New Challenge for Policy Analysis." *Policy and Politics,* vol.11, no. 2: 123–143.

———, 1993. "Governing Failures and the Problem of Governability: Some Comments on a Theoretical Paradigm." In Jan Kooiman, ed., *Modern Governance: New Government-Society Interactions.* London: Sage, 9–20.

Ostrom, Vincent, 1972. *Polycentricity.* Bloomington, IN: Workshop in Political Theory and Policy Analysis.

Ostrom, Vincent, and Elinor Ostrom, 1965. "A Behavioral Approach to the Study of Intergovernmental Relations." *Annals of the American Academy of Political and Social Science* (May) 137–146.

Pressman, Jeffery L., and Aaron B. Wildavsky, 1973. *Implementation.* Berkeley: University of California Press.

Scharpf, Fritz W., 1989. "Politische Steuerung und politische Institutionen." *Politische Vierteljahrsschrift,* vol. 30, no. 1: 10–22.

Scharpf, Fritz W., et al., 1976. *Politikverflechtung: Theorie und Empirie des kooperativen Föderalismus in der Bundesrepublik.* Kronberg: Scriptor.

Simon, Herbert A., 1947. *Administrative Behaviour: A Study of Decision-making Processes in Administrative Organization.* New York: MacMillan.

———, 1957. *Models of Man.* New York: Wiley.

Teubner, Gunther, 1993. *Law as an Autopoietic System.* Oxford: Blackwell.

Thelen, Kathleen A., and Sven Steinmo, 1992. In Sven Steinmo et al., eds., *Structuring Politics. Historical Institutionalism in Comparative Analysis.* New York: Cambridge University Press, 1–32.

Van der Eyden, Antonius P. J., 1980. *Overheidskunde en Overheidswetenschap.* Deventer: Kluwer.

Weber, Max, 1947. *The Theory of Social and Economic Organization,* Part 1 of "Writschaft und Gesellschaft," trans. A. M. Henderson and T. Parsons, ed. T. Parsons. New York: Free Press.

Willke, Helmut, 1985. "Three Types of Legal Structure: The Conditional, the Purposive, and the Relational Program." In Gunther Teubner, ed., *Dilemmas of Law in the Welfare State.* Berlin/New York: de Gruyter, 281–298.

———, 1992. *Ironie des Staates: Grundlinien einer Staatstheorie polyzentrischer Gesellschaft.* Frankfurt am Main: Suhrkamp.

Works by Luhmann

Habermas, Jürgen, and Niklas Luhmann, 1971. *Theorie der Gesellschaft oder Sozialtechnologie—Was leistet die Systemforschung?* Frankfurt: Suhrkamp.

Luhmann, Niklas, 1964. *Funktionen und Folgen formaler Organisation.* Berlin: Duncker & Humblot.

———, 1966. *Theorie der Verwaltungswissenschaft. Bestandsaufnahme und Entwuf.* Köln/Berlin: Grote.

———, 1968. *Vertrauen. Ein Mechanismus der Reduktion sozialer Komplexität.* Stuttgart: Enke Verlag.

———, 1969. *Legitimation durch Verfahren.* Neuwied/Berlin: Luchterhand.

———, 1970. *Soziologische Aufklärung 1. Aufsätze zur Theorie sozialer Systeme.* Opladen: Westdeutscher Verlag.

———, 1971. *Politische Planung. Aufsätze zur Soziologie von Politik und Verwaltung.* Opladen: Westdeutscher Verlag.

———, 1975a. *Macht.* Stuttgart: Enke.

———, 1975b. *Soziologische Aufklärung 2. Aufsätze zur Theorie der Gesellschaft.* Opladen: Westdeutscher Verlag.

———, 1981a. *Politische Theorie im Wohlfahrtsstaat.* München/Wien: Olzog.

———, 1981b. *Soziologische Aufklärung 3. Soziales System, Gesellechaft, Organisation.* Opladen: Westdeutscher Verlag.

———, 1982a. "Autopoiesis, Handlung und kommunicative Verständigung." *Zeitschrift für Soziologie,* vol. 11, no. 4: 366–379.

———, 1982b. *The Differentiation of Society,* transl. Stephen Holmes and Charles Larmore. New York: Columbia University Press.

———, 1989. *Gesellschaftsstruktur und Semantik. Studien zur Wissenssoziologie der modernen Gesellschaft. Band 3.* Frankfurt: Suhrkamp.

———, 1990a. *Political Theory in the Welfare State.* Trans. and introduced by John Bednarz, Jr. Berlin/New York: de Gruyter.

———, 1990b. *Die Wissenschaft der Gesellschaft.* Frankfurt: Suhrkamp.

———, 1991. "Am Ende der Kritischen Soziologie." *Zeitschrift für Soziologie,* vol. 20, no. 2: 147–152.

LYING WITH STATISTICS.

The misuse in communication of data in print or presentation, either intentionally or unintentionally, the result of which misleads those to whom the communication is directed.

A classic example of associating statistics with lying is attributed to British Prime Minister Disraeli, who declared, "There are three kinds of lies: lies, damned lies, and statistics." More contemporary and book length efforts to explore lying and statistics include Darrel Huff's (1954) *How to Lie with Statistics* and Robert Hooke's (1983) *How to Tell the Liars from the Statisticians*. Neither of these books were intended to be primers for lying but, rather, light-hearted guides for nonstatisticians in how to distinguish between complete statistical disclosure and good statistical reasoning on the one hand and misleading or malicious reporting of data on the other.

Increasingly, we rely on statistics to determine trends, to judge public opinion, and even to learn which toothpaste reduces cavity production. Hooke (1983) distinguishes between statistics in the plural and in the singular. Most people think of statistics as plural—as sets of numbers and figures and data. Statisticians think of it as singular—a subject matter that allows one to understand chance, cause and effect, correlation, and the scientific method. People who gather data (statistics plural) are not necessarily statisticians. If these "data pushers," as Hooke refers to them, use the data in an incomplete or uninformed manner, then their manipulation, intended or not intended, is considered lying.

When someone is lying with statistics, they are unaware of or purposely ignoring statistical assumptions or rules and then make incorrect interpretations about what the data infer. An oftentimes cited example of violating statistical assumptions resulting in an incorrect result was the 1936 *Literary Digest* magazine presidential preference poll that predicted Alf Landon would defeat Franklin Roosevelt in a landslide. Roosevelt won the election. So, what went wrong?

The pollsters at the *Literary Digest* used a biased sample. According to statistics, one can only make predictions from a random sample of the population, in this case, of all eligible voters. In random sampling, each person in the population must have an equal and nonzero chance of being included in the sample. Potential respondents to the *Literary Digest* poll were readers of the magazine and people who had telephones. The poll was taken during the Great Depression when most poor people did not have phones. The sample was biased against poor people. In addition, the poll was biased in favor of people with higher educations; they read the literary magazine. Wealthy people and those better educated tended to be Republicans, Landon's party. The "data" indicated Landon would win; the data, and those reporting them, lied.

Closely related to biased samples are those "lies" which are generated by using a small number of cases, or the "small N" problem. Consumers presented with a statement of the type "Seventy-five percent of citizens are satisfied with local services" should also be given information about the number of cases in the sample and whether the sample was drawn randomly. If a city manager can pick the citizens he or she wants to ask about the quality of services (biased sampling) and there are only four citizens in the sample (small N), then the assumptions of statistics cannot be used to make inferences about citizens' evaluation of services. Probability theory allows statisticians to make inferences from random samples to populations only if the number of cases is large enough. There are mathematical equations to determine how large the number should be to be confident about the findings. In studies involving citizens and public administration, a sample of four is never large enough.

Pollsters should also report the margin of error of their findings. For example, let us say a school district is interested in finding out if voters would support a levy (tax increase) to secure funding for extracurricular activities. A responsible survey researcher finds that the randomly selected sample of 1,500 voters indicated that 55 percent of the voters supported the levy. Without a report of the margin for error, the "lie" might be that there is good support for the levy, and the school district officials should be comfortable with the campaign. However, if the margin for error is plus or minus 7 percent, the support may be as high as 62 percent but as low as 48 percent (losing). Probability theory allows statisticians to determine how confident the researcher is that the sample reflects the population and the margin for error around the statistic—in this case, percent of support. Therefore, consumers of this information should be given information about the randomness of the sample, the number of cases included in the sample, the confidence level, and the margin of error in the statistic in order to evaluate the "truth" of the statistics. Hooke (1983) implies that failure to report these figures should be interpreted as hiding them or lying with them.

Another problem concerns the reporting of the averages. Take the following statement, for example, "The average citizen consumes 38 pounds of rice a year." A savvy statistical consumer would want to know what kind of average is being reported. The median is the point at which 50 percent of the cases are below it and 50 percent of the cases are above it. The arithmetic mean is affected by extreme scores either low or high. When the cases are normally distributed, the median and mean are similar. However, when there are outliers, the mean is pulled in the direction of the extreme scores. In the example above, if the unit of analysis is a city that has a small section inhabited predominantly by ethnic groups whose diets revolve around rice and their average consumption is 100 pounds a year, then the mean for all citizens could be 38 while the median might be 10 pounds. In cases where the distribution may be affected by extreme scores, the median is usually the best measure of the "average." In any case, the particular statistic used should be reported.

When statistics are reported, the consumer should be concerned with how the data compare with other statistics. Comparison is a fundamental enterprise in science. Therefore, when data are reported, they should be explained in comparison to something else. That something else may be a temporal trend, another group of cases, or some baseline so that the consumer can evaluate the worth of the statistic.

However, just comparison is not enough. Probability theory allows us to determine whether differences seen in data are true differences. This is what is meant by something being "statistically significantly" different from something else. Tests of statistical significance can tell whether a group's having an average income of $30,000 is significantly different than a group's having one of $29,500. To avoid the appearance of lying, data should be reported revealing whether the differences are statistically significant.

Comparisons are also made between variables in studies. The statistics often used to estimate the strength of relationships between variables are called correlations. A positive 1.0 correlation indicates a perfect positive relationship; as one variable takes on a higher value, the other one also takes on a higher value. A negative 1.0 is a perfect negative relationship; as one variable increases in value, the other one decreases in value. No relationship results in a 0.0 correlation. One way one could lie with a correlation statistic is to report a correlation that is statistically insignificant. When correlations do not achieve significance, it means that there is no real relationship at all.

However, when the number of cases increases, almost any correlation can be statistically significant—it is an artifact of the mathematics involved. Therefore, the strength of the association becomes even more significant than statistical significance. The correlation coefficient itself is the measure of the strength of the association.

One of the lies made by using correlations is the assumption that all things that are correlated are causally related. Correlation does not equal causation. This is true especially in light of large numbers of cases and their effect on statistical significance. Correlation is a necessary, though not sufficient, condition for inferring causation. The others are temporal sequencing (one variable occurs before the other), the association makes theoretical sense, and all other variables have been ruled out as causal agents (the relationship is not "spurious").

A widely used example makes this point. There is a strong, statistically significant association between the number of storks migrating to Sweden in the fall and the birth rate of children in the country during that season. If one assumes correlation is the same as causation, then the inference can be made that storks "cause" babies in Sweden. Obviously this is not the case.

Another method to lie with statistics is to distort tabular presentations. With the widespread use of computer-generated tables and figures, this is an important lie about which a statistics consumer should be skeptical. One example is changing the units of measure on a trend line by changing the scale on the abscissa or ordinate (X- or Y-axis) in order to accentuate a trend or to smooth one out. Another is cutting out the middle of charts for no apparent reason than to accentuate an apparent increase or decrease of interest. Either way, this represents altering a scale to comport with one's desired visual findings.

Increasingly, popular media have been using one-dimensional pictures to graphically display statistics. For example, one subgroup of a population makes a certain income, displayed by a money bag. If another subpopulation makes double that amount, then their money bag is pictured twice as high. This makes intuitive sense. However, while increasing the height, the width is also increased, making it twice as wide. In actuality, the second figure is actually occupying four times as much area as the first. This distortion can leave a big, though untrue, impression regarding the status of the first group relative to the second.

There are many and varied methods one can use to "lie" with statistics. However, most public administrators are not that unethical and would not knowingly distort findings for citizens. Huff (1954) suggests that consumers of statistics should be active participants in the data-relaying process; they should ask questions and challenge the reporter to verify the statistics presented. He suggests that consumers should "look a phoney statistic in the eye and face it down" but also "recognize sound and usable data in the wilderness of fraud," which may be out there (p. 122). He proposes five simple questions consumers may pose when confronting the veracity of statistics:

1. *Who says so?* Who generated the statistics and do they stand behind them? Or are the implications from the statistics subject to a reporter's interpretation of them?
2. *How does he or she know?* Was the sample biased? Is the N large enough to permit a reliable conclusion? Is the statistical significance reported?
3. *What's missing?* Is the number of cases reported? What about the standard error? Which average is being reported? Are expected comparisons or baselines missing?
4. *Did somebody change the subject?* Did the incidence of a condition increase over time or are the data gathered more carefully now? Did crime rate go up or are newspapers competing by reporting more crime in print? Have definitions of a condition changed over time?
5. *Does it make sense?* Are impressively precise figures reported that contradict commonsense? Are extrapolations from the statistics reasonable given what is known about the culture?

The best defense against those accused of lying with statistics is caveat emptor—let the informed consumer beware.

CLAIRE FELBINGER

BIBLIOGRAPHY

Hooke, Robert, 1983. *How to Tell the Liars from the Statisticians.* New York: Marcel Dekker.
Huff, Darrell, 1954. *How to Lie with Statistics.* New York: W. W. Norton.

M

MACHIAVELLI. Florentine administrator, diplomat, and statesman whose name in popular usage has become synonymous with ruthless and devious political calculations. Niccolo di Bernardo dei Machiavelli, 1469–1527, on exclusion from public office by the ruling Medici family after 1512, turned his attention to the study of politics, statecraft, and war. It is his published works rather than his conduct of public affairs for which he is most renowned. His writings include *The Prince* (his most famous work), *Discourses on the First Decade of Livy, The Art of War,* and *The History of Florence* (Bondanella and Musa 1979).

These classics of Renaissance literature represent important contributions to the development of politics as an area of academic focus. Indeed, Machiavelli has often been described as the founder of modern "political science." While this is perhaps an exaggeration, he undoubtedly employed empirical methods, relying heavily on his own observations and experiences as a foundation for his analysis of politics within the Italian peninsula in general and his own city-state of Florence in particular. He certainly believed that through the rigorous analysis of man's past actions, it should be possible to predict future behavior.

Machiavelli was not a philosopher who deliberately set out to posit or develop theory; he was more an experienced practitioner prescribing a distinctive approach to government and the conduct of state business. He first took up public office in 1498 in Florence's Second Chancery, which had involvement in both foreign and domestic affairs. He remained in office for 14 years, during which he helped raise the Florentine militia and traveled abroad on several diplomatic missions. Most significant of these excursions were three visits paid to Cesare Borgia in the years 1502 and 1503. Machiavelli came to admire Pope Alexander VI's illegitimate son, who, at that time, posed a serious threat to Florentine territorial integrity. It was Cesare Borgia's guile and determination that forged in Machiavelli's mind the character of the ideal ruler who was to be the central figure in *The Prince.*

Machiavelli lost his office in 1512 on the fall of the Florentine Republic and the return to power of the Medici family. Initially imprisoned and tortured, he was eventually allowed to retire to his estates, dying in 1527. During the whole of his life, the Italian states were locked in political and military struggles. The Italian wars involved not only the states of the peninsula itself but also intervening powers that sought to impose their hegemony over the region. Most notable of these were France and the Holy Roman Empire of the Hapsburgs. In the year of Machiavelli's death, Rome was sacked by the Hapsburg army while its leader looked helplessly on. If Machiavelli was anything at all, he was certainly a product of his times.

While not setting out to become a philosopher, there is no doubt that he became one of importance and substance. Machiavelli's philosophical starting point is a grimly pessimistic assessment of human nature. Fundamentally selfish, mankind is motivated entirely by its own self-interest. This renders fear a far more effective force for progress than love. Ventures undertaken out of love will invariably be abandoned if the consequences threaten self-interest or if a better outcome can be pursued. Fear of punishment, by contrast, will drive one on to meet one's commitments because it would clearly not be in one's interests to fail to meet them. One can therefore trust someone motivated by fear rather more than one can trust someone motivated by love.

While Machiavelli was pessimistic about human nature, he was optimistic about the future of human society. If self-interest will invariably prevail, as he believed it would, then man's actions can be analyzed, future behavior can be predicted, citizens and other rulers can be manipulated, and society can be organized by an astute ruler to maximize the benefit to all, especially, of course, himself. That ruler will recognize the essentially conflictual nature of politics—all politics, both domestic and international—and use that understanding to advantage.

Unfortunately for Machiavelli, his views on human nature have given him a bad name. The extent to which he was influenced by Cesare Borgia, a man of grossly evil reputation, has done nothing over the centuries to enhance his own standing. His reliance on the manipulative potential of an astute, self-interested ruler is fundamentally unattractive to the liberal mind, regardless of the actual outcome of that ruler's conduct. So too is the apparent detaching of the conduct of politics from immediate questions of ethics and morality. Universal benefit is unacceptable if the methods used to achieve it are repulsive. Machiavelli's own name has often been regarded as synonymous with evil. If a person is described as "Machiavellian," one can assume that that person is regarded as devious, immoral, two-faced, manipulative, and untrustworthy.

And yet, Machiavelli was a champion of republicanism and of liberty. Far from being immoral, it was arguably his morality that motivated him to seek out a way of overcoming the profound shortcomings he discerned in human nature. In the final chapter of *The Prince,* he exhorts, by implication, Lorenzo di Medici to "liberate Italy from the Barbarians." The message was straightforward: Achieve power by the only way possible and then use that power to good advantage. Machiavelli was a realist who saw the possibility of security and a well-ordered society in which citizens would enjoy liberty through the necessary manipulation and utilization of mankind's inherent selfishness.

Machiavelli remains a profoundly controversial figure, more maligned than read, more misinterpreted than understood. Ironically, if he had been more "Machiavellian" himself, he may well have enjoyed a further official career under the Medici and may never have had the inclination to write those works that secured his reputation.

STEVEN HAINES

BIBLIOGRAPHY

Bondanella, P., and M. Musa, eds., 1979. *The Portable Machiavelli.* New York: Penguin Books.

Gilbert, F., 1986. "Machiavelli: The Renaissance of the Art of War." In P. Paret, ed., *Makers of Modern Strategy from Machiavelli to the Nuclear Age.* Oxford: Clarendon Press.

Wight, M., 1991. *International Theory: The Three Traditions.* Leicester: Leicester University Press.

MACHINERY OF GOVERNMENT. The structure of departments and agencies through which the functions of government are delivered.

Origins and Definition

The term "machinery of government" may be traced to the appointment by the British government in 1917 of a "Committee on the Machinery of Government" headed by Viscount Haldane. The purpose of the committee was to provide recommendations as to the best way to structure government departments in the period of reconstruction following World War I. Since then, particularly in countries within the Westminster tradition, the term has come to mean the structure of departments and agencies created from time to time to deliver government programs and services. The election of a new government frequently gives rise to a recasting of "machinery of government arrangements" to better reflect new priorities and altered cabinet responsibilities, although the machinery of government may also evolve by changes made in between elections.

United Kingdom: The Haldane Report

The Haldane Committee addressed itself to the question, "Upon what principle are the functions of departments to be determined and allocated?" It concluded that there were two alternatives–distributing functions according to the classes of persons served or according to the services provided. It firmly recommended the latter in its report, published in 1918.

Influence of the Haldane Report

The Haldane Report was of importance for drawing attention to the fact that arrangements for delivering government services are not immutable but are capable of being freshly designed and altered to meet changing needs and to overcome overlap and duplication. The report had a big influence on both sides of the Atlantic. In the United States, it was frequently cited by public administration scholars, and it influenced Luther Gulick, later a member of the Brownlow Committee, which was appointed by the president to comprehensively review the U.S. machinery of government.

USA: The Brownlow Committee

The Brownlow Committee was appointed by President Franklin D. Roosevelt in 1936 in the wake of the profusion of government programs and services during the New Deal. Like its English counterpart, the committee had the opportunity to take a comprehensive view of the problem of machinery of government. Its report, presented in 1937, recommended strengthening the provision of support to the presidency, as well as a major reorganization of the executive branch, implemented through the Reorganization Act of 1939. Among other things, this legislation brought into being the Executive Office of the President and the Bureau of the Budget.

Australia: Constitutional Origins of Machinery of Government

In Australia, machinery of government arrangements at the national level were shaped not by a committee but by the provisions of the federal constitution adopted in 1901. This constitution anticipated the creation of departments by the national government, but the first cabinet governed through just seven agencies. By the 1960s, this had grown to 24 departments covering most aspects of national policy and peaked with 37 departments during the 1970s.

Successive Machinery of Government Reforms

Since the pioneering work of the Haldane and Brownlow Committees, there have been periodic attempts to reform the machinery of government at national and state levels in most advanced countries. In the United States, the Hoover Commissions of 1948 and 1953, President Reagan's Private Sector Survey on Cost Control in 1982 (the "Grace Commission"), and Vice President Gore's National Performance Review of 1993 all addressed machinery of government reforms. In the United Kingdom, very significant changes occurred to the machinery of government during the 1980s as a result of the Thatcher government's privatization program, and after 1988, through the Next Steps program, by the creation of executive agencies to undertake specified functions with substantial autonomy. These models have parallels in New Zealand and Canada and form part of the process of reducing state spending.

Conclusion

The reform of state institutional arrangements—of the machinery of government—has formed a central theme of public sector reform in many countries in recent decades, with many local variations. Generally speaking, efficiency in government initiatives have precipitated institutional change toward leaner, more economic structures. Machinery of government reform today is typically linked to economic as much as to political agendas.

E. W. RUSSELL

BIBLIOGRAPHY

Australian Government, 1992. *The Australian Public Service Reformed.* Task Force on Management Improvement.
Brownlow, Louis, 1958. *A Passion for Anonymity: The Autobiography of Louis Brownlow.* University of Chicago Press.
Great Britain, House of Commons, Parliamentary Papers, 1918. *Report of the Machinery of Government Committee,* Cd9230 (the "Haldane Report").

MACHINERY OF GOVERNMENT, AUSTRALIA.

The pattern of organization of Australian national government.

"Machinery of government" is a term customarily associated with the British-derived systems of parliamentary democracy. It refers to the grouping of government functions into a relatively few, large and long-lived departments. Such departments are sometimes called the "core public service" because they answer directly to ministers. Outside the departmental framework reside the many publicly funded but independent, specialist bodies and agencies that characterize the modern state.

The appropriate architecture for machinery of government has long been debated within nations sharing Westminster-style institutions. The Haldane Report of 1918 in Britain and the 1962 Glassco Commission in Canada each offer detailed recommendations on how the activities of the core public service might be organized. The issue also arose in various Australian reports and finds its most common expression in the justifications offered by governments each time departments are reorganized.

Following the British model, Australian executives deploy their career public servants in functional departments. Each department is headed by a secretary, typically a career public servant, who answers to a minister. The Australian Public Service (APS) has not followed the pattern of extensive political appointees found in the United States, although traffic between the bureaucracy and the private political offices of ministers has increased over the last two decades.

The responsibilities of the Commonwealth of Australia are enumerated in the national constitution, and departmental duties originally reflected that document.

However, for over half a century the Commonwealth has asserted authority over numerous new policy domains and so the federal bureaucracy now duplicates many areas, such as health and education, which are nominally preserved for the states.

This expanding role has encouraged frequent changes to the configuration, duties, and title of the APS. Australian machinery changes are swift to execute and are used frequently to accommodate ambitious ministers, to appease pressure group demands, or to solve personnel problems within the public service. Consequently, institutional maps of recent Australian governments—as elsewhere in similar systems—suggest a moveable feast, as organizational structures and responsibilities bend to circumstance.

Origins

The federal divide that followed nationhood in 1901 was intended to keep the national government small, with most service delivery functions retained by the former colonies, now states. The national constitution anticipated the creation of departments by the national government, but the first Cabinet felt able to administer with just seven agencies—Departments of External Affairs, Defense, Trade and Customs, Home Affairs, the Treasury, the Attorney General, and the Postmaster General.

As Commonwealth responsibilities grew, so did the national bureaucracy. A Prime Minister's Department was created in 1911, and by the 1960s some 24 Commonwealth departments covered most aspects of national policy. Departmental numbers peaked at 37 in the following decade. As Fin Crisp (1978) noted in his magisterial study *Australian National Government,* the departmental titles of 1972 "were an eloquent indication of the Commonwealth's latter-day leadership in the economic and social aspects of national life" (p. 436).

Continuous Change

If growth has been one constant in Australian machinery of government, regular machinery change remains the other. There have been some stretches of stability in institutional arrangements. During the reign of Prime Minister Robert Menzies (1949–1966), only three new departments were created and name changes remained modest. His successors, Prime Ministers Holt, Gorton, and McMahon (1966–1972), made more changes in the next 6 years than had Menzies in the previous 16.

Dramatic volatility in APS structures began in December 1972. First the Whitlam Labor government (1972–1975), then the Fraser Liberal/National Country Party government (1975–1983) imposed endless structural variations to the public service. Public servants employed by the Department of the Postmaster General in 1972, for example, could find themselves working successively for the Department of the Media, the Department of Posts and Telecommunications, and the Department of Communications, all within less than a decade and possibly all without moving a desk. Even the central agencies were not immune, with the Treasury split in 1976 and the long-standing Public Service Board abolished a decade later. Until 1987, APS structures were continuously shuffled, cut and played.

The Search for Principles

Instability in Australian machinery of government reflected the lack of underlying principles guiding structural choices. Putting together functional areas—all health services in one portfolio, all education in another, and so on—does not resolve overlap and inconsistency or provide guidance when emerging social concerns, such as consumer affairs, inspire new machinery that cuts across existing portfolios.

Further, structural change is easy to achieve in the Australian context. With a single administrative order, approved by the governor general, an Australian prime minister can recast the entire machinery of government. Small and unimportant portfolios can be created to accommodate less able ministers. In some cases the tight tenure provisions of senior public servants made it easier to abolish a department and then reconstitute it with a new title and slightly amended responsibilities than to seek the dismissal of the chief executive. The machinery of government, in sum, served greater political and administrative goals and was not seen as significant in itself, despite constant complaints from public servants about the costs of endless restructuring and the difficulty of improving policy and programs when all energy is focused on organizational change.

In 1987, the Hawke Labor government (1983–1991) sought to break the cycle. It argued that structures should follow policy, and Prime Minister Hawke used an election victory to initiate the single largest consolidation of the Commonwealth machinery in Australian administrative history. Some 28 departments were amalgamated into just 16 agencies, each with wide policy responsibilities. Many of the new agencies reflected the government's agenda of microeconomic reform, with combinations such as a Department of Employment, Education, and Training and a Department of Transport and Communications. In the social policy arena, related services were drawn together in a Department of Health, Housing, and Community Services. Australian machinery of government thus drew toward the American model of fewer but larger agencies with wide policy portfolios. The underlying policy objective of economic reform provided a common foundation not found in earlier reshuffles, and senior officials expressed hope the new structures would prove more enduring than their predecessors.

A Return to the Past

The 1987 changes represented the first Australian attempt at a coherent and defensible set of administrative arrangements, structured around major policy rather than functional objectives. Yet, even within this new model incongruities survived, such as linking immigration and local government. The 1987 changes did provide some years of relative stability in organizational structures; however, when Hawke lost office in late 1991, his tightly bound organization of the Australian machinery of government began to unravel.

The return to the traditional pattern of growth but instability reflects the underlying realities of machinery of government. As the Glassco inquiry found, organizational theorists "with a passion for neatness" who argue for more predictable structures fail to grasp the political context of public administration. What suits one group of players may disadvantage another. Demanding that departments be coherent and attuned to ministerial interests sets up potential contradictions. Add a requirement that portfolios also be efficient, accountable, and meet functional, symbolic, and cabinet representative needs, and any prospect for a single organizing principle is surrendered.

Given that public sector structures are subservient to political ends, a slide back to ad hoc and incremental recasting of the Australian machinery of government seems likely, with 1987 a rare pause in an otherwise endless card game.

Yet, the past will not return entirely. The push for microeconomic reform that inspired the 1987 APS amalgamations has also encouraged the shedding of many traditional public sector functions. Some have become government-owned trading enterprises, others have been sold entirely. Large numbers of former Commonwealth employees are now outside the public sector, working in corporatized communications and financial institutions (Telecom, Australia Post, the Commonwealth Bank) or in agencies moving rapidly toward privatization (Qantas, Australian National Lines). The scope and size of government machinery is thus retracting, with surviving core agencies becoming more focused on policy formulation than extensive service delivery. This recasting around policy concerns is likely to preserve the trend to fewer, larger portfolios. The 16 departments established in 1987 may expand slightly in number, but the APS is unlikely to regain its previous dimensions or degree of continuous structural change.

GLYN DAVIS

BIBLIOGRAPHY

Codd, M., 1988. "Recent Changes in the Machinery of Government." *Canberra Bulletin of Public Administration*, vol. 54: 25–30.

Crisp, L. F., 1978. *Australian National Government,* 4th ed. Melbourne: Longman Cheshire.

MAB, 1993. *The Australian Public Sector Reformed: An Evaluation of a Decade of Management Reform.* Report prepared for the Commonwealth Government's Management Advisory Board. Canberra: AGPS.

Weller, P., J. Forster, and G. Davis, eds., 1993. *Restructuring the Public Service: Lessons from Recent Experience.* Melbourne: Macmillan.

MALAYSIAN ADMINISTRATIVE TRADITION.

The traditional administrative system, culture, and practices of Malaysia, which is a product of its historical, social, and political environment.

The Federation

Malaysia is a plural society in which the native Malays form the largest proportion (49 percent), followed by the Chinese (37 percent) and Indians (10 percent). These last two groups immigrated to the country for the most part during the early twentieth century. The Federation of Malaysia comprises the 11 states of the Malay Peninsula (known as West Malaysia), which stretches from the northern border with Thailand to the southern border with Singapore, and the 2 states of Sabah and Sarawak (both known as East Malaysia) on the northern part of the island of Borneo. Malaysia gained its independence from the British in 1957.

The system of administration follows closely the pattern of the modern Western bureaucratic administration, which was inherited from the British during the colonial period. However, even though the forms of the Western system are outwardly observed, there appears to be a widespread discrepancy between form and reality.

Colonial Administration

The British established administrative hegemony over Malaya (currently known as West Malaysia) in three stages. The first stage was between 1786 and 1867 when Penang, Singapore, and Malacca were established to form the Colony of the Straits Settlements. The second stage was between 1874 and 1895 when Britain entered into treaties with the rulers of Perak, Selangor, Negeri Sembilan, and Pahang whereby these four states were formed into a federation known as the Federated Malay States to be administered under the advice and protection of the British government. The third stage was reached in 1909 when, by the Siamese Treaty of 1909, Siam agreed to relinquish its rights over the northern Malay states of Kedah, Perlis, Kelantan, and Trengganu. These states and the southern state of Johore were collectively referred to as the Unfederated Malay States.

Prior to the independence of Malaysia, the civil service was a political bureaucracy that was not limited to narrow law and order functions but made policy decisions as well. The Malayan Civil Service (MCS), staffed almost exclusively by British officers, was the key policymaking service (Esman, 1972). However, the supporting services included the local natives and the Chinese and Indian population.

The political objective of obtaining the acceptance and support of the natives led the British to preserve the traditional Malay system of local government with its *penghulu* (headman) and *mukim* (parish) structure (Puthucheary 1978). The *penghulu* service became a subordinate civil service, which helped the British MCS officers when they became district officers to cover their respective *mukims*. The Malay Administrative Service (MAS) was created with its members selected from among the Malays to form a subordinate service to the MCS at the federal and state level (Puthucheary 1978; Sidhu 1980, p. 137). In addition, in the Unfederated Malay States, provisions were also made for the creation of separate state civil services staffed by the respective state population to assist the British in the administration of the states.

The MCS was an elite policymaking service and staffed almost entirely by British officers. The MAS, in contrast, was staffed mainly by Malays from the upper classes. Hence, when MAS officers were promoted to MCS, or when they assumed the duties of MCS upon independence, the elitist nature and prestige of the MCS was preserved (Esman 1972; Puthucheary 1978; Tilman 1964).

Administrative Culture

The racial composition of the current Malaysian civil service, in which the Malays are dominant, is the key to understanding the pattern and style of its administration. Despite the formal acceptance of a career system of administration based on a high degree of professionalism and freedom from political interference, the saliency of ethnic values over bureaucratic values creates a style of administrative behavior that is highly politicized (Puthucheary 1978).

One of the mutual agreements made between the leaders of the different ethnic groups was that citizenship status would be given to all immigrant Chinese and Indians upon independence. In return, the Constitution of Malaysia would provide that the composition of the MCS, renamed the Malaysian Administrative and Diplomatic Service (ADS) in 1973, should be in the ratio of 4:1 in favor of the Malays. However, non-Malays would be selected if qualified Malays were not available. The overall ethnic representation of the whole public service has been dominated by Malays, who occupy between 60 percent and 67 percent of the service.

Consequently, Malay culture has been dominant in the civil service. For example, the traditional Malay authority structure provides a clear division between the ruling class and the ruled, where all persons know their place in the social system and show respect for authority and deference to those of superior status. This cultural attitude has been extended to the administrative sphere. Hence, there is a psychological and social distance between senior and junior officers, with the complete subordination of organization members to their superiors (Sidhu 1980, p. 3; Muzzafar 1989), as well as between the civil service and the citizen or clients. As regularly voiced by many frustrated citizen-customers, instead of public officials being the "servants," they are, in practice, the masters.

This is not formality in the Weberian sense (Weber 1946). Within the formal organizational relationship, "there is little separation of official and private life especially at the state and local levels where it is likely that one's superior is also a member of the traditional elite" (Puthucheary 1978, p. 90). Hence, decisionmaking and other administrative practices are also influenced by both status within the administrative hierarchy as well as status in the society.

Structure

Structurally, the public services of the federation are derived from British colonial administration. Thus, today, one of the striking characteristics of the administrative system is that each of the five former Unfederated Malay States (as well as Sabah and Sarawak) has both a state civil service and a state clerical service; they have both senior and junior civil servants of their own. However, each of the four formerly Federated Malay states has its own state clerical service but no state civil service (Ahmad 1987); the senior posts in these states would be filled up by federal officers. This whole complex web of federal-state public services is legally held together by a quasi treaty between the federal government, on the one hand, and each of the states individually, on the other.

On the surface at least, there appears to be a remarkable order in the relationship of the two services. To a great extent, this has been accomplished by standardizing salary scales and conditions of services. Coordination, interaction, and exchange of officers are made possible by mechanisms such as committees and especially by the fact that the ruling political party at the federal level is also the ruling party in all but one of the states.

Another characteristic of the present-day civil service reminiscent of its colonial heritage is that it is highly centralized with powers concentrated in the central agencies, especially the Public Service Department, or PSD (the former Federal Establishment Office), the various service commissions (Public Service Commission, Education Service Commission, Police Service Commission, etc.), and the Treasury (Ahmad 1987).

The federal civil service structure is also divided into separate services with the ADS (the former MCS) at the top and the other services (including professional services such as medical doctors, engineers, etc.) at the lower levels. A special position in the civil service structure continues to be accorded to the ADS (Ahmad 1987, p. 6). Following the British tradition, the generalist ADS officers are to be found assigned to key positions in every ministry as well as in the state secretariats and district offices of the six states. ADS officers are the most senior officers in every federal ministry and in the six states. This has resulted in frequent friction between professional officers (including other non-ADS officers) and ADS officers, and between operating agencies with the central agencies. Through their powers in the central agencies (the secretariats) to make decisions on policy matters, the ADS maintains control over the operating departments. This emphasis on control (a feature of the colonial administrative style) is one of the reasons for the highly centralized administrative structure.

Civil Service Neutrality

The Malaysian constitution provided for a civil service that was meant to be impartially selected on the basis of merit and was to be politically neutral (Chee 1989). Although it seldom happens that the administrators interfere in partisan political matters, it is common for elected politicians at the federal, state, and local levels to interfere in policy implementation and administrative processes (Puthucheary 1978). Despite the fact that an increasing number of the administrative and professional members of the civil service receive their postgraduate education and training in the United States and the fact that several "renovations" of the administrative system have taken place since independence (Taib and Mat 1992), the bureaucracy continues to be influenced by its colonial experience and its highly politicized local environment.

SHARIFUDDIN ZAINUDDIN

BIBLIOGRAPHY

Ahmad, Zakaria Haji, ed., 1987. *Government and Politics of Malaysia.* Singapore: Oxford University Press.
Chee, Stephen, 1989. *Public Accountability in Malaysia: Form and Substance.* Paper presented at the EROPA 13th General Assembly and Conference, Kathmandu, Nepal.
Esman, Milton J., 1972. *Administration and Development in Malaysia.* Ithaca, NY: Cornell University Press.
Muzafar, Chandra, 1989. *Challenges and Choices in Malaysian Politics and Society.* Penang, Malaysia: Aliran.
Puthucheary, Marvis, 1978. *The Politics of Administration: The Malaysian Experience.* Kuala Lumpur, Malaysia: Oxford University Press.

Sidhu, Jagjit Singh, 1980. *Administration in the Federated Malay States 1896–1920.* Kuala Lumpur, Malaysia: Oxford University Press.

Taib, Tan Sri Mahmood bin, and Johari Mat, 1992. "Administrative Reforms in Malaysia: Toward Enhancing Public Service Performance." *Governance,* vol. 5, no. 4 (Oct.) 423–437.

Tilman, Robert O., 1964. *Bureaucratic Transition in Malaya.* Cambridge, England: Cambridge University Press.

Weber, Max, 1946. "Bureaucracy." In H. H. Gerth and C. Wright Mills., eds., *Essays in Sociology.* Oxford, England: Oxford University Press.

MANAGEMENT AUDIT. The assessment of an organization's efficiency and economy of resource utilization to evaluate the adequacy of administrative policies and actions and to determine the suitability of organizational structures and procedures. These audits are conducted periodically by employees within an agency to provide information to management and to help maintain and improve managerial control over operations.

Management audit is rapidly becoming an internationally applied concept. In the United States, Edward Wheat (1991) reports that two-thirds of the states as well as many cities, counties, and special districts now have in-house units that regularly produce audit reports that are quite different from traditional financial preaudits and postaudits (p. 386).

Also, throughout the industrial world and in many developing countries one finds persistent efforts to restructure public institutions and to reform their managerial practices, particularly in the area of financial management. The common feature in all this is the growing emphasis on results and outputs. Almost all new major administrative reform initiatives in these countries pursue the goals of attaining higher efficiencies and greater effectiveness of public services. The process of reform almost always entails performance monitoring that provides periodic information on outcomes and impacts of activities. Hence, the most frequently mentioned terms in these reforming prescriptions are connected to performance: audit, evaluation, measurement, and improvement.

Certainly, the end purpose of management audits is to ascertain whether program objectives are being met, and the desired benefits are being achieved, while verifying management's current operating proficiency. This proficiency encompasses organizational processes and all of the coordinate methods and measures adopted to safeguard assets, to confirm the reliability of the accounting data, to promote operational efficiency, and to encourage adherence to prescribed managerial policies.

As C. William Garner (1991) points out, the "manager audit" is conducted on budget and accounting systems of the operating unit as well as the activities associated with these systems such as policies and procedures. Usually these audits are brief, focused, and remedial, and they generate data that can be used in an ongoing financial analysis program. They are conducted by a manager or an internal audit committee according to an established framework designed to fit the type of organization in which they are conducted (pp. 229–235).

Whatever the specific design, Garner (1991) points out, all management audits will use the same basic methods and examine the same elements, such as accounting forms, budget forms, budget plans, authorization and approval practices and procedures, budget reports, inventory records, inventory reports, petty cash receipts, financial statements, and so forth (p. 230). All these elements cannot and should not be examined each time an audit is implemented; rather, selections should be made in advance.

It is important that management audit is not viewed or considered as a policing function carried out to catch embezzlers or to discover fraud. Although sometimes the motivation behind the audit is discovering dishonest employees or uncovering false transactions, the purpose of most management audits is to determine possibilities of operational improvements. Findings of these audits are expected to primarily reveal weaknesses and suggest refinements in the managerial processes. Recommended changes vary; they range from procedures to policies and from adapting the organizational structure to adoption of a new technology. Invariably, the aim is to make organizations function better and the individuals in them operate more effectively.

Management Audit Compared to Financial Audit

Management audit and financial audit are relatively distinct, despite considerable overlapping in purpose and in process:

1. A major distinction is that management audit does not have to abide by generally accepted accounting principles (GAAP), determined by the accounting profession or by generally accepted government auditing standards (GAGAS), determined by appropriate government authority. Financial audit, by contrast, is bound by GAAP and GAGAS as applicable to government transactions (Herbert, Killough, and Steiss 1984).

2. Management audit is future-oriented, seeking improvements and change in future operations. Financial audit mainly attempts to discover mistakes and errors that have taken place in past actions.

3. Management audit is a tool, providing information mainly for internal management purposes. Actually, management often undertakes multiple audits to assess specific components of a program and to make adequate data available before major decisions are made. In order to guide planned action, audits may

focus on programs, objectives, elements of a program, indicators or intended benefits. In contrast, financial audit is essentially an independent, external process of verification of compliance and examination of transactions of an administrative unit or an entity. Results of financial audits also are reported to various users within and without the government.

4. Management audit is not limited to utilizing financial data but may employ information about any aspect of the unit or the program. It may seek relevant knowledge from within and without the management field to define, explain, and solve management problems and impediments.

5. Both types of audit largely depend on the quality of staffs conducting them. Unless management auditors are selected on the basis of knowledge, technical skills, and ethical standards, there is no assurance that they will display the necessary detachment and independence of judgment. Nevertheless, management auditors, in their analysis and recommendations, frequently are found to be protective and supportive of their superiors and peers at the workplace. In addition, the focus of internal auditors tends to stay on the side of legal and financial compliance rather than branching out to develop a broad and integrated vision of overall managerial functions. In contrast, financial auditors generally exhibit greater autonomy and persistence in their investigation and verification of data as they are more detached from the operations of the unit and specifically targeted in their tasks.

Global Claims of Management Reform

A recent trend, clearly demonstrated in the United States and in many other countries, is making individual agencies responsible for their own review and control systems. A significant element in almost every administrative reform program proposed in recent years in developed as well as developing countries has been to decentralize authority and to empower administrative structures. The assumption is that authority and responsibility for the task must be lodged at the level at which the job is to be accomplished. The rationale frequently given includes considerations of inducement and morale as well as know-how and expertise.

In the United States in particular, agencies are involved in ensuring that obligations they incur and the resulting outlays adhere to provisions in the authorizing and appropriations legislation as well as to other laws and regulations governing the obligations of expenditures of funds. The U.S. Inspector General Act of 1978, as amended, established agency inspectors general to provide policy direction and to conduct, supervise, and coordinate audits and investigations relating to agency programs and operations. The focus on outcomes of public management has been unmistakable after several recent public policy initiatives including Al Gore's Report of the National Performance Review (1993).

The U.S. Chief Financial Officers Act of 1990 established agency officers to oversee all financial management activities relating to agency programs and operations. The U.S. Office of Management and Budgeting exercises its review responsibility by appraising program and financial reports and by keeping abreast of agencies' efforts to attain program objectives. Moreover, the U.S. General Accounting Office, as an agency responsible to Congress, regularly audits, examines, and evaluates government programs. Its findings and recommendations for corrective action are made to Congress and to other government agencies and institutions.

During the 1980s, Britain's administrative reform programs converged on developing performance measures to be able to relate outputs to costs and to ensure that the public receives value for public expenditures. This meant initiating long-term efforts to change not only financial management processes but also the managerial culture itself. Spurring managerial initiative within broad guidelines gave each department the freedom to develop the management system most suitable for its own mission and circumstances. Throughout the administrative machinery of government, financial powers newly delegated to operations' levels were intended to give sufficient flexibility and incentive to produce value for the money spent.

Similarly, in Canada, Australia, New Zealand, and other countries, reforming public administration meant stressing the performance of public service agencies and developing internal capacities to carry out new mandates. In the restructured administrative systems, departments are held accountable for performance expectations established in advance by central authorities approving the funding requirements. Public agencies must show results commensurate with funding allocated to them. Consequently, money is allocated for a purpose and evidence of achieving that purpose is a condition for gaining the money. Input-output or cost-benefit are not mutually exclusive considerations in public management. The imperative is to develop managerial capacities to implement the new strategies. In the process, management audits are potentially powerful tools for strengthening administrative discretion and self-review.

In developing countries in general, the vital role of auditing is neither recognized nor understood. Managerial decisions remain highly centralized, government accountability is limited, and transparency of financial transactions is the exception. In these developing countries, accounting systems do not lend themselves to processes of validation to determine correctness of operations or to verify the accuracy of financial information.

Internal managerial audits are a form of self-study that synthesizes concepts of organizational development and change with a drive toward managerial self-renewal. The conceptual backdrop often integrates some ideas of performance audit and program evaluation techniques with views and prescriptions from Total Quality Management. Generally, management audits are not rigidly defined in purpose or in process. These audits allow their enforcers greater latitude and flexibility to induce innovation and to encourage experimentation.

Consequently, the professionalism and skills of the staff are crucial, not only in terms of obtaining and evaluating evidence from management but also in demonstrating independence of judgment and high ethical standards. Here resides a serious problem for many developing countries that attempted management audits with existing staffs who were often not qualified or equipped to carry out such responsibility. Moreover, in highly centralized systems, professional considerations easily give way to hierarchical restrictions. Employees face extreme difficulties in revealing abuses of authority, waste of resources, or fraud by their superiors or peers.

Many deficiencies of public management in developing countries are manifested in public financial management. Yet, as James Wesberry, Jr. (1990) reports on Latin America, accounting for government is not emphasized in many of these countries; it appears to have been accorded the lowest possible priority (pp. 345–346). Most of the reasons offered to explain this condition in Latin America are applicable to other developing countries:

1. The accountancy profession is weak and commands little respect. Few talented young people therefore seek to enter it, thus perpetuating its weakness.
2. Public sector financial management in general is lax and rarely professional, partly owing to the low priority it receives. Government accountants are often not really accountants but persons given posts through contacts; they then learn the existing practices on a repetitive basis without understanding them or having the capacity or desire to improve them.
3. Government accounting is completely overshadowed by the budget function. Priority and emphasis are placed on budgeting. Budget people frequently maintain their own separate accounting records, which are more accurate, timely, and useful than those of accounting offices.
4. Government accounting is so poor in quality, inadequate in content, and late in presentations that it generates little or no impact. It serves primarily the legal purpose of documenting and summarizing receipts and expenditures in a formal report that is presented several years after the execution of the transactions reported.
5. Centralization of authority in financial management and lack of documentation and transparency of public financial transactions compound the difficulties of

management audit. When financial records do not provide an accurate snapshot of government activities or financial status, determining accountability becomes a daunting quest.

Thus, in developing countries, audits that could offer significant ideas or findings are those detached from operating agencies, such as external audits. The trouble is these semiautonomous accounting establishments entrusted with external postaudits have reduced their tasks to routine action and enforcement of procedures that appear mainly complementary to standard operating procedures of the administrative units. Rarely have ideas of change or dramatic findings resulted from audits by these accounting agencies in developing countries. (This is not to say that their actions have not resulted in some prevention of fraud and waste.)

Almost every country in the Middle East, for example, has some type of a general accounting office enjoying a measure of autonomy (at least more than do line agencies). Many Asian and Latin American countries have been attempting to reform their financial managements through a variety of ideas and approaches. In the two decades after World War II, the Philippines, India, Indonesia, Malaysia, Singapore, and others have attempted to apply performance-oriented financial administrative systems. Performance and program budgeting also have been on the agenda of most Asian and Latin American countries.

All these efforts have resulted only in modest accomplishments. Reforming financial systems to improve their utility, to make them accountable, to simplify verification of achievement, and to improve public services delivery proved to be lofty goals but troublesome in implementation. Thus, strengthening management capacity to act, as a concept, is universally accepted. For an administrative unit, however, to actually develop the ability to monitor its operations, diagnose its problems, and recommend solutions is entirely a different matter.

Yet, the pressure is on. Administrative reform efforts as well as demands for democratization and citizens participation in public policy decisions have helped to put the issues of accountability and good government in the forefront of change. Internal audits have served to offer indications of the seriousness of response by public agencies to these demands. Internal and external audits increasingly are used as effective means for establishing credibility and building trust in public decisions.

The success of management audits is crucial for the evolution of good government everywhere. The compelling question at this time, therefore, is to define the particulars that contribute to this success as well as the contextual preconditions that must prevail.

The particulars are (1) the availability or the successful development of an accounting system with fairly elaborate mechanisms of financial reporting and documentation of service efforts and accomplishments; (2) professional, neutral competence within staff to exert the authority of its expert knowledge and professional ethics in overseeing, monitoring, proposing, and ushering in new ideas and improvements, and (3) senior management that is understanding of the role of management audit in achieving overall improvements and better accountability.

The contextual factors include elements that envelop and influence management such as the quality of political leadership and its willingness to allow professional management to apply sound managerial principles and techniques in making decisions. Such concerns cannot be separated from existing managerial cultures, traditions, and levels of integrity and ethics applied in the conduct of government functions at large.

In specifying conditions of success, one must also recognize most common problems and difficulties. At all levels of government, political considerations are paramount, often outweighing the desire for economy and efficiency. Interest in program costs is often of greater concern to managers than to politicians. Elected officials are always hesitant to make long-term decisions based largely on financial considerations.

Perhaps the most agreed upon concern regarding the practicality of management audits is the public's concern with expenditures. The benefits of professional monitoring will eventually outweigh all costs associated with its implementation, which initially could be expensive. Although monitoring managerial performance is not a goal without difficulties; it is important that realized benefits outweigh any problems associated with implementation.

JAMIL E. JREISAT

BIBLIOGRAPHY

Garner, C. William, 1991. *Accounting and Budgeting in Public and Nonprofit Organizations: A Manager's Guide.* San Francisco, CA: Jossey-Bass.

Herbert, L., L. N. Killough, and A.W. Steiss, 1984. *Governmental Accounting and Control.* Monterey, CA: Brooks/Cole.

Wesberry, James P., Jr., 1990. "Government Accounting and Financial Management in Latin American Countries." In *Government Financial Management: Issues and Country Studies.* Washington, DC: International Monetary Fund.

Wheat, Edward M., 1991. "The Activist Auditor: A New Player in State and Local Politics." *Public Administration Review,* vol. 51, no. 5 (September–October).

MANAGEMENT BY FEAR.

The use of threats (implicit or explicit), coercion, intimidation, and tyranny by managers in their quest to get employees to accomplish organizational tasks.

Introduction

Fear, one of the most intense emotions known to humans, evokes physiological changes in individuals who feel threatened either physically or psychologically. What is the motivation for creating such an environment and treating people in this manner?

Central to the practice of management and leadership is motivation, since management is concerned with getting work done with the assistance of others. Whether or not we accept the premise that leaders and managers are different in the way they view organizational life, virtually everyone agrees that both leaders and managers do not exist without followers and/or subordinates and that both leaders and managers are capable of using fear to accomplish personal as well as organizational goals.

The use of fear to accomplish work is well documented. Throughout history various philosophies have been espoused to express the need to oppress workers, thereby maintaining control and achieving certain levels of productivity. Slavery, which has existed since recorded history, is the best-known example of managing by fear. In this extreme case of management of workers, the slaves were removed from familiar surroundings, stripped of their feelings of self-worth, their identity, and their independence, and subjected to unwarranted and unpredictable punishment. The separation from one's homeland and all that was familiar, including the language spoken, brought about a reaction—fear and the concomitant response of fight or flight. In every system of slavery, there are numerous reports about those who attempted to get away and by so doing gain freedom, and there are an equal number of reports of those who fought back in a variety of ways. However, escape and resistance in any form could not be tolerated, and therefore punishment for any deviation from the master's wishes was generally swift, severe, and public. In addition, punishment was often administered for no apparent reason and slaves were sold to other owners in order to discourage support systems among the slaves, thus keeping slaves in a constant state of fear of the unknown and making control more easily attainable.

The motivation to work in order to avoid punishment was strong among slaves, but so too was the motivation to sabotage the operation. Subtle and not so subtle acts of sabotage were frequent.

As the need for slavery declined, thus leading to its demise, the need of some to utilize fear tactics in the workplace did not decline. As societies became more enlightened, organizations acted on the belief that workers were not to be trusted and therefore had to be coerced into performing at the desired level; this Theory X view of workers, as Douglas McGregor called it, it assuredly the one that was held by slaveholders and owners of company towns.

Ostensibly, it has been replaced by a modern view of management, but if actions are the determining factor, there are numerous organizations that still operate (or subtly applaud the actions of those who manage) as though Theory X is an accurate depiction of workers.

Management by fear is by no means limited to any particular sector of the world of work. Perhaps it is no surprise that it existed in the private sector where the profit motive outweighs all other considerations. Although not explicitly stated in any research, it is very likely that at least one of the reasons for the development of the Human Relations School was an attempt to find a solution to the problem of managers who used intimidation and fear. As organizational and motivational theory evolved, there was greater recognition of the "crazy boss" syndrome, although for the most part it was thought to be an individual rather than an organizational problem.

The existence and the prevalence of this philosophy of managing employees by fear and intimidation in the public sector is perhaps much more surprising, but no less real. If we look at the history of public administration, it may be less of a surprise that managers have been able to use coercive power to keep employees in line.

Public administration began during a time of limited political participation, and therefore positions were filled on the basis of patronage rather than merit. During the first 40 years of public administration in the United States, government personnel came from the elite, those who had a certain social standing and advanced education (Gordon 1982). As the country expanded and as the interest in government service increased, individuals from classes other than the elite became involved in government service. Government positions were still mainly patronage positions based on loyalty to the winning party. Since partisan affiliation was the basis for an appointment, employees were fearful of the personal impact of not following the party line or of their party losing a subsequent election. Managers in this type of situation are able to take advantage of the security concerns of the employees and to coerce them to participate in campaign and other nonjob-related activities.

The creation of the civil service system was not only a response to the spoils system, where patronage took precedence over merit, but was also a response to the systematic intimidation of workers and the massive turnover of personnel that occurred at the change of each administration. However, in every civil service jurisdiction, there are numerous "at will" employees who serve at the pleasure of the appointing authority (a designated individual or office within that jurisdiction). Although the reforms of the past indicated a need for some measure of fitness for duty that would be nonpartisan and would afford all an equal opportunity to compete for government positions based on job-related skills, these individuals do not participate in the competitive process. For the most part, they understand the rules of the game (that they are expected to leave office when there is a change in the administration) and are often unable to make the decisions or implement the actions that would be beneficial to the public because of political, and therefore, employment, ramifications. Fear of losing one's job can place the public good in a low priority position. Somewhat surprisingly, the number of "at will" employees has been on the rise while public sector employment, particularly at the state and federal levels, has been on the decline.

Several other factors have made management by fear acceptable in the public sector. According to Gerome Evans (1978), "the California voters clearly displayed their distrust of state and local officials and a waning appreciation for the services provided by cities, counties, school districts and special districts" (p. 79). The public outcry that began with Proposition 13 in California could be credited with making all public sector employees "at will" and creating an environment that had not existed in the public sector. Managers who believed in Theory X found a new battle cry—that citizens do not want to pay for lazy, unproductive, irresponsible and nonresponsive individuals. And citizens who previously would have been shocked at any attempt to dismantle the civil service system were heading the movement to eliminate the protections once cited as essential and to privatize as many services as possible. If the problems of productivity and waste were confined to the public sector, then the arguments put forth for privatization could be seen as having some validity. However, the private sector is plagued by similar problems and Theory X managers operate in this arena as well.

When the air traffic controllers went on strike in 1981 and were subsequently fired by President Reagan, a whole new era of management by fear was born in the public sector. Now both the public and the private sectors use what Richard Kazis and Richard Grossman (1982) term "job blackmail." Employees in the private sector are told that government regulations, on such issues as environmental safety, pollution, and public health, are too costly and therefore the organization must lay off workers. The employees are forced to choose between their immediate livelihood and the results of decisions that may not be evident for many years. Using the government as a scapegoat increases the distrust of the government, and since the workers do not have access to all of the information, they make their decisions based on limited information. Employees in the public sector are viewed as costs rather than resources, and therefore they are thought of as something to cut. The fear of having one's agency privatized is rampant and has created an atmosphere of mistrust and low morale, which has a negative impact on productivity and serves only to increase the public's anger with public sector employees.

Neurotic organizations (Kets deVries and Miller 1984) exist in all sectors, and it is the personality types of the leaders and managers that form the commonality of these organizations. These leaders and managers have a particular disposition, including beliefs about the organization (bureaucratic orientation), about subordinates (Theory X orientation), and about self (self-esteem), and they have their own preferences for action (Ashforth 1994). Combinations of these factors are the antecedent conditions for "petty tyrants" to operate with virtual impunity (Ashforth 1994). Combined with the stresses created by a global economy, the stockholders cry for increased profits and the public cry for accountability and lower taxes, organizations are often willing to ignore the actions of tyrants in favor of increased productivity, even when the increases are only temporary.

It appears that individuals who have a high need for controlling the actions of others are prone to operate as Theory X managers, and the easiest way to control others is to instill in them a sense of fear. Since one's job provides either the basics (i.e., the means for obtaining food, shelter, and clothing) or some higher-level need such as self-esteem or self-actualization, the prospect of losing one's job can be a traumatizing experience. Thus, we can draw a parallel between management by fear and power over one's employees. Those who rule by fear or the use of coercive power are most likely to horde power rather than to share power. Empowerment is not likely to be a serious topic of discussion within organizational units where the managers believe that they must instill a sense of fear in their employees. This does not mean that lip service is not given to the popular ideas of teamwork, participative management, total quality management, and so forth. Often, there is a great deal of planning to implement these concepts, but for one reason for another the plans are never finalized or implemented.

As with any system that is based on fear rather than commitment, the gains are always short term. Today's organizations require a sustained effort of excellence that is not possible when individuals are demeaned and apprehensive.

Organizations that wish to alter the balance of power away from those who use their positions to execute a reign of terror on workers will have to pay close attention to their reward systems. High levels of productivity can be achieved in oppressive environments, such as the levels of productivity achieved during any period of slavery or in any neurotic organization. However, the long-term effect of organizational terrorism will be detrimental to organizational success. In healthy organizations, tyrants will be cut off from the mainstream and will eventually leave for jobs in organizations more conducive to their style. In a sick organization, or one that is under intense pressure, where people live in fear of their lives and no general standards or

proper management exist, the tyrant will find a home in which to flourish (Bing, p. 25, 1992). It is important to state that, as Bing points out, "the existence of a 'crazy boss' near you is evidence that something is wrong up above"; the problem is institutional, not personal.

This problem is exacerbated in the public sector because of the protections afforded to civil servants and the distrust of appointed officials for careerists. Once an individual gains tenure in a position, it is very difficult to remove that individual without "good cause." Since fear is likely, in the short term, to result in a high producing work group, and since this is the desired result, the means are often ignored. When an appointed official is the perpetrator, the typical attitude is that the bureaucrats are laggards and need to be threatened in order to produce at the level desired by the current administration. In this situation, the workers do not have as many alternatives since there is generally no higher internal authority to appeal to for some relief. Ultimately, the more competent workers will leave the organization, creating a brain drain and setting the organization on a downward productivity spiral.

The trend toward downsizing has created an atmosphere of fear in both the private and public sectors. In both sectors, however, for the first time managers are targets of this effort. The public sector once again is attempting to follow the path of the private sector and is trying to act more like a business. If businesses should be "lean and mean," then government should aspire to the same goal. While some bureaucrats do not see the need for change, most would agree that government operations need to be revisited and revised with new and more efficient systems put in place. The fear of many bureaucrats, however, is that government will be lean and mean to careerists while feathering the pockets of the politically active, special interests. It is feared that the tyrants will be given even more latitude to carry out their dysfunctional activities as the charges continue to be leveled as to government's inability to respond in a timely fashion, to cut the red tape, and to cut costs while preserving services.

By all reports, management by fear is alive and well in the public sector. As a policy issue, it is important that those who study public administration, as well as those who practice in the arena of public administration, must ask themselves and their colleagues if this methodology is an appropriate strategy for the sector that represents the "public good." Do the ends justify the means? Are short-term benefits sufficient to allow neurotic organizations to multiply? If we ignore the problem and pretend that we do not know that it exists, can we claim to believe in the principles of constitutional democracy? Can public administration survive the current Theory X managers?

ALMA M. JOSEPH

BIBLIOGRAPHY

Ashforth, Blake, 1994. "Petty Tyranny in Organizations." *Human Relations,* vol. 47: 775–778.

Bing, Stanley, 1992. "Crazy Bosses." *Across the Board,* vol. 29: 22–25.

deVries Kets, F. R. Manfred, and Danny Miller, 1984. *The Neurotic Organization.* San Francisco, California: Jossey-Bass.

Evans, Gerome, 1978. "Proposition 13: The Morning After." *State Government,* vol. 51: 74–80.

Gordon, George, J., 1982. *Public Administration in America.* New York: St. Martin's.

Kazis, Richard, and Richard L. Grossman, 1982. *Fear at Work.* New York: Pilgrim Press.

McGregor, Douglas M., 1960. *The Human Side of Enterprise.* New York: McGraw-Hill.

Rosenbloom, David H., 1993. *Public Administration Understanding Management, Politics, and Law in the Public Sector.* New York: McGraw-Hill.

MANAGEMENT BY OBJECTIVES (MBO).

A management system based on the identification and measurement of specific output objectives. The approach is credited to Peter Drucker (1954), who believed that the manager's job required the balancing of an organization's needs and goals in every area in which it must perform. By the 1970s, MBO was the gospel at Harvard Business School, the accepted approach in most businesses, and even the operational system for the U.S. government. As a descendant of Taylor's Scientific Management (1911), it held out the hope that any organizational activity could be managed if it were properly defined, measured, and monitored. MBO's adherents promised better strategies, better decisionmaking, more control, and more motivated employees.

For ten years, MBO was the predominant approach to management. By the 1980s, it had fallen out of favor as a management approach largely because it failed to deliver the results that many promised it would. Nevertheless, its systematic methods changed the way in which managers viewed their work, and its effects can be seen in more modern management approaches such as Total Quality Management.

MBO requires an organization to be directed toward a common goal. It is the responsibility of top management to identify a goal or goals to guide the organization. From those goals organizationwide objectives are established. At each subordinate level, these objectives are further refined to reflect the activities and responsibilities of that level. At the lowest level of the organization—the frontline employee—objectives become individual or team performance objectives. Thus, all employees should understand their specific job expectations and the manner in which their work relates to the organization as a whole.

MBO requires that objectives be specific (delineating the particular area of performance), individual (identifying the specific responsibilities of each employee), measurable (quantifiable at best, or at least with some measure of progress), and realistic (achievable). It requires that objectives be put in writing so that there is no "guesswork" about what an individual supervisor or the organization as a whole expects of an employee. This has also been called "performance targeting."

MBO also requires that objectives be monitored regularly and that individuals' performance be evaluated based on the extent to which they have met those objectives. This means that MBO requires the involvement of both superiors and subordinates. The superior must be able to direct and counsel subordinates on expected results. This helps to focus the employees' attention on the most important outcomes of work and allows them some decisionmaking role in how they perform that work. Other efforts at participatory management also seek to have this kind of employee input, involvement, and initiative.

In its best applications, MBO improves organizational performance by focusing on short- and long-range planning and the monitoring of work progress and results. It strengthens effective employee involvement, improves the commitment of employees and managers at all levels to the goals of the organization, and increases employees' sense of being a part of an organization. It improves the clarity of the manager's job and increases communication between superiors and subordinates. Finally, it improves organizational climate in general by focusing on performance rather than on personality.

Unfortunately, the potential of MBO often becomes another form of industrial engineering. Heavy-handed, top-down MBO systems fail because they (1) view jobs as static, (2) allow little or no employee discretion, (3) do not reflect the interdependence of most jobs, (4) ignore issues of organizational climate or a manager's interpersonal competence, (5) set and measure objectives in a time frame that is too short to reflect organizational and environmental realities, and (6) place performance appraisal, the least-liked and perhaps least-well-done part of a supervisor's job, at the center of the management process.

While MBO can be applied in situations in which there are adequate or scarce resources, it is inappropriately used in a crisis situation. For example, in recent years, the credibility of public organizations or their fiscal situation has been threatened. In the midst of this chaos, some managers have looked to MBO to replace the certainty which has been lost. Usually they are not successful. Most private-sector organizations put aside MBO systems during recessions and concentrate on essential capital spending and centralized decisionmaking.

To be successful, MBO systems must be introduced across the organization, from top to bottom. There are three critical components: participatory decisionmaking, goal setting, and objective feedback. Studies of MBO efforts have found that MBO success is influenced by (1) the amount of influence all employees have in the goal-setting process, (2) the relevance of feedback given to employees on their performance, and (3) top-level goal setting and support for the program (Alpin and Schoderbek 1976). Because the concept of MBO appears to be relatively simple and straightforward, it may be adopted without fully using these three elements. Then it falls short of expectations.

In addition, successful MBO systems require organizationwide trust—what Douglas McGregor (1960) has termed a "Theory Y Organization." Both employers and employees must believe that all people in the organization are working for the best interests of the group and that individuals will rise above self-interest to achieve organizational goals. This management philosophy is incompatible with a measurement-oriented, scientific management philosophy that often accompanies MBO efforts.

MBO came into vogue in government in the early 1970s, primarily as a budgeting technique. Circular A-11 (1975) of the federal Office of Management and Budget (OMB) required the submission of agency objectives along with budget estimates. Two years later, MBO was dropped at the federal level when the OMB replaced MBO with zero-based budgeting.

MBO systems were tried in many public organizations at the federal, state, and local levels. They were abandoned because managers discovered that the processes were difficult and demanding and researchers found that "productivity improvement is a likely, though not certain, outcome of MBO." (Guzzo and Bondy 1983, p. 22). More recent reanalysis has found that MBO can account for productivity gains if it is fully implemented and there is high commitment from top-level managers (Rodgers and Hunter 1992). Further, MBO can be as effective in public-sector organizations as it has been in the private sector.

Though generally discredited, the elements of MBO are present in many modern management systems. Most notable among these is Total Quality Management, where the MBO elements of goal setting, participation, and feedback are also critical. MBO is not a comprehensive system for management, but rather a management tactic that can deal with planning, coordination, and performance measurement.

SUSAN C PADDOCK

BIBLIOGRAPHY

Alpin, John C., and Peter P. Schoderbeck, 1976. "MBO: Requisites for Success in the Public Sector." *Human Resource Management,* vol. 15 (Summer) 30–36.
Drucker, Peter F., 1954. *The Practice of Management.* New York: Harper and Row.
Guzzo, Richard A, and Jeffrey S. Bondy, 1983. *A Guide to Worker Productivity Experiments in the United States, 1976–1981.* New York: Pergamon Press, 22.
McGregor, Douglas, 1960. *The Human Side of Enterprise.* New York: McGraw-Hill.
Rodgers, Robert, and John E. Hunter, 1992, "A Foundation of Good Management Practice in Government: Management by Objectives." *Public Administration Review,* vol. 52, no. 1 (January–February) 27–37.
Taylor, Frederick Winslow, 1911. *The Principles of Scientific Management.* New York: Harper and Brothers.

MANAGEMENT CONTROL.
A results-oriented process used by management to assure that resources are obtained and used effectively and efficiently to further the goals of an organization.

Perhaps the best-known definition of management control is that presented by Robert Anthony (1965) in his book *Planning and Control Systems: A Framework for Analysis.* He defines management control as "the process by which managers assure that resources are obtained and used effectively and efficiently in the accomplishment of the organization's objectives" (p. 17). This definition emphasizes that the function of management control is to facilitate the accomplishment of organizational goals by implementing previously identified strategies. Geert Hofstede (1981) in an article in *Accounting, Organizations, and Society* provides another useful definition of management control, defining it "as a pragmatic concern for results, obtained through people" (p. 193). The value of Hofstede's definition lies in the emphasis on three important aspects of management control: pragmatism, results, and people.

Briefly let us consider these in turn. First, management control is pragmatic. It is not an abstract description or process. The purpose of management control is to achieve goals within the specific environment in which it operates. Second, management control focuses on results, which are defined as reaching the goals or objectives both of the specific operation at hand and of the larger organization. Third, and probably the most important aspect of management control, is that it is concerned with people and organizations. People are the reason management control has significance and, ultimately, it is they who make an organization successful or not.

Management control has four major components: measurement, planning, control, evaluation. Measurement is a necessary condition for planning, control, and evaluation to occur. Information is needed for carrying out the other functions in management control—planning, control, and evaluation. That information generally is in quantitative form (e.g., number of X rays performed, number of airplane landings, number of individuals counseled, number of audits completed) and is the result of some measurement process. Although sometimes taken for granted, the measurement process is central to the operation of effective and efficient planning, control, or evaluation of a system. Seemingly well-designed systems can produce undesired results because of a poor choice of the attributes measured. Planning generates specifications of how the organization is intended to affect the future. Planning identifies key organizational goals and objectives and the means by which the organization aligns its resources to reach the goals and objectives. Planning is the road map that helps the organization identify key resources and constraints in the pursuit of its goals and objectives. Control keeps the organization headed in the right direction. Control happens when components of the management control system are used to ensure that desired outputs are generated. Control is primarily concerned with the relationship between causal factors (e.g., budgets, decisions, hierarchy) and actual effects of the system (output attributes that are measured). Control and control mechanisms can be found almost everywhere. The type of control of interest here is the type that affects and is affected by managers. This type of control is not of much value to the organization or its members if it does not result in individuals behaving in the desired fashion; controls, therefore, must address behavior directly. Control requires comparing behavior to a standard (without a standard, any performance is good performance) and then taking some action based on the comparison. In management control systems, control occurs as an ongoing process that supports performance, which is defined by the attributes measured of specific outputs of the organization. Evaluation takes place in the comparison of actual outputs with desired outputs. Evaluation is primarily concerned with the relationship between actual outputs or effects and desired outputs or effects (such as performance as specified by the goals and objectives).

Although the purpose of the management control system is to determine how best to achieve the goals and objectives of the organization, one should not assume that the management control system cannot facilitate and influence the setting of goals and objectives. Robert Simons (1991) in an article in the *Strategic Management Journal* argues that the management control system can become and possibly should become an active influence in guiding the organization. The control system can focus management and at least partially define the reality that management must address, thereby influencing the goals and objectives selected.

The specificity of the goals and objectives affects the success of the management control system. Poorly specified goals and objectives will create difficulty because of the resulting uncertainty and ambiguity. However, precisely stated goals and objectives also can be a problem because specific statements of purpose may be short run. Philip Bromiley and K. J. Euske (1986) in an article in *Financial Accountability & Management* point out that although specific short-run statements of purpose may be met, long-run statements of purpose may be ignored. For instance, a health-care agency may have the long-run goal of eradicating tuberculosis among the homeless in San Francisco. Such a goal is difficult to use for evaluating the performance of treatment units. Therefore, a short-term

goal that is easier to monitor may be used. A goal such as performing Y number of X rays per period could become the operational measure of success of the program. Performing X rays does not necessarily assure the achievement or even progress toward the agency's long-term goal of eradicating tuberculosis.

The segregation of management control into four components—measurement, planning, control, and evaluation—is useful for pedagogical purposes, but in practice these functions cannot be separated. You measure in order to have the information to plan, control, and evaluate; you plan in order to know where you are going; you control so you can get there; you evaluate in order to know whether you have arrived. Although there is no guarantee that the management control system will work until it is implemented, a successful management control system helps ensure that the right behaviors occur and provides information to correct behaviors when deviations occur. Even if the management control system does not provide the behavioral control, the information generated may still be useful in improving the management control system. The information generated by a failed system may provide an indication of why the failure occurred and suggest guidance for the design and implementation of an improved system.

KEN J. EUSKE

BIBLIOGRAPHY

Anthony, Robert, 1965. *Planning and Control Systems: A Framework for Analysis.* Boston: Graduate School of Business Administration, Harvard University.

Bromiley, Philip, and K. J. Euske, 1986. "The Use of Rational Systems in Bounded Rationality Organizations: A Dilemma for Financial Managers." *Financial Accountability & Management*, vol. 2, no. 4 (Winter) 311–320.

Churchman, C. West, and Philburn Ratoosh, 1962. *Measurement, Definitions, and Theories.* New York: Wiley.

Hofstede, Geert, 1981. "Management Control of Public and Not-for-Profit Activities." *Accounting, Organizations, and Society*, vol. 6, no. 3: 193–211.

Simons, Robert, 1991. "Strategic Orientation and Top Management Attention to Control Systems." *Strategic Management Journal*, vol. 12, no. 1: 49–62.

MANAGEMENT INFORMATION SYSTEM (MIS).

Any formal system for collecting, processing, and supplying information that is used by managers to enhance operational control and management of an organization. When used in a formal sense, management information systems use input, processing, and outputs for regulating the system. Inputs capture facts or data, processing transforms the data into information, and output provides the information to management to assist in decisionmaking. Some of this output is feedback data, which report on the performance or status of the system. Feedback information allows management to determine if the system is moving toward its goal and make corrections. MIS has a narrow meaning, which refers to the least complex type of information systems providing management with control and exception reports. MIS may also refer to the organizational unit responsible for information resources. Finally, MIS is also an academic discipline or course of study, which investigates the role of information technologies in the organization.

In recent years, the rapid growth of information and constant adaptations of technology have made it difficult to develop a concise standard definition of terms used to describe information systems. The terms "information system" (IS), "computer information system" (CIS), and "computer-based information system" (CBIS) are generally synonyms for the broad definition of MIS above.

Types of Information Systems

Information systems are designed to assist managers in making all types of decisions. The grid in Figure I shows that decisions can be classified by organizational level: strategic decisionmaking, management control, and operational control. Strategic decisionmaking is carried out by top executives of the organization. Their decisions assure the long-term future of the organization. In response to internal and external environment pressures, they establish the company's long-term objectives and policies. Middle managers are responsible for controlling and monitoring operational units to meet objectives and policies. Operational control involves selecting the best methods to carry out the tasks required by strategic and middle managers. Types of decisions at each organizational level may be further classified as structured, semistructured, or unstructured. Structured decisions are routine decisions with predefined procedures for completing them. Unstructured decisions are nonroutine, which require the decisionmaker to use judgment. In reality, few decisions are solely structured or unstructured.

Figure I shows four major types of information systems. The various types of information systems have become more complex and more pervasive moving from structured to unstructured and operational control to strategic as computer technology has developed. Each type of information system is focused on a particular organization level and decision type but may overlap other information system types.

Transaction processing systems (TPSs) were the original, and only, type of information system developed in the early 1960s. It remains an important part of present information systems. A TPS supports structured decisions at the operational level. These systems link the organization to the external environment. A TPS captures and updates data required for sales, manufacturing, human resources, or any other area. It collects detailed data about orders, payments, inventory, employees, patients, and so forth.

The TPS for a mail order company records and updates basic facts about inventory, orders, payments, and customers. It is hard to conceive of an organization from a local dry cleaning establishment to a multinational corporation without such systems. The TPS is the primary source of data for other types of information systems.

A management information system (MIS narrow definition) was an immediate extension of TPSs. The MIS focuses on the general information and decision needs of numerous middle managers. It primarily supports structured management decisions related to monitoring and meeting organizational objectives. Therefore, an MIS requires only limited analytical capabilities. It provides standard periodic exception reports or online files for monitoring and controlling system performance. An MIS does not collect information from the external environment but relies on data collected by one or more of the organizational TPS databases. An MIS for a mail order company provides summary reports on sales, returned items, and account receivables reports.

Until the mid-1970s, the only types of information systems available were TPSs and MISs (narrow definition), designed primarily for structured decisions. Many organizational problems are semistructured, which cannot be programmed in advance. A decision support system (DSS) is a group of computing facilities designed to assist a manager or a small group of managers make better decisions when facing semistructured problems. DSS facilities include databases, programs or query languages to extract data, mathematical models, report preparation programs, and a graphical user interface program to facilitate gathering data and modeling organizational processes. A small company manager may use a PC-based database and spreadsheets as models in the DSS. A large corporation may develop a comprehensive set of capabilities with specialized DSS databases, models, a graphical user interface, and technical support staff. Often organizations have many different DSSs. The manager, perhaps with technical assistants, has a major role in developing, revising, and using the DSS.

A typical DSS applies mathematical and statistical models to simulate one or more operations of the firm using databases created by the organizations TPS or MIS and to project the future. Models may simulate future production requirements or the impact of a marketing strategy on future sales and profitability. Some DSS models produce an optimum solution, but many allow managers to play the "what-if game" by changing decision variables and observing the impact.

Group decision support systems (GDSSs), which focus on improving group decisionmaking and communication may also be part of a DSS. GDSSs, developed in the late 1980s, rely on special rooms with a networked PC for each participant and specialized software that supports processes such as electronic brainstorming, ranking/rating

FIGURE I. ORGANIZATIONAL LEVEL, DECISIONS AND INFORMATION SYSTEMS TYPES

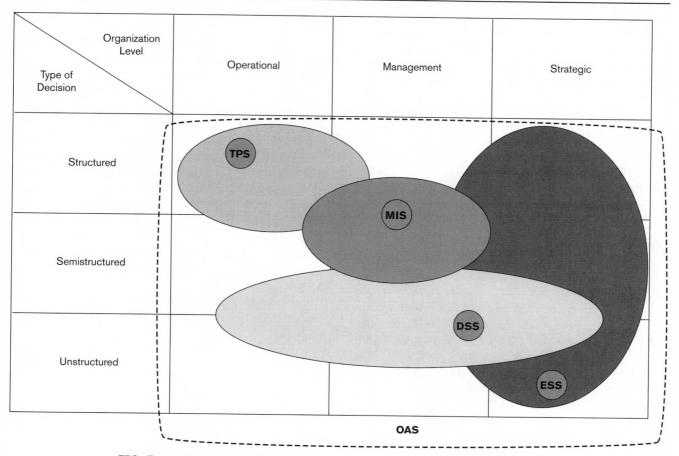

TPS - Transaction Processing System
MIS - Management Information System
OAS - Office Automation System

DSS - Decision Support System
ESS - Executive Support System

Source: Adapted from G. Anthony Gorry and Michael S. Scott Morton, 1971. "A Framework for Management Information Systems." *Sloan Management Review* (Fall).

ideas, anonymous voting, and so forth. These systems may include modeling and other software used by managers to develop their DSS.

Executive support systems (ESSs) assist strategic decisionmaking. These systems are designed to meet the executive's need for external and, to a lesser extent, internal information and communication. ESSs emphasize generalized computing and telecommunications rather than focusing on solving specific problems. An ESS is designed by working with the executive to identify critical internal and external events plus indicators that track these events. The software can notify the executive when critical events occur. Executives may have graphical access to aggregated organizational data, which can be "drilled" (viewed in increasing and minute detail). Some prewritten ESS software packages are available. When a large company develops its own software, a significant staff and even mainframe computers may be required to maintain it. ESSs are the least used of all information system types.

An office automation system (OAS) is also known as an office information system (OIS). An OAS serves as the link between all other types of information systems. It facilitates communication between systems in the organization and members of the organization. OASs began growing rapidly in the mid-1980s with the introduction of personal computers and local area networks connecting personal computers and other office equipment. An ideal OAS would be a computer network based system that allows any employee of an organization to communicate with any medium: voice, data, images, or video. An OAS focuses on developing technologies for managing documents, messages, conferences, and group activities. Document management includes word processing, publishing, text filing systems, and microfilm. Message systems include voice mail, facsimile, and electronic mail. Conferencing includes group conferences with telephone, video or networked PCs, and electronic bulletin boards. OASs also support group calendaring, project management, and other group activities. Building an OAS is hampered by a lack of organizational, national, and international standards for connecting office automation equipment.

Knowledge work systems (KWSs) are systems developed to support knowledge workers for professionals such as engineers, architects, and doctors. They are responsible for the creation of new knowledge such as bioengineering services, computer software, and other high-technology industries. KWSs use powerful computer workstations with specialized software.

The Sociotechnical Nature of the MIS Practice and Discipline

Organizations can acquire great wealth and power from the use of computer technology. However, information systems can and do fail to achieve their potential. Failures often result from not fully understanding the impact technology can have on the organization and its people. New systems may alter the power of key individuals or groups resulting in conflict and reduced efficiency. If a new information system fails to match the education, skills, or learning style of the people in the organization, the information system may be resisted or fall into disuse. Successful MIS practitioners have learned that the design of any significant information system must knit together a unique set of technological, organizational, and employee characteristics. When these three factors are expertly crafted, organizational efficiency and effectiveness are greatly enhanced.

Scholars have long recognized the sociotechnical nature of MISs. The discipline of MIS is a pragmatic discipline that draws on the experience of MIS practitioners, technical disciplines, and behavioral fields. The technical disciplines contributing to MIS are computer science, management science, and operations research. These disciplines stress mathematically based models. Computer science is particularly important as a source of powerful technologies that shape organizations. But new technologies cannot be placed in organizations without political, social, and psychological impacts. Theories in these disciplines are used to improve systems design, acceptance, and use. Since the 1980s, larger and larger parts of the organization have been redesigned to take advantage of computer technologies. As a result, a growing part of MIS is concerned with behavioral issues.

Sources of Information

Because MIS is a pragmatic sociotechnical discipline, there is a wide range and depth of sources of information. The leading journals focusing on the sociotechnical nature of MIS are the *MIS Quarterly, Journal of Management Information, Information Systems Research*, and *Management Science*. A wide range of emerging sociotechnical issues in the practice of MIS are reported in *Datamation, Infosystems, Com-*

puterworld, and *Information Week*. The impact and use of MIS in organizations is reported in the *Harvard Business Review, Sloan Management Review*, and the *Administrative Science Quarterly*.

Computer science is the leading source of new hardware and software technologies applied in MIS systems. Methodologies for engineering complex programs have led to new methodologies for developing MIS systems. Development of relational database concepts and techniques have given end users direct access to organization databases scattered throughout the world. Developments in computer science can be followed in the *Communications of the Association for Computing Machinery* (ACM). Studies of the behavioral aspects of MIS can be followed in the *American Sociological Review, Administrative Science Quarterly, American Political Science Review*, and the *Journal of Psychology*.

As MIS develops, the changes are reflected in educational and training programs. Both the Data Processing Management Association (DPMA) and the Association for Computing Machinery (ACM) periodically publish model curricula for educational institutions and technical institutes.

WILLIAM A. PERRY

BIBLIOGRAPHY

Davis, Gordon B., and Margrethe H. Olson, 1985. *Management Information Systems: Conceptual Foundation, Structure, and Development.* New York: McGraw-Hill.
Laudon, Kenneth C., and Jane P. Laudon, 1994. *Management Information Systems: Organization and Technology.* New York: Macmillan.
McLoad, Raymond, Jr., 1994. *Management Information Systems: A Study of Computer-Based Information Systems.* New York: Macmillan.
Zwass, Vladimir, 1992. *Management Information Systems.* Dubuque: Wm. C. Brown

MANAGEMENT SCIENCE.

An interdisciplinary field comprising elements of mathematics, economics, computer science, and engineering. It is primarily concerned with the development and application of quantitative analyses to find solutions to problems faced by managers of public and private organizations.

History

Although quantitative analysis to solve managerial problems can be identified as having been used by very early civilizations, the generally agreed upon beginning of management science, as a field of study, dates to World War II. In the early 1940s, P. M. S. Blackett, a Nobel Prize–winning physicist, was asked by the British government to convene a group of scientists to study operational problems such as optimal deployment of convoy vessels, tactic of anti-submarine warfare, and strategies of civilian defense. This group included physicists, astrophysicists, mathematicians, physiologists, surveyors, mathematical physicists, and army officers. It was officially known as the Army Operations Research Group; unofficially the group was called Blackett's Circus. This diverse group successfully found solutions to complex military problems and led to the creation of similar "operations analysis" groups in all branches of the military in Britain and the United States.

Operations research was the original term used to describe the work of a group of mathematicians and scientists who collaborated in attempting to apply scientific principles to solve business and industrial problems. However, a division among the practitioners of this new discipline developed early in the life of the discipline between those who were oriented toward business and those who focused on industry or engineering. Consequently, two terms emerged to reflect the divergent applications. Management science emphasized the application of scientific principles to management problems, whereas operations research was grounded in civil and industrial engineering, thus emphasizing production problems and nonbusiness applications. Today the terms are used interchangeably.

After World War II, some of the scientists involved in the operations analysis groups began to apply the techniques, developed as part of those groups, to business and national security problems. However, their efforts did not really take off until computers became commercially available in the 1950s. In fact, industrial applications of operations analysis are largely attributed to two events: the availability of high-speed computers and the development of linear programming by George Dantzig.

The dependence of management science on computers cannot be underestimated. Solutions to complex business and industry problems frequently require the ability to perform numerous calculations and keep track of large data sets. The commercial availability of computers in the 1950s, even though these early computers were puny by today's standards, provided firms large enough to afford computers the ability to apply the advances in analytic decisionmaking developed to aid the war effort. Computers were an invaluable tool for management science and operations research as it developed into a profession.

In 1947, George Dantzig developed the simplex method of solving linear programming problems. This technique is an algebraic procedure that can be used to solve a system of simultaneous linear equations to determine the optimal allocation of resources. Dantzig's work gave business a powerful tool to analyze many large-scale resource allocation problems. When coupled with the rapid development of computers, linear programming applications spread throughout the private sector, and it became an important tool for business and industry. It exemplified the application of scientific techniques that supported the overwhelming success of American business after World War II.

Reflecting the wartime roots of management science, public sector development and application of management science was dominated by the military in the 1940s and 1950s. The navy, in cooperation with the consulting firm of Booz, Allen, and Hamilton, developed PERT (Program, Evaluation, and Review Technique) to assist in the planning and control of large-scale projects or networks. PERT is credited with delivering the navy's Polaris submarine two years ahead of schedule. This development exercise is an early example of successful public-private cooperation.

The nonmilitary public sector began to employ management science in the late 1960s and early 1970s. City governments perform tasks such as sanitation, fire, and police management that are particularly suited to the application of management science techniques. And as software packages became available, local governments increasingly took advantage of the opportunity to use linear programming, integer programming, and decision analysis to manage government operations more efficiently.

Management Science Techniques

Management science provides a methodology to assist managerial decisionmaking. The techniques used in management science help to provide a more rational and scientific basis for making these decisions. Over time the techniques that make up the field have grown to reflect the large-scale computing capacities available and to make use of the new communication and transportation technologies.

The content of the field in the 1950s was dominated by linear and dynamic programming, network analysis, inventory control, and queuing theory. The 1960s introduced decision analysis and goal and multiobjective linear programming. In the 1970s, the management science efforts focused on artificial intelligence and expert systems. Also during the 1970s, small computers became increasingly available to businesses and the general public and work began to focus on management information systems. Since the 1980s, with the increased availability of personal computers, management science techniques have not just been within the purview of business anymore. Increasingly, the tools of management science are available to anyone who wants to use them. Some emphasis has been placed on adapting the techniques to make them more user-friendly for general use.

Professional Associations

The establishment of operations research and management science as a profession was indicated by two events: the development of academic programs to train individuals specifically for management science positions and the formation of professional associations. Academic programs were developed in the late 1950s and early 1960s based on recommendations by the Carnegie and Ford foundations. The first graduate to receive a Ph.D. in Operations Research was Lawrence Freidman, who received his degree from Case Western in 1957. MIT, Stanford, UC at Berkeley, and Cornell were the early leaders in formalizing the study of operations research or management science.

The growth of professional associations to facilitate research and development, to enhance communication among members, and to act as advocate for the emerging profession occurred very early. In 1952, the Operations Research Society of America (ORSA) was formed, followed in 1953 by the creation of the Institute of Management Science (TIMS). The original membership of these two associations reflected the different types of application being emphasized. However, over time the distinction became less meaningful and the two groups merged in 1995. The new group is called the Institute for Operations Research and Management Science (INFORMS), and its mission is to "serve as an international network to facilitate improvements in operational processes, decisionmaking, and management by individuals and organizations through the use of operations research, the management sciences and related methods" (INFORMS brochure). Presently, the association consists of 135,000 members in more than 80 countries from a variety of fields such as government, computer science, engineering, and economics. INFORMS sponsors international meetings and publishes ten professional journals or magazines: *Interfaces, Management Science, Operations Research, Information Systems Research, Journal on Computing, Organizational Science, Marketing Science, Mathematics of Operations Research, Transportation Science,* and *OR/MS Today.*

DOROTHY OLSHFSKI AND MICHELE COLLINS

MANAGEMENT ACCOUNTING. The process

of identification, measurement, accumulation, analysis, preparation, interpretation, and communication of information (both financial and nonfinancial) used by management or controlling authority for planning, control, and decisionmaking within an organization.

The purpose of management accounting is to provide managers with information on planning, resourcing, controlling, and reviewing the current operations of an entity, and for decisionmaking over future activities. It is primarily concerned with the internal use of information, which distinguishes it from financial accounting, which focuses on external reporting and accountability of an entity. The accounting data and sources are often the same as for financial accounting (see Figure I); however, the information needs of management lead to more detailed and spe-

cialized reporting. The term "cost accounting" has also been used to describe internal accounting procedures; however, costing is now considered a specialized area within the broader management accounting function.

Figure I sets out the sources of data for a management accounting system and for financial accounting and reporting. It shows how the two different objectives of reporting are met.

History of Management Accounting

The development of management accounting is traced to pioneering nineteenth-century industries including railroads, textile making, pottery manufacturing, and retail distribution. Accounting systems were developed to facilitate internal economic exchange and hence to improve efficiency and performance. Control of costs became more important as organizations grew and diversified, and the emphasis was placed on profit calculation and competitive behavior. Management accounting has evolved in response to business needs, developing the relationship between capital and financial performance and introducing modern measurement techniques such as standard costing, activity-based costing, capital evaluation models, and the use of statistical analysis to control inventories and distribution.

Role of Management Accounting

The role of management accounting is to provide information in the following areas.

Setting Operational Targets and Applying Managerial Control

Managers need to know whether goods and services are supplied efficiently and to measure their performance against internal targets and against other entities (benchmarking). Management accounting information provides the data to exercise these product and organization financial controls, ranging from a gross margin analysis (sales less costs of production), product mix, the relationship of marketing, administration and finance expenditure to revenues through to total final profit or loss (surplus/deficiency) breakdowns by business unit, division, and for the overall entity.

The information is incorporated in initial budgets and management reports comparing actual revenues and expenditures to the budget. The sources of information are primarily the accounting records but include input from other systems involving human resources, manufacturing, inventory, and planning and corporate systems.

Resource Allocations

Determining the allocation of operational or capital funds (budgeting) is a key role for the management accountant. The management accounting system is critical in providing

FIGURE I. SOURCE, PROCESS, AND OUTPUT OF ACCOUNTING SYSTEMS

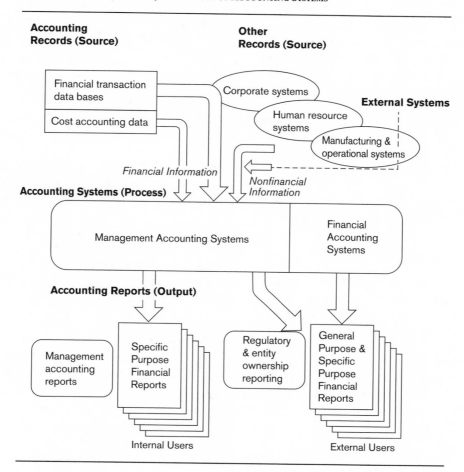

financial data in conjunction with strategic and corporate plans to set financial targets. The techniques of budgeting require detailed expenditure and revenue estimates by product or service to be accumulated by organizational unit. The aggregation of these estimates and presentation in a business plan or entity operational plan is then used for managerial control and for the raising of funds, either internally from an entity's own reserves or from the external financial providers. The accuracy and relevance of the budget is a key component of an organization's continuity.

Capital budgeting is a special area of management accounting where measurement techniques have been developed to give more assurance on risk investment funds, including net-present value calculation, benefit–cost or cost effectiveness analysis, and so forth.

Pricing of Goods and Services

The pricing of goods and services in a market economy is determined by both supply and demand, the competitive structure (perfect competition through to monopoly), and the financial constraints of the entity providing the products. Management accounts provide fundamental input to pricing decisions through accurate cost of production per

unit, the marginal cost of production (the additional cost of producing the next unit), and the likely future effect of changing prices and/or product mixes (differential costing). The use of these data can lead to efficient resource allocation through appropriate pricing decisions.

Strategic Analysis

Management constantly needs to make decisions about retaining or deleting products, outsourcing or internally providing, making or buying, purchasing or leasing, investing or divesting, and so forth. Management accounting provides the tools for decisionmaking through a variety of cost systems and techniques. Cost-volume-profit calculation techniques enable managers to evaluate the effect of varying volume, cost, prices, or mix of products on profit or output maximization. The analysis of variances from standard, average, or historical costs provides information on whether operations are efficient or inefficient, controllable or noncontrollable, significant or immaterial to performance. The availability of such cost and management information combined with management accounting techniques provides the basis for effective strategic management.

Bases of Cost Measurement and Cost Accounting Categories and Terms

Management accounting is not subject to external regulation or standard setters; therefore, a wide variety of methods and bases have been adopted to meet individual business needs for information. For example, the basis of recording in a management accounting system can be historical cost (where each transaction is recorded at the transaction date amount), standard cost (a predetermined or budgeted cost), current cost (measuring the service potential of assets), or an average of costs using any of these bases.

Categories of costs and terms that have general acceptance under management accounting include the following:

Functional classification of costs:

- *Direct costs:* those costs that are essential inputs or outputs in a process, such as materials and labor.
- *Indirect costs:* those costs that are incurred necessary to complete a process but not directly associated with outputs, such as power and depreciation.
- *Overhead costs:* those costs not associated with product or process but nevertheless necessary for the continuance of the entity, such as governance and senior management salaries.

Behavioral classification of costs:

- *Variable costs:* those costs that vary wholly or proportionately with an increase or decrease in output, such as cost of materials.
- *Fixed costs:* those costs that remain unchanged as output or activity increases or decreases, such as rent and depreciation.

Scope of Management Accounting

Management accounting applications are used extensively in private-sector, not-for-profit, and government entities. The objectives and purpose of entities determine the type of management accounting used and the reports produced. Because management accounting is a function of management, it will evolve continuously in line with needs of managers for information and the technology available to produce it.

GRAEME MACMILLAN

BIBLIOGRAPHY

Anthony, Robert N., and James S. Reece, 1975. *Management Accounting: Text and Cases.* Irwin-Dorsey International.
Hansen, D., and M. Mowen, 1992. *Management Accounting.* Cincinnati: South-Western Publishing.
Henke, E., and C. W. Spoede, 1991. *Cost Accounting: Managerial Use of Accounting.* Boston: PWS-Kent.
International Management Accounting Practice 1: Management Accounting Concepts, 1989. International Federation of Accountants.
Johnson, H. Thomas, and Robert Kaplan, 1987. *Relevance Lost: The Rise and Fall of Management Accounting.* HBS Press.
Langfield-Smith, K., H. Thorne, and R. W. Hilton, 1995. *Management Accounting: An Australian Perspective.* Melbourne: McGraw Hill.

MANAGEMENT, CONTINGENCY.

"Contingency," the idea that one thing depends on other things, is the core of the contingency management theory, which emphasizes that there is no one best management approach to all organizational situations and that the organization's various situational variables dictate the correct choice of a management approach. Contingency management theory can be succinctly defined as a theory of "it all depends" or an "if-then theory."

Introduction

No two organizations are alike. Problems arise when they are treated alike, as were the cases of traditional administrative principles and bureaucratic approaches to organization, which tried to design all organizations alike. The contingency approach emerged to help managers determine what approach or practice, when and under what situation, is most applicable for attainment of the organization's goals.

The contingency approach does not deny the usefulness of traditional and human relations theories, but it does deny the notion of "one best way" of managing regardless of situation. A particular theory may be chosen to best suit a particular managerial situation, but this same theory may not fit another situation. Therefore, the contingency approach implies that either being right or wrong in applying a particular theory depends upon the particulars of a given organizational situation.

In adopting a contingency theory for practical application, the manager should take a logical, step-by-step approach. First, managers should assess the reality in the organizational situation; second, they should grasp every pertinent aspect of the implications of various management theories at their disposal; and third, they should determine the best fit between the organization's situational requirements and a particular management theory.

Contingency theorists have delineated several major situational variables that tend to be highly correlated with the structure of organizations and the choice of courses of action, which include the organization's technology, environment, size, and strategy. Also, they have identified other important situational variables, including leader-member relationships, task structure, and the leader's position power, all of which tend to have impact on managerial leadership. The relationships among these situational variables have been found to be complex and interdependent.

Development and Theoretical Framework

Mary Parker Follett (1868–1933) proposed the original idea of contingency as "the law of situation" in the early 1920s. She advocated that different situations required different kinds of knowledge and that the person possessing the knowledge demanded by a certain situation tended to best manage the business and to become the leader of the moment.

Chester Barnard (1886–1961) did not use the term "contingency management" but implied in his book *The Functions of the Executive* in 1938 that the subordinates' acceptance of executive authority is contingent upon four conditions: (1) subordinates' understanding of communicated directive, (2) their belief that the authority is consistent with the purpose of the organization, (3) their belief that the authority is compatible with their own personal interests, and (4) their physical and mental ability to comply with the authority.

The theoretical framework of the contingency approach, backed by Joan Woodward's empirical findings, had not been developed until the late 1950s and 1960s. Instead, the framework evolved as a synthesis of pertinent prior theories of management as an alternative to the systems approach. The theory refined its basic assumptions and predictions by integrating key characteristics of an open systems theory, a practical research orientation, and a multivariate approach in the 1970s. Specifically, it relates to how the organization structure adjusts to fit with the internal and the external environment.

Researchers have been searching for the most appropriate way of designing an organization structure that varies with critical contingency factors such as the technology, environment, size, and strategy. Some of the most significant research studies were conducted by Joan Woodward (1958) on technology; Tom Burns and George Stalker (1961) and Paul Lawrence and Jay Lorsch (1969) on environment; Derek Pugh, David Hickson, and others (1969; 1976); Peter Blau and Richard Schoenherr (1971); and John Child and Roger Mansfield (1972) on size; and Alfred Chandler, Jr. (1962), on strategy.

In the area of leadership, the failure of the trait and traditional approach to leadership in identifying the universal prototype of effective leadership turned the attention of researchers to the situational aspects of leadership. The contingency model of leadership effectiveness was an outgrowth of a program of research begun at the University of Illinois by Fred Fiedler (1967), who sought to determine the relationship between the leadership style and the favorableness or unfavorableness of a situation. Fiedler's model

stimulated a great deal of research, inspiring the formulation of more refined or alternative contingency theories.

Contingency Approach to Organization

Technology

Woodward: Technology and Structure. Beginning in 1953, Joan Woodward, a British industrial sociologist at the South Essex College of Technology in Great Britain, and her research team conducted a series of research studies on technology and organization. She made a great contribution to the study of contingency management. Her most significant finding (1958) was that each organization's success and effectiveness were directly related to a proper match between technology and organizational structure and process. Technology was defined as the techniques or processes used to transform labor, knowledge, and raw materials into the finished product or services. Based on large-scale research involving 100 firms of widely diverse lines of business in South Essex, England, the researchers identified each firm with one of the three types of production technology: (1) unit/small-batch production (custom-made production such as special ordered clothing, machine tools and goods, etc.), (2) mass production/large-batch (large volumes of standardized goods such as cars, appliances, and textile mills, etc.), and (3) process/continuous-flow production (most mechanized and automated production such as oil refineries, large breweries and paper mills, etc.).

Woodward (1958) found that technology was related to the organization's structure and process in the following manner:

1. *Unit/small-batch production firms* tended to exhibit the following: lines of authority were flexible; departmentalization was a product type; degree of specialization was low; decisionmaking was decentralized; and span of control was small.
2. *Mass/large-batch production firms* tended to exhibit the following: lines of authority were rigidly adhered to; departmentalization was functional; degree of specialization was high; decisionmaking was centralized; and span of control was large.
3. *Process/continuous-flow production firms* tended to exhibit the following: lines of authority were flexible; departmentalization was a product type; degree of specialization was low; decisionmaking was decentralized; and span of control was small.

Woodward also found that firms with unit/small-batch and process/continuous technologies tended to make greater use of informal, ad hoc, verbal communications, whereas mass/large-batch production firms tended to rely more on formal, written communications. The mass production firms tended to adhere to the traditional, more dichotomous line-staff type of organization, in which line managers engaged in direct supervision of workers, while staff personnel provided technical assistance and advice. Line managers in unit and process expected to have greater technical expertise and to be able to make technical decisions. There were more skilled workers in unit and process firms than in mass production firms. The number of management levels increased as technical complexity increased from unit production of continuous process. Other characteristics such as span of control, formalized procedures, and centralization were high for mass-production technology but low for other technologies because the work was standardized. Woodward concluded that technology dictated the design of the organization's structure.

Environment

Burns and Stalker: Environment and Structure. Tom Burns and George Stalker (1961), British behavioral scientists, studied 20 industrial firms in England, focusing on the relationships between environmental factors and the structures of organization. They identified two different environmental conditions–changing and stable–and categorized two types of organization structure–mechanistic and organic.

The mechanistic structure of organization was characterized by the rigid hierarchy of authority, standardized procedures, rules and regulations, the division of labor, precisely defined tasks and responsibilities, and centralized authority; whereas the organic structure was characterized by flexibility, minimum rules and regulations, team work, and decentralized authority.

Burns and Stalker found that organizations in stable, unchanging environments tended to develop structures that were mechanistic and formal, whereas organizations in unstable, changing environments tended to develop structures that were organic and informal. In reality, however, there is no clearly defined distinction between the purely mechanistic or the purely organic structure of an organization, but most combine characteristics of both.

Lawrence and Lorsch: Differentiation and Integration. Paul Lawrence and Jay Lorsch (1969) from Harvard University conducted research of ten U.S. firms on the relationship between an organization's environment and its structure. Their two-step research involved plastics, food, and container industries, which were selected in view of their marked differences in environmental uncertainty. In the first study, they examined the relationship between the uncertainty of an organization's environment and its internal structure. In the second study, the relationship between the uncertainty of an organization's subsystem, or "department," and its own internal structure was investigated.

Lawrence and Lorsch found that in large, multidepartment organizations, each department had its own unique environment to contend with and its own organizational

substructure suited to this task. They also found that the differences in the subenvironments were reflected within their organization's substructures, contributing to differentiation of the organization. This differentiation compelled each subsystem's effort at integration for the purpose of achieving unity of the organization, which was essential for the attainment of the organization's goals.

Their findings are summarized as follows:

1. *Lines of authority:* Where tasks were routine and predictable, lines of authority were very clear, and the chain of authority was strictly enforced. Where tasks were more ambiguous and unpredictable, lines of authority were not so clear, and the chain of command was loosely enforced.
2. *Departmentalization:* Where tasks were routine and predictable, functional types of departmentalization prevailed. Where tasks were ambiguous and unpredictable, product types of departmentalization prevailed.
3. *Degree of specialization of jobs:* Where tasks were routine and predictable, jobs were much more specialized. Where tasks were ambiguous and unpredictable, jobs were more enlarged.
4. *Delegation and decentralization:* Where tasks were routine and predictable, decisionmaking was centralized at the top of the hierarchy. Where tasks were ambiguous and unpredictable, more delegation of authority and decentralization prevailed.
5. *Span of control:* Where tasks were routine and predictable, a narrower span of control seemed appropriate. Where tasks were ambiguous and unpredictable, wider spans prevailed.
6. *Coordination:* Where tasks were routine and predictable, coordination was achieved through rules and adherence to the chain of command. Where tasks were ambiguous and unpredictable, coordination was achieved through special coordinators or integrators, whose job was to facilitate communication across the organizational hierarchy.

These findings concurred with the findings of Burns and Stalker (1961) that organizations in a stable and predictable environment tended to develop structures that were mechanistic and formal, whereas those that must deal with a more unstable and dynamic environment developed more organic and flexible structures. The findings suggested that in order to be successful and effective, organizations in stable, predictable environments are required to design mechanistic and formal structures while those in more unstable and uncertain environments develop a more organic and flexible structure.

Thus, Lawrence and Lorsch concluded that the characteristics of the external environment are a powerful determinant of organizational structure and that if the external environment is very diverse and highly uncertain and the internal environment is highly differentiated, there needs to be a highly elaborated integrating mechanism within the organization's structure.

Size

Aston Studies. A group of researchers led by Derek S. Pugh and associated with the Industrial Administration Research Center at the University of Aston in Birmingham, England, conducted a series of research studies of organization theory, known as "the Aston studies" (1969 and 1976). From the literature, they distilled seven organizational dimensions particularly relevant to studies of organizations: (1) origin and history, (2) ownership and control, (3) size, (4) character, (5) technology, (6) location, and (7) dependence.

The results of the Aston studies indicated that organization size was the best predictor of organization structure. The correlation between organization size and specialization, standardization, formalization, and centralization of decisions was consistently higher than that between any other dimensions or variables and measures of organizational structure.

Blau and Schoenherr Study. Peter Blau and Richard Schoenherr (1971), the University of Chicago based researchers and contemporaries of the Aston study group, independently conducted a large-scale study aimed at understanding the structural dimensions of organizations and their interrelationships. Their study included 53 state and territorial employment security agencies with 387 of their major divisions and 1,201 of their local offices.

From the data obtained by interviews, questionnaires, and review of records, Blau and Schoenherr delineated a total of 85 variables or dimensions of organizational structure. They analyzed the interrelationships between the structural variables to learn how these variables were related to one another.

Blau and Schoenherr found that most structural variables were highly correlated with the organization size and that size was the single most powerful predictor of the rest of the structure of the organization. Reinforcing the findings of the Aston studies, they concluded that size was more important than technology in predicting organization structure, especially the organizational dimension of differentiation.

Child: National Study. John Child (1972) replicated the Aston studies, using the same measurements and procedures that had been used with a national sample drawn from the firms in England and Scotland. His study, also known as the National study, found that organization size was substantially and positively related to specialization of role and function, standardization, formalization, and span of control, and negatively related to centralization.

Child later compared the findings with those of the Aston studies, the Blau and Schoenherr study, and two other studies that shared similar measures. The comparative analysis involving five studies on size and structural variables revealed that larger organizations tended to be more specialized, formal with more rules and documentation, and had more extended hierarchies and greater decentralization of the decisionmaking process as compared with smaller organizations.

Child also found that the nature of the relationship between size and structure was curvilinear and that, as size increased, specialization, formalization, and vertical span also increased, but at a declining rate. His study described the relationships between size and other organizational variables with improved specificity.

Strategy

Alfred Chandler (1962), a business historian at Harvard University, studied the histories of approximately 100 of America's largest organizations, including General Motors, Westinghouse, Sears, and Du Pont. He analyzed information obtained from annual reports, articles, and government publications, as well as from interviews with senior executives.

Chandler found that strategy was the determinant of an organization's long-term goals, the choice of courses of action, and the allocation of resources toward the goals. Also, strategy determined its technology and helped determine the nature of its environment, such as its clientele, competition, diversity and rate of change. Environment, in turn, had an impact on the structure of the organization accordingly. Thus, strategy ultimately determined organizational structure.

Contingency Approach to Leadership

Fiedler: Contingency Theory of Leadership Effectiveness

Fred Fiedler (1967) sought to discover the relationship between leadership style and the favorableness of managerial situation. He classified leadership styles into two categories: (1) the task-oriented, or demanding, style (similar to job-centered and initiating-structure leadership style) and (2) the human relations, or lenient, style (similar to employee-centered and consideration leadership style). Situational favorableness was defined in terms of three dimensions: (1) the leader-member relationship, (2) the degree of task structure, and (3) the leader's position power.

Fiedler found that the effectiveness of the leadership style was contingent upon the favorableness or unfavorableness of the situation. When under very favorable or very unfavorable situations, the task-oriented type of leader was most effective; when the situation was only moderately favorable or unfavorable, the human relations type of leader was most effective. Based on his contingency model of leadership effectiveness, Fiedler and his associates developed a training program called "leader match." The essence of this program is that by manipulating the three situational dimensions—leader-member relationship, task structure, and the leader's position power—leaders can change the situation to best suit their individual management style.

Fiedler's work underscores the importance of fitting leaders to the reality of their management situation. His leader match research findings indicate that training leaders on how to change leader-member relations or to choose the best situations suited to the managerial style can improve effectiveness of the leadership. Although Fiedler and his associates claim substantial research support for their contingency model, some of the supportive findings may have been due mainly to the "Hawthorne effect." While awaiting more methodologically refined research studies, Fiedler deserves a major credit for the current, widely shared conception of leadership as being situationally based.

House: Path-Goal Theory of Leadership

Another recognized theory of leadership developed from a contingency approach is the path-goal theory. This theory stemmed from the expectancy framework of motivation theory, which states that motivation is a function of a person's ability to accomplish the task and the person's desire to do so. Robert House (1971) proposed a theory of leadership that emphasizes the situational nature of the leader behavior.

According to House, the important functions of a leader consist largely of increasing personal rewards for subordinates for the attainment of goals and of making the path to these goals easier for them to follow by clarifying goals, clearing roadblocks and pitfalls, and increasing the opportunities for personal satisfaction en route. In essence, the path-goal theory attempts to explain the impact of the leader's behavior on subordinates' motivation, satisfaction, and performance.

The path-goal theory identifies four major styles of leadership, which can be employed by the same leader in different situations:

1. *Directive leadership:* The leader is authoritarian, directive, and autocratic.
2. *Supportive leadership:* The leader is friendly, approachable, and has genuine concern for subordinates.
3. *Participatory leadership:* The leader encourages suggestions from subordinates in decisionmaking.
4. *Achievement-oriented leadership:* The leader sets challenging goals for subordinates and shows confidence in their ability to achieve them.

The leader may choose one of the four leadership styles contingent upon two situational factors: (1) the characteristics of subordinates and (2) the environmental pressures and demands facing the subordinates. With respect to the first factor, the path-goal theory asserts that leader behavior will be accepted by subordinates if they perceive it to be a source of their immediate satisfaction or instrumental to future satisfaction. With respect to the second situational factor, the theory predicts that the leader behavior will increase subordinate effort if it complements the subordinates' environment by providing needed coaching, guidance, and support.

House's work has been credited for putting theories of leadership, expectancy, and motivation into a coherent perspective. His main thesis that the leader's function is to clarify goals and to facilitate subordinates' efforts at achieving them has implications for progressive human resources management. House's contentions that clearing roadblocks, facilitating group performance, and instituting functional structure are important leader behaviors that have implications for leadership training.

Despite a relatively high degree of acceptance of the contingency and path-goal theories of leadership and a substantial amount of research that has been conducted to test their validity, the field of leadership research is still quite hazy as it suffers from conceptual, methodological, and applicational shortcomings. A number of other, newer theories, including the charismatic, transformational, social learning, and substitute theories have emerged in recent years to supplement or complement existing theories.

JAE TAIK KIM

BIBLIOGRAPHY

Barnard, Chester, 1938. *The Functions of the Executive.* Cambridge, MA: Harvard University Press.
Bedeian, Arthur G., and Raymond F. Zammuto, 1991. *Organizations: Theory and Design.* Chicago: Dryden Press.
Blau, Peter M., and Richard Schoenherr, 1971. *The Structure of Organizations.* New York: Basic Books.
Burns, Tom, and George M. Stalker, 1961. *The Management of Innovation.* London: Tavistock.
Chandler, Alfred D., Jr., 1962. *Strategy and Structure: Chapters in the History of the American Industrial Enterprise.* Cambridge, MA: MIT Press.
Child, John, 1972. "Organizational Structure, Environment, and Performance: The Role of Strategic Choice." *Sociology,* vol. 6 (Jan.) 1–22.
Child, John, and Roger Mansfield, 1972. "Technology, Size, and Organizations Structure." *Sociology,* vol. 6: 369–393.
Fiedler, Fred E., 1967. *A Theory of Leadership Effectiveness.* New York: McGraw-Hill.
House, Robert J., 1971. "A Path-Goal Theory of Leader Effectiveness." *Administrative Science Quarterly,* vol. 16: 321–338.
Lawrence, Paul R., and Jay W. Lorsch, 1969. *Organization and Environment.* Homewood, IL: Richard D. Irwin.
Luthans, Fred, 1995. *Organizational Behavior,* 7th ed. New York: McGraw-Hill.
Mintzberg, Henry, 1979. *The Structuring of Organizations.* Englewood Cliffs, NJ: Prentice-Hall.
Pugh, Derek S., and David J. Hickson, 1976. *Organization Structure in Its Context: The Aston Programme.* Lexington, MA: D. C. Heath.

Pugh, Derek S., *et al.*, 1969. "The Context of Organizational Structures." *Administrative Science Quarterly*, vol. 14: 91–114.

Woodward, Joan, 1958. *Management and Technology.* London: Her Majesty's Stationery Office.

———, 1965. *Industrial Organization: Theory and Practice.* London: Oxford University Press.

MANAGEMENT, PRINCIPLES OF.

The universal processes and general standards prescribing the functions of management and the designing of organizational structure that are applicable to all types of organizations regardless of the nature and the size of an organization—public or private, military or church, large or small. These principles were intended as a guide for a manager or administrator to choose an appropriate course of managerial action in an efficient and effective way for achievement of organizational goals. These are also referred to as the universal principles of general management or the administrative principles categorized under the traditional or classical management theory.

Development of the Principles of Management

In the record of the ancient history of management practiced in Egyptian, Greek, Roman, and Chinese societies, the need of administration and organization was recognized in governing state affairs, in overseeing the church, and in supervising the military. Egyptians used planning and coordination principles to build the great pyramids. Greeks treated management as an art that should be separated from technical knowledge and experience, and they promoted management principles of specialization. The Roman Empire expanded the small city administration of Rome to a great empire with an efficient management and a well-structured organization by effectively utilizing the scalar principle and the delegation of authority. The Chinese civil service adopted merit principles that suggested the pattern of public administration.

Religious institutions, particularly the Roman Catholic church, contributed to the principles of management, developing the hierarchy of authority with its scalar territorial organization. The military was forced to create and develop the principles managing gigantic masses of troops, dispersed units, and sophisticated military operations to win wars. The core principles of modern management practice, such as the unity of command, the chain of command, the delegation of authority, and staff principles were instituted by the military, especially from the Roman to the Prussian armies to solve such management problems.

In addition, the Industrial Revolution in the late eighteenth century was characterized by the rapid emergence and growth of large manufacturing organizations that led to enormous problems of making management efficient and effective in competition among organizations. These management problems were quite different from those encountered before. Naturally, these problems brought about the need for new management theories, concepts, and principles. Scientific management and the principles of management were popularized in practice and accepted as a respectable discipline of management study.

Although the study of management practice from a conceptual perspective accepted as modern management began with the work of Frederick Taylor (who led the scientific management movement from 1885 to 1911, concentrating on managerial philosophy and techniques addressing lower levels of management), the basic attempts to develop a top management view of organization did not appear until Henri Fayol, a French industrial consultant, promulgated his 5 elements of administration and 14 principles of administration in 1916. Fayol and subsequent writers on management principles, including James Mooney and Allan Reiley, Luther Gulick and Lyndall Urwick, who were considered modern management pioneers, constructed the essential managerial functions and principles of planning, organizing, and control in a theoretical framework. Their agreement on the management functions directed their thoughts into a common pattern. They endeavored to prescribe management functions and principles in choosing a course of efficient managerial action toward achievement of organizational objectives. They also asserted that management should be considered as a separate discipline, a field parallel to law, medicine, and other professional studies, and should be practiced according to the established principles that managers learn and practice.

With the commonalties in their independently arrived at conclusions about management, they tended to regard their statements as more than mere personal reflections on relevant experiences and to refer to them as universal principles applicable to all managerial situations. The principles of management are grouped into three perspectives according to the level of focus:

1. the perspective of management functions and principles led by Henri Fayol;
2. the perspective of general principles of organization led by James Mooney and Allan Reiley; and
3. the perspectives of a synthesis of management, organization, and public administration, led by Luther Gulick and Lyndall Urwick.

Fayol: Management Functions and Principles

Henri Fayol (1841–1925), a pioneer of the principles of management and the father of modern management, prescribed management functions and principles in detail, laying the foundation for management theories. First hired as a mining engineer at the level of a junior executive of a French mining and metallurgical company in 1860, he rose to a position of a managing director and successfully transformed the financially troubled company to a profitable business firm in 1886. He remained in the firm as an administrator and practical management writer until his retirement in 1918.

In 1916, at the age of 75, Fayol wrote the book *Administration Industrielle et Generale,* reflecting on his managerial career. The book was translated into English in 1929, and its American version, *General and Industrial Management,* was published in 1949. In his book, Fayol examined management activities from the point of view of top management. Management was seen as omnipresent in every human organization—military, government, industries, business, church, large or small. Management was considered as a process that is common to all organizations, regardless of the type, nature, and size of the organization.

Fayol found that all activities of business operation or industrial undertaking could be divided into 6 activities, 5 management functions, and 14 principles.

The six business activities are as follows:

1. *Technical:* producing and manufacturing products;
2. *Commercial:* buying raw materials, selling products and exchange goods;
3. *Financial:* acquiring and using capital, searching for optimum use of capital;
4. *Security:* protecting employees and property;
5. *Accounting:* recording and taking stock of costs, calculating profit and liabilities, keeping balance sheets, and compiling statistics; and
6. *Managerial:* planning, organizing, commanding, coordinating, and controlling.

Fayol elaborated the managerial process by identifying five duties or functions of management:

1. *Planning:* formulating objectives for the future, selecting approaches for accomplishing the objectives, and setting the direction in which the management is headed;
2. *Organizing:* defining and setting up the general structure of the organization according to its objectives, means of operation, and future course as determined by planning;
3. *Command:* executing of plans to carry out the operations in an orderly and rational manner;
4. *Coordination:* uniting, correlating, and synchronizing persons and activities to maximize the organization's performance;
5. *Control:* checking of actual performance with the rules and instructions that have been set and provided.

Fayol viewed planning and organizing as being essential to the preparation of organizational operations. The functions of command, coordination, and control logically follow the first two functions or duties to carry out necessary operations.

Fayol's 14 principles of management were intended to show managers how to carry out their functional duties. He felt that these principles could be universally applicable to all management situations, including business, government, military, religious, and financial organizations. The 14 management principles, aimed at promoting efficiency, order, stability, and fairness in management process, are as follows:

1. *Division of work* permits specialization of work and reduces the number of objects or concerns to which an employee's attention and effort must be directed. Dividing labor into specialized units reduces inefficiency through less waste and increased productivity.
2. *Authority* is the power or right to give commands, enforce orders or obedience, and take action or make final decisions. Authority may be formal, backed by position, or informal, supported by authoritative knowledge or skills in a certain profession or trade.
3. *Discipline* is control to enforce obedience, respect, and efficiency. The best ways to foster good discipline are: assignment of good superiors at all levels, agreements between the organization and employees as clear and fair as possible, and application of sanctions and penalties in a judicious manner.
4. *Unity of command* refers to the idea that the chain of command must be singular: An employee should receive orders from only one superior. This practice streamlines communication within an organization.
5. *Unity of direction* refers to the idea that a group of activities having the same objective must be adhered to as one plan and commanded by one boss. This practice ensures clarity and uniformity in goal direction.
6. *Subordination* of individual interest to general interest: The whole is greater than the sum of its parts; a group interest takes precedence over individual interest.
7. *Remuneration* of personnel concerns a policy of fair pay and rewards. The rate of remuneration depends on many factors and circumstances that are often independent of the worth of the employee or the will of the employer.
8. *Centralization/decentralization:* Centralization refers to one central place in the organization where a final decision is made. Decentralization means that certain decisionmaking authorities are delegated to lower levels of the organization. In large organizations, decentralization is necessary in practice. An increase in the role of the subordinate contributes to decentralization, whereas a decrease in the subordinate's role contributes to centralization.
9. *Scalar chain* is the unbroken chain of superiors, ranging from the highest to the lowest ranks. However, in large organizations, it is too lengthy to follow this chain. As an alternative, a "gang plank" is suggested. It is a proper routing of the line of authority and formal

communication channels to improve efficiency in transactions between managers and their superiors.

10. *Order* is the sequence or arrangement of things, events, and persons, which ensures a place for every thing, every happening, and everyone. A chart, or plan, can clarify the sequence or arrangement more vividly for everybody.

11. *Equity* is equality and fairness in dealing with employees; it results from kindness and justice.

12. *Stability* of tenure for personnel is steadiness in personnel policy, which ensures continuity and security of employment for employees.

13. *Initiative* is the motivation of employees to originate new ideas or to apply their uppermost efforts and energies toward the achievement of the organization's goals. It can be inspired by much tact and integrity on the part of the superior.

14. *Esprit de corps* is the harmony and unity within the organization. It should be stressed to strengthen the positive spirits of the organization.

Implications for Practice

Fayol, one of the first and foremost contributors to early administrative management thinking, responded to the growing need to understand the overall management process in a systematic manner. In so doing, he identified 5 universal managerial functions, which, with some modification, can still be widely used in business management and public administration as a rational means of studying and understanding the manager's tasks. His 14 principles of management have been found to be of practical value as guides to managers in any field.

Fayol's principles of management were enthusiastically received by many public-sector organizations in European nations. Thus, the Ministry of National Defense in Belgium and the Ministry of Posts, Telegraphs, and Telephones in France adopted his principles as the foremost principal guides to managerial actions. The enthusiasm for Fayol's principles of management extended to the United States, where they were incorporated into the classical school of American public administration by Luther H. Gulick and his British colleague, Lyndall F. Urwick, as the gospel of administrative efficiency such as Planning, Organizing, Staffing, Directing, Coordinating, Reporting, and Budgeting (POSDCORB). Intended to be general and broad, Fayol's principles of management lack logical clarity since they suggest nothing about the primacy of certain principles or mediating situational factors in these principles. The principles, however, offered a conceptual basis for further exploration and elaboration and a new dimension by subsequent writers such as Mooney and Reiley.

Mooney and Reiley: Organization Principles

A major initiative to provide a conceptual framework of organization principles, similar to that of Fayol's management, was undertaken in the United States by James Mooney (1884–1957) and Allan Reiley (1869–1947), two executives of General Motors during the decade from 1930 to 1940. Mooney and Reiley first published *Onward Industry* in 1931, later revised in 1939 under its new title *The Principles of Organization*. A later edition in 1947 appeared with only Mooney as author.

Mooney and Reiley, advancing their thoughts on administration, characterized organization as a whole by the thesis that there are fundamental principles of organization that can be identified in every form of human groups and that efficient management of the organization depends on a conscious use of these principles in the pursuit of all industrial endeavors. An efficient organization must have its formalism, and this formalism must be based on principles. The essence of Mooney and Reiley complements and supplements Fayol's work.

The framework by Mooney (1947) was built around four major principles:

1. *The coordinative principle* is the all-inclusive principle that directs attention to the unity of action in pursuit of a common purpose. Coordination is achieved not only through the hierarchy of authority and leadership but also through the unifying forces of doctrine, spirit, and morale.

2. *The scalar principle* refers to the vertical flow of authority and corresponding responsibility and definite assignment of duties to subunits of organization. There shall be a clearly defined and tangible process through which coordinating authority operates from the top to the bottom.

3. *The functional principle* stresses the importance of specialization in the grouping of duties. "Functionalism" involves differentiation between duties, which aims at correlating three important functions: the determinative, the applicative, and the interpretative. To improve efficiency, distinct components of jobs must be identified, correlated, and coordinated.

4. *The line and staff principle:* The line represents authority and command; the staff represents advice and counsel. The line is synonymous with the "scalar chain," as distinguished from the more adjective (indirect) staff functions. However, the dichotomy of the line and staff should not lead to a double-track organization, and every staff function must adhere to some line duty in a dependent relationship.

All four of Mooney's principles were found, to a various degree, in the military, the Roman Catholic church, the state, and industry. Mooney's personal experience with the navy during World War II was reflected in his 1947 edition, which dealt with the military organization. The military and the church were viewed by Mooney as being most efficient in their application of the coordinative principles, owing to their heavy reliance on indoctrination as well as moral and spiritual factors.

Implications for Practice

Mooney and Reiley viewed management as a technique for directing and inspiring other people. Organization, by contrast, was considered the technique of relating specific duties or functions in a coordinated manner. The primary purpose of management was to devise an appropriate organization.

Mooney's personal experience and his expert knowledge of organization in government, church, military, and industrial institutions led him to believe that natural laws of organizing existed, and it was these natural laws, or principles, that he sought to discover through logic. Although his analysis of the organizing function was all-inclusive, there remained the task of synthesizing the vast field of classical management theories for those who followed.

Gulick and Urwick: A Synthesis of Management and Organization and Public Administration

Luther Gulick (1892–1993) is widely known as a distinguished American scholar who contributed to the development of public administration as the inventor of the acronym POSDCORB, as director of the Institute of Public Administration as Eaton Professor of Municipal Science and Administration, at Columbia University, and as a member of President Roosevelt's Committee on Administrative Management of 1937 (commonly known as the Brownlow Committee). Lyndall Urwick (1891–1983) was Lt. Colonel of the British Army, director of the International Management Institute at Geneva, and an industrial consultant. Gulick and Urwick codified much early management and organization knowledge by combining their efforts at synthesizing various perspectives of the functions of management and principles of organization into one conceptual framework of general management and organization, and also contributed much in the area of public administration.

Like Fayol, Mooney and Reiley, as well as Taylor, Gulick and Urwick believed that there are universal principles of management and that management is a matter of technique applicable to all management situations irrespective of particular circumstances of the organization. The management principles concentrated on the method of subdividing work, specialization of skills, and allocating individuals to the various jobs in such a way as to maximize the efficiency of management.

Gulick and Urwick emphasized homogeneity of tasks within each department so that the department could have only a limited number of skills and processes to coordinate in the most economic and efficient way to achieve organizational goals. Not only would that specialization of skills prevail within the department, but also there would be specialists at the head of departments coordinating and relating departments with each other, thereby combining units of work that could be identified as homogeneous under a single director who would have total responsibility and control.

Gulick described managerial activities common to all organization. In so doing, he developed "POSDCORB," an acronym which stands for planning, organizing, staffing, directing, coordinating, reporting, and budgeting. POSDCORB aimed at turning "principles" of administrative theory into actual administrative practice in the private and public sector. Its primary concern was how organizations might actually be structured and what the activities of their administrators should be.

POSDCORB is elaborated as follows:

1. *Planning:* drawing a broad scheme for those things that need to be done and the methods for carrying them out to accomplish the organization's purpose;
2. *Organizing:* establishing the formal structure of authority through which work is defined and subdivided;
3. *Staffing:* recruiting and training a group of people to do the work and providing favorable working conditions for them;
4. *Directing:* making decisions and giving orders and directions to subordinates, thereby taking the role of a leader;
5. *Coordinating:* interrelating the various parts of the work units of the organization;
6. *Reporting:* informing those to whom the manager is responsible and having oneself and one's subordinates continuously informed of the process and progress of the work by keeping records, conducting research, and inspecting job performance; and
7. *Budgeting:* fiscal planning and accounting.

In addition to POSDCORB, Gulick suggested the four ways for grouping work units into similar or associated activities: (1) the major purpose to be served, such as providing transportation, fighting crime, or conducting education; (2) the process to be used, such as engineering, medicine, or accounting; (3) the persons or materials to be dealt with or served, such as soldiers, veterans, students, or automobiles; and (4) the place where the activities will proceed, such as California, New York, town, school, library, or store. While the primary basis of grouping activities is of great importance, choice has to depend on the results desired at a given time and place, the developmental stage of the organization or department, the technology used, the size of the workforce, and geographical distribution.

Gulick forcefully advocated the principle of unity of command that was drawn from Fayol's management principles, asserting that a workman could not serve two masters and that he could not receive orders from separate foremen concerning different matters. A work unit based on specialization should not be given technical direction by a layman. The executive can personally direct only a few persons, who, in turn, must direct others. This process continues until the last person in the organization is reached.

Gulick and Urwick made an attempt at synthesizing the contributions of the main writers on administration, advocating the convergence of theories in this field. They considered administering to be a technical skill, consisting of principles and methods. They believed in the eventual emergence of a "true science of management." The organization must be structured for continuation of activities into the future, and administrative process must be bound by clearly defined principles, standards, and duties.

Urwick endeavored to provide guidance on methods, especially the ways in which executive functions should be differentiated. He emphasized clear boundaries between groups of activities to avoid overlapping, duplication, and confusion. He distinguished between three methods of defining the boundaries in functional differentiation: the unitary, the serial, and the subjectival method: (1) *The unitary method:* The limits of boundaries are determined by persons, things, or areas; (2) *The serial method:* The boundaries are determined by a range of departments, each carrying out some closely related processes; and (3) *The subjectival method:* Activities are bounded with reference to a particular subject or an aspect of management that requires "specialized authority" possessing specialized knowledge.

Urwick was credited for popularizing the "span of control principle," also proposed by French management consultant V. A. Graicunas in 1937. The principle pertaining to a manager's span of control prescribes that the number of subordinates reporting to a superior should be limited to five or six. This number, however, may vary depending on the hierarchy of the manager involved. At the top of the hierarchy, the span should be more limited, to about three; at the lower levels it may be larger, about five or six.

Implications for Practice

There are criticisms that have been echoed by academicians and practitioners of business management and public administration who have made serious attempts at understanding and applying principles to practical situations. The main criticisms appear to have been mainly on the following grounds: (1) the principles are mere common sense, (2) they are based on false assumptions, and (3) they are ambiguous and impractical for application. Gulick

changed his acronym from POSDCORB to POSDECORB, with the "E" standing for evaluation. He also strengthened POSDCORB by emphasizing the importance of "decentralization, delegation, and the participation of workers and clients in work." Certain concepts are indeed quite ambiguous. For example, it is not at all clear what exactly Fayol meant by the term "principle," which he adopted very loosely, as an equivalent to concept, element, proposition, or recommendation. Also, some of the principles, such as the one advanced by Gulick concerning the bases for grouping work units or activities, give no practical clue as to which of the four competing bases (purpose, process, persons or material, and place) is applicable in a specific managerial situation. One may argue that the principles of management have not been refined enough to claim the status of "true science." The nature and complexity of administering modern organizations are such that they may never be distilled into sets of truly scientific principles. Specificity and practicability are generally significantly lacking.

Despite such criticisms, the principles of management are still widely applied and taught as fundamentals to management practice in the field of business and public administration because there are no better alternatives to managing organizations. Although they are often regarded as no more than "common sense" based generalizations, the principles provide starting points for the meaningful conceptual advancement of management.

The important features of the principles of management developed from reflections of managers, consultants, and academicians on their experiences in running and/or studying various organizations. Their reflections are analyzed and described in a logical manner, without having been subjected to empirically rigorous validation. Current trends suggest that, more and more, management professionals, public administrators, teaching and research academicians demand better empirical support for the principles of management as a foundation and base. Until more data-based revisions or elaborations emerge, the principles may remain as practical guides for management and central administrative concepts to be taught in school as well as useful hypotheses for future research. There is no doubt that the principles of management are going to be long lived and omnipresent in the field of business and public administration as the primer of modern management and organization theory.

JAE TAIK KIM

BIBLIOGRAPHY

Fayol, Henri, 1916. *Administration Industrielle et Generale.* Paris: The Societe del l'Industrielle Minerale. First trans. into English by J. A. Coubrough, 1929. *General and Industrial Management.* Geneva: International Management Institute. Later trans. by Constance Storrs, 1949. New York: Pitman.

Graham, Cole Blease, Jr., and Steven W. Hays, 1991. "Management Functions and Public Administration–POSDCORB Revisited." In J. Steven Ott, Albert C. Hyde, and Jay M. Shafritz, eds., *Public Management*. Chicago: Lyceum Books/Nelson-Hall.

Graicunas, V. A., 1937. "Relationship in Organization." Bulletin of the International Management Institute. Geneva: International Labour Office. In Luther H. Gulick and Lyndall F. Urwick, eds., *Papers on the Science of Administration*. New York: Columbia University, Institute of Public Administration.

Gulick, Luther H., 1983. "The Dynamics of Public Administration Today as Guidelines for the Future." *Public Administration Review,* vol. 43 (May–June) 193–198.

Gulick, Luther H., and Lyndall F. Urwick, eds., 1937. *Papers on the Science of Administration.* New York: Columbia University, Institute of Public Administration.

Koontz, Harold, and Cyril O'Donnell, 1972. *Principles of Management.* New York: McGraw-Hill.

March, James G., 1965. *Handbook of Organizations.* Chicago: Rand McNally.

Mooney, James D., 1947. *The Principles of Organization,* rev. ed. New York: Harper & Row.

Mooney, James D., and Allan C. Reiley, 1931. *Onward Industry.* New York: Harper & Brothers. (*The Principles of Organization,* 1939, rev. under new title.)

Pfiffner, John M., and Frank P. Sherwood, 1960. *Administrative Organization.* Englewood Cliffs, NJ: Prentice-Hall.

Taylor, Frederick W., 1911. *The Principles of Scientific Management.* New York: Harper & Row.

Urwick, Lyndall F., 1944. *The Elements of Administration.* Pitman and New York: Harper and Row.

MANAGERIALISM.

A set of beliefs and practices that allows for the taking of responsibility for the performance of a system and that assumes that "better" management results in more effective solutions for organizational or societal problems.

The word and concept of "management" is derived from "manage" (maneggio, maneggiare), which is related to "manege." Originally the training and handling of horses (manage) happened privately or in a riding school (manege). This activity was reduced to its core element, that is, the action or art of conducting and supervising someone or something, and it kept its original semantic label.

Historically, according to L. Gunn, the 1950s and early 1960s were times of "public administration," the late 1960s and early 1970s were the decade of "public policy," and the late 1970s up to today are about "public management" (Gunn 1987). J. Perry and K. Kraemer, referring to N. Henry's famous "paradigms of public administration," also suggest these stages (Henry 1975; Perry and Kraemer 1983). Public management could then be defined as a concern for rules and procedures and the results obtained (Parry 1992). In the late 1980s and early 1990s, public management became the common terminology (Halachmi and Bouckaert 1995; Trosa 1995).

Literature refers to a set of related labels such as "managerialism" (Pollitt 1993), "new public service managerial-ism" (Farnham and Horton 1993), and "new public management" (Hood 1991; Hughes 1993).

Pollitt defines "managerialism" as "a set of beliefs and practices, at the core of which burns the seldom-tested assumption that better management will prove an effective solvent for a wide range of economic and social ills" (Pollitt 1993, p. 1). He refers to it as Gulick's and Urwick's newly dressed POSDCORB (planning, organizing, staffing, directing, coordinating, reporting, and budgeting).

D. Farnham and S. Horton (1993) define "new managerialism" as "the structural, organizational and managerial changes which have taken place in the public services in recent years. In essence, it incorporates the application of private sector management systems and managerial techniques into the public services" (p. 237). Traditional features of administration (i.e., bureaucratic, incremental, particular) are transcended and transformed into new characteristics of managerialism (i.e., economic, rational, and generic) (Farnham and Horton 1993, p. 47).

The economic focus is derived from a "value for money" approach that includes a focus, among other things, on delegation of financial competencies, awareness of price-quality ratios, tenders, and adapted monitoring systems (e.g., unit cost, efficiency indicators, quantity and quality measures). The rational focus results in objectives, strategies, and business plans. The generic approach results in powerful general managers rather than in specialists and professionals. Goal orientation is stronger than problem orientedness. Facilitating behavior is more important than preventing events. Also, environmental incentives are overruling internal ones. Managers are guided by goals and objectives, plans, and performance-related budgets. In Pollitt's (1993) terms, this is part of the "litany of managerialism" (p. 83).

The discussion about whether management in the public sector is generic management (Farnham and Horton 1993, p. 49) or an expression of general management functions (Hughes 1993, p. 63) has implications for the position of public management itself, as well as for the public manager. Public management as generic management means that there is no difference between management in the public and the private sector. The locus of activities is without importance. Managers can be exchanged without limits between public and private sectors. By contrast, public management as a coherent elaboration of general management functions implies that there are common management functions; yet, they are subject to specific contingencies. This discussion may shift to whether these contingencies and differences are significant or not. A possible consequence is that managers may not be so substitutable as expected.

Managers are responsible for the performance of systems. This is influenced by the political system. Integrating rational techniques in the public sector could seem like a paradox since political governance relies more on rhetoric. According to O. Hughes (1993) "under the public management model the relationship between politicians and managers is more fluid and is closer than before" (p. 72). Also Bozeman and Straussman (1990) say that public management is not identical to government management or to public administration. Public management involved management under the influence of political authority. . . . Political authority leaves its stamp on organizations in any of a variety of forms: red tape (or, depending on your perspective, public accountability), shared power and interdependence, fragmentation, sensitivity to political cycles. The result is that public management is distinctive from management not similarly influenced by political authority (pp. 27–28). Public managers should be able to handle politicians and vice versa. According to Hughes (1993), "The traditional model tried to de-politicize what is essentially political. New public management recognizes the essential political character of government; public servants work with politicians in an interactive process called management" (p. 73). The traditional dichotomy between politics and administration is removed. As a consequence new types of accountability are emerging, such as, direct accountability between managers and the public, as a result of a customer focus and for greater responsiveness to outside groups and individuals.

Origins

According to Pollitt, neo-Taylorism is an important origin of managerialism. The focus on quality allows it to go "beyond Taylorism." According to Hood, the origins of new public management are modern Taylorism and institutional economics (Hood 1991). This twin origin means on the one hand, public choice, transaction cost approaches, and principal-agent models, and on the other hand, scientific management based, business-oriented techniques. This allows to combine concepts as customer choice, transparency, and incentive structures, and also professional management, technical expertise, and degrees of freedom to obtain results. According to P. Aucoin (1990), the origins of new public management are managerialism and public choice. This allows it to combine "the need to reestablish the primacy of managerial principles over bureaucracy" and "the need to reestablish the primacy of representative government over bureaucracy" (p. 115). Managerialism will be more oriented toward decentralization, deregulation, and delegation. Public choice will focus more on centralization, coordination, and control. According to Aucoin, this could result in some unavoidable paradoxes and ambiguities like, for instance, the diagnosis and solution for the bureaucratic problem, the dichotomy of politics and administration, and the combination of representation, responsiveness, and accountability. J. Alford tries to develop the new public management from the opposite views on contingencies and norms of "manageri-

alists" and their critics. A contingency approach of managerialism means, first, that there is "not a single managerial paradigm but rather a repertoire of prescriptions" and, second, "a concomitant set of understandings, attributes and skills on the part of public sector managers" (Alford 1993, pp. 143–144). Alford thinks of three specific features of public managers: first, "awareness of and sensitivity to the nature of value to the public and other stakeholders, and of how it is affected by different mixes of public resources and capabilities;" second, "creativity and imagination in tapping productive capabilities;" and third, "political awareness and skills" (p. 144).

Geert Bouckaert

Bibliography

Alford, John, 1993. "Towards a New Public Management Model: Beyond 'Managerialism' and Its Critics." *Australian Journal of Public Administration,* vol. 52, no. 2:135–148.

Aucoin, Peter, 1990. "Administrative Reform in Public Management: Paradigms, Principles, Paradoxes, and Pendulums." *Governance,* vol. 3 no. 2: 115–137.

Bozeman, Barry, and Jeffrey Staussman, 1990. *Public Management Strategies. Guidelines for Managerial Effectiveness.* San Francisco: Jossey-Bass.

Farnham, David, and Sylvia Horton, 1993. *Managing the New Public Services.* London: Macmillan.

Gunn, Lewis, 1987. "Perspectives on Public Management." In Jan Kooiman and Kjell Eliassen, eds., *Managing Public Organizations: Lessons from Contemporary European Experience.* London: Sage.

Halachmi, Arie, and Geert Bouckaert, eds., 1995. *The Enduring Challenges in Public Management: Surviving and Excelling in a Changing World.* San Francisco: Jossey-Bass.

Henry, Niclas, 1975. "Paradigms for Public Administration." *Public Administration Review,* vol. 3: 387–396.

Hood, Christopher, 1991. "A Public Management for all Seasons?" *Public Administration,* vol. 69: 3–19.

Hughes, Owen, 1993. *Public Management and Administration: An Introduction.* London: St. Martin's.

Parry, Richard, 1992. "Concepts and Assumptions of Public Management." In Colin Duncan, ed., *The Evolution of Public Management: Concepts and Techniques for the 1990s.* London: Macmillan.

Perry, James, and Kenneth Kraemer, eds., 1983. *Public Management: Public and Private Perspectives.* Mountain View, CA: Mayfield.

Pollitt, Christopher, 1993. *Managerialism and the Public Services,* 2d ed. London: Blackwell.

Trosa, Sylvie, 1995. *Moderniser l'Administration. Comment font les autres?* Paris: Les éditions d'organisation.

MANDATES. Impositions by higher-level governments on lower-level governments that require the lower-level governments to do something or refrain from doing something under the threat of criminal or civil sanction and/or the removal of funds. They take the form of procedures, responsibilities, and activities that must be carried out by the lower-level government. The sources of the mandates are the federal and state constitutions, statutes, administrative rules and procedures and court orders. Mandates may be "direct orders" or they may be "conditions of aid" (Catherine Lovell and Charles Tobin 1981).

Mandates are the subject of much political, legal, and fiscal debate in the United States because of their number, penetration, and cost throughout the intergovernmental system. To understand mandates, it is first necessary to have a comprehensive classification of the different types that exist. Catherine Lovell and Charles Tobin (1981) have provided the following useful classification of the myriad mandates that exist in the U.S. intergovernmental system. The following draws heavily from their work.

The first way to think about mandates is to consider the requirements that mandates impose, the method that is used to impose them, and the application of the mandates.

Requirements

Requirements may be either programmatic or procedural. Programmatic mandates specify the content of what should be done. They may identify the quality or the quantity of the content. For example, a federally funded school lunch program that is implemented at the local level may specify nutritional standards that must be met by the school districts that receive the federal funds. Programmatic quantity mandates require specific amounts of a government service that is financed, in part or in whole, by a higher-level government. An example is the Davis Bacon Act, which requires that local contractors pay union wages when federal funds are involved in construction projects.

Programmatic mandates may also be procedural. An example here would be personnel requirements such as equal opportunity and affirmative action steps that must be taken to fill public personnel vacancies. Personnel requirements may also pertain to the skills and education of employees hired with funds from a higher-level government. An example would be the requirement that bilingual teachers be hired with federal funds. State government education departments routinely regulate local school district teacher hiring through mandated educational specifications and licensing requirements.

Constraints

Mandates impose constraints on governments. Mandate constraints are particularly noticeable in the areas of taxing and spending. State finance laws, for instance, specify the kinds of property that are exempt from local property taxation. This means that some local governments find that more than half of the real property in their jurisdiction—government buildings, religious institutions, and nonprofit organizations—are not subject to property taxation. Such property tax restrictions act as a revenue base constraint since they limit the aggregate value of taxable property in the jurisdiction. Similarly, state governments also set limits on revenue rates for various types of taxes. One example is a state limit on the rate that a local government may set on a gross utility tax, which is a tax on the consumption of energy. State referenda that have established tax and/or expenditure limitations apply not only to the fiscal environment of the state but to local governments as well. These limitations may try to limit the growth of property taxation at the local level, restrict the annual growth of state government expenditures, and/or limit the growth of state revenues by tying revenues to changes in personal income.

How Mandates Are Imposed

Mandates are imposed as "direct orders" or "conditions of aid." A direct order comes from either a regulation imposed by an administrative agency or a statute. When direct orders are imposed by the federal government on state and local governments, the failure to comply with them carries the threat of criminal and/or civil penalties. One illustration is the Equal Opportunity Act of 1972. This statute prohibits state and local governments from discriminating on the basis of sex, race, color, religion, or national origin. In addition to public employment, direct orders prohibiting certain types of actions are commonly found in the area of environmental protection. Wastewater treatment standards defined by the Clean Water Act are a case in point. When the federal government sets minimum standards in various environmental programs, this is also known as "partial preemption." For example, the federal government's Clean Air Act establishes emission levels and requires that the state governments administer and enforce the statute.

Some mandates are "crosscutting." Mandates that are attached to all federally funded programs would have this characteristic. An example is a mandate that prohibits discrimination in hiring. Similarly, some mandates apply "crossover sanctions" to federal funding sources when the statute allows the federal government to withdraw funds from the states for noncompliance. A good example is federal highway funds. Here, the federal government has threatened state governments with the loss of funds if they do not enforce federal government speed limits, the regulation of the legal drinking age, billboard regulations, and the implementation of the Clean Air Act.

Mandates may also be attached to programs as conditions of aid. This means that when lower-level governments accept funding from a higher-level government, the lower-level government must agree to implement specific requirements that accompany the funds. For instance, a

local government that accepts mass transit funds from the federal government must ensure that a given percentage of the buses are accessible to the physically handicapped. The distinction, however, between conditions of aid and direct orders is not so straightforward in practice. Consider the following situation. The federal government may offer grant funds for subsidized housing. If a local government receives the grant funds, it is required to implement mandates such as nondiscrimination provisions. Suppose a local government objects to what it interprets as excessive federal government interference with local preferences. Logically, the local government can simply forego the grant funds and thereby avoid the mandates. However, in such a case the federal government may initiate litigation against the recalcitrant local government for circumventing a crosscutting mandate (a nondiscrimination requirement in this example).

Why Mandates Are So Controversial

Edward Koch, a former mayor of the City of New York wrote a now famous article in 1980 in which he complained that "a maze of complex statutory and administrative directives has come to threaten both the initiative and the financial health of local governments throughout the country" (p. 42). Koch's criticism has been echoed by local government officials who have continually complained about the intrusiveness, inflexibility, and burden of state and local government mandates. The first complaint is one of classic federalism; higher-level governments are said to intrude into activities that are better left to the discretion of lower-level governments. Critics of mandates often point out that the high governmental level of intrusion via the imposition of mandates is coercive and out of character with "grassroots" democracy. The burden, measured simply as the number of federal mandates on state and local governments, is significant. As of 1992, it was estimated that there were 172 separate pieces of federal legislation that imposed mandates on state and local governments (*National Performance Review,* "Strengthening the Partnership in Intergovernmental Service Delivery, September 1993, p. 13). The myriad number of mandates is also criticized for inflexibility. State and local governments have complained that some federal mandates fail to take account of the unique conditions of some jurisdictions and therefore require action that is unproductive.

Furthermore, mandates are criticized for being vague. Consider the Americans with Disabilities Act (ADA), which, among other things, requires state and local governments to make new facilities and renovated facilities accessible to the disabled. However, the federal courts are filled with cases that are contesting what it means to be a renovated facility and what it means to make a facility accessible. A good example comes from Philadelphia, where

the federal courts held that street resurfacing qualified as a renovation, which therefore required the city to improve accessibility. All street resurfacing projects had to add curb cuts to comply with ADA, obviously increasing the cost of the projects

The most consistent criticism of mandates focuses on their budgetary burden. Although the charge is uniformly shared by local governments, estimates of the budgetary burden of mandates are difficult to make and suspect to conceptual and empirical challenges. For example, in a 1970s study of mandate costs, researchers from the Urban Institute in Washington, DC, estimated the cost impact of six federal government mandates on seven local governments (Fix and Fix 1990, pp. 35–37). Costs ranged from US $6 per capita to US $51.50, with an average per capita cost of US $25. The study, however, did not standardize different compensation costs, and the costs did not include overhead expenses. Some budgetary burdens may be due to local fiscal conditions rather than direct mandate costs. Finally, no attempt was made to estimate the benefits of mandate compliance.

A more recent survey of 314 cities was conducted by Price Waterhouse in 1993 for the U.S. Conference of Mayors. The survey examined the financial impact of ten federal government mandates: Underground Storage Tanks, Clean Water Act, Clean Air Act, Resource Conservation and Recovery Act, Safe Drinking Water Act, Asbestos Abatement, Lead Paint Abatement, Endangered Species Act, Americans with Disabilities Act, and Fair Labor Standards Act. The survey found that 1993 cost estimates for the ten mandates totaled US $5.6 billion for the 314 cities. The study provided a five-year total (1994 to 1998) of US $54 billion. Environmental mandates (Clean Water Act, Solid Waste Disposal, and Safe Drinking Water Act) were the most costly (Hearing, United States Senate, Committee on Governmental Affairs, 1993, pp. 125–126).

A study by the Advisory Commission on Intergovernmental Relations (ACIR) assessed the impact of federal mandates on state and local governments. Several conceptual and methodological issues hamper precise estimates of mandate burdens. First, some mandates are clearly unfunded (where the entire cost is borne by the local government), whereas others are embedded in grant conditions. In the latter case, mandate costs should be separated from the grant so that one could estimate the net budgetary increment of federal funding. Some mandate costs may be passed along to users of services in the form of fees; others are covered by local taxes. Both should be included in any estimate of per capita mandate costs; however, only the latter would be included in an estimate of fiscal or budgetary burden. Similarly, some mandates are known to have future local budget costs (based on start-up dates) but may not have current costs. Public officials need to clarify what is counted and when mandates are included in local cost estimates (Dearborn 1994, p. 22).

Conceptual and methodological issues concerning mandate cost estimating were examined by the ACIR. Consider the following illustration. In 1995, 20 states taxed food sales. However, purchases of food with food stamps are exempt from state sales taxes. Therefore, the mandate, which in this case is a prohibition, clearly has a cost implication for those 20 states in the form of uncollected sales tax revenues (Dearborn 1994, p. 24). Multiyear capital costs are particularly difficult to estimate. The ACIR study offered the Americans with Disabilities Act as an example. To comply with the act, some governments must implement substantial physical improvements that are multiyear and frequently require local governments to incur debt from the issuance of municipal bonds. Since capital spending is not linear, estimating year-to-year costs of this type of mandate is difficult.

The budgetary impact of mandates varies greatly depending on whether one looks at actual budgeted costs or estimates based on full compliance. The ACIR illustrated this point with reference to the city of Lewiston, Maine. In 1992, Lewiston budgeted US $414,000 to comply with safe drinking water, clean water, and occupational safety federal mandates. This represented 0.8 percent of a US $53 million budget in 1992. Full compliance with (then) existing mandates was estimated at US $1.6 million, or 3.1 percent of the budget. A third estimate was the amount needed to comply with proposed federal mandates. This was estimated at US $7.7 million, or 14.5 percent of the budget. If all of the proposed mandates were enacted by the federal government, it would mean that the city would be spending 18.4 percent of the budget on federal mandates (Dearborn 1994, pp. 24–25).

Despite obvious conceptual and methodological problems in estimating the fiscal impact of mandates, there is little disagreement that the federal government imposes budgetary burdens on lower-level governments. Often cited figures from the Congressional Budget Office compared total mandate costs in 1986 of US $225 million with US $2.8 billion in 1991. Aggregate estimates like this mask the real criticism of mandates from local government officials–that mandates distort local government spending priorities. Testimony by Gregory S. Lashutka, Mayor of Columbus, Ohio, before the Senate Committee on Governmental Affairs on November 3, 1993, is telling:

[T]he U.S. EPA requires removal of many of our city's underground fuel tanks. Incidentally, we are going to do this well above what we believe will be further regulations coming about that won't tell us whether we are doing it correctly above the ground. Our Columbus fire division will have to spend over $800,000 to move those tanks. That means to us we could have hired 24 new firefighters or buy two new engines and ladder trucks for that amount. I didn't get to make that decision. It was forced on us by the Environmental Protection Agency (Hearing,

United States Senate, Committee on Governmental Affairs, 1993, p. 27).

The previous reference to the curb cuts in Philadelphia required under ADA regulatory guidelines is also instructive of the budgetary pressures faced by local officials. During Senate testimony, Philadelphia Mayor Edward Rendell complained that the implementation of the curb cuts requirement would cost US $140 million over a two-year period when the total annual capital budget (in 1993) was US $95 million (Hearing, United States Senate, Committee of Governmental Affairs, 1993, pp. 30–31).

Advantages of Mandates: Are There Any?

There are few defenders of mandates when they are said to impose regulatory and budgetary burdens on lower level governments. The strongest defense of some federal mandates is that they promote laudable national objectives. Civil rights, certain health care regulations, environmental mandates that are designed to monitor pollution, and constitutional guarantees for the incarcerated—all require national enforcement. Advocates of vigorous federal action would claim that, in the absence of mandates, state and local governments would be lax in the enforcement of many national objectives. The continuing debate, therefore, is over three broad features of mandates: (1) the amount of flexibility that will be given to lower-level governments in their administration and enforcement, (2) a careful accounting of the benefits of mandates compared with their costs, and (3) the appropriate sharing of the burden in the intergovernmental system of the United States.

JEFFREY D. STRAUSSMAN

BIBLIOGRAPHY

Advisory Commission on Intergovernmental Relations, 1994. *Regulatory Federalism: Policy, Process, Impact, and Reform.* Washington, D.C.

Dearborn, Philip M., 1994. *Local Government Responsibilities in Health Care.* Washington, DC: U.S. Advisory Commission on Intergovernmental Relations.

Fix, Michael, and Daphne Fix, eds., 1990. *Coping with Mandates.* Washington, DC: Urban Institute Press.

Koch, Edward, 1980. "The Mandate Millstone." *The Public Interest,* no. 61 (Fall): 42.

Lovell, Catherine, and Charles Tobin, 1981. "The Mandate Issue," *Public Administration Reviews* vol.41, (May/June) 318–331.

United States House of Representatives, Committee on Science, Space, and Technology, 1994. *Unfunded Federal Mandates: Who Should Pick Up the Tab?* Hearing, March 22.

United States Senate, Committee on Governmental Affairs, 1993. *Federal Mandates on State and Local Governments.* Hearing, November 3.

Wright, Deil, 1988. *Understanding Intergovernmental Relations,* 3d ed. Pacific Grove, CA: Brooks/Cole.

THE MANHATTAN PROJECT.

The World War II crash project undertaken in the United States from mid-1942 to mid-1945 with the objective of producing the first atomic bomb. The Manhattan Project was one of the most complex undertakings in governmental administration during the twentieth century and established many organizational principles that have guided subsequent large-scale endeavors.

Two major technical hurdles had to be overcome in order to achieve this objective. First, a sufficient amount of fissionable material had to be produced to fuel the bomb. The fissionable material could not be separated from its natural constituent, uranium 238, using simple mechanical means. Consequently, its production required the development of extraction procedures of great power and complexity, never before attempted on a large scale.

Second, project leaders had to devise a method that would cause the fissionable material to attain the supercritical mass necessary to produce an uncontrolled chain reaction. The highly radioactive material had to be reduced to pure metal and shaped in such a way as to remain inert until the moment of detonation. At that point, sufficient mass had to be brought together for the chain reaction to begin, with its commensurate release of energy. All this had to be accomplished within a bomb casing of reasonable size and operated by remote control.

Project work was carried out at a number of locations. Much of the early work on fissionable material separation had been conducted at Columbia University in New York City. Separation methods were explored at the University of Chicago and the University of California at Berkeley. Large-scale production efforts employing these methods were undertaken at futuristic engineering sites constructed in rural locations at Oak Ridge, Tennessee, and Hanford, Washington. Design of the bomb itself took place at an isolated laboratory in Los Alamos, New Mexico.

Prior to 1942, preliminary work in the United States was carried out through a loose collection of laboratories under the supervision of the National Bureau of Standards, the President's Office of Scientific Research and Development, and the military departments. In September 1942, Brigadier General Leslie R. Groves of the U.S. Army Corps of Engineers was placed in charge of the construction activities necessary to produce the bomb. The gruff, 46-year-old West Point graduate, whose previous assignments had included the construction of the Pentagon, quickly took charge of the day-to-day management of the project. Three months earlier the Manhattan District of the U.S. Army Corps of Engineers in New York had been assigned responsibility for initial construction work, hence the code name "Manhattan Project." Groves worked out of Washington, D.C., under the supervision of a three-person Military Policy Committee.

The Manhattan Project required a maximum amount of creativity in an undertaking fraught with uncertainty. Although the theoretical work was sound, when the project began no one knew how to produce sufficient fuel to power an atomic explosion or how to fabricate a bomb that would cause the explosion to take place when specified. The scope of the project required a guiding organization of considerable force. Combining the creativity necessary for technological discovery with a strong organization in a single, large-scale undertaking proved to be its central administrative legacy.

Groves and his staff used a number of techniques to accomplish this. First, Groves clearly specified the objectives of the project. The primary objective (to produce an atomic bomb as rapidly as possible) was compartmentalized into subobjectives, both to preserve secrecy and to keep participants focused on their own contribution. The objectives, moreover, were finite, in the sense that work on each objective ended once it was accomplished. (Facilities constructed at Los Alamos and elsewhere continued to support further development of nuclear weapons once the Manhattan Project ended.)

Project leaders pursued parallel lines of research and development simultaneously. Four separate methods for producing the fissionable material were intensively explored. This created competition among the staff, amplifying the motivation to succeed already excited by the knowledge that their efforts could hasten the end of the war and that the Germans were conducting similar research.

Groves had sufficient resources to accomplish all necessary phases of the project. The undertaking cost an estimated US $2 billion, a huge sum by standards of that day. President Franklin Roosevelt and congressional leaders approved the funds in secret with hardly a complaint.

Groves did not build up a large bureaucracy to supervise the project. He assembled a small headquarters staff, which for most of the project's duration fit inside five rooms in a building in Washington, D.C. To carry out the project, Groves relied upon the best laboratories, contractors, and supporting organizations he could find. The nation's best physicists were recruited from universities and laboratories, with the expectation that they would return to their regular jobs when the project was over. Groves relied extensively upon private contractors to carry out construction and production work, as was the Corps's organizational style. This philosophy established the central principle of what became known as project management: reliance upon outside organizations and individuals mobilized to make a finite contribution to a specific objective coordinated by a small project staff. Said Groves (1963) in a paper prepared for *Science, Technology, and Management*: "We never did anything ourselves that we could have anyone else do for us" (pp. 39–40).

Although people working on the project agreed with its objectives, they frequently fought over technical and organizational matters. This was especially true of the scientists at the Los Alamos facility, directed by physicist J. Robert Oppenheimer. They fought with each other over the physics of the bomb and with Groves over issues such as secrecy and compartmentalization. Battles got nasty and personal. Conflict and the ability to express different points of view are healthy signs in an innovation organization.

The first atomic bomb was exploded before dawn on July 16, 1945, at a test site in the New Mexico desert. A few weeks later, the United States dropped two other bombs produced by the project on the Japanese cities of Hiroshima and Nagasaki. In late 1946, in a ceremony in President Harry Truman's office, Groves symbolically transferred control over the nuclear domain to the newly created Atomic Energy Commission.

HOWARD E. MCCURDY

BIBLIOGRAPHY

Groves, Leslie R., 1963. "The A-Bomb Program." In Fremont E. Kast and James E. Rosenzweig, eds., *Science, Technology, and Management*. New York: McGraw-Hill.

Rhodes, Richard, 1986. *The Making of the Atomic Bomb*. New York: Simon and Schuster.

MARKUP.

The drafting of legislation as it occurs within a committee of the U.S. Congress. When the detailed language of legislation is originally written and approved by senators or representatives acting as members of a committee, the legislation is said to be marked up. Members vote to approve specific measures as well as the complete and final legislation when markup is complete. Committees mark up legislation on matters falling within the jurisdiction of the committee as determined by the rules of Congress. Markup usually follows hearings during which the committee receives testimony and other evidence relevant to the legislation, and the committee debates the issues involved. Legislation includes bills, resolutions, and other matters that are to be first developed and approved by a committee, followed by full consideration by the House or Senate. A markup session may be open to the public or closed, depending upon congressional and committee rules, the subject under consideration, and the wishes of the chairman.

Markup may occur at two levels within a committee. In some cases, subcommittees mark up legislation followed by another markup session conducted by the full committee, which may alter the work of the subcommittee. Full committee markup of legislation previously marked up by a subcommittee is usually less comprehensive than the work of the subcommittee. If a bill that was marked up and reported out by a committee is then substantially changed by the full House of Senate—which is the exception—it is said that such a measure was marked up on the floor.

While a markup session may produce an original document, it is not unusual for a committee to work from a draft. The "chairman's mark" is a draft version of legislation provided to the committee by its chairman. Because chairmen typically enjoy significant influence over the work of the committees, the chairman's mark is an important starting point for markup. Committees and subcommittees may also mark up from drafts submitted by the president, typically written by the agency of the executive branch most affected by the legislation, or, in the Senate, from legislation already passed by the House.

At all levels of committee markup, congressional staff plays a critical role. It provides technical information, suggests policy implications, interprets separate provisions and proposed changes, and redrafts the legislation in accordance with the decisions of committee members during markup. Prior to and during markup, committee staff may communicate with groups affected by the legislation as well as with the executive branch and staff of other committees affected by matters in the legislation. Depending upon the nature of the legislation, staff from the Office of Legislative Counsel may provide the committee with legal assistance during markup.

RICHARD DOYLE

BIBLIOGRAPHY

Cohn, Mary, ed., 1991. *How Congress Works*. Washington, D.C.: Congressional Quarterly.

Davidson, Roger, and Walter Oleszek, 1994. *Congress and Its Members*. Washington, D.C.: Congressional Quarterly.

Kravitz, Walter, 1993. *American Congressional Dictionary*. Washington, D.C.: Congressional Quarterly.

MARKET SOCIALISM.

The combination of the socialist principles of collective ownership and of limited inequality in the distribution of the national income and wealth with the use of markets and prices to allocate resources and goods. However, around this central core, there are various possible ways for the combination of planners' and consumers' sovereignty, the method of price formation, the scope of market, the nature of enterprise management, and other features of the economic system. The term is often used in contrast to centralized planned economy.

Although market socialism has been initially defined in economic terms, it requires political management to ensure that the system as a whole conforms to preset ethical criteria. The idea of market socialism thus invokes deeper philosophical issues related to the nature and role of the state.

One can distinguish at least three markedly different approaches to and origins of market socialism. The first ideas for market socialism originated around the turn of the twentieth century in response to some theoretical arguments that rational economic calculation and thus efficient allocation of resources were, in principle, impossible in a socialist economy based on the social ownership of resources and central planning. This line of interpretation is basically a formal exercise in general equilibrium theory and welfare economics and had little effect on the actual functioning of the "socialist" (centrally planned) economies.

A second significant line of contribution to this term emerged during the debates about reforming the over-centralized, bureaucratic form of central planning that evolved in the Soviet-type socialist (communist) countries. Market socialism in this context has emerged as an attempt to overcome practical defects encountered in state socialism (bureaucratic central planning). Market socialism has been used in this context both as a theoretical concept and to indicate the character of the economies of Yugoslavia after 1965, Hungary after 1968, and the People's Republic of China after 1978.

The third approach to market socialism can be identified with the system of the advanced welfare states (such as Sweden or Norway). This view is in a way a retreat to, and the revision of, the original Marxian idea, that socialism is the outcome of the socioeconomic development in efficient market economies. Unlike Marx, however, the proponents of this approach see this process as a gradual transition through reforms rather than a change brought about by a revolution. Also, in times of economic problems, socialist values are easily put aside as untimely issues.

The first historical debates about market socialism were initiated by some prominent economists who argued that without private ownership of the means of production, there is no market for capital goods, no prices on those goods, and consequently no way of determining rationally how they are to be employed. In 1908, Enrico Barone had developed a model to show how a socialist government might rationally plan production. Barone himself acknowledged, as did his later critics (e.g., Ludwig von Mises, Lionel Robbins, and Friedrich A. Hayek), that his solution did not provide a practical method of deciding what outputs should be turned out with the means of production.

Hayek, for example, argued that in order to construct a good plan, a planning body would have to collect a detailed set of information and solve hundreds of thousands of simultaneous equations that were impossible to realize in practice. Such a task, even if implementable, would require so much time that the results would be outdated by changes taking place in the economy in the meantime. (The difficulties that the centrally planned economies have encountered over the years in achieving consistency and efficiency lend support to the contentions of Hayek and others.)

Others, for example, Oskar Lange and Fred M. Taylor (1938), developed models in which they tried to show that by imitating the working of the market and combining it with central planning, efficient allocation of resources is compatible with the collective ownership of the means of production. These theoretical models can be regarded as the first examples and foundations of what has come to be known as "market socialism."

In the centrally planned countries, Lange's model has become the best-known. Lange demonstrated that a central planning board could, through trial and error, find such prices for the recourses that would reflect their scarcity and that rational decisions in response to conditions of scarcity could be made in such a system. In his model, there is a genuine market for consumer goods and labor. Their prices and quantities are thus decided by the law of demand and supply. But there is no market for capital goods and productive resources outside of labor. Instead, a central planning board sets accounting prices for them, adjusting them from time to time in an effort to equate the supply and demand for each good.

The prices for consumer goods (set directly by the market) and for producer goods (set by the central planning board imitating the market) are to be considered "parametric" (given) for the managers of socialist enterprises. In light of these prices, they must combine factors of production so as to minimize average cost and select an output level at which the marginal cost of the enterprise equals the parametric price. These two rules secure the efficiency of social production. The central planning board also decides the rate of investment for the economy as a whole. It then sets an interest rate on investment funds that equates the demand for them, on the part of socialist managers, to the amount available. Finally, the central planning board distributes to the population, the owners of the means of production, a social dividend based on the surplus collectively produced.

In Lange's model, enterprises are run by state-appointed managers following common broad rules dictated by economic efficiency considerations. In the "participatory" version of a socialist market economy, originated by Jaroslav Vanek, each firm is managed by its workers. In this model, the enterprises are not subject to central planning. Instead, elected workers' representatives and management hired from outside run the firm in response to price and profit signals. The key characteristics of the participatory economy are workers management, income sharing, payment for the use of society's capital, free markets, and freedom of employment. The labor-managed firm's aim is the maximization of income for each of its members.

The reform ideas put forward in the centrally planned economies have referred to the models presented here only as abstract theoretical predecessors. The issues on the agenda included complex problems that these stylized models could not effectively handle. Apart from the question of how to obtain the efficiency advantages of markets in the production of goods and services, the issues addressed involved questions such as how to confine the economic role of the state in a way that makes democratic government feasible, how to protect the autonomy of workers, both as individuals and members of self-managed enterprises and the like.

Proponents of social and economic reforms in centrally planned economies were originally led in their examinations by traditional socialist values such as equality, community interest, and rationality on the social level, which marked out the direction as well as the limits of reforms. Many of them gradually realized that the socialist ideals hit against the hard economic realities and became advocates of switching to a capitalist market economy. In this way, market socialism turned out to be a terminal in the process of transition to a market economy

MIHÁLY HÕGYE AND ERNÕ ZALAI

BIBLIOGRAPHY

Bornstein, Morris, ed., 1994. *Comparative Economic Systems, Models, and Cases*. Burr Ridge, IL: Irwin.
Kornai, János, 1991. *The Socialist System: The Political Economy of Communism*. Princeton, NJ: Princeton University Press.
Lange, Oskar, and Fred M. Taylor, 1938. *On the Economic Theory of Socialism*. Minneapolis: University of Minnesota Press.
Le Grand, Julian, and Saul Estrin, eds., 1989. *Market Socialism*. Oxford: Clarendon Press.
Miller, David, 1990. *Market, State, and Community: Theoretical Foundations of Market Socialism*. Oxford: Clarendon Press.
Vanek, Jaroslav, 1971. *The Participatory Economy: An Evolutionary Hypothesis and a Strategy for Development*. Ithaca, NY: Cornell University Press.
Yunker, James A., 1992. *Socialism Revised and Modernized: The Case for Pragmatic Market Socialism*. New York: Praeger.

MARKET TESTING.

The policy of exposing public-sector activities previously conducted in-house by directly employed personnel to periodic competition from external organizations. Market testing can result in the activity remaining in-house or being contracted out (transferring the function to an external organization) after the competitive bidding process.

Origins and Subsequent History

Market testing has been applied most extensively in the United Kingdom, but it has also attracted attention throughout North America and Europe. British public bodies have always relied on private-sector organizations to supply goods and services. Before the late 1970s, however, the majority of government functions were provided by in-house units. The dominant political ethos that public-sector organizations were the most "effective" form of provision meant that in-house units were immune from private-sector competition.

Since the 1970s, market testing policies have been actively pursued. Policy has been premised on its potential for reducing public-sector expenditure, early evidence of cost savings from pilot market testing schemes, and the ideological influence of "Thatcherism" and "public choice" economics. Market testing currently affects a wide range of functions in municipal authorities, central government, and the National Health Service.

Theory and Prospects

Advocates of market testing assume cost savings and efficiency improvements in public-service delivery from periodic rivalry. As S. Domberger *et al.* (1986) point out, traditional public-sector, in-house provision in the absence of competition "removes, to a significant extent, the constraints that apply to firms operating under competitive market conditions" (p. 69). *De facto* monopoly-supply, it is argued, creates disincentives for the unit to seek lower-cost methods of work because operating costs are met from government budget allocations. In addition, monopoly arrangements create an asymmetry of information between the service provider and the policymaker because comparative cost data are unavailable. As "public choice" economists have argued, these factors have enabled in-house units to pursue economic rents and dissipate rents through lower efficiency (see, for example, Mitchell 1988).

Proponents claim market testing resolves these deficiencies. First, competitive tendering—the process of bidding—furnishes the policymaker with comparative cost information on alternative sources of supply. On this basis, accurate assessments can be made of competitively determined productivity levels and unit costs. Second, periodic competition and the threat of substitution creates incentives for the in-house unit and potential market entrants to minimize costs at the bidding phase. And third, writing specifications and requirements in terms of outputs that tendering implies may identify inappropriate, existing service standards and thus facilitate allocative efficiency gains.

Critics of market testing point to the dangers of market testing for service quality and "hidden costs" of competition and contracting out. First, concern has arisen over loss of control and flexibility of contract staff, risks of contractor exploitation when in-house units are disbanded, and the potential for reduced quality after the market testing process. Second, critics claim that in practice, "transaction costs" (administrative overheads incurred in organiz-

ing competitions and monitoring contractor performance) and "anticompetitive factors" (collusion between bidders, loss-leading behavior, etc.) significantly undermine theoretical efficiency gains from competition.

The implication of these claims and counterclaims has been that market testing in the United Kingdom has remained a highly controversial area of public policy (see Uttley 1993; Chaundy and Uttley 1993). A result has been that policy implementation has generally been limited to ancillary or "noncore" areas of public-sector activity.

MATTHEW R. H. UTTLEY

BIBLIOGRAPHY

Chaundy, D, and M. R. H. Uttley, 1993. "The Economics of Compulsory Competitive Tendering: Issues, Evidence, and the Case of Municipal Refuse Collection." *Public Policy and Administration*, vol. 8, no. 2: 25–41.
Domberger, S., S. A. Meadowcroft, and D. J. Thompson, 1986. "Competitive Tendering and Efficiency: The Case of Refuse Collection." *Fiscal Studies*, vol. 7, no. 4: 69–87.
Mitchell, W. C., 1988. "Government as It Is." *Hobart Paper 109.* London: Institute of Economic Affairs.
Uttley, M. R. H., 1993. "Competition in the Provision of Defense Support Services: The UK Experience." *Defense Analysis*, vol. 9, no. 3: 271–288.

MARTIAL LAW. Military government by which the ordinary law is suspended and the military authorities are empowered to arrest and punish offenders at their discretion.

Martial law implies not so much the use of the military to police the civilian population and keep order, which historically was often the norm before civilian police forces became commonplace and which may well be ancillary to the imposition of martial law, as the power of the military authorities, either given to them or assumed by them, to try and punish offenders for breaches of laws imposed by those authorities. Such laws may be a mixture of the existing criminal codes and new rules or regulations imposed by the military authorities. Martial law must be distinguished from military rule in which a small number of senior military officers rule a country using the army only to ensure compliance by existing police, judicial, and administrative authorities with their laws or decrees.

The main distinction between martial law and military rule is, therefore, that where martial law exists there will also exist military tribunals of some sort to enforce it, either in place of or in parallel with the existing court and judicial structure. Military rulers, on the other hand, may either impose martial law or may leave the existing judicial and police structure to enforce the existing laws and any additional ones that they may pass. Furthermore, martial

law may be imposed to a limited extent, either geographically or in relation to specific laws or regulations.

Complete martial law is rare. It usually has to come into existence either as a result of conquest because the old legal and judicial structure has ceased to exist, as for example in Germany in the immediate aftermath of World War II, or of a coup when the civil government is deposed, as for example in Pakistan in 1958. It may, however, be imposed by the existing civil authorities either generally or specifically. For example, after the Easter Rising in Ireland in 1916, the military authorities were empowered to try the leaders by secret court-martial and then execute them. The imposition of martial law by a conquering army is likely to be because initially the conquering military power possesses the only means of imposing any rule of law and the only administrative machinery, the original organs of the conquered state, having ceased to exist. Historically, occupying powers have usually very quickly replaced martial law with a new form of civil administration and law, often based on the preexisting civil and criminal codes and on the preexisting court structures.

Where martial law has come into force as a result of a military coup, it has often been as a result of a perception by the senior military authorities of a state that democratic rule has failed, either because authority has broken down or because the elected government has become unacceptably corrupt, or in some cases because the economy of the country has disintegrated. Military coups have been frequent in Africa and in South America but are not unknown in Europe, an example being the coup organized by the Greek colonels in 1967. In such a case, it is not unusual for the coup leaders to assert that democratic rule will be reestablished as soon as conditions permit. In states where there are strong tribal or religious divergent forces, the army has frequently been the only cohesive force.

True martial law does not exist unless the military leaders are able to enforce their rule of law, through their own organs, on the civil population. Thus after the second coup in two days in Sierra Leone in 1968, the coup leader, Brigadier Juxon-Smith, declared, "Whoever it is in Sierra Leone, wherever you may be, who is planning trouble, let me warn you, in your own interest, in the interest of your family, to go back home. Regardless of your rank or status, regardless of your personality, you will be immediately apprehended, you will be tried by court martial, and you will be shot by firing squad. That is what martial law means" (Fisher 1989, p. 635). Within a month, however, Juxon-Smith was himself deposed by a group of NCOs and warrant officers.

Martial law may also be imposed by the civil authorities in a limited area or for limited purposes. Thus, if there is serious civil unrest in a province that the police are unable to control, often because of secessionist tendencies, the central government may use the military to reassert its authority, investing the military authorities with either general or limited powers.

An example of the successful imposition of martial law occurred in Pakistan in October 1958. The Proclamation by the President, Major General Iskander Mirza, began as follows:

> For the past two years I have been watching, with the deepest anxiety, the ruthless struggle for power, corruption, the shameful exploitation of our simple, honest, patriotic and industrious masses, the lack of decorum, and the prostitution of Islam for political ends . . . .
>
> Despite my repeated endeavours, no serious attempt has been made to tackle the food crises. Food has been a problem of life and death for us in a country which should be really surplus . . . .

It concluded as follows:

> . . . I have therefore decided that:-
> (a) The Constitution . . . will be abrogated.
> . . .
> (d) All political parties will be abolished.
> (e) Until alternative arrangements are made, Pakistan will come under Martial Law. . . .
>
> To the valiant Armed Forces of Pakistan, I have to say . . . . Do your job without fear or favour and may God help you (Feldman 1967, pp. 213–215).

Martial Law Regulations were published a week later dividing the country into zones and setting up Special Military and Summary Military Courts with power to try and punish any person for contravention of Martial Law Regulations or orders or for offenses under the ordinary law. The criminal courts were also given power to try and punish both ordinary law offenses and contraventions of Martial Law Regulations and orders. Twenty-five activities were specifically prohibited by the regulations. Some, such as damaging property, were clearly already crimes under the ordinary law; others, such as striking in educational institutions, were not previously offenses. Martial law in Pakistan lasted for nearly four years until a new constitution was proclaimed.

From this, one can see that there is a spectrum from the imposition of full martial law, with only military tribunals having power to enforce laws laid down by the military authorities, to the use by civil authorities of the military to enforce laws laid down by those civil authorities. The top end of the spectrum is seldom seen and even more seldom seen for any length of time. This is probably because generally military authorities are neither trained for nor keen to undertake the imposition of criminal law on civilian populations. It is not unusual, however, to see the imposition of martial law at a lower point in the spectrum, with military authorities having power to try civilians for breaches of certain laws imposed by those authorities, but

with the normal civilian criminal courts continuing to function in relation to ordinary crime, as happened extensively in occupied countries during World War II.

JOHN F. T. BAYLISS

BIBLIOGRAPHY

Feldman, Herbert, 1967. *Revolution in Pakistan–A Study of the Martial Law Administration*. Oxford: Oxford University Press.

Fisher, H., 1989. "Elections and Coups in Sierra Leone." *Journal of Modern African Studies* (December 7).

Simon, Sheldon W., ed, 1978. *The Military and Security in the Third World: Domestic and International Impacts*. Boulder, CO: Westview.

MASLOW, ABRAHAM H. (1908–1970).

Author of one of the most prominent and influential theories of human motivation, based on a hierarchy of needs and motives, and one of the intellectual leaders in the development of Humanistic Psychology in the 1960s. His theory of human needs elevated the term "self-actualization" into prominence in social scientific and popular discourse. His theory clearly influenced other major theoretical developments in the social, administrative, and policy sciences.

Born in Brooklyn, New York, Maslow began his undergraduate education at the City College of New York, ultimately completing his B.A. degree, master's degree, and doctorate (1934) from the University of Wisconsin. He spent most of his academic career at Brandeis University. His most influential books include *Motivation and Personality* (1954), *Toward a Psychology of Being* (1962), and *Eupsychian Management* (1965).

Maslow's need hierarchy theory of motivation involved a "hierarchy of prepotency" among five levels of needs or motives. The levels were the physiological needs, the security and safety needs, the social or love needs, the esteem needs, and the self-actualization needs. The theory contends that the levels of need fall into a hierarchy of prepotency from lower-order to higher-order needs. Beginning with the lowest level, the physiological needs–for relief from extremes of temperature, for food and shelter–dominate the person's motivation until that need is satisfied to some sufficient extent. In other words, a person who is deprived of food and extremely hungry will concentrate more on acquiring food than on the higher levels of need. Once a particular level is satisfied, the next higher need becomes dominant, and so on through the hierarchy.

After the most basic physiological needs, the next level includes the needs for safety and security of person, against threats and dangers. Then, the love and belongingness needs include the needs for satisfactory social relations with others and love relationships. Next, the esteem needs include the needs for the respect of others. The highest order of needs, the self-actualization needs, is almost certainly the most widely noted concept in Maslow's theory. According to Maslow, this level includes needs to fulfill one's potential, to maximize attainment in a chosen domain of activity or interest. Maslow argued that such motives appear in managers and executives seeking to exert some ultimate influence or make some ultimate contribution.

Later, in his book *Eupsychian Management* (1965), Maslow further developed his ideas about self-actualization and its association with work, duty, and group or communal benefits. Partly in response to the widespread, diverse, and occasionally dubious use of the concept of self-actualization that followed his earlier work, he sharply rejected some of the usages. He rejected conceptions of self-actualization as self-absorbed concern with one's emotional salvation or personal satisfaction, especially through merely shedding inhibitions or social controls. Maslow depicted self-actualized persons as achieving this ultimate mode of satisfaction through hardworking dedication to a duty, from work or a mission, that serves higher values than one's simple self-satisfaction and that benefits others or society. Genuine personal contentment and emotional salvation, he argued, come as by-products of such dedication. In *Eupsychian Management*, Maslow also conceived the levels of need not as separate steps or phases from which one successively departs. Rather, he treated them as cumulative phases of a growth toward self-actualization, a motive which grows out of satisfaction of social and esteem needs and also builds on them.

Maslow's ideas have had a significant impact on many social scientists, but his model has received limited support from empirical researchers attempting to validate it. Researchers attempting to devise measures of the needs and to test the theory have not confirmed the existence of a five-step hierarchy. Studies have tended to find a two-step hierarchy in which lower-level employees show more concern with material and security rewards. Higher-level employees place more emphasis on achievement and challenge. Of course, these studies may fail to support the theory simply because of our limited ability to operationalize and test the concepts and dynamics of the theory. For example, as implied by the findings mentioned here, the tests often compare lower-level to higher-level employees, and this provides only a static assessment of a process that the theory treats as dynamic. In addition, since the concept of self-actualization is quite complex, questionnaire items in the studies may not capture this complexity.

More important, scholars point to theoretical problems with Maslow's model, as did Maslow himself. He said that more than one need may determine behavior, that some needs may disappear, and even that some behavior is not determined by needs. Other critics emphasized ambiguities in the behavioral implications of need deprivation. Need deprivation may induce discomfort, but it does not tell the person what to do about it, and therefore the behavioral implications of the theory remain amorphous. The vague conception of self-actualization also impedes testing of the theory.

Still, Maslow's theory retains a strong plausibility and attractiveness. Maslow contributed to a growing recognition of the importance of motives for growth, development, and actualization among members of organizations. The influences of his ideas have followed some interesting paths. For example, Douglas McGregor's conception of *Theory X* and *Theory Y* management—like self-actualization, one of the most widely repeated ideas in organizational and managerial discourse—shows a very clear relation to Maslow's need hierarchy in such places as McGregor's (1960) *The Human Side of Enterprise*. As another example, in his seminal writings on "transformational leadership," James MacGregor Burns (in *Leadership*, 1978) drew on Maslow's concepts of a hierarchy of needs and of higher-order needs such as self-actualization. Burns observed that "transformational" leaders—that is, leaders who bring about major transformations in society—do not engage in simple exchanges of benefits with their followers. Rather, they elicit higher-order motives in the population, including forms of self-actualization motives tied to societal ends, with visions of a society transformed in ways that fulfill such motives. As a political scientist, Burns analyzed political and societal leaders, but writers on organizational leadership have acknowledged his influence on recent writings about transformational leadership in organizations. In addition, Maslow's later writings on self-actualization in work settings foreshadowed and influenced many aspects of the current topics of organizational mission and culture, empowerment of workers, and highly participative forms of management.

HAL G. RAINEY

BIBLIOGRAPHY

Bass, Bernard M., 1985. *Leadership and Performance beyond Expectations.* New York: Free Press.
Burns, James MacGregor, 1978. *Leadership.* New York: Harper & Row.
Hoffman, Edward, 1988. *The Right to Be Human: A Biography of Abraham Maslow.* Los Angeles: Jeremy P. Tarcher.
Locke, Edwin A., and David Henne, 1986. "Work Motivation Theories." In C. L. Cooper and I. Robertson, eds., *International Review of Industrial and Organizational Psychology.* New York: John Wiley and Sons, 1–35.
Maslow, Abraham H., 1954. *Motivation and Personality.* New York: Harper and Row.
———, 1962. *Toward a Psychology of Being.* Princeton, NJ: Van Nostrand.

Maslow, Abraham H., 1965. *Eupsychian Management.* Home-wood, IL: Richard D. Irwin.

McGregor , Douglas M., 1960. *The Human Side of Enterprise.* New York: McGraw-Hill.

Pinder, Craig C., 1984. *Work Motivation.* Glenview, IL.: Scott, Foresman.

MASTER OF PUBLIC ADMINISTRATION (MPA).

The typical designation for the professional degree in public policy and administration. The MPA is a postbaccalaureate degree awarded by universities upon the completion of a prescribed course of graduate study. The abbreviation MPA is often used generically for all such degrees, although official degree titles for similar courses of study include not only master of public administration, but also master of public affairs, master of public management, master of public policy, and master of arts or master of science in areas such as public administration, policy analysis, and urban policy.

The MPA is usually awarded following a two-year course of study. The MPA curriculum typically includes study of techniques for analyzing public policies and for managing public programs, as well as study of the economic, legal, political, and social contexts and purposes in which, through which, and for which public programs work. Although special areas of expertise are emphasized in some MPA curricula, many MPA programs emphasize generalist preparation for executive responsibility in a variety of careers in government and nonprofit agencies.

By 1995, more than 200 universities in the United States offered the MPA or similar degree. Most of these institutions belong to the National Association of Schools of Public Affairs and Administration (NASPAA). In 1993, 218 NASPAA member universities reported awarding 7,867 professional masters degrees. They reported 26,679 master's-degree students enrolled that year. (Because many students pursue the MPA degree part time, the average student takes more than two years to complete MPA degree requirements.)

MPA programs are variously organized in U.S. universities. In 1993, 15 percent were housed in separate schools of public administration, public affairs, or public policy; 2 percent in combined schools of management and business administration; 37 percent in departments of public administration, affairs, or policy; 32 percent in departments of political science; 3 percent in other departments; and 10 percent were organized under an interdisciplinary curriculum committee or other arrangement. MPA programs range in size from fewer than 20 students to more than 500 students enrolled annually.

Origins

In the United States, university-based professional graduate education in public administration began at Syracuse University with the founding of the Maxwell School of Citizenship and Public Affairs in 1924. The Syracuse Master of Science in Public Administration program was based on the Training School for Public Service developed after 1911 by the New York Bureau of Municipal Research. The curriculum reflected the tenets of Scientific Management and the Progressive Reform Movement and focused on skills and knowledge directly applicable to managing city government. The Syracuse program clearly produced public service generalists, however. Despite its local government focus, most graduates of the Syracuse program even during its first dozen years were employed by state or federal governments or by nongovernmental public service agencies. Reviewing the careers of early Syracuse graduates, George Graham reported that fewer than 15 percent worked for local governments in 1938.

At first only a few other universities followed Syracuse's lead and set up professional masters programs for public administration. The rapid expansion of government programs in the mid-1930s, however, encouraged the development of several new public service education programs. By 1940, more than 70 U.S. colleges and universities offered some sort of preparation in public administration. Several of these were undergraduate majors. Others were collections of courses with no organized degree program. There was even considerable diversity of approaches among the 40 or so universities offering graduate-level professional degrees in public administration. Some, like Syracuse and the University of Cincinnati, had highly structured programs requiring a specific set of courses. Others, like the University of Michigan and Harvard, permitted students to design their own programs from among many relevant courses offered throughout the university, but especially in political science. All were administrative generalist programs, preparing their students for what Graham called "managerial work" in government. Practical experience was an important part of many of these programs. They commonly assigned students to work in public agencies or to research public problems. Regardless of program format, "administrative science" was their intellectual core.

Stagnation

In the two decades following World War II, there was only a very slow increase in the number of universities offering graduate professional education in public administration. At the same time, there was a growing disenchantment with "administrative science" among public administration scholars. In 1958, Stephen Sweeny edited a symposium on contemporary public administration education in the United States. These discussions emphasized the importance of studying the political, economic, and social environment of public administration, the psychological and social dimensions of organizations, and the policy-shaping roles of public agencies. While such broader concerns of public service leadership were being incorporated into professional public administration masters degrees, organization and management, public personnel, and public finance were the subjects most often required. Only a few programs required a course in statistics. More common were courses in such administrative techniques as accounting, budgeting, planning, or purchasing. Only half of the programs required an internship.

As a report prepared by John Honey for the American Society for Public Administration (ASPA) clearly shows, MPA education seemed to many to be stagnating by the mid-1960s. Honey noted widespread lack of resources for MPA programs, general confusion among MPA faculty about intellectual foundations and direction and about the field's professional competence and status, and weak external respect and acceptance of the field among both university colleagues and the public. Although there were now more than 70 graduate public administration programs in the United States, many were quite small: only about 400 graduate degrees in public administration were awarded annually.

New Initiatives

The post–World War II malaise was broken by a variety of initiatives. During the last years of the 1960s, new intellectual approaches reinvigorated graduate public administration education and new organizations fostered and supported program initiation, renewal, and growth. The intellectual ferment of this period included both the "New Public Administration" and "Policy Analysis." While the former emphasized moral purposes of public service, the centrality of community, and equity and responsiveness as core values, the latter stressed rationality of program design, the centrality of the market, and effectiveness and economic efficiency as core values.

During this period the first of the public policy programs were begun, often explicitly to replace public administration programs. The public policy programs (frequently offering a master of public policy–MPP) emphasized microeconomics, benefit-cost analysis, statistics and systems analysis. The Association for Public Policy Analysis and Management (APPAM) was organized and provided a forum for developing and disseminating this new approach to professional public service education.

At the same time, the traditional MPA curriculum also began to change, reflecting concerns of both the New Public Administration and of Policy Analysis. Classes in ethics and citizen participation, on the one hand, and statistics and program planning and evaluation on the other became more common in MPA programs.

The National Association of Schools of Public Affairs and Administration (NASPAA) was founded in 1970, and an early priority was discussion of graduate program curricula. NASPAA soon included among its members almost all the MPA and MPP programs in the United States. Although many of the policy programs identified more strongly with APPAM, their participation in NASPAA permitted ongoing discussion about professional graduate education in public administration and public policy. By 1973, NASPAA had 101 member schools. In that year, they awarded 2,403 masters degrees (up from about 400 less than ten years before).

Expansion and Growth

The next two decades saw rapid expansion of MPA programs and a growing sense of professional identity. By 1983, NASPAA had 186 member programs, and they awarded 6,209 masters degrees. In 1993, 218 NASPAA programs awarded 7,867 masters degrees, (This included 30 programs that also belonged to APPAM. Another 11 APPAM schools were not NASPAA members.) Much of the sharp distinction between policy analysis and public administration programs has become blurred as policy programs have added courses in administrative processes and administration programs have added courses in policy analysis. Still, major contrasts remain between programs that emphasize economic models and analytic techniques and those that focus primarily on how public services can be well designed, organized, and managed.

The MPA is no longer seen as preparation solely for government employment. Traditionally, MPA programs focused their instruction on government programs and policies. Increasingly, however, public service is understood to include the work of nonprofit organizations and even the work of many for-profit businesses as they carry out public programs under governmental contract, mandate, or partnership. Several MPA programs have developed specializations in nonprofit management. An ongoing challenge is how to incorporate into the MPA curriculum understanding of public-private partnerships and other alternative ways of organizing programs for the public good.

Various organizations have helped foster a professional identity for public administration/policy graduate students. For example, the American Public Works Association (APWA) and the International City/County Management Association (ICMA) have each joined NASPAA in developing guidelines for MPA specializations to prepare students for careers in their professions. ICMA, ASPA, APPAM, the International Personnel Management Association, and other organizations of practicing professionals have student memberships and encourage student participation at their meetings. A number of government agencies have established internship programs for professional masters students, and increasing numbers of job descriptions specify the MPA or similar degree.

Finally, NASPAA has been recognized since 1986 by the Council on Postsecondary Accreditation to accredit masters degree programs in public affairs and administration. The process of designing and implementing standards for MPA programs, which NASPAA began in 1974, helped MPA faculty at many universities develop their programs' identities, curricula, and resources on a par with other professional degrees. By 1994, 117 MPA programs were on NASPAA's list of accredited programs.

GORDON P. WHITAKER

BIBLIOGRAPHY

Averch, H., and M. Dluhy, 1991. "Teaching Public Administration, Public Management, and Policy Analysis." *Journal of Policy Analysis and Management,* vol. 11: 541–551.

Birkhead, Guthrie S., and James D. Carroll, eds., 1980. *Education for Public Service, 1980.* Syracuse, NY: Maxwell School of Citizenship and Public Affairs, Syracuse University.

Crecine, John P., ed., 1982. *The New Educational Programs in Public Policy: The First Decade.* Greenwich, CT: JAI Press.

Graham, George A., 1941. *Education for Public Administration.* Chicago: Public Administration Service.

Honey, John C., 1966. *Higher Education for Public Service.* Washington, D.C.: American Society for Public Administration.

Jennings, Edward T., Jr., 1989. "Accountability, Program Quality, Outcome Assessment, and Graduate Education for Public Affairs and Administration." *Public Administration Review,* vol. 49 (September-October) 438–446.

National Association of Schools of Public Affairs and Administration, 1994. *1994 Directory of Programs.* Washington, D.C.: NASPAA.

Roeder, Phillip W., and Gordon Whitaker, 1993. "Education for the Public Service: Policy Analysis and Administration in the MPA Core Curriculum." *Administration and Society,* vol. 24 (February) 512–540.

Sweeney, Stephen B., ed., 1958. *Education for Administrative Careers in Government Service.* Philadelphia: University of Pennsylvania Press.

MASTERS OF NONPROFIT MANAGEMENT.

Masters degrees exclusively devoted to or including a concentration devoted to the management of private nongovernmental agencies as a generic group. A concentration typically includes nine or more semester units. Generic programs focus on all types of nonprofit agencies rather than one type, such as arts, religious, health care, or social service.

Although the management of complex enterprises such as wars, the building of pyramids, and the governing of secular and ecclesiastical empires has been evident for thousands of years, formal management education is only a century old. The first programs focused on training the managers of business enterprises. As government spending grew, the field of public administration came into being.

Specialized offshoots of management education developed in fields like health care, the arts, social work, education, and religion. In the 1980s, generic nonprofit management education was added to the higher education curriculum. In little more than a decade, this new field has grown rapidly in the United States and is beginning to take root in several other nations. Yet, its full acceptance and permanence are by no means assured.

History

Educational change is partly a function of economic and social change. This relationship is clear in the beginnings of formal education in ancient Egypt, Mesopotamia, and China; in the rise of the university in Europe during the eleventh and twelfth centuries; and in the vast economic, social, and educational changes in nineteenth-century America. The growth of management education has followed a similar pattern. Theories and research on management, and the first business administration programs, were triggered in large part by the development of the factory system and the rise of the modern corporation. Public administration programs began, not coincidentally, during a time of sharp increase in government spending.

Nonprofit management education arose in the 1980s, following an economic boom in the nonprofit sector. In the United States, this boom began in the two decades after World War II, with dramatic growth in private nonprofit health care and research, education, social services, and religion. Even more dramatic growth took place from 1965 to the late 1970s, due to U.S. President Lyndon Johnson's "Great Society" programs, many of which contracted with nonprofit agencies to deliver services. Other causes of nonprofit growth included a sharp increase in advocacy work (civil rights, anti-Vietnam and other peace efforts, environmentalism, the women's movement, gay-lesbian liberation, and so forth), the reopening of the United States to significant immigration (always a stimulus of nonprofit activity), the growth of the American economy, and tax policies favorable to charitable giving. The number of nonreligious nonprofits increased from 27,500 in 1946 to more than 1 million in 1994 (Hall 1994, p. 31; Internal Revenue Service 1995, Table 25). An Internal Revenue Service study reported: "Between 1975 and 1990, assets of tax-exempt organizations increased in real terms by over 150 percent while revenues increased by over 227 percent. This is in comparison to a growth in [U.S.] real GDP of 52 percent over the same period" (Skelly 1993, p. 556). By 1990, the sector employed 8 million people (more than the federal government and 50 state governments combined, not counting military employees), received the volunteer services of 80 million people, had total annual revenues of US $500 billion, and received charitable contributions of

US $125 billion, more than the combined profit of all Fortune 500 corporations.

The rapid growth of the nonprofit sector during the half century since World War II created the need for more and better trained managers. Universities were not the first to respond to this need. A host of consultants and training agencies offered nonprofits a variety of services. For instance, the Support Centers of the United States, a nonprofit technical assistance organization serving nonprofit organizations in 13 cities, provided workshops for 40,000 people in 1993. The Fund Raising School and the Grantsmanship Center train thousands each year. Large nonprofits such as the American Red Cross and YMCA have developed sophisticated in-house management training programs.

This first university-based nonprofit management education programs appeared in the 1980s. The University of Missouri at Kansas City launched a nonprofit management concentration within its master of public administration program in 1981. The University of San Francisco began a similar concentration in 1983; two years later it became the nation's first free-standing master of nonprofit administration program. George Washington University started a master of association management degree in 1984; this unique program is aimed primarily at managers of nonprofit trade and professional associations in the nation's capital. The University of Colorado in Denver created nonprofit management concentrations within both master and doctoral public administration degrees in the early 1980s. The New School for Social Research converted its master of professional studies in fund-raising management (which started in 1979) to a master of science in nonprofit management in 1986. The State University of New York at Stony Brook created a nonprofit management concentration in 1986. Case Western Reserve University began its master of nonprofit organizations program in 1989. One report concluded that there were 32 such programs in the United States by 1992–1993 (Wish 1993, pp. 22–23).

There were parallel developments in other nations. In Canada, York University in Toronto inaugurated a voluntary sector management concentration in its MBA program in 1983. In 1984, England's Brunel University began a voluntary sector concentration area in its master of arts in public and social administration. The London School of Economics and Political Science created a master of science in voluntary sector organization in 1987. Australia's University of Technology at Sydney began a master of management in community management in 1991.

Although this discussion deals specifically with master's degree programs in nonprofit administration, several related developments should be noted. In addition to approximately 20 nonprofit master's degree programs, at least a 100 universities offer one or more courses on some aspect of nonprofit management (Kaziol 1993). There are at least 20 nonprofit certificate programs in the United States and Canada (Donaldson and Wentz 1992), the pioneer being a certificate offered since 1977 by Columbia University's Institute for Not-for-Profit Management. There is one doctoral program, at the Union Institute for Experimenting Colleges and Universities based in Cincinnati, Ohio (the doctoral major at the University of Colorado has been discontinued). Indiana University has a master of arts in philanthropic studies, focusing on general rather than professional education. There has been a general absence of nonprofit management course work on the undergraduate level (as contrasted with the plethora of undergraduate business administration programs), but Indiana University's business school inaugurated such a concentration area in 1995, and a few dozen universities have offered coursework in philanthropic studies. Of great importance to nonprofit management education has been the development at several universities of research centers in nonprofit and philanthropic studies. The first, Yale University's Program on Nonprofit Organizations, was founded in 1977 and by 1995 had produced more than 200 working papers and several articles and books. Other research centers have been established at Boston College, the City University of New York, Duke University, Johns Hopkins University, Indiana University, the New York University School of Law, and the Queensland University of Technology in Brisbane, Australia. Additionally, some of the institutions that offer masters degrees, such as Case Western Reserve University, the London School of Economics, the University of San Francisco, and the University of Technology at Sydney, also have active research programs. The 1980s and 1990s have seen an explosion of publications about voluntary, nonprofit, and philanthropic issues. Jossey-Bass, the Foundation Center, Oxford University Press, Indiana University Press, Yale University Press, Johns Hopkins University Press, and other book publishers have developed nonprofit series. Three scholarly journals, *Nonprofit Management and Leadership*, *Voluntas*, and *Nonprofit and Voluntary Sector Quarterly* (formerly the *Journal of Voluntary Action Research*) serve the field, and there are several popular journals and newspapers, such as the *Chronicle of Philanthropy* and *Foundation News*. There are two associations of scholars: the Association for Research on Nonprofit Organizations and Voluntary Action (ARNOVA) and the International Society for Third-Sector Research (ISTR). The National Association of Schools of Public Affairs and Administration (NASPAA), the organization that accredits U.S. public administration degrees, now includes a section on nonprofit management. Independent Sector, a U.S. coalition of national nonprofit organizations and foundations, has actively supported the growth of nonprofit management programs. The Ford Foundation and several other funders joined to create the Nonprofit Sector Research Fund at the Aspen Institute.

Rationale

Leaving aside the interesting question of whether there should be formal management education at all, one may ask why there should be separate programs for administrators of nonprofit agencies. This question is analogous to the long-debated questions of whether there should be separate degrees for business and government managers or separate degrees for educational, arts, religious, health care, and social service administrators. Some hold that management concepts and skills are sufficiently similar from one situation to another that all managers should take the same management degree. Advocates of separate nonprofit management programs contend that nonprofit agencies, while similar in many respects to other organizations, are unique in important ways and that these differences call for somewhat different preparation (O'Neill and Young 1988, pp. 3–8, generally Mason 1984, pp. 21–22). They hold that

- nonprofits differ from business organizations in that revenue, particularly net revenue, is the goal of for-profit organizations, whereas in nonprofits revenue is a means to the end of providing some service or public benefit. A corollary is that nonprofits have more complex and ambiguous measures of success, or "bottom line," than do for-profit firms.
- nonprofits are often value oriented. Religious congregations, advocacy organizations, and many educational, social service, mutual benefit, and other nonprofits are strongly and explicitly permeated by values. Although values exist to some extent in business and government organizations, values have a uniquely important role in many nonprofits. A corollary is that many people who work for nonprofits, paid or unpaid, do so in large part for value-related reasons.
- most nonprofits depend heavily on an unpaid workforce, with 80 million volunteers contributing an estimated 20 billion hours of work time per year in the United States. Managing a largely volunteer workforce calls for a significantly different approach to incentive systems, work scheduling, long-range planning, and the like.
- in general, paid staff in nonprofit organizations is significantly more likely to be female, professional, and college educated than workers in business or government (although these differences tend to disappear in particular industries such as education and health care). Significantly different personnel characteristics have implications for management.
- resource acquisition is significantly different in nonprofit and for-profit agencies. In the latter, clients or customers pay for the goods and services they receive; this is the principal and often sole method of resource acquisition in for-profit firms. Nonprofits acquire resources from clients, members, individual donors,

foundations, corporations, the government, and other sources. Nonprofit managers must be skilled in widely different types of resource acquisition. Additionally, since the direct recipient of the nonprofit's services is only one (and often not a particularly important one) of many different resource providers, the organization-client relationship is significantly different than in most for-profit firms.

Although it is easy to find exceptions to these and other differences between nonprofit and other organizations (for instance, the differences between nonprofit, for-profit, and government hospitals and nursing homes seem to be decreasing rapidly), proponents of nonprofit management degrees hold that such differences, and their implications for management, justify the existence of separate management education programs.

Issues

Beyond the central issue addressed here—whether nonprofit management education should exist as a separate endeavor—several other questions have been central to the development of this new academic field.

Academic Setting

Should nonprofit management education be part of a master of business administration, part of a master of public administration, part of some other degree, or a freestanding program? A conference and book on nonprofit management education (O'Neill and Young 1988, p. 20) concluded that there is no "one best way" to offer nonprofit management education and that much depends on local needs, institutional priorities, and academic politics. The empirical answer has been similarly mixed: Existing programs are approximately equally distributed across the four models, with a few more programs using the MPA base than the others.

Curriculum

Nonprofit degree programs primarily offer courses in functional areas of management (marketing, fund-raising, personnel, finance) as well as a few general courses (history, economics, ethics), with a variety of capstone requirements (thesis, project, comprehensive examination, internship). There is a high degree of curricular consensus in this new academic field. For instance, three-fourths of the courses in three prominent free-standing programs (Case Western Reserve University, New School for Social Research, University of San Francisco) are the same, allowing for minor differences in terminology (see also Rubin, Adamski, and Block 1989). Curriculum in the MBA–and MPA-based programs is largely determined by traditions and accreditation bodies related to those two degrees. As of 1995, there had been no serious consideration of a new accreditation body to accredit free-standing masters of nonprofit management degrees, probably because of the newness and small number of such programs.

Students

Most of the masters programs have focused on midcareer, nonprofit staff members who take evening or weekend courses while continuing to work. The median age of these students is between 30 and 35. About two-thirds are female, and about 20 percent are minority, reflecting the U.S. nonprofit workforce generally. The students come from a variety of academic backgrounds and work for a wide variety of organizations, most of them human and social service organizations. Many students hold midlevel or top management positions. This focus on adult working students appears to be largely pragmatic on both sides: The students have made a firm career commitment to the nonprofit sector, and the universities find them a more responsive market. However, an increasing number of younger, less experienced students are enrolling in such programs.

Faculty

As with any field of professional education, there is ongoing debate as to the relative role of full-time, research-oriented faculty and part-time, practice-oriented faculty. Most of the nonprofit management degree programs are taught by a mix of the two, though the mix differs widely from one institution to another, from very few to more than 75 percent of courses taught by adjunct faculty (Crowder and Hodgkinson 1993, pp. 56–57).

Passing Fad or Permanent Fixture?

Academia has seen many new specialties come and go; recent examples include urban studies, women's studies, ethnic studies and various branches thereof, environmental studies, peace studies, and so forth. It is probably too early to tell whether nonprofit management and, more generally, nonprofit and philanthropic studies will become permanent fixtures in higher education. There are many signs of emerging permanence: more than 600 members in the two scholarly associations; a significant increase in the number of books, articles, working papers, and other scholarly productions focusing on nonprofit organizations and voluntary action; rapid increase in the number of courses and programs being offered; and steady growth in the number of students enrolling in such offerings. However, there is little evidence of mainline, long-term institutional support for the field. Only two endowed chairs have been established (at Case Western Reserve University and the University of Missouri, Kansas City). Apart from the directors of nonprofit management programs, there are very few full-time faculty positions—perhaps fewer than ten in the

United States—allocated to nonprofit masters degrees; the vast majority of courses are taught by adjunct faculty and full-time faculty "borrowed" from other departments. The quantity and quality of scholarship in the field has grown rapidly, but there are still only three journals devoted to the field. A few national foundations (Kellogg, Ford, Rockefeller Brothers Fund, Lilly, Mott) have been consistently supportive, but foundation, corporate, and government support of such programs remains thin. The first generation of nonprofit management masters programs has been characterized by energetic and creative program development in response to increasingly obvious needs. If this promising new field of professional education is to achieve stability, longevity, and respect, its second generation will need to be characterized by scholarly depth and skills in resource acquisition and academic politics.

MICHAEL O'NEILL

BIBLIOGRAPHY

Crowder, Nancy L., and Virginia A. Hodgkinson, 1993. *Academic Centers and Programs: Focusing on the Study of Philanthropy, Voluntarism, and Not-for-Profit Activities*, 3d ed. Washington, D.C.: Independent Sector.

Donaldson, Judie, and Melanie Wentz, 1992. *Survey of Nonprofit Certificate Programs*. San Francisco: Institute for Nonprofit Organization Management, University of San Francisco.

Hall, Peter D., 1994. "Historical Perspectives on Nonprofit Organizations." In Robert D. Herman and Associates, *The Jossey-Bass Handbook of Nonprofit Leadership and Management*. San Francisco: Jossey-Bass.

Internal Revenue Service, 1995. *Annual Report: Commissioner of Internal Revenue*. Washington, D.C.: Internal Revenue Service.

Kaziol, Ken, 1993. *Nonprofit Management Syllabi Collection*. San Francisco: Institute for Nonprofit Organization Management, University of San Francisco.

Mason, David E., 1984. *Voluntary Nonprofit Enterprise Management*. New York: Plenum.

O'Neill, Michael, and Dennis R. Young, 1988. *Educating Managers of Nonprofit Organizations*. New York: Praeger.

Rubin, Hank, Laura Adamski, and Stephen R. Block, 1989. "Toward a Discipline of Nonprofit Administration: Report from the Clarion Conference." *Nonprofit and Voluntary Sector Quarterly*, vol. 18, no. 3 (Fall) 279–286.

Skelly, Daniel F., 1993. "Tax-Based Research and Data on Nonprofit Organizations." *Voluntas*, vol. 4, no. 4: 555–568.

Wish, Naomi B., 1993. "Colleges Offering More Nonprofit Graduate Programs." *Nonprofit Times* (June) 22–23.

MATRIX ORGANIZATION.

A form of organizational structure that simultaneously overlays functional and goal-oriented units in a relatively permanent alteration of the traditional hierarchical model of organization.

Matrix organization originated in the United States aerospace industry during the 1950s and 1960s as an alternative organizational form that grouped teams of specialists to facilitate the completion of projects. Project teams cut across vertical lines of command typically found in hierarchical organizations to accomplish complex tasks whose quality and timeliness benefited from marshalling specialized information and expertise.

Utilized primarily by corporations with multiple product lines operating in high-pressure, volatile markets, matrix organization has slowly found its way into public-sector agencies where the nature of work and environmental characteristics demand flexibility and quick response. The relatively few examples of enduring, public-sector applications of matrix organization may be due to formalization and rigidity frequently found in government agencies and the restrictive nature of the civil service. However, where matrix management has been utilized in public organizations, benefits frequently have been gained.

Given the widespread use of bureaucracy and its hierarchically arranged lines of authority, there appears to be no one part of the world that has capitalized on matrix more than other parts. A decision to utilize this innovative design is predicated more upon the characteristics of individual organizations and their environments rather than on prevailing cultural norms. A hospitable climate for matrix organization consists of leadership willing to take risks and experience higher cost in order to benefit from improved responsiveness and creativity that results from project- or problem-oriented teams. A primary risk occurs in violating the time-honored unity of command principle. Project team members have two bosses which may cause confusion and anxiety. Where managers perceive the benefits to outweigh these types of disadvantages, matrix management is used to respond to environmentally dictated constraints and contingencies, which defy adequate response from traditional bureaucracies.

Matrix organization gains its name from the resulting rectangular arrangement of units in rows and columns on an organizational chart when horizontally depicted project teams are superimposed on vertically oriented functional departments. The matrix is referred to as a simultaneous structure because it utilizes the elements of the bureaucratic structure at the same time that it employs the elements of the organic structure. The former represents a highly predictable, steady, rule-bound structure better suited for accomplishing routine tasks, whereas the latter is characterized by decentralization, collaboration, and high flexibility for producing creative solutions.

Stanley Davis and Paul Lawrence, authors of a widely read study on matrix management simply titled *Matrix* (1977) postulated three "necessary and sufficient" conditions that must exist if the benefits of matrix are to outweigh the costs: (1) outside pressure for dual focus such as satisfying two different client groups, (2) high uncertainty combined with interrelated or interdependent tasks, and (3) pressure to share limited or specialized resources among organizational subunits. Application in the public sector may appear evident, based on these criteria. Massive urban

development projects requiring rapid, comprehensive government action, for example, might qualify. A federal agency threatened by massive budget recision might well utilize a matrix approach.

Despite the apparent preference for such an innovative strategy, most agencies defer. Beyond the natural aversion to change and a desire for security, public officials may hesitate because matrix organization is likely to create confusion and ambiguity, foster power struggles, and place increased stress on individuals. For example, when project team members must respond to directions from two bosses, they are likely to struggle with prioritizing those orders. Ambiguity and uncertainty increase, which can lead to conflict. Likewise, disagreement may occur if project managers fight over getting the best specialists assigned to their teams. Meanwhile, individual team members may wrestle with role conflict, unclear expectations, and competing work assignments.

Advocates of matrix organization, while acknowledging its limited success in the public sector, contend that much of the problem lies not in the design but in the implementation of this innovative approach. Like all change strategies enacted in organizations, the matrix model depends on leadership to create a supportive culture that encourages cooperation, trust, openness, and interpersonal responsibility. These admirable traits may be even more critical for the effective use of matrix management because of the natural tensions created by greatly diverse project and functional orientations. In such a supportive internal environment, benefits such as creative solutions to problems, enhanced risk taking, faster response to environmental demands, improved communications and information transfer across functional boundaries, and job and professional enrichment are possible.

The ideal or pure form of matrix exists when there is a balance of priority and authority between functional bureau chiefs and project managers. Further, most students of this innovative form would contend that permanence, not a temporary task force approach, characterizes a true matrix organization. Given these rigorous requirements, strictly defined matrix structures are even less likely to exist. Failure to achieve such a pinnacle, however, does not negate the various derivatives of the pure form.

Jay Galbraith (1977), who has written extensively on matrix and complex organizational designs, contends that a number of transition stages exist between functional and product dominance. He found that there is a "continuous range of distribution of influence between product and functional orientations (p. 117)," not a dichotomous arrangement. With reference to industrial organizations, Galbraith observed that diversity and new product introductions are best managed through product-oriented structures. A need for increased interdependence among functional departments or heightened responsiveness to the market likewise favored a project approach. On the other side of the continuum, economies of scale, a concentration of expertise, and career paths for specialists encouraged favoring the functional organization. The point where product and function are of equal power is called the matrix organization.

Galbraith and others have found that the matrix is a transitional structure that should be adopted when conditions merit and discarded when those conditions no longer prevail. Simultaneous structures are flexible structures that can and should be fine-tuned by altering the power distribution as environmental changes and internal strategies dictate. Hence, the role of the organizational executive is one of power balancing.

DAVID W. SINK

BIBLIOGRAPHY

Burns, Lawton R., 1989. "Matrix Management in Hospitals: Testing Theories of Matrix Structure and Development." *Administrative Science Quarterly,* vol. 34: 349–368.

Chadwin, Mark Lincoln, 1983. "Managing Program Headquarters Units: The Importance of Matrixing." *Public Administration Review,* vol. 43 (July-August) 305–314.

Davis, Stanley M., and Paul R. Lawrence, 1977. *Matrix.* Reading, MA: Addison-Wesley.

Galbraith, Jay, 1977. *Organization Design.* Reading, MA: Addison-Wesley.

Kolodny, Harvey F., 1979. "Evolution to a Matrix Organization." *Academy of Management Review,* vol. 4: 543–553.

MCGREGOR, DOUGLAS M. (1906–1964).

A Harvard-trained social psychologist, former president of Antioch College, and professor of industrial management at MIT, who is considered part of the human relations tradition in organization theory. His elaboration of alternative leadership styles in his seminal book *The Human Side of Enterprise* (1960) is his principal contribution to management theory. Less known, but also important, is his pioneering involvement in "organizational development" (OD). McGregor's thinking has had enormous influence on management teaching, research, and practice.

McGregor's classic work *The Human Side of Enterprise* was written in the late 1950s. It was based on a speech by the same title delivered at the Fifth Anniversary Convocation of MIT's Alfred P. Sloan School of Management in April 1957. The book's central theme was that administrative practice was driven by theoretical assumptions managers held about the nature of people. McGregor felt that managers do not react to an objective world, but to one created out of their own beliefs about what the world is like.

McGregor believed that traditional management practices were based on erroneous assumptions about human nature. He characterized the set of suppositions supporting traditional management patterns as "Theory X." According

to McGregor (1960), Theory X was based on the following questionable propositions:

1. The average human being has an inherent dislike of work and will avoid it if possible.
2. Because of this human characteristic of dislike of work, most people must be coerced, controlled, directed, or threatened with punishment to put forth adequate effort toward the achievement of organizational objectives.
3. The average human being prefers to be directed, wishes to avoid responsibility, has relatively little ambition, wants security above all (pp. 33–34).

McGregor believed that traditional management beliefs about the nature of workers was wrongheaded, self-fulfilling, and inconsistent with developments in behavioral science research.

McGregor was greatly influenced by the work of Abraham Maslow (1954) and Frederick Herzberg (Herzberg et al. 1959) that suggested higher-order needs, such as social, ego, esteem, growth, and fulfillment drives, were most powerful in arousing and sustaining motivation. These urges were seen as intrinsic, energized by the nature of the work itself. To trigger higher-order needs, persons must be given the opportunity to engage in interesting, meaningful, and challenging labor.

Theory X was a "carrot and stick" theory of motivation that appealed only to lower-order extrinsic needs like pay, supervision, and physical working conditions. Research had shown that these were hardly more than mere satisfiers and had at best only narrow motivational potential. The premises underlying Theory X, according to McGregor, reflected an imperfect understanding of human motivation and the management methods that inevitably followed from these beliefs limited the productivity and creative energy of people.

McGregor (1960) argued that developments in social science research about human behavior made possible a new theory of managing people; one different from Theory X. This nontraditional theory that he labeled "Theory Y" was based on the following propositions:

1. The expenditure of physical and mental effort in work is as natural as play or rest.
2. External control and the threat of punishment are not the only means for bringing about effort toward organizational objectives. Mankind will exercise self-direction and self-control in the service of objectives to which one is committed.
3. Commitment to objectives is a function of the rewards associated with their achievement.
4. The average human being learns, under proper conditions, not only to accept but to seek responsibility.
5. The capacity to exercise a relatively high degree of imagination, ingenuity, and creativity in the solution

of organizational problems is widely, not narrowly, distributed in the population.

6. Under conditions of modern industrial life, the intellectual potentialities of the average human being are only partially utilized (pp. 47–48).

McGregor concluded that the problem in attaining human collaboration at work was not because of something inherently flawed about human nature, but because of the failure of management to take advantage of the full capabilities of its workforce. McGregor contended that managers were not reality-centered but trapped by a set of incorrect assumptions about their employees. *The Human Side of Enterprise* was a plea for a different approach, one relying on employee self-control and self-direction.

The central organizing principle arising from the high trust assumptions of Theory Y is that of "integration" or creating conditions where the organization's and the individual's needs are legitimized. The idea is to build employee commitment to organizational objectives by giving staff a role in setting goals, determining means to achieve them, and identifying methods of evaluating performance. Using this management-by-objective (MBO) plan, administrators can count on employees accepting greater responsibility and accomplishing more.

Five years after introducing Theory X and Theory Y, McGregor expressed concern that he was misinterpreted. He tried to make clear that his two theories were not alternative management "strategies," but underlying beliefs about the nature of man that "influenced" management methods. In *The Professional Manager,* a volume in progress at the time of his death, McGregor (1967) wrote, "It seems to me to be far less important to categorize and label managerial cosmologies than it is to understand their development, their impact on managerial strategies, and the implications for them of behavioral science knowledge" (p. 80). He was always encouraging managers to be introspective about what they were doing. That message, more than an argument for or against any particular management style, was constantly at the heart of his work.

McGregor was a pioneer in the field of organizational development (OD). He helped Kurt Lewin establish the Research Center for Group Dynamics at MIT, applied Lewin's ideas when he was president of Antioch College, and recruited to MIT the team of Richard Beckhard, Warren Bennis, Mason Haire, Joseph Scanlon, and Edgar Schein—a group generally credited with setting the boundaries, practices, and values of OD. He is recognized, along with Beckhard, for coining the term "organizational development" (Weisbord 1987).

McGregor was one of the first management thinkers to appreciate the importance of work teams and group dynamics. Since his writing was directed toward practicing managers, he applied his ideas about groups and team building to the development of management groups. What he had to say about the elements of effective teams, however, has value for team activities at every level of contemporary organizations.

According to McGregor (1967), effective teams are based upon:

1. *understanding the primary task of the group.* Well before strategic planning came into vogue, McGregor thought that answering the question "what business are we in" was a powerful way to develop mutual agreement and common purpose in a work group.

2. *open communications.* The influence of OD thinking is also evident in McGregor's appreciation of the salutary effects of open communications in team building. He understood that intellectual ideas, neutral facts, and the use of logical arguments were not the only elements of a superior communications system. He also encouraged the open expression of feelings in order to surface emotional data essential for teamwork.

3. *mutual trust.* McGregor grasped the importance of trust for shared influence, creativity, and effective problem solving. He appreciated that mistrust impaired group performance by adding social uncertainty to the objective uncertainty in every problem situation.

4. *mutual support.* Support, according to McGregor, ranged from a negative to a positive extreme. At its most negative, the absence of support encouraged defensive behavior. At the other extreme, too much support encouraged dependency. In both cases, group functioning was disabled. McGregor believed mutual support meant a predictable absence of either hostility or indifference between group members, allowing individuals to be authentic with one another.

5. *management of human differences.* McGregor anticipated the increasing importance of work teams and the general challenge of managing diversity in modern organizations. He acknowledged the paradoxical problems generated by individual differences in groups. If group members are too much alike, for instance, they are prone to groupthinking. If they are too different, they may engage in dysfunctional conflict. According to McGregor, maintaining a constructive tension in the group, without its losing discriminating judgment or falling apart, is a crucial task of productive team management.

6. *selective use of the team.* McGregor was a contingency theorist; that is, he did not advocate the use of teams in every problem situation; only in those where their use was appropriate. He recognized that several contingencies such as nature of the task, group maturity, and group atmosphere conditioned whether teams should be delegated responsibility.

7. *appropriate member skills.* The skills McGregor identified as important to group performance are familiar to students of organizational behavior. They are "task" and

"maintenance" capabilities. Task functions mean helping to get the job done by seeking and giving information, summarizing and evaluating ideas, and testing the feasibility of actions. Maintenance behaviors are related to sustaining the group as a viable system by encouraging members to participate, relieving tension through the use of humor, and mediating and testing for consensus and commitment. McGregor appreciated that not every member of the group had to perform each of these roles, but that these activities had to be accomplished if the group was to be efficient.

8. *leadership*. Unlike most thinking about leadership, McGregor saw it as a necessary element, but not the most vital, in determining the quality of group performance. Leaders might subvert the set of contingencies described above that led to high levels of group accomplishment, but leaders alone could not create these conditions independent from the group's collective capacity to interact constructively. The synergy at the core of group dynamics persuaded McGregor that leaders were constrained in creating such physics through their normal tools of power.

What might summarize McGregor's legacy to the study and practice of management? First, his juxtaposition of the two worldviews, Theory X and Theory Y, remains a powerful influence on generations of managers and students. Second, McGregor was well ahead of his time when it came to criticisms about performance appraisal, the limitations of command and control methods of administration, the value of teamwork, the importance of diversity, and the significance of managing conflict. His writing remains relevant although it dates back almost 30 years. Third, McGregor wrote not just about how to manage, but he advanced a philosophy in which people, the human side of organizations, are respected, valued, and encouraged to develop their fullest potential. These values are evident in his writing, teaching, and his own leadership style. McGregor remains a force for human values in an organizational society.

DAVID CARNAVALE

BIBLIOGRAPHY

Herzberg, Frederick, Bernard Mausner, and Barbara Bloch, 1959. *The Motivation to Work.* New York: John Wiley & Sons.
Maslow, Abraham H., 1954. *Motivation and Personality.* New York: Harper & Row.
McGregor, Douglas M., 1960. *The Human Side of Enterprise.* New York: McGraw-Hill.
———, 1967. *The Professional Manager.* New York: McGraw-Hill.
Weisbord, Marvin, 1987. *Productive Work Places.* San Francisco: Jossey-Bass.

MEDIATING INSTITUTIONS.

Those social institutions standing between the individual in private life and the large institutions of public life, providing alternative, more personalized, and diverse welfare-state services—thereby empowering individuals in a diverse society—and providing venues for civic discourse, a concept given popular currency by Peter Berger and Richard Neuhaus in a 1977 essay entitled *To Empower People: The Role of Mediating Structures in Public Policy.* The authors identified four types of mediating structures—the neighborhood, family, church, and voluntary associations—and argued that public policy should protect and foster mediating structures, and utilize them for the realization of social purposes.

The concept is most frequently associated with the goals of the social welfare state, and the weaknesses inherent in the delivery of welfare services by large, state-run bureaucracies. Berger and Neuhaus argued that public megastructures—whether government, big business, or big labor—are, by their very nature, devoid of personal meaning, alienating, and viewed as unreal or even harmful. Citizens have come to desire certain services from the modern welfare state but also harbor suspicion and distrust against government and other megastructures. Meaning and personal identity, by contrast, are associated with private life. But the individual is provided with little institutional support in private life, and achievement of basic needs and meaning is, therefore, a fragile enterprise. What is required, Berger and Neuhaus maintain, is a means of bridging or mediating the two spheres of life in the modern bureaucratic state, private and public. These "mediating structures" would be sufficiently personalized to give private life a measure of stability and sufficiently public to provide meaning and value to megastructures.

The need for mediating institutions is a particular challenge for democracy, the authors said. Totalitarian states overcome the division of private and public life by imposing one order of meaning over all. The danger in the bureaucratic democracy, where public and private life continue to be separated without mediating structures, is that the consequent wholesale cynicism toward public institutions will destroy the state. Between the polar extremes of totalitarianism (value is imbedded in the institutions of the state) and the breakdown of democracy (through cynicism engendered by the absence of values in its institutions), there is a requirement for mediating (private, but with a public purpose) structures that generate and maintain social values.

The Berger and Neuhaus essay began a debate that can be said to have had two principal impacts on later scholars. First, voluntary sector theorists have alternately suggested that their work argued there is an inherent conflict between the state and voluntary organizations that act as mediating structures (Gidron *et al.* 1992; Salamon 1994), and that the functions of the modern welfare state and voluntary organizations that act as mediating structures are cooperative or complementary (Van Til 1988). This apparent confusion over the essay's conclusions about the natural relationship between the state and the voluntary sector likely arises from Berger and Neuhaus' reflections on political theory. Liberalism, they suggest, has been blind to the need for mediating structures since its Enlightenment roots. Focused on the rights of the individual and the need for a just public order, mediating communal structures have been seen by liberalism as irrelevant, anachronistic, or obstructive. The argument that private behavior can have public consequences has found little support in U.S. law and jurisprudence, for example, and private rights have frequently been defended against mediating structures (e.g., children's rights against the family, the rights of sexual deviants against neighborhoods, etc.). Even the American liberal commitment to religious liberty, the authors say, is defended as a right to privatized religion. Similarly, they suggest, modern conservatism has rejected mediating structures, preferring the alienations of big business to those of big government. In another portion of the essay, however, they argue that the concept of mediating institutions supports empowerment of individual citizens through pluralism. The use of the term "pluralism" usually refers to a variant of liberalism that promotes competition between social interests to achieve an overall balance or compromise in democratically determined public policy. Applying this traditional meaning to the use of "pluralism"—when combined with the authors' comments on the antipathy of liberalism and modern conservatism to mediating structures—would lead the reader to assume Berger and Neuhaus referred to a natural condition of conflict between the state and the voluntary sector (or other mediating structures). A more careful reading, however, indicates the authors are not using "pluralism" as a technical term of political theory, but as both a surrogate description for (1) a process of local political dialogue leading to consensus (or a new particularity) that arises from diverse perspectives in the first instance and (2) a condition of political life which encourages the non-competitive co-existence of local mediating structures based on differing, but often symbiotic, community values. Taken with the authors' overall enthusiasm for the complementarity of mediating institutions with a healthy democratic state, this latter reading of the comments on pluralism would conclude that Berger and Neuhaus do not see conflict as the natural relationship between the state and the voluntary sector.

The second principal impact of the Berger and Neuhaus essay, and its concept of mediating institutions, relates to the contemporary critique of liberalism. Their essay is one of the earliest to decry classical liberalism's reliance upon an ahistorical and contingent definition of self and, therefore, its perceived overemphasis on the rights of individuals without due regard to the welfare of the wider community. Citing social commentators ranging from Alexis de Tocqueville and Edmund Burke to Max Weber

and Thorstein Veblen, Berger and Neuhaus argue that the loss of community threatens the future of American democracy. Their proposed remedy—encouragement of private mediating structures with a public purpose—is echoed in later writers associated with the communitarian movement, who have viewed mediating structures as a venue for civic discourse about the nature of, and appropriate remedies for, social problems, in addition to their role in the direct provision of public services (Kemmis 1990; Barber 1984; McCollough 1991).

JACQUELYN THAYER SCOTT

Barber, Benjamin, 1984. *Strong Democracy.* Berkeley: University of California Press.
Berger, Peter L., and Richard John Neuhaus, 1977. *To Empower People: The Role of Mediating Structures in Public Policy.* Washington, DC: American Enterprise Institute for Public Policy Research.
Gidron, Benjamin, Ralph M. Kramer, and Lester M. Salamon, eds., 1992. *Government and the Third Sector: Emerging Relationships in Welfare States.* San Francisco CA: Jossey-Bass.
Kemmis, Daniel, 1990. *Community and the Politics of Place.* Norman: University of Oklahoma Press.
McCollough, Thomas E., 1991. *The Moral Imagination and Public Life: Raising the Ethical Question.* Chatham, NJ: Chatham House.
Salamon, Lester M., 1994. "The Nonprofit Sector and the Evolution of the American Welfare State." In Robert D. Herman, ed., *The Jossey-Bass Handbook of Nonprofit Leadership and Management.* San Francisco CA: Jossey-Bass, 83–99.
Van Til, Jon, 1988. *Mapping the Third Sector: Voluntarism in a Changing Social Economy.* New York: Foundation Center.

MENTORING. The use of more experienced employees to assist with the orientation, training, and career advancement of newer workers. A "mentor" is "someone with whom you had a relationship at any stage of your career in which he or she took a personal interest in your career and helped to promote you and who guided or sponsored you" (Roche 1979, p. 14). As such, mentoring is an inexpensive and relatively unstructured means of career development. Understandably, it is extremely commonplace. One survey found that over 70 percent of all public managers benefit from two or more mentors during their careers (Henderson 1985).

The vast majority of mentoring relationships arise spontaneously. Older workers take younger workers "under their wings" in order to "show them the ropes." This approach is called informal mentoring; it probably occurs every day in every organization. Often, the contact is so subtle that one or even both of the participants may not recognize that mentoring is taking place. Helpful information concerning organizational norms and professional expectations is transferred, but neither party consciously considers the relationship to be that of mentor/protégé. In many other situations, conversely, employees may aggres-

sively seek out a mentor (also referred to as "patron" or "sponsor") for direction and support. Similarly, some senior managers derive great satisfaction from the mentor role; they continuously search for new subordinates on whom they can "leave their stamp."

Formal mentoring, in contrast, occurs when an organization expressly assigns experienced employees to serve as teachers and role models for subordinates (and, in some cases, for newly arriving peers). Whereas informal mentorships are not managed, structured, or technically recognized by the organization, formal mentor programs are intentionally designed to fulfill specific career management objectives. Some agencies, for example, assign mentors to all junior management personnel, or to anyone newly promoted to a supervisory position, as part of their orientation and socialization efforts. Recently, the practice of assigning senior faculty members to mentor junior faculty has almost become routine in higher education. As the advantages of mentoring programs have become known, formal efforts to foster mentor/protégé relationships have ballooned throughout government.

Historical Background

For something as ubiquitous as mentor relationships, it is not possible to ascertain specific historical stages or momentous events. Mentoring has always "just happened," a reality that is evident in literature and history. Virtually any chronicle of human behavior, from the Bible to Machiavelli's *The Prince,* contains plentiful allusions to mentors and protégés. The term itself is borrowed from the *Odyssey;* Mentor was the wise guardian who was appointed by Odysseus to protect Telemachus as he departed for the Trojan War.

Because mentoring is closely related to affiliation and friendship—differentiated only by the fact that it occurs within an organizational context—it is a pervasive phenomenon that cannot easily be studied. Thus, the management literature has only recently begun to take notice of the inherent significance that mentoring can play in an individual's professional development. Whereas research on mentors was once exceedingly sparse, greatly increased attention has been devoted to the topic during the past 10 to 15 years.

Without question, the primary catalyst for the growing interest in mentoring was the widespread influx of women and minorities into management positions. By the 1970s, researchers were preoccupied with identifying the organizational factors that enhance or impede the career progress of nontraditional managers. The mentor/protégé relationship was soon identified as a potential problem area for two reasons. Since women and minorities are sometimes viewed as interlopers (or, at a minimum, as "different"), they are thought to be less likely to attract the services of mentors. This dilemma is exacerbated by the paucity of women and minorities in high-level positions. With few white male volunteers, and with a shortage of role models who are available to serve in a mentor capacity, women and minorities appear to operate at a decided disadvantage to the white male managers, who typically enjoy plentiful mentor opportunities. Concern over this situation has heightened as research reveals the many advantages that accrue to well-mentored subordinates.

Functions and Benefits of Mentoring

If, as the adage goes, "experience is the best teacher," then mentoring is clearly an effective way to communicate knowledge to new workers. An immediate advantage that appeals to most managers is that a mentor system is virtually cost-free. Because mentoring activities occur on-the-job, there is no "down-time" while a worker is sent elsewhere for job-specific training. Likewise, even a sophisticated mentor program can be established with little outlay of resources. Once mentors and protégés are matched together, the organization's role is largely confined to monitoring progress and (in a highly progressive setting) rewarding employees who prove to be enthusiastic and effective mentors. Otherwise, little proactive effort is required on the organization's part.

The work context in which it takes place also makes mentoring an attractive training technique. The trainer and apprentice may work side-by-side, allowing for instantaneous feedback and reinforcement as complex tasks are learned. One frequently cited example is that of police patrol teams, in which a rookie is paired with an experienced officer. Under this apprentice-like system, job skills are learned while the employee is making a productive contribution to the agency's mission.

For the employee who is lucky enough to have an attentive mentor, the benefits can be profound. According to K. E. Kram (1985), the mentoring process consists of both a "career" function and a "psychosocial" function. The career activities are related to such services as coaching, being shielded from adverse assignments, and receiving access to important networks or work teams. The psychosocial function is reflected in the provision of a nurturing environment is which the mentor provides advice and guidance in a relatively nonjudgmental mode.

The specific benefits of a mentoring relationship have been summarized as follows: (1) acquisition of organizational norms and values, (2) socialization into the organization, (3) coping with structural barriers in the organization, (4) gaining information on career path experience, and (5) advancement (Hale 1992, p. 89). To this impressive list can be added such related advantages as exposure and visibility, counseling, protection, friendship, and the acquisition of challenging assignments.

A considerable body of research suggests that these benefits of mentoring are real. Individuals who receive personal attention from mentors report significantly higher levels of career success and satisfaction than employees who are not mentored. Extensive mentorship experience also correlates with the absolute number of promotions and with salary growth (Dreher and Ash 1990). These striking advantages of mentorship are thought to be related to the assistance that mentors give their protégés in the area of organizational socialization. They "guide and protect" the subordinate and "convey the necessary knowledge and information concerning organizational history, politics, people, and performance" (Chao *et al.*, 1992, p. 622). Clearly, workers who have access to this type of information concerning their organization's "realpolitik" have a marked advantage over those who do not.

In summarizing much of the research, Mary Hale (1992) concludes that the career enhancement benefits of mentoring are largely attributable to four factors. First, mentored workers are more successful at "coping successfully with organizational barriers" (p. 92), thanks to the advice and counsel of individuals who have already negotiated the bureaucratic maze. Second, because of the access provided by their mentors, they are better able to cultivate linkages with influential decisionmakers and to gain membership on successful teams. Third, they are more likely than unmentored workers to be aware of critical information that assists them in making career choices. Knowledge about career options, salary expectations, and professional development opportunities provides them with a tactical advantage over their competitors. Finally, mentoring relationships have been found to enhance workers' job and career satisfaction. Dee Henderson (1985) found that mentored employees enjoy their jobs more than other workers, are more likely to risk relocating during their careers, and tend to reach executive levels at earlier ages. In sum, the evidence is overwhelming that mentors provide a valuable service to workers striving to climb the organizational ladder.

Although most research attention has focused on the advantages to workers, the mentors themselves also derive certain benefits from the relationships. The psychosocial rewards are mutual in that both the superior and subordinate can enjoy the friendship and comradery that often exist between teacher and protégé. Many individuals are also motivated by the simple satisfaction that is gained from passing on wisdom and developing the next generation of managers (Aldag and Stearns 1987). Their interactions with subordinates, meanwhile, usually intensify the workers' loyalty to the mentor. Thus, managers who are generous with their mentoring talents are usually quite popular among subordinates.

Another important consideration is that one's reputation as a manager, both inside and outside the organization, can be greatly embellished through the mentoring process. Employees who are known for cultivating and

nurturing the skills of their subordinates are treasured commodities. They have no difficulty attracting the best assistants to work with them, and they are in great demand by other organizations. One needs only to look at the coaching fraternity to appreciate these realities. The most successful coaches—those who are "household names"—are almost always the best mentors, as evidenced by the number of former assistants who have gone on to productive careers of their own. Interestingly, an identical phenomenon exists in city management, where a few beloved "deans" of the profession are nationally known for developing and refining their former assistants' skills.

Other Research Findings

In general, mentor relationships are most common—and probably most helpful—early in one's career. However, even older managers report significant levels of mentor involvement in many settings. Public executives are more likely than their private-sector counterparts to acquire external mentors, such as college professors or acquaintances in different organizations. Also, the organizational rank of public-sector mentors tends to be higher than those in business and industry. Public managers are much more likely to receive tutoring from a top official—such as an agency director or city manager—than is the typical business worker. Reduced levels of competition, coupled with the public service ethos, have been suggested as possible explanations for this phenomenon.

As mentioned earlier, women reportedly face a particularly difficult challenge in finding effective mentors. Much of the evidence is inconclusive and/or contradictory concerning the severity of this problem. It appears as if women generally have mentors with about the same frequency as men (Hale 1992), or perhaps at even a slightly higher frequency (Henderson 1985).

The primary difference between the two genders is that there is a strong same-sex bias. That is, both men and women prefer to have mentors of their own sex. This preference is partly attributable to sexual tensions between opposite gender pairs. Women are reluctant to initiate mentoring relationships with men because their action may be misconstrued as sexual advances (Ragins and Cotton 1993). Also, same-sex pairings are thought to be more effective because women and men need and expect different types of support from their mentors. Women are in greater need of assistance in such areas as building self-confidence, improving self-awareness of management style, and balancing career and family obligations (Hale 1992, p. 101). Men, in contrast, are more often concerned with tactical considerations and improving task-related skills. The chief consequence of these preferences is that successful women managers are overburdened with requests for mentor assistance from their female subordinates.

Designing Mentor Programs

Managers seeking to maximize the benefits of mentor programs need to consider the differences between the formal and informal approaches. Although having any mentor program is better than not having one at all, mentoring relationships engineered through a formal program are less fruitful than those that arise naturally from personal attraction (Chao *et al.* 1992). The satisfaction level of workers in informal arrangements is higher, and they report more promotions and salary increases than those in formally sanctioned programs. These differences may be linked to the bad matches that will inevitably result when mentors are assigned and to resentment that is probably generated on both sides of the relationship. The mentor may resent the time and energy demands of the assignment, while the protégé may feel uncomfortable (or even demeaned) by the arrangement. Another potential dilemma is that mentoring may result in a mutual dependency relationship under which the employee loses self-sufficiency and the mentor refuses to "let go" (Vertz 1985). For these reasons, managers who simply assign mentors to new workers are probably following the least effective path.

Short of assigning mentors to all upwardly mobile employees, then, what can management safely do to encourage these relationships? First, most experts agree that managers should target certain groups of workers. One logical application is to the transitional employee who has just been promoted to a managerial position from a technical or professional specialty. Whenever such mentorships are arranged, however, participation should be strictly voluntary for both teacher and protégé. Moreover, the mentorship program should be part of a broader career-planning effort (Phillips-Jones 1983) that also includes peer counseling and structured professional development opportunities.

Another step that managers can take to promote the development of mentor activities is to elevate their visibility within the organization. Perhaps the most effective strategy is to provide potential mentors with training on their roles and responsibilities. This might be supplemented with sessions designed to sensitize managers to the gender-based problems that sometimes surface between opposite-sex pairs.

Some organizations have also discovered that they can foster mentorships by providing increased opportunities for worker interaction. Networking breakfasts and weekend retreats can place workers in situations that encourage informal associations. Often, the truly meaningful mentorships arise from these types of low-pressure contact between superiors and subordinates.

A final step that might be taken to solidify the importance of mentor programs in managers' minds is to include them in the organization's incentive system. If managers receive formal recognition for their mentoring efforts, more are likely to volunteer and to invest the requisite energies in the task. Thus, the inclusion of mentorships in the annual evaluation process, or in salary determinations, is a nonintrusive but highly effective means of encouraging this form of employee development activity.

STEVEN W. HAYS

BIBLIOGRAPHY

Aldag, R. J., and T. M. Stearns, 1987. *Management.* Cincinnati, OH: South-Western Publishing, 834–835.

Chao, G., P. Walz, and P. Gardner, 1992. "Formal and Informal Mentorships: A Comparison of the Mentoring Functions and Contrasts with Nonmentored Counterparts." *Personnel Psychology*, vol. 45 (Autumn) 619–636.

Dreher, F., and R. Ash, 1990. "A Comparative Study of Mentoring among Men and Women in Managerial, Professional, and Technical Positions." *Journal of Applied Psychology*, vol. 75 (Summer) 539–546.

Hale, Mary M., 1992. "Mentoring." In Mary E. Guy, ed., *Women and Men of the States*. Armonk, New York: M. E. Sharpe, 89–108.

Hays, Steve W., and Richard C. Kearney, 1995. "Promotion of Personnel—Career Advancement." In Jack Rabin, Thomas Vocino, W. Bartley Hildreth, and Gerald Miller, eds., *Handbook of Public Personnel Administration*. New York: Marcel Dekker, 499–529.

Henderson, Dee, 1985. "Enlightened Mentoring: A Characteristic of Public Management Professionalism." *Public Administration Review*, vol. 45 (November-December) 857–863.

Kram, K. E., 1985. *Mentoring at Work: Developmental Relationships in Organizational Life*. Glenview, IL: Scott, Foresman.

Phillips-Jones, L., 1983. "Establishing a Formalized Mentoring Program." *Training and Development Journal* (February) 38–42.

Ragins, Belle R., and John L. Cotton, 1993. "Wanted: Mentors for Women." *Personnel Journal* (April) 20.

Roche, G., 1979. "Much Ado About Mentors." *Harvard Business Review*, vol. 57 (January–February) 14–28.

Vertz, L., 1985. "Women, Occupational Advancement, and Mentoring: An Analysis of One Public Organization." *Public Administration Review*, vol. 45 (May–June) 415–422.

MERIT SYSTEM.

An employment system in which decisions regarding entrance into the system and decisions regarding the allocation of rewards to employees within the system are based upon merit criteria rather than family lineage, spoils, political partisanship, or other possible decisionmaking standards.

Whereas the public service is a more general concept composed of elected officials, political appointees, and career civil servants, the merit system is a subdivision of the public service and includes only those public servants chosen through competitive merit-based selection processes and evaluated and promoted based on similar merit-based criteria.

A merit system may be established as a "closed" system with promotions only granted from within—that is, to employees already a part of the system (English model)—or it may permit entry from outside the system at different levels within the bureaucratic structure depending on a candidate's level of merit (American model).

In the United States, the percentage of federal positions that are a part of some merit system has constantly grown since the passage of the Pendleton Act of 1883 establishing the original merit system. Following the passage of this act, the percentage of federal civil service positions that were a part of merit systems grew from 10 percent in the 1880s to around 90 percent by the 1990s.

Two components closely associated with merit systems are job security and political neutrality. One idea behind the establishment of the original merit system in the national government was to ensure some continuity in governmental service even with the change of presidential administrations. Thus, when employees are first placed in a merit system position, they must successfully complete a probationary period in which they demonstrate their competence on the job. After this competence has been demonstrated, they are given permanent status and job security. This means that they have some legal rights to the job and cannot be dismissed without these due process rights (*Board of Regents v. Roth* 1972).

Employees within merit systems, in exchange for job security, are expected to carry out in a neutral manner the policies of the incumbent administration, no matter which political party the president and the president's appointees may represent. This concept of political neutrality for merit system employees in the United States was addressed in part by the Pendleton Act through provisions prohibiting officials from using their authority to coerce political action from others, and provisions making mandatory political contributions for merit system employees illegal. Later, in the Hatch Acts of 1939 and 1940, federal employees, as well as state and local employees working in federal programs, were specifically prohibited from active participation in partisan political campaigns. Many state governments, following the national governments' example, passed similar state legislation enacting such prohibitions for state and local employees.

These legal restrictions were enacted to guarantee the public the right to treatment by its servants free from prejudices caused by partisanship, and in order to protect public employees from being forced by elected officials into mandated partisan campaign efforts. Yet, since their passage, these restrictions have been controversial. Public-employee organizations in the United States have generally opposed Hatch Act restrictions on partisan activities, and in 1994 Congress responded to some of these complaints by amending the Hatch Act to allow more freedom of political participation, even in partisan campaigns, for federal employees. Merit system employee rights are still not the same as general citizen rights under the First Amendment, but they are certainly greater now than prior to the 1994 amendments.

Thus, merit systems rest on competence-based selection and allocation of rewards, on employee probationary periods followed by guarantees of job security for successful employees, and on the concept of a neutral delivery of nonpartisan services to the general public.

ROBERT H. ELLIOTT

BIBLIOGRAPHY

"An Act to Regulate and Improve the Civil Service of the United States," 1883 (The Pendleton Act). United States Congress, 22 Stat. 27.
Board of Regents v. Roth, 408 U.S. 564, 1972.
Elliott, Robert H., 1985. *Public Personnel Administration: A Values Perspective.* Reston, VA: Reston.
Pearson, William M., and David S. Castle, 1993. "Expanding the Opportunity for Partisan Activity among Government Employees: Potential Effects on Federal Executives' Political Involvement." *International Journal of Public Administration*, vol. 16 (April) 511–525.

METAPHOR, ORGANIZATIONAL.

A means by which organizational writers and scholars use metaphors (a word or phrase literally denoting one kind of object or idea in place of another used in order to suggest a likeness between them) in attempts to capture and communicate the essence of organizations (Trice and Beyer 1993). These comparisons are used to reach an "understanding and an experiencing of one kind of thing in terms of another" (Lakoff and Johnson 1980, p. 43).

The use of organizational metaphors implies ways of thinking about or of perceiving reality in and about organizations and their environments (Morgan 1986). "Current studies of metaphor recognize that it is not simply a stylistic embellishment of literal language, but actually shapes the experience of social actors. . . . Metaphors serve to produce and reproduce the organizational structure that they describe" (Mumby 1988, p. 18). For example, "an organization is a machine," or "an organization is a living organism." The primary value or purpose for using organizational metaphors is to help people—particularly participants in an organization—to frame reality. Organizations are complex societies that are characterized by ambiguity, politics of interpretation, and conflicting interests. Thus, "participants are presented with slogans and metaphors ("Tech is a bottom-up company," or "We are a football team") with which the complex reality that is Tech is to be expressed" (Kunda 1992, p. 154).

For years, metaphors have been used to portray organizations as orderly, machine-like entities. "The development of theories of organization [was] the history of the metaphor of orderliness" (Meadows 1967, p. 82). Classical organization theory dominated organization theory from the industrial revolution of the 1700s well into the 1930s and remains highly influential today (Merkle 1980). The basic tenets and assumptions of classical organization theory are grounded in the machine-like professions of mechanical engineering, industrial engineering, and economics:

1. "Organizations exist to accomplish production-related and economic goals.
2. There is one best way to organize for production, and that way can be found through systematic, scientific inquiry.
3. Production is maximized through specialization and division of labor.
4. People and organizations act in accordance with rational economic principles" (Shafritz and Ott 1996, p. 31).

In several more recent theories of organization, metaphors serve different purposes. For example, the primary purpose that metaphors serve in symbolic or cultural theories is to help organizational participants create shared meanings or engage in "sensemaking." Organizations are complex and rapidly shifting minisocieties in which "reality" can be difficult or impossible to discern (Smircich 1983; Weick 1995). "Sensemaking is about plausibility, coherence, and reasonableness. . . . In an equivocal, postmodern world, infused with the politics of interpretation and conflicting interests and inhabited by people with multiple shifting identities, an obsession with accuracy seems fruitless, and not of much practical help, either. Of much more help are the symbolic trappings of sensemaking, trappings such as myths, metaphors, platitudes, fables, epics, and paradigms" (Weick 1995, p. 61). Metaphors help organizational members to infuse their organizational experiences with meaning and to resolve dilemmas and paradoxes. "The use of metaphors helps to couple the organization, to tie its parts together into some kind of meaningful whole; that is, metaphors help to organize the objective facts of the situation in the minds of the participants. . . . Metaphors serve as models *of* the situation and models *for* the situation" (Pondy 1983, p. 157).

Some current systems theorists have adopted an organic metaphor of organization that shares some similarities with classical theory's machine metaphor—but also endows the machine with life. "Organizations in this view retain many machine-like properties, but their internal processes and their relationships with their environments now become 'dynamic.' As living entities, organizations not only have bodies but sense and response systems as well. Like all organisms, they must learn to adapt themselves to increasingly complex and changing environments or face the penalty that nature exacts from any species ill adapted to its environment—extinction. . . . The organic metaphor is seen in the view that speaks of the 'health' of

organizations, of 'organizational personality,' and of 'organizational climate'" (Greenfield 1984, pp. 148–149).

Gareth Morgan's 1986 book *Images of Organization* brought metaphors to "center stage" of organization theory. In it, organizations are described as eight metaphors: as machines, as organisms, as brains, as cultures, as political systems, as psychic prisons, as flux and transformation, and as instruments of domination. Morgan describes *images* as "a treatise on metaphorical thinking" (p. 16) about complex, ambiguous, and paradoxical organizations, not as an exhaustive list of metaphorical possibilities.

J. STEVEN OTT

BIBLIOGRAPHY

Greenfield, Thomas B., 1984. "Leaders and Schools: Willfulness and Nonnatural Order in Organizations." In T. J. Sergiovanni and J. E. Corbally, eds., *Leadership and Organizational Culture.* Urbana: University of Illinois Press.

Kunda, Gideon, 1992. *Engineering Culture: Control and Commitment in a High-Tech Corporation Engineering Culture: Control and Commitment in a High-Tech Corporation.* Philadelphia: Temple University Press.

Lakoff, George, and Mark Johnson, 1980. *Metaphors We Live By.* Chicago: University of Chicago Press.

Meadows, Paul, 1967. "The Metaphor of Order: Toward a Taxonomy of Organization Theory." In Gross and Lewellyn, eds., *Sociological Theory: Inquiries and Paradigms.* New York: Harper & Row.

Merkle, Judith A., 1980. *Management and Ideology.* Berkeley: University of California Press.

Morgan, Gareth, 1986. *Images of Organization.* Beverly Hills, CA: Sage.

Mumby, Dennis K., 1988. *Communication and Power in Organizations: Discourse, Ideology, and Domination.* Norwood, NJ: Ablex.

Pondy, Louis R., 1983. "The Role of Metaphors and Myths in Organization and in the Facilitation of Change." In L. R. Pondy, G. Morgan, P. J. Frost, and T. C. Dandridge, eds., *Organizational Symbolism.* Greenwich, CT: JAI Press.

Shafritz, Jay M., and J. Steven Ott, eds., 1996. *Classics of Organization Theory,* 4th ed. Ft. Worth, TX: Harcourt Brace.

Smircich, Linda, 1983. "Organizations as Shared Meanings." In L. R. Pondy, G. Morgan, P. J. Frost, and T. C. Dandridge, eds., *Organizational Symbolism.* Greenwich, CT: JAI Press.

Trice, Harrison M., and Janice M. Beyer, 1993. *The Cultures of Work Organizations.* Englewood Cliffs, NJ: Prentice-Hall.

Weick, Karl E., 1995. *Sensemaking in Organizations.* Thousand Oaks, CA: Sage.

METROPOLITAN ORGANIZATION. Implies, combined with governance, the centralization of some service functions as well as aspects of the governing mechanism in the hands of a newly created metropolitanwide political unit.

One of the major characteristics of government in metropolitan areas is "fragmentation." Metropolitan areas are divided into a large and diverse number of overlapping governmental units: municipalities, counties, authorities, and special districts, including school districts, community college districts, water and sewer districts, library districts, and park districts. Even without being aware of it, citizens in the metropolis are receiving public services from several different local governmental bodies.

Such multiple responsibility for service provision often leads to chaos and confusion. With so many governments, effective, coordinated action and service delivery are not always possible. Citizens cannot easily see where their tax money is going or who is to blame for service inadequacies. By contrast, some argue that fragmentation allows for the highest values to be placed on consumer choice by allowing residents to vote with their feet in determining which communities in the metropolitan area provide the right mix of services and taxes for each family.

Some urbanists have called for a system of "metropolitan government" to rationalize governmental structure and service delivery in the metropolis. Under metropolitan government a number of important decisionmaking powers would be taken away from the existing local governments and given to a new centralized metropolitan body capable of acting in the interest of the metropolis as a whole.

Yet, the establishment of a metropolitan government possessing significant authority has been realized in only a few urban areas across the United States. Incorporated suburban governments refuse to sacrifice their autonomy for the ideal of establishing a new centralized regional governing institution. In most metropolitan areas, cities and suburbs cooperated with one another only on a limited and, to a great degree, voluntary basis.

Interlocal cooperation has taken a wide variety of forms. Informal cooperation, intergovernmental contracting, and the creation of special districts are among the most popular mechanisms that contiguous suburbs have resorted to in an attempt to improve the provision of schooling, water supply, sewage disposal, transportation, and other services to their citizens. This variety of cooperative solutions allows suburbs to enhance service delivery without threatening their autonomy.

But critics charge that the institutionalization of this vast variety of interlocal cooperative arrangements compounds certain problems of governing metropolitan regions. For instance, the increasing resort to special districts and independent authorities has shifted broad areas of public policymaking responsibility from locally elected officials to the relatively invisible and insulated program specialists who populate the boards and agencies of these special districts and service areas. Interlocal cooperation can also be time-consuming and cumbersome. Critics further point out that local jurisdictions will cooperate only to the extent they find it convenient to do so. Many urbanists,

then, continue to call for the establishment of strong, centralized, metropolitan governments. But as we shall see, the political opposition to metropolitan government remains so strong that, in all but a few cases, the enactment of truly effective regional governing structures remains an impossibility.

Three Forms of Metropolitan Government

Proposals for metropolitanwide governments entail boundary changes, which carry with them an implicit alteration in power relationships. Suburban residents and local officials generally do not want to cede power to new regional governing institutions. Americans are also a generally conservative people who prefer their existing fragmented and flawed governmental arrangements instead of the proposed changes that might be brought about by more comprehensive governmental reform.

Yet, a number of metropolitan areas, including Jacksonville, Baton Rouge, Nashville, Lexington (Kentucky), Indianapolis, Miami, Portland, and Minneapolis–St. Paul, do have some form of metropolitan government. Special circumstances help to explain how centralized regional governments were established in these areas despite widespread opposition to their enactment. I will identify three forms of metropolitan government: city-county consolidation, the two-tier plan, and the three-tier plan.

Under city-county consolidation, a county and the cities within it merge to form a single governmental unit. The county, in effect, becomes the government of the entire metropolitan region as other local governments are eliminated. In some cases, existing local governments are allowed to keep their identities after consolidation, but their powers are curtailed as increased authority is transferred to the enhanced countywide unit. The achievement of consolidation usually requires state legislative approval as well as approval at the polls by voters in both the central city and contiguous political units in the metropolitan area.

While consolidations in a number of smaller urban areas have been realized, the great majority of all consolidation plans never achieve enactment. Three important consolidation efforts that did succeed were in Nashville-Davidson County, Tennessee (1962); Jacksonville-Duval County, Florida (1967), and Unigov in Indianapolis-Marion County (1969). In Jacksonville-Duval County, Florida, the metropolitan reform movement was triggered by public concern over criminal indictments of numerous public officials. Unigov, or the merger of Indianapolis with Marion County, was aided by a number of special circumstances: the unique political alignment of forces, the leadership efforts of the mayor of the city of Indianapolis at the time, and the absence of a strong home rule tradition in Indiana.

What can be concluded from a review of city-county consolidation efforts throughout the United States? First of all, consolidation is quite difficult to achieve; most consolidation efforts fail. Second, the consolidation of multi-county areas is a virtual impossibility. Third, an important impetus to reform exists where suburban areas desire improved service levels or where reorganization is perceived as a means of getting rid of corrupt or incompetent officials. City-county consolidation is also to a great extent a regional phenomenon, occuring mostly in the south.

Under two-tier restructuring, two levels of government are established in a metropolitan area. Areawide functions are assigned to an areawide, or metropolitan, government with boundaries that encompass all the individual local government units. More localized functions, however, are left to the existing municipalities; there is no consolidation or merger of governments. A variation of this restructuring is commonly called the "federation plan"; local governments retain their existence but, in effect, are represented in a new federation that handles areawide concerns. Metropolitan Toronto and Winnipeg are two prominent Canadian examples of the federation plan; their local unit members are referred to as "boroughs."

In the United States, Metro Miami-Dade County, established in 1957, is the only important example of a two-tired system. The creation of Metro Miami was facilitated by a number of special circumstances. At the time of Metro's formation, many of the residents of Dade County's suburbs were not long-time residents of the region; as a result, they had little time to develop strong attachments to their communities or strong resentment against the city of Miami. Yet, the implementation of the two-tiered plan in Miami-Dade County has not always been easy. The wealthier communities in the county opposed the plan from the beginning. The creation of Metro Miami was marked by severe conflict and debate. Still, over the years, Metro has gained increased acceptance.

The three-tier reform is a rarely used approach that tried to deal with the problems of multicounty areas. It derives its name from the fact that it keeps the existing county and municipal levels of government but seeks to add an areawide coordinating agency with some real power on top. The three-tier reform is a plan for limited metropolitan government that seeks to avoid the hostility that often greets more comprehensive unification efforts. The two most prominent examples of this approach are the Greater Portland (Oregon) Metropolitan Service District, an elected body, and the Twin Cities (Minneapolis–St. Paul) Metropolitan Council, an appointed body. The Metropolitan Council represents a much praised approach to regional government. Yet, it is a model that is not likely to be replicated in a great many other metropolitan areas across the United States. Portland, on the other hand, has just strengthened the powers and scope of its Metropolitan

Service District in many of the capital-intensive, nonsocial issues.

Is Metropolitan Government Desirable?

There exists a sharp debate between two schools of thought regarding the desirability of metropolitan reform. "Metropolitanists" seek a consolidation of some or all of the local governments in the metropolitan area in order to provide more uniform resource and service distribution over a wide range of communities. The more comprehensive forms of metropolitan reorganization are quite difficult to realize. Yet, a second school of thought questions whether the achievement of more comprehensive metropolitan government is really worth the effort. These "polycentrists" favor the status quo, whereby a multitude of autonomous governments continue to exist in a metropolitan area. The polycentrists believe that a multicentered or polycentric metropolis can better serve its citizens. Each local government can provide a different quantity and quality of service as demanded by its constituents. This permits families to "shop" in the metropolitan market for the mix of services that best meets their needs at a specific time.

Political Power and Metropolitan Reform

Future prospects for comprehensive reform are not very good. Except when special circumstances facilitate their creation, the achievement of one-tier, two-tier, and three-tier governments in most American metropolitan areas remains a serious political challenge. Too many powerful interests, including minorities, suburban residents, and suburban business interests coalesce and keep a watchful eye on proposals for metropolitan reform.

Given the strong constellation of powers that usually opposes metropolitan reform, it takes a unique situation and the organization of a countervailing coalition to bring about reform. Outside power is often necessary to bring about metropolitan reform. The residents of the Toronto, Indianapolis, and Minneapolis–St. Paul Twin Cities areas all had new metropolitan arrangements imposed on them from above by state (or provincial) governments.

Complete metropolitan reform represents a major political test. Metropolitanists will have to settle for something less. Perhaps the best that can be hoped for is an intermediate level of reform. Voluntary, cooperative solutions do provide certain benefits. They increase communications among jurisdictions, they encourage joint problem solving, and they save money by realizing economies of scale. Even in the absence of a centralized metropolitan government, metropolitan governance still takes place. I will now turn to an analysis of these more commonplace forms of intergovernmental cooperation.

The Easiest Means
of Metropolitan Cooperation

"Informal cooperation" represents the desire on the part of officials from two or more local governments to cooperate to improve service. It might entail nothing more than the sharing or exchanging of information; or it may entail an unwritten agreement whereby one jurisdiction is allowed to use equipment owned by another. Informal cooperation is clearly the most pragmatic, and probably the most widely practiced, approach to regionalism. However, what can be accomplished through informal collaboration is greatly limited. Such collaboration rarely requires fiscal actions and only rarely involves matters of regional or even subregional significance, let alone a realignment of power in the region.

"Interlocal service contracts" are legally binding agreements entered into by two (or more) governments under which one government agrees to provide a service that the other pays for upon receiving it. Smaller jurisdictions are able to obtain a service, such as water or sewage disposal, that they could never hope to provide for themselves except at a very high cost. These jurisdictions can also choose just what quantity and quality of service they wish to pay for.

One very interesting example of intergovernmental contracting is provided by the *Lakewood Plan*. The plan takes its name from the suburban Los Angeles community, which incorporated in the mid-1950s after Los Angeles County's enactment of this plan. The Lakewood Plan offers such a wide range of services to participating jurisdictions that a locality can choose to purchase all or nearly all of its services from the county. One advantage of the Lakewood Plan and service contracting is the economy of scale that is offered. Yet, the Lakewood Plan is also the target of severe criticism. Some have argued that the county, as the dominant service provider, exercises too much influence in determining the quantity, quality, price, and style of the services delivered. The Lakewood Plan also exacerbates the problem of metropolitan fragmentation.

Under "joint powers agreements" two or more units of local government agree to work together in the financing and delivery of a service to their citizens. A variation of the joint powers agreement is "parallel action" whereby two or more governments pursue their agreed-upon commitments separately, even though the results are designed to benefit both parties.

"Extraterritorial powers" are allowed in cities in 35 U.S. states. Under these powers, certain cities in a state are given authority outside their boundaries over some of the actions of contiguous unincorporated areas. Texas state law, for instance, grants the state's cities the right to regulate subdivisions on unincorporated land lying adjacent to the city.

The "councils of governments" (COGs) approach essentially consists of bringing together on a voluntary basis the top elected officials of municipalities in a metropolitan area. These officials, or their representatives, meet on a regular basis to discuss problems of mutual interest and to share information and ideas. One of the primary concerns of COGs has been the preparation and implementation of a comprehensive plan for regional growth and development.

The COG approach was initiated with great hopes. Yet, the weaknesses of COGs soon became apparent. First, COGs are only advisory in nature. They possess no substantial legislative power or authority. Second, COGs are voluntary organizations from which members can withdraw at any time. Third, COGs have few independent sources of revenue; they are dependent to a great extent on the financial contributions of their members as well as on federal and/or state grant-in-aid programs. COGs are heavily dependent upon federal funding. Reductions in federal support are not generally compensated for by increased local contributions, as few localities see COG operations and regionalism as major priorities.

Fourth, many COGs are quite understaffed. Fifth, the "one government, one vote" rule of many COGs gives disproportionate power to smaller jurisdictions at the expense of central cities and larger suburbs. On the whole, COGs remain very weak mechanisms of metropolitan cooperation. Like the United Nations, they can debate, discuss, and suggest, but they cannot enforce action on any of their numbers.

"Federally encouraged single-purpose regional bodies" are planning agencies established in such areas as economic development, job training, metropolitan transportation, and assistance to Appalachia, as a result of federal aid requirements.

"State planning and development districts" (SPDDs) were established as states sought to attain some control over federal spending in metropolitan areas. In the 1980s, SPDDs took on the responsibilities of the regional clearinghouse function as a result of Reagan's efforts to decentralize and devolve decisionmaking to subnational units of governing.

During the Bush administration, Congress passed the Intermodal Surface Transportation Efficiency Act (ISTEA). This legislation redirected federal transportation policy from states to metropolitan planning organizations, thereby encouraging greater flexibility within individual projects.

Contracting with the private sector follows the same logic as intergovernmental service contracts; only here municipal governments enter into agreements with private-sector firms, not with other governmental jurisdictions for the provision of specified services. Public-sector unions, in particular, oppose private-sector contracting, fearing that municipalities will issue such contracts in order to circumvent union protections and undermine municipal workforce wage structures.

Structural Changes

David Walker identifies six other approaches to metropolitan service delivery that are a bit more difficult to achieve than the easiest six. Each of these means of structural reform represents a more stable way to effectively align governmental and service delivery boundaries without asking regions to turn to metropolitan government. Nevertheless, they do represent an alteration in existing power relationships.

"Local special districts" are units of government that provide a specific service or a related set of services. The overwhelming number of special districts provide a special service. Special districts have proved to be a flexible means of providing services. Special district boundaries can crosscut municipal, county, and even state lines. District size can vary with the service provided and the needs that are identified. The growth in the number of special districts over the years is due to the advantage of economies of scale and the fact that local governments do not have to change their boundaries or surrender their autonomy.

A "transfer of functions" entails a permanent shift in the responsibility of providing a service from one jurisdiction to another that is better able to handle the service or realize the economies of scale. Despite the increased use of the mechanism in recent years, the intergovernmental reassignment of functions still faces some serious limitations. Less than half the states authorize such shifts; and half the states require voter approval before any transfer is finalized. Furthermore, political rivalries can stand in the way of service transfer.

"Annexation" is the acquisition of additional territory to enlarge the existing governmental jurisdiction. Annexation occurs when a municipality extends its boundaries outward, thereby absorbing a contiguous area. Annexations are almost always of areas that are still unincorporated. This is because most states seek to protect the sovereignty of incorporated municipalities. When the annexation of an incorporated area is attempted, state laws usually require "dual referenda"—that is, citizens in both jurisdictions must approve of the proposed consolidation. This requirement greatly impedes the ability of older cities surrounded by incorporated suburban municipalities to annex new land. Even in the Sunbelt, aggressive annexation is no longer universal.

"Regional special districts and authorities" are large areawide institutions that usually are established by state law. Where interstate agreements are negotiated, such regional authorities can even provide services across state borders. The metropolitan authority usually has the power to issue revenue bonds, but not the power to tax. But even these large regional units of government are not the perfect answer to the metropolitan fragmentation problem. Such authorities are difficult to set up as they require special state enactment and may face opposition by more local-ized units of government that fear a loss of power to the larger unit.

"Metropolitan multipurpose districts" are regional districts set up to provide a diverse variety of services. However, this regional governance mechanism has proved to be among the most difficult to set up. Only a few states authorize the creation of such broadly empowered districts but still restrict the range of services to be offered. Metro Seattle represents the classic case study of this structural innovation.

The "reformed urban county" is often suggested as an institution that can provide improved services, particularly to the suburban and fringe portions of the metropolis. Suburban residents have increasingly come to expect higher levels of urban service delivery. To meet these new service expectations, urban and suburban counties have had to modernize their structures. Yet, even the modernized county does not provide the answer to all the problems posed by the metropolitan fragmentation problem.

Conclusion

Suburban residents are opposed not just to the idea of metropolitan government but to any interlocal cooperative plan that might result in increased local taxes. Local businesses, too, will oppose intergovernmental cooperative arrangements that threaten to raise their taxes. Yet, a wide variety of interlocal accommodative arrangements does exist. Even the residents of affluent bedroom communities have recognized the benefits that can be brought by joint action. Business interests, too, will press for metropolitan reform measures that are in their financial interests.

In areas such as pollution control, economic development, and mass transit construction, new regional problem-solving efforts are being attempted. Some suburbs have even begun informally to cooperate with central cities in very limited school and housing integration plans. Other areas are collaborating in recreation, land use, and public safety. Yet, for the most part, voluntary intergovernmental cooperation has been lacking in social welfare matters and other service areas where the shared benefits of joint action are less apparent. Paradoxically, metropolitan governance is alive and well but still quite limited in what it can achieve.

BERNARD H. ROSS

BIBLIOGRAPHY

Bish, Robert L., and Vincent Ostrom, 1973. *Understanding Urban Government: Metropolitan Reform Reconsidered.* Washington, DC: American Enterprise Institute.

Cion, Richard M., 1971. "Accommodation par Excellence: The Lakewood Plan." In Michael N. Danielson, ed., *Metropolitan Politics: A Reader,* 2d ed. Boston: Little Brown.

Downs, Anthony, 1994. *New Vision for Metropolitan America.* Washington, DC: Brookings Institution.

Florestano, Patricia S., and Stephen B. Gordon, 1981. "A Survey of City and County Use of Private Contracting." *Urban Interest,* vol. 3 (Spring).

Harrigan, John J., 1993. *Political Change in the Metropolis,* 5th ed. New York: HarperCollins.

Lyons, W. E., David Lowery, and Ruth Hoogland DeHoog, 1992. *The Politics of Dissatisfaction: Citizens, Services, and Urban Institutions.* Armonk, NY: M. E. Sharpe.

Marando, Vincent L., 1979. "City-County Consolidation: Reform, Regionalism, Referenda, and Requiem." *Western Political Quarterly,* vol. 32 (December).

Ostrom, Vincent, Charles Tiebout, and Robert Warren, 1961. "The Organization of Government in Metropolitan Areas." *American Political Science Review,* vol. 55 (December) 831–842.

Rusk, David, 1994. *Cities without Suburbs.* Baltimore: Johns Hopkins University Press.

Scott, Stanley, and John Corzine, 1971. "Special Districts in the Bay Area." In Michael N. Danielson, ed. *Metropolitan Politics: A Reader,* 2d ed. Boston: Little Brown.

Sofen, Edward, 1963. *The Miami Metropolitan Experiment.* Bloomington: University of Indiana Press.

Stein, Robert, 1990. *Urban Alternatives: Public and Private Markets in the Provision of Local Services.* Pittsburgh: University of Pittsburgh Press.

Walker, David, 1987. "Snow White and the 17 Dwarfs: From Metro Cooperation to Governance." *National Civic Review,* vol. 76 (January-February).

———, 1995. *The Rebirth of Federalism; Slouching Toward Washington.* Chatham, NJ: Chatham House.

MEXICAN ADMINISTRATIVE TRADITION.

The management practices and administrative cultures of Mexico.

Historical Overview of Mexican Public Administration

Colonial Administration (1521–1821)

The central and southern regions of the current Mexican territory were inhabited by various civilizations. The Aztecs (1325–1521) ruled over a vast empire of indigenous peoples that was finally defeated by the conqueror Hernán Cortés.

Since its beginning, Spanish rule over the Kingdom of the New Spain was acknowledged as being part of the two main components of the Christian world: the *Ecclesia Universalis* and the *Imperium Universale*. In accordance with the European conception of conquest, the Spaniards developed an ambition for a universal political society, the *Respublica Christiana,* that summarized church and empire, reflecting the Christian aspiration toward the unity of humankind. Since 1519, Emperor Carlos V has been the sole incarnation of this cosmogonic view and ancient tradition that made him the *Dominus Mundi,* with supreme

rights above all, rulers and vassels as well. The conquest of Mexico was achieved under this conception, under his name, advocacy, inspiration, and authority. Under this belief, Cortés presented himself as the envoy of the Master of the World, urging the natives to submit to their lord at once and to embrace the Catholic faith, by will or by force.

Throughout 300 years of Spanish domination (1521–1821), centralization of power was the main characteristic of the New Spain colonial government (present-day Mexico). Regarding the colony as a source of wealth and as a place for Christianization, the Habsburgs (1524) ruled the colony from Spain through the Indias Council (*Consejo de Indias*). The council was the central agency in charge of administration, supervision, and regulation of financial, judicial, political, military, commercial, and church businesses of the colony. Later on, with the arrival of the first viceroy of New Spain, Antonio de Mendoza (1535), a process of power concentration started, benefiting mainly the viceroy and the colonial officials. This process determined the centralized way of organizing public administration, which would endure and label the entire colonial time. The government of New Spain ended up operating in total independence from the metropolis. In the long run, this administrative independence made it very difficult to coordinate the colonial governmental actions with the Crown's orders.

The Catholic Church is also an important element to understand colonial public administration; it influenced the society with its norms and hierarchy, and the economy with its wealth and possessions. The spiritual and economic power of the church would turn it into a major competitor to the Crown. This struggle between the government and the church started during colonial times and continued during the first decades of independent Mexico.

By 1700, the colonial government organization had visible malfunctions. Colonial public administration was a complex and sluggish apparatus in solving administrative problems. This fact and the centralized scheme of the viceroy's government made the Spanish Crown lose control over the colony. That is why, as other colonial powers did, the new royal house in Spain—the Bourbons—considered it necessary to make a deep reform to liberate the economy from the strict colonial control and to decentralize the administration.

The Bourbons ruled with the absolutist and mercantilistic ideas of their time. They opposed the existence of corporate or private powers, which could be rivals to the Spanish Crown's own power. One of the first tasks of Carlos III (1750) was to gain back for the Crown the prerogatives that the Habsburgs had lost by virtue of corporations and traders. In the political domain, the most important action was the king's decision to subordinate the church's power by making it submit to the Crown. He expelled the Jesuits from Spain and its colonies (1767) and passed a royal law (1804) that restricted the church's power to purchase real estate. Regarding the economy, free trade norms were established in order to finish with trade monopolies, such as the Commercial Consulate of Mexico City (*Consulado Commercial de la Ciudad de México*) used to control the colony's internal trade.

To improve the old bureaucracy inherited from the Habsburgs and to implement the so-called Bourbonic reforms, the Bourbons reorganized colonial administration. The objective was to create a professional administration directly subordinated to the king. In order to counterbalance the viceroy's power, the Crown created the *intendencias*, which were territorial administrative and political units headed by *intendentes*, or general governors. This would weaken his competence and prerogatives by decentralizing them. The *intendentes* were then responsible for the finance, justice, and military businesses within their territorial jurisdiction. Their main functions were to rebuild the political order, maintain the unity of the Spanish Empire, fight against administrative corruption, promote industry, trade, and agriculture, as well as better the tax-collecting system and prevent illegal trading.

The importance of Bourbonic reforms lies in the fact that they unraveled the structural contradictions within the Spanish colonial system and made more acute the rivalries among the most prominent members of New Spain's elite. This in turn caused problems that could not be possibly solved through the previously established institutional ways. That is why these reforms triggered a process that made the whole system lose stability and worked against their own interests. This instability was manifested in the rise of nationalist oriented movements that demanded New Spain's independence from the metropolis. The Napoleonic invasion to Spain (1808) and the resulting Spanish monarchy crisis allowed these movements to achieve their intentions. The national independence movement headed by the priest Miguel Hidalgo started in 1810 and ended 11 years later (1821). During that time trade, mining, and agricultural production were reduced to a minimum. This fact and the lack of an effective public administration left the country in a precarious situation that constituted the distinctive feature of Mexico in the nineteenth century.

Administration in Independent Mexico (1821–1910)

After the War of Independence, Mexico submerged into a 55-year stage (1821–1876) during which a nation-state emerged. This period was a turbulent and bloody process because of the struggle between different and contrasting ways of envisioning the political constitution of a national state: either empire or republic, federal or central system, civic rights or corporate privileges. The constant internal conflicts produced high social, political, and economic costs that prevented the national state from establishing an efficient administrative organization, which in time would strengthen the state itself.

The first administrative and political organization attempted in independent Mexico took an imperial structure (1822–1823), headed by Agustín de Iturbide. The empire organized its administration on four ministries: Interior and Exterior Relations, Justice and Church Businesses, Treasury, War and Navy. However, the empire ended, unable to untangle the chaotic political situation. In 1824, the country's first political constitution was promulgated and it organized the newly born state as a federal republic.

The federal system was substituted by a new central order established in the Seven Laws (1843) and in the Organic Basis (1843). This legal proviso did not contradict the idea of building a republic, but a centralist one. The internal struggle between centralists and federalists caused the province of Texas to secede from the country in 1836 and provoked the United States invasion of 1847, which resulted in the loss of almost half of the Mexican territory in the northern region and forced the Mexican government to make war compensations at a time when the country had no economic resources to confront that obligation.

There were constant changes at the top of the national government by reason of various regional revolts and the lack of a legitimate centralized power with effective administrative and military command. The ephemeral duration and the multiple failures of the first Mexican governments reflected the tough polemic between the two dominant groups: Liberals and Conservatives. The Liberals insisted that a federal republic, based upon the recognition of civil rights, would be ideal for Mexico. In contrast, the Conservatives insisted that the new state should be built on the basis of the colonial institutions and the established corporations. What both groups really wanted was to shape a national state that would make a solid government possible. The Liberals, headed by Benito Juárez, tried to build a firm government by passing the Reform Laws (*Leyes de Reforma*)—which established a definite separation between the Mexican state and the Catholic Church—and the republican and federal Constitution of 1857. The Conservatives, supported by the church and corporations, tried to establish a new empire headed by a European aristocrat. Due to their different points of view, there were two parallel governments in those years: the Mexican Empire led by Maximilian Von Habsburg (1861–1867) and the liberal constitutional government led by Benito Juárez. However, neither of them was able to establish an efficient and coordinated administrative system because the continuous battling created a state of anarchy during those years. In the end, the French invasion of Mexico, ordered by Napoleon III to support the Emperor Maximilian, was defeated militarily by the Liberals and institutionally by their 1857 Constitution.

With General Porfirio Díaz as president in 1876, a long period of authoritarianism began, enabling the federal administration to become more organized and centralized. This brought peace and progress to Mexico until the year 1910. The federal public administration of those years was not only oriented to the customary areas of government (internal affairs, external relations, defense, justice, and tax collection). Besides these public functions, it added other functions related to enforce economic growth and created the Secretariat of Development, Industry, and Trade in 1853, allowing the government the promotion of agriculture, industry, and commerce.

The favorable conditions created by the Porfirian period known as "Pax Porfiriana" allowed foreign investment (mainly American and British) to pour into Mexico in order to exploit mines and oil and railroad construction. The political stability, supported by an incipient professional administration, made it possible for the country to grow economically. There were improvements to the governmental agencies in charge of economic affairs, mainly the ones in charge of finance and communications. The permanence of Porfirio Díaz in the presidency fostered the integration in 1890 of a small group of public officials who had been educated abroad. Such a group was the core of the "scientific" Porfirian public administration.

The Mexican Revolution and the Postrevolutionary Governments: The Centralized Pattern of Public Management (1910–1940)

The centralist and authoritarian government of Porfirio Díaz stimulated the building of a national state with a modern economy, but based upon feeble social and political foundations. At the beginning of the twentieth century, Mexico was basically a rural country marked by inequality among regions and individuals. There were dispossessed peasants, small rural and urban middle classes displeased with their economic situation with no means of political participation, and a land-owning class that was concerned with their loss of political power during the Porfirian years. Under those circumstances, various regional leaders, some of them with national prominence (Francisco Villa, Emiliano Zapata, Francisco I. Madero) ignited the uprisings with demands of democracy and social justice, particularly in the agrarian sector. What started as mere isolated revolts gave way to the most important social movement of this century in the country: the Mexican Revolution, the founding event of contemporary Mexico.

The political instability during the revolution (1910–1917) was translated into administrative chaos and continuous changes of residence of the executive. The different leaders who temporarily held power implemented operational changes with little success in the realm of a disordered state apparatus with no real capacity of action. Venustiano Carranza, leader of the Constitutionalist Army, was a key figure in bringing institutional order into the upheaval of the revolutionary time.

When the constitutionalist movement triumphed, the first steps toward a new state organization and legality were taken. The 1917 Constitution–prevailing today–envisioned a republican, representative, democratic, and federal republic, divided vertically into three government jurisdictions (federal, state, and municipal) and three horizontal autonomous branches (executive, legislative, and judicial). The new Mexican political system was structured around a strong presidency with extensive faculties. In general terms, the president is the head of the state and the government, commander in chief of the army, headman of foreign policy. His functions include the making of the substantive decisions on public expenditure and debt, taxes, monetary, agrarian, work, education, energy, and communication matters. Besides, the president also has the power to name and remove the members of his cabinet, the diplomatic representatives, and the directors of state-owned enterprises.

Simultaneously, the new Constitution laid the foundations of a strong and socially active state; with large faculties to intervene in economic, land ownership, work, public education, and health matters. Articles 25 and 28 established that the state would be the leader of national economic development and would have some exclusive areas of intervention (oil and basic petrochemicals, coinage and bill emission, mail, telegraphs, etc.). Article 27 assigned the ownership of the land to the nation and made the state the sole regulating agent of land ownership. Article 123, searching for an equilibrium in worker-employer relations by means of state regulating actions, established a maximum of hours for a day's work, minimum wage, work protection for women and minors, compulsory periodic holidays, a share of the companies' profits for the workers, association and strike rights for workers and employers, among other measures. Article 3 established the right of every individual to receive elementary education. Furthermore, the article stated that education would be free, secular, compulsory, and provided by the state. These articles set the legal basis of a social state responsible for the improvement of general living standards and welfare of society.

The ideological and political transformation of the country, as a product of the Revolution, made it compulsory to reorganize the administrative apparatus. That is the reason for Article 90–to determine that the federal executive power required two kinds of agencies in order to fulfill its responsibilities: the state secretariats and the administrative departments. The former would be in charge of the relevant administrative and political decisionmaking, while the latter would only carry out operative functions. The Law of Secretariats and Administrative Departments, issued in 1917, organized the federal public administration into six secretariats—Internal Government; Foreign Relations; Treasury and Public Credit; War and Navy; Agriculture and Development; Communications and Public Works; Industry, Trade, and Work—and five departments—University and Fine Arts, Public Health, Factories, Military Procurement, and the Comptroller's Office.

From 1920 to 1934, national government priority was to bring peace to the country by centralizing the political power and setting up an efficient federal public administration. However, the differences among the revolutionary leaders inhibited the peacemaking process. The first steps toward a centralization and institutionalization of the political power were taken by President Plutarco Elías Calles in 1929 when he founded the National Revolutionary Party (*Partido Revolucionario Nacional*, PNR) that grouped together the different revolutionary factions and leaders. During his government (1924–1928), Calles carried out several important measures in order to rebuild the federal public administration: the Treasury and Public Credit Secretariat functions were reorganized and the Bank of Mexico, the central bank, was created in 1926 with the purpose of centralizing and making uniform the credit, monetary, and exchange rate policies in the country.

In 1933, central planning was introduced to Mexico as a tool for government efficiency, molded after the emerging socialist countries. The new president, Lázaro Cárdenas (1934–1940) considered central planning to be the most effective administrative instrument in order to achieve the social and nationalistic claims of the postrevolutionary state. At the same time, he created the political conditions that would give support to his idea of government. He reorganized the dominant party—PNR—into four sectors (workers, peasants, populace—integrated by small traders, artisans, professionals and employees—and military), which would organize the masses for sustaining the emerging new political system and his social policies. That way, in 1938 the PNR became the Mexican Revolution Party (*Partido de la Revolución Mexicana*, PRM) with a new corporatist arrangement that integrated the militance of different backgrounds and diverse interests in a new structure that made it possible for the regime to interchange social and economic benefits for loyalty, cooperation, and political support. The transformation of the official party modified the Mexican political system. The personalized way of governing was left behind, and the new style was supported by a strong presidential institution and by a popular political pact that integrated the country's different social organizations. In addition, the public administrative apparatus that Cárdenas received was insufficient to accomplish his project. That is why in 1935 a new Law of Secretariats and Administrative Departments was passed by Congress; it included the creation of agrarian, health, and Indian affairs departments, among others.

During Cárdenas' administration, World War II stimulated industrial development. The increase of an external demand for goods, services, raw materials, and commodities, especially by North America, and the diminishing of imports added as an incentive to the country's private sector to exploit raw materials and invest in industry. There was a close association between public and private sectors, the government providing infrastructure and the private entrepreneurs investing in the domestic market. That way, by the end of the 1930s, the government had built new roads and railways, improved mail, telephone, telegraph, and radio services, and impulsed aviation. The construction of dams and irrigation channels was intensified, along with the generation and distribution of electric energy.

During that period, there was a visible insufficiency of internal savings, which did not allow the expansion of private investment as desired. To avoid that obstacle, the National Bank of International Trade (*Banco Nacional de Comercio Exterior*) and the National Financing Bank (*Nacional Financiera*) were created. To promote the industrialization process, state-owned enterprises were created in several fields of economic activity, such as steel, iron, heavy machinery, electric machinery, fertilizers, copper, and coal, providing the private industry with the necessary resources.

In 1938, the government made the decision of expropriating the oil industry from foreign companies in order to protect the national natural resources and to guarantee Mexican sovereignity in such an important field. Since then, *Petróleos Mexicanos* (PEMEX) has taken the responsibility of administering, exploring, extracting, commercializing, and distributing oil in Mexico, becoming the most important public-owned enterprise in the country.

Interventionism: The Growth of the State (1940–1982)

By the 1940s, the political institutions in Mexico had achieved their basic profile. To complete the consolidation of the system, a new reform of the party was undertaken. The PRM changed its structure and its name, becoming the still dominant Institutional Revolutionary Party (*Partido Revolucionario Institucional*, PRI). Now, the main governmental objective was economic growth. In order to accomplish this goal, a highly centralized, control-free, and discretionary management style was outlined. The federal government tightly controlled the whole political system, including public policies' formulation and implementation.

The growth of the administrative apparatus came as a natural consequence. The state enlargement was a necessary output, if we consider that the system's legitimacy was based primarily upon the provision of social and economic benefits and not upon the citizens' independent vote, though periodic elections were held. Trading economic and political benefits for political support, such a system relied more on short-term solutions than structural changes for the long run. While the economic growth persisted, governmental performance was not challenged by individual discontent.

After 1940, an economic development model was implemented, called "import substitution" or "inner growth." This model, influenced by economic ideas developed in the United Nation's Economic Commission for Latin America (*Comisión Económica para América Latina*, CEPAL), translated into the Mexican government's direct participation to create basic infrastructure and to enhance private investment by means of imposing protectionist policies and subsidies. Trade closed to the exterior by levying permits, quotas, and high taxes on imports. This model, together with the centralized government pattern, paved the way to a rapid growth of state-owned enterprises. Between 1940 and 1950, that number increased from 57 to 158. There was an outstanding creation of around 80 public-owned firms and companies in the sugar, paper, petrochemicals, and metal mechanics industries. By the end of the 1950s, 251 public enterprises existed already.

As the size of the economy and the government involvement grew, management and coordination problems arose. The Secretariat of the Presidency was created in 1958 in order to assist the president in the integral coordination of the different branches of public action.

In 1970, the number of state-owned enterprises was 491. The social ideology of the Mexican Revolution called for economic growth and redistributive policies that the private businesses could not fulfill. Public enterprises contributed directly to employment generation and the production of heavily subsidized goods and services, which strove to give the economic development a social orientation. And their number increased further when the government bought private enterprises that had gone into bankruptcy in order to protect employment and family income.

Besides creating state-owned enterprises, other governmental organizations in charge of fulfilling the state social functions were created. The passing of the Law of Social Security in 1943 founded the Mexican Social Security Institute (*Instituto Mexicano del Seguro Scocial*, IMSS) to provide health services and social security to the working population in the private sector. The IMSS combined government, employers, and workers representatives in a three-party covenant. After the constitutional reform to Article 123—which defined the state workers' legal status—in 1960, the Institute of Social Security and Services for the State Workers (*Instituto de Seguridad y Servicios Sociales para los Trabajadores del Estado*, ISSSTE) was created. This institute was in charge of providing social security services to public servants. Furthermore, to ameliorate the living conditions in the countryside, the federal government created the National Company of Popular Provisions (*Compañia Nacional de Subsistencias Populares*, Conasupo) in order to regulate the price, industrialization, and distribution of commodities, as well as to sell these goods with subsidized prices through a national outlet system. Although its functions have been recently revised and some of its parts were disvested, this company is currently operating and constitutes a pillar of the governmental social policy.

The state apparatus enlargement brought about a considerable increase in the number of public employees. The Mexican public sector comprises two basic categories of public employees: unionized and appointees. By 1965, there were 230,749 public employees in both categories—who worked mainly for the federal public sector—registered in the ISSSTE. By 1970, there were already 371,489.

Public spending started to grow without tax revenues increasing accordingly (in 1960 the public sector's total expenditure was 13.39 percent of the GNP, while in 1970 the percentage was 24.59). There was also a problem of inefficiency in public management due to improvisation and poor coordination between resource allocation, agencies, and programs. That forced the creation in 1965 of the Public Administration Commission (*Comisón de Administración Pública*, CAP) whose task it was to submit a reorganization scheme in order to improve the performance of public administration.

On economic grounds, the import substitution model was successful. Between 1940 and 1970, the GNP annual growth rate was 6.43 percent, which was almost the same as in most developed economies. From 1954 to 1970, real wages and the inflation rate grew by almost 5 percent and 3.5 percent respectively. Control over the inflation rate was achieved by adequate managing of public finances: The budget deficits were deterred by a firm control of public expenditure and financed with a moderate increase of external debt. Nevertheless, at the end of the 1960s, this development model produced several structural problems that jeopardized the price stability and the economic growth achieved in previous decades. The main problems were the stagnation of agricultural development, distortions in the national consumer goods' prices as compared to the international ones, the narrowing of the internal market, technological obsolescence, low internal saving and investment rates, and above all, the unequal distribution of income and wealth and noticeable differences in regional development.

The political reaction against the social outcomes of the economic development was expressed in popular demonstrations, strong criticism by the middle class, and rural guerrilla outbursts. The government, in response to this upheaval, developed a social activism, leaving aside the core questions about the authoritarian structure of the political system and the highly centralized pattern of public decisionmaking. Distributive policies through public expenditure and direct state intervention were strongly developed, causing a rapid increase in the number of federal government enterprises, programs, and bureaucrats. In order to overcome the insufficiency of private firms and the inefficiency of markets, the state-owned enterprises and the social programs undertaken would become strategic means for overcoming the impasse of a stagnant national development.

During the administration of President Luis Echeverría Álvarez (1970–1976), the number of state-owned enterprises was almost doubled, from 491 to 845, and the number of public employees went up from 371,489 to 870,392. Even though Álvarez's political program comprised an administrative reform, the results did not come out the way it was expected. All the attempts to control public administration's overgrowth and disarray were insufficient. That motivated the creation of an office in charge of the Administrative Studies for the Presidency (*Dirección de Estudios Administrativos de la Presidencia de la República*). The office which did administrative studies replaced CAP in 1971. The studies served as basis for the Federal Executive Administrative Reform Program in 1971–1976.

In order to face the problems of public administration's enlargement and its poor performance, President José López Portillo (1976–1982) proposed a new program, known in general as the "administrative reform." This was the first serious attempt of governmental self-correction. It strove to revise the public administration structure and process, introducing instruments for coordination, budgeting, programming, follow-up, and evaluation of programs and results. These administrative and legal changes occurred in (1) the passing of the Organic Law of Federal Public Administration (*Ley Orgánica de la Administración Pública Federal*, LOAPF) and the Law of Budgeting, Accounting, and Public Expenditure (*Ley de Presupuesto, Contabilidad y Presupuesto Público*), (2) the creation of a Secretariat of Programming and Budgeting (*Secretaría de Programación y Presupuesto*, SPP), which was expected to solve the problem of planning, budget, and programming disorder, (3) a new sectorial reorganization of the public agencies, which was basically oriented to reassign functions and responsibilities between secretariats, administrative departments, and public-owned enterprises in order to prevent waste, overlapping, duplication, and dispersion of functions, and (4) the creation of a General Coordination for the Evaluation National System (*Coordinación General del Sistema Nacional de Evaluación*) to monitor the governmental programs and to evaluate their performance.

Crisis and Reforms: Toward an Innovative State and Public Management Style (1982–1994)

The administrative reforms of the 1970s did not accomplish their objectives. On the contrary, the lack of coordination and inefficiency prevailed. Also, the number of state-owned enterprises and governmental entities grew: between 1976 and 1982, from 845 to 1155. In spite of a rapid economic growth during the administration of President López Portillo, a serious state fiscal crisis, the collapse of the national economy and a feeling of general social unrest were the results of poor management and excessive public expenditure on too many programs. Hence, at the beginning of 1982, his government was left with no international reserves and could not hold the exchange rate, so it was forced to devalue the peso by 470 percent in December of that year. The public expenditure growth rate fell from 25 percent of the GNP in 1981 to 3.7 percent in 1982. The six-year governmental period ended with the signature of a stabilizing program with the International Monetary Fund (IMF), no international reserves, an almost 100 percent inflation rate, a fall of 0.5 percent in the real GNP, a public deficit of almost 18 percent of the GNP, and a foreign debt of US $92,400 million.

The fiscal crisis brought the prevailing government and its management style to their limits. The six decades of government intervention in almost every sphere of the social and economic activities ended up shaping a government style characterized by (1) the preeminence of the federal government over the state and municipal levels, (2) a public decisionmaking process with great autonomy, (3) direct provision of goods and services to citizens as the first source of political legitimacy, (4) overregulation of the economic activity, (5) public management structured according to loyalties and personal arrangements, (6) fiscal irresponsibility.

The 1982 fiscal crisis, however, allowed the government to recognize that its failures were rooted deeper than the public administration and organization levels. They lay on the structure of the political system itself. This crisis forced the beginning of a new political and administrative period. It was a spur for renewing the society's claim for the democratization of the regime and a revision of the public role of the state. The liberalization of political life, through a sequence of profound electoral reforms and the *redimensionamiento* (downsizing) of the state, with the arrival of Miguel De la Madrid to the presidency (1982–1988), were the timely responses to the changed circumstances of Mexican society. The downsizing process, which would later become known as the *reform of the state*, consisted in liquidation, merging, closure, and selling as part of the privatization process of the state-owned enterprises, as well as the introduction of new forms of public services provisions. Several social programs and public services started to be implemented in collaboration with nongovernmental, private, and social organizations, profit or nonprofit. The process questioned once again the proper realm of the state and its role: its intervention, administration, performance, and its subjects.

At the beginning of President Miguel De la Madrid's administration, it was urgent to work toward the stabilization and recovery of the Mexican economy. In addition to the economic recovery policies implemented, it was also necessary to make the public administration structures and practices more efficient. That is why the government instrumented a series of measures in order to accomplish an administrative modernization. The leading principles of President Miguel de la Madrid's government were "moral renovation and administrative simplification." The former motivated the creation of a Federation General Comptroller Secretariat (*Secretaría de la Contraloría General de la Federación,* SECOGEF) in order to control authority abuses, fight administrative corruption, and evaluate government actions. The latter established that the governmental agencies should simplify the procedures that citizens had to carry out in order to receive services in a more efficient and fast manner.

Miguel de la Madrid's government also made some important constitutional amendments to facilitate the public administration transformation. These legal reforms attempted to activate local governments by amending Article 115 of the Constitution so as to decentralize the responsibilities of an exhausted central administration. Article 26 established the general guidelines to enforce a Democratic National Planning System (*Sistema Nacional de Planeación Democrática,* SNPD) and set forward the obligation to govern in accordance with a National Development Plan (*Plan Nacional de Desarrollo,* PND), making planning the main requisite for the rationalization of governmental action, objectives, means, and resources. The amendment to Article 25 redefined the state intervention: It validated its economic leadership of national development and its exclusive management of certain strategic areas of economic activity (electricity, trains, oil, basic petrochemicals, etc.), while other economic sectors were opened to the market competition.

This constitutional reform made possible for the government to start a process by which the number of state-owned enterprises would be reduced. That process was called *desincorporación,* "taking away from the corpus of the state." As mentioned before, this divestiture process meant the closure of enterprises with no economic purpose or with objectives that were already achieved, the mergers to take more advantage of the resources involved, the transfer of federal enterprises with regional relevance to the state governments and the sale of nonstrategic enterprises.

The divestiture process (*desincorporación*) started in 1983, but it was accelerated since 1985 due to a new fall in the international oil price and an increase of the national inflation rate (63 percent at the end of 1984). Consequently, in December 1982, there were 1,155 state-owned enterprises, whereas six years later, there were only 618. The contribution made by selling the public-owned enterprises was not very significant in terms of the gross national product, but it allowed the creation of a "contingencies fund" (*Fondo de Contingencia*) to help pay for the foreign public debt. In summary, the experience acquired by privatizing will be important for major endeavors in the future.

Although the biggest public enterprises (*Petóleos Mexicanos, Comisión Federal de Electricidad, Compaña Nacional de Subsistencias Populares, Teléfonos de México, Ferrocarriles Nacionales, Fertilizantes de México,* among others) were left out of this process, it proved to be a fundamental issue in putting public finances in order and a decisive step in redefining a completely different type of state involvement, modifying its intervening nature of previous decades and altering the public management pattern that was traditionally used to govern Mexico. In this way, the crisis of the 1980s brought a change in administration and government style, which in turn altered the style of policymaking, the way in which groups and leaders represent their interests and demands, and the traditional manner of solving conflicts and obtaining legitimacy from social organizations.

Carlos Salinas de Gortari took office in December 1988. The novelty during his administration (1988–1994) lay in making the *redimensionamiento* (downsizing) process of the state a political and institutional concept and argument. The idea was not only to stabilize the public finances or to restructure the state-owned enterprises or to be an economic recovery program. The real purpose was to bring to an end the notion of an owner and entrepreneurial state, which had overseen basic public functions, mainly social ones, that the 1917 Constitution established as its main duties. The idea was to root out a state that had become more preoccupied with administering its own assets than taking care of urgent social needs.

With the perception that an "owner state is not necessarily a fair state," the government started a deep reform. The results speak for themselves: By the end of 1993, there were only 258 state-owned enterprises, of which 48 were to be privatized. There were successful privatizations of major companies such as the two main national airlines (*Mexicana de Aviación* and *Aereoméxico*), one of the biggest copper mines in the world (*Compaña Minera de Cananea*), the national telephone company (*Teléfonos de Méxcio*), and all of the banks that had been nationalized in 1982 by President López Portillo. The decision of reprivatizing the commercial banks in May 1990 was the clearest sign of how determined the liberalization, divestiture, and privatizion effort was.

President Salinas continued with economic recovery and price stabilizing policies. On the one hand, in 1989 the foreign debt was renegotiated allowing a drastic decrease in the service of foreign debt. One the other hand, the Mexican government and the labor and private corporations signed a yearly pact, with the purposes of reducing the annual inflation rate to one digit, recovering the economic growth in a rate higher than the population growth, and reducing the external resource transfer as a requisite to grow again in a sustained manner with price stability. There were also great advances in the opening of the economy, which altered the endogenous model of the previous industrial development. The North American Free Trade Agreement (NAFTA), signed with the United States and Canada in November 1993, was a great achievement in making the Mexican economy more open and competitive.

The reform of the state was also materialized in two outcomes: a deregulation process and the adoption of proxy measures for governing. The first took place in the transport, finance, and commercial services. The second involved a broader participation of society in the services management and provision: The government gave concessions or contracted out services to private organizations or to nongovernmental organizations capable of undertaking social functions. Furthermore, innovative mechanisms in social policy were implemented to promote citizen involvement in solving their social problems and needs. The National Solidarity Program (*Programa Nacional de Solidaridad*, PRONASOL) was the government's instrument to fight extreme poverty and used these mechanisms with great success. PRONASOL is a social program supported by joint efforts from the benefited communities and the government to produce the social goods and local infrastructure needed to achieve higher standards of living. Under this scheme, each community is in charge of handling and managing the resources allocated through small committees integrated by the benefited neighbors. This way, the government departs from the across-the-board public subsidies approach and adopts an innovative focused social expenditure policy.

There is an obvious conclusion that rises out of Miguel de la Madrid's and Carlos Salinas' reformism: Rather than reforming public administration as an apparatus, the goal was a deep transformation of the relations between state and society, the view and scope of the public and private spheres. More than a mere administrative reorganization, the aim was to attain an authentic reform of the state.

The Discipline of Public Administration

The study of public administration in Mexico has been influenced by several schools. The Institutional, Administrative Process, Sociological, Systemic, Organizational, Public Policy, and New Public Management schools have been the most influential. Nevertheless, major transformations in Mexico's public administration have always been ahead of the discipline: The first thrust to research on this field has essentially come from the government, and therefore the academic works have been more explanatory descriptions of government initiatives than studies with real impact on the administrative functioning of public agencies.

The Institutional School studied the government agencies' formal administrative structures and the principles and regulations established by the administrative public law. This school prevailed until the 1960s when two Sociological School currents—Weberian and Marxist—started to develop in the academic environment in Mexico, basically with scarce influence on the real public administration process. At the same time, the Administrative Process and Systemic Schools became stronger and competed in the academic realm with the other two schools, the Institutional and the Sociological. In essence, no school dominated clearly over the others. This situation lasted until the late 1980s, when the Public Policy and the New Public Management approaches burst strongly into the academic environment and normed government praxis.

The Institutional School, concerned with legal compliance within the administrative performance and an unbiased treatment of citizens, privileged the study of laws and formal guidelines, distribution of faculties and competences, and responsibility areas in the government agencies. In a country where discretional and patrimonialist ways of a traditional public administration were being abandoned, the merit of this school was to contribute to the foundations of a government of laws and to introduce a strict legal character in administrative behavior. However, it was not emphatic enough on the need of administrative process efficiency, or on the linkage of administration with real political life and actual government practices. Its outcomes—fine comments on law and administrative responsibilities—always left the impression of describing or prescribing an impeccable formal world that had hardly anything to do with public administration as it really worked and was organized and where there was a tendency to make discretional and patrimonialist decisions and to freely recruit civil servants.

Although this school was left behind several years ago in the Anglo-Saxon countries, there are two reasons that can explain its permanence in Mexico: First, the preeminence of a legal tradition in the Mexican public administration stemming from the last century and the significant weight that lawyers had in the decisionmaking process of government agencies in the 1960s; second, a relative isolation of the Mexican academy from the contemporary advances of the management sciences. However, even as the legal-formal perspective was necessary, it was insufficient for organizing a growing administrative sector that became more and more complex as well as incapable of theoretically explaining its real functioning and improving the public personnel's behavior.

Counterbalancing the institutional approach, this situation caused other professional groups (particularly, economists and engineers), interested in the administrative process itself, to begin to develop and introduce managerial techniques in order to make the public sector more efficient. These professional contributions were molded after the American Administrative Process School. Even though the administrative ideas were developed in the United States at the beginning of this century, they were adopted in Mexico by the late 1950s, when public administration was getting bigger and more complex. Wilson's ideas about the separation between government and administration, as well as Gullick and Urwick's POSDCORB, offered a theoretical framework for a second generation of professionals and scholars working on public administration.

Although this new approach brought a scientific and technical character to public management, its influence was scarce and restricted to a small circle of experts and academics. Its low impact at the moment of its reception was due to the fact that the Mexican academy had something else at the core of its interests: the problems of the regime's authoritarianism and the social differences not yet solved and worsened by the processes of industrialization and urbanization of the country. In spite of that, the Mexican public administration structure, influenced by the managerial approach, carried out some reforms during the late 1970s and the early 1980s, such as the creation of organization and methods departments in almost all government agencies, as well as an ambitious National System of Planning, Evaluation, and Control.

There also appeared new influences that went farther than the approach of the Institutional School with administrative nuances. Herbert Simon and his "administrative behavior" thesis, although late, brought into Mexico innovative key concepts such as decision, organization, and bounded rationality, which made possible to link wisely politics with administration, value and factual judgments, and to understand administration as an ongoing decision-making process. Administration was no longer considered only as the executing arm of former political authority decisions.

The social and political issues preeminent in the public agenda gave birth to the Sociological Public Administration School in Mexico. This school was divided into two currents which used the theoretical concepts developed by Karl Marx and Max Weber, respectively. Although the Marxist critical theory was hyperactive in the academic environment, it never made it through to explain public administration's functioning in general, and Mexican public administration's functioning in particular. They clung to the idea of a structural crisis in the capitalist societies, which would inevitably lead to a global state crisis as the "dominant class apparatus." This made Mexican Marxists write general propositions that were declarations of principles rather than analytical studies. Besides, the Marxist

school hindered its own evolution by not recognizing that the Mexican state strongly intervened by regulating market exchanges and by carrying out mass welfare policies. The major deficiency of the Marxist approach was that it never focused its attention on the Mexican public administration's actual performance and its attempted reforms. This in turn opened a gap between the public administration academy and the professionals, the former criticizing the public officers' acts and the latter rejecting those criticisms. The final result was a scarce and limited influence of Marxism on the actual public administration, the way it was organized, and its outcomes.

The other sociological current is the Weberian one. Its main influence was Weber's political theory on "domination types." In a country changing from a traditional to a modern society, with strong popular leaders, the Weberian concepts on charismatic, traditional, and legal-bureaucratic domination are important to analyze the political-administrative processes that take place and their associated problems. This approach threw light on the functioning of traditional political communities present in many indigenous and rural zones, and it helped explain, as well as criticize, the patrimonialistic way of political power. It also offered the legal, organizational, and professional traits of modern government and its bureaucracy.

The Weberian concept of bureaucracy was left as an abstract concept with little reference to the actual Mexican public administration or as an organizing ideal to strive for. At least, it was useful to show the distance between the real action of Mexican public organizations and the modern concept of its behavior. Two other Weberian concepts also had some influence: his "rational action" concept (the capacity to previously calculate the most effective accomplishment of ends on the basis of available means and resources) and his classic distinction between the politician and the scientist. On the one hand, his emphasis on rationality contributed to discussions of the need for efficacy, efficiency, and responsibility in administrative performance and hence for the requirement for expert professional personnel. On the other hand, his distinction between politics and science/technique was useful to show the inconveniences of an overpoliticized public administration, which served as a warning on the risk involved in doing the contrary, placing technocrats at the head of the government, when they are fairly insensitive to political processes.

The Weberian views of bureaucracy as the proper way of organizing modern public administration, as well as the criticizing Marxist statements on the biased capitalist state bureaucracy, made the sociological viewpoint quite popular within the academic environment. We can even talk about a "sociologization" of public administration study. This helped the discipline to attain greater depth, as public administration study was placed in a broader political and economic system and social structural frame, but at the price of diluting this field into a social one. This school therefore did not pay much attention to the institutional and managerial aspects of public administration either.

However, the sociological approach paved the way for the scientific community to assume the more specific "organization sociology" and "organization theory" approach. An academic wing, integrated by a few people only but all of them convinced that the organizational approach was valid to analyze the public administration structure and functioning, held on to this theoretical current in the 1980s and carried out important research and case studies. This is still a developing theory that has included in its research framework the "new economy organization" approaches (Coase, Williamson, Ouchi) and the "new institutionalism" approach (North, Selznick) besides the pioneer studies (Crozier, Perrow, Pfeffer, Mintzberg). However, today's impact of these approaches has been more scholarly than professional.

In contrast, the Systemic Theory School was highly influential in Mexican public administration study and reform during the 1970s. The systemic approach applied to public administration made it possible to consider the set of public organizations as a complex whole from the internal viewpoint and, above all, it linked its relations with the environment where they took place. The Institutional School gained importance isolated from political and social phenomena outside the administrative apparatus. The Systemic School emergence in Mexico made it easier to study the processes within the public administration system, as well as the relations among themselves and with the environment in which they interacted, to make public administration function more adequately and flexibly, to respond efficiently to the growing social and political demands of its environment (Deutsch, Katz and Kahn, Sharkansky).

The systemic viewpoint permeated Mexican administrative studies visibly. This theory's main assumption claimed that public administration could be defined as a complex and open system oriented to solve and regulate problems and tensions generated within its political, economic, and social environment. These ideas were put into practice in the Administrative Reform during the 1970s, combined with the institutional tradition. In spite of this approach's attempt to bring order on the set of public organizations and to arrange them according to the social and political system inputs and claims, its concrete results were scarce. The out-of-proportion growth of public enterprises and government agencies of those years and the careless public expenditure that led the state to a traumatic bankruptcy frustrated the purposes of the reform and its systemic assumptions. This also showed clearly that the Mexican government had ended in a self-contained and closed system with a compulsory logic of action, without enough control mechanisms, and low political participation.

The 1982 fiscal crisis, which society blamed for the economy's collapse, unveiled the limits of this style of government. On the one hand, this crisis showed that it was necessary to submit governmental decisions to law control and a democratic way of life. On the other hand, it showed the need for improving the quality of public decision processes in order to prevent future mistakes. Most miscalculations basically came from a strong presidential discretional power and severe faults in the information systems, policy modeling, and design. The issues of public decision quality and public policy design were raised and made central once again in the 1980s. If claims for citizen participation and agreement on government decisions awakened the interest in democratic transition, claims for rationality and effectiveness of public decisionmaking awakened academic interest in the study of public policymaking.

Although policy sciences and policy analysis were born and developed in the United States since the 1950s, their value for the study of public administration was unknown to Mexico and many other countries. Their emphasis on analyzing the key components of governmental decisions and to maximize their outcomes with scarce public resources was a recrimination in time to conventional public administration study and practice in Mexico.

Due to the influence of the Wilsonian dichotomy between politics and administration, Mexican public administration was not interested in the governmental decision quality and was only, or mainly, devoted to study how to carry out decisions (the implementation process). Public administration studies did not consider the components of the public decisionmaking process as their subject of knowledge until policy analysis appeared. When citizens and scholars turned their attention to the decisionmaking process, it became the target of severe criticism due to its former mistakes and miscalculations. The only available theoretical developments were basically the American policy sciences, stressing decision analysis, its multidisciplinary nature, and its problem-solving character. If later in the 1970s, American implementation studies gave more significance to the political and administrative process after decisions had been made, the need for analysis to correct and maximize an optimum impact of governmental decisions did not lose its importance.

This was the way in which the academy became interested in policy studies in the 1990s. Some enthusiastic scholars even reduced the study and research of public administration to policy studies, while others considered wisely that policy analysis was a basic complement but not the single approach to administrative studies. The success of this approach in Mexico is largely explained by the idea that it restores and reclaims the public character of administration. It is also partly explained by the demand to abandon an old governmental decision style that was generic and uniform when facing problems and needs, and favored efficient decisions tailored to the size and nature of public problems.

The best academic conditions for the development of the public policy approach appeared at the same time as the so-called reform of the state took place. This did not only mean to decrease the public finances deficit by reducing the number of state-owned enterprises and public programs and personnel. It meant, above all, to create a responsible and efficient public administration that every democratic government should have. Under the theoretical and institutional assumption that the public character of administration is not necessarily equivalent to its governmental character, some scholars then insisted that the state could fulfill its public functions not only by means of governmental agencies but also by means of private and social organizations, profit or nonprofit ones. The idea evolved that government should set regulations and guidelines, and coordinate, follow up, audit, and evaluate the agencies in charge of public interest actions; and the parallel idea evolved that it need not necessarily undertake directly the operation of every public program. Today it could be said that we assist an intellectual revolution of public administration that is rapidly developing and giving a place to society action and participation. Several organizations, private and social, and the so-called third sector government, or government by proxy (NGOs, QUANGOs), are being accepted as providers of some public services.

The emphasis in public-sector efficiency and in a better equilibrium between social benefit and cost has made public administration scholars and professionals turn their eyes toward organization and managerial instruments that have proved to be successful in private enterprises. In Mexico, just as in other countries, there have been scholars and schools that make a drastic distinction between public and private administration and consider that there should not be extrapolation of ideas and techniques from the private to the public world. In spite of that, other scholars and professionals have found in the new public management ideas a framework for research and praxis. In recent years, several innovations in administrative processes and organizational methods found their impulse in strategic planning, total quality management, process reengineering, and so forth. A new promising wind blows in universities and government agencies.

In conclusion, one can say that until the beginning of the 1990s, Mexican public administration was regarded as a set of procedures and transformations within the government structure. As a consequence, academic study never went ahead of public administrative functions and hardly had a significant influence on government. Academic research became a sort of public problem diagnosis instead of being propositive or innovative. It always followed behind governmental actions to study them once they were implemented. However, in the 1990s, public policy and new public management schools have started to modify the relation between research and praxis, making the study of public administration more influential in the public service.

LUIS F. AGUILAR VILLANEUVA

BIBLIOGRAPHY

Aguilar, Villanueva Luis F., 1982. *Política y racionalidad administrativa*. Mexico: Instituto Nacional de Administración Pública (INAP).
———, 1992a. *El estudio de las políticas públicas*. Mexico: M. A. Porrúa.
———, 1992b. "Gestión gubernamental y reforma del estado." In Mauricio Merino, comp., *Cambio político y gobernabilidad*. Mexico: CONACYT-Colegio Nacional de Ciencia Política y Administración Pública.
———, 1992c. "Las reformas mexicanas: hechos y agenda." In Barry B. Levin, comp., *El desafío neoliberal*. Bogotá: Norma.
Argüelles, Antonio, 1992. *La desconcentración en el proceso de modernización económica de México; el caso SECOFI*. Mexico: Porrúa.
Aspe Armella, Pedro, 1993. *El camino mexicano de la transformación económica*. Mexico: Fondo de Cultura Económica (FCE).
Bazdresch, Carlos, and Santiago Levy, 1992. "El populismo y la política económica en México, 1970–1982." In Carlos Bazdresch *et al., Macroeconomía del populismo en la América Latina*. Mexico: FCE.
Cabrero, Enrique, 1992. *Evolución y cambio en la administración pública. Del administrador al gerente público*. Mexico: INAP.
Carrillo Castro, Alejandro, 1978. *La reforma administrativa en México*. Mexico: INAP.
Carrillo Castro, Alejandro, and Sergio García Ramírez, 1983. *Las empresas públicas en México*. Mexico: M. A. Porrúa.
Fernández Santillán José, 1980. *Política y administración pública en México*. Mexico: INAP.
Flores Caballero, Romeo, 1988. *Administración y política en la historia de México*. Mexico: FCE-INAP.
Fraga, Gabino, 1991. *Derecho Administrativo*. 30th ed., Mexico: Porrúa.
Guerrero, Omar, 1989. *El estado y la administración pública en México*. Mexico: INAP.
Méndez, José Luis, 1993. "La política como variable dependiente: hacia un análisis más integral de las políticas públicas." *Foro Internacional*, vol. 23, Mexico: El Colegio de México, 111–144.
Pardo, María del Carmen, 1992. *La modernización administrativa en México*. Mexico: El Colegio de México-INAP.
———, 1993. "La administración pública en México, su desarrollo como disciplina." *Foro Internacional*, vol. 23, Mexico: El Colegio de México, 12–29.
Rebolledo, Juan, 1994. *La reforma del Estado en México; una visión de la modernización en México*. México: FCE.
Uvalle, Ricardo, 1984. *El gobierno en acción. La formación del régimen presidencial de la administración pública*. Mexico: FCE.
Vázquez Nava, María Elena, coord., 1993. *La administración pública contemporánea en México*. México: Secretaría de la Controlaría General de la Federación (SECOGEF)-FCE.

MICROECONOMIC REFORM.
A shorthand description of the measures taken at the microeconomic level that are supposedly necessary to improve productive economic efficiency for any given set of inputs.

Microeconomic reform can subsume notions such as deregulation, privatization, and out-sourcing. It can simply be shifting publicly owned utilities from cost-plus to marginal costing regimes or applying opportunity cost to their capital investment. In application, microeconomic reform is often an imprecise concept, often being used to cover notions such as making the economy more flexible and responsive to new economic trends. Occasionally, it is interchangeable with structural adjustment, which often involves government subsidization or direction of industry and so is, *prima facie,* not about the free operation of economic markets at all.

Origin and Subsequent History

Microeconomic reform as a policy agenda was a consequence of the end of the long postwar Keynesian boom. The eruption of economic "stagflation" during the 1970s raised concerns about improving the efficiency of Western capitalist economies. At the macroeconomic level, it led to monetarism, supply-side economics, the "winding-back" of the state (packages labeled as "Reaganism" or "Thatcherism"). Following upon these phenomena, microeconomic reform emerged as a concern with the productive efficiency of individual industry sectors. From the late 1980s, the movement toward trade liberalization–initiated by the Uruguay round of the General Agreement on Tariffs and Trade (GATT) negotiations and carried on by the World Trade Organization (WTO)–provided further justifications for microeconimic reform.

Underlying Theoretical Framework

The theoretical exposition of microeconomic reform derived from Mancur Olson (1965). Olson's description of distributional coalitions–such as regulatory capture alliances between workers and capitalists to shelter behind tariffs, and public services being organized to benefit producers and managers and not efficient or client-oriented delivery–seemed to explain long-term declines in efficiency. In that sense, it was an application of the public-choice approach, interpreting state activity as analogous to a political market. This mode of analysis was extended to explain relative national economic decline (Olson 1982). Microeconomic reform was a policy reaction to this critique of economic and political inefficiency.

Microeconomic reform is based upon neoclassical economic market assumptions. From this demonstrable theoretical set, however, it goes further to assert that the whole economy benefits, if all its individual components are operating, at maximum productive efficiency. But this makes unsustainable assumptions about the consequences of the interaction between economic and political markets.

For example, governments may impose pollution taxes so that the environmental costs of various industries are more efficiently allocated (i. e., the producers pay the cost of pollution rather than the taxpayers). But this may reduce the gross domestic product (GDP), the conventional measure of an economy's efficiency. Similarly, health investment by governments may reduce morbidity but at the same time could reduce measurable GDP.

Practice Internationally

The international application of microeconomic reform has been varied. In part this has been a function of historical legacies. For example, countries that historically had state-regulated, privately owned gas and electricity utilities (like the U.S.) concentrated upon improving market contestibility. Countries like the UK, where the utilities were state owned, focused upon privatization strategies. In Australia, where electricity utilities were owned by state governments, a mixture of strategies was used–some states privatizing some utilities, others merely corporatizing them–while the federal government sought to make the market more contestible nationally.

Variations in the application of microeconomic reform do not appear to correlate to national institutional structure (i.e., presidential versus parliamentary; unitary versus federal). And they do not appear to correlate to the governments' ideological bases. There has been little cross-national analysis of microeconomic reform. What comparative evidence exists, suggests wide variation in its application, even between governments supposedly of the same ideological persuasion (Easton and Gerritsen 1995). Generally, from the early 1980s, most Western governments initiated measures to improve microeconomic efficiency. Some of these measures–deregulation and competition policy–were applied across all regime types, whether social democratic or conservative (OECD 1994a).

Telecommunications Case Study

Microeconomic reform of telecommunications (usually owned by the state prior to 1980, though the United States had a privately owned, publicly regulated supplier) has involved liberalizing entry into telecommunications markets. This process of liberalization began in the United States in 1982, with the breakup of AT&T into regional operators and the separation of the market into local and long-distance operators. The UK soon followed with the entry of Mercury, to challenge the British Telecom (BT) monopoly, and the eventual full privatization of BT by 1993. Japan partly privatized its telecommunications in 1985, also introducing a two-part industry structure. In 1989, New Zealand fully privatized is telecommunications agency and removed restrictions on service type and entry. In 1993, Canada deregulated its long-distance service monopoly. Australian deregulation is geared to the complete removal of entry barriers by 1997.

The Europeans have been much more hesitant about microeconomic reform of telecommunications. Up to the mid-1990s, partial privatization was the usual mode of reform. The European Union has decided to liberalize the provision of public voice telephony by 1998 (with five years grace for the less-developed states). This will involve trans-border simple resale necessary for the development of trans-border European networks and integrating manufacturing and service components of the industry (OECD 1994b).

During the 1990s, the increasing convergence between telecommunications and broadcasting changed the policy parameters of microeconomic reform of this sector. This has been encouraged by the importance governments place upon the economic and social concomitants of these technologies. National advantage is increasingly seen in securing domestic competition but with national control/access to the manufacturing technologies. Within such a contradiction, microeconomic reform of this sector is likely to be limited in the twenty-first century.

Conclusion

Microeconomic reform was a label attached to the improvement of the productive efficiency of ailing industry sectors in the two decades from 1980. In that sense, it is analogous to the reform of the Corn Laws in nineteenth-century Britain. Future microeconomic reform will be episodic, related to the complex interaction between politics, national industrial, and sectoral decline and the associated rise and fall of interest groups. It will never be uniformly applied, ultimately being related to economic transformation, the power configurations of the state, and the creation and management of global policy agendas.

ROLF GERRITSEN

BIBLIOGRAPHY

Easton, Brian, and Rolf Gerritsen, 1995. "Economic Reform: Parallels and Divergences." In F. G. Castles, Rolf Gerritsen, and J. Vowles, eds., *The Great Experiment: Labour Parties and Public Policy Transformation in Australia and New Zealand.* Sydney: Allen & Unwin, 14–38.
Forsyth, Peter, 1992. "A Perspective on Microeconomic Reform." In Peter Forsyth, ed., *Microeconomic Reform in Australia.* Sydney: Allen & Unwin, 3–23.
OECD (Organisation for Economic Cooperation and Development), 1994a. *Competition Policy in OECD Countries.* Paris: OECD.
———, 1994b. *Communications Outlook–Draft Report,* Working Party on Telecommunications and Information Services Policies, Committee for Information, Computer and Communications Policy, DSTI/ICCP/TISP (94) 5, 2 June, Paris.
Olson, Mancur, 1965. *The Logic of Collective Action.* Cambridge: Harvard University Press.
———, 1982. *The Rise and Decline of Nations: Economic Growth Stagflation, and Social Rigidities.* New Haven: Yale University Press.

MICROMANAGEMENT.

A form of supervision in which attention to detail is extreme and reliance on control mechanisms is high.

Usage and History

The term "micromanagement" has come into use only in recent decades, but the concept is universal. What some people view as responsible oversight and direction, others view as needlessly extreme—that is, micromanagement. It is a subjective determination. This article discusses tools and practices used for micromanagement, how micromanagement takes place in various public administration settings, and who is involved.

Although the term "micromanagement" applies in organizational surroundings, the practice can be observed at every level of society. At the family level, for example, most teenagers at some point accuse a parent of micromanagement: "I'm old enough to know what to do and what not to do! Please stop checking on me and telling me how to run my life." At a society's broadest level, totalitarian governments are characterized by the pervasive domination and highly restrictive controls they impose on their citizens. Micromanagement even surfaces as a theme in literary works, such as the dystopian novels of George Orwell (1946) and Aldous Huxley (1932), Charles Dickens' artfully drawn antagonists Fagin in *Oliver Twist* (1839) and Scrooge in *A Christmas Carol* (1843), and Laura's protective mother Amanda Wingfield in playwright Tennessee Williams' *The Glass Menagerie* (1945).

In the context of public policy and administration, micromanagement is deeply imbedded in concepts laid out by nineteenth-century German sociologist Max Weber. He conceived of bureaucratic organizations as hierarchies wherein the lower level of the organization performed specialized, routine tasks that comprised the fundamental work of the organization. The middle level of the organization coordinated those tasks. The top level was the part of the organization that truly understood what was going on in the organization, what was supposed to go on, and why—only top elements of the organization had the knowledge and authority necessary to manage the organization's activities wisely. As the size of an organization increased and its work became more complex, the top level had to

absorb increasing detail to keep the organization effective—management by limited delegation, while useful and even essential, was not necessarily sufficient. Hence, under this bureaucratic paradigm, micromanagement became an inevitable consequence.

The practice of micromanagement was given a boost early in the twentieth century with the concept, articulated by American industrial consultant Frederick Winslow Taylor, of finding the one best way of performing each specialized task. An axiom of scientific management, the "one best way" particularly applied to work done at the lowest level of the organization; but it was identified and prescribed by officials at the top level—the repository of trustworthy knowledge about the organization. By the second half of the century, researchers had become well aware that organizations were crosscurrents of many behaviors. Douglas Murray McGregor posited a Theory X/Theory Y distinction wherein Theory X managers naturally favored micromanagement-like oversight of their subordinates whereas Theory Y managers perceived their subordinates as, by and large, both willing and able to perform without pervasive supervision. Building on the observations of McGregor and others, later researchers such as Paul Hersey and Kenneth Blanchard analyzed management styles in which—unlike Theory X/Theory Y—the level of attention a supervisor might devote to a subordinate's work skills and performance varied independently of attention to the subordinate's social needs. To date, however, little has been written about micromanagement as a subject of direct study.

Natural Settings

Although the term "micromanagement" bears a decisively negative connotation, micromangement can be an appropriate and necessary management practice among some players and within some settings. Micromanagement is especially likely to take place in environments that are small, unskilled, and untrusting—environmental characteristics that are mutually compatible.

In small organizational settings, one or a few individuals may be the source of knowledge and experience essential for accomplishing the tasks and objectives of the organization. Other members of the organization serve as extra hands to enable the master individual to achieve the objective or to increase output. In that setting, all but the most routine activities come under the close surveillance of the master, with the "extra hands" sometimes being individuals in apprentice capacities. Examples of such settings include "mom and pop" business, small printing operations, and offices supplemented with volunteer workers.

Unskilled organizational settings use similar surveillance and oversight for similar reasons. The number of individuals may be substantial if most are unskilled. Such organizational environments are typically concerned with output volume and use unskilled workers to increase the volume produced. Workers are monitored closely to assure reasonable quality. Task specialization, an organizational characteristic likely in larger unskilled settings, often encourages micromanagement to assure reasonable coordination among activities. Examples of such settings include manufacturing production lines, fast-food operations, and high-volume manual information-processing environments (e.g., cataloging and shelving library acquisitions, receiving and recording tax return data).

Whereas small and unskilled organizational environments may be micromanaged, untrusting environments will, with certainty, be micromanaged. Two such organizational settings are typical. The first is where labor and management have come to regard one another as adversaries, with much of the labor force often formally represented through labor unions; in this instance, micromanagement may be either an effect or a contributing cause of the adversarial relationship. The second setting is where the workforce is captive, either literally or figuratively. Prison labor is an example of a truly captive workforce. Military settings (especially during combat, on maneuvers, or at sea) involve a virtually captive workforce. Temporary labor, especially migrant agricultural labor, is essentially captive. Single-industry towns sustain a largely captive workforce (and, for some localities, "government" can be the dominating industry), although micromanagement of the workforce is not necessarily an outcome in such settings.

As a management approach, micromanagement has identifiable strengths as well as significant weaknesses. Its strengths are innate to human interactions and, as such, give immortality to micromanagement, though not vitality. As management paradigms evolve, however, the weaknesses of micromanagement become both more serious and more apparent.

Strengths

Micromanagement has a number of positive characteristics. Prime among them is that micromanagement reflects two facets of human nature: the need to be aware of one's environment and the need to control what takes place in that environment. We all display these needs even though their intensity varies with the individual and the situation. Because micromanagement addresses those needs, it will always be one of the ways we interact with others in group settings.

Micromanagement has operational and theory-based advantages as well. Operationally, micromanagement permits production through unwilling or untrained workers; it extends ability for short-term and temporary changes in production levels; and, under some circumstances, it may preserve secrecy. In terms of theory, micromanagement accommodates the paradigm of scientific management (e.g., Luther Gulick's POSDCORB—planning, organizing, staffing, directing, coordinating, reporting, budgeting); more fundamentally, it plays to the view that human nature is inherently self-oriented.

Weaknesses

International business practices in recent years have found micromanagement wanting. Private- and public-sector organizations increasingly rely on placing decision authority and responsibility as close to the operating levels of the organization as possible, seeking the counsel of front-line employees in running and improving operations, and valuing independent expertise and judgment within the workforce rather than imposed upon it. This is an uncomfortable environment for micromangement because it exacerbates rather than diffuses micromanagement's limitation.

Among its weaknesses, micromanagement demands extreme attention on the part of the manager. It typically requires continued or frequent physical proximity of manager and worker. It dampens individual initiative, innovation, entrepreneurialism. It can generate resentment from subordinate workers subjected to micromanagement practices. It runs counter to trends toward worker empowerment, self-managed work groups, work at home (telecommuting), flexible work scheduling, and so forth. Perhaps most important, micromanaged organizations and organizational activities tend to distance the worker (firsthand service deliverer) from direct accountability with the customer, which, in a fundamental sense, is the reverse of the effectiveness that micromanagement strives to achieve.

U.S. Practice

Micromanagement takes place both among and within organizations. Within organizations, micromanagement may involve all aspects of organizational activity; in most circumstances, however, only selected activities are likely to be micromanaged—usually the most lucrative, significant, politically sensitive, or disrespected. Micromanagement is most likely to occur in specific situations: (1) along targeted programmatic and funding lines, (2) where problems have surfaced, (3) to set an example for other elements within the organization, and (4) to portray "responsible concern" to parties outside the organization. Moreover, micromanagement may take place between some organizational levels and yet not involve all levels of the organization.

The following discussion focuses on the federal government, but the same considerations apply at state and local levels in the United States. Those considerations also apply in other settings.

Executive Branch

Within the executive branch, departments and agencies traditionally impose a disproportionately intense level of scrutiny and control on specific spending categories—budgets for travel, training, and office supplies are often highly controlled. Several factors encourage this attention: These funding areas are frequently more decentralized than other funding categories, are perceived as discretionary, are suspected of being open to abuse, and are narrowly defined (i.e., it is clear what the money is being spent on).

Micromanagement of one organization by another can take place when a pecking order exists among the organizations involved. Adding staff at higher organizational levels, such as within the Executive Office of the President, enables the upper-level component to exert more detailed control over lower-level organizations. The purview of high-level staff may remain broad (e.g., the president's chief domestic adviser) or may evolve into a microcosm of a lower-level organizational component (e.g., the president's national security staff and its influence over the Departments of State and Defense). Such shadow staffs make micromanagement in those areas inevitable.

At the federal level, a natural pecking order exists from the Office of Management and Budget (OMB) down to the departments and independent agencies that comprise the bulk of the executive branch, on down to the bureaus within each department. Two strongly related types of leverage enable an oversight organization such as OMB to micromanage another public organization: The first is hierarchical authority; the second is budgetary influence.

The Office of Management and Budget provides technical policy alignment and budgetary direction for the executive branch. The director of OMB does not have line authority over cabinet members or agency heads. Often, however, the OMB director speaks with the voice of the president—informally by asserting that such-and-such must be brought into line with the president's policy or political agenda or formally by issuing an OMB circular with which agency heads must comply.

The second mechanism, at least as powerful as the first, is the power of the purse. Every year OMB constructs the president's budget for the coming fiscal year (which runs from October through September). The budget document is presented to Congress within a few weeks after the president delivers a state of the union message to a joint session of Congress—and to the nation—in late January or early February. The voluminous document reflects the administration's budget strategies and priorities for the coming fiscal year and the four years that follow. It provides both a big-picture look at the proposed budget and an extremely detailed look that includes staffing and spending details for each independent agency, cabinet-level department, and bureau. Because OMB controls the budget development process, officials within OMB exert extensive authority over how funding is apportioned among the departments and agencies, within those agencies, within the bureaus of a department; and how the proposed funding within each bureau is to be spent—that is, what programs, what staffing levels, and what technology and other investment costs are funded. Congress also establishes legislative requirements that OMB micromanage certain executive branch activities; a prime example of this is the Paperwork Reduction Act of 1978 and subsequent legislation, which, in part, requires OMB to review and approve every government form that solicits information from the public and every change to any form.

Department heads, in their turn, use budgetary influence and line authority to micromanage bureaus within the agency and programs of interest within each bureau—a level of attention that bureau heads are likely to resist. In writing laws, Congress frequently inserts language that permits a department head to retain or delegate specified authority to lower organizational levels (e.g., "The secretary may, at his or her discretion, delegate. . . . "). Policy formulation is typically retained at the department- or agency-head level, while policy-execution authority is delegated to bureau heads and their subordinate offices. Even so, non-routine operational decisions often must first be cleared above the bureau level; those decisions may, it is argued, affect policy. In addition to policy-impact rationales and budget formulation approval, a third technique used by the upper echelons of a bureaucratic organization to micromanage lower echelons is filtering its formal access to Congress. Access control takes place in numerous ways, among them prior approval of testimony a bureau-level executive intends to give during a congressional subcommittee hearing, review and approval of answers to written questions from subcommittee staff preparing for hearings, and culling legislative proposals bureau executives wish to submit that deal with the administrative features of existing or prospective legislation.

Congress

Micromanagement occurs between branches of government as well as within branches. In the United States, the legislative branch has long held a reputation for micromanaging programs—and sometimes agencies—within the executive branch. When Congress micromanages, it most frequently does so through House and Senate oversight committees and subcommittees through appropriations action, or both.

The U.S. Congress is often seen to micromanage specific federal agencies and programs. Ironically, much of the bureaucracy within the executive branch—particularly its independent agencies—was created by the legislative branch as a means of keeping at arms length from day-to-day, case-by-case, administration of the law. A principal reason Congress established the Interstate Commerce Commission (ICC) was that the members of Congress felt inundated when attempting to deal with the rapidly expanding rail lines of that era. The ICC, established in 1887 and now near abolishment, was the first federal independent agency. Members of Congress, even at that time, did not appreciate having to provide separate legislative remedies about rates, services, and rights of way in each dispute among rail companies or between a rail company and the states through which it wished to build new tracks. By creating the ICC, Congress could use legislation to set forth basic guidance and then turn over to ICC—an administrative body—interpreting the law, filling in details lacking in the legislation, and resolving the squabbles among dissatisfied parties—except, of course, whenever Congress might choose to intervene.

Congress micromanages agencies in several ways. Among them are funding, conscribing legislation, reports accompanying legislation, hearings and guidance, and investigations such as those by the General Accounting Office (GAO).

Funding is simultaneously the most basic and most complex among methods of micromanaging. The most common method is by requiring most of an agency's budget to consist of an annual appropriation from Congress rather than an open-ended appropriation (e.g., for the life of a project or length of an acquisition) or through self-funding mechanisms (e.g., an agency's retaining service fees for government loans it administers). Other dominant forms of micromanagement by funding are either through restricting an agency from using appropriated funds in a certain way (e.g., "zero funding" an ongoing program or a project authorized by another congressional committee) or by specifying that the agency spend a particular minimum amount for a given purpose. What can make this form of micromanagement complicated is that appropriations originate in a different set of subcommittees from enabling legislation, which deals with program content. sometimes the goals or tactics of the committees conflict with one another; when that happens, the negative position usually wins.

Legislation that conscribes (i.e., restricts) an agency from taking certain actions that, otherwise, would fall within the agency's administrative jurisdiction is a second technique Congress uses to micromanage agencies within the executive branch. This happens in hundreds of small ways every year, with only a handful receiving widespread public attention. At various times, Congress has forbidden the Food and Drug Administration, a part of the Department of Health and Human Services, from making or enforcing regulations against the tobacco industry; the Federal Trade Administration, an arm of the Department of Commerce, from imposing new regulations on the insurance industry or the funeral industry; and the Internal Revenue Service, a bureau within the Department of the Treasury, from enforcing certain then-current tax laws as they applied to church-run colleges or from issuing regulations that define "employer" and "employee" for tax purposes. These prohibitions are frequently initiated in response to pressure from special interests and may be followed, one or several years later, by detailed legislation redirecting how the executive branch is to administer the areas in question. The statutory language can be direct or it can be deliberately obscure, defining a particular situation or set of conditions under which private-sector organizations are exempted from a specific law or regulation—those conditions are intentionally restrictive so that, at times, only a single company or individual qualifies for the exemption. Congress may also threaten legislation if an agency does not agree to redirect its efforts voluntarily, or it may seemingly empower an agency while requiring the implementing agency to secure prior written approval from a specified subcommittee before undertaking certain actions or spending particular funds.

Reports accompanying legislation are valuable tools enabling public administrators to understand the intent of Congress as it enacts legislation. Although details explained in these reports do not technically have the force of law, they carry almost as much weight. Consequently, such reports enable congressional micromanagement that is less obvious than when done directly through legislation or appropriations. The reports explain the background of a piece of legislation; they may also define studies, specific reporting requirements, deadlines expected of the implementing agency or agencies; and they may provide more details than included in the law itself about how the legislation is to be implemented and administered.

Congressional hearings and guidance are powerful micromanagement tools. Congressional committees and subcommittees traditionally hold two kinds of hearings annually to review each department and agency: One set of hearings, called oversight hearings, looks at the workings and impact of the agency; the other set of hearings, held by appropriations subcommittees, reviews the agency's proposed budget and its spending history. House and Senate hearings are held separately. In addition, a subcommittee may hold *ad hoc* hearings to probe a specific topic. Through written questions to the agencies that precede the hearings, discussion and questions put to agency officials during the hearings, and follow-up contacts, members of Congress can burrow deeply into both the operations and objectives of agencies, significantly influencing how the agency and its programs are run. Even without hearings, members of Congress have great latitude in corresponding with agency heads to make clear their thoughts and concerns about anything within the agency's jurisdiction.

Members of Congress can also ask the General Accounting Office to review programs within and across agencies, publish a written report of their findings, offer recommendations for change through legislation and through operational modifications, and testify before House and Senate hearings. GAO is part of the legislative branch. Most of GAO's reviews within the executive branch concern operational, record-keeping, budgetary, regulatory, and law enforcement aspects of agency activities rather than policy-level issues. GAO invites the agency under review to respond to a draft version of the report and incorporates or summarizes the comments in the report's final version, which is submitted to the requesting subcommittee or member of Congress. Reports may contribute to hearings and can become the focal point for a hearing. The agency must respond to the report with a description of how the GAO recommendations will be or have been implemented; or, if the agency disagrees, the agency must present reasons and defend its position.

Federal-State and Other Relations

Other major sets of micromanagement-prone relationships occur between levels of government and between governmental entities and the public. Here, too, funding is frequently a key element, often taking the form of transfer payments. Transfer payments include categorical and block grants-in-aid; they also include social services payments, such as unemployment and medicaid, as well as loans and loan guarantees, such as for housing, higher education, and small business ventures.

Transfer payments typically come with "strings attached"—that is, requirements or conditions that must be met in order to qualify for the money. With categorical grants-in-aid from the federal government to states and localities, the conditions are likely to involve matching funds from the recipient, meeting minimum qualification standards, adhering to specified time frames, submitting to periodic inspections, and providing detailed reports. All are devices for micromanaging projects. Block grants involve fewer strings, but they are never condition-free. (Federal revenue-sharing, which involved almost no conditions, was abandoned in the 1980s.) Direct payments to individuals and businesses are likewise accompanied by detailed conditions. Direct and federally backed student loans, for example, set requirements based on identified need, student and family income, past and current academic performance, university accreditation, student course load, playback agreement schedules, and other factors. Funding recipients are likely to criticize strings as costly, burdensome, and even counterproductive; consequently, some potential recipients elect not to participate because of such concerns.

But micromanagement can occur without funding, too. State sometimes refer to certain federally imposed requirements (usually involving health and safety) as "unfunded mandates." Complicated or pervasive government rules and regulations—whether issued by a federal agency, a state government, or a local jurisdiction—can have the effect of micromanaging whoever is being regulated (e.g., wetlands restoration, smoking bans in public areas, residential zoning restrictions, school busing plans). Moreover, as these examples suggest, the label of "micromanagement" is more likely to be invoked by parties who disagree with the intended objective of a regulation or ordinance than by those who agree with its intent.

Finally, although this discussion has focused on micromanagement in the political sphere, micromanagement occurs as readily in business and other walks of contemporary life—anywhere where one party has the ability to impose its influence on another party: Subsidiaries of conglomerate corporations may find they have no choice but to conform to edicts from the parent company. Franchise businesses may find themselves restricted to a select set of suppliers and a host of company rules. Mortgage bankers may require an exhaustive array of information from borrowers. Community associations may impose oppressive limitations on what homeowners shall and shall not do to the exteriors of their homes. Labor unions, through negotiated contracts, may require an employer to submit detailed information on every employee promotion or termination. The list is endless.

Micromanagement is a practice and a tool. In selected situations, it can be used advantageously; in most situations, it is a poor choice. Micromanagement is antithetical to many contemporary management practices, such as employee empowerment and entrepreneurial organizations. Nevertheless, micromanagement is a manifestation of the very human need for control over others and our environment. Consequently, micromanagement will be with us for a long, long time.

KENNETH L. NICHOLS

BIBLIOGRAPHY

Dickens, Charles, 1843. *A Christmas Carol*. London: Chapman and Hall.
———, 1839. *Oliver Twist*. London: Chapman and Hall.
Gerth, Hans H., and C. Wright Mills, trans. and eds., 1946. *From Max Weber: Essays in Sociology*. New York: Oxford University Press. Most of Weber's observations about bureaucracy are drawn from *Wirtschaft and Gesellschaft*, segments of which were published from 1917 into the 1920s.
Gulick, Luther H., and Lyndall F. Urwick, 1938 [1969]. *Papers on the Science of Administration*. New York: A. M. Kelley.
Hersey, Paul, and Kenneth H. Blanchard, 1982. *Management of Organizational Behavior*, 4th ed. Englewood Cliffs, NJ: Prentice-Hall.
Huxley, Aldous, 1932. *Brave New World*. London: Chatto and Windus.
McGregor, Douglas M., 1960. *The Human Side of Enterprise*. New York: McGraw-Hill.
Orwell, George, 1946. *Animal Farm*. New York: Harcourt, Brace.
Taylor, Frederick W., 1947. *The Principles of Scientific Management*. New York: Norton.
Williams, Tennessee, 1945. *The Glass Menagerie, a Play*. New York: Random House.
Wilson, James Q., 1989. *Bureaucracy: What Government Agencies Do and Why They Do It*. New York: Basic Books.

MIDDLE MANAGEMENT.

The level of management between senior and first-line management. Senior, or executive, managers generally are responsible for long-term, strategic management of the organization, including the setting of organizational policy and direction. First-line, or supervisory, managers are responsible for directing, controlling, and evaluating the work of first-line service, or production workers.

The responsibilities of middle managers overlap those of both senior and first-line management. Middle managers find themselves responsible for developing and communicating organizational policies and programs and, at the same time, for the supervision of supervisors. As a member of the program and policy team, the middle manager can provide a valuable organizational perspective on proposed policies and strategies. For example, the middle manager may be able to evaluate more accurately the capacity of an organization's workforce to respond to a new direction. In addition, the middle manager usually serves as the primary spokesperson for organizational programs and policies that affect the workforce or workplace.

As a member of the service team, the middle manager assists and support first-line managers in their supervision of employees. The manager's primary roles are as coach, counselor, and team leader. The roles of middle managers in both policy and service pose three significant challenges: they have a boss's responsibility without a boss's authority; they must function as both specialists and generalists; and they must meet the conflicting demands of superiors, subordinates, and peers and still get the job done (Uyterhoeven 1989). Middle managers must assume "the bilingual role of translating the strategic language of . . . superiors into the operational language of subordinates in order to get results" (Uyterhoeven 1989, p. 138). They also must make explicit the network of relationships that support policies, procedures, and programs.

In a study for the American Management Association, Boyatzis (1983) identified four major competency areas for middle managers. They were (1) the use of socialized power, or the ability to build alliances and networks; (2) the management of group processes, including the skills in team building and the ability to have subordinates adhere to a common objective; (3) accurate self-assessment, or a candid assessment of personal strengths and weakness; and (4) positive regard, or a positive belief in others. The stamina, adaptability, and self-control identified as aspects of positive regard reflect the powerful demands of middle management. Training for middle managers generally reflects these needs and competencies, emphasizing, for example, the need to "collaborate and coordinate rather than command and control" (Van Wart *et al.* 1993, p. 13).

Mintzberg (1990, p. 164) describes middle managers as working in "real time at an unrelenting pace." He identifies managers' activities as occurring in three role areas: interpersonal, informational, and decisional. Interpersonal roles (figurehead, leader, liaison) seem unrelated to organizational objectives but are critical for their achievement. Informational roles (monitor, disseminator, spokesperson) require a reliance on verbal media rather than written documents. Decisional roles (entrepreneur, disturbance handler, resource allocator, negotiator) depend on using judgment and intuition.

Despite their importance to organizational success, middle managers in the public sector have received little attention. There is limited research on how they express leadership and their management philosophy, or on how they establish effective working relationships with politically appointed senior managers and with legislative bodies. Three things appear to distinguish middle managers in the public sector from those in business and industry. First, they may be the highest level of career employee in the organization. Their superiors often are appointed by elected chief executives and reflect the political climate and will of the time. True organizational leadership thus may fall on the shoulders of middle managers.

Second, as career bureaucrats, middle managers hold the organizational memory. This knowledge is critical in establishing or changing the corporate culture and in integrating innovative approaches into established procedures. Finally, because of their unique relationships to politically appointed senior managers and their long-term knowledge of the organization, government middle managers play a pivotal role in organizational change. They can serve as change agents, using their professional expertise to support and encourage change efforts. Alternatively, they can serve as barriers to change, particularly if they believe that a change sought by a superior or the political system is inconsistent with their personal or organizational philosophy. Because they are protected by civil service rules, their ability to derail change is far more significant than it is in the private sector.

Once seen as the avenue to senior management, middle management now has become a career terminus for many individuals. Demographics—especially the aging of the baby-boom generation—have, in part, caused this, as fewer senior management spots become available to middle-aged middle managers. Politics also have played a part, as an increasing number of formerly career management positions have become subject to appointment by the chief executive officer.

Finally, economics have been important in changing the nature of middle management and reducing the opportunities for advancement to or from that rank. "Reinventing," "streamlining," "downsizing," and other current attempts to make government more efficient and effective have had significant effect on middle managers. Middle managers may find their positions eliminated as new management strategies push decisionmaking and other traditional middle-management responsibilities to the frontline employees.

Middle managers who remain in the organization often find themselves directly on the firing line when new methods are tried, and they may be asked to learn entirely new management approaches (Labich 1989). Those middle managers are challenged to learn and change rapidly. Those unable to adapt may find themselves spending "surprisingly little time managing and quite a lot of time at routine clerical tasks" (Schellhardt 1990, p. B1).

Retaining middle managers in this environment requires attention to both their compensation and their challenges. Compensation plans that are not tied to rigid salary structures serve to motivate middle managers (Cowan 1987). Even more important are professional challenges such as task force assignments and lateral transfers to new areas of the organization. These encourage middle managers to continue to learn and to develop within their careers.

SUSAN C PADDOCK

BIBLIOGRAPHY

Boyatzis, Richard, 1982. *The Competent Manager.* New York: John Wiley and Sons.

Cowan, Robert A., 1987. "How Not to Lose the Most Talented Middle Managers." *Boardroom Reports* (August 1) 3.

Labich, Kenneth, 1989. "Making Over Middle Managers." *Fortune* (May 2) 58–64.

Mintzberg, Henry, 1990. "The Manager's Job: Folklore and Fact." *Harvard Business Review,* vol. 68, no. 2 (March-April) 163–175.

Schellhardt, Timothy D., 1990. "Middle Managers Get Mired in the Middle." *Wall Street Journal* (November 28).

Uyterhoeven, Hugo, 1989. "General Managers in the Middle." *Harvard Business Review,* vol. 67, no. 5 (September-October) 136–145.

Van Wart, Montgomery, N. Joseph Cayer, and Steve Cook, 1993. *Handbook of Training and Development for the Public Sector.* San Francisco: Jossey-Bass.

MILES'S LAW. A maxim that evolved from a theory developed by Rufus E. Miles when he managed a branch of the Federal Bureau of the Budget responsible for labor and welfare in the late 1940s. Miles's Law states, "Where you stand depends on where you sit." The law theorizes that there is a direct correlation between the position an individual takes on a particular issue and the title or position that individual holds in the organization.

Development of the Theory

Although Miles himself admitted the "concept was as old as Plato," the "phraseology" evolved after a sequence of events that took place while Miles was supervising a group of middle-level federal employees at the Bureau of the Budget. One of Miles's employees, a budget examiner, was offered a position in a federal agency over which Miles's group had the power of budgetary review. The subordinate explained to Miles that he was concerned about working at a new agency that he did not perceive as very efficient. The subordinate also had been critical of this particular agency in his capacity as an examiner. The job, however, was a grade higher than the position of examiner the subordinate currently held and the income increase based on the job's higher grade was attractive to the employee. The employee informed Miles that he would like to remain in his current position as an examiner but with the increased salary of the position he had been offered at the other agency. Miles, while expressing appreciation for the employee's loyalty, refused to increase the individual's pay and the employee resigned his position with Miles to accept the position at the other agency. After the employee left the bureau, Miles remarked to his fellow workers that in a very short time, the former employee would become a defender of the very policies he had been critical of when he was in the position of an examiner because "where you stand depends on where you sit."

Lessons to Be Learned from Miles's Law

Miles determined there are three lessons that can be drawn from Miles's Law and its impact on organizations. The first lesson is that when individuals change positions in an organization, their position on issues impacting the area of their new area of responsibility will evolve to reflect the needs of that area. An example of such an evolution exists with the case of John Gardner, Chairman of President Johnson's Task Force on Education. Gardner, President of the Carnegie Corporation, was asked to chair a task force on education in 1964. The task force under Gardner's leadership concluded that the Department of Health, Education, and Welfare (HEW) as constituted in 1964 could not adequately address the needs of education. The task force was split as to whether a separate cabinet-level Department of Education should be established. Less than a year later, Gardner accepted the position of Secretary of Health, Education, and Welfare. When asked in his new position if education should be removed from HEW, Gardner replied with an emphatic no. Now that Gardner was the secretary and no longer simply a detached evaluator, his position of the issue was reversed. He did not wish to see his responsibilities decreased or his opportunities limited. In the case of Gardner, where he stood on the issue was now a direct result of the perspectives of his new position at HEW.

The second more subtle lesson that can be learned is that no individual can serve objectively on a committee or task force that is called upon to evaluate the agency or commission of which the individual is an integral part.

This is the problem that impacts internal committees that are called together to assess and evaluate their own agency's efficiency and effectiveness. Miles believes that no person from within the organization can "totally rise" above the individual concerns and issues of the agency they are called upon to evaluate if this individual is a part of the organization. Such individuals will be unable to make sound recommendations as they will always be concerned about the impact of their recommendations on the organization to which they eventually return. Miles feels that people should be placed in a position where they are asked to render a recommendation or decision that will impact their own future.

The third implication of Miles's Law concerns communication. The head of an agency or organization must constantly evaluate the channels of communication from which data are received within the organization. No subordinate, according to Miles's Law, is able to give a superior information that is not partially biased in favor of the messenger's agenda. Even the most trustworthy subordinates cannot help but flavor their communications to their superior with the essence of their own opinions or biases. Miles noted that Franklin Roosevelt was an excellent user of the multichannel communication process, as he gathered information from many sources within his organization. Richard Nixon, on the other hand, drew his data from a select few with disastrous results.

Impact of Miles's Law

Miles's Law makes it clear that no individual can be divorced from the perspectives of the responsibilities of the position they hold. These perspectives will change when the individual assumes a new capacity in a different agency and these revised perspectives can legitimately be the opposite of previous positions taken by the individual because "where you stand depends on where you sit."

JEFFERY K. GUILER

BIBLIOGRAPHY

Miles, Jr., Rufus E., 1976. *Awakening from the American Dream.* New York: Universe Books.
———, 1978. "The Origins and Meanings of Miles's Law." *Public Administration Review* (September-October) 399–403.
———, 1979. "Miles Six Other Maxims of Management." *Organizational Dynamics* (Summer).

MILITARY-INDUSTRIAL COMPLEX.

All the offices, organizations, trade associations, and business enterprises operating in a country's domestic armaments market, in both defense procurement (the demand side of the market) and military production (the supply side).

Prior to World War II, most countries maintained comparatively small standing forces (navies and armies until World War I, afterward air arms as well), and comparatively small sectors of their economies were engaged in supplying those forces with material and equipment. Apart from a number of dockyards, arsenals, and ordnance factories, typically owned and operated by the state, there were virtually no entire industries and very few individual plants devoted solely to weapons development and manufacture. When it was necessary to employ armed forces to a degree beyond the capacity of the standing contingents and to produce arms for a war effort, the adult male population and the country's industrial capacity were mobilized for military duty; and once the crisis had passed–the war won or otherwise terminated–there was demobilization. Sailors and soldiers returned to civilian life. Factories reverted to making products for civil markets.

During the cold war (1945–1989), for almost all countries in the northern hemisphere, things were completely different. Following the defeat of Nazi Germany, the Soviet Union and Eastern bloc countries did not demobilize completely. Quite the contrary: They kept substantial forces-in-being, whose war-fighting capability they took pains to preserve and, indeed, constantly to improve. In the United States and Western Europe, demobilization did proceed in the second half of the 1940s. But it was soon halted, and governments approved rearmament so as to be able to match the might of the USSR and its allies. It appeared important to all to establish and sustain a military balance in and around Europe. Both East and West judged it prudent to develop and maintain the means to deter aggression by the other and to defend against invasion if deterrence failed–and, as a result, became engaged in an arms competition (if not, at times, an arms race).

Conditions were thus created that led each of the leading powers–the United States, the United Kingdom, and France on the Western side, the Soviet Union on the Eastern side–to establish what has been termed a "permanent war economy." Each kept substantial numbers of troops under arms plus significant research and development (R&D), technological and manufacturing capacity committed to military work, with large bureaucracies to define what the one would require from the other and to supervise its provision.

Moreover, under the circumstances, within each country the corps of bureaucrats–uniformed and civilian–responsible for procuring weapons made common cause with the scientists, engineers, and managers in industry whose business was producing weapons. The former were interested in obtaining the most effective and up-to-date equipment for the forces. The latter were interested in making such equipment, the more the better. To all appearances these groups were, respectively, the buyers and sellers in the armaments marketplace. But their conduct came to resemble that of partners in a shared mission to apply to weapons acquisition as much money as could be wrested from legislatures; and it appeared to many observers that the nominal purchasers and nominal providers were acting in collusion to extract more funds year by year to pay for successively more complex and costly weapon systems.

The term "military-industrial complex" (MIC) was coined to capture the sense of common cause, the suggestion of collusion, even the whiff of conspiracy present in this state of affairs. In this area of public business those responsible for spending taxpayers' money were for all practical purposes in league with those to whom they were channeling it. The institutional and individual operators on the demand and supply sides of the armaments market were not performing the distinct and essentially adversarial roles that economic logic and constitutional propriety required. Distinctions were blurred, adversarial behavior absent. There was, as it were, a solitary actor on a stage designed for an entire cast of players.

That there was common cause, collusion, even conspiracy in the American weapons acquisition process during the 1950s and 1960s is not in question. The evidence in the literature is extensive and persuasive. Furthermore, did not so distinguished and respected a figure as President Dwight D. Eisenhower warn, in a celebrated valedictory speech, of the disturbing power of the MIC and its potential for distorting national priorities? Also there is little doubt that in France the distinction between arms buyers and arms sellers was not only blurred but nonexistent. After all, the same government body–the *Direction Generale d'Armement*–was both procurement agency and either production company itself (through its *Directions Techniques* for naval and land-forces armaments) or patron of state-owned enterprises (notably the *Sociétés Nationales* in the aerospace industry). Note, though, that it was a deliberate choice of French policymakers to manage military procurement and production together, under the rubric of a resources strategy expressly designed to safeguard national technical competence and competitiveness in key areas–partly to promote indigenous technology, partly to preserve France's freedom to pursue an independent grand strategy. The position in Britain was more ambiguous. As in France, a symbiotic relationship between purchasers and suppliers existed in some sectors, while in others the fact that the single (state) purchaser typically confronted a sole "preferred supplier" was similarly conducive to recognition of a certain identity of interest and purpose. At the same time, no one in Britain ever took military-industrial conspiracy theories particularly seriously; and at no time did British governments adopt the same single-minded approach to defense-industrial policy as their counterparts in France. As for the

Soviet Union, the absence of an armaments market being a fact of life (or, rather, ideology), the existence of a national MIC was proclaimed as a matter of pride and never regarded as a possible cause for concern (not in the 1950s and 1960s, that is).

By the time the USSR and other Eastern bloc states had begun to see the socialist MIC—and its appetite for financial and technological resources—as a liability rather than an asset (in the 1980s), the United States and the West Europeans had already gone a long way in addressing the dangers of which Eisenhower and others had warned during the years of rearmament for the cold war: by scrutinizing their forces' operational requirements more intensively; by insisting on more stringent cost-effectiveness analyses before embarking on new development programs; by promoting more open competition for most military R&D and production business; by striking tougher bargains with suppliers on all procurement contracts (largely abandoning cost-plus-fixed-fee terms in favor of fixed-price deals on manufacturing work); and by regulating such practices as "revolving door" employment (i.e., curtailing the freedom accorded to top military officers and defense officials to retire from public office to lucrative employment with private-sector armaments firms to whom they had previously awarded contracts, or at least being more attentive to the potential for corrupt practice that exists wherever such transitions are permitted). Indeed, by the later 1980s and early 1990s, the prime concern in Western defense ministries was not so much how to control the MIC in order to prevent abuses of power but rather how to safeguard R&D and production capacity threatened by the shrinkage in military spending—and especially military investment spending—that accompanied the cold war's end. While in the former Eastern bloc it appeared that the authorities could not dismantle the MIC rapidly enough, and the talk was all of procurement reform, output diversification, and plant conversion, in North America and Western Europe governments were now asking themselves how best to ensure retention of a viable "defense technology and industrial base" (DTIB).

In the United States—and elsewhere, but to a lesser extent elsewhere—the DTIB issue so overshadowed any residual MIC anxieties in the immediate post–cold war period that the latter all but disappeared from the political agenda. For the purposes of this new American debate, the DTIB was defined, in a 1992 study, as "the combination of people, institutions, technological know-how and facilities used to design, develop, manufacture and maintain the weapons and supporting equipment needed to meet US national security objectives" (U.S. Congress Office of Technology Assessment 1992, p. 4). For all practical purposes this describes the supply side of the armaments and material market, whose underpinning shrinking defense budgets had been placed under threat.

So far as the main lines of the debate are concerned, the "Building Future Security" investigation drew the important conclusion that, while the capacity of the (then) current DTIB exceeded foreseeable requirements, restructuring of the base rather than "proportional downsizing" was required, even though "powerful military, economic and political interests support downsizing . . . in a manner that allows the maximum number of firms and organizations to survive" (p. 6)—clear echoes there of earlier MIC concerns. It further urged that elements of the future DTIB be better integrated "to achieve the best use of resources for the DTIB as a whole" (p. 6); that the Defense Department adopt a "new paradigm" for procurement, resting on "a willingness to purchase knowledge rather than hardware in many cases" (p. 7); that attention be paid to promoting "flexibility in development and manufacture" (p. 7); that effort be put into identifying the "defense industrial sectors in which R&D alone is sufficient, those in which warm production lines must be preserved and those in which other alternatives may exist" (p. 7); and, most interestingly (and representing a potential death blow to the conspiratorial MIC), that the Defense Department be disabused of any notion that it should be "at the forefront of all defense-related product and process technologies" (p. 7). On this final point, the study noted that "defense-relevant technologies are increasingly developed in the civil sector and by other countries" (p. 7).

Similar themes featured in a parallel debate that took place in Europe during the first half of the 1990s. Governments acknowledged the need for structural adjustment and nationalization of the DTIB (which, indeed, proceeded apace). They also acknowledged the need for imaginative thinking about how best to retain adequate, but not excessive, productive capacity through periods of lean demand. Most important, they came to recognize that in advanced technology the once-pronounced civil-military divide had effectively disappeared and the era of "dual-use" technologies had arrived.

In the latter development, perhaps, lies the key reason for the diminished concern about malignant MICs. When there are fewer laboratories and factories whose fortunes depend on defense-related business, and when there is less military work anyhow, it is hard for procurement bureaucracies and armaments manufacturers to make common cause, collude, and conspire. This raises an intriguing general question. Maybe we have witnessed the end of the "permanent war economy" and are poised for a return to pre–World War II conditions in military-industrial affairs. With reduced budgets, smaller standing forces, no entire industries, and few individual plants devoted solely to weapons development and production, revival of the mobilization-demobilization approach to security provision is certainly possible. If that happens, the expression "military-industrial complex" could go out of fashion altogether or remain in use only to denote a cold war concept describing a cold war phenomenon.

DAVID E. GREENWOOD

BIBLIOGRAPHY

Brosza M., and P. Lock, 1992. *Restructuring of Arms Production in Western Europe.* Oxford: Oxford University Press (for the Stockholm International Peace Research Institute (SIPRI).

Duscha, Julius, 1967. *Arms, Money, and Politics.* New York: Ives Washburn.

Faramazyan, R., 1974. *USA, Militarism, and the Economy.* Moscow: Progress Publishers (Russian edition, 1970).

Melman, Seymour, 1971. *The War Economy of the United States: Readings in Military Industry and Economy.* New York: Praeger.

Rosen, Stephen, ed, 1973. *Testing the Theory of the Military-Industrial Complex.* Lexington, MA: Prentice-Hall.

Sarkesian, Sam C., ed, 1972. *The Military-Industrial Complex: A Reassessment.* Beverley Hills, CA: Sage.

Stevenson, Paul, 1973. "The Military-Industrial Complex: An Examination of Corporate Capitalism in America." *Journal of Political and Military Sociology,* vol. 1: 247–259.

U.S. Congress Office of Technology Assessment, 1992. *Building Future Security,* OTA-ISC-530. Washington, DC: U.S. Government Printing Office.

MINISTERIAL ADVISERS.

Members of the personal staff of a minister who are responsible for providing advice for that person's term of office.

The concept of the ministerial adviser covers a range of appointees who perform a number of tasks in serving a minister. This role, or broadly similar roles—*inter alia* ministerial assistant, special(ist) adviser, ministerial consultant—exists in a number of countries. The common element is that as a political appointee, the adviser is subject to the survival of the minister, and the position has no existence or status independent of the minister. The advisers also need to be distinguished from public servants—historically the minister's main policy advisers—who normally occupy a position that has traditionally been distinguished by permanence and other public service features.

The role of the adviser to political leaders has a long history, but the ministerial adviser is a particular product of the expansion of the administrative state in the twentieth century that conferred greater discretion and independence on public service. Once ministers sought to reinforce (or to retrieve) their power, they had as one option the expansion of the resources of their private office. The ministerial adviser became a prominent addition to executive branches in Westminster-based bureaucracies over recent decades as a means of extending the influence of the ministerial office and the political realm within the executive. This suggests the main rationale for the ministerial adviser: to provide support to the minister in carrying out functions that cannot be delegated to departments without handing over responsibilities deemed to be ministerial; to augment the resources available to ministers in carrying out their tasks, thereby strengthening ministerial control; and to provide alternative advice to that available from the public service.

The propensity to use ministerial advisers varies between countries. As a means of influencing and mediating between the political executive and the bureaucracy, it is possible to distinguish systems that rely on ministerial advisers and others that rely on political appointments, although some use both. Ministerial advisers have been a principal means of influencing public service in countries that have maintained a clear distinction between political and public service careers, such as Westminster-derived systems, but they may also have a pivotal role in countries where the career streams are not so clearly separated.

Countries that use ministerial advisers have varied in their willingness to develop this form of advisory system for ministers. Thus, the British arrangements have been less developed than those of Australia or Canada. The former has experimented with two advisers per minister but has otherwise tended to employ them on a selective basis. Australia and Canada have taken the concept further in developing the minister's office. The ministerial cabinet, used in France (and other European countries), is perhaps the most distinctive expression of the idea of having a group of advisers operating out of the minister's office, but in this case there is a much greater need for ministerial direction because there is no head of department, and the directive role is significant. The members of the cabinet have generally been public servants who resume other administrative roles once their term is finished.

Ministerial advisers perform a number of functions that cover the spectrum ranging from advice on political matters through substantive policy to routine operational and strategic considerations. The main forms of political advice cover the cabinet process and departmental policy proposals and operations. In addition, there are partisan relationships: liaison with the parliamentary party caucus on policy matters and the national and subnational party organization. There is also liaison with departments and agencies, other ministerial offices, and interest groups. Another area is the media and promotional functions, which involve advice on communication matters such as press releases and speeches and the handling of media appearances.

It can be seen that policy advice is only one component. Advisers may play a definable and specific policy role, which may reflect their expertise, but a generalist role is possibly more usual. The adviser can exercise a major influence on policy processes, if not always on the content of policy. Observers of Australian and Canadian advisers have discounted their actual contribution to policy; the policy process has been depicted as a collective exercise with the contribution of the ministerial actors being significant as a "group enterprise" but indeterminate individually (Walter 1986, p. 58). High-level policy advisers are more likely to be in the offices of senior ministers such as the prime minister or treasurer.

It is common for the main functions to be associated with specialized roles, for advisers are often located within a ministerial advisory system that consists of a range of specialist tasks designed to support the minister. Advisers may be generalists or specialists, political or nonpolitical, and their work might normally include political, policy, and other activities of some strategic significance. New governments may rely more on political advisers and outsiders but appreciate the contribution of public servants as they become more comfortable in office. The minister's office will employ specialists for handling the media (perhaps a former journalist), a party liaison (possibly a party member), or for a departmental liaison (often a public servant on secondment). There have also been experiments with chiefs of staff, the most ambitious and somewhat problematic being those for Canadian ministerial offices in the 1980s, whose status was almost equal with that of the department head.

The size of the minister's office varies widely between countries and portfolios. There has been a tendency for them to expand over time with the growing complexity of government and the increasing specialization of roles. They range in size from a single adviser through the more substantial European offices to the large prime minister's offices (PMOs) of Canada and the United Kingdom with over 100 staff members. The distinctive roles are most clearly apparent in a larger PMO, such as Britain's Number 10 Downing Street, where the main elements are the private office, the political office, the press office, the policy unit, and special advisers.

Ministerial advisers are part of a network of key political and administrative relationships in many countries. The experience indicates that it is possible for ministerial staff and public servants to work harmoniously and effectively together provided that they recognize their distinctive functions. Ministerial advisers have become an accepted, even integral component of modern government.

JOHN HALLIGAN

BIBLIOGRAPHY

Plasse, Micheline, 1994. *Ministerial Chiefs of Staff in the Federal Government in 1990: Profiles, Recruitment, Duties, and Relations with Senior Public Servants.* Ottawa: Canadian Centre for Management Development.
Plowden, William, ed., 1987. *Advising the Rulers.* Oxford: Basil Blackwell.
Savoie, Donald J., 1983. "The Minister's Staff: The Need for Reform." *Canadian Public Administration,* vol. 26, no. 4 (Winter) 509–524.
Walter, James, 1986. *The Ministers' Minders: Personal Advisers in National Government.* Melbourne: Oxford University Press.

MINISTERIAL RESPONSIBILITY. The accountability linkage between the executive and the legislature in parliamentary systems based on the Westminster model. These systems are found in Britain and many of its former colonies, such as Canada, Australia, and New Zealand. Under this model, ministers, who are always members of the legislature unlike U.S. cabinet secretaries, are under an obligation to answer for the policies and actions of their departments within Parliament and, where serious policy or administrative failures occur, resign from the ministry.

Unlike the U.S. model, where the executive and legislative branches are elected separately and are constitutional equals in the sense that neither is subordinate to the other or removable by the other (except through the rarely used powers of presidential impeachment), a "responsible" executive is removable and responsible to the legislature or Parliament.

The convention dates back to the late nineteenth century when the political parties acquired greater importance and the British civil service became a permanent, nonpartisan service (following the implementation of the Northcote-Trevelyan civil service reforms in the 1870s). As a result, the division between politicians and officials became much sharper than before. Thus, for practical and constitutional reasons, civil servants ceased to be directly responsible to Parliament, whereas ministers came to be held individually responsible for the actions of their departments.

Over recent years, many academics and practitioners have questioned the effectiveness of ministerial responsibility as an accountability device. Ministerial accountability may well have been a plausible and workable principle in the nineteenth-century minimalist state. However, as government bureaucracies have mushroomed, particularly since World War II, the notion of one person being held responsible for everything (the principle of direct responsibility) that occurs within a bureaucracy employing thousands of people and spending large sums of money has lost plausibility. Most commentators would agree that ministers should be held responsible for major "policy" decisions, but the extent to which they should be held responsible for "operational" or "administrative" failures has been widely debated. Moreover, recent developments in public management have further eroded the traditional notion of ministerial responsibility; in particular, where semi-independent bodies (such as the British 1988 *Next Steps* reorganizations) have been created outside traditional bureaucratic structures.

The doctrine has also been criticized because of the weakness of Parliaments. The presence of disciplined political parties in Westminster-type Parliaments enables the executive or government of the day to dominate Parliament, unlike the U.S. case, where the executive is quite separate from the legislature and characterized by weak party discipline. Consequently, ministers can usually rely on the support of their party backbenchers in Parliament. Backbenchers are unwilling to denigrate their own government, particularly as ministerial advancement depends on their loyalty to senior government ministers and the prime minister.

The infrequency of ministerial resignations has also been cited as evidence of the weakness of the convention. Yet, interest in the convention has revived during the 1980s. In Britain, a wave of ministerial resignation, that Woodhouse attributes to the principle, occurred during the Margaret Thatcher and John Major Conservative Governments (10 between 1979 and 1992 compared with 11 over the previous 35 years from 1945 to 1979) (Woodhouse 1994, p. 43).

However, of these ten resignations, only four involved departmental fault in which the minister was involved. The best known was that of Lord Carrington, the foreign secretary, and two of his junior ministers who resigned in 1982 following the Foreign Office's failure to anticipate the Argentinian invasion of the Falkland Islands. Three other ministers resigned over personal fault, for example in 1990 Nicholas Ridley, then Secretary of the State for Trade and Industry, made several offensive remarks about the Germans in a magazine interview, which was widely seen within government and Parliament as a major political misjudgment. Finally, three ministers resigned over personal faults of a private nature. For example, Cecil Parkinson, then Secretary of State for Trade and Industry, resigned in 1983 following revelations that he had an affair, which resulted in the imminent birth of a child, although his decision to end the affair, despite having given an earlier promise to divorce his wife and marry his mistress, appears to have been more damaging than the actual affair.

The evidence suggests that resignation is most likely to occur when ministers have committed serious personal indiscretions (although more appears to be required than just an extramarital affair) and/or displayed extremely poor political judgment. The seriousness of these failings and whether there is a political requirement for resignation is usually determined by the strength of feeling within the majority parliamentary party, often despite prime ministerial attempts to prevent the resignation. The majority party in Britain, certainly the Conservative Parliamentary Party, has shown itself to be more vigilant in the case of personal indiscretion rather than departmental or policy failures.

Although the convention may have been effective in policing the morals of Conservative Party ministers in Britain, it is less so in sheeting home policy and manage-

ment responsibility to ministers. Ministers enjoy considerable latitude in evading responsibility despite the convention. Ministers can exploit the unclear division between "policy" and "administration" or "operational" matters to disclaim responsibility for failures within their department. For instance, during the 1990s, two British home secretaries were able to evade responsibility for major prison escapes, which, they argued, were purely "operational" and not "policy" failures. Ministers can also refuse to divulge information and their reasons for taking a course of action on the grounds of national security, public interest, or confidentiality. They can then use their party support within Parliament to prevent any moves to censure them.

The British judiciary, too, in reviewing ministerial decisions has failed to challenge the view that ministerial responsibility is an effective restraint on the irresponsible exercise of ministerial power. In contrast, the Australian High Court, which identifies much less with the executive than its British equivalents, has raised questions over the adequacy of the convention.

Ministerial Responsibility and the Civil Service

The convention has important implications for the work of civil servants. Ministerial responsibility has encouraged the development of centralized controls and standardized systems as ministers, and senior civil servants on their behalf, try to minimize the possibility of politically embarrassing mistakes by the department or, more often, the possibility of awkward information leaking out. In this way, the convention does not sit comfortably with the more recent demand that public sector managers should be autonomous and be less risk averse.

Civil servants exercise power in law and by convention on behalf of their ministers. They are permanent and do not change when the government changes. The traditional nineteenth-century departmental model, on which the convention rests, assumes that ministers have direct control over their civil servants. However, as the size and complexity of government has increased, so has the power of officials and the difficulties ministers face in asserting themselves over their departments. The convention has been questioned especially as many commentators and indeed former ministers have argued that civil servants can easily capture ministers and frustrate government policy. It is seen by these critics as a smoke-screen for civil service power rather than a means of ensuring responsible government.

In addition, the tradition of civil service anonymity, the other side of ministerial responsibility, has also declined as civil servants have increasingly been questioned by parliamentary committees and been identified publicly with government policy. Ministerial responsibility has traditionally protected them by making ministers, not civil servants, responsible for justifying government policy. Civil servants cannot publicly defend their actions or answer allegations of misconduct or incompetence. However, concern has been expressed, not least by civil service unions, that individual civil servants are increasingly maned and blamed by ministers and parliamentary committees yet denied the right of reply.

Recent Developments in Public Management

Recent developments in public management are posing a serious challenge to the convention of ministerial responsibility. In Britain, under the *Next Steps* reorganizations (named after the 1988 White Paper *The Next Steps*), ministerial departments have been broken up into agencies to deliver most of the services of government; about three-quarters of the civil service now work in these agencies. The government introduced these agencies to increase the efficiency of service delivery either, where possible, through privatization or the introduction of private-sector business methods. In addition, the government has argued that the agencies enable accountability and blame to be better located than in the traditional, large ministerial departments.

The chief executives of these new agencies are responsible for managing them on the basis of framework documents agreed on with the minister. Despite the recommendation in the original *Next Steps* report that the convention of ministerial responsibility be modified, the Conservative government insisted on retaining a conventional view of ministerial responsibility. Thus, despite recognizing the individual responsibility of the chief executive, the government has insisted that he or she only works and speaks on behalf of the minister. Some commentators have argued that the retention of the convention contradicts the main point of having agencies, which was to have a chief executive with personal responsibility for carrying out delegated powers. The suggestion has been made that ministers are trying to get the best of both worlds—retaining control over the agencies, yet using the agency concept to justify any refusal on their part to take responsibility for mistakes committed within an agency.

Moreover, the chief executives, quite unlike agency heads in the U.S. government, do not personally have the constitutional authority to account to parliamentary select committees for their delegated responsibilities (except in the narrow role as accounting officers). At best, they can only provide information or evidence to these committees on behalf of their minister. To date only one has resigned following management failings. The chief executive of the Child Support Agency resigned in September 1994, following fierce criticism of its pursuit of absent fathers.

Nevertheless, the agency chief executives have ceased to be anonymous civil servants and have acquired a much more public identity than has been usual for British civil servants. Chief executives, especially those appointed from outside the civil service, are acquiring a greater public presence and beginning to account directly to parliamentary select committees. Some chief executives have begun to defend their management performance before these committees and in the media. Indeed in the future some chief executives might come to pose a significant challenge to ministers, in much the same way as bureau chiefs in the United States can usually defy the cabinet secretary, who is their nominal superior.

Despite the government's constitutional conservatism, the agencies potentially could significantly clarify the relationships of accountability within British government. The framework documents, signed by the responsible minister and the chief executive, do mark a significant step toward greater openness and specificity in allocating responsibility for decisions.

At the same time, no administrative law procedures have been established to deal with individual grievance. Such grievances are still left to the individual citizen to take up through members of Parliament or the ombudsman (parliamentary commissioner) in much the same way as prior to the introduction of agencies.

Developments in Other Westminster Systems

Inspired by the British example, similar agencies (special operating agencies) were introduced in Canada after 1989 but in a more half-hearted way. At least until 1994, the Canadian government has followed their British equivalents in arguing that any accompanying constitutional change was unnecessary. In contrast, comparable reforms in New Zealand under the State Sector Act of 1988 have been accompanied by significant constitutional changes. New Zealand department heads have been restyled "chief executives" and appointed on five-year contracts and for many purposes are the employers of all staff within the department. In addition, these chief executives are required to report directly to Parliament on the performance and outputs of their departments as well as to their minister.

In Australia, comparable organizational changes have not been introduced. However, some recent reforms do reflect a wider conception of public accountability as more than just ministerial accountability. Additional mechanisms of accountability to the public have been introduced, such as freedom of information, administrative review tribunals, and the Commonwealth ombudsman (commissioner for administration). Nevertheless, as for the other three countries, ministerial responsibility, despite its imperfections, remains the dominant form of political accountability.

MARTIN LAFFIN

BIBLIOGRAPHY

Boston, Jonathon, 1992. "Assessing the Performance of Departmental Chief Executives." *Public Administration*, vol. 65: 423–442.
Drewry, Gavin, and Tony Butcher, 1991. *The Civil Service Today*, 2d ed. Oxford: Blackwell.
Marshall, Geoffrey, ed., 1989. *Ministerial Responsibility*. Oxford: Oxford University Press.
O'Toole, Barry J., and Richard A. Chapman, 1995. "Parliamentary Accountability." In Barry J. O'Toole and Grant Jordan, eds., *Next Steps: Improving Management in Government?* Aldershot: Dartmouth.
Woodhouse, Diana, 1994. *Ministers and Parliament: Accountability in Theory and Practice*. New York: Oxford University Press.

MINORITY SET-ASIDE.

A procedure in which purchasing or contracting provisions allocate or set aside a certain percentage of expenditures for minority-controlled businesses. The Public Works Act of 1977 included a provision requiring that 10 percent of the federal funds expended for local public works projects must be used to procure supplies or services from minority-owned businesses. The use of set-asides was challenged under the equal protection component of the Due Process Clause of the Fifth Amendment to the Constitution in the 1980 case of Fullilove v. Klutznick. The Supreme Court upheld the set-aside provision with a 6-3 vote.

Proponents see set-asides as a way of increasing the competitiveness of minority-owned businesses, creating jobs in high unemployment areas, and showing impartiality in the public bidding and contracting process. Opponents tend to view set-asides as reverse discrimination in violation of the principles of competition, fairness, and efficiency.

Despite opposition to minority set-asides, by 1989 there were 234 set-aside programs operating in state and local governments across the country. In general, those eligible were traditional affirmative-action groups such as blacks, Hispanics, Asian Americans, Native Americans, and women, who were added to the list in 1987. The arrangements used to increase the number of contracts for women business enterprises (WBEs) and minority business enterprises (MBEs) varied from state to state and from city to city. For example, Washington, D.C., had a 35 percent statutory set-aside. Further, various federal agencies, such as the Department of Energy and the Federal Highway Administration, required the establishment of goals or set-asides for MBEs and WBEs by state and local governments as a condition for receiving federal funds.

The 1989 Supreme Court decision in City of Richmond v. Croson had distinct ramifications on set-aside programs. In 1983, Richmond established a set-aside program for city contracts. Shortly thereafter, the J. A. Croson Company was the lowest bidder on a contract, but it was not awarded to them because of the set-aside program. Croson filed suit and the case made its way to the Supreme Court. The Court ruled in favor of Croson saying that the set-aside provision violated Croson's Fourteenth Amendment right to equal protection. Further, the Court declared the use of racial classifications by state and local governments to be subject to "strict scrutiny." Essentially, this meant that racial categories could only be used to remedy identified discrimination; and the remedies had to be narrowly tailored and employed only after race-neutral efforts had been tried and failed. Past societal discrimination could no longer be used to justify the application of racial classifications in public contracting at the state and local level.

An example of a federal government set-aside program is the U.S. Small Business Administration's 8(a) program, authorized by the Small Business Act, which channels federal government contracts to socially and economically disadvantaged small business owners. A recent Supreme Court case, however, challenged the Small Business Act. In the 1995 case of Adarand Constructors Co. v. Pena, the Supreme Court ruled that strict scrutiny standards must be applied to any federal affirmative-action program, including minority set-asides. The Court remanded the case for reevaluation under this test without deciding the constitutionality of the program at issue.

KAY MATHEWS

BIBLIOGRAPHY

Adarand Constructors Co. v. Pena, 1995. 115 S. Ct. 2097.
City of Richmond v. J.A. Croson Co., 1989. 488 U.S. 469.
Fullilove v. Klutznick, 1980. 448 U.S. 488, 100 S. Ct. 2758.
McCoy, Frank, 1994. "Will the High Court End Federal Set-Asides? The Supreme Court Is Set to Hear Case That Challenges Set-Asides." *Black Enterprise*, vol. 25 (December) 24–25.

MISSION STATEMENT.

A brief written statement of an organization's purpose, goals, operating philosophy, and aspirations—hence, the mission statement provides a guide for decisionmaking and planning within the organization and also can be used as a contract of accountability for citizens, clients, and other external constituencies.

Purposes of a Mission Statement

An effective mission statement should serve three essential purposes. First, it should provide constituencies inside and outside the organization with a commonly understood interpretation of the organization's legal mandate.

The mandate and the mission statement, while related, are not the same (Bryson 1991, pp. 93–95). The organization's mandate specifies the obligations to which it is legally bound and often is expressed in the form of a charter, articles of incorporation, bylaws, authorizing legislation, statutes, ordinances, or administrative regulations. Often, the mandate will outline in excruciating detail nearly all facets of the organization's functions, its structure, its policymaking procedures, and the sources of its revenue. For example, the Borough Code for the Commonwealth of Pennsylvania—a typical mandate—is a document of several hundred pages covering everything from the allowable sources of tax revenue to procedures for awarding public contracts.

Technically, the mandate is a public document, but generally it is not widely distributed and is not expressed in terms that the general public can understand. The mission statement, therefore, should provide a concise interpretation of the mandate in terms that people can easily understand. What business are we in? What are our principle products and services? Who are our primary clients or beneficiaries? What needs do we fill? What operating philosophies do we follow? What are our priorities for the future? As such, the mission statement should dwell less on technical or legal obligations and more on what the organization is committing itself to do within whatever discretionary authority is granted by the mandate.

Second, the mission statement should provide a guide to daily decisionmaking and long-term planning. In other words, an effective mission statement should provide much more than eloquent, but meaningless, rhetoric about the organization's purpose. Rather, it should provide an explicit statement of the organization's operating philosophy and core values. For example, the mission statement of a prestigious research university contains a section that states, among other things, that the institution will pursue only those initiatives in which it has a "comparative advantage" and that all of its activities in teaching and research will be designed to enhance its position of national leadership by influencing the behavior of other institutions. In other words, the institution is publicly stating, to both internal and external audiences, that it will not attempt to be all things to all people. Such an explicit operating philosophy clearly can have a powerful impact on strategic decisionmaking and long-term resource allocation.

Some operating philosophies may have immediate effects on short-term (versus long-term) decisionmaking. For example, the mission statement may say something about the organization's commitment to employee development, to measuring the quality of client services, or to a certain philosophy of resource management.

Third, and finally, the mission statement should be linked to the organization's strategic plan by providing a concise and general statement of the organization's goals and aspirations for the future. Often, the strategic direction of the organization is expressed in a separate vision statement appended to the mission. Whether as a separate vision statement or incorporated into the mission statement, the organization should publicly state its priorities and the strategic direction in which it is heading.

Thus, the mission statement should include at least three distinct sections as follows:

1. the purpose of the organization expressed in terms of products, services, targeted customers, and needs filled;
2. the operating philosophies and values expressed in terms of the organization's self-image, how it perceives its niche or distinctive characteristics in the marketplace, how it makes decisions and manages resources to preserve or enhance its self-image; and
3. the aspirations for the future, expressed in terms of broad strategic goals and priorities.

Developing a Mission Statement

Occasionally, decisionmakers express skepticism about the value of mission statements, especially in government organizations where the prevailing belief may be that the mandate is the mission. "Why should we develop a mission statement when everything we need to know is contained in our authorizing legislation or in the administrative regulations which guide us?" Missions are slightly more fluid and dynamic than mandates because they reflect the organization's interpretation of its role in society, its relationship to its constituents, its position in the marketplace, and its aspirations for the future. Also, old mission can be accomplished and new missions can be formulated to take their place, all within the context of an unchanging mandate.

Additionally, there are several "triggers," or symptoms, that may suggest that the mandate alone is not sufficient and, therefore, that effort should be invested in the development of a mission statement:

1. recurring and unproductive debates within the organization (e.g., line versus staff, headquarters versus field offices) regarding interpretation of the mandate—core purpose, resource allocation, operating philosophies, and goals;

2. a pattern of apparently *ad hoc* decisionmaking at the top of the organization or "goal displacement" in the middle of the organization wherein key decisions do not seem to be guided by an overarching purpose or vision;

3. a portfolio of services or products, with shifting priorities among them, which appear haphazard or disjointed; and

4. a pattern of confusion or misunderstanding among key constituencies—elected officials, oversight agencies, citizens, and funders—regarding the core purpose and goals of the organization.

Any of these symptoms may suggest that the organization should develop or refine its mission statement. The process of developing a mission statement should include a variety of stakeholders—executive staff, middle management, and key external constituencies. In general, the following steps will provide useful input in the development of a mission statement (see also Bryson 1991, pp. 106–116; Espy 1986, pp. 21–41):

1. a thorough review of the organization's mandate—what it is legally obligated to do—and how that mandate has evolved since its inception;

2. a survey of key stakeholders regarding their expectations of the organization, which may or may not be perfectly consistent with its mandate;

3. an assessment of external trends, which present either opportunities or challenges for the organization, accompanied by an evaluation of the organization's current strengths and weaknesses in responding to those trends (Kearns 1992);

4. a list of operating philosophies and values, generated by executives and staff, which they believe should guide the organization; and

5. a summary statement of the strategic goals derived from the long-range plan of the organization.

Although the process of gathering and interpreting this information should involve a diverse set of stakeholders, the task of actually drafting the mission statement should probably be assigned to one person or a small team of people. The drafts should then be circulated, edited, and finalized with input from the broader set of stakeholders.

Generally, the mission statement should be formally reviewed every five years or so, consistent with the organization's strategic planning cycle. Often it is suggested that the mission statement be drafted as the first step in the strategic planning process. But decisionmakers should keep in mind that certain portions of the mission statement (e.g., priorities and aspirations) cannot be drafted until the strategic plan is nearly complete. Clearly, there is a delicate trade-off between a mission statement that is so broad and general that it is never changed and one which is so specific and focused that it quickly becomes obsolete. This trade-off can be addressed by asking, "Is this draft mission statement capable of providing a useful, but not overly confining, guide to decisionmaking over the next five years or so?"

Missions Statements, Performance, and Accountability

Like the mandate, the mission statement is a powerful instrument of accountability. Peter Drucker (1990) goes further by suggesting that the mission statement is the instrument of accountability for nonprofit organizations, since they do not have a "bottom line" of performance like profit and loss: "(Nonprofits) must therefore have a clear mission that is translated into operational goals and provides guides for effective action. Of course, businesses also deteriorate if they do not have a clear mission. . . . But, in good times a business can muddle through for a while with no other lodestar than the financial bottom line. A nonprofit institution will start to flounder almost immediately unless it clearly defines its mission and emphasizes that mission again and again" (p. 8).

Consequently, the mission statement may be the organization's primary accountability contract with the public. It is the document in which we essentially say to the public, "Here is what we promise to do for you. You may hold us accountable for this."

KEVIN P. KEARNS

BIBLIOGRAPHY

Bryson, John M., 1991. *Strategic Planning for Public and Nonprofit Organizations.* San Francisco: Jossey-Bass. (See especially Chapter 5, "Clarifying Organizational Mandates and Missions.")

Drucker, Peter F., 1990. "Lessons for Successful Nonprofit Governance." *Nonprofit Management and Leadership*, vol. 1, no. 1: 7–14.

Espy, Siri N., 1986. *Handbook of Strategic Planning for Nonprofit Organizations.* New York: Praeger. (See especially Chapter 3, "Corporate Identity and Directions.")

Kearns, Kevin P., 1992. "From Comparative Advantage to Damage Control: Clarifying Strategic Issues Using SWOT Analysis." *Nonprofit Management and Leadership*, vol. 3, no. 1: 3–22.

MIXED ECONOMY.

An economy in which key economic, political, and social roles are shared between government and the market.

In a mixed economy, government resorts to a range of devices to steer the economy toward a desired direction in the public interest, which would not happen if left to unregulated free market forces. The use of such devices ranges from controls over entry and prices, regulation of businesses to promote the public interest, encouragement of indigenous industry through subsidies or tax incentives and ultimately resorting to public ownership. Robert Dahl (1993) identifies "a mixed-economy as one in which markets are limited, controlled, regulated, or modified by government intervention" (p. 260).

In Western democratic countries, the institutions of government and the market play a significant role in the economy. During different historical periods and in different countries that balance between their roles varies, governed by a variety of circumstances. Where there is a demand for greater freedom for the market, governments are likely to play a minimal role. Where the demand for restraining the free play of market forces is more dominant, governments play a more active role in the economy. Whichever way the balance lies, in as much as the functioning of markets relies on a framework of political institutions that provide the legal and political framework, then, irrespective of the role the government plays in the economy, such economies are best described as mixed economies. In such mixed economies, both the public and private sectors of the economy are entrusted with distinct decisional and operational roles within the framework of the market. In such political systems, the state or government plays two distinct roles: (1) the responsibility to govern and thus maintain the public order so that citizens can act freely while transacting in the market and (2) intervention when such markets function imperfectly. While the first function is essential to a civilized society and is referred to as the universal role of the state (Nelson 1989), the second role—that of intervention in the economy—is relative to the nature of market malfunctioning and dictates the nature of public-private mix, varying between countries generally categorized as industrialized capitalist economies, or mixed economies.

The Approach

While this broadbased approach to the role of the state in market economies is referred to as mixed economy, some authors prefer to narrow the term (mixed economy) essentially to "government ownership and operation of a substantial number of firms and in which a large number of investment decisions are in public hands" (Freeman 1989, p. ix). In suggesting that mixed economies are largely a product of democratic societies, Dahl suggests that the advocates of government intervention justify it as superior to unregulated markets (Dahl 1993, p. 272). However, a broader definition would recognize the variety of influences that government policies bring to bear on the functioning of the economy without having to resort to public ownership. Illustrative of this is the significant role of the state in the economic development of Japan and other East Asian economies outside of resorting to public ownership, thus prompting the use of the term "developmental state"

(Johnson 1985). If such a focus broadens the term mixed economy to include varieties of state intervention, the forms of public ownership then become increasingly confused contributing to the growing trend toward hybridization (Wettenhall 1992) and degovernmentalization (Siedman 1992). For instance, the United States, which is often referred to as a country whose citizens prefer private enterprise to public ownership, had in 1990 US$800 billion public investment in government-sponsored enterprises, generally considered as operating outside the jurisdiction of the United States government (Mascarenhas 1992), thereby making it difficult to assess the true extent of public ownership. In fact, the use of a range of policies coupled with mechanisms for intervention makes any separation of private markets from government increasingly difficult. Horowitz (1989) sees an interlocking relationship between government and the economy as the fabric of an advanced civilization and not as forces facing each other (p. 41).

Therefore, in mixed economies government intervenes to influence the actions of various participants in the economy using a variety of policies and instruments. Such intervention is generally categorized into macro- and microintervention. While the former is identified with monetary and fiscal policies, the latter affects a specific sector and is identified as industrial policy. Governments of different complexions adopt a mix of these interventions primarily to meet a variety of situations and without any apparent consistency. Such policies differ in terms of how much consensus exists, what ends governments should pursue and how it ought to achieve them. Notwithstanding these variations in approach, it is generally recognized that governments should intervene to set right market failures like natural monopolies, public goods, and externalities.

While these are conditions generally regarded as sufficient for state intervention, the nature of intervention is often dictated by ideological preferences, historical influences, pressure groups, and regime characteristics. In line with this, we see a distinct preference for regulation of business in the United States, whereas countries in Europe have been willing to adopt a range of interventions including public ownership. Between these extremes, governments in these countries have since the 1920s resorted to such a range of options to promote the public interest that the distinction between the public and the private has become increasingly blurred. The New Deal in the United States in the 1930s, the nationalization of industries in Britain and France in the late 1940s and the organization of primary producers into producer monopolies in Australia and New Zealand in the 1930s and 1940s are indicative of the extensive role played by the state in what are generally regarded as market or capitalist economies. A similar wave of state intervention in all these countries was witnessed during the energy crisis of the 1970s.

The period of the 1950s to the mid-1970s was described by Hobsbawm (*The Age of Hobsbawm, The Indepen-*

dent, 1994) as "the Golden years," when the gigantic success of the capitalist "mixed economy" (not the free market) changed the conditions of the human race more rapidly, completely, and irrevocably than ever before.

Whereas the above verdict credits such success to the mixed economy, other critics attribute the decline of economic performance in the 1970s in the form of low economic growth, high inflation, high levels of unemployment, and the increased power of unions to state intervention arising out of the Keynesian entitlement. For such critics, the target of attack has been the state, the reducing or cutting back of which became the central issue in the 1980s, spearheaded by Margaret Thatcher in Britain and Ronald Reagan in the United States. This conservative reaction has led to what has come to be known as "the rolling back of the state" by adopting policies of divestment, user pays, contracting, and so forth. While the response to the crisis of the decade was load shedding, the real issues arising out of the globalization of the economy were in actual fact unmanageable, with governments lacking the power to operate in such an economy by reverting to free market policies. This was associated with (1) short-term growth at the expense of long-term investments in education, health, and infrastructure; (2) technological sophistication leading to endemic unemployment; and (3) decline of social institutions like the family, the church, and unions, which encourage social belonging (*The Independent,* October 1, 1994).

However, this phenomenon of indifferent economic performance of the mid-1970s associated with a growing public sector seems to have affected only the Anglo-American group of countries like the United States, Britain, Canada, Australia, and New Zealand. During the same period, countries like Japan, France, and Germany, where the state played an active role in the economy, showed improved performance. That the performance of different economies is governed by factors other than the public-private enterprise mix becomes evident when one examines different political economies. In fact, Freeman (1989) identifies the character of state administration, the development and workings of capital markets, the degree of societal discensus over the ends and means of government market intervention and the citizens' willingness and ability to exercise public ownership rights through certain political institutions as critical determining factors (p. x). These factors not only help to explain relative economic performance of economies but also provide an insight into why some countries view government's role as complementary or supportive of private enterprise, whereas others regard the relationship as adversarial. Whereas West Germany's social market, Japan's developmental state, and France's dirigisme reflect the former, the United States typifies the latter.

Essentially, an understanding of a modern economy rests on whether one views the role of the state as residual to the market in a predominantly capitalist economy or whether one adopts a positive theory of state intervention in which the role of the state is more central to the functioning of the economy. Despite a reversion to a neoclassical market model as the dominant paradigm of the academic discourse in economics, the alternative is a broadbased political economy approach. In a political economy approach the state provides the environment within which markets function. It also intervenes using a variety of instruments or mechanisms. The problems faced by Anglo-American countries have been brought about by their failure to develop proper institutions for effective state intervention (Mascarenhas 1992; Nelson 1989).

Although governments intervene to complement or support private markets, they also protect citizens against the uncertainty and inhuman aspects of the market by adopting a range of protectionist measures. Such measures range from social security, accident and unemployment benefits to compensation against injustices, price supports, and subsidies. Despite these measures, the personal insecurity caused by market uncertainty particularly in terms of their social costs to the community cannot be easily measured. The closure of an industry means that the community loses a whole person who then moves away with certain skills. The dynamism of the market contributes to temporariness, high uncertainty, and high risk in addition to inefficiencies caused by imperfections or market failures.

Changing the Nature of Capitalism

Neoclassical economists and economic rationalists, who maintain the distinction between private enterprise and mixed economies, continue to assume the existence of proprietory capitalism although it has long been overtaken by managerial capitalism, a feature of which is the separation of ownership from management (Galbraith 1967; Schonfield 1965). Such managerial capitalism, which contributed to the postwar economic performance of Western Europe and the United States, has now been overtaken by collective capitalism, predominantly the Japanese variant. Under collective capitalism, there is growing cooperation between competing firms to promote a national industry. In promoting such cooperation the state plays an active role by encouraging cooperation in the area of research and development among competitors, assuring access to inexpensive finance and providing a highly educated workforce. This organizational integration of private sector manufacturing with an activist role for the state provides an environment for the development of a "qualitative new mode of business organisation in the evolution of capitalism" (Lazonick 1993, pp. 36–38).

While the term collective capitalism expresses in capsule the growing interrelationship between competing enterprises with the active support of public agencies, similar trends are observed in the working of industrial districts in Italy, Germany, France, and the Silicon Valley in the United States. Each industrial district reputed for manufacturing specialized products like ceramics, leather goods, furniture, machine tools, and so forth attempts to combine sophisticated technology with craftlike skills to cater to custom-built consumers. Again studies reveal that these enterprises operating in industrial districts lay "heavy emphasis upon the role of cooperation and community that one finds in every single ethnographic study of industrial districts and in the corporate enterprises which are being used by big business as models for their reform" (Piore 1992, p. 308).

Such industrial districts adopt flexible manufacturing described as diversified quality production for which, according to Streek, a regime of free markets and private hierarchies is not enough. In this pursuit of "islands of excellence," Streek places significant responsibility on public institutions (in Elam 1993, pp. 22–23).

In view of the historical developments discussed above, the efforts to distinguish private from public and free market economies from mixed economies seem far from realistic. Such distinctions have been obliterated by the growing convergence moving along a continuum of private to public, wherein the government plays a significant role relative to the demands and situations within each economy. Historically that role is minimal in the Anglo-American set of countries but more visible in countries like Japan, Germany, and France. It is recognized that private enterprise cannot create the conditions required without public intervention, and the wealth of capitalist nations in the late twentieth century is attributed to the growing power of collective capitalism (Lazonick 1993, p. 58).

Conclusion

This analysis of mixed economies confined largely to Western industrial democracies adopts a contingent approach to state intervention within predominantly market-oriented economies. The differing historical evolution can be observed of two distinct groups of countries: (1) the Anglo-American countries, where the relation between government and business is adversarial and (2) the countries typified by Japan, France, and Germany, where the relationship is more cooperative. Although this categorization broadly reflects the trends observed from World War II to the mid-1970s, the two sets of countries seem to have moved apart since then. While the Anglo-American group is seeking to return to the neoclassical free market model characteristic of the early proprietory capitalism, the Japanese appear to be moving toward greater cooperation characteristic of collective capitalism. The failure of English-speaking countries to observe such changes can be attributed to the framework of analysis adopted by main-

stream economists who continue to ignore the evolutionary approach adopted by economic historians (North 1994).

REGINALD C. MASCARENHAS

BIBLIOGRAPHY

Dahl, Robert A., 1993. "Why All Democratic Countries Have Mixed Economies." In John W. Chapman and Ian Schampiora, eds., *Democratic Communities, Nomos, Yearbook of the American Society for Political and Legal Philosophy*, vol. 35. New York: New York University Press.

Elam, Mark, 1993. "Markets, Morals, and Powers of Innovation." *Economy and Society*, vol. 22: 1–41.

Freeman, John R., 1989. *Democracy and Markets: The Politics of Mixed Economies*. Ithaca, NY: Cornell University Press.

Galbraith, John Kenneth, 1967. *The New Industrial State*. England: Penguin.

Horowitz, Irving Louis, 1989. "The Public Costs of Private Blessings." *Studies in International Comparative Development*. vol. 24: 39–46.

Johnson, Chalmers, 1985. MITI (Ministry for International Trade and Industry) *The Japanese Miracle*. Berkeley: University of California Press.

Lazonick, William, 1993. *Business Organisation and the Myth of the Market Economy*. London: Cambridge University Press.

Mascarenhas, R. C., 1992. "State Intervention in the Economy: Why Is the United States Different from Other Mixed Economies?" *Australian Journal of Public Administration.*, vol. 51: 387–397.

Nelson, Richard R., 1989. "Role of Government in a Mixed Economy." *Journal of Policy Analysis and Management*, vol. 6: 541–547.

North, Douglas C., 1994. "Economic Performance through Time." *The American Economic Review*. vol. 84: 359–368.

Piore, Michael, 1992. "Work, Labour, and Action Work Experience in a System of Flexible Production." In Thomas A. Kochan and Michael Useem, eds., *Transforming Organisations*. Oxford: Oxford University Press, 307–319.

Schonfield, Andrew, 1965. *Modern Capitalism: The Changing Balance of Public and Private Power*. Oxford: Oxford University Press.

Siedman, Harold, 1992. "Public Enterprise versus Privatisation in the United States." *International Review of Administrative Sciences*, vol. 56: 15–28.

"The Age of Hobsbawm," 1994. *The Independent* (October 1). London.

Wettenhall, Roger, 1992. "Where Stands Public Enterprise in the Privatisation Revolution?" Australasian Political Studies Conference, Canberra, September 30–October 1.

MONASH, SIR JOHN (1865–1931).

Engineer, soldier and public enterprise pioneer; was born in Melbourne, Australia, son of Jewish migrants from Prussia. His father prospered temporarily as a rural storekeeper and sent John to Scotch College, Melbourne, where he became equal dux, excelling in mathematics, logic, languages, and literature. In 1882, he began arts and engineering at the University of Melbourne, passed two years, and abandoned his course because of his mother's long fatal illness and the need to provide for his two younger sisters. He found employment building a major bridge, then constructing a suburban railway, during which he completed his engineering degree with honors, by cramming without attending lectures. He then earned arts and law degrees. Since 1886, he had been an officer in the militia. He married in 1891; a daughter was born in 1893.

Around 1890, the Colony of Victoria fell into severe depression. Monash found a haven in the Melbourne Harbor Trust, practicing occasionally in the courts as an expert witness. In 1894, he boldly launched a civil engineering practice with Joshua Anderson. Having gained the local patent rights for Monier-reinforced concrete construction, they concentrated on contracting for bridge building. However, when a client refused to make a large final payment, they lost all their capital. The partnership dissolved, and Monash grimly worked off his debt. In 1905, backed by business associates, he formed the Reinforced Concrete & Monier Pipe Construction Co. and largely switched to building construction. He soon became wealthy.

Monash had had no important patron or guide in business or administrative matters, let alone any specific training. Although engaged as engineering superintendent of the railway project, his contractor-employers gave him full charge of the works. He soon assessed the limitations of knowledge of his employers, became friendly with the government inspector, and found a military parallel when he deputed detailed supervision to the gangers and foremen, similar to noncommissioned military officers. He had adopted his lifetime practice of preparing a daily agenda, striking out each item when disposed of, then drawing a vertical line through the whole. "The possession of absolute administrative power, and the conscientious attempt to make each administrative action . . . depend on logical analysis . . . is a new and delightful experience" (Serle, 1983 p. 83). The Monash & Anderson practice was a long lesson in endurance. Later, in the Reinforced Concrete Co., Monash was more in touch with business leaders and entrepreneurs. His first overseas visit to Europe and the United States of America in 1910 was highly educative.

For 20 years, Monash had been in a military backwater, the coastal artillery. In 1908, however, he joined the Australian Intelligence Corps at the center of military activity, studied military history, and in 1913 won command of an infantry brigade. When war broke out, he was just young enough to lead an infantry brigade in the Australian Imperial Force. After enduring the Gallipoli campaign with mixed success, he was appointed to command a division in 1916 and in May 1918 the Australian corps of five divisions, which from August 8 was perhaps the leading spearhead of the British Army in an astonishing series of victories. Monash was by no means negligible as a battle commander and tactician, but the higher he rose, the greater was his success as his qualities as an administrator were demonstrated. In later 1918, the battletroops were at last sure that all was right behind them in terms of supply, reinforcement, transport, and medical facilities.

Monash earned the undying respect of almost all his superiors, his senior subordinates, and staff. He won some reputation as "the best man in France" (Serle, 1983, p. 376); some even believed that he might become commander-in-chief of the British Army, but it is inconceivable that a colonial Jewish militiaman of German extraction could have been acceptable. His particular strengths were personal diplomacy, great teamwork with his chief of staff, wide consultation about battleplans, meticulous attention to detail, a creed of optimism, openness to technological innovation, ability to stand up to higher commanders, attention to publicity for his men's achievements, moral courage, articulateness, fairness and courtesy, a reputation as "the absolute antithesis of the unapproachable, self-conscious brass-hat." In short, a democratic, considerate man-manager, unusual among generals, who restrained expression of his intellectual superiority. He carried out the repatriation of 160,000 soldiers with speed, efficiency, and humanity.

Monash returned from the war a national hero, widely accepted as the greatest living Australian. He briefly considered politics, a defense posting, or continuing his own business but in mid-1920 accepted the managership of the State Electricity Commission of Victoria (SEC), which potentially was one of the most important jobs in the country. Victoria held 28 percent of the Australian population of 5.4 million. Australia's was a weak federation; central intervention in the states' largely separate economies was minimal. Melbourne, a city of 800,000, was the most important industrial and manufacturing center but was hampered by tardy development of the electricity industry and dependent on the unreliable supply of black coal from neighboring New South Wales. However, there was a vast brown-coal deposit in Gippsland, about 100 miles east. The task was to make abundant cheap power available. Monash was attracted by the combination of administrative, financial, and engineering functions involved. The SEC, founded in 1918, was a statutory corporation, an example of Victoria's "state socialism," similar to the Railways and Tramways. The commission had already committed itself to development of brown coal rather than hydro works.

Monash was immediately appointed chairman of commissioners as well as general manager. The objectives were to develop open-cut mining, build statewide installations, take over existing electricity makers, and establish a system of distribution and sale. From the start, vested interests, some politicians, and a section of the press provided powerful opposition. However, power from Gippsland was "turned on" in 1924 when "briquettes," the popular domestic and industrial fuel, were also freely on sale. Yallourn, the "company town," was a model of advanced town planning. But the broad scheme was still in jeopardy because the problem of high moisture content in the coal had not been entirely solved: two different seams had been confused; the boilers for the main powerhouse had to be redesigned. Monash and his fellow commissioners succeeded in concealing the dangers, thus avoiding a possible major scandal, until in 1926 they could safely claim the problem had been solved. Little was known locally about brown-coal technology and, despite all prejudices, German advice and employment had to be sought. Helped by the brilliant Hyman Herman and other senior technicians, expert German employees were found and the scale of operations raised.

For three years, Monash had had an entirely supportive ministerial chief. For another two and a half, he had the stubborn F. W. Eggleston, later a famous diplomat and political theorist, who was determined to bring him under control. In 1925, criticism of the SEC led the commissioners to request a formal inquiry. In preparation, Monash wrote a masterly memorandum on the situation and had the terms of the inquiry revised, for he "believed in winning the battle before the barrage opened" (Serle, 1983, p. 450). An American, W. H. Sawyer, expert in the electricity business but ignorant of brown coal, was appointed. His report in 1926 judged the SEC to be economically sound but was pessimistic about its paying its way anytime soon, recommended marking time, and considered that Monash was too much in control. The government adopted the report; the commission defied it. Monash had calculated correctly: In 1927, the SEC showed a profit. The battle was won; the grid was almost complete; Eggleston had been destroyed as a politician; the SEC was another successful state enterprise and had established (for some 50 years) its independence of the government.

Above all, Monash was the SEC's superb champion, convincingly addressing innumerable gatherings including Parliament and its select committees, where several times, by sheer force of argument, he butchered his opponents. When the enemy was securely entrenched, the old general was spurred to attack them decisively. When he appeared before cabinet, the future prime minister R. G. Menzies recalled, "We all stood up instinctively" (Serle, 1983, p. 460) In labor relations, Monash was a fair dealer whose paternalism combined nicely with his worker's pride in a public enterprise.

Monash's achievements in establishing the success of the SEC were materially important in consolidating an extensive Australian commitment to a major role for public enterprise that helped shape and distinguish the Australian economy for the remainder of the twentieth century. The model of the engineer–public enterprise manager he provided was emulated widely, although not all who sought to follow it could combine technical excellence, leadership, and political acumen in so seamless a style.

Monash was a legendary figure to SEC employees. He led and did not drive his senior colleagues, exacting their best and making them his personal friends. He was approachable and open to argument. He listened carefully, "then with a breath blew away the chaff and gave a decision that everyone knew was right" (Serle, 1983, p. 461) He often opened a memorandum, "In order to crystallize a discussion . . . , I set out hereunder certain views." Herman summed him up as "the only *real* leader I have encountered . . . a genius in getting to the heart of any problem and finding its solution" (Serle, 1983, p. 462) At Yallourn, or on the train from Melbourne, he would chat unaffectedly and cheerily with all and sundry. In later years, his egotism was well under control; he was a rare case of supreme breadth of intellect combined with pragmatism and consideration for his fellows.

As acting Chancellor of the University of Melbourne for a year, Monash concluded that "the University is about as difficult to manage–if not more so–than an army" (Serle, 1983, p. 479) Despite his failing health, he would not withdraw from the SEC. Monash died in Melbourne on October 8, 1931.

GEOFFREY SERLE

BIBLIOGRAPHY

Holmes, Jean, 1970. "Administrative Style and Sir John Monash." *Public Administration* (Sydney), vol. 29 (September).
Monash Papers, National Library of Australia, Canberra.
Serle, Geoffrey, 1982. *John Monash: A Biography.* Melbourne: Melbourne University Press.

MONETARY POLICY. Involves changing the nation's money supply to influence macroeconomic performance, including unemployment, inflation, and economic growth. Monetary policy is conducted by the nation's central bank, the Federal Reserve System in the United States (see **Federal Reserve System**). Changes in the supply of money relative to its demand affect financial market conditions, including interest and exchange rates. These changes alter investment, consumption, and net export demand, which in turn influence macroeconomic performance.

Increasing the money supply relative to its demand creates an excess supply of money. Individuals will spend some of this money on consumption goods and save the rest in savings accounts or by investing in stocks, bonds, and other interest-bearing assets. Savings reduce interest rates. Capital market competition and arbitrage ensure that the lower interest rates spread across all short-run financial markets. As interest rates fall, investment demand and consumer durable purchases increase. Finally, lower interest rates affect exchange rates. As domestic interest rates fall relative to international interest rates, domestic investment shifts to foreign markets; foreign investment in domestic capital markets also decreases. This increases the supply of dollars relative to demand in the international currency markets, lowering the price of a dollar. Lower exchange rates stimulate U.S. exports and reduce imports into the United States. Thus, increasing the money supply increases aggregate demand for consumption, investment, and net exports.

Monetary policy, like fiscal policy, is a demand side macroeconomic policy (see **fiscal policy**). In particular, monetary policy indirectly affects aggregate demand and macroeconomic performance through the financial markets. Fiscal policy, which involves changes in government expenditures and taxes, directly affects aggregate demand. Government expenditures influence government demand; tax policy influences both consumption and investment demand.

Demand-side macroeconomic policies are often used to offset business cycles and to stabilize economic performance, particularly prices and unemployment. If the economy is operating below full employment, monetary and fiscal policies can be used to increase aggregate demand.

Presumably, businesses will increase output to satisfy the increase in aggregate demand. If there are unemployed resources, including human, capital, and natural resources, output can increase without significantly increasing prices. As the economy approaches full employment, and there are few slack resources, increases in aggregate demand primarily affect wages and prices. Businesses must compete against one another for the limited supply of resources; product prices increase with wages and input prices. Given these responses, expansionary monetary and fiscal policy can stimulate employment during an economic downturn; contractionary monetary and fiscal policy can alleviate inflationary pressures when the economy is overheated.

Macroeconomic stabilization is generally considered a short-run policy. In the long run, market prices for capital, labor, and other inputs adjust to ensure full employment. Thus, the economy automatically converges to full employment in the long run. In contrast, supply-side economics addresses long-run economic performance. Supply-side economics emphasizes aggregate supply (see **supply-side economics**). Supply-side economics hypothesizes that long-run economic growth requires expanding productive capacity. In the supply-side model, reducing marginal tax rates increases productive capacity by increasing the labor supply and capital investment. Increasing economic capacity enables the economy to accommodate growth while reducing inflationary pressures.

Discretionary Monetary Policy Options

In the United States, monetary policy is conducted by the Federal Reserve (Fed), the United States's central bank (see **Federal Reserve System**). In contrast, fiscal policy is conducted by the executive and legislative branches of the government. The Fed was specifically established as an independent institution. Its decisions do not have to be ratified by either the executive or the legislative branch. This separates control over monetary and fiscal policy, providing some checks and balances. However, the Fed is not completely isolated. Its highest-ranking members are appointed to overlapping 14-year terms by the president and confirmed by the Senate. The Federal Reserve's chairman regularly reports to Congress concerning Fed policy. Finally, the Fed chairman meets regularly with the secretary of the Treasury and the chairman of the President's Council of Economic Advisors.

The Fed has three policy tools for manipulating the money supply: conducting open market operations (buying and selling U.S. government securities and securities from other federal agencies), setting the discount rate (the interest rate at which banks can borrow from the Fed), and setting the required reserve ratio (the percent of bank deposits that must be held as deposits with the Fed or in the bank's vaults). These policies all work by influencing commercial banks' reserve positions. Commercial banks are only required to hold a fraction of their deposits as reserves (cash in the banks' vaults and balances maintained with the Fed). The remainder of the banks' reserves can be lent out or invested in interest-earning assets. As banks lend out their excess reserves, they "create money." Thus, any change in commercial banks' reserve position affects the money supply.

The Fed typically purchases or sells government securities to influence the money supply (open market operations). The Fed can only buy or sell preexisting government securities, not newly issued securities. When they purchase a preexisting security, they create a cash deposit in a commercial bank in exchange for an interest-bearing asset. This directly increases the money supply by an amount equal to the cash deposit. Under a fractional reserve system, commercial banks only need to hold a fraction of their deposits as reserves. They can loan out the excess reserves. As banks loan their excess reserves, they create additional commercial bank deposits (money), much of which become additional excess reserves. The process continues until the banking system absorbs all excess reserves. As illustrated in Table I, if the required reserve ratio is 20 percent and the Fed purchases a US $100 government security, the money supply can expand by up to US $500. The initial purchase will have a smaller impact on the money supply if banks decide to hold some of their excess reserves rather than lending them out. The opposite multiplicative effect occurs when the Fed sells government securities.

The Fed can also influence the money supply by changing the discount rate. The discount rate is the interest rate commercial banks pay on short-term loans from the Fed. Commercial banks borrow from the Fed if their re-

TABLE I. EFFECT OF $100 OPEN MARKET PURCHASE (20% REQUIRED RESERVE RATIO)

Bank	New Deposits	Required Reserves	Excess Reserves
First bank	US $100.00	US $20.00	US $80.00
Second bank	80.00	16.00	64.00
Third bank	64.00	12.80	51.20
Fourth bank	51.20	10.24	40.96
Fifth bank	40.96	8.19	32.77
Sixth bank	32.77	6.55	26.21
Seventh bank	26.21	5.24	20.97
All other banks	104.86	20.97	83.89
Total	US $500.00	US $100.00	US $400.00

serves fall short of the required reserve ratio. If the Fed lowers the discount rate, it reduces the cost of borrowing from the Fed. Banks lend out more of their excess reserves as it becomes cheaper to cover temporary reserve shortages by borrowing from the Fed. This increases the money supply. Conversely, if the Fed increases the discount rate, banks hold more of their excess reserves, decreasing the money supply. Commercial banks can also borrow funds from other commercial banks. The federal funds rate is the interest paid on short-term loans between commercial banks. The Fed tends to keep the discount rate roughly equal to the federal funds rate.

Finally, the Fed can influence the money supply by changing the required reserve ratio. A decrease in the required reserve ratio creates excess reserves. The money supply increases as banks lend out these excess reserves. Conversely, increasing the reserve requirement decreases the money supply. Because a fractional reserve banking system introduces a multiplier effect on the money supply, small changes in the reserve requirement can cause large changes in the money supply. Thus, this policy option is a blunt instrument and is used infrequently.

The Evolution of Monetary Policy

Monetary policy has its roots in classical economics, the predominant economic theory prior to 1936, the year John Maynard Keynes published his book *General Theory of Employment, Interest, and Money*. Classical economics is characterized by at least two central themes: the quantity theory of money and the flexibility of market prices. The quantity theory is represented by the relationship $P*Q = M*V$, where P represents prices, Q represents the quantity of output, M represents the supply of money, and V represents

the velocity of money (i.e., the number of times per period a dollar changes hands). The left-hand side of the quantity of money relationship represents the nominal value of aggregate output (i.e., gross domestic product, or GDP). The right-hand side represents the total nominal value of the money that was exchanged during a period. In every market transaction, the buyer gives money to the seller in exchange for a good or service. Therefore, the total nominal value of market transactions can be measured by either the nominal value of the goods and services or the nominal value of the money exchanged.

Classical economists believe that V and Q are independent of the money supply, M. In particular, V is determined by the efficiency with which financial institutions operate. V is predictable over time, increasing about 3 percent annually from the end of World War II to the early 1980s. Similarly, classical economists believe that Q is determined by the economy's productive capacity. Productive capacity depends largely on the available quantity of productive resources (e.g., labor, capital, and natural resources). If the economy is operating below economic capacity, classical economists believe that market prices will fall for the underemployed resources. Falling resource prices reduce production costs, encouraging firms to increase output. If the demand for resources exceeds the available supply, resource prices increase, increasing production costs and reducing output. Thus, flexible market prices ensure that the quantity of goods and services produced, Q, always equals the economy's economic capacity.

If Q and V are independent of M, then changes in M only affect prices, P. If M grows faster than Q, P increases; if M grows more slowly than Q, P falls. This conclusion has at least two policy implications: M should grow at a steady rate over time, and monetary policy to stabilize economic performance is unnecessary. Classical economists believe that M should grow at a constant rate over time. P is stable over time if the growth of M is tied to the long-term growth of Q (as determined by the growth of productive capacity). Furthermore, resource and product price flexibility ensure full employment, so monetary policy need not be used to stabilize economic performance.

Keynes, writing during the Great Depression, challenged the classical view on two accounts: price flexibility and the effect of pessimistic expectations (see **fiscal policy**). Specifically, Keynes believed that prices adjust slowly, particularly for price decreases, and that lower resource prices might not increase production. Producers only produce output if they expect to sell it. If producers and consumers have pessimistic expectations regarding future economic conditions, producers probably will not increase output as resource prices fall. If prices adjust slowly and expectations are pessimistic, the economy can experience prolonged periods of high unemployment, as in the Great Depression. Early Keynesians recommended countercyclical fiscal policy to stimulate the economy during economic downturns. Keynesians believe that expansionary fiscal policy could increase GDP, without significantly increasing prices, if there are slack resources. In contrast, early Keynesians did not support expansionary monetary policy. With pessimistic expectations, early Keynesians believed that consumers would save rather than spend any additional money and that businesses would not increase investment as interest rates fell. Thus, monetary policy would be ineffective. (This is called the Keynesian "Liquidity trap.")

Economic performance during the 1950s and 1960s seemed to validate the Keynesian view (see Figure I). Excluding the Korean War years, the economy was near full employment, and inflation rates remained relatively modest during much of this period. (For policy purposes, full employment does not imply zero unemployment. Full employment requires eliminating the unemployment associated with business cycle contractions. However, it allows for the "natural unemployment" associated with individuals voluntarily seeking better jobs or transitioning out of declining industries. During the 1950s and 1960s, 4 percent unemployment was considered full employment.) As the economy expanded beyond full employment, inflation increased. As the economy contracted below full employment, inflation decreased.

The Phillips curve depicts the Keynesian trade-off between inflation and unemployment (see Figure II). As such, the Phillips curve represents an important policy trade-off for early Keynesians. It implied that expansionary economic policies could indefinitely sustain the economy above full employment if policymakers were willing to accept higher inflation rates. Macroeconomic policy debates frequently considered the appropriate balance between unemployment and inflation. Unemployment imposes significant costs on relatively few individuals; inflation redistributes income across a broad range of individuals. Early Keynesians tended to view unemployment as more serious than inflation.

During the 1970s and 1980s, inflation and unemployment diverged from the Phillips curve relationship, which Keynesian economists had trouble explaining (it was generally attributed to an outward shift in the Phillips curve over time due to oil price shocks and structural economic changes; see Figure III). Monetary policy enjoyed a resurgence, led by Milton Friedman and the monetarist economists. The monetarists reaffirmed the quantity theory of money and reemphasized price stability as the preeminent macroeconomic policy objective. The monetarists' work, including empirical analysis regarding monetary policy's historical impact, established monetary policy as an important macroeconomic policy tool. In addition, monetarists offered a plausible explanation for the inflation and unemployment pattern observed in the 1970s and 1980s.

The monetarists' explanation involves the natural rate of unemployment. If market dynamics always move resource markets toward full employment, the long-run unemployment rate is independent of the inflation rate and unaffected by fiscal and monetary policy. In the short run, expansionary macroeconomic policy can reduce unemployment. However, expansionary macroeconomic policy

FIGURE I. INFLATION VERSUS UNEMPLOYMENT: 1954–1969

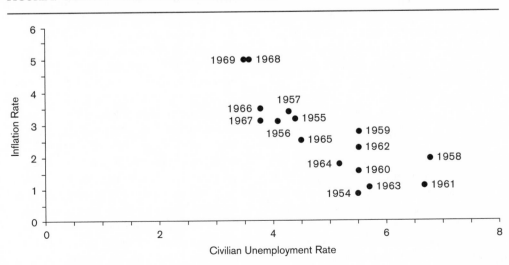

Source: Economic Report of the President, 1995.

FIGURE II. PHILLIPS CURVE: 1954–1969

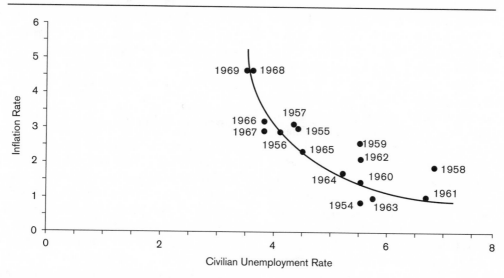

Source: Economic Report of the President, 1995.

FIGURE III. INFLATION VERSUS UNEMPLOYMENT: 1954–1994

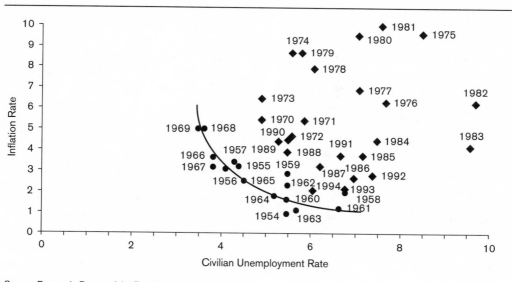

Source: Economic Report of the President, 1995.

increasingly affects prices, as resource markets naturally adjust to full employment. If expansionary policies persist in the long run, inflation accelerates. Anticipating future inflation, individuals take precautionary measures (e.g., building expected inflation into future wage and price agreements and interest rates). This creates an accelerating inflationary spiral (called the "acceleration principal"). The only way to sustain long-run GDP above its full employment level is to increase aggregate demand faster than inflation.

Monetarists believe that monetary policy can be an effective short-run macroeconomic stabilization tool (they also believe that fiscal policy is ineffective; see fiscal policy). However, they argue against any kind of stabilization policy. This conclusion is based on at least three related considerations: inherent economic stability, inaccurate economic forecasting, and policy implementation lags. As with the classical economists, monetarists believe that the economy is inherently stable. Flexible resource prices quickly move the economy to full employment; prolonged periods of unemployment are unlikely. In addition, monetarists believe that economic forecasting models cannot predict future economic contractions with enough accuracy to justify preemptive countercyclical policies. Finally, monetarists believe that countercyclical monetary and fiscal policies affect the economy with lags of 18 months or more. If contractions cannot be predicted in advance and stabilization policies have lagged effects, countercyclical policies may not be felt until after the economy naturally corrects itself. Countercyclical macroeconomic policies will become procyclical and destabilize rather than stabilize the economy. (In fact, empirical analysis by monetarists largely attributes business cycles to miss-timed government stabilization policies.)

Rational expectations, the recent new classical extension to the classical and monetarist schools, implies countercyclical monetary policy is ineffective in both the short and long run. Rational expectations hypothesizes that decisionmakers select actions considering all available information concerning the probable effects of current and expected future economic policies. According to this logic, anticipated monetary policy is ineffective. To illustrate, consider expansionary monetary policy. Decisionmakers rationally expect expansionary fiscal policy to aggravate inflation in the long run. The public adjusts wages, prices, and interest rates in anticipation. Thus, anticipated expansionary monetary policy will not affect real prices or real GDP. Monetary policy is only effective in the short run when it is entirely unanticipated. This makes monetary policy ineffective as a stabilization tool. Countercyclical monetary policy cannot be unanticipated. Monetary policy is only unanticipated if it is purely random; random monetary policy clearly does not increase macroeconomic stability.

Monetary policy's resurgence in the 1970s and 1980s has affected Keynesian economics but not repudiated it. Keynesians have accepted that monetary policy does affect economic performance, and they rely largely on monetary policy for short-run macroeconomic stabilization. Although they consider fiscal policy a distinct demand-side policy instrument, government expenditures and tax policy have become increasingly cumbersome and overtaken by concern for the federal budget deficit. This makes fiscal policy ineffective for short-run stabilization. However, Keynesians continue to believe that the federal government should actively stabilize macroeconomic performance. To explain the economy's short-run instability, Keynesians emphasize frictions retarding the adjustment

process and misperceptions regarding current economic conditions (mistakes in extrapolating from personal and local to general economic conditions). If these imperfections are significant, the economy can experience prolonged unemployment, justifying countercyclical monetary policy. Recent Keynesian research has tried to explain price frictions in resource markets (see **fiscal policy**).

Monetary Policy Targets

Part of the monetary policy debate involves the appropriate policy target. There are at least three classes of targets: quantitative money supply measures, financial market performance measures (e.g., interest and exchange rates), and macroeconomic performance measures (e.g., GDP growth, inflation, unemployment). The Fed has the most direct control over the money supply and the least control over macroeconomic performance (macroeconomic performance is influenced by several factors besides domestic monetary policy, including domestic fiscal policy and international monetary and fiscal policy). Thus, the debate over monetary policy targets in part considers whether it is better to have targets that correspond more closely to the Fed's direct span of control or that reflect the overall performance with which the Fed is concerned.

As expected, the preference for monetary policy targets varies across macroeconomic schools of thought. The classical-based economists (including classical, monetarist, and new classical economists) generally prefer quantitative money supply measures. In their view, monetary policy should not, or cannot, be used for short-run stabilization purposes. Instead, they believe in rigid monetary policy rules. Considering the quantity theory of money, $P*Q = M*V$, if V is stable and M and Q grow at the same long-run rate, prices will be stable. Thus classical-based economists believe that the money supply should grow at a constant rate over time, equal to the long-run growth in GDP. They believe that the Fed should adhere to this rule, regardless of short-run fluctuations in GDP. In fact, the new classical economists (rational expectations) maintain that this nondiscretionary monetary policy rule has an added benefit for price stability; it creates a price stability expectation. If decisionmakers believe prices will be stable, they will adjust their actions accordingly. These adjustments help stabilize prices.

One difficulty in implementing money supply targets concerns the definition of money. There are at least three major definitions of the money supply, M1, M2, and M3. M1 is the narrowest definition of money and includes only the most liquid assets: currency (coins and paper bills), traveler's checks, checking deposits in commercial banks, and other interest-earning checking deposits. M2 is slightly broader and includes less liquid assets: M1 plus savings and small denomination time deposits (less than US

$100,000), money market mutual fund shares and deposit accounts, repurchase agreements (overnight loans from customers to commercial banks), and Eurodollar deposits of U.S. residents. M3 is the broadest definition and includes the least liquid assets: M2 plus large denomination time deposits and longer-term loans from customers to commercial banks. In terms of a monetary policy target, the Fed controls M1 most directly, but financial market innovations, including electronic banking, have made M1, M2, and M3 closer and closer substitutes. Historically, M1 received the greatest emphasis. More recently, M2 and M3 have received increasing attention.

Typically, Keynesians target financial market and overall macroeconomic performance. This preference is based on at least two beliefs: The velocity of money has recently been unstable, and monetary policy should stabilize short-run macroeconomic performance. While V increased steadily from the end of World War II to the early 1980s, it has been unstable recently. This instability has been attributed to financial market innovations and deposit deregulation. If V is unstable, there is no direct link between M and P. Quantitative monetary targets do not capture the complex processes through which changes in the money supply are translated to financial markets and overall macroeconomic performance. Furthermore, Keynesians generally view monetary policy as the government's most effective short-run macroeconomic stabilization tool. Monetary policy targets should reflect that monetary policy bears the macroeconomic stabilization burden. These two considerations shift the emphasis to financial market and macroeconomic performance targets. Because the Fed has only limited control over macroeconomic performance, interest rates are generally emphasized. Inflation, unemployment, and GDP growth provide feedback to ensure the interest rate targets are consistent with the desired macroeconomic performance.

Typically, the Fed has followed the Keynesian prescription, though money supply targets received increasing attention during the 1970s as inflation increased and monetarism gained popularity. The primary exception to the Keynesian prescription came between 1979 and 1982, when Paul Volcker was chairman of the Fed. In an anti-inflationary move, Volcker announced that the Fed would target the money supply, allowing financial market supply and demand to determine interest rates. Unfortunately, the stability of V decreased at the same time. The expected volatility in interest rates was exacerbated by the instability in V. Because of the interest rate instability, Volcker abandoned the experiment and reemphasized interest rates in 1982. Monetarists maintain that the Fed's control over the money supply was too inconsistent, even during this period, to qualify as an actual test of monetarist economics.

The debate over the appropriate role for monetary policy is far from resolved. Classical-based economists (in-cluding classical, monetarist, and new classical economists) maintain that monetary policy should follow a strict, nondiscretionary rule: allowing the money supply to increase at the same rate as full employment GDP. In other words, growth in the money supply should be tied to the growth in the economy's productive capacity. This view is based on three related beliefs: the economy's inherent stability, the inadequacy of economic forecasting models, and the lengthy lags before monetary policy affects macroeconomic performance. Keynesians do not believe that the economy is inherently stable. Thus, the federal government has a responsibility to conduct countercyclical macroeconomic stabilization policy. Monetary policy is the most effective short-run policy. Thus, Keynesians believe that the Fed should conduct discretionary monetary policy, targeting interest rates with feedback from unemployment, inflation, and GDP growth rates. The Keynesian view is supported by the recent instability in the velocity of money. Unfortunately, it has been impossible to validate either position empirically or in practice. Sophisticated empirical analyses have been used to support both positions. Furthermore, the results of the U.S. "monetarist experiment," from 1979 to 1982, are dubious because the Fed's control over the money supply was inconsistent.

WILLIAM R. GATES

BIBLIOGRAPHY

Baumol, William J., and Alan S. Blinder, 1994. *Macroeconomics: Principals and Policy*, 6th ed. Fort Worth: Dryden Press.

Biven, W. Carl, 1989. *Who Killed John Maynard Keynes?* Homewood, IL: Dow Jones-Irwin.

Federal Reserve Bank of Kansas City, 1989. *Monetary Policy in the 1990s*.

Friedman, Milton, 1968. "The Role of Monetary Policy." Presidential address at the 80th Annual Meeting of the American Economic Association, December 1967; published in *American Economic Review*, vol. 58 (March 1968) 1–17.

Friedman, Milton, and Anna Schwartz, 1963. *A Monetary History of the United States, 1867–1960*. Princeton: Princeton University Press.

Gwartney, James D., and Richard L. Stroup, 1995. *Macroeconomics: Private and Public Choice*, 7th ed. Fort Worth: Dryden Press.

Keynes, John Maynard, 1936. The General Theory of Employment Interest, and Money. London: Macmillian.

Samuelson, Paul A., and William D. Nordhaus, 1992. *Macroeconomics*, 14th ed. New York: McGraw-Hill.

MONNET, JEAN (1888–1979).

The so-called Father of the European Community, an ardent European federalist whose influence on interstate relations in postwar Europe in terms of encouraging and instigating

European cooperation and integration was profound and enduring. He drafted the Schuman Plan, which is called the birth certificate of the European Community as it gave rise to the first of the three European Communities, namely, the European Coal and Steel Community; he also inspired the two other communities, namely, the European Economic Community and the European Atomic Energy Community, more commonly known as Euratom. The three communities were generally referred to collectively as the European Community from 1967 onward as they were served by common institutions.

Born in 1888 in the Cognac region of France where his father was a cognac merchant, the young Monnet's formal education ended at an early age and, instead of going to university, he traveled extensively for his father's business. It was in meeting lawyers, bankers, and other merchants that Monnet imbibed the spirit of initiative and enterprise and acquired a thorough knowledge of business and politics.

Monnet's career was lengthy and remarkable. His career began in 1914 when, at the age of 26, Monnet argued his way to seeing the French prime minister. Monnet was alarmed at what he observed on his frequent visits between France and Britain. French and British ships were supplying separately the Allied troops at the front; Monnet warned that the lack of coordination was dissipating scarce resources. He was accordingly assigned the task of organizing and coordinating war supplies between the two countries. In 1921, at the age of 33, Monnet was appointed deputy secretary-general of the League of Nations. In 1926, he went to the United States to set up an international commercial bank and traveled widely in Europe and also to China, where he helped to modernize the railway system. In the 1930s, he returned to public service in France, uneasy at the rise of Hitler and Nazism in Germany. In 1938, Monnet was charged by the French prime minister to order war planes from the United States. As the United States was bound by the Neutrality Act not to supply weapons to nations at war, the mission was a delicate one. The planes were ordered and delivered in time and, when France fell, they were given to Britain, where they played a crucial role in the Battle of Britain. In the opinion of the economist John Maynard Keynes, such supplies helped to shorten the war by a year. This was the first occasion on which Monnet met President Franklin D. Roosevelt, to whom Monnet was to become a trusted adviser particularly regarding the Victory Program, which mobilized the U.S. war effort. Roosevelt's phrase that "America must become the arsenal of democracy" originated with Monnet.

In 1940, Monnet proposed a plan for a Franco-British Union, which was accepted by both Sir Winston Churchill and General Charles de Gaulle. The plan provided for an indissoluble union between both countries involving joint organs of defense, foreign, financial, and economic policies. The purpose of the union was to present a united force vis-a-vis the common enemy and to win the war. This far-reaching plan was formally endorsed on June 16, 1940 only to be aborted the following day when France fell to Nazi Germany. The notions of joint action and of pooling national sovereignty were to foreshadow Monnet's future proposals for European integration.

Monnet's lasting contribution to European affairs came in 1950 when the plan he drafted for the French foreign minister, Robert Schuman, was announced. The Schuman Plan of May 5, 1950 proposed the integration of the coal and steel industries of France and Germany through the creation of a new supranational organization. The plan was underpinned by both economic and political motives. German economic recovery depended on the revitalization of its heavy industry; the proposed creation of a common market in coal and steel between France and Germany was calculated to liberalize trade and to stimulate growth in these sectors. Politically, the plan was based on a reconciliation of two arch enemies, France and Germany. The choice of coal and steel was significant since these are known as the industries of war; it is not possible to make war in modern times without steel and to make steel, it is necessary to have coal and iron ore. The proposal set out to make the possibility of war between these two states not only unthinkable but materially impossible. Furthermore, both Monnet and Schuman regarded the new organization as the first step toward a European federation. The plan was enthusiastically greeted beforehand by Konrad Adenauer, the German chancellor, who was unhappy with the International Ruhr Authority set up by the allies to manage the German steel industry after the war. Four institutions were established under the Paris Treaty, namely, the High Authority, which is now known as the European Commission, the Council of Ministers, the Common Assembly, now known as the European Parliament, and the Court of Justice. Monnet served as the first president of the High Authority of the new organization.

Shortly after the Schuman Plan was announced, France came under pressure from the United States to find a means of rearming Germany. The Korean War had broken out and the United States, concerned about European security, wanted to see Germany join the North Atlantic Treaty Organization. Based on one of Monnet's ideas, René Pleven, the French prime minister, proposed a European Defense Community modeled on the European Coal and Steel Community. The treaty was signed on May 27, 1952 but failed to be ratified by the French National Assembly in 1954. As a result of the failure of this premature attempt at political integration, Monnet resigned as president of the High Authority of the European Coal and Steel

Community in order to devote himself full-time from 1955 to 1973 to a pressure group he created, namely, the Action Committee for the United States of Europe.

A recurrent theme throughout Monnet's career was the need to utterly transform interstate relations in Europe by limiting national sovereignty. Nationalism in its extreme form bred distrust and confrontation between states. Monnet once noted that "there will be no peace in Europe if States are reconstructed on the basis of national sovereignty, with all that that implies in terms of prestige politics and economic protectionism. . . . Prosperity and vital progress will remain elusive until the nations of Europe form a federation or a 'European entity' which forge them into a single economic unit."

Moreover, for Monnet, institutions played a role of paramount importance in the process of integration. He often quoted the Swiss philosopher Henri-Frédéric Amiel: "Each man's experience starts again from the beginning. Only institutions grow wiser: they accumulate collective experience; and, owing to this experience and this wisdom, men subject to the same rules will not see their own nature changing, but their behaviour gradually transformed."

Monnet remains a source of inspiration for European integrationists. In recognition of his contribution to the process of European integration, the European Council on April 2, 1976 named Jean Monnet "honorary citizen of Europe," the only person to have been conferred with this title.

MARGARET MARY MALONE

BIBLIOGRAPHY

Fontaine, Pascal, 1988. *Jean Monnet: l'inspirateur.* Paris: Ed. Jacques Grancher.
Kohnstamm, Max, 1981. "Jean Monnet: The Power of the Imagination." Florence, November 23, European University Institute.
Monnet, Jean, 1978. *Memoirs.* Trans. Richard Mayne. London: Collins.
Monnet, Jean, and Robert Schuman, 1986. *Correspondance 1947–1953.* Lausanne: Fondation Jean Monnet pour l'Europe, Centre de Recherches Européennes.

MORALE. The work-related mental state of individual employees and employee groups. Because it is used generically to describe the overall condition of employee attitudes in a work setting, morale is ordinarily defined by proxy. That is, the worker traits and behaviors that are thought to occur under different levels of morale are used as definitions for the concept itself. Work groups with high morale are generally expected to exhibit such traits as cheerfulness, discipline, enthusiasm, and willingness to endure hardship for the good of the organization. Low morale, in contrast, is usually associated with such dysfunctional behaviors as insubordination, apathy, incessant complaining, and bickering over relatively trivial matters. As is the case with many terms dealing with the human condition, the struggle to define morale is much like that experienced by Supreme Court Justice Potter Stewart when he tried to define pornography: Potter reportedly deadpanned, "I can't define it, but I know it when I see it!"

Morale Versus Motivation

Morale and motivation are often used interchangeably. The blending of the two concepts is easily understandable in light of the fact that both are affected by the same organizational attributes. The conditions that promote motivation among workers are also intuitively linked to morale. Progressive leadership practices, equitable treatment of workers, and the ability to gain intrinsic rewards from one's work have all been correlated with both motivation and morale.

Despite this undeniable link, the two concepts can be quite distinct. Motivation refers to the goal-directed activities of workers, whereas morale simply describes the overall level of employee esprit de corps. As such, it is closely related to the concept of job satisfaction. Workers who appear to be happy with the terms and conditions of their employment ordinarily are said to have high morale. The critical difference is that high morale does not necessarily imply that there is a correspondingly high level of goal-directed activity. Work environments that provide good pay, solid job security, and fair treatment will probably contain workers with good morale, but there is no guarantee that those individuals will be motivated to perform (Imundo 1992). In fact, pleasant work settings may be filled with complacent employees who are completely unconcerned with accomplishing anything. By the same token, workers with very low morale may–through threats, intimidation, or fear of termination–be highly motivated to produce.

The essential difference is that motivation to produce is imposed, either intentionally or by happenstance, by management's manipulation of varying intrinsic and extrinsic incentives. Morale can also be influenced by management's actions, but it does not always correlate with either motivation or productivity. There will always be some type of morale, be it good or bad, whether or not management intervenes in any way. True motivation to perform, in constrast, rarely occurs in the absence of proactive steps on the part of supervisors. Management has a responsibility to foster good morale and then to harness it in a fashion that results in improved productivity. In many ways, morale is the more fragile and elusive of the two concepts.

The Current Morale Crisis

One of the most persistent themes of contemporary public administration is that there is a "quiet crisis" in the civil service. Public employees are said to be suffering from "plummeting morale" (Volcker Commission 1989, T. xxiii), a phenomenon that is manifested in high attrition rates and endless numbers of related maladies. Research confirms that, at a minimum, low morale almost always translates into excessive turnover and heightened rates of absenteeism, grievances, stress-related illness, and workplace accidents (Vroom 1964).

The causes for this international phenomenon are diverse but generally center on the antigovernment rhetoric that dominates political discourse throughout the industrialized world. Political leaders in England, Canada, Australia, Brazil, Japan, and most other developed countries have been waging war against the public service. Buzzwords such as "privatization," "downsizing," "debureaucratization," and "managerialism" reflect a pervasive desire to reduce the power and privileges of civil servants.

For the typical public employee, the by-products of this assault on government include reduced professional opportunities (i.e., fewer promotions, infrequent salary increases, lessened transfer options), increased monitoring from external groups, more stringent accountability standards, and greatly heightened output and productivity expectations. Additionally, the citizenry's irritation with "bureaucracy" is often translated into personalized attacks on anyone who works for government. As a consequence, civil servants are almost made to feel guilty or apologetic for their jobs. Government employment has unquestionably become less attractive and rewarding as these trends have accelerated. The devastating impact that these developments may have on workers is best examined by looking at the various antecedents to high morale.

Antecedents to Morale

Research on the variables that influence worker morale tends to confirm the concept's close relationship to job satisfaction. Both tend to be greatly influenced by a wide array of exogenous and job-specific factors. Among the characteristics of the work setting that are most influential, compensation, working conditions, and interpersonal relationships with one's superiors tend to be especially important (Bacharach and Bamberger 1992). The degree of "procedural justice" present in the organization is also critical. To maintain morale, the organization's system of recognizing and rewarding workers for their contributions must be perceived as fair and equitable (Folger and Konovsky 1989). Morale is also affected by the sense of group cohesion that prevails. If the workers feel as if they are part of a community, or that they are contributing to an important cause, then they are much more likely to have high morale. The pride that workers have in their organizations, coupled with the prestige that the job brings them, are essential components of this complex recipe.

In addition to these contextual factors, morale is also affected by the nature of the work itself. As much of the motivational literature demonstrates, workers are most inclined to be happy when their jobs allow for flexibility, achievement, and recognition. Also, low levels of role stress—i.e., ambiguity and conflict over duties and expectations—are correlated with job satisfaction and morale (Hom, Griffeth, and Carson 1995). All of these conditions are potentially influenced by the organization's overall levels of decentralizaton, as well as the amount of trust and respect that management gives its labor force.

When weighed against this list of antecedents, contemporary public employment comes up short by almost any standard. Except for the much-touted efforts to "empower" civil servants (a movement that some have referred to as a "disempowerment" strategy), the entire tone and direction of public management in the late twentieth century tends to diminish morale-inducing variables.

The effects of budget cuts and widespread assaults on the bureaucracy have been to erode all of the contextual incentives that once were available to civil servants. In addition to lessened salary and promotional opportunities, job security and virtually all related perquisites of employment have deteriorated. Likewise, the workers' sense of pride and accomplishment from contributing to public service objectives has undoubtedly suffered from the avalanche of negative public opinion concerning government and bureaucracy. These factors are compounded in many jurisdictions by extreme pressures to economize and "produce." The typical organizational response in such settings is not to decentralize and enrich work but to add increasing layers of procedures and controls designed to ensure that resources are not wasted. Within this context, then, both extrinsic and intrinsic sources of job satisfaction are probably discouraged.

Practical Steps to Improve Morale

Given the depth of public impatience with bureaucracy and government, the current crisis in public employment morale is likely to persist for the forseeable future. There are no simple solutions to the problem of low employee morale. As a result, government will probably continue to encounter problems in attracting and retaining talented employees. Likewise, creating a rewarding and interesting work environment for civil servants will continue to challenge even the most imaginative public managers.

Despite this well-founded pessimism, however, there are a few steps that can be taken by almost any manager to improve worker morale. For the most part, these measures are simply applications of common sense that spring naturally from the research findings detailed here. For example, because morale is so closely tied to workers' perceptions of the organization in which they are employed, effective recruitment and orientation are essential preliminary steps. Finding workers who are most likely to internalize the goals of the organization and then properly training and orienting them concerning workplace norms and expectations are some of the most effective means of promoting high morale. Because "problem employees" can reduce the job satisfaction of the entire workforce, weeding out job applicants who are likely to be chronic complainers needs to be a high priority of all managers. Similarly, managers will be well rewarded if they devote some attention to educating their workers about the agency's mission and significance. Taking care to provide civil servants with a sense of their jobs' underlying worth is an important element of the morale puzzle.

Another step that managers can take to enhance morale is to remember that workers are highly attentive judges of workplace equity and fairness. The supervisor-subordinate relationship is one of the foundation stones of a comfortable work environment; treating one's coworkers with dignity and respect is thus a low-cost means of aiding morale. These benefits can be compounded when the supervisor tries to provide challenging yet reasonable assignments, expresses appreciation for accomplishments, distributes rewards fairly and on the basis of agreed-upon criteria, and respects honest differences of opinion among the work group. Although most public managers are not in a position to improve their workers' salaries and fringe benefit packages, they can see to it that the workplace is administered in a just and caring manner.

One additional managerial contribution to worker morale deserves brief attention. Because the inherent joy of work within the public sector is often sacrificed on the altar of bureaucratic procedure, managers have an obligation to strive to keep red tape from blocking employees from doing their jobs (Imundo 1992, p. 46). This is one area in which efforts to "reinvent government" can actually benefit civil servants, since a truly reinvented workplace would be far less rule-oriented than is presently the case. At the same time, if managers were to reduce their subordinates' job stress by clearly delineating priorities and responsibilities, then the intrinsic satisfactions of much public work would certainly be enhanced.

STEVEN W. HAYS

BIBLIOGRAPHY

Bacharach, S., and P. Bamberger, 1992. "Causal Models of Role Stressor Antecedents and Consequences." *Journal of Vocational Behavior,* vol. 41: 13–34.

Folger, R., and M. A. Konovsky, 1989. "Effects of Procedural and Distributive Justice on Reactions to Pay Raise Decisions." *Academy of Management Journal,* vol. 32: 115–130.
Hom, Peter, Rodger Griffeth, and Paula Carson, 1995. "Turnover of Personnel." In Jack Rabin, Thomas Vocino, W. B. Hildreth, and Gerald Miller, eds., *Handbook of Public Personnel Administration.* New York: Marcel Dekker, 531–582.
Imundo, Louis, 1992. *The Effective Supervisor's Handbook.* Chicago: American Management Association.
Volcker Commission, 1989. *Leadership for America: Rebuilding the Public Service.* Lexington, MA: Lexington Books.
Vroom, Victor, 1964. *Some Personality Determinants of the Effects of Participation.* Englewood Cliffs, NJ: Prentice-Hall.

MOSES, ROBERT (1888–1981).

The state and municipal official who through his appointment to a number of independent public authorities and special posts controlled the physical development of the New York metropolitan area. He used his political skills to complete a massive network of parks, roads, bridges, tunnels, and housing projects, one of the largest building programs in the history of public administration. Although never elected to public office, Moses exercised as much power as the various governors and mayors with whom he served.

Moses was born on December 18, 1888, in New Haven, Connecticut. His father was a prosperous department store owner in New Haven, whose strong-willed wife forced him to retire in 1897 at the age of 46 so that the family could move to New York City. There Bella Moses played a leading role in the Settlement House Movement, helping to aid Jewish immigrants pouring into New York from eastern Europe.

In 1905, Moses returned to New Haven from his Manhattan home to attend Yale University. Following his graduation from Yale in 1909, he attended Oxford University in England, where his interest in public service and conservative political thought emerged. He graduated with honors from Oxford in 1911 and completed a Ph.D. in political science from Columbia University in New York in 1913. His thesis on the civil service of great Britain argued for a higher class of civil servants free from outside influence.

Armed with his philosophy, Moses in 1913 joined the teaching staff at the Bureau of Municipal Research, one of the leading public administration reform organizations in the United States. Moses and his colleagues agitated for personnel and budgetary reform and departmental reorganization. In 1919, Governor Alfred Smith appointed Moses to be chief of staff of the governor's Citizens Committee on Reorganization in the state government. After the state legislature finally approved the reorganization plan, Smith placed Moses in charge of the effort to develop the state system of public parks.

As a reformer, Moses had embraced the principle that agency heads should report directly to the governor. As the prospective president of the state park commission for Long Island, Moses drafted legislation that gave the president a six-year term (three times as long as the governor's) and virtual immunity from removal. The commission, moreover, received wide-ranging powers to obtain land and construct parkways along which city dwellers could drive to their parks.

Moses perfected the use of the public authority as a device for completing government-sponsored projects with minimum political interference. In 1933, New York mayor Fiorello LaGuardia appointed Moses head of the Triborough Bridge Authority. Working through the New York state legislature, Moses amended the enabling legislation so as to give to the Authority the same powers as a business corporation. The Authority could issue bonds, make contracts, collect tolls, acquire real estate (through the power of eminent domain), and make laws. The rules and regulations of the Authority, once placed in a contract with bondholders, could not be repealed by the state. Moses controlled the Authority until 1968.

In 1934, Moses ran for governor of New York, his only attempt at elected office. Nominated by the Republican State Convention, he ran a disastrous campaign in a year when Republican candidates did poorly nationwide and received only 35 percent of the votes cast.

Although his strong-willed personality antagonized many people, mayors and governors continued to appoint Moses to the posts that gave him power. In 1946, New York City Mayor William O'Dwyer appointed Moses to the undefined position of city coordinator of construction. Designed as a temporary post, Moses used the position for 14 years to guide the progress of city roads and slum removal projects by acting as the liaison between the city and federal funding agencies.

As with positions before it, Moses used the post of city construction coordinator to broker relationships between funding sources, construction companies, labor unions, bankers, civic leaders, and politicians. He often drafted the laws for the positions he held, ensuring that they maximized his authority. He drew up elaborate plans and ruthlessly pursued them. In his early years, with the park issue, he had public opinion on his side. For much of his career his allies included the press, which viewed Moses as an idol of technical competence in a sea of urban bureaucracy and greed. His ability to get things done, along with the financial resources his organizations generated through tolls and federal grants, remained a precious resource in the eyes of politicians with whom he worked and whom he often irritated.

Moses did not achieve these accomplishments alone. In addition to his role as a broker between various urban and state interests, he led a legion of supporters equally committed to public works. They helped him manage the interlocking network of organizations on which he sat. Among the organizations that Moses directly controlled

during his public career were the Long Island State Park Commission, the State Council of Parks, the Jones Beach State Parkway and Bethpage Park authorities, the variously named Triborough Bridge and New York City Tunnel authorities, and the offices of the New York City park commissioner and the New York City construction coordinator. In 1934, for example, Moses simultaneously oversaw seven separate government organizations concerned with parks and roads in the New York metropolitan area.

By the late 1950s, his bullish construction techniques had earned Moses the enmity of the same type of civic associations from which he earlier had launched his public career. A heavy-handed battle with uptown residents over a small parking lot in Central Park for restaurant patrons and the drawn-out effort to build a Lower Manhattan Expressway (both unsuccessful) tarnished his public image. In 1959, city leaders convinced the 70-year-old Moses that he could resurrect his fame by taking charge of the 1964–1965 New York World's Fair. The financially mismanaged fair lost money and destroyed what was left of Moses' reputation.

In 1968, New York Governor Nelson Rockefeller stripped Moses of his last base of power by merging the Triborough Bridge and Tunnel Authority into a collection of regional transportation agencies. Rockefeller promised the 79-year old Moses a leading role in the new authority but delivered only an advisory post after Moses gave the reorganization his blessing. The event marked the end of Moses' public career. He died on July 28, 1981.

HOWARD E. MCCURDY

BIBLIOGRAPHY

Caro, Robert A., 1974. *The Power Broker: Robert Moses and the Fall of New York.* New York: Vintage Books.
Kaufman, Herbert, 1975. "Robert Moses: Charismatic Bureaucrat." *Political Science Quarterly*, vol. 90 (Fall) 521–538.

MOTIVATION-HYGIENE THEORY (MHT).

A theory that holds that human beings have two sets of needs that tend to operate independently in dynamically different ways: (1) the motivator need to seek growth and satisfaction and (2) the hygiene need to avoid pain and dissatisfaction. Based on job satisfaction studies of critical events in the workplace, which revealed two independent sets of factors, MHT is sometimes called the two-factor theory.

History

Secondary research, directed by Frederick Herzberg et al. (1957) at Psychological Services of Pittsburgh, brought together classification of the problem areas of job attitudes in a review of over 2,000 writings—virtually everything that had been published on the subject from 1900 to 1955. The goal of the study was to definitively answer the question, What do workers want from their jobs?

Results were contradictory, but one clue emerged from 15 studies involving 28,000 employees who were asked to indicate what made them satisfied or dissatisfied on the job. Four studies discussed only positive contributors to satisfaction, six only negative contributions, and five studies discussed both sides. There appeared to be some difference in the primacy of factors, depending upon whether the investigator was looking for things the workers liked or disliked about their jobs. The concept that there might be some factors that were "satisfiers" and others that were "dissatisfiers" was suggested by this finding.

Primary research for *Motivation to Work* (1959) was based on the hypothesis that the factors leading to positive attitudes and those leading to negative attitudes would differ. The critical event method, first developed by John Flanagan, was adapted for the study. Two hundred accountants and engineers were interviewed and asked (1) to describe a time when they felt very good on the job and (2) to describe a time when they felt very bad on the job.

For quantification, the procedure of content analysis, as developed by students of political science and of public opinion, such as Paul Laswell and Bernard Berelson, was used.

Results revealed that (1) good events involved chiefly intrinsic factors: achievement, recognition for achievement, work itself, responsibility, and growth, whereas (2) bad events involved chiefly extrinsic factors: company policy and administration, supervision, interpersonal relations, salary, working conditions, security. Feelings of satisfaction from the intrinsic factors also lasted significantly longer than feelings of dissatisfaction from extrinsic factors.

The theory derived from this study named the satisfiers "motivators" because these factors involve intrinsics of what people do on the job. It named the dissatisfiers "hygienes" because these factors involved extrinsics of the job environment.

The satisfier "achievement" had been given relatively little emphasis in previous research on job satisfaction. The results of this study appear to show that behavior (achievement-performance) leads to satisfaction and attitude change rather than the previously held assumption that attitude leads to behavior.

The *Motivation to Work* study became the most replicated in industrial-organizational psychology of the 1960s. It also became one of the most controversial since it called into question traditional single scales, which are incapable of revealing the two sets of factors (see Figure I).

Replications of the *Motivation to Work* study were reported in Frederick Herzberg's 1966 book *Work and the Nature of Man* and in his 1968 article in the *Harvard Business Review*, "One More Time: How Do You Motivate Employ-

FIGURE I. Contrast of Traditional Single Scale with M-H Scales

Dissatisfaction------------Satisfaction

Traditional Scale

No Satisfaction-----MOTIVATORS----- Satisfaction
Dissatisfaction------HYGIENE------No Dissatisfaction

M-H Scales

ees?" The first 12 studies utilizing the critical events method on 17 populations revealed the distinction between satisfiers and dissatisfiers first shown in *Motivation to Work*. These included lower-level supervisors, professional women, agricultural administrators, men about to retire from management positions, hospital maintenance personnel, manufacturing supervisors, nurses, food handlers, engineers, scientists, housekeepers, teachers, technicians, female assemblers, accountants, Finnish foremen, and Hungarian engineers (see Figure II).

Underlying Framework

MHT agrees with other humanist theories in psychology that motivation of human beings to grow psychologically (self-actualize) is unique in the animal realm. MHT disagrees with Maslow's Hierarchical Theory (to which it is often compared) that physical and social needs (hygiene) must be satisfied to a large extent before growth needs (motivators) become operational. Indeed, MHT research studies show that hygiene needs seldom lead to satisfaction and that motivators and hygienes operate simultaneously. The normal motivation-hygiene nature of the individual is summarized in *Work and the Nature of Man* (1966) as made up of two Biblical archetypes: Adam—avoiding pain from the environment—and Abraham—seeking happiness from achieving and growing.

Hygiene

The underlying dynamic of hygiene is the avoidance of pain from the environment (APE) or, in organizational terms, job dissatisfaction. There are infinite sources of pain. Man has a limitless variety of dissatisfaction from which to choose. With 10 billion nerve cells in the central nervous system, man has a potential for misery unheralded in the history of biological life forms.

The Dynamics of Hygiene

- The psychological basis of hygiene needs is the avoidance of pain from the environment—APE.
- There are infinite sources of pain in the environment.

FIGURE II. Factors Affecting Job Attitudes as Reported in the First 12 Investigations

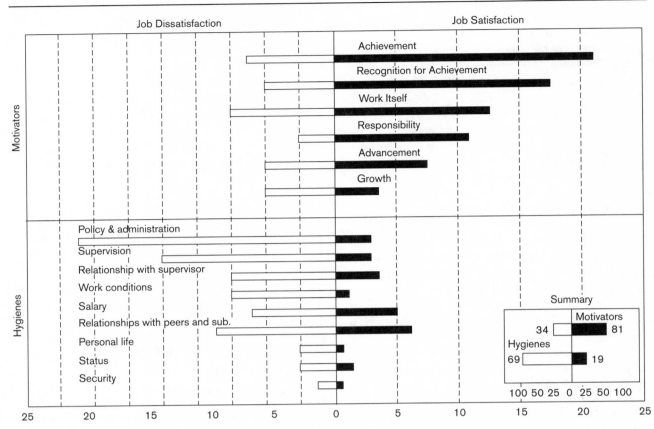

Source: Frederick Herzberg, 1986,"One More Time: How Do You Motivate Employees?" *Harvard Business Review,* (January)

- Hygiene improvements have short-term effects.
- Hygiene needs are cyclical in nature.
- Hygiene needs have an escalating zero point.
- There is no final answer to hygiene needs.

In summary, hygiene is short-term and cyclical in nature. The zero point of pain relief escalates, and the hygiene problem is, "How do you treat people well?"

Motivators

The dynamics of motivators are in direct contrast to the dynamics of hygiene.

The Dynamics of Motivation

- The psychological basis of motivation is the need for personal growth.
- There are limited sources of motivator satisfaction.
- Motivator improvements have long-term effects.
- Motivators are additive in nature.
- Motivator needs have a nonescalating zero point.
- There are answers to motivator needs.

Motivation is chiefly a result of internal abilities. People want to use their abilities. The following formula suggests the strategy for motivation based on MHT:

$$\text{Motivation} = \text{Ability} + \text{Intrinsic Reward}$$

The first variable, ability, says that the more someone is capable of doing, the more one can be motivated; therefore selection and training are important in MHT. The second variable, intrinsic reward (the work itself), contrasts with extrinsic reward (money and "attaboys") used by behaviorist strategies. MHT therefore holds that design of the work itself, or job content, is essential to motivation.

Influence and Applications

Mental Health

MHT research in mental health/mental illness conducted at veterans hospitals and on college campuses showed that the hospitalized patients were finding the few events that made them feel good from environmental (hygiene) factors before and since their hospitalization. In contrast, the events that made the college students feel good came chiefly from the content of what they were doing, achieving and learning, the motivators. The motivational pattern of college students was similar to that of functioning populations at work, who had previously been studied.

The researchers concluded that the mentally ill were functioning only on the hygiene or pain-avoidance dynamic and that they could never become mentally healthy unless they began functioning on the motivator dynamic—doing something with content that interested them. Roy Hamlin, a psychologist with the Veterans Administration hospitals began applying this deduction from MHT in activity therapy for his hospital patients—teaching them to play golf and giving them the opportunity to develop skills in the game. These studies had a great influence on activity therapy, what later came to be known as reality therapy.

Job Enrichment

The major application of MHT has been job enrichment, which translates the motivator factor into specifics for job redesign (see Table I).

The term "job enrichment" was first introduced in a 1968 article in the *Harvard Business Review* as an application of MHT, which has been tested in the workplace. This article reported specifically on job enrichment studies at AT&T, where motivators had been systematically introduced into the jobs of stockholder correspondents and others without additional pay or other hygiene rewards. After an initial drop in performance attributed to the learning curve, those in enriched jobs far outperformed those in the control groups. Job satisfaction and positive attitudes also increased dramatically. The vertical loading of job enrichment (pushing down responsibility for clients) was contrasted with horizontal loading-adding more variety of tasks at the same level "washing dishes, then washing silverware." "One More Time" became the most reprinted article in the history of the *Harvard Business Review;* over 1.7 million copies sold. Job enrichment was applied in scores of other organizations, most notably Imperial Chemicals, Inc. in Great Britain on jobs at all levels.

In late 1978, Al Alber surveyed 186 companies and 6 agencies of the federal government about their job enrichment programs. Two-thirds of the companies reported improvements in quality, three-fourths reported improvements in productivity, and the goal of reduced absenteeism and/or turnover was achieved 80 percent of the time. The major cost of job enrichment is in training costs, and Alber found that many organizations had failed to invest in the training necessary for enriched jobs.

Job enrichment applications of Motivation-Hygiene Theory became the most influential job design strategy of the 1970s but was often confused with horizontal loading, or with human relations changes in the job environment.

In the 1980s, the quality circles movement spread to the United States from Japan, where it had been greatly influenced by Motivation-Hygiene Theory and its job enrichment strategy of pushing down responsibility for quality to the worker level. In the United States, quality circle training materials cited four of the job enrichment ingredients: new learning, direct feedback, authority to communicate, and accountability. The central ingredient of the client relationship was notably absent.

In the 1990s, the quality circle strategy was replaced by a focus on client-customer feedback on quality and on worker empowerment. In 1994, the Society for Industrial and Organizational Psychology recognized Frederick Herzberg as a pioneer in contemporary worker empowerment through application of Motivation-Hygiene Theory (see Figure III).

Cross-Cultural Studies

Figure III shows some of the critical events studies conducted around the world. Most appear to support the distinction between motivators and hygiene. The U.S. profile summarizes events in the lives of 1,685 employees in 12 job event studies. Only 19 percent of the satisfying job events involve external incentives. In contrast, 69 percent of the dissatisfying job events relate to external incentives and only 31 percent to motivator failure to achieve and grow.

The next profile summarizes job events of 253 workers in public and private sector jobs in Japan. Contrary to all the conventional wisdom that has grown up about differences between American and Japanese workers, their profiles are quite similar. Like their counterparts in the United States, Japanese workers tend to be made happy by their own achievement and growth. Finland in Northern Europe and Hungary in Central Europe have similar motivation patterns.

TABLE I. Motivation Factors and Job Enrichment Ingredients

Motivator Factors	Job Enrichment Ingredients
Achievement	New learning (from performance and on-the-job training)
Recognition for achievement	Direct feedback (from client and product, where possible)
Work itself	Client/product relationship
Responsibility	Accountability, control of resources, self-scheduling, and authority to communicate directly
Advancement-growth	Unique expertise (responsibility for training others)

FIGURE III. CROSS-CULTURAL MOTIVATION-HYGIENE STUDIES

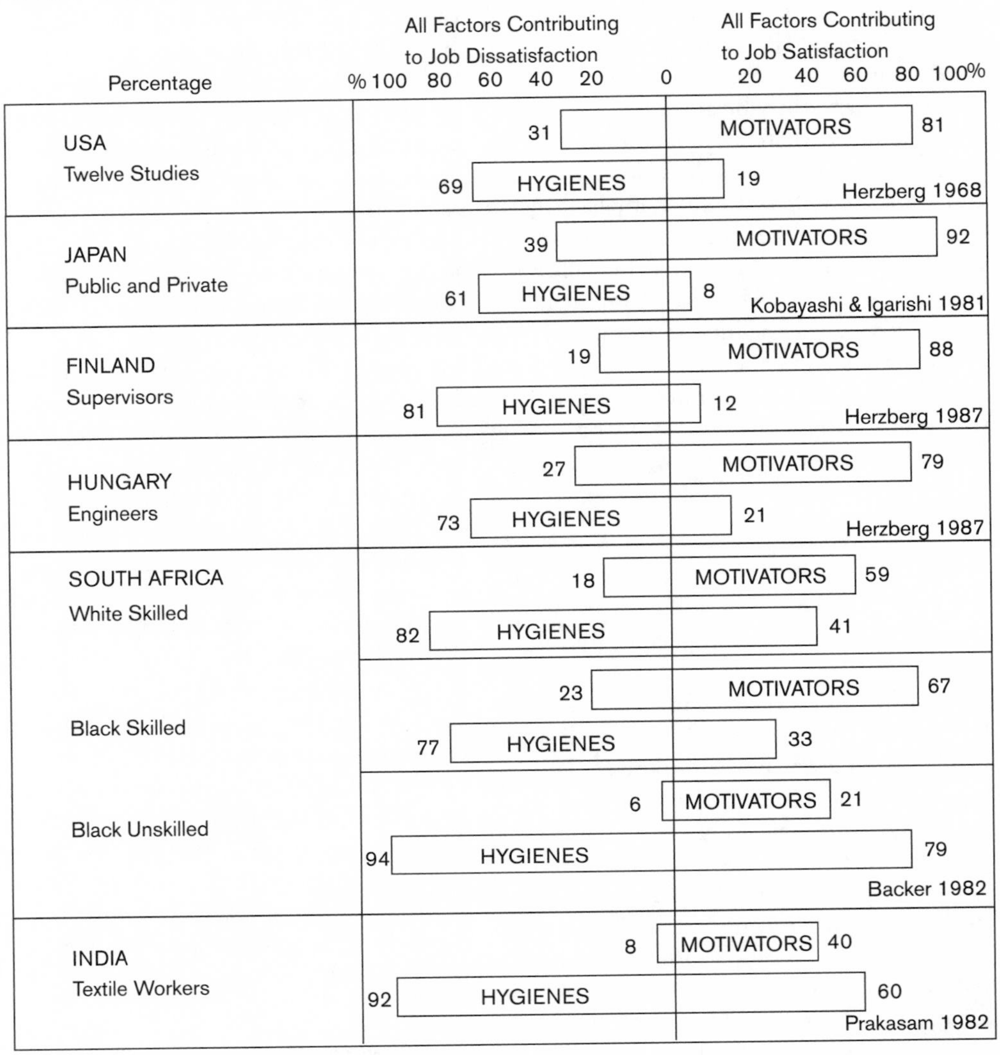

Percentage	All Factors Contributing to Job Dissatisfaction (%)	Factor	All Factors Contributing to Job Satisfaction (%)	Source
USA Twelve Studies	31	MOTIVATORS	81	
	69	HYGIENES	19	Herzberg 1968
JAPAN Public and Private	39	MOTIVATORS	92	
	61	HYGIENES	8	Kobayashi & Igarishi 1981
FINLAND Supervisors	19	MOTIVATORS	88	
	81	HYGIENES	12	Herzberg 1987
HUNGARY Engineers	27	MOTIVATORS	79	
	73	HYGIENES	21	Herzberg 1987
SOUTH AFRICA White Skilled	18	MOTIVATORS	59	
	82	HYGIENES	41	
Black Skilled	23	MOTIVATORS	67	
	77	HYGIENES	33	
Black Unskilled	6	MOTIVATORS	21	
	94	HYGIENES	79	Backer 1982
INDIA Textile Workers	8	MOTIVATORS	40	
	92	HYGIENES	60	Prakasam 1982

The South African profiles of skilled black and white workers follow the predicted pattern, but the 789 unskilled blacks sampled from various ethnic groups employed in a number of companies show job satisfaction being dependent on external incentives. The researcher, Luther Backer, says that the impoverished nature of the unskilled workers' jobs has not afforded these workers with motivators.

The profile of 300 textile mill workers in Bombay, India, also shows lack of normal motivator satisfaction on the job. Such abnormal profiles tend to predict strikes and labor unrest. In the case of the Indian textile workers, they went on strike soon after this study was conducted in 1981. The government finally had to take over the mills in 1983, after they had lain idle for 21 months.

When human beings are denied motivating work or decent hygiene treatment, they will express their rage somehow in strikes or passive hostility and slowdowns on the job (see Figure IV).

Figure IV summarizes a study of 341 public- and private-sector workers from a variety of job levels in 11 organizations in the developing country of Zambia. Instead of analyzing events that made workers feel very good or bad, the researchers of this study asked about times when workers put forth either very great effort or very little effort. The resulting profile is very similar to job satisfaction-dissatisfaction profiles. The work itself appeared to bring forth great effort, while external incentives appeared to bring forth little effort.

FIGURE IV. ZAMBIA: PUBLIC AND PRIVATE SECTORS

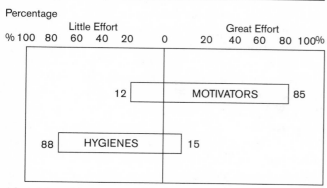

Adapted from: Machunga and Schmitt, 1983, "Work Motivation in a Developing Country," *JAP,* vol. 68.

FIGURE V. BRITISH AND NIGERIAN PROFILES

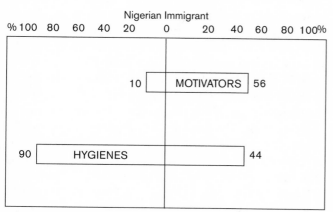

Adapted from: Adigun and Stephenson, 1992, "Sources of Job Motivation and Satisfaction among British and Nigerian Employees," *Journal of Social Psychology,* vol. 132, no. 3.

A 1993 study (Figure V) contrasted events in the work lives of native British workers and Nigerian immigrant workers. Not surprisingly, the native British work-ers, who are under less stress from an alien hygiene environment, had a much more normal satisfaction profile. Motivation-Hygiene Theory would not accept the immigrant profile as mere cultural differences, but as evidence of the need for more training and job enrichment for immigrants so they can experience more motivation satisfaction and less feeling of dependence on hygiene. In a world where managers must deal with more and more immigrant workers, Motivation-Hygiene Theory offers some universal principles.

FREDERICK I. HERZBERG

BIBLIOGRAPHY

Adigun, Isaac O. and Geoffrey M. Stephenson, 1992. "Sources of Job Motivation and Satisfaction Among British and Nigerian Employees." *Journal of Social Psychology,* vol. 132, no. 3. pp. 369–376.

Alber, Al, 1979, "The Real Cost of Job Enrichment." *Business Horizons* (February). University of Indiana Press, 62–72.

Backer, Luther, 1982. "An Intercultural Study of Work Motivation—A Useful Instrument in Industrial Relations." *Journal of Labour Relations,* vol. 6: 49–65.

Bockman, Valerie, 1971. "The Herzberg Controversy." *Personnel Psychology,* vol. 24: 155–189.

Ford, Robert, 1970. *Motivation through the Work Itself.* New York: American Management Association.

Grigaliunas, B., and Y. Wiener, 1974. "Has the Research Challenge to Motivation-Hygiene Theory Been Conclusive? An Analysis of Critical Studies." *Human Relations,* vol. 27, no. 9.

Herzberg, Frederick I. 1966. *Work and the Nature of Man.* New York: Thomas Crowell.

———, 1968. "One More Time: How Do You Motivate Employees?" *Harvard Business Review* (January-February).

———, 1976. *The Managerial Choice: To Be Efficient and to Be Human.* Homewood, IL: Dow Jones-Irwin. 2d rev. ed., Salt Lake City, Utah: Olympus Publishing Company, 1982.

———, 1979. "Motivation and Innovation: Who Are Your Employees Serving?" *California Management Review* (June).

———, 1987. "Workers' Needs: The Same Around the World." *Industry Week* (September).

———, 1991. "Herzberg's Motivation-Hygiene Theory." In Richard Trahair, ed., *"Eponyms in Social Science: A Dictionary and Sourcebook.* Australia: Greenwood Press.

Herzberg, F., and R. Hamlin., 1963. "Motivation-Hygiene Concept and Psychotherapy." *Mental Hygiene,* vol. 47.

Herzberg, F., B. Mausner, R. Peterson, and D. Capwell, 1957. *Job Attitudes: Research and Opinion.* Pittsburgh, PA: Psychological Services of Pittsburgh.

Herzberg, F., B. Mausner, and B. Snyderman, 1959. *The Motivation to Work.* New York: John Wiley & Sons. Reprinted as Management Classic with a new introductory chapter. Transaction Publishers (Rutgers University), 1993.

Herzberg, Frederick I. and M. Minger, 1990. "Motivation to Work versus Incentive to Labor." *Journal of Sociological Studies,* USSR Academy of Science, Moscow.

Kobayashi, Y., and H. Igarishi, 1981. "An Empirical Test of the Herzberg Theory about Job Satisfaction." *Tohuku Psychological Folia,* vol. 40: 74–83.

Machungwa, Peter D., and Neal Schmitt, 1983. "Work Motivation in a Developing Country." *Journal of Applied Psychology*, vol. 68, no. 1: 31–42.

Paul, William James, and Keith B. Robertson, 1970. *Job Enrichment and Employee Motivation*. London: Gower Press.

Prakasam, R., 1982. "Employee Attitudes in High and Low Productivity Mills: An Application of Two-Factor Theory," vol. 43, *Indian Journal of Social Work*.

Quality Circle Syllabus, Norfolk Naval Shipyard, 1981.

Zdravomyslov, A., and V.A. Yadov, 1964. "A Case Study of Attitude to Labor." *Problems of Philosophy* (Moscow), vol. 4.

MUCKRAKERS. A group of American writers who documented abuses on many levels of society in the early twentieth century.

Closely associated with the Progressive Movement, muckrakers were noted for exposing corruption in business and politics and were most active during the decade from 1902 to 1912. Although many were journalists, muckraking writers included novelists, poets, jurists, and other professionals. Their exposures of the abuses of capitalism and corrupt government led to wide-ranging political and social reforms and contributed to the significant impact made by the Progressives on American history.

Although "yellow journalism" had been practiced at least since 1835, when James Gordon Bennett founded the *New York Herald*, the incisive investigative reporting of the muckraking era revolutionized American journalism. The muckraking press was influential, albeit essential, to the Progressive Movement and supplied both the fact and fiction needed to gain public support for sweeping reforms. New printing technology at the turn of the century allowed the publication of inexpensive magazines reaching a much wider readership. At least ten magazines with a total circulation of over 3 million engaged in muckraking, including *Cosmopolitan*, *McClure's*, and *Collier's*. Newspapers such as Joseph Pulitzer's *New York World* and those in the William Randolph Hearst chain devoted much of their journalistic energy to muckraking. Muckrakers published roughly 2,000 articles over the progressive years. Novelists whose previous literature was one of fantasy and polite manners turned increasingly to the reality of muckraking issues. Edith Wharton's *House of Mirth* (1905) and Jack London's *Martin Eden* (1909), for example, both struck progressive notes.

Regarded as the leader of the muckraking writers was Charles Edward Russell, who at times had been a journalist, socialist, and poet. Russell's prolific writings uncovered abuses in areas such as prison conditions in Georgia, squalor in New York inner-city tenements, and corruption within journalism, while his books exposed the beef monopoly (*The Greatest Trust in the World*, 1905) and social dislocation (*The Uprising of the Many*, 1907). Ida Tarbell was another important, early muckraker whose 1902 series of

McClure's articles on John D. Rockefeller's Standard Oil Company launched a relentless muckraker attack on the large corporate trusts. She was joined by other influential muckrakers of the period, including Lincoln Steffens writing on corruption in state and municipal governments (*The Shame of the Cities*, 1904), Samuel Hopkins Adams on dangerous medicines (*Great American Fraud*, 1906), Brand Whitlock on capital punishment (*The Turn of the Balance*, 1907), Ray Stannard Baker on racial discrimination (*Following the Color Line*, 1908), Edwin Markham on child labor (*Children in Bondage*, 1914), Thomas Lawson on Wall Street stock manipulations (*Frenzied Finance*, 1905), and Thomas Mott Osborne on prison reform (*Within Prison Walls*, 1914).

Most notorious of the muckrakers was journalist-turned-novelist David Graham Phillips. Many of Phillips' 23 novels were muckraking fictions based on true front-page stories. His most successful novel, *The Plum Tree* (1905), uncovered political corruption in a loose blend of fact and fiction. From March through November 1906, Phillips published a series of articles in Hearst's *Cosmopolitan* titled "The Treason of the Senate," in which he attacked 18 prominent U.S. senators. So popular was the series that *Cosmopolitan*'s circulation rose from 300,000 to 450,000. At the same time Phillips was attacking the Senate, Upton Sinclair published *The Jungle* (1906). Sinclair's graphic descriptions of unsanitary conditions in the meatpacking industry caused a public outcry and a demand for government controls. Sinclair's *The Jungle*, and his later book *The Brass Check* (1919), which accused large corporations of controlling the newspaper profession, each sold over 100,000 copies.

Muckraking reached its climax in 1906 with the publication of "Treason" and *The Jungle*. Criticism began to mount over the unbridled muckraker attacks on almost every aspect of government, business, and society. Even the progressive Theodore Roosevelt concluded that the muckrakers had gone too far, especially Phillips and Sinclair. In a speech on April 14, 1906, Roosevelt recognized the value of the reform writer in provoking change, but he saw grave dangers from their negative attacks on society. Quoting from John Bunyan's *The Pilgrim's Progress* (1678), the president warned of "the Man with the Muckrake, the man who could look no way but downward." To many writers, Roosevelt's creation of the muckrake label was derisive, but others such as the socialist Sinclair wore the title as a badge of honor.

Despite the overzealousness of the muckrakers, the list of reforms they prompted is nevertheless an impressive one. Among the more significant reforms were the adoption of child labor laws, mothers' pensions, workers' compensation, and women's suffrage. Spurred by the work of Sinclair and Samuel Hopkins Adams, Congress passed the Pure Food and Drug Act in 1906. Many states reformed their prison systems and abolished peonage. Muckrakers assisted the early conversation movement by promoting laws setting aside forest preserves and by saving Niagara Falls from corporation control. Muckrakers prompted an unprecedented set of government reforms, including the federal income tax, direct popular election of U.S. senators, and direct legislation through the initiative, referendum, and recall. They caused countless local reforms, for example, Russell's exposure of New York's venerable Trinity Church as the owner of some of the city's worst slums, prompting the church to destroy the unsanitary tenements.

By 1910, muckraking began to decline. In many ways, muckraking was an epiphenomenon that may have been destroyed by its own success. The public tired of the relentless attacks on government and business. Progressivism was also declining and would not survive the resurgence of conservatism during World War I. At the same time, newspaper and magazine publishers became reluctant to publish muckraking articles. Corporations, weary of muckrakers' attacks, withheld advertising from their publications, and a surge of libel suits made journalists more accountable for their copy. The symbolic end of muckraking came tragically in 1911 when a man presumed slandered by a David Graham Phillips' article assassinated the writer in New York City.

Although in some ways muckraking was a passing fad, it made an indelible imprint on the increasingly influential role that journalism would play in public affairs. Ahead of their time, the early muckrakers left a legacy of investigative reporting that has been in vogue in recent years. Strong similarities exist between the early muckrakers and the more recent work of television pioneer Edward Murrow, consumer advocate Ralph Nader, investigative journalist Jack Anderson, and the reporters investigating the Watergate scandal.

RICHARD D. WHITE, JR.

BIBLIOGRAPHY

Chalmers, David M., 1964. *The Social and Political Ideas of the Muckrakers.* New York: Citadel Press.

———, 1974. *The Muckrake Years.* New York: Van Nostrand.

Filler, Louis, 1976. *Appointment at Armageddon: Muckraking and Progressivism in the American Tradition.* Westport, CT: Greenwood Press.

Miraldi, Robert, 1990. *Muckraking and Objectivity: Journalism's Colliding Traditions.* New York: Greenwood Press.

Regier, Cornelius C., 1932. *The Era of the Muckrakers.* Chapel Hill: University of North Carolina Press.

Shapiro, Herbert, 1968. *The Muckrakers and American Society.* Boston: D. C. Heath.

Swados, Harvey, ed., 1962. *Tears of Conscience: The Muckrakers.* New York: Meridian Books.

MUDDLING THROUGH. "To achieve a degree of success without much planning or effort" (Webster's Ninth New Collegiate Dictionary, p. 778).

Introduction

Despite decades of prescriptions to "plan, coordinate, and control," it is evident that many administrators plan little and control less. This is particularly so in agencies that suffer from financial stress (e.g., many public schools) or intense political conflict (e.g., the Occupational Safety and Health Administration) or that are chronically understaffed (e.g., the Immigration and Naturalization Service) or endure sudden shocks in their task environments (e.g., military organizations) or that must adapt to new and difficult tasks (e.g., the Social Security Agency; Derthick 1990). . . . In short, in most agencies most of the time even capable administrators usually seem to "muddle through" rather than engage in comprehensive, systematic decisionmaking.

This point is at the core of Charles Lindblom's theory of incrementalism (1959). Together with David Braybrooke (1963), Lindblom built a theory of decisionmaking that made far less "heroic" assumptions about the cognitive abilities of individual decisionmakers and the constraints imposed by politics than was true of advice traditionally given to public administrators. This entry explains and analyzes Lindblom's theory.

The Basic Argument

Although the details of the theory are complex, as we shall see, the basic argument is straightforward. Lindblom (1959) describes the conventional method for making policy decisions—which he presumes is consistent with a theory of rational choice—as consisting of the following steps (p. 79). First, decisionmakers identify the set of objectives they are trying to reach, including all the trade-offs among these goals. Second, they list all possible alternatives for attaining these goals. Third, they evaluate the alternatives and their consequences in terms of their objectives. Fourth and finally, they select the best alternative. (If this sounds uninteresting and even banal, it is because it still captures the conventional wisdom about decisionmaking, which implies that Lindblom's critique is still relevant). All this he calls the synoptic method of decisionmaking. Other terms that he uses are the "rational-comprehensive," or the "root," method.

Lindblom's critique of the synoptic method is based on his taking it seriously. In particular, he takes seriously the injunction to identify all possible (feasible) alternatives for reaching a set of objectives and to identify their consequences. This injunction is thus a requirement of comprehensiveness. Lindblom's analysis of why policy analysis cannot be comprehensive is the core of his thesis.

> Ideally, rational-comprehensive analysis leaves out nothing important. But it is impossible to take everything important into consideration unless "important" is so narrowly defined that analysis is in fact quite limited. Limits on human intellectual capacities and on available information set definite limits to man's capacity to be comprehensive. In actual fact, therefore, *no one can practice the rational comprehensive method for really complex problems, and every administrator faced with a sufficiently complex problem must find ways drastically to simplify* (1959, p. 84; emphasis added).

To this he adds political constraints, which often make large policy changes difficult or impossible. He argues that these political constraints reinforce the cognitive ones: Why waste valuable and scarce resources of information-gathering, analysis, and problem solving on schemes that the political system will reject out of hand?

Essentially, the paragraph here quoted focuses on decisionmakers' cognitive limits; given that the field of cognitive psychology was just getting under way when Lindblom wrote this article, this passage has a startlingly modern flavor. A scholar writing today about the implications of cognitive psychology for policymaking would not have to change it much at all. Perhaps the only change would be terminological: the word "heuristics" is now commonly used to refer to rules of thumb that "simplify sufficiently complex problems." Lindblom's formulation bears a strong resemblance, as he recognized, to Herbert Simon's pioneering work on bounded rationality (1947, 1957; March and Simon 1958. See especially the foreword to the second edition of *Administrative Behavior,* pp. xxv–xxvi, and March and Simon, chapter 6).

As used in cognitive psychology, "heuristic" has two significant connotations. First, it is a rule of thumb that makes complex problems manageable. (There is, however, no guarantee that a heuristic is optimal). Second, since a heuristic is only a guide to action, it need not be comprehensive: It need not specify what to do under all contingencies. For example, the budgetary rule of "in normal times, ask for a fixed percentage increase over the current year's budget" is a heuristic rather than a complete strategy because it does not say what do to in abnormal times.

Some of the heuristics that Lindblom analyzed include the following: remediality (ameliorating problems rather than trying to move toward ideal states), seriality (making and remaking policy in an endless series), redundancy (adding decisionmakers to tasks where, in principle, one would suffice), and most famous of all, incremental search (designing new policies that differ only marginally from the status quo policy).

It is important to keep in mind that a key part of Lindblom's theory is that of decision context. He argues that the above heuristics are needed when the problem at hand is "sufficiently complex." What is sufficiently complex is an important empirical issue, but his idea can be illustrated by comparing decisionmaking in two games, chess and tic-tac-toe.

These games are similar in several ways: They are zero-sum (win-lose-draw) games with everything "on the table" (nothing is hidden, as it is in poker). However, their complexity differs dramatically. Indeed, tic-tac-toe is so simple that heuristics are unnecessary: Most adults or teenagers can develop comprehensive strategies—"if she moves first into a corner, I'll take the center; if she then . . . etc."—that say what the player will do in every contingency. Moreover, each player can think about all possible strategies (alternatives), evaluate them, and choose the best one. Thus, few adults play the game, as it is well known that when both sides play optimally—which all adults of normal mental ability can do easily—the outcome is always a draw. Hence there is no point in playing.

Chess is another matter, for no complete strategy for playing an entire game of chess has ever been produced by either carbon-based or silicon-based players. Computer scientists do not even expect the fastest computers to develop complete strategies for chess in the foreseeable future. The reason is simple: The entire game is too complex. (It is possible to be comprehensive in endgames of chess. For example, even a duffer can force mate if at the end she has a king and a rook to her opponent's king, no matter what her opponent does, and both players should be able to anticipate this. Thus, the feasibility of synoptics can vary over time within the same task.) As decision theorists put it, the decision tree describing the sequence of possible moves explodes. White has 20 possible opening moves, Black has 20 possible replies, so there are 400 possible sequences by the end of the first full turn. Analysts have estimated that there are over 10^{120} possible games of chess.

In this context, Lindblom is absolutely correct. Comprehensiveness is out of reach even for grandmasters for two reasons: They cannot construct even one complete strategy, much less compare and evaluate all possible complete strategies. Accordingly, although experts observing the beginning of a game might be able to agree that move A is better or more promising than move B, even the very best experts could not identify the optimal move, since doing so would require constructing and comparing all possible complete strategies, which is impossible. Thus even grandmasters must be content with heuristics, which are incomplete, and with a small set of heuristics at that—small, that is, relative to the set of all possible heuristics. (Of course grandmasters and novices use different heuristics. And learning to become a better chess player involves, in large measure, learning more sophisticated heuristics.)

Thus, one might rewrite the previous passage as follows: "If a policy problem is chesslike, then advice to 'consider all possible alternatives' is useless. In fact, whoever gives such advice reveals that they do not grasp the complexity of the problem about which they are purportedly giving advice."

Replies by Advocates of the Synoptic Method

Lindblom's argument caused quite a stir. Advocates of synoptic decisionmaking have made several rejoinders.

(1) "We didn't really mean *all* alternatives." A common response to Lindblom's critique is that he took the synoptic method too seriously and thus created a strawman. In particular, synopticists did not mean literally all possible alternatives; that is of course impossible. What is really recommended is only that all promising alternatives be generated.

Braybrooke and Lindblom (1963) have little patience with this line of retreat: "What does the ideal actually specify when we read that 'all alternatives are to be considered' . . . if the specification cannot really mean 'all'? An ideal that either specifies the impossible or fails to specify at all is a dubious ideal" (p. 44). They could have followed that up by noting that once the advice is restricted to "important" alternatives, then like it or not, synopticists are playing the heuristics game: They will need rules of thumb to help generate the subset of alternatives that are promising. (Again the psychologists' study of chess is instructive. Apparently, grandmasters are highly selective: They think about only a very small subset of all possible moves. Somehow they have learned how to generate a short list of promising possibilities.)

Further, this reply—"we didn't really mean it"—does not address the issue of what is involved in describing even the set of important alternatives. Or, in short, what is an alternative? If "comprehensiveness" extends to the specification of alternatives—they should be complete strategies—then as noted earlier, no one has seen or will ever see a fully worked out alternative in chess. So the synopticists could not have meant this kind of comprehensiveness literally either. But then how will we know when to stop describing an alternative? Again, heuristics beckon.

(2) "The synoptic method doesn't describe what real decisionmakers do; it is an ideal toward which they should strive."

This reply proposes a peaceful intellectual division of labor: Muddling through is a descriptive theory; synoptics is prescriptive. Under this interpretation, the relation of muddling through to traditional public administration recommendations is straightforward: Administrators rarely make long-term or comprehensive plans (description); they

should do so much more (prescription). Accepting this interpretation makes Lindblom's argument much less controversial. Most scholars in public administration could have just nodded and said, "Yes, indeed, most bureaus muddle through; we should expect more from them." Claims about what is need not conflict at all with claims about what ought to be.

But Lindblom rejects a peaceful division of labor between incrementalism as description and synoptics as prescription. His argument is that for "sufficiently complex" (chesslike) policy problems, it is not just that synoptic does not describe how decisionmakers currently behave; it does not describe how they could behave. That is, the method is infeasible for such problems. And as moral philosophers say, "ought implies can." As Braybrooke and Lindblom (1963) remarked, "An ideal that . . . specifies the impossible is a dubious ideal" (p. 44).

For this class of problems, the synopticist is thrown back on a more controversial version of reply (2): "If you try to be comprehensive—even when *we know in advance that you will fail*—your decisions will be better than if you had muddled through." Now the battle is truly joined. I think that the reply is probably wrong—being deliberately selective would probably work better when comprehensiveness is clearly impossible—but the issue has not been investigated very much, although Braybrooke and Lindblom (1963) do cite some evidence on the point (pp. 42–43).

(3) "Comprehensiveness is in the eye [model] of the beholder." This last reply is the most sophisticated and, I believe, the best. It claims that a decisionmaker can be comprehensive only relative to one's model of the situation. Even in tic-tac-toe—which is so simple that constructing a model seems unnecessary—a mental image of the situation is necessary. For example, each person must have a model that bounds the situation by the rules of tic-tac-toe: The alternative of "winning" by punching the other player is rarely considered. Thus, even in simple choices, strategizing is comprehensive only in relation to a frame.

Hence, confronted by a complex policy issue that apparently defies comprehensive decisionmaking, an advocate of synoptics could argue that one should construct (an admittedly simplified) model of the situation and optimize with respect to that. This recommendation has at least one significant merit: It is feasible. No matter how complex the policy question, one can always construct a model that is sufficiently simple so that one can comprehensively analyze all possible strategies—possible, that is, within the confines of the model—and select the best one. But as Simon (1972) has pointed out, this procedure presumes that the model "approximates the actual [situation] in some appropriate sense" (p. 166). Otherwise, "The optimal decision in the approximated world is not necessarily even a good decision in the real world" (ibid., p. 167). Indeed, if the approximation is poor, one will wind up solving the wrong problem. The fact that the decisionmaker analyzes alternatives comprehensively, given the drastically simplified model, and selects the optimal one, out of this drastically reduced set, will then be cold comfort. As Simon notes, essentially what has happened is that cognitive constraints are still having a major impact, but in a different phase of the decision process: in the symbolic representation of the situation

Criticizing Muddling Through on Its Own Terms

In this section we will accept, for purposes of argument, Lindblom's central assertion: that for an important class of policy problems–indeed, for most policy problems that are considered important–synoptics is infeasible. We will also accept his thesis that striving to do something that is impossible is unlikely to produce better decisions than working within known cognitive and political constraints. Instead, this section will criticize incrementalism on its own terms.

I see two significant problems. First, it is unclear whether muddling through constitutes a strategy of decisionmaking or merely a list of loosely connected heuristics. Lindblom's position is that it is the former; indeed, the title of his and Braybrooke's book *A Strategy of Decision* (Braybrooke and Lindblom 1963) shows the strength of his conviction. But the argument is less than compelling. Further, new work has demonstrated that some of the elements of muddling through do not interact in the way hypothesized by Lindblom. In particular, if a system uses enough redundancy, then it should not search locally; instead, it should search nonincrementally (Bendor 1995, Theorem 8). This result suggests that we do not understand the internal structure of muddling through very well. Therefore, at present it may be wise to consider it a list of heuristics, connected by the common aim of making complex policy problems manageable, rather than a strategy with a tightly articulated structure. And if this view is correct, then we should ask, Why these heuristics and not others? Discovering other heuristics used by effective policymakers should be a major task of researchers.

Second, why should we believe that these heuristics help decisionmakers? The theory could use a tighter connection between diagnostics, identifying cognitive constraints or political properties that cause problems in decisionmaking, and prescription, heuristics that purportedly address the problems. This connection is often made too casually by those working in the Lindblomian tradition. (For example, psychologists have clearly established that all decisionmakers have sharply limited short-term memory, and some scholars have concluded that this helps to explain the span of control of executives. But long-term memory has no known limits on storage, and whether the president can remember that he has an Interior Department to control depends on long-term memory, not short-term memory.)

And we could also use tighter arguments as to why and when certain heuristics are supposed to help. For example, exactly why is incremental (local) search supposed to be better than nonlocal search? Lindblom is not very clear about this. The basic idea is that nonlocal policy design creates more uncertainty. (The following is taken from Bendor 1995.) However, more than one type of uncertainty might arise. First, nonincremental search by definition involves more policy innovation, and although policy innovations might turn out to be big improvements on the status quo, they could turn out to be much worse. In this sense, nonlocal search is riskier than incremental search: the latter, by generating new alternatives that are similar to the status quo, is less likely to produce a new option that is far worse or far better than the current policy. Second, the evaluation of any one new alternative might depend on how much it differs from the status quo: The more it differs, the more error-prone is evaluation.

Lindblom's work suggests that both kinds of uncertainty rise as search becomes less incremental. But these two different types of uncertainty have the opposite impact on policy outcomes: Whereas more uncertainty in policy evaluation does have the harmful effect anticipated by Lindblom, the increased riskiness of a new set of options–wonderful and terrible new policies both more likely–is benign if decisionmakers are trying to maximize the expected value of their choice (Bendor 1995). And it is hard to know, a priori, which effect will predominate. For example, suppose incremental search produces, with equal likelihood, new alternatives that are worth 2 or -2, relative to a status quo worth zero, whereas nonincremental search produces options that are worth either 10 or -10, with equal likelihood. Assume that the decisionmaker chooses correctly 90 percent of the time when faced with alternatives that differ only incrementally from the status quo but is right only 60 percent of the time when trying to evaluate radically different policies. Then the expected value of searching locally equals $.5[.9(2) + 1(0)] + .5[.1(+2) + .9(0)] = .5[.9(2) - 1(2)] = .8$, whereas the expected value of nonincremental search is $.5[.6(10) + 4(0)] + .5[.4(-10) + .6(0)] = .5[.6(10) + .4(10)] = 1.0$. Thus, in this example, bold search's benign effect predominates.

Now consider the effect of a second heuristic, seriality. It turns out that the usefulness of seriality depends strongly on how new alternatives affect different policy dimensions (Bendor 1995). Suppose a group of decisionmakers in an agency gives advice to a superior about a project. Their advice must take the form, "The majority of this committee thinks that the agency should proceed with this project." The decisionmakers specialize by evaluating different aspects of the project. So if this were, for instance, a proposed dam for the Army Corps of Engineers, one decisionmaker might specialize in flood control, another in recreational effects, and a third in environmental impact. Due to cognitive limitations, all specialists ignore the project's impact on areas outside their jurisdiction. The group will evaluate a sequence of projects, giving a recommendation on each.

Let us normalize the status quo to have a value of zero on each dimension: If a policy has three dimensions, then the status quo is worth $(0,0,0)$. A new proposal that is worth $(5,5,-1)$ is objectively better than the status quo on dimensions one and two but worse on dimension three. Suppose that relative to this normalized status quo, the new types of proposals are worth $(8,8,-1)$, $(8,-1,8)$, $(-1,8,8)$, $(-8,1,-8)$, and $(1,-8,-8)$. Each of these new proposals arrives in the policy "queue" with a chance of one-sixth.

What will happen over time? Will the outcome be better or worse, on average, than the starting point of $(0,0,0)$? It turns out that the expected outcome gets better the longer this process continues. To see why, assume for the moment that all decisionmakers are narrow-minded but infallible within their own speciality. Then a majority of them recommend accepting each of $(8,8,-1)$, $(8,-1,8)$, $(-1,8,8)$ while rejecting $(-8,-8,1)$, $(-8,1,-8)$, and $(1,-8,-8)$. Therefore, the expected payoff for, say, dimension one in any decisionmaking period is just $\frac{1}{6}(8) + \frac{1}{6}(8) + \frac{1}{6}(-1)$, which equals $+2.5$. So, since expected payoffs per period are positive, the longer this process goes on, the higher the total payoff. (The same result holds if the decisionmakers are fallible, sometimes voting against good projects or for bad ones, so long as they are right more than half the time.) In this case, the decisionmakers' narrow-mindedness, or lack of comprehensiveness, dovetails nicely with how the new options affect different policy dimensions. That is, in this example, whenever a new alternative is better than the status quo on a majority of dimensions, it helps those dimensions much more than it hurts the minority dimension. Conversely, whenever a new alternative is worse than the status quo on a majority of dimensions, it hurts those dimensions much more than it helps the minority dimension. Hence, if the three policy dimensions are more or less equally important, citizens would like the decisionmakers to accept the first kind of alternative (which improves most dimensions) and to reject the second (which impairs most). And because the collective choice process—giving recommendations via majority rule—fits perfectly with the distribution of alternatives' costs and benefits across different policy dimensions, this is exactly what happens.

But of course we have no guarantee that the distribution of costs and benefits across policy dimensions will follow the above pattern. Suppose the opposite pattern obtains: When a majority of dimensions are improved, the benefits are small compared to the devastation wreaked upon the minority dimension, and when a majority is hurt, the costs are small compared to the benefits conferred on the minority dimension. Specifically, consider an example in which the new types of proposals are worth $(-7,1,1)$, $(1,-7,1)$, $(1,1,-7)$, $(7,-1,-1)$, $(-1,7,-1)$, and $(-1,-1,7)$; again each type of proposal occurs with a one-sixth chance. Because each decisionmaker is narrow-minded, the group will recommended rejecting options like $(7,-1-1)$, whereas those that are good on two dimensions, such as $(1,1,-7)$, will be supported. But if the agency implements proposals $(1,1,-7)$, $(1,-7,1)$, and $(-7,1,1)$, overall each policy dimension will degrade.

Similar problems attend the heuristic of redundancy: When there is a mismatch between how many dimensions are helped or hurt by an alternative and how much they are helped or hurt, then adding decisionmakers, in order to have more minds working on a complex problem, can make things worse rather than better. Suppose, for example, every decisionmaker is right 90 percent of the time about the effect of an alternative on the decisionmaker's particular speciality. The agency, recognizing that everyone is fallible, decides to have three specialists in every area (flood control, recreation, and the environment) , and every department's recommendation is based on the opinion of a majority of its specialists. If new alternatives come in the pattern of $(-7,1,1,)$, $(1,-7,1)$, ..., $(-1,-1,7)$, the status quo policy will degrade faster than it would if each department had only one specialist (Bendor 1995).

Conclusion

There is little doubt that most administrators "muddle through" when working on complex problems. But we should not let the comfortable familiarity of that phrase fool us into thinking that we know more than we do. Exactly which heuristics are commonly used by bureaucrats, and which heuristics are effective, remain open questions. Lindblom's pioneering work raised but did not settle these issues.

JONATHAN BENDOR

BIBLIOGRAPHY

Bendor, Jonathan, 1995. "A Model of Muddling Through." *American Political Science Review,* vol. 89, no. 4 (December).

Braybrooke, David, and Charles Lindblom, 1963. *A Strategy of Decision.* New York: Free Press.

Derthick, Martha, 1990. *Agency under Stress.* Washington, DC: Brookings.

Lindblom, Charles, 1959. "The Science of 'Muddling Through'". *Public Administration Review,* vol. 19 (Spring) 79–88.

March, James, and Herbert Simon, 1958. *Organizations.* New York: Wiley.

Simon, Herbert, 1947. *Administrative Behavior.* New York: Macmillan.

———, 1957. *Models of Man: Social and Rational.* New York: Wiley.

———, 1972. "Theories of Bounded Rationality." In C. B. McGuire and Roy Radner, eds., *Decision and Organization: A Volume in Honor of Jacob Marschak.* Amsterdam: North-Holland.

MULTICOMMUNITY PARTNERSHIPS.

Alliances of public private, and/or nonprofit sector organizations across two or more communities to share resources to deliver services or to solve problems.

There are a variety of ways to organize the delivery of services, solve problems, and develop the capacity to compete in the global economy. One such mechanism, multicommunity partnerships, can be depicted along a continuum of relationships that ranges from networks to cooperation to coordination to collaboration. Each type on the continuum differs in complexity or purposes (information sharing versus complicated, joint problem solving), intensity of linkages (based on common goals, decision rules, shared tasks, and resource commitments), and the formality of agreements reached (informality versus formality of rules guiding operating structures, policies, and procedures).

Loosely linked organizations that work together, primarily for information exchange, are called networks. Members can join or disconnect with ease and without threatening the partnership's existence. Informality governs procedural and structural patterns, including resource sharing.

Cooperation can also be relatively simple in terms of organizational purpose, with relatively low levels of intensity in linkages and agreements that can range from informal to somewhat formal. This type of multicommunity partnership poses marginal costs for participants and entails the use of relatively few resources.

More closely linked connections among organizations that work together are coordinating partnerships that entail specific shared, common goals, a greater commitment of resources, and more formality. Some loss of autonomy is agreed to by participating units, with the consequences of member units leaving having a possible negative effect on the organization.

The fourth partnership type, collaboration, involves strong linkages among members and specific, often complex, and usually long-term purposes. Processes are more formal, as is resource commitment. Member units delegate considerable autonomy to the collaboration and the addition or reduction of members could have significant and often detrimental effects on the partnership, including its failure.

Multicommunity partnerships of any type are complex organizational forms because they occur among multiple sector and multiple communities. Truly collaborative ventures are system changing because they require a recasting of the fundamental structure or purpose of the participating units, their culture, incentive and sanction system, and their core processes.

My research (1992) has focused on the organizational factors associated with the emergence and maintenance of multicommunity partnerships, especially those leading to genuine collaboration. Several preconditions dominate the activities of communities that participate in these partnerships. Preconditions associated with the local context include a disaster occurrence, community fiscal stress or perceived stress, the presence of a political constituency for cooperation, supportive capacity-building programs of technical or other assistance provided by state government, professional associations or universities. Preconditions related to local organizational decisionmaking include early and continued support by local officials and civic leaders, a clear demonstration of advantages to participating organizations or governments, the emergence of a policy entrepreneur or entrepreneurs to promote partnerships, an early focus on visible and effective strategies, and an emphasis on collaborative skills building by and for those involved in partnerships.

Origins

Historically, both small rural areas and densely populated urban regions have been highly competitive. Interjurisdictional competition, not cooperation, dominated relationships. As rural areas have lost population, businesses, and jobs, and suffered revenue declines, cooperation has emerged as an alternative way to deal with changing economic and demographic forces. Similarly, communities in urban areas have begun to realize that it is difficult to engage in community and economic development in the global economy as strictly autonomous units with the resources to tackle problems which spillover jurisdictional boundaries. Multicommunity partnerships began to appear throughout the United States in the late 1980s and proliferated at a quickened pace in the 1990s. Government and foundation-funding policies have spurred cooperative efforts by either requiring or awarding more funds if communities develop partnerships. Similarly, national or state legal mandates may spawn multicommunity partnerships. One example is solid waste management, in which multiple communities may develop a regional landfill. With the appropriate combination of preconditions, grassroots partnerships can emerge, for example, to encourage small business development or to revitalize a downtown shopping area. Often, the impetus comes from the business community. Chambers of Commerce within an area may regionalize, thus paving the way for more formal cooperation by local communities to deliver services, solve problems, and/or make policies.

Current Practice

The midwestern region of the United States is notable for its multicommunity partnerships. After midwestern farm communities suffered declines in population, jobs, businesses, and revenues in the 1980s, a number of systematic efforts were made to promote multicommunity partnerships. Many of these efforts were sparked by cooperative extensions, state government, universities, and foundations through the development of leadership training programs, community visioning and strategic planning processes. As a result, clusters of communities in Iowa, Nebraska, Kansas, Minnesota, and other states have well established multicommunity partnerships. These cover the range of partnership types—networking, cooperation, coordination, and collaboration. The southern states (e.g., Georgia, South Carolina, and Virginia) also have developed significant multicommunity organizations and activities, as has the southern tier of New York state and some parts of rural New England. Rural areas have emerged as especially likely to participate in multicommunity partnerships, compared to their urban counterparts. This may be due to the complexity of problems and the greater number of actors in urban areas, as well as greater resource disparities among communities. An entire rural region, including all of its constituent communities, may be financially depressed. It is less likely that even a declining urban region will have sweeping uniformity in terms of distress of all of its governments. Similarly, multiple rural communities might be cooperative to develop a multicommunity event—a fair, picnic, or other celebration—whereas urban communities might resist even that much loosening of identity and autonomy.

BEVERLY A. CIGLER

BIBLIOGRAPHY

Cigler, Beverly A., 1992. "Pre-Conditions for Multicommunity Collaboration." In Peter F. Korsching, Timothy O. Borich, and Julie Stewart, eds., *Multicommunity Collaboration: An Evolving Rural Revitalization Strategy.* Ames, IA: Northwest Central Regional Center For Rural Development, 53–74.
Cigler, Beverly A., Anicca Jansen, Vern Ryan, and Jack R. Stabler, 1992. "In Search of Multicommunity collaboration: Three Case Studies." In Peter F. Korsching, Timothy O. Borich, and Julie Stewart, eds., *Multicommunity Collaboration: An Evolving Rural Revitalization Strategy.* Ames, IA: Northwest Central Regional Center for Rural Development, 13–52.
Gilroy, N., and J. Swan, eds., 1984. *Building Networks.* Dubuque, IA: Kendall/Hunt.
Habana-Hafner, S., H. B. Reed & Associates, 1989. *Partnerships for Community Development: Resources for Practitioners and Trainers.* Amherst, MA: Center for Organizational and Community Development, University of Massachusetts.
Sokolow, Alvin D., 1986. "Management without the Manager: The Administrative Work of Legislators in Rural Local Governments." In J. Seroka, ed., *Rural Public Administration: Problems and Prospects.* New York: Greenwood Press, 59–76.

MULTICULTURALISM.

A conceptual model that sets out principles for public policy and national identity in societies affected by increasing ethnocultural diversity. Multiculturalism generally means the public acceptance of immigrant and minority groups as distinct communities that are distinguishable from the majority population with regard to language, culture, and social behavior and that have their own associations and social infrastructure. Multiculturalism implies that members of such groups should be granted equal rights in all spheres of society, without being expected to give up their diversity, although usually with an expectation of conformity to certain key values.

Multiculturalism has been an explicit government policy in Canada since 1971 and in Australia since about 1973. The Swedish "immigrant policy" (introduced in 1975) has strong elements of multiculturalism. The Dutch "minorities policy" (introduced in the early 1980s) was originally concerned with recognition of minority group cultures but has since been modified to stress socioeconomic integration. Other countries have introduced multicultural policies in specific sectors, such as education and social work. In the United States of America, the debate on multiculturalism has taken a different form: It has been mainly about the reinterpretation of history and culture to recognize the role of ethnic minorities and women. Cultural maintenance is seen largely as a private matter, rather than an area of public policy. However, any state in the United States does have the role of guaranteeing equality of rights, which may involve special measures to overcome discrimination toward specific racial or ethnic groups.

Ways of Managing Ethnocultural Diversity

Multiculturalism is a topic of intense public debate in virtually all highly developed countries, even where such policies are generally rejected—as for example in France and Japan. This is because cultural diversity and the need for policies and institutions to manage it are central characteristics of contemporary societies, linked to economic and cultural globalization. Ethnoculturally heterogeneous populations may be the result of international migration, which has escalated in volume and scope since 1945. They may also arise from growing group awareness and mobilization of older minorities, including indigenous peoples in former settler colonies (such as the United States of America, Canada, Australia, New Zealand), descendants of slaves or indentured workers (e.g., in the United States and the Caribbean) as well as ethnic groups incorporated into expanding nation-states (e.g., Hispanics in the southwestern United States, Catalans in Spain). Many countries have all these types of diversity, giving rise to complex "national mosaics."

Ethnocultural diversity questions prevailing ideas derived from eighteenth- and nineteenth-century nationalism, which postulated nation-states with relatively homogeneous populations, sharing a common heritage, language, and culture. This was the basis of a concept of citizenship involving equality of rights, obligations, and treatment by the state for all members of society. Such homogeneity was always a myth, for it ignored historical processes of integration of diverse groups into expanding nation-states, as well as schisms based on class and gender. Twentieth-century labor movements sought to extend citizenship to include the working class, while the issue of full citizenship for women was raised by feminist movements. However, the implications of ethnocultural diversity for citizenship and participation were largely ignored until the emergence of the U.S. civil rights movement in the 1960s and the growing mobilization of people of immigrant origin in Western Europe, North America, and Australia from the 1970s.

The idea of common culture values and heritage as the basis of national cohesion and identity is hard to sustain when 10 to 20 percent of the population is of minority ethnic background, as is the case in most advanced countries (Australia is the extreme with 44 percent of the population of first or second generation immigrant background and 2 percent of aboriginal background in 1991). Ethnocultural diversity is particularly problematic when membership of a minority group is linked to social disadvantage or exclusion. Where immigrants get only the jobs nobody else wants, or indigenous people have been deprived of their land, assertion of cultural difference is often a form of symbolic mobilization to achieve social, economic, or political goals.

The emergence of multiculturalism is largely the result of difficulties with two alternative approaches to cultural diversity: (1) Differential exclusion, which means admitting immigrants or ethnic minorities only to certain societal subsystems, especially the labor market, while excluding them from others, such as legal rights, the welfare system, or political participation. Groups treated in this way include African Americans in the United States of America up to the 1960s; indigenous people in Australia and Canada up to the 1960s; contract workers in Germany and other Western European countries in the 1960s and 1970s, and in some Middle-East and Asian labor importing countries today; and undocumented migrant workers in countries like the United States, Italy, and Japan. Differen-

tial exclusion means state-endorsed discrimination and repression of minorities. It is problematic and generally unsustainable in democratic states because it leads to racism, conflict, and split societies and violates the principle of equal treatment and participation for all members of society.

(2) Assimilation, the policy of incorporating immigrants and minorities into society through a one-sided process of adaptation, in which they are meant to give up their distinctive cultural characteristics and become indistinguishable from the majority population. The assimilation model has been applied at various times in most advanced countries, sometimes as a response to failure of differential exclusion. The role of public policy is to create conditions for successful assimilation through granting equal rights and through facilitating cultural adaptation, especially through the school system. Assimilation policies break down where they fail to counteract processes of socioeconomic differentiation through which ethnic minorities take on inferior positions. These often provide the conditions for ethnic community formation and mobilization, which negate the idea of individual assimilation. This has happened in most countries with ethnoculturally diverse populations.

Dimensions of Multiculturalism

Multiculturalism emerged from the 1970s in response to the recognition that social incorporation of minorities is a gradual process in which group cohesion and culture play an important part. In Canada, Australia, and Sweden, there is a consensus of most major political forces on multiculturalism—albeit with variations in emphasis. Typically, multicultural policies have two main public dimensions: The first is concerned with cultural and linguistic maintenance and the role of the "ethnic community"; the second is concerned with equality, participation, and the removal of social barriers encountered by minority groups.

The cultural maintenance dimension is based on the idea that knowledge of their linguistic and cultural heritage is vital for the self-esteem and psychosocial development of minority children. The passing on of group values is seen as crucial for intergenerational cohesion, as well as for success in the wider society. In terms of public policy, this implies multicultural education policies, mother-tongue learning programs, and official acceptance of minority religions, festivals, and other types of cultural expression. Such policies can be found in the Canadian Multiculturalism Act of 1989, the Australian National policy on Languages of 1987, and in the Swedish mother-tongue schooling policy. The cultural maintenance dimension also has political implications for the acceptance by the state of ethnic associations as legitimate representatives of group concerns. Leaders of such associations may be consulted by government on specific issues or involved in government consultative bodies. Multicultural countries also often provide financial support for ethnic associations.

The equality dimension of multiculturalism involves a wide range of public policies. Perhaps the most important is facilitating admission to citizenship for immigrants (after two years' residence in Australia and five years in Canada and Sweden). This is combined with rules that automatically grant citizenship to children of immigrants or at least give them a right to it (in the case of Sweden). It is hard to imagine multiculturalism functioning where immigrants and their children find it very hard to become citizens, as in Germany or Switzerland. But citizenship does not in itself imply multiculturalism: For instance, France offers citizenship to most immigrants, but rejects cultural pluralism. Sweden introduced local voting rights for resident noncitizens in 1975 and was followed by the Netherlands in 1983. Another set of policies is concerned with socioeconomic integration: measures to help members of minorities to learn the majority language, to gain vocational skills, and to get recognition of overseas qualification. This is linked to measures to eliminate workplace discrimination (such as the Canadian Employment Equity Act of 1986), as well as to laws outlawing discrimination in public places and racial violence or vilification. In Australia, all federal government agencies have to carry out "access and equity" policies to ensure that their services meet the need of all groups of society.

Overarching these two public policy dimensions is a more general discourse on the role of multiculturalism for identity. In Canada, this has taken the form of symbolically defining national identity as a synthesis of a wide range of influences that make up the "Canadian mosaic." French Canadians argue, however, that multiculturalism has been a ploy to counter demands for Quebec's independence by submerging the British-French cultural conflict in an amorphous pluralism. In Australia, multiculturalism is officially seen as a way of reshaping identity at a time when historical links with Britain have become unviable and the nation has to find a new position within the Asia-Pacific region. Here the skepticism comes from indigenous people, who feel that multiculturalism neglects the issue of their historical dispossession. It is easy to understand the need for rethinking identity in former colonies, now cut off from their European "mother country," but Sweden is interesting as a country with a high degree of cultural and religious homogeneity prior to post-1945 immigration. Here, the acceptance of diverse cultural identities is probably more about achieving long-term integration into the welfare state than about the perceived need for a new national identity.

Multiculturalism has taken on many institutional forms: In Canada, multiculturalism is laid down in several laws as well as in the 1982 Charter of Rights and Freedoms, while Australia's main policy blueprint is the 1989 National Agenda for a Multicultural Australia. Canada had a Ministry of Multiculturalism and Citizenship until 1993, but this was then incorporated into a subministry for Citizenship and Canadian Identity by the newly elected liberal government. Australia's multicultural policies are coordinated both by the Department of Immigration and Ethnic Affairs and the Office of Multicultural Affairs in the Department of Prime Minister and Cabinet. All three countries have large numbers of special agencies or sections within ministries concerned with specific aspects of multicultural policy, such as social welfare, health, women's issues, equal opportunities, antidiscrimination, multicultural education, and cultural affairs. Countries without general policies of multiculturalism have also introduced agencies and policies concerned with multicultural policies in specific areas. For instance, Britain has had multicultural education and social work policies in some areas since the 1970s. Some German education authorities also speak of multicultural education despite the rejection of the approach by government.

The Dilemma of Universality and Differentiation

Multiculturalism has been criticized from various perspectives. Some members of the majority group feel that it waters down national culture, leading to what they portray as a "nation of tribes." Such fears are most developed where there are large Islamic minorities, which are seen as a threat to a secular culture based on Christian values and bureaucratic rationality. However, it is often exclusionary or assimilationist policies that lead to a form of reactive isolationism by minorities. Some members of minority groups argue that multiculturalism is little more than tokenism designed to mask continuing cultural domination by the majority group. This argument is taken up in another form by those who argue that recognition of cultural difference and group identities does little to address the issues of socioeconomic disadvantage and political exclusion of some ethnic minorities. In response to these critiques, a shift can be observed in several countries, especially Canada and Australia: If the main emphasis was on the cultural maintenance dimension of muticulturalism in the 1970s, it had clearly shifted to the equality dimension by the late 1980s. The changes in the Dutch minorities policy were motivated by similar considerations. Multiculturalism thus appears to be developing from an "ethnic group model" to a "citizenship model," which stresses the conditions and meaning of citizenship in ethnoculturally diverse societies.

In the context of liberal-democratic ideas of citizenship, multiculturalism clearly contains a contradiction: the universalistic ideal of equality of all citizens as individuals and the demand for the recognition of difference based on group belonging. The former requires equal treatment of all by the state, whereas the latter gives rise to the demand for differential treatment of people with different needs, values, and interests. There is no easy solution to this contradiction: It is a reflection of the transformation of liberal-democratic societies in the era of globalization. In its attempt to address both the need for cultural identity and the principle of equality within modern democratic society, multiculturalism offers at least a provisional answer to the dilemma.

STEPHEN CASTLES

BIBLIOGRAPHY

Ålund, Aleksandra, and Carl-Ulrik Schierup, 1991. *Paradoxes of Multiculturalism.* Aldershot: Avebury.

Bauböck, Rainer, ed., 1994. *From Aliens to Citizens: Redefining the Status of Immigrants in Europe.* Aldershot: Avebury.

Breton, Raymond, W. W. Isajiw, Warren E. Kalbach, and Jeffrey G. Reitz, 1990. *Ethnic Identity and Equality.* Toronto: University of Toronto Press.

Castles, Stephen, and Mark J. Miller, 1993. *The Age of Migration: International Population Movements in the Modern World.* London and Melbourne: Macmillan Education; New York: Guilford Books.

Costa-Lascoux, Jacqueline, and Patrick Weil, eds., 1992. *Logiques d'États et Immigrations.* Paris: Éditions Kimé.

Freeman, Gary P., and James Jupp, eds. 1992. *Nations of Immigrants: Australia, the United States, and International Migration.* Melbourne: Oxford University Press.

Hammar, Tomas, 1990. *Democracy and the Nation-State: Aliens, Denizens, and Citizens in a World of International Migration.* Aldershot: Avebury.

Young, Iris Marion, 1990. *Justice and the Politics of Difference.* Princeton, NJ: Princeton University Press.

MULTICULTURALISM POLICY.

Official state policy that recognizes and promotes cultural diversity and pluralism in a society.

It is useful first to distinguish between multiculturalism as a description of a society and multiculturalism as a public policy. As a description of a society, multiculturalism is a society featuring a multiplicity of cultures based on ethnic and religious diversity rather than one prevailing culture (uniculturalism) or two cultures (biculturalism). Such diversity and pluralism may be celebrated or regretted, but it is a sociological reality nevertheless. As public policy, the state officially recognizes and promotes cultural pluralism and diversity. Here, multiculturalism not only is officially endorsed, but it is also actively encouraged through state support and public funding.

Policies of multiculturalism are a recent development, emerging in large-scale immigrant, multiethnic, and multiracial societies such as in Canada, the United States,

the United Kingdom, Australia, and New Zealand. In its strongest form, multiculturalism is a proclaimed policy of the state that is officially dedicated to preserving and promoting cultural differences. This involves laws and programs with the objective of managing cultural diversity, encouraging harmonious ethnic and race relations, eliminating discrimination based on race and ethnicity, assisting members of minorities in preserving their language and culture, and educating the public about the value of tolerance and the economic and political benefits of cultural diversity. In milder forms of the policy, some of these elements are missing.

Canada is a leading example of a country with a strong multiculturalism policy. Officially declared in 1971, Canada's policy is now enshrined in the 1982 constitutional Charter of Rights, embodied in the 1988 Multiculturalism Act, and implemented by designated government departments (now Canadian Heritage). Beginning in 1971 with the primary aim of recognizing and promoting cultural diversity and heritage, the policy has expanded to pursue the aims of reducing discrimination and racism, enhancing intercultural awareness and understanding, and encouraging culturally sensitive institutional change. Policy has shifted from one of cultural preservation and a folkloric focus in the 1970s to one of removing all barriers to the effective integration of cultural minorities into the Canadian mainstream. Greater focus now is on achieving equal economic opportunity, promoting an educational system that reflects Canada's cultural diversity, and promoting changes in institutions so that they better respond to Canada's different cultures. Canadian policy is not limited to the federal level. Most provinces and many municipalities also have a policy of multiculturalism, actively developing educational and heritage language programs similar to the federal ones.

Australia and New Zealand are examples of countries with a moderately strong policy. In Australia, while not entrenched in the constitution or established in special legislation as in Canada, an official policy of multiculturalism has been put into effect since 1975. Under the policy, the Australian Institute of Multicultural Affairs was established in 1979 to increase public awareness, appreciation of cultural pluralism, and the value of tolerance. Television broadcasting policy was altered as well to improve ethnic broadcasting, and education policy was changed to increase the teaching of languages and cultures in ethnic schools and universities. The policy was justified in terms not only of social justice but also economic benefits—that different languages and cultures could be key assets in creating a more prosperous Australia. As in Canada, the policy did not end at the federal level. Most states have developed policies and programs as well, especially New South Wales. In New Zealand, although not pursued as far, multiculturalism also emerged as official policy during the

1970s. In response to pressures from the indigenous Maori population, Polynesian islanders, and Pacific Rim immigrants, New Zealand's policy became one of encouraging tolerance and cultural diversity as a positive value and of modifying institutions so that they reflect the cultural and racial diversity of New Zealand. But in contrast to Australia, the policy has not continued to expand.

The United States and the United Kingdom are examples of countries with a relatively mild policy. Despite the concept of the melting pot, American policy informally recognizes the reality of cultural diversity and the virtues of pluralism. Most attention has been focused on the removal of discriminatory barriers. As a component of the Civil Rights Acts and education programs, policy has given recognition to the pluralistic nature of American society, the contributions of cultural minorities, and the need to uphold the principle of equal opportunity. Similarly, in the United Kingdom, while there is not an official policy of multiculturalism, attention has been given to the removal of discriminatory barriers and to multicultural education. Under race relations acts since 1965, policy goals have included the elimination of discrimination, the spread of cultural awareness, and the establishment of racially sensitive law enforcement. In schools, beginning with initiatives by the Department of Education in 1974, steps have been taken to remedy educational disadvantages facing minority children, to assist in teacher education for a multiethnic classroom, and to ensure that schools and the curriculum reflect the multicultural reality. With the unrest and ethnic tensions of the early 1980s, initiatives in multicultural education have been accelerated.

Multiculturalism has its critics and its defenders. A common criticism is that the policy undermines the unity of a nation and encourages ethnic separation rather than common purpose and solidarity. While laws against discrimination are necessary, say the critics, an official policy of promoting cultural diversity is not. If groups want to preserve and promote their cultures, they should do so on a private basis rather than through public support. Moreover, argue the critics, such a policy can undermine the reality of a bicultural country. This has been a complaint of Maori leaders in New Zealand and francophone Quebecers in Canada who see multiculturalism as undermining the concept of New Zealand and Canada as the partnership of two founding nations. In contrast, the policy is defended on the basis that it fits in with the reality of a multicultural society and makes minorities feel more at home in the society. As the cultures of all groups are recognized and encouraged, this works to bolster national unity rather than erode it. Multiculturalism, say the defenders, is the expression of an open and tolerant society, respectful of cultural differences and appreciative of the enrichment that cultural diversity brings.

R. BRIAN HOWE

BIBLIOGRAPHY

Fleras, Augie, and Jean Elliott, 1992. *Multiculturalism in Canada: The Challenge of Diversity.* Toronto: Nelson Canada.

Foster, Lois, and Anne Seitz, 1989. "The Politicization of Language Issues in 'Multicultural' Societies: Some Australian and Canadian Comparisons." *Canadian Ethnic Studies,* vol. 21, no. 3: 55–73.

Horton, John, ed., 1993. *Liberalism, Multiculturalism, and Toleration.* Basingstoke: Macmillan.

Hudson, Michael, 1987. "Multiculturalism, Government Policy, and Constitutional Entrenchment–A Comparative Study." In Canadian Human Rights Foundation, ed., *Multiculturalism and the Charter: A Legal Perspective.* Toronto: Carswell.

Richmond, Anthony H., 1991. "Immigration and Multiculturalism in Canada and Australia." *International Journal of Canadian Studies,* vol. 3 (Spring) 87–109.

Troyna, Barry, 1988. "Education and Racism." In Ellis Cashmore, ed., *Dictionary of Race and Ethnic Relations.* London: Routledge.

MUNICIPAL BONDS. The interest-bearing obligations of state or local governments. One way governments raise money is by borrowing and incurring a debt. Consider the example of a government wanting to buy a new fire station. That government might borrow the money to pay for the fire station by finding investors willing to loan them money based on the promise of repayment over a specified period of time, with interest. Interest is the compensation paid to investors for the use of their money. The interest rate paid is also called the coupon rate. The issuer also pays the face amount of the bond called the principal amount. Debt service is the aggregate principal and interest payments. Maturity is the date the principal is due and payable; the maturity schedule is the amount of principal maturing each year. Financial intermediaries, called underwriters, provide the link between the investors and the government.

What revenue stream is promised to bondholders for repayment? The particulars of the promise to repay bondholders are the bond's security provisions or the security pledge. There are seemingly endless ways to design repayment to bondholders (see **municipal bonds: security**). The most basic security is the general obligation (GO) bond. A general obligation unlimited tax (GOULT) security pledges the government's full faith and credit, including a pledge to raise property taxes unlimited as to rate or amount necessary to repay the bond. A general obligation limited tax security (GOLT) pledges that property taxes will be raised if necessary, but only up to some taxing limit (many states have limits on property taxes).

The chief aspect of municipal bonds that makes them distinct from other types of capital market securities is their federal tax exemption. Investors' income from interest on most types of municipal bonds is exempt from federal income taxation. Indeed, municipal bonds are also referred to as tax-exempt bonds. Often the interest on municipal bonds is also exempt from state and local income taxes, although it is typical for states to exempt only those obligations issued within their own borders. There are some types of municipal bonds that are not tax exempt due to the provisions of the Tax Reform Act of 1986. This will be discussed in more detail later.

The tax exemption enjoyed by municipal bonds leads to interest rate savings for issuers. Because investors do not have to pay income tax on municipal bond interest, they are willing to accept a lower rate. Consider the example of an investor in the 31 percent marginal tax bracket (that is, additional income is taxed at 31 percent). For a taxable bond that pays US $100 annually, the investor only keeps US $69 dollars since the federal government takes US $31 dollars in taxes. To that investor, the exemption from the income tax afforded municipal bonds is worth 31 percent of the yield. The investor would do just as well purchasing a tax-exempt bond that pays 6.9 percent as a taxable one that pays 10 percent. The benefit of the tax exemption increases with higher marginal tax brackets, and the advantage of tax exemption increases for investors in states that have state and/or local income taxes. The tax-exempt nature of municipal bonds provides a sizable subsidy to state and local governments. In fact, the 1991 annual tax-exempt interest reported by individuals in the United States totaled a whopping US $44.4 *billion* (PSA 1993).

What Are Municipal Bonds Issued For?

There are three historic reasons to issue municipal securities: for capital projects, for cash flow purposes, and to refinance existing debt.

Financing capital projects is the primary use of municipal bonds. The definition of a capital project varies from state to state but generally requires that the item being financed have a useful life exceeding at least the current operating year. Examples of capital projects that have been funded by municipal bonds include government buildings such as fire stations or schools; road and bridge construction; airports; trash burning facilities; college and university construction; hospitals; housing construction; mass transit, sports arenas, and convention centers; port facilities; sewer, water, and electric facilities; even vehicles and computer equipment.

Borrowing for cash flow purposes is another important use for municipal securities. Many governments face mismatched timing of revenues and expenditures. For instance, certain school districts in New York State do not receive the bulk of their property tax revenue until November, four months into their fiscal year that starts on July 1. How do they pay expenses until the tax money arrives? One way is to issue a note, pay the expenditures, and then retire the note when the tax money is received. A note is a short-term obligation and is typically secured by a specific revenue such as property taxes or intergovernmental aid. Another, less pleasant purpose for cash flow borrowing is to bail out troubled governments. There have been occasions where municipal securities have been used to reduce or eliminate government budget deficits. For example, the New York State Municipal Assistance Corporation (MAC) used bonds to help finance New York City's budget deficit.

Finally, municipal bonds may be issued to retire existing debt. The new bonds are called "refunding" bonds; the bonds being retired are called "refunded" bonds. There are two types of refunding: current refunding and advance refunding. A current refunding is when the obligations being refunded are paid off immediately. Often, however, the bonds can only be retired at a specific time in the future. For an advance refunding, the refunding bond proceeds are invested, typically in U.S. government securities. These investments are then used to pay the principal and interest on the refunded bonds. Why would a government issue new bonds to pay off old ones? There are several reasons. Typically bonds are refunded to realize interest rate savings. Savings occur when the current interest rates are lower than those carried by the existing bonds plus the cost of issuing the new bonds. Another reason is to change the terms of the agreement between the issuer and the bondholder. Once the bonds are issued it is very difficult for the government to alter, say, the maturity schedule or other promises made to the investors. It is often easier to simply refund the bonds.

A Brief History of Municipal Bonds

Despite the size of the current municipal bond market, its history is one checkered with defaults. A default is when a government fails to make principal and interest payments in full and on time. Indeed, "one conclusion that can be made at the outset is that we have a long and rich history of municipal bond defaults" (Feldstein and Fabozzi 1987, p. 26).

Borrowing by state governments began in earnest in the 1820s and 1830s for infrastructure improvements such as canals, roads, and railways. In 1837, however, there was a severe depression that continued into the 1840s and several states and municipalities defaulted. The earliest municipal default took place in Mobile in 1839, when the effects of the 1837 depression, two major fires, and a yellow fever epidemic led to the city being unable to pay its debts (Feldstein and Fabozzi 1987). Mobile defaulted again in the 1870s.

Following the civil war, local government debt was used to finance internal improvements, typically railways. The 1873 panic and the following years of depression led to widespread defaults that may have totaled as much as 20 percent of outstanding municipal bonds (Aronson and Hilley 1986; Hillhouse 1936). These defaults led to changes in state constitutions and statutes that govern municipal debt, typically in the form of debt limits, usually set as a debt to property value ratio.

Debt issuance continued at an accelerating pace from the turn of the century into the 1930s and the Great Depression when, again, there were a significant number of defaults—perhaps as much as 10 percent of the total and including the bonds of the State of Arkansas (Aronson and Hilley 1986). From the end of World War II to the present, the amount of state and local debt has continued to swell, and 1993 was a record year for municipal bond issuance. However, although defaults are not frequent, they continue to happen, punctuated by default on general obligation notes by New York City in 1975 and Cleveland in 1978, and the biggest default in history—the Washington Public Power Supply System (WPPSS) 1983 default on US $2.25 billion of debt.

Who Issues Municipal Bonds?

Of the approximately 80,000 local governments in the United States, 50,000 have issued municipal securities (PSA 1990). Municipal bonds are issued by states, counties, municipalities, school and other special districts, and authorities. Authorities such as the Port Authority of New York and New Jersey and the New Jersey Turnpike Authority account for by far the largest percentage of long-term borrowing (PSA 1990, p. 57). State and local governments began to create these debt-issuing authorities around the turn of the century often to deliver services to an area that crossed several political boundaries. Usually, the debt of these authorities is not subject to local debt limit restrictions.

What is Involved with Selling Municipal Bonds and Who Are the Actors?

The process of selling debt is governed by state and local constitutions and statutes. The sale of municipal bonds involves a plethora of steps and rules and a constellation of private consultants.

The first step in selling bonds for capital purposes is to have a capital plan. The capital improvement program (CIP) is the primary capital planning document used by state and local governments. Typically, the CIP covers long-term capital planning, usually over at least five years, and generally sets out the government's projects, establishes priorities and project timing, and identifies funding. The CIP at a minimum "addresses current unmet service requirements and the need for expansion, replacement, or renewal of existing facilities" (Moody's Investors Service 1991, p. 32). There are several possible funding sources for capital projects, including grants, current operating funds, other specific revenues such as user fees, and municipal bond proceeds. The CIP is an important document because, when done thoroughly and completely, it shows how the government's capital priorities interact with its financing constraints. The CIP should be updated frequently so that the information does not grow stale or outdated.

Governments frequently use consultants for capital planning. Feasibility or engineering studies examine the technical details of a specific project, its cost and possible funding, and may include an analysis of local economic development benefits. These studies are usually done by independent consulting engineers.

Following a decision to move forward with a capital program, and the debt requirements decided, the next step in the debt issuance process is to obtain legal authorization. The way debt is authorized varies from state to state. Typically, for GO bonds, voter approval is required; however, sometimes approval of the governing body, such as the city council, is all that is needed. Public hearings may also be required.

The rampant defaults of the late nineteenth century led not only to the widespread establishment of local debt limits, they also generated the need for legal opinions. Some of the defaulting issuers had successfully avoided their payment obligation by arguing that the bonds had not been authorized or properly issued (PSA 1990). Legal opinions were sought by issuers to restore market confidence and, to this day, virtually every municipal bond is accompanied by an approving legal opinion of a bond counsel. The legal opinion confirms that the issuer has conformed to the applicable legal requirements, that all the necessary procedural steps have been completed, and that the debt is a validly authorized obligation. The legal opinion also attests to the bond's tax status. In addition, bond counsel must reveal any litigation that could affect the validity of the bond.

There are two ways to sell municipal bonds: by competitive sale or through negotiation. For a competitive sale, underwriters bid to purchase the bonds, and the bid with the lowest interest cost wins the bonds. In a competitive sale, the government structures the sale itself, usually with the assistance and advice of an expert financial adviser. The issuer and the financial adviser decide on the timing of the sale, the amount, the maturity schedule, bidding specifications, and all other particulars of the sale. These requirements are usually listed in a notice of sale that is published typically in a financial industry periodical such as *The Bond*

Buyer and, sometimes, in a local newspaper. The underwriters must submit a bid that conforms with the published requirements. When the bids are opened, the underwriter bidding the lowest interest rate wins the bonds. When the low bid is accepted, it becomes the contract of sale at the conditions specified in the bid. After the bonds are purchased by the underwriter, they are typically resold to investors. The difference between what the underwriter pays to the issuer and the selling price to investors is called "the gross underwriter spread," or simply "the spread." The underwriter's expenses, commissions, and profit are paid out of the spread.

For a negotiated sale the underwriter is chosen beforehand by the issuer. The interest costs and the particulars of the offering for a negotiated sale are determined by the terms of the agreement between the underwriter and the issuer. (More on competitive versus negotiated sales can be found in the entry on **municipal bonds: policy and strategy**.)

If the sale is large enough, several underwriters may get together and form a syndicate and collectively purchase the bonds. Syndicates are formed to raise sufficient resources to purchase the bonds and share the risks of underwriting the issue. One or two of the underwriter firms will be the lead manager(s), or senior manager(s), that administer the operations of the syndicate.

Municipal bonds are often issued as serial maturities, where bonds are payable in consecutive years. This makes the calculation of interest cost more complex. There are two common ways of calculating interest cost: net interest cost (NIC) and true interest cost (TIC). Calculating NIC is computationally simpler than TIC; however, NIC ignores the time value of money. NIC is calculated by adding the total interest payments over the life of the issue, divided by the bond years. Bond years equal the amount of the bonds multiplied by the years they are outstanding. Sometimes bonds are sold at a discount (when bonds are sold at less than the face value) or a premium (when bonds are sold at more than the face value). Discounts or premiums are treated as if they were interest payments, as follows:

$$\text{NIC} = \frac{\text{Total interest payments plus discount or less premium}}{\text{Bond years}}$$

NIC is, therefore, the ratio of debt cost to outstanding principal, but it treats all dollars the same whether they are paid next year or 20 years from now. Two bids could have the same NIC, but one bid may have most of the interest payments front-loaded, that is higher interest rates for earlier maturities. The front-loaded bid, even though it has the same NIC, is inferior since it requires the issuer to relinquish resources earlier that could have been used to earn a return. The key benefit of NIC is its relative ease of calculation by hand.

TIC, or Canadian interest cost (CIC) as it is sometimes called, is more complex to calculate since it accounts for the timing of payments. TIC is the internal rate of return paid by the issuer. That is, it is the interest rate that equates the amount received by the issuer with the interest and principal payments over the life of the issue (Mikesell 1991). Although this is complex to do by hand, particularly for larger offerings, computers can calculate a bid's TIC almost instantaneously.

TIC is superior to NIC because it accounts for the time value of money, although certain restrictions can be required that bring NIC more in line with TIC. NIC remains the most common method, despite its drawbacks and the availability of computers to calculate TIC (PSA 1990).

For virtually every municipal offering a prospectus or official statement (OS) is prepared. The issuer, the financial adviser, the underwriter, and the bond counsel are usually involved in the preparation of the OS, which is the primary document used to disclose information about the bond offering and the issuer. According to Moody's Investors Service (1991), an official statement typically includes the following: Specifications for competitive bidding,

> "An introduction to the official statement including the identification of the issuer, legal security and purpose; the securities being offered and a comprehensive examination of legal structure; a description of the issuer and the community served including demographic and economic data; a discussion of the issuer's debt structure and outstanding short- and long-term debt; authorized but unissued debt and debt service schedules; financial information; legal matters; and miscellaneous items. . . . The official statement typically includes one or more years of audited financial statements, summaries of budgets, capital plans and pertinent legal documents, including the form of the legal opinion to be printed on the bonds or notes" (p. 35).

A preliminary official statement (POS), also called a red herring, is circulated before the sale. The final official statement is produced after the bonds are purchased and the particulars of the sale are decided.

The issuer may also apply to get the bonds rated by one or more of the bond rating agencies. Most large issues that sell on a national market are rated, but smaller issues are sometimes marketed locally on a nonrated basis. The bond rating is a measure of the relative riskiness of the bond issue. There are two key firms that provide bond ratings for municipal bonds: Moody's Investors Service, which has been rating municipal bonds since 1919, and Standard and Poor's Corporation (S&P), which began in 1940. Fitch Investors Service is another rating agency, which has been rating bonds since 1923. For a fee, these firms will prepare an opinion of the credit worthiness of a debt obligation. These ratings have a major influence on issuers' borrowing costs, with the more highly rated (less risky) bonds on average having lower interest rates than lower rated bonds.

Bond ratings are expressed as symbols that provide a simple system to note the relative credit qualities of bonds. The highest long-term rating is noted as Aaa by Moody's (AAA by S&P and by Fitch). These bonds carry the lowest degree of investment risk. The lowest rating is C by Moody's (D by S&P and by Fitch). Moody's defines bonds rated C as "the lowest class of bonds, issues so rated can be regarded as having extremely poor prospects of ever attaining any real investment standing" (Moody's Investors Service 1991, p. 48). Bonds rated D by S&P are in default, and bonds rated D by Fitch are either in default or expected to be in default.

Bonds that are rated higher than Baa by Moody's and BBB by S&P and by Fitch are known as investment grade, signifying that the bonds have a high probability of being paid. The ratings in the investment grade category by Moody's include: Aaa, the best quality; Aa, high quality but with smaller margins of protection than Aaa; A, upper medium grade with adequate security to principal and interest, but elements exist that suggest a susceptibility to impairment some time in the future; and Baa, medium grade, neither highly protected nor poorly secured, lacking outstanding investment characteristics and, in fact, have speculative characteristics as well (Moody's Investors Service 1991). S&P and Fitch have similarly defined investment grade rating categories.

Debt issues can be structured in several different ways, depending upon the needs of the government and the needs of the investors. Bonds can have serial or term maturities. A term maturity is when all of the bonds mature at the same time. A 20-year term bond would have all of the principal repaid in one payment maturing in 20 years. Typically, for term bonds, the issuer is required to make mandatory payments into a sinking fund that put money away as if it were a serial structure. Term bonds are used to attract long-term buyers, such as bond funds or individuals (Moody's Investors Service 1991). For term bonds, the debt service requirements include the sinking fund payments.

Municipal bonds are sometimes sold with a call or redemption feature. A call feature is the issuer's right to buy back, or call, the bonds at a specified date at a specified amount. A call feature helps the issuer take advantage of a decline in interest rates, and, typically, the issuer sells refunding bonds to provide the money to retire the bonds being called.

Investors' demand for high quality, safe securities has led to the development of credit enhancement or third party debt service guarantees. These debt service guarantees can be bank letters of credit (LOC), municipal bond insurance, or guarantees from other governments.

A municipal bond insurance policy is a noncancelable guarantee to protect bond holders from issuer nonpayment (PSA 1990). In the event an issuer does not make debt service payments, those payments will be made by the insurer. The issuer pays the insurer an up-front premium for the bond insurance. The issuer can realize savings if the premium paid to the insurer is less than the interest rate savings from having the additional credit from the insurer. Not all issues qualify for insurance, however, since the insurers have criteria for whether they will provide a policy. Municipal bond insurance is offered by several firms and insured issues accounted for about 40 percent of the municipal market in 1993 (Task 1994).

With a typical LOC, the bank pledges its credit to cover bond payments, providing investors with liquidity and default protection. A LOC from a highly rated bank can benefit a government with lower rated debt, since the government may gain advantage from the bank's rating. The small number of highly rated domestic banks has limited the use of LOC's for credit enhancement (Mikesell 1991).

Other governments sometimes provide credit enhancement. The credit enhancement can be as strong as a full, faith and credit unlimited tax pledge, as Montgomery County, Maryland, has done for certain debt of the Montgomery County Housing Opportunities Commission (Simonsen 1989). Or the credit enhancement can be less strong with a more limited pledge. The State of New Jersey's "qualified bond" programs are examples of state-provided credit enhancement. For certain general obligation bonds of some municipalities and school districts, the Treasurer of the State of New Jersey pays selected state aid monies directly to the bond-paying agent, which can improve the credit standing of those bonds (Feldstein, Fabozzi, and Pollack 1983).

Finally, the closing culminates the sale. At the closing, bonds are delivered and the proceeds paid to the issuer. Sometimes a book entry system is used and no bonds are delivered to the investor, rather it is all done electronically (Moody's Investors Service 1991). After the closing, the issuer is responsible for managing the debt and paying the investors. Typically, a paying agent is employed by the issuer to actually make the required payments to the bondholders.

Tax Reform Act of 1986

When the federal income tax was established in 1913 it contained specific provisions exempting interest on state and local bonds. This seemingly reflected the doctrine of intergovernmental tax immunity, established in the *McCullouch v. Maryland* ruling in 1819. This ruling contained Justice Marshall's famous statement, "The power to tax is the power to destroy" (PSA 1990). *The Pollock v. Farmers Loan and Trust Company* decision in 1895 applied this doctrine to municipal securities and, incidently, also produced the need for a constitutional amendment authorizing the federal income tax (PSA 1990). Consideration of federal taxation of municipal bond interest, however, happened almost immediately:

> In mid-1918, for example, *The Daily Bond Buyer,* as it was then styled, carried a story on the House Ways and Means Committee's move to tax state and municipal bonds. The debate dragged on for months, until in October the newspaper reported that the Senate Finance Committee killed the so-called "municipal bond tax" because it thought the measure was unconstitutional. (Marlin and Mysak 1991)

Continued attacks on municipal bonds' tax exemption may have been inevitable, however. Because of the tax exemption, governments could borrow at artificially low rates, providing a subsidy to local governments and lost revenue to the federal government. Further, the distinction between private and public purposes became blurred when, in 1936, in the midst of the depression, Mississippi "innovated the use of industrial development bonds (IDBs), a mechanism whereby a tax-exempt borrower constructed a plant for a private firm and serviced the debt with lease payments from the firm" (Mikesell 1991, p. 407). The federal treasury made several attempts to eliminate the tax exemption and in 1942 proposed abolishing the tax exemption not only for future issues, but for outstanding issues as well. In 1967, the Treasury ruled that IDBs were subject to income taxation, but this was overturned by Congress in 1968 when the Revenue and Expenditure Control Act exempted certain kinds of IDBs from taxation (Marlin and Mysak 1991, p. 37).

The use of IDBs continued to grow and by 1982 accounted for 57 percent of the tax-exempt debt sold, financing everything from factories and industrial parks to sports facilities and motels (Marlin and Mysak 1991). It was largely in reaction to the use of tax exemption benefiting private activities that the Tax Reform Act of 1986 was born.

The 1986 act is very complex, but simply put, it divides municipal debt into two categories: taxable private activity and tax-exempt pubic purpose (Mikesell 1991). The act established certain tests as to whether a bond is classified as private activity. Some private activity bonds can still be tax exempt—subject to a volume cap allocated to each state. Examples of private activity bonds subject to this cap include multifamily rental housing; some student loans; and some water, gas, and electric facilities—while private activity bonds for airports, docks, wharves, and solid waste facilities are outside of the cap (Mikesell 1991).

The act also created bank-qualified and alternative minimum tax bonds. Alternative minimum tax bonds are subject to tax when held by certain individuals and corporations, whereas bank-qualified bonds are the only bonds

of which commercial banks can still deduct 80 percent of the interest they incur to carry municipal bonds on their inventory (Marlin and Mysak 1991, p. 37). Issues are bank qualified if the issuer reasonably expects to sell less than US $10 million of tax-exempt bonds a year.

These and other provisions of the Tax Reform Act of 1986 had a profound affect on the municipal bond market. The long-term new issue volume fell from US $222 billion in 1985 to US $152 billion in 1986 and US $106 billion in 1987 (PSA 1990). The decline in volume led to reduced underwriter spreads and some of the biggest players in the municipal bond market leaving the business, including Salomon Brothers Inc.

Finally, in 1989, the Supreme Court ruled in the *South Carolina v. Baker* case that the Constitution does not protect the tax-exempt status of municipal bonds, overruling the earlier *Pollack* decision (PSA 1990). The tax exemption for municipal bonds is now subject to the federal legislative process, and as federal budgets continue to be tight, municipal bonds' income tax exemption is likely to continue to be a target.

WILLIAM SIMONSEN

BIBLIOGRAPHY

Aronson, J. Richard, and John L. Hilley, 1986. *Financing State and Local Governments,* 4th ed. Washington, DC: Brookings Institution.

Doran, John J., 1994. "Gross Spreads Tumbled in 1993, Despite Banner Year for Bonds." *Bond Buyer* (January 31), 2A.

Feldstein, Sylvan G., and Frank J. Fabozzi, 1987. *The Dow Jones-Irwin Guide to Municipal Bonds,* Homewood IL: Dow Jones-Irwin.

Feldstein, Sylvan G., Frank J. Fabozzi, and Irving M. Pollack, 1983. *The Municipal Bond Handbook,* Vol. 2. Homewood, IL: Dow Jones-Irwin.

Hillhouse, Albert M., 1936. *Municipal Bonds: A Century of Experience.* Englewood Cliffs, NJ: Prentice-Hall.

Marlin, George J., and Joe Mysak. 1991. *The Guide to Municipal Bonds: The History, the Industry, the Mechanics.* New York: American Banker/Bond Buyer.

Mikesell, John L., 1991. *Fiscal Administration: Analysis and Applications for the Public Sector,* 3rd ed. Pacific Grove, CA: Brooks/Cole.

Moody's Investors Service, 1991. *Moody's on Municipals: An Introduction to Issuing Debt.* New York: Moody's Investors Service.

Public Securities Association, 1990. *Fundamentals of Municipal Bonds,* 4th ed. New York: Public Securities Association.

———, 1993. "Tax-Exempt Interest Reported by Individuals Totals $44.4 Billion." *Municipal Market Developments* (August) 1, 6.

Simonsen, William, 1989. *Municipal Credit Report on the Montgomery County Housing Opportunities Commission, Maryland* (May 30). New York: Moody's Investors Service.

Stone, Peter M., 1994. "Bonds of Gold." *National Journal,* vol. 26, no. 5 (January 29) 238.

Task, Aaron, 1994. "Bond Insurers Expecting to Face sharper Competition in 94." *American Banker* vol. 8, no.1 (January) 10.

MUNICIPAL BONDS: POLICY AND STRATEGY.

The strategy of bringing bond issues to market which requires a multitude of decisions and involves several different actors. Selling bonds means that issuers must make judgments about, for instance, the method of sale, issue demand features, and maturity schedule. Typically, the issuer's expert advisers are involved, since these decisions are complex and require specialized technical expertise and knowledge of the market.

How Should the Decisions Be Made?

It is very important for the issuer to develop a set of principles to provide a guide for decisionmaking. Producing such a set of principles provides the issuer with a road map through the complex and often perplexing decisions around debt issuance. These principles should be based on notions of efficiency, administrative concerns, and ethics.

Resource allocation and least cost financing are key concepts of efficiency. An obvious efficiency issue is financing improvements at the lowest possible cost. Therefore, issuers need to care about how the market will react to decisions about such important choices as the design of the maturity schedules or bond security provisions. The issuers' expert advisers can provide them with guidance about navigating the municipal bond market.

A less obvious efficiency issue concerns how financing alternatives influence the way the public sector allocates its limited resources (Petersen and Strachota 1991). Consider the example of financing a water treatment facility, where revenue bonds or general obligation bonds may be used. Assuming the water rates are based on consumption, a self-supporting revenue bond paid for by increased water rates is more likely to lead to further conservation of water and a more efficient use of resources than would a general obligation bond secured by general taxation. Using water rates better informs the consumers about the actual comprehensive cost of the service, and they make their decisions about how much to use accordingly.

Administrative concerns, flexibility, and the impact on the organization should also be part of the decision process. For instance, bond covenants for revenue bonds can sometimes prove restrictive, requiring for example, investments in only certain types of securities or establishing of funds for replacement or maintenance. Changing promises given to bondholders is difficult, and therefore the obligations that these promises create need to be carefully weighed, even though they may produce interest cost savings.

Last but not least, ethical concerns should be considered. What do I mean by ethics? The notion of ethics can be defined simply as principles of right and wrong behavior (Lewis 1988). The huge size of the municipal bond market and the large amounts of money changing hands makes it a magnet for ethical dilemmas for finance officers and local officials. This suggests the need to link ethical obligations with governmental power. One way to link these notions is through laws or regulation, another way may be through the development of ethical codes and standards. Within the idea of ethics lie the twin notions of equity and accountability.

The idea of equity suggests some analysis of winners and losers from a policy or decision. The various ways that municipal bonds may be structured raises some equity issues. One key notion of equity pertains to the ability to pay. For instance, let us return to the choice of revenue or general obligation (GO) bonds for a water project. Choosing revenue bonds secured through fees, rather than using property taxes, has different implications for who ultimately pays the bill. Using fees to pay off bonds may be in conflict with the notion of ability to pay and could result in higher burdens for lower income groups. Another equity principle is that those who benefit from an improvement should pay for it in relation to how much they use, called benefit equity. The use of fees based on consumption to secure a revenue bond for water improvements would more likely meet the benefit equity criterion than would using GO bonds paid by the general populace. However, some services benefit society in general, such as police or fire protection, and this widespread value provides the rationale for broad-based payment for these services.

Accountability revolves around the notion of government employees having many bosses. To whom is the finance officer responsible? Many groups are potentially affected by the finance officer's decisions. These groups include taxpayers (both current and future), citizen, business, or other neighborhood groups, elected officials, the citizens generally, and users of the service where the improvement is paid for by the bonds. In fact, the increasing distrust of government adds salience to considering ethical concerns. Only 6 percent of respondents to a survey done by the U.S. Advisory Commission on Intergovernmental Relations (1992) said they had a great deal of confidence that local governments do a good job in carrying out their responsibilities. Issuers need to be mindful of appearances of impropriety or risk further erosion of the public trust.

The notions of efficiency, administrative concerns, and ethics can be at odds with each other. Examples include use of restrictive revenue bond covenants that may lead to lower interest rates but put an undue burden on organizational management, or the use of fee-based revenue bonds aiding resource allocation but placing an increased burden on lower-income consumers. The conflicting nature of these ideas suggests careful analysis and consideration of alternatives.

Debt Policy

Debt policies set out the "fiscal and management practices that seek to integrate a community's long-term physical needs with available finance resources" (Petersen and

Strachota 1991, p. 271). The key notion behind a debt policy is that it is a plan for how future debt financing will be treated given the recognition of the ongoing need to address capital requirements. According to John Petersen and Dennis Strachota (1991) debt policies typically include "acceptable levels of indebtedness, priorities among types of projects being financed, policies regarding the use of tax-supported versus self-supporting debt, the mix between current revenues and borrowing, and the appropriateness of and acceptable levels of short term indebtedness" (p. 271).

A debt policy provides guidance for finance officers as they try to sort through the implications of various options. As such, a community's debt policy may be an appropriate place to articulate the guiding principles about efficiency, administrative concerns, and ethics. Another key reason for a debt policy is to provide comfort to interested parties about the jurisdiction's commitment to sound debt practices. Debt policies should be considered and approved by the government's elected body to enhance its legitimacy to the public, rating agencies and prospective bondholders.

Pay-as-You-Go Versus Pay-as-You-Use

One possible component of a debt policy is the appropriate mix of capital improvements paid for out of current operating revenues and through debt financing. Funding projects out of current revenues is often called pay-as-you-go (sometimes pay-as-you-acquire) financing, whereas using debt is known as pay-as-you-use financing.

There are four key arguments for some amount of pay-as-you-go financing (Petersen and Strachota 1991):

1. Using current funds may provide budget flexibility if less of the budget is committed to debt service payments.
2. The savings from lower interest payments can be used to provide additional services or result in a lower tax rate.
3. Lower levels of borrowing can conserve debt capacity and perhaps lead to an enhanced credit rating.
4. Finally, pay-as-you-go financing leaves a legacy to future generations of infrastructure that is already paid.

There are also two key arguments in favor of debt financing. As a practical matter, it may be unrealistic to consider raising enough money up front to pay for expensive capital items, such as a sewer or water treatment plant. Using debt spreads the cost over the length of the bond issue. Spreading the cost over the useful life of the improvement meets the benefit equity criterion—those who benefit from the improvement pay for it, as it is consumed over time. The "great mobility of individuals and families in American society makes this argument particularly persuasive" (Petersen and Strachota 1991, p. 271).

Choosing a Method of Sale

Municipal bonds can be sold either by competitive bid or through negotiation (see **municipal bonds**). In a competitive sale, underwriters bid for the bonds that are then awarded to the firm bidding the lowest interest cost. For a negotiated sale, the issuer chooses the underwriter before the sale and negotiates the terms and conditions of the sale, including the interest rate. There are several factors to consider when deciding whether to sell bonds through negotiation or by competition.

Competitive sales provide some assurance that the bonds have been sold at the lowest possible interest rate. The evidence from the empirical research of the municipal bond market suggests that issuers' interest costs are typically lower and competitive sales compared to negotiated sales, all else equal. This difference increases as the intensity of bidding increases—that is, the higher the number of bids received, the lower the issuer's interest costs, all else equal. This difference can be quite substantial. Recent research on method of sale and interest costs for general obligation bonds in Oregon found that competitive sales with six or more bids, on average and all else equal, resulted in true interest costs (TICs) about one-half an interest rate point lower than negotiated sales (Simonsen and Robbins 1996). For a typical general obligation bond sale in Oregon (about US $6 million), this difference in interest rates means annual debt service payments would be about US$20,000 higher for negotiated sales.

Another key advantage of competitive sales is that they promote the reality and appearance of an open and fair process. In recent years, the municipal bond industry has been battered by several scandals and alleged improprieties. Several of these allegations involved the use of negotiated bond sales.

In May 1993, New Jersey Governor James Florio required that state and authority bond issues be sold through competitive bidding (Gasparino 1993a). The governor was responding to allegations of malfeasance in a New Jersey Turnpike bond issue. This was a US $2.8 billion negotiated deal in which Merrill Lynch allegedly channeled money to Armacon, a small New Jersey firm, in exchange for the position of chief underwriter. Armacon was owned by Governor Florio's chief of staff and a close political ally (Fitzgibbons and Monsarret 1993).

In Massachusetts, state investigators are concerned about an arrangement where Lazard Freres' Mark Ferber allegedly received an annual retainer from Merrill Lynch of US $1 million. State officials are investigating whether this was payment for recommending Merrill Lynch to underwrite interest rate swaps with the Massachusetts Water Resources Authority (MWRA) and other clients for whom Ferber and Lazard were financial advisers (Kurkjian 1993). The Massachusetts inspector general alleges that Ferber provided Merrill Lynch & Co. with an "unfair advantage," basically assuring that the firm would be selected to underwrite certain large MWRA issues (Fitzgibbons 1993).

Another controversy exploded in Chicago when the *Bond Buyer* reported that Mayor Daley's brother Michael was allegedly paid US $15,000 a month by Smith Barney for help in obtaining lead underwriter status for some of Chicago's and Cook County's largest bond deals (Gasparino 1993b; Pierog 1994). In response, a city alderman proposed revisions in local laws requiring competitive bids on all debt issues (Hornung 1994).

Following these and other allegations of impropriety, the Securities and Exchange Commission (SEC) asked several underwriting firms to report their political contributions at the municipal level (Stamas and Dickson 1993). In a March 1994 statement of its views, the SEC said that "increased attention needs to be directed at disclosure of potential conflicts of interest and material financial relationships among issuers, advisers and underwriters, including those arising from political contributions" (*Bond Buyer* 1994, p. 22).

On April 6, 1994, the SEC voted to adopt proposal G-37 of the Municipal Securities Rulemaking Board (MSRB) addressing these issues. This order bars firms from participating in negotiated underwriting with an issuer for two years after making political contributions to officials who could influence the awarding of bond business (Stamas 1994). According to the GFOA (1994):

> competitive sales promote the appearance of an open, fair process. A growing concern of negotiated sales, whether real or apparent, is that underwriting firms may be awarded business to reward them for campaign contributions or for other political reasons. Competitive sales, if conducted properly, can remove the appearance of impropriety in the bond sale process (p. 4).

There are circumstances where a negotiated sale may have an advantage over competitive issuance. One advantage of negotiated sales cited by the GFOA (1994) is flexibility. For a negotiated sale, the timing or the features of an issue can be adjusted more quickly to better meet investors' needs when there are changing or unsettled market conditions.

Also, there are circumstances where competition for the bonds may be limited and presale marketing would help generate investor demand. With competitive sale, the underwriter's sales force does not know whether it will win the bid and get the bonds and, therefore, may be reluctant to spend much time marketing the bonds. For negotiated sales, the underwriter is chosen beforehand and assured the bonds and as a result may have a greater incentive to engage in presale marketing. According to the GFOA (1994), "for certain issuers, such as those experiencing financial difficulty or those contemplating a structure not well understood by investors, pre-sale marketing efforts may enhance investor demand for their securities" (p. 5).

Variable Rate Demand Obligations

A variable rate demand obligation (VRDO) combines features of a bond and a note. A VRDO has two characteristics (Moody's Investors Service 1991). First VRDOs have a demand feature whereby the investor can require the issuer to purchase the obligation at its par (face) value plus accrued interest (called a tender, or put). In other words, the investor can choose to give back the obligation to the issuer. Second, they also have an interest rate that varies periodically. The primary benefit is that VRDOs carry short-term interest rates (which are typically lower than long-term rates) because of the demand feature. Should the bondholders exercise the tender option, the bonds are hopefully remarketed to other buyers. Typically, there is an agreement with a bank to provide liquidity to purchase the obligations in case the remarketing fails.

VRDOs are more complex than fixed rate bonds and carry several risks. First, debt service payments are predictable for fixed rate bonds but vary for VRDOs. In the case of rapidly rising market interest rates, the issuer may be faced with escalating interest payments and, in the event of a failed remarketing, may be required to purchase the obligations. Because of these concerns "poor structuring of VRDOs may have a negative effect on issuer creditworthiness, with consequent effect on both long- and short-term ratings of debt" (Moody's Investors Service 1991, p. 21).

Choosing a Maturity Schedule

Structuring a municipal bond offering requires decisions about its maturity schedule. The structure of the maturity schedule is of importance to municipalities for several reasons. First, the maturity schedule determines, in part, the debt service requirements. The longer the issuer takes to retire the issue, the lower, on average, the annual debt service payments—for example, a 30-year repayment schedule will result in lower yearly debt service payments than would a 15-year schedule, all else equal. Issuers may be tempted to extend the maturities as much as possible. However, it is a bad practice for the length of the debt to exceed the useful life of the improvement—or the issuer faces the risk of paying for both a used up improvement and its replacement.

The debt service payments also depend on the schedule of principal repayment. Level debt service (or equal annual payments) requires that the principal payments are lower initially and increase over the life of the issue. This is similar to the payment schedule of a home mortgage. Principal payments may also be front loaded, resulting in higher initial debt service payments that decline over the life of the issue. Maturity schedules that result in ascending annual debt service requirements push out the payment requirements. If this is done to provide budget relief in tight times, it is likely to be viewed negatively by the rating agencies.

Capital appreciation bonds, relatively new to the municipal market, are sold at a deep discount with the interest figured into the value of the bond at its term maturity. These bonds may be attractive to institutional investors (such as bond funds) and certain individual investors interested in capital gains rather than current income and where all earnings are reinvested (Moody's Investors Service 1991). Future income compound securities combine the features of serial bonds with capital appreciation bonds. Future income compound securities are capital appreciation bonds that revert to serial bonds at some future date, providing investors with both long-term capital gains and future income (Moody's Investors Service 1991).

These are only a few of the seemingly limitless possibilities for structuring repayment. Issuers can look to their debt policy (if there is one) and market factors for guidance on how to structure individual issues.

Importance of Planning

The importance of wise capital improvement planning and development of sensible debt policies cannot be understated. The task of financing capital improvements is complex and the workings of the municipal bond market can be obscure to those without substantial previous experience.

The long-term nature of capital financing commits future generations to current decisions—both through multiyear payment of debt and the long life of capital assets. Consequently, poor choices can have repercussions long into the future. Perhaps the most spectacular example of faulty planning resulted in the Washington Public Power Supply System (WPPSS) default on US $2.25 billion of municipal bonds for projects 4 and 5. WPPSS projected need for electricity was far greater than what ultimately materialized, and the power from projects 4 and 5 was not needed. Howard Gleckman (in Feldstein, Fabozzi, and Pollack 1983) summed up the WPPSS planning process as follows: "the forecasts were grossly wrong" (p. 654). (For several examples of defaults and other related problems see Feldstein, Fabozzi, and Pollack 1983, pp. 640–690.) A jurisdiction, therefore, benefits greatly from a well conceived and thought out capital plan and a set of financing principles articulated in a comprehensive debt policy.

The Orange County, California, bankruptcy provides another example of the importance of a debt policy and planning. Orange County is one of the wealthiest counties in the nation, and its population of about 2.6 million people makes it the fifth largest U.S. County (Lemov 1995). On December 6, 1994, Orange County filed for bankruptcy under Chapter 9 of the Federal Bankruptcy Code. Orange County is well known for its political conservatism—it gave Ronald Reagan the largest margin of victory in his presidential races of any of the nation's counties (Greenwald 1994). How could one of the wealthiest and most populated counties in the nation go bankrupt?

The county managed an investment pool with deposits totaling about US $7.4 billion. The deposits came from the county itself, 187 other governments in California, and 400 individuals. The county treasurer's, Robert Citron's, investment policy was based on interest rates remaining low. This strategy was successful for several years, earning a higher rate of return compared to other California investment pools (Greenwald 1994). A significant portion of the pool was invested in highly interest rate sensitive derivative products called inverse floaters. The term "derivative" includes a wide range of financial products that derive their value from other products, prices, or indexes—such as options and futures, swaps, and forwards (Levitt 1995). Inverse floaters are structured to provide a rate of return equal to a fixed rate less a multiple of a floating rate index. According to Arthur Levitt (1995), Chairman of the SEC,

> this rate feature makes the market value of the inverse floaters much more sensitive to interest rate fluctuations than traditional fixed or floating rate obligations. If interest rates decrease or remain stable, the inverse floaters provide a high rate of return. In the few years of declining rates prior to 1994, this would have contributed to the high rate of return achieved by the [investment] Pools. When rates increase, however, the interest return is reduced sharply, causing a corresponding drop in market or "liquidation" value of the note (p. 6).

In pursuit of this investment strategy, the county borrowed an additional US $12.5 billion in reverse repurchase agreements at short-term rates and took long-term rate positions that pay higher interest. A repurchase agreement provides for the sale of securities by a dealer to a customer, with the agreement that the customer will resell the securities back to the dealer at a later date. Reverse repurchase agreements are initiated by the dealer, where the dealer agrees to buy securities from the customer in exchange for funds, and the customer agrees to buy back the securities at a later date (Levitt 1995).

However, this strategy, like inverse floaters, is very sensitive to interest rate movements. As rates increased during 1994, returns on the long-term obligations were no longer higher than the money borrowed through the reverse repurchase agreements. As interest rates rose, the decline in market value required the commitments of more and more securities (similar to collateral). On December 1, 1994, Orange County disclosed that the investment pool had suffered a "paper" loss of US $1.5 billion, and on December 6, the county did not meet its obligation under a reverse repurchase agreement with First Boston, and First Boston proceeded to liquidate about US $2.6 billion in securities it held under the reverse repurchase agreements (Levitt 1995). Later that day, the county filed for Chapter 9 bankruptcy. The investment pool's losses are now estimated at about US $1.7 billion. Actually, two bankruptcies were filed, one for the investment pool and one for the county itself (Vartabedian 1995). In an effort to recoup some of the losses, the county has sued Merrill Lynch—for selling to the county 70 percent of its high-risk investments (Vartabedian 1995).

County Treasurer Citron pleaded guilty to six felony charges of misleading investors and misrepresenting interest earnings from the investment fund. Citron admitted to, among other things, diverting to county accounts more than US $80 million in interest earned by pool participants, improperly transferring securities from a county fund to one including other investors, using false and misleading financial statements to sell securities, and using false statements about the condition and earnings of the county pool to sell about US $1.4 billion worth of bonds and notes.

A hypothetical situation may help explain what happened with Orange County (loosely based on an example by Ritter 1994; dollars not necessarily U.S. dollars—could be any currency). You are very frugal and manage to save $10,000. You decide to gamble on interest rates, and so you use it as collateral to borrow $100,000 for one year at 3 percent interest. With your borrowed $100,000 you invest in $100,000 of five-year U.S. securities paying 5 percent annually. At the end of one year, you will have made $5,000 in interest, paid $3,000 interest on the loan, and your profit is $2,000, or a 20 percent return ($2,000/your original $10,000). But soon after you make your investment, interest rates start rising and keep rising all year. Your return (5 percent) is locked in for five years, but you must roll over the loan every year. If short-term rates jump to 6 percent, it would cost you $6,000 in interest on the $100,000 loan, but you only receive $5,000 in interest from the U.S. securities that are locked in for five years. You lose $1,000, or 10 percent of your original $100,000 investment. You may decide to sell your U.S. securities. But five-year rates have also gone up, so your U.S. securities have plunged in value to compensate to, say, $90,000. You are wiped out. If you sold the U.S. securities, you would need your entire $10,000 original investment to pay off the loan. Although the circumstances were much more complex for Orange County, the basic principle applies—"betting" on interest rates can be a risky venture.

Along with inverse floaters and reverse repurchases agreements, the county also borrowed US $600 million from the municipal market as part of its investment strategy. These notes were not income tax–exempt and were is-

sued for arbitrage purposes (Johnston 1995). Arbitrage is the practice of investing at rates higher than the rates paid to borrow the money. These notes came due July 10, 1995; indeed, the county had US $1.2 billion of short-term notes due between June and August 1995.

Unfortunately, many of the 187 local government participants in the investment pool also borrowed taxable notes to invest in the investment pool. The City of Irvine borrowed US $62 million and invested it in the pool, which had historically yielded a higher rate of return than paid on the notes. Payment of the notes were due in July. Irvine received an emergency release of funds from the investment pool sufficient to pay about half the notes, and reached an agreement with note holders to retire some of the debt and extend the remainder for several months (Johnston 1995).

School districts in the county were required to invest virtually all of their cash in the pool (Johnston 1995). Some also borrowed to invest in the pool, such as the Irvine Unified School District, which had US $54.6 million of taxable arbitrage notes and had an additional US $48 million of operating cash invested in the pool.

Montebello, California, provides another example of a local government gambling on interest rate arbitrage through borrowing to invest in the pool. Montebello's US $25 million taxable arbitrage note (equal in size to about four times their fiscal 1993 fund balance) came due December 30, 1994. The city received an emergency release of funds from the investment pool sufficient to pay about half the notes and reached an agreement with note holders to retire some of the debt and extend the remainder to April 1995 (Johnston 1995). Montebello's fiscal operations are likely to be affected for several years because of their attempt to use arbitrage having gone amiss.

In June 1996, Orange County sold about $800 million of insured certificate of participation that provided for payment of the county's bankruptcy claims. Although this action helped the county regain some immediate fiscal stability, residents will be paying off this debt for 30 years. In addition, the county was forced to make significant budget cuts, with services used by the poor hit the hardest (Weikel and Marquis, 1994; Richardson 1995).

Perhaps one of the most insidious outcomes of the county's fiscal collapse is the influence it has had on feelings about government. A public opinion poll conducted by Mark Baldassare and Associates from January 20 to January 23, 1995, for the *Los Angeles Times* asked county residents about the impact of the bankruptcy. Here are some of the questions and the responses (Ellingwood 1995):

■ How worried are you that you or a family member will be hurt financially as a result of the crisis involving the county's investment fund?
17% very worried, 30% somewhat worried

- Do you think the investment fund losses will hurt quality:
  - of life in Orange County?
    17% a lot, 57% somewhat
  - of life in your city or community?
    12% a lot, 48% somewhat
  - of education in your school district?
    22% a lot, 41% somewhat
  - Others say the financial crisis came about in part because county government was overstaffed and wasted taxpayers' money for years. Do you agree or disagree with this view?
    67% agree

The Orange County bankruptcy provides a spectacular example of the importance of planning, debt policies, and guiding principles about the use of debt. For instance, key elements of a debt policy are the appropriate uses of long- and short-term debt. Local governments using taxable arbitrage notes to, essentially, gamble on interest rates is at best a questionable policy. A debt policy should provide clear guidance about the appropriateness of this practice. The guiding principles forming debt policies should include ethical concerns and incorporate the notions of accountability and appearances of impropriety. Appearances of impropriety (indeed, real impropriety in the case of Citron) adversely affects the public trust, as seen from the public opinion poll results presented here. It may be that one of the most difficult to overcome legacies of the county's bankruptcy will be the reforging of trust with the citizens.

WILLIAM SIMONSEN

BIBLIOGRAPHY

Ellingwood, Ken, 1995. "Waste–Not Prop. 13–Is Blamed." Los Angeles Times. (January 21).

Feldstein, Sylvan G., Frank J. Fabozzi and Irving M. Pollack, 1983. *The Municipal Bond Handbook*, Vol. 2. Homewood, IL: Dow Jones–Irwin.

Fitzgibbons, Patrick M., 1993. "When Know-How Is Not Enough: The Many Friends of Mark Ferber." *Bond Buyer* (December 30), 1.

Fitzgibbons, Patrick M., and Sean Monsarret, 1993. "Investigation into New Jersey Bond Refunding Triggers Wary Reaction in Municipal Market." *Bond Buyer* (May 10), 1.

Gasparino, Charles, 1993a. "NYC's Stein Urges Mayor, Comptroller to Copy New Jersey, Ban Negotiated Debt." *Bond Buyer* (May 12), 1.

———, 1993b. "The Market May Be Getting Serious about Campaign Contributions, But There Is More Than One Way to Peddle Influence." *Bond Buyer* (November 16), 1.

Government Finance Officers Association (GFOA), 1994. *Competitive v. Negotiated: How to Choose the Method of Sale for Tax-Exempt Bonds*. Chicago, IL: Government Finance Officers Association.

Greenwald, John, 1994. "The California Wipeout." *Time* (December 19), 55–56.

Hornung, Mark N., 1994. "Put Municipal Financing Out to Bid." *Chicago Sun Times* (March 4), 37.

Johnson, Greg, and Susan Marquez Owen, 1995. "Bankruptcy Court OKs $5.7 Billion O.C. Pool Payout." *Los Angeles Times* (May 3), 1, A12.

Johnston, Michael, 1995. *Municipal Report on Orange County, California* (January 10). New York: Sandler O'Neill & Partners, L.P.

Kurkjian, Stephen, 1993. "Papers Show Links Between Ferber, Firm." *Boston Globe* (December 17), 1.

Lemov, Penelope, 1995. "After the Fiscal Quake." *Governing* (February) 34–35.

Levitt, Arthur, 1995. "Testimony of Arthur Levitt, Chairman U.S. Securities and Exchange Commission Concerning Municipal Bond and Government Securities Markets before the Committee on Banking, Housing, and Urban Affairs, United States Senate" (January 5).

Lewis, Carol W., 1988. "Ethics and the Public Finance Function." *Government Finance Review* (October) 7–12.

Moody's Investors Service, 1991. *Moody's on Municipals: An Introduction to Issuing Debt*. New York: Moody's Investors Service.

Petersen, John E., and Dennis R. Strachota, 1991. *Local Government Finance: Concepts and Practices*. Chicago, IL: Government Finance Officers Association.

Pierog, Karen, 1994. "Chicago Alderman Pushes for Probe of Daley's Dealings with Smith Barney." *Bond Buyer* (February 10), 1.

Richardson, Lisa, 1995. "Latest Layoffs Hit Hard at Social Service Agency." *Los Angeles Times* (April 14), A12–A13.

Ritter, Hal, 1994. "Interest Rate Hikes + Speculation = Trouble." *USA Today* (December 8), 2A.

Simonsen, William, and Mark D. Robbins, 1996. Does It Make Any Difference Anymore? Competitive Versus Negotiated Municipal Bond Issuance." *Public Administration Review*. (Jan/Feb). Vol 56, No. 1 (57–64).

Stamas, Vicky, 1994. "MSRB Bans Gifts by Dealers, Firms to Go into Effect Monday, April 25." *Bond Buyer* (April 14), 1.

Stamas, Vicky, and Steven Dickson, 1993. "SEC Questions Underwriters, Probes Political Contributions." *Bond Buyer* (June 9), 1.

U.S. Advisory Commission on Intergovernmental Relations, 1992. *Changing Public Attitudes on Governments and Taxes*. ACIR.

Vartabedian, Ralph, 1995. "Bankruptcy Suits Could Keep Armies of Lawyers Busy Years." *Los Angeles Times* (January 30), A1, A14, A15.

Weikel, Dan, and Julie Marquis, 1994. "Services Used by Poor Are Hit Hardest." *Los Angeles Times* (December 14), 1, A32.

Wilgoren, Jodi, and Shelby Grad, 1995. "O.C. Settlement Support Given; Judge's OK Is Next." *Los Angeles Times* (April 13), A1, A17, A18.

MUNICIPAL BONDS: SECURITY.

The formal financial arrangements for the repayment of state and local government debt. Municipal bonds are contracts between debt issuers and the purchasers of that debt. Investors buying municipal bonds are essentially creditors to which the government owes money. Security refers to the manner in which the payment of principal and interest on this debt is promised and how it is structured. The numerous elements of security include the format and timing of payments, the source of the revenues used to make the payments and other provisions.

General Obligation Bonds

The first and most basic form of municipal bond security is the general obligation (GO). General obligation bonds are backed by the full faith and credit of the issuer. Such a pledge is a legally enforceable promise to bring the resources of the municipality to bear in honoring the debt. In addition to this pledge, the government issuing a general obligation is supporting their promise of repayment with the specific ability to levy the taxes necessary to do so. In the words of Wade Smith (1979), "Whatever else it may possess in the way of attributes, a bond is not a general obligation if it does not possess both of these [features], and if it does, it is" (p. 180).

Government borrowing based on this form of security dates back to the early nineteenth century when state and local governments were financing large infrastructure projects (Aronson and Hilley 1986). The size and rate of growth of this borrowing has closely followed the economic cycles of the nation. Following the depression of 1873 and a number of defaults, many governments began restricting the types and amounts of borrowing. As a result, the rate of borrowing slowed for a time. In the years prior to the depression in the 1930s, however, municipal bond volume was increasing again. Once the depression hit, tax revenues were in many cases inadequate to cover interest and principal payments and defaults were common. Since World War II, the growth of municipal debt has continued, with 1993 being a record year for bond issuance.

Over time, with the growth of tax limitation measures and a growing national debt, general obligation bonds have decreased as a proportion of overall municipal bond sales. For various reasons, including avoiding the voter approval process and specific debt limits of local governments, much of government borrowing has shifted to instruments with dedicated revenue streams such as revenue bonds (see enterprise revenue bonds later in this entry).

Types of General Obligations

One type of general obligation bond is the general obligation unlimited tax (GOULT) bond. These bonds are backed by the full faith and credit of the issuing municipality, which has an ability to tax unconstrained by statutory or constitutional limits. Governments issuing these bonds are pledging all available sources of revenue to pay for the debt, without qualification.

General obligation limited tax (GOLT) bonds are issued under the constraint of restrictions that limit the amount that taxes can be raised in order to make payments on the debt. In several states, constitutional amendments have passed limiting the degree to which municipalities can increase property taxes. In such cases, governments issuing bonds are limited in their ability to raise revenues to make principal and interest payments. In theory, this level of security is different from GOULT bonds. In practice, GOLT bonds may or may not be rated lower than GOULT bonds from the same jurisdiction, depending upon the issuer's overall credit characteristics. A key issue here is how much taxes can be raised until reaching any existing tax limit. If there is substantial room under the limit, the GOLT bonds may be nearly as strong as the GOULT bonds.

There are many advantages to the use of general obligation bonds. Among these advantages is the strength of the pledge backing the issue. The full faith and credit unlimited tax pledge is considered the strongest commitment to repayment available and generally results in the lowest interest cost to the issuer. Another advantage of general obligation bonds is the fiscal restraint and accountability forced upon municipalities, which typically must put such issues to a vote. General obligation bonds are the simplest of bonds to sell, and the easiest to understand. This can result in cost savings for the issuer.

General obligation bonds also have disadvantages associated with them. The most serious of these is the possible overburdening of the full faith and credit pledge that may come with heavy use of this type of debt (Moak 1982). Correspondingly, the reliance upon debt supported by general tax revenues may insulate users from an appreciation of the true costs of a service and inadvertently encourage overuse. Consider the case of a local electric utility. If the capital costs of a municipal electricity-generating station were paid for out of property taxes as opposed to rate payments, rates would be lower and one might expect usage to be higher than if such improvements were supported solely by utility fees.

Along with the restraint that may result from the voter approval requirement of some issues come corresponding sacrifices in flexibility and timing. Waiting for such approval may result in costly delays, particularly when interest rates are moving upward. Finally, the rejection of a particular bond measure by the electorate does not of itself assure the prudent stewardship of a given government's financial resources. The inability of a government to make a compelling case for a particular capital project may not obviate the public need for such improvements.

Lease-Rental Bonds

There are three parties involved in lease-rental debt. The first is the authority or agency issuing the bonds. This party acts as a lessor, leasing some facility or property to a lessee. The second party is the lessee, generally a government that makes payments to the authority or lessor for use of the funded facility. These payments are used to pay the principal and interest on the debt. The third party is the investor who buys the lease-rental bonds and is paid back by the lessor from the lease payments. Ultimately, the lease payments are paid by a government from the proceeds of taxes or other revenues. They may even be secured by the full faith and credit pledge and tax authority of a local government.

Among the general advantages of lease-rental bonds is the ability to borrow outside of the general obligation debt limit. This enables municipalities to maintain the ability to issue GO debt later for other projects. Another potential advantage of this security type is that it typically avoids the process of voter approval associated with general obligation debt in some states. The higher interest rates frequently associated with lease rental bonds is the primary disadvantage related to them (Moak 1982). In addition to the increased costs, such financing may raise concerns with the electorate about circumventing their approval authority in issuing debt.

The key legal document for holders of lease-rental bonds is the lease agreement, since the security for the repayment of the bonds are the lease payments. The provisions for these payments (schedule and sources) are established in the lease agreement. Specific security arrangements vary with the type of lease-rental bond. Several of these are explained here.

Common Examples of Lease-Backed Financing

Certificates of Participation (COPs) are typically used for the purchase or improvement of real property or equipment. COPs are one form of lease-backed financing. Instead of buying bonds, investors purchase certificates entitling them to a share of the lease payments associated with a specific endeavor. The proceeds of the lease payments less operations expenses and reserve payments are paid to investors through a trustee, who issues the certificates, monitors the project and distributes the money back to certificate holders (PSA 1990). The strength of the lease varies from state to state.

In order to avoid a debt classification, the issue normally must be structured in such a way as to avoid the establishment of an unqualified liability to the government. This is accomplished through the use of legal language that limits the government's promise of repayment subject to appropriations and catastrophic events, establishing an agreement similar to a renewable lease. Investors are typically protected by insurance and covenants against cata-

strophic loss. Many municipalities in states with restrictive guidelines for general obligations rely on COPs as they are not considered to be debt. This preserves any GO borrowing limit for other projects.

Single Family Mortgage Revenue Bonds are secured by mortgages and mortgage loan repayments on single family homes. These bonds are sold by a governmental authority or administration (such as the Veterans Administration) that uses mortgage payments as the revenue from which to make principal and interest payments on the debt. In 1968, Congress approved statutes allowing states to create authorities to make available low cost mortgages to homeowners. These provisions promoted an enormous volume of related bond issues. Following the Tax Reform Act of 1986, limits were set on the number of these issues allowed. As a result, volume went from US $37.2 billion in 1985 to US $8.6 billion in 1989 (Marlin and Mysak 1991).

Multifamily mortgage revenue bonds are commonly issued by housing authorities or agencies seeking to establish low income or senior citizen housing. Such borrowing was authorized by the Housing Act of 1937 (Marlin and Mysak 1991). In addition to the rental income (which is generally inadequate to meet operating expenses in addition to principal and interest payments), such arrangements normally include some form of government operating or interest cost subsidies (Feldstein and Fabozzi 1987).

Hospital bonds have been used to support both public and private hospitals and health care facilities. A hospital or hospital authority sells the bonds, which are repaid from the income of hospital services. The debt is typically structured like a mortgage with various provisions established to assure payments from the hospital's revenues, fund-raising, and reserves (Moak 1982). In the case of public and charitable hospitals, such income may be insufficient to cover principal and interest payments. In such instances, some portion of these payments may come from a government's tax contributions.

Public bonding authority is commonly used to issue education bonds for private as well as public institutions of higher education. In many states, separate financing authorities exist that issue the debt backed by the revenue pledge of the institution by rents or mortgages on facilities, the tax pledge of a government, or some combination of these.

Industrial development bonds (IDBs) are used to provide capital for a variety of projects with typically private uses such as airports, industrial parks, or pollution-control facilities. In some instances, a government or authority will lease the facilities to a private enterprise and pay the debt with the proceeds. In other cases, the funds are turned over directly to the private entity using them. The advantage to the private enterprise is the lower interest costs associated with tax-exempt borrowing. The advantage for governments involved in IDBs is generally associated with a perceived public benefit such as improved access to markets, job creation, or cleaner air or water (PSA 1990).

The industrial development bond accounted for 57 percent of the tax-exempt debt sold in 1982 (Marlin and Mysak 1991). This debt was so heavily used for private purposes that the federal government ultimately limited its use through the Tax Reform Act of 1986. This legislation places a cap on the type and amount of private activity debt that can be issued with tax exemptions.

Special Tax Bonds

Special tax bonds are secured by some portion of tax revenues dedicated specifically to them. In such cases, the debt for a capital project might be backed by an excise tax or a sales or income tax. Unlike general obligations, special tax bonds do not carry the unlimited tax pledge of the issuing municipality. As a result, the security is generally considered to be weaker than that of GO debt, and subsequently more expensive (Moody's Investors Service 1991). The use of such a security allows governments to avoid any GO debt limits and leaves the general revenues of a government unencumbered. Special tax bonds may be structured to facilitate the taxation of nonresidents, a practice of great appeal for many voters (Moak 1982).

Enterprise Revenue Bonds

Instead of securing municipal debt as a general obligation of a government, many issuers identify a specific revenue stream related to the borrowing and dedicate it toward the repayment of the debt. These enterprise revenue bonds are paid from the proceeds of governmental enterprises. They are used for a broad variety of revenue-producing purposes such as the building of electric generation facilities, waste water treatment plants, and bridges. The principal and interest payments are made from the fees, rents or tolls associated with such endeavors. Because property taxes are not being used to pay for these projects they often may be approved without a vote of the electorate. Because they do not characterize "debt" in the legal sense (they are not a liability to the government), they do not count toward the debt limits commonly imposed on municipalities (Smith 1979; PSA 1990). These advantages have led to the increased popularity and use of revenue bonds in the United States.

Revenue bonds were initially used for purposes that could be understood in the most narrow interpretation of "revenue-producing" enterprises, such as toll roads and utilities. In an effort to stimulate the construction of public works projects in the 1930s, the Public Works Admin-

istration encouraged state and local governments to approve revenue bonds for broader uses (Aronson and Hilley 1986). As a result of this encouragement and growing statutory limits on borrowing with full faith and credit as security, enterprise revenue bonds as well as lease-rental bonds have grown as a portion of the nation's municipal debt.

Enterprise revenue bonds are structured differently from general obligations. General obligations constitute the full faith and credit pledge of the municipality and back this with specific taxing authority. Revenue bonds pledge a specific revenue stream. The particulars of this security are principally established in the contract between the issuer and the bond holder. This contract, called the bond trust indenture, delineates the flow of funds and any covenants associated with the issue. The flow of funds establishes the order and priority of payment. This language typically indicates the amount of funds to be dedicated to operations, debt service, and reserves. Also indicated is whether bond holders are to be paid first out of the revenues of the endeavor (gross revenue pledge) or after other expenses are paid (net revenue pledge).

In addition to a statement describing the flow of funds, covenants are often included as part of the security structure of enterprise revenue bonds. Such covenants commit the issuer to establishing rates high enough to assure funding for the full variety of ongoing expenses, including debt service (PSA 1990). These expenses might include maintenance, capital reserves, insurance, and other items that may serve to protect the investor.

There are several advantages that enterprise bonds offer, the most significant of which are the conservation of borrowing power, equity, and discipline, which the use of such financing may provide (Moak 1982). Bonds secured by the revenues of a utility or other similar operation leave untouched the general obligation borrowing power of the municipality. The ability to issue general obligation debt in the future may be significant as important or urgent projects arise. Furthermore, the limited use of a government's debt limit is one indicator of financial stability that may contribute to the ease in which a government can sell its debt cheaply.

Enterprise revenue bonds are paid back directly from the proceeds of a government activity. This arrangement is an example of benefit equity, because the users of a service are the ones bearing the cost of the debt, usually in some proportion to their use of the service (see **municipal bonds: policy and strategy**). Because the costs of service are directly associated with the source of financing, a more disciplined spending pattern may be encouraged.

There are also some disadvantages to enterprise revenue bonds. The security of a specific revenue stream may not be considered by investors and rating agencies to be as strong a pledge as the full faith and credit and tax authority of a government. As a result, the interest costs associated with such issues tend to be higher than for general obligations (Moak 1982). Another potential disadvantage of enterprise revenue bonds are the costs associated with their issuance. Because of their complexity, many parties are involved in bringing an enterprise issue to market. These parties may include attorneys, engineers, and financial consultants, to name a few. The money that these participants are paid increases the overall cost of this type of debt.

Double-barrelled bonds are secured by the revenue from some enterprise or lease-rental agreement and further backed by the taxing powers of a municipality. They often carry with them at least some of the legal protections and covenants of revenue bonds. An example of such an arrangement might be a municipal waste water treatment facility that, in addition to water and sewer revenues, backs its bonds with the tax authority of the county in which it resides. These arrangements create a more secure form of debt because of the tax pledge, and the reduced risk associated with them may present lower interest costs for the issuer. Where they are secured by the full faith and credit and the tax pledge of a government they become general obligations, and may or may not be subject to any applicable debt limits or other statutory or constitutional restrictions. In this manner, municipalities using double barrelled bonds may enjoy the best features of each security, gaining the added benefit of a general obligation pledge while being able to exclude the debt from any GO limits (Moody's Investors Service 1991).

Moral Obligation Bonds

Moral obligations are an understanding that a state (or an authority or other) government has a "moral obligation" to appropriate the necessary funds to cover a default of various agencies and authorities. If the government making the moral obligation pledge fails to appropriate adequate funds to repay bond investors, they are not in default, they have simply broken a nonbinding promise. This type of debt has been issued extensively by the State of New York and other states to finance public housing and other projects (Feldstein and Fabozzi 1987; Moak 1982; PSA 1990).

John Mitchell came up with the idea of moral obligations as added security to debt as the bond counsel to New York's Governor Nelson Rockefeller in the 1960s. In an effort to get around the voter approval process and to obtain the lowest possible interest costs for the state, Mitchell attached language to the offerings that indicated New York State's intent to meet bond payments of an agency even though it was not obligated to do so (Marlin and Mysak 1991).

George Marlin and Joe Mysak (1991) quote Mitchell in an interview with the *Bond Buyer* about his role in creating this innovation over 20 years later. After being asked to respond to the concerns of some that moral obligations represent a "form of political elitism that bypasses the voter's right to a referendum or an initiative," Mitchell responded laconically: "That's exactly the purpose of them" (p. 24).

Moral obligations are treated differently by different rating agencies. The Public Securities Association (1990) notes that "Standard and Poor's usually assigns a lower rating to a moral obligation bond than it would assign to a full faith and credit bond of the same guarantor, unless the project can be rated better on its own. Moody's simply ignores the moral obligation and rates the issue on its own pledged revenue support" (p. 127).

BANs, TANs, and RANs

In addition to the long-term debt represented by general obligation and revenue bonds, there exists a variety of short-term or interim debt commonly used by governments as part of their overall debt management strategy. Bond anticipation notes (BANS) are a form of short-term debt issues by governments that are expecting to put together a bond offering in the immediate future. BANs are designed to provide the issuer with temporary capital until the issue is sold. The notes are then paid with the proceeds of the bond sale. In some instances, BANs are issued for a project that needs to be initiated but for which the precise amount of borrowing needed remains undetermined (Moak 1982). This is most common with construction projects where time is a critical element in order to complete building on schedule, but where the total amount of construction loans remains uncertain. BANs are also issued at the other end of a project when delays or expense overruns have created the need for short-term capital that has not been previously anticipated in the original bond issue. Such devices allow a government to continue a project while arranging its long-term financing (Moak 1982; Smith 1979).

Other reasons for the issuance of BANs are circumstances where some legal or technical delay has prevented the completion of a complete general obligation offering, such as the need to hold the issue over to another year to avoid exceeding debt limits in the present period. The debt is secured in these instruments by the issuer's ability to sell long-term securities or substitute new BANs once the current set matures.

Tax anticipation notes (TANs) are another form of short-term debt issued by governments. As the name suggests, this form of financing allows municipalities to borrow against anticipated tax revenues. For many municipalities, taxes are paid only infrequently during the year while expenses accrue continuously. In order to remain faithful to its other financial obligations, a government may find it necessary to issue TANs. This form of debt is secured by a specific tax. At the local level, these are typically property taxes (Smith 1979). The notes are repayable once tax collections are complete.

Revenue anticipation notes (RANs) are issued in anticipation of other revenues such as intergovernmental transfers, excise taxes, or revenue sharing. These notes are secured by the specifically indicated revenue stream and are repaid once those revenues are realized. TANs and RANs are often sold directly to banks.

Tax-Exempt Commercial Paper

Tax-exempt commercial paper (TECP) is another short-term borrowing instrument. TECP is commonly used to provide working capital for governments and government-sponsored projects. The security for this paper is typically a bank letter or line of credit backed up by project revenues or the general obligation pledge of a sponsoring municipality. Unlike tax or revenue anticipation notes, TECP maturities are flexible, usually lasting from periods of 1 to 270 days (Feldstein and Fabozzi 1987). Such flexibility facilitates quick repayment or extensions, based on the needs of the issuer. TECP may also be rolled over any number of times. Because of the short-term nature of these arrangements, interest costs are typically lower than those for longer-term municipal bonds. Due to the complexity and novelty of this kind of security, however, administrative as well as counsel and underwriting costs for TECP may be significantly greater than those associated with more traditional forms of financing (Marlin and Mysak 1991).

MARK D. ROBBINS

BIBLIOGRAPHY

Aronson, J. Richard, and John L. Hilley, 1986. *Financing State and Local Governments,* 4th ed. Washington, DC: Brookings Institution.

Feldstein, Sylvan G., and Frank J. Fabozzi, 1987. *The Dow Jones-Irwin Guide to Municipal Bonds.* Homewood, IL: Dow Jones–Irwin.

Marlin, George J., and Joe Mysak, 1991. *The Guide to Municipal Bonds: The History, the Industry, the Mechanics.* New York: American Banker/Bond Buyer.

Moak, Lennox L., 1982. *Municipal Bonds: Planning, Sale, and Administration.* Chicago: Municipal Finance Officers Association.

Moody's Investors Service, 1991. *Moody's on Municipals: An Introduction to Issuing Debt.* New York: Moody's Investors Service.

Public Securities Association (PSA), 1990. *Fundamentals of Municipal Bonds,* 4th ed. New York: Public Securities Association.

Smith, Wade S., 1979. *The Appraisal of Municipal Credit Risk.* New York: Moody's Investors Service.

MUNICIPAL HOUSEKEEPING.

A term used during the Progressive Reform Period in the United States (c. 1900–1920) to refer to the municipal betterment and reform efforts of middle-class clubwomen—activities so described because women's work for municipal improvement was seen as a natural extension of their primary social role as homemakers and guardians of domestic virtue. Women's clubs, originally formed to drink tea and read great works of literature, soon shifted their focus.

Very early the club women became unwilling to discuss Dante and Browning over the teacups, at a meeting of their peers in some lady's drawing room, while unsightly heaps of rubbish flanked the paths over which they had passed in their journeys thither. They began to realize that the one calling in which they were, as a body, proficient, that of housekeeping and homemaking, had its outdoor as well as its indoor application (Wood 1914, p. 79).

Thus, clubwomen moved into reform activities not by turning away from housework but by widening their understanding of "home."

First steps usually included such activities as neighborhood clean-up days, providing trash buckets, giving prizes for backyard improvement, installing window boxes, or advocating for the establishment of a small park. Gradually, such work grew into campaigns for better garbage collection, eradication of flies and mosquitos, the clearing of alleys, and other sanitation efforts. As women's interests continued to broaden, they took on issues such as pure food and milk, the development of recreational facilities, the conditions of local jails, and occupational safety. Clubwomen helped gather vital statistics, investigated housing conditions, formulated and recommended social welfare measures, raised funds for experimental social programs, and pushed for improvements in local schools. Many women became experts on particular issues and were called on by government officials to study problems and recommend solutions.

Once the conceptual wall between the private, domestic sphere and the public sector was breached, women's reform work led them to increasingly critical perspectives on the conditions in cities. They moved step by step from playgrounds to child labor practices to factory and shop conditions in general, "back to the whole underlying industrial situation, and to the economic conditions which have begotten it" (Woodruff 1912, p. 717). As Mary Ritter Beard (1914) put it, women who once would have been grateful for any sort of water coming out of a faucet, now found their minds reaching out "through the long chain of circumstances that connect the faucet and tub with the gentlemen who sit in aldermanic conclave" (p. 206). Thus, as they realized that the causes of urban ills went beyond what any group of volunteers, no matter how committed, could ameliorate, clubwomen eventually found themselves testifying and lobbying for a wide range of social welfare policies and for administrative efficiencies to support them. In addition, of course, since women had the franchise in only a few states, they redoubled their suffrage campaigns in order to be able to have a more direct say in who would control city governments.

Skocpol (1992) argued that women's clubs, organized in national networks, achieved a unique, cross-class "maternalist political consciousness" that, at a time when U.S. industrial workers were not politically class-conscious, enabled reform women to succeed on a range of issues—mothers' pensions, for example—that extended the social welfare responsibilities of first local, then state and national governments to an extent that men's groups were unable to achieve. "Municipal housekeeping" provided both a legitimating rationale for women's activities and policy proposals and a way of linking together women of differing economic levels, though regrettably not women of different races: African American women, barred from white women's clubs and from the hearing rooms and public meeting platforms to which white women had access, devoted themselves to institution building within their own communities, an activity at which they achieved extraordinary successes.

The attainment of the national franchise for women, with the passage of the Twentieth Amendment to the U.S. Constitution in 1920, had the unfortunate effect of draining energy from women's club reform efforts. In addition, as many of the measures women had sought were implemented as policies, administration of them was taken over largely by men. Chambers (1967) has argued, however, that the efforts of women reformers, both club women and settlement house residents, laid the policy groundwork for a number of key New Deal programs put in place in the 1930s.

CAMILLA STIVERS

BIBLIOGRAPHY

Beard, Mary Ritter, 1914. *Women's Work in Municipalities.* New York: D. Appleton.
Chambers, Clarke A., 1967. *Seedtime of Reform: American Social Service and Social Action 1918-1933.* Ann Arbor, MI: University of Michigan Press.
Hine, Darlene Clark, 1990. "'We Specialize in the Wholly Impossible': The Philanthropic Work of Black Women." In McCarthy, Kathleen D., ed., *Lady Bountiful Revisited: Women, Philanthropy, and Power.* New Brunswick, NJ: Rutgers University Press.
Muncy, Robyn, 1991. *Creating a Female Dominion in American Reform 1890-1935.* New York: Oxford University Press.
Skocpol, Theda, 1992. *Protecting Soldiers and Mothers: The Political Origins of Social Policy in the United States.* Cambridge, MA: Belknap Press of Harvard University Press.
Wood, Mary I., 1914. "Civic Activities of Women's Clubs." *Annals of the American Academy of Political and Social Science,* vol. 56 (November) 78–87.
Woodruff, Clinton Rogers, 1912. "American Municipal Tendencies." *National Municipal Review,* vol. 1, no. 1 (January) 3–20.

MUNICIPAL RESEARCH BUREAUS.

Private, nonprofit organizations established in the early twentieth century to further municipal government reform through research into effective and efficient administrative methods. Typical of Progressivism in its emphasis on fact gathering and science rather than "simple moralism" as bases for advocating governmental reform, the "bureau movement" (Waldo 1948, p. 32) played a key role in the emergence of public administration as a field of scholarly study and professional education.

History

The first municipal research bureau was formed in New York City in 1906. At that time, nearly 250 nonpartisan good government organizations were calling for the reform of U.S. city governments dominated by political machines like New York's Tammany Hall; but their efforts were blocked by party success in winning elections and filling government agencies with party loyalists. A somewhat reform-minded New York mayor had formed a commission on financial administration and accounting; its investigative efforts, however, were blocked by agency incumbents not eager to submit their work to the scrutiny of what they considered meddling do-gooders. In a brilliant end-run around the bureaucracy, the fledgling New York Bureau conducted a field study of the condition of New York streets, comparing them with available information about repair contracts. Bureau director Henry Bruere, who led the study, found that many streets recorded as repaired had had no work done; in some cases, streets that were supposed to have been repaved several times had no paving at all. Study results, published as a pamphlet entitled "How Manhattan Is Governed," hit New York like a bombshell, leading to an investigation and the eventual forced resignation of the Manhattan borough president.

Success in New York quickly produced similar bureaus in a host of other cities: for example, Philadelphia, Cincinnati, Chicago, Dayton, Milwaukee, Minneapolis, Akron, Kansas City, and San Francisco. With some ebbs and flows in their fortunes occasioned by World War I and the depression, municipal research bureaus remained active until the 1940s, when universities, legislatures, and state and local governments began to establish their own research institutes, whose activities gradually diminished the perceived need for private, nonprofit organizations in this arena.

Typical Activities

Municipal research bureaus were engaged in a wide range of efforts, including the development of municipal budgeting and uniform accounting methods; the establishment of guidelines for statistical charts; standardization of personnel procedures such as time sheets, job descriptions, work routines, performance tests, and retirement systems; the design of organization charts; uniform crime statistics; in-service training of city employees; revamped billing procedures for water systems; improved garbage collection and sanitary inspection methods; improved purchasing and inventory control procedures; reforms in housing inspection, milk inspection, and medical inspection of school children; and the systematization of records in all areas of government.

The centerpiece of bureau activity, however, was the establishment of the executive budget. The first public budget in the United States was adopted by the New York City Department of Health in 1907 after a study by the New York Bureau demonstrated the need for it. At that time, government expenditures were generally authorized on a piecemeal basis and appropriations made without reference to available revenues or projected expenses; special revenue bonds took care of revenue shortfalls. In general, the bureaus saw the lack of an executive budget as the root cause of inefficient administration; as a result, budgeting became perhaps their central concern. Out of it, they developed an entire political philosophy that entailed shifting power from the legislature to the chief executive in order for the latter to be able to propose and execute effective policies.

Citizen education was another of the bureaus' key activities on the theory that informed citizens would hold governments accountable and demand economy and effective use of tax dollars. Thus, many of the bureaus published periodic bulletins describing their activities and findings, bureau staff members addressed civic groups, and some bureaus maintained public information services. Combining public education with their interest in budgeting, some bureaus organized budget exhibits, displaying graphs that showed the costs and benefits of various government activities, as well as more tangible items like 6-cent hat hooks for which the city government had paid US $0.65 apiece. The first exhibit, held in New York City in 1908, was attended by 50,000 people and received considerable press coverage.

Philosophy

Despite its rhetoric of nonpartisan neutrality, the bureau movement had a well-developed political philosophy with a clear set of values. Perhaps the most central was the idea that democratic accountability in governmental administration required not just good men but good methods as well—hence their emphasis on the objective, scientific study of administrative procedure in order to achieve maximum efficiency and effectiveness. Scientific study was believed to develop factual information about government operations that would enable citizens to hold officials accountable for the expenditure of tax dollars.

A related belief was the value of expertise. Government activities should be conducted by people who were chosen not on the basis of their loyalty to a particular party but according to their knowledge and skills. Effective government, based on factual analysis and rational planning, would require professionalism based on training and administrative experience.

Belief in science and expertise led bureau partisans to develop a theory of government that moved away from the separated powers, checks and balances theory of the framers of the Constitution, toward a view of government that emphasized the need for centralized control and rational decisionmaking, hence the desirability of a stronger chief executive. Adopting the idea of a dichotomy between politics and administration, especially as formulated by Frank Goodnow's *Politics and Administration* (1900), adherents of the bureau philosophy saw separated powers as weakening the executive branch by depriving it of a policy role; therefore, they called for such reforms as the executive budget and staff-versus-line distinctions in order to make it possible for the executive to centralize and rationalize control over government processes.

Several observers, including Donald Stone and Alice Stone (1975) and Frederick Mosher (1968), view the bureau movement as the source of scholarly research in public administration. Emphasis on the importance of facts and objective analysis, together with the use of field research into administrative processes, produced a prototype form of systematic investigation that became the model for scholarly work once university public administration programs were established.

Professional Education

Early on, the bureau emphasis on scientific and managerial expertise produced a parallel interest in training administrators for government work. The spread of the bureau movement from its New York source to other cities also created a felt need for experts in municipal research and analysis.

In 1911, the New York Bureau established the Training School for Public Service with the help of a donation from Mrs. E. H. Harriman. The initial class of 25 students included several engineers, businessmen, a lawyer, a school superintendent, and 8 Ph.D.s. The students were given specific work assignments, generally involving them directly in city agencies. Each students was required to participate in the budgetmaking process, to take an accountancy course, and to do routine administrative work for the Bureau itself. No official time limit for the training was set, though two years was considered advisable. Over time the amount of required reading increased, and formal lectures were introduced. In 1921, the Training School and the Bureau were reorganized as the National Institute of Public Administration, under the leadership of Luther Gulick.

Many graduates of the Training School became directors or staff members of other research bureaus, producing considerable continuity and uniformity of interest and approach across the entire bureau movement. In addition, Dahlberg (1966) credits the New York Training School with being the catalyst for university education in public administration. In 1914, the University of Michigan established a Master of Arts degree in public administration, a program headed by former New York Bureau men. Dr. Gulick provided important advice to the nascent Maxwell School of Citizenship and Public Affairs at Syracuse University and selected its first dean, William E. Mosher, who had taught at the Training School. The first Maxwell School class consisted of Training School students who transferred there along with Mosher. Thus, the Training School can be considered the seedbed for modern public administration education.

CAMILLA STIVERS

BIBLIOGRAPHY

Crane, R. T., 1923. "Research Agencies and Equipment." *American Political Science Review,* vol. 42 (May) 295–303.

Dahlberg, Jane, 1966. *The New York Bureau of Municipal Research: Pioneer in Government Administration.* New York: New York University Press.

Gaus, John M., 1930. *A Survey of Research in Public Administration.* New York: Social Science Research Council.

Gill, Norman N., 1944. *Municipal Research Bureaus: A Study of the Nation's Leading Citizen-Supported Agencies.* Washington, DC: American Council on Public Affairs.

Goodnow, Frank J., 1900. *Politics and Administration.* New York: Macmillan.

Mosher, Frederick C., 1968. *Democracy and the Public Service.* New York: Oxford University Press.

Stone, Donald C., and Alice B. Stone, 1975. "Early Development of Education in Public Administration." In Frederick C. Mosher, ed., *American Public Administration: Past, Present, Future.* Tuscaloosa: University of Alabama Press, 11–48.

Waldo, Dwight, 1948. *The Administrative State.* New York: Ronald Press.

MUTUAL BENEFIT ORGANIZATION.   A private, nonprofit group whose primary or exclusive purpose is to benefit or represent the individuals or entities that are members of the group.

In 1993, there were approximately 1.2 million tax-exempt organizations registered with the U.S. Internal Revenue Service, not including about 300,000 religious congregations, which are not required to register, and including about 400,000 entities other than "charitable" or "public benefit" nonprofit organizations, most of which are classified under Internal Revenue Code section 501(c)(3). These other groups are referred to in the legal systems of several states as "mutual benefit organizations" (MBOs). Principal types of MBOs include fraternal beneficiary societies, labor and agricultural organizations, business leagues and chambers of commerce, social and recreation clubs, pension funds and credit unions, and veterans' groups. The legal distinction between public and mutual benefit derives from the primary purpose of the organization, but in practice there is much mixing of the two: Many charitable nonprofits include some private benefit, and many mutual benefit nonprofits help nonmembers (O'Neill 1994; Smith 1991, 1993). Religious congregations include characteristics of both mutual benefit and public benefit organizations (Smith 1991; Biddle 1992, p. 93).

History

Anthropologists have documented the existence of voluntary associations with many of the characteristics of MBOs as far back as the neolithic period, beginning in the seventh or eighth millennium B.C.E. (Anderson 1971; Banton 1968; Kerri 1974; Lowie 1948; Ross 1976; Smith and Freedman 1972). Ancient China, Egypt, Greece, and Rome had merchants' associations, cooperative loan societies, associations for visiting the sick and burying the dead, religious cults, and clublike groups. The medieval period saw the widespread development of merchant and craft guilds, occupation-based groups that provided to their members many work-related and other benefits. The demise of the guilds in Europe and England opened the way for the "friendly societies," workingmen's associations that performed many of the functions that the guilds had (Gosden 1974).

In seventeenth- and eighteenth-century America, population dispersion and colonial status discouraged associational activity. The few voluntary associations of the preindependence period—such as the Scots Charitable Society (1657), the Massachusetts Charitable Society (1672), the Charitable Irish Society (1737), and the fire societies of the eighteenth century—exhibited a combination of public-benefit and mutual-benefit purposes. After independence, and as the nation experienced mass immigration, the rapid growth of cities, and westward expansion, Americans created a large array of voluntary associations, many of which would now be termed MBOs. All social classes, women and men, immigrants and the host society, whites and minorities created MBOs for self-improvement, companionship, business and social advancement, protection against sudden economic loss, protection against discrimination, and other purposes. Some MBOs, like today's self-help groups, focused on members' personal problems. For instance, by 1835 there were 1.2 million members of the American Temperance Society in 8,000 local affiliates.

Fraternal beneficiary societies played several important roles, especially among the lower social classes. Immigrants and people of color formed mutual benefit societies to maintain their cultural heritage, find jobs and apartments, get insurance and credit, socialize, gain protection against discrimination, and be assured of a proper burial.

Agriculture, labor, and business organizations grew rapidly, especially following the Civil War. One example was the Order of Patrons of Husbandry, more commonly known as the Grange, founded in 1867; by 1875, there were 800,000 Grange members in 20,000 local chapters. Workingmen's associations and labor unions, as well as business leagues and chambers of commerce, proliferated throughout the United States.

The nineteenth and early twentieth centuries also saw the development of many social and recreational organizations such as private clubs, self-improvement associations, and "service" clubs such as the Rotary, Kiwanis, Elks, and Knights of Columbus.

Trade and professional associations were established during this period, including the American Statistical Association (1839), the American Ethnological Society (1842), the American Medical Association (1847), the American Society of Engineers and Architects (1852), the American Entomological Society (1859), and the American Bar Association (1878). These MBOs represented and provided benefits to their members as well as performing public benefit functions such as research and development, professional education and training, licensing and accreditation, publications and conferences for members and for the general public and scholarship and fellowship programs.

Veterans' organizations grew out of each of the nation's wars, providing mechanisms for members to cope with the effects of, and sometimes prolong, their shared military experiences.

In recent decades, new types of MBOs have been added, including homeowner associations, computer clubs, and self-help groups of many types. However, among incorporated nonprofits, the rate of growth of MBOs was only 22 percent from 1976 to 1993, compared with a growth rate of 86 percent for public benefit organizations (Internal Revenue Service 1978, p. 101; Internal Revenue Service 1993, Table 25). The "nation of joiners" syndrome that Alexis de Tocqueville had discussed and Sinclair Lewis' "Babbit" had pilloried, was clearly in decline.

Current Dimensions

While federal law on tax-exempt entities does not use the term "mutual benefit organization," Table I presents U.S. statistics on the types and numbers of incorporated nonprofit organizations recognized by several states as MBOs. (It is also useful to remember that there are many unincorporated voluntary associations—ostomy and cancer self-help groups, women's consciousness-raising groups, book clubs, neighborhood associations, and the like—that function in a way similar to incorporated MBOs. The number of such MBO associations is estimated to be in the hundreds of thousands, or even millions, in the United States [Gartner and Reissman 1994; Smith 1984].

Fraternal beneficiary societies remain the largest type of MBO, numbering about 115,000 organizations combining 501(c)(8) and 501(c)(10). Although such societies are commonly associated with the mass immigration periods of the nineteenth and early twentieth centuries, and with the values and customs of a less urbanized "main street" America, they are still a major presence. However, the number of such organizations has declined by 25 percent since 1976 (Internal Revenue Service 1978, p. 101; Internal Revenue Service 1993, Table 25).

Reflecting the downward trend in organized labor that has been documented in many studies, the number of labor and agriculture MBOs [501(c)(5)] has dropped by 20 percent since the mid-1970s. The number of business leagues [501(c)(6)], by contrast, grew by 75 percent during the same period and now stands as the second largest type of MBO.

The third largest type of MBO is that of social and recreation clubs [501(c)(7)], the number of which grew by 36 percent since 1976. Veterans' organizations [501(c)(19)], the fourth largest type, grew in number by 40 percent in the fifteen years between 1978 and 1993. Employee benefit associations [501(c)(9)] constitute the fifth largest type and have also been growing steadily since the mid-1970s.

Financial Statistics

Table II presents selected financial information on MBOs reporting to the U.S. Internal Revenue Service in 1990.

In 1990, these five types of MBOs had assets of US $105 billion and revenue of about US $100 billion. This compares with 1990 assets of US $732 billion and revenue

TABLE I. Non-501(c)(1) to (c)(4) Tax-Exempt Organizations Registered with Internal Revenue Service, 1993

Internal Revenue Code Section 501(c)		No. of Organizations
(5)	Labor, agriculture, horticulture orgs.	70,416
(6)	Business leagues, chambers of commerce, etc.	72,901
(7)	Social and recreation clubs	64,924
(8)	Fraternal beneficiary societies	93,728
(9)	Voluntary employees' beneficiary societies	15,048
(10)	Domestic fraternal beneficiary societies	20,827
(11)	Teachers' retirement funds	11
(12)	Benevolent life insurance associations	6,177
(13)	Cemetery companies	9,184
(14)	Credit unions	5,637
(15)	Mutual insurance companies	1,165
(16)	Corporations to finance crop operation	22
(17)	Supplemental unemployment benefit trusts	611
(18)	Employee funded pension trusts	4
(19)	War veterans' organizations	29,974
(20)	Legal service organizations	213
(21)	Black lung benefit trusts	22
(22)	Mutli-employer pension plans	0
(23)	Veterans associations (created before 1880)	2
(24)	Trusts described in section 4049 of ERISA	1
(25)	Holding companies for pensions, etc.	374
501(d)	Religious and apostolic organizations	96
501(e)	Cooperative hospital service organizations	69
501(f)	Cooperative service organizations of operating educational organizations	1
521(a)	Farmers' cooperative associations	1,950
Total		393,357

SOURCE: Internal Revenue Service, *Annual Report*, 1993, Table 25.

of US $461 billion for public benefit [501(c)(3) and 501(c)(4)] organizations, not counting private foundations and religious organizations (Hilgert 1994). By far the largest MBO revenue recipients were the employee benefit associations [501(c)(9)], with revenue of US $55 billion. It is interesting to note that fraternal beneficiary societies [501(c)(8)] have an asset-revenue ratio of 4:1, quite unlike the other four categories. This may reflect the accumulated historical wealth of such entities as well as recent decline in membership.

Activities and Societal Role

Much has been written about the activities and societal role of certain types of MBOs, such as labor unions, chambers of commerce, immigrant mutual aid societies, elite social clubs, and veterans organizations. The range of MBO activity parallels the wide diversity of nonprofit

public benefit work. For instance, some trade and professional associations wield great political power, while other MBOs, like small burial associations, are virtually ignored by the wider society. A Hudson Institute study commissioned by the American Society of Association Executives found that trade and professional associations engage in lobbying and other government relations, member and public education, training, research, conventions and other meetings, setting and enforcing standards, formulating professional and ethical codes, and a variety of other activities (*Value* 1990). The report also argued that trade and professional associations improve the functioning of the market system by increasing the quantity and quality of information available to consumers on the market's goods and services, for example, the quality of various types of engine oil. The report also argued that some associations, such as the American Medical Association, protect the public by standards, licensing, education and train-

TABLE II. SELECTED FINANCIAL DATA ON MUTUAL BENEFIT ORGANIZATIONS, 1990

(FIGURES IN US $000)

I.R.C. Section 501(c)	Assets	Revenue	Expenses
(5)	13,718,661	12,351,900	12,651,595
(6)	19,320,022	18,038,500	18,160,585
(7)	9,343,543	6,089,846	6,178,570
(8)	29,993,563	7,230,390	7,071,160
(9)	33,011,258	55,189,838	54,044,660
Totals	105,387,047	98,900,480	98,106,570

SOURCE: Cecilia Hilgert, 1994, "Charities and Others Tax-Exempt Organizations, 1990," *Statistics of Income Bulletin*, vol. 14, no. 2 (Fall), Tables 1 and 2.

ing, research, and practitioner regulation. Others, of course, take a somewhat more skeptical view of such matters and view trade and professional associations as working to benefit their members at all costs, including costs to consumers and the public.

Member education is a prime focus of trade and professional organizations. These associations annually sponsor hundreds of thousands of conventions, seminars, and workshops on everything from truck tire quality to the information superhighway. Research and publications aimed at both members and the general public are also principal activities of these MBOs. Ethical and professional codes have been present in some occupational groups (physicians, social workers, accountants) for many years; code-making is a significant activity in associations. There are codes for engineers, realtors, optometrists, city managers, police officers, plastic surgeons, and insurance agents.

Lobbying is an important activity in many MBOs. Not only the oil and computer industries but also music publishers and physical therapists fill the halls of Congress and state legislatures with lobbyists. MBOs file lawsuits, testify before congressional subcommittees, donate to political causes and candidates, and spend millions attempting to persuade the public of their point of view. There are widely different perceptions of such MBO activity. Some, in the tradition of James Madison's attack on "factions," see MBO lobbying as pernicious self-interest; others view it as generally beneficial to the political system, analogues to the role MBOs play in the market system.

Although by definition established primarily to benefit their members, MBOs also engage in public benefit work. MBOs create scholarships and student loan programs; give aid to camps, libraries, archives, hospitals, churches, museums, schools, and colleges; support institutions for the blind, orphans, retarded children, handicapped, aged, war victims, and substance abusers; donate to medical research, disaster relief, and international assistance programs; and

provide volunteer service of many types. Social and "service" clubs such as the Shriners, Elks, and Kiwanis support many public benefit programs. For instance, in an effort to fight drug abuse, "Kiwanis International . . . mounted a far-reaching public awareness campaign, using 5,500 billboards, 500 prime-time network airings of a public service announcement, a 14-week radio series, and advertising in *Time, Newsweek,* and *Sports Illustrated*" (*Value* 1990, p. 104). Chambers of commerce and other business-related MBOs provide technical expertise, meeting space, mailing lists, and other assistance to charitable nonprofits.

Any discussion of mutual benefit organizations must, however, begin and end with the role these groups play in providing economic, social, and other benefits to members, whether the members are individuals or organizations. For example, the fastest-growing type of MBO, in terms of revenue, is the 501(c)(9) voluntary employee beneficiary association; through group benefit plans, these entities provide economic benefits to their members. While both history and present practice illustrate the difficulty of separating completely the mutual benefit and public benefit functions, MBOs are, true to their name, principally and sometimes exclusively involved in providing certain specific benefits for their members.

MICHAEL O'NEILL

BIBLIOGRAPHY

Anderson, R. T., 1971. "Voluntary Associations in History." *American Anthropologist*, vol. 73, no.: 1: 209–222.

Banton, M., 1968. "Voluntary Associations: Anthropological Aspects." In D. L. Sills, ed., *International Encyclopedia of the Social Sciences*. New York: Macmillan.

Biddle, J. E., 1992. "Religious Organizations." In C. T. Clotfelter, ed., *Who Benefits from the Nonprofit Sector?* Chicago: University of Chicago Press.

Gartner, A., and F. Reissman, eds., 1984. *The Self-Help Revolution.* New York: Human Sciences Press.

Gosden, P. H. J. H., 1974. *Self-Help: Voluntary Associations in 19th-Century Britain.* New York: Barnes and Noble.

Hilgert, Cecilia, 1994. "Charities and Other Tax-Exempt Organizations, 1990." *Statistics of Income Bulletin*, vol. 14, no. 2 (Fall) 132–138.

Internal Revenue Service, 1978. *Annual Report: Commissioner of Internal Revenue.* Washington, DC: Internal Revenue Service.

———, 1993. *Annual Report: Commissioner of Internal Revenue.* Washington, DC: Internal Revenue Service.

Kerri, J. N., 1974. "Anthropological Studies of Voluntary Associations and Voluntary Action: A Review." *Journal of Voluntary Action Research*, vol. 3, no. 1: 10–25.

Lowie, R. H., 1948. *Social Organization.* New York: Rinehart.

O'Neill, Michael, 1994. "Philanthropic Dimensions of Mutual Benefit Organizations." *Nonprofit and Voluntary Sector Quarterly*, vol. 23, no. 1 (Spring) 3–20.

Ross, J. C., 1976. "Anthropological Studies of Voluntary Associations and Voluntary Action: A Reassessment." *Journal of Voluntary Action Research*, vol. 5, no. 1: 27–32.

Smith, C., and A. Freedman, 1972. *Voluntary Associations: Perspectives on the Literature*. Cambridge, MA: Harvard University Press.

Smith, D. H., 1991. "Four Sectors or Five? Retaining the Membership Sector." *Nonprofit and Voluntary Sector Quarterly*, vol. 20, no. 2: 137–150.

———, 1993. "Public Benefit and Member Benefit Nonprofit, Voluntary Groups." *Nonprofit and Voluntary Sector Quarterly*, vol. 22, no. 1: 53–68.

The Value of Associations to American Society: A Report by the Hudson Institute, 1990. Washington, DC: American Society of Association Executives.

N

NATIONAL CHARITIES INFORMATION BUREAU (NCIB).

An independent, nonprofit organization that encourages informed charitable giving by evaluating and reporting on the performance and behavior of major charities soliciting contributions or operating in the United States. The NCIB, itself a charitable organization (under section 501(c)(3) of the Internal Revenue Service Code), is one of several "watchdog" organizations operating in the United States (see also **Philanthropic Advisory Service**). These watchdog organizations all seek to educate and inform potential donors and encourage ethical and responsible behavior by charities and other nonprofit organizations.

The NCIB was founded in 1918 by national leaders wishing to ensure that Americans' contributions to war relief and similar charitable organizations were used well and responsibly. The mission of the NCIB, as stated in its "Wise Giving Guide," (p. 2) is to promote informed giving. "The NCIB believes that donors are entitled to accurate information about the charitable organizations that seek their support. NCIB also believes that well-informed givers will ask questions and make judgments that will lead to an improved level of performance by charitable organizations."

The NCIB judges an organization's accountability and performance by applying its "NCIB Standards in Philanthropy," a set of nine criteria developed in the late 1980s to become the basis for assessing governance, policymaking, financial management, and reporting. In keeping with the emphasis of financial accountability, many of the standards focus on the organization's willingness to maintain and share complete, accurate, and verifiable financial information. The Standards in Philanthropy in effect in 1994 comprise the following (consult with the NCIB for the most current and complete statements of its standards):

(1) Board Governance: The board is responsible for policy setting, fiscal guidance, and ongoing governance and should regularly review the organization's policies, programs, and operations. The standard specifies several subcriteria by which to assess governance, including no compensation for board service.

(2) Purpose: The organization's purpose, approved by the board, should be formally and specifically stated.

(3) Programs: The organization's activities should be consistent with its statement of purpose.

(4) Information: Promotion, fund-raising, and public information should describe accurately the organization's identity, purpose, programs, and financial needs.

(5) Financial Support and Related Activities: The board is accountable for all authorized activities generating financial support on the organization's behalf. Three subcriteria further detail this standard, including open disclosure of all program and financial information for the organization and any subsidiaries.

(6) Use of Funds: The organization's use of funds should reflect consideration of current and future needs and resources in planning for program continuity. Subcriteria further specify that a charity should spend at least 60 percent of its annual expenses on program activities, not have excessive fund-raising costs, maintain net assets for the following year that do not exceed twice the current year's expenses or the next year's budget (whichever is greater), and not have a significant deficit in the unrestricted fund balance.

(7) Annual Reporting: An annual report should be available on request and key elements are identified that should be included in such a report, including audited financial statements or a comprehensive financial summary.

(8) Accountability: An organization should supply on request complete financial statements; four elements of such accountability are specified:
   - preparation of financial information in conformity with generally accepted accounting principles (GAAP), accompanied by a report of an independent certified public accountant and reviewed by the charity's board;
   - full disclosure of economic resources and obligations, including transactions with related parties and affiliated organizations;
   - statement of functional allocation of expenses;
   - a national organization with local affiliates should prepare combined financial statements of such financial information.

(9) Budget: The organization should prepare a detailed annual budget consistent with the major classifications in the audited financial statements; the budget should then be approved by the board.

The NCIB standards are intended to offer a common measure of accountability and management for all charities, although young organizations (i.e., less than three years old) and those with less than US $100,000 in annual budget are granted somewhat greater leeway in meeting the standards. The NCIB monitors charities by reviewing information from a variety of documents, ranging from charities' annual reports, IRS tax returns, and audited financial statements to solicitation scripts and funder contracts. It also asks subject charities to complete disclosure forms on board and staff members and their compensation. Evaluated charities are offered an opportunity to review and respond to the NCIB's report on them.

Over 300 detailed reports on charities were prepared by the NCIB in 1994, according to bureau officials, and over 75 percent of these met all of the 9 standards. Detailed evaluative reports present information on a given charity's programs, board chair and staff executive names, budget and salary ranges, analysis of financial statements, tax deductibility, and the NCIB's own evaluation of the charity. NCIB also tracks several hundred other charities, but does not prepare such detailed reports.

Funding for the NCIB comes primarily from contributions, plus a minimal amount of earned income. The NCIB's annual report states that its 1994 annual budget was US $1.14 million. Forty-six percent of the bureau's revenue was from individual contributors, and nearly all remaining revenue was from foundations and corporations with giving programs.

The NCIB communicates with the public and potential donors via reports on specific nonprofit organizations and via its quarterly publication, the "Wise Giving Guide." The National Charities Information Bureau may be contacted at

19 Union Square West
New York, New York 10003
(212) 929–6300

DAVID O. RENZ

BIBLIOGRAPHY

National Charities Information Bureau, 1994. "Wise Giving Guide." New York: National Charities Information Bureau.

NATIONAL INTEREST. The basic term deployed by foreign policymakers to describe the long-term core, collective objectives of the state. Generally, in descending order of priority, the collective objectives are deemed to comprise the security and survival of the state, economic prosperity and wealth maximization, and the sustenance and propagation of the social and political values of the society of the state. Normally, governments will claim that these objectives constitute the fundamental, immutable interests of all the citizens of the state, regardless of social rank, party political affiliation, or wealth. These nationwide, collective objectives are seen to reflect the vital interests of the whole state whereas the sectional objectives of subnational groups probably do not. There may be occasions when the interests of some sectional groups could be in the wider interests of the collective citizenry of the state, but this is normally not the case. Often the interests of sectional groups compete, and the successful achievement of one group's interests damage another group. A simple example of this would be a tariff on imports to protect a domestic industry that would raise the price of such goods to the customers requiring that product. Such clashes of interests prevent any simple aggregation of sectional interests constituting the national interest.

Nonetheless, as the term national interest is imbued with a high ethical condition, sectional groups like to attach the epithet to their side of any argument. Clearly, what is in the national interest in any debate over free trade versus protectionism in the case of any single industry is far from obvious and may be very ambiguous. Yet, the alacrity with which protagonists in domestic political and economic controversies claim that the national interest is on their side contributes to the cynicism surrounding the whole notion and the suspicions about the validity of the concept even when deployed by national governments. Owing to the supposed moral virtue of the condition known as national interest, governments throughout the international system are inclined to damage the integrity of the concept by attaching it to short-term foreign policies, which may be of less than vital interest to the state and may be mutually contradictory, in attempts to win popular support. National interest is a term liable to exploitation by governments and interest groups of all political complexions. Of course, how accurate an accusation of exploitation may be usually depends upon which side any commentator takes on any argument.

But even if the term national interest is restricted to perceived, core, long-term, collective objectives, there are grounds for controversy and debate. The so-called collective objectives may have inherent inner contradictions or may be incompatible. In the Realist School of international politics, national security is at the heart of national interest, and the quest for power is a perpetual national interest in order to address state security needs. However, more liberal schools would argue that the unceasing search for power advantage over other states may, in many instances, create more enemies than it deters. In other words, to assign national security priority as a national interest may be to the detriment of national security. Indeed, there may be incompatibilities between the core, collective objectives. The "guns versus butter" debate in nearly all modern societies illustrates this point. To what extent defense spending, while enhancing military security, damages civilian economic growth and social welfare provision was a salient domestic political issue throughout the cold war and remains so to this day. Another instance of how problematic it may be to reconcile incompatibilities in the collective objectives of national interest is the question of individual freedoms in a national security state. Sustaining the traditional freedoms of individual expression, freedom of movement and employment, and open, accountable government is normally deemed a national interest of Western democracies, yet the exigencies of total war and cold war illustrated the incompatibility of these values with the survival of the state.

There is the assumption that the bland, core objectives of national interest have been constant throughout the evolution of the state system and are immutable. Some critics argue that this is a false impression and that there may be occasions when the interests of the citizens of a state may not be in the continuance of the state. It is quite conceivable that it would benefit a national society more to integrate voluntarily with a neighboring state than to continue as a separate state, as happened when Scotland chose parliamentary union with England in 1707 and the young republic of Texas supported annexation by the United States in 1845. The very close strategic, economic, and cultural links between many states in the contemporary international system make the debate over survival of the state as a real national interest a practical as well as an academic issue, not least within West Europe.

Increasing economic and social regionalization in the Western developed world does pose a genuine conundrum over the exact role of the traditional state in serving its citizens needs, especially when the needs and demands of citizens are going through such a rapid transition. There is a respectable argument that free access to a wider employment market better serves the needs of a West European or North American citizen at the turn of the twentieth century than a strong national defense policy. There is a strong political lobby within the European Union, including many national governments, which chooses to interpret national interest as best served by increasing political and economic integration, aimed at the decline of the old European nation-states as viable sovereign entities. This liberal view sees the state as merely an instrument to satisfy the needs of the citizens, and if the citizens needs can be better served outside the state, then it is in the national interest for the state to wither. The contrary, conservative argument, which may be entitled the "Hegelian" view, is that the state is the supreme guarantor of citizens' rights and prospects and that any development that weakens the power of the state is against the national interest. In their fundamentals, the two camps contribute to the confusion about what national interest really is, but sometimes compromise may be achieved. Conservative foreign policy makers may identify some ways to strengthen the state by allowing some concessions to external organizations. To date, British membership of the European Union may be seen in this light, but clearly there is a strong lobby across British political life that would see further concessions beyond the 1992 Treaty of Maastricht as weakening the British state and hence against the British national interest. Liberal foreign policy makers may pull back from the strategy that cooperation best serves the citizens and retreat to strengthen the state when dire threats against the well-being of the people are identified. In the late 1930s, after a generation of foreign policy makers had put their faith in disarmament, appeasement and collective security, Britain hastily rearmed in the face of the Nazi threat.

However, generally, political leaders are guided by their intuitive notions of national interest. The conservative inclines to strengthening the state and defending against threats. If international conditions are hostile to core objectives, then power will be sought and deployed to attempt to change these conditions. Only in stable, predictable circumstances will a more liberal interpretation of national interest be considered. The instinct of the small liberal, or "Kantian," foreign policy maker is to look to cooperation and association as an answer to threats to the values and needs of the citizenry. In modern times, this worldview is fueled by the rash of transnational challenges such as environmental pollution, international terrorism, and cross-border criminality, which appear beyond the capabilities of any single state or even ad hoc coalitions to manage. Only in the most dangerous of circumstances is there an expedient retreat into a robust, nationalistic defense posture.

What constitutes the values of a state is another area of dispute over the nature of national interest. In the modern world of social movement and transition, the exact, or even general, moral, religious, and ideological characteristics the protection of which contributes to a country's national interest is more open to debate than ever. This is particularly the case in heterogeneous democracies, of which the United States is the best example. Whether or not the United States should proactively encourage the spread of democracy in the post–cold war world or, automatically, combat militant Islamic revivalism wherever it challenges secular government are but two contemporary issues that illustrate the quandaries that surround the values component of United States national interest.

Whatever the core, collective objective is deemed to be, who makes that decision is a further feature of the concept of national interest open to question. Critics often argue that a salient weakness in the concept derives from the narrowness of the elite who decides what constitutes national interest. The high foreign policy pursued in the national interest is determined by a small band of the politically influential. This is particularly so in the nondemocratic societies but is also usually the case in democracies as well. Claiming special expertise and privileged access to information, determining national interest is in the hands of a small elite of political leaders and government officials, sometimes influenced by their peer group in business, the media, and academic life. It is this elite that has established and perpetuated the ranking of national security first, economic advancement second, and national values third as the core, collective objectives of national interest for most states. An "interested public" of no more than approximately 10 percent of the population concurs with this framework and, most of the rest of the time, the vast bulk of the nation pursue their lives oblivious to what the elite has decided is in their national interest. Only in peculiar and rare circumstances, when the high costs of a foreign policy seem to outweigh any advantages, does a nation exhibit a mass influence on what is deemed to be in the national interest. Such an instance was the widespread opposition to the United States ground war in Vietnam in the late 1960s.

However, it should not be assumed that foreign policy elites always have coherent, lucid conceptions of what is the national interest. Most of the time, they inherit traditional frameworks and view the outside world through prisms bequeathed by their country's history. Most foreign policy makers are too busy responding to immediate pressures to work out new collective objectives and devise grand strategies to achieve them. Some notable exceptions to this trend have existed. Arguably, Napoleon Bonaparte, Adolf Hitler, Charles de Gaulle, and perhaps Presidents Reagan and Gorbachev devised their own distinctive, coherent vision of national interest, but most foreign policies are no more than ad hoc responses in the light of a general awareness of the national interest rather than major redefinitions of that national interest.

The national interest is a vague and abstract concept over which there has been prolonged scholarly debate. At first sight, the notion of a clutch of core, collective objectives for a state seems self-evident and self-supporting. But upon a closer examination, there are some inherent contradictions, incompatibilities, competing perspectives, and mistaken assumptions permeating the general concept. Awareness of these conceptual weaknesses causes some observers to suspect frequent political manipulation of what may be an emotive symbol for the mass of the uninformed public. Nonetheless, despite conceptual inadequacies and accusations of ruthless exploitation, political leaders and foreign policy makers insist that there is such a thing as the national interest, whether it is a set of vague ideals or a catalog of vital objectives, and that they know it when they meet it.

JAMES H. WYLLIE

BIBLIOGRAPHY

Dougherty, James E., and Robert L. Pfaltzgraff, Jr., 1990. *Contending Theories of International Relations.* New York: HarperCollins.

Frankel, Joseph, 1973. *International Politics, Conflict, and Harmony.* Harmondsworth: Pelican.

Holsti, K. J., 1974. *International Politics, A Framework for Analysis.* London: Prentice-Hall International.

Kegley, Jr., Charles W., and Eugune R. Wittkopf, 1993. *World Politics, Trend, and Transition.* New York: St. Martin's.

Reynolds, Philip A., 1971. *An Introduction to International Relations.* London: Longman.

Taylor, Trevor, ed., 1978. *Approaches and Theory in International Relations.* London: Longman.

NATIONAL SECURITY. The objective of protecting and preserving the state. In whatever kind of collective unit mankind has found itself, the safety of that unit from destruction or conquest has been the oldest preoccupation of leaderships. This has been the case whether the units have been small tribes, city-states, large nations, or empires. The behavior of states engaged in the recent cold war clearly illustrated this classic maxim of government. The cold war is over, there is a variety of less well-defined threats, and public discussion of protection of the state has diminished. Yet, a major feature of state behavior has been the cautious and gradual readjustment of defense policies, the continuation of relatively high defense budgets, and the determination not to abandon successful security policies with imprudent haste.

It may be understated in the post–cold war, Western, developed world, but the constant quest for security remains the primary and fundamental purpose of government. In the less-developed world, for instance the Middle East and the burgeoning industrial societies of East Asia, the salience of security is not understated. Large defense budgets pursuant to the dilution of cold war stabilities and predictabilities are testimony to that reality. Throughout the history of the international system, strong and resilient states have been expected to provide the two most important and related components of security: defense of the people within their borders and the promotion of economic well-being.

So far, the international system remains a competitive and basically anarchic system of states. Submersion of all security requirements in multinational organizations that aspire to supranationalism, such as the European Union and the United Nations, has been shown to be ineffective for most states. There is no authority providing comprehensive protection against the hostile intentions of other states higher than the government of the state. In all but the rarest exceptions, states cannot abrogate responsibility for their own protection. It is the policies which governments devise and pursue that deliver whatever degree of security is attainable. States seek power in order to address the need for security. Without security, other achievements and values of the state are vulnerable. Distrust and suspicion amongst states has been an unchanging characteristic of the ancient and modern worlds. The paradox is that as more power is sought to achieve a level of security, which can never be absolute, then the greater the degree of insecurity felt by other states. One state's relative security being another state's insecurity is the security dilemma that produces vicious circles of anxiety about national security. Hence, states are preoccupied with security.

But it is difficult for states to measure their real level of security. Security is a debatable concept—ambiguous, flexible, and open to wide interpretation. There is a distinct psychological dimension to notions of security. Feeling safe from attack against values and possessions is a vital element of security, even when objective realities could suggest great vulnerability. Measured only by objective criteria, Canada ought to feel extremely insecure vis-à-vis the United States. It does not, and it feels very much at ease with its giant neighbor. It is the history, for over 100 years, of benign United States intentions toward Canada that induces that deep sense of security, regardless of the severe imbalance in national capabilities. In most parts of the international system, such an imbalance of capabilities as between the United States and Canada would induce a deep sense of insecurity. Usually, security is assumed to comprise an absence, or at least a manageable level, of physical threat and the confidence that any level of threat to the state can be defeated or repulsed. But any appreciation of the security enjoyed by a state hinges on a correct assessment of the character of the animosity toward the state, externally and domestically, and honest measure of the weaknesses of the state. History is littered with instances where states got this wrong and suffered terrible consequences. And, on the other side of the coin, perhaps there have been many instances when states misperceived threats and subsequently wasted valuable national resources on needlessly high defense budgets. On the whole, security is negative in nature in that it stops nasty things from happening, and it is often difficult to prove that nasty things were going to happen anyway. Nonetheless, the historical record does show that although states may often be uncertain as to the level of national security they enjoy, in times of jeopardy they certainly know when they feel unsafe, whether or not feelings are an objective measure of reality.

The highly subjective element to feelings of security explains why so many considerations may be incorporated in any measure of security. What makes one person or state feel insecure may make another feel secure. The public debate in the West in the 1980s over the virtues and vices of nuclear deterrence illustrated this feature of national security. Clearly, national security is an inexact concept. Many variables contribute to and detract from national security. Identifying all the relevant variables is problematic, measuring them even more so. Traditionally, military considerations are deemed the most important element. Military force is the only governmental instrument sustained directly for attack or defense against rival states. Military power ought to be, and usually is, the monopoly of the government, and it is only through the military instrument that one state may conquer another. A state may be secure in political, economic, and social terms, but failure on the battlefield can expose all these achievements to absolute vulnerability. However, military superiority alone does not provide a high level of relative security. In the modern world, a strong, vibrant technological and economic base is essential to provide advanced military hardware and the means to pay for it. A legitimate political system and a popular consensus in support of the security policy vital for a robust, durable level of national security. If the state is homogeneous, normally there is a deeper sense of loyalty, and it is stronger internally. If multinational, it is more

prone to internal divisions, it is weaker domestically, and a consequence may be a heightened sense of external vulnerability. Ancillary variables such as strong allies, access to raw materials, sea borders or undefended borders with historically friendly neighbors, a free trading system, and cultural interests similar to other states all have a role to play in national security.

A holistic view of national security would argue that as well as defense policy and most foreign policy, large elements of domestic policy such as education and social welfare have vital national security functions. In effect, all government policy carries national security implications. This is a view particularly popular in the welfarist societies of Scandinavia. Indeed, all states have their own national security cultures, which are reflections of their history and strategic circumstances but which, by way of reputation, govern the security perceptions of their neighbors. Some states traditionally, such as Russia, are seen as expansive, belligerent, and proud. Others, such as Canada and Denmark, have collectivist, liberal, low defense-spending cultures. The self-perception of states as well as the prism through which the rest of the international system views individual states color assessments of security.

To be effective, a national security policy must be dynamic. Just as power is a relative concept, and meaningless unless related to countervailing power, then so is national security. A state's security is of a different quality depending upon the state to which it is related. And the strengths and the weaknesses of all states are in constant, often rapid, change. In the international system, nothing is immutable. The nature of challenges changes, capabilities change, and opponents may become allies, and old allies transform into rivals. National security is a condition, not a framed set of policies. Policies must be flexible to address the desirable condition called national security. States use a variety of policies to seek security, not all of which are military in nature. If there is insecurity over access to raw materials in unstable, faraway countries, then stockpiling reserves, the use of substitutes, conservation, and diversifying suppliers could be a more cost-effective way of improving security than deploying a military expeditionary force to a hostile and distance environment. If, when measured in objective capabilities, a state is relatively weak, then diplomatic arrangements with states that share a mutual view of how the international system should be shaped may be pursued.

JAMES H. WYLLIE

BIBLIOGRAPHY

Bull, Hedley, 1977. *The Anarchical Society.* London: Macmillan.
Buzan, Barry, 1983. *People, States, and Fear.* Brighton, Sussex: Wheatsheaf Books.
Freedman, Lawrence, ed., 1994. *War.* Oxford: Oxford University Press.
Herz, John, 1951. *Political Realism and Political Idealism.* Chicago: University of Chicago Press.

Jervis, Robert, 1976. *Perception and Misperception in International Politics.* Princeton, NJ: Princeton University Press.

Waltz, Kenneth N., 1959. *Man, the State, and War.* New York: Columbia University Press.

Wolfers, Arnold, 1962. *Discord and Collaboration.* Baltimore, MD: Johns Hopkins University Press.

NATIONAL SOCIETY OF FUND RAISING EXECUTIVES (NSFRE).

An association of professionals working on behalf of nonprofit organizations in the area of development.

The National Society of Fund Raising Executives was founded in 1960 for the purposes of "improving the climate for fund-raising and instilling professional standards." Through programs of advocacy, training, and education, the society serves nearly 18,000 international members; thus, it is the world's largest organization representing the interests of philanthropy.

NSFRE has five different kinds of membership:
Regular: those having more than one year's experience.
Student: full-time students working in philanthropy.
Intern: those with less than one year's experience.
Retired: individuals who have retired.
Affiliate: those who work in fields related to fund-raising or who share mutual interests.

NSFRE offers a wide variety of benefits to members, including executive search, a resource library, fundamental and advanced continuing education courses, publications, pro-philanthropy lobbying, professional achievement recognition, and both basic and advanced certification.

The NSFRE Foundation, funded largely through the contributions of members and project grants, provides scholarship assistance for educational programs, research on philanthropy, and service efforts to advance philanthropy.

The National Society of Fund Raising Executives is located at

1101 King Street, Suite 700
Alexandria, VA 22314
Ph.: (703) 684-0410; Fax: (703) 684-0540

ROBERT W. BUCHANAN AND WILLIAM BERGOSH

NATIONALIZATION.

A process of transferring an industry or enterprise from private to state ownership.

Defense-related enterprises such as munitions production and naval shipyards and postal services were established as royal or government monopolies from the sixteenth to the eighteenth centuries. But it was in the nineteenth century that the word and concept of "nationalization" became current. In Great Britain, common ownership of the railroads, land, and coal mines was advocated or considered by some in the mainstream of politics as well as those with more radical views. From 1844, when W. E. Gladstone, as president of the Board of Trade, promoted the Railways Act, which opened the way for government purchase of railroads, to 1867, when the question of nationalization was rejected by the Royal Commission on Railways, the issue was significant in political debate. In 1881, the Land Nationalization Society was formed and subsequently labor unions became committed to this objective. However, of more lasting significance was the rise of the union-backed modern British Labour Party at the beginning of the twentieth century. Labour Members of Parliament introduced nationalization bills, without success, in 1906 (Mines, Canals, Railways, and Tramways) and similar bills, excluding mines, in 1908, 1911, and 1912, a Mines and Minerals Bill in 1913 and a Railways Bill in 1914. On the eve of World War I, the public control of industrial activity was restricted to local government-run water, gas, and electricity utilities and to tramway transport services.

Clause IV of the British Labour Party's 1918 constitution defined as an objective "the common ownership of the means of production, distribution, and exchange"—an objective that was abrogated only in the mid 1990s. In common with other countries, the issue of nationalization was placed back on the agenda of debate and action in the inter–World War period. The Bolshevik Revolution in October 1917 brought to power, in the new Soviet Russia, a government that was to improvise its way through economic, financial, industrial, and political chaos to the nationalization of private assets. The establishment of the Supreme Council of the National Economy (Vesankha) in December 1917, with the right to confiscate and control industry, trade, and finance, prepared the way for its command of nationalized industries. The merchant fleet and land were nationalized in early 1918 and these were followed in March by confirmation that the state-controlled railways under the Tsars would pass to the new government. Banks were nationalized by the end of the year as were all factories. Up to February 1921, under the banner of "war communism," nationalization was pursued vigorously. Although disputed, even workshops of less than five employees were placed under state control. The chaotic, anarchic outcome led to a shift away from the extremes of workshop nationalization in the New Economic Policy (NEP) from 1921 to 1923 and to an acceptance that small-scale private trade, manufacturing, and agricultural enterprises would operate within a predominantly state-controlled system.

In capitalist countries in the 1920s and 1930s, industries in economic difficulties, for example, railroads in France, and facing bankruptcy, such as Italian investment banks, were brought under state control. Other emerging and successful industries, such as electricity and radio broadcasting, were also brought into the state sector with the creation of the UK National Grid and the Central Electricity Board in 1926 and, for example, the British Broadcasting Corporation in 1927. The Tennessee Valley Authority created in 1933 is a rare American example of a state enterprise. Mexico's 1917 constitution claimed "subsoil" resources as state property and this was given force by the expropriation of foreign oil companies' assets in 1938. This is a precursor of subsequent, postwar, expropriations in many other developing countries.

It was in the period after World War II that the greatest surge of nationalization took place in many capitalist economies. France took into state ownership the fuel utilities (1946), banks (1948), and the Renault automobile organization (1945). The British Labour Government 1945–1951 placed under state control the Bank of England and Civil Aviation (1946), Coal (1947), Transport and Electricity (1948), Gas (1949), and Iron and Steel (1951). This process increased public-sector employment in the UK by 2 million workers and placed about 10 percent of the workforce in nationalized concerns. Until the 1980s mixed economies with a significant state sector were accepted with relatively little criticism. The creation of command economies on the Soviet model in the period after 1945, in Eastern Europe, China, and elsewhere resulted in the confiscation of private assets and the creation of large nationalized sectors. Not until the collapse of the Soviet bloc in the early 1990s was there a beginning of a wholesale return of industry to the private sector.

In the postwar world, new states, anxious to assert their sovereign power, nationalized foreign-owned assets. Persian nationalization of the Anglo-Iranian Oil Company in 1951, given the world preeminence of its tanker fleet, its refinery capacity, and its financial contribution to the British economy, make this a renowned example. Other oil industry nationalizations such as the Kuwait Petroleum Company and Petroleos de Venezuela in 1975 further illustrate this widening process. The nationalization of the Anglo-French Suez Canal Company by the Egyptian government in 1956 created an international political crisis, suggesting that such nationalization decisions are controversial to an extent not normally experienced in domestic nationalization programs.

The justification of nationalization is partly dependent on time and place. Arguments range from the abstract to the highly pragmatic but are mainly concerned with the perceived failures of private enterprise and free market operations. The economic, political, and social consequences of such failure require, it is argued, nationalization.

The normative motivation of socialist advocates relies heavily on Marx's labor theory of value, which contends that the value of output depends on the quantity of labor embodied in production. Since only part of that value is paid in the form of wages to the labor force, the remainder, known as "surplus value" accrues to the capitalists. This is regarded as illegitimate expropriation. Marxists assert that only by removing production from private ownership can the appetite for surplus value be eliminated and the workers be rewarded appropriately. There is also a rich nonsocialist British literature that recognized the failing of capitalism in providing the luxuries of the few before the necessities of the many, for example, the philosopher John Stuart Mill, the political economist Henry Sidgwick, and social critics Thomas Carlyle and John Ruskin. Less explicitly, all these ideas emerge as suspicion of, or objection to, the concept of private capitalist firms. These formal and informal reasons were expressed, amongst others, in the Soviet, East European, Chinese, British, and French programs of nationalization.

Related to these arguments are those that are critical of the distribution of income in private industry. The intention is to shift the rewards of the profits of private owners and management to consumers, in the form of lower prices, and employees, in the form of higher wages and improved working conditions. Similarly, the nationalization of foreign-owned assets is justified as a legitimate exercise of national sovereignty in shifting income and control away from foreign investors for the benefit of the domestic economy. Cross-subsidization of production is also possible under nationalization to compensate for social costs generated by private-sector profit maximizing activity. The loss of railroads in dependent rural communities could be cited as an example of such a social cost.

Another justification relates to the desire to control the cyclical fluctuations of the economy. In order to protect the whole economy from the buffeting of market forces and excessive fluctuations of economic activity, it is argued that the basic industrial infrastructure, "the commanding heights of the economy," should be placed in the hands of the government where expenditure decisions would be made with longer-term economic and political interests in mind. French indicative planning in the 1950s and 1960s was able to use the state sector as a basic part of its programming mechanism. A similar theme with a long pedigree advocated the extension of state control for strategic industries, significant in national defense, in order to separate them from market forces. A third argument in this group of market vulnerable industries concerns the preservation of depletable resources. This, too, can be effected by nationalization, as illustrated by Norway's control of its oil extraction industry.

Finally, nationalization is justified as a response to the market failure associated with private oligopoly or monopoly. The pricing and production level decisions of private firms may give rise to long-term "excess" profits. In state hands, different pricing and production rules may be implemented to reduce adverse allocative consequences. A "natural monopoly" has frequently been cited as a particular example of market concentration for which nationalization would be a solution. Such monopolies are derived from economies of scale, which result in falling average costs the larger the output of the firm. A single firm can produce the entire output of the industry at lower costs than could any larger number of firms. Water, gas, and electricity are often quoted as examples of natural monopolies.

Socialist-style command states confiscate the privately owned assets without compensation. In mixed capitalist economies, the democratic decision to nationalize is followed by legal and administrative arrangements of great complexity upon which the subsequent success of the process depends. Each industry has a different history and structure and each requires individual attention. For example, the British nationalization of the coal industry involved translating 800 operating management units and over three quarters of a million employees into a single management organization. At the same time, Road Haulage only employed 80,000 workers yet had nearly 4,000 management units before nationalization. These industries were relatively competitive before nationalization. Others, such as Gas or Electricity, were monopolies. Whatever the structure, nationalization requires a definition of the industry; the valuation of its assets; the nature and form of compensation to the former owners; the timing and organization of the transfer of operations; the local, regional, and national organizational and power structure of management; a statement of the objectives of the industry; financial operating rules, including the criteria for pricing and investment decisions; arrangements for worker consultation, for pay and conditions, and for pension provision; and the question of political and operational accountability. All have to be enshrined in legislation or operating rules.

The British experience of nationalization in the postwar period provided a noncommunist model, which was widely copied. They created public corporations to run the industries as distinct from a state enterprise where the shares were owned by the government. These public corporations, in general, were expected to break even after meeting current costs of production. The Treasury provided finance for investment. The chairman and board of management were responsible for day-to-day operations and were answerable to the relevant minister in Parliament, where policy was determined. This policy was not concerned merely with financial objectives as is implied by the arguments for nationalization outlined here. In many particulars, practice departed from this simple model, not least in periodic ministerial interference, for political reasons, in the operational decisions of the corporations.

The postwar flush of nationalization gave way to subsequent debate about the adequacy of the performance of the industries and of government control in the 1950s. In the 1960s and 1970s, in the light of experience, a great deal of attention was paid to the criteria and techniques for pricing and investment decisions on the grounds that resource allocation could only be effectively accomplished if these decisions were themselves properly analyzed (see,

for example, "Nationalised Industries: A Review of Financial and Economic Objectives," Cmnd 3437, HMSO, London). These developments were concerned with putting in place, in a dynamic system, rules that would control the behavior of industries not subject to the controls of the capital and product market.

Much empirical research sought to identify the relative efficiency of public-sector and private-sector business. The evidence is not one-sided. Although research confirms that loss making lasts longer in state-owned business and that innovation is weaker in state industries, there is contrary evidence on cost and productivity levels. However, increasingly the political perception that these industries were performing poorly and that government control was inadequate led analysts to contemplate alternatives to nationalization such as state ownership without monopoly protection; unregulated privatized monopoly; regulated private monopoly; and the breakup of the nationalized industry into two or more private firms.

At the same time, developments in economic theory began to question some of the underlying arguments for nationalization. Thus, the static assumptions of natural monopoly theory fail to recognize the significance of dynamic change in, for example, technology that can create competitive forces, as in telecommunications and postal services. Also, imperfect information may make effective control of nationalized industries impossible. W. J. Baumol's 1982 notion of contestable markets goes further in suggesting that the threat of the entry of a new firm may be enough to bring prices of a monopolist down to competitive levels.

The resurgence of faith in the power of the market at the same time as a growth in the belief in the failure of bureaucratic and government administration and control in the 1970s and 1980s led to a widespread rejection of nationalization in capitalist countries and in the former socialist countries of the Soviet empire and the advocacy of privatization or denationalization.

RICHARD M. ALEXANDER

BIBLIOGRAPHY

Chester, N., 1975. *The Nationalisation of British Industry*. London: HMSO.

Hanson, A. H., ed., 1963. *Nationalization: A Book of Readings*. London: George Allen and Unwin (for the Royal Institute of Public Administration).

Pryke, R., 1971. *Public Enterprise in Practice: The British Experience of Nationalisation over Two Decades*. London: MacGibbons and Key.

Ramanadham, V. V., 1991. *The Economics of Public Enterprise*. London: Routledge.

NATURAL LAW. A complex philosophical concept that holds essentially that the laws of society must be consistent with the higher natural laws or conditions of

man, or peace and happiness within society cannot be obtained. Natural law is significant in contemporary legal thought (Marske *et al.* 1978). Its significance is evident in the evolution of natural law theories from antiquity in Stoic philosophy to current conceptions of the role of prevailing mind sets, worldviews, background assumptions, and values in positive law in Western civilization. The concept is found in contemporary public administration literature in discussions that range from moral antecedents of positive law to judicial activism. Although the term's classical meaning and relevance may be rejected by most students of society (Strauss 1968, p. 80), it nonetheless has had an impact on the way students of law and society view the role of law, governing institutions, and the courts in establishing, maintaining, and legitimating forms and directions of social order.

In the contemporary context, there are at least three different views associated with the concept of natural law. Perhaps the more common view is associated with the Roman Catholic Church's doctrine of divine law and the moral imperative of following church precepts. Another view is deeply embedded in Western legal theory and concerns the existence of a higher law from which positive law emanates. This perspective is juxtaposed to positivistic philosophies of law, which contend that the science of lawmaking and application is grounded in scientific knowledge and sufficient for explaining the existence and operation of law. Yet another view of natural law is available from the social sciences, which take into account the issues of competing values, beliefs, power, and authority relations in the development, implementation, and ongoing legitimation of legal precepts. In this view, natural law refers to the values, beliefs, and background assumptions that adhere to lawmaking, the operation of the legal profession, and the social context of adjudication.

Although each of these perspectives offers a different view of natural law, there is considerable overlap. At the core of these perspectives is a common set of values and assumptions of social order, which reflects some of the deepest beliefs about human nature and society. Thus, conceptions of natural law are found in the writings of some of the earliest Western philosophers, including Plato and Aristotle. However, the term acquired a distinct philosophical theme in Stoicism.

Philosophical Conceptions

Natural law in Stoic philosophy referred to physical laws of the universe. Specifically, these natural laws embodied God's rationale for structuring the universe, which transcended temporal social and political orders. According to the Stoics, rational beings were able to comprehend God's rationality. Wisdom was evident in such a comprehension, which viewed the common elements of man's existence as

a way of understanding God's reasoning in natural laws. Preoccupied with a view of the unifying elements of man's existence, the Stoics were able to compare prevailing forms of social organizations to natural laws that led them to debunk inconsistent and arbitrary fiats of kings and emperors while attacking tribalism, chauvinism, class distinctions, and social differences rooted in political organization. The validity of positive law rested universally upon its intrinsic rationality, which the Stoics considered to be an essential element of the natural order. Positive laws contradicting the natural laws of mankind's unity were held to be invalid. In this philosophical conceptualization, natural law and the law of nations were merged. Also, the notion of natural law as the source of legitimate positive laws took shape. The enactment of a law was viewed as a discovery of an element of God's universe and a manifestation of his reason and order in the world. The Stoic notions of natural law were fundamental in the Roman philosophical concepts of *ius naturale,* as well as in the Roman legal system, *ius gentium* (Marske *et al.* 1978, p. 63).

A legacy of the Stoic concept of natural law is found in the work of Thomas Aquinas and Christian natural law teaching during the Middle Ages. It was Aquinas who consolidated the metaphysical writings of Aristotle into a view of the world as a manifestation of God's reason or law. This law or natural laws is discovered by man's divine faculty of reason; thus, it becomes God's law as man can know it (Marske et al. 1978, p. 64). Social and moral order is predicated on the understanding of natural law, which is both morally binding since it stems from God and instructional in that it personifies His intellect.

Aquinas wrote extensively on the law of nature and the inherent ordering of each part of creation, from the simplest elements to suprahuman elements. Human beings occupy a special position in this hierarchy with their unique capacities to exercise free will and reason. These characteristics provide the capability of human beings to understand God's reasoning in structuring the universe. Thus, God's laws of nature remain immutable objects of reason to be understood by mankind in satisfying needs and desires, preserving life, and continuing the species (Haakonssen 1992, pp. 886–887).

During the seventeenth and eighteenth centuries, conceptions of natural law began to lose their clerical overtones. Natural law began to be associated with man's natural state prior to the imposition of contracts from social and governmental institutions. Locke, for example, drew distinctions between man in society with the social contract and man's natural state in nature, which was governed by natural law. The philosophical link between the two was natural right of self-preservation, which in civil society was unlimited property acquisition through labor and capital accumulation. Rousseau, the prophet and inspiration of the French Revolution, viewed man in a natural state as noble, savage, simple, and peaceful. As a matter of self-preservation, men entered into a contract to constitute society. The means of preservation was judged to be the societal contract that guaranteed freedom and equality. Thus, there was no need for a higher law than positive laws that legitimately guaranteed freedom and equality among men.

Legalistic Conceptions

Although enduring, the concept of natural law in legal science has been discounted, rejected, and maligned. Under the influence of positivism, reference to natural law became unfashionable. In both legal education and practice, positivism rejected natural law arguments on the basis that case-by-case development of law was sufficient to explain its emergence and legitimacy in the social and political order. These sentiments are reflected in the following excerpt taken from Dabin (1966): "It is contradictory to speak of natural(-law) jurisprudence, because 'jurisprudence' down to its more general rules and their aims—not only the useful but also the good and the just—is a matter of prudence, and prudence is a matter of rational appraisal according to the cases and not a matter of inclination" (p. 32). Accordingly, legal scientific scholarship would necessarily limit the scope of legal inquiry to precedent and exclude notions of moral antecedents.

During the latter half of the nineteenth century and during the early twentieth century, a new direction in legal theory began to emerge with the development of the comparative, historical, and sociological schools of jurisprudence. These perspectives analyzed laws in action and compared and contrasted their actual and intended effects. Positive laws were evaluated according to their ability to satisfy social wants and needs. The legal realism movement in jurisprudence focused intently on the "life of the law," that is the intentions of public policy, the shared assumptions, beliefs, and fallacies that become embedded in laws governing human relations. Theories of natural law compared the "is" with the "ought to be" and found applicability in the moral and less predictable dimensions of legal decisionmaking. Harry Jones (1966), for example, commented that every legal precept creates zones of certainty and uncertainty and points to the need for analyzing the moral dimension of law in managing uncertainty. Also, proponents of natural law theory are quick to point to the moral precepts embedded in the amendments to the U.S. Constitution and the Bill of Rights, which provide the guiding principles for the enactment and judicial review of laws. According to Brendan Brown (1960), the high-water mark of natural-law thinking in the United States is the "emergence and survival of the doctrine of judicial supremacy which subjects positive law to the inhibition of the moral order, constitutionally implemented" (p. 31).

Social Science Conceptions

The social sciences take aim at the moral, ethical, social, and/or political underpinnings of law with the hope of understanding the role of values, beliefs, and assumptions in the design and implementation of legal systems and public administration. These value and belief systems are reflective of both existential assumptions about how things are and normative assumptions of how things ought to be. As a set of background assumptions reflecting fundamental values associated with the exercise of power, the mechanics of governing, and the foundations of legitimation systems, natural law issues are raised in a variety of public administration and policy contexts. These include, for example, the questions of the validity of laws apart from their moral underpinnings, the allocation of responsibility for making law and justice effective where positive laws fall short in prescribing courses of action or remedies, and the inherent limitations of positive law as the context for the use of natural law theory by an active judiciary. Russell Hittinger (1993, p. 10) writes that there are at least three different kinds of questions that crop up in debates over the relationship between natural and human positive law. The first concerns the philosophical debate as to whether natural law exists and the validity of human law to moral principles. The second concerns the constitutional issues of lawmaking and law adjudicating. The third concerns the decisions of judges with respect to procedural rules of prudence and art or interpretation. A secular social-scientific view of natural law has something to offer to each of these arguments.

The proposed secular view of natural law as a set of background assumptions and values that adhere to the formulation and operation of positive law clearly accepts the limitations of specific laws to address the unique facts and circumstances of particular cases. The dichotomy between values and knowledge in legal science is, in fact, a particular world view about the nature of knowledge and its role in adjudication and the legal profession. Although philosophers, logicians, and social scientists have argued that separating values and beliefs from the context of knowledge and science is unreasonable, there still remain certain values and intentions of attributing cause and effect certainty to the development of case law and the use of the scientific method in analyzing political institutions. Similarities between belief systems and perspectives on positive law and legal institutions have legitimated decisions in public administration and have had a bearing on the development of public policy.

Accepting the premise that natural law exists or emanates from assumptions, worldviews, and belief systems, the question begged by natural law theory concerns which branch of government is more effective in promoting and realizing these values in human collective action. Is it the legislature, the role of the judiciary, or some combination of the two? Although the enactment of positive law is the function of the legislative branch, the judiciary is responsible for applying and in some instances interpreting the law.

This point raises questions concerning judicial activism (in a pejorative sense) and adjudication as a means of ferreting out the moral intent of law. Part of the problem clearly lies in deficiencies in the art of legislation and the recognized inadequacy of the written word to express and convey moral intentions. Adjudication frequently involves the search for basic principles in law and public policy to arrive at an appropriate, just, and sustainable conclusion. However, the search for moral principles in law is a consequence of recognizing the importance of values and beliefs in applying the law, realizing justice, and ultimately substantiating the underlying values and beliefs that legitimize the law. In short, the life of the law is natural law. As Oliver Wendell Holmes (1963) wrote

The life of the law has not been logic; it has been experience. The felt necessities of the times, the prevalent moral and political theories, intentions of public policy, avowed or unconscious, even the prejudices which judges share with their fellow men, have had a good deal more to do than the syllogisms in determining the rules by which men should be governed (p. 5).

CHARLES P. KOFRON

BIBLIOGRAPHY

Brown, Brendan, 1960. *The Natural Law Reader.* New York: Oceana Press.

Dabin, 1966. "Is There a Juridical Natural Law?" In M. Golding, ed., *The Nature of Law, Readings in Legal Philosophy.* New York: Random House, 25–32.

Haakonssen, Knud, 1992. "Natural Law." In Lawrence C. Becker and Charlotte B. Becker, eds., *Encyclopedia of Ethics,* Volume 2. New York: Garland Publishing, 884–890.

Hittinger, Russell, 1993. "Natural Law in the Positive Laws: A Legislative or Adjudicative Issue?" *The Review of Politics,* vol. 1: 5–34.

Holmes, Oliver Wendell, 1963. *The Common Law.* Cambridge: Belknap Press of Harvard University Press.

Jones, Harry W., 1966. "Legal Realism and Natural Law." In M. Golding, ed., *The Nature of Law, Readings in Legal Philosophy.* New York: Random House, 261–269.

Marske, Charles E., Charles P. Kofron, and Seven Vago, 1978. "The Significance of Natural Law in Contemporary Legal Thought." 24 *The Catholic Lawyer,* vol. 1: 60–76.

Strauss, Leo, 1968. "Natural Law." In David L. Sills, ed., *International Encyclopedia of the Social Sciences,* vol. 2. New York: Macmillan and Free Press, 80–85.

NATURAL RESOURCE POLICY.   Policies relating to the appropriate use of natural resources, including

the rate at which resources are exploited or completely withdrawn from use in the name of environmental protection.

Contemporary natural resource policymaking has become a highly complex and potentially controversial area, particularly in those nations where there has been a rising community demand for the conservation and preservation of scarce or environmentally significant resources. The potential diversity of matters that can come under the rubric of resource policy exacerbates the policy area's degree of difficulty. As nearly all nation-states view natural resources as the property of the community rather than any individual or company, matters dealing with mining, forestry, fisheries, and the management of state-owned lands clearly occupy important positions on the agenda. So, too, do matters pertaining to a host of elementary resources such as air and water, the fulsome availability of which is as important for the life expectations of human beings as they are as resources for the use of industry.

In the times before heightened public sensitivity about environmental protection, natural resource policy had been dominated by rather more simple economic cost-benefit analyses; save for the most aesthetically significant land areas that were protected by nature reserves or parks, the decision to exploit natural resources tended to be dominated by assessment of the extent to which profits offset the costs incurred in their extraction. In a number of nations, the location of important exploitable natural resources, including minerals and forest products, in regions remote from the major metropolitan centers contributed to two important features of natural resource policy politics: first, natural resource exploitation became critical to the local economies of typically isolated and/or sparsely populated communities; and, second, a close working relationship began to emerge between companies and individuals extracting resources and the locally based government agencies responsible for managing resources owned by the community. In conjunction with the importance of the private sector to state or national economies, these factors placed extraction and exploitation at the center of natural resource policymaking.

Natural Resources and Environmental Sensitivity

In the 1960s, the predominance of the exploitationist approach came under serious challenge, and a greater national and international focus on natural resource issues occurred. In 1972, the United Nations held one of its first international meetings on the problem of environmental damage when the Conference on Human Environment was convened in Stockholm. The perceived need for multilateral discussion of environmental matters emanated from arguments by scientists and scholars that the industrial world had become profligate in its use of finite natural resources. On the argument that profligacy could lead to exhaustion, governments were urged to consider incorporating conservation into their resources policies. The international sensitivity to the finite nature of many natural resources was reinforced by the "energy crisis" that profoundly impacted upon Western economies in 1976. Although in reality this was a shortage brought about by politics rather than ecology, policy planners were given a taste of what a shortage of a key resource like oil could mean for an industrial economy, and accordingly they began to seriously address resource conservation as a policy option.

From the growing awareness of industrial society's capacity to pollute emerged a new concern about the finite nature of a set of natural resources usually taken for granted as being inexhaustible. These resources included clean water, fresh air, diversity in species of flora and fauna, and an aesthetically pleasing living environment. Once again, policymakers now had to confront the problem that these commodities that had hitherto been impossible to value in money terms were now emerging as precious resources. The old approaches to resource exploitation were no longer appropriate. In their place policymakers now had to consider enacting laws designed to protect air and water quality, put in place administrative regimes capable of regulating the use of scarce resources, and seek ways in which the noneconomic values of environmental qualities could be incorporated into the decision making process.

In the 1980s, the natural resource policy debate was made all the more complicated by the emergence of "environmentalism." Although it is true that environmental "pressure groups" have had a long-standing presence in the political landscape of Western Europe, Australia, Canada, and the United States, in recent times there has been the onset of a greater community concern about a wide range of environmental issues that had all the characteristics of being a broad social movement. As such, the agenda that was now being addressed by environmentalists broadened substantially. To the usual debates about the real value of seemingly infinite resources such as air and water were added quite complex debates about humanity's appropriate relationship to the entire environment—sometimes referred to as the "biosphere."

Here some of the philosophical debates that began to gain a wider public audience presented two important arguments: First, environmentalists began to question that which had been enacted by governments by way of resource policy based on the assumption that humanity naturally sits atop of the hierarchy of species and that resources are valued according to how they meet the material needs of human beings. This approach, the philosophical element in the movement argued, was "anthropocentric"— that is, it placed humanity above other species and above the very biosphere itself. Second, environmentalists were beginning to argue that the "anthropocentric" approach to policy had meant that humanity, rather than living in balance with its environment, had attempted to establish its mastery over the biosphere with disastrous consequences for may species of flora and fauna. The philosophy of environmentalism argued that living out of balance with the environment would lead to an acceleration of the rate of extinction of species, which, if allowed to continue unabated, would threaten the existence of the human species itself.

The Challenge for Developers and the State

These approaches have presented a direct challenge to the perspectives of developers and governments for whom the value of natural resources lay in that which their exploitation could contribute to economic growth. Developers and governments have traditionally viewed natural resources as community resources and held that decisions to conserve them have to be made from an assessment of whether the community can afford the economic cost conservation brings. The search for material advancement is a task common to governments the world over regardless of their ideological disposition. For developer interests, perceptions of community good are intimately linked with perceptions of the need to achieve material security. In all nations, resource policy debates have become acutely problematic as environmentalists on one side advocate the need to value (and preserve) natural resources in a bid to achieve an ecological balance, while developers argue the case for exploiting resources to generate the wealth necessary to give the community material security.

Whichever of these approaches is correct, the new "environmentalism" that clearly emerged throughout the world in the last decade has presented policymakers with a host of complex challenges. The rise of environmentalism has had its political corollary. In many nations, there has been a substantial growth in community demands for a more environmentally sensitive approach to resource policy decision-making. In liberal democracies, "green" political parties have emerged to either seek to influence voting patterns or to win parliamentary representation. Governments that seek to make policy with the participation of interest groups have also found land-use policy dynamics complicated by a proliferation of seemingly radical environmental interest groups who, unlike established groups like the Sierra Club in the United States or the Australian Conservation Foundation in Australia, are less willing to enter into dialogue with governments, preferring instead to undertake direct action. Thus, resource politics out in the field have become much more radical, much more activist, and much more confrontationalist, as major land-use disputes have become characterized by demonstrations, vigils, blockades, and, in the United States at least, incidents of sabotage.

Values and Policymaking

Bureaucratic policymaking actors have also been seriously affected by the changing nature of the environmental debate. Policymaking never goes on in a vacuum of values and philosophies, and natural resource policy making is no exception. However, as a result of the impact of "environmentalism"–and especially of the argument about the need to achieve "ecology"–government departments and state agencies have been forced to at least review their approach, particularly given their propensity to either disregard environmental value inputs, or to consider them as something of an after-thought. Not even the prior existence of agencies designed to put the environmental view on policy matters has sufficed, for invariably such environment-oriented departments have found themselves to be less influential in the decisionmaking process than their developer-oriented counterparts. In seeking to address the implications of responding to the new environmentalism, bureaucratic actors have found other problems besides interdepartmental rivalry: With the politicization of the values and assumptions surrounding the land-use debate has come a politicization of the technical and scientific debate. Once the domain of the bureaucracy, the question of who shall advise the government and with what technical and scientific data has become one of the more hotly contested issues between the protagonist interest groups.

The new social movement-type environmentalism has also succeeded in bringing a much broader regional focus to natural resource policy issues. Although it is true that environmental debates in the 1960s and 1970s had an international dimension, contemporary environmentalism links its ecological approach to a critique of relations between rich and poor nations. Environmentalism's claim that the wealthy industrial nations should consume less in order that the chronic poverty in the rest of the world might be addressed by a more equitable distribution of resources has been taken up by the political leaders or poorer nations. Herein lies just another example of how the new environmentalism is a much broader political phenomenon, with the consequence being that, unlike the past in which it had a strong local dimension, natural resource issues are now the concern of national government and the subject of international relations.

The Response of Government

Governments have tried to meet the challenge presented by the new environmentalism by seeking to incorporate environmentalists and some of their agendas into the policymaking process. In response to the allegation that policy decisions have tended to consider environmentalist values as an after-thought, governments have sought to incorporate ecological perspective at the formative stage of the decisionmaking process. There have also been attempts to create mechanisms and government agencies to find ways of bringing the otherwise fundamentally opposed interest groups from the development-environmentalist divide together. In so doing, governments have demonstrated their belief in the possibility of bringing consensus to the natural resource policy arena, particularly where in matters such as the need for clean air, clean water, and land protection there appear to be interests in common between these groups.

In international relations, developing nations have sought to link arguments about environmental protection and equitable resource distribution with perceptions of their being unfairly treated by industrialized countries. The demand for international ecological equity has subsequently been taken to international forums such as the various agencies of the United Nations (UN). Indeed, UN initiatives on the protection of important land areas in the name of preserving the "world heritage" have been used to stop developments and resource exploitation in a number of countries. In this way, the United Nations Economic, Social, and Cultural Organization's (UNESCO) covenant on world heritage protection has been used by governments to pass laws to protect significant areas in the name of international cooperation–a further example of how environmental issues have been transformed from a regional to a global concern.

Toward International Resource Policy?

Attempts have been made at taking an international approach to addressing key environmental issues such as the preservation of significant land areas, control of dangerous industrial emissions, addressing the problem of global warming, and regulation of the use of dangerous chemicals. Two of these attempts have been particularly noteworthy: In 1987 under the auspices of the UN, the World Commission on Environment and Development, otherwise known as the Brundlandt Commission, studied the problem of how policymakers might reconcile their pursuit of economic growth with growing concern about the environmental costs of development and growth. Its response was the concept of "Ecologically Sustainable Development" (or ESD) in which, it was argued, governments could and should strive to achieve economic growth that exists in balance with environmental protection. The concept also sought to explain the idea of inter- and intragenerational equity in resource policy. Intragenerational equity would require policymakers to acknowledge the need for the costs associated with environmental protection to be born equally within societies and between nations (thereby ensuring protection for the poor), while intergenerational equity requires this generation to bequeath a rich, diverse, and life-sustaining biosphere to future generations. Importantly, the Brundlandt Commission's work did not advocate (as many environmentalists hoped that it would) that economic growth itself was no longer sustainable. Rather, ESD was articulated as a concept about "balance" between the pursuit of material advancement for society and the need for environmental protection.

Meanwhile, the convening of the "Earth Summit" in June 1992 in Rio de Janeiro was the second important international approach to environmental matters. At this meeting, general discussions about the need for greater international sensitivity to environmental protection occurred alongside the addressing of specific matters such as the depletion of the earth's ozone layer and the prospect of global warming resulting from carbon dioxide emissions (the so-called greenhouse syndrome). The greenhouse issue in particular had been the subject of previous multilateral discussions and agreements, including protocols established in Montreal in 1987 and 1990, in which participants had agreed in principle to reduce the level of "greenhouse gas" emissions. In the context of these prior agreements, the Rio summit was considered to be less than successful, however, particularly in the light of the refusal of the U.S. government to accept harsher cuts. Still, the meeting did indicate that international cooperation on such matters was viewed as important and that domestic politicians would need to ensure that the policies formed back in their home countries would be influenced by decisions made at the international level.

In response to these challenges, many states have resorted to the search for policies capable of finding "balance" between societal demands for both environmental preservation and economic development. Once again, the Brundlandt Commission's approach to ESD has provided the basis for this. Adopting a fair amount of ecological rhetoric, the commission's report nonetheless declared that the pursuit of economic growth was vital particularly as a means to alleviating the poverty of the developing world. Such a view is seized upon by states for whom economic matters are still of critical social and political importance. Even in the advanced industrial states, with their burgeoning community sensitivity toward environmental protection, policymakers still fear the political consequences of low growth and rising unemployment. Despite writings by many "green" economists to the contrary, environmental protection is still regarded as something that involves an economic cost by way of foregone material returns on that resource being preserved. The environmental movement's approach to "balance" is based on perceptions of the need for humanity to live with, rather than dominate, its natural environment. Policymakers, however, view "balance" as the need to try to reconcile contradictory ide-

ological and philosophical positions in debates about resource use in an attempt to have both development and environmental protection.

NICHOLAS M. ECONOMOU

BIBLIOGRAPHY

Commission for the Future, 1990. *Our Common Future: The World Commission on Environment and Development.* Oxford: Oxford University Press.

Dryzek, John S., 1983. *Conflict and Choice in Resource Management: The Case of Alaska.* Boulder, Co: Westview.

———, 1987. *Rational Ecology: Environment and Political Economy.* Oxford: Basil Blackwell.

Eckersley, Robyn, 1992. *Environmentalism and Political Theory: Towards an Ecocentric Approach.* New York: State University of New York Press.

Inglehart, Ronald, 1977. *The Silent Revolution: Changing Values and Political Styles among Western Publics.* Princeton, NJ: Princeton University Press.

Melucci, Alberto Princeton, 1989. *Nomads of the Present: Social Movements and Individual Needs in Contemporary Society.* London: Hutchison.

Offe, Claus, 1985. "New Social Movements: Challenging the Boundaries of Institutional Politics." *Social Research,* vol. 52, no. 4 (Winter) 817–868.

Porritt, Jonathon, 1984. *Seeing Green: The Politics of Ecology Explained.* Oxford: Basil Blackwell.

Spretnak, Charlene, and Fritjof Capra, 1984. *Green Politics: The Global Promise.* London: Paladin.

Stretton, Hugh, 1976. *Capitalism, Socialism, and the Environment.* London: Cambridge University Press.

Touraine, Alain, 1981. *The Voice and the Eye: An Analysis of Social Movements.* Cambridge: Cambridge University Press.

Young, Oran, 1981. *Natural Resources and the State: the Political Economy of Resource Management.* Berkeley: University of California Press.

———, 1982. *Resource Regimes: Natural Resources and Social Institutions.* Berkeley: University of California Press.

NEEDS ASSESSMENT. One or more of a set of analytic techniques that identifies, measures, and/or evaluates priorities or resource and service deficiencies within specified programs or target populations.

Needs assessment gained currency in the United States during the late 1960s and 1970s as a result of citizen advocacy, which not only illuminated social conditions but placed greater emphasis upon resource allocation and the determination of service provision priorities. Passage of federal legislation such as Public Law 94-63 in 1975, which assigned community health centers the responsibility of researching and responding to local area needs, contributed to this impetus. Various service delivery agencies have increasingly been required to identify "at-risk" populations and justify the resources necessary to improve services or ameliorate underlying social problems. Public-sector entities, which rely upon needs assessment for data gathering and analysis, include social and human services, planning organizations, recreational and leisure programs, educational institutions, and municipal governments.

Purposes needs assessment may serve include the gathering and evaluation of information, the formalization of information flow, the identification and definition of deficiencies or problems, the reduction of uncertainty, the formulation of goals, and the facilitation of communication, perhaps most particularly between agencies and clientele. "Endogenous" needs assessment may be conducted internally to examine the feasibility or capability of a program to meet goals and objectives, or to obtain resources, while "exogenous" needs assessment may be employed to identify and evaluate the needs of an external clientele or population. Depending upon the nature of the particular approach adopted, the research may rely exclusively upon professional staff, involve outside expertise, or require extensive public participation.

Needs

Needs can be an important consideration in the agenda setting and prioritization components of the policy formulation process. The definitions of "needs" is fundamental to the particular assessment approach adopted and to the concept itself. Needs have been understood in a variety of ways, although most definitions utilized in practice share "values" and "problems" as constructs, usually relative to a given time and place. Values are normative and reflect prevalent orientations and judgments about proper or attainable levels of service delivery, client well-being, community standards, and so forth. Orientations that contrast "what is" with "what should be," or judgments concerning the resolution of such discrepancies, are indicative of the problem aspect of the definition.

One classification breaks the subject into four types of needs. The first category, "normative" need, is based upon the evaluation of experts and geared toward the formulation of adequate levels of service and desirable outcomes. Often expressed as ratios, standards are set, with individuals, groups, or programs falling short of attainment labeled as being "in need." The next category, "perceived" or "felt" need, reflects the perspectives of members of a group about their own needs. They identify and articulate the levels of service or outcomes they feel satisfactory for themselves. The objective is to match existing conditions and available resources with expectations.

"Expressed" need can be defined as the difference between the demand for services and the existing levels of service provision. If demand is higher than actual utilization, then expressed need can be said to exist. "Comparative" or "relative" need does not set fixed standards but seeks to provide equitable services relative to differences in location and conditions. Particular attention is paid to

characteristics that might invalidate generalizations upon which standards have been predicated.

Models

A number of models for conducting needs assessment have been developed. These include the participatory method, which features some form of comparatively structured or unstructured participatory process, whereby input into the prioritization and decisionmaking process is solicited. Community forums or public hearings constitute relatively unstructured examples of the participatory approach.

A more structured variant is the discrepancy model, which consists of three stages: goal setting, or the identification of what should be, performance measurement, or the definition of what is, and the identification and ordering of discrepancies between performance and goals. An expert group, such as a Delphi panel, is frequently employed as the source from which data are gathered. The decisionmaking model has been identified as an even more structured, and predominantly quantitative, method for assessing needs. Needs are identified through a problem modeling process. The decision problem is considered relative to options and fixed types of information known as attributes, such as social indicators, key informant survey results, and the costs of program implementation associated with the various identified options.

Survey research techniques have formed the core of one of the most widely employed approaches to needs assessment. Survey instruments such as questionnaires are used to obtain primary data about specific topics predetermined by researchers. One of the most popular examples of this model is "community needs assessment." conducted by municipal government officials to solicit information about funding and service priorities. An approach closely related to survey research relies upon social indicators as the source of secondary data. Data gathered by other governmental or private organizations are accessed and analyzed relative to areas of predefined research interest.

The marketing model is a feedback approach that focuses upon ensuring the organization is effectively delivering the goods and services desired by its clientele. The relationship is predicated upon exchange, in other words, organizational goods and services are marketed on the basis of resources the clients are able to provide for the organization. Similarly, the Rates Under Treatment model seeks to establish and measure the relationship between estimated target population and service utilization rates within a specific locale.

There are additionally a considerable number of techniques that are closely related and may be utilized in conjunction with needs assessment. These include problem analyses, resource inventories, service use analyses, values clarification, client analyses, citizen participation, community organization, the nominal group technique, and brainstorming. A number of standard statistical routines can be brought to bear upon data generated through needs assessment, such as cross-tabulation tables, frequencies, factor analyses, indexing, and scaling. Needs assessment may also be used as a component of program planning and forecasting. One of the areas where needs assessment may be the most critical is program evaluation. Needs assessment may be used to set forth the measures and criteria that ultimately will be used for output and outcome evaluations.

Conclusion

Needs assessment certainly possesses inherent limitations, such as the uncertainty or unreliability of estimates, and the nonavailability or noncomparability of data. To be utilized most effectively, needs assessment must be a cyclical process, repeated every several years at a minimum. Even with shortcomings such as these, needs assessment provides a cost-effective methodology whereby public-sector agencies and programs can determine their own priorities and resource deficiencies as well as the nature and level of services required by constituencies.

JAY D. JURIE

BIBLIOGRAPHY

Bradshaw, Jonathan, 1972. "The Concept of Social Need." *New Society,* vol. 30 (March) 640–643.
Howe, Elizabeth, 1988, "Social Aspects of Physical Planning." In Frank S. So and Judith Getzels, eds., *The Practice of Local Government Planning,* 2d ed. Washington, DC: ICMA, 330–362.
McKillip, Jack, 1987. *Need Analysis: Tools for the Human Services and Education.* Newbury Park, CA: Sage.
Moroney, Robert M., 1977. "Needs Assessment for Human Services." In Wayne F. Anderson and Bernard J. Frieden, eds., *Managing Human Services.* Washington, DC: ICMA, 128–154.
Neuber, Keith A., William T. Atkins, James A. Jacobson, and Nicholas A. Reuterman, 1980. *Needs Assessment: A Model for Community Planning.* Beverly Hills, CA: Sage.
Nickens, John M., Adelbert J. Purga, III, and Penny P. Noriega, 1980. *Research Methods for Needs Assessment.* Washington, DC: University Press of America.
Parsons, Robert J., Dee W. Henderson, James M. Palazzo, Ralph Garn, and Bill Hulterstrom, 1990. "Community Needs Assessment: An Integrated Approach." *National Civic Review,* vol. 79, no. 5: 426–435.

NEIGHBORHOOD-BASED ORGANIZATIONS (NBOs). Participatory associations of residents that serve or are identified with a certain geographic area, usually a neighborhood or residential community. Active and successful NBOs are not just ad hoc groups, but rather represent a significant citizen infrastructure in communities where they exist. Many NBOs address major issues in distressed urban society. Their often confrontational, multi-issue struggles center around protecting the interests of their members and seeking to tackle powerful political and economic interests in their communities. Not all play highly activist or politicized roles in their communities. They include everything from food co-ops and cultural associations to neighborhood revitalization groups, free schools, and block clubs concerned with crime control. Those found in older urban inner cities are often engaged in complex programs to rehabilitate housing, clean up lots, improve transportation services, and provide health, family, and senior services. And not all NBOs operate in distressed urban areas. Homeowners associations operate in newer suburbs with agendas no more complicated than those of garden clubs that maintain small neighborhood public plantings.

A Definition of NBOs

More specifically and following a definition created by Carl Milofsky (1987; 1988), NBOs have these characteristics:

(1) They often provide social services and/or serve as a setting in which social or cultural activities may take place.
(2) They are often organized to act as an agent of advocacy or governance for a particular neighborhood or constituency.
(3) Some are incorporated as nonprofits while others are too small or informal to be incorporated. Sometimes they are incorporated as cooperatives although as such they do not have the goal of making profit for members.
(4) Usually, their commitment is to represent the interests of the community. NBOs are often committed to the values of democratic governance and have policies and procedures to include community members in policymaking and the administration of programs.
(5) NBOs are often small and loosely structured with few layers of hierarchy. They rarely have bureaucratic structures organized into formal departments.

NBOs as Open Systems

NBOs have highly permeable boundaries or are what social scientist call "open systems" (Milofsky 1988). Many NBOs are small, fluid, and loosely structured with uncertain fuzzy boundaries. They can be short lived with rapid turnover in membership and leadership. Their basis of legitimacy rests within a community and reflects the changing community involvement in their affairs. They are participatory organizations with roots in the social fabric of neighborhoods and community institutions. As such, their composition and objectives are a reflection of the often changing interests of different volunteer members and the demographic, political flux of a community. This does not mean that some NBOs have not sustained long and viable roles in their communities or that they have not evolved into organizations with a formal structure. This happens most often when dependable grants or other sources of funding allow for planning, continuity in (paid) staff and ongoing, regular support and participation by volunteer members, and effective volunteer leadership.

A History of NBOs

Historically in the United States, NBOs arose in ethnic communities where they were a focus of community life, mutual benefit, and community betterment. Many churches, with their concerns for a sense of community and benefit to others, have served as initiators of NBOs and then as partners in community-building activities, providing not only moral support but meeting space and administrative services. During the city reform movement in local government in America, from 1920 to 1940, NBOs often were promoted by reformers as organizations that could both model and teach residents about "good" government and the future of urban communities based on effective and efficient local government.

By the 1960s, "community control" became a leading principle in revitalization of urban America. Creation of the Model Cities program and the War on Poverty in the United States, conducted by the Office of Economic Opportunity (OEO) through its Community Action Program (CAP) and the use of categorical grants programs, transferred many social service functions to small, local nonprofit organizations and thereby created a special role for community-based NBOs.

These federal categorical grants allocated by Congress are distributed and overseen by specialized offices in Washington to which NBOs must submit proposals if they wish to receive grants. Critics argue that the process places a premium on grant-writing skills and knowledge of the priorities of specialized offices of the federal government. Residents of low-income neighborhoods are less likely to have either grant-writing or the political skills and must compete with large social service agencies that can hire experienced and educated grant-writing staff.

State governments have not played a major role in funding NBOs. However, federal block grants to the states in the 1980s increasingly replaced categorical grants as the federal government sought to decentralize the distribution of social service dollars intended for community use. Block grants have been accompanied by substantial funding cuts as the decade of the 1990s portends an uncertain future for funding of NBOs in the twenty-first century.

Foundations and NBOs

Many foundations pursue comprehensive, neighborhood-based programs, typically focusing on housing and economic development. These initiatives are worked through NBOs to help neighborhoods become cohesive communities—addressing common local problems and concerns. Foundations are not susceptible to the same sort of political pressure as is government. But NBOs face the same kind of challenge to develop grant-writing skills to access foundation grants. NBO leaders must be able to cultivate contacts beyond their communities and learn the funding priorities of the foundation community.

Leadership of NBOs

NBOs are ofttimes led by individuals with political ambitions where leadership skills are honed, building consensus and advancing community interests. Other leaders are zealots with particular causes who flash as brightly as meteors and die off as quickly. Neighborhood leaders may have narrow special interests and to survive must foster the loyalty of others. Some may have broader community-building interests and identify with neighbors who share simply the dedication to ensure a community as a decent and safe place to live. All leaders of NBOs share the common interest in building solidarity among community residents and thereby provide ways for citizens to become integrated into the broader democratic political culture (Dahl 1961). Some are obviously more skillful at this than others. As Dennis Young (1987) has shown, previously ailing NBOs can be revived when entrepreneurial leaders take charge.

The Future of NBOs

Today across the United States, in every decaying city and distressed rural area, the need for community revitalization continues. To respond to this need, increasing numbers of community leaders, philanthropists, policymakers and planners have once again committed themselves to the potential of comprehensive, neighborhood-based, community empowerment initiatives. The role of NBOs in these initiatives is central. In many cities, these organizations are successful at establishing themselves as major players in community decisionmaking. They are found at the table in communitywide revitalization efforts, playing a major role in building healthy communities and presenting challenges to others to operate in new, increasingly collaborative ways.

Sharp reductions in social program funding from the federal government as both a conservative political agenda and the pressures of deficit reduction take hold in the 1990s, suggesting a substantial challenge for the future of NBOs. Despite the funding challenge, NBOs are a means by which a spirit of community thrives within a residential area. NBOs foster a commitment to those who share common concerns. Thus, NBOs will certainly continue to play a role in shaping the lives of those for whom there is a commitment to a sense of place.

RICHARD D. HEIMOVICS

BIBLIOGRAPHY

Dahl, Robert, 1961. *Who Governs? Democracy and Power in an American City.* New Haven, CT: Yale University Press.
Milofsky, Carl, 1987. "Neighborhood-Based Organization: A Market Analogy." In Walter W. Powell, ed., *The Nonprofit Sector: A Research Handbook.* New Haven CT: Yale University Press, 277–295.
———, 1988, ed., *Community Organizations: Studies in Mobilization and Exchange.* New York: Oxford University Press.
Young, Dennis, 1987. "Executive Leadership in Nonprofit Organizations." In Walter W. Powell, ed., *The Nonprofit Sector: A Research Handbook.* New Haven, CT: Yale University Press, 167–179.

NEOCORPORATISM.

A form of democratic political theory that asserts three powerful interests—business, government, and labor (but to a lesser degree than the other two)—should dominate public decisionmaking through political arrangement; often used in conjunction with, or synonymously for, neoconservatism.

Philosophically, neocorporatism draws on several streams of thought, including those of Herbert Spencer (1820–1903), Georges Sorel (1847–1922), Georg Wilhelm Friedrich Hegel (1770–1831), and Edmund Burke (1729–1797). From Spencer, among others, comes the notion of Social Darwinism, which sought to apply the theories of Charles Darwin (1809–1882) to human society. Spencer interpreted Darwin's work to mean that life is an "open struggle," and "survival of the fittest" is the result of "natural selection." Within a national society, the struggle among groups assures that leadership resides in those sectors that have established a firm base of power; in industrial society, these are government, business, and labor. Sorel's work offered the proposition that a social myth is required to accomplish social objectives. Thus, for labor, the social myth must be created that a general strike will lead to improving conditions of workers. The myth need not be based in reality, Sorel wrote, but it must express determination to take strong action and capture the emotions and will of the masses. Hegelian philosophy emphasized the irrational and chaotic nature of life and the relative unimportance, therefore, of reason, logic, and intelligence

in human behavior. Intuition, instinct, and emotion are required to bind together peoples for social and political action. Burke's views also were based on a pessimistic view of human nature and abilities; he extolled the virtues of national/cultural tradition, arguing that political, familial, and religious structures should maintain stability and order.

In other words, neocorporatism—as its precursor, corporatism—may be seen as an elitist critique of classical theory: people (whatever the nature and structure of their government) have always been ruled by powerful minority interests; the idea of a "public good" is a mythical and intuitive concept rather than an objective reality; human conduct is more often governed by emotion and habit than by deliberate and rational choice; and stability and order are best achieved through political arrangements among powerful structures.

The principal twentieth-century experiment with corporatism was conducted by Benito Mussolini (1883–1945) in pre–World War II fascist Italy, during which pubic policy was formulated and implemented through a series of elite political arrangements among "corporate" sectors, both business and labor, with government. During the latter half of the twentieth century, this philosophical resurgence was labeled "neocorporatist" and appeared in the political regimes of Margaret Thatcher, elected British prime minister in 1979; Ronald Reagan, elected U.S. president in 1980; and Brian Mulroney, elected Canadian prime minister in 1984. All three regimes were characterized by (1) formal involvement of private-sector business in government policymaking processes; (2) a lesser formal role for organized labor, in policymaking or as part of the construction of social myth; (3) emotional public rhetoric about the virtues of self-reliance; (4) vastly reduced/reallocated levels of spending on programs associated with the social welfare state; (5) deregulation of "public good" services (e.g., airlines); and (6) devolution of public (or Crown) corporations to the private sector and privatization of social services delivery. In all three countries, during these regimes, the economic gap between rich and poor increased significantly.

JACQUELYN THAYER SCOTT

BIBLIOGRAPHY

Bachrach, Peter, 1967. *The Theory of Democratic Elitism.* Boston: Little Brown.
Held, David, 1991. *Political Theory Today.* Stanford: Stanford University Press.
Honneth, Axel. 1990. "Atomism and Ethical Life: On Hegel's Critique of the French Revolution." In David Rasmussen, ed., *Universalism vs. Communitarianism: Contemporary Debates in Ethics.* Cambridge, MA: MIT Press, 129–138.
Rejai, Mostafa, 1984. *Comparative Political Ideologies.* New York: St. Martin's.
Winter, Herbert, 1992. *Political Science and Theory.* New York: HarperCollins.

NEPOTISM. The practice of employing relatives in public-sector organizations. Rules regulating the employment of relatives within public-sector organizations are called antinepotism rules.

Historically, it was not uncommon in democracies throughout the world for elected officials to hire wives, aunts, uncles, and cousins into public-sector positions. Public jobs were used by elected officials to pad the family income or as favors to be given to relatives. In more modern times, in the "goldfish bowl" atmosphere of public employment even the appearance of impropriety or conflicts of interest can cause major public relations problems. As merit systems became more common and as taxpaying citizens demanded more and more competence from public servants, antinepotism laws were passed prohibiting the appointment of family members to public-sector positions.

In the private sector, managers became concerned that the employment of more than one family member within the same organization could become disruptive to smooth operations as family members brought their family-based quarrels with them to the office or as family members formed coalitions favoring their own interest within the organization. Therefore, in the private sector antinepotism policies became common.

These policies in both the public and private sectors can be very broadly based or very narrowly tailored. Broadly based antinepotism rules prohibit the employment of more than one family member within the same organization. More narrowly tailored policies allow the employment of more than one family member in the same organization but prohibit one family member from being in the direct supervisory chain-of-command over another family member.

In recent years, antinepotism policies have come under increased criticism for being discriminatory against women. The contention is that because women typically enter the workforce later than men and often have to drop out and reenter the workforce during their childbearing years, antinepotism policies cause them a greater hardship. Since they may enter the workforce later than their husbands or reenter after childbearing, they may be prohibited a job in the same company as their husband. Men, by their greater longevity with an organization, are more likely to be promoted to supervisory positions. Organizational antinepotism policies then may result in a woman having to transfer to another location or be terminated if she is left in a subordinate chain-of-command relationship with her husband.

In the United States, the above criticism has led many individuals affected by such rules to challenge their legality in court, although such challenges have usually fallen on unsympathetic judicial ears. Nearly all such challenges have resulted in a general trend toward deference to administrative interests in employee rights cases. In fact, in recent years the federal courts have almost uniformly dis- missed these law suits concluding that antinepotism rules, which seek to prevent conflicts of interest and promote employee harmony and productivity, are reasonable and justified even though they may work a hardship on the careers of married couples.

ROBERT H. ELLIOTT

BIBLIOGRAPHY

Aronoff, Craig E., and John L. Ward, 1993. "Rules for Nepotism." *Nation's Business*, vol. 81, no. 1 (January), 64–65.
Reed, Christine M., and Willa M. Bruce, 1993. "Dual-Career Couples in the Public Sector: A Survey of Personnel Policies and Practices." *Public Personnel Management*, vol. 22, no. 2 (Summer) 187–199.
Reed, Christine M., and Linda J. Cohen, 1989. "Anti-Nepotism Rules: The Legal Rights of Married Co-workers." *Public Personnel Management*, vol. 18, no. 1 (Spring) 37–44.

NEW PUBLIC MANAGEMENT. A concerted program of public sector reform aimed at replacing administration by management, replacing formal bureaucracy by markets or contracts as far as possible, and reducing the size and scale of the public sector.

The 1980s and 1990s saw major changes to the public sectors of most advanced countries, best characterized as a change from traditional public administration to new public management (Hughes 1994). There are other names for the transition including "managerialism" (Pollitt 1990), "market-based public administration" (Lan and Rosenbloom 1992), or "entrepreneurial government" (Osborne and Gaebler 1992). New public management has some advantages over these as a description of what has taken place.

New public management, as a term, derives from the United Kingdom and is different from the earlier American usage of public management as a technical subfield of public administration. For example, U.S. authors J. Steven Ott, Albert Hyde, and Jay Shafritz (1991) see public management as a branch of the larger field of public administration or public affairs; the part that "overviews the art and science of applied methodologies for public administrative program design and organisational restructuring, policy and management planning, resource allocations through budgeting systems, financial management, human resources management, and program evaluation and audit" (p. ix). In other countries than the United States, the 1980s saw the eclipse of the public administrator, a decline in public administration as a field, and the rise of the public manager. The new term is appropriate as there are differences in meaning between "administration" and "management" with the latter more about gaining results and the personal responsibility for doing so than the former, which is more narrowly concerned with following instructions.

Christopher Hood (1991)–the popularizer of the term "new public management"–argued the managerial program comprises seven main points. First, there should be "hands-on professional management in the public sector." This means letting the managers manage or, as Hood puts it "active, visible, discretionary control of organisations from named persons at the top." The typical justification for this is that "accountability requires clear assignment of responsibility for action." Second, there should be "a focus on explicit standards and measures of performance." This requires goals to be defined and performance targets to be set, and it is justified by proponents as "accountability requires clear statement of goals; efficiency requires a 'hard look' at objectives." Third, "a greater emphasis on output controls." Resources are directed to areas according to measured performance, because of the "need to stress results rather than procedures." Fourth, a "shift to disaggregation" of units in the public sector. This involves the breaking up of large entities into "corporatised units around products," funded separately and "dealing with one another on an 'arm's-length' basis." This is justified on the need to create manageable units and "to gain the efficiency advantages of franchise arrangements *inside* as well as outside the public sector." Fifth, "a shift to greater competition" in the public sector. This involves "the move to term contracts and public tendering procedures" and is justified as using "rivalry as the key to lower costs and better standards." Sixth, a stress on "private sector styles" of management practice. This involves a "move away from military-style 'public service ethic'" and "flexibility in hiring and rewards," which is justified by "need to use 'proven' private sector management tools in the public sector." Seventh, a stress on "greater discipline and parsimony" in resource use. Hood sees this as "cutting direct costs, raising labour discipline, resisting union demands, limiting 'compliance costs' to business" and is typically justified by the "need to check resource demands" of the public sector and "do more with less (pp. 4–5)."

The listing by Hood is thorough, but could be summarized as, first, a shift from traditional public administration with far greater attention paid to the achievement of results and the personal responsibility of managers and, second, a replacement of bureaucracy by markets. Organizations, personnel, and employment terms and conditions are to be more flexible with such traditional public administration conditions of service as a job for life disappearing. Organizational and personal objectives are to be set clearly to enable measurement of their achievement through performance indicators, and there is to be more systematic evaluation of programs. Senior staff is more likely to be politically committed to the government of day rather than nonpartisan or neutral. Government functions are more likely to face market tests, such as contracting out. Also, government involvement in an area need not always mean government provision through bureaucratic means. Finally, there is also a trend toward reducing government functions. This may not necessarily be part of the managerial program, as managerial reforms could conceivably occur without reducing the scope of government, but it is occurring at the same time.

New public management is a serious challenge to traditional public administration and is so for three reasons. First, it appears to be better based in a theoretical sense, being drawn from economics and management in the private sector, while traditional public administration's theory of bureaucracy, service to the state, and separation of politics from administration theories seem outdated. Second, it promises a great reduction in the role of public sector as function after function is contracted out or is regarded as unnecessary. In an age in which public servants and high taxes are reputedly unpopular, this has some electoral benefit for politicians. Third, new public management may be the harbinger of a form of genericism whereby there is nothing particularly novel or different about the management of government compared to any other form of management.

It is hard to know what will be the end result of the widespread adoption of new public management. Critics, particularly from a public administration tradition, argue that the good parts of the old model–high ethical standards, service to the state–are being cast aside in the headlong rush to adopt the new theory. Presumably an increase in corruption will lead to the reassertion of the traditional model of public administration for the same reason it was adopted in the nineteenth century. By contrast, it could be argued that the public administration model was moribund and ineffective. Greater productivity is being achieved by the adoption of new public management and many of the parts of the old model such as political neutrality or employment for life were no longer necessary. However, the change to a managerial form of government has been accompanied by an even greater disenchantment with the political system and its ability to solve or ameliorate social ills.

What remains to be seen is if the best parts of the old model of administration–professionalism, impartiality, high ethical standards, the absence of corruption–can be maintained, along with the improved performance a managerial model promises.

OWEN E. HUGHES

BIBLIOGRAPHY

Hood, Christopher, 1991. "A Public Management for All Seasons?" *Public Administration*, vol. 69, no. 1: 3–19.
Hughes, Owen E., 1994. *Public Management and Administration*. London: Macmillan.
Lan, Zhiyong, and David H. Rosenbloom, 1992. "Editorial." *Public Administration Review*, vol. 52: 6.

Osborne, David, and Ted Gaebler, 1992. *Reinventing Government: How the Entrepreneurial Spirit Is Transforming the Public Sector.* Reading, MA: Addison-Wesley.

Ott, J. Steven, Albert C. Hyde, and Jay M. Shafritz, eds., 1991. *Public Management: The Essential Readings.* Chicago: Lyceum Books/Nelson Hall.

Pollitt, Christopher, 1990. *Managerialism and the Public Services: The Anglo-American Experience.* Oxford: Basil Blackwell.

NEW URBANISM. An approach to building cities which reemphasises qualities of urbanity rather than suburban qualities. It combines design for higher housing densities and greater diversity in housing choice with mixed land use to integrate a greater range of urban services within walking distance. It stresses traditional streets, focused toward a town center linked by a good transit system. It is a reaction to 50 years of city building that has created significant loss of urban community and heavy dependence on the automobile.

The Problem Addressed by New Urbanism

Elmer Johnson (1993), the former executive vice president and director of General Motors (GM), chaired a panel of eminent U.S. urban transportation policy experts in 1993 called together to assess the extent of the problem of the automobile. His report begins: "Can we avoid the collision of cities and cars? Is it possible to have good transportation and great cities as well? . . . Urbanites should have good basic access to people, goods, and services whether or not they drive cars. They should have transportation systems that enable them to move about in ways that are secure, commodious, efficient and hassle-free; to view clear skies and breathe clean air; and to choose from among a variety of mobility modes, including walking and bicycling in a safer, non-intimidating environment".

Johnson's question has become a central policy issue for American cities as they approach the twenty-first century. The significance of Johnson's report was not in its condemnation of American automobile dependence, which has been attacked by many commentators and citizen groups for a long time, but it signified that the issue had become mainstream for industry and government. When a former GM executive (advised by 26 of the nation's transportation and urban policy experts) says that there are "serious problems" with cars and American cities, that we are "at a crossroads similar to that described by Rachel Carson in *Silent Spring* in 1962," then the issue is surely on the public-policy agenda.

This is not just an American phenomenon. The British government's Royal Commission on Environmental Pollution in 1994 made a complete reassessment of how it was managing the issue of the automobile in the city and concluded: "The need for a change in direction and a new

TABLE I. PROBLEMS OF AUTOMOBILE DEPENDENCE

Environmental	Economic	Social
Oil vulnerability	Congestion costs	Loss of street life
Urban sprawl	High infra-structure costs	Loss of community
Photochemical smog	Loss of productive rural land	Loss of public safety
Lead, Benzene, other toxics	Loss of urban land to bitumen	Isolation in remote suburbs
High greenhouse gas contributions		Access problems for carless people and those with disabilities
Greater storm-water problems		
Traffic problems—noise, community severance.		

strategy is starkly highlighted by forecasts of road traffic growth and by the road building programs...we do not regard this cycle of continual road building facilitating continual growth of road traffic as environmentally sustainable." (Royal Commission on Environmental Pollution, 1994, p. xiii).

Reports like these are showing that cars are colliding with the environment of cities in obvious ways, but they are also now being seen to be the source of much economic inefficiency and social unrest to the city in general. Although recognizing the obvious attraction of cars to individuals, urban policy makers are faced in the 1990s with a raft of problems from dependence on the automobile that rapidly threatens to swamp them. Cities in every part of the world are facing the same issue, from Los Angeles to Lima, from Budapest to Bangkok. The problems that are highlighted by this debate are summarized in Table I.

The dilemma over the automobile is not new; it is essentially the moral dilemma that has always faced cities between providing for individual desires and providing for the good of the whole community (Ellul 1970). The automobile is a technology that offers significant attractions to individuals in terms of freedom and power, but in large numbers it is associated with the loss of many public realm attributes in cities. The reclaiming of the urban "commons" is critical to the New Urbanism movement. It has tried to provide a policy framework for resolving the dilemma of the automobile in cities.

Underlying Theoretical Framework

Three different approaches to avoiding the collision between cars and cities are open to policymakers: "cleaning up the car", "charging for the car", or "providing options to the car".

Automobile Technology—"Cleaning up the Car"

American public policy and administration since the 1960s has emphasized the cleaning up of the automobile. Powerful regulatory frameworks have been established for cleaning up the emissions, reducing the fuel consumption, controlling the noise, and improving the safety of automobiles. Considerable progress has been made and much more can be done with technology, though there is growing awareness that some thermodynamic limits may make future progress less spectacular. Johnson's (1993) report concludes that the next technological gains will be "more difficult and costly to attain" (p. 28). There is also awareness that the multiple goals required of technology are often conflicting; for example, the new "supercars" of the future are extremely lightweight but may not be popular from a safety point of view, especially when the trend in freight technology is to go for bigger, heavier trucks.

As well there is now widespread awareness that the problems of the automobile go beyond these technological approaches. Even with completely clean automobiles, American cities still are on collision course with cars. The sheer space occupied by cars with their associated roads and parking has created "black top wildernesses" out of so much of the modern city. Johnson's report concludes that "Cities are ill-equipped to accommodate the space demands of cars" (p. 20). The land requirements of the car feed urban sprawl and have helped make urban growth management a major American urban issue (Richmond 1994). The economic and social issues listed in Table I are all related to excessive car use and dependence, not to failures in car technology.

Thus in the 1990s, American public policy and administration has begun to look in other directions as to how it can avoid the collision between cars and cities. The major policy response, and the one favored by Johnson and his team of public policy advisers, has been to use economic measures. They believe excessive car use in occurring because it is too cheap. Thus, the mood is shifting toward "charging for the car" rather than "cleaning up the car" as the focus for public policy and administration in this area.

Economics—"Charging for the Car"

Several economic studies on the automobile in America (Apogee Research 1994; Litman 1992; Mackenzie, Dower, and Cheng 1992; Moffet 1991; Voorhees 1992) and in other countries (Royal Commission on Environmental Pollution 1994; Kageson 1993; Laube and Lynch 1994; UPI 1991) reveal that there are many hidden subsidies on cars and their use.

The average is around US $4,000 per vehicle per year from roads, parking, health costs, pollution costs, and so forth. Although there is awareness that transit is subsi-

dized, the policy community has only in these recent studies discovered that the car subsidy is much greater.

Thus, the main push by policy analysts in America attempting to address the problem of cars in cities has become the need to have a more appropriate price for gasoline, for car parking and for road use (through tools and as yet untried electronic techniques of pricing).

Johnson's (1993) report concludes:

> When a good as central to American life as the automobile remains underpriced for several decades, that good tends to be used more than it otherwise would be. Habits become ingrained and are hard to break. They are reinforced by the present urban infrastructure designed to exploit the full possibilities of private car mobility. The legacy is a built environment and a deeply rooted culture that for the next ten to twenty years leave the nation with little choice but to continue to rely on the motor vehicle for both private and pubic transportation in urban areas. Moreover, because one in six American workers is employed in an automotive-related industry, there is an enormous interest that works against major reform except over the long term.
>
> Accordingly the nation must devise strategies to change the habits of the driving public by signalling the true social costs of vehicle use (p. 11).

This is good economic sense and at least partly explains why European cities have much less car usage than American cities (Newman and Kenworthy 1989b). However, it is not good political sense. It is hard to achieve any significant increases in the cost of driving when Congress is always cutting transit but has no plans for hitting the motorist. In a car-dependent city, it is the poor who suffer most from this pricing approach. Cities built around car use cannot easily provide other options in the short term. True social costs in the short term will mean that people and firms just spend more money on travel, resulting in inflation and social pain at lower incomes.

As it is not politically acceptable to use large price increases to change car use behavior, the view develops that nothing can be done. The result is a kind of policy despair. Charles Lave (1992) concludes that "The desire for personal mobility seems to be unstoppable; it is perhaps the 'Irresistible Force'" (p. 10). The implication is that there is nothing to avoid the collision of the car with cities; we can merely adjust a little at the margin.

Into this policy vacuum has come a renewed interest in the potential for urban planning to provide alternatives to the car in cities.

Planning/the New Urbanism—"Providing Options to the Car"

The views of most transportation and urban policymakers in America over the past few decades seem to have been that it is not possible to control use of the automobile through planning, that urban planning is just not an appropriate area for policy initiatives in managing the automobile (Wachs and Crawford 1991; Altshuler *et al.* 1984; Meyer and Gomez-Ibanez 1981; Meyer, Kain, and Wohl 1965). Alternatives have been rare (e.g. Pushkarev and Zupan 1977; Schneider 1979; Cervero 1986; Pucher 1988) so that when our research on 32 global cities and their automobile dependence was published in the *Journal of the American Planning Association* (Newman and Kenworthy 1989a) suggesting an important role for planning, there was an immediate and powerful response in the next issue:

> Newman and Kenworthy's world is the Kafkaesque nightmare that Hayek (1945) always dreaded, a world in which consumers have no voice, relative prices have no role and planners are tyrants . . . Fortunately, the United States remains a free society where consumers and group interests retain sufficient power and influence to restrain draconian means of intervention. . . . Perhaps Newman and Kenworthy would be well advised to seek out another planet, preferably unpopulated, where they can build their compact cities from scratch with solar-powered transit (Gordon and Richardson 1989, p. 345).

There has however been a growing movement for managing the automobile through urban planning that is now loosely called New Urbanism. It has a number of key texts (Katz 1994; Calthorpe 1993; Duany and Plater-Zybeck 1991; Engwicht 1993; Trancik 1986; Rabinowitz *et al.* 1991). Although it has its academic champions, the main momentum of New Urbanism is coming from citizen groups in the cities. They have no doubt that American cities have been and are being planned, but the assumptions are too oriented toward automobile dependence. For example, the Portland group 1000 Friends of Oregon concludes:

> During the past 40 years, the number of cars and light trucks, and the number of miles Americans have driven them, have increased at a rate roughly three times that of population growth. With this increasing dependence on automobile travel has come an increasing awareness of the mobility, energy, air quality and social impacts associated with extensive auto use.

> Although we have made great strides in making our cars cleaner and more fuel efficient, these steps alone have not cured the negative side effects of automobile use.

> ■ Despite a doubling of the miles per gallon rating for new cars between 1973 and 1988, transportation oil consumption during the same period increased nearly 20%.

> ■ While increased tail pipe emissions standards are expected to result in a 10% reduction in carbon monoxide, nitrous oxides, and hydrocarbons between 1989 and 2000, the same pollutants are expected to increase by 30% between 1989–2000.

> The reason energy and air policies have not been more successful is that the increase in the number of vehicle miles travelled each year has completely outstripped any advances produced by these measures. We must face the fact that to protect the quality of the air we breathe, the sustainability of our economy, and the mobility of our society, we must drive less" (LUTRAQ Fact Sheet #1, 1000 Friends of Oregon).

The suggested solutions from 1000 Friends of Oregon are as follows:

■ Density: Only when residential densities are more than 8 net units per acre can there by a competitive transit service, and more walking/cycling will be feasible.

■ Designation: If a more market-oriented zoning could be designated for suburbs, then car trips would be around 25 percent less.

■ Design: Land use needs to be designed around transit and has to be pedestrian friendly; such development corridors can more than halve car use.

The group, like many others in American cities, spends much of its time and resources trying to stop highways and provide scenarios for the future where such expensive infrastructure is not needed. Its input to the policy process has been sophisticated and successful, winning most of its legal battles for a different and less car dependent city. Portland is rapidly becoming one of the icons of New Urbanism together with a number of smaller developments such as Seaside (Florida), Laguna West (California), Kentlands (Maryland), Brentwood (California), Bamberton (British Columbia), and Windsor (Florida).

Many examples of New Urbanism are also found in Australian and Canadian cities where a fertile audience has developed for such ideas in recent years (Cervero 1986; Kenworthy and Newman 1993; Newman, Kenworthy, and Robinson, 1992). Transit-oriented planning of this kind is a well established part of many European and Asian cities. However, New Urbanism has given an extra credibility to policymakers in these cities as well. The Organization for Economic Cooperation and Development (OECD), the ECE, the United Nations (UN), and other international agencies are all pushing a combination of pricing and planning as their recommended strategies for managing the automobile. Even the World Bank is recognizing that land-use planning is a major process in managing traffic (Serageldin and Barrett 1993) that contains a range of economic and social policy considerations. Sources of hope are thus found across the world (Newman 1995) and are characterized by a strong belief that urban citizens are more than just isolated consumers (Newman, Kenworthy, and Vintila 1993).

U.S. Urban Policy

Despite the overwhelming advice from American transportation and urban policy theorists not to use urban planning to help cities in their struggle to manage the automobile, America did move to a more substantial commitment and belief in urban planning—at least at a federal level. The Intermodal Surface Transportation Efficiency Act (ISTEA) of 1992 was largely developed from citizens groups (a coalition called Surface Transportation Policy Project) who felt the lack of policy in their cities and who did not feel it was a lost cause to involve planning. It largely took the transportation and planning policy community by surprise when Congress and the Senate overwhelmingly supported it. The act gives flexibility to cities in how they spend transportation funds, but they must show compliance with the Clean Air Act, which requires a reduction in car use to be demonstrated. The act depends on regional strategies at the metropolitan level and thus reasserts the importance of long-range strategic urban planning.

Despite the new required commitment to planning, there has not been as much use of the ISTEA legislation in U.S. cities as the proponents of the act expected. Partly this is because American cities had lost much of their planning infrastructure in the 1980s, partly because there were few planners trained in the past 20 years to demonstrate less car-dependent options and partly because local communities were unaware of the potential in the act to contribute to this process. There appears now to be a gathering momentum that is providing some of the New Urbanism agenda, but the 1980s and early 1990s in America seem to have been largely lost opportunities compared to many other cities around the world (Kenworthy and Newman 1993).

The debate on the collision between cars and cities is thus highlighting the importance of public policy and administration in American cities. The private desires of individuals for the mobility and freedom that are promised by the automobile are colliding with the public dimension of cities—their streets and neighborhoods, their air, their surrounding forest and farmland, and perhaps even their climate. The growth of New Urbanism and the strength of citizen involvement in the future of their cities has led to a revival in the belief that public policy and administration does provide the potential to overcome many of the apparently intractable problems of cities, including the collision with the automobile.

This has however run hard up against the new Republican Congress in the mid-1990s with its mandate to reduce government. Thus, creative solutions using public-private partnerships are being found such as "enterprise districts" used to help revive old areas or the "city center districts," with their local knowledge and their commitment to local improvement. However, for truly sustainable solutions that can genuinely avoid the collision between cars and cities, there need to be metropolitanwide plans that can deliver real alternatives to car dependence and will inevitably involve all levels of public policy and administration. New Urbanism is beginning to work out what this may mean in an America that if it does not change is facing a doubling of car numbers in its cities over the next generation together with an even greater increase in car use.

Policies of New Urbanism

New Urbanism is fundamentally a revival in the belief that city planning can address many of the problems of the modern city. It suggests that to manage the automobile in modern cities is not easy, but it is also not impossible.

Cities that are seen to have had some success point to a combination of policies that have worked for them. Thus, the public policy and administration agenda being set by New Urbanism to manage the car in cities appears to involve the following:

- *Reducing Road and Parking Infrastructure:* Cities that are serious about managing the car need to implement policies to stop major road proposals and to begin reducing parking and implement regulations concerning parking provisions. The reclaiming of black top for more creative urban activity is a feature of such cities (Trancik 1986).
- *New Transit Infrastructure:* Cities need high profile transit infrastructure that can help shape the city as well as ease traffic problems. If transit is just left to be a supplementary process in streets designed for the automobile, there will be no resolution of the transport dilemma. This highlights the importance of electric rail systems, which can go directly into the center of urban activity taking up to 50 times less space than car-based transportation and providing a travel experience that can also rival if not surpass that provided by the automobile—particularly an automobile caught up in traffic. Modern light rail systems that run in streets as well as on separate rights of way are providing many cities with the cost-effective and high profile solution they are looking for (ECMT 1994). Demand-responsive mini buses that use satellite tracking and electronic communication systems are likely to provide the links to fixed track rail services in local suburbs. Evidence on the commercial value for city centers of mass transit is provided by Portland, which went from 5 percent to 30 percent of the city's retail turnover after investing in light rail.
- *Pedestrian/Cycle Orientation:* Cities need to provide for the most efficient, equitable, and human form of transport. This means a city needs specific infrastructure for cycling, and it is critical to provide good walking space on streets and public places. Traffic calming,

which deliberately slows traffic to provide better access for nonmotorized modes is proving to be environmentally, socially, and economically successful (Roberts 1989). Urban design in the city needs to have the perspective of what is best to make lively and attractive streets. Any city that neglects this dimension is predicted to find social and economic problems as well as the obvious environmental ones.

- *Density and Mixed Land Use:* Cities need to maintain land use efficiency, which is linked closely to transport. Dispersing land uses at low density in uniformly zoned areas creates automobile dependence. Dense, mixed-use urban villages linked by transit create the opportunity for pedestrian and transit-oriented characteristics to be introduced into the automobile-dominated city. Reversing the density trends of car-based cities can begin by redeveloping older industrial and warehouse sites in inner areas and old office sites in city centers. However, the biggest challenge is to begin building urban villages in transit-oriented suburban centers and to prevent the unnecessary spread of urban development into surrounding forest and farmland.

Evidence that density and mixed land use has commercial advantages is coming from the Bank of America (1994) report, which is suggesting there are limits to urban sprawl and from Equitable Real Estate Investment Management Inc. (1995), a top real estate adviser, who says the future will favor "24-hour cities." They emphasize that livability is the key to a safe investment:

> "Attractive neighbourhoods lie within hailing distance of the office, and at the very least, you don't have to spend a major fraction of your life commuting to work. It's a short walk to take the kids to a park. The supermarket is within easy reach, you can pick up a quart of milk just about any time. There are movie theatres and museums in town. Good schools–preferably public–are mainstays. You feel relatively safe–it's OK to stroll around the block at night without a Rottweiler."

There is increasing awareness that such urbanity and services are very limited unless there is sufficient density and mixed use.

- *Planning Control:* All of the above policy areas have strong market pressures behind them but require planning to facilitate. This planning is not heavy-handed bureaucracy but is an expression of any city's cultural values–it highlights the priority on urbanity and access to the city's services for all people, that is, to a greater degree of community activity. All cities have some commitment to this social value, but it is most obvious in those cities that are seen as pioneers of New Urbanism. The control of automobile dependence

through conscious planning is seen as essential, otherwise it will destroy almost every attempt to maintain vital community life in an urban setting. This is seen to apply to strong neighborhoods, which need to be protected from the dispersing and disruptive aspects of the automobile, whereas in many cities the policy of reducing automobile dependence is seen to be part of a process of reclaiming neighborhoods.

- *Strategic Participative Plans:* Apart from local plans, the critical role of a strategic plan for a city-region is seen as central to New Urbanism. Such plans need to involve the populace in every stage so that the tendency to optimize only for particular neighborhoods is eased if not overcome. The importance of long-term plans with a focus on sustainability as required by ISTEA and the UN Agenda 21 is another motivating factor in these cities.

Conclusion

New Urbanism is the third stage in the public policy and administration agenda for managing the automobile in American cities. Obviously, it does not see its agenda as replacing the other two; improved auto technology and better pricing of car use will be needed as much as possible. But the inability of the other approaches to deliver a full solution has driven policy toward New Urbanism.

Perhaps the most important contribution of New Urbanism is that it is providing a different level of hope in the whole policy process as it relates to cities. The strength of feeling it is generating among citizen groups and students is akin to the early days of the environmental movement. Whether it is as successful in becoming an established part of urban public policy and practice remains to be seen, but the dearth of other options for avoiding the collision between cities and cars would suggest it will be given a fair trial over the next generation in American cities.

PETER NEWMAN

BIBLIOGRAPHY

Altshuler, A., J. R. Pucher, and J. Womack, 1979. *The Urban Transportation Problem: Politics and Policy Innovation.* Cambridge, MA: MIT Press.

Altshuler, A., M. Anderson, D. Jones, D. Roos, and J. Wormack, 1984. *The Future of the Automobile: Report of MIT's International Automobile Program.* Cambridge, MA: MIT Press.

Apogee Research, 1994. *The Costs of Transportation.* Boston: Conservation Law Foundation.

Bank of America, 1994. *Beyond Sprawl.* San Francisco: Bank of America.

Calthorpe, P., 1993. *The Next American Metropolis: Ecology Unity and the American Dream.* New York: Princeton Architectural Press.

Cervero, R., 1986. *Suburban Gridlock.* New Brunswick: Rutgers Center for Urban Policy Research.

Duany, A., and E. Plater Zybeck, 1991. *Towns and Town-Making Principles.* New York: Rizzoli.

ECMT, 1994. *Light Rail Transit Systems.* Paris: European Conference of Ministers of Transport and OECD.

Ellul J., 1970. *The Meaning of the City.* London: Eerdmans.

Engwicht, D., 1993. *Towards an Ecocity: Calming the Traffic.* Sydney: Envirobook.

Equitable Real Estate Investment Management Inc., 1995. *Emerging Trends.* Chicago: Real Estate Research Corporation.

Gordon, P., and H. Richardson, 1989. "Gasoline Consumption and Cities: A Reply." *Journal of the American Planning Association,* vol. 55, no. 2 : 342–346.

Johnson, E., 1993. *Avoiding the Collision of Cities and Cars.* Chicago: American Academy of Arts and Sciences with the Aspen Institute.

Kageson, P., 1993. *Getting the Prices Right: A European Scheme for Making Transport Pay Its True Cost.* Stockholm, Brussels: European Federation for Transport and Environment.

Katz, P., 1994. *The New Urbanism: Toward an Architecture of Community.* New York: McGraw Hill.

Kenworthy, J. R., and P. W. G. Newman, 1993. *Automobile Dependence: The Irresistible Force?* Perth: ISTP Murdoch University.

Ketcham, B., and C. Komanoff, 1992. *Win-Win Transportation: A Loser's Approach to Financing Transport in New York City and the Region.* New York: Ketcham, Komanoff and Associates.

Laube, F. and M. Lynch, 1994. *Costs and Benefits of Motor Vehicle Traffic in Western Australia.* Perth: ISTP Murdoch University.

Lave, C., 1992. "Cars and Demographics." *Access,* vol. 1:4–11.

Litman, T., 1992. *Transportation Efficiency and Equity: An Economic Analysis,* masters dissertation, TESC, Victoria, BC.

Mackenzie, J., R. Dower and D. Cheng, 1992. *The Going Rate: What It Really Costs to Drive.* Washington, DC: World Resources Institute.

Meyer, J., and A. Gomez-Ibanez, 1981. *Autos, Transit, and Cities.* Cambridge: Harvard University Press.

Meyer, J., J. Kain, and M. Wohl, 1965. *The Urban Transportation Problem.* Cambridge: Harvard University Press.

Meyer, John, and Anthony Gomez-Ibane, 1981. *Auto's Transit and Cities.* Cambridge: Harvard University Press.

Moffet, J., 1991. *The Price of Mobility.* San Francisco: Natural Resources Defence Council.

Newman, P. W. G., 1995. "Transport." In *UN Global Report on Human Settlements.* Nairobi: Habitat and UNEP.

Newman, P. W. G., and J. R. Kenworthy, 1989a. "Gasoline Consumption and Cities: A Comparison of US Cities with a Global Survey and Its Implications." *Journal of the American Planning Association,* vol. 55, no. 1: 24–37.

———, 1989b. *Cities and Automobile Dependence: An International Sourcebook.* Aldershoot: Grower.

Newman, P. W. G., J. R. Kenworthy, and L. Robinson, 1992. *Winning Back the Cities.* Sydney: Pluto Press.

Newman, P. W. G., J. R. Kenworthy, and P. Vintila, 1993. "Can We Overcome Autombile Dependence: Physical Planning in an Age of Urban Cynicism." *Cities,* vol. 12, no. 1: 53–65.

Pucher, J., 1988. "Urban Travel Behavior as the Outcome of Public Policy: The Example of Modal-Split Western Europe and North America." *Journal of the American Planning Association,* vol. 54 (Autumn) : 509–520.

Pushkarev, W. and J. M. Zupan 1977. *Public Transportation and Land Use Policy.* Indiana Press: Bloomington and London.

Rabinowitz, H., E. Beimborn, C. Mrotek, S. Yan, and P. Gugliotta, 1991. *The New Suburb.* U.S. Dept. of Transportation, Report DOT-T-91-12.

Richmond, H. R. 1994. *The Prospects for Land Use Reform in America: Storm Clouds Silver Lining?* National Growth Management Alliance, Portland, Oregon.

Roberts J., 1989. *User-Friendly Cities: What Britain Can Learn from Mainland Europe.* London: TEST.

Royal Commission on Environmental Pollution, 1994. *Transport and the Environment.* London: HMSO.

Schneider, K. R., 1979. *On the Nature of Cities.* San Francisco: Jossey-Bass.

Serageldin, I., and R. Barrett, 1993. *Environmentally Sustainable Urban Transport: Defining a Global Policy.* Washington, D.C.: World Bank.

Trancik, R., 1986. *Finding Lost Space: Theories of Urban Design.* New York: Van Nostrand.

UPI, 1991. *Unweltwirkungen von Finanzinstrumenten in Verkehrsbereich.* Heidelberg: Umwelt und Prognose-Institut.

Voorhees, M., 1992. *The True Costs of the Automobile to Society.* Boulder, CO: Westview.

Wachs, M., and M. Crawford, 1991. *The Car and the City: The Automobile, the Built Environment, and Daily Urban Life.* Ann Arbor: University of Michigan Press.

NEW ZEALAND MODEL.

Arguably, the purest and most developed example of managerialism to emerge in the public sector by the mid-1990s. This article surveys the origins, nature, and merits of this model.

Introduction

Prior to the mid-1980s, New Zealand had a highly centralized and heavily regulated system of public administration. Human resource management, including pay fixing, was controlled by the State Services Commission (SSC). Government agencies were funded via a cash-based, program-oriented budgeting system with strict controls on inputs. Most departments were multifunctional in nature and provided a range of services, such as policy advice to ministers and the delivery of governmental program. Many departments also undertook significant commercial activities. Since the mid-1980s, the fourth Labour government (1984–1990) and the subsequent National government (1990–) have made far-reaching changes to the design and management of the public sector. These reforms have included a vigorous program of commercialization, corporatization, and asset sales, as well as radical changes to human resource management, financial management, the machinery of government, and the structure and organization of subnational government (see Boston *et al.* 1991, 1996; OECD 1990; Scott, Bushnell, and Sallee 1990). Most of the reforms have conformed to the principles and practices of managerialism or the "new public management" (Hood 1990; Hood and Jackson 1991).

The Political System

New Zealand is a small, unitary state, with a unicameral parliament and a system of cabinet government based on the Westminster model (see Mulgan 1994). Accordingly, the doctrines of collective responsibility and individual ministerial responsibility are key constitutional conventions. The sovereign, the Queen of New Zealand, appoints the governor-general on the recommendation of the prime minister. The legal system is based on the British model. Until 1993, New Zealand had a first-past-the-post electoral system. This generally produced single-party governments with clear parliamentary majorities. As a result of a referendum in late 1993, a new system of proportional representation—based on the German model—has been introduced. The majority of future governments are likely to be coalitions.

Since the early twentieth century, the public service has been nonpartisan in nature with recruitment at all levels based on the principle of merit. The heads of ministries and departments, referred to as chief executives since 1988, are appointed by the government, normally on the recommendation of the State Services commissioner, and are placed on performance-based contracts for (renewable) terms of up to five years. In accordance with the conventions of the Westminster system, it is expected that chief executives and their staff will serve the government of the day efficiently, competently, and loyally and provide policy advice that is "free and frank."

Most important areas of public policy—including the funding and administration of education, health care, housing, social welfare, and policing—are the responsibility of the central government. At the subnational level, there are 17 regional councils (including unitary councils) and over 70 territorial authorities, all of which are elected. The regional councils have a primary responsibility for resource management; the territorial authorities have a wider range of functions such as land-use planning, the regulation of building, parking, and transportation, the provision of local public goods (e.g., roads, parks and reserves, etc.), and the provision of public services (e.g., passenger transport, water supply, sewerage and rubbish disposal, and pensioner housing).

The Public Sector Reforms

New Zealand's public sector reforms, which commenced in earnest in the mid-1980s, were part of a comprehensive and radical program of economic stabilization and liberalization (Bollard 1994). The liberalization program was prompted primarily by economic considerations: serious fiscal difficulties, a substantial public debt, poor economic growth, high inflation, rising unemployment, a poorly performing state-trading sector, and declining living standards. As in many other jurisdictions, the key aims of the public-sector reforms were to improve the efficiency, effectiveness, and accountability of the bureaucracy. Supplementary objectives included curbing public expenditure, reducing the number of government employees, clarifying departmental objectives, improving the quality of the goods and services produced by public agencies, and making public services more accessible and culturally sensitive (especially for the indigenous Maori population). The public-sector reforms began tentatively but quickly expanded from a series of largely administrative changes to a comprehensive program of "reinvention."

In designing this program, policymakers were influenced not merely by overseas models (especially Australia and Britain) and previous New Zealand experience but also by at least four distinct theoretical traditions: managerialism, public choice theory, property-rights theory, and the new economics of organizations (i.e., agency theory and transaction cost analysis) (see Boston 1991; Scott and Gorringe 1989). The strong theoretical influence on New Zealand's reforms has contributed to their conceptual rigor, coherence, and distinctiveness. Among other things, it has led to

1. a heavy emphasis on contracting out and the contestable provision of publicly funded services (including policy advice);
2. an extensive use of contracts of various kinds, both within and between organizations;
3. an emphasis on the avoidance of provider (or bureaucratic) capture in organizational design;
4. a significant devolution of management responsibilities; and
5. the quest for governance arrangements and incentive structures that minimize agency costs and transaction costs.

In accordance with the new model, the relationships between voters, politicians, and bureaucrats are regarded as a cascading series of agent-principal relationships. Voters, as the ultimate principal, contract with politicians to provide a range of services. Cabinet ministers, who are both agents and principals, purchase outputs from various suppliers, such as government agencies and private-sector organizations, in order to achieve their desired outcomes. Departmental chief executives, in turn, are accountable to their portfolio minister for the efficient management of the Crown's ownership and purchaser interests in their departments. If they do not perform adequately, they risk the nonrenewal—or worse, the termination—of their employment contract.

A central, and related, feature of the new approach is an emphasis on written contracts and agreements rather than informal understandings and implicit contracts. The legal status of these documents varies. Whereas some are legally binding, others are in the nature of mutual undertakings and simply provide another instrument for clarifying expectations and exercising hierarchical control. Examples of the various kinds of "contracts" that have been introduced include annual performance agreements between ministers and departmental chief executives, purchase agreements between ministers and their departments, performance agreements between managers and their staff at all levels within public agencies, and contracts between public agencies (e.g., between funders and purchasers, funders and providers, and purchasers and providers). To illustrate, the minister of health has an annual performance agreement and a purchase agreement with the chief executive of the ministry in health, and funding agreements with the boards of the four regional health authorities. These latter organizations purchase health services, via annual provider contracts, from the 23 Crown Health Enterprises and various private suppliers (including voluntary organizations).

The rationale for using written agreements rests on the assumption that the performance, accountability, and control of individuals and organizations are enhanced where the respective obligations of principals and agents are made explicit. Although the new approach is proving to be reasonably robust, it is not without its limitations. For instance, it is not always possible for a principal to specify in advance precisely what is required of an agent. The attempt to prepare and negotiate detailed contracts can be time consuming and costly. A strict adherence to imperfectly specified agreements can be counterproductive (e.g., it can reduce innovation and flexibility). The monitoring and enforcement of many contracts is difficult. There is a risk of goal displacing behavior with agents focusing on those outputs (or contract provisions) that are observable and measurable at the expense of those that are not. And a heavy reliance upon legally binding contracts between public agencies runs the risk of judicializing the process of policymaking and implementation.

In the interests of minimizing agency costs and enhancing accountability, the public-sector reforms have been designed to ensure that, wherever possible, each bureaucratic agent serves only one principal. This has led, among other things, to a bias against combining central and local democratic control of public services, or situations where local government delivers centrally funded services. Accordingly, Area Health Boards, which comprised locally elected and centrally appointed members, were abolished in 1993 and replaced with separate purchaser and provider organizations, the boards of which are wholly appointed by the government. Likewise, plans to devolve the provision of a number of key government services to iwi authorities (i.e., Maori tribal organizations) have been abandoned. As it stands, the provision of public education (via early childhood education centers, schools, and tertiary institutions) is the only major governmental activity that still entails dual accountability: locally elected boards are responsible both to their constituents and to the central government (as funder and owner). Although the desire to minimize situations in which agents serve multiple principals may have merit in

terms of managerial accountability, it limits the choice of governance arrangements and tends to reduce opportunities for participation by citizens in the design and delivery of publicly funded services.

The influence of managerialism upon the New Zealand model is evident in various ways. As in many other jurisdictions, there has been a significant devolution of management responsibilities in the interests of productive efficiency, innovation, and client responsiveness. Coupled with this, there has been a marked improvement in performance management systems. Under the State Sector Act (1988), departmental chief executives acquired the SSC's responsibilities for human resource management. Chief executives are now the employers of their staff and, as such, are responsible for all personnel functions. The SSC, however, has retained its role as the employer party for bargaining purposes in some sectors. As a result of the State Sector Act and other legislative changes, uniform, servicewide employment and remuneration determinations have ceased and the principle of fair relativity with the private sector has been abandoned. Compulsory arbitration has also been abolished, but final offer arbitration is available under certain conditions. Wage bargaining is now conducted on a decentralized basis, an increasing number of public servants are covered by individual contracts rather than collective agreements, and there has been a greater reliance on fixed-term appointments and performance-based remuneration systems.

Public choice theory has made at least two major contributions to the New Zealand model. First, it has led to a preoccupation in certain quarters, especially the Treasury (1987), with the avoidance of provider capture. A particular concern has been to minimize conflicting responsibilities or conflicts of interest within departments (such as advising ministers on the delivery of services that the department itself produces) and to ensure that advice from producer departments is contestable (i.e., complemented by advice from other departments). The objective of decoupling potentially conflicting departmental functions has led to substantial institutional fragmentation. Wherever feasible, commercial and noncommercial functions have been separated; commercial functions have either been privatized or placed in state-owned enterprises (SOEs) based on company structures. Likewise, in many cases departments' advisory, delivery, and regulatory functions have been decoupled, as have their roles as funders, purchasers, and providers. In some sectors, especially education, health care, scientific research, and transport, this process has resulted in the creation of a plethora of functionally distinct organizations. Although the new approach has given many government departments and Crown-owned entities a greater clarity of purpose, it has intensified the problems of policy coordination. In some cases, it has also produced substantial interorganization conflict (Ewart and Boston 1993). Another problem arising from institutional fragmentation is that the end users of certain government services (i.e., citizens and consumers) have to deal with a plethora of separate organizations. For various reasons, the full separation of advisory and delivery activities has not been attempted in all cases. Hence, some departments have retained a range of functional responsibilities. Even where agencies have no specific mandate to provide policy advice, some have nonetheless formed policy units and have contributed significantly to policy development.

A second manifestation of the influence of public choice theory has been the various efforts to minimize opportunities for ministerial discretion in the detailed operations of public agencies (especially commercial ones). This has been coupled with the introduction of new mechanisms to make ministerial interventions more transparent and hence—in theory, if not in practice—more politically accountable. A notable example is the Reserve Bank Act (1989). Under this statute, the Reserve Bank is responsible for the management of monetary policy and is charged with pursuing price stability (defined currently as between 0 and 2 percent inflation). If the government wishes to change the definition of price stability or intervene in the bank's implementation of its statutory responsibilities, it can do so, but such interventions must be made public. Similarly, if the government wants an SOE to undertake a function that is not commercially viable, then in accordance with the State-Owned Enterprises Act (1988) it must provide an appropriate subsidy and its actions must be transparent.

New Zealand's financial management reform (FMR) has been particularly distinctive and innovative (see Boston et al. 1991; Pallot 1993). For instance, New Zealand was the first country to introduce accrual accounting and impose capital charges throughout the public sector. It was also the first country to produce comprehensive financial statements on an accruals basis, including a consolidated balance sheet and an operating statement for the whole central government. Another distinctive feature of the FMR is the new appropriations system. Pivotal here is the distinction, on the one hand, between outcomes and outputs and, on the other, between the Crown's purchaser and ownership interests. Such distinctions, although well known in the accounting literature, have not been used previously as the basis for determining the departmental appropriations. And governments elsewhere have not sought to treat all the goods and services produced by public agencies, including policy advice, diplomatic services, and contingent military capabilities, as commodities to which prices can and should be fixed. Among the reporting procedures introduced under the FMR is the requirement for all departments to produce "statements of service performance." These must include financial and nonfinancial information, in particular, the quality, quantity, timeliness, and price of the outputs produced and the level of ministerial satisfaction with their agencies' services.

The Current Structure of the Public Sector

In mid-1995, the agencies of the central government comprised 43 departments (including the New Zealand Defence Force, the Police, the Office of the Clerk, the Parliamentary Counsel Office, and the Parliamentary Service) and three Offices of Parliament (the Office of the Ombudsman, the Parliamentary Commissioner for the Environment, and the Office of the Controller and Auditor-General). In addition, there were over 3,000 Crown entities and other public bodies (e.g., school boards of trustees, tertiary institutions, Crown Health Enterprises, Crown Research Institutes, SOEs, Maori Trust Boards, etc.) As of June 30, 1992, there were around 260,000 staff members employed in central government and nearly 41,000 employed in local government (OECD 1993, p. 220). Of those employed in central government, just under 43,000 worked in the "core" public service (i.e., government departments). By December 1994, this number had fallen to just over 33,000, under half the number employed in the mid-1980s. The reduction in staffing levels in the core public service has been due primarily to corporatization, privatization, contracting-out, and the loss of functions.

Among these, privatization has proved to be of considerable significance and has become a central feature of the New Zealand model. Since the tentative commencement of the privatization program in 1987, over 20 SOEs and other substantial assets have been sold, representing well over a half of the state's commercial assets (both in number and value). The program of asset sales is continuing: A number of SOEs are being prepared for sale, while others are selling some of their assets. The future of the country's largest SOE, the Electricity Corporation of New Zealand, has been under review for a number of years, but it is unlikely to be fully privatized.

Results

It is too early to assess the success of some of the reforms, especially those in the area of health care delivery and scientific research. Nonetheless, there can be little doubt that the reforms introduced in the mid- to late 1980s have been reasonably successful in meeting most of their objectives (Boston et al. 1991, 1996; Duncan and Bollard 1992; Scott, Bushnell, and Sallee 1990; Steering Group 1991). Virtually all the SOEs have experienced marked gains in labor productivity and profitability; there is also evidence of significant improvements in customer services and consumer satisfaction. At the departmental level, substantial savings in administration costs have been recorded, as have improvements in the quality of many services. In addition, the financial management reforms have greatly enhanced management information systems with consequent improvements in the quality of information available to policymakers. As a result, there have been gains in managerial accountability and the opportunity for better policy decisions. There is also general agreement that the new framework of public-sector management has given ministers greater control over the bureaucracy and enhanced their strategic planning capability.

Against this, the public-sector reforms—and the wider economic liberalization program of which they were a part—have had some very negative social consequences, especially for the Maori and the Pacific Islanders, low-income groups, and some rural communities. They have also contributed to a weakening of the egalitarian values that guided policymaking in New Zealand for much of the twentieth century. At another level, while the State Sector Act has arguably enhanced vertical accountability relationships between departments and ministers, horizontal relationships within the executive have been weakened with corresponding implications for policy coordination and the collective interest (Steering Group 1991). A related concern is that ministers have been increasingly reluctant to take political responsibility for activities of their departments (Martin 1994). Similarly, questions have been raised about the way in which organizational fragmentation, the increasing use of consultants, and the heavy reliance on "contracts" may be undermining political control and accountability. The magnitude of the organizational changes to which the public sector has been subjected has also prompted concerns about the loss of institutional memory, the damage to staff morale, and the costs of the reform program (Boston et al. 1991). In addition, it is suggested that the managerialist ethos, which now pervades the public sector, is weakening traditional ethical norms and conventions (Martin 1994). On another front, there are continuing difficulties with the performance management system, including problems with output specification and monitoring, and the application of rewards and sanctions. Finally, the various efforts over the past decade to accommodate Maori interests and to ensure that public agencies are sensitive to the needs of different cultural groups have not been entirely successful. Indeed, the problems that cultural pluralism poses to managerialism are among its greatest challenges.

Overall, the New Zealand model provides a robust and coherent approach to public-sector management. Although doubts persist over the merits of some aspects of the model and although further modifications are inevitable, the major reforms since the mid-1980s in the areas of human resource management, financial management, and machinery of government are widely supported by senior public servants and the main political parties. The impending introduction of proportional representation, therefore, is unlikely to bring substantial policy reversals in these areas. It will, however, alter the style and process of policymaking and as such may have significant implications for the management of policy-oriented departments.

JONATHAN BOSTON

BIBLIOGRAPHY

Bollard, A., 1994. "New Zealand." In J. Williamson, ed., *The Political Economy of Policy Reform*. Washington, DC: Institute for International Economics.

Boston, J., 1991. "The Theoretical Underpinnings of Public Sector Restructuring." In J. Boston, J. Martin, J. Pallot, and P. Walsh, eds., *Reshaping the State: New Zealand's Bureaucratic Revolution*. Auckland: Oxford University Press.

Boston, J., J. Martin, J. Pallot, and P. Walsh, eds. 1991. *Reshaping the State: New Zealand's Bureaucratic Revolution*. Auckland: Oxford University Press.

Boston, J., J. Pallot, and P. Walsh, 1996. *Public Management: The New Zealand Model*. Auckland: Oxford University Press.

Duncan, I., and A. Bollard, 1992. *Corporatization and Privatization: Lessons from New Zealand*. Auckland: Oxford University Press.

Ewart, B., and J. Boston, 1993. "The Separation of Policy Advice from Operations: The Case of Defence Restructuring in New Zealand." *Australian Journal of Public Administration*, vol. 52 (June) 223–240.

Hood, C., 1990. "De-Sir Humphreyfying the Westminster Model of Bureaucracy: A New Style of Governance?" *Governance*, vol. 3 (April) 205–214.

Hood, C., and M. Jackson, 1991. *Administrative Argument*. Aldershot: Dartmouth.

Martin, J., 1994. "The Role of the State in Administration." In A. Sharp, ed., *Leap into the Dark*. Auckland: Auckland University Press.

Mulgan, R., 1994. *Politics in New Zealand*. Auckland: Auckland University Press.

OECD, 1990. *Public Management Developments: Survey—1990*. Paris: OECD.

———, 1993. *Public Management: OECD Country Profiles*. Paris: OECD.

Pallot, J., 1993. "Specifying and Monitoring Government Performance in New Zealand: An Evaluation of Performance to Date." In E. Buschor and K. Schedler, eds., *Perspectives on Performance Measurement and Public Sector Accounting*. Berne: Paul Haupt.

Scott, G., and P. Gorringe, 1989. "Reform of the Core Public Sector: The New Zealand Experience." *Australian Journal of Public Administration*, vol. 48 (March) 81–92.

Scott, G., P. Bushnell, and N. Sallee, 1990. "Reform of the Core Public Sector: New Zealand Experience." *Governance*, vol. 3 (April) 138–167.

Steering Group, 1991. *Review of State Sector Reforms*. Wellington: State Services Commission.

Treasury, 1987. *Government Management*. Wellington: Government Printer.

NOBLESSE OBLIGE.

A French term commonly translated as "rights imply duties." More specifically, it refers to the moral imperative that the possession of, or claim to, rights, statuses, or powers entails corresponding moral duties—duties that are voluntarily assumed by the possessor or the claimant. The sources of such moral obligations are various. For some, the obligation originates in their religious beliefs. Thus, a Christian might argue that having taken upon herself the name of Christ, she is obligated to love others. For some, the obligation originates in their beliefs about class. Thus, a Prussian Junker might argue that as a member of a militaristic aristocracy, he is obligated to be a soldier.

More recently, there has grown an assumption that certain moral obligations are entailed by the character of our innate human nature, which dictates that we can only be fully human by becoming progressively more virtuous. Therefore, every individual is under the imperative of constantly seeking moral nobility.

Since noblesse oblige can take a number of forms, three of the most important will be discussed herein: the noblesse oblige of elitism, the noblesse oblige of power, and the noblesse oblige of good character.

The Noblesse Oblige of Elitism

This form is rooted in the belief in an elite, selected and prepared by nature or deity, with specific and superior necessary characteristics: military elites, spiritual elites, intellectual elites, blood-line elites, or economic elites, to name a few. Whatever the specific nature of their elitism, their overriding moral obligation is to dominate and rule their societies. To resist such "chosen" rulers is an offense against nature or deity and, certainly, against good sense.

Although such elitism still has some defenders, it has been too often discredited to be defensible. This is not to deny the existence of genius in its many guises. Correctly understood and employed, genius can be of the greatest benefit to society. But the assumption that such individuals should be the natural rulers is both morally wrong and destructive.

One illustration should suffice. In some parts of the world, the last two centuries witnessed a romantic revival of a class-based conception of nobility, in which the dominant imperative was a militant defense of one's honor. Such noblesse oblige was central to the romantic novels of Sir Walter Scott or Raphael Sabitini.

The practical results of such beliefs have been most unfortunate, from idealizing dueling to justifying war for the sake of honor. In American history, this can be seen in the misconceived chivalry of the self-styled gentry in the antebellum South. Mark Twain, in *Life on the Mississippi* (1883), went so far as to blame the Civil War upon "the Sir Walter [Scott] disease, which . . . sets the world in love with dreams and phantoms; . . . with the sillinesses and emptinesses, sham grandeurs, sham gauds, and sham chivalries of a brainless and worthless long-vanished society" (p. 375). He concluded: "Sir Walter had so large a hand in making Southern character, as it existed before the [Civil War], that he is in great measure responsible for the war" (p. 376). That may be a bit strong, but it is not entirely off the mark.

The point is that assumptions of a natural superiority based upon genetics, gender, race, or history has produced epic human tragedies. Rightfully, this form of noblesse oblige should be completely rejected.

The Noblesse Oblige of Power

This can be a more beneficial form of noblesse oblige. Here it is assumed that when one is favored by good fortune with power, whether from wealth or position, the recipient is morally obligated to return something to society.

To illustrate the point concerning wealth, some of the self-made American millionaires of the late nineteenth and early twentieth centuries believed great wealth carried with it the obligation to promote the civil welfare. They reasoned that because they were beneficiaries of the economic system of their society, they should return something to that society. Some (but not all) of them made that obligation a reality. Thus, and whatever their ethical failings elsewhere, the philanthropies of Andrew Carnegie, John D. Rockefeller, among others, have benefited many Americans.

The noblesse oblige of holding a position of power, whether through appointment (a CEO, a bureau chief, or a general) or election (a president, a governor, a senator), derives from the fact that power is both addictive and corruptive to both the exercisers and the exercisees. In Lord Acton's familiar phrase, "power tends to corrupt and absolute power corrupts absolutely." The corrective is the voluntary acceptance by the powerful that their power carries with it the moral obligation to conduct themselves according to a higher moral code: to be braver, or kinder, or wiser than those over whom they have power.

Unfortunately, the noblesse oblige of power has been demonstrated more in the breach than in the observance. Nonetheless, the ideal still stands and although it has been sadly neglected in organizational theory and practice, fortunately the military has continued to emphasize it. Hopefully, more organizational theorists and practitioners will understand the importance of the moral obligations of power.

The Noblesse Oblige of Good Character

This form of noblesse oblige derives moral obligations from the moral necessities of human nature. For instance, some virtue ethicists argue that the highest levels of human-ness, of human flourishing, can only be achieved through the progressive development of good moral character. They believe that nature has so designed human beings that virtue is essential to the attainment of full humanity: to be amoral or immoral is to be less than fully human.

This form of noblesse oblige is, both individually and socially, the most significant because, unlike the elitist and the power arguments, good character can be achieved by all people. This makes it the most egalitarian form of noblesse oblige. Because good character cannot be developed in isolation, one must be good in association with others, to the general benefit. The British utilitarian John Stuart

Mill (1806–1873) noted the benefits of this connection in *Utilitarianism* (1863): "And if it may possibly be doubted whether a noble character is always the happier for its nobleness, there can be no doubt that it makes other people happier, and that the world in general is immensely the gainer by it" (p. 14).

This form of noblesse oblige requires individuals to constantly improve their moral character and, as that character improves, their moral actions must likewise always improve. Furthermore, for the noblesse oblige of good character to be effective, it must be both intentional and voluntary. In other words, the sinner does not have the right to demand goodness from the saint. The moral force of the noblesse oblige of good character lies in its intentionality and voluntarism: There can be no external compulsion to goodness.

Morally superior individuals do not owe goodness to others, because all individuals have the potential of developing their character to the highest levels. Rather, the obligation to act morally derives from the fact that such actions are the epitome of our human-ness. One assumes the burdens of moral obligation freely and with no sense of being bound: It is a gift given freely and joyously.

Noblesse oblige is not often overtly discussed by contemporary moral philosophers, but it is implied in the works of many of them, particularly David Norton. The same is true for organizational theorists. For instance, although they do not specifically mention the term, the works of Abraham Maslow, W. Edwards Deming, Amitai Etzioni, and William G. Scott assume a noblesse oblige of good character. In public administration, the same is true for the works of Dwight Waldo and John Rohr.

In conclusion, there is no place for a noblesse oblige of elitism in any part of a democratic society. With respect to public administration, the other two forms of noblesse oblige have an important place. The noblesse oblige of power in relation to the exercise of public power should be quite clear: Because of the terms of their oath of office, public servants must treat the possession of power as an obligation to a heightened morality.

Further, given the moral implications of the adjective "public," public servants should also be committed to the noblesse oblige of good character. The acceptance of these two forms of noblesse oblige would ensure that, as public servants move up the promotional ladder, they would become moral exemplars, which would redound to the benefit of all citizens.

DAVID KIRKWOOD HART

BIBLIOGRAPHY

Deming, W. Edwards, 1986. *Out of the Crisis.* Cambridge, MA: Massachusetts Institute of Technology Press.

Etzioni, Amitai, 1988. *The Moral Dimension.* New York: Free Press.
Maslow, Abraham H., 1970. *Motivation and Personality,* 2d ed. New York: Harper & Row.
Mill, John Stuart, [1863] 1950. "Utilitarianism" in John Stuart Mill's *Utilitarianism, Liberty, and Representative Government.* New York: E. P. Dutton.
Norton, David L., 1976. *Personal Destinies.* Princeton, NJ: Princeton University Press.
Rohr, John A., 1989. *Ethics for Bureaucrats,* 2d ed. New York: Marcel Dekker.
Scott, William G., and David Kirkwood Hart, 1989. *Organizational Values in America.* New Brunswick, NJ: Transaction Publishers.
Twain, Mark, [1883] 1993. *Life on the Mississippi.* New York: Quality Paper Back Bookclub.
Waldo, Dwight, 1948. *The Administrative State.* New York: Ronald Press.

NONDISTRIBUTION CONSTRAINT.

The prohibition against the sharing of profits or dividends or the distribution of income or earnings among a nonprofit organization's owners, trustees, or members beyond reasonable compensation for services or contractual obligations. Although limited by this constraint in what they may do with profits, nonprofit organizations are not legally prescribed from profit earning. Instead, the earnings must be devoted entirely to financing further production of the organization's services or to furthering its mission (Hansmann 1981, p. 553).

The constraint is a concept and derives from state statutes, often guided by the Model [nonprofit] Act, the New York Act, or the California Act (Hansmann 1981). It addresses legal limitations placed on nonprofit enterprise. The law does not allow the sale of stock and dividend payments common in the for-profit sector; similarly it disallows distributions common among cooperatives. The term, perhaps more than any other, serves to define the overriding distinction between for-profit and nonprofit firms or organizations. First proffered by Henry Hansmann (1980) it is often shortened in discussion or writing to (simply) "nondistribution" as in "nondistribution requires that . . . ."

ERNA GELLES

BIBLIOGRAPHY

Hansmann, Henry, 1980. "The Role of Nonprofit Enterprise." *Yale Law Journal,* vol. 89: 835–901.
———, 1981. "Reforming Nonprofit Corporation Law." *University of Pennsylvania Law Review,* vol. 129: 497–623.

NONFEASANCE.

Omission of some act that ought to have been done. In the context of public administration, it refers to not having done what is law or custom due to laziness, ignorance, want of care for charges, or through corrupt influence.

Overfeasance, by contrast, comes from "over," meaning advanced or beyond, and "feasance," meaning the doing or execution of a condition or obligation. Together in public administration they refer to some action undertaken beyond what law and custom oblige or empower.

Nonfeasance and malfeasance trace their origins to legal scholarship. Nonfeasance is tied intimately to the work of Sir Francis Bacon in 1596. Bacon uses this term in conjunction with the concept misfeasance to express violations of the law. Misfeasance, by definition, is the wrongful exercise of lawful authority. Together nonfeasance and misfeasance are powerful concepts to explain both legal and administrative behavior.

Nonfeasance, overfeasance, and malfeasance are terms by Herman Finer, a British scholar, to build a case for administrative responsibility and what controls over bureaucracies are necessary to ensure its proper function in American government. Finer, rather than using Bacon's term misfeasance, coined the term overfeasance to express the phenomenon. Overfeasance addresses the problem of bureaucratic action beyond what is warranted, typically by law or tradition. Nonfeasance refers to the problem of inaction in bureaucracies.

Nonfeasance and overfeasance are a part of a broader discussion of administrative control and responsibility. Finer builds the case for external controls over bureaucratic behavior, while his American counterpart proposes greater discretion and internal controls. These classic debates give intellectual currency to malfeasance, nonfeasance, and overfeasance in public administration through Finer's work "Administrative Responsibility in Democratic Government," published in 1941. Finer, in these series of debates, argues that without external controls over bureaucracies, overfeasance, nonfeasance, and malfeasance will run rampant, hindering the efficiency of any bureaucracy.

The problem of nonfeasance, according to Finer, does not directly raise concerns about a politicized bureaucracy. Rather, nonfeasance is a concern about the level of professionalism due to a reduction in the efficient conduct of the wishes of elected officials. This inaction by bureaucracy lends support to the argument for a professional, dispassionate bureaucracy that is efficient. This lack of action by a bureaucracy is consistent with Finer's parliamentary background and underlying views about the role of bureaucracies.

Overfeasance is based on the premise that an administrator exceeds the limits of this power regardless of whether the action is for good or ill. This undermines any legitimacy or political position that bureaucracies would have in the eyes of both the public and elected officials. When overfeasance goes unchecked, it enables unchecked power to override the smooth function of bureaucracies and violates the premise of the three branches of government, designed to prevent despotic rule. This unchecked action, according to Finer, can be a function of ambition, temperament, or honest zeal. The idea that overfeasance can go unaddressed implies that there is no legal method to check bureaucratic action.

Concerns about nonfeasance and overfeasance directly and indirectly influence current scholarship in public administration. Larry Terry (1995) directly revisits the dilemma of nonfeasance and overfeasance to help support his argument for the administrator as conservator. He indicates that overfeasance and nonfeasance are still real concerns when examining violations of the spirit of the law, providing examples of when bureaucracies overstep their authority, raising questions of overfeasance. He provides further examples of nonfeasance, associated with negligent management of bureaucratic programs. Terry also indicates that problems of nonfeasance and overfeasance can be corrected or prevented by an organizational leadership that is the conservator of the values of an agency.

Finer's concerns about nonfeasance and overfeasance indirectly influence current debates about legitimacy and discretion. Both Charles Jones (1994) and Louis Fisher (1993) argue that this concern for overfeasance is not justified, proposing instead that bureaucracies do have checks on their power through the structure of American governance. The authors differ in opinions about which branch is charged with the leading role. Some scholars of public administration support the arguments of Jones and Fisher about the limits of bureaucratic power further challenging Finer's position. Jones would support Finer's notion of efficiency, though not Finer's concern about the overfeasance.

Currently, the legacy of nonfeasance and overfeasance clearly influences literature on administrative ethics. Work by the scholars Terry Cooper, Robert Denhardt, and Edward Jennings are but a few examples of this. They all argue, in different ways, that overfeasance and nonfeasance are preventable through ethical leadership in practice. These scholars support internal controls on behavior rather than the external ones proposed by Finer. Denhardt and Cooper both forward arguments concerning virtuous leadership and how it promotes responsible administration. This prevents or at least mitigates the problems associated with nonfeasance and overfeasance.

The legacy of Herman Finer still influences current debates in public administration. They range from questions about the role of bureaucracy in American government and leadership to current discourse about ethical controls used to enforce professional behavior in public administration. Ironically, the position that Finer examined during his discourse about public administration over 50 years ago has not changed much, although it has been clarified through study and scholarship in the field. Heated debates still rage over the discretionary power of bureaucracies, their role in governance, efficiency, bureaucratic leadership, and the ongoing debate over the role of politics in administration. These concerns about nonfeasance and overfeasance either explicitly, or implicitly, still touch many facets of modern scholarship in public administration.

ARTHUR J. SEMENTELLI

BIBLIOGRAPHY

Bowman, James S., ed., 1991. *Ethical Frontiers in Public Management.* San Francisco, CA: Jossey-Bass.

The Compact Oxford English Dictionary, 1991. Oxford, England: Oxford University Press.

Finer, Herman, 1941. "Administrative Responsibility in Democratic Government." *Public Administration Review,* vol. 1 (Summer) 335–350.

Fisher, Louis, 1993. *The Politics of Shared Power: Congress and the Executive.* Washington, D.C.: Congressional Quarterly.

Jones, Charles O., 1994. *The Presidency in a Separated System.* Washington, D.C.: Brookings Institution.

Terry, Larry D., 1995. *Leadership of Public Bureaucracies: The Administrator as Conservator.* Thousand Oaks, CA: Sage.

NONGOVERNMENTAL ORGANIZATION.

A group brought together by common aims and with a basic organizational structure; it does not rely upon governments for its formation or for most of the resources for its continued existence, and it is not profitmaking in its aim. The Economic and Social Council (ECOSOC) of the United Nations describes any international organization not established by intergovernmental agreement as a nongovernmental organization (NGO) and includes those organizations that accept members designated by government authorities, provided that does not affect the organization's free expression of views.

Origins

The existence of nongovernmental organizations mirrors that of the growth of the state and governments. When the task of government was primarily that of protection, whether against internal disorder or external attack, other aspects of public life could be left to the family or to organized groups not directly under governmental control. Whether in biblical times or in Ancient Greece and Rome, this often involved religion, although because of the power of religious organizations, there was at least a tension between them and the state authorities and often an attempt by the secular power to control the power of religious groups. In the Middle Ages until the Reformation, the Catholic Church represented the strongest nongovernmental organization in most European states, although this church—with the Pope at its head—gradually obtained temporal power and governmental responsibilities, especially in the form of papal states in Italy. Furthermore, Christian rulers considered themselves subordinate to God and regarded the Catholic Church as the deity's earthly representative, thereby blurring the dividing line between government and church. The Reformation in Europe led to a sharper distinction between state and church and gave the opportunity for the latter to develop into a distinct nongovernmental agency in many countries.

Meanwhile other nongovernmental organizations had sprung up in economic and social life in Europe. Perhaps the most important were the guilds and, later, Masonic organizations. The guilds offered a network of support for tradesmen and skilled workers and also controlled entry into the major crafts. They provided a form of social stability and of economic well-being, and their relationship with government was often ambiguous as they requested special rights and favors normally in exchange for money and taxes, yet they were outside governmental control.

The industrial revolution in Europe in the last eighteenth and nineteenth century and subsequent growth in urbanization increased the opportunity for nongovernmental agencies, such as friendly societies providing basic insurance cover, savings clubs, and trade unions. The power of the latter grew particularly in the industrializing societies of the United Kingdom, Germany, France, and in the big cities of the United States.

Also during the nineteenth century, governments in Europe and the United States became more involved in the economic and social life of their citizens. This took power away from church and guild organizations as the state became more involved in welfare issues. It also encouraged the growth of pressure groups, the aim of which was to influence public opinion and government policy on particular issues. Early examples were the antislavery leagues in, for instance, the United Kingdom and the United States.

As communications improved and as governments increased their involvement in building the foundations of an international society with rules and norms for activities such as trade and commerce, travel and transport, health services and even warfare, so the potential arose for international nongovernmental organizations (INGOs). These bodies represented nongovernmental organizations working across frontiers to particular ends. Early INGOs were often humanitarian, such as the Universal Peace Congress or the World Anti-Slavery Convention. An impact was made by the International Committee of the Red Cross (ICRC), which, based in Switzerland, arranged agreements between governments on the treatment of the wounded and of civilians in wartime (the Geneva Conventions of 1864, 1906, 1929, and 1949). The ICRC, the national societies, and the International Federation of Red Cross and Red Crescent Societies make up the Red Cross and Red Crescent Movement, which has provided assistance to those visited by warfare or natural disaster. The twentieth century, with its rapid improvement in communications, has seen a massive increase in INGOs. While between 1909 and 1994 the number of intergovernmental organizations–those established by governments across frontiers–rose from 37 to 263, the number of INGOs increased from 176 to 4,928 (*Yearbook of International Organizations 1994/1995*, 1994, p. 1625). A substantial part of this growth came after World War II and has been associated with political movements (for example the Liberal International, established in 1947), education and research (the International Association of Universities), the move to encourage peace (International Christian Service for Peace), and environmental bodies such as Friends of the Earth International, Conservation International, Greenpeace International, and the Worldwide Fund for Nature International.

Theory

The roles and functions attributed to nongovernmental organizations and their international manifestation depend mainly on concepts of the state and of international relations. A view of the state based on, for example, the U.S. Constitution might see it as a servant of the people and their needs. Insofar as these needs can be achieved by other means–by the use of the market or by voluntary associations–then the state has less to do and private enterprise and civil society are to the fore. The role of nongovernmental organizations increases in importance as they undertake operational activities (charitable actions, education, research) and also form competing pressure groups (for and against smoking or abortion). In a totalitarian state, the ruling party may wish to control not only political and economic activity but also that in the social, religious, and family sphere. Such governments have thus been opposed to the existence of independent nongovernmental organizations. Many organizations in the Soviet Union–such as peace movements, cultural activities, and churches–were strictly monitored by the government and were often "front" organizations mirroring government views. A government that believes it has the monopoly of wisdom–as well as power–has little time for nongovernmental organizations. Likewise the role given to such organizations on the world stage depends on the importance attached to the state in international affairs. If it is believed that the most important relations across international frontiers are those conducted or controlled by sovereign states, then little importance will be attached to

INGOs. This "realist" perspective can be contrasted to a more "pluralist" view that attaches greater import to the growing number of INGOs. They are seen as affecting the functioning of the international political system, especially in its norms and rulemaking (e.g., Anti-Apartheid Movement, Amnesty International, the many environmental organizations), and in a number of operational activities, such as those by the Red Cross and Red Crescent Movement, and Caritas, Save the Children.

Current Practice in the United States

The *Yearbook of International Organizations 1994/1995* (Volume 2, 1994, p. 1683) notes the growth of membership in INGOs by the United States and its citizens from 612 in 1960 to 1,106 in 1977 to 2,273 in 1990. This latter figure, while high, compares unfavorably with the larger European states such as France (3,038), Germany (2,974), and the United Kingdom (2,846), and even Canada with 2,043 in 1990. However, a slightly different picture is given when considering the national nongovernmental organizations in the United States. The *Encyclopedia of Associations* (1995, p. vii) claims that the United States has some 5,500 associations, although their definition is drawn to cover local nongovernmental organizations, nonmembership, and for-profit organizations. It reports that seven out of ten Americans belong to at least one such association, 90 percent of which offer educational courses to the public. Associations employ 8.6 million people and spend US $14.5 billion on industrial standard setting each year, some 400 times the amount spent by the U.S. government on setting and enforcing product and safety standards every year. They also provide some 100 million hours each year of community service. These figures demonstrate the importance of nongovernmental organizations in American life. A trend to notice is the move away from organizations and toward much looser networks. These are less structured than NGOs and are made possible on a countrywide–and international–basis by modern technology.

Variation of Practice in Other Areas

Statistics show that Europe is still the bastion of nongovernmental organizations, but the largest growth has been experienced in Africa. Using a wide definition of NGOs, the *Yearbook of International Organizations 1994/1995* (1994, Volume 2, pp. 1682–1685) showed that Europe participated in 57,081 in 1990 (up from 13,023 in 1960), whereas Africa saw an increase to 19,384 from 1,994 during the same period. The Pacific area's participation increased from 720 in 1960 to 4,878 in 1990, Asia's from 3,342 to 21,269 for the same years. The increase in the Americas was from 5,057 to 23,420 from 1960 to 1990. The dramatic rise in the African, Asian, and Pacific participation can be explained by low starting figures, by the growth of new states and civil societies in these areas, and—in some cases—by NGOs filling the obvious gaps in welfare, education, and economic activity left by the state. It is worth noting that while the citizens of the Soviet Union participated in 433 NGOs in 1977, those of Russia were in 822 by 1990. A further growth can be expected with the Russian Federation having achieved full sovereignty in 1991 and with the economic and political changes in the country.

Representation in International Organizations

The UN's ECOSOC has had a special relationship with NGOs since 1945 and now almost every UN department and specialized agency offers some link with them. A 1988 survey shows some 1,500 NGOs associated formally with the UN and an interdepartmental working group on relations between the NGOs and the UN makes recommendations to the secretary-general of the UN. Article 71 of the UN Charter states that ECOSOC should make suitable arrangements to consult with international, and internationally oriented, NGOs that are concerned with matters within its competence. ECOSOC recognizes three types of relations: Category I, with organizations with basic interests in most of the activities of the council (such as the International Council of Women and the International Parliamentary Union); Category II, being organizations with special competence but concerned only with a few of the council's activities (e.g., Anti-Apartheid Movement, Anti-Slavery International); and the roster on which NGOs are placed for ad hoc consultation, either by ECOSOC, other UN bodies or specialized agencies, or by the secretary-general. All NGOs that have a consultative status can meet in the Conference on Nongovernmental Organizations in Consultation Status with the United Nations ECOSOC (CONGO). There is also formal representation given to NGOs in the European Communities (EC—now part of the European Union, EU), although this is not the case in the decisionmaking of the other two "pillars" of the EU, the Common Foreign and Security Policy and Justice and Home Affairs, both of which are primarily intergovernmental in their approach. The EC has as part of its decisionmaking process a requirement to send most draft legislation to the Economic and Social Committee. This is made up of representatives of the main strands of economic and social interest groups throughout the EC. Each state is allotted a number of seats on the committee, but these are divided between the representatives of employers, employees, consumers, and other groups such as professional organizations. The committee is consultative, but it can influence details by applying expert knowledge. EC-wide interests—such as ETUC, the trade union organizations, and UNICE, the employers' organization—also operate and influence decisions at the various stages of the policymaking process.

CLIVE ARCHER

BIBLIOGRAPHY

Archer, Clive, 1992. *International Organizations*, 2d ed. London and New York: Routledge.
Haas, Peter M., ed., 1992. "Knowledge, Power, and International Policy Coordination." Special edition of *International Organization*, vol. 46, no. 1.
Jacobsen, Harold, 1984. *Networks of Interdependence: International Organizations and the Global Political System*. New York: Alfred Knopf.
Lador-Lederer, J. J., 1963. *International Non-Governmental Organizations and Economic Entities*. Leyden: A. W. Sythoff.
Princen, Thomas, and Matthias Finger, 1994. *Environmental NGOs in World Politics. Linking the Local and the Global*. London and New York: Routledge.
Schwartz, Carol A., and Rebecca L. Turner, eds., 1994. *Encyclopedia of Associations 1995*. Volume 1, *National Organizations of the US*. Detroit; Washington, D.C.; London: Gale Research, Inc.
Union of International Associations, ed., 1994. *Yearbook of International Organizations 1994/1995*, Volumes 1, 2, and 3. Munich, New Providence, London, Paris: K. G. Saur.
Willets, Peter, ed., 1982. *Pressure Groups in the Global System: The Transnational Relations of Issue-Oriented Non-Governmental Organizations*. London: Pinter.

NONPROFIT ENTREPRENEURSHIP.
A proactive style of management through which leaders of nonprofit organizations seek to implement change through new organizational and programmatic initiatives. The term "entrepreneurship" is commonly associated with the establishment of new ventures in the business sector. However, as a generic concept, entrepreneurship is equally applicable to the nonprofit sector and, in fact, is an intrinsic aspect of successful management and leadership of public organizations.

Entrepreneurship and Innovation

The classic definition of entrepreneurship was given by Joseph Schumpeter (1949), who called it the implementation of "new combinations of the means of production." Schumpeter, who studied economic development, identified five types of entrepreneurial activity, including the introduction of a new economic good or service, the introduction of a new method of production, the opening of a new market, the conquest of a new source of raw materials, and the reorganization of an industry such as the creation or breaking up of a monopoly. The thrust of Schumpeter's definition is the "implementation of change." Thus, the establishment of a new organization, the making of profits, or the taking of risks per se—all characteristics commonly associated with entrepreneurship—are not its essence. Peter Drucker's (1985) words echo the emphasis on implementation of change as the defining characteristic: "Innovation is the specific tool of entrepreneurs, the means by which they exploit change as an opportunity for a different business or a different service" (p. 19). Firstenberg (1986) adds, however, that risk taking is intrinsic to bringing about change through entrepreneurship: "I label certain organizations 'entrepreneurial' because, in order to reap the benefits that flow from innovative change, they are willing to accept the uncertainty inherent in new endeavors and the possibility of disappointing results" (pp. 211–212).

Evidence of Nonprofit Entrepreneurship

Drucker (1985) cities developments in the nonprofit sector as prime examples of entrepreneurship, including the creation of the modern university in the late nineteenth century, the establishment of new private and metropolitan universities after World War II, the establishment of the modern hospital and the community hospital in the late eighteenth century, the development of specialized health clinics in the early twentieth century, and new program developments in a number of specific organizations in the social services, religion, health care, and professional societies. Dennis Young (1985) documents several different forms that nonprofit entrepreneurial ventures can take, including the establishment of new organizations designed to implement new service concepts, new organizations parented by existing organizations—through mergers or spinoffs, and new program initiatives undertaken within the framework of existing organizations. Overall, numerous examples and case studies of nonprofit entrepreneurship are documented in the literature (Young 1983, 1985, 1990, 1991; Drucker 1985).

Other signs also point to the importance of entrepreneurship as an intrinsic force in the nonprofit sector. First, the nonprofit sector is a fast-growing segment of the overall economy in the United States. In terms of income and employment, the sector's growth has paralleled and often exceeded the growth of government and business over the past two decades (Hodgkinson et al. 1992). Such aggregate growth, while underpinned by the commitment of new public and private resources, suggests the presence of considerable entrepreneurial effort to transform these resources into operating programs.

Second, 57 percent of existing charitable nonprofits came into existence only within the last 20 years (Hodgkinson et al. 1993), and the number of new public charities has increased at a rate of 6.5 percent between 1965 and 1990 (Bowen et al. 1994). These statistics reflect the classic mode of nonprofit entrepreneurship—individuals or groups motivated to address a social, health, environmental, or other issue, unsatisfied with existing services and aware of potential resources to support their interests, forming their own organizations. The fact that the nonprofit sector exhibits a steady entry of new organizations and is populated largely by young, small organizations bears witness to its entrepreneurial character. Although older, larger organizations also nurture entrepreneurial activity, smaller, younger organizations are its principal venue.

Third, many nonprofit organizations are established explicitly to bring about change. Indeed, social welfare advocacy organizations are designated with their own tax code [501(c)4] precisely to enable this function. More broadly, the missions of many foundations and charitable nonprofits are framed in terms of finding solutions to social, health, or environmental problems, supporting new means of expression in the arts or implementing new concepts of service delivery. Although its entrepreneurial character may not be the basic explanation for the nonprofit sector's dynamism, it appears to be a necessary element in the sector's ability to transform concern over social issues and the availability of governmental and private resources into new operating programs and services.

Motivation for Nonprofit Entrepreneurship

In the classical business context, the lure of profits and potential wealth is often assumed to be the primary motivating force behind entrepreneurship. This raises the question, what takes the place of profits in motivating entrepreneurship in the nonprofit sector? The answer to this question can be presented in three steps: (1) Profit is not the sole motivator for entrepreneurship, even in the business sector; (2) profit does sometimes play a role in nonprofit entrepreneurship and (3) other motivators are more important than profit or wealth in motivating nonprofit entrepreneurship.

Motivation for entrepreneurship in the business sector was studied by David McClelland (1973), who found that business entrepreneurs were "achievement oriented" and driven primarily by the need for accomplishment. McClelland also identified the needs for power and affiliation as sources of entrepreneurial motivation, especially in other sectors than business.

In the nonprofit sector, several scholars have studied entrepreneurial motivations. Estelle James (1987) cited promotion of one's own religious values as a key source of nonprofit entrepreneurship; thus, people form educational, social service, and health organizations in order to create environments that allow them to transmit their religious values to others or to maintain those values within their own group. Alternatively, Henry Hansmann (1980) identifies the quest for income and the desire to lead institutions of high quality as dual sources of nonprofit entrepreneurial motivation in nonprofits, especially those in education, health care, or social services, where professionals play an important role. Studying a range of nonprofit, governmental, and business ventures in the social service, Young (1983) identified a spectrum of entrepreneurial motivations including craftmanship and pride of creative accomplishment, acclaim of professional peers, belief in a cause, search for personal identity, need for autonomy and independence, desire to preserve a cherished organization, need for power or control, and desire for personal wealth. In this schema, motivations are correlated with sector, whereby income seeking is more heavily associated with entrepreneurship in the business sector, power seeking more heavily found in the public sector, and other motivations tending to cluster in the nonprofit sector.

Although the seeking of personal wealth is apparently a minor factor in motivating nonprofit-sector entrepreneurship, the role of profits generated by the entrepreneurial activities of nonprofit organizations is nonetheless potentially important. In particular, the undertaking of commercial ventures with the intent of generating financial surpluses has become an increasingly common nonprofit-sector phenomenon (Crimmins and Keil 1983; Skloot 1987; Starkweather 1993). Indeed, such activity has stirred up a storm of controversy in the small business sector over the issue of "unfair competition" (Wellford and Gallagher 1988; Bennett and DiLorenzo 1989). The growth of commercial ventures in the nonprofit sector has paralleled the more general usage of fees to finance nonprofit-sector services. Fee income, consisting of conventional service fees as well as other commercial income, accounted for over half the growth of the nonprofit sector between 1977 and 1989 (Salamon 1992).

The rationale for the undertaking of commercial ventures by nonprofit organizations is twofold: Some activities, such as university sporting events or sales of art reproductions by museums, may contribute directly to the mission and work of the organization. For example, sporting events are presumably a part of a well-rounded physical education program whereas art reproductions help educate people about great works of art. However, other nonprofit commercial activities are not directly related to mission but generate profits that can be allocated to support mission-related services. Profits from such "unrelated business income" are subject to federal unrelated business income tax (UBIT), which is similar to a corporate profits tax. Studies suggest that most nonprofit commercial ventures are related to mission (Skloot 1988). Moreover, relatively little UBIT is actually paid, although such collections and the level of unrelated nonprofit commercial activity are increasing (Schiff and Weisbrod 1991).

Because wealth seeking does not appear to be the primary force, the motivation for nonprofit entrepreneurship is a key question in the development of theory to explain why nonprofits are found to contribute to important parts of the economy. Most economic theory of the nonprofit sector (see **contract failure, government failure,** and **third party government**) focuses on "demand," attempting to explain why people want and will pay for the services of nonprofit organizations. However, demand-side theory leaves open the question of how such demand is translated into the actual supply of services. In the business sector, it is assumed by standard economic theory that supply will manifest itself in the form of new firms or expansion of existing firms, implicitly driven by profit-seeking entrepreneurs. As noted, for the nonprofit sector, theorists such as James (1987), Hansmann (1980), and Young (1983) have proposed a variety of entrepreneurial motivations to explain the manifestation of supply. Alternatively, Avner Ben-Ner and Theresa Van Hoomissen (1993) postulate that coalitions of stakeholders (consumers, donors, sponsors) assume much of the entrepreneurial initiative in nonprofit organizations, motivated by the desire to closely control the quality and character of services they consider important (see **contract failure**).

Requirements for Success

Aside from the significance of entrepreneurship as an element in nonprofit theory, understanding the conditions and skills of entrepreneurship is important to successful management of nonprofit organizations. Drucker (1985) identified four conditions or organizational "policies" for successful entrepreneurship in what he called "public-service institutions": (1) a clear definition of mission, (2) a realistic statement of goals, (3) willingness to question the validity of objectives that are not achieved after repeated attempts, and (4) constant search for innovative opportunities.

Paul Firstenberg's (1986) list focuses more specifically on the style of an organization's management. His ten characteristics are (1) coherent aims and values, (2) focus on comparative advantage, (3) intuitive decisionmaking, (4) an adaptive (internal) environment, (5) excellence of execution, (6) staying power, (7) marshalling exceptional talent, (8) finesse with diverse constituencies, (9) having a sense of where the action is, and (10) active-positive leadership.

Young's (1985, 1991) analysis focuses more specifically on the skills and knowledge of the entrepreneurial leader, in the context of an existing organization or in the process of building a new one. These capabilities are (1) developing a sense of mission, (2) problem-solving ability, (3) applying creativity and ingenuity, (4) identifying opportunities and good timing, (5) analyzing risks, (6) consensus and team building, (7) mobilizing resources, and (8) persistence. There is a clear nexus between Drucker's, Firstenberg's, and

Young's requirements in the areas of mission focus and proactive searching for opportunities, although Drucker's principles more clearly emphasize the role of organizational culture and policy in creating the context for entrepreneurial management, Firstenberg's focus is on the management style, and Young's focus more heavily on the capacities of entrepreneurs themselves. All three sets of requirements raise the issue of whether entrepreneurial management is a subject that can be taught or whether it relies essentially on the innate talents of individuals. Young's emphasis on creativity, a good sense of timing, problem solving, and persistence and Firstenberg's stress on intuition and talent suggest that much depends on individual capacities. Drucker (1985), however, argues that "entrepreneurship and innovation can be achieved by any business. But they must be consciously striven for. They can be learned, but it requires effort. Entrepreneurial businesses treat entrepreneurship as a duty. They are disciplined about it.... They work at it.... They practice it" (p. 150).

DENNIS R. YOUNG

BIBLIOGRAPHY

Ben-Ner, Avner, and Theresa Van Hoomissen, 1993. "Nonprofit Organizations in the Mixed Economy: A Demand and Supply Analysis." In Avner Ben-Ner and Benedetto Gui, eds. *The Nonprofit Sector in the Mixed Economy.* Ann Arbor: University of Michigan Press.

Bennett, James T., and Thomas J. DiLorenzo, 1989. *Unfair Competition.* Lanham, MD: Hamilton Press.

Bowen, William G., Thomas I. Nygren, Sarah E. Turner, and Elizabeth Duffy, 1994. *The Charitable Nonprofits.* San Francisco: Jossey-Bass.

Crimmins, James C., and Mary Keil, 1983. *Enterprise in the Nonprofit Sector.* Washington, DC: Partners for Liveable Places.

Drucker, Peter F., 1985. *Innovation and Entrepreneurship.* New York: Harper and Row.

Firstenberg, Paul B., 1986. *Managing for Profit in the Nonprofit World.* New York: Foundation Center.

Hansmann, Henry B., 1980. "The Role of Nonprofit Enterprise." *Yale Law Journal,* vol. 89: 835–898.

Hodgkinson, Virginia A., Murray S. Weitzman, Stephen M. Noga, and Heather Gorski, 1993. *A Portrait of the Independent Sector.* Washington, DC: Independent Sector.

Hodgkinson, Virginia A., Murray S. Weitzman, Christopher M. Toppe, and Stephen M. Noga, 1992. *Nonprofit Almanac: 1992–1993.* San Francisco: Jossey-Bass.

James, Estelle, 1983. "How Nonprofits Grow." *Journal of Policy Analysis and Management,* vol. 2: 350–375.

———, 1987. "The Nonprofit Sector in Comparative Perspective." In Walter W. Powell , ed., *The Nonprofit Sector: A Research Handbook.* New Haven, CT: Yale University Press, 397–415.

McClelland, David C., 1973. "The Two Faces of Power." Chapter 19 in David C. McClelland and Robert S. Steele, eds., *Human Motivation.* Morris, NJ: General Learning Press.

Salamon, Lester M., 1992. *America's Nonprofit Sector.* New York: Foundation Center.

Schiff, Jerald, and Burton A. Weisbrod, 1991. "Competition between For-Profit and Non-Profit Organizations in Commercial Activities." *Annals of Public and Cooperative Economics,* vol. 62.

Schumpeter, Joseph, 1949. *The Theory of Economic Development.* Cambridge, MA: Harvard University Press.

Skloot, Edward, 1987. "Enterprise and Commerce in Nonprofit Organizations." In Walter W. Powell, ed., *The Nonprofit Sector: A Research Handbook.* New Haven, CT: Yale University Press, 380–396.

———, 1988. *The Nonprofit Entrepreneur.* New York: Foundation Center.

Starkweather, David B., 1993. "Profit Making by Nonprofit Hospitals." In David C. Hammack and Dennis R. Young, eds., *Nonprofit Organizations in a Market Economy.* San Francisco: Jossey-Bass 105–137.

Wellford, W. Harrison, and Janne G. Gallagher, 1988. *Unfair Competition?* Washington, DC: National Assembly.

Young, Dennis R., 1983. *If Not for Profit, for What?* Lexington, MA: D. C. Heath.

———, 1985. *Casebook of Management for Nonprofit Organizations.* New York: Haworth Press.

———, 1990. "Champions of Change: Entrepreneurs in Social Work." In Harold H. Weissman, ed., *Serious Play.* Silver Spring, MD: National Association of Social Workers, 126–135.

———, 1991. "Providing Entrepreneurial Leadership." In Richard L. Edwards and John A. Yankey, *Skills for Effective Human Service Management.* Silver Spring, MD: NASW Press, 62–75.

NONPROFIT ORGANIZATION.

A grouping of individuals who collectively form a social unit–an organization–to accomplish some public or societal purpose.

Organizations are pandemic; they are an everyday, everywhere occurrence. Organizations exist in three economic sectors: government, nonprofit, and private for-profit. Nonprofit organizations exist in both the private and public sectors. Public-sector organizations are government entities that are funded by taxes and include schools, firehouses, police stations, municipal courts, social services, and numerous others.

Private nonprofit organizations are nongovernmental entities and are usually funded by an array of resources, such as individual contributions, fees for service, government, corporate, and foundation grants. Private nonprofit organizations are also very numerous; some examples are religious institutions, educational institutions, health care programs, museums, civic and arts groups.

A commonality found among private and public nonprofit organizations is that their existence is predicated on having a public purpose or mission. In fact, some economists suggest that the existence of private nonprofit organizations results from market failure. Consumers who lack confidence in for-profit services provide opportunities for nonprofit organizations to exist, especially when the consumer places greater trust in the same services provided by mission-oriented nonprofits. Additionally, nonprofit organizations emerge when governmental interventions are impeded or fail, or when for-profit businesses see no method for generating profits from certain activities.

Private nonprofit organizations may be incorporated under state laws, but they may not be owned by individuals or stockholders. Governmental organizations, by contrast are founded by legislative bodies. Currently, there are about 1.5 million private nonprofit organizations in the United States of America with combined expenditures of approximately US \$400 billion.

There are circa 85,000 governmental entities, which comprise less than 1 percent of all organizations operating in the USA. In comparison, organizations in the private nonprofit sector including an estimated 350,000 religious organizations represent nearly 6.0 percent of all organizations. In contrast, organizations in the private for-profit sector tower over the nonprofit sector with close to 22 million, or 94 percent of all organizations operating in the USA.

Forming a Nonprofit Organization

The formation of a private nonprofit organization usually starts with a community issue that needs an organized response. Concerned and interested citizens voluntarily come together to solve problems in a fashion that Alex de Tocquville in 1835 referred to as uniquely American. Solving problems sometimes requires money, materials, and visibility, which are not always available through a loose association of individuals. Therefore, interested citizens form an organization to represent them collectively.

Tax-exempt status is not automatically granted to nonprofit organizations that endeavor to serve their community. After state incorporation, a nonprofit organization may begin to seek recognition as an entity exempt from paying federal taxes by filing Form 1023 with the Internal Revenue Service (IRS). Exemption from state and local taxes requires approval from those taxing authorities.

By their very nature, nonprofit organizations are formed to benefit society or members of specific groups by providing program services in areas such as prevention, education, counseling, scientific research, religion, housing, the environment, and advocacy.

Individuals starting nonprofit organizations often focus their attention on program development, service delivery, and fund-raising, while spending less time on organizational management and governance concerns such as determining strategic direction, identifying organizational values, and establishing management information systems. Over time, organizations that are not managed or governed effectively may encounter critical problems, which are identified by the following symptoms. The organization

- has insufficient funds;
- relies on one funding source;

- has an unclear direction;
- experiences ongoing crises;
- cannot recruit volunteers;
- loses active volunteers;
- does not attract appropriate board members;
- has disinterested or inattentive board members;
- does not have adequate financial data for making appropriate decisions;
- does not know whether services are making a difference.

The development of a strong, vibrant, purposeful nonprofit organization should start before the organization is incorporated. With early and appropriate planning, nonprofit organizations could avoid many pitfalls. In the planning process, the organization should

- determine its central purpose and vision;
- analyze the internal and external environment in which it would operate, including identifying stakeholders, competitors, and potential collaborators;
- identify strategic obstacles;
- establish goals, objectives, and tasks;
- determine financial and human resources needed for task implementation;
- allocate the necessary resources;
- implement the tasks;
- evaluate the progress of task implementation and assess the barriers that interfere with task achievement;
- revise or reaffirm objectives and tasks in response to strategic obstacles.

The Mission

A nonprofit organization must have a solid foundation on which to base decisions and program delivery. Thus, it is essential to develop a mission that defines the organization's identity and purpose for existence. The mission statement outlines a vision for guiding the board, staff, and other volunteers. It states the purpose of the organization, who it serves, and its geographical boundaries. It reflects the culture, values, and beliefs of the organization.

Incorporating the Organization

Incorporation of a nonprofit organization bestows protections and benefits designated in state statutes, such as perpetual life, an ability to hold and convey property, and limited personal liability. The process for becoming a corporation is not difficult. A processing fee is paid and articles of incorporation are filed with a state government agency—in most states, the Secretary of State.

Most states provide application forms with instructions on how to incorporate a nonprofit organization. Forms for a nonprofit organization may be different from those for a for-profit entity. In each state, statutes guide the specific type of information needed in articles of incorporation. The following eight provisions are generally required in articles of incorporation:

(1) Name of the organization.
(2) The purpose of the organization.
(3) How long the organization will exist.
(4) The location of the organization and the name and address of its registered agent.
(5) The names and addresses of the initial board of directors.
(6) The names and addresses of each incorporator.
(7) A statement that the board of directors will not personally gain financially or share in the profits of the organization.
(8) Provisions for dissolving the organization and distributing its assets.

If the articles of incorporation are complete, the filing fee is paid, and a search shows that the chosen organizational name is not protected or in use by another corporation, a certificate of incorporation can be issued. The date on the certificate is considered the official date of incorporation.

Occasionally, a nonprofit corporation will find it necessary to amend information that was filed in the original articles of incorporation. This is particularly true if the purpose statement requires significant changes or if there is a change of registered office, or agent, or organizational name.

The Bylaws

Nonprofit organizations require another governing document known as bylaws, which serve as the constitution and provide guidelines and rules for governing and managing the organization. The following 25 provisions are representative of the type of information found in bylaws of a nonprofit organization:

(1) Organization name.
(2) Principal location.
(3) Enumeration of duties (i.e., powers of the board of directors and its officers).
(4) The number of board members and officers.
(5) Annual meetings.
(6) Required notice of meetings.
(7) Quorum requirements.
(8) Voting rights.
(9) Proxy requirements.
(10) Board terms of office.

(11) Nominating procedures.
(12) Attendance requirements.
(13) Resignation and expulsion.
(14) Waivers of notice.
(15) Board liability.
(16) Committee establishment.
(17) Dues of the organization.
(18) Authority to sign corporate contracts.
(19) Authority to spend and sign checks on behalf of the organization.
(20) Indemnification.
(21) Requirements for keeping records.
(22) Corporate seal designation.
(23) Fiscal year designation.
(24) Procedures for amending the bylaws.
(25) Procedures for dissolution.

A responsibility incurred when creating or maintaining an organization is the implementation of a system for the safe keeping of all important organizational records detailing policy decisions such as bylaws, articles of incorporation, and meeting minutes. The latter provide a historical account of board and committee activities and decisions.

Tax Exemption

When the term "nonprofit organization" is used, most individuals envision charitable [501(c)(3)], tax-exempt organizations. There are, however, approximately 30 types of nonprofit organizations that are classified as exempt from federal taxes:

Categories of Exempt Organizations	Purpose of Organizations
IRC § 501(c)(1)	Instrumentalities of the United States
IRC § 501(c)(2)	Title-holding corporations
IRC § 501(c)(3)	Charitable, educational, religious, scientific, literary, public safety testing, prevention of cruelty to children or animals, amateur sports, and some cooperative service organizations
IRC § 501(c)(4)	Social welfare, civic leagues
IRC § 501(c)(5)	Labor, horticultural, agricultural
IRC § 501(c)(6)	Chambers of commerce, business leagues, trade associations
IRC § 501(c)(7)	Social clubs
IRC § 501(c)(8)	Fraternal organizations
IRC § 501(c)(9)	Voluntary employees' beneficiary associations
IRC § 501(c)(10)	Domestic fraternal societies
IRC § 501(c)(11)	Teachers' retirement fund associations
IRC § 501(c)(12)	Benevolent or mutual associations

Categories of Exempt Organizations	Purpose of Organizations
IRC § 501(c)(13)	Cemetery companies
IRC § 501(c)(14)	State-chartered credit unions
IRC § 501(c)(15)	Mutual insurance companies or associations
IRC § 501(c)(16)	Crop financing corporations
IRC § 501(c)(17)	Supplemental unemployment benefit trusts
IRC § 501(c)(18)	Funded pension trusts (created before June 25, 1959)
IRC § 501(c)(19)	Organizations for veterans
IRC § 501(c)(20)	Group legal service
IRC § 501(c)(21)	Black lung benefits trusts
IRC § 501(c)(22)	Multiemployer pension plan trusts
IRC § 501(c)(23)	Pre-1880 veterans organizations
IRC § 501(c)(24)	Employee trusts
IRC § 501(d)	Religious and apostolic associations
IRC § 501(e)	Cooperative hospital service
IRC § 501(f)	Cooperative service groups of operating, educational organizations
IRC § 501(k)	Treatment of certain child care
IRC § 521	Farmers' cooperatives
IRC § 526	Ship owners' protection and indemnity associations
IRC § 528	Homeowners' associations

This list of tax-exempt organizations is likely to grow. Currently, there are more than 20 different types of nonprofit organizations seeking statutory recognition as tax-exempt entities.

The most preferred tax-exempt recognition is the 501(c)(3), an Internal Revenue Service designation for an organization with a charitable purpose. The 501(c)(3) label not only provides the organization with exemption from paying taxes on related income but also allows donors to deduct a portion of their gifts on their own personal tax return. Donor deduction is considered to be an incentive for charitable giving among individuals. Additionally, some granting institutions, corporations, and foundations will not consider making a financial contribution unless the nonprofit organization has received its recognition as a 501(c)(3).

When an organization seeks federal tax-exempt status, the IRS may test the applicant's responses and attachments to Form 1023 to determine whether the nonprofit corporation fits the IRS code profile of a charitable, tax-exempt organization. There are at least three tests that can be used at this stage of the application process. One test determines whether the nonprofit organization's purpose and mission statement is compatible with the IRS codes categories of exempt organizations, which are as follows: charitable, education, science, health, human services, religion, testing for public safety, the prevention of cruelty to children or animals, or fostering national or international amateur sports competition (excepting the provision of athletic facilities or equipment).

In a second test, Form 1023 responses are used to determine whether the organization was formed to engage in political campaigns or ballot initiatives. Lobbying to influence public policy cannot be a central activity of the nonprofit that is recognized as a 501(c)(3). Although some legislative lobbying is permitted, an intent to engage in extensive organizational lobbying must be declared.

A third test determines whether the organization intends to distribute organizational assets to board members or other individuals. This test may include a review of the bylaws and/or articles of incorporation to ensure that a dissolution provision exists, stating that assets would be distributed to similar mission-oriented nonprofit organizations or to government entities. Unlike for-profit corporations, nonprofits may not distribute annual earnings to their directors; therefore, the IRS will be interested in responses to Form 1023 questions about the trustees' handling of excess revenues. The expectation is that excess revenues will be reinvested in staff salaries, operational expenses, safe investments, and program services.

All 501(c)(3) organizations must be categorized as either private foundations or public charities; organizational testing can be used to sort private foundations from publicly supported charities. Private foundations do not experience all of the same benefits as publicly supported charities. By law, the private foundation must annually distribute a percentage of its assets to other charitable organizations; it may be taxed on certain investments; and it is subject to very strict rules that subject its trustees and executive director to harsh fines for violations. Therefore, charitable organizations would want to avoid this private foundation classification (unless, of course, the organization is truly seeking a private foundation classification).

As part of the Form 1023 review, the IRS may ask for financial statements that report assets, liabilities, revenues, and expenditures, especially if the organization has been operating for a year or more. An existing organizational budget or a proposed budget will be reviewed to determine fund-raising projections and methods. The IRS is particularly interested in whether the organization plans to generate revenues mainly from public support or from fees for services. This distinction is used to further classify nonprofit organizations according to their primary means of generating revenues; publicly supported charities are classified as 501(c)(3), 509(a)(1), and organizations relying on fees for service are classified as 501(c)(3), 509(a)(2).

If the IRS is satisfied with the information in Form 1023, the organization will receive a ruling letter recognizing it as a tax-exempt organization. This status is retroactive only if Form 1023 was filed within 15 months of incorporation. If the form was filled after the 15-month period, recognition is granted from the date of the application, not the date of incorporation. Understanding the limited time frame may be important. Missing the 15-month deadline can adversely impact donors who expected deduction privileges for their gifts. Timing is also critical for the organization seeking exemption from taxes on revenues generated from the organization's inception through its 15-month filing deadline. If tax-exempt recognition occurs after the 15-month filing deadline, the nonprofit organization will have a tax burden on its income up until the date of tax-exempt recognition.

Organizations in which the missions are human service oriented and which have been in existence longer than 15 months may apply for recognition as a 501(c)(4), a social welfare organization. The 501(c)(4) has tax-exempt privileges, although it does not offer deduction privileges to donors. Receiving a 501(c)(4) ruling is advantageous for late application filers because the recognition is retroactive to the organization's inception. The 501(c)(4) nonprofit organization may be relieved of all prior tax obligations. Once excused of its tax burdens, the organization can file Form 1023 for recognition as a 501(c)(3) organization. If recognized, it can add donor deduction privileges to its fund-raising arsenal, effective as of the Form 1023 application date.

Other Forms of Tax Relief

IRS recognition does not guarantee tax exemption from any other taxing authority. Therefore, nonprofit organizations should also apply for tax relief from state, city, and county taxing authorities. Some states, cities, and counties have very narrow definitions of charitable organizations, making it difficult to secure tax exemption on organizational revenues, purchases, and property. Additionally, tax exemption may not excuse an agency from paying taxes on revenues if the income was derived from activities not directly related to the organization's purpose and mission. Earnings of US $1,000 or more from unrelated business usually create a tax liability, and earnings that exceed one-third of an organization's budget may even trigger examination by the IRS to determine whether the tax-exempt status should be revoked.

Similar to the obligations of for-profit businesses, nonprofits also have tax collection and tax payment obligations. The nonprofit organization, for example, is required to pay taxes for unemployment insurance programs, workers' compensation, social security, and medicare. Some states permit nonprofit organizations to purchase a bond or use a letter of credit in lieu of paying state unemployment taxes. Under these circumstances, the nonprofit would be responsible for reimbursing the state

for any financial payments awarded by the state to former employees of the nonprofit.

Expenditures by nonprofit organizations for unemployment insurance and workers' compensation fees are usually affected by the number of claims made against the organization's insurance policies. Workers' compensation insurance fees are also calculated by a formula that considers number of employees, amount of annual payroll, and the type and degree of risks associated with employee job responsibilities.

Although nonprofit organizations may be exempt from paying taxes, its employees are not. Employees will have social security taxes, medicare taxes, as well as federal, state, and local income taxes withheld from their paychecks. As an employer, a tax-exempt nonprofit organization is not exempted from matching its employees' share of social security and medicare taxes.

Nonprofit, tax-exempt organizations have certain tax-reporting obligations. Specifically, the organization is required to file Form 990, an end-of-year tax return filed by organizations with annual revenues of at least US $25,000. Form 990 must be filed no later than five and a half months after the end of the organization's fiscal year.

Form 990 can be used by the Internal Revenue Service to review an organization's revenue base, source of revenues, fund-raising methods, lobbying expenditures, and major salary and benefit expenditures. It can also be used to help demonstrate whether the nonprofit has experienced adequate public support for the Internal Revenue Service's continued recognition of the organization as a tax-exempt entity. The 990 information can serve as the basis for invoking the "public support test."

With a minimum of four years of operating experience, the nonprofit organization may be scrutinized by the IRS seeking proof of public support under the organization's (509)(a) classification. Failing the support test can lead to the loss of tax-exempt recognition. There are two related tests: the one-third support test and the 10 percent support and facts and circumstances test.

An organization classified as a 501(c)(3), 509(a)(1) must demonstrate that during a preceding four-year period, at least one-third of its support came from the general public, or government, or a combination of public and government funding. In the calculation of support, a nonprofit organization may not count any individual contribution to the extent it exceeds 2 percent of the organization's total support. This restriction severely limits the ability of the organization to pass the one-third test on the basis of a few large contributions.

If the organization fails the one-third test, it may be reviewed under a more subjective analysis, the 10 percent test, showing 10 percent of the organization's support coming from the general public. In addition, the IRS may look at other facts and circumstances. For example, the organization may evidence a large pool of community volunteers and board members from diverse backgrounds. The IRS has the authority to determine whether certain facts and circumstances can be evidence of public support.

Nonprofit organizations with 501(c)(3), 509(a)(2) designations have a similar obligation to demonstrate public support, proving that more than one-third of its public support is from contributions, fees, and program-related business income. Passing the public support test should be a matter of concern for any organization. If a nonprofit organization is unable to muster a diverse funding base, volunteer participation, or cross section of community representatives on its board of directors, it risks the loss of its special tax-exempt status.

Community Support

The principal purpose of the nonprofit organization is to serve its community, to have a public purpose rather than existing for an individual's self-interest. Starting, organizing, and perpetuating a nonprofit organization is an important but difficult job. In order to protect the community's interests and its cash investments—whether in the form of direct financial contributions or the organization's tax-exempt status—the organization must be under the stewardship of a responsible board of directors.

As a result of the important role that nonprofit organizations have in society, communities expect (and establish through their laws) that boards of directors will monitor their organizations, protect their assets, and ensure that they operate in the general public interest.

STEPHEN R. BLOCK

BIBLIOGRAPHY

Billis, David, 1993. "What Can Nonprofits and Businesses Learn from Each Other?" In David C. Hammack and Dennis R. Young, eds., *Nonprofit Organizations in a Market Economy.* San Francisco: Jossey-Bass, 319–343.
Block, Stephen R., and Katherine Carol, 1994. "From Visions to Reality: Transforming Community through a Transformed Organization." In Cary Griffin, Katherine Carol, and Roger Van Lieshout, eds., *Vision, Innovation, and Competence: The Annual Management Mentoring Monograph.* Greeley, CO: Center for Technical Assistance and Training, University of Northern Colorado.
Block, Stephen R., and Jeffrey W. Pryor, 1991. *Improving Nonprofit Management Practice: A Handbook for Community-Based Organizations.* Rockville, MD: OSAP/Public Health Service, U.S. Dept. of Health and Human Services.
Bookman, Mark, 1992. *Protecting Your Organization's Tax-Exempt Status.* San Francisco: Jossey-Bass.
Dayton, Kenneth N., 1987. "Governance is Governance." *An Independent Sector Occasional Paper,* Washington DC: Independent Sector.
Hall, Peter Dobkin, 1994. "Historical Perspectives on Nonprofit Organizations." In Robert D. Herman, ed., *The Jossey-Bass Handbook of Nonprofit Leadership and Management.* San Francisco: Jossey-Bass, 3–43.
Hansmann, Henry, 1987. "Economic Theories of Nonprofit Organization." In Walter W. Powell, ed., *The Nonprofit Sector: A Research Handbook.* New Haven, CT: Yale University Press, 27–42.
Hodgkinson, Virginia Ann, et al., 1992. *Nonprofit Almanac, 1992–1993: Dimensions of the Independent Sector.* San Francisco: Jossey-Bass.
Milofsky, Carl, 1987. "Neighborhood-Based Organizations: A Market Analogy." In Walter W. Powell, ed., *The Nonprofit Sector: A Research Handbook.* New Haven, CT: Yale University Press, 277–295.
Ostrom, Elinor, and Gina Davis, 1993. "Nonprofit Organizations as Alternatives and Complements in a Mixed Economy." In David C. Hammack and Dennis R. Young, eds., *Nonprofit Organizations in a Market Economy.* San Francisco: Jossey-Bass, 23–56.
Van Til, Jon, 1988. *Mapping the Third Sector.* New York: Foundation Center.
———, 1994. "Nonprofit Organizations and Social Institutions." In Robert D. Herman, ed., *The Jossey-Bass Handbook of Nonprofit Leadership and Management.* San Francisco: Jossey-Bass, 44–64.

NONPROFIT SECTOR RESEARCH FUND.

The first grantmaking fund dedicated to supporting research on nonprofit organizations and philanthropy in the United States and other countries. The Nonprofit Sector Research Fund was created in 1991 as a program of the Aspen Institute, an international organization known for its classic leadership development program, public policy conferences, and related programs. The fund makes grants of almost US $1 million available per year through its national program and through state-based programs in California and Michigan. Financial support for the fund is contributed by philanthropic foundations, individuals, and organizations.

The Nonprofit Sector Research Fund seeks to increase the quality and quantity of research on nonprofit organizations and to enhance the legitimacy and visibility of nonprofit scholarship. With the input of peer reviewers, the fund's governing council makes the final decisions on grant awards. Recipients include researchers from academia and nonprofit organizations, as well as independent scholars and doctoral candidates.

The fund gives preference to research in the following areas: the role of nonprofits in fostering democratic values and practices, the role of the nonprofit sector compared to business and government, the nature and effectiveness of nonprofit advocacy, philanthropy, governance issues; public accountability, financing issues, the nonprofit sector workforce, including volunteers, and international dimensions of nonprofits and philanthropy.

Central to the fund's mission is the dissemination of research findings to boards and staffs of nonprofit organizations, to policymakers and the general public through its newsletter, *Nonprofit Research News,* and through conferences and working papers.

The Nonprofit Sector Research Fund was formed after several years of debate about the need for an independent institution to support research on the nonprofit sector. A white paper written by David Arnold of the Ford Foundation set out the rationale for the program and presented options. A group of donors including the Ford Foundation, the Rockefeller Brothers Fund, the Charles Stewart Mott Foundation, the AAFRC Trust for Philanthropy, and anonymous donors provided the initial grant money.

The fund's first governing council was chaired by Tom Kessinger, President of Haverford College, and its first staff director was Elizabeth Boris, former Vice President for Research at the Council on Foundations.

ELIZABETH T. BORIS

BIBLIOGRAPHY

Nonprofit Sector Research Fund, 1993. *The Nonprofit Sector Coming of Age: Inaugural Report on Fund Directions and Activities 1991–1992.* Washington, DC: Aspen Institute.

NORTHCOTE-TREVELYAN REPORT. The radical report of a British government commission published in February 1854, which provided the foundations of the modern British Civil Service. The report, coauthored by Sir Charles Trevelyan and Sir Stafford Northcote, squarely addressed the issues of the organization of, and qualification for, public service. John Stuart Mill remarked that it represented "one of those great public improvements, the adoption of which would form an era in history;" *The Times* of London commented, perhaps a little prematurely, that with its acceptance an era had ended in which gentlemen were *ipso facto* considered capable of anything and everything (Reader 1981, p. 7). Although implementation was a long drawn-out process, the contents of the report have had a lasting impact well beyond the nineteenth-century British experience.

The setting up of the commission of inquiry seems, with hindsight, a natural and even inevitable step for the British ruling elite to have taken. The Parliamentary Reform Act of 1832 had ushered in not merely a more democratic House of Commons; it began a series of reforming pieces of legislation that stretched into many new areas of national life. Local government, factory conditions, school grants, a new Poor Law, and more were all subject to parliamentary attention. The supposed virtues of patronage began to be challenged by the notion of competition. "Whom you know" could not, in such a climate, forever outweigh the claims of "what you know." But there was more to it than that. The Great Britain of the 1840s had been powerfully shaped by the religious and moral revival of the previous century; corruption in public life had become endemic, or at least embarrassingly obvious. Oxford and Cambridge, forcing houses for the new elite, had become (not without a fight) imbued with the benefits of competition; providing the recruitment pool, as they did, meant that such an ethos would spread. Napoleon had been defeated at Waterloo, but the cry of "Career open to talent!" was not silenced thereby. The effort to defeat the French may have reduced criticism of government policy in wartime but doubts about the prudence of wartime spending priorities were aimed at government employees. The revolutions of 1848, while not directly expressed in Britain with the overthrow, however temporarily, of the *status quo,* had given the system a challenge only reform could address. Not surprisingly therefore, both the Treasury and the authorities responsible for education began to experiment with examinations as the preferred method of professional entry. To that extent, the reforming Northcote-Trevelyan Report can be seen as a natural development.

The interpretation of that reforming zeal can be overdone. The authors of the report—largely, in fact, Trevelyan—made what they called "a proper distinction between intellectual and mechanical labour" (Northcote-Trevelyan Report 1854, p. 17). This became the well-known split between the policy and administrative functions of government. To be sure, examinations were recommended for both classes of civil servant but the social opportunities of this division heavily weighted the outcome in favor of the existing power structures. Those with the opportunities of getting an education—and doing well—would have available to themselves the "policy" design functions of the state rather than the less socially significant "executive" activities. However, such a critique can itself go too far. The imposition of an examination for entry to the civil service was a big change; so was the idea that promotion should be on merit. Examinations were to be conducted, the report recommended, by an independent educational body. Full-time employment would depend on the successful completion of a period of probation. Personal advancement would be conditional upon some form of staff reporting system. The report was clear: Personal merit and integrity should be the measures of recruitment and promotion. It pointed out the dangers of a system in which "numerous instances might be given in which personal or political considerations have led to the appointment of men of very slender ability, and perhaps of questionable character, to situations of considerable emolument" (Northcote-Trevelyan Report 1854, p. 4).

As would be expected, vested interests delayed the imposition of these ideas as mainstream to the British Civil Service for several decades. Nevertheless, their incorporation occurred, not least because the intellectual case so to do was irrefutable. The British have long since had time to reflect on the benefits of this report. The massive expansion of the government's range of activities from World War I through the Great Depression absolutely depended upon a level of public probity and service that is directly attributable to those values inherent in the Northcote-Trevelyan Report of the 1850s. However, it is notable that the civil service accepted, with the onset of what was to become World War II, that it would not be able to deal successfully with the requirements of another total war. It therefore, and very successfully, prepared itself for that conflict by recruiting in advance key personnel from the private sector. From the mid-1930s, such individuals agreed—a good example being Patrick Ashley Cooper, the British-born governor of the Hudson's Bay Company, who went straight into the Ministry of Supply—that in the event of hostilities, they would immediately make their talent, managerial experience, and contacts available to the British state, leaving their private interests to one side for the duration of the war.

Ironically perhaps, such groups were themselves powerfully imbued by the sense that public service constituted a higher calling that personal profit. (Indeed, they belonged largely to the same social milieu as those in what used to be called the "administrative class.") Today, such a value system is seen as a largely irrelevant to the business of the British state; the managerial ethos has dismantled that. The growth of executive agencies and quangos has attracted a different kind of official to those proposed in the 1850s. To this extent, the Northcote-Trevelyan Report now represents, perhaps, a fading influence on the theory and practice of public administration.

PETER FOOT

BIBLIOGRAPHY

Fry, G. Kingdom, 1969. *Statesmen in Disguise: The Changing Role of the Administrative Class of the British Home Civil Service 1853–1966.* London: Macmillan.

Hennessy, Peter, 1995. *The Hidden Wiring: Unearthing the British Constitution.* London: Gollancz.

Northcote-Trevelyan Report, 1854. *The Organisation of the Permanent Civil Service,* c. 1713, London.

Reader, K. M., 1981. *The Civil Service Commission 1855–1975.* London: HMSO.

O

OBJECTIVE SETTING. The process of establishing statements for people within an organization, either as individuals, as members of organizational units, or as members of the organization as a whole, that make it clear what ends they are expected to serve and what results they are expected to achieve.

Objective setting by government first became an active topic in respect of the regulation of public enterprises, initially in the 1920s in Soviet economics with the advent of the Five-Year Plans and then in the 1930s in Western economics when Oscar Lange and Abba P. Lerner (building on the general equilibrium model of Wassily W. Leontief) attempted to show how socialist enterprises could be regulated to produce welfare results equivalent to those claimed for competitive market economies (Kowalik 1990). This debate spawned the continuing theory and practice of utility regulation, which continues to focus mainly on economic objectives, generally of the type "to set price equal to marginal cost."

The detailed exposition of objective setting as a major responsibility of managers within an organization dates back only to Peter Drucker in the 1950s. Earlier management writers tended to pay little explicit attention to objectives. Frederick Taylor (1911, reissued 1947) suggested that "the principal object of management should be to secure the maximum prosperity for the employer, coupled with the maximum prosperity of each employee," but this is more of a mission statement than a set of operation objectives—and it does little to help managers in nonprofit sectors. Although Chester Barnard (1938) wrote extensively on mission statements as embodiments of organizational purpose and argued strongly that it was the role of the executive to ensure that all members of an organization were indoctrinated with its general purposes, he did not explore how this knowledge could be cascaded down into objectives for units within the organization. In public administration, the work of Max Weber and Herbert Simon both characterized organizations as goal seeking, but Weber suggested that bureaucrats were more concerned with setting and following rules than objectives, and Simon focused on the desire of managers to use rules of thumb for programmed decisions and their use of judgement, intuition, and creativity for making unprogrammed decisions.

Drucker (1954, 1955) sharpened up the vague statements made by previous writers. He attacked the simplistic notion that the objective of business was to make profits and suggested instead that profit is simply the test of the validity of the business enterprise. Furthermore, it is not realistic to think of an organization as having a single objective; rather management always involves balancing the different possible objectives and deciding the priorities to be put on them. He suggested that the need for juggling these multiple objectives in complex departmentalized organizations required "Management by Objectives" (MBO).

Drucker argued that objective in a business enterprise would enable management to explain, predict, and control activities to a much greater extent than was possible with unidimensional ideas like profit maximization.

- They help an organization to model the central factors affecting its prosperity in a small number of general statements.
- They make easier the testing of these statements in the light of experience.
- They embody past lessons in such a way as to allow the prediction of future behavior.
- They allow the soundness of decisions to be examined while those decisions are still being made, rather than after the event.
- They force detailed planning, focused on what the business should aim at and how it might effectively achieve these aims.
- They, therefore, enable performance in the future to be improved through the analysis of past experience.

Right from the outset, MBO was seen as an approach that should attempt to cement the interests of individual staff to those of their team and the overall organization. Through setting objectives, and the subsequent feedback of information on performance, it was expected that management by self-control would be developed and would replace management by domination, leading to greater motivation and more efficient learning.

These ideas were quickly incorporated into management textbooks and management practice. While MBO mushroomed at first in the private sector, in 1961 the U.S. Department of Defense introduced a planning, programming, and budgeting system (PPB) system, which incorporated objective setting as a major element. In 1965, PPB was imposed on all major agencies of U.S. federal government, and in early 1970s the Nixon administration imposed "presidential MBO" governmentwide. Thereafter, it rapidly spread to many state and local governments (Poister and Streib 1995). By 1966, MBO had spread to the United Kingdom, with its adoption by the Greater London Council.

However, a substantial body of criticism soon built up, from a number of different perspectives, on the grounds that this conception of objective-led management may

- focus upon official and management objectives to the exclusion of the objectives of other stakeholders;
- neglect implicit, latent, hidden, or informal objectives;

- neglect the multiple, conflicting, and even, sometimes, contradictory nature of organizational objectives;

- neglect environmental influences, which sometimes mean that it is the environment, not the management, which "selects" the objectives of successful organizations;

- fail to recognize explicitly that organizational objectives are often retrospective and serve mainly to justify organizational action, not to direct it;

- fail to recognize that organizational objectives change as contextual factors and organizational behavior change.

In addition, it has often been obvious that objectives, as set out in practice by organizations, have suffered from being bland (almost to the point of meaninglessness, as in "motherhood and apple pie" statements), vague (or even outrightly ambiguous), incomplete (sometimes deliberately, in order not to alienate important stakeholders who must feel "ownership" of them), complex and interacting (so that each objective has important effects on several others), difficult to assess (in terms of whether they have been achieved), and symbolic (in the sense that they are intended to signify the adoption of a certain management style or organizational culture rather than being meant to be taken literally as guidelines for action).

In these circumstances, it is easy to dismiss objective setting as a purely notional exercise, engaged in by top management mainly to satisfy external stakeholders that strategic direction and control is being exercised, complied with by lower management to show they are "playing the game," and perpetuated by all stakeholders owing to a dominant belief system that insists upon the language of the rational cycle of decisionmaking, however remote it may be from practice.

However, this view may be too pessimistic. Some of the objections to traditional methods of objective setting can be overcome by technical means, using the technique of the "hierarchy of objectives." Furthermore, some may be overcome by ensuring that an organization separates out the role of objective setting for internal learning purposes, as distinct from external control purposes. These possibilities are now explored in turn.

Although most authors on objective setting stress that objectives should cascade down an organization, from corporate objectives at the top to individual objectives at the bottom, few show how this might be done, other than by constructing lists of objectives for each level of management or each organizational unit. H. Igor Ansoff (1969) showed how this might work in principle, but concentrated on hierarchies of performance indicators and targets rather than hierarchies of objectives. In the private sector, the hierarchy of objectives technique has become known as a "tree diagram" and is strongly associated with the work of W. Elwards Deming and other quality management practitioners (Oakland 1989). This approach, based on extensive practice in U.K. local government, was spelled out in detail in Tony Bovaird and Ian Mallinson (1988).

The use of the "hierarchy of objectives" technique is illustrated in Figure I, in relation to an aspect of policing services. By adopting this approach, the interrelationships between different objectives are spelt out in a cause-and-effect chain. As one goes from the top to the bottom of the hierarchy, one is asking, How is this objective going to be achieved? The objectives at the next level down indicate the means by which the higher-level aspiration will be met. Again, moving up the picture from bottom to top, one is

FIGURE I. A HIERARCHY OF OBJECTIVES FOR REASSURING THE PUBLIC ON PUBLIC SAFETY

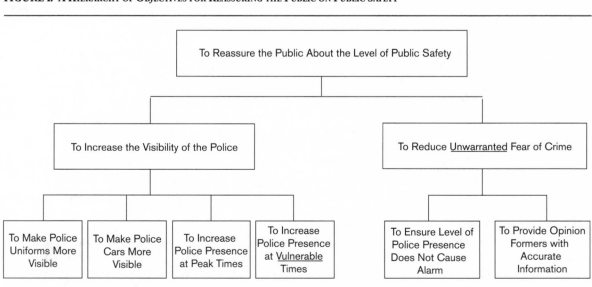

asking, Why are we interested in this objective? The objective at the next level up indicates the reason why the lower-level objective is of interest.

Although a hierarchy of objectives is certainly more complicated than a straightforward list of objectives, the approach meets most of the technical objections to objective setting. It clearly models the interrelationship of objectives, it moderates the blandness of top-level objectives by specifying their implications in more detail at lower levels, it invites measurement of the achievement of objectives at each level (so that, even in circumstances where the achievement of top-level objectives cannot easily be assessed, achievements of lower-level objectives should normally be easier and more acceptable to assess), and it shows that all objectives are potentially in conflict, at least in the sense that managers must prioritize between subobjectives at each level.

Clearly, any hierarchy of objectives can be expanded into a much larger picture with only a little effort. Those objectives toward the top of the picture, which refer to the top-level impacts of the service, can be spelled out in greater detail, as can those objectives toward the bottom, which demonstrate some of the logistics by means of which the higher level objectives will be achieved. Indeed, it may be useful to keep this distinction in mind when formulating a set of objectives: Some should be framed in terms of the impacts to be achieved (top-level objectives) and others should be in terms of the logistical prerequisites without which achievement of the other objectives is not feasible (the lowest-level objectives).

However, managers may not wish to or need to work with a very elaborate set of objectives. Any picture such as Figure 1 merely provides one window into the possible set of objectives, which might be spelled out in detail. Normally, for a manager undertaking any given management task, only a few key objectives need to be highlighted in such a window and overelaborate detail would be counterproductive.

Having a clear set of objectives is only the starting point—the big payoff to a manager will come when it is possible to show how many of the key objectives have been achieved, to what extent, and whether it is likely that the achievement was indeed related to the organization's intervention. Thus each objective needs to have a performance indicator attached to it. There is little point in having objectives without assessing whether they are being met and how they might better be achieved. But similarly, there is little point in having performance indicators if the basic set of objectives is unusable. Often the exercise is taken to greater levels of quantification, in target setting, when target levels of performance indicators are specified, to be achieved within given periods of time. (The terminology associated with these concepts is, unfortunately, far from standard—for example, Ansoff (1965) uses the term "yardstick" instead of performance indicator and "goal" in-

stead of target, although Ansoff does not insist that each goal have a specified time period for its achievement. However, one of the advantages of the hierarchy-of-objectives formulation is that it becomes immediately clear that there are no hard-and-fast distinctions to be made between levels of objectives and subobjectives, or aims or subaims, as they are all linked in a seamless web).

This discussion has stressed that the cause-and-effect chain embedded in any hierarchy of objectives is simply a model, or set of hypotheses. These hypotheses can—and should—be tested. Different levels of staff should be involved in discussing the logic of the proposed cause-and-effect chains, and where staff differs in its views, evidence-gathering procedures should be devised, agreed on, and implemented.

Indeed, this hypothesis-testing approach may be able to turn objective setting from a control instrument, which is potentially mechanistic, contentious, and dysfunctional into a tool for enhancing organizational learning. It attempts to make explicit the mechanisms through which professional and managerial practices are related to the final set of outcomes desired by policymakers, to reveal that there are differences of opinion on some aspects of the model (sometimes associated with particular stakeholder perspectives) and that there is substantial ignorance about many aspects of the model, including even the extent to which top-level objectives might be achieved by much cheaper or very different resource inputs and processes.

This learning process is likely to be more effective if an organization recognizes, and does not attempt to hide, the differences between stakeholders on the priority attached to certain objectives and on the best way of achieving these objectives. Indeed, Aaron Wildavsky (1975) has argued that attempting to set objectives without explicit reference to the configuration of stakeholders is foolish. "Goals may well be the product of interaction among key participants rather than some *deus ex machina*. . . . What we call goals or objectives may, in large part, be operationally determined by policies we can agree on. The mixtures of values found in complex policies may have to be taken in packages, so that policies may determine goals at least as much as general objectives determine policies. In a political, situation, then, the need for support assumes central importance" (p. 332).

Yet, acceptance of the diversity of stakeholder interests and perspectives is unlikely to characterize a control-fixated organization. This is perhaps why many public-sector organizations (and in particular operations-oriented departments like police, fire, highways, etc.) appear to be more comfortable with target setting, which is a relatively narrow and short-term approach and often successfully masks any underlying conflicts between stakeholders, than they are with the wider and more strategic approach of objective setting. However, organizations that wish to legitimate create thinking about their desired outcomes and to shape rather than rigidly control the mechanisms by which these outcomes are brought about might well find construction of a hierarchy of objectives, as a joint effort by multiple stakeholders, a valuable framework to surface these debates and to structure the evidence-gathering process.

Since objective setting is an integral part of the rational cycle of decisionmaking, which has almost universal acceptance as a logical way to analyze past decisions, it is not surprising to find that objective setting, too, is widely practiced in the public sectors of most countries. Moreover, its logic appears applicable in all types of organizational cultures and structures. However, the arguments above would suggest that its use to actually inform or determine decisions in the public sector may be very much less than might appear from official documentation or the public utterances of politicians and public-sector managers.

In light of these contrasting experiences, it is consistent to argue that objective setting could indeed be an invaluable management tool, while at the same time recommending that many organizations should desist on the grounds that their current approach to objective setting is dysfunctional.

TONY BOVAIRD

BIBLIOGRAPHY

Ansoff, H. Igor, 1965. *Business Strategy.* Harmondsworth: Penguin Books.
Barnard, Chester, 1938. *The Functions of the Executive.* Cambridge, MA: Harvard University Press.
Bovaird, Tony, and Ian Mallinson, 1988. "Setting Objectives and Increasing Achievement in Social Care." *British Journal of Social Work,* vol. 18 (July).
Drucker, Peter F., 1954. *The Practice of Management.* New York: Harper and Row.
———, 1955. *Management by Objectives.* Englewood Cliffs, NJ: Prentice-Hall.
Kowalik, Tadeusz, 1990. "Lange-Lerner Mechanism." In John Eatwell, Murray Milgate, and Peter Newman, 1990. *Problems of the Planned Economy.* London: Macmillan.
Oakland, John S., 1989. *Total Quality Management.* Oxford: Butterworth Heinemann.
Poister, Theodore H., and Gregory Streib, 1995. "MbO in Municipal Government: Variations on a Traditional Management Tool." *Public Administration Review,* vol. 55, no. 1.
Taylor, Frederick W., 1911 (reissued 1947). *Scientific Management.* New York: Harper and Row.
Wildavsky, A., 1975. *Budgeting: A Comparative Theory of Budgetary Process.* Boston: Little, Brown.

OCCUPATIONAL SAFETY AND HEALTH.

Governmental efforts to diminish rates and severity of occupational injuries and illness.

The economic argument for public regulation of occupational safety and health is essentially the following.

Employees face the risk of injury and illness from their work, just as capital equipment in firms suffers wear and tear in the course of production. Similarly, just as efficiency requires that firms try to conserve capital equipment by routine maintenance, firms should try to conserve labor resources by taking steps to prevent occupational health and safety hazards. The costs of the injuries and illnesses, which nevertheless do occur, should be reflected in the price of the firm's products, providing a continuous incentive to minimize potential hazards. Otherwise, workers' physical well-being, like any underpriced resource used in production, is wasted. Even unregulated firms bear some costs when employees are injured or made ill; workers must be replaced, their replacements may need to be paid more to accept risks, production is slowed, and so forth. Unregulated firms, however, would be able to pass a large share of these costs onto workers without compensation, as injured or ill employees personally carry most of the costs away from the firm. These firms commonly would accept their relatively minor share of the costs of injuries and illnesses in order to avoid the investments required to prevent the injuries or illnesses in the first place. Accordingly, government regulation directs firms to invest in the safety and health measures they would take if they bore all of these costs. The argument does not speak of eliminating all injuries or illnesses, but of reducing them to a level one could reasonably expect if firms were forced to internalize all the costs of wear and tear incurred by workers—just as firms need to bear the costs of replacing equipment (leaving aside the question of tax laws).

The social and political argument for public regulation of occupational safety and health is less concerned with balancing the marginal costs and benefits of injury/illness prevention and appeals to general sentiments of what is ethical, equitable, or moral in industrial society. The social and political argument is that a situation in which large numbers of workers are forced to trade off their health and safety in order to hold a job is objectionable on its face. This was the most prominent argument during the debate over the Occupational Safety and Health Act in 1969.

The Occupational Safety and Health Act

Prior to 1970, state governments had the main responsibility for regulating occupational safety and health conditions, but for a variety of reasons many states failed to do so effectively. The Occupational Safety and Health (OSH) Act of 1970 (PL 91-596) thus was part of the major wave of regulatory legislation in the United States in the late 1960s and early 1970s. The OSH Act established the Occupational Safety and Health Administration (OSHA) in the United States Department of Labor as the central federal agency concerned with workplace safety and health.

The law established other activities besides those in OSHA. The Bureau of Labor Statistics in the Department of Labor was to prepare an annual survey of injuries and illnesses, and a new National Institute for Occupational Safety and Health (NIOSH) in the Department of Health, Education, and Welfare (now in the Department of Health and Human Services) was to conduct research on occupational safety and health hazards and provide OSHA with technical guidance in OSHA's standards development. The law also created the Occupational Safety and Health Review Commission (OSHRC) as an indecent body to adjudicate enforcement disputes (Section 12). Enforcement and adjudication were split between OSHA and OSHRC as a compromise between those who wanted the Department of Labor to carry all administrative responsibilities for the law and business groups who were suspicious of the department's links with organized labor and who therefore wanted the OSH Act to be implemented by an independent commission, such as the Federal Trade Commission. Thus, OSHA would develop and enforce regulations, but appeals of citations would be heard by OSHRC.

In addition, given that states had carried the main responsibilities for occupational safety and health regulation in the past, and that some might want to continued to do so under the federal law, the OSH Act permitted states to retain their regulatory role if they mounted a regulatory program that was "at least as effective" [Section 18(c)(2)] as the federal program, with OSHA to approve the plans. In 1994, 21 states covered both private and public sector employees under federally approved OSH programs, and New York and Connecticut covered state and local employees but not the private sector. In fiscal year 1993, US $67 million of OSHA's US $288 million appropriation directly supported state programs. The federal program covered the remainder of the workforce in the nation.

The law set a high standard for worker protection. One especially consequential phrase instructed the secretary of the Department of Labor, through the Occupational Safety and Health Administration, "in promulgating standards dealing with toxic materials or harmful physical agents under this subsection, [to] set the standard which most adequately assures, to the extent feasible, on the basis of the best available evidence, that no employee will suffer material impairment of health or functional capacity even if such employee has regular exposure to the hazard dealt with by such standard for the period of his working life" [Section 6(b)(5)]. This phrase, first, implied an aspiration that all employees would be protected from health and safety hazards on the job. Second, it specified that when OSHA did promulgate a pertinent rule, it was to reduce the hazard to the point virtually safeguarding workers from harm, subject to a loose "feasibility" constraint. The phrase did not require that benefits and costs of a regulation be balanced even approximately. OSHA thus was mandated to force thou-

sands of firms of insulate from injury and illness millions of workers dealing with thousands of potentially hazardous substances and processes. OSHA's development since 1970 reflects the debate over how this relatively small agency can and should cope with this overwhelmingly difficult task in a contentious environment. In this entry, three issues are noted surfacing in the practice of, and research on, occupational safety and health. First, how should regulations be designed? Second, how should regulations be implemented? Third, how much does the regulatory program actually improve occupational safety and health?

The Design of Regulations

Since the early 1970s, OSHA has been at the center of a debate over how agencies should weigh the benefits and costs of their regulations. As noted above, the law mandated that OSHA should design its regulations to be highly protective, subject to a loose feasibility constraint; the law suggested that the agency should not be concerned with balancing carefully their benefits and costs. Supporters of this approach have argued that the Occupational Safety and Health Act committed the United States to strive continuously for a more complete protection of its workforce from job safety and health hazards. They maintain that a policy of trying to balance regulations' costs and benefits in more than a very general sense would be unrealistic because the requisite technical information usually is unavailable and, in the case of health hazards with long-term effects, probably unattainable. Furthermore, such a policy would create potentially endless debates over ambiguous scientific and technical issues in each case and thus give self-interested parties a tool to stalemate sensible and just protections for employees.

In contrast, others have maintained that OSHA should carefully weigh the costs and benefits of alternative regulations. They point out that, regardless of the OSH Act's mandate, the economic and technical problems of designing, implementing, and enforcing regulations force OSHA to be selective in choosing hazards to regulate and how stringently it will regulate them. Thus, it is important for the agency to direct its attention to initiatives with the highest "payoffs," even if this means foregoing regulations for hazards confronting few employees, or hazards facing many employees but posing minimal risk; the agency should act on the basis of rational analysis rather than responsiveness to "crises of the moment" or political pressures from influential sectors of industry or labor. Supporters of this approach acknowledge that the Occupational Safety and Health Act did not favor such risk assessment—indeed, the law's spirit tends to conflict with it—but stress that in reality OSHA must embrace such a policy in order to function effectively.

Generally, OSHA has come to behave somewhere between these two positions. OSHA has not tried to balance economic costs and benefits of rules as an overriding principle, but it has weighed such analyses heavily in its decisionmaking. How far it leans one way or the other has varied by administration. This uneven institutionalization of economic analysis in the agency has reflected pressure from the Executive Office of the President for greater use of economic analysis, balanced by congressional concerns about spreading presidential control of agency rulemaking; a series of judicial decisions (notably, *Industrial Union Department, AFL-CIO v. American Petroleum Institute*, 1980, 448 U.S. 607, and *American Textile Manufacturers, Inc. v. Donovan*, 1978, 452 U.S. 408; has added tension between the evident economic costs of regulation and the social aversion to insidious if unmeasurable health risks.

The Implementation of Regulations

The Occupational Safety and Health Administration's most visible activity has been its own inspections of firms. Yet, state governments conduct much of the enforcement of the Occupational Safety and Health Act. Also, efforts to increase the involvement of labor-management committees in safety and health programs are now widespread.

Direct Federal Inspections

The intensity of OSHA's inspection program has varied in striking ways through the agency's history. In its first years, OSHA conducted large numbers of relatively low-cost inspections, an organizationally expedient but ineffective strategy. Beginning in the mid-1970s, the agency shifted to a program of fewer but more intensive inspections, often of larger employers, with greater attention to potential health hazards. The first years of the Reagan administration saw an abrupt shift to a "conciliatory" OSHA inspection program, with the number and intensity of inspections dropping dramatically. That, however, was largely reversed by the mid-1980s, as the program again became more publicly assertive. For example, in the late 1980s the agency imposed numerous large fines—in the hundreds of thousands, or even millions of, dollars—although these fines consistently were reduced by 50 percent or more following negotiations. By the 1990s, the political climate continued to favor an assertive enforcement program by OSHA. In 1990, Congress authorized a sevenfold increase in OSHA's maximum allowable penalties, and some subsequent legislative proposals to strengthen OSHA's enforcement program were so strong that they were opposed by the agency.

OSHA, and certainly its critics, have always been aware of the flaws of the inspection program. The agency can inspect relatively few firms; its technical resources are extremely limited compared to those of the firms it inspects; and, given these limited resources, it is in an unfavorable position to manage the routine challenges to its citations (thus emerges the pattern in which large fines are levied, but ultimately negotiated to a fraction of original amounts). A perennial challenge for OSHA has been the design and management of the inspection program under exceptionally difficult resource constraints.

State Plans

The federal OSHA inspection is not the only mechanism for enforcing the Occupational Safety and Health Act. The relative effectiveness and role of state plans is a matter of great interest for those working in the area. As noted earlier, 21 states have responsibilities to enforce the Occupational Safety and Health Act in their private and public sectors, two states cover the public sector, and support of state plans accounted for about one-quarter of OSHA's US$288 million appropriation in fiscal year 1993–1994.

Organized labor generally has been suspicious of state plans—keep in mind that the OSH Act was enacted partly to compensate for historical weaknesses in state enforcement of job safety laws. Furthermore, given that OSHA has had difficulty managing, overseeing, and evaluating its own regulatory operations, it is not surprising that it has had great difficulty overseeing the operations of the 23 state programs. The "dangers" of relying heavily on state programs are noted whenever a catastrophe occurs in such a state. For example, in 1991 a fire in a poultry plant in North Carolina—a state operating such a plan—reinforced calls for much stronger centralized enforcement.

Yet, there is no clear evidence that regulatory programs operating in state plan states are less effective than the federal program—the question cannot be answered either way because data on the subject are limited. Furthermore, states have been able to experiment with different styles of enforcement in ways OSHA, because of its tight political constraints, cannot. Most notably, the states have been laboratories for the development of labor-management safety committees.

Labor-Management Safety Committees

From 1991 to 1994, the worker's compensation programs in 32 states moved to actively encourage or require worker involvement in safety plans, and 6 states operating state plans enacted or strengthened requirements for labor-management safety committees. Many analysts have pointed out the advantages of such cooperation if employees are given the information and internal leverage to participate effectively in the committees. Regulatory issues settled locally are more likely to be adapted to the specifics of the local situation and more likely to be implemented in good faith. Indeed, such cooperation on health-safety matters can go a long way toward remedying the market failures justifying regulation in the firm itself, as neither party's interests would be subordinated in health-safety issues. Supporters of these systems point out that occupational safety and health regulation is conducted in a more adversarial manner in the United States than in most other Western nations and that the institutionalization of labor-management safety committees—which play a prominent role in other industrial democracies—would provide a more constructive way to deal with conflicts over safety and health matters within firms. (For a comparative discussion of a labor involvement in occupational health and safety regulation, see Korostoff, Zimmerman, and Ryan 1991.)

The idea of labor-management committees appeals to managers, who see them as a way to minimize external regulators' intrusions. The committees also appeal to many labor representatives, who see committees potentially as a way to enhance employees' influence within the firm. Labor, however, stresses that managers will allow employees such effective "voice" only if managers see strong external regulation as an unappealing alternative should the arrangements break down. Thus, although the development of labor-management safety committees is perhaps the most important regulatory innovation in this area in the 1990s, no one expects such programs to supplant external regulation.

The Impacts of Occupational Safety and Health Regulation

Have occupational safety and health conditions improved in the 25 years since the enactment of the Occupational Safety and Health Act? Several factors confound evaluations of this issue. The measurement of the incidence of occupational injuries and, particularly, illnesses is extremely difficult because of reporting and methodological problems. For example, constructing widely accepted illness rates becomes virtually impossible when the latency period of diseases from particular exposures can range from less than 1 year to 20 years or more. Furthermore, even if one could cleanly determine injury and illness rates, regulation is only one factor influencing the rates. The demographic composition of the active workforce, changes in technology, and changes in workers' compensation programs all influence injury and illness experience, probably in interacting ways not easily held constant in statistical research. Thus, no consensus view on the impact of occupational safety and health regulation is likely to emerge.

An interesting pattern in the extant evaluations, however, is a split between the results of qualitative as opposed to quantitative evaluations. Qualitative, or perceptual, data suggest that OSHA has had a considerable impact on occupational safety and health conditions. Surveys or workers and managers report fairly consistently that since OSHA was established, managers have assigned a higher priority to plant safety, workers are more able to influence safety conditions, and safety efforts generally have been strengthened. Yet, quantitative research, which has examined in painstaking ways the statistical effects of OSHA enforcement on injury rates, produce generally negative results, although some recent research indicates substantial effects (for example, compare Ruser and Smith 1991 with Gray and Scholz 1993).

Still, it is difficult to believe that the 25 years of activity since the Occupational Safety and Health Act was passed has not affected the ways managers and employees approach health and safety questions, at least in the majority of firms. The results of the current widespread interest in developing labor-management safety committees should provide useful information for both practitioners and scholars concerned with this area.

DAVID P. MCCAFFREY

BIBLIOGRAPHY

Ashford, Nicholas A., 1976. *Crisis in the Workplace: Occupational Disease and Injury.* Cambridge, MA: MIT Press.

Breyer, Stephen, 1993. *Breaking the Vicious Circle: Toward Effective Risk Regulation.* Cambridge, MA: Harvard University Press.

Gray, Wayne B., and John T. Scholz, 1993. "Does Regulatory Enforcement Work? A Panel Analysis of OSHA Enforcement." *Law and Society Review,* vol. 27: 177–213.

Korostoff, Julie, Linda Zimmerman, and Carolyn Ryan, 1991. "Rethinking the OSHA Approach to Workplace Safety: A Look at Worker Participation in the Enforcement of Safety Regulations in Sweden, France, and Great Britain." *Comparative Labor Law Journal,* vol. 13: 45–95.

McGarity, Thomas O., and Sidney A. Shapiro, 1993. *Workers at Risk: The Failed Promise of the Occupational Safety and Health Administration.* Westport, CT: Praeger.

Mendeloff, John, 1988. *The Dilemma of Toxic Substance Regulation.* Cambridge, MA: MIT Press.

Rees, Joseph, 1988. *Reforming the Workplace: A Study of Self-Regulation in Occupational Safety.* Philadelphia: University of Pennsylvania Press.

Ruser, John W., and Robert W. Smith, 1991. "Reestimating OSHA's Effects: Have the Data Changed?" *Journal of Human Resources,* vol. 26 (Spring) 212–235.

United States Congress, Senate Committee on Labor and Human Resources, 1991. *Hearing on the OSHA Criminal Penalty Reform Act.* Washington, DC: U.S. Government Printing Office.

United States General Accounting Office, 1994. *Occupational Safety and Health: Changes Needed in the Combined Federal-State Approach* (GAO/HEHS-94-10) (February). Washington, DC: U.S. General Accounting Office.

Viscusi, W. Kip, 1992. *Fatal Tradeoffs: Public and Private Responsibilities for Risk.* New York: Oxford University Press.

ORGANIZATION FOR ECONOMIC COOPERATION AND DEVELOPMENT (OECD).

An intergovernmental organization that provides opportunities for the governments of industrialized democracies to monitor, study, discuss and make recommendations about social and economic policies.

The OECD

The Organization of Economic Cooperation and Development (OECD) was established on September 30, 1961. It replaced the Organization for European Economic Cooperation, which was founded on April 16, 1948, to administer the United States' aid program for European economic recovery known as the Marshall Plan. The OECD is an intergovernmental organization that provides opportunities for the governments of the world's industrialized democracies to monitor, to study, to discuss, and to make recommendations for the best possible social and economic policies.

There are currently 25 member countries. The 20 founding members were Austria, Belgium, Canada, Denmark, the Federal Republic of Germany, France, Greece, Iceland, Ireland, Italy, Luxembourg, the Netherlands, Norway, Portugal, Spain, Sweden, Switzerland, Turkey, the United Kingdom, and the United States. Since the founding of the OECD, 5 other countries have become members: Japan (1964), Finland (1969), Australia (1971), New Zealand (1973), and Mexico (1994). Additionally, over 30 nonmember countries and the Commission of the European Union participate in certain OECD activities.

The basic aims of the OECD are outlined in the *Convention on the Organization for Economic Cooperation and Development*, which was signed on December 14, 1960. Article 1 of the convention states that the OECD will promote policies designed (a) to achieve the highest sustainable economic growth and employment and a rising standard of living in member countries, while maintaining financial stability, and thus to contribute to the development of the world economy, (b) to contribute to sound economic expansion in member as well as nonmember countries in the process of economic development, and (c) to contribute to the expansion of world trade on a multilateral, nondiscriminatory basis in accordance with international obligations.

The OECD differs from other intergovernmental organizations. The OECD's strength is that it provides a forum for direct policy dialogue between governments of member countries; it has neither supranational legal powers nor financial resources at its disposal for the purposes of granting loans or subsidies. Cooperation is based on common values and principles, notably support for democratic systems of governance, the market economy, open multilateral trade, and the fostering of social equity and justice. The work of the OECD is multidisciplinary, reflecting a horizontal or integrated approach to social and economic questions.

The supreme body of the OECD is the council, which is composed of one representative for each member country. Each country maintains a permanent delegation, which is established as a normal diplomatic mission and headed by an ambassador. The member countries' ambassadors represent their countries at council meetings held under the chairmanship of the secretary-general. The council operates on the principle of consensus. It produces decisions and recommendations, approves the program of work and budget, and appoints the secretary-general.

OECD's Committees

It is in the committees that the major part of the OECD's work is prepared and carried out. There are over 150 specialized committees and working groups that meet regularly between two and four times a year. They are composed of representatives from member country capitals and are often high-ranking government officials, technical experts, or members of the permanent delegations to the OECD. Approximately 20,000 delegates attend OECD meetings each year. The main committees are as follows: Economic Policy; Economic and Development Review; Development Assistance; Trade; Capital Movements and Invisible Transactions; Financial Markets; Insurance; Fiscal Affairs; Competition Law and Policy; Consumer Policy; Tourism; Maritime Transport; International Investment and Multinational Enterprises; Industry; Steel; Scientific and Technology Policy; Information, Computer, and Communications Policy; Education, Labor and Social Affairs; Environment; Agriculture; Fisheries; and Public Management.

The International Secretariat

The work of these committees and working groups is supported by the staff of the OECD secretariat. The staff works in two official languages—English and French—and is drawn from all the member countries. The OECD employs around 1,800 staff members of which nearly 600 are policy analysts. These analysts prepare studies and facilitate the exchange of information between member government officials. One of the major tasks of the secretariat is to gather data and policy information from all member countries and to standardize this information into an internationally comparable form. The secretariat is organized to reflect the OECD committee structure, which itself is a reflection of the major economic and social ministries in member countries. They are as follows: the Economics and Statistics Department; the Environment Directorate; the Development Cooperation Directorate; the Public Management Service; the Trade Directorate; the Directorate for Financial, Fiscal, and Enterprise Affairs; the Directorate for Science, Technology, and Industry; the Directorate for Education, Employment, and Social Affairs; the Directorate for Food, Agriculture, and Fisheries; and the Territorial Development Service.

There are also several autonomous and semiautonomous bodies that operate within the OECD framework, each with its own governing committee. These are the International Energy Agency, the Nuclear Energy Agency, the Development Center, and the Center for Educational Research and Innovation. To respond to changes in Eastern Europe and to coordinate the OECD's cooperation with the former centrally planned economies in that region, the Center for Cooperation with Economies in Transition was created in 1990.

The work of the secretariat in these areas often leads to publications that are made available to the public. Given the focus on economic and social policy and the frequent use of statistics, a proportion of the published output of the OECD is statistical in nature. Examples include the basic economic statistics published in the monthly *Main Economic Indicators* and the annual *National Accounts*. Twice a year, the Economics Department produces a detailed economic forecast for all OECD countries, which is published under the title *OECD Economic Outlook*. The OECD also publishes a bimonthly magazine, *The OECD Observer*, which offers articles relating to current activities and forthcoming publications.

OECD's Public Management Committee

The OECD's work in the field of governance and public administration is carried out by the Public Management Committee. The committee is made up of senior officials from central management agencies in member countries, who attend meetings twice a year. The mission of this committee is threefold: to provide information and analysis on public management issues to policymakers in member countries and to the OECD; to facilitate contact and exchange of experience among public management practitioners, particularly those working in central management agencies in government; and to report regularly to policymakers and the public on developments in the public sector and on its role in economic and social development. In summary, the committee works to help countries improve decision making and policy processes, the choice and use of instruments to implement public policies, and the management of financial and human resources.

Committee activities are carried out by specialist groups of senior managers responsible for administrative reform, budgeting and financial management, human resources, the policy process, and regulatory systems, who meet to consider analysis of specific management issues. These meetings offer public-sector managers an opportunity to exchange ideas and experiences and to discuss promising practice in dealing with shared problems. They also provide a forum for addressing broad strategic questions such as how improved public management can contribute to overall economic performance and further structural adjustment (*Serving the Economy Better* 1991).

The Public Management Service, or "PUMA"

The committee is served by the OECD Secretariat's Public Management Service (PUMA), whose work program is shaped and directed by the committee. PUMA deals with the capacity to govern and the ability of public authorities to make policy, to set rules, and to select the right mix of instruments to implement decisions effectively. There are currently six major areas in which PUMA works: monitoring and reporting on developments in public management; management of policymaking; budgeting and financial management; performance, accountability, and control; managing human resources; and regulatory management and reform.

Reporting on Public Management

With regard to monitoring developments in public management, the broad objectives are threefold: (1) to contribute to developing a capacity within the OECD for consistent analysis and reporting on the public sector and its management; (2) to produce surveys and profiles on public management and institutional change, which are of direct use to policymakers and which include progressively higher quality statistical information; (3) to develop ways of assessing public-sector performance in order to aid national decisionmaking. PUMA conducts triennial surveys of public management developments, which are supplemented by yearly updates (*Public Management Developments*, Update 1995). The country profiles (*Public Management: OECD Country Profiles*, 1992) describe the diverse structures of public administration and the public sector in OECD countries. Monitoring also involves analyzing trends in public management reform, including the multitude of pressures behind those reforms and the economic and political context in which they were introduced. In this regard, PUMA has prepared a report entitled *Governance in Transition: Public Management Reforms in OECD Countries 1995*. It also puts out a regular series of *Occasional Papers* reporting on work conducted with member countries or reproducing expert papers.

Management of Policymaking

The second major work area in PUMA is the management of policymaking. Governments in OECD countries continue to seek better ways to coordinate policy development, decisionmaking, and implementation. Effective policy management requires a better understanding of the linkages between horizontal, vertical, and temporal elements in decisionmaking. The main objective is to identify ways in which governments can improve cost-effective policy coherence and responsiveness in order to better meet interconnected and multisectoral goals. The focus, therefore, is on examining different aspects of policy management and decisionmaking at the center of government, since the primary responsibility for promoting policy a necessary degree of coherence rests with the head of government. Work in the management of policymaking concentrates in three areas; (1) overseeing the full range of policymaking activities, including budgetary policies, and maintaining a strategic perspective on the government's overall political and economic agenda; (2) ensuring that day-to-day decisions are consistent with the government's strategic and longer-term policy objectives and that the implementation of decisions takes place in a timely and integrated manner; and (3) promoting institutional change to improve coordination and encouraging the development of nonorganizational factors that enhance coherence, such as a more consultation-oriented and collaborative management culture.

Budgeting and Financial Management

Budgeting and financial management is the third principal work area in PUMA. This field demands careful attention because the budget is the main mechanism through which governments give effect to their economic and social priorities. Moreover, the nature of the rules, procedures, and incentives inherent in budgeting systems condition the manner in which public-sector activities are viewed and managed. A reflection of this relationship is the fact that reforms of the budgetary process have been a major element in most member countries' strategies for public sector reform. PUMA work in this area entails examining techniques and policies to control public expenditures and promote efficiency and effectiveness in service provision (see in this respect, *Budgeting for Results,* 1995, which also includes profiles of each member country's budget process). More specifically, the four main objectives are (1) to facilitate exchanges of information and experience on the institutional arrangements, practices, and tools employed in the formulation and management of expenditure budgets; (2) to provide a forum for the generation of innovative ideas and to analyze trends in policy design and expenditure management structures and techniques; (3) to highlight the role of the budget process and related financial management practices in effecting consolidation of public finances and in promoting the goals of efficient and effective public services; and (4) to develop quantitative and qualitative comparative data on key aspects related to budgetary processes and expenditure management.

Performance Management

The fourth major work area deals with performance management, accountability, and consultation. Performance-based public management involves a shift away from the traditional focus on adherence to rules and administrative procedures toward a framework oriented toward result and the outcomes of public programs. The activities in this area are concerned with examining ways to improve performance in a decentralized and discretionary management environment; they have examined the technical aspects of performance measurement and the extent to which measurement can be used as a management tool for improving performance. The case study approach has been employed to examine management issues in selected member countries. Work under this theme has three primary objectives: (1) to collect information and to provide a forum for the exchange of country experience in performance management and related changes to accountability and control mechanisms; (2) to identify and analyze emerging performance management initiatives such as service quality, corporate planning, benchmarking, and performance measurement in OECD countries; and (3) to conduct comparative assessments of these experiences to highlight promising practices, so as to support further reforms in member countries. A range of reports have been published on performance management as well as one on *Managing with Market-Type Mechanisms* (1993).

Human Resources Management

A fifth PUMA work area is the management of human resources. Effective management of human resources is integral to achieving the improvements in productivity and standards of public service that governments in OECD countries are pursuing. Public-management reforms imply some fundamental changes in human resource management policies and systems. The work in this area, therefore, is designed to support the efforts of member countries in developing human resource management systems that are appropriate for the current and anticipated needs of the public sector. In this regard, the capacity to implement more flexible, performance-oriented human resource management practices and the capacity to provide high standards of leadership and management are likely to be critical to the overall performance of public-sector organizations in the years ahead. The objectives of the work in this area are (1) to identify and analyze current and emerging issues and problems in public sector human resource management, thereby helping to clarify policy options and to formulate implementation strategies (*Flexible Personnel Management in the Public Service,* 1990); (2) to develop, as appropriate, and to disseminate comparative data on key aspects of human resource management such as pay, where an annual report on trends is now being produced as well as monographs on pay flexibility and performance related pay; (3) to assess reform experience and exchange ideas and information among human resources managers; and (4) to make clear the role human resource management can play in achieving the objectives of public sector management reform.

Regulatory Management and Reform

The sixth major work area is regulatory management and reform. Regulatory reform initiatives in member countries have improved substantially the capacities for governments to address the issues of poor economic growth, business development, and fiscal constraints. Member countries have taken varied approaches that include deregulation, administrative simplification, debureaucratization, improving the quality of new regulations, increasing openness, and integrating rules into regional or international regulatory systems. In this last respect, see *Regulatory Cooperation for an Interdependent World*, 1994. The overall trend in all reform initiatives is that the reform of individual rules has evolved into the need to improve the overall management of the regulatory system. PUMA work in this area, including a Regulatory Management and Reform series of published papers, seeks to support the diverse activities under way to improve regulatory processes and to enhance understanding of the costs and benefits of various regulatory reform strategies. The main objectives are (1) to examine institutional and procedural strategies for improving the quality of regulation, which has included approval of the *OECD Reference Checklist for Regulatory Decision-Making*, 1995; (2) to support the development of more effective management of the regulatory system in order to reduce regulatory inflation and costs, improve consistency, and increase openness; (3) to promote understanding of the ways in which alternative instruments can be used to advance regulatory objectives; (4) to highlight the role of regulatory management and reform; and (5) to support efforts to minimize the administrative and compliance burden on private enterprise and to reduce economic disincentives to the private sector.

Supporting Public Management Reform in Central and Eastern Europe

PUMA has also been playing a role in the economic and political reforms in Central and Eastern Europe through the program for Support for Improvement in Governance and Management (SIGMA). This is a joint initiative of the OECD and the Commission of the European Communities financed mainly by the commission programme for assistance to Central and Eastern European countries known as PHARE. SIGMA started work with the signing of a convention between the OECD and the commission on May 25, 1992. The original countries in the SIGMA program were Bulgaria, the Czech Republic, Hungary, Poland, Romania, and the Slovak Republic. In 1994, the program was renewed, and Albania, Estonia, Latvia, Lithuania, and Slovenia were added to the list of SIGMA countries.

SIGMA is able to draw directly as a resource on the accumulating experience of the OECD countries through the work of the Public Management Committee. The five major work areas mirror closely the PUMA program. First, SIGMA seeks help build capacities for leading change and reform. SIGMA has given priority to marketing reform and communication skills and has helped by holding meetings with governments, media, and business. Managing policymaking has been a second focus of SIGMA work. This has involved efforts to improve the structure of meetings of the council of ministers and to ensure proper preparation of decisions. A training workshop was also used to build skills in regulatory analysis and to improve the quality of legal norms. A third activity has been to improve budget management. The SIGMA countries have confirmed that budgeting was one of the most important areas for reform, also one of the most difficult given the pressure on budget offices. SIGMA has provided documentation and advice through workshops, multicountry seminars, and research on control of semi-independent bodies. A fourth activity focuses on human resources management. SIGMA has concentrated its support on design and implementation of legal frameworks and on training strategies. It has also stressed the importance of establishing a civil service as a function that should be common to all ministries and managed according to common standards. Administrative supervision is a fifth work area. Although most countries have formal oversight systems in place, a need for reform remains. For example, there is a need to strengthen bodies such as audit bureaus, inspectorates, constitutional courts, parliamentary review mechanisms, and administrative courts.

Better Public Management: A Political Issue

Through the Public Management Service and its program for Support for Improvement in Governance and Management in Central and Eastern Europe, the OECD addresses key areas of public management. These have become vital political issues today because of the ways in which government activities touch the everyday lives of all citizens and influence the day-to-day running of businesses. Government policies in OECD countries underline the need for a cost-effective public sector to help achieve economic growth and social development, two principal goals of the OECD. Hence current reforms in public-sector management are an integral part of the structural reform programs being pursued in OECD as well as in many other countries.

DERRY ORMOND

BIBLIOGRAPHY

Occasional Papers on Public Management

Accounting for What? The Value of Accrual Accounting to the Public Sector, 1993. OCDE/GD(93)178.
Aspects of Managing the Centre of Government, 1990.
Financing Public Expenditures Through User Charges, 1990.
Information Technology in Government: Management Challenges, 1993. OCDE/GD(92)194.
Internal Management Consultancy in Government, 1993. OCDE/GD/(92)185.

Performance Appraisal: Practice, Problems, and Issues, 1993.
OCDE/GD(93)177.

Performance Pay and Related Compensation Practices in Australian State Public Sector Organisations: A Summary of the Experience with Pay for Performance in the United States, 1991.

Public Management and Private Enterprise: Administrative Responsiveness and the Needs of Small Firms, 1990.

Serving the Economy Better, 1991.

Value and Vision: Management Development in a Climate of Civil Service Change, 1993. OCDE/GD(92)186.

Market-Type Mechanisms Series

No. 1: *Issues and Strategy: Managerial Aspects, 1992.* OCDE/GD(92)64.

No. 2: *The United States Experience with Contracting Out: User Charges for Prescription Drugs in Italy; Market-type Mechanisms and Health Services in the UK, 1992.* OCDE/GD(91)205.

No. 3: *Property Rights Modifications in Fisheries, 1992.* OCDE/GD(92)132.

No. 4: *Vouchers: Social Housing and Nursing Homes, 1992.* OCDE/GD(92)133.

No. 5: *Complex Contracting Out Information Technology Services, 1992.* OCDE/GD(92) 134.

No. 6: *Internal Markets, 1993.* OCDE/GD(93)135.

No. 7: *Market Emulations in Hospitals, 1993.* OCDE/GD(92) 193.

Regulatory Management and Reform Series

No. 1: *Current Concerns in OECD Countries, 1992.* OCDE/GD(92)58.

No. 2: *Controlling Regulatory Costs: The Use of Regulatory Budgeting, 1992.* OCDE/GD(92)176.

No. 3: *Improving Regulatory Compliance: Strategies and Practical Applications in OECD Countries, 1993.* OCDE/GD(93)63.

No. 4: *The Design and Use of Regulatory Checklists in OECD Countries, 1993.* OCDE/GD(93)181.

Other Publications

Assessment of Reforms in Human Resource Management, 1995.

Budgeting in a Performance Environment–The Control and Management of Government Expenditure, 1995.

Flexible Personnel Management in the Public Service, 1990.

Managing with Market-type Mechanisms, 1993.

Opening Up Regulation: Public Consultation in Ten OECD Countries, 1995.

Pay Flexibility in the Public Sector, 1993.

Private Pay for Public Work: Performance Related Pay Schemes for Public Sector Managers, 1993.

Public Management Developments: Survey and Updates for 1990, 1991, 1992, 1993, and 1994.

Public Management: OECD Country Profiles, 1993.

Regulatory Co-operation for an Interdependent World, 1994.

Service Quality in Government, 1995.

Statistical Sources on Public Sector Employment, 1994.

The Control and Management of Government Regulation, 1995.

The Governance in Transition, 1995.

1994 Series of "Occasional Papers on Public Management"

No. 1: *Trends in Public Sector Pay: A Study on Nine OECD Countries 1985–1990.*

No. 2: *Public Service Pay Determination and Pay Systems in OECD Countries.*

No. 3: *Performance Management in Government: Performance Measurement and Results-Oriented Management.*

No. 4: *Senior Civil Service Pay: A Study of Eleven OECD Countries 1980–1991.*

No. 5: *Performance Measurement in Government: Issues and Illustrations.*

No. 6: *New Ways of Managing Infrastructures Provision. Market-type Mechanisms Series No. 8.*

No. 7: *Forecasting and Control of the Costs of Transfer Programme.*

No. 8: *Regulatory Management and Information Systems.*

OFF-BUDGET.

OFF-BUDGET. A financial transaction of the government that is neither included in the main budget document nor in budget totals.

Government budgets are supposed to support numerous goals, including allocation of limited resources among many competing uses and stabilization of the economy. Comprehensiveness is therefore greatly desirable for government budgets. The process of allocation should work best when all feasible alternatives are compared; a budget that excluded some uses of funds would not necessarily allow decisionmakers to rank alternatives accurately and to fund the better ones. Nor could stabilization activities be fully successful if some of the government's fiscal activities were ignored.

In 1969, the United States federal government adopted a comprehensive budget format known as the "unified budget" (see **unified budget**). Since that time, the goal of a comprehensive budget has generally been met. However, some financial transactions still were not included in the unified budget even though many observers believed they should have been; these exceptions were said to be "off budget."

To be excluded from the budget has three practical interpretations. The most complete is a financial transaction that neither shows in the budget nor affects the budget totals. A second alternative is that the transaction is not detailed in the budget presentation in the main budget document but is still included implicitly in the budget totals. For example, the costs of tax expenditures are reflected in the budget totals but are not displayed prominently–rather, the main discussion of tax expenditures is relegated to a supplementary analysis. Similarly, the operating expenses of the Federal Reserve Banks are not displayed in the budget , but since the Federal Reserves transfers its profits (its revenues net of these expenses) to the Treasury, the budget totals are not distorted.

The third off-budget practice is the near reverse of the second–a full presentation of the details of the transaction, but exclusion from the budget totals. From the mid-1970s to the mid-1980s, for example, some off-budget accounts were completely displayed in the off-budget section of the Budget Appendix but were not tallied in the totals. More recently, the Social Security funds have been fully integrated into the budget displays, except for a few summary tables that distinguish between the "off-budget" Social Security funds and the "on-budget" remainder of the "total budget".

One of the most important reasons for creating off-budget status is political. When a transaction is not included in the main budget document, it is not visible, making it difficult for opponents of a program to dramatize its budgetary costs. When a transaction is not included in budget totals, eliminating the transaction will not affect the reported deficit. Off-budget status therefore enables some financial transactions to escape budgetary controls. Consequently, astute supporters of an agency, program, or subsidy may decide that an attractive political tactic is to seek to have it placed off budget.

A second justification for off-budget status is the harm that might result if an agency was subject to the constraints of the budget process. For agencies that intend to operate like a business, or that carry out activities of perceived great importance, off-budget status is thought to give necessary flexibility. For a good example of the use of the former rationale, the urgent need to finance the costs of paying off depositors in insolvent savings and loan associations was partially met by the creation of the off-budget Resolution Finance Corporation. For an example of the use of the latter rationale, the expenses of the intelligence establishment—the Central Intelligence Agency, National Security Agency, National Reconnaissance Office, and others—have always been hidden in other budget accounts. This practice was expanded significantly in the 1980s by the Pentagon's creation of so-called black accounts for selected high-technology research and development and procurement spending, notably for stealthy aircraft.

A third reason why transactions are placed off budget is technical uncertainty. Many financial transactions are highly complex and may not fit well within a simplistic budgetary accounting system. Some involve joint action by the private and public sectors, a result of the process commonly known as "sector blurring." It may be difficult to draw the line between cases that belong on budget and those in which the federal government's involvement is so minimal that off-budget status is more appropriate. "Government-sponsored enterprises" lie on or close to this line, and the normal resolution of this quandary has been to exclude them from the budget totals. The costs borne by regulated state and local governments, businesses, and citizens are also generally excluded from the budget because they are not considered to be federal fiscal costs.

Another technical complication is an "apples versus oranges" problem or, more abstractly, the difficulty of developing a reliable metric. The cost of tax expenditures, for example, is relatively more difficult to estimate than the costs of grants, loans, and contracts, the normal methods of regular government spending that are featured in the budget. In part because sufficient attention has not been paid to reducing estimating uncertainties, the budget does not include a reliable side-by-side presentation of regular spending and tax expenditures within each functional area of the budget.

The remainder of this entry first discusses the off-budget treatment of standard programs and agencies and then turns to the off-budget treatment of government-sponsored enterprises, tax expenditures, and regulations. The off-budget practices of U.S. state and local governments and other countries are then described briefly.

Standard Programs and Agencies

It was not long after the adoption of the unified budget in 1969 that some important programs and agencies were placed off budget by statute. Four of the leading examples during the 1970s were the Export-Import Bank (off-budget 1971–1975), the Rural Electrification Administration (off-budget from 1973–1985), the Postal Service (off-budget 1974–1985 and then again in the latter 1980s), and the Section 202 Housing for the Elderly and Handicapped program (off-budget 1974–1977). The practice continued in 1981, when the Strategic Petroleum Reserve was placed off-budget.

The most important source of off-budget treatment was the Federal Financing Bank (FFB). The FFB was created in 1973 to sell "agency debt," the bonds sold by agencies rather than the Treasury. Agency-borrowing authority was usually granted by statute as a partial substitute for appropriations and other types of budget authority. Unfortunately, agencies that sold bonds directly almost always had to pay more than the Treasury did, for several reasons. First, the issuance costs were far greater per dollar borrowed, for the agencies could not match the economies of scale available to the Treasury. Second, agency debt was less liquid, fewer agency securities being available than Treasury securities. This led security purchasers to charge the agencies a premium, which compensated the purchasers for the possible greater difficulty in selling the agency securities. Finally, the strength of the pledges by agencies to make good on their debt was sometimes unclear to investors, which again led them to charge a premium when purchasing agency securities.

The Treasury decided if the FFB could serve as the sales agent for Treasury debt, these costs could be minimized. The initial mechanism was that the FFB would borrow funds and then loan them to agencies. To prevent double counting of budget authority, the FFB was defined as off budget. But shortly after the FFB made its initial sales, it began to borrow directly from the Treasury rather than sell agency debt. This practice, combined with the FFB's definition as off budget and with accounting rules adopted by Congress and the Office of Management and Budget, had the practical effect of excluding agency borrowing through the FFB from the budget. Numerous agencies took advantage of this opportunity, and the result was a substantial underreporting of the deficit. An analysis by the Congressional Budget Office (CBO) in 1982 calculated that US $82.3 billion of actual deficit spending went unreported because the FFB was off budget.

Most statutory off-budgets, including the FFB, were placed back on budget in 1985. The machinations of reunifying the budget were almost as Machiavellian as the tactics used to place these programs off budget. In the 1985 budget, President Reagan, following the lead of Office of Management and Budget (OMB) Director David Stockman, proposed legislation that would strip almost all off-budget programs and agencies of their special status. Reagan also proposed to cut much of the spending of those agencies that borrowed through the FFB. By doing this, he could claim budgetary savings despite the previous off-budget status of the affected agencies. The proposed repeals were adopted in the Balanced Budget Act of 1985, popularly known as "Gramm-Rudman-Hollings."

Being explicitly placed off budget by statutes had often been an invitation for extra scrutiny by budgetary controllers. Following the off-budget repeals, budgetary controllers strengthened their resolve that standard programs and agencies belong on budget. Fiscal stress continued, however, and the resulting imposition of new budget process controls, particularly in the Budget Enforcement Act of 1990, motivated some advocates of threatened agencies and programs to seek off-budget status. This tactic was especially attractive to the advocates of highway and aviation programs, which are typically financed out of so-called trust funds. Claiming that the dedicated revenues intended for highway and aviation programs were in fact being reserved to reduce the deficit temporarily, they argued that only placing these funds off budget would serve as protection. These proposals were turned down in several close votes in Congress.

Government-Sponsored Enterprises

A government-sponsored enterprise (GSE) is a privately owned organization that has quasi-governmental status. This status comes from the charter granted the GSE by the government. Although the charters given to the different GSEs vary, most charters exempt the GSEs from some laws and regulations that normally apply to privately owned businesses. Some charters also grant lines of credit with the Treasury to the GSEs. These privileges are interpreted by credit market participants as conveying an implicit guarantee of GSE debt by the government. Due to this guarantee, GSE debt trades at only a small premium above Treasury rates and is collectively known in credit markets as "agency debt."

These financing advantages are conveyed by the government in return for the expectation that each GSE will channel funds to favored sectors of the economy. For example, the Federal National Mortgage Association (FNMA) and the Federal Home Loan Mortgage Corporation (Freddie Mac) are intended to benefit purchasers of residences by lowering financing costs. These financial

benefits for homeowners take a different form than direct grants from the Farmers Home Administration and tax preferences under the Internal Revenue Code, but they are valuable nonetheless.

GSEs deliver services in two ways that are significantly different from regular programs, however. First, since GSEs are privately owned, they are not considered governmental organizations. According to the "complete private ownership rule" that was developed from the President's Commission on Budget Concepts (see **unified budget**), GSEs are excluded from the budget. Second, GSEs tend to make profits, and in the case of FNMA in recent years, huge profits. Although management efficiencies have contributed to profits, GSE profits are also the result of risk taking. Since GSEs have an implicit federal guarantee of their debt, they need not attract much capital relative to the investments that they make. This high degree of leveraging, however, also exposes the federal government to financial risk—that is, the managers of GSEs might bet the bank and lose, requiring the government to step in to remedy financial problems. The government now seeks to control this risk for housing GSEs with a new agency—the Office of Federal Housing Enterprise Oversight. The budget agencies developed estimates of the subsidies conveyed to GSEs during the long process of reforming budgetary treatment of credit programs, and some consideration was given to incorporating these subsidy costs into the budget. The only budgetary coverage of GSEs to date, however, is a short display of GSE finances at the end of the Budget Appendix.

Tax Expenditures

The Congressional Budget Act defined tax expenditures as "those revenues attributable to provisions of the federal tax laws which allow a special exclusion, exemption, or deduction from gross income or which provide a special credit, a preferential rate of tax, or a deferral of tax liability." This definition itself illustrates the difficulty of dealing with tax expenditures in the budget—there are a variety of ways of creating preferences in the tax code, almost all of which are difficult to understand. Moreover, tax expenditures represent money that is "spent," in effect, because it is not collected by the Internal Revenue Service (IRS), rather than money that is collected and then spent by government agencies. Estimation of what is not collected depends on having a clear concept of what would be, and should be, collected in the absence of the tax preference. However, philosophical disputes about the design of the "normal" and "reference" tax bases have prevented agreement on a list of tax expenditures and their magnitude.

The U.S. government does not release aggregate estimates of tax expenditures; to do so would ignore some technical features of tax expenditures, such as the high interdependency of some preferences, that make aggregate estimates highly suspect. The costs of selected tax expenditures are clearly very large, however. For example, revenues lost in 1994 from the exclusion of pension benefits, the exclusion of health insurance benefits, and the deductibility of home mortgage interest and property taxes, were, respectively, over US $55 billion, over US $50 billion, and over US $65 billion. All of these costs are reflected in the budget totals, but they need not be regularly authorized in budget laws; instead, almost all tax preferences are permanent until changed by law. The visibility of tax expenditures in budget documents is also very low—tax expenditures were not compared to regular spending programs in the functional descriptions of the budget. Congressional committee jurisdictions are not designed to force competition between tax preferences and regular spending programs. These factors have often made tax preferences an attractive form of program delivery, particularly when fiscal stress threatens regular spending with cutbacks. Historically, only when the number and cost of tax preferences became very large were tax preferences under threat, as occurred from 1984 until 1986, which produced the tax-expenditure-cutting Tax Reform Act of 1986. The 1990 passage of the Budget Enforcement Act placed another constraint on tax expenditures—the "pay-as-you-go" requirement, which forces proponents of new spending or tax cuts to pay for these changes with offsetting deficit reductions. Less popular tax expenditures have been exposed to cuts under this procedure.

Regulatory Costs

Regulations, like budgets, impose costs on some members of society and convey benefits to others. Some experts have therefore advocated that these transactions be included in the budget, rather than be placed off budget, as is the current practice. A related proposal for a separate "regulatory budget" was made during the deregulation movement of the latter 1970s and early 1980s. This budget would have set annual targets for regulatory costs; a similar approach was considered by Congress in 1995.

The common rationale for excluding regulatory transactions from the budget is that they are not fiscal ones. Unlike spending and taxing, which are direct uses and sources of the government's financial resources, regulatory costs and benefits are borne and enjoyed by private citizens and businesses without channeling money through government accounts. During the debate over the Clinton health care reform proposal, however, the Congressional Budget Office suggested that the regulatory costs of this plan should be included within the budget. The plan established an employer mandate to provide health insurance and required employers to pay premiums to health care alliances. CBO argued that the mandate was effectively like a tax and that the alliances were effectively governmental organizations and, therefore, that almost all of society's health care expenditures belonged on budget. This recommendation was never

debated fully, as there was insufficient support for the Clinton plan to bring it to the floor of Congress.

The Practices of U.S. State and Local Governments and Other Countries

In the United States, only the federal government follows a unified budget structure. State and local governments use a diversified fund structure, with funds classified into different categories like operating, special, proprietary (businesslike), and fiduciary funds. "Generally accepted accounting principles" for state and local governments, which are established by the Government Accounting Standards Board, allow substantial leeway for the classification of certain expenditures. Many states have used this leeway to place certain programs effectively off budget. The most popular tactic is to use a "public authority," an organization that is partially insulated from direct control by elected officials. These authorities often need not receive approval for their budgets each year and have executives whose fixed, long terms cannot be terminated at the pleasure of elected officials. Although most authorities must raise the bulk of their revenues from their operations, they resemble regular government agencies in several crucial respects: Their activities are often indistinguishable from those of regular government agencies, and they borrow funds as a legally chartered entity of the government. Despite these similarities, the relative independence of public authorities has often placed them outside of the regular budget structure. Some elected officials have taken advantage of this status by selling the assets or transferring the responsibilities of regular agencies to public authorities and claiming operating budget savings from these acts. For example, several states have sold highways owned by departments of transportation to thruway authorities, a practice that did not change the governmental nature of these roads but did affect their budgetary status. The temptation to engage in such fraudulent budgetary accounting is often constrained by the reactions of bond raters, who regularly collate on-budget and off-budget components of state finances in order to guage the risks presented to bondholders from state operations.

Countries other than the United States typically also have a more diversified budget structure. Unfortunately, little summary information on the off-budget practices of other countries is publicly available. (This topic is discussed briefly in the entry on the unified budget.)

ROY T. MEYERS

BIBLIOGRAPHY

Congressional Budget Office, 1991. *Controlling the Risks of Government-Sponsored Enterprises.*
———, 1994. *An Analysis of the Administration's Health Proposal.*
Meyers, Roy T., 1994. *Strategic Budgeting.* Ann Arbor: University of Michigan Press, 69–83.
President's Commission on Budget Concepts, 1967. *Report of the President's Commission on Budget Concepts* (October) 1–35.

Surrey, Stanley, and Paul R. McDaniel, 1985. *Tax Expenditures.* Cambridge, MA: Harvard University Press.

OFFICIAL IMMUNITY.

An exemption from civil liability extended to government officials with regard to acts performed in their official conduct. This exemption applies to both domestic and foreign entities.

Domestic Official Immunity

Under common law, government officials enjoyed no immunity. All citizens were equal before the law and public authorities could just as anyone else be sued for damage caused by actions that the law did not authorize. They were liable even if they acted in good faith (*Miller v. Horton*, Massachusetts, 1891) in the course of their official functions. This insured public-servant accountability. An exception, however, was always made for judges in order to protect their independence in the administration of justice; but the courts eventually proceeded to grant immunity to broader and broader categories of administrative officers and, in effect, abandoned the common law rule of equality before the law.

The United States Supreme Court in *Spalding v. Vilas* (1896) started the trend toward official immunity when it held that heads of executive departments should receive the same immunity from civil suits for damages arising from acts done in the performance of their duties as judges did. "The head of an executive department, keeping within the limits of his authority, should not be under an apprehension that the motives that control his official conduct may at any time become subject of inquiry in a civil suit for damages. It would seriously cripple the proper and effective administration of public affairs . . . if he were subjected to any such restraint" (161 U.S. 498). The motive of the public servant is "wholly immaterial" (ibid., p. 499), the official remains absolutely immune from damage suits even when acting maliciously with intention of causing harm.

As David Rosenbloom observed, this was a dangerous extension of the doctrine of official immunity as the role of state bureaucracy was becoming more pervasive in modern society (*Public Administration Review* 1980, p. 168). What the public needed was protection against state administrators acting in bad faith. But the broadening of absolute official immunity continued for another half century. Such a development was made easier by the fact that courts frequently tied official immunity to the sovereign immunity of the government and its agencies (see **sovereign immunity**). Thus, the Supreme Court held in *Larson v. Domestic and Foreign Commerce Corp.* (1949) that suits against public officials should in most cases be dismissed because they are protected by the government's sovereign immunity. Kenneth Warren (1996) points out that this opinion set the tone for many other court decisions (p. 468).

The final opening of the flood gates came with *Barr v. Matteo* (1959), when the Supreme Court extended absolute immunity to virtually all public officials in the performance of their duties. The Court acknowledged that it was faced with two sharply conflicting objectives: protecting private individuals against pecuniary damages caused by oppressive or malicious administrative action and protecting governmental officials against the threat of harassment and hazards of damage suits, some of them possibly ill-founded or vindictive. The Court decided for the protection of administrators in the name of vigorous and effective administration in the public interest. The Court recognized that "there may be occasional instances of actual injustice which will go unredressed, but we think that price a necessary one to pay for the greater good" (360 U.S. 576), since suits against public administrators "would consume time and energies which would otherwise be devoted to governmental service and the threat of which might appreciably inhibit the fearless, vigorous, and effective administration of policies of government" (ibid, p. 571).

In the wake of the *Barr* decision, federal courts granted absolute immunity even to low-ranking federal public servants such as an Internal Revenue Service tax collector or a deputy U.S. marshal (see **absolute immunity**). This carried official immunity to unwarranted extremes, thus denying means of redress in cases of flagrant abuse at a time when the public was facing a growing and more intrusive government bureaucracy. Limits, long overdue, were eventually devised.

Section 1983 of the Civil Rights Act of 1871 was used to provide a foundation for a multiplicity of damage actions against state officials, but not federal public servants. Indeed, it specifies that persons who under color or any state law deprive anyone of any rights secured by the U.S. Constitution and laws will be liable to judicial proceedings for redress. In *Scheuer v. Rhodes* (1974), for instance, the Supreme Court held that in a Section 1983 action, public officials were not entitled to absolute immunity. They could, however, receive a "qualified immunity" of "varying scope," depending upon the level of discretion and responsibilities of the office and all circumstances. The grant of immunity was also contingent upon whether these officials could show that they acted reasonably and in good faith (416 U.S. 248). These were significant restrictions, even if limited to state officials (see **qualified immunity**).

The Supreme Court later qualified the immunity of federal public servants, but without the help of a federal statute. In its landmark case, *Bivens v. Six Unknown Federal Narcotics Agents* (1971), the Court ruled that federal officials could be sued for damages resulting from their violation of plaintiff's constitutional rights. It justified its new approach with a principle enunciated in the classic *Marbury v. Madison* (1803). "The very essence of civil liberty certainly consists in the right of every individual to claim the protection of the law, whenever [this individual] receives an injury"; and the Court emphasized that "federal courts may use any available remedy to make good the wrong done" (403 U.S. 396). One wonders why it took so long to remember this fundamental principle of justice.

The Supreme Court ruled that the damage suit was appropriate and that the federal courts could provide relief by ordering money damages to be paid to the plaintiff. The case was remanded to the Second Circuit Court of Appeals, which decided that although governmental officials should be protected by the official immunity doctrine, they were not entitled to immunity form tort action in all situations, particularly when their actions violated constitutional rights. The appeals court thus established a qualified official immunity standard based on circumstances: Federal officials could be held liable for damages if their actions deprived persons of their constitutional rights, even in the absence of federal statutes authorizing such remedies. Stephen Breyer and Richard Stewart note that the courts have made the *Bivens* type of action an effective way of initiating against federal public servants the same kind of constitutionally based damage action made possible by Section 1983 of the Civil Rights Act against state officers (*Administrative Law and Regulatory Policy* 1992, p. 1002). Absolute immunity, however, is still available to a substantial number of public officers (e.g., judges, prosecutors, and legislators).

In Britain, official immunity is very limited. A few statutes exempt some local officials from personal liability for acts committed in good faith (in which case the local agency itself can be made liable). Some immunity is given to persons executing the orders of courts, such as police officers; but anyone wrongfully arrested by the police may bring an ordinary action in tort for damages against any officer who carried out the arrest, or who ordered it, just as if the police were private individuals.

Administrative officials have no immunity. What they do under statutory authority does not give any ground for action, even when the injury is the inevitable consequence of what the law ordered. But any act not statutorily authorized entails full personal liability, even if the act is the most reasonable possible in the public interest. All officials, government ministers included, who participate in a wrongful act are equally liable; superior orders are no defense.

The French legal system is more complex but provides an even higher guarantee of compensation to all aggrieved parties. Two distinctions are made: (1) between ordinary courts and administrative courts and (2) between personal fault and fault in the performance of one's official duties. In the case of personal fault (i.e., not linked to the official's public service), the public servant can be sued personally in ordinary courts. In the case of a fault in the performance of one's official duties, the public servant benefits from official immunity before the ordinary courts because of the separation of powers in the court system, which prohibits the ordinary courts from receiving actions against government institutions or their public officials. Such actions must be brought before the administrative courts where government institutions are totally liable for the faults of their officers. It is interesting to note that under the principle of general liability of all public authorities, the state is liable and must provide reparation for any injury, even when no fault has been committed by public officials.

The main patterns of the French administrative law system have been widely adopted around the world, not only in countries in continental Europe and other regions (e.g., Latin America).

Foreign Official Immunity

Immunity is available to foreign sovereigns and high government officials, members of foreign armed forces and foreign diplomatic personnel, unless the governments concerned waive their immunity. This immunity is rooted in the sovereign immunity of the national state (see sovereign immunity). To this day, the head of a foreign state is entitled to absolute immunity even for acts performed in a private capacity. In addition, according to Section 66 of the Restatement (Second), Foreign Relations Law of the United States (1965), immunity is also extended to the head of a state's government, its foreign minister and any public minister, official, or agent of the state with respect to acts performed in an official capacity if the effect of exercising jurisdiction would be to enforce a rule of law against the foreign state.

With regard to armed forces stationed abroad with the consent of the host state, a fairly widespread occurrence after World War II, under a variety of collective defense agreements such as the North Atlantic Treaty Organization (NATO), the states involved have endeavored to reduce the problems resulting from the impact of foreign troops on the local communities by negotiating status of forces agreements generally giving the local authorities a limited amount of control, in effect restricting the troops' immunity. But in the absence of such treaty arrangements, the members of foreign forces are protected by absolute immunity.

Diplomatic immunity is provided by international custom supplemented by a number of international agreements negotiated under the aegis of the United Nations (UN). A pragmatic functional approach is beginning to replace the traditionally absolute immunity doctrine; but the law remains exceedingly traditional, retaining forms of immunity, which a strictly functional approach would have eliminated. Several categories of personnel are now identified receiving different levels of immunity. Members of the service staff (chauffeurs, etc.) have very limited immunity for acts performed in the exercise of their functions. Members of diplomatic rank and their families enjoy almost absolute immunity, except, for example, for acts relating to any professional or commercial activity exercised outside their official duties. Other categories of diplomatic personnel, including now UN officials such as the secretary-general, have a comparable immunity, but somewhat more limited, for example, not extending to acts performed outside official duties.

All immunities can be waived, but waivers pertaining to civil or administrative proceedings do not apply to the execution of judgments for which a separate waiver is necessary. Under the 1946 Convention on the Privileges and Immunities of the United Nations, member states have the duty to waive the immunity of their representatives in any case where, in their opinion, such immunity would impede the course of justice. The UN secretary-general has a similar duty with regard to his officers. Obviously, it should not be left to their final, and possibly self-serving, judgment.

With the vast expansion of international relations, the number of public officials involved in foreign affairs has kept growing, and so has the number of public servants protected by official immunity. Absolute protection denies injured parties legitimate means of redress (see **absolute immunity**). The trend is now toward limiting official immunity (see **qualified immunity**). However, much more progress in this direction has been made at the domestic level than at the international level, where sovereign states insist on very extensive immunity for their personnel abroad. Admittedly, state officials on foreign missions need some immunity to be effective, particularly in politically sensitive tasks. But states often go beyond reasonable protection in their continuing obsession with national sovereignty.

JEAN-ROBERT LEGUEY-FEILLEUX

BIBLIOGRAPHY

Brown, L. Neville, and John S. Bell, 1993. *French Administrative Law*, 4th ed. Oxford: Clarendon Press.

Davis, Kenneth Culp, and Richard J. Pierce, Jr., 1994. *Administrative Law Treatise*, 3d ed. 3 vols. with 1994 supplement. Boston: Little, Brown.

Henkin, Louis, Richard Crawford Pugh, Oscar Schachter, and Hans Smit, 1993. *International Law*, 3d ed. St. Paul, MN: West Publishing.

Lee, D. W., 1993. "Qualified Immunity Under 42 U.S.C. Section 1983 for Public Officials." *The Urban Lawyer*, vol. 2 (Winter) 97–115.

Libby, S., 1992. "When Off-Duty State Officials Act Under Color of State Law for the Purposes of Section 1983." *Memphis State University Law Review*, vol. 22 (Summer) 725–754.

Nordin, J. E., II, 1994. "The Constitutional Liability of Federal Employees: Bivens [*Bivens v. Six Unknown Named Agents of the Federal Bureau of Narcotics*, 91 S. Ct. 1999 (1971)] Claim." *Federal Bar News and Journal*, vol. 41 (June) 340ff.

Schwartz, Bernard, 1994. *Administrative Law*, 4th ed. Boston: Little, Brown.

Wade, Sir William, and Christopher Forsyth, 1994. *Administrative Law*. Oxford: Clarendon Press.

Warren, Kenneth F., 1996. *Administrative Law in the Political System*, 3d ed. Upper Saddle River, NJ: Prentice-Hall.

Whomersley, C. A., 1992. "Some Reflections on the Immunity of Individuals for Official Act." *International and Comparative Law Quarterly*, vol. 41 (October) 848–858.

OFFSETTING COLLECTIONS.

As used in the budget of the United States government (the "federal budget"), this term refers to income recorded as a deduction in computing spending ("outlays") rather than recorded as a receipt.

The practice of offsetting collections has a major impact in determining the recorded size and composition of the federal budget. In recent years, offsetting collections from the public (i.e., excluding intragovernmental collections) have been equal to about 18 percent of the amount of collections recorded as federal (governmental) receipts.

Both of the words "offsetting" and "collections" are key to understanding these transactions.

"Collections" consist of money received by the government that is budgetary in nature. Income to the government—such as tax collections, interest received, proceeds from the sale of postage stamps, fines, penalties, and forfeitures—constitutes collections that are budgetary in nature.

Not all money received by the government is budgetary. For example, when the government borrows, the money it collects is not income. Money collected and money paid by the government that is not budgetary in nature is entitled "means of financing," since such transactions provide the means to finance the deficit (or, conversely, in cases of a surplus, they constitute the use of the proceeds from the surplus). (See, for example, Table 13-2 of the 1996 federal budget document entitled "Analytical Perspectives.")

"Offsetting" means that the collections are recorded in the federal budget as offsets to outlays rather than as receipts.

The coverage of the federal budget (i.e., the determination of what activities are deemed to belong within the federal budget) has varied over time. "Budgetary" and "the budget" in this context refer to any activities that are officially recognized as belonging in the federal budget under current budget concepts. At various times, programs that are budgetary in nature have been required by law to be excluded from the budget (i.e., "on budget") totals. Currently, the social security (but not medicare) funds and the Postal Service fund are required by law to be excluded from the official budget totals. In current practice, when activities are recognized as being budgetary in nature (i.e., belong within the budget according to current budget concepts) but are required by law to be excluded from the official budget totals, they are classified as being "off budget," and the off-budget transactions are accounted for in the same way as on-budget transactions. Off-budget programs (especially the Postal Service) frequently have offsetting collections.

Development of the Practice of Offsetting Collections

The practice extends back to the nineteenth century, when the federal government began to create "revolving funds." In principle, a revolving fund is a business-type enterprise operated by the federal government. The Tennessee Valley Authority (TVA), the Postal Service, and the Bank Insurance fund are examples.

Under federal law, any income to a revolving fund is (1) automatically credited to the fund and (2) recorded as offsets in computing the fund's outlays rather than recorded as receipts.

For example, the TVA collected US $6.1 billion of income in fiscal year 1994–1995, primarily from the sale of electric power and disbursed (spent) US $7.3 billion for salaries, materials, construction, and so forth. The budget recorded TVA "gross" outlays of US $7.3 billion, offsetting collections of US $6.1 billion, and "net" outlays of US $1.2 billion. All of these transactions were recorded within budget outlays—none of the collections were recorded as receipts.

In addition to funds that are designated as being revolving funds, a significant number of expenditure accounts are authorized by law to perform services on a reimbursable basis and to record the reimbursements as offsets to outlays rather than as receipts.

The Census Bureau is financed primarily from general fund appropriations, so it is not a revolving fund. However, the bureau is authorized by law to contract to perform special censuses, provide technical assistance, and so forth. The bureau is authorized to offset the fees charged for such services against the cost of performing the services, so the net outlay totals for the bureau reflect the amounts financed from general fund appropriations.

The term "offsetting collections" refers to any collections offset within the budget or off-budget totals, regardless of whether they come from outside the government (i.e., "the public" or "nonfederal sources") or from payments by government accounts to other government accounts (i.e., "intragovernmental transactions"). The primary categories of offsetting collections are described in the General Accounting Office (GAO 1993) *Glossary of Terms Used in the Federal Budget Process.*

Extension of the Concept Under the "Unified Budget"

In 1967, President Johnson appointed the President's Commission on Budget Concepts (PCBC) to review the basic concepts used in the federal budget and to recommend changes in budgetary usage. The PCBC issued a report, and to a great extent the recommendations contained in that report continue to guide federal budget concepts.

By the time that the PCBC came into existence, the practice of offsetting collections was widespread and longstanding, but it was not applied uniformly. In cases where the law called for offsetting collections within expenditure accounts, the collections were offset rather than being counted as receipts. However, in all other cases, the collections were recorded as receipts, even if they were of the same nature as the income commonly offset within expenditure accounts.

Both the Employees and Retired Employees Health Benefits (EHB) fund and the Supplemental Medical Insurance (SMI) fund finance health care services, and both collect noncompulsory insurance premiums. By law, the EHB fund is constituted as a revolving-EHB fund, so its insurance premiums and other income are offset within the expenditure account. In contrast, the SMI fund is not authorized by law to be treated as a revolving fund and is not authorized to offset its premiums within the expenditure account, so its income is recorded in receipt accounts. According to the rules for recording income prior to the PCBC, the EHB collections would be offset against spending whereas the SMI collections would be included in budget receipts.

The PCBC concluded that the classification of income as budget receipts or as offsetting collections should be carried out on as consistent a basis as is feasible.

It concluded that the most important focus should be on what the government does as government (i.e., net of its business-type activities). As a result, it said that for computations of the size and composition of the federal budget (i.e., receipts and outlays), the focus should be on what the government does through exercise of its sovereign power. Thus, budget receipts should include all taxes (including social insurance taxes, such as for social security), customs duties, fines, penalties, and any other income arising as a result of the government's exercise of its sovereign power. In turn, any income that does not arise as a result of the government's sovereign power should be offset in computing budget outlays, regardless of whether it is credited to an expenditure account or recorded in a receipt account. This approach was put in place in the 1969 budget and (with exceptions discussed later) has been used ever since.

The budget does not always adhere to these rules—there are cases where legislation requires that compulsory assessments be treated as offsetting collections—but to the extent that the budget adheres to these classification rules, the budget measures the size of the federal government "as government."

Starting with the 1992 budget, the budget documents began displaying a category of offsetting collections classified as "offsetting governmental receipts." The U.S. Office of Management and Budget (OMB) defines them as follows: "These receipts are governmental in nature but are required by law or other reasons to be treated as offsetting" (OMB Circular A-11, July 6, 1994, p. 38). Starting with the 1996 budget, the budget also began to identify collections that the OMB deems to be governmental in nature but that are credited to (i.e., offset within) expenditure accounts. Thus, the budget documents officially identify a body of offsetting collections that they label as being offsetting but should not be offsetting (i.e., they are "governmental" in nature and, under budget concepts, they should be recorded as budget receipts).

For example, the budget classified the cash contributions by foreign governments to help finance Operations Desert Shield and Desert Storm (the Persian Gulf War) as offsetting governmental receipts. The decision to classify these as offsetting (rather than budget) receipts was made by executive branch officials, not law. (The argument for classifying these collections as budget receipts is that they were payments to the federal government arising from its sovereign capacity in waging war; the argument for classifying them as offsetting collections is that they constituted voluntary cost-sharing payments by foreign governments.)

The existence of the offsetting governmental collections category illustrates (1) the fact that legislation can overrule budget concepts: if the law requires compulsory collections to be classified as offsetting collections, the budget must conform to the law; and (2) the fact that not all such classification decisions are easy—there are inevitably controversial borderline calls that someone must make and with which others may disagree.

Principal Controversies Concerning the Practice of Offsetting Collections

Although the practice of offsetting collections in the federal budget has existed for around a century, and the unified budget concepts have been in use since 1968, this approach has some major criticisms. Aside from arguments over borderline classification issues, the principal controversies are as follows:

(1) It is frequently argued that the practice of offsetting collections understates the size of the government (i.e., federal receipts and outlays).

Some critics argue that budget receipts should include all income to the government, regardless of its nature, and that budget outlays should focus on gross, not net, spending.

Should budgetary presentations highlight the magnitude of tax collections, or should they highlight revenue totals that include income from the sale of commercial services? Should intragovernmental collections (i.e., payments from one government account to another) be recorded as budget outlays of the paying account and budget receipts of the collecting account? When the budget reports the cost of agency operations (such as comparing the cost of revolving funds, such as TVA and the Postal Service, to the cost of programs financed largely through taxes, such as the Defense Department), should the focus be on gross disbursements or on the amounts that have to be financed from taxes and borrowing?

Current budget concepts call for focusing on the size of what the government collects and spends as "government" and, therefore, for measuring the budget totals and major components on a net basis (with displays of the gross flows and the netting transactions provided in subsidiary tables). Critics argue that this focus is misleading—that it understates the size and misstates the composition of the federal budget.

(2) A second set of criticisms is directed at the concept of the unified budget. This is not a direct criticism of the practice of offsetting collections, but it has important ramifications for the determination of the amounts that the budget records as offsetting collections.

Most such critics argue that the federal budget should be confined to the "federal funds" component of the unified budget. They argue that whenever the government levies taxes to finance specific programs—such as social security—and designates the funds as being "trust funds," the taxes and associated spending should be excluded from the budget totals.

Excluding "trust funds" from the budget would have a major impact on the recorded size and composition of offsetting collections.

Consider, for example, the functional category entitled "net interest." Net interest is composed of interest payments (largely interest on the public debt) offset by interest received. In fiscal year 1994–1995, for example, interest on the public debt amounted to US $296.3 billion. However, the net outlay total (on budget and off budget) for the function was US $203.0 billion, because it included US $85.7 billion of offsetting receipts of funds that are classified as being "trust funds," US $14.0 billion of other offsetting receipts, largely interest or loans to the public, and US $6.4 billion of interest payments (such as interest on tax refunds). If the trust funds had been excluded from the total, only the US $14.0 billion would have been recorded as offsetting collections.

The current budget approach (i.e., the approach that includes the trust funds in the budget and that combines the on-budget and off-budget amounts into a consolidated total) was recommended by the PCBC. That commission concluded that since most of the "trust funds" are actually carrying out federal taxing and spending activities, failure to include them within the budget totals would seriously understate the size and composition of federal fiscal activities. (That is, it proposed to focus on the totality of federal taxes and spending and leave information about the fund classification to subordinate data displays.) The approach recommended by the PCBC is to provide as comprehensive a measure of what is "budgetary" as is feasible. Critics of the unified budget concept argue that the current approach is misleading–that the budget should focus on the size and operations of the general fund and associated funds.

(3) The other primary criticism of current practice comes from critics who argue that the budget does not do enough offsetting.

These critics argue that since user charges are collected to finance services rendered, they should be offset against the cost of the services that they finance, even if the collections arise from compulsory assessments.

Under current budget concepts, the question of whether a particular source of income arises from user charges is irrelevant to the question of whether the collection should be recorded as budget receipts or as offsetting collections. If user changes flow from the government's use of its sovereign power (such as levying excise taxes to finance the highway trust fund), the concepts call for the budget to record the income as receipts.

In recent years, a number of laws have been enacted that require nonfederal parties to use services provided by the government (such as inspection and regulatory services) and pay charges to finance the cost of the services; the resultant collections are then to be recorded as offsetting collections. Current budget concepts call for treating such collections as budget receipts (since they arise from the government's exercise of its sovereign power), but the budget must conform to the requirements of law, so in these cases the collections are recorded as offsetting collections. However, as noted earlier, in such cases the budget identifies them as "offsetting governmental collections."

Confusion Between "Offsetting Collections" and "Offsetting Receipts"

The authority to offset any collections in expenditure accounts is dependent upon law. Absent legislated authority, the collecting agency is required to deposit collections into "receipt accounts."

However, unless legislation overrules, the OMB, acting under presidential authority, is free to classify receipt accounts as being composed of "governmental" receipts (i.e., income arising from the government's exercise of its sovereign power and, hence, to be recorded as budget receipts) or as offsetting receipts (i.e., income that is to be offset in computing outlays).

Offsetting receipts are any collections deposited into receipt accounts that are recorded as offsets in computing outlays. There is usually no substantive difference between offsetting receipts and the types of collections that are offset within expenditure accounts.

For example, interest income arises from commercial-type activities, so it is recorded as offsetting collections. Large amounts of interest income are offset within expenditure accounts because the law calls for such treatment. However, larger amounts of interest income are recorded in receipt accounts because there is no legal authority to offset the income within expenditure accounts. The receipt accounts used to record interest income are classified as offsetting receipt accounts so that such income is treated as offsetting receipts.

In standard OMB usage, offsetting receipts are a subset of offsetting collections. That is, OMB generally uses the term "offsetting collections" to refer both to collections offset within expenditure accounts and to offsetting receipts. In contrast, in congressional usage, the term "offsetting collections" is most commonly used to refer only to collections that are offset within expenditure accounts (i.e., congressional usage normally refers to "offsetting receipts" as being separate from offsetting collections). There is no substantive difference between the OMB and congressional treatment of the transactions, but the differences in the way the terms are used frequently causes confusion.

THOMAS J. CUNY

BIBLIOGRAPHY

Congressional Budget Office, 1993, *The Growth of Federal User Charges.* Washington, D.C.: Congressional Budget Office (August).
Cuny, Thomas J., 1991. "Offsetting Collections in the Federal Budget." *Public Budgeting & Finance*, vol. 8, no. 3 (Autumn) 96–110.
General Accounting Office, 1993. *A Glossary of Terms Used in the Federal Budget Process.* Washington, D.C.: GAO/AMFD-2. 1.1.
Office of Management and Budget, *Budget of the United States Government* (various documents and various years). Washington, D.C.: Government Printing Office.
———, Circular A-1 1, rev. July 6, 1994. *Preparation and Submission of Budget Estimates.* Washington, D.C.: Government Printing Office.
Report of the President's Commission on Budget Concepts, 1967. Washington, D.C.: Government Printing Office (October).

OMAR IBN-AL-KHATTAB (ALSO UMAR OO' MÄR) (581–644) was the second Muslim "caliph" (*Khalifa*). His ten-year reign (634–644) witnessed the phenomenal expansion of the Islamic state as well as the development of the nation *(ummah)* as a political, economic, and social entity through the establishment of effective military, administrative, and judicial institutions.

Omar embraced Islam in 615. During Abu Bakr's first caliphate, which lasted for two years (632–634), Omar was his adviser as well as being the first judge *(Qadi)* in the Islamic State.

Army Administration and Expansion of the Islamic State

To Omar goes the credit of extending the reach of the Islamic state beyond the boundaries of the Arabian peninsula. Despite the fact that there were other factors that contributed to the defeat of the Eastern Roman Empire and the Persian Empire, the vital factor behind the success of these conquests was attributed to Omar's military genius and his ability to organize, coordinate, and maintain these invasions. The detailed accounts of these conquests clearly indicate that the march of the Muslim army from one front to another was centrally orchestrated by Omar. He had in all expeditions fixed the stages that the army should follow, developed a systematic reporting system to keep him fully informed about the actions in the battlefield, and continued to dispatch instructions to lead and determine the strategic and tactical movements of the Muslim forces.

Many innovations were introduced by Omar in the army administration. Main among these was the fact that expeditions were decided upon with due consideration to climate; thus, military forces were sent to cold territories in the summer and to hot territories in the winter. To ensure efficient administrative practice an auxiliary staff backup for every expedition had its designated professional staff, which included a treasurer, interpreters, physicians, surgeons, and a judge. To keep his troops prepared for emergency and to prevent them from mixing the native population, he founded three camp towns *(amsār)*, Basra and Kūfa in Iraq, and Fusṭāṭ in Egypt. He gave special attention to soldiers' training, and a center was established for that purpose in Medina, the state capital, to be under his direct supervision.

Developing a Decentralized Administrative System

The Islamic state under Omar had increased enormously covering vast areas with indigenous people of different races, customs, values, modes of living, types of government, and degrees of civilization. To safeguard effective and efficient administration of this proliferating variety of territories, Omar developed a decentralized system of administration, which gave due consideration to the peculiar conditions of each territory; yet, he maintained a central tight rein on the governors *(Walis)* of these provinces

through continued directives, reporting systems, inquiries, and investigations.

The decentralized administrative system that had been developed under the strict guidance of Omar consisted of eight provinces *(Williat* or *Imart)*, namely, Makkah, Madinah, Syria, Jazirah, Baṣrah, Kūfah, Egypt, and Palestine. He also retained the administrative divisions of Persia, which existed before the Islamic conquest. These add three more provinces: Khurāsān, Ādharbāijān, and Fārs. The chief administrative officer in each province, the governor *(Wali)*, was entrusted with functions of representing the caliph in all religious, political, and civil matters, as well as being the commander-in-chief of the provincial army. The *Wali* was assisted by six officers, namely, the chief secretary, the treasury officer, the chief secretary of the army bureau, the revenue collector, the police officer, and the judge.

Establishing Central Bureaus

The administrative apparatus was further institutionalized at the central level by adopting the Persian concept of *diwān*, meaning register or bureau. He had developed four central bureaus *(diwāns)*: *Diwān-ul-Jund*, which dealt with army register, payroll, ammunition, and related matters; *Diwān-ul-Atta*, entrusted with the register to pay the ruling elite and the Muslims from Prophet Muhammad's family on down in order of embracing Islam; *Diwān-ar-Rasā'il*, concerned with preparation of messages, sealing and dispatching letters, and keeping copies; *Diwān-ul-Jibāya* to deal with revenue administration.

The headquarters of these four bureaus *(diwāns)* were at Medina, the state capital, while the provincial capital had branches undertaking the same functions in full coordination with the central bureaus.

Selection and Control of Public Officials

To ensure efficient and effective performance of the substantive executive departments both at the central and the provincial levels, Omar developed a system for the selection of suitable officers that ensured equality throughout the Islamic state and established a code for administrative practice to guide their performance and behavior. The selection of officers for different positions was free from favoritism and substantiated by the capabilities of an individual that match the requirements of the assignment.

Introducing the *Hijra* Calendar

Main among Omar's administrative innovations was the introduction of a lunar calendar universally known as the *Hijra* calendar, which began with the emigration of

Prophet Muhammad to Medinah, a landmark which brought Islam to the forefront as a religious, political, and social force.

Administrative of Justice

Early in his reign, Omar separated the judiciary from the executive. He established courts of justice at the central, provincial, and district levels. He appointed the judges and continued to dispatch directives and judgements *(fatāws)* on difficult issues that ultimately comprised the fundamental principles of judicial procedure and practice.

The appointment of judges was often made after a practical test of the candidate's ability in reaching a sound judgment on a difficult question. Their salaries were comparatively high to avoid the need for additional income, taking into consideration that they were not permitted to engage in trade or any other profession that could influence their judgments.

Two specialized courts of justice received special consideration during his reign. These were *Williāt-ul-Māzalim* and *Williāt-ul-Hisbah*. The overall objective of the first was to look into the suits of the subjects against the provincial governors or any government official. It was an administrative judicial system that corresponds to the modern concepts of administrative courts and the Scandinavian ombudsman. *Williāt-ul-Hisbah* was created by Omar to promote law and discipline in the Muslims' daily life and to punish offenders on the spot.

Omar was stabbed to death by a Persian slave in November 644 in the mosque at Medinah.

HASSAN A. EL TAYEB

BIBLIOGRAPHY

The first four books are in Arabic. The last book's original text is in Urdu.

–Al-Agad, Abbas M., 1969. *Abgariat Omar.* Beruit: Dar Al-Kitab Al-Zahabi.
–Al-Tantawi, Ali, and Nagi Al-Tantawi, 1973. *Akhbar Omar Wa Akhbar Abdullah ibn Omar.* Beruit: Dar Al-Fikr.
–Ibn-Algawzi, Abi Al-Farag A., 1980. *Managib Amir-ul-Mu'minin Omar ibn-al-Khattab,* ed. Zainab I-Al-Garout. Beruit: Dar Al-Kutub Al-Ilmia.
–Magdalawi, Farouq, 1991. *Al-Idarah Al-Islamia Fi Ahd Omar ibn-al-Khattab.* Beruit: Dar Al Nahdah Al-Arabia.
–Nu'mani, Shamsul'Ulama A., 1976. *Umar the Great (The Second Caliph of Islam).* Volumes 1 and 2, Trans. Maulana Zafar Ali Khan. Lahore: Ashraf Press.

OMBUDSMAN.

An official appointed by the legislature to receive, investigate, and report upon complaints and grievances from members of the public regarding actions or decisions taken by government agencies.

Background

"Ombudsman" is a Swedish word meaning a legal representative or agent of a group or people. It can typically refer to an individual appointed to represent the legal interest of a trade union or business. The term acquired its more broadly understood meaning from *justitieombudsman*–an officer appointed by the Swedish Parliament to investigate complaints against government agencies, the court system, and, initially, the armed services. The *justitieombudsman* was appointed under Sweden's first democratic constitution in 1809 and replaced the Chancellor of Justice–an appointee of the Swedish king, whose task it had been to investigate complaints against royal officials.

The concept did not move beyond Sweden's borders until neighboring Finland incorporated a similar function into its machinery of government when it achieved independence from Russia in 1919. Prior to its incorporation into the Russian Empire in 1809, Finland had been ruled for over 500 years by Sweden and had in that time been well exposed to the notions of citizen-state relations and general principles of governance embodied in the *justitieombudsman*.

For many years, the notion of a parliamentary watchdog who could fearlessly take on those responsible for maladministration in government was considered to be an essentially Scandinavian response that would not necessarily translate well into other jurisdictions. Grievances that citizens might harbor in relation to perceived unreasonable, unjust, oppressive, discriminatory, unfair, inequitable, or wrong behavior by officers of public agencies were expected to be dealt with and remedied where appropriate, by either of two courses of action. The first involved making direct representations through the elected legislature via one or more of its members. The second involved application of administrative law via the court system. In reality, neither of these avenues was fully effective or adequate. Appeals to elected representatives operating in highly political environments and with multiple competing demands on their time and energy provided no guarantee of satisfactory resolution for the aggrieved citizen. Additionally, the use of administrative law and the court system generally proved too costly and complex for many ordinary citizens to contemplate.

A growing awareness of these limitations that led to the increasing acceptance of the ombudsman concept and its progressive adoption by other countries, beginning with Norway in 1952, Denmark in 1955, and New Zealand in 1962. Since then, the idea has spread across different levels of government into different areas of government activity and is now even being adopted as a grievance resolution mechanism in the private sector by such industries as banking and insurance.

The function is known by many names. It is called the *Médiateur* (mediator) in France, the Parliamentary Commissioner for Administration in the United Kingdom, the *Protecteur du citoyen* (public protector) in the Canadian province of Quebec, the Commissioner for Complaints from the Public in Israel, the Commissioner for Investigations in Zambia, the *Difensore Civico* (ombudsman) in the Italian region of Tuscany, the Defender of the People in Spain, the Permanent Commission of Enquiry in Tanzania, the *Lokayukta* (people's commissioner) in the Indian states of Bihar, Maharashtra, and Rajasthan, the Public Counsel in the American state of Nebraska, and simply the ombudsman in Scandinavia, Australia, Fiji, Guyana, Mauritius, Papua New Guinea, the German state of Rheinland-Pfalz, and several of the Canadian provinces.

U.S. Practice

Only a very small number of American states, cities, and counties have appointed ombudsmen. Legislators in the United States have mostly remained resistant to the idea, and the reasons for this are complex. There is some concern that the idea is not compatible with a federal system, despite the example of Australia, where there are ombudsmen at state and national levels of government. There is also some fear that because of the size of the American civil service, a U.S. ombudsman would inevitably become a bureaucratic nightmare. Again, international comparisons do not suggest that ombudsmen require large armies of staff behind them to be effective. Finally, there is a view that an ombudsman is better suited to a parliamentary system of government and that an ombudsman reporting to Congress would somehow interfere with the strict separation of powers established under the U.S. Constitution. This, too, does not seem justified as there is no reason why an ombudsman without executive or quasi-judicial powers should in any way unbalance the relationships between the legislature, the executive, and the courts.

Key Characteristics

While the adoption of the ombudsman concept has been accompanied by considerable regional variation, in each case there are several key characteristics that link to the central idea of the ombudsman. As defined by Rowat (1985) these are as follows:

- the creation of an independent and nonpartisan office of the legislature under the provisions of either the constitution or a specific law to oversight government administration;
- a focus on complaints and grievances from members of the public regarding particular instances of per-

ceived maladministration or injustice at the hands of government agencies and their staff; and

- the power to investigate, review, and report upon—but not, unilaterally, to overturn, vary, or require reconsideration of—the actions and decisions of government agencies and their staff.

Beyond these three key features, there can be broad differences in jurisdiction, powers, mode of operation, tenure, removal procedures, qualifications, salary, and access to government documents. For example, the scope of an ombudsman's jurisdiction varies according to the legislative charter establishing the office. In some instances, the ombudsman will have jurisdiction over every area of government; in others, the scope will be more tightly defined. Some ombudsmen have jurisdiction over local government, but few have jurisdiction over the courts or the military.

Powers

The powers of ombudsmen are similarly varied. Sweden, Finland, Denmark, and France have vested their ombudsmen with the power to initiate legal action against public officials, but other countries have tended not to follow suit. The norm is for the ombudsman to have the power to refer a matter of significant concern to an officer of appropriately senior rank—such as the political or administrative head of an agency—and to recommend a course of action, which the recipient of such advice must then make a decision upon. Most ombudsmen have the power to initiate investigations on the grounds that genuine cause for concern exists. However, this is perhaps seen more realistically as a reserve power, since it is infrequently used except in the Scandinavian countries and a small number of other jurisdictions.

Operating Arrangements

The *modus operandi* of the ombudsman generally observes a number of common practices. Members of the public with grievances against the decisions or actions of government agencies submit their complaints, which are then subject to a preliminary assessment before any decision is taken to proceed further. With only one exception (an Indian state that imposes a small stamp duty, which can be waived), there are no financial charges incurred by the complainant. A complaint formally investigated and found to have substance will be reported to the agency concerned. Each year, an annual report is prepared, which documents grievances received, investigations undertaken, and conclusions reached. This annual report is submitted either directly to the legislature or to the head of state for presentation to the legislature and attracts considerable media and political interest.

Very few ombudsmen will accept verbal complaints, but all, with the exception of the United Kingdom and France, receive written complaints and representations directly from the public. In the United Kingdom, the Parliamentary Commissioner for Administration can only receive complaints—which must specifically refer to alleged acts of maladministration via members of Parliament. The Parliamentary Commissioner in turn reports back in each case to the parliamentarian who initially referred the complaint. In France, the *Mediateur* also can only receive complaints via the senators and deputies of the French parliamentary system. In both countries, the number of complaints received is far fewer than those received in many much smaller countries.

The ombudsman's terms of appointment vary. Some countries appoint their ombudsman for a set term; others are appointed for the duration of a parliamentary term; others can serve only a limited number of terms; and others still are appointed until they reach a predetermined retirement age. Few countries have imposed any qualification requirements for the post, although in many cases the appointee is an individual with a legal background. Given the essentially apolitical nature of the ombudsman's office, removal from office is rarely contemplated and can only proceed in accordance with statutory requirements that usually involve a vote by the legislature.

All ombudsmen will generally have access to a very broad range of documents—the files, working papers, and minutes of government agencies—in order to pursue investigations. But very few ombudsmen have unrestricted access to all government documents. Where an ombudsman is denied access to material, it is usually because the document/s concerned fall into one or more of the following categories: state secrets, security interests, defense matters, international relations, international trade, cabinet or cabinet subcommittee deliberations, investigation or detection of a crime, or any other similarly sensitive matter where the disclosure of information could be argued to be against the public interest.

Outcomes

Proponents of the ombudsman concept claim many advantages flow from its implementation. Because the ombudsman is not part of the political framework and tends to operate in a low-key way, it is possible for many grievances to be satisfactorily resolved with minimum fuss or publicity away from the glare of the political spotlight and without political point scoring. If a matter cannot be resolved, the sanction of reporting either to a political authority or to a legislature can be employed in such a way as to facilitate a resolution, as government agencies must then decide if they are prepared to endure any resulting political opprobrium or negative publicity arising from their dealings with the ombudsman. When such advice repeatedly relates to one particular organization, or a part thereof, the government may be alerted to serious problems, which can then be rectified.

It is also widely claimed that the activities of the ombudsman have led to improved decisionmaking within public management. When an ombudsman investigates a matter, the agency responding to the ombudsman's questions is required to reassess its original decision and how it was reached. In the process, new material or additional relevant factors may surface. As a consequence, a more appropriate course of action may emerge, resolving the issue at hand and enhancing the quality of future decisions. In the same way, the review process and recommendations resulting from an ombudsman's inquiry can lead to improvements in administrative practices within government agencies. It is similarly possible for the work of an ombudsman to influence government policies and the laws supporting them, although the ombudsman is not intended to assume a political role.

Finally, it can be argued that the existence of the ombudsman strengthens the bond of trust that must exist between the citizen and the state. The review function performed by the ombudsman invariably helps to reinforce this trust. As the British Parliamentary Commissioner has observed, "A grievance investigated is a resentment relieved even if it be dismissed in the end" (Select Committee 1979–1980 p. 2).

In an age where governments everywhere are searching for better and more effective ways of delivering services to the community, and those working within government are being held more and more accountable for their actions, the ombudsman has increasingly become a permanent feature of many political systems around the world. The concept of the ombudsman offers an independent, inexpensive, and relatively straightforward means of resolving problems and misunderstandings between the citizen and the state.

DEIRDRE O'NEILL

BIBLIOGRAPHY

Pearce, Dennis, 1990. "The Commonwealth Ombudsman: Present Operation and Future Developments." In Papers on Parliament, No. 7, *Unchaining the Watchdogs*. Canberra: Department of the Senate, 31–53.

Rowat, Donald C., 1985. *The Ombudsman Plan*. Lanham, MD: University Press of America.

Select Committee on the Parliamentary Commissioner for Administration, 1979-1980. *Second Report, The System of Ombudsmen in the United Kingdom*. London: House of Commons 254.

Stacy, Frank, 1978. *Ombudsmen Compared*. Oxford: Oxford University Press.

Weeks, Kent M., 1978. *Ombudsmen around the World*, 2d ed. Berkeley, CA: Institute of Governmental Studies.

OPPORTUNITY COST.

A concept which helps us make decisions by focusing explicitly on the relative merit of one action versus another. The opportunity cost of an action is the value of the best alternative use of the

TABLE I. Opportunity Cost of Investment: The Case of the Fixer-Upper

Resources Used in the House Investment			Benefits of the Resources When Used in the Best Alternative[1]		
Cash Resource		Noncash Resource	Cash Resources	Noncash Resources	Total Resources
House	Material	Tools &Human Equip.Capital	Total cash	Tools &Human Equip.[2] Capital[2]	**Opportunity cost**
$60,000	$20,000	1 year 1 year	$88,000	$12,000 $50,000	**$150,000**

[1]Alternative benefits are measured in future values (one year from the house purchase). It is, therefore, valid to compare them to the benefit of the action, selling the house, which also accrues one year from the purchase date.

[2]Since both of these resources are capital goods, we must include not only the rental benefits of the services they render but also the relative differences in the valuation after the usage. The opportunity cost for tools and equipment is $12,000 = $13,000 − $1,000. The opportunity cost for the investor's time is $50,000 = $40,000+$10,000.

associated resources. Opportunity cost measures the resource costs of an action in terms of the benefits that must be sacrificed to use the resource in this selected action. An action becomes efficient when its benefits exceed its opportunity cost. This concept serves as a convenient tool for efficient resource allocation and is the most important cost concept in economics.

Examples

Opportunity costs include explicit expenditures on resources and much more. For a simple example, consider the cost of a student going to see a movie instead of studying for a test. The opportunity cost includes the ticket price for the movie. It also includes the benefit of the studying that the student sacrificed in order to see the movie.

For a more detailed example, consider an investor who purchases a $60,000 house considered a "fixer-upper" to sell a year from now. (A hypothetical example–not necessarily U.S. dollars.) Suppose the investor spends an extra $20,000 on materials and 12 months of his time to refurbish the house. The investor owns the tools and equipment used for this job. The explicit out of pocket expenses for the investment come to $80,000. They are part of the opportunity cost of investing in the house. They are not, however, the only elements of the opportunity cost. Suppose the investor's best alternative investment pays a 10 percent return with the same risk as the house investment. The opportunity cost of the $80,000 in the house investment is $88,000. Similarly, the tools and equipment and 12 months' time have opportunity costs. They could be used for other activities. Suppose the best alternative use of the tools and equipment is to rent them to another contractor for the year. The rental earns $13,000 but with a diminished property value due to their increased usage during the rental. If the reduction due to the increased usage is $1,000, then the opportunity cost of the tools and equipment in the house investment is $12,000 ($13,000−$1,000). Suppose the investor's best alternative use of time earns $40,000, and his total future prospective earning is improved by $10,000 due to the special experience of the job. Then the opportunity cost of his time in the house investment is $50,000 ($40,000 + $10,000). The total opportunity cost of the house investment equals $150,000 ($88,000 + $12,000 + $50,000). This means that the house investment is profitable only if the benefits of the action exceed $150,000. The purchase price of $60,000, or the explicit cash outlay of $80,000, is not really the relevant cost with which to evaluate the investment.

Opportunity cost, as in this example, can differ from the explicit expenditure. The opportunity cost can also vary from individual to individual, reflecting their different forgone opportunities. Table I summarizes the opportunity cost for the house investment example.

Relation of Opportunity Costs to Competitive Prices

In a competitive market equilibrium, all fully traded goods and services are paid their opportunity costs. The same price will prevail for the goods and services with the same characteristics. Competition and unrestricted entry and exit in markets are critical for ensuring that prices reflect opportunity costs. If prices exceed opportunity cost, new firms will enter the industry to capture a share of the excess profit. If prices are less than opportunity costs, firms will leave the industry to pursue more lucrative alternative opportunities. Effective restrictions on prices, such as rent control or minimum wages, will prevent the prices from reflecting the opportunity cost of the resources involved. This leads to economic inefficiency.

K. L. Terasawa

OPTIMIZING PRINCIPLES. Eight principles of optimizing analysis especially applicable to public administration. Those principles can be divided into ones that deal with the essence of optimizing analysis and ones that deal with overcoming objections to optimizing analysis. The essence relates to key elements, sources of information, the overall goal, and the basic methodology. The objections relate to subjectivity, missing information, multiplicity of alternatives, and general complexity.

The Essence of Optimizing Analysis Applied to Public Administration

Elements

Principle #1. Optimizing analysis refers to procedures for arriving at the best or a desirable policy or combination of policies for achieving a set of goals with various weights, constraints, and relations between the policies and the goals.

Goals are whatever effects one is seeking to achieve or avoid. Desired effects are benefits to be maximized. Undesired effects are costs to be minimized. In legal policy analysis, there are six frequently mentioned goals. The three E's are generally associated with economics. They are (1) effectiveness, or the quantity of benefits achieved, (2) efficiency, or the cost at which the benefits are achieved, and (3) equity, or the distribution of the benefits and the costs among person, groups, or places. The three P's are generally associated with political science. They are (1) public participation, or the extent to which majority and minority elements of the public have a part in making the decisions, (2) predictability, or the extent to which the decisions are consistent with constitutional principles and reasonable expectations, and (3) procedural due process, or the extent to which those allegedly hurt by the decisions can seek meaningful redress or exoneration.

Policies can be referred to as laws, decisions, options, projects, programs, or other words for alternatives. Public policies tend to be divided into those that have (1) a political science emphasis, such as foreign policy, defense policy, electoral policy, legislative reform, and civil liberties, (2) an economics emphasis, such as economic regulation, labor policy, communications, taxing/spending, and agricultural policy, (3) a sociology/psychology emphasis, such as poverty/welfare, minorities, criminal justice, education, and population policy, (4) an urban and regional planning emphasis, such as land use, transportation, and environmental protection, or (5) a natural science or engineering emphasis, such as technological innovation, health policy, energy policy, and biomedical policy.

The relations between policies and goals can be positive or negative, strong or weak, expressed in absolute or relative terms, or derived from a variety of sources, as mentioned later. The relations can also be linear or constant, as contrasted to nonlinear or exhibiting diminishing returns. Establishing relations is of the most difficult pact of optimizing analysis, although difficulty also occurs in establishing the relative weights of the goals and in drawing conclusions from the goals, policies, and relations.

There are basically four forms for drawing conclusions from goals, policies, and relations as to which policy or combination is best, depending on the nature of the problem. The four forms can be referred to as optimum choice, risk, level, and mix analysis. Optimum choice analysis (or basic benefit-cost analysis) involves lump-sum alternatives that do not allow for adopting a fraction of an alternative or more than one of the same alternative. Optimum risk analysis (or decision theory) also involves lump-sum alternatives, but whether they produce benefits (or costs) is contingent on the occurrence of one or more probabilistic or risky events. Optimum level analysis involves a policy which can take many positions along a continuum, but doing too much or too little is considered undesirable. Optimum mix analysis (or allocation theory) involves multiple policies, places, activities, persons, or other entities to which budget, time, or other scarce resources are to be allocated.

For further details on optimizing analysis in terms of goals, policies, relations, and conclusions, see Stuart Nagel, *Public Policy: Goals, Means, and Methods* (1984) and Edward Quade, *Analysis for Public Decisions* (1982). These two books could be referred to for any of the eight principles. The first book uses numerous legal examples. Other books that take an optimizing perspective toward law include Richard Posner, *Economic Analysis of Law* (1977) and Gordon Tullock, *The Logic of the Law* (1971).

Sources

Principle #2. The relations, policies, and goals tend to come from authority, inductive observation, deductive reasoning, or guesswork subject to seeing how sensitive the conclusions are to alternative guesses.

Consulting authority can be a big timesaver over establishing goals, policies, or relations through statistical analysis or deductive reasoning. More important, it can often provide greater validity. Goals have validity if they are the goals of the decisionmakers who are responsible for choosing among the alternatives. The best way to determine their goals my often be to ask them, especially where they are interested in arriving at a policy that will maximize their goals. Likewise, the decisionmakers or other knowledgeable insiders may be the best source of information for a list of feasible policy alternatives. Even on relations, knowledgeable insiders can often provide greater validity than statistical analysis, which tends to be confounded by the interactions between policies, goals, and other variables.

Deductive reasoning can be especially valuable in policy analysis because it may provide insights into the deduced effects of policies before they are adopted. Statistical analysis, on the other hand, generally requires policies to be adopted before they can be evaluated. That could allow bureaucratic inertia and vested interests to set in and also cause harm before the evaluation occurs. Deductive reasoning enables one to control for confounding variables by way of reasonable assumptions that statistical analysis may not allow for.

Statistical observation does have the advantage of being more explicitly based on empirical reality. That should be the ultimate test of how well the relations have been determined or the conclusions reached, provided that the test can be well designed. That gets into problems of measurement, sampling, controls, prediction, causal analysis, and other aspects of designing empirical research. In policy evaluation, the units of analysis are often states, cities, or countries that have adopted different policies, rather than individuals. Such units may require special methods of analysis to attempt to offset (1) the lack of randomness in being assigned to a treatment or control group, (2) the smallness of the sample sizes, and (3) the lack of meaningfulness as to what universe of units one is generalizing to.

Sensitivity analysis is an especially useful source of information about goals, policies, and relations in policy evaluation when authority, statistics, and deduction do not provide clear answers as to the goals/weights, policies, or relations. Sensitivity or threshold analysis enables one to determine how much room for error there is in weighting the goals, listing the policies, or measuring the relations. Often the controversy over precision on those matters is wasted controversy because within the range in which the controversy occurs, the overall conclusion is still the same as to which policy or combination is best. Sensitivity analysis also enables the policy evaluator to convert difficult questions about goals, policies, and relations into relatively easy questions of the form, is a given weight, policy, or relation above or below some threshold? rather than, What is the exact weight, policy score, or relation?

For further details on the sources of relations, policies, and goals in a public policy context, see E. E. Schattschneider, Victor Jones, and Stephen Bailey, *A Guide to the Study of Public Affairs* (1952) (authority); Martin Greenberger, Matthew Crenson, and Brian Crissey, *Models in the Policy Process: Public Decision Making in the Computer Era* (1976) (deductive reasoning); David Hoaglin *et al.*, *Data for Decisions: Information Strategies for Policy Makers* (1982) (statistical observation); and Carl Moore, *Profitable Applications of the Break-Even System* (1971) (sensitivity analysis). In the legal context, see Myron Jacobstein and Roy Mersky, *Fundamentals of Legal Research* (1977) (authority); Clarence Morris, *How Lawyers Think* (1937) (deductive reasoning); and David Barnes, *Statistics as Proof: Fundamentals of Quantitative Evidence* (1983) (statistical observation).

The Overall Goal

Principle #3. The overall goal in optimizing analysis is to maximize benefits minus costs, or the satisfaction from the good effects of adopting a policy minus the dissatisfaction from the bad effects.

Minimizing costs subject to a safety net or minimum benefit constraint is an alternative popular with the Reagan administration. That kind of alternative, however, produces undesirable results. For example, if there is a 50-unit minimum benefit constraint, then Project A, which costs less than Project B, will be favored over Project B if Project A produces more than 50 benefit units. This is so even though Project B may produce many more benefit units and is thus much more profitable. Likewise, maximizing benefits subject to a maximum cost constraint also produces undesirable results. For example, if there is a 60-unit maximum cost constraint, then Project A will still be favored over Project B if Project B exceeds the 60-unit cost constraint, even though Project B may be much more profitable.

Picking projects because they have high benefit/cost ratios also produces undesirable results. The results will not be undesirable if the project that is highest on B/C is also highest on B − C. That will happen if the cost or benefits for both projects are the same. If one project is better on benefits, but worse on costs, as is often the case, then one project may be higher on B − C but lower on B/C. Business people judge projects and firms on income minus expenses, not on income divided by expenses. The project with the better B/C ration is likely to have unspent funds, which might be spendable elsewhere. If doing so brings in enough additional profit, then the combination of Project A plus the additional Project C may be better than Project B because the combination of the two is more profitable, not because Project A had a higher B/C ratio than Project B. Like the other alternatives to maximizing benefits minus costs, the B/C ratio is often resorted to rather than coming to grips with the problem of subtracting monetary costs from nonmonetary benefits.

On the overall goal of maximizing benefits minus costs, see Edith Stokey and Richard Zeckhauser, *A Primer for Policy Analysis* (1978), especially Chapter 9 on "Project Evaluation: Benefit-Cost Analysis"; and John Cohagan, *Quantitative Analysis for Public Policy* (1980), especially Chapter 10 on "Economic Evaluation Methods."

The Basic Methodology

Principle #4. List the benefits minus costs for each alternative and then pick the alternative that is highest on B − C, or find a shortcut or indirect method for arriving at the same result. The ideal way in theory to arrive at the policy or combination of policies which maximizes benefits minus costs is to determine the benefits minus costs for each policy, and choose the policy that scores the highest.

In practice, that approach may not work where (1) the benefits are nonmonetary and the costs are monetary, which may make the subtraction process meaningless, (2) some or all of the benefits, the costs, and/or the weights of the goals may be unknown, (3) the number of alternatives may be huge, as where one is allocating a large number of resource units to a substantial number of activities, places, or persons, or (4) the relations between each policy and each benefit or cost may be highly complex. Those four conditions are the basis of the four objections to optimizing analysis applied to law or applied to almost any subject matter.

On the basic methodology of enumerating alternatives or finding shortcuts or indirect methods for doing so, see Michael White *et al.*, *Managing Public Systems: Analytic Techniques for Public Administration* (1980), especially Chapter 14 on "Marginal Analysis for Public System," and Samuel Richmond, *Operations Research for Management Decisions* (1968), especially Chapter 1 on "Models and Decisions."

Overcoming Objections to Optimizing Analysis Applied to Law

Subjectivity, Especially Nonmonetary Goals

Principle #5. If the incremental nonmonetary benefits are valued more than the incremental cost saving, then one should choose the policy that produces more benefits. Otherwise, go with the policy that produces more cost saving, as is illustrated by the data in Table I.

If Policy 1 will result in 100 crimes solved at a cost of $20, and Policy 2 will result in 60 crimes solved at a cost of $15, which is the better policy? (A hypothetical example—not necessarily U.S. dollars.) One cannot subtract $20 from 100 crimes or $15 from 60 crimes to determine a B − C figure. Doing so, however, is not necessary, since all the decisionmaker needs to know is which policy is better on B − C, not the score of each policy on B ≤ C. All one, therefore, needs to decide is which increment is preferred between the additional 40 crimes solved or the additional $5 saved. If the decisionmakers prefer an additional 40 crimes solved on a base of 60 over an additional $5 saved on a base of $20, then they should go with Policy 1, since it solves the additional 40 crimes. Otherwise they should go with Policy 2, since it saves the $5.

If Policy 2 solved no crimes, but it resulted in 12 civil cases processed and Policy 1 processed no civil cases, then which policy is better? Now we cannot even determine the incremental benefits since we cannot subtract cases from crimes, or dollars from either cases or crimes. If, however, the decisionmaker would prefer the 12 civil cases processed to the 100 crimes solved independent of the cost, then Policy 2 is clearly better on B − C since it is better on both benefits and costs. If however, the 100 crimes solved of Policy 1 is preferred over the 12 civil cases processed of Policy 2, then the decisionmaker should decide whether the incremental satisfaction from the 100 crimes solved is more or less than the incremental satisfaction from the $5 saved. If more, then adopt Policy 1. If less, then adopt Policy 2.

If a third policy were to be added, one could compare the incremental gains of the first policy with the incremental gains of the second policy. Whichever policy wins that comparison would then be compared with the third policy. Whichever policy is left uneliminated is best on B − C after going through a series of $N − 1$ comparisons where there are N policies. That series of comparisons tells the decisionmaker which policy is best, although not necessarily the rank order or the B − C score of each policy. That detailed information, however, is not especially relevant information where one only needs to know which policy or combination is best.

On dealing with nonmonetary benefits and costs, see Mark Thompson, *Benefit-Cost Analysis for Program Evaluation* (1980), and Edward Gramlich, *Benefit-Cost Analysis of*

TABLE I. DATA TO ILLUSTRATE PRINCIPLES OVERCOMING OBJECTIONS TO OPTIMIZING ANALYSIS

	Crimes Solved (B)	Dollar Cost (C)	B − C	Civil Cases Processed	% Sum
Policy 1	100	$20	?	0	
	(62%)	(57%)			119%
Policy 2	60	$15	?	12	
	(38%)	(43%)			81%
Difference (increment)	40	$5	?	12	38%
Total (whole)	160	$35	?	12	200%

Government Programs (1981), although they may overemphasize monetizing nonmonetary variables, rather than working with them in their original form or close to it.

Missing Information, Especially Weights and Relations

Principle #6. Convert questions as to the quantity of B, C, or P into questions as to whether B, C, or P are above or below a go/nogo threshold or a conflicting-choice threshold, or else work in terms of a reasonable error around the values of B, C, or P.

The above principle can be illustrated in the data from Table I. Suppose, for example, we just the two goals of increasing crimes solved and decreasing dollar cost. Suppose further that any one of those four numbers is missing information, such as the 60 crimes solved of Policy 2. Then which policy is better? The problem would be relatively easy if the benefits were $100 and $60 for each of the two policies rather than 100 crimes solved and 60 crimes solved. One would then say Policy 1 is better if Policy 2 is considered incapable of generating more than $95 in benefit units. By contrast, Policy 2 is better if it is considered capable of generating more than $95 in benefit units. The $95 is the threshold value of the benefits of Policy 2. Such a value is arrived at by solving for one unknown in a threshold equation in which the benefits minus costs of one policy are set equal to the benefits minus costs of the second policy. In this context, that means what does X have to be where $100 - 200 = X - 15$? The answer is logically 95. It is generally much easier to decide whether a policy will generate more or less benefits or costs than a threshold value than it is to decide how many benefits or costs a policy will generate.

If the benefits are nonmonetary like 100 crimes, then which policy is better if we do not know how many crimes Policy 2 will solve? In resolving that matter, one should note that Policy 2 does have a $5 advantage over Policy 1 on dollar cost. The question then becomes, at what incremental number of crimes solved will there be a tie in the decisionmaker's preferences between incremental crimes solved and an incremental cost saving of $5? If the answer is 30 crimes solved, that means an incremental $5 is worth as much as an incremental 30 crimes solved. More important, it means Policy 2 must result in more than 70 crimes solved in order to be better than Policy 1. It is clearly easier to determine whether Policy 2 can result in more or less than 70 crimes solved than to determine how many crimes Policy 2 will solve.

This kind of threshold analysis, or break-even analysis, for dealing with missing information can be extended to situations where more than one key variable is missing, such as the benefits of Policy 2 and the costs of Policy 1. That extension involves the concept of a threshold curve rather than a threshold point. If the Policy 2 benefits and the Policy 1 costs are above the threshold curve then adopt Policy 2. If the Policy 2 benefits and the Policy 1 costs are below the threshold curve, then adopt Policy 1. The equation for the threshold curve is derived from the basic threshold equation, which is B1 − C1 = B2 − C2. To derive the curve, we substitute the known values and obtain, 100 crimes − C1 = B2 − $15. We then simplify the equation to B2 = 100 crimes +$15 − C1. To carry it further, the decisionmaker has to indicate the dollar value of 100 crimes, although not the dollar value of a whole range of crimes, which is much harder. If the decisionmaker says there is an equal tradeoff at $50, then the equation for the threshold curve is B2 = $65 − C1. That curve or straight line can be easily plotted on a two-dimensional graph, with B2 on the vertical axis and C1 on the horizontal axis. That graph can be a useful visual aid in deciding whether the combination of B2 and C1 are above or below the threshold curve. This analysis can be extended to further unknowns by talking in terms of a threshold band rather than a threshold curve and to multiple threshold bands, but seldom if ever is missing information that missing.

One can also work with a range on each input rather than a fixed number. For each numerical value that relates to Policy 1, there can be an endpoint on the range that favors Policy 1 and an opposite endpoint that disfavors Policy 1. When working with ranges like that for each policy, one can arrive at bottom-line percentages that also ranges. Knowing those ranges can facilitate compromise between the extremes in deciding among policies or budgeting for activities.

On dealing with missing information without having to gather additional information, see Mark Thompson, *Decision Analysis for Program Evaluation* (1982), and Clifford Harris, *The Break-Even Handbook* (1978).

Multiplicity of Policies, Especially in Allocation Problems

Principle #7. Use part/whole percentaging to convert raw scores on goals, so a summation allocation percentage can be calculated for each activity, place, person, or group to which scarce resources are being allocated.

Suppose we change the problem in Table I from a problem of which policy is best to a problem of how to allocate a $300 budget between two activities. One activity scores 100 on the first goal and 20 on the second goal, and the second activity scores 60 on the first goal and 15 on the second goal. Assume for the sake of simplicity that both goals are scored like bowling, where high scores are good, rather than like golf, where high scores are bad. There are 301 ways that one can allocate $300 to two activities. They include all $300 to the first activity and $0 to the second, $299 to the first activity and $1 to the second, and so on down to $0 to the first activity and $300 to the second. With N dollars, there are $N - 1$ ways of allocating to two activities, meaning there are 1,000,001 ways of allocating $1,000,000 to two activities. There are far more than

1,000,001 ways of allocating $1,000,000 to three or four major activities.

In spite of that multiplicity objection, allocation problems are relatively easy to deal with through part/whole percentaging. All one needs to do is note that the part/whole percentaging scores on the first goal are 62 percent and 38 percent for Policies 1 and 2, respectively and that the scores are 57 percent and 43 percent on the second goal. One can sum those percentages across each policy and obtain 119 percent and 81 percent. By then dividing those percentage sums by 2, one obtains allocation percentages of 60 percent and 40 percent. Applying those percentages to the $300 budget means giving $180 to the first activity and $120 to the second activity. If one wants to give extra weight to the second goal in recognition that it is twice as important as the first goal, then we add 114 percent to 62 percent to get a weighted percentage sum of 176 percent for Activity 1, and we add 86 percent to 38 percent to get 124 percent for Activity 2. Likewise, one could specify as part of the budgeting problem that Activity 1 should get a minimum of $80 off the top of the $300 before there is any allocating in proportion to the part/whole percentages, and Activity 2 should get a minimum of $90. That would leave $130 to be allocated in proportion to the part/whole percentages. The $80 and $90 minimums may have been derived by saying each activity should get at least 70 percent of the allocations that each received in the previous year. Those minimums can simultaneously consider equity, constitutional constraints, incremental budgeting, and other factor the part/whole percentaging might not adequately consider.

On diverse methods for dealing with the multiplicity of alternatives in allocation problems, see Philip Kotler, *Marketing Decision Making: A Model Building Approach* (1971) (calculus and statistical analysis); Claude McMillan, *Mathematical Programming: An Introduction to the Design and Application of Optimal Decision Machines* (1970) (reiterative guessing and operations research); and Stuart Nagel, *Policy Evaluation: Making Optimum Decisions* (1982) (variations on part/whole percentaging in Chapters 10–13).

Complexity of Policy Analysis

Principle #8. Use a policies/goals, or PC, table to relate policies to goals with words rather than numbers to express the relations if numbers are not readily available through authority, deduction, observation, or guesswork plus sensitivity analysis.

Table I is a PG table since it shows the alternative policies on the rows, the relevant goals on the columns, and the relations in the cells. Where no numbers are available, one can go down one goal column at a time and discuss each relation, and then go across each policy row to make an overall statement about each policy. One can then conclude by noting which policy or combination of policies is best in light of the goals and relations. PG tables can be ap-

plied to problems that involve optimum choice, risk, level, mix, or other forms or combinations of optimizing. This analysis is extremely simple yet can be quite useful in generating insights. Those insights can be furthered by a microcomputer where a TV screen provides prompting and shows how the results change as a result of changing the goals, their weights, the policies, their constraints, the relations, and their measurement.

One qualitative methods for relating policies to goals and drawing optimizing conclusions, see William Dunn, *Public Policy Analysis: An Introduction* (1981); Ruth Mack, *Planning on Uncertainty: Decision Making in Business and Government Administration* (1971); and Egon Guba and Yvonna Lincoln, *Effective Evaluation: Improving Evaluation through Naturalistic Approaches* (1981).

In view of the relative ease of meaningfully dealing with the objections to optimizing analysis (as applied to governmental decisionmaking), one should be able to conclude that optimizing policies is methodologically feasible. More important, one should be able to conclude that the benefits of applying optimizing analysis will generally outweigh the costs. The costs include being more explicitly thoughtful in reaching decisions than one might otherwise be. The benefits include having more effective and efficient government agencies. Those benefits do outweigh the costs, especially since being explicitly more thoughtful may be more of a benefit than a cost.

STUART S. NAGEL

BIBLIOGRAPHY

Barnes, David, 1983. *Statistics as Proof: Fundamentals of Quantitative Evidence.* Boston: Little Brown.

Cohagan, John, 1980. *Quantitative Analysis for Public Policy.* New York: McGraw-Hill.

Dunn, William, 1981. *Public Policy Analysis: An Introduction.* Englewood Cliffs, N.J.: Prentice-Hall.

Gramlich, Edward, 1981. *Benefit-Cost Analysis of Government Programs.* Englewood Cliffs, N.J.: Prentice-Hall.

Greenberger, Martin, Matthew Crenson, and Brian Crissey, 1976. *Models in the Policy Process: Public Decision Making in the Computer Era.* New York: Russell Sage.

Guba, Egon, and Yvonna Lincoln, 1981. *Effective Evaluation: Improving Evaluation through Naturalistic Approaches.* San Francisco, CA: Jossey-Bass.

Harris, Clifford, 1978. *The Break-Even Handbook.* Englewood Cliffs, NJ: Prentice-Hall.

Hoaglin, David, *et al.,* 1982. *Data for Decisions: Information Strategies for Policy Makers.* Cambridge, MA: Abt Books.

Jacobstein, Myron, and Roy Mersky, 1977. *Fundamentals of Legal Research.* Mineola, NY: Foundation.

Kotler, Philip, 1971. *Marketing Decision Making: A Model Building Approach.* New York: Holt.

Mack, Ruth, 1971. *Planning on Uncertainty: Decision Making in Business and Government Administration.* New York: Wiley.

McMillan, Claude, 1970. *Mathematical Programming: An Introduction to the Design and Application of Optimal Decision Machines.* New York: Wiley.

Moore, Carl, 1971. *Profitable Applications of the Break-Even System.* Englewood Cliffs, NJ: Prentice-Hall.

Morris, Clarence, 1937. *How Lawyers Think.* Cambridge, MA: Harvard University Press.

Nagel, Stuart, 1982. *Policy Evaluation: Making Optimum Decisions.* New York: Praeger.

———, 1984. *Public Policy: Goals, Means, and Methods.* New York: St. Martin's.

Posner, Richard, 1977. *Economic Analysis of Law,* Boston, MA: Little, Brown.

Quade, Edward, 1982. *Analysis for Public Decisions.* Amsterdam: North Holland.

Richmond, Samuel, 1968. *Operations Research for Management Decisions.* New York: Ronald.

Schattschneider, E. E., Victor Jones, and Stephen Bailey, 1952. *A Guide to the Study of Public Affairs.* New York: Dryden.

Stokey, Edith, and Richard Zeckhauser, 1978. *A Primer for Policy Analysis.* New York: Norton.

Thompson, Mark, 1980. *Benefit-Cost Analysis for Program Evaluation.* Beverly Hills, CA: Sage.

———, 1982. *Decision Analysis for Program Evaluation.* Cambridge, MA: Ballinger.

Tullock, Gordon, 1971. *The Logic of the Law.* New York: Basic Books.

White, Michael, *et al.,* 1980. *Managing Public Systems: Analytic Techniques for Public Administration.* Scituate, MA: Duxbury.

ORGANIZATION DEVELOPMENT.

An evolving approach to improving the effectiveness of human systems by applying behavioral science knowledge in accord with humanistic principles. A subfield of organization theory, organization development (OD) emerged in the United States after World War II. It is a form of planned change historically focused on interaction processes and culture within formal organizations. Typically, a professionally trained consultant intervenes to help organization members identify behaviors, beliefs, and norms which are interfering with performance and then decide what actions to take to improve job satisfaction and productivity. Recently, more OD practitioners have focused on organizational structure, policy, or strategy as well as, or even instead of, interaction processes and culture. Intervention techniques have burgeoned. Moreover, practice has expanded—from mostly business corporations to public and nonprofit organizations, and even inter-organizational, community, and international settings.

Origin and Subsequent History

Organization development emerged gradually from four streams of applied behavioral science. Laboratory training, survey research and feedback, and action research developed mostly in the United States in the 1940s and were associated with social scientist Kurt Lewin. They embodied the humanistic values that soon distinguished OD. The sociotechnical system (STS) approach to organizations and related quality of worklife (QWL) movement began soon after in Northern Europe. Although also embracing humanistic values, they looked to structural change more than OD did. Organization development achieved classic expression in the early 1970s. It then incorporated new practices and perspectives, for example from the STS approach and QWL movement. It also extended into additional organizational and cultural settings. Debate about organization development's identity and efficacy has persisted while some essential elements have been revitalized and even incorporated into other fields.

Genesis and Early Development

In the 25 years after World War II, progress in four areas of applied behavioral science contributed to OD. Many individuals and organizations associated with these developments continued to shape the developing field.

In 1946, Lewin and his colleagues at Massachusetts Institute of Technology (MIT) agreed to give human relations training to a number of community leaders in Connecticut. The first T group (training group, laboratory training group, sensitivity training group, or encounter group) appeared when some of the community leaders joined in the staff review of the workshop sessions. Although the focus of T groups has varied—for example, race relations, interpersonal competence, or intrapersonal awareness—the general form was set. Trained facilitators help perhaps 20 individuals learn by analyzing how they behave toward each other in temporary, unstructured groups. The intention is to increase participants' skills in analyzing and coping with interpersonal and group dynamics so that they can be more effective when they return to real-life situations, generally at work.

Full-fledged T groups took place in Bethel, Maine, the next summer, shortly after Lewin died. Sponsors included the National Education Association (NEA), Teachers College of Columbia University, University of California at Los Angeles (UCLA), and Cornell University. National Training Laboratories (NTL), which three directors of the Connecticut workshops—Kenneth Benne, Leland Bradford, and Ronald Lippitt—had just founded, ran the sessions. NTL soon offered expanded programs and regional laboratories. Hoping to increase the transfer of learning back to the job, businesses began sending work teams to NTL training. In the late 1950s and early 1960s, Douglas McGregor, Herbert Shepard, Robert Blake, and Richard Beckhard set up training programs in corporations, including Union Carbide, General Mills, and what is now Exxon. Team-building was the name given to applying T-group methods to organizations; organization development connoted broader efforts. Emphasizing that participants learn directly from experience in collaboration with consultants, and espousing values such as open communication, democratic participation, authentic expression, and inquiry, laboratory training was the main precursor of organization development. The process-consultation approach which laboratory training used became a defining characteristic of OD.

In 1947, Lewin's MIT colleagues moved to the University of Michigan, locating in the new Institute for Social Research, which Rensis Likert headed. In 1948, Likert and Floyd Mann began to survey the attitudes of 3,000 managers and employees at the Detroit Edison Company. Using questionnaires to collect data allowed them to study the whole organization, not just selected managers or work groups. Scientifically advanced techniques for constructing, administering, and analyzing the questionnaires allowed them to report survey results back to participants without violating confidentiality. Reporting the data back to groups at all organizational levels gave members common information for devising solutions to problems. Follow-up surveys enabled researchers and participants to assess changes. Later evaluations of survey-feedback interventions suggest that they can not only produce valid data about participants' attitudes but also prompt organizational change.

Community studies and Lewin's work at Harwood Manufacturing Company in the mid-1940s produced action research. In action research, organization members collaborate with a trained researcher in a cyclical process of collecting data about the organization's functioning, analyzing the data so as to understand problems which hinder performance, using the data to guide planning and implementing of actions to solve the problems, and monitoring and assessing results of the actions to determine what to do next. That research should guide action and the consequences of actions should be assessed before taking further actions became tenets of OD. Actively involving clients at each stage of the action research process reinforced the collaborative theme common to laboratory training and survey feedback.

In the 1950s, Eric Trist and his colleagues at the Tavistock Institute of Human Relations in England introduced the sociotechnical systems approach to redesigning work. It seems to improve both productivity and the quality of worklife by understanding and integrating two independent systems which jointly comprise the work organization. The social system involves the knowledge, skills, and needs of organization members and how they work together to produce a product or service. The technical system involves techniques and methods of production. Neither system is fixed; either, or both, should be adjusted so as to satisfy, both social and technical needs and optimize organizational effectiveness. The STS approach also calls attention to the environmental context of organizations. Associated with European industrial democracy, the STS approach and QWL movement were more comfortable with politics, production workers, and unions, less focused on interpersonal processes and managers, and more oriented toward structural change than was the OD movement emerging in the United States. Some OD researchers cooperated with Tavistock researchers; but not until the mid-1970s did the STS approach and QWL movement gain momentum in North America. Then they challenged and enriched OD.

Classic Expression

By 1970, the outlines of classic OD had appeared. Techniques were developing, the number of practitioners was growing, and professional support structures were evolving.

Arguably, OD came of age in 1969 when Addison-Wesley publishers launched a major series exploring the field. Editors Warren Bennis, Edgar Schein, and, Richard Beckhard contributed classic statements. Bennis viewed OD as a complex, experiential, educational strategy for increasing the quantity and quality of organizational choices in times of growing environmental turbulence. Changing an organization required changing its culture, that is, its accepted beliefs, values, and norms. In order to generate the shared data and experience necessary to change the culture and improve decisions, a change agent (consultant, or interventionist) trained in behavioral sciences collaborated with organization members. Schein distinguished the process-consultation model of consulting from the purchase model, in which a manager buys from an outside expert information which the manager specifies, and also from the doctor-patient model, in which a consultant diagnoses the organization's problems and prescribes remedies. Process consultation focuses on human processes. It entails joint diagnosis by consultant and clients. And it aims to help clients understand and cope with group and intergroup dynamics by increasing their skills in diagnosis and action. Beckhard, who had developed the confrontation meeting in which employees at all organizational levels may raise issues, further expanded OD into large-scale interventions. He also raised awareness of environmental factors.

Such discussions and practices in the field reveal the contours of classic OD:

- Focus on a formal organization;
- Effort to balance individual and organizational needs and goals;
- Focus on human interactions;
- Attempts to enhance the problem-solving capabilities of individuals, groups, and the organization, not just solve immediate problems;

- Focus on managers;
- Preference for planned, systematic application of behavioral science knowledge;
- Focus on incremental change;
- Preference for adaptive change strategies informed by data-based diagnosis of the organization;
- Emphasis on collaborative, democratic processes, open communication, and trust among participants and between participants and a facilitating consultant;
- Use of experienced behavior rather than just intellectual education to change behavior and culture;
- Preference for systemwide, long-term change efforts; and
- Willingness to borrow from many disciplines and experiment with practices.

By no means did most OD applications meet these criteria. Indeed, the field was merging with management training. Furthermore, market forces exerted a growing impact. When the Managerial Grid program developed in the early 1960s by Robert Blake and Jane Mouton evoked corporate enthusiasm, more consultants, many not affiliated with universities, promoted packaged programs. In addition, consultants gave workshops on managerial practices not selected on the basis of research in the organization at hand. Competition increased as more companies set up internal OD departments, and consulting firms and divisions of major accounting firms also began to sell OD services. Focus began to shift toward organizational effectiveness and efficiency and away from the humanistic values that typically had marked the OD efforts of academic researchers.

The growing array of OD techniques focused on different organizational elements and ranged from simple to highly complex. For example, laboratory learning and stress management focused on the individual. Team-building and role analysis targeted work groups. Intergroup development and organization mirror activities addressed relations between work groups. Management by objectives and survey feedback often reached the whole organization. Some techniques, such as Managerial Grid and job enrichment, were applied at several organizational levels, as were the underlying action-research and process-consultation approaches. Interventions differed in complexity: from training individuals to listen actively; to counseling two feuding managers and coaching them in how to manage conflict; to developing long-term, comprehensive strategies to renew the whole organization.

Universities, publications, and professional organizations fostered professionalism among the several thousand persons who identified themselves as OD practitioners. In 1960, Shepard began the first doctoral program in OD at what is now Case Western Reserve University. Graduate programs followed at many other universities, including those mentioned before. Robert Tannenbaum, who likely had invented team-building, helped start the first nondegree university training program in 1967 at UCLA. NTL and University Associates taught process observation. Since beginning in 1954 and 1948 respectively, NTL's *Journal of Applied Behavioral Science* and Tavistock's *Human Relations* have remained major journals of research related to OD. Additional journals and book publishers began to cover the field. NTL pressed for higher professional standards. Formed in 1964 after talks at Case among Shepard, Mann, and leaders of corporations, including TRW, the OD Network published *OD Practitioner*. In 1968, the American Society for Training and Development formed an OD division, as did the Academy of Management in 1971. The Division of Industrial and Organizational Psychology in the American Psychological Association also served OD practitioners.

Post-Classic Expansion and Renewal

Beginning in the mid-1970s, mounting pressures on managers worldwide, criticisms of OD practice, and competing movements challenged OD. In response, it incorporated new practices and elements of other approaches. Theorists reaffirmed OD's core values and improved research. OD expanded into new settings, too. Although stretched so far that it risked formlessness, organization development revitalized itself and saw some of its basic elements adopted as routine practices in some other fields, including community development.

Global economic, technological, and social changes in the 1970s prompted managers to demand quick, measurable improvements in efficiency. Competition grew among the several thousand practitioners, some lacking formal training in OD. Academic researchers were tempted to turn from long-term projects and action research to limited interventions based on expert diagnoses and promising measurable results.

Critics roundly attacked. For example, concentrating on managers and retreating from action research could make consultants agents of management, not change. In practice, interventions seldom were organizationwide or long-term. Consultants bowed to market pressures and promoted "fads." Interventions usually focused on a few processes, mostly interpersonal. OD had failed to demonstrate positive impact on organizational effectiveness, efficiency, or profitability. The research was weak, perhaps even self-serving. Nor was it clear that OD, formed largely in corporations in the stable and affluent postwar United States, was suited to poorer organizations, organizations in countries with different cultures, or any organization in any culture under severe economic constraints.

In response, OD theorists added more aspects of systems theory, sociotechnical design, and anthropology to their knowledge base. Some used more advanced quantitative techniques. Others added new qualitative approaches, such as ethnomethodology, or more participatory and collaborative forms of action research. Others developed techniques in new areas, such as multicultural training and strategic planning. OD also at least partially absorbed three growing movements and became more sensitive to power.

Total Quality Management (TQM) sought to increase customer satisfaction and cut costs by improving the efficiency and reliability of work processes. As TQM gained popularity, some OD consultants began to serve as TQM content experts. Others addressed issues central to QWL, worked with lower-level employees, and incorporated techniques directly involving work methods, such as quality circles and job redesign. Asserting that employees could achieve exceptional results if they felt a compelling purpose, the organizational transformation (OT) movement concentrated less than OD on data-based diagnosis and more on a strong leader envisioning a better future. It fitted with the growing conviction that many organizations needed to change radically. Eventually, most OD proponents granted that OT might be appropriate sometimes, and many adopted some OT techniques. Appropriating much of the QWL and OT movements and certain additional techniques, such as strategic planning, increased OD's appreciation of political factors. So did decades of experience showing that organizational politics could affect OD interventions and the spread of OD into the public sector, where politics generally are more overt than in the business or nonprofit sectors. Moreover, OD was melding with community development—not only in North America, where Shepard had pioneered its use in the early 1960s, but also on other continents, where class fissures are wider and cultures obscure power relations less.

Greater understanding of power and confrontation enriched OD, but at the risk of increasing the use of power-coercive tactics antithetical to OD values. Consequently, attending to politics had the effect of both meeting some criticisms and raising questions about the identity of organization development. So did absorbing new practices. To what extent could practitioners substitute universal solutions for action research and still be said to practice OD? How much could they use expert models, not process consultation? If they used only structural interventions, was it still OD?

Also beginning in the mid-1970s, leading theorists reaffirmed the primacy of OD's core values and approaches. For example, Newton Margulies, Anthony Raia, Warner Burke, Robert Golembiewski, and Edgar Schein warned that techniques and market forces were driving the field. OD risked emphasizing efficiency and effectiveness over core principles. Margulies and Raia urged a Janusian perspective, looking both to the organization's

need to survive and to members' needs which OD values expressed.

Closely related was concern about professional standards. By the late 1970s, perhaps 8,000 firms offered OD services and corporations increasingly assigned OD tasks to employees in variously labeled units, from human resources development to quality management. But the field required no certification or licensing. Nor was there a code of ethics. In the early 1980s, with support from the OD Network and National Science Foundation, a consortium of researchers issued "A Statement of Values and Ethics by Professionals in Organization and Human Systems Development." Presented as ideals and a catalyst for dialogue, the "Statement of Values" reasserted basic OD values concerning desired relationships in organizations and how to attain them.

Not incidentally because it was associated with academics, OD generated many evaluation studies. These generally concluded that interventions had been successful. But demonstrating success is not easy. No one authoritative definition of organizational effectiveness ever emerged, and most organizational changes seem to have many contributing causes. Critics found the research suspect for other reasons, too. Typically, it rested on a few cases—sometimes one. It used "soft" indicators, for example, changes in participants' reports about their attitudes. It seldom linked changes in specified variables to greater profitability. Or, it might be biased because the evaluators had conducted the intervention. At any rate, early studies were neither comprehensive nor compelling enough to establish the efficacy of OD.

Jerry Porras and Robert Golembiewski contributed significantly to the quality of the research. Beginning in the late 1970s, Porras drew attention to flaws in design, measurement, and analysis. He also suggested that the major impact of OD interventions was on participants as individuals, not on human or organizational processes. Golembiewski analyzed the success of reported OD interventions using very large, sophisticated panel studies. He found high success rates in all contexts—public or private sectors, affluent or poor settings, and industrialized or less developed countries. Acknowledging that the reported research had deficiencies, in particular, few experimental designs and long-term studies, Golembiewski noted that other areas of behavioral science had similar shortcomings. Moreover, the high success rates he and other scholars reported might even be artificially low because OD, in effect, could change the psychological scales participants used to evaluate organizational conditions. For instance, OD activities might raise participants' expectations, causing them to judge similar conditions more harshly after the intervention. But although Golembiewski argued that OD often was effective, he worried that it might not be efficient enough in some contexts.

Theoretical Framework

Although organization development has not yet produced a fully unifying theory, it has a distinct framework. Major elements include underlying values, assumptions about social processes, and models of intervention.

Humanistic values always have been central, so much so that Golembiewski defines the field in terms of accepting those values as the basis for relationships among people, especially at work. The seminal value is the dignity of the human person. As elaborated in "A Statement of Values," a person has fundamental rights, including rights to life, to justice, to the pursuit of happiness, and to experience responsible freedom and self-control. Individuals have potential to grow and develop their capacities. Fully functioning individuals are authentic, act consistently with their feelings, are honest and appropriately open, and accept others who behave similarly. They act on their environment, and they change themselves. It is important that people learn and develop, cooperate, experience community, honor diversity, participate in making decisions affecting them, and achieve desired results in ways that coordinate the energies, needs, and desires of people in their systems. Consequently, organizations should treat individuals as having complex needs. They should provide them with opportunities to learn, fulfill their potential, find challenging work, engage in cooperative relationships, and influence their environment. The design of work should promote growth, involvement, and responsibility.

Major assumptions about social life derive from organizational humanism, open systems theory, and experiential learning theory. Organizational humanism differs from the human relations tradition preceding it in valuing personal development as much as organizational productivity, if not more. Abraham Maslow's "growth psychology" sees human needs arrayed in a hierarchy culminating in self-actualization. Douglas McGregor applied Maslow's theories to industrial organizations and distinguished Theory X from Theory Y assumptions about workers. Theory Y assumptions infuse OD. Chris Argyris (1970) developed organizational learning theory and elaborated the role of the interventionist. Bennis espoused democratic principles, and Golembiewski saw democratic choice in moral terms. Organization development was the way to reconcile conflicts between the needs of organizations and their members. The consultant would help members recognize and overcome negative relationships and situations hindering mutual benefit.

According to open systems theory, organizations can respond to external and internal catalysts for change. They are social systems composed of subsystems, which more or less affect one another. The subsystems have some autonomy and can develop values, norms, perceptions, and behaviors which may reduce the effectiveness of the organization as a whole. Because subsystems interrelate and

systems tend toward equilibrium, it is difficult to change just one part of the organization. Thus, systems thinking encourages comprehensive OD interventions as well as attention to environmental factors.

Experiential learning theory undergirded Lewin's laboratory training and action research and distinguishes process consultation. Akin to adult learning theory, it reflects John Dewey's principles of humanistic education, as well as work by Maslow and Carl Rogers. In fact, OD pioneers Bradford and Benne studied Dewey's educational philosophy. Experiential learning emphasizes continuous learning grounded in experience in real-life situations. The learner actively participates intellectually and emotionally. Thus, OD is a normative-reeducative strategy of planned change.

Organizational humanism, open systems theory, and experiential learning theory infused OD with optimistic assumptions:

- Human beings and human systems are interdependent;
- Individuals and organizations can adapt;
- Organizations are open to change initiatives—the more comprehensive, the more effective generally;
- Organizations are essentially unified: having few basic conflicts of values, and able to agree on goals, members share common cause in improving organizational performance;
- Needs of individuals and organizations are compatible enough to permit design of mutually beneficial arrangements;
- Technical and social processes have no one best form; specific contexts count;
- Some conflict is natural and can be managed;
- Most conflict is largely psychological;
- Individuals want to grow, develop themselves, and help organizations reach their goals;
- Fulfilling employee needs and empowering them releases creative energies and improves organizational efficiency and effectiveness;
- Democratic participation enhances an organization's decisions and its workers' commitment;
- Democratic participation helps individuals mature psychologically;
- Freely committed workers accomplish more organizational work better;
- Open communication promotes awareness of self and others, increases trust and self-esteem, and promotes positive relationships and organizational commitment;
- Top management's culture affects an organization's ability to change;
- Collaboration helps organizations attain objectives better than coercion;

- Uncovering and correcting organizational pathologies may require a trained consultant, usually from outside;
- Changing organizational behavior may require new norms, attitudes, values, skills, and relationships, as well as knowledge; and
- Changing organizational culture requires active involvement of members.

Correspondingly, three propositions underlie the OD perspective on interventions. First, data-based diagnosis of the organization's problems should guide the choice of intervention techniques and corrective actions. Second, organizational members should participate with the consultant in diagnosing problems and planning actions. Third, the consultant should help members become better able to diagnose problems and act in the future.

These propositions define process consultation, whereby the consultant acts as a catalyst and facilitator regarding organizational processes, including decisionmaking and communications. Rather than letting clients become dependent, process consultants try to enhance their ability to find and solve problems on their own. The model assumes that members have relevant knowledge, will accept valid information, and will implement informed decisions in which they participate. It also assumes that experience observing and reflecting increases the ability of members and the organization to learn. Process consultation underlies specific intervention techniques, including survey feedback and team building.

An extension of process consultation, action research involves joint participation by members and a consultant in a continuous, cyclical process intended to improve the client system's behavior and also to develop behavioral science knowledge. Interviews, observations, questionnaires, and various kinds of organizational records can provide data. Action research can help consultants avoid getting trapped in top management's view and indicates to organization members that their views count.

In addition to the process-consultation and action-research approaches, Lippitt's scheme of stages of interventions and Lewin's model of changing social systems are important OD models of intervention. Lippitt elaborated stages of intervention, which may overlap: initial scouting, entry, diagnosis, planning, action, stabilization, evaluation, and termination. Lewin suggested that social systems change in three stages. First, the array of forces in an existing system alters so that the system "unfreezes," becoming open to change. Next, a planned, managed intervention moves the system to an improved state of being. Finally, the new improved state is locked in place, or "refrozen." Both models reflect a rational-instrumental perspective. A change agent intentionally takes actions and manipulates forces so as to achieve progressive, desired change in a relatively stable organization, within a relatively predictable environment.

Current Practice

Still most common in the United States, OD now is used by business, government, nongovernmental, and international organizations throughout the world. In some countries, OD practices go by other names, however. In addition, in many countries in Latin America, Africa, and Asia, a greater portion of OD efforts involves interorganizational settings, community development, and community organizing than in the United States.

In the United States, numerous businesses, public agencies, and nonprofit organizations use organization development. There have been projects in many industries: oil, chemicals, automobiles, defense, general consumer products, insurance, banking, communications, utilities, food processing, and high technology. TRW's efforts have lasted 30 years, employed multiple techniques, and gotten many line managers to use OD practices routinely. Governmental agencies at all levels—local, county, state, and national—use OD: local police departments, county mental health agencies, state departments of social services, the U.S. Food and Drug Administration, and all branches of the U.S. armed forces. OD is strong in education, health care, and human services. Many suburban public schools long have used OD. Recently, more urban schools, colleges, and universities have followed suit, likewise hospitals, clinics, after-care facilities, health planning agencies, social welfare agencies, and interagency human services planning organizations. Among nonprofits, professional, religious, and youth organizations have been especially hospitable. The fields of organization development and community development have basic affinity, and community development has incorporated many OD elements. Less confrontational kinds of community organizing also use OD practices.

About 50 OD techniques now are used. Businesses favor laboratory training and the Managerial Grid less than before, but they often use team-building, which is developing in the direction of training participants to think in terms of systems and envision desired futures. The future conference is one technique linking OD to strategic planning. Community development often employs action research and large-group techniques, such as decision conferencing and future search conferences.

OD projects have occurred in Canada, England, Japan, Norway, Sweden, Finland, Australia, New Zealand, Germany, Yugoslavia, Israel, Mexico, the Netherlands, and more than 30 less-developed countries. Especially in Canada and Northern Europe, corporations have undertaken major OD efforts. Generally, however, outside the United States community development and community organizing make up a higher proportion of significant OD enterprises. Such projects have been notable, too. In Norway, regional economic development enterprises have used participatory action research, search conferences, and action planning. In Sweden, the technique of democratic dialogue has linked more than 100 organizations in mutual support of their self-directed development efforts. In Asia, efforts to strengthen communities and organizations have used participatory action research. In one instance, the Institute for Development Research fostered nongovernmental organizations throughout the region by helping their directors collectively reflect upon their experiences. The search conference has been used at the national level in Australia.

A number of researchers and nonprofit organizations in the United States and several U.S. government agencies have fostered international applications. The World Bank undertook an extensive OD effort to improve its own performance. The Management Development Program in the United Nations Development Program has encouraged recipients of aid to use process consultants, assuming that the consultants can help local administrators adjust development plans to local situations and build their own capacity to implement the plans. The grandest international application of OD may be the series of dialogue conferences held by the Partnerships for Development program. To foster economic development, officials from developed and less-developed countries, international organizations, and multinational corporations participated in sessions employing strategic planning, team-building, and action planning.

Although many evaluations of international OD efforts have been positive, notable failures also have been reported. Questions remain about how relevant OD is in poorer settings, more authoritarian societies, or cultures less permeated by ideas associated with the Enlightenment and Protestant ethic. International efforts also underscore questions about the identity of the field. For example, the very term organization development seems ill-applied to work increasingly set among international organizations or in community systems. Additional problems attend the use of OD in community organizing, which historically has been more oriented toward power-coercive strategies and tactics. Nonetheless, international applications, like recent developments in the United States, demonstrate the potency of the action-research and process-consultation approaches and many of OD's techniques.

MARY ELIZABETH CARROLL

BIBLIOGRAPHY

Adams, John, ed., 1984. *Transforming Work*. Alexandria, VA: Miles River Press.

Argyris, Chris, 1970. *Intervention Theory and Method: A Behavioral Science View*. Reading, MA: Addison-Wesley.

Beckhard, Richard, 1969. *Organization Development: Strategies and Models*. Reading, MA: Addison-Wesley.

Bennis, Warren G., 1969. *Organization Development: Its Nature, Origins, and Prospects*. Reading, MA: Addison-Wesley.

Blake, R. R., and J. S. Mouton. 1964. *The Management Grid*. Houston: Gulf Publishing Co.

Bradford, L., J. R. Gibb, and K. D., Benne, Eds., 1964. *T-Group Theory and Laboratory Method: Innovation in Re-Education*. New York: Wiley.

Burke, W. Warner, 1987. *Organization Development: A Normative View*. Reading, MA: Addison-Wesley.

French, Wendell L., and Cecil H. Bell, 1995. *Organization Development: Behavioral Science Interventions for Organization Improvement*. 5th ed. Englewood Cliffs, NJ: Prentice-Hall.

Golembiewski, Robert T., 1990. *Organization Development: Ideas and Issues*. New Brunswick, NJ: Transaction.

———, 1993. *Handbook of Organizational Consultation*. New York: Marcel Dekker.

Lewin, K. 1951. *Field Theory in Social Science*. New York: Harper.

Lippitt, R., J. Watson, and B. Westley, 1958. *The Dynamics of Planned Change*. New York: Harcourt Brace Jovanovich.

Margulies, N., and A. Raia. 1972. *Organization Development: Valves, Process and Technology*.

Maslow, A. H. 1943. "A Theory of Human Motivation." *Psychological Review*, vol. 50.

Massarik, Fred, ed., 1990. *Advances in Organization Development*. Vol. I. Norwood, N. J.: Ablex Publication.

McGregor, D. M. 1960. *The Human Side of Enterprise*. New York: McGraw-Hill.

Porras, J. I. April 1979. "The Comparative Impact of Different Ad Techniques and Their Results in 23 Organizations." *Journal of Applied Behavioral Science*, vol. 15.

Schein, Edgar H., 1969. *Process Consultation: Its Role in Organization Development*. Reading, MA: Addison-Wesley.

Senge, Peter, 1990. *The Fifth Discipline: The Art and Practice of the Learning Organization*. New York: Currency Doubleday.

Trist, E. L. 1960. *Socio-technical Systems*. London: Trivistock Institute of Human Relations.

Weisbord, Marvin R., 1989. *Productive Workplaces: Organizing and Managing for Dignity, Meaning, and Community*. San Francisco: Jossey-Bass.

ORGANIZATION THEORY.

A body of social theory concerned with explaining the conduct and operations of human organizations, especially large and complex organizations. Generally speaking, organization theory focuses on "macro" concerns, such as organizational structure, organizational design, or organization culture. That is, organization theory tries to understand the organization as a unit of analysis, as opposed to the "micro" approach that concentrates on individual behavior in organizations. However, the two approaches are inevitably intertwined, making any clear distinction difficult if not impossible. Indeed, some of the more recent theories of organization quite clearly seek to understand and build upon the interaction of individual and organizational concerns.

A discipline contributed to by scholars in both business and public administration, as well political scientists, sociologists, psychologists, and those from many other disciplines, organization theory has been of great value to students of public administration as they have sought to understand the distinctive nature of public organizations. Rather than attempting a comprehensive review of work in organization theory, this entry will present representative schools and models that have been of special interest to students of public administration over the years. We will conclude with some special comments on the possibility of building theories of organization that are distinctively public in their orientation.

Max Weber

Every student of organization theory begins with the German sociologist Max Weber, who lived and wrote in the late nineteenth and early twentieth century, but whose works were largely unknown to American scholars until mid-century. Weber was concerned with a large range of social, economic, and political issues, but particularly interested in interpreting the social order. As one tool to do so, Weber attempted to construct "ideal types," abstractions of particular sets of elements or events that have special significance in terms of providing meaning and structure to human experience. (Note that the use of the word "ideal" here does not imply a value preference for any particular type but rather signifies the prominence the type holds in social, economic, or political life.) Of special interest to students of public administration is Weber's ideal-type bureaucracy.

Weber approached this issue from a discussion of patterns of authority or domination in society, in which he noted that every system of authority must somehow establish a basis for its own legitimacy. Specifically, he suggested three types of legitimate authority: (1) legal authority, based on the belief in the legality of certain patterns or rules and in the right of those in positions of legal authority to issue commands; (2) traditional authority, based on a belief in the importance of enduring traditions and those who rule within such traditions; and (3) charismatic authority, based on an emotional attachment or devotion to a specific individual. Weber found the first of these types, legal authority, to be typically associated with the use of a bureaucratic administrative staff.

Note that Weber's use of the word "bureaucracy" was not pejorative, as it might be today, but merely descriptive of a particular type, a type Weber saw characterized by the following features:

- They are personally free and are subject to authority only with respect to their impersonal official obligations.
- They are organized in a clearly defined hierarchy of offices.
- Each office has a clearly defined sphere of competence, in the legal sense.

- The office is filled by a free contractual relationship. Thus, in principle, there is free selection.
- Candidates are selected on the basis of technical qualifications. In the most rational case, these qualifications are tested by examination, guaranteed by diplomas certifying technical training, or both. Candidates are appointed, not elected.
- They are remunerated by fixed salaries in money, for the most part with a right to pensions. Only under certain circumstances does the employing authority, especially in private organizations, have a right to terminate the appointment, but in addition to this criterion, the responsibility of the position and the requirements of the incumbent's social status may be taken into account.
- The office is treated as the sole, or at least the primary, occupation of the incumbent.
- The office constitutes a career. Promotion is based on seniority, achievement, or both and depends on the judgment of the superiors.
- Officials work entirely separate from ownership of the means of administration and without appropriation of their positions.
- They are subject to strict and systematic discipline and control in the conduct of the office (Weber 1947, p. 328).

As a practical matter, Weber found that bureaucratic organizations were able to order and arrange human actions in a way that seemed most "rational" in the accomplishment of human goals. For example, Weber (1947) wrote, "Experience tends universally to show that the purely bureaucratic type is . . . capable of attaining the highest degree of efficiency and is in this sense formally the most rational known means of carrying out imperative control over human beings" (pp. 333–334). While Weber did not neglect the potential negative consequences of bureaucracy, his characterization was seen by many as constituting an endorsement. In any case, Weber clearly captured the prevailing form of administration during the period of his writing.

Frederick W. Taylor and Mary Parker Follett

Dramatically different views of organizational life in the early twentieth century were presented by Frederick W. Taylor and Mark Parker Follett. Taylor, known as the father of "scientific management," argued that a scientific approach should be used to guide the actions of practicing managers as they went about their work. Taylor held that such an approach could be used at the technical level to identify the best practices or most productive behaviors of individual workers, so that such knowledge might be extended to other workers and other groups. Whether the work being done was office work or shoveling dirt, Taylor sought to analyze work processes in a scientifically rigorous fashion, so that the "one best way" of performing would be known to all. Obviously, in such an effort, individual workers would only be seen as production machines, whose performance was to be tuned to peak efficiency.

Beyond the technical level, however, Taylor sought to extend scientific analysis throughout the organization. Indeed, in his view, the scientific imperative held that managers should not merely be observers and regulators of their workers' behaviors, but that their job was to make the organization more efficient through the application of scientific principles to all work processes. The management group would be the primary proponents of the scientific philosophy as it moved through the organization. Their work would be the scientific work of making the machinery of the organization—including its human machinery—more efficient and more productive.

In contrast to Taylor's mechanistic model of management, Mary Parker Follett sought to introduce psychological concepts to the study of organizations. She emphasized the importance of an individual's motivating desires within the organization. Interested in the maintenance of human cooperation, Mary Parker Follett detached herself from the traditional structural approach to the problems of organizational life. As a result, she was considered as having ideas much ahead of her time.

Follett argued that, while at work, the individual is activated by habits and desires similar to those that are involved in that person's personal life. It was based on this idea that she saw the individual and human relationships as the foundation of organizations. According to her, the business organization is a part of a larger, holistic human organization which makes up society.

Follett held that organizational problems within government or private enterprise stem from the organization's inability to build and maintain dynamic and harmonious human relations. In her view, an individual's past life, beliefs, prejudices, emotions, and desires are combined to form "habits of mind." In order to change behavior in the workplace, managers need to influence these habit patterns. Throughout her work, one can see evidence of her strong belief that smoothly operating organizations are based on strong psychological foundations.

While the humanistic essence of her ideas can be viewed in contrast to Taylor's contributions, Follett does give credit to certain aspects of the scientific management philosophy. In particular, she agreed with the concept of superiors' depersonalizing orders given to subordinates. In giving orders, Follett claimed that rather than attempting to get employees to obey orders, superiors ought to devise methods for the employee to discover the order specific to

a situation. She refers to this depersonalization of orders as finding the "law of the situation."

In sum, Mary Parker Follett was convinced of three things: (1) all problems, whenever they occur, are fundamentally problems in human relations; (2) while every human being is different, there is a sufficiently large common factor in human reactions to similar situations to permit the development of principles of administration; (3) these principles should be sought and applied wherever human endeavors are required in the pursuit of a common objective (Metcalf and Urwick 1940, p. 24).

The Rational Model of Administration

Most organization theory in the first half of the twentieth century tended to follow Taylor more than Follett, at least in the sense that the primary focus was on efficiency in the production process and ways in which organization control mechanisms could increase the productivity of the organization. A series of studies conducted at the Hawthorne works of Western Electric, however, began to call into question the mechanistic and structural approach of earlier times. The research program originally was undertaken as an exercise in scientific management, one designed to determine under which working conditions (heat, light, etc.) workers were more productive (less subject to fatigue, etc.). What the researchers found, however, was that workers responded positively under a variety of conditions, leading to the conclusion that the attention being given to them by the researchers was more important than other conditions of work. The study suggested, in other words, that there was an informal organization existing alongside the formal organization and capable of greatly influencing what happens in the organization. Indeed, the researchers concluded that "the limits of human collaboration are determined far more by the informal than the formal organization" (Roethlisberger and Dickson 1940, p. 568).

Among the writers who soon followed, Chester Barnard best captured the new direction of organization theory in this book, *The Functions of the Executive*. Barnard defines a formal organization as a "system of consciously coordinated activities or forces of two or more individuals" (1948, p. 81). Since such coordination is dependent upon the individual being willing to make certain contributions, Barnard recognizes that the needs and desires of the individual, whether rational or not, have to be met at least to a degree in order for the individual to continue to contribute. Similarly, in order for authority to be exercised, orders must fall within the individual's "zone of indifference." Otherwise, the individual will refuse to go along. In either case, "If the individual finds his motives being satisfied by what he does, he continues his cooperative effort; otherwise he does not" (p. 57).

Interestingly, Barnard began by arguing that theories of organization always imply a certain view of the individual, either a view of the individual as a function of social forces or a view of the individual as having greater freedom of choice or will. While Barnard did not himself take a position along these lines, the two approaches we examine in this section and the next seem quite clearly to differentiate in this way.

Herbert Simon, perhaps the leading public administration scholar contributing to the broader field of organization theory, began his work by attacking the "pseudoscience" of earlier organization theory, then developing a comprehensive system for understanding "rational" behavior in organizational settings. In *Administrative Behavior* (1957) and *Models of Man* (1958), written with James March, Simon elaborated a positivist view of organizations, one presumably based on observation of the objective facts of organizational life, one paying little attention to values. Simon begins by arguing that human beings bring only limited or "bounded" rationality with them to organizations, but as a rule they act as much as they can based on an assessment of what is rationally in their interest. For example, following Barnard, if members of the organization feel they are receiving sufficient inducements, they will contribute to the work of the organization.

The keys for management in seeking to move efficiently toward the goals of the organization are (1) how to get people to join the organization, and (2) how to get them to contribute. Each is approached through a rational (or nearly rational) calculation of individual costs and benefits. To secure greater participation and greater contributions, management must offer more attractive inducements, whether money, status, prestige, or whatever. "It may be postulated," writes Simon, "that each participant will remain in the organization, if the satisfaction (or utility) he derives is greater than the satisfaction he could obtain if he withdrew. The zero-point in such a 'satisfaction-function' is defined, therefore, in terms of the opportunity cost of participation" (1958, p. 173). A similar calculation occurs in determining the "zone of acceptance," within which individuals will carry out orders from those in positions of authority.

While Simon's formulation is said to be dependent on individual decision "premises," there are clearly ways in which the organization can begin to displace the values of the individual with those of the organization and, obviously, it is in the interest of the organization's "controlling group" to make this happen. To the extent that these organizational values, which are, in Simon's view, clearly more rational than those of the individual, begin to dominate, the individual will become subordinated to the organization, something Simon apparently approves. "Since these institutions largely determine the mental sets of the participants, they set the conditions for the exercise of docility, and hence rationality, in human society" (1957a, p. 198).

Organizational Humanism

While Simon clearly saw the individual as a function of social forces, other writers at the same time and soon after saw the individual as having much greater choice in organizational matters. Chris Argyris, writing in *Personality and Organization* (1957), argued that traditional organizational practices are often quite at odds with the natural developmental tendencies of human beings. Reviewing studies of personality development, Argyris pointed out that people, in their growth from infancy to adulthood, tend to move from passivity to activity, from dependency to independence, from a limited to a greater range of behaviors, from shallow to deeper interests, from a shorter to a longer time perspective, from a subordinate position to one of equality, and from a lack of awareness to greater awareness.

In contrast, traditional assumptions about management tend to thwart the development of the healthy adult personality. For example, people are given little control over their work and are expected to be, like infants, dependent and submissive. Under these restrictions on adult development, employees may react in terms of hostility and aggression. When this happens, management is likely to "crack down" further, leading to a vicious and negative cycle of interactions. A healthier approach, according to Argyris, would be one that would recognize the developmental needs of individuals, then seek ways in which the needs of individuals would be "fused" with those of the organization. The manager's task is exactly that of finding a congruence between individual needs and organizational demands, a task far different from that prescribed by Taylor or Simon, and a task that may be aided by the help of an outside interventionist.

Such an interventionist, or specialist in organization development, should not impose solutions from the outside, but should assist those in the organization to reduce sources of anxiety and defensiveness so that they may arrive at mutually agreed-upon solutions to their problems. Argyris writes that the task of the interventionists are three: (1) to help generate valid and useful information; (2) to create conditions in which clients can make informed and free choices; and (3) to help clients develop an internal commitment to their choice (1970).

Similar themes were pursued by Douglas McGregor in *The Human Side of Enterprise* (1960). McGregor held that the traditional approach to management—which he called Theory X—seemed to be based on several assumptions: that most people dislike work, that they must be coerced and controlled, and that they actually prefer to be directed and to avoid responsibility. A more effective approach, he suggests, would be one based on assumptions such as these:

- The expenditure of physical and mental effort in work is as natural as play or rest.
- Humans will exercise self-direction and self-control in the service of objectives to which they are committed.
- The average human being learns . . . not only to accept but to seek responsibility.
- The capacity to exercise a relatively high degree of imagination, ingenuity, and creativity in the solution of organizational problems is widely, not narrowly distributed in society.

As with Argyris, these assumptions point directly toward the creation of circumstances under which the needs of the individual would be integrated with those of the organization.

Systems Theory and Contingency Theory

Following trends in both the natural sciences and in other social sciences, organization theorists in the 1960s and 1970s began to explore the implications of viewing organizations as systems, that is, wholes made up of many interrelated parts, separated from other systems by definable boundaries, and operating according to a set of general principles common to all natural and social systems. Organizations, like other open systems depend on interactions with their environment in order to survive. Katz and Kahn (1978) identified a variety of characteristics that govern the operations of open systems. These include:

- *The importation of energy*—Organizations, as open systems, energize themselves by taking in energy or inputs from their environment. For example, organizations need inputs of people, materials, financial resources, and so on in order to operate. One special input that organizations require is information.
- *Throughput*—Organizations as systems treat inputs with processes that convert these input into acceptable outputs, including projects or services. Basically, these processes are the sum of the internal operations of the organization—what they do to affect the inputs.
- *Outputs*—The outputs produced by the organization are returned to the environment. Obviously any system must produce a needed product or service, as evaluated by those in the environment, in order to continue in operation. Failing to meet needs or demands will result in the loss of inputs necessary to the survival of the system.
- *Negative entropy*—Entropy suggests that all organized forms move toward disorganization and demise. The effect of entropy can be halted by the organization's taking in excess energy from the environment and storing it for future use: negative entropy.
- *Steady state*—A steady state is reached when the cycle of input, output, and feedback continues in a balanced fashion over time. In an effort to achieve a steady state, organizations often seek to control greater portions of their environment and seek to integrate various subsystems that may need coordination.

James Thompson (1967, pp. 10–11) sought a balance of open systems concepts with the idea of closed systems, those with less integration and hence more control over events. Basing his work on the ideas of sociologist Talcott Parsons, Thompson suggested three organizational levels of responsibility and control: the technical, managerial, and institutional. The technical portion of the organization is concerned with the efficient performance of the actual task of the organization; the managerial portion is concerned with mediating between the technical groups and clients of the organization and with providing the resources necessary to perform the work; the institutional portion of the organization is concerned with the relationship between the organization as an institution and the wider social system of which it is a part. According to Thompson, the logic of closed systems, which would allow a greater insistence on technical efficiency, would seem more appropriate to the technical core. The logic of open systems, focusing on interactions with the environment, would seem more appropriate to the institutional level. The managerial subsystem would be required to mediate between the two other levels of the organization.

The open systems view also led to considerable attention among organization theorists to issues of interorganizational relations. Kast and Rosenzweig (1974) suggest that there are certain general environmental features that affect all organizations, among them factors that are cultural, technological, educational, political, legal, natural resource, demographic, sociological, and economic. All organizations would be affected in some way by all these factors. Specific organizations, however, face different task environments, which might include their relations to customers, suppliers, or competitors.

Various authors have pointed out the obvious: that certain environments can be hostile to an organization while others might be quite benign. Emery and Trist (1965) suggested that environments vary according to the among of change taking place in them and the complexity of knowledge required to operate successfully. Their resulting typology ranges from environments that are called placid, to those that are disturbed, to those that are turbulent. Depending on the type of environment within which an organization is operating, different approaches to both boundary spanning and internal management might be called for. Seeking to guide organizations in adapting to their environments, organization theorists have described various mechanisms for successfully interacting with the organization's environment, including such concepts as buffering, integrating, and specifying organization sets.

Alternative Epistemologies

The positivist model of science that supported most organization theory through the first half of the twentieth century and well into the second half began to come under attack in the late 1960s and early 1970s. Pointing out that human beings don't react to events in the same way as billiard balls on a table, but rather through expressing hopes, aspirations, and values in their actions, the critics suggested that the models of the natural sciences simply weren't applicable to the study of human beings and human organizations. Rather, they suggested, an approach was needed that allowed a more substantial accounting of the fact that humans bring meaning to social situations and that they operate in a world of values, values quite different from rational calculations.

Drawing on work in phenomenology and interpretive theory, one group sought a clearer understanding of human meaning in organizational life. For example, David Silverman (1971) described organizations as being socially constructed and maintained by virtue of the fact that people assign meaning to their actions and those meanings are the basis for intentional action. Under such circumstances, the key to organizational change, as one example, is the flow of meanings generated by interacting individuals. In a related vein, Karl Weick (1969) described organizations as being "enacted," that is, created through the interactions and dominant meanings that various people and groups assign to their work. For example, those at the organization's boundary wishing to relate effectively to that environment must be careful not to have views imposed on them from outside.

Other theorists developed theories based in critical social theory, an approach that suggests a value-critical understanding of organizational life (Denhardt 1981). Organizations, as human constructions, are seen as imposing certain "blinders" on their members, the removal of which would open individuals to new possibilities for freedom and self-expression. In this approach, the role of the manager is an "educative" one, helping people see the possibilities for greater meaning that lie beyond the limitations of that which currently exists. Incidentally, both the interpretive and critical approaches supported an important movement in organizational studies away from a preoccupation with quantitative studies to more openness to qualitative, field-based research, research that would allow the interpretation and critique of human meaning in organizational settings.

Organizational Culture and Organizational Learning

The interaction between the organization and its members—at least in terms of general norms, beliefs, and values—has been the focal point of some fairly recent theorizing that centers on the concept of organizational culture and the related idea of organizational learning. The idea of organizational culture reflects the anthropological understanding of more general cultures and thus includes such ideas as the norms that underlie the operation of working groups, the general philosophy and unstated policies that guide the organization, and the "rules of the game" for getting things done. Edgar Schein (1987) argues that these ideas reflect an organization's culture, but are not the essence of culture. Instead, he holds that "the term 'culture' should be reserved for the deeper level of basic assumptions and beliefs that are shared by members of an organization, that operate unconsciously, and that define an organization's view of itself and its environment" (p. 6).

Interestingly, the concept of culture has been used in various ways to suggest strategies for change or even transformation in organizations, both public and private. Some authors use culture in an instrumental fashion, merely trying to manipulate culture to produce desired ends. Others, much more respectful of the real nature of culture, suggest ways in which organizations can assist persons throughout the organizations in asserting meaning and in producing cultural change. (Linda Smircich [1983] has described these two uses as "culture as a variable" and "culture as a metaphor.") Many who appear to prefer the latter interpretation have focused on the question of organizational learning.

Change can be described as another word for learning; organizations that undergo change of a cultural nature can be described as going through the learning process. The learning organization is explained as having two meanings. It can mean an organization which learns and it can mean an organization that encourages learning in its people (Handy 1989). Learning organizations have also been defined as organizations where people continually expand their capacity to create the results they truly desire, where new and expansive patterns of thinking are nurtured, where collective aspirations are set free, and where people are continually learning how to learn together (Senge 1990, p. 3).

The concept of a learning organization is based on the premise that all humans are naturally learners. Infants do not have to be taught to speak, walk, or eat. Humans are thought of as being innately inquisitive—we ask ourselves questions, we come up with ideas, we test those ideas, then we reflect on the results. Learning, then, can be conceptualized as a process by which we assimilate new thoughts, ideas, and beliefs into our basic assumptions of life. An organization that learns goes through a similar process of posing questions, generating theories, testing the theories, and reflecting on the results.

Chris Argyris and Donald Schön (1978) have studied how organizations learn or fail to learn. They make the distinction between three types of organizational learning. "Single-loop" learning takes place when the detection and correction of an error still permits the organization to achieve its objectives without modifying the organizational norms. If the error is detected and the correction does involve modifying the organization's policies and norms, it has said to have undergone "double-loop" learning. Third, when the organization conducts an inquiry into the learning system by which they go about detecting and correcting errors, the learning is categorized as "deutero-learning."

Just as humans are inflicted with learning disabilities, organizations too can be disabled in certain ways. Peter Senge (1990) describes several types of learning disabilities. For example, the "I am my position" disability refers to the tendency of employees to define themselves and their powers in relation to their specific job. As a result, they may perceive themselves as having no influence in the organization and may feel they must cope with forces out of their control. This type of disability, along with others of different kinds, limits the individual and the organization's ability to learn and achieve new goals. Senge suggests five learning "disciplines" that are helpful in building a "learning organization." These are personal mastery, mental models, shared vision, team learning, and systems thinking.

Conclusion: Building Theories of Public Organization

While the most significant portion of organization theory has been built by scholars outside the field of public administration, those in public administration have drawn on that material extensively. One question that remains is whether public administration scholars will continue "borrowing" from other disciplines or whether a distinctive set of theories of public organization can be developed. The latter is suggested by Denhardt (1993), who argues that defining public administration in terms of "managing change in pursuit of publicly defined values" offers the possibility of a distinctive theoretical understanding of public organizations as opposed to organizations more generally. While a fully developed theory built along these lines still remains to be constructed, there are certainly hints of that possibility occurring over the coming years.

ROBERT B. DENHARDT

BIBLIOGRAPHY

Argyris, Chris, 1957. *Personality and Organization.* New York: Harper & Row.
———, 1970. *Intervention Theory and Method: A Behavioral Science View.* Reading, MA: Addison-Wesley.
Argyris, Chris, and Donald A. Schön, 1978. *Organizational Learning: A Theory of Action Perspective.* Reading, MA: Addison-Wesley.
Barnard, Chester I., 1948. *The Functions of the Executive.* Cambridge, MA: Harvard University Press.
Denhardt, Robert B., 1981. *In the Shadow of Organization.* Lawrence: Regents Press of Kansas.
———, 1993. *The Pursuit of Significance: Strategies for Managerial Success in Public Organizations.* Belmont, CA: Wadsworth.
Emery, F. E., and Eric L. Trist, 1965. "Causal Texture of Organizational Environments." *Human Relations,* vol. 18 (February) 21–32.
Handy, Charles, 1989. *The Age of Unreason.* Boston: Harvard Business School Press.
Kast, F. E., and J. E. Rosenzweig, 1974. *Contingency Views of Organizations and Management.* Chicago: Science and Research Associates.
Katz, Daniel, and Robert L. Kahn, 1978. *The Social Psychology of Organizing.* 2d. ed. New York: John Wiley.
March, James G., and Herbert A. Simon, 1957. *Models of Man.* New York: Wiley.
McGregor, Douglas M., 1960. *The Human Side of Enterprise.* New York: McGraw-Hill.
Metcalf, Henry C., and L. Urwick, eds., 1940. *Dynamic Administration.* New York: Harper & Row.
Roethlisberger, Fritz, and William Dickson, 1940. *Management and the Worker.* Cambridge, MA: Harvard University Press.
Schein, Edgar H., 1987. *The Art of Managing Human Resources.* New York: Oxford University Press.
Senge, Peter M., 1990. *The Fifth Discipline: The Art and Practice of the Learning Organization.* New York: Doubleday/Currency.
Silverman, David, 1971. *The Theory of Organizations.* New York: Basic Books.
Simon, Herbert A., 1957. *Administrative Behavior.* New York: Macmillan.
———, 1958. *Models of Man: Social and Rational.* New York: Wiley.
Smircich, Linda, 1983. "Concepts of Culture and Organizational Analysis," *Administrative Science Quarterly,* vol. 28: 339–358.
Thompson, James A., 1967. *Organizations in Action.* New York: McGraw-Hill.
Weber, Max, 1947. *The Theory of Social and Economic Organization.* New York: Oxford University Press.
Weick, Karl, 1969. *The Social Psychology of Organizing.* Reading, MA: Addison-Wesley.

ORGANIZATIONAL ARCHITECTURE. A term that captures the interaction of structure with behavior; it combines command and control elements that create the shape of an organization with the cultural components that form its milieu. Architectural elements include the authority structure, reporting mechanisms, communication channels, position classification system, work flow, unit grouping, cultural norms, and the processes for selection, socialization, and development of personnel. As a concept, it captures those qualities that differentiate one workplace from another, based on the composite effects of mission, size, shape, history, structure, norms, and staff. It is the most holistic means of describing the characteristics of an organization, especially in the post-modern context (Bergquist 1993). The term encompasses aspects as intangible as culture and as tangible as the formal lines of authority.

There are architectural characteristics of an established workplace that are accepted as givens and that serve to structure interactions among individuals and departments. These structures hold systems in place and resist change. They are submerged within the daily activities on the job, they are commonplace, and they are rarely questioned, if even noticed.

Theoretical Context

First popularized by Nadler, Gerstein, Shaw, and Associates (1992), the term replaces a simplistic focus on organizational structure with a holistic focus on the interaction between structure, people, mission, and behavior. A well-designed organization is one in which the architectural elements are congruent with one another. This means that communication channels transmit information as quickly and as accurately as necessary, that workers have the skills and resources necessary to perform their tasks, that units within the organization contribute in the intended way to the goals of the organization, and that the organization's interactions with constituents are conducive to its mission.

An architectural analysis of an organization is the first step in identifying key variables that affect and interact with one another. Such an analysis is particularly effective as a precursor to organization development initiatives that require alterations in architectural elements. For example, flattening hierarchies to delete middle management positions alters the way decisions are made and who makes them. This, in turn, changes the form that communication takes and the degree of worker participation. Alterations in one series of elements produce changes in additional elements and have implications for the overall architecture. Like tipping the first in a line of dominoes, a change in one produces changes in many others.

The evolution of organization theory through the twentieth century demonstrates the shift in emphasis from specific architectural elements to the interconnectedness of structural and cultural components. The writings of Frederick Taylor, Woodrow Wilson, Max Weber, Mary Parker Follett, Henri Fayol, Chester Barnard, Anthony Downs, James March and Herbert Simon, among others, address architectural components that each theorist considered to be important in the overall functioning of an organization. (See, for example, Wilson 1887; Weber 1946; Fry 1989). While earlier writers (Wilson, Taylor, Weber, Fayol) focused on the structural elements of organizations, later writers introduced additional elements into organizational design. For example, interactions among workers, decision processes, personal motivation, informal groups, cultural components, and external environmental factors were included in the writings of Mary Parker Follett, Chester Barnard, Elton Mayo, Anthony Downs, Herbert Simon, and others. By the late 1990s, organization theorists were emphasizing organizational culture, with its focus on informal interaction, values, traditions, and rituals (see, for example, Deal and Kennedy 1982; Ott 1989). This shift reflects the changes that have occurred over the past century in the way organization theorists think about the architecture of organizations. As the workforce becomes more educated and as organizations adopt more participatory management styles, the architecture changes and the pre-eminence of various architectural components changes.

Architectural Differences Between Government and Business Organizations

The architecture of large bureaucracies, such as those found in most governmental agencies, includes the following elements: reliance on formal chains of command, a hierarchical alignment of power and responsibility, and resistance to change. In addition to these elements are those that are unique to government, including deference to authority; the simultaneous trust and mistrust that citizens have of government; partisan politics; rigid hiring, firing, and promotion schedules; citizen demands for accountability; risk aversion so as not to offend elected officials; Freedom of Information statutes; and safeguards against corrupt practices.

TABLE I. ARCHITECTURAL COMPONENTS OF PUBLIC ORGANIZATIONS

Mission

Structure

Culture

Workforce characteristics

Incentive systems

Size

Communication channels

Partisan politics

Public trust

Time horizon

Policies and procedures

Decisionmaking processes

Although not exhaustive, Table I displays elements that exist in the organizational architecture of public organizations.

Each component interacts with the others to produce a unique organization. As changes occur in the elements of one, a ripple effect is produced in other elements, ultimately changing the architecture of the organization. Government organizations include architectural components not found in private sector organizations because public agencies (1) are usually large, (2) are well-established with a long history, (3) change leadership and priorities as political cycles change, and (4) must respond to constituencies driven by political motives rather than market motives. This environment presents differentiating elements: political culture, partisan politics, public trust, and democratic representativeness. A brief description of each follows.

Political Culture

The organizational architecture of governmental agencies contains elements that reflect political culture. In the U.S., this means that governmental agencies must function within constraints rather than freedoms in terms of the actions they may undertake. These constraints reflect the public's demand for accountability, predictability, reliance on routines, and access to information. Citizens and the press exercise their right to know about the actions of their government, which injects nonmarket-based accountability mechanisms into the architecture of public agencies. These are reflected in laws requiring public meetings, duplicative reporting, and programs that must balance competing political values.

Partisan Politics

Partisan politics is an architectural component in public organizations that changes with political cycles. In the two-party system of the U.S., the party that controls the presidency also controls all executive agencies. Thus, the directors of agencies and the policies they pursue change with elections. Agencies must adapt to differing initiatives rather suddenly, thus creating waves of change throughout the agency on a periodic basis. What would be too chaotic to manage in a for-profit company must be treated as business as usual in a government agency.

Time Horizon

Closely linked with election cycles is the time horizon, meaning the extent to which people in an agency define "short-term" or "long-term" in terms of days, weeks, months, or years. The speed with which an organization is accustomed to acting differentiates the type of long-term planning and short-term planning that is required, the kinds of skills required, and the kinds of workers that are necessary. Likewise, length of tenure in office for key posi-

tions is another aspect of organizational architecture. When staffing changes at each political cycle, the architecture of the organization must be able to adapt to new directions, or to steer the organization during transition periods in leadership.

Public Trust

Trust, and lack of it, is a part of the architecture of government. While business organizations exist to create wealth, government organizations exist to advance and promote the interests of agreed-upon political values. Citizens value the actions of government differently than they value the work of the business sector. A government that is too responsive to partisan politics fails to provide the checks and balance to executive zealotry. Because partisan politics determines who is appointed to lead public agencies, public employees are protected against patronage by myriad rules and procedures. While these safeguards have beneficial effects, they also stymie agency directors' flexibility to appoint subordinates, thus producing an additional difference in the architecture of public as compared to private organizations.

Democratic Representativeness

Public agencies are designed to serve as a conversion process from what voters want to what they receive. Agencies transform resources in the form of tax revenues into output, in the form of policies and programs. The composition of the workforce is a component of the architecture. While some organizations in the U.S. predominantly hire and promote white males, the dominant group in power, into decisionmaking positions, other agencies employ a more balanced workforce with representation of women and racial and ethnic minorities (Guy 1994). The amount of diversity in the workforce makes a difference in the organization in terms of communication, inculcation of organizational values, and response of the external environment to the organization's actions.

Summary

Public organizations are designed to conceive, connect, and confirm. Conceiving is the act of deciding how to implement policies. Connecting is the process of converting policy-level strategic decisions into workable programs. Confirming is the process of determining that agency action is in compliance with laws, regulations, and legislative intent. These functions affect, and are affected by, the organizational architecture of public agencies the tangled web of formal and informal structures and processes that produces the footprint of each agency.

MARY E. GUY

BIBLIOGRAPHY

Bergquist, William H., 1993. *The Postmodern Organization: Mastering the Art of Irreversible Change.* San Francisco, CA: Jossey-Bass.

Deal, Terrence E., and Allan A. Kennedy, 1982. *Corporate Cultures.* Reading, MA: Addison-Wesley.

Fry, Brian, 1989. *Mastering Public Administration: From Max Weber to Dwight Waldo.* Chatham, NJ: Chatham House.

Guy, Mary E., 1994. "Organizational Architecture, Gender and Women's Careers." *Review of Public Personnel Administration,* 14:2, 77–90.

Nadler, David A., Marc S. Gerstein, Robert B. Shaw, and Associates, 1992. *Organizational Architecture: Designs for Changing Organizations.* San Francisco, CA: Jossey-Bass.

Ott, J. Steven, 1989. *The Organizational Culture Perspective.* Chicago, IL: Dorsey Press.

Weber, Max, 1946. "Bureaucracy." In H. H. Gerth and C. W. Mills, trans. and eds., *From Max Weber: Essays in Sociology.* New York: Oxford University Press.

Wilson, Woodrow, 1887. "The Study of Administration." *Political Science Quarterly,* vol. 2: 197–222.

ORGANIZATIONAL BEHAVIOR.

A field of research, theory, and practice in the social and administrative sciences that concentrates on the behaviors of individuals and groups in organizations. No precise definition clearly differentiates this field from related ones, such as organization theory, and usage of such labels as organizational behavior and organization theory varies widely. Fairly commonly, however, organization theory serves as a general field that focuses on the analysis of organizations, with organizational behavior referring to a closely related field concentrating on human behaviors in organizations.

The titles and coverage of textbooks and of divisions in professional associations often imply or explicitly indicate that organization theory refers to organizational analysis in general, but also can refer to the study of organizations as the primary unit of analysis (as opposed to concentrating on persons in organizations as the unit of analysis). The study of organizations as units of analysis, usually regarded as the domain of organization theory, has important origins in sociology, where scholars began analysis of large and complex organizations in society at least in the latter part of the nineteenth century. While references to complex organizational forms and their leadership, management, and societal roles are as old as human letters, with references in the Bible and other ancient sources, scholars often date the systematic study of organizations from the work of Max Weber in the late nineteenth and early twentieth centuries. Weber wrote, among many other topics, analytical discussions of bureaucracy. Later sociologists further pursued research and theory on complex organizations and bureaucracies, with emphasis on their structural characteristics, their operating effectiveness, their changefulness or resistance to change, their environments, goals, power relations, and many related topics.

In the field of psychology, researchers analyze the behaviors of workers and work groups in organizations, also a classic topic that has received sporadic attention in various forms since antiquity. As with the study of organizations, behaviors within organizations became a more focused and intensive field of inquiry within the social sciences in the latter part of the nineteenth century and especially in the early decades of the twentieth century. The subfields of industrial psychology and social psychology further developed a specialized focus on behaviors, attitudes, and impacts of persons in organizations and groups. In various usages, one began to encounter references to industrial/organizational (I/O) psychology across the century, and texts and university departments may have titles referring to I/O psychology.

Similarly, across the century references to organizational behavior (OB) appeared more frequently, and now texts, journals, divisions of professional associations (such as the Organizational Behavior Division of the Academy of Management in the United States), and university units and courses include organizational behavior in their titles.

The utilization of OB in these titles appears to be related to the broadening involvement of professionals outside the field of psychology, such as researchers in business schools. In addition, the movement away from the title of industrial psychology probably reflects a move away from the technical and industrial implications of that title, toward recognition that the field concerns many matters besides, for example, human-machine or human-instrumentation topics, and many locations in addition to industry, such as service firms, nonprofit and government organizations, and educational and medical organizations.

OB texts and journals, and OB sections of professional associations, typically cover individual and group-level topics such as the following:

- Individual and group productivity and performance.
- Individual and group psychological processes in organizational settings, such as interpersonal perception and attribution, individual learning, cognitive and emotional development, and dynamics in organizations.
- Motivation to work, and its determinants and outcomes such as productivity and individual effectiveness.
- Incentives and reward systems, and their influences on organization members.
- Work-related attitudes and reactions such as satisfaction with work and the job, commitment to an organization, and individual psychological stress.
- Leadership processes and effectiveness, including characteristics and behaviors of effective leaders.

- Group dynamics and influences, including the effectiveness of work groups, their influences on members, and processes within them such as communication and decisionmaking.
- Interpersonal and group conflict and its management and resolution, and negotiation processes.
- Processes of organizational change, with emphasis on individual psychology and behavior in this process.
- Decisionmaking and communication, with emphasis on individual and psychological processes.

Organizational behavior texts and journals will often cover topics such as organizational structure and design, organizational effectiveness, and other topics referring to organizations as the unit of analysis. In the very imprecise and evolving definition of the field, however, these topics tend to receive less emphasis than in journals, texts, and professional activities devoted to organization theory.

In addition, the field constantly evolves to cover additional and newly developing topics. Currently, information technology (including computerization and communication technology) and its behavioral and work-related effects in organizations receive increasing attention. Also, workforce diversity (diversity of race and ethnicity, gender, age, national origin or culture, and life circumstance such as parenthood) receives increasing attention.

HAL G. RAINEY

BIBLIOGRAPHY

Dunnette, Marvin D., and Leaetta M. Hough, eds., 1990. *Handbook of Industrial and Organizational Psychology.* Palo Alto, CA: Consulting Psychologists Press.
Golembiewski, Robert T., ed., 1993. *Handbook of Organizational Behavior.* New York: Marcel Dekker.
Gordon, Judith R., 1993. *A Diagnostic Approach to Organizational Behavior.* Needham Heights, MA: Allyn and Bacon.
Hellriegel, Don, John W. Slocum, Jr., and Richard W. Woodman, 1995. *Organizational Behavior.* 7th ed. St. Paul, MN: West Publishing Company.
Lorsch, Jay W., ed., 1987. *Handbook of Organizational Behavior.* Englewood Cliffs, N.J.: Prentice-Hall.

ORGANIZATIONAL CHANGE.

The philosophies, processes, values, and assumptions which determine the response of organizations and institutions to changing conditions in their environment. Five traditional and emergent paradigms of organizational change are described: process, rational, pragmatic, chaos, and continuous organizational learning models.

Introduction

Providing a review of approaches to organizational change is a daunting task. An argument could be made that this concept includes most of the discipline's literature on organizational behavior and administrative theory. The au-

thor is tempted to refer the reader to two excellent anthologies by Ott (1996) and Shafritz and Ott (1996) and leave it at that. The complexity of the task is made worse by the explosion of literature in the last five years on fundamental organizational change—especially with respect to organizational learning, high performance organizations, quality management, participatory management, and values-based management.

This essay attempts to provide a historical and future-oriented framework for thinking about this literature. It examines five models or approaches to organizational and institutional change that capture several of the intellectual traditions within the field. To make this task more manageable, the primary focus of this article is on models which address organizational change from a policymaking perspective. That is, how do organizations and institutions change in order to improve their capacity for policymaking and decisionmaking? The essay does not address such topics as individual change, group dynamics, or the role of leadership, except when such concepts are central to the five broad models of change. Nor does it try to identify all contributors to a given model. Rather, the scope is primarily conceptual; while several major authors are identified, no attempt is made to give a comprehensive review of the literature.

Five models of organizational change are discussed: process, rational choice, pragmatic rationality, chaos, and continuous organizational learning approaches. These models are grounded in divergent literatures, ranging from the policy sciences to human relations and quantum mechanics. The first three represent the "traditional paradigms" of the last several decades; they have been the most commonly used approaches to understanding how organizations respond to changing policy environments. These three are based on assumptions of hierarchical organizations, control and stability. The last two models, chaos and organizational learning, are "emergent paradigms" in the sense that they are based on assumptions and perspectives which are fundamentally different. They reflect conditions of large and rapid change, unpredictable external environments, and an inability to understand or control organizations through linear approaches. They emphasize the need for rapid learning, adaptation, and survival. After each approach is described, the five models are compared according to their assumptions, primary contribution, how they characterize organizational functions, mechanisms for change, and weaknesses.

Traditional Models

Traditional approaches are built on the "machine model" (Morgan 1986), accepting bureaucratization, hierarchy, and routinization as dominant characteristics of the organization. However, they have very different views of what constitutes "good decisionmaking," the importance of information and analysis, and how organizations interact with their environment.

Process

The primary contribution of process models of change is their understanding of democratic participation and, especially, how organizations respond to multiple demands from competing stakeholders and interest groups. While process models are frequently criticized for their status quo bias, they nevertheless describe the forces driving compromise in our political system as well as the importance and positive contributions of "special interests." Process models emphasize pluralism as a primary determinant of organizational decisionmaking; the more pluralistic the society, the better the ability of the organization to develop compromises which keep groups active in and supportive of democracy. For these models, change is largely a reactive process, caused by the continuous interplay of demands made by interest groups on public institutions.

The most well-known process model is Lindblom's incrementalism (Lindblom 1959, 1968; Lindblom and Cohen 1979). Incrementalism is based on three assumptions: (1) social values are unknown, conflicting, and/or too complex to allow for precise or rational choices among competing alternatives; (2) knowledge of policy outcomes is so limited, in a predictive sense, that policymakers cannot rationally design the future; and (3) policymaking in a democratic society requires continuous compromise among competing interest groups in order to provide stability and to maintain their continuous political participation.

For Lindblom, good public policy is that for which agreement or consensus can be obtained. Incremental change, therefore, is both a descriptive and a normative model–it is the natural result of bargaining and compromise among competing interests, it is the best policy because it facilitates participation of interest groups in a pluralistic society, and it minimizes costs and risks associated with making decisions under conditions of uncertainty.

Lindblom has much to say about the relationship between interest groups and public organizations. The role of public organizations is to react to their environment–that is, the demands made by interest groups (Archibald 1970, p. 77). Lindblom accepts hierarchical organizational structure, including the downward flow of decisionmaking. However, organizations are also decentralized, in the sense that lower levels of the organization play the key role of collecting and transmitting information from the environment to the top of the organization (Archibald 1970, p. 76). Analysis (knowledge) is relatively unimportant to incrementalism, except as a mechanism to improve the capacity of interest groups to make demands on the organization.

Kash (1989) and Kash and Rycroft (1984) add substantially to our understanding of the value of interest groups, which they characterize as experts with a continuing stake in the outcomes of public decisions. Hence, they provide two important values, stability and continuous innovation and growth in their "policy subsystem." Stability results from the ability of special interests to manage routine change within established institutions and processes. They are able to do this over long periods of time because they possess specialized technical knowledge about what change is feasible; they agree on legitimate members of the policy community; and they typically have several norms which govern their interaction, such as agreement on objectives and institutional responsibility, a fear of outsiders, and agreement not to intervene in other policy arenas. Special interests have vested interests in the sense that they maintain control over a policy area as long as they are able to respond effectively to emerging issues, disruptions in their policy area, and environmental demands. The primary mechanism for doing this is expansion of the boundaries of their subsystem, usually through technological innovation. As long as special interests can create new options for problem solving, they maintain control of their policy area.

Stable policy systems are the norm in the U.S. political system, in large part because the complexity, fragmentation (see Weiss and Gruber 1984), and pluralism of our society dictate that change be controlled by substantive experts in specific problem areas. The exception is when a crisis or new problem emerges that goes beyond the management capacity of special interests. This requires the intervention of what Kash and Rycroft call the "presidential-congressional policy system," which controls policymaking until stability is restored and a new special interest system is established. When it is reestablished, decisionmaking is returned to the special interests and incremental change is the norm.

Rational Choice

The primary contributions of rational choice models are their outcome orientation and their recognition of the importance of information and analysis to improve decisionmaking and organizational change processes. Current attention to such tools as performance contracting and benchmarking are direct derivatives of the rational model and, indeed, are largely minor modifications of decisionmaking innovations of the 1960s and 1970s.

Many forms of rational choice models, such as systems analysis (see Schick 1969; Quade and Boucher 1968), systems budgeting, cost-benefit analysis, input-output analysis and rational-comprehensive decisionmaking (see Archibald 1970), have emerged in response to the weaknesses of process models. Three major weaknesses in process models are perceived by adherents to rational models: (1) a conservative bias towards the status quo; (2) an inability to manage new problems effectively, and (3) inattention to how policymaking affects the clients of the organization. Rationalists' fundamental questions about policy change are whether conditions are getting better or worse and what the organization can do to correct the deficiencies of society, especially those related to the disproportionate influence of elites.

The driving force behind rational choice models is not the need for accommodation in democratic processes, but the power of knowledge to direct planned change (Rivlin 1971). Hence, rationalists assume that social conditions are understandable and that effective policy options can be identified to respond to these conditions. The generalized sequence of activities in rational choice models is as follows:

- Recognize the existence of a problem;
- Identify the nature of the problem through investigation;
- Identify all policy alternatives for addressing the problem;
- Identify criteria for evaluating policy alternatives;
- Evaluate the advantages and disadvantages of alternatives;
- Make a policy decision based on the results of the analysis (choose the option which will maximize outcomes).

Rational choice models have several perspectives on public institutions and policy change. First, they favor centralized decisionmaking and hierarchical organizations, largely because this improves their ability to influence decisions and to establish clear goals and objectives for policy change. Second, in contrast to incrementalism, rationalists see public organizations as changing and determining their environment (e.g., interest groups) rather than reacting to it. Rationalists are much more interested in the effectiveness and efficiency of decisions than they are the process of decisionmaking; they see the give and take of political bargaining as counterproductive to achieving desired social end states. Finally, rationalists are usually very critical of bureaucracies because they represent narrow and parochial interests and because implementation processes often alter the decisions derived from rational analysis at the top of the organization (Archibald 1970, p. 75). Knowledge is the key mechanism in exerting control and directing change to overcome the inertia of special interests.

Pragmatic Rationality

The contribution of pragmatic models is to integrate the reality of process models with the idealism of pure rational approaches. Pragmatists understand well the limits of analysis within organizations (see Wildavsky 1984) and the role of noncognitive influences on decisionmaking (Lindblom

and Cohen 1979). Weaknesses of the pure rational choice model are obvious (see Hoos 1972). Rationalists tend to ignore what happens after a decision is made and reject the inevitability of social interaction in the policymaking process (Lindblom and Cohen 1979). They discount the important role of implementation and tend to depreciate internal organizational communication that links implementation to decisionmaking. The informational requirements for rational choice are often beyond the capacities or realities of decisionmaking. Rationalists assume that social conditions are knowable, that analysis will be precise, and that criteria for selecting policy options are unambiguous or that the single criterion of efficiency is preferable for determining the relative strengths of the alternatives.

In response to these weaknesses, pragmatic approaches have evolved which have two common characteristics: (1) they accept the rational idea that organizational decisionmaking can be improved by rational understanding; but (2) they identify several political and organizational realities which constrain and condition the application of rational analysis in policy processes and institutions. "Pragmatic rationality" includes satisficing, mixed scanning, and clinical decisionmaking.

"Satisficing" is attributable to Herbert Simon (1955), who is the most sympathetic of the pragmatists to pure rationality. Satisficing suggests that policymaking is the product of efforts to select alternatives that are "good enough," rather than those that maximize or optimize. Simon characterizes the political world as one of "bounded rationality"—mixtures of rational and nonrational behavior. For example, rationality is limited by the quality of information and by the psychology of decisionmaking, or different perceptions and values about the same factual base. In such a system, satisficing is simply the best that can be achieved.

Amitai Etzioni (1967) developed the concept of mixed scanning in an effort to combine rational and incremental aspects of decisionmaking. Mixed scanning begins with a generalized monitoring of the broad policy system in order to detect trouble spots, such as new demands from interest groups or social conditions which have been unnoticed. This allows distinctions to be made between routine and nonroutine problems. Phase two is an examination of the nonroutine problems—a detailed, comprehensive, and largely rational analysis of significant problems. In such cases, Etzioni recommends a cursory review of a broad range of options, followed by a detailed analysis of the most promising options. This is intended to allow for innovation without requiring comprehensive searches in every case. Decisions are also mixed. For example, several incremental decisions may follow a more fundamental or radical choice. Etzioni characterizes mixed scanning as descriptive in that fundamental change is more common than can be accounted for by the incremental method. It is also prescriptive in its criticism of incrementalism and in its emphasis on the importance of fundamental value-oriented policies.

The clinical model of decisionmaking has roots in medicine, psychiatry, planned change (Bennis, Benne, Chin, and Corey 1976) and human relations (Archibald 1970). This approach suggests that effective policy change requires two-way communication between policy elites and clients–those intended to benefit from public policies (Archibald 1970). The clinical model identifies two primary weaknesses in rational decisionmaking: (l) a failure to understand policy implementation and how to use information to facilitate implementation (Weiss and Gruber 1984); and (2) a failure to understand communication process within an organization and between clients and change agents. This approach represents an early version of quality management in the sense that client (or customer) needs drive organizational processes.

The clinical model, similar to process models, recognizes the messiness of the policy environment, including conflicting values, competing demands and imprecise understanding of future conditions. The clinical approach to dealing with this confusion is to focus on the clients or constituents by improving their capacity to function. Thus, the clinical model emphasizes the need to change the structure and processes of the client system (Archibald 1970, p. 80).

The clinical model views public organizations as being anticipatory. By developing ongoing relationships with customers, the organization not only understands how well current policies are working but more importantly their emerging needs. Communications and perceptions within an organization are critical for understanding problems and achieving effective change. For the clinical approach, internal acceptability of decisions is more important than political feasibility or economic rationality because of the need to improve the implementation process. These ideas are closely aligned with new paradigms in leadership theory which emphasize contextual and relational world views, organizational heterarchy, perspectual rather than objective rationality, and mutual rather than linear causality (Rogers 1988). In many respects, then, the clinical model bridges the traditional models with emergent concepts of chaos, learning, and continuous improvement (Ballard 1992).

Emergent Models

New concepts of organizational change began to emerge as the external environment began to change and as new "images" of organizational function and design gained legitimacy (Morgan 1986). Five specific factors directly challenged the relevancy of traditional models:

1. Crises which threatened organizational viability and survival, first in the private sector (Peters and Water-

man 1982) and increasingly in the public sector (Osborne and Gaebler 1992);

2. Technological changes, especially related to information and communication processes, which have empowered individual members and made control through information policy virtually impossible (Cleveland 1985);

3. Realization that effective organizations require more than having the best and the brightest at the top of the organization; rather, success often depends on the capability of the average worker (Walton 1986);

4. Emergent models of leadership, characterizing effective leaders not so much as decisionmakers but as energizers, coaches, enablers, and catalysts (Rogers 1988); and

5. Complexity and rapid change in the external environment; thus, organizational survival increasingly requires adaptability, flexibility, and sophisticated learning capacity for the individual, team, and organization.

Chaos

Chaos theory has intellectual roots in the work of March and Olsen, especially their characterization of the messiness and randomness of policy change. This model views change as a garbage can into which various problems and solutions are dumped by participants. The mix of choices is often random and can change very quickly, depending on the "labels attached to the alternative cans; what garbage is being produced at the moment, the mix of cans available, and the speed with which garbage is collected and removed from the scene" (March and Olsen 1979, p. 26).

Policy institutions are characterized as "organized anarchy" in which personal preferences are unclear, learning is by trial and error, and policy participants change frequently due to personnel turnover and task reassignment (Kingdon 1984, pp. 89–91). These factors are similar to the characteristics of more recent approaches to chaos theory (see below). However, other aspects of the March and Olsen approach suggest inadvertent happenstance in organizational response and thus are less consistent with chaos approaches. For example, March and Olsen say the system is biased against change and that decisions tend to emerge by default which is considerably different than chaos theory.

More recent approaches borrow theoretically from the physical sciences. Chaotic systems are characterized by:

1. Inherent unpredictability and nonlinear relationships; outcomes of decisions cannot be anticipated (Peters 1987);

2. Boundaries on all systems, even though events within the boundaries seem random; "chaos has a shape" (Wheatley 1992, p. 122);

3. Iteration, or the constant process of information feedback, is critical to system performance (Kiel 1994);

4. Iterations that can take the system in any direction—even very small changes can have very large effects (the butterfly effect); hence, small change cannot be neglected (Wheatley 1992, pp. 126–127); and

5. Challenge of understanding: because of the importance of small changes and iteration, the wholeness of the system cannot be understood by precise measurement of its minute parts; understanding the organization requires the study of shapes, patterns, and themes.

The importance of chaos theory became apparent in the 1980s as the private sector responded to global economic conditions which were changing all the ground rules. Peters's book in 1987, *Thriving on Chaos*, not only identified the factors which called for fundamental reengineering of private organizations, but also identified the components necessary for organizations to thrive: customer responsiveness, fast-paced innovation, empowerment of people, redesign of leadership, and the creation of holistic response systems. Peters successfully challenged such ideas as "bigger is better" and specialization of labor. In chaotic environments, the rate of change forces organizations to maximize flexibility rather than stability, to create redundancy in place of stability, and to train employees to perform multiple complex tasks rather than simple and routine ones.

While all of these ideas are important, perhaps the largest contribution of chaos models is in identifying the importance of transformational leadership styles. In chaotic environments, leaders simply cannot control an organization or its members. According to Wheatley (1992), orderliness comes from relationships among members who are empowered to respond to the complexity of their environments. Hence, the primary role of leadership is to provide the conditions necessary for individual and team empowerment. As Peters (1987) states: "The chief job of the leader, at all levels, is to oversee the dismantling of dysfunctional old truths and to prepare people and organizations to deal with—to love, to develop affection for—change per se, as innovations are proposed, tested, rejected, modified and adopted" (p. 486).

Continuous Organizational Learning

Once it becomes clear that old paradigms are ill-suited to the realities of rapidly changing environments, organizations can then devote their energies to continuous learning. These models are logical extensions of chaos models, even if they do not necessarily recognize all five characteristics of the chaos approach. These approaches are closely linked to quality management, high performance organizations, and participatory management approaches. The primary contribution of the continuous organizational learning models is their emphasis on the internal change mechanisms necessary for rapid response and adaptability. These internal mechanisms include transformational leadership, developing group values, team decisionmaking and team competencies, and redesigned evaluation and reward systems. The purpose of these mechanisms is to create "self-organizing" organizations (Rogers and Ballard 1994).

Again, this approach to organizational change has intellectual roots in classic literature. In particular, Argyris and Shön (1974, 1978) have made significant contributions to organizational learning as more than individual learning. Of particular consequence is their explication of "double-loop" learning. This contribution is also clear in Argyris's most recent book (1993), *Knowledge for Action: A Guide to Overcoming Barriers to Organizational Change*. Single-loop learning is a behavioral change in response to a particular problem (ad hoc problem solving). Of much more consequence is double-loop learning, or value changes which direct behavioral changes. Morgan (1986) has also contributed to the concept of double-loop learning, which he characterizes as a process by which organization members reflect on how well they have achieved their purposes and also whether those purposes themselves remain relevant and appropriate. It requires of managers and staff alike an "ability to remain open to changes in the environment and an ability to challenge operating assumptions in a most fundamental way (p. 91)."

A significant difference between continuous learning approaches and traditional models is the role of values in helping to direct organizational change. As expressed in vision statements (Block 1987) or aspirations statements (Rogers and Ballard 1994), values help to provide orderliness in organizations that have been destructured. As organizational members are able to identify shared values, they develop congruent images of what the organization is about and where it is headed. Values then become internal controls for member behavior. Rather than the manager enforcing rules, staff monitor their own behavior based on their shared values (Rogers and Ballard 1994).

As expressed by Howard (1990): "In a more volatile and dynamic business environment, the controls have to be conceptual. They can't be human anymore . . . values provide a common language for aligning a company's leadership and its people" (p. 134).

Another important contribution of the continuous learning approach is the emphasis on team learning as well as on the capacity of each individual. While core competencies for each individual are a necessary component (Senge 1990), team capacity must also be emphasized. Empowered teams require effective communication skills, group and interpersonal skills, collaborative approaches, and an ability to understand the big picture about the purposes of the organization and to monitor the environment in light of those purposes (Rogers and Ballard 1994).

According to Giddens (1990), effective team decisionmaking requires such competencies as:

- Group leadership/membership skills: Each employee must understand both the process and task in accomplishing work. The ability to verbalize and to participate in establishing group norms is essential;
- Group productivity and product/service excellence: Members must know what a good job is and how to measure success;
- The ability to link self and group to the system: Empowered employees can recognize that individual actions affect organizational performance;
- Interdependence, linkages, and collaboration: Empowered employees encourage networking and look for "win-win" opportunities; and
- Interpersonal competency: Including mature and open interaction, ability to listen and reflect, to give and receive feedback, to confront and disagree, and to support and encourage.

The result of building such internal learning mechanisms is self-organizing organizations. Such organizations place primary value in people as the basis of organizational functioning and success. This contrasts sharply with conventional organizations, which assume people must be controlled and managed in order to perform according to minimum standards. For conventional organizations, it is assumed that failure results from bad people. For self-organizing organizations, people are the source of growth, learning, environmental responsiveness, and adaptability.

Comparison and Summary

Table I compares and summarizes several key points about each model of organizational change. Each approach makes important, and largely separate, contributions to our understanding of change. Process models challenge the assumption that large (comprehensive) change is necessarily a value; they emphasize, instead, that bargaining and

TABLE I. A COMPARISON OF APPROACHES TO ORGANIZATIONAL CHANGE

CHARACTERISTIC	TRADITIONAL MODELS			EMERGENT MODELS	
	Process	Rational	Pragmatic	Chaos	Continuous Learning
Key Assumption	Society is pluralistic Interest groups have equal capacity to participate	Society is stable Hierarchical organizations are a given No limits on information capabilities	Hierarchical organizations are a given Environment of the organization is predictable	Environment of the organization is not predictable Change is rapid	Change is rapid No preferable organizational designs exist Organizations reengineer continuously
Primary Contribution	Value of compromise Interest groups provide stability	Focus on outcomes (performance-based) Importance of information in decisionmaking	Focus on the importance of implementation Understand the limits of analysis Anticipate the need for destructured organizations (clinical)	Impact of unpredictable environment on organizational design Specialization of labor is an anachronism Significance of transformational leadership	Emphasis on internal change mechanisms (values, teams, etc.) People are the key to effectiveness
Primary Organizational Function	Respond to its environment; change driven externally; the organization must limit the degree of change	Improve the welfare of clients; change determined internally	Interact with its client group; change is a mutually adaptive process	Survival; change is a rapid and continuous response to a range of factors	Learn how to learn; the organization must be flexible and adaptable

(Continued)

TABLE I. (Continued)

Characteristic	Traditional Models			Emergent Models	
	Process	Rational	Pragmatic	Chaos	Continuous Learning
Mechanisms for Change	Continuous negotiation and the selection of demand of interest group Empowering interest groups as solution to unequal power distribution	Information and analysis; rational preferable policy instruments Focus of efficiency to resolve competing demands	Careful balancing of political and environment capabilities Understanding the needs of clients/customers Trial and error	Understanding patterns and themes in the environment Leadership which is empowering Customer responsiveness Creating new organizational designs and structures	Values of organizational members Increasing team competencies Creating self-organizing organizations Changing organizational cultures
Weakness	Status quo bias Organizations are only reactive Minimizes the importance of outcomes and change; unresponsive to new conditions	Difficulty in dealing with uncertainty; looks for deterministic outcomes Ignores critical role of implementation in determining organizational success Underestimates noncognitive factors in the change process	Not suitable for dealing with crises Difficulty in responding to multiple customers Requires stable environments and business-as-usual conditions	Situations with high degrees of ambiguity cannot be tolerated Traditional leaders motivated by power Difficult to determine organizational success	Organizations are only as good as weakest member Threatening to members who need stability or routinization Requires investments in competency development

compromise are inherent in the process and, more importantly, help provide the stability necessary not only to maintain the system but also to solve problems within the boundaries of existing problems, processes, and institutions. Process models are less concerned with change than with the responsiveness of the organization to its environment and especially to client groups.

Rational models have one important similarity with emergent models; they appreciate the capacity of public institutions for purposeful change. However, they approach change in fundamentally different ways. The rational approach emphasizes information and analysis within a highly centralized and controlled organizational environment—presumably necessary to identify the optimal policy choice and ensure the policy is adopted throughout the organization. In contrast, emergent models do not propose to be the driving force behind change in their environments. Rather these models see environmental condi-

tions as forcing the public organization to structure itself differently in order to survive. Effectiveness in dealing with rapidly changing conditions and perpetual uncertainty cause the public organization to destructure, restructure, or reengineer.

In some ways, the clinical approach was a precursor to emergent models. The primary contribution of the clinical model is its understanding of client/customer relationships. The customer-responsiveness component of total quality management and other emergent models is a direct derivative of the clinical model. The clinical model also anticipated the destructuring of the hierarchical organization as both necessary, to develop customer relationships, and appropriate, as the capabilities of members at all levels of the organization became apparent.

In spite of these linkages between traditional and emergent models of change, it is also quite apparent that they represent two different paradigms based on different assumptions, different conditions within the larger society and culture, and therefore, they present very different pictures of how organizations should operate. Chaos and learning models emphasize holistic, systemic change within the organization. Hence, participatory organizations, team decisionmaking, investment in the competencies of organizational members, and transformational leadership are key characteristics of the organization under these models. Further, chaos and organizational learning paradigms clearly suggest that none of these innovations are sufficient by themselves. A holistic philosophy of continuous learning and adaption is called for by the emergent models.

Which of the two paradigms has the largest influence on the design and behavior of the public organization in the mid-1990s and beyond? Two answers are in order. First, traditional models still dominate the public sector. In part this is because all paradigm shifts are threatening; while it is frequently easy to identify the weaknesses of the old paradigm, we hesitate to adopt the new until we are certain either that it will be an improvement or that we have no realistic choice. Indeed, the latter condition had much to do with adoption of emergent models in the private sector (Peters 1987). One is reminded of the Fosbury Flop, perhaps the most radical innovation ever introduced into high-jumping. Today, of course, all world class high jumpers use the technique, or slight modifications of it, developed by Dick Fosbury in the 1960s. Even though it added 10 inches to the world record, it was strenuously resisted for 6 years by the entire U.S. Olympic institutional structure.

The second answer is that many indicators suggest that the public sector is now in a position similar to that of many businesses in the 1970s; the external environment has changed radically and leaders now realize that our institutions and organizations must respond to new realities. Among the conditions driving the reexamination are public cynicism, continuing fiscal crises, the political upheaval of the 1994 elections, and the rapid growth of intellectual attention devoted to reinventing, reengineering, and restructuring. The combination of these factors strongly suggest that emergent models will be increasingly significant to the process of change in the public organization.

STEVEN BALLARD

BIBLIOGRAPHY

Archibald, K. A., 1970. "Three Views of the Expert's Role in Policymaking: Systems Analysis, Incrementalism, and the Clinical Approach." *Policy Sciences* 1 (1) (Spring) 73–86.

Argyris, Chris, 1993. *Knowledge for Action: A Guide to Overcoming Barriers to Organizational Change.* San Francisco: Jossey-Bass.

Argyris, Chris and D. A. Schön, 1974. *Theory in Practice.* San Francisco: Jossey-Bass.

———, 1978. *Organizational Learning.* Reading, MA: Addison-Wesley.

Ballard, Steven, 1992. "High Performance Organizations: Designing Change in the Public Sector." *Policy Papers* 92-01. Orono, ME: Margaret Chase Smith Center for Public Policy.

Bennis, Warren G., Kenneth D. Benne, Robert Chin, and Kenneth E. Corey, 1976. *The Planning of Change.* 3d ed. New York: Holt, Rinehart and Winston.

Block, Peter, 1987. *The Empowered Manager: Positive Political Skills at Work.* San Francisco: Jossey-Bass.

Cleveland, Harlan, 1985. "The Twilight of Hierarchy: Speculations on the Global Information Society." *Public Administration Review* 20 (January-February) 185–195.

Etzioni, Amitai, 1967. "Mixed Scanning: A Third Approach to Decision Making." *Public Administration Review* 27 (6) (December) 385–392.

Giddens, P., 1990. *Recommendations for Basic Skills Required for Empowerment.* Unpublished report to the Secretary's Commission on Achieving Necessary Skills, U.S. Department of Labor.

Howard, R., 1990. "Values Make the Company: An Interview with Robert Haas." *Harvard Business Review* 68 (5):133–144.

Hoos, Ida, 1972. *Systems Analysis in Public Policy: A Critique.* Berkeley: University of California Press.

Kash, Don E., 1989. *Perpetual Innovation: The New World of Competition.* New York: Basic Books, Inc.

Kash, Don E. and Robert Rycroft, 1984. *U.S. Energy Policy: Crisis and Complacency.* Norman, OK: University of Oklahoma Press.

Kiel, L. Douglas, 1994. "Current Thinking About Chaos Theory." *PA Times* 17 (11) (November 1) 4, 9.

Kingdon, John W., 1984. *Agendas, Alternatives, and Public Policies.* Boston: Little Brown.

Lindblom, Charles E., 1968. *The Policymaking Process.* Englewood Cliffs, NJ: Prentice-Hall.

———, 1959. "The Science of Muddling Through." *Public Administration Review* 19 (Spring) 79–88.

Lindblom, Charles E. and David K. Cohen, 1979. *Usable Knowledge: Social Science and Social Problem-Solving.* New Haven: Yale University Press.

March, James and Johan Olsen, eds., 1979. *Ambiguity and Choice in Organizations.* Bergen, Norway: Universitetsforlaget.

Morgan, Gareth, 1986. *Images of Organization.* Beverly Hills, CA: Sage.

Osborne, David and Ted Gaebler, 1992. *Reinventing Government: How the Entrepreneurial Spirit Is Transforming the Public Sector.* Reading, MA: Addison-Wesley.

Ott, J. Steven, ed., 1996. *Classic Readings in Organizational Behavior.* (2nd. ed). Ft. Worth, TX: Harcourt Brace.

Peters, Tom, 1987. *Thriving on Chaos: Handbook for a Management Revolution.* New York: Harper and Row.

Peters, Tom and R. H. Waterman, 1982. *In Search of Excellence.* New York: HarperCollins.

Quade, E. S. and W. I. Boucher, 1968. *Systems Analysis and Policy Planning.* New York: American Elsevier Publishing.

Rivlin, Alice M., 1971. *Systematic Thinking for Social Action.* Washington, D.C.: The Brookings Institution.

Rogers, Judy L., 1988. "New Paradigm Leadership: Integrating the Female Ethos." *Journal of NAWDAC* 51 (9): 1–8.

Rogers, Judy L. and Steven Ballard, 1994. "Aspirational Management: Building Effective Organizations Through Shared Values." *NASPA Journal* 31 (4):215–231.

Schick, Allen, 1969. "Systems Politics and Systems Budgeting." *Public Administration Review* 29(2) (March-April) 137–151.

Shafritz, Jay M. and J. Steven Ott, eds., 1996. *Classics of Organizational Theory.*(4th ed). Ft. Worth, TX: Harcourt Brace.

Senge, Peter M., 1990. *The Fifth Discipline: The Art and Practice of the Learning Organization.* New York: Doubleday.

Simon, Herbert A., 1955. "A Behavioral Model of Rational Choice." *Quarterly Journal of Economics* 69 (February) 99–118.

Walton, Mary, 1986. *Deming Management at Work.* New York: Harper and Row.

Weiss, Janet and Judith E. Gruber, 1984. "Using Knowledge for Control in Fragmented Policy Arenas." *Journal of Policy Analysis and Management* 3 (2) (Winter) 225–247.

Wheatley, Margaret, 1992. *Leadership and the New Science.* San Francisco: Berrett-Koehler.

Wildavsky, Aaron, 1984. *The Politics of the Budgetary Process.* 4th ed. Boston: Little, Brown.

ORGANIZATIONAL CULTURE.

A concept in or an approach to the study of organizations focusing on elements thought to be overlooked by the more prevalent functional and rational approaches such as organizational design, human relations, systems, and organizational politics. The study may focus on organizational artifacts, such as stories, symbols, ceremonies, rituals, myths, sagas, tales, heroes, taboos, jargon, slang, metaphors, gestures, signs, humor, gossip, rumor, and proverbs, and/or on the values, beliefs, and feelings that are seen as underlying such artifacts; and/or on the context-specific meanings made by members of the organization and other organizationally relevant publics, as well as researchers' interpretations of those meanings. Which of these is seen as defining organizational culture depends on the way "culture" is understood. Organizational culture studies developed largely in the 1980s, although there are earlier works that can be included under this heading. Simultaneous developments in Europe and the U.S. largely followed distinct themes.

Origins, Definitions, and Early History

Culture as a concept has historically been the concern of anthropologists, who, however, have developed no consensus on its definition. Various schools of thought and methodologies within anthropology have influenced definitions and treatments of organizational culture. For example, anthropologists Kroeber and Kluckhohn (1952) developed a functionalist perspective, while Levi-Strauss (1964) pursued a structural approach. Their influences and others from anthropology can be seen in the five perspectives on organizational culture presented in Smircich (1983). Two of the perspectives she discusses construe culture as a variable: one examines differences between organizations across national cultures (with culture as an independent variable), while the other looks at culture as a dependent variable within particular organizations (the corporate culture approach). The remaining three approaches treat "culture" metaphorically, as a way of seeing organizations. These include a symbolic approach; a clinical, psychodynamic approach; and a cognitive approach. This early framework still accurately describes the range of current approaches to organizational cultures.

The notion of culture in an organizational context goes back at least as far as a 1951 study by Elliott Jaques. The English sociologist Barry A. Turner made the first extensive use of the concept of culture in studying organizations in 1971. Within public administration, some of the early work of the institutionalist school has much in common with later work in organizational culture. Selznick (1949) and Kaufman (1960) are two examples.

The Recent Development of Organizational Culture

Current work in organizational culture developed rapidly at the end of the 1970s and early 1980s. In the later 1970s, the Organizational Symbolism Network, a group of primarily U.S. academics, was formed. In the early 1980s in Europe, the Standing Conference on Organizational Symbolism (SCOS) was started (a part of EGOS, the European Group on Organization Studies, the counterpart of the U.S. Academy of Management). A 1979 conference at the University of Illinois led to the publication of a collection of essays, edited by Louis A. Pondy and others (1983). Beginning in 1981, several iterations of a summer conference on "Interpretive Approaches to the Study of Organizations" were held through the auspices of the Communications Department at the University of Utah. In 1983, Michael Owen Jones and others organized a conference entitled "Myth, Symbols and Folklore: Expanding the Analysis of Organizations" at the University of California-Los Angeles. This was followed by another conference in 1984, "Organizational Culture and the Meaning of Life in the Workplace." Held at the University of British Columbia in Canada, it was the first institutional naming of the field as organizational culture (the essays are collected in Frost *et al.* 1985). Two other conferences were also held in 1984: "Corporate Culture: From the Native's Point of View," in California, and "Managing Corporate Cultures" at the University of Pittsburgh. Others followed. Five influential academic journals devoted entire issues to the topic of organizational culture. The first was the *Administrative Science Quarterly* in Fall 1983. It was followed by the *Journal of Management* and *Organizational Dynamics* in Spring and Fall 1984, respectively, and the *Journal of Management Studies* and *Organization Studies,* two European journals, in 1986.

This early outpouring of work developed into two fairly distinct schools of thought. One evolved out of comparisons between increasingly more successful Japanese firms and lagging U.S. productivity at the time. Largely developed in the U.S., it came to be known as the "corporate culture" school. Today, its scholars are often searching for quantitative measures of culture, and many European and other non-U.S. scholars are active in this stream.

The second school of thought evolved out of a more diffuse dissatisfaction with traditional theories of organization and management, on the one hand by those taking qualitative, field-based methodological approaches to studying organizations, on the other hand by those with concerns rooted in the philosophy of science (including social science), which were receiving increasing attention in a wide variety of disciplines (including cultural anthropology, social history, literary criticism, qualitative sociology). This latter approach, in particular, has been more extensively developed by European scholars and professional associations. Largely under the influence of their work, it has come to be known as the "organizational symbolism" school.

Between them has emerged a third camp, the more general "organizational culture" school, that seeks to develop generalizable typologies of cultures informed by context-specific data. These three streams will be examined in turn.

Corporate Culture

Much of the attention, both popular and academic, to organizational culture studies dates to the publication of several popular books in the early 1980s. Two books concerning Japanese management styles are often included in this historical reckoning: Ouchi's *Theory Z* (1981) and Peters and Waterman's *In Search of Excellence* (1982). But it was Deal and Kennedy's *Corporate Cultures* (1982) that gave the field one of its names and established a framework for debate. The authors identified various rituals, symbols, and heroes of contemporary corporate American life and prescribed their adoption by other companies wishing to be "successful." This book and other work in the same vein seem to treat culture almost as if it were souvenirs for corporate tourists: collections of departmental celebrations, retirement mementos, office costumes, phrasebook terminologies, and the like, which were claimed to be unique to the culture in which they were found. These authors argued that organizational leaders and managers could develop successful companies and agencies by creating, deploying, and managing these cultural artifacts.

Among other things, the discovery that identical stories, appeared in different organizations led to a broadening of this view of culture. It led, for example, to a new line of inquiry exploring whether "industries" could be said to have unique cultures. An interesting variant of this re-search seeks to determine whether a geographic region further distinguishes among organizations within a single industry: for example, are Silicon Valley (California) electronics firms different culturally from Route 128 (Massachusetts) electronics firms (Weiss and Delbecq 1987)?

The question of regional influence has its parallel in studies that seek to determine the intersections of national cultural effects and organizational cultural effects, of which Geert Hofstede, the Dutch organizational scholar, has been the central figure. His research in multinational corporations (MNCs) claims that even within a single MNC, employees in different national offices reflect national culture more than corporate culture (e.g., Hofstede 1984). Others, however, have been unable to replicate Hofstede's research, suggesting that he was also finding the effects of a particular profession's culture (in this case, engineers).

Organizational Culture

Edgar A. Schein, the MIT organizational psychologist, has produced the best known writing within this stream. The ideas that first appeared in a number of working papers and journal articles are developed in *Organizational Culture and Leadership,* first published in 1985 and expanded and revised in a second edition in 1992. Schein's analysis was then, and the second edition still is, the most through conceptual treatment of the subject, albeit from the standpoint of a social psychologist interested in client-driven research (what he calls a "clinical" perspective), as distinct from research driven by the researcher's interests. His treatment reflects the functionalist approach to culture developed by Kluckhohn alongside Schein's own open systems approach, developed in his earlier work in organizational psychology. The 1992 edition retains the chapter entitled "Ethical Problems in Studying Organizational Cultures" (chapter 10), still the best (and perhaps only) discussion of what it means from the client's point of view to have a consultant/researcher make public that which is organizationally private (if not tacit) knowledge.

Schein begins by defining organizational culture, giving an archeology of levels of culture from the more visible "artifacts" to the "espoused values" that underlie them (the strategies, goals, philosophies) to the more deeply buried "basic underlying assumptions," the "unconscious, taken-for-granted beliefs, perceptions, thoughts, and feelings" that are the "ultimate source of values and action" (1992, p. 17). When it first appeared, Schein's theoretical argument raised several of the issues that still mark debate in the field today. As his title indicates, he considers organizational leaders to be the active creators of organizational cultures, a position logical–as he himself has remarked–in the context of his own access as a consultant to top organizational levels.

This leader-focused approach was adopted by many scholars. It raised a key conceptual question: are organizational cultures established *only* by leaders at the top of the organization? A second conceptual issue derives from this top-down view: whether there is a one-to-one relationship between organizational boundaries and culture—one organization, one unitary culture. There is no room in this view for subcultures or countercultures. Both of these assumptions, shared by the corporate culture school, have been challenged by other researchers who have studied culture on the shop floor, among employees and midlevel managers, and in occupational and professional subcultures. Most organizational culture theorists (e.g., Sackmann 1991; Trice and Beyer 1993) now accept that any organization may contain multiple cultures or subcultures, not all of them created by organizational leaders or managers.

These later studies move closer to a phenomenological point of view, seeing artifacts as the expressions of less visible values, beliefs, feelings, meanings. Yet the approach is still a positivist view that sees the reality of culture *in* the organization, rather than in the researcher's *view* of the organization. It is an approach that seeks to discover universally applicable rules.

Organizational Symbolism and Cultural Studies of Organizations

Some organizational culture scholars have followed the "interpretive turn" made by many in reaction against the perceived limitations of positivist science. This represents an ontological shift to a view that organizational cultures are perceived, not factual, realities. More recently, others have made a "narrative turn" to focus on language and rhetorical issues (see, e.g., Czarniawska-Joerges 1997; Golden-Biddle and Locke 1993; Hatch 1996; O'Connor 1995; Smircich 1995; Van Maanen 1995; White 1992; Yanow 1995). This includes attention to forms of (re)presentation of field work, parallel to developments in anthropology that explore how the writing up of field notes can, itself, create (a view of) culture.

Those following these paths make a radical departure from earlier treatments of the concept of culture. Here, integral questions of reality, knowledge, and methodology are being worked out. If culture is understood to be "real," then it can be studied and known through objective fact-gathering means such as those specified by positivism and the scientific method, and researchers can generate "laws" or principles about organizational culture that are generalizable across organizations. But an interpretive position argues that this is not the case: that culture, rather than being "real," is a way of seeing organizations that entails methodological implications as well. Cultural analyses of organizations generate situation-specific knowledge that reflects organizational actors' understandings of their situations and researchers' interpretations of those understandings as well as of their own experiences. Both the subject of study and the researcher are understood to be situated in specific contexts. Generalizable typologies are not possible, in this view.

Initial arguments about the distinctions between positivist and interpretive theories cast them as differences between quantitative and qualitative methods. But that is a misleading distinction: researchers who conduct open-ended interviews or who act as participant observers also quantify when it is necessary. Neither quantitative nor qualitative methods inherently require the researcher to turn away from the ontological and epistemological assumptions of positivist science.

The interpretive turn in organizational culture has rested, in part, on the question of unitary versus multiple cultures. Seeing organizations from the perspective of agency executives implied that there was only one legitimate view of each organization's culture—and that culture was singular. When researchers looked at the organization from other positions—from the shop floor, for example, or from inside various departments—cultural singularity disappeared in the face of the meanings made of organizational actions by employees in the situation. The interpretive turn places the problem of *meaning* at the center of research: meanings made by organizational actors, as well as meanings made by researchers who interpret actors' meanings.

Seeing organizational cultures from different vantage points introduced a world of multiple realities. Organizational reality was no longer seen to exist external to the person perceiving that reality, whether that person is an employee or a researcher. Knowledge came to be seen as a creation by subjects in a situation; it is subjective knowledge (in the sense that it pertains to the subject), not objective (externally derived) knowledge. Following on or recreating the thinking of European philosophers (Schutz and phenomenology, Ricoeur and hermeneutics) and their U.S. counterparts (Garfinkel and ethnomethodology, Goffman and Mead and symbolic interactionism), theorists working from this view see a representational relationship between cultural beliefs, values, and feelings and the artifacts that express them. This view has led them to focus on symbolic objects, language, and acts as representations or embodiments of meanings. This school of thought is often referred to as "organizational symbolism."

Much of this work has been done by European and other non-U.S. researchers, particularly within the Standing Conference on Organisational Symbolism (SCOS) formed over a decade ago. Two edited collections of SCOS conference papers, Gagliardi (1990) and Turner (1990), are noteworthy both in their symbolic-interpretive approach to the subject and in their inclusion of public agencies as subjects of study (the Danish Ministry of Domestic Affairs, NASA's Space Shuttle, the Luneberg, Germany, municipal saltworks, the Washington State Ferry System, an English prison, and so forth).

In the U.S. most of the work from a symbolic perspective has appeared in academic journals. One exception is Ott (1989), who places symbolism at the heart of what culture is all about, while building on Schein's three-part cultural structure. Another is the work of Ingersoll and Adams (1992), an ethnography of the takeover of the Washington State Ferry System by the state's Department of Transportation (DOT). Theirs is a view of culture as cognition, including its tacit aspects, taking a cultural approach to the study of the ferry system—one that focuses on meanings made by actors in the situation—rather than seeing the organization's culture as a set of objects or rituals. In a related vein, Yanow (1996) explores ways in which the organizational metaphors, buildings, and acts of a public agency, the Israel Corporation of Community Centers, were symbolic representations of policy and organizational meanings, thereby communicating those meanings, even as tacit knowledge, to multiple audiences or "readers." Kunda (1992) may also be considered a cultural approach. Finding that managerial uses of corporate culture concepts have produced feelings of alienation among middle- and lower-level employees, without necessarily enabling greater control over them, Kunda addresses the moral responsibility of culture researchers providing managers with tools to alter workers' realities. The question of meanings made by the actors in the organizational situation is central to these analyses.

Turning to culture as an approach, rather than a variable to be studied, situates methodological concerns within their related questions of knowledge and reality. This links cultural studies of organizations to other recent theoretical developments: feminist, critical, literary, and postmodern theoretical approaches. Feminist and critical theorists (e.g., Minow 1990) have called attention to the fact that much of what is presented as neutral and universal knowledge is actually based on an assumed norm. (For feminist theorists, that norm has been seen typically as male; for critical theorists, the norm is seen to embody a power-based status, resting typically on class and/or race and/or, lately, gender.) These critiques call attention to the context of the researcher producing knowledge, as well as to the subject of knowledge. In narrative, rhetorical, and literary critical theories, this point appears in analyses of writing that argue that the text is as much a representation of the author as a reflection of the subject (see, e.g., Golden-Biddle and Locke 1993; Van Maanen 1988). In anthropology, for example, the language used by ethnographers convinces (or fails to convince) the reader that the ethnographer was truly present in and conversant with the

place that is being presented. Such analyses invoke methods of literary criticism to analyze representations of culture as narratives that use rhetorical tools to persuade the reader of the veracity of the account. By extension, organizational practices may also be "read" as "texts" intended to convince multiple audiences ("readers"), who may read those texts quite differently. To judge from recent scholarly work in economics, policy analysis, and other fields, this is an important new direction that cultural analyses of organizational theories and practices are now taking.

DVORA YANOW AND
GUY B. ADAMS

BIBLIOGRAPHY

Czarniawska-Joerges, Barbara, 1997. *Narrating the Organization.* Chicago: University of Chicago Press.

Deal, Terrence E. and Allen A. Kennedy, 1982. *Corporate Cultures.* Reading, MA: Addison-Wesley.

Frost, Peter J., Larry F. Moore, Meryl Reis Louis, Craig C. Lundberg, and Joanne Martin, 1985. *Organizational Culture.* Newbury Park, CA: Sage.

Gagliardi, Pasquale, ed., 1990. *Symbols and Artifacts.* New York: Walter de Gruyter.

Golden-Biddle, Karen and Karen Locke, 1993. "Appealing Work: An Investigation in How Ethnographic Texts Convince." *Organization Science* 4:4 (November).

Hatch, Mary Jo, 1996. "The Role of the Researcher: An Analysis of Narrative Position in Organizational Theory." *Journal of Management Inquiry* vol. 5, no. 4: 359–374.

Hofstede, Geert, 1984. *Culture's Consequences.* Abridged edition. London: Sage.

Ingersoll, Virginia Hill and Guy B. Adams, 1992. *The Tacit Organization.* Greenwich, CT: JAI Press.

Jaques, Elliott, 1951. *The Changing Culture of a Factory.* London: Tavistock.

Kaufman, Herbert, 1960. *The Forest Ranger.* Baltimore: Johns Hopkins Press.

Kroeber, Clyde and Theodore Kluckhohn, 1952. *Culture: A Critical Review of Concepts and Definitions.* Cambridge, MA: Harvard University Press.

Kunda, Gideon, 1992. *Engineering Culture.* Philadelphia: Temple University Press.

Levi-Strauss, Claude, 1964. *Structural Anthropology.* New York: Basic Books.

Minow, Martha, 1990. *Making All the Difference.* Ithaca, NY: Cornell University Press.

O'Connor, Ellen, 1995. "Paradoxes of Participation: A Literary Analysis of Case Studies on Employee Involvement." *Organization Studies* 15:2.

O'Connor, Ellen, with Mary Jo Hatch, Hayden White, and Mayer Zald, 1995. "Undisciplining Organizational Studies: A Conversation Across Domains, Methods, and Beliefs." *Journal of Management Inquiry* 4:2, 119–136.

Ott, J. Steven, 1989. *The Organizational Culture Perspective.* Pacific Grove, CA: Brooks/Cole.

Ouchi, William, 1981. *Theory Z.* Reading, MA: Addison-Wesley.

Peters, Thomas J. and Robert H. Waterman, 1982. *In Search of Excellence.* New York: Harper and Row.

Pondy, Louis A., Peter N. Frost, Gareth Morgan, and Thomas C. Dandridge eds., 1983. *Organizational Symbolism.* Greenwich, CT: JAI Press.

Sackmann, Sonja A., 1991. *Cultural Knowledge in Organizations: Exploring the Collective Mind.* Newbury Park, CA: Sage.

Schein, Edgar H., 1985. *Organizational Culture and Leadership.* San Francisco: Jossey-Bass.

———, 1992. *Organizational Culture and Leadership*, 2d ed. San Francisco: Jossey-Bass.

Selznick, Philip, 1949. *TVA and the Grass Roots.* New York: Harper and Row.

Smircich, Linda, 1983. "Concepts of Culture and Organizational Analysis." *Administrative Science Quarterly* 28:3, 339–358.

———, 1995. "Writing Organizational Tales: Reflections on Three Books on Organizational Culture." *Organization Science* 6:2, 232–237.

Trice, Harrison M. and Janice M. Beyer, 1993. *The Cultures of Work Organizations.* Englewood Cliffs, NJ: Prentice-Hall.

Turner, Barry A., 1971. *Exploring the Industrial Subculture.* London: Herder and Herder.

———, ed., 1990. *Organizational Symbolism.* New York: Walter de Gruyter.

Van Maanen, John, 1988. *Tales of the Field.* Chicago: University of Chicago Press.

———, 1995. "Style as Theory." *Organization Science* 6:1.

Weiss, Joseph and Andre Delbecq, 1987. "High-technology Cultures and Management." *Group and Organization Studies* 12, 39-54.

White, Jay D., 1992. "Taking Language Seriously: Toward a Narrative Theory of Knowledge for Administrative Research." *American Review of Public Administration* 22:2 (June).

Yanow, Dvora, 1995. "Writing Organizational Tales: Four Authors and Their Stories About Culture." *Organization Science* 6:2, 225–226.

———, 1996. *How Does a Policy Mean? Interpreting Policy and Organizational Actions.* Washington, D.C.: Georgetown University Press.

ORGANIZATIONAL LEARNING.

A process of detecting and correcting errors in an organization's decisionmaking process or modifying organizational goals in response to various changes in the external environment; the methods an organization uses to improve its survival potential by increasing its readiness to cope with new changes and opportunities.

Organizational learning has gained increasing attention among administrative theorists as an important approach to such concepts as public policy, managerial decisionmaking, strategic planning, marketing strategies, organizational change, and leadership, to mention just a few. However, like any new theoretical approach its intellectual (and practical) viability depends, somewhat, upon how it is defined and conceptualized (see Bennis & Nanus 1985; Ventriss and Luke 1988). Unfortunately, there has not emerged, as of yet, any accepted consensus of what organizational learning actually means. More important, it has been argued that because the concept of learning first originated in the fields of education and individual psychology, many administrative theorists have ignored the salient issue of reification; that is, "granting the concept of organization anthropomorphic [human] characteristics if

does not possess. The question thus emerges as to whether it is possible for organizations to learn, except in a purely metamorphical or figurative sense" (Bedeian 1986, p. 194).

Notwithstanding the ambiguity of learning as applied to organizations and the paucity of empirical studies dealing with organizational learning, it still is regarded–to use Donald Schön's (1983) term–as an idea in good currency. According to Schön, organizational learning raises some central issues of organizational life. "Is our learning capacity adequate to the challenges that confront us? How can we learn to cope with change? What have we learned from past experiences?" (pp. 115–127). As critical as these questions seem to be, there is still a conceptual confusion concerning learning due to its varied meaning. Generally speaking, there are three broad categories of organizational learning.

The first approach is called "assumption sharing" (Shrivastava 1983). This approach is epitomized by the works of Chris Argyris and Donald Schön (1978) who make a distinction between single-loop and double-loop learning. The latter concept focuses on the detection and correction of error by critically questioning the underlying organizational culture and behavioral norms that are contributing to the original organizational dysfunction. The former term, on the other hand, detects and corrects error through an organizational adjustment that does not question the organizational norms or internal governing variables through which these goals are pursued. They contend that while single-loop learning is the most predominant mode of learning in organizations, double-loop learning (which they favor) examines the tacit values that guide administrative action.

The second broad category is illustrated by Richard Cyert and James March's (1963) theoretical work as well as others that view learning under the conditions of ambiguity. March and Cyert, for example, contend that organizational learning is a means of adapting to the environment by appropriately adjusting organizational goals and search rules. This approach to learning, in short, contends that organizations change their goals and structure on the basis of this learning experience. This kind of organizational learning also emphasizes how individuals interpret environmental responses and update their beliefs in regards to this relationship (Sinkula 1994).

The third approach to organizational learning stresses the development of what is called the "knowledge base" of the organization. This view, as Shrivastava (1983) argues, focuses on the "interpretative routines used by decisionmakers to detect problems, define priorities, and develop an understanding of how to deal with performance discrepancies" (pp. 13–14). This perspective articulates the importance of the role of knowledge in improving managerial and policy decisionmaking. In particular, this approach to organizational learning refers to how to improve such factors as management information systems, strategic decisionmaking, and budgetary control systems.

Although this typology is helpful in understanding the various approaches to organizational learning, C. Marlene Foil and Marjorie Lyles (1985) have asserted that the present literature on organizational learning can be classified under the rubric of either lower-level learning or higher-level learning. Lower-level learning, they posit, "tends to take place in organizational contexts that are well understood and in which management thinks it can control situations" (p. 807). Conversely, higher-level learning attempts to adjust or revise overall rules and norms rather than specific activities or behavior. In other words, higher-level learning tries to create new insights, new skill development, and new knowledge into the organization that will result in more effective decisionmaking. One characteristic of higher-level learning, therefore, is how organizations can "unlearn" previous practices (and procedures) and develop new cognitive frameworks in addressing organizational problems (Nystrom and Starbuck 1984).

It should be noted that much of what would fall under the rubric of higher-level learning is similar to the laboratory approach to individual learning developed initially by Kurt Lewin as well as what is referred to in the literature as organizational development (OD). In fact, according to Frank Friedlander (1983), "organizational change and learning are interwoven in OD" (p. 194). Warren Bennis and Burt Nanus (1985) have introduced another twist to this view by their focus on what they aptly call "innovative learning." They declare that when organizations engage in innovative learning "they will reconfigure themselves, replace old rules, improve their information flows, and revitalize their creative abilities" (p. 203). Moreover, they contend that there are six types of innovative learning: (1) examination of the organization's history in light of new markets; (2) an emphasis on training and education for organizational members; (3) the unlearning of old behavioral habits and processes; (4) continuous monitoring of trends in the external environment; (5) experimentation with new services and products and new organizational configurations; and (6) observation of other organizations and the ability to learn from such experiences.

Also worth noting in this regard is social learning. This view of learning emphasizes, among other things, how to democratize organizations that allow—and encourage—client/program interface and the redesign of organizational forms congruent with a strategic approach to foster collaborative policy initiatives. For example, David Korten (1980) and Clarence Stone (1985)—building upon the views articulated by Donald Michael (1993)—have emphasized the importance of social learning in order to redesign political and administrative institutions to expand citizen involvement in the policy process. Social learning, in part, is an endeavor to create the conditions for a mutual learning process between organizations and the public they serve.

One of the most salient contributions to organizational learning has come from Peter Senge's book, *The Fifth Discipline: The Art and Practice of the Learning Organization* (1990). While this book concentrates on the private sector, it can also be applied to the public sector. Senge divides learning into five domains: personal mastery (training and education), shared vision, team learning, cognitive formation, and finally, systems learning. Systems learning, he tells us, serves as an integrative process of linking these other domains of learning together. From a somewhat similar theoretical angle, Argyris (1993) builds upon his extensive research work on organizational learning, but with more explicit attention given to how certain factors can inhibit double-loop learning. His primary goal here is on developing intervention strategies that can confront the debilitating conflicts that single-loop learning cannot adequately resolve, both at the individual and organizational level. Argyris again reminds us that double-loop learning is a requisite process for improving organizational performance. He proposes that intervention strategies require a learning that tries to change the "framework" in which organizational problems and issues are placed.

While this is only a sampling of some of the relevant literature in organizational learning, a nagging question about this perspective must be posed, even given its diverse usage in the literature: is organizational learning most effective (from the organization's perspective) when it does not encourage organizational members to question critically the basic goals and activities of the organization?

It has been argued that the major goals of these different views to organizational learning feature the following tacit assumptions: (1) a preoccupation with organizational adjustment and the necessary adjustments of action in order to reach established organizational goals and objectives; (2) a goal of learning new techniques that contribute to the more efficient achievement of intended organizational goals; (3) an emphasis on organizational means to larger organizational ends that are typically assumed as given; (4) a focus on the immediate moment, on immediate organizational needs predicaments, or errors of immediate practical interest (the future orientation of innovative learning and other similar perspectives, which at first appear to be exceptions, is still aimed at ensuring organizational survival and growth in its immediate environment); and (5) a focus on managerial processes for guiding or motivating individual behavior for organizational purposes of efficiency, effectiveness, and adaptation (Ventriss and Luke 1988, pp. 347–348).

Assuming the general validity of these assumptions associated with organizational learning, some have raised the critical issue of whether promoting learning in organizations can actually take place, especially higher-level learning, given the constraints of an instrument value system that underlies the functional norms and goals of organizations. In partial response to this question, Gareth Morgan (1986) has proposed a "holographic organization" which incorporates the following elements: (1) a redundancy of functions (the design of wholes into parts by creating redundancy and at the same time both specialization and generalization); (2) minimum critical specification (the design of new forms to achieve self-organization); (3) requisite variety (the development of activities to deal with the external environment in a holistic and integrated manner); and (4) learning to learn (the encouragement of organizational members to question and challenge institutional activities).

Morgan suggests that a "holographic learning organization," by definition, necessitates innovation: "For unless an organization is able to change itself to accommodate the ideas it produces and values, it is likely eventually to block its own innovations" (p. 105). Yet, Michael Crozier (1965, p. 186) cynically concludes that bureaucratic organizations "cannot correct their behavior by learning from their errors." Others have argued that we need to distinguish organizational learning not based upon lower or higher levels of learning, but rather whether learning is instrumental or substantive (Ramos 1981). For instance, instrumental learning "refers to how a formal organization can incorporate new knowledge that can help it adapt or shape the environment–a process, however, that would limit learning to instrumental issues and never call into question the primordial goals of the organization" (Ventriss and Luke 1988, p. 794). Substantive learning, on the other hand, is defined as a normative or ethical inquiry that encourages the questioning and examination of organizational norms and practices that are incidental to the issues of efficiency, effectiveness, and maintenance. Substantive learning is somewhat closely related to Gregory Bateson's concept of deutero-learning–a concept that has also influenced both Schön's and Argyris's works–which refers to the process of learning about learning. Specifically, it applies to how individuals can invent new strategies or approaches for learning, particularly strategies that can facilitate creativity in the problem solving process. In brief, substantive learning tries to promote new possibilities for both public dialogue and public action that are not bound to instrumental considerations. This kind of learning, as it has been proposed in reference to public organizations, would exhibit the following characteristics:

1. It assumes that public organizations are more than mere technical instruments to produce goods and services: they provide a mechanism for political decision-making in a democratic polity;
2. It assumes that organizations exist in an environment rich with both subtle and direct interconnection, networks, and ripple effects;
3. Although organizations themselves are no more than means to ends, organizational learning requires critical analysis of those substantive ends and outcomes of organizational action;
4. It focuses on social values, seeks critical reflective awareness on the part of organizational members in order to identify intended and indirect outcomes, or other normative consequences on the environmental context in which the organization exists; and
5. It focuses on past, present, and future policy choices for the purposes of human betterment, rather than developing administrative means to implement enacted policy. As such, it is value-creating rather than value-conserving (Ramos 1981; Ventriss and Luke 1988, pp. 348–349).

While substantive learning and other similar approaches are still in their theoretical embryonic stage of development, the concept of organizational learning will most likely remain as an idea in good currency. Yet, the parameters of what constitutes, or does not constitute, learning in organizations has not been clearly clarified. These issues, for example, include the unit of analysis (individual vs. organizational learning), definitional ambiguity, and more significantly, the social and political barriers of knowledge to initiate organizational and policy change. Even given these difficulties, organizational learning as an area rich in conceptual diversity has become an important approach in dealing with the central issues of organization theory and structure.

CURTIS VENTRISS

BIBLIOGRAPHY

Argyris, Chris, 1976. "Single-Loop and Double-Loop Learning in Research and Decision-making." *Administrative Science Quarterly,* vol. 21:366–367.

———, 1993. *Knowledge for Action: A Guide to Overcoming Barriers to Organizational Change.* San Francisco, CA: Jossey-Bass.

Argyris, Chris and Donald Schön, 1978. *Organizational Learning: A Theory of Action Perspective.* Reading, MA: Addison-Wesley.

Bedeian, A. G., 1986. "Contemporary Challenges in the Study of Organizations." *Journal of Management,* vol. 12:185–201.

Bennis, Warren and Bert Nanus, 1985. *Leaders: The Strategies for Taking Charge.* New York: Harper and Row.

Crozier, Michael, 1965. *The Bureaucratic Phenomenon.* London: Oxford University Press.

Cyert, Richard and James March, 1963. *A Behavioral Theory of the Firm.* Englewood Cliffs, NJ: Prentice-Hall.

Foil, C. Marlene and Marjorie Lyles, 1985. "Organizational Learning." *Academy of Management,* vol. 10:803–813.

Friedlander, Frank, 1983. "Patterns of Individual and Organizational Learning." In S. Shrivastva, ed., *The Executive Mind.* San Francisco, CA: Jossey-Bass.

Korten, David, 1980. "Community Organization and Rural Development: A Learning Process Approach." *Public Administration Review,* vol. 40:480–512.

Michael, Donald, 1993. *On Learning to Plan and Planning to Learn.* San Francisco, CA: Jossey-Bass.

Morgan, Gareth, 1986. *Images of Organization.* Beverly Hills, CA: Sage.

Nystrom, P. C. and W. H. Starbuck, 1984. "To Avoid Organizational Crises, Unlearn." *Organizational Dynamics,* vol. 12:53–65.

Ramos, A. G., 1981. *The New Science of Organizations.* Toronto: University of Toronto Press.

Schön, Donald, 1983. "Organizational Learning." In G. Morgan, ed., *Beyond Method: Strategies for Social Research.* Beverly Hills, CA: Sage.

Senge, Peter, 1990. *The Fifth Discipline: The Art and Practice of the Learning Organization.* New York: Doubleday.

Shrivastava, P., 1983. "A Typology of Organizational Learning Systems." *Journal of Management Studies,* vol. 20:8–28.

Sinkula, James, 1994. "Market Information Processing and Organizational Learning." *Journal of Marketing,* vol. 58:35–45.

Stone, Clarence, 1985. "Efficiency Versus Social Learning: A Reconsideration of the Implementation Process." *Policy Studies Review,* vol. 4:484–496.

Ventriss, Curtis and Jeff Luke, 1988. "Organizational Learning and Public Policy." *American Review of Public Administration,* vol. 18:337–357.

ORGANIZATIONAL PSYCHODYNAMICS.

The study of unconscious patterns of work relations and their influence on leadership, role formation, group dynamics, organizational structure, strategy, and culture.

Organizations are produced and perpetuated by people who come together in order to accomplish something that they cannot achieve alone. Whether their purpose is to defend national boundaries, govern and collect taxes, build homes, roads, and schools, or provide health care and education, complex organizations are permanent fixtures of contemporary life. Thus, an in-depth understanding and evaluation of organizational life can be of great value.

Whether in the minds of members or customers, organizations (companies, public agencies, and associations) signify different things to different people. Organizations are, thereby, meaningful to both those on the inside and those on the outside. Organizational symbols emerge from the internalized world of participants' experiences and emotions. These private images of interpersonal, group, and organizational life shape members' expectations and desires at work. For example, when one joins an association one does so for a purpose: It is anticipated that one's membership will satisfy certain needs, whether for income, security, knowledge, power, intimacy, mastery, dependency, aggression, spirituality, or identity.

Organizational sociologists, economists, and political scientists typically pay attention to the structural dynamics of management-worker relations, coalitions of power and authority, hierarchies, markets, or power strategies for interdependence between and among organizations. They also assume that people make only conscious choices, and interact only on the basis of self-interest and cost-benefit exchanges. From the vantage point of observing and participating in large, complex organizations, that assumption is incorrect. Social and behavioral scientists typically apply technical and instrumental rationality in their investigations and descriptions of organizational behavior. Their studies may be methodologically rigorous and statistically sophisticated. But are they relevant to the world of practice, a reality that is uncertain, unpredictable, and unique from one moment to the next? Do they unwittingly discourage individual reflectivity, systemic learning, and critical awareness? Can they account for, and explain, incidents of irrationality and irresponsibility?

Organizations are social settings where people can, ideally, express their true selves; however, they are often authoritarian cultures that promote false and inauthentic actions, which consequently suppress the potential for learning, problem solving, and organizational culture change. Whether or not organizations facilitate genuine and productive human relations depends upon the values, ambitions, ideals, talents, and skills of key participants, members of powerful organizational coalitions, and their host political culture. If one acknowledges the influence of personality on power relations and decisionmaking in organizations, then one must look beyond traditional organization theories.

What, then, does organizational psychodynamics look at? What can it teach us? And what are its methods?

Suppression, Defense, and the Unconscious in Organizations

Analyzing an organization is not the same as analyzing an individual. Granted individuals are complex creatures who may act defensively, anxiously, and paradoxically. People are not always aware of why they do what they do, nor why they feel what they feel. From one moment to the next, they may deny or forget the occurrence of a critical incident, a thought, idea, or name of a friend or colleague. Certain experiences and relationships may trigger specific anxieties or attributions of which they are seemingly unaware. Accepting that individuals are perplexing subjects of analysis (not to mention imperfect and at times irrational), it follows that organizations might be expected to present overwhelming complexity to the prospective analyst.

One does not psychoanalyze the organization as one would an individual on the couch—although there are similarities. Rather, one analyzes patterns of relationships (intersubjectivity) and individual perceptions of organizational experiences—that which is called organizational identity (Diamond 1993). For example, individuals in the organization often forget (or some might say deny and suppress) critical incidents in the organization's history. In fact, it is commonplace for organizational member to push out of awareness (by means of suppression) painful organizational realities such as the effects of retrenchment, leadership transitions, reorganization, shifting budgetary procedures and evaluations, changing task environments, and conflicts among executives, managers, and staff. People may go about their business despite the turmoil, and often do so with diminishing effectiveness.

Suppressed incidents and denial of reality affect people and their organizational operations. Errors are repeated. Problems are unsolved. Conflicts are avoided. Organizational members are demoralized, and organizational viability is jeopardized. Suppression and denial negatively affect morale and diminish organizational effectiveness. These activities are part of the unconscious dimension of organizational culture—or what is sometimes called organizational identity.

Like psychoanalytic patients, organizational members often passively experience critical incidents such as those mentioned above. They characteristically feel victimized by constant change and transition. Seeing themselves as powerless and helpless, they suppress their anger and come to rely upon ritualistic defenses and routines at work. That way they can deny and avoid confronting their problems of coping and adaptation, and succumb to cynicism. It is this pessimism and negativity that organizational analysts are confronted with in trying to extract pertinent information, and facilitate collaboration and change. And, quite possibly, it is this experience that led many organization theorists back to Freud.

The Relevance of Freud's Findings for Organization Theory

Freud's discovery of the unconscious coincided with his finding that people repress painful thoughts, ideas, and experiences. People shut out of awareness certain emotionally loaded, anxiety-producing information, rendering it unconscious. Individuals cope with perceived dangers by defending themselves in this way. They may physically or psychologically flee or withdraw from a relationship or situation viewed as dangerous. However, people are suppressing thoughts, feelings, ideas and defending themselves against anxiety, not organizations.

While there is unconscious life in organizations, there is no organizational unconscious per se. The intricacy of organizational psychology in contrast to individual psychology seems enormous. Understanding behavior in organizations, however, rests in ferreting out the meanings of interpersonal and group relationships, which collectively comprise the identity of the organization.

Individual psychology is at the same time social psychology (Freud 1921). Despite his intense focus on instincts and drives (the aims of bodily stimulus and tension reduction), Freud understood the impact of social and in-

terpersonal phenomena on the construction of personality. To understand the individual, one must comprehend the character of one's relationship to others and the context of interactions.

Adherents of contemporary psychoanalytic thinking emphasize patterns of relationships, both conscious and unconscious, and view individuals as object-seeking rather than instinctually driven (Greenberg and Mitchell 1983; Mitchell 1988). Analysts with the assistance of organizational members are thereby encouraged to make public the intersubjective meaning of patterns of relationships, values, attitudes, frames of mind, and personality characteristics found to be unique to the organizational culture under investigation.

In order to distinguish the peculiarities from one organization to the next, the analyst must evaluate the nature of leadership and interpersonal and group activities in their cultural, historical, political, and environmental context. Psychoanalytic knowledge of organizations is acquired from the in-depth study of human activities and relationships, whose meaning is communicated through the verbal expression of individual feelings, fantasies, and perceptions of the participants.

It could be further argued that one rarely, if ever, reaches the unconscious life of organizational members; it is more often the case that the application of psychodynamic theories to organizational behavior helps to elicit what is more accurately termed valuable preconscious data—the unexamined, undiscussed, avoided, and denied issues of organizational experience. Preconscious data—the result of suppression—are more accessible than unconscious material—the consequence of repression. Organizational participants may deny and suppress problems that were at one time conscious, and of which they may be partially aware. Not surprisingly, acts of suppression and defense occur often in organizations—a fact ignored by mainstream organization theory.

On the other hand, if one takes seriously the notion that people enter organizations as adults with their personalities complete, then one might assume unconscious processes will influence role performance. That is, one's identity, psychoanalytically speaking, results from the internalization of significant interpersonal relationships, particularly those of infancy and childhood. One might assume, therefore, that early interpersonal experiences unconsciously affect interactions at work. That is why the concept of transference is central to the understanding of the psychodynamics of everyday organizational life.

Transference and Organizational Hierarchy

Transference is the unconscious sharing of emotions between two (or more) persons in which one projects feelings and attitudes from past relationships (to parent, sibling, etc.) onto another person in the present. According to Ralph Greenson (1978), "Transference is the experiencing of feelings, drives, attitudes, fantasies, and defenses toward a person in the present that are inappropriate to that person and are a repetition, a displacement of reactions originating in regard to significant persons of early childhood" (p. 201). Such unconscious reactions are bound to occur in adult life, particularly in the context of authority relations that tend to trigger unconscious expectations.

For example, a subordinate may come to idealize his or her superior as a consequence of frustrated idealization of parents during childhood. Kohut (1977, 1984) stresses the child's need for greatness, strength, and calmness to be found in his or her identification with a parent. If thwarted, the need for idealization becomes exaggerated, and if left unfulfilled it provokes an unconscious search for such traits in adult relationships. The idealizing subordinate, thereby, comes to view his or her boss as superhuman and infallible. Children with parents who are not worth idealizing, for whatever reason, continue searching, often obsessively, for substitutes.

A superordinate, on the other hand, may require idealizing subordinates as a consequence of frustrated needs for acceptance by parents during childhood. His own narcissistic needs went unmet. Kohut (1977, 1984) stresses the child's developmental need to be the center of his or her parents' universe, to feel loved and admired, and to satisfy his exhibitionistic demands. In the case of unresponsive or overly indulgent parents, the child's need for recognition and acceptance (what Kohut calls mirroring) will motivate him or her in the selection and maintenance of adult relationships. The mirror hungry superordinate, for instance, will require idealizing, loving, and admiring subordinates.

What is most relevant for organizational life in the concept of transference (and countertransference) is not so much the childhood origins of participants' relational conflicts as their awareness of interactional patterns in the present that limit their abilities to change and work effectively with others. Childhood experiences shape individual perceptions of roles in the workplace. "Here-and-now" relational patterns are the result of personalities in roles, and hierarchies encourage transference dynamics between and among organizational members—power and authority relations stoke the fire of internal parental images whether real or fantasized. Participants interpret hierarchic positions, tasks, and roles differently and often unconsciously. Gaining insights into the emotional dimensions of their relations can enable them with the help of an organizational analyst to clarify and resolve differences, improve coordination, and thereby to consider alternative ways of interacting at work. Organizational psychodynamics views feelings as the unconscious foundation on which everything else emerges in the context of organizational culture.

Summary

Psychoanalysis is a theory of interpretation for understanding the significance of human feelings and actions. Its application to examining organizational life moves us beyond the scientific search for observable facts and truths; rather, if offers a theory and practice for assertaining the meaning of human relations and experiences at work—meanings found in the unconscious and latent processes of social systems.

Psychoanalytic research attempts to locate the intent of human experience by focusing on psychic reality in contrast to objective reality. Acquisition of psychic reality is at the center of psychoanalytic work—referring to subjective and, especially, unconscious meaning. "Its usefulness resides in its reminding us that psychoanalytic explanation depends on our knowing what an event, action, or object means to the subject; it is the specifically psychoanalytic alternative to descriptive classification by a behavioristic observer" (Schafer 1976, p. 89). Here, one finds the relevance and contribution of psychoanalysis for organization theory.

Organizational psychodynamics explores the significance of, and the reasons for, the private images people hold of organizational life—the participant's psychic reality. That includes unconscious fantasies, expectations, attributions, assumptions, fears, and anxieties about themselves and others in their mutual organizational roles. Psychoanalytic organizational researchers work to understand the meaning of critical incidents, and the collective patterns of response to those events. Organizational psychodynamics assume that the mysteries of organizational life reside in the intersubjective world of organizational members' experience—their particular organizational identity.

People use their organizations for unconscious reasons such as defending themselves against certain anxieties; renewing a sense of lost omnipotence; enhancing their self-esteem; resolving incomplete developmental issues; serving as targets of aggression; and utilizing them and as a psychological space for play and imagination, to name a few. The personal meaning of organizational experience, discovered in organizational identity, helps to explain the unconscious intentions of those who plan and structure organizational action. How people, particularly those in power, use their experiences with and fantasies about organizational membership affects their relationships, and ultimately their collective image of organization. Awareness of the structure of intersubjectivity and the relational patterns organizing experience and action, transference being one major component in that analysis, helps to explain human behavior.

Organizations, however, are not analyzable as a single entity, an organism with its own psyche, but as a consequence of interpreting the patterns of human interactions and perceptions of members in their respective roles and groups. Collective patterns of private images and interactions may be distinguished from one organization to the next, rendering coherent what otherwise seems chaotic and unreasonable. Organizations are more than the sum total of members' collective projections; that is, organizations are psychological containers for members' individual and shared experiences, fantasies, and expectations. Organizational images, psychoanalytically speaking, are neither real nor fantasy: they are the product of imagination, and in this potential space between reality and fantasy the riddles of organizational life reside. This is not meant to deny the objective reality of organizations, but to emphasize the psychodynamic position that the understanding of organizational dynamics rests in the psychic reality of organizational participants. Interpreting their individual stories, images, experiences, and perceptions of organizational reality is what matters.

Drawing upon ideas from psychoanalytic theory and practice helps organizational researchers to understand the experience of organizational members—experiences held in members' private images of organization. Meaningful private images occur as a result of one's internalization of events before and after entry into an organization. These intra- and interpersonal, group, and organizational events are incorporated into preconscious thoughts and, if repressed, reside as unconscious memory traces. Hence, organizational psychodynamics is the study of the internalized world of organizational life.

MICHAEL A. DIAMOND

BIBLIOGRAPHY

Diamond, Michael A., 1993. *The Unconscious Life of Organizations*. Westport, CT: Quorum Books, Greenwood Publishing Group.
Freud, Sigmund, 1921. *Group Psychology and the Analysis of the Ego*. New York: W. W. Norton & Company.
Greenberg, Jay R. and Stephen A. Mitchell, 1983. *Object Relations in Psychoanalytic Theory*. Cambridge, MA: Harvard University Press.
Greenson, Ralph, 1978. *Explorations in Psychoanalysis*. New York: International Universities Press.
Kohut, Heinz, 1977. *The Restoration of the Self*. New York: International Universities Press.
———, 1984. *How Does Analysis Cure?* Chicago: University of Chicago Press.
Mitchell, Stephen A., 1988. *Relational Concepts in Psychoanalysis*. Cambridge, MA: Harvard University Press.
Schafer, Roy, 1976. *A New Language for Psychoanalysis*. New Haven, CT: Yale University Press.

ORGANIZATIONAL RENEWAL.

Systemwide management interventions designed to dramatically improve the quality and productivity of public organizations. As organizations of today become increasingly more complex in both their systems and functions, a need grows to understand the changes about us and to find ways in which organizations can most productively direct themselves towards the results they desire. In order to meet public demands to do more with less or simply to improve a worn public image, many public managers are undertaking new programs of change or renewal. In many cases, organizations are finding it necessary to transform their basic underlying assumptions, beliefs, and values in order to increase quality and productivity. This article will consider two representative examples of contemporary thinking on this topic.

Among the most contemporary approaches to organizational transformation, there is an emphasis on bringing people together in collective thinking, finding new ways of thinking about old problems, and establishing clear visions for the future. Peter Senge (1990) claims that organizations need to change or transform themselves into "learning organizations." He proposes that many organizations of today are in need of change due to the disastrous effects of learning disabilities. These disabilities prevent organizations from being able to identify the opportunities available as well as the factors potentially threatening to them. In order to transform an organization into a "learning organization," one that prevents learning disabilities from occurring, Senge suggests that five disciplines ought to be continually pursued.

The first discipline, personal mastery, is described as an essential cornerstone to the learning organization. It is the discipline of constantly clarifying and deepening one's personal vision, focusing energies, developing patience, and seeing reality objectively. Senge characterizes people with a high level of personal mastery as individuals who realize the results that matter most deeply to them and who are committed to their own lifelong learning. He claims that unfortunately organizations do not encourage their employees to grow in such a way. The disability that develops as a result is a loss of employee commitment, a loss of the sense of mission, and a loss of excitement for their careers.

Senge proposes that analyzing one's own mental models is an additional discipline that must be pursued on a regular basis. Mental models are defined as deeply ingrained assumptions, generalizations, or images that influence how we understand the world and how we take action. According to him, very often individuals are not aware of how these models affect the way that they behave. While working on this discipline, individuals start by turning a mirror inwards in order to learn about the mental models they live by. In addition, once the mental models have been unveiled, they ought to be scrutinized so that alternative ways of thinking about the world can be considered.

The third discipline espoused by Senge concerns the idea of building a shared vision. Organizations need to bring people together around a common identity and a common sense of destiny. "When there is a genuine vision, people excel and learn, not because they are told to, but because they want to" (Senge 1990, p. 9). Practicing this discipline involves moving away from emphasizing the vision of one leader to finding shared "pictures of the future" that everyone can be guided by.

The fourth discipline, team learning, stresses the importance of dialogue and the capacity of members to genuinely think together. Embedded here is the idea that the intelligence of a team exceeds the intelligence of any one member of that team. Team learning involves uncovering patterns of defensiveness that are oftentimes firmly ingrained in behavior.

Making up the fifth discipline, systems thinking integrates all of the other disciplines together into a coherent body of theory and practice. According to Senge, learning disabilities related to any of the other disciplines stem from the inability to think systematically. Organizations need to think about and understand the forces and interrelationships that shape the behavior of systems. Change within organizations will come about more effectively if individuals understand and act more in tune with the larger processes around them. In sum, systems thinking offers individuals a greater understanding of how they perceive themselves, their organization, and their world. Peter Senge suggests that these disciplines, when enhanced, help to transform organizations into organizations that truly learn and have the ability to realize their highest potentials.

An example of similar work set in the public sector is Robert Denhardt's *The Pursuit of Significance* (1993). Successful organizational change involves the use of managerial approaches strikingly different than traditional management practices that have typically emphasized rule-bound hierarchical structures. Based on interviews with "revolutionary" public managers, Denhardt suggests five specific strategies that managers of public organizations can use to facilitate an organizational change geared towards increasing the quality and productivity: a commitment to a common purpose, a concern for serving the public promptly and well, empowerment and shared leadership, pragmatic incrementalism, and a dedication to public service. Utilizing these approaches, managers can make dramatic improvements to the quality and productivity of their organizations.

First, the best public managers seek organizational change less by attention to structure than by developing a pervasive commitment to the mission and values of the organization, especially the values of professionalism and integrity, service and quality. Values should be clearly articulated by the chief executive and shared by those throughout the organization. Thus, change is focused less on the organization's structure and more on the underlying basic assumptions or culture of the organization. With a commitment to values, an organization can successfully direct itself into experiencing the future it envisions itself as having.

Second, managers should give priority in service to both clients and citizens. That priority ought to be supported by high standards of performance and accountability, and by a constant emphasis on quality. Most important, managers should recognize that technical efforts alone will fail unless equal or even greater attention is given to the human side. In addition, managers must pay attention to what happens outside the organization and establish effective and cooperative relationships with other groups and organizations.

Third, managers ought to encourage a high level of participation and involvement on the part of all members of the organization in the effort to improve the quality and productivity of the organization. The concept of leadership needs to be understood in terms of shifting the distribution of power and responsibility to members throughout the organization. The sharing of leadership and the empowerment of employees will open channels of communication across all levels of the organization. Leadership should not be defined in terms of one particular position; instead, it ought to be conceptualized as a function or process that must be developed and extended throughout the organization.

Fourth, the best public managers seem to approach change through pragmatic incrementalism. As a strategy for organizational change, pragmatic incrementalism suggests that managers need a clear vision but do not always need a plan for getting there. The idea of rationally planning an organization's future and exercising unilateral control over its direction represents an inappropriate approach in today's complex and unpredictable world. Change should be viewed as a natural feature of organizational life and as a free-flowing process by which managers can pursue unexpected opportunities and endeavors.

The fifth and final strategy for improving the quality and productivity of public organizations involves a strong emphasis on the dedication to serve the public. Individuals throughout the organization should understand and appreciate the special character of the public service, especially the role of public organizations in the process of democratic governance. Managers need to insist that members of the organization maintain high ethical standards and must encourage them to make their organization a model of integrity for similarly situated groups.

As both Senge and Denhardt suggest, organizational change is required if the envisioned future of the organization is to be obtained. Organizations will be forced to abandon the traditional management philosophies that stifle learning and inhibit growth and creativity.

ROBERT B. DENHARDT

BIBLIOGRAPHY

Denhardt, Robert B., 1993. *The Pursuit of Significance: Strategies for Managerial Success in Public Organizations.* Belmont, CA: Wadsworth.

Senge, Peter M., 1990. *The Fifth Discipline: The Art and Practice of the Learning Organization.* New York: Doubleday/Currency.

ORGANIZATIONAL TRUST. Faith or confidence in the intentions and actions of a person or group to be ethical, fair, predictable, and nonthreatening concerning the rights and interests of others in social exchange relationships (Carnevale 1988). It means a willingness to place oneself at risk, to become vulnerable, or to make a commitment even if one's dependency might be exploited. It involves a leap of faith or giving the benefit of the doubt to another in a situation beyond one's control. Conversely, mistrust is based on feelings of being threatened; or that the intentions and motives of another cannot be relied upon.

"Organizational trust" then, is a distinct work-related attitude and may be defined as "an employee's belief that the organization can be depended on, that it will act in a nonexploitive manner, that it will be consistent and predictable in the application of work-related policies and procedures, and that it will treat both organizational members and external stakeholders in a trustworthy manner (Carnevale and Wechsler 1992, p. 474).

Levels of trust have a profound effect on organizational performance. For example, higher levels of trust reduce conflict and encourage cooperation (Deutsch 1973), foster labor-management cooperation (Carnevale 1993), enhance group problem solving (Zand 1972), and diminish individual stress and burnout (Golembiewski, Munzenrider, and Stevenson 1986). Trust is an important integrative mechanism that promotes and sustains solidarity and cohesion in social systems (Barber 1983; Blau 1964). In high trust organizations, people show greater commitment (Buchanan 1974), motivation (Locke, Latham, and Erez 1988), and job satisfaction (Cook and Wall 1980). High levels of trust are a form of social capital and a measure of organizational power because of the positive relationship of trust to individual, group, and organizational achievement.

Trust is manifest in an organization's rules, roles, and relations (Fox 1974). It is at the heart of every management philosophy. The type of organization structure, nature of job design, labor-management relations pattern, communication climate, extent of employee involvement, and the character of reward and incentive systems are just some of the cues about the disposition of trust in an organization.

It is true that people come to work with predispositions about trust, but the most powerful determinants are within the control of the organization.

The Physics of Trust

Trust is a reciprocal attitude, which means people get back what they give when it comes to trust. In other words, outlooks about trust are often self-fulfilling. When people see others acting in ways that show trust, for instance, they are more disposed to reciprocate those feelings. Conversely, when faced with actions that are expressions of distrust, people tend to return the same sentiments. This reciprocal dynamic means that trust begets trust and distrust engenders distrust. Trust and distrust feed on themselves. Once a cycle is started, it tends to intensify and reinforce itself.

The significance of the reciprocal nature of trust, in the organizational case, works as follows: how system authorities choose to operate symbolizes and informs staff how much they are trusted. Staff interpret the amount and kind of trust directed toward them and respond in kind. High-trust methods beget high trust and low-trust techniques lead to low-trust reactions. When a high-trust sequence is in effect, trust is self-heightening or "regenerative." The regenerative trust cycle has positive effects on individual, group, and organizational performance. During low-trust cycles, trust is "degenerative" as organizational performance progressively deteriorates (Golembiewski and McConkie 1975).

One way to understand trust is to consider its antithesis—mistrust. Mistrust creates fear and "defensive routines" in people. Gibb (1978) details the behavioral implications of fear, the distinctive signature of mistrust:

> When fears are high, relative to trust level, I tend to try to control my reactions and yours. My energies are directed towards discovering and creating boundaries, legalities, rules, contracts, protective devices, and various structures that will embody the controls that seem necessary to keep life in order. . . . Fear predisposes a person to overperceive and overreact to the significance of authority and power figures, and the importance of management and control (pp. 31–32).

Fearful, low-trust people are preoccupied with managing the impression that they are making on others. They either try to dominate or avoid situations to protect themselves from the level of social uncertainty that is created in low-trust organizational climates. They engage in distancing, camouflaging, mask maintenance, and role-barricading behaviors. They close themselves off from the reality of experiences that produces learning (Carnevale 1995).

Of all the effects of trust in organizations, the most important may be how conditions of trust affect learning. Contemporary organizations are increasingly understanding from experience to improve awareness and actions. Learning means adapting and surviving. It requires the ability to process and build upon new information to innovate and create. It relies on authenticity and the willingness to deal with the truth of a situation. Organizations only learn through individuals and groups who learn. Organizational learning is seriously impaired when levels of trust are low among individuals, groups, and organizations because of the behavior patterns that arise in reaction to mistrust (Senge 1990).

Assumptions About Human Nature and Trust

Different philosophies of human nature bear directly on organizational trust formation and the management methods created in response to those beliefs. For example, if people are perceived as self-reliant, altruistic, and trustworthy, they are granted more authority, responsibility, and control over their work. If, on the other hand, it is believed that people are dependent, conformist, and untrustworthy, management systems are designed to coerce, control, and manipulate their behavior. The classic description of these attitudes is McGregor's (1960) Theory X and Theory Y typology, which deals with the management philosophies that arise from assumptions about human nature and the extent to which it may be controlled.

The Theory X view is decidedly low-trust. It envisions people as disliking work and responsibility, eschewing ambition, and prizing security above all. It is therefore logical, given this perspective, to establish management models where people are coerced, controlled, and threatened with punishment to get them to perform.

The Theory Y outlook sees people as enjoying work, seeking responsibility, and being self-motivated. Management methods consistent with this high-trust perception are empowering. They provide employees greater charge over their work.

For most of this century management philosophies have been based on Theory X assumptions that have spawned decidedly low-trust administrative methods. The low-trust approach has been somewhat effective as long as organizational success depended upon producing standardized goods and services. After all, deviations from the approved way of doing things increased variation and costs. Controlling management patterns based on low-trust assumptions about the potential contributions of workers worked when the principal competitive standards were only quantity, efficiency, and economy.

In the contemporary organization, competitive standards have changed. It is now increasingly understood that conformity and control subvert modern measures of organization success like quality, variety, customization, speed, and convenience. Today's organizations are aware that meeting the new set of performance standards cannot be realized without trusting people down the line with more authority and responsibility in deciding how the work should be done.

The evidence that organizational philosophies about work and workers are changing can be found in the core assumptions at the heart of all recent management reforms. For instance, management by objectives (MBO) techniques, quality circles, various excellence strategies, total quality management (TQM) plans, and the expanding use of autonomous and self-directed work teams are premised on the idea that organizational success is dependent on trusting personnel at the point of production by increasing their scope of action in doing work.

In addition to changing assumptions about the nature of work and workers, what other elements leverage trust in organizations? Research shows that (1) enriched job design, (2) open communications, (3) elevated levels of employee participation, (4) ethical management of politics, power, and conflict, and (5) fairness in the administration of rewards and punishments engender higher levels of organizational trust.

Work Roles and Trust

Building trust requires giving people power over work processes and procedures. The nature of work roles says something to employees about how much they are trusted. Narrowly specified jobs significantly reduce the scope of action of workers and let employees know that they are not trusted to impose their own judgments on how the work should be performed. Conversely, enriched job designs provide employees with greater control over the conception and execution of their work and reflects more faith in people to use their judgment about what a situation calls for—how the work wants to be done. Allowing staff greater latitude in deciding the appropriate working moves in a situation signifies greater confidences in their knowledge, motivation, and capabilities. It paves the way for better decisions and quality.

Communications and Trust

Research shows a strong connection between levels of trust and open communications (Roberts and O'Reilly 1974). When it comes to communications, all of the prescriptive literature advocates increasing trust. Trust in communications means that people can speak their minds without fear of reprisal. Trust and communications operate together. Trust encourages a person to be candid about information and feelings. When being open is not punished or when confidences are not violated, the individual is encouraged to continue to be frank. As long as openness is supported, this self-heightening dynamic between trust and open communications continues. When there is low trust, system performance is disabled because of the suppression of the free flow of information.

Participation and Trust

Increasing opportunities to participate expands trust in organizations. Participatory work cultures also encourage learning. Enlarging chances for participation increases people's sense of self-efficacy or internal locus of control by giving them greater information, power, responsibility, and authority. Creating conditions for employee participation works much like enriched job characteristics and open communications. It too is an expression of confidence in the motivation and know-how of staff. It is reciprocated by higher levels of trust in the organization and better system performance.

Ethical Politics, Power, and Conflict Resolution

Power, politics, and conflict are interrelated, inevitable facts of life in organizations. These energies are neither inherently good nor bad. They are natural forces created by inevitable disagreements over what goals to establish and the types of methods that should be used to achieve them.

Trust is affected by whether organizations deal ethically with the certainty of conflict, politics, and the necessary use of power. Trust is elevated when people assert their interests, form coalitions, and try to solve differences without resorting to coercion and autocratic rule. Trust is raised when influence strategies are open, honest, and civil. On the other hand, when the expression of disagreements are not permitted or where conflict is dysfunctional and zero-sum, trust is lessened. As with other organizational processes, how these forces are handled predict the kind of trust climate that is established.

Fairness and Trust

Fairness in the administration of rewards and disciplinary policies is a significant predictor of organizational trust. Employees are especially sensitive to fairness at work and closely monitor organizational practices for clues about trust. When staff feel that reward and punishment decisions are arbitrary or inequitable, or when their expectancies are mismanaged, they lose trust. When they are denied effective voice or procedural due process about the nature of such judgments, their faith and confidence in the organization ebb.

Bureaucracy, Governance, and Trust

The U.S. workplace is designed around the bureaucratic mass production model established in the early 1900s. In terms of developing trust and high performance over the long haul, the influence of bureaucratic structures is deadly. That is why all recent efforts at transforming bureaucratic work systems are designed to overcome the bureaucracy's low-trust, degenerative legacy. Bureaucracy is explicitly unfriendly to the idea of trust because it typically features impoverished work roles, close supervision, hierarchical authority structures, and few opportunities for effective employee voice and participation. Bureaucracy is a monument to mistrust.

Organizational trust is leveraged by more than structural arrangements. Organizations can be understood as societies and how they are managed represents a political theory as much as an administrative doctrine. When it comes to trust, a particular kind of government or social order involving a special set of expectations, mutual obligations, and a special combination of rights and duties among people is required.

In high-trust work cultures, staff experience (1) effective voice or freedom of speech, (2) opportunities to participate in decisionmaking, (3) enforceable protections or procedural due process when they are evaluated, rewarded, and especially when they are disciplined, (4) expectations that politics and conflict will be ethically managed, and (5) the belief that power will not be legitimated through force. Taken together, these high-trust dynamics can be reconceptualized as representing the fundamental norms of a democratic work culture (Carnevale 1995).

Democracy is founded upon trust. In democratic structures, there is a measure of faith and confidence in the nature and potential of people. It is acknowledged that people are not necessarily angels, but there is a companion belief that governance systems can be crafted that take advantage of people's best, not their worst, tendencies.

An organization serves democratic values to the extent that it reflects five interacting factors (Bernstein 1980):

1. Participation by all relevant organization members in decisionmaking, either directly or indirectly through representatives.
2. Frequent feedback of the results or organizational performance, not only in terms of information but also in terms of variable rewards keyed to performance.
3. Sharing of both management-level information and expertise throughout the organization.
4. Guarantees of individual rights, which correspond essentially to the basic political liberties that are so commonly unavailable in both public and business organizations.
5. The availability of appeal or recourse in cases of intractable disputes, decision units of which will at least in part be composed of peers.

These considerations can be characterized as participation, free speech, constitutionalism, opportunities for individual self-development, sharing of information, and the chance to exercise control over one's activities. These elements are at once fundamental determinants of democracy and trust.

Some of the reasons low-trust bureaucracy endures are because (1) change threatens existing power arrangements;

(2) elected officials mistrust expanding the role of un-elected bureaucrats in the policy process; (3) the impetus for reform is often driven by economic crises and the price of transforming bureaucratic organizations often requires more investment in people, not less; (4) because recent management reforms like the Civil Service Reform Act of 1978, Grace Commission, Volcker Commission, Winter Commission, Total Quality Management (TQM), quality circles, and reinventing government have all delivered less than promised, there is a growing cynicism about reform as faddish and ineffective, and (5) the public at large continues to prefer slashing the size and cost of bureaucracy rather than tackling the difficult task of reforming it; and (6) elected officials have short time horizons and fundamental system change takes a long time to accomplish.

In summary, organizational trust is a highly differentiated work attitude that bears on individual, group, and organizational performance. Its main contribution to performance centers around its impact on learning. In high-trust climates, staff are more willing to deal with the truth of a working situation, which means that organizational learning and achievement are enhanced. The key to building trust in organization is the development of a high-trust system that fosters enlarged authority of front-line employees, increased opportunities for staff involvement in decision-making, fundamental fairness in how employment decisions are handled, open communications, and a bias for more democratic governance. The basic idea behind building trust is to establish administrative methods and work processes that symbolize faith and confidence in people with the expectation that these attitudes will be reciprocated by more positive employee attitudes and better performance.

The Future of Trust Research

Three approaches can be distinguished in the study of trust. The first is "inferential" because researchers infer the amount of trust present in a situation from other forms of behavior. For instance, willingness to involve staff in decisionmaking can be interpreted as high trust. The second method is "experimental" because it features game theory applications such as the Prisoner's Dilemma to gauge trust. The third approach relies on "direct reports" where degrees of trust are measured as a directly experienced or affective reaction by means of self-report scales (Cook and Wall 1980).

No matter what investigative method is used to explore trust in organizations, very little research so far has examined the relationship of trust to organizational outcomes such as staff absenteeism and turnover. Moreover, there needs to be more research on group dynamics and trust, particularly relating to the effectiveness of work teams. The role of trust in labor relations is getting increasing attention, but more needs to be known about its role in labor-management cooperation, collective bargaining, and dispute resolution. More study of trust as a factor in organizational change interventions is yet another promising area of future inquiry. The relationship of trust to various personality traits such as locus of control, Machiavellianism, and authoritarianism represent promising areas of analysis. There are a host of other individual difference variables that have yet to be tested to determine if they are significant predictors of trust. Finally, continued work needs to be done on the trust-learning relationship.

DAVID CARNEVALE

BIBLIOGRAPHY

Barber, Bernard, 1983. *The Logic and Limits of Trust.* New Brunswick, N.J.: Rutgers University Press.

Bernstein, Paul, 1980. *Workplace Democratization: Its Internal Dynamics.* New Brunswick, NJ: Transaction Books.

Blau, Peter, 1964. *Exchange and Power in Social Life.* New York: John Wiley.

Buchanan, Bruce, 1974. "Building Organizational Commitment: The Socialization of Managers in Work Organizations." *Administrative Science Quarterly,* vol. 19:533–546.

Carnevale, David G., 1988. "A Model of Organizational Trust: A Case Study in Florida State Government." Unpublished Dissertation. Department of Public Administration. Tallahasse: Florida State University.

———, 1993. "Root Dynamics of Alternative Dispute Resolution: An Illustrative Case in the U.S. Postal Service." *Public Administration Review,* vol. 53:1–7.

———, 1995. *Trustworthy Government.* San Francisco: Jossey-Bass.

Carnevale, David G. and Barton Wechsler, 1992. "Trust in the Public Sector: Individual and Organizational Determinants." *Administration and Society,* vol. 23:471–494.

Cook, James and Toby Wall, 1980. "New Work Attitude Measures of Trust, Organizational Commitment and Personal Need Fulfillment." *Journal of Occupational Psychology,* vol. 53:39–52.

Deutsch, Morton., 1973. *The Resolution of Conflict.* New Haven, CT: Yale University Press.

Fox, Alan, 1974. *Beyond Contract: Work, Power, and Trust Relations.* London: Faber & Faber.

Gibb, Jack, 1978. *Trust: A New View of Personal and Organizational Development.* Los Angeles: Guild Press.

Golembiewski, Robert, Robert Munzenrider, and Jerry Stevenson, 1986. *Stress in Organizations: Toward a Model of Burnout.* New York: Praeger.

Golembiewski, Robert and Mark McConkie, 1975. "The Centrality of Interpersonal Trust in Group Processes." In C. L. Cooper, ed., *Theories of Group Processes.* New York: John Wiley.

Locke, Edwin, Gray Latham, and Miriam Erez, 1988. "The Determinants of Goal Commitment." *Academy of Management Review,* vol. 13:23–39.

McGregor, Douglas, 1960. *The Human Side of Enterprise.* New York: McGraw-Hill.

Roberts, Karelene and Charles O'Reilly, 1974. "Measuring Organizational Communication." *Journal of Applied Psychology,* vol. 59:321–326.

Senge, Peter, 1990. *The Fifth Discipline: The Art and Practice of the Learning Organization.* New York: Doubleday Currency.

Zand, Dale, 1972. "Trust and Managerial Problem Solving." *Administrative Science Quarterly,* vol. 17:229–239.

ORIGINAL INTENT. In U.S. jurisprudence, what the framers of the 1787 U.S. Constitution understood the document to mean. In the United States, there has long been a debate over the meaning of the Constitution and, since the New Deal, over the principles of constructing that meaning. At issue in this debate is the role of the judiciary in democratic government versus the role of the majoritarian forces, the elected legislators.

Since the Constitution is not completely majoritarian, some limitation of the majority is inherent in it. The question becomes, "What kind of limitation is consistent with democracy?" Those who oppose judicial intervention in the policymaking process argue that judges too often choose to limit the majority by using their own personal values as a standard for judicial review of the constitutionality of legislation. They limit elected legislators by casting themselves as unelected legislators. From this perspective, a standard for review that is more consistent with constitutional democracy is the framers' original intent, a standard which minimizes restrictions on the legislature and maximizes restrictions on the judiciary. Prominent examples of existing judge-made law that would have been precluded by strict adherence to original intent can be found in cases on school desegregation, abortion, and reapportionment. The ultimate effect of original intent as a standard in constitutional adjudication is deference to the will of the legislature.

History

While the controversy over original intent in the United States is novel in the history of law, the general practice of interpreting law according to the intent of the lawmaker is neither novel nor controversial. Commentators trace reliance on intent as a standard for interpretation to Aristotle's distinction between equity and legal justice, which was followed by medieval jurists. Equity was intended to address the gap between the spirit and the letter of the law. It dictated that, where the words were deficient, law should be interpreted according to spirit, or intent. In the beginning, equity involved applying a general rule to a specific instance by referring to what the lawmaker would have intended if he or she had foreseen that particular case. From this initial use to correct law that was deficient because of its generality, later on equity was extended to correct law that was deficient because of its specificity. Both English common law authorities such as Blackstone, and Continental authorities on the law of nations such as Grotius, were rooted in this tradition and agreed that the intent of lawmakers should guide legal interpretation.

Early U.S. jurists followed suit. As Gregory Bassham (1992) has observed,

> When Chief Justice John Marshall, writing in defense of his landmark decision in *McCulloch v. Maryland,* re-

marked that 'the great duty of a judge who construes an instrument, is to fit the intention of its maker,' his words reflected an orthodoxy that had prevailed in Western jurisprudence for centuries (pp. 3–4).

Less orthodox was the status of the U.S. Constitution as a written higher law, and the responsibility of the judiciary to ensure that ordinary laws passed by legislatures did not violate that higher law. These conditions laid the foundation for the current debate over original intent.

The reason is that original intent differs from the generic intent-of-the-lawmaker standard of interpretation in relating solely to higher law. Original intent becomes an issue, then, only with the rise of modern judicial review, which rests on a higher law, articulated through a written constitution and preserved as sovereign by a judiciary vested with the legal responsibility for passing on the constitutionality of statutory laws. These conditions have developed to the greatest degree in the United States.

While the first precedent of a written higher law for government was the Magna Carta of 1215, the English have never translated this beginning into a written constitution. They consider themselves guided by an unwritten constitution that has evolved over time. This unwritten constitution has not provided a central role for judicial review. It fell to the framers of the U.S. Constitution, who were influenced by Lockean natural rights concepts, the natural law notion of a higher moral law, and their own experience having acts of the colonial legislatures reviewed by the English Privy Council, to write higher law into a constitution that was intended to prevail over ordinary law. Some commentators argue, based on Federalist No. 78, that the framers intended that the judiciary have the authority to review the constitutionality of acts of Congress. Whether or not that was the framers' intention, the judiciary's power to review legislation was established early on, by the Supreme Court itself, in the 1803 case *Marbury v. Madison.*

Since that time, there has been periodic debate over how judges should use original intent to justify their review of legislation. Arguably, nearly all jurists look to some version of original intent as a standard for interpreting the constitution. In fact, that was the view of constitutional interpretation that dominated Supreme Court decisions until the late nineteenth century. Not that there was no controversy; however, according to Christopher Wolfe, there was general agreement that the Court exercised only judgment, and not will. The justices interpreted law; they did not make it. As Wolfe (1994, p. 71) has described them, the Court's decisions were "based on the words of the document in light of the subject matter, context, and intent, and interpretation [was] still understood to be an ascertainment of the principles embodied in the Constitution".

Around the turn of the century, the Supreme Court exchanged its defense of constitutional principles for a defense of natural law, which it defined primarily in terms of property rights. The Court's defense of "liberty of contract," justified as interpretation of the due process clause of the Fifth and Fourteenth Amendments to the Constitution, was used to strike down legislative attempts to regulate economic matters. A school of legal realists developed to challenge this laissez-faire approach as inherently legislative, not, as its advocates still claimed, a mere interpretation of existing constitutional principles.

With the rise of the New Deal and Franklin Roosevelt's famous battle with the Court over its resistance to New Deal legislation, the legal realists' view of judicial decisions as legislative in character became dominant. In the 1950s, the Warren Court ushered in an era of overt judicial activism, during which the Court used the Fourteenth Amendment to apply many Bill of Rights provisions to the states and to justify judges' formulation of rules for carrying out those provisions. The result was extensive judge-made policy in the areas of school desegregation, apportionment of legislative districts, and expansion of the rights of defendants in criminal trials.

Contemporary Debate

In the 1970s, a reaction to the Warren Court's activism began in academic circles. Among the chief proponents were Robert Bork and Raoul Berger, who posited as an alternative a return to original intent, strictly conceived. Their writings led to the more recent public controversy over original intent, which began with an indirect exchange in 1985 between U.S. Attorney General Edwin Meese and Supreme Court Justice William Brennan. After Mr. Meese served notice that the Reagan administration intended to use a "jurisprudence of original intention" to mount an attack on the Supreme Court's incorporation of the Bill of Rights as applicable to the states through the Fourteenth Amendment, Justice Brennan defended judicial activism as a means of protecting individual rights. As Professor Murray Dry explained in a 1987 commentary,

> For Justice Brennan and his supporters, the choice is between being ruled by the dead hand of the past or the living present: for Attorney General Meese and his supporters, the choice is between courts that say what the law is, which is their job, and courts that make law and policy, which is the job of legislatures (quoted by Farber, 1988 p. 1085).

In the current debate, there are two general schools of thought. Originalists, also called interpretivists or intentionalists, believe that judges should use the Constitution as a higher law standard for determining the legitimacy of positive laws and that they should interpret the Constitution in accordance with the best evidence of the framers' intent. Nonoriginalists do not believe that recourse to original intent is either possible or desirable, though, in this belief, they often are rejecting the originalists' narrow definition of original intent.

As categorized by Daniel Farber, arguments for originalism are: (1) Nonoriginalist approaches, in relying on the judges' own values rather than on relatively fixed constitutional standards, undermine the majority rule on which legitimate democratic government rests; (2) originalism can be defined in a broader way by looking to the Constitution as a legal text with implicit goals, instead of looking for historical evidence about the intent of the framers; (3) it is difficult to find an alternative basis for principled judicial review, since there appears to be no consensus on sources such as natural law or moral philosophy.

Arguments against originalism are: (1) Historical evidence about the framers' intent is unreliable; (2) the framers may not have understood their own intent (as opposed to the ratifiers' intent) to be authoritative; (3) in the Ninth Amendment and other open-ended clauses, the framers anticipated that courts would define unspecified human rights; (4) knowledge of the framers' views on a specific topic is not reasonable basis for projecting how they would react today; (5) original intent is too unchangeable to adapt to changing times.

Originalism and nonoriginalism often are discussed in terms of judicial restraint and judicial activism. Activism requires judges to interpret the moral principles embodied in the Constitution, to look more to the spirit than the letter of the law, when they are applying constitutional requirements to legislative acts. Restraint requires the reverse. Advocates of judicial restraint tend to look not to the spirit of the Constitution, broadly conceived, but to the specific intent of the framers at the time they wrote the Constitution, because that standard restricts the interpretive leeway of judges and reduces the opportunity for judges to substitute their will for the will of elected legislators.

Questions surrounding original intent have not been the center of debate in other countries that have developed versions of judicial review. In these cases, judicial review generally operates in the context of parliamentary democracy and does not challenge the majoritarian assumptions on which that system rests. Because judges in parliamentary regimes have not acquired the independent policy-making authority associated with judges in the United States, they do not have the same need for original intent to legitimize opposition to the will of legislators.

To illustrate: In English common law, judicial review related to administrative action. In the United Kingdom today, judicial review still is concerned primarily with administration action rather than with the review of legislative action which defines the phenomenon of modern judicial review. And when legislation is reviewed, there is no superior principle, firmly established in text, to limit Parliament.

Israel, like England, has no written constitution; but it does have a set of Basic Laws in light of which the Supreme Court assesses ordinary legislation. In a formal sense, then,

Israel has a system of judicial review. However, as Aaron Barak, a Justice of the Israeli Supreme Court has observed (1990), without a written constitution, the Court's rulings are effective only if the Knesset chooses not to alter them. Where there is a written constitution, the formal legitimacy of judicial decisions rests on ties to this text. If judges appear to move away from the text, their decisions lose legitimacy. These are the circumstances that produced the debate in the United States over original intent. As Barak has stated, Israel is "not faced with this problem" (pp. 291–292). It does not have to struggle with the original intent of a set of founders, because its version of higher law does not seek a standard for limiting the majority. It operates in the context of Israel's parliamentary system.

Also likely to ignore original intent is the kind of abstract judicial review that has evolved in several European countries–Austria, Portugal, Spain, Germany, and France–since 1950. Recent scholarship challenges the traditional notion that judicial review of the legislature's will does not occur in European parliamentary system, where constitutions, written or unwritten, are not legally established as superior to ordinary statutes. However, the irrelevance of original intent to these versions of judicial review shows the difference between them and the majority-limiting version that has developed in the United States.

Abstract review does not serve the same purpose as judicial review in the United States. Under the system of abstract constitutional review, politicians refer laws to special constitutional courts for examination, sometimes before and sometimes after promulgation. But in either case, the examination is simply of the text of the statute, not of a concrete instance where an individual seeks protection from the majority. The influence of abstract constitutional review on legislation is at its strongest in France and Germany, where politicians have exploited the possibility of censure by the courts to alter the outcome of the legislative process. As Alec Stone explains, this means that the constitutional courts function, in effect, as a final step in the legislative process; they offer a "final reading" of the law to which legislators can respond (1992 p. 45). This type of judicial review still fits the majoritarian legal culture of parliamentary systems. Functioning as part of the legislative process, it has less need of a defense for being undemocratic than does the American version of judicial review. For this reason, and also because it is of recent vintage, abstract constitutional review is unlikely to provoke the controversy over original intent that has arisen in the United States.

WYNNE WALKER MOSKOP

BIBLIOGRAPHY

Barak, Aaron, 1990. "Judicial Perspectives: The View from Israel." In Schlomo Slonim, ed., *The Constitutional Bases of Political and Social Change in the United States.* New York: Praeger.

Bassham, Gregory, 1992. *Original Intent and the Constitution: A Philosophical Study.* Lanham, MD: Rowman and Littlefield.

Berger, Raoul, 1977. *Government by Judiciary: The Transformation of the Fourteenth Amendment.* Cambridge, MA: Harvard University Press.

Dworkin, Ronald, 1978. *Taking Rights Seriously.* Cambridge, MA: Harvard University Press.

Farber, Daniel A., 1988. "The Originalism Debate: A Guide for the Perplexed." *Ohio State Law Journal,* vol. 49:1085–1106.

Hamilton, Alexander, John Jay, and James Madison, N.D. *The Federalist: A Commentary on the Constitution of the United States.* New York: Modern Library, Number 78.

Jackson, Donald W. and C. Neal Tate, eds., 1992. *Comparative Judicial Review and Public Policy.* Westport, CT: Greenwood Press.

Levy, Leonard W., 1988. *Original Intent and the Framers' Constitution.* New York: MacMillan.

Marbury v. Madison, 1803. 1 Cranch 137.

Rakove, Jack N., ed., 1990. *Interpreting the Constitution: The Debate over Original Intent.* Boston: Northeastern University Press.

Stone, Alec, 1992. "Abstract Constitutional Review and Public Policy-Making in Western Europe." In Donald U. Jackson and C. Neal Tate, eds., *Comparative Judicial Review and Public Policy.* Westport, CT: Greenwood.

Wolfe, Christopher, 1994. *The Rise of Modern Judicial Review: From Constitutional Interpretation to Judge-Made Law.* Lanham, MD: Rowman and Littlefield.

OUTSOURCING. The practice, in both private and public sectors, of a producer of a service or product contracting out some functions of its activity to another firm or organization, usually a private entity; also known as contracting out for services; purchasing of services; subcontracting; privatization.

Outsourcing is generally hailed as a key to increased effectiveness and efficiency, and is becoming a more popular practice in both the private and public sectors. Because of new technologies (particularly in the fields of information processing and telecommunications), proponents of outsourcing argue, vertical integration of traditional corporations that enabled the control of every step of production is no longer necessary (Quinn *et al.* 1990). Instead, they insist, companies should concentrate on activities (and not on the product) they are good at as their core business and outsource everything else. Others propose contingency tables of "strategic sourcing" (e.g., based on competitiveness of key technology across the market and maturity of technology process), specifying when it makes sense to outsource, when to produce a product or service, and when to make an R&D effort to develop a technology (Welch and Nayak 1992). The notion that outsourcing is an already efficient and cost-effective option to internal production of goods or services due simply to the

specialization of the subcontractor is not only hailed, but is also attacked. It is mainly criticized on the grounds that it erodes organizational capacities.

Outsourcing can restrict the flexibility of the organization (either public or private)—its ability to adjust to the demand—and can hinder the gains from intraorganizational cooperation where economies of scale (the reduction of costs due to mass production) and scope (the reduction of costs due to a complementary line of services, though not necessarily specialized and not necessarily of superior quality) are possible, and where the costs of contracting out (monitoring and evaluation of contractor's performance) are high (Prager 1994). Outsourcing has also been criticized as an "invisible" incremental process, through which an erosion of capabilities and decline of competitive edge is taking place, and which ultimately may bring destruction to a domestic industry (Bettis et al. 1992).

This topic has appeared in the economic literature since the 1930s. One of the topics institutional economics examines is the "efficiency properties of alternative contracting modes" (Williamson 1975, p. xi). This is often called the issue of transaction costs, and its origins are traced to a famous paper by Coase, "The Nature of the Firm" (1937). The paper has a central proposition that markets do not operate without costs, and that the higher the costs of transacting across markets, the greater will be the comparative advantage of organizing resources within a firm (Krusselberg 1991). It is argued that firms (i.e., internal production in the firms) exist because they provide better means of coping with shirking (free-rider behavior) in a cooperative effort than the markets do (Alchian and Demsetz 1972).

The practice of outsourcing is also known as purchase of services, contracting out for services, and privatization. Although the term privatization is very often used as a substitute for outsourcing, it describes a much wider phenomenon and has a different emphasis. Privatization includes, but is not identical with, the practice of outsourcing in the public sector. Privatization implies contracting out services to private, for-profit organizations, or even nonprofit organizations, while outsourcing per se can include contracting services to public organizations. Also, privatization can take many other forms than contracting out for services. Privatization is broadly defined by Savas (1992) as "the act of reducing the role of the government, or increasing the role of the private sector, in an activity or in ownership of assets" (p. 81). This definition includes divestment of state-owned enterprises and assets; delegation of service production via contracts, franchises, and vouchers; and displacement of government activities by allowing private alternatives to emerge in deregulated marketplaces. Traditionally, because of the historically limited character of the public sector and other forms of privatization in the U.S., outsourcing in the United States is generally identified

with privatization (e.g. Kemp 1991), and very often is only a part of a larger discussion concerning the size and the scope of the government.

A more systematic definition of privatization and outsourcing in the public sector is given by authors who argue that the choice between public and private delivery of services has two basic dimensions: financing and performance (ownership, operation) (Wamsley and Zald 1973; Kolderie 1986; Donahue 1989). The first dimension is an answer to the question: how should we pay for services we get, individually or collectively? The second dimension asks the question: should the good be produced or the service delivered by a governmental organization or a nongovernmental organization? Thus, we have two axes and four possible cells describing the public-private relationship in the production of goods and services. The first cell is the delivery of services (also goods, but hereafter for simplicity we will call them only services) paid for collectively and delivered by public sector organizations. This cell contains what is usually referred to as government—public schools, Veterans' Administration, Army, etc. The second cell describes the activities that are privately financed but publicly delivered. This cell describes such widespread activities as delivery of mail through the U.S. Postal Service, launching of commercial satellites by NASA, and so forth. The third cell is the delivery of services that are paid for individually and delivered individually, and is referred to as the market. And finally, the last cell is the one with public financing and private delivery. This cell covers a range of activities from contracting out of municipal garbage collection to the production of intercontinental ballistic missiles. The activities embraced here constitute nearly half of all government spending on goods and services, and usually describe the practices the most in the United States refer as privatization.

	GOVERNMENTAL OPERATION	NONGOVERNMENTAL OPERATION
COLLECTIVE FINANCING	Government	Privatization
INDIVIDUAL FINANCING	User fees for government services	Market

One weakness of this definition is its assumption of dichotomy between public and private financing, as well as the dichotomy between governmental and nongovernmental organizations or governmental and nongovernmental delivery of services. In reality, there is a continuum in both cases, and different organizations have varying degrees of political and economic authority (Bozeman 1987). Many organizations are financed both from user fees and government subsidies, and from private donations and subsidies. The issue of government vs. nongovernment dichotomy is even less clear, where the rise of "paragovernment" organizations, or "quangos" (quasi-nongovernmental organizations) is considered to be one of the most important phenomena in modern societies. The most complete taxonomy of organizations is offered by Perry and Rainey, which cross-classifies organizations according to ownership (operation), funding, and mode of social control (Rainey 1991).

Contracting out for services can be described also from the viewpoint of degrees of relevance to the mission (core) of the organization (Halachmi and Holzer 1993). They are : (1) none; (2) contracting ancillary services unrelated to the mission of the organization (e.g., cafeterias); (3) contracting support services related to the mission (e.g., clerical staff); (4) contracting part of mission implementation (e.g., prison guards); (5) contracting core components of mission implementation (e.g., social services); and (6) contracting aspects of mission determination (e.g., private prisons).

Managerial and institutional aspects of the situation—the independence of the agency or organization, strength and relevance of competitors, relations with regulating organizations and different jurisdictions of power, the extent of the regulation in the field, the funding of the organization, relevance of the outsourced service to the core (mission) of organization—rather than the public-private dimension of the issue at hand are key starting points when discussing outsourcing and privatization decisions.

History and Practice of Outsourcing Public Sector Services in the U.S.

Contracting out of services has a long history in the United States. Mail delivery was contracted out before the Constitution and continued to be a common practice throughout the nineteenth century. Even activities usually conceived of as enforcement and not as delivery of services, such as tax collection, were contracted out (NAPA 1989), although corruption and scandals were also common (Hanrahan 1983, p. 79). It is worthy to note that in each case of making a decision about nationalization or "governmentalization" of the services, the decision by the president or Congress—or both—followed some problem or scandal involving the contractors (NAPA 1989, p. 9).

The scope and scale of government activities expanded greatly during the Progressive movement and especially with the New Deal. Although the expansion of the government was based on a positivist faith in scientific management and government's ability to solve problems, this expansion was accompanied by growing cooperation of the government with the private sector. This tendency of government growth, along with increased cooperation with the private sector, was apparent also in the 1960s, when such public-private programs as Medicare and Medicaid were enacted (NAPA 1989).

The first major attempt on behalf of the federal government to encourage contracting out instead of its own

production came after World War II. During the war, along with increased government production, the biggest fusion of the government and private sector happened. After the war many companies tried to maintain their contracting relationships with the government—a large and credible client. While during the Truman administration two major statutes (the Armed Forces Procurement Act of 1947 and the Federal Property and Administrative Services Act of 1949) were passed that regulated the federal procurement process, it was the Eisenhower administration that began the first assault on public production and called for substituting contracting out in place of governmental commercial and industrial production. By the time Kennedy succeeded Eisenhower in the office, there had been a number of cases when companies with government research and consulting contracts had made recommendations that resulted in renewed contracts. These conflicts of interest caused Kennedy to appoint a commission, which warned that the government was losing its capability to evaluate contracted services, and urged that "management and control of such programs must be firmly in the hands of full-time government officials clearly responsible to the president and Congress" (as quoted in Hanrahan 1983, p. 88).

In 1966, the Bureau of the Budget issued Circular A-76, which called for an accelerated pace of contracting government industrial and commercial goods and services. This circular, which was revised in 1967 and 1979, has continued to be the basic contracting guideline since.

Because the United States government has never owned telephone, airline, or other industries, as the governments do in other industrialized countries, the privatization agenda in the United States almost always boils down to the issue of contracting.

The history of privatization and contracting out for services, or purchase of services, on the state and local level is diverse and is not as well documented as the same activities on the federal level. As Nelson (1980, p. 428) notes, the provision of local services has undergone two transformations since colonial times. Early in that period, the only providers of services such as fire protection were private firms. As the cities grew, the first transformation occurred, and public provision of services became a norm. The purchase of services by local government always existed, but the trend of contracting for sanitation services, for example, did not become popular until the late 1960s, when the second transformation occurred. Contracting for human and social services is also a new phenomenon (Nelson 1980; Kettl 1993). A survey of city and county governments in 1987 found that almost 60 percent of them were doing at least some purchasing of services, and experimenting with other forms of privatization (NAPA 1989). Drawing from survey data for 1988–1989, Savas maintains that "virtually every jurisdiction in the United States contracts for one or more services," and that an average service from the list of 48 different services ranging form public works to health and human services is contracted out by 20 percent of those communities responding to the questionnaire (1992).

Privatization literature usually addresses the issue either on the federal level or on the local level, and studies dealing with privatization of the state level are rare. In 1993, the Council of State Governments initiated a national survey to fill is this gap. The study found an increased frequency of privatization projects recently, outsourcing being the most popular form of privatization (Chi 1994).

Although in centrally planned economies outsourcing was virtually nonexistent, it in now taking place in post-communist transition economies. While the government is withdrawing from immediate production of goods in factories by selling of the companies to the public, on the local level some services are being outsourced. In other countries outsourcing is an established practice. Throughout the 1980s, different governments responded to fiscal stress in different ways—some outsourced more services through competitive bidding, while others "privatized" the government enterprises that provide the service (e.g., water distribution)—that is, they sold them to investors. In Europe and former communist countries privatization usually means selling of government assets rather than outsourcing, as in the U. S.

Although surveys are a widely used tool for evaluating the state of outsourcing, survey results can often be distorted. While almost all surveys rightly show the scope of privatization (i.e., what services are being privatized and what forms of privatization are taking place), the assessed scale of privatization may be inflated, mainly because most surveys do not mention what portion of the activity is outsourced.

Arguments for and Against Outsourcing (Privatization)

Because outsourcing is the most widespread form of privatization in the United States, it is often identified with privatization, and the debate over outsourcing in the public sector usually is argued in the framework of privatization. Arguments for and against outsourcing (privatization) are either ideological or practical. The ideological arguments are coming from commonly held beliefs that privatization reduces the size of the government and that the smaller the government the better; that privatization can help stimulate the economy and lower the taxes; that government agencies are less efficient; that private sector managers manage better; that government agencies, because of their monopolistic position, lack incentives to cut costs; that the government should not deliver services the private sector can provide (Buchanan 1977; Johnston 1990; Henig 1989–1990).

Practical arguments for privatization are: the need for filling short-term project needs; the necessity to adjust for limited resources; the pressure to lower the cost of services, while improving their quality and improving the operation of government (Johnston 1990).

Opponents of privatization argue both against the ideological and practical arguments. The ones who argue against ideology maintain that small government is not compatible with the welfare state, and that the private sector does not automatically mean competition and efficiency. They maintain the private, single, large providers of services are no better than public agencies which have a monopoly or which are assumed to have a monopoly. Another line of argument holds that while outsourcing emphasizes the value of efficiency, it overlooks the values of accountability, equity, service equality, and governmental capacity. Many observers mention that privatization studies overlook the issue of quality. The other argument against contracting out for services is that there is a possibility of "creaming"—when private providers of services tend to overlook "unprofitable" customers—and that privatization will result in no service or low quality service for this "disadvantaged population," who happen to live further away, be poorer, and so on. It is argued also that a significant part of savings from outsourcing comes from lower wage levels and greater use of part-time workers, which reduces the fringe benefits of employees (Kettl 1993). This is especially significant in state and local government, where the biggest share of expenditures is spent on personnel.

Critics warn against taking contractors' bidding prices as real on the following grounds. Economists distinguish between marginal costs and fully distributed costs. Marginal costs are the costs when the firm calculates only the direct costs of providing a service, usually an extension of existing operations, (e.g., servicing new communities along the same railroad), and fully distributed costs are the costs when the service is assigned a "fair share" or the firm's total costs according to some formula. When firms in the market compete in prices that are close to marginal costs rather that to fully distributed costs, it can lead into snowballing negligence of infrastructure and capital assets, and can eventually lead to a self-destructive competition (Baumol and Blinder 1988), or the decreased safety and service quality (Thayer 1987). The possibility of self-destructive competition, along with economies of scale and scope; the desire for providing universal services for all parts of the population; and protection of the consumers are the rationales economists provide for the justification of regulation (Baumol and Blinder 1988).

Thus, critics of outsourcing argue, in case of bidding that is close to the marginal cost of the service (which is usually the case when government contracts out services and is a result of the monopoly of the government as buyer), two consequences are possible: (1) inattention to assets, and as a consequence, lower safety and lower quality of services; and (2) transfer of the costs from one product to another or from one group of consumers to another.

In many cases of contracting, they claim, there is no real competition. Usually, the government requires that services should be contracted if there is a "reasonable fit" of the bidder to perform the wanted job. In most cases, because of large investments required to perform the large-scale government contract, there is only one firm having the capacities in place to provide the service (usually the firm previously having the contract), or the bidding firms have to negotiate a common price (which can be a violation of law) for parts of the contract (instead of the whole contract) in order to be able to survive the possible loss of a renewable contract, which will be impossible if the firm having the whole contract builds up massive capacities for which there is no demand otherwise (Thayer 1987). Thus, the argument goes, in cases when we have either monopoly of demand or monopoly of supply, contracting may end in two extremes: either a private monopoly, or competitive bidding that leads to low safety and service inequality.

Another line of criticism of contracting out services is that competitive bidding leads to corruption of public officials, because managers of private companies have incentives to bribe both public institutions (e.g., gifts to the agency) and public officials in order to assure their firms' survival (Thayer 1987).

The proponents of outsourcing answer these charges by arguing that privatization studies usually control for variables such as the size of the municipalities, wages levels, amount of the work performed, quality levels, and so on. They, in turn, argue that ordinary, commonsense comparisons overlook some problems and deflate the real costs of the services provided for government agencies (Savas 1992). For instance, they argue, in most cases in the cost estimates of services performed by the government cost of the buildings is not included, which significantly lowers the overall cost of services. They also argue that opportunity costs for the assets the government uses (e.g., the same buildings) are not taken into consideration while calculating the cost of the services. Another criticism is that some agencies in government use general services provided by the central administration, which they again fail to include in costs. It is also argued that in many cases studies mention figures for the costs of government-delivered services, which are drawn not from actual budget expenditures, but from forecasted ones, and that the latter figure is usually lower. The proponents of privatization refute the idea that the scheme of "low-ball bids" works. The "low-ball bids" idea maintains that a firm will offer a low competitive price, then make the government dependent on the firm, and then raise dramatically the price when the terms of the contract are renegotiated. And, finally, the argument holds, if every other condition is equal, and the private firm and government agency bid

for the same price and promise the same quality of service delivery, it is always preferable to award the contract to the private firm, because the private firm will also pay taxes and, thus, contribute to public welfare to a greater extent.

There have been numerous empirical studies comparing costs of services provided by public and private organizations. The studies are mostly performed for local services, and although the researchers maintain that they took into account different factors, such as the size of the municipality, comparability of services, cuts in wages, and so forth, the methodology is often contested (Donahue 1989). Probably, the most studied service is solid waste collection (Savas 1977; Stevens 1984); studies generally conclude that collection of solid waste by a public agency is more expensive than contracting it out, although less expensive than a totally private (market) provision of the service. Studies comparing delivery of several services both by agencies and contractors by and large find that private contractors are more effective (e.g., Stevens 1984), although in the case of natural monopolies (utilities) government provision seems to be less costly (Baumol and Blinder 1988; Donahue 1989).

Some proponents of privatization (outsourcing) see it as a universal tool, a panacea for all the problems the public faces. Most of the authors treating the subject of privatization, and some proponents of it, however, do not hold necessarily that privatization and outsourcing are an end by themselves and a cure for all ills. Most of them qualify their call for privatization, emphasizing the actual arrangements under which the service is delivered. Hatry warns that success of privatization is highly situational, and that other than efficiency factors should be discussed as well as when deciding to outsource services (Hatry 1988). Goodman and Loveman (1991) find it more useful to "move the debate away from the ideological ground of private versus public to the more pragmatic ground of managerial behavior and accountability," and argue that "the pros and cons of privatization can be measured against the standards of good management: regardless of ownership" (p. 28). They conclude that what matters is competition and a set of institutional arrangements that will induce managers to work for the public interest. Competition rather than ownership is what matters—this is a theme that is shared by the majority of students of outsourcing and privatization. Osborne and Gaebler (1992) call for competitive government. They do not limit the competitiveness only to markets or only between private firms that bid for contracts, but also call for competitiveness between public and private, and between public agencies.

Savas (1987) recognizes the government's role in providing essential services, and discusses the best ways of service delivery. He distinguishes between four types of goods and services: private, toll, common and collective, and identifies ten types of service arrangements: (1) government service, (2) government vending, (3) intergovernmental agreement, (4) contracts, (5) franchises, (6) grants, (7) vouchers, (8) market systems, (9) voluntary service, and (10) self-service. Savas maintains that the appropriateness of each arrangement for provision of a certain type of service or good should be judged according to the following criteria: (1) service specificity, or how specifically the service can be defined so that the guidelines of private producers of the service can be exact; (2) availability of competitors; (3) efficiency and effectiveness; (4) the scale of the service, or how large the organization should be to produce the service efficiently; (5) relationship of benefits and costs, or the calculation of the degree to which those who use the service pay directly for its benefits; (6) responsiveness to consumers; (7) susceptibility to fraud; (8) economic equity; (9) equity for minorities; (10) responsiveness to government direction; (11) the size of the government required by service arrangement (Osborne and Gaebler 1992, pp. 343–344). Others basically agree with this framework, also adding that outsourcing makes sense when transaction costs are low (Donahue 1990; Prager 1994). Osborne and Gaebler (1992, pp. 347–348) elaborate on Savas' framework and come up with a table that contains recommendations for what kinds of tasks are best suited for different sectors—public, private and not-for-profit. The tasks best suited for public sector are policy management, regulation, enforcement of equity, prevention of discrimination, prevention of exploitation, and promotion of social cohesion. The tasks best suited for the private sector include economic and investment tasks, profit generation and promotion of self-sufficiency. The tasks more appropriate for the third sector are the social tasks, tasks that require volunteer labor, tasks that generate little profit, promotion of individual responsibility, promotion of community, and promotion of commitment to welfare of others.

Conclusion

Outsourcing is taking place—both in private and public sectors—and it is taking place at an increased pace. In most cases, outsourcing of government services to the private sector is cost-effective. It is not effective because the private sector per se is better, more efficient, and more effective. The reason for cost savings is the special institutional arrangement, where private firms compete with each other or with public agencies and are duly monitored by the contracting jurisdiction.

Privatization in the form of outsourcing of services should not be considered as the ultimately efficient available option for the increasingly complex problems that government faces. It should be viewed as an alternative arrangement of service delivery that can be more efficient and effective under certain conditions. The decision about privatization should be adopted after careful consideration of a host of factors, ranging from technical characteristics (e.g., size for which that operation becomes efficient), organizational structure, and competitiveness of the environment, to the management's capacity of monitoring, costs of monitoring, and the relation of the outsourced service to the agency's mission. Gains in cost savings should not be at the expense of other values of the government, such as equity, fairness, and public trust. Because of an increased possibility of corruption, outsourcing requires constant feedback and reinforcement of accountability practices. And finally, privatization in the form of outsourcing should not be pursued for goals other than cost savings, such as reducing the government or decreasing service levels.

VATCHE GABRIELIAN

BIBLIOGRAPHY

Alchian, Armen, A., and Harold Demsetz, 1972. "Production, Information Costs and Economic Organization." *American Economic Review* (December) 777–795.

Baumol, William J. and Alan S. Blinder, 1988. *Economics: Principles and Policy: Microeconomics*. 4th ed. San Diego, CA: Harcourt Brace Jovanovich.

Bettis, Richard A., Stephen P. Bradley and Gray Hamel, 1992. "Outsourcing and Industrial Decline." *The Executive,* vol. 6, no.1 (February) 7–22.

Bozeman, Barry, 1987. *All Organizations Are Public: Bridging Public and Private Organizational Theories*. San Francisco, CA: Jossey-Bass.

Buchanan, James, 1977. "Why Does Government Grow?" In Borcherding, Thomas E., ed., *Budgets and Bureaucrats: The Sources of Government Growth*. Durham NC: Duke University Press.

Chi, Keon S., 1994. "Privatization in State Government: Trends and Issues." Paper presented at ASPA's 55th National Training Conference, Kansas City, MO: July 23–27.

Coase, Ronald, 1937. "The Nature of the Firm." *Economica* (November) 386–405.

Donahue, John D. 1989. *The Privatization Decision: Public Ends, Private Means*. New York: Basic Books.

Goodman, John B. and Gary W. Loveman, 1991. "Does Privatization Serve the Public Interest?" *Harvard Business Review* (November-December) 26–38.

Halachmi, Arie and Marc Hozler, 1993. "Toward a Competitive Public Administration." *International Review of Administrative Science*, vol. 59, no. 1 (March) 29–45.

Hanke, S. H., ed., 1987. *Prospects for Privatization*. Academy of Political Science, New York.

Hanrahan, John, 1983. *Government by Contract*. New York: Norton.

Hatry, Harry P., 1988. "Privatization Presents Problems." *National Civic Review*, vol. 77, no. 2 (March-April).

Henig, Jeffrey R., 1989–90. "Privatization in the United States: Theory and Practice." *Political Science Quarterly*, vol. 104, no. 4: 649–670.

Johnston, Van R., 1990. "Privatization of Prisons: Management, Productivity, and Governance Concerns." *Public Productivity and Management Review*, vol. XIV, no. 2 (Winter) 189–201.

Kemp, Roger L., ed., 1991. *Privatization: Provision of Public Services by the Private Sector.* Jefferson, NC: McFarland.

Kettl, Donald F., 1993. "The Myths, Realities, and Challenges of Privatization." In Frank J. Thompson, ed., *Revitalizing State and Local Public Service: Strengthening Performance, Accountability and Citizen Confidence.* San Francisco: Jossey-Bass, 246–279.

Kolderie, Ted, 1986. "The Two Different Concepts of Privatization." *Public Administration Review,* vol. 46, no. 4 (July-August).

Krusselberg, Hans-Gunter, 1991. "Markets and Hierarchies: About the Dialectics of Their Antagonism and Compatibility." In F.-X. Kaufman, ed., *The Public Sector: Challenge for Education and Learning.* Berlin: de Gruyter, pp. 376–369.

National Academy of Public Administration (NAPA), 1989. *Privatization: The Challenge to Public Management: A Report by an Academy Panel.* Washington D.C.: NAPA.

Nelson, Barbara J., 1980. "Purchase of Services." In G. J. Washnis, ed., *Productivity Improvement Handbook for State and Local Governments.* New York: Wiley.

Osborne, David and Ted Gaebler, 1992. *Reinventing Government: How the Entrepreneurial Spirit Is Transforming the Public Sector.* Reading, MA: Addison-Wesley.

Prager, Jonas, 1994. "Contracting Out Government Services: Lessons from the Private Sector." *Public Administration Review,* vol. 54, no. 2 (March-April) 176–185.

Quinn, James Brian, Thomas L. Doorley, and Penny C. Paquette, 1990. "Beyond Products: Service-Based Strategy." *Harvard Business Review* (March-April) 58–68.

Rainey, Hal G., 1991. *Understanding and Managing Public Organizations.* San Francisco: Jossey-Bass.

Savas, E. S., 1992. "Privatization and Productivity." In Marc Holzer, ed., *Public Productivity Handbook.* Dekker, NY: 79–99.

Savas, E. S., 1987. *Privatization: The Key to Better Government.* Chatham House.

Savas, E. S., 1977. *The Organization and Efficiency of Solid Waste Collection.* Lexington Books.

Stevens, Barbara J., 1984. "Comparing Public- and Private-Sector Efficiency: An Analysis of Eight Activities." *National Productivity Review* Lexington, MA: (Autumn).

Stevens, Barbara J., 1977. "Scale, Market Structure and the Cost of Refuse Collection." *Review of Economics and Statistics* 60 (March).

Thayer, Frederick C., 1987. "Privatization: Carnage, Chaos and Corruption." In B. J. Carroll et al., eds., *Private Means Public Ends: Private Business in Social Service Delivery.* NY: Praeger, pp. 146–147.

Wamsley, G. L. and M. N. Zald, 1973. *The Political Economy of Public Organizations.* Lexington, MA: Heath.

Welch, James A. and P. Ranganath Nayak, 1992. "Strategic Sourcing: A Progressive Approach to the Make-or-Buy Decision." *The Executive,* vol. 6, no. 1 (February) 23–31.

Williamson, Oliver E., 1975. *Markets and Hierarchies. Analysis and Antitrust Implications.* New York: Free Press.

P

PARKINSON'S LAW. The proposition that work expands to fill the time made available for its completion. The idea was first set out formally by the British social theorist and political scientist, C. Northcote Parkinson, in his book *Parkinson's Law*, published in 1957. Like a number of popular studies, its main function is to suggest that the more severe theorists of management practice ought not to take themselves too seriously.

Parkinson was what used to be called an Admiralty civil servant: a British official seconded to the Royal Navy. It was during an investigation of work practices in the British Naval Service that he became impressed by the phenomenon expressed in the principle that was ever after to bear his name. Regardless of management structure or an incentive- or reward-based system, individuals seemed to make their own choices as to how fast a job could be completed. The work would be completed on time—the "time" being defined as the moment when adverse effects would be visited upon the employee for late delivery. As interesting is Parkinson's analysis of how employees respond to repeated difficulties in meeting deadlines. In effect, Parkinson argues that employees conspire against their employers by increasing the size of the hierarchy, aggrandizing their own position in the process, at the expense of those who pay them. He tended to assume that supervisors tended to conspire against the employer; that employees (acting individually or in concert) would injure themselves to the point where the paymaster is brought to the brink of bankruptcy; that less spent on wages will maximize profits. While challenging, none of these are self-evidently true. Parkinson, as with many who have a particular insight—in this case the one that is encapsulated in the definition above—took the point too far in his published theoretical work, to the extent where other theorists had more to say on the questions that he was addressing. Unlike them, however, he has achieved his own immortality.

PETER FOOT

BIBLIOGRAPHY

Parkinson, C. N., 1957. *Parkinson's Law and Other Studies in Administration.* Boston: Houghton Mifflin.

PARLIAMENTARY APPROPRIATION. The appropriation by a parliament of a government's proposed budget, based on strict conformity to legislative processes through which executive proposals are examined and, if appropriate, amended before being granted legal authority; or, in a more restricted sense, the approval process for the internal budget of a parliament itself. The latter process varies considerably among parliamentary systems, displaying different degrees of legislative independence and financial autonomy. Generally, the greater the degree of financial autonomy, the greater the degree of independent parliamentary control over an executive's budget proposals. Thus the state of the former provides clues on the effectiveness of the latter.

Appropriation processes are typically reactive, involving parliamentary consideration of budget proposals or estimates initiated by an executive. Parliaments vary in their formal emphasis, but a common convention is to have the estimates detailed so that they are allocated to identifiable activities or programs, with separate "votes" or units of appropriation each attracting separate legislative endorsement. The specific articulation of program aims serves a traditional parliamentary purpose, even in the era of program budgeting: governments may spend public money only on those activities or programs duly authorized by parliament.

British parliamentary history displays the basic appropriation function that is adapted to different structures in different parliamentary systems. From its earliest meetings, the House of Commons was convened and constituted in response to the demands of executive governments, for whom periodic parliamentary consent was the necessary price of their continued legitimacy. At first the Crown, then later cabinet executives, accepted that their popular legitimacy required that access to public money rests on the consent and taxation authority of a popular body. Faced with requests for their consent, parliaments soon appreciated that their greatest power was the threat of refusal of "supply" to a needy executive. Armed with this ultimate power of refusal to open the public purse, parliaments became the basic authority over the supply of public expenditure to government.

Fundamental to the grievances listed in the Bill of Rights of 1689 is that the executive levied money "by pretence of prerogative . . . in other manner, than . . . was granted by Parliament." But there is a world of difference between a constitutional requirement for government appropriations by annual consent of Parliament and an institutional capacity to control the budget process. The model is one of informed consent rather than of initiative and control. Parliamentary systems have tended to follow the British lead in establishing a consolidated fund, a system of annual estimates with audited accounts, and control facilities of the kind represented by a parliamentary public accounts committee and an independent auditor-general reporting directly to Parliament. As reactive mechanisms, these facilities are only as good as the information provided by the initiating executive.

Executive governments have retained primary control over the policy directions of funds appropriated. Parliaments are presented with a bill of charges, and typically even the most assiduous appropriation processes fail to amend other than at the expenditure margins. It is a commonplace that parliamentary appropriations committees achieve modest influence compared to their U.S. counterparts. Jennings (1940) long ago stated their characteristic defects: government rules preclude them from examining issues of policy; governments provide them with insufficient time, especially for detailed estimates examination; and unlike either the Treasury or the Auditor-General, they have few professional staff (pp. 309–311).

Two important features reveal enduring institutional tensions within the appropriations process: bicameralism and executive recommendations. The British solution has been to deny, since the bicameral crisis of 1909–1911, any effective responsibility to the unelected House of Lords. The UK Parliament Act stipulates that core appropriations bills certified by the Speaker as "money bills" may not be held up by the Lords for longer than one month. Westminster-derived parliaments differ, with Canada, with its unelected Senate, forshadowing British practice while Australia, with its elected Senate, conferred virtually equal legislative responsibility on both houses. New Zealand abolished its upper house in the late 1940s.

British constitutional development also provides that, unlike all other legislation, appropriation bills may not pass into law unless accompanied by an executive recommendation of support. This device virtually protects appropriation law as an executive monopoly, justified by appeal to fears of fiscal extravagence by a misguided democracy of backbench "demagogues and republicans" (Reid 1966, p. 40; cf. pp. 35–45). In marked contrast to the U.S. situation, Westminster-derived parliaments generally accept this principle of party government under which public expenditure is primarily the responsibility of the government of the day, subject to their retention of the confidence of the House and thereby their continued delegation of executive responsibilities.

The contrast with the U.S. appropriations process is instructive. Article 1, section 9 of the U.S. Constitution provides for "appropriations made by law." Specialist appropriations committees in both houses hold detailed hearings with affected agencies in the process of initiating appropriations bills, complementing the work of separate authorization committees which determine core agency programs. The U.S. system tests the fiscal determination of executive and legislative interests. The classic 1950s study by Beer, *Treasury Control*, concluded that British political and bureaucratic executives face fewer risks of public scrutiny by the legislature than do their U.S. counterparts. Sadly, the British model now "appears to mean authorizing spending in general without any discussion and occasionally closely scrutinizing a particular item of expenditure without any coherent analytical framework" (Garrett 1992, p. 108).

Processes for the determination of a parliament's own appropriations defy easy summary. The trend is toward a parliamentary commission of senior parliamentarians and the finance minister, which sets an agreed amount for inclusion in the government's estimates. Independent forms can mask substantial dependencies. Australia, for instance, lacks such a strong advisory commission, but does have a separate appropriation bill covering Parliament, albeit one effectively determined by the government of the day.

JOHN UHR

BIBLIOGRAPHY

Beer, S., 1956. *Treasury Control*. Oxford: Clarendon Press.
Garrett, J., 1992. *Westminster: Does It Work?* London: Gollancz.
Jennings, I., 1940. *Parliament*. Cambridge, England: Cambridge University Press.
Reid, G., 1966. *The Politics of Financial Control*. London: Hutchinson.
Wildavsky, A., 1981. *The Politics of the Budgetary Process*. Boston: Little Brown.

PARLIAMENTARY PROCEDURE.

Rules governing the conduct of deliberative assemblies. The deliberative assemblies may be national parliaments with the power of giving effect to laws but any established body that proceeds by discussion, rather than vote or diktat alone, falls within the rubric. A student debating body may thus adopt parliamentary procedure.

The rules governing the conduct of proceedings have the distinguishing characteristics of being established and enforced. That is, proceedings take place within an established framework of rules and those rules are enforced on members of the assembly. The form in which the rules are expressed can vary. Some are embodied in a formal code. It is common for legislatures, for example, to adopt standing orders. These are agreed and then published. Other rules derive from practice and tradition. Some may be maintained on the basis of an oral tradition but almost always they will be written down, though not necessarily carry legal force.

At the heart of parliamentary procedure, then, is the parliamentary rule book, though the book may not be a single document. In the British Parliament, the standing orders adapted by each of the two Houses are contained in relatively brief documents. However, the procedural practices derived from precedent are so extensive that the rules and practices are published in a volume that exceeds a thousand pages. Known formally as *Erskine May's Treatise on the Law, Privileges, Proceedings and Usage of Parliament*—and more popularly by the short title of *Erskine May*—it brings together all the rules established by standing order and precedent. First compiled by a nineteenth-century clerk of the House of Commons called Erskine May, it is now in its twenty-first edition (Boulton 1989) and runs to 1,079 pages. Though the work has no legal force, it is relied upon by members of Parliament and by the parliamentary authorities in determining what is permissible and what is not.

Methods of enforcement also vary. Power to enforce the rules is normally vested in a presiding officer. This presiding officer may be a neutral figure with no partisan affiliation—as in the British House of Commons—or a partisan figure with the power to utilize the rules in a politically self-serving manner, as in the U.S. House of Representatives or the Russian Parliament. However, in some cases enforcement is left to members themselves. In the British House of Lords, for example, the presiding officer (the Lord Chancellor) has no formal powers, members of the House being responsible for ensuring the rules are followed. In practice, guidance is normally given by a leading figure in the House, the Leader of the House, but it is no more than guidance.

In addition to rules that are known and enforceable, the term may also be used to convey substantive procedural rights, principally for both sides of an argument to be heard. Typically, provision will be made for a motion to be proposed and then for a response by someone opposed to the motion. Parliamentary procedure derived from British experience will normally provide for speakers for both sides to be heard at the beginning of a debate and for speakers from both sides to make closing speeches. In the British House of Commons, a government motion will be moved by a government minister; a member of the Opposition front bench will then respond; members of the House will then rise to "catch the Speaker's eye" and the Speaker will call members from the back benches—usually from alternate sides of the House—to speak before a member of the Opposition front bench makes a closing speech for the Opposition and a minister makes the final speech on behalf of the government. If the motion is contested, a vote then takes place.

In terms of ensuring some balance between the rights of the majority and the rights of the minority, parliamentary procedure varies. Typically, a member will have some right to intervene, or to seek to intervene, during a speech by another member. Members may also have the power to filibuster—that is, to continue speaking at length, moving procedural motions or raising points of order, for the purpose of delaying proceedings, in the hope that the motion before the house will be dropped, thus allowing the house to move on to other business. The use of the filibuster is associated especially with the U.S. Senate. In 1957, one senator—Storm Thurmond—held the floor for 24 hours and 18 minutes. (A member of the Senate in the Texas state legislature once spoke for more than 28 hours.) A minority of members may also be empowered to block a particular motion, especially a procedural motion, or conversely may

have the power to trigger a particular procedure. In the U.S. House of Representatives and the Senate, one-fifth of the members present can require a roll-call vote, though in the Senate a request by a single senator for a roll call vote is usually not denied. In the British House of Commons, two members are sufficient to force a vote (known as a division) in which members' votes are recorded.

The majority of members will be able to get their way in a vote and there may also be particular procedures that allow the will of the majority to prevail over attempts at obstruction by a minority of members. Parliamentary procedure will normally provide for minority voices to be heard—but not endlessly. Provision will typically exist for debate to be limited, either through formal advance timetabling or through provision for a closure motion, the latter—if carried—requiring an immediate vote on the substantive motion or limiting the remaining period of debate. In the U.S. Senate, a closure motion requires support of three-fifths of the senators. Limits may also be set on the length of individual speeches. In the Canadian House of Commons, for example, when the Speaker is in the chair, no member—with certain exceptions, such as the prime minister and leader of the opposition—"shall speak for more than twenty minutes at a time in any debate."

In order to ensure that deliberation is relevant and tempered, it is common but not universal to require that speeches are germane to the motion under consideration. The U.S. Senate, though not the House of Representatives, is one of the exceptions. Members may also be prohibited from using "unparliamentary language," though what is unparliamentary in one debating body may not be in another. In the Australian House of Representatives, for example, personal invective tends to be allowed, whereas in the British House of Commons it is normally ruled out of order. In the Indian Lok Sabha, defamatory, indecent, unparliamentary, or undignified words can be ordered to be expunged by the presiding officer.

Once debate is concluded, a vote may then take place on the motion. Methods of voting vary considerably. Some legislatures allow for a voice vote, the presiding officer deciding which side has the advantage (though usually with provision for the assessment to be challenged and a more formal method of voting employed); some for members to vote by raising their hands; some for members to rise in their places and be counted; some for a secret ballot; some for electronic voting, with the voting figures only being displayed or announced; and some for a roll call vote, with names being read out, or with members physically voting in lobbies, or with members voting electronically and their names being recorded. A Number of these methods may be employed by a single legislature. Most will have some provision for a voice vote or vote by show of hands. Secret balloting is variously employed, though the practice is probably less frequent now than in previous decades. In 1989, for example, the provision in the Italian Parliament for secret voting on request for most bills was abolished. Even so, the use of voting that does not require the names of members to be recorded is common. The two houses of the British Parliament are unusual in the extent to which roll-call votes–members voting by going into an "aye" or "no" lobby–are taken whenever a motion is contested.

Characteristically, parliamentary procedure entails debate on a motion. However, parliaments have generally deviated from this rule by increasingly making provision for a period of questions, when there is no motion before the House and when members may ask questions of members of the executive or of other members who are not members of the executive (for example, those who chair parliamentary bodies). In almost all parliamentary assemblies, according to Gaston Bruyneel (1978) in a report adopted by the Association of Secretaries General of Parliaments, "it is possible to ask oral questions which are either introduced by written notice and then sometimes are read out, or put orally by means of an organized procedure, or by using a point of order" (p. 84). These questions then receive a reply given in public session by the appropriate minister. A fixed period for questions–Question Time–is a feature of many parliaments. In some countries, such as Austria and Finland, the procedure for asking questions is even enshrined in the constitution.

Though question time may deviate from the usual rule that there must be a motion for debate, it falls within the rubric of parliamentary procedure because it exists within a parliamentary arena–dating, in the British Parliament, from the eighteenth century–and because it takes place within an organized procedure.

PHILIP NORTON

BIBLIOGRAPHY

Boulton, Clifford J., ed., 1989. *Erskine May's Treatise on the Law, Privileges, Proceedings and Usage of Parliament.* 21st ed. London: Butterworths.
Bradshaw, Kenneth and David Pring, 1981. *Parliament and Congress.* Rev. ed. London: Quartet Books.
Bruyneel, G., 1978. *Interpellations, Questions and Analogous Procedures for the Control of Government Actions and Challenging the Responsibility of the Government.* Report adopted by the Association of Secretaries General of Parliaments.
Loewenberg, Gerhard and Samuel C. Patterson, 1979. *Comparing Legislatures.* Lanham, MA: University Press of America.
Olson, David M., 1980. *The Legislative Process: A Comparative Analysis.* New York: Harper & Row.

PARLIAMENTARY SCRUTINY. The process by which legislatures in the parliamentary tradition undertake oversight of administrative processes.

In the parliamentary tradition, the preeminent roles of Parliament are to provide the focus of responsible government, the forum which a party must dominate in order to form government, the place where proposed legislation is debated and budgets approved, the group from which the cabinet is chosen, and the assembly whose confidence must be retained for authority to continue. However, the roles of Parliament in the scrutiny of executive and administrative actions have become increasingly important over the last century.

Importance of Parliamentary Scrutiny

The scrutiny of administrative actions is an important function for parliaments. It provides opportunities for members of parliaments to gain firsthand knowledge of administrative problems and issues, and should lead to more informed debate and heightened accountability. When problems arise, the authority of Parliament can be an appropriate basis from which to conduct an authoritative investigation. Sometimes the broad base of parliamentary representation can facilitate a form of scrutiny whose credibility allows contentious social issues to be explored.

Dimensions of Parliamentary Scrutiny

The principal means by which Parliament scrutinizes administrative and executive actions include parliamentary questions (with or without notice); requirements for administrative agencies to present annual or other reports and returns to Parliament; the activities of investigative units such as auditors-general or monitors which report to Parliament on administrative actions; and the inquiries of select or standing committees of Parliament, which may scrutinize administrative actions through hearings, field visits, consultancy inquiries, and the receipt of submissions and other evidence.

Parliamentary Questions

Most parliamentary procedures schedule regular times at which members can pose questions, "with or without notice," to ministers of the government. Ministers are expected, by reason of their responsibility for a portfolio, to respond spontaneously to a question without notice, or to provide a prepared response to a question on notice, concerning policies or administrative actions within their portfolios.

At best, these procedures can epitomize accountability, requiring ministers to have at their command a sound knowledge of their areas of responsibility. The requirement to provide a written answer itself can draw issues and information about administrative performance into the public arena. The requirement for ministers to answer questions has become an important means of making public information about administrative actions which might otherwise be secret.

Procedures for parliamentary questions are open to abuse. Particularly if question time is broadcast or televised, politicians may exploit the segment for publicity purposes with grandstanding, abuse, or dramatic interplay with opposing politicians. Government members may ask pre-agreed questions (or "dorothy dixers") whose aim is not to elicit information but to provide the signal for a government statement. Ministers may respond to questions with lengthy political diatribes rather than answering the questions asked. And, under conditions of the commercialization of public enterprise, they may refuse to answer questions on the basis of the supposed commercial confidentiality of the enterprise in question.

Parliamentary questions form an important opportunity for a degree of parliamentary scrutiny, albeit an opportunity likely to be superficial and open to political manipulation.

Annual Reporting Requirements

A form of parliamentary scrutiny less open to abuse is the imposition of mandatory requirements for public departments and agencies to provide formal annual reports or returns to parliament. Such a requirement is strengthened if the requirement specifies the form in which financial reports are to be made, and stipulates other matters which must be reported—such as performance data, the names of senior office holders, the corporate objectives of the organization, details of borrowings, consultancies, and so forth.

Objections are sometimes levelled at these requirements based on the cost of providing the reports required, the charge that politicians do not seem to read or debate the contents of the reports at a level which justifies the cost and difficulty in preparing them, and in the case of commercial organizations, that they do not wish to report their operations in the level of detail required. Despite these objections, an annual reporting requirement based on Parliament's scrutiny function is critical if systematic information about public sector bodies is to be brought into the public arena.

Auditors-General and Monitors

Because of the complex demands on the time of parliamentarians and the need in some areas such as financial management for painstaking inquiry before judgments can be made, most parliaments are assisted in their scrutiny role by specialized investigators, such as auditors-general or monitors (ombuds). Such investigators have statutory powers and their own investigative staff. They may or may not form part of parliamentary administration, though if they do not, the executive government of the day may through direction or financial constraint offer real or potential threats to their independence or capability.

Contemporary auditors-general, in extending their role beyond financial or compliance audit to performance audit, program evaluation, and comprehensive audit, may provide parliaments with information critical to their scrutiny function.

Parliamentary Committees

As is the case with the U.S. Congress, parliaments today often have an extensive committee system supported by professional research support. While some committees are devoted to consideration of prospective legislation and initiatives, some parliamentary committees are usually devoted to the scrutiny of administration. The UK House of Commons in 1861 pioneered the concept of a Committee of Public Accounts, whose role is to focus on the financial management of public agencies, often using reports received from the auditor-general as a trigger. Other committees are often created to examine government operations or to oversight public bodies and government business enterprises. The appearance of civil servants before committees as witnesses can raise concerns as to confidentiality and the operation of ministerial responsibility, and explicit guidelines often exist to govern such situations.

Parliamentary committees at their best can provide parliamentary scrutiny with a powerful cutting edge, exposing inefficiency and providing parliamentarians (and future ministers) with a tough grounding in administrative practice and malpractice. Effective parliamentary committees, however, can make executive governments nervous, and the dominance of Parliament as well as executive government by the ministry in the parliamentary tradition affords scope for a threatened government to draw the teeth of potential critics. Accordingly parliamentary committees in some regimes and at some periods of time are tame cats which draw no blood.

Overview

Parliamentarians have diverse functions, and the scrutiny of administration and the executive is not the top priority of all. Nonetheless, an effective parliament is one which has a meaningful scrutiny function, presided over by parliamentarians who understand the importance of this role for effective democracy. Parliamentary democracy is well served when the organs of scrutiny—question time, formal reporting, committees, and the investigative jurisdictions—are playing their part well.

E. W. RUSSELL

BIBLIOGRAPHY

Augment, S., 1991. "Annual Reporting by Commonwealth Departments and Statutory Authorities: The Cornerstone of Executive Accountability to the Parliament." *Legislative Studies,* vol. 61, no. 8.

Drewry, G., 1989. *The New Select Committees: A Study of the 1979 Reforms.* Oxford, England: Oxford University Press.

Marsh, Ian, 1992. *Parliamentary Oversight of Public Service Performance: Australian Developments: UK and US Perspectives.* Canberra: Task Force on Management Improvement.

Normanton, E. L., 1966. *Accountability and Audit of Governments: A Comparative Study.* Manchester: Manchester University Press.

Thynne, I. and John Goldring, 1987. *Accountability and Control, Government Officials and the Exercise of Power.* Sydney: Law Book Co.

Uhr, J. 1991. "Annual Reports and Parliamentary Committees." *Legislative Studies,* vol. 6, no. 1.

PARLIAMENTARY SYSTEM.

1. A system of government based on a deliberative assembly. This distinguishes it from government by a dictator or a junta or one by plebiscite. The term is sometimes qualified, as in "parliamentary democracy", thus distinguishing a democracy with a deliberative assembly from those political systems which either do not have a deliberative assembly or do not have one that is freely chosen by the electors. 2. A particular system of government in which government and deliberative assembly do not enjoy mutually autonomous existences. In this—the more common—usage, there are three defining characteristics. First, the government is drawn from the legislature. Second, the government remains dependent on the legislature for its continuance in office. And, third, the government proceeds by collective deliberation and answers for its actions as a collective body. These distinguish it from a presidential system in which there is the separate election of executive and legislature, each enjoying autonomy of the other, and with the powers of government being exercised formally by an individual and not a collective body.

These characteristics are the defining characteristics of a parliamentary system. Such a system, though, has usually a number of other features, though none constituting a defining characteristic. In a parliamentary system, there is a separation of head of state and head of government, ministers will usually remain within the legislature, and the head of government will usually have the power to call or request a dissolution of the legislature.

Defining Characteristics

Indirect Election

Government in a parliamentary system is drawn from the legislature. There is therefore the indirect election of the government. Those political leaders who are to head the government are elected but they are elected on the same basis as other members of the legislature. Electors may vote for the party they wish to form the government, or be in government, but they have no power to exercise a direct choice in electing the head of government. They may know who is likely to be head of government as a result of how they vote, but the name of that individual does not appear on the ballot paper as a candidate for that office.

Dependence on the Confidence of the Legislature

Once in office, the executive remains dependent on the confidence of the legislature. It requires a majority to get its measures passed, but that is not a feature peculiar to a parliamentary system. What is peculiar to the system is the capacity of the legislature to turn the executive out of office by a vote of no confidence.

The form such an expression of no confidence may take varies. The simplest form is an explicit vote of no confidence ("That this House has no confidence in the Government") with no attendant qualifications. In some systems, the motion must embody the reasons for the action. Thus, for example, under Article 94 of the Italian constitution: "Each House grants or withdraws its confidence by a motion in which reasons are set forth and which is submitted to a roll-call vote." In some countries, such as Germany, the constitution stipulates that a constructive vote of no confidence is required: that is, that the legislature cannot simply turn out the head of government, but has to agree on the replacement.

In some systems, votes may be deemed to constitute implicit votes of confidence—such as the vote approving the government's budget—or the government may declare that votes on substantive issues are to be treated as votes of confidence. In 1972, for example, British prime minister Edward Heath (1970–74) declared that the vote on the second reading (the vote on the principle of the measure) of the European Communities Bill, providing the legal basis for British membership of the European Community, was to constitute a vote of confidence. He told the House of Commons that, if the government lost the vote, "this Parliament cannot sensibly continue." If a vote of no confidence is carried, then a government may be replaced by another—predetermined in the case of a constructive vote of no confidence—or it may have the choice, as in the United Kingdom, of resigning office (leaving it to the head of state to select a new head of government) or of seeking the election of a new legislature.

Constitutional provisions also vary as to whether, in bicameral legislatures, the government is dependent on the confidence of one or both houses. In Italy, for example, the constitution stipulates that "The Government must enjoy the confidence of the two Houses." In Canada and the United Kingdom, where neither second chamber is elected, the government depends on the confidence solely of the elected lower House.

Collective Government

The third defining characteristic is that of a collective government. This has two elements: collective decisionmaking and collective responsibility. Though some parliamentary systems may have very powerful heads of government, each head governs through a collective decisionmaking body. The principal measures of public policy to be placed before the legislature for approval are agreed upon by the collective body of government leaders, commonly called a cabinet.

In 1918 a Machinery of Government Committee in Britain delineated three main functions of the British cabinet: (1) the final determination of the policy to be submitted to Parliament; (2) the supreme control of the national executive in accordance with the policy prescribed by Parliament; and (3) the continuous coordination and delimitation of the authorities of the several departments of state. Those functions remain extant and have general applicability. Some cabinets may be dominated by the prime minister but the cabinet has the ultimate authority in determining government policy and may, if it wishes, overrule the prime minister. Even the most powerful of prime ministers in Britain, such as Winston Churchill in wartime (1940–45) and Margaret Thatcher (1979–90), have not always managed to carry their cabinets with them. No such capacity to overrule the head of government exists in a presidential system.

There is collective deliberation and there is collective responsibility. That is, ministers collectively are answerable for the policy of the government. If the legislature disapproves, then it has the option not just of negating the policy but of expressing its lack of confidence in the government. In that event, then the whole government goes. When in November 1994, British prime minister John Major (1990–) made a vote on a bill a vote of confidence, some Conservative members of parliament claimed that a government defeat would not necessarily require the resignation of the government. It was made clear by the chancellor of the exchequer that, if the vote was lost, the entire government would resign.

Separation of Head of Government and State

A government is formed from the party or parties able to command a majority following elections to the legislature. The leader of the coalition or of the majority party then becomes the head of government, though not—as in a presidential system—head of state. A parliamentary system will typically have a head of state with few if any political powers, fulfilling primarily a symbolic role. The head of state may have some latitude in calling on a party leader to form a government, but will usually be bound by specific provisions of the constitution or by convention. The Greek constitution, for example, lays down precise rules for the choice of prime minister. "The leader of the party having the absolute majority of seats in Parliament shall be appointed Prime Minister.... If no party has an absolute majority of parliamentary seats, the President of the Republic shall assign to the leader of the party with a relative majority an exploratory mandate." In the United Kingdom, the choice is determined not by law but by convention.

Ministers Remain Within the Legislature

In parliamentary systems, government ministers are usually drawn from, and remain within, the legislature. It is not axiomatic that they are members of the legislature. In some parliamentary systems, such as the Netherlands, there is a constitutional bar on ministers serving as members of parliament. Even in the United Kingdom, the exemplar of a parliamentary system, there is no legal requirement that ministers be members of parliament. On occasion, some ministers are appointed who are not members of the House of Commons or House of Lords and, more exceptionally, continue to serve while members of neither House. The occasions, though, are rare. It makes political, as well as constitutional, sense for ministers to be in Parliament. They are in a position to promote and defend government policy, rally supporters, and contribute to the government's majority when a vote takes place and, by virtue of their presence, are able to answer to the legislature for the conduct of government.

Even in those parliamentary systems in which ministers are not formally members of the legislature, it is common for them to be permitted to take part in parliamentary debates. Insofar as they are thus able to be present and take part in the deliberations they may be deemed to be "within" the legislature.

Head of Government Can Call an Election

In parliamentary systems, the head of state is usually empowered to dissolve the legislature and call an election. In certain limited cases, the head of state may be able to exercise independent choice in doing so. Usually, the action is taken on the advice of the head of government. The capacity to call an election is often not unrestricted. A time limit may be and usually is set on the maximum period a legislature may serve before being subject to election again. There may be limits on the number of times the legislature may be dissolved or on the circumstances in which it may be dissolved. The essential point, though, is that there is some leeway for new legislative elections to be called by the head of state, acting on the advice of the head of government. This distinguishes it from a strictly presidential system, where no such capacity exists.

Some writers, such as Douglas Verney in *The Analysis of Political Systems* (1959), have listed other characteristics of a parliamentary system, but they are either historical features or largely compounds or consequences of the six characteristics just enumerated. Verney notes that in a parliamentary system, Parliament itself is supreme—the outputs of Parliament cannot be overturned by the executive—but that within Parliament the component parts are dependent on one another. What he means is that government and the institution from which it is drawn are largely dependent on one another. The government depends for its continuance in office on the support of the legislature. The legislature looks to the government for leadership and itself may be dissolved on the decision of the government. The majority party in the legislature will also look to the government for policy that proves electorally popular. The relationship is thus symbiotic. Legislature and government depend on one another in a way that they do not in a presidential system.

Incidence

Parliamentary systems are numerous and tend to predominate in particular parts of the world. Arend Lijphart, in the introduction to his edited volume *Parliamentary Versus Presidential Government* (1992), identifies parliamentary systems as predominating in two particular groups of countries. One grouping is geographical and the other political. The geographical concentration is in Western Europe, where all the countries—with the exception of the semipresidential system of France—fall into the category. The political grouping is the Commonwealth, where British influence has been pronounced. All the principal countries (Australia, Canada, India, and New Zealand), as well as some of the smaller member countries, such as Jamaica, have parliamentary forms of government. (Nigeria, from 1960 to 1966, also falls within this category.) In addition to these two groups, there are a number of geographically disparate countries that have parliamentary systems, including most notably Japan and Israel. There is a dearth of parliamentary systems in Latin America, where a presidential system is dominant.

Strengths

The choice of a particular system of government will be influenced by historical and cultural variables. Each system has a number of strengths and none is problem free. Compared with a presidential system of government, a parliamentary system can claim five particular strengths: those of accountability, flexibility, structured conflict, political apprenticeship and productivity, though the last one is challenged by the findings of recent studies.

Accountability

The government is drawn from the legislature and is formed usually from the party, or parties, able to command a majority. That majority then passes the measures put forward by the government. There is thus a clearly identifiable body—the party or coalition in government—that electors can hold accountable for those measures at the next election. If electors disapprove of the public policy enacted during a particular Parliament, they can identify the body

to be turned out. In a presidential system, electors are potentially less able to identify a single body responsible for public policy. Is it the elected president or is it the majority party within the separately elected legislature?

Flexibility

If a government proves unable to command a parliamentary majority, or simply falls apart politically, the opportunity exists for new elections to take place and for the return of a party or parties able to form a new government. There is no need to wait until a fixed term is completed. There is flexibility also in the selection of a head of government. If a head of government proves to be politically incompetent or no longer acceptable to the government's supporters in the legislature, then he or she may be eased out of office by the governing party, or by the partners in the coalition, and replaced by a new head. Unlike an elected president, the head of government has no independent mandate and no independent legitimacy derived from direct election.

The flexibility in the system may result in the same party remaining in power, but with a new leader—as in the United Kingdom in 1990, when Margaret Thatcher was replaced as Conservative prime minister by John Major—or in a new party taking over the reins of government, with or without new elections. In Ireland in 1994, for example, a switch of allegiance by the Labour Party resulted in a new prime minister and a new coalition of parties in government, but without an election being called.

Structured Conflict

What this refers to is the fact that a parliamentary system provides a structure within which a clearly defined body of opposition can operate. Within Parliament, there is the party or parties that form the government and there is a party or parties not in government. The "out" party or parties form an opposition, usually an organized opposition. Within a parliamentary system, there is typically a prime minister and a leader of the opposition. The leader of the opposition may have a team of shadow ministers, to cover and comment on the policies and actions of ministers. Government is thus open to regular scrutiny and criticism.

Structured Apprenticeship

Where ministers are drawn from the parliament, aspirant ministers have to serve a political apprenticeship. Serving in Parliament provides an opportunity for them to display their parliamentary and political skills. Parliament constitutes a testing ground. It also constitutes a learning opportunity, members having an opportunity to see how ministers operate in a parliamentary context. When it comes to the selection of ministers, members of the parliament constitute known quantities. The prime minister has some idea of the particular skills—and limitations—of those he or she is putting in government.

This apprenticeship may also help contribute to cooperation and stability in the relationship between the legislature and that part of it which forms the executive. Ministers are socialized within the legislature. They understand the system and they are familiar with the problems facing members of the legislature. They may therefore be more responsive to requests for particular action from members of the legislature than in the case of ministers in presidential systems with no experience of service in the legislature.

Productivity

Given that the government is formed from a party or parties commanding a parliamentary majority, the government is likely to get its measures passed by the legislature. Thus, for instance, of 202 bills introduced by the British government in the Parliament of 1987–92, all but 11 were passed into law, and of the small number not passed most fell because of the calling of a general election. (Of 519 bills introduced by private members, only 65 were passed.) It is argued therefore that a parliamentary system is likely to be more productive in terms of policy output than a presidential system, where there is the potential for conflict, and hence stalemate, between the executive and the legislature. However, two recent studies—R. Kent Weaver and Bert A. Rockman, eds., *Do Institutions Matter?* (1993), and Hans-Dieter Klingemann, Richard Hofferbert, and Ian Budge, *Parties, Policies, and Democracy* (1994)—suggest that the difference between the systems is not as great as popularly supposed, the Westminster model of majoritarian party control not consistently performing better than other systems in translating programs into public policy.

Limitations

Parliamentary systems are also seen to have their negative side. Relative to presidential systems, the three principal limitations are those of executive dominance, instability, and limited legitimacy. In those systems in which ministers are drawn from Parliament, there is also the problem of a narrow base of recruitment to ministerial office.

Executive Dominance

Governments are formed from the party or parties able to command a majority of votes in the parliament. The government is therefore normally able to get its measures passed by that majority. There is no legislature independent of the executive; the relationship is symbiotic. Within that relationship, the government dominates. Members of the—or a—governing party support the party because they usually agree with what it is doing, because they were elected to support their party, and because failure to do so may result in the party losing power at the next election.

Command of a parliamentary majority may result in an executive that is not only dominant but one that is subject to no effective constraint. The term "elective dictatorship" was employed in a public lecture in 1976 by a leading parliamentarian, Lord Hailsham, to describe the situation in the United Kingdom.

Instability

The fact that parliaments may be dissolved and new elections held can be seen in both a positive and a negative light. The positive and negative characteristics are, respectively, flexibility and instability. If a governing coalition falls apart or loses a parliamentary vote of confidence, a new government is formed or fresh elections may be called. If negotiations between parties or a new election fail to produce a government able to command a majority, there may be a period of weak government and demands for fresh elections. "There is no doubt," according to Lijphart (1992) "that the cabinet's dependence on the legislature's confidence makes potential cabinet instability an inherent and inevitable feature of parliamentary systems" (p. 11). The exemplar of an unstable parliamentary system is Italy. Since 1945, it has averaged roughly one new government every year.

Limited Legitimacy

The fact that government derives from the parliament gives it some legitimacy but it lacks the legitimacy that derives from direct election. There is not the same democratic legitimacy as vests in a president elected directly by the people. In a parliamentary system, no elector votes definitively for the executive. The elector votes only for one or more members of the legislature. By voting for members of a particular party, electors may express a preference for a particular party to form the executive but have no power formally through the ballot box to determine directly who is to head the government or form the collective decisionmaking body. In a presidential system, the elector exercises a choice (voting for the executive and for members of the legislature) denied the elector in a parliamentary system.

Limited Pool for Recruitment

In a parliamentary system in which ministers are drawn from the legislature, the head of government has a narrow pool of talent from which to make the selection. In the United Kingdom, for instance, ministers are by convention drawn from Parliament and, again by convention, drawn predominantly from the elected chamber, the House of Commons. The pool of talent from which the prime minister may draw ministers is thus limited by constitutional convention. The choice is further limited in practice by a political imperative. The prime minister's selection is confined to members of his or her own party (or, in the event of a coalition, to members of the parties in the coalition). What this means, in practice, is that in the United Kingdom, the prime minister will choose the leading figures in government from a pool of 300 or so members of Parliament. The rest of the population is largely excluded from consideration.

Conclusion

Parliamentary systems are the antithesis of presidential systems. Each system has particular strengths and limitations. Nonetheless, the distinction is not always as sharp as our foregoing analysis may suggest. There are differences within parliamentary systems. As G. Bingham Powell, Jr. has shown, in *Contemporary Democracies: Participation, Stability and Violence* (1982), there is a distinction to be drawn between majoritarian parliamentary systems and representational parliamentary systems, the former being based on single-member electoral districts (or districts with few members) and the latter on multiple members per district. He found that presidential and majoritarian parliamentary systems were significantly more stable (in terms of the duration of government in office) than representational parliamentary systems. Representational parliamentary systems produced much higher voter turnout than majoritarian parliamentary–and presidential–systems. Furthermore, as the studies by Weaver and Rockman (1993) and Hans-Dieter Klingemann and his associates (1994) have shown, the distinction between parliamentary and presidential systems is often of little if any utility in explaining the capability of a system to generate public policy. There are thus dangers in seeking to generalize about parliamentary systems. The systems differ. Nonetheless, there is a particular political system that can be described as a parliamentary system, a system that has clear defining characteristics.

PHILIP NORTON

BIBLIOGRAPHY

Hailsham, Lord, 1976. *Elective Dictatorship.* London: British Broadcasting Corporation.

Klingemann, Hans-Dieter, Richard I. Hofferbert, and Ian Budge, 1994. *Parties, Policies, and Democracy.* Boulder, CO: Westview Press.

Lijphart, Arend, ed., 1992. *Parliamentary Versus Presidential Government.* Oxford: Oxford University Press.

Linz, Juan J., 1990. "The Virtues of Parliamentarianism." *Journal of Democracy,* 1(4):84–91.

Powell, Jr. G. Bingham, 1982. *Contemporary Democracies: Participation, Stability, and Violence.* Cambridge, MA: Harvard University Press.

Verney, Douglas V., 1959. *The Analysis of Political Systems.* London: Routledge & Kegan Paul.

Weaver, R. Kent and Bert A. Rockman, eds., 1993. *Do Institutions Matter?* Washington, D.C.: The Brookings Institution.

PAROLE. A criminal justice policy that provides a form of conditional release to a prisoner after having served a portion of his or her sentence in a correctional facility. Parole does not release the parolee from custody; it merely grants permission to a prisoner to serve a portion of the sentence outside the prison. The original sentence remains in full force and parolees can have their parole revoked if they do not comply with its conditions. All parolees remain under the supervision of a parole officer who is responsible for monitoring the parolee's conduct in the community.

Historical Background

The first concept of parole originated in the British penal colony in Australasia in 1840. It was conceived by Royal Navy Captain Alexander Maconochie (1787–1860) on Norfolk Island (a small island approximately one thousand miles east of Sydney, Australia). Maconochie's system required inmates to pass through five stages under an indefinite sentence. Each stage carried an increasing degree of responsibility and the prisoner had to successfully earn "marks" for labor, study, and favorable conduct in order to get promoted to the next stage. The five stages were: (1) strict imprisonment; (2) labor on government work gangs; (3) freedom within a limited area; (4) "ticket of leave" (parole); and (5) full restoration of liberty. Maconochie's system of parole was a radical departure from the past. This was the first major program where penal discipline was to be achieved by hope rather than fear.

The British system of parole was soon adopted in Ireland. It spread to Germany in 1842. Spain used a similar parole system in the mid-1840s. France adopted a parole policy in 1847 at the urging of the public prosecutor of Versailles. All of these countries continue to maintain a system of conditional release for prisoners.

A parole policy was first implemented in the United States at the Elmira Reformatory, in New York, in 1876. Early advocates thought that parole was best implemented in conjunction with an indeterminate sentence. Inmates were incarcerated without being told how long they had to remain in prison. The only way to get out of prison was to obtain a conditional release on parole. In its purest form, the inmate was kept under close supervision in the community for a period of time. Only after successfully meeting the terms of his or her parole (i.e., generally, maintaining viable employment, an acceptable residence, and crime-free behavior), would a parolee be released from the jurisdiction of the corrections authorities.

The initial form of parole was undermined in the United States when indeterminate sentencing fell into disfavor during the 1960s and was replaced by the "minimum/maximum" sentence. Inmates were required to serve their minimum sentence before being considered for parole. If their institutional adjustment was not satisfactory, they could be held in custody until their maximum sentence expired, at which time they had to be released from correctional authority. In many states, parole eligibility at the minimum date became automatic in order to make the parole process more impartial. Parole policy gradually came under criticism as a liberal notion that was responsible for letting criminals out of prison early. The problem was compounded by an overwhelmed parole system that could not adequately supervise the number of inmates being released. In many jurisdictions, the problem of overburdened parole officers continues.

Current Policy

Contemporary parole policy is composed of three fundamental processes: preparation, selection, and supervision. Preparation begins when the inmate is interviewed and his or her case history is examined. Among the factors considered are the committing offense, prior criminal record, prior institutional adjustment record, prior employment history, mental health status, and physical condition. An individualized treatment plan is prepared that outlines the therapeutic expectations for the inmate during incarceration. The preparation for parole really starts when the inmate becomes actively engaged in the prescriptive program plan.

The selection process for parole begins when the inmate first becomes eligible. The correctional staff review the inmate's degree of compliance with the treatment plan. They make a recommendation to the parole authorities whether or not to parole the inmate. Generally, the correctional staff are required to present a prognosis for success. The ability of corrections authorities to predict future criminal behavior has always been the subject of considerable debate. The debate notwithstanding, parole authorities must select the candidates that they believe are the most likely to reintegrate successfully into the community.

Once selected for parole, the parolee is returned to the community under the supervison of a parole officer. The parole officer develops a parole program that addresses the same issues considered by the correctional authorities. Parolees are expected to maintain suitable housing, viable employment, and a crime-free lifestyle. Generally the supervision is frequent and intense initially, gradually reducing in frequency and intensity as the parolee demonstrates consistent compliance with the parole terms. Should the parolee violate some condition of parole, he or she is given a due process hearing to consider the revocation of parole. If parole is revoked, the parolee is returned to prison. The parole authorities generally establish a new date upon

which the parole violator will again become eligible for parole based on the seriousness of the violation.

Parole policy must consider the question: Who should be selected for parole? The answer is: All inmates who are expected to be returned to society. Since 95 percent of all inmates are eventually released into the community, it would seem prudent that those persons should be released under supervision. The question then becomes not who will be paroled, but when they will be paroled. Parole eligibility varies from state to state in the United States. The majority of states set parole eligibility at the minimum sentence. Once the eligibility date is established, the question of when to parole an inmate is determined by assessing his or her degree of preparation and readiness to return to the community. The parole plan should include a sponsor (someone who agrees to provide community support), bona fide employment, a supportive social network, and a program that addresses the parolee's needs and develops his or her potential.

The crux of a successful parole policy is in the supervision process. Without meaningful supervision, the conditional aspect of the release to the community is diminished. Some jurisdictions merely require parolees to return postcards monthly attesting to the fact that they are maintaining the same parole address and their approved employment. Due primarily to the size of the parole officers' caseloads, parolees know that the chances of getting caught violating parole with this system are minimal. Many jurisdictions have now established an intensive form of supervision for the highest-risk parolees. Intensive supervision generally entails frequent reporting, random urinalysis (for illegal drug detection), and surprise visits from the parole officer at the parolee's home and place of employment. The certainty of getting caught for a parole violation is greatly increased with intensive supervision; which theoretically provides greater deterrence to illegal behavior and greater incentive for acceptable conduct.

Predicting the probability of success on parole in the community is the most difficult aspect of the parole process. Persons making decisions about parole generally consider the following information before granting approval for parole:

- institutional adjustment and recommendation;
- institutional program participation;
- community sensitivity and victim input;
- judge and/or district attorney recommendation;
- committing offense(s);
- length of sentence versus actual prison time served;
- previous criminal history;
- prior parole adjustment;
- prior community adjustment; and
- present social support network and parole plan.

Favorable responses to the majority of these factors are generally considered to be good predictors of the probability of success while on parole in the community.

Statistical Notes and Sources

State parole statistics in the United States reveal that the percentage of sentence served in prison has increased from 1988 to 1992. In 1988, the average inmate served 32 percent of his or her total prison sentence before being released on parole. In 1992, the average inmate served 34 percent of his or her prison sentence. The state parole statistics reveal that the success rate of parolees increased during the period from 1988 to 1992. A successful parole discharge is when the parolee completes his or her period of parole and is discharged from correctional authority. Unsuccessful parole discharges are largely due to parole violations that result in the revocation of parole and subsequent return to prison. Table I below highlights the percent of successful and unsuccessful state parole discharges from 1988 to 1992.

The statistics from the federal United States Parole Commission in Table II illustrate a somewhat higher success rate for parolees and some interesting comparisons between the sexes and the races.

The United States Parole Commission statistics also reveal that there has been a significant increase in the percentage of prisoners granted parole by the federal au-

TABLE I. STATE PAROLE DISCHARGES BY TYPE, 1988–1992

Type of Parole Discharge	1988	1991	1992
Successful	35.1%	40.6%	49.2%
Unsuccessful (All)	64.9%	59.4%	50.8%
*Returned to Prison	61.8%	57.0%	48.2%
Death	1.0%	1.1%	1.1%
Absconded	0.5%	0.7%	0.8%
Transfer	0.2%	0.1%	0.1%
Other	1.4%	0.5%	0.6%

*Includes those returned to prison with a new sentence, technical parole violation, and those returned pending parole revocation or new charges.

SOURCE: Adapted from Perkins 1994, p. 90.

TABLE II. FEDERAL PAROLE DISCHARGES BY SEX AND RACE, 1991

Type of Parole Discharge	SEX		RACE		
	Male	Female	White	Black	Other
Successful	63.1%	70.5%	70.0%	48.4%	68.7%
Unsuccessful	36.9%	29.5%	30.0%	51.6%	31.3%

SOURCE: Adapted from Maguire and Pastore 1994, p. 656.

TABLE III. PERCENT OF U.S. FEDERAL INMATES GRANTED PAROLE, 1977–1993

Year	Percent
1977	44.1%
1979	65.8%
1981	64.8%
1983	64.0%
1985	59.0%
1987	62.9%
1989	65.8%
1991	69.3%
1993	69.8%

SOURCE: Adapted from Maguire and Pastore 1994, p. 658.

thorities from 1977 to 1993. The percentages indicated in Table III are in relation to the total number of inmates considered for parole that year.

Trends

The latest trend in parole policy is known as "presumptive release." This is a derivation of automatic eligibility for parole at the minimum sentence date; however, presumptive release automatically places the inmate on parole at his or her minimum date. The parolee is then monitored on parole until the expiration of the maximum sentence date. Mandatory institutional program participation is deemphasized. There are provisions for delaying parole in the event of serious institutional misconduct or strenuous objection from a victim, but absent that, the inmate is paroled at the expiration of his or her minimum sentence.

Another growing trend that is bound to have an impact on the parole process is the increasing recognition of victims' rights. Victims are being given greater input into parole decisions. While it is too early to determine the impact of victims' rights input on the percentage of inmates who are paroled, it would seem intuitively that objections from victims would serve to increase the percentage of the prison sentence served before parole is granted and reduce the percentage of paroles granted each year.

Well-structured parole policies have certain characteristics. They include a meaningful preparation phase that allows inmates to address their needs and develop their assets while they are incarcerated. The preparation phase includes academic/vocational programming, medical/mental health treatment, and therapeutic intervention. Sound parole policy must also provide for a selection process that maximizes the probability that the persons granted parole will successfully reintegrate into the community. A thorough review of the individual case file that considers all pertinent factors is required. Adequate housing and viable employment are prerequisites to selection for parole. Community supervision is extremely important to a successful parole strategy. Parolees must know that parole revocation will be swift and certain if the conditions of parole are violated.

The concept of parole as a conditional release from incarceration is a criminal justice policy that is both cost-effective and relatively successful when applied properly. It makes sense that supervision of the offender in the community is preferable to simply letting the inmate return to the community directly from prison without supervision. The more meaningful the supervision, and the greater the certainty of parole revocation for parole violations, the more effective the program will be.

Without parole as an incentive for inmates, prisons would be more difficult places to control. Without parole, inmates would serve longer prison sentences. The prison population would increase significantly, which would require increased expenditures for the construction and operation of more prisons. The average age of the inmate population would rise as longer sentences were served. There are increased health care costs associated with increased age, while at the same time, there is a positive correlation between age and public risk (i.e., as age increases, public risk declines). Overall, parole is an essential component of the criminal justice infrastructure. Parole provides a conditional release to a prisoner with supervision in the community while generally ensuring the safety of the public.

JOHN S. SHAFFER

BIBLIOGRAPHY

Barnes, Harry Elmer and Negley K. Teeters, 1947. *New Horizons in Criminology.* New York: Prentice Hall.

Harrison, William, 1995. Discussion with the Director of the Pennsylvania Department of Corrections, Bureau of Inmate Services, held on February 9, 1995, at the State Correctional Institution at Somerset, Pennsylvania.

Maguire, Kathleen and Ann L. Pastore, eds., 1994. *Sourcebook of Criminal Justice Statistics–1993.* Washington, D.C.: U.S. Department of Justice, The Hindelang Criminal Justice Research Center, NCJ-148211.

Perkins, Craig, 1994. *National Corrections Reporting Program, 1992.* Washington, D.C.: U.S. Department of Justice, (October), NCJ-145862.

PARTICIPATION MANAGEMENT.

A philosophy and concept of management based on the empowerment and involvement of employees, usually working in teams, to ensure effective decisions on matters that affect the company and their jobs. Participation management provides an opportunity for employees to share organizational responsibility, risk, and success.

Participation management in the United States was an outgrowth of failed post–World War II plant-level labor-management committees and theories of organizational behavior and industrial psychology. Following the path of the research on the reorganization of work by Elton Mayo and his associates in the 1930s, the new theorists of the 1950s and 1960s began a human relations movement that enhanced employee participation and empowerment. This new generation of industrial psychologists, which included Abraham Maslow, Douglas McGregor, Frederick Hertzberg, Rensis Likert, and Chris Argyris, advanced various behavioral-oriented human relations theories and approaches, and argued that employee-centered work environments would increase job satisfaction, job performance, productivity, efficiency, and quality.

In the United States, recessions in the late 1950s and early 1960s, combined with government pressure for price restraints and the beginning of foreign import competition, began to force management to seek greater efficiencies in the workplace. By the mid-1960s, managers of many organizations began to experiment with some of the emerging human relations concepts in reorganizing their work environment.

For example, overly simplified and routinized jobs were redesigned by adding tasks. This attempt to increase the duties of employees at the same skill level was known as job enlargement. Also, select employees were given more discretion in performing their jobs, which was termed job enrichment. Furthermore, organizations applied various forms of matrix management, which allowed crossing traditional barriers of the chain of command in the hierarchy of divisions and departments to enhance communication, interaction, collaboration, and cooperation at the upper, middle, and lower levels of management.

The human relations work innovations of the 1960s paved the way toward greater worker participation in managerial decisions at the work level. During this period, Sid Rubinstein and other intellectuals conducted research on worker participation in the context of management structure, the organization of work, and union-management relations. This participation management approach continued until in 1972, at a conference at Harriman, New York, Louis Davis of the University of California first introduced the term quality of worklife (QWL), which led to experiments with various forms of worker participation through team-oriented, problem-solving work groups. About that time employees began to experiment with team-oriented small study groups to enhance quality control, known as quality control circles.

Quality circles are small worker groups that voluntarily meet to provide input for solving quality or production problems. They are a way of extending participative decisionmaking into teams. Quality circles usually are generated from the bottom up; that is, they provide advice to managers who still retain decisionmaking authority. As such, quality circles are not empowered to implement their own recommendations. However, managers often listen to recommendations from quality circles and implement the suggestions. Rewards for the suggestions are shared and can be financial in nature, but more often they are intrinsic, with involvement in the decisionmaking process as the primary reward.

By the late 1970s and early 1980s, the United States began to take notice of Japan's development of the quality circle concept and Japanese management's ability to gain labor's cooperation on the shop floor. In Japan, quality circles have been integrated into the organization instead of operating as an experimental alternative (which is often only for the short term). This may be one reason for Japan's success with this technique. The Japanese model involves a committee of workers and floor supervisors who meet weekly to discuss and solve production problems relating to quality. It is a long-term, ongoing process.

Quality circles spread rapidly in U.S. industry from 1979 on. One survey found that 713 companies had installed 12,424 quality circles in 1,572 locations by 1982. Recent estimates suggested that more than 90 percent of the Fortune 500 companies have quality circle programs, while a study of Fortune 1,000 companies over the period 1987–90 revealed that all forms of employee participation and power-sharing practices involving work redesign are on the rise.

Results of the Fortune 1,000 study are summarized by Lawler, Mohrman, and Ledford in *Employee Involvement and Total Quality Management* (1992). The authors focused on which types of employee involvement practices were being adopted by Fortune 1,000 corporations and how these companies viewed the effectiveness of these practices. The results of the study provided a benchmark of the degree to which employee involvement practices were actually used by Fortune 1,000 corporations. The authors maintained that participation management and employee involvement encompass four key features—information, knowledge, rewards, and power—factors relevant to any organization's performance. The contemporary view of participation management is that employees at all levels need to possess these in order to participate effectively in the organization, and true involvement requires that all four of these features are present at the lowest level of the organization.

Participation management in the 1990s has taken on many forms. In the book *A Better Idea* (1991), Donald Petersen and John Hillkirk describe the work of a task force which conducted an in-depth study of six of the most outstanding companies in the United States that practiced participation management. Among the findings of this task force were those practices these companies had in

common relative to participation management. Some of the practices included the circulation and communication of corporate goals and values to employees; the importance of respect for each employee; trust, in place of strict rules and controls; customer satisfaction; teamwork; reduction in the levels of management; free, open, face-to-face communication; peer and subordinate evaluations; and management training.

Contemporary applications of participation management in the private and public sectors in the United States have been characterized by team-based and shared management systems. In these systems, both the team and individuals are empowered to make important decisions regarding scheduling, quality maintenance, and other issues that had previously been the sole province of management. Employees in this team-based system share in the decisionmaking and responsibilities that directly affect their work. The earlier preoccupation with quality circles that included meaningful and shared decisionmaking gave rise to team-based systems which included quality teams.

Quality teams, in contrast to quality circles, are included in total quality management and other quality improvement efforts as part of a change in the organization's structure. Quality teams are generated from the top down and are empowered to act on their own recommendations. Whereas quality circles emphasize the generation of ideas, quality teams make data-based decisions about improving product and service quality. Various decisionmaking techniques are employed within quality teams. Brainstorming, flowcharts, and cause-and-effect diagrams are utilized to help pinpoint problems that affect quality.

While quality circles and quality teams are methods for using groups in the decisionmaking process, self-managed teams take the concept of participation one step further. Decisionmaking activities of self-managed teams are more broadly focused than those of quality circles and quality teams, which usually emphasize quality and production problems. Self-managed teams make many of the decisions that were once reserved for managers, such as work scheduling, job assignments, and staffing. Unlike quality circles, whose role is an advisory one, self-managed teams are delegated authority in the organization's decisionmaking process.

Many organizations have claimed success with self-managed teams. Preliminary research evidence is supportive of self-managed teams. An analysis of 70 studies concluded that self-managed teams positively affected productivity and attitudes toward self-management. However, the analysis indicated no significant effects of self-managed teams on job satisfaction, absenteeism, or turnover.

Research studies suggest that decisions that concern quality or production would benefit from the advice of quality circles or the empowered decisions of quality teams. In addition, a manager who wants to provide total empowerment to a group might consider self-managed teams.

Participation management based on teams requires that members of the team have the information to make decisions, the autonomy to carry them out, an organization structure which supports this behavior, and managers who can operate within this framework. In a recent case study, the Government Accounting Office (GAO) surveyed the 1,000 largest corporations in the United States. Its report indicates that 80 percent of the firms have some type of employee involvement effort in place, but only 25 percent have made significant changes in the way people are managed.

Many government officials and outside analysts believe that if the federal bureaucracy adopted a comprehensive productivity and quality program it would be easier for businesses and citizens to deal with federal agencies and the resulting cost savings could ultimately cut the deficit and lower taxes. Several billion dollars have already been saved due to employee suggestions and the increased use of participation management techniques adopted from private industry.

Skeptics say that participation management is not possible in a government bureaucracy, partly because of the sheer size of government. In addition, the National Association of Government Employees, the federal workers' union, is generally opposed to the approach and its concepts, such as merit pay programs, quality circles, and other total quality management (TQM) components.

Nevertheless, in June 1988 efforts to improve government productivity through extensive employee involvement programs intensified with the formation of the Federal Quality Institute, whose mission is to apply the principles of TQM. Also, the Office of Personnel Management continues to explore the adoption of select participation management techniques and the use of incentives to reward employees.

Other examples of participation management in the United States federal government include a pilot project in the Department of Agriculture. Although government research organizations vary, they share a number of common problems, such as poor public perception of goals or mission. The United States Department of Agriculture's Forest Service initiated a pilot test program to explore new ways to enhance a creative and innovative work environment in two of its research stations. In one of the stations, the Northeastern Forest Experiment Station, an employee-driven program was implemented as a pilot test and was kept as informal and nonbureaucratic as possible. Employees ranging from the short-term temporary to the station director participated in the pilot test, so that the ideas for change took on an organizational rather than an individual perspective. Instead of operating within a narrowly defined problem area and delivering bits and pieces of a bigger puzzle, a team of researchers from several disciplines ad-

dressed broad and clearly defined problems. Although limited in scope in comparison to the innovations of participation management in the private sector, this experiment indicates a growing awareness of the need for human relations approaches in the federal government.

An example of participation management in the public sector at the state level includes experiences of the City of Chula Vista, California, and those of San Bernardino County, California. This effort focused on three critical factors for success: being mindful of the three generations of participation management efforts, understanding the key differences between the public and private sectors, and knowing some management rules to make participation management successful. The study revealed that considerable mistrust, misinformation, and disinformation are the most troublesome impediments to participation management efforts in the public realm. In addition, there are also three different domains with values frequently in conflict that directly affect any participative efforts: the publicly elected domain, the administrative domain, and the professional-technical domain. The study concluded that to transform a public sector organization into a highly successful participative workplace, the following six principles must be addressed: wholeness, self-design, representation, empowerment, integration, and equality.

In the public sector, participation management in the form of team-oriented study groups has met with some success in the case of one city in Florida. Since implementing a quality improvement (QI) process called TEAM into its work environment in 1986, the city of Fort Lauderdale, Florida, has experienced increased employee moral, reduced absenteeism, a significant decrease in red tape, and an annual savings of about $300,000. The city currently has 55 all-volunteer QI teams mainly working on problems that affect work in the volunteers' particular functional areas.

For instance, in the water division of the city's department of utilities, a team of six employees was formed to reduce the occurrence of shocks from electrified water meters. Following the seven-step QI process developed by the team, it analyzed the root causes of the problem and designed a copper bypass wire and daily procedures to use to address shock prevention. Since the team's solution and established safety procedures were put into effect, no injuries due to shocks have occurred.

Several state governments in the northeastern section of the United States have also experimented with participation management. One example is the Pennsylvania Department of Transportation (PennDOT), which promotes and uses participative methods that provide employees with the opportunity to participate in decisionmaking, identify and propose solutions to work-related problems, and communicate freely and openly with department managers and supervisors. These methods are an integral part of the manager' roles in setting standards, defining performance expectations, and meeting PennDOT objectives.

The public sectors of other countries have created pilot projects, and in some cases have adopted various forms of participation management. In 1990 the Canadian government declared that as part of the renewal of the Public Service of Canada all departments were to put people first. In the Ontario Region of Environment (Canada) in the 1980s, management teams worked with clients to set policy objectives as to what was to be done in the future.

A recent study focused on the participants in the management teams of the Ontario Region and was based on a series of interviews with key participants. This study, which evaluated the effectiveness of the innovations and assessed the impact of the new directions on the policy process, found that managers in the teams tried to move the region simultaneously along three continua: (1) in terms of structure, to encourage and reward team behaviors and purposes, instead of maintaining hierarchical ones; (2) in terms of decisionmaking processes, to move along the continuum from hierarchic toward more participatory methods; and (3) in terms of culture, to place priority on people rather than on systems. A common feeling among managers was that they should not only provide leadership and direct policy, but should act as supporters of ideas and be cheerleaders to promote the spawning of new ideas.

In the 1970s some experiments with participation management, known as participatory design (PD) movements, got under way in Europe. Since that time participatory design movements such as those developed in Norway have influenced a wide range of private sector organizations, including banks and hospitals, and public sector organizations, including government offices and schools.

ROSS PRIZZIA

BIBLIOGRAPHY

Axelrod, Dick, 1992. "Are You Ready for Team-Based Management?" *Journal for Quality & Participation,* vol. 5 (December) 12–17.

Eisman, Regina, 1990. "Government Gridlock." *Incentive,* vol. 164 (January) 24–28.

Kelsell, John E., Mario E. DeSimone and George G. Mulamoottil, 1991–1992. "Some PS 2000 Principles Have Been Tested." *Optimum,* vol. 22 (1991–1992) 25–30.

Kline, Robert M. and Noreen C. Young, 1994. "Our Road to Quality Is Paved with Employee Involvement." *Journal for Quality & Participation,* vol. 17 (January-February) 20–24.

Lawler III, E. E., S. A. Mohrman, and G. E. Ledford, Jr., 1992. *Employee Involvement and Total Quality Management.* San Francisco, CA: Jossey-Bass Publishers.

Lewis, Robert and William F. DeLaney, 1991. "Promoting Innovation and Creativity." *Research-Technology Management,* vol. 34 (May-June) 21–25.

Moore, Ernest D., 1990. "Transforming People and a City." *Journal for Quality & Participation* (July-August) 74–76.

Nelson, Martin E. and Nancy H. Taylor, 1990. "Conceptual Tools to Make Participation Work for You." *Journal for Quality & Participation* (July-August) 46–49.

Petersen, Donald E. and John Hillkirk, 1991. *A Better Idea—Redefining the Way Americans Work.* Boston: Houghton Mifflin Company.

Plunkett, Lorne C. and Robert Fournier, 1991. *Participative Management—Implementing Empowerment.* New York: John Wiley & Sons, Inc.

Rubinstein, Sidney P., ed., 1987. *Participative Systems at Work—Creating Quality and Employment Security.* New York: Human Sciences Press, Inc.

PATRONAGE. Used in the context of the civil service, refers to governmental positions or other favors distributed by political authorities. Most political systems along a full spectrum from monarchies to democracies to communist contain elements of patronage. Indeed, it has many times been an essential element for the maintenance and continuation of a wide variety of the world's governmental systems.

In the United States patronage jobs were the lifeblood of political parties, party officials, and elected officials who jointly or individually exercised control over them as rewards for their loyal followers. These grants of governmental jobs were in turn insurance of political support from the job holders at the next election.

Throughout history governmental officials have reserved for themselves the right to distribute certain governmental positions based on criteria such as loyalty or political expediency. In the United States patronage has served as one basis for the development of what are called "political machines"–political party organizations which dominate a given jurisdiction's political power and control election results through the use of this patronage power. Common examples of such political party machines are the Tammany organization of New York City, the Crump political machine in the city of Memphis, Tennessee, or the Richard Daley machine in the city of Chicago, Illinois.

While the percentage of United States governmental jobs distributed as patronage was high in the nineteenth century, with the passage of the Pendleton Act in 1883 and the development of merit systems and the use of written tests, patronage declined as a tool of political power into the twentieth century. By the 1970s and 1980s the U.S. courts had further limited the use of patronage to high level policymaking type positions in decisions such as *Elrod v. Burns, Branti v. Finkel,* and *Rutan v. Republican Party of Illinois.* In the *Elrod* decision the Supreme Court held that patronage dismissals of rank and file employees of the

Cook County, Illinois, sheriff's department were unconstitutional violations of public employees' First Amendment rights, severely restricting political beliefs and political associations. Patronage dismissals were to be limited to employees clearly in policymaking type positions. Later, in *Branti*, the Supreme Court went even further in limiting dismissals. In this case the legitimacy of dismissals was limited to employees where "the hiring authority can demonstrate that party affiliation is an appropriate requirement for the effective performance of the public office involved." And finally, in *Rutan*, the Supreme Court went even further in protecting public employees from partisan treatment in employment by expanding the *Branti* and *Rutan* standards beyond dismissals into other personnel areas such as initial hiring and promotions.

Throughout this process of narrowing the powers of elected officials in distributing political patronage-based rewards, the power of political organizations has suffered. At one time in our history, during the heyday of spoils politics, political party organizations derived enormous power from the arbitrary dispensing of patronage jobs and other party favors. Jobs-based patronage is no longer a large source of party power.

Patronage occurs in forms other than jobs and many of these types of patronage are still surviving today. The favorable consideration of party service in the dispensing of government contracts, the making of government purchases involving huge sums with private companies, the granting of government licenses, and many other forms of preferential treatment have not been eliminated. While in many jurisdictions these practices are subject to rules and regulation, patronage—an integral part of the United States and world political scene—is far from a thing of the past.

ROBERT H. ELLIOTT

BIBLIOGRAPHY

Branti v. Finkel, 445 U.S. 507 1980.
Elrod v. Burns, 427 U.S. 347 1976.
Riordon, William L., 1963. *Plunkett of Tammany Hall*. New York: Dutton.
Rutan v. Republican Party of Illinois, 58 LW 4872 1990.

PAY-FOR-PERFORMANCE.

The use of extrinsic monetary incentives to motivate increased or enhanced employee effort and performance (see also **performance appraisal**).

Generally, pay-for-performance is an intricate part of the industrial revolution wherein workers' wages were linked explicitly to the production of specific quantities of a product (piecework). These concerns were reemphasized under Frederick Winslow Taylor's (1856–1915) scientific management movement and the advent of industrial engineering at the end of the nineteenth century (see **Taylor, Frederick W.** and **scientific management**). While Taylor focused on the introduction of productivity-enhancing processes and techniques, later efforts were directed at means of acquiring worker compliance with and motivation in their use.

Very little application of incentive systems was made in the United Stated to the public sector (outside of the blue-collar, manufacturing functions performed mainly for the military). Since efficiency still had to compete with notions of government as a threat to individual liberty, a highly motivated and effective civil service was not necessarily seen as desirable. Furthermore, market theorists preferred incentive structures that drew the more dynamic individuals to productive business occupations. Insofar as individuals pursuing public employment were concerned, public interest purposes and patriotism were the preferred motivators rather than pecuniary gain.

Even so, merit pay was introduced as part of the positivistic administrative management reforms introduced with the Classification Act of 1923. Exceptional performance was to be rewarded through merit step increases and grade promotion. However, restrictions to prevent favoritism and abuse limited their use. Merit pay soon devolved into a system of automatic annual increases rewarding longevity/loyalty and a means of providing an inflationary cost of living adjustment (COLA).

Pay-for-performance is an application of expectancy theory (see **expectancy theory**). Employee motivation is deemed to be extrinsic and follow the outlines of B. F. Skinner's (1904–1990) operant conditioning models. Expectancy theory posits that employees will be motivated to the extent to which their calculation of the desirability of rewards, the effort required to perform a task, and the probability of successful performance (and of the organization paying off) are viewed favorably. Pay-for-performance schemes concentrate on providing or determining the right balance between extrinsic reward (pay and required effort–performance).

A wide array of extrinsic pay-for-performance schemes exist. The modern pay-for-performance scheme builds upon a base pay system. The salary or wage put "at risk" is such to encourage or motivate the worker without jeopardizing his or her basic financial security. One can address overall individual performance or specific instances; focus can be on group performance at the organizational or team level. Individual systems based on merit pay step increases, annuities, bonuses, and suggestion awards as well as skill-or competency-based approaches abound. In addition group or organization rewards are the focus of gain or goal sharing programs. Performance appraisal systems are the trigger instrument for operationalizing pay-for-performance. The individual performance rating is used to determine which employees are eligible for individual and group awards as well as the amount of reward an individual is entitled to. Management by objectives systems (see **management by objectives**) may also serve as the measurement instrument for a pay-for-performance system (appraisal by objectives formally incorporates MBO into the performance appraisal process).

Merit Pay

Merit step increases, even in systems that are primarily across-the-board longevity awards, are today often modified by the requirement that an employee obtain a minimum (average or fully satisfactory) performance rating in order to be eligible. Mild as such requirements are (less than 5 percent of covered employees are likely to be ineligible), they serve as an incentive encouraging poor performers to improve or to seek opportunities elsewhere.

Merit pay annuities reward the individual's overall performance by an addition to base salary (hence, the term annuity). Because the increased base salary pays dividends throughout the employee's future years, the amount of the pay-for-performance award need be only half that associated with lump-sum bonuses. Currently, a minimum figure of 2.5 percent is suggested (although 5 percent was widely advocated only a few years ago). However, there is little in the way of empirical evidence supporting these figures; they remain, for the most part, the guesses of compensation and benefits experts. What is essential is that the amount be substantial enough from the employee's perspective to serve as a motivating factor. This is likely to depend on both the economic situation and on the individual's relevant equity comparisons. Merit pay annuities may be applied as a set percentage (or dollar) increase added to all who achieve a specified performance rating. On the other hand, different performance rating levels may trigger different percentage (or dollar) increases.

Bonus

The bonus (like the single event suggestion award) is a lump-sum payment. Its advantage is that it recognizes exceptional performance occurring during the year without entailing a commitment to continuous future payments. Because they are one-time rewards, bonuses need to be more substantial than merit pay annuities. A minimum figure of 5 percent is currently suggested; however, results are more likely if bonuses are more on the order of 10 percent or one month's salary at a minimum. Bonuses, like merit pay annuities, can also be prorated to correspond with differing performance rating levels.

While merit annuities and bonuses award overall behavior and results, suggestion systems are attached to spe-

cific items. Awards tend to be in the order of 10 percent of the first year's savings or productivity gain. Suggestion programs may also entail various intrinsic rewards (e.g., recognition in newsletters or official meetings in addition to symbolic mementos and trophies). Suggestion systems are designed to unleash the innovative and creative talents of the everyday employee. Successful suggestion systems need to demonstrate that they seriously consider all the suggestions submitted. This may entail offering rewards for meritorious, workable ideas that upper management chooses not to implement. Suggestion systems often limit awards to 10 percent or a maximum of $10,000. While most ideas are not affected by such limits, it sets a discouraging tone to the whole suggestion program. Mega-awards for extraordinary ideas are analogous to the lottery "big winner." They serve as a very visible public relations advertisement for the success of the suggestion program and encourage others to try their "luck."

Skill-Based Pay

Skill- and competency-based pay rewards employees more for organizational potential than for actual performance. In a way it is a expanded variation of "on-call" pay. Employees are paid extra for possessing the ability to step in and use their acquired skill or competency. In fact, they are paid even if they are never called upon the use their additional skills and competencies. As personnel technicians have narrowly defined "skills," the broader term "competency" has been introduced to represent desired capabilities. The organizational advantage is that needed talent is on call in case of emergency or special circumstances. It allows the organization the ability to temporarily (or permanently) transfer individuals to more needed tasks. In addition to the extra pay, individuals benefit from the intrinsic motivation and revitalization inherent in the learning process and job rotation. They also are able to explore career options without having to abandon their current jobs. Skill- and competency-based pay is also associated with the broadbanding of jobs. An organization's management determines what extra skills or competencies the organization wants or needs. It then pays employees extra who have acquired those skills or competencies; the organization is also very likely to assist employees in acquiring the designated skills or competencies. To continue receiving the extra pay, employees are required periodically to demonstrate proficiency in their skill or competency; the list of needed skills and competencies is also periodically reevaluated by the organization.

One serious problem faced by most pay-for-performance schemes in the public sector is the tendency to cap awards. Locked into older notions of classification pay grades, those who have obtained the maximum pay allowed within their official pay grade may be deemed ineligible for merit annuities or bonuses. Since these awards are touted as being earned through meritorious performance, their denial greatly undermines perceptions not only of the program's efficacy but of organizational fairness as well.

Gain Sharing

Most pay-for-performance systems focus primarily on the individual; however, growing concern for the group or team aspects of the work process is directing attention to group incentives. Total Quality Management (TQM) movements have brought these concerns to the forefront in recent years (see **performance appraisal** for discussion of TQM). While W. Edwards Deming (1900–1993) insisted that the only rewards necessary for TQM were intrinsic, other advocates also embrace the use of extrinsic group rewards.

Gain sharing or goal sharing is the primary group or team incentive system employed to measure and reward organizational performance. It is an outgrowth or refinement of the profit-sharing plans (such as Scanlon, Rucker, or Improshare). Profit sharing focuses on the entire organization and rewards individuals on the basis of its overall performance. Since individual employees materially share in the organization's success, this is expected to motivate their performance.

However, for large or diversified organizations, individuals often do not see how their individual efforts could influence the overall results. Individuals in internal services or staff units also have difficulty in relating their efforts to the overall organization's purpose. Gain sharing addresses those concerns by focusing on organizational subunits instead of the overall organization. Using the organization's budget process and performance management system, savings or productivity gains (in addition to profits) can be used as the basis for group rewards. This enables rewards to be dispensed for staff and service units that reduce costs as well as for units that have made improvements in productivity even if they are still technically losing money.

Gain sharing is quite appealing to public sector organizations. It capitalizes on both the public sector's lack of a profit system and its greater reliance on group processes. As such, gain sharing complements Total Quality Management efforts by providing a mechanism for extrinsic rewards.

A recent refinement to gain sharing has been the notion of goal sharing. Instead of rewards based on documented budget savings, they are tied to the achievement of specified group or team goals. Goals derived from TQM (or strategic planning or MBO) programs are thereby linked to extrinsic rewards for the individual. This serves to assure the individual's attention and motivation.

For gain sharing or goal sharing to be effective, the goals or savings gains must be based on measurable factors under control of employees in the unit. Individual employees must understand what the goals are and feel that they are indeed obtainable through their group's combined teamwork. Employee participation in the selection of the goals is an added means for ensuring understanding and sense of stakeholder status.

Related to this is the requirement that payout pools for gain sharing or goal sharing rewards also be readily understood. Complex formulas or the manipulation of payout formulas undermine confidence in the system's efficacy. Upward adjustments or the ratcheting of expected performance rates or goals also undermine employee confidence.

Payout pools should link together an identifiable "community of interest." Employees must see the people in their pool as being part of a team. the distribution of gain sharing or goal sharing rewards can be across the board (in terms of actual dollars or percentages). It can be linked to individual performance appraisals as an eligibility factor or as a prorating device. It can even be left for the employees themselves to decide.

Variations

The application of pay-for-performance is, at best, erratic if not somewhat faddish. While at any one time many governmental jurisdictions claim to employ one or another of the pay-for-performance schemes, most efforts are limited to short one to two-year experiments. Comparatively few long-term examples exist. Merit pay systems which are the most often cited examples are seldom more than annual longevity awards or across-the-board pay increases (little distinguished from cost of living adjustments).

The market-oriented, pay-for-performance concept has its strongest appeal in the United States. Other nations currently showing an interest in this concept tend to rely upon U.S. examples. In many other countries the public service already represents one of the more highly prestigious and paid occupations, often a generalist administrative elite drawn predominantly from their society's upper and educated classes. Without recruitment and retention problems extrinsic pay-for-performance systems are not as necessary. With greater emphasis placed upon public or community interests, intrinsic rewards and honors serve as more substantial motivators. These intrinsic factors are reinforced by the somewhat elitist or "aristocratic" aspect of these societies. In nations such as France and Japan, for example, extrinsic awards in the form of highly paid "early retirement" job placements exist. Group rewards and bonuses, albeit relatively small in size, are found in some nations such as Japan.

DENNIS M. DALEY

BIBLIOGRAPHY

Graham-Moore, Brian and Timothy L. Ross, 1990. *Gainsharing: Plans for Improving Performance.* Washington, D.C.: BNA Books.

Greiner, John M., Harry P. Hatry, Margo P. Koss, Annie P. Millar, and Jane P. Woodward, 1981. *Productivity and Motivation: A Review of State and Local Government Initiatives.* Washington, D.C.: Urban Institute.

Lawler III, Edward E., 1990. *Strategic Pay: Aligning Organizational Strategies and Pay Systems.* San Francisco, CA: Jossey-Bass.

Milkovich, George T. and Alexandra K. Wigdor, eds., with Ranae F. Broderick and Anne S. Mavor, 1991. *Pay for Performance: Evaluating Performance Appraisal and Merit Pay.* Washington, D.C.: National Academy Press.

PERFORMANCE APPRAISAL. A formal assessment or evaluation of an individual's efforts at or potential for carrying out the tasks of a specific job (see **pay-for-performance** and **incentive pay**).

The modern performance appraisal or rating arose in the mid-nineteenth century from the British Indian Civil Service's system of duty reports (itself a carryover from traditional Indian administrative practices). In conjunction with the administrative science movement at the turn of the century associated with Henri Fayol (1841–1925) and Frederick W. Taylor (1856–1915), the written essay format was transformed into graphic rating scales in which a job's tasks along with the necessary worker traits were separated into identifiable components (see **Fayol, Henri** and **Taylor, Frederick W.**). The last 50 years have witnessed repeated, continuous efforts at perfecting these into objective measurements of work behaviors (processes) or results (outcomes).

Underlying the nineteenth-century development of performance appraisal systems in the public sector is the notion of legal accountability. The United States's constitutional limits on governmental behavior and European traditions of administrative law seek to hold individual officials responsible for their acts. This entails a formal system wherein each official's responsibilities and duties are clearly outlined. During the twentieth century, positivistic management concerns have linked performance appraisal to motivational concepts, especially as a goal-setting and communications instrument in Victor Vroom's (1932–) and Edward Lawler's (1938–) expectancy theory.

Performance appraisal is used as an aid in making judgment decisions pertaining to promotion, demotion, retention, transfer, and pay. It is also employed as a developmental guide for training needs assessment and employee feedback. Performance appraisal also aids with a number of more general organizational functions as a means for validating selection and hiring procedures, promoting employee-supervisor understanding, and supporting an organization's culture. Modern performance appraisal systems combine an objective appraisal instrument with supervisory and employee training in its proper use.

Legal Criteria for Effective Appraisal Systems

Since the enactment of the Civil Rights Act of 1964, the courts and administrative practitioners have worked out a series of six criteria for designing an effective and objective performance appraisal process. Job analysis delineates the job duties and responsibilities required of an employee, which are the appropriate basis upon which to assess an individual (see **job analysis** and **evaluation**). A job analysis informs employees what is expected from them and reminds supervisors of what it is their employees are being asked to do. The specific evaluation factors used in an appraisal instrument are designed to measure the performance of the tasks indicated by the job analysis.

Related to this criterion is the focus on work behaviors. Public administration has always placed emphasis on job-relatedness. Job-specific work behaviors serve as the basis for the evaluation of an employee's performance.

Communication is essential to performance appraisal. United States notions of due process and fairness are clearly evident here. Individuals must be aware of the performance standards used to evaluate them. Feedback is essential for the improvement of performance.

Supervisory training focuses on another behavioral criterion. Supervisors cannot be left without any guidance in the application of the performance appraisal processes. As with any tool, performance appraisal requires instruction in its proper and safe use.

Documentation addresses the somewhat more negative issue of legal defensibility. The importance attached to an individual's job is such that the courts have extended the rules of evidence to cover the employment of performance appraisal systems. Organizations must be able to produce evidence in support of their personnel decisions, especially in those incidences wherein severe sanctions and job loss are imposed.

Due process considerations also underlie the requirement for monitoring. Organizations must not only check to see that their appraisal systems are up-to-date but also that they are not being abused. Performance appraisal standards based on out-of-date job analyses fail to reflect current job requirements. In addition, liability litigation documents numerous cases involving the abuse of authority. Grievance and discipline appeal provisions can build in safeguards against the abuse of the performance appraisal process.

Objective Appraisal Systems

Two formats dominate the arena of objective appraisal techniques: behaviorally anchored rating scales (BARS) and management by objectives (MBO, see **management by objectives**). Behaviorally anchored rating scales and management by objectives approaches essentially involve the same components; however, the objective components which are common in both approaches are introduced into the appraisal process in a somewhat different order. BARS appraisals work best with large groups and subgroups and individuals whose job descriptions can be standardized; MBO, on the other hand, is more suited to cases that can be tailored to each individual job. MBO is best when it is focused on the results to be expected from job performance; BARS handles behavioral processes where outputs are more identifiable and assurable than outcomes. Both employ variations on participative management in order to guarantee their effectiveness. A somewhat more passive approach to participation guides BARS, while a more proactive style is found in MBO.

While the use of objective appraisal instruments is recommended, many jurisdictions still employ subjective graphic rating scales. Although invalid, for the most part, they are relatively inexpensive and prove adequate "paper systems" for jurisdictions wherein performance appraisal is not realistically relied upon as an aid in decisionmaking. Often effective and trusted supervisors can compensate for the shortcomings of inadequate systems. Unfortunately, supervisory (and employee) training in the proper use of the appraisal process tends to lag significantly. This often results in systems failures in that the advantages of an objective appraisal are dissipated through assorted managerial mistakes and rater errors.

Rater Errors

While the employment of objective appraisal instruments greatly enhances the efficacy of the performance appraisal process, they alone cannot guarantee acceptable results. Performance appraisal is conducted by individuals on individuals; it is a human process. The skills which supervisors and employees bring to this process are quite crucial to its success. Training individuals to handle appraisal is a necessary rather than an optional aspect of the performance appraisal process.

Information on what the appraisal process is and how to use it is only the beginning to the training program. Troubleshooting or diagnostic skills in rater error avoidance are also called for. If supervisors are to be taught how to employ performance appraisal correctly, what must be taught is how the human mind actually operates.

Errors are committed whenever the responsibilities inherent in the job itself are substituted for a measure of the incumbent's job performance. Similarly, individuals working in a critical unit may benefit from the perceived centrality or significance of their part of the organization. In neither instance is the individual's job performance actually measured.

Contrast errors arise through interpersonal comparisons. Individuals are not assessed on their job performance but on their performance compared to someone else's performance, or, as is more often the case, someone else's personal traits and characteristics (e.g., social and leadership traits, demographic characteristics, or social, ethnic, and gender differences). These social differentiation or similar-to-me approaches, even when based on examples of successful employees, exclude people who may be successful or potentially successful from receiving a fair and accurate evaluation.

In unidimensional errors one item dominates the evaluation process to such an extent that other, critical factors are ignored. Traits and characteristics as age, longevity, or loyalty can be the basis for an overall evaluation even when other factors are formally specified in the appraisal instrument. The unidimensional response eliminates the sought-after balance that the international introduction of the other factors are designed to achieve. Similarly, the vividness of one event can overshadow all other incidents. A halo effect occurs when a good performance in one aspect of a job becomes the basis for overall assessment; a horns effect indicates that an incident perceived as negative was the basis of the evaluation (see **halo and horns effect**). First impression or recency error is introduced when early or late events are given extraordinary weight in the evaluation. Supervisors may also exhibit a central tendency (i.e., awarding everyone middle-range or average ratings) or restricted range (i.e., extremely good and bad ratings are not awarded) problem in which all employees receive the same rating or very close and similar ratings. Constant error also occurs when supervisors exhibit tendencies toward awarding consistently high or low ratings or are overly lenient or strict in their rating evaluations.

Interpersonal biases introduce intentional distortions into the appraisal process. The greater the extent to which a supervisor's own performance and career is dependent upon a subordinate's performance, the more likely it is that favorable ratings will be awarded. Squeaky wheels may benefit with higher ratings than they otherwise deserve in order to avoid any unpleasantness. However, employees deemed difficult, as well as those who make use of the organization's grievance process, are likely to receive more critical attention in future performance appraisals. Interpersonal biases are also the source of abuse rather than of errors. They may entail worksite politics wherein ratings are adjusted in order to support or hinder an employee's opportunity for advancement and reward. Lower than deserved ratings can be awarded in an effort to selfishly retain a valued and productive employee. Lower than deserved ratings are also a means for "taking out" someone seen as a potential competitor. Similarly, appraisal ratings can be affected by factors entirely extraneous to the working relationship. External preferences vis-à-vis politics, religion, and sex may be furthered through the manipulation of the performance appraisal process.

TQM and Performance Appraisal

The introduction of Total Quality Management, especially those approaches emphasizing W. Edwards Deming's (1900–1993) practices, focus on systemic or group-level factors rather than on individual performance. Given the extensive compliance and rater error problems associated with performance appraisal systems, TQM concentrates on reengineering the processes rather than repair. TQM advocates also claim that it is more future focused while performance appraisal is bogged down in recording past activities.

The United States, with its ideological emphasis upon the individual, is the leading proponent and model for performance appraisal systems. Many jurisdictions (including many in the United States) still retain patronage systems or personalistic/crony employment patterns (see **patronage**). Cultures wherein TQM approaches have found favor also places less emphasis upon individual performance appraisal. In contrast, many of these jurisdictions place far more stringency on the recruitment and selection process.

DENNIS M. DALEY

BIBLIOGRAPHY

Daley, Dennis M., 1992. *Performance Appraisal in the Public Sector: Techniques and Applications.* Westport, CT: Quorum Books.

Milkovich, George T. and Alexandra K. Wigdor, eds., with Ranae F. Broderick and Anne S. Mavor, 1991. *Pay for Performance: Evaluating Performance Appraisal and Merit Pay.* Washington, D.C.: National Academy Press.

Mohrman, Jr., Allan M., Susan M. Resnick-West, and Edward E. Lawler III, 1989. *Designing Performance Appraisal Systems: Aligning Appraisals and Organizational Realities.* San Francisco, CA: Jossey-Bass.

PERFORMANCE AUDIT. The examination and evaluation of performance data to determine efficiency and effectiveness of government operations and programs, fidelity of administrators to jurisdictional specifications, and adherence to public policy intent. It is a relatively recent development and a natural extension of financial post-audit in procedure and purpose.

Performance audit is also viewed as an outcome of the general change in political and administrative values and approaches that unfolded in the United States in the late 1960s. Revenue shortfalls and huge budget deficits prompted the need for fiscal constraint. Continuing fiscal stress, management cutbacks, competition for decreasing resources, and citizens' growing expectations of accountability in government—all have fostered and expanded the demand for finding "better ways" to manage government policies and programs. Citizens and elected officials exerted and continue to exert pressures on public administrators to "stretch tax dollars" by increasing the efficiency and effectiveness of public management. Consequently, monitoring, evaluating, and auditing performance have become significant tools assisting the heightened emphasis on outcomes.

While concerns with performance of public programs and activities are universal, performance audit remains mainly a U.S. invention. In its short history, performance audit itself has undergone dramatic changes in format, content, and importance. Moreover, performance budgeting and the constant effort to measure, audit, or improve organizational outputs and program results have become global pursuits. It is not surprising, therefore, that performance audit in the 1990s is one of the most promising management concepts.

In the United States, for example, most states and many cities, counties, and special districts have adopted new methods and procedures for scrutinizing performance. They have regularly produced audit reports that are quite different from traditional financial pre-audits and post-audits. State and local elected officials and public managers increasingly confront and interact with auditors in all phases of policy and budget processes.

The earliest methodical application of performance audit in the United States was in 1972, when the U.S. General Accounting Office (GAO) popularized it by publishing "Standard for Audit of Government Organizations, Programs, Activities and Functions." Currently, this reference is called *Government Auditing Standards,* popularly known as "the yellow book." In a 1994 revised edition, it defines performance audit as "an objective and systematic examination of evidence for the purpose of providing an independent assessment of the performance of a government organization, program, activity, or function in order to provide information to improve public accountability and facilitate decisionmaking by parties with responsibility to oversee or initiate corrective action" (p. 14).

Thus, performance audit emphasizes economy and efficiency of programs. These include: (1) whether the entity is acquiring, protecting, and using its resources (personnel, property, and space) economically and efficiently, (2) the causes of inefficiencies and wasteful practices, and (3) whether the entity is complying with laws and regulations on matters of economy and efficiency.

The basic premise here is that organizations have objectives that they seek to attain through activities and programs. Management essentially is responsible for selecting activities and programs that provide the most efficient and effective results. By selecting a program or designating a certain activity from among several competing alternatives, management is obligated, by this selection, to relate cost to benefit (input to output). Mainly, this is accomplished through the budgetary process, but not limited to it. Concern with the relationship between the cost of a program and its results also are reflected in other managerial processes such as the accounting system in use, financial reporting, mechanisms of financial control, and performance measurements.

Traditional budgetary decisions have been preoccupied with the input side of the equation, where managers habitually emphasize financial needs (costs) of programs more than their outputs. Today, the performance of a program is crucial. In developing programs, more and more expectations are that management spells out performance standards by which it determines when the objectives have or have not been met. It is assumed that standards to be met include quality and quantity of performance that are definable and measurable. Auditors conducting a performance review are supposed to be familiar with these standards and the conditions surrounding them.

In brief, through examination and analysis audits primarily aim to establish whether desired benefits or results (as established by authorizing legislation) are being achieved. They evaluate organizational activities and functions in terms of realizing program goals. In the process, a performance audit is unalterably obligated to determine if the entity has complied with applicable laws and significant regulations.

Process

The process of an audit is a course of several interrelated steps and events that unfold over a period of time to achieve a defined purpose or goal. Such a process is not mechanical in the sense of being a sequence of exact procedures. Rather, it is a progression of steps that outlines how an audit is carried out in a flexible and adaptive form. As a dynamic activity, a well-conceived audit is a unique design of how to proceed in order to accomplish what to be done.

The initial phase of a performance audit requires setting forth a broad framework for planning the audit and agreeing on its purpose and procedures. Because of a range of possible approaches, initiators of the audit must decide what the audit should accomplish before the process is activated. They may examine any aspect of the organization or the program that relates to performance such as procurement practices, resources used, cost, duplication of employees' efforts, overstaffing, operating procedures, and so forth. Typically, a program audit attempts to identify bottlenecks, waste, conflicts, and factors that inhibit or reduce efficiency and effectiveness of operations.

An important rule is that careful implementation requires evaluating evidence before formulating final opinions. Such evidence involves written or verbal confirmation of the presence and effective functioning of internal controls and records. The task of auditors is simplified with the availability of authoritative and valid documents in support of recorded transactions. Verification of information usually entails physical examination, visual observation, and/or oral testimony by parties inside or outside the organization being audited. Whatever the form or the method, it is imperative that auditors evaluate sufficient

competent evidence as a condition for maintaining fairness.

A professionally managed audit also seeks to obtain and evaluate evidence from management in order to ascertain the degree of correspondence between what is claimed and what is carried out. Effective auditors exhibit cooperative and supportive attitudes toward management in their search for common grounds, with the goal of bringing about improvements. Turning the process into a policing act creates conditions conducive to distortion and misrepresentation. Negative audits drive the staff into being concerned with surviving the ordeal rather than learning from it. Mutual trust and confidence between auditors and managers improve the definition of problems and enhance opportunities for solving them.

Thus, discussions between auditors and management of the agency under review, through two-way communication and give-and-take sessions, greatly strengthen auditors' effectiveness and increase the value of their recommendations. Customarily, before a report is published, which is the primary product of a performance audit, it is made available to the agency concerned for comments and reactions. This could be decisive for improving the chances of implementing the report's recommendations.

Moreover, seeking the agency's reaction often results in rectifying any factual errors and removing an agency's pretext for criticizing the report on grounds of inaccuracy. Frequently, an audit is concluded with a seminar at the agency's premises where a dialogue and constructive interaction may produce deeper understanding of the issues. Certainly, convincing management to accept auditors' conclusions, or at least minimizing the force of initial resistance, are worthy objectives.

The auditors' final report, containing findings and recommendations, is presented in clear and straightforward language with financial and numerical data employed only to illustrate the analysis and recommendations. Reports of performance audit represent the independent judgment of the auditors and thus have a considerable normative stance.

A Comparative Perspective on Performance Audit

It should be understood that many approaches and techniques exist for conducting a performance audit. Some audits are nearly indistinguishable from program evaluation. Others overlap in their concerns with management or financial audits. But the most common approach is a problem-solving orientation that focuses on identifying, defining, and analyzing the problem before recommending solutions. In this regard, the constant objective remains improving the quality of service, increasing the effectiveness of programs, and reducing the cost of operations.

Not surprising, the scope of performance audit has changed over the years. During the inception phase, performance audit was narrowly focused and vaguely conceived. Since 1972, with extensive experience at various levels of government in the United States as well as in several other countries, performance audit and performance measurement have expanded to include many previously excluded management and public policy issues. These changes are further explained by comparing performance audit with program evaluation.

Unlike program evaluation, which grew out of the social sciences, performance auditing is an extension of accounting and financial audits. The usual distinctions between performance audit and program evaluation, however, are rapidly disappearing. The contention that program evaluation measures a wide range of social concerns, rather than the narrow managerial efficiency focus of the performance audit, is a superfluous argument in light of the comprehensive coverage of current performance audits. Similarly, the derivative notion that performance audit is of utility only to line managers is false.

Actually, performance audit and program evaluation share the same ultimate objective, that of improving the performance of a program or a whole organization. As practiced over the past several years, performance audit has extended its purview far beyond the concerns of traditional accounting and budget analysis, which have failed to offer policymakers and managers the help they need. Namely, how do we develop responsive and efficient management of public service agencies in an environment of financial stress? This question includes the administrative commitment to improving the chances of implementation of legislatively mandated programs.

At least one primary difference between performance audit and program evaluation is worth noting. Performance audit, unlike an evaluation, can never be regarded as complete upon the mere statement of disclosed or unveiled problems. Usually, its presentations are accompanied by proposals for solutions to specific problems or improvements in overall effectiveness.

Far from being a narrow accounting tool, performance audit in its most comprehensive content encompasses analysis of policy, monitoring of programs, measurement of results, and development of alternative processes to deliver public services. Within this expansive mode, performance audit also may be regarded as a catalyst for organizational change, functioning as a vehicle for implementing Total Quality Management (TQM) in public agencies. This means that performance audit must succeed where other approaches have failed: namely, attain a radical shift in management philosophy and operations by developing a permanent commitment to quality improvements in all processes and at all levels of public organizations.

The continual extension of coverage and inclusion of functions, however, do not always mark vitality or confirm strength of performance audits. It is a serious concern whether performance audit is becoming an umbrella concept organized around the public inquiry: "What are we getting for our money?" A potential consequence of this view is that performance audit, by becoming anything its conductors want, risks being nothing in particular. Worse, such dispersion carries the seeds of disintegration over time.

In a global context, deficit spending and the heavy burden of public debt in most countries have prompted a variety of remedial proposals. The most frequently recommended solutions by reformers in contemporary states are privatizing public enterprises, and building the administrative capacities of the state in order to improve the performance of public service agencies.

Also, focus on performance has been globally touted as an obligation of modern management. The success of private organizations that transformed themselves into flexible, lean operations through the adaptation of innovative management concepts provides a powerful impetus for public sector programs. By restructuring the public sector and its system of financial management, governments of Germany, Britain, Canada, Australia, and New Zealand as well as the United States sought to give public managers greater authority and responsibility. At the same time these managers are held accountable for results by instituting a variety of efficiency checks and installing financial management systems stressing performance measurement and accountability.

Reforms of these public services illustrate a managerial culture that has become one of inducements and incentives, performance measurement and improvement, and attention to quality of services and to citizens' demands. In the new environment, accent is on organizational knowledge, managerial skills, and professional ethics. Success in converging knowledge, skills, and ethics in managing modern organizations is most likely when applied democratically and in the context of participatory decisionmaking and team-building.

Britain launched its Financial Management Initiatives (FMI) in 1982 as a long-term effort for measuring performance and assessing whether programs are providing "value for money" (Schick 1990, pp. 26–34). Within broad guidelines, FMI impels each department to have a clear view of its objectives and to develop the means to assess and to measure performance in relation to these objectives. Departments are free to develop their managerial systems to this end, according to their own specific circumstances. A principal issue is the extent to which data on output and results should be linked to the budget.

Britain's experience is particularly relevant for two reasons: First, it has influenced many of the changes introduced afterward in Canada, Australia, and New Zealand. Second, it has underscored the importance of performance audit and the continuous challenge to develop methods and techniques for measuring performance of public activities as an essential element in the allocation of resources.

In summary, global practices indicate that performance audit is conceived of differently: with a narrow accounting mission, as a catalyst of overall quality management, or as an umbrella that arches over a variety of interests and perspectives. Regardless, it is commonly held that objectives of the audit determine the type of information needed, and a successful audit remains flexible and creative. It utilizes adequate background information about the entity being reviewed and selects the appropriate approach from a number of possible perspectives.

Obstacles and Impediments

At all levels of government, political considerations are paramount, often outweighing the desire for economy and efficiency. Interest in program costs is often of greater concern to managers than to politicians. Elected officials primarily are interested in their reelection and in what they consider to be the will of their constituents. While performance audits are of most value when the long-term effects of measurement are considered, it is always difficult for elected officials to make long-range decisions based largely on financial considerations.

Generally, public administrators are less than enthusiastic about having their departments or agencies undergo the scrutiny of either elected officials or the public. This sort of oversight by elected officials might result in a perceived micromanagement of agencies by legislators. Similarly, public knowledge of performance measurement of individual departments without the benefit of a thorough understanding of the department's goals and objectives might encourage public managers to consider misrepresenting financial matters in order to manage public opinion.

Judgments made by the public and by elected officials as a result of performance measurements become troublesome when comparisons are made between departments. The value of comparisons between the performance measurement of the Department of Interior and the Department of Defense is unclear. And yet such comparisons must be made when considering the effective use of public funds. Both the public and elected officials need to realize that performance measurement cannot be the only factors considered in determining an organization's value.

Conversely, to set these types of examinations and evaluations aside is to suggest that effectiveness of organizations cannot be evaluated. Yet performance measurements and evaluation have developed under the presumption that effectiveness can be monitored and periodically assessed. Measurement is the key to any performance improvement process and an essential means for controlling quality and quantity of output—this despite the fact that many related questions of measurement have not been satisfactorily answered. Also, performance budgeting has not mastered the need for stronger connection between performance and revenue allocations. What can or may be measured in government operations? Who makes the measurement? What interpretation can be made from the raw data? How can these data be correlated with budgeted dollars so that the public may readily understand service agency performance? Notwithstanding progress achieved in measuring outputs of public programs in the past few years, these and similar questions remain troublesome.

Interest in measurement is not to deny the valid claim that the most important aspect of performance auditing of public service agencies lies not in quantitative analytical methods but rather in the internal and external politics affecting service improvement—the ultimate goal. At the same time, it seems that the public will be observing and evaluating public service agencies in terms of performance versus tax dollars as well as the quality of service delivered.

Among the results of recent changes in performance auditing are a growing interest in public policy and an increasing orientation toward a problem-solving approach. Such a trend has not received universal support or acceptance, however. Debates over the role of the U.S. General Accounting Office in 1994 illustrate the political sensitivity of legislators toward an independent, professional analysis of public policies. Lawmakers continually cite the accounting office's findings in deciding whether to create, abolish, cut or revise programs. Yet, as *The New York Times* notes (October 17, 1994, p. A1), lawmakers of both parties have expressed concern that GAO sometimes seemed more eager to make policy pronouncements than simply provide information.

The GAO produces reports on many volatile issues, including health care, defense-related procurement, immigration, and trade. It alerted Congress to problems in the savings and loan industry long before most people were aware of them. It has documented problems in dozens of weapons programs. Federal agencies accept three-fourths of its recommendation, and Congress follows more than half of its suggestions for legislative action (*The New York Times*, October 17, 1994, p. A1). A study by a panel of experts from the National Academy of Public Administration, a nonprofit organization chartered by Congress to increase the effectiveness of federal, state, and local government, describes the GAO as an invaluable institution and found "no evidence of deliberate partisan bias" in its work. But the study said the GAO "seems to be exceeding its appropriate role" by venturing into the analysis and development of public policy (*The New York Times*, October 17, 1994, p. A12).

Clearly, role definition is vital for any organization involved in performance audit. Until performance audit is universally accepted and practiced, such a task will face criticism, if not hostility, from political as well as administrative sources. Perhaps the most widely acknowledged apprehension regarding the practicality of performance monitoring is the public's concern with expenditures. The benefits of professional monitoring will eventually outweigh all costs associated with its implementation, which initially will be expensive. Considering the current financial condition of both federal and local governments in the United States and most other governments of the world, it is imperative that such programs be presented in a manner that ensures political acceptance of the required additional expenditures.

For developing countries, the crucial factor is to build capacities of public agencies and to develop employees' knowledge and skills to be able to conduct performance audits. These systems are facing a dearth of professional neutral competence among staffs, essential for exerting the authority of expert knowledge and professional ethics in monitoring, proposing, and ushering in new ideas and improvements. So far senior public managers have not developed sufficient appreciation of the positive role of audits and their potential contributions to achieving overall improvements or better accountability.

While there is no simple formula for realizing such necessary changes in developing countries, faithful execution of performance audits is not likely without them. Thus, a sort of managerial vicious cycle continues to keep in check all potential disruptions of the status quo. To carry out a performance audit plan effectively in these developing systems, therefore, presence of certain preconditions is vital:

1. Unwavering support of the political leadership, which is essential. Corrupt and uninspired leadership constitutes the single greatest discouragement of efforts to study and analyze government practices. Such leaders may praise popular activities that claim to reform existing conditions, only to bury them at the implementation and monitoring phases. The political order is the context that envelops and influences management in numerous ways. Political leadership is able to induce or stifle professional management and thus is a contributor to existing managerial culture, tradition, and level of integrity and ethics applied in the conduct of government functions at large.

2. Greater recognition and appreciation of the vital role of accounting standards and performance measurement practices in public programs. This entails enriching the accountancy profession with new talents and according at high priority in public policies. Government accounting in developing countries is completely overshadowed by the budget function, which is emphasized and granted preeminence. Budget people frequently maintain their own separate accounting records, which are more accurate, timely, and useful than those of accounting offices. Government accounting is poor in quality, inadequate in content, and late in presenting data that are easily ignored (Wesberry 1990). Typically, accounting in developing coun-

tries has been limited primarily to serving the legal purpose of documenting and summarizing receipts and expenditures in a formal report that is presented several years after the execution of the transactions reported. When financial records do not provide an accurate snapshot of government activities or financial status, determining accountability becomes a daunting quest.

3. Empowering employees at the operational levels through substantive decentralization of decisionmaking. Unquestionably, existing staffs in most developing countries are not qualified or equipped to carry out responsibilities of auditing the performance of public programs. Consequently, improving their professional standards is a fundamental step, not only in terms of obtaining and evaluating evidence but also in demonstrating independence, reliability, and ethical conduct. In highly centralized systems, professional considerations easily give way to hierarchical restrictions. Particularly, in organizational environments that emphasize conformance and obedience, it is not customary for employees readily to reveal corruption or waste by people of high authority.

4. Transparency of financial transactions so that accounting processes lend themselves to measures of validation of correct operations or verification of the accuracy of financial information. Issues of accountability and good government usually are strengthened when an administrative unit actually develops the ability to monitor its operations, diagnose its problems, and recommend solutions for them—all in the public eye and with democratic means.

Currently operating accounting systems in developing countries rarely introduce change or propose dramatic conclusions in their audits. This is not to say that their actions have not resulted in some prevention of fraud and waste. Many Asian and Latin American countries have been attempting to reform their financial managements through a variety of approaches. In the two decades after World War II, the Philippines, India, Indonesia, Malaysia, Singapore, and others have attempted to apply performance-oriented financial administrative systems. Performance and program budgeting also have been on the agenda of most Asian and Latin American countries.

So far these efforts have resulted only in modest accomplishments. Success of management audits may be important for the evolution of any good government; achieving it, however, has proved to be illusive for most governments. Consequently, this discussion is concerned with defining the particulars that contributed to effective auditing as well as the contextual preconditions that facilitate its competent discharge. Despite the obvious advantages to conducting performance auditing, it is sometimes disparaged for perceived deficiencies: lacking clear criteria, second-guessing management, and placing auditors in judgment roles. Moreover, despite progress made in setting standards and defining processes, performance audit continues to carry an element of subjectivity and personal judgment.

JAMIL E. JREISAT

BIBLIOGRAPHY

Garner, C. William, 1991. *Accounting and Budgeting in Public and Nonprofit Organizations: A Manager's Guide.* San Francisco, CA: Jossey-Bass Publishers.

Herbert, L., L. N. Killough, and A. W. Steiss, 1984. *Governmental Accounting and Control.* Monterey, CA: Brooks/Cole.

Mascarenhas, R. C., 1993. "Building an Enterprise Culture in the Public Sector in Australia, Britain, and New Zealand." *Public Administration Review,* 53(4) (July-August).

Schick, Allen, 1990. "Budgeting for Results: Recent Developments in Five Industrialized Countries." *Public Administration Review,* 50(1) (January-February).

U.S. General Accounting Office, 1994. *Government Auditing Standards.* Washington, D.C.: Government Printing Office.

Wesberry, James P., Jr., 1990. "Government Accounting and Financial Management in Latin American Countries." *Government Financial Management: Issues and Country Studies.* Washington, D.C.: International Monetary Fund.

Wheat, Edward M., 1991. "The Activist Auditor: A New Player in State and Local Politics." *Public Administration Review,* 51(5) (September-October).

PERFORMANCE BUDGET.

A budget which emphasizes activities performed and their costs and includes various performance measures in the budget to document what is gained from what is spent. These measures usually include unit cost comparisons over time or between jurisdictions. Performance budgeting tends to emphasize measures of efficiency and effectiveness. Broader measures (outcome) are often difficult to define and measure, particularly in human service functions. Nonetheless performance budget concepts have proven persistent.

History of Performance Budgeting

General acceptance of the concepts of performance budgeting may be dated in the U.S. from the recommendations of the Commission on Organization of the Executive Branch of the Government (commonly called the Hoover Commission) in 1949. Among other recommendations, the Commission recommended that "a budget based on functions, activities, and projects, called a 'performance budget,' be adopted" (Hoover Commission 1949, p. 8). The Commission observed that if the federal budget were prepared on a performance basis, focusing attention on the amount of work to be achieved, and the cost of this work, congressional action and executive direction of the scope and magnitude of different federal activities could then be appropriately emphasized and compared in the resource allocation process. Additionally, the costs and achievements of the federal government would be furnished to Congress and the people.

Performance budgeting was initially mandated by amendments to the National Security Act in 1949. These amendments required the Department of Defense to install performance budgeting in the three services (63 Stat 412, 1949). The federal government as a whole entered into performance budgeting as a consequence of the Budget and Accounting Procedures Act of 1950. This act required the heads of each agency to support "budget justifications by information on performance and program cost by organizational unit" (64 Stat 946, 1950).

While the federal government was developing performance measures and moving toward performance budgeting, some state and local governments quickly adopted the concept. Early attempts included Detroit, Michigan, Kissimmee, Florida, San Diego, California, and various states including Oklahoma, California, and Maryland (Seckler-Hudson 1953, pp. 5–9). The City of Los Angeles has provided a noteworthy case study of this era from 1952 to 1958.

In 1951, Los Angeles created the position of City Administrative Officer (CAO) and filled it with Samuel Leask, Jr. Just one year after his appointment, Leask had instituted a performance budget system throughout the city. The heart of the Los Angeles system was a performance contract. This contract was based on goals and targets developed in the budget process. The parties to this contract were the mayor, city council and the CAO, on the one hand, and department administrators on the other. These performance contracts were monitored by the CAO during budget execution to ensure goals were being achieved (Eghtedari and Sherwood 1960, p. 83).

The contracts were based upon work programs that became the starting point from which questions about timing, size, and nature of expenditures could be framed. Departmental appropriations were based on work programs and a governmentwide reporting system was used to compare units of work performed to hours expended in the budget execution process. This was the final check on actual versus proposed performance (Eghetdari and Sherwood 1960, p. 83).

A study of this system conducted primarily in the building, safety, and library departments found that the performance approach resulted in a strengthening of the executive budget, program planning, and central control of decisions going into the executive budget. Measurement of work in a governmental jurisdiction was found to be practical and feasible, with positive benefits gained from such measurements (Eghtedari 1959, p. 82–88). In this case perhaps the major finding of the study was in the value of creating and staffing the Office of City Administrative Officer (CAO). The study found that the CAO had ". . . improved the quality of program planning, had brought about a higher degree of coordination among the essentially independent departments than ever before existed, and has made some contribution to the overall efficiency of municipal operations" (Eghtedari and Sherwood 1960, p. 82). Additionally, the new budget process assisted in increased control for the city administrator by creating the performance contracts. Perhaps the most important result of the Los Angeles experiment was the proof that a performance style budget in a governmental agency was feasible and beneficial.

During this period, the United States was not alone in its recognition of the potential of performance budgeting. As various state and local governments continued to experiment with versions of performance budgeting, nearly 50 countries implemented various aspects of performance budgets in the 1960s. Among the leaders in this endeavor were Sweden, Britain, Canada, and France. Most attempts in foreign nations merely supplemented the traditional budget and were usually issued as separate documents (Axelrod 1988, pp. 272–273). Meanwhile the performance budget experiment in the U.S. Department of Defense (DOD) was integrated first into program budgeting (see **program budgeting**) and then planning, programming, budgeting (see **budgeting**).

Performance Budgeting Described

Performance budgeting requires an administrator to break down his or her program into the basic activities in which the agency engages, decide what measures best fit each activity, and develop budget costs for each measure. The typical performance budget has narrative describing what the unit does, performance measures which indicate activities and trends, and a breakdown by typical budget category. Exhibit I is a typical, if hypothetical, performance budget. A "pure" performance budget would consist of activity classifications, workload data, other measures of performance, unit costing data, and program goals. Other data

EXHIBIT I. NARRATIVE

This unit is responsible for evaluating, inspecting, and licensing potential widget makers. As a result of dedicated analytic efforts all our unit cost indicators have shown a decrease from last year to this year.

Activity and Performance Measures

Activity	Items	Budget	Unit Cost This Year	Unit Cost Last Year
Evaluating	800	$15,000	$18.75	$19.00
Inspecting	18,500	$40,000	$2.18	$2.30
Licensing	2,600	$16,475	$6.34	$6.50
Total		$71,875		

Budget Accounts

Personal Services	$57,500
Supporting Expenses	$14,375
Capital Outlay	0
Total	$71,875

typically found in budgets that are modeled after performance budgets consist of narratives discussing the activity or program, several years of data, mission statements, and outcomes desired. It should be noted most budgets that are called performance budgets are not of the pure format.

Once programs have been broken down into activities, measurements for performance must be generated for program evaluation. There are five generic performance measures used with performance budgeting. These include input, workload, efficiency ("doing the thing right"), effectiveness ("doing the right thing,") and impact or outcome measures. Input measures describe the resources, time, and personnel used for a program. They typically appear in the budget as dollars for salary and supporting expenses. They also might be presented as staff training hours and number of person years expended on an activity.

Workload measures are volumetric measures of what an agency does. Such items as number of audits done, returns filed, checks issued, number of arrests made, or miles of highway constructed are typical workload measures. Workload measures are the lowest form of performance measurement. The trouble with workload measures is that there are a lot of them and they do not tell anyone very much without further analysis. While workload measures do describe the activities of a program, they do not define how well the program is accomplishing its mission. To do this, workload measures must be converted into measures of efficiency, effectiveness, and outcome.

Efficiency measures take workload data and merge it with cost data to develop unit cost measures. Then efficiency can be gauged on such items as the cost per arrest made, the cost of issuing a check, or the cost of flying an aircraft per hour. Efficiency is a much better indicator of performance than simple workload data since it gives outputs a direct cost relationship. These costs per unit can then be compared over time or against other similar activities to gauge competitiveness or improvement. This is important since it allows administrators a simple way to keep track of complex programs. At higher levels, the legislature can track efficiency measures to keep costs down, and the public can be assured its taxes are being spent efficiently. Efficiency, however, does not necessarily indicate effectiveness.

Effectiveness measures are used to mark output conformance to specified characteristics. Such items as quality, timeliness, and customer satisfaction fall into this category. These measures require managers to determine goals for the particular program activity and to identify who their customers are and what type of characteristics customers would want within the products or services delivered to them. Then effectiveness measures indicate how well the agency is satisfying these needs. Effectiveness measures are better than efficiency measures in that the primary focus of effectiveness is on the customers, whereas the primary focus of efficiency is the organization. If efficiency focuses on cost per unit, effectiveness measures tend to focus on rates of accomplishment, such as percentage of satisfied clients, or ratio of clients helped as opposed to ratio of clients seen. Effectiveness is associated with the quality of service and includes such things as responsiveness, timeliness, accessibility, availability, participation, safety, and client satisfaction. If efficiency measures are largely internal, effectiveness measures connect the operator to his clientele, the citizen to her government.

Outcome measures are the most difficult level of measure used in a performance budget system. These are measures of outcome, impact, or result. They attempt to capture performance based on achieving what the program was intended to do as a whole. Simply put, they ask if the program achieved the mission it set out to accomplish from the start. Has the city become cleaner, the streets safer, students more knowledgeable, and customers more satisfied? In the 1970s several cities took pictures of their city streets and used a standardized photograph rating scale to judge if their streets were actually getting cleaner as a result of sanitation efforts. This information could then be compared against historical data or against a rating for a different neighborhood. After all, it is possible to collect many more tons of trash and to have the unit cost drop, but have the city streets getting dirtier. The photo scale technique was meant to provide an outcome measure.

As a practical matter, outcome measures have proved to be very difficult to develop and maintain. They tend to be particularly difficult in human service areas, such as education or public safety, where global statements are easy, but precise measurement difficult. Additionally, in the budget process, even where measurement is easy, sometimes it is difficult for policymakers to decide how many dollars it will take to move up an increment or two on a rating scale and if it is worth it. This further assumes more clarity in cause and effect relationships than may be possible in the real world. Constructing and evaluating measures adds technical difficulty to the budget process, which many participants view as complicated enough in terms of determination of cost and political preference.

Early versions of performance budgeting focused simply on measures of workload and efficiency. In other words, the indicators focused primarily on the agency itself and were primarily internal measures of what the agency did and what it cost. These were input and workload measures, such as salary cost and tons of trash collected, with efficiency ratios developed to measure the change in cost of collecting a ton of trash from one year to the next. Recent attempts at performance budgeting include measures of effectiveness and outcomes or results and have a focus on the clients and customers of the agency, with some measures constructed to evaluate client or customer satisfaction or response time to customer demand. Whatever measures are used, they are compared to similar agencies or over several years to measure competitiveness or improvement.

This type of budget aims to assist managers in spending wisely such that maximum output is achieved with as little input as possible, with the focus shifting from objects of expenditure to program activities as the basis for budgeting. Therefore, instead of budgeting for salaries, utilities, and travel expenses, the manager would base the budget upon the activities the unit performs and policymakers would judge which activities should be increased or decreased.

GPRA and Performance Measurement

On August 3, 1993, Congress passed P.L. 103-62, the Government Performance and Results Act of 1993 (GPRA). The purpose of the act was to shift the focus of government management from inputs to outputs and outcomes, from process to results, from compliance to performance, and from management control to managerial initiative (P.L. 103-62, 1993).

The significance of this act is evident in the Office of Management and Budget's (OMB) FY96 Circular No. A-11 (Preparation and Submission of Budget Estimates). Under these guidelines, justification of programs and program funding will require the use of performance indicators and goals as set forth by the GPRA. In issuing Circular A-11 in 1994 to control the preparation of the FY96 budget, OMB said: "Without performance indicators, performance goals, or some other type of performance data, agency requests for significant funding to continue or increase an ongoing program are difficult to justify" (OMB 1994, p. 2).

For the FY96 budget submission, OMB encouraged agencies to use output- and outcome-based performance measures in the budget decisionmaking process and budget justification statements. These guidelines agree with the general provisions of the GPRA.

The apparent long-term goal for GPRA is to implement performance budgeting as a means of resource allocation for all federal agencies. Performance budget pilot projects are to be conducted for FY98 and FY99 under the auspices of GPRA (P.L. 103-62, 1993). In the meantime, several performance planning and reporting pilot projects were gotten underway, to be used to evaluate the ability of federal agencies to build plans based upon performance indicators as an initial step toward performance budgeting.

In the Department of Defense seven units were selected as pilot projects. The units had to volunteer, be selected by the Secretary of Defense, and then be approved by the Director, Office of Management and Budget (OMB, 1995). The pilots nominated and selected were the Defense Logistics Agency (DLA); Defense Commissary Agency (DeCA); Air Combat Command (ACC); Army Research Laboratory (ARL); Commander-in-Chief, U.S. Atlantic Fleet (CINCLANTFLT), Carrier Battle Group; the Department of the Army, Army Audit Agency (AAA); and the U.S. Army Corps of Engineers Civil Works Operation.

Of the commands selected, two are major combatant commands, one is a research facility and the others can be classified as service-oriented agencies. This diversification in types of commands will be beneficial in finding out what types of agencies will be conducive to performance measurement and what types will have problems with these measures. One might speculate that it will be easier for the service agencies than the research or operational commands to develop performance plans/reports. The difficulty with performance measurement in the research and operational cases lies in outcome measurement.

A comparative analysis of the first set of plans submitted by each agency was conducted. In doing so the definitions of the performance measures given earlier will be used in comparing the measures used by the pilots.

Table I is a synopsis of the analysis results. The first column indicates the command or agency engaged in the pilot project. The second column indicates the primary orientation of the command (i.e., is the pilot unit service-oriented, operational, or research?). The third and fourth columns show the level of resources used by the agency in the form of budget and personnel. Column five shows the total number of measures included within the pilots' first performance plans.

The last five columns of Table I represent the five types of performance measures as described earlier. They are arranged on a spectrum from least difficult to capture (input) to the most difficult (outcome). Indicated for each pilot is the percentage this measure takes of the total number of measures in its plan. (Percentages may not add up to 100 percent since they were rounded to the nearest whole percent.) For example, ARL included six output measures in its FY95 plan. This makes up approximately 32 percent of the total measures in the plan.

Some rather interesting results can be gleaned from Table I. First, a comparison of the agency size with the number of measures used might be useful. By far, the largest pilot as measured by resources used is DLA. It is approximately three times the size of the nearest pilot in both budget and personnel. Twenty-two measures for an agency this size does not seem unreasonable. However, DLA does not have the largest plan with regard to number of measures. ACC tops the list with 32 measures in all. The budget authority covered by these 32 measures is less than one-tenth that of DLA's. ARL also has a large measure/resource ratio (which is simply the number of measures divided by the resources employed) as compared to DLA. With 19 measures, just short of DLA's 22, ARL is measuring the performance of resources with a value of about 5 percent of DLA's. In fact, DLA has the lowest measure to resource ratio of all the plans. Overall, the trend appears to be toward more, rather than fewer, numbers of performance measures in this group.

Another interesting result taken from Table I is how different types of agencies chose measures in the spectrum of those available. The service type commands tended to choose measures more evenly distributed across the entire spectrum of measures. This contrasts with the research and operational commands. The research command, ARL, included 84 percent of its measures in the input/output categories. The operational command shifted to the opposite end of the spectrum in that 72 percent of its measures were effectiveness and efficiency indicators. However, one exception to this generality was the Army Corps of Engineers, which used four of six measures of effectiveness. As seen by the bottom row of Table I, the plans as a whole spread across the spectrum evenly. Input, output, and efficiency measures all have about 20 percent of the total. Effectiveness measures are used approximately twice as often as the others. The one glaring exception is the lack of outcome measures provided. Despite the shortage of outcome measures, the plans consisted of almost 60 percent higher order measures (i.e., efficiency and effectiveness). The other problem with the measurement choices was the use

TABLE I. PILOT PERFORMANCE MEASURE COMPARISON

Command Agency	Type	Budget	Employees	Total Measures	Input Measures	Output Measures	Efficiency	Effectiveness	Outcome
DLA	Service	$14.6 Billion	~58,000	22	0%	36%	27%	36%	0%
DeCA	Service	$5.9 Billion	~20,000	11	27%	27%	18%	27%	0%
ARL	Research	$570 Million	~3,600	19	52%	32%	5%	11%	0%
AAA***	Service	$44 Million	~700	7	14%	14%	29%	43%	0%
Corp of Engineers	Service	$1.7 Billion	~14,000	6	0%	17%	17%	67%	0%
ACC	Operations	$120* Million	13,500*	32	19%	6%	22%	50%	3%
Total/ Avg %	N/A	N/A	N/A	97	21%	22%	20%	37%	1%

*These resources represent only those being applied to the pilot project air wings, not the entire commands available resources.

**CINCLANTFLT had not yet submitted a performance plan at the time of this analysis and thus is not included in Table I.

***Department of Army, Army Audit Agency.

of input measures about 20 percent of the time. Input measures are not required under GPRA, but they are easy to construct and do represent some measure of effort for a unit. In any case, they seem to remain an attractive starting point for performance measurement efforts.

An analysis of the pilot project plans uncovered some additional strengths and weaknesses. The strengths seemed to lie in goal linkage and target identification.

Goal Linkage

Several plans were able to relate performance measures directly with overall strategic goals. This is extremely important since the efficient and effective accomplishment of the primary goals of an organization is what the writers of GPRA desired. For example, DeCA (1994, p. 5) arranged its plan such that the goal and measure were identified together:

Goal: *Maximize Customer Satisfaction*
Objective: *Improve customer service at the commissary level.*
Performance Indicator: *Customer Service Evaluation System. (CSES).*
Performance Goal: *Annual increase in CSES.*
Baseline: *FY94 average CSES score is 86%.*

This allows the administrator to identify the overall corporate goal with which the performance indicator is most closely associated.

Target/Goal Identification

A few agencies found ways to articulate the goals and targets for performance indicators. Providing baseline data and targets for the current and future years allows administrators to see trends in the program instead of raw current year workload numbers. This also provides a means for asking intelligent questions about the program's activities and the associated performance. DLA and ARL seemed to have displays that were exceptional. An excerpt from the ARL FY95 plan shows this arrangement (ARL 1994, p. 24).

Metric:	Actual FY93	Goal FY94	Actual FY94	Goal FY95	Long-term goal (5 + yr)
No. of invention disclosures	166	100	84*	100	10

(*YTD as of May 31, 1994)

As can be seen, ARL expected their workload for Invention Disclosures to decline from its FY93 level. The baseline shown in FY93 is considerably higher than the goals set for the next several years. Also indicated is the fact they have completed 84 percent of this year's goal eight months into the fiscal year. Reviewers might be stimulated to ask questions about this profile.

The plans seemed to have had two primary weaknesses.

Measures Difficult to Capture

Some plans included measures that would be inherently unmeasurable. These types of measures have goals that simply state "reduce," "minimize," or "develop" some aspect of a program. A prime example of this is the Army Corps of Engineers "Industry delay cost due to unscheduled closures" measurement. The goal associated with this measure is to minimize the cost to the navigation industry resulting from unscheduled lock closures (U.S. Army Corps of Engineers 1994, p. 5). No targets or baseline data were provided beyond this. Several plans took this type of measure only one step farther in that they attached a numerical goal to the measure such as "increase by 10 percent." One such example comes from the FY95 DeCA p. 8 plan. The performance indicator in question was the "DeCA regional work force diversity." The goal associated with the measure was to simply "get a 2 percent increase in categories that have an imbalance."

Bulk

Several plans were extremely large and discussed items not directly related to the performance measures contained in the plan. A couple of plans appeared to be overwhelming in size. The initial DLA plan was 120 pages long. Only 40 of those pages dealt directly with the FY94 performance plan itself. The remainder of the plan was used to describe the 30-plus strategic initiatives currently in progress at DLA. When GPRA legally mandated plans are to be submitted in 1997, if the individual agency plans are as large in sheer volume as some pilots this will impose a heavy burden on plan reviewers. One of the major problems for the budget process has always been information overload, and a system which adds even more information to the process risks confusing the decision process with an avalanche of data.

A Case Study: Adapting to the New Performance Measurement System

The Defense Logistics Agency was the first agency chosen within DOD to act as a pilot under the auspices of the GPRA; consequently by 1995 it had two years worth of experience with the new requirements. DLA is the logistics division of the DOD and provides material and logistical services to all the military services. Figure I presents the strategic mission statement, vision statement, and goals as indicated by the DLA Corporate Plan. DLA began the pilot project on October 22, 1993, and had produced two annual reports on its performance measurement efforts by 1995.

DLA's FY95 performance plan is arranged into three sections, one for each of its major business areas. Each section contains a description of the business area, the budget relationship, the associated performance indicators that

FIGURE I. DLA MISSION AND VISION STATEMENTS

DLA Mission: The Defense Logistics Agency is a combat support agency responsible for worldwide logistics support throughout the Department of Defense. The primary focus of the Agency is to support the warfighter in time of war and in peace, and to provide relief efforts during times of national emergency.

DLA Vision: To be the provider of choice, around the clock—around the world . . . providing the logistics readiness and enabling weapon systems acquisition at reduced cost . . . by leveraging our corporate resources against global logistics targets . . . and finding savings through teams, improved business practices, and technological breakthroughs.

DLA Strategic Goals:

- Put customers first
- Improve the process of delivering logistics support
- Empower employees to get results
- Meet customer readiness and weapon systems acquisition requirements at reduced cost

DLA Customer-Oriented Goals:

- Responsiveness
- Quality
- Financial Performance
- Timeliness
- Operating Efficiency
- Customer Satisfaction

SOURCE: *The DLA Corporate Plan, 1994.*

apply to the area, and definitions of the various performance measures.

The most important parts of the plan are the performance measures. The GPRA requires that each agency "establish performance goals to define the level of performance to be achieved by a program activity" and "establish performance indicators to be used in measuring or assessing the relevant outputs, service levels, and outcomes of each program activity" (P.L. 103-62, 1993). These measures are provided in the annual performance plan. In order to comply with this requirement, DLA first had to identify the major activities in which it engages. Then it had to arrange these activities by major business area. The next step was to specify performance measures for each activity.

DLA has submitted two performance plans to date. A comparison of the performance measures contained in each plan gives some interesting results.

Table II contains the results of this comparison. Starting with the left-hand column, the two DLA plans are represented. The next column is the total number of measures used in the plan. The next five columns represent the percentage of each type of measure used in the plan.

TABLE II. DLA FY94–FY95 COMPARISON

DLA	Total	Input	Output	Efficiency	Effectiveness	Outcome
FY94	41*	17%	22%	29%	12%	20%
FY95	24	16%	16%	4%	13%	50%

*Total measures used in performance plan.

There are three significant results that can be observed in Table II. First, DLA has shifted from several lower-order measures (input, output, efficiency) to more higher-order measures in its second plan. The FY95 plan contains a majority of outcome measures. Simple input and output (workload) measures are of limited use; however, when comparing them to standards or costs they become much more useful for managers. This is an indication of DLA's desire to shift more toward customer-oriented type measures.

However, the second result gleaned from this table is the fact that DLA still uses about the same percentage of input measures. This testifies to the extreme difficulty in getting agencies to shift to a result-oriented mentality.

Lastly, DLA has significantly reduced the number of measures it intends to use for performance measure reporting. Though many of the FY94 measures had not yet been established, DLA realized that this was going to be far too many measures for purposes of external reporting. Thus, many measures were dropped without ever having been officially included in the plans.

Advantages and Disadvantages

Just as with any budget format, performance budgets have many advantages and disadvantages associated with them. Some advantages mentioned by participants in the pilot projects included improved planning, more effective administrative control, decentralized decisionmaking, improved public relations from clearer program information, better focus on the activities of the organization, and provision of more precise quantitative measures, if pertinent and feasible, which are better than vague generalities. Some disadvantages were also noted. Performance budgeting is not equally applicable to all agencies. For example, an agency involved in basic research such as the Army Research Laboratory does not have workload data that is easily quantifiable.

Second, efficiency is not guaranteed by using unit cost data. Legislators and administrators can use a performance budget to identify problem areas or wasteful agencies, but this by itself does not increase efficiency. Third, it is very difficult to settle in on an appropriate set of measurements for such things as workload. In practice many indicators have proven to be inappropriate and an agency may have to go through several iterations before a good set of measures is found. Fourth, the end product of many agencies is not measurable by any known means. Measures of effectiveness and outcome or impact are extremely difficult to develop. Last, this type of budgeting may not be practicable for relatively small agencies. The staffing time and costs associated with monitoring several indicators year round might inhibit smaller agencies from effectively using performance budgets.

This reincarnation of performance measurement has focused from the start on external relations. Every person interviewed in DLA identified customer satisfaction measures as a major strength of the new performance measurement system. Many also mentioned the value of having a shared sense of vision from the top to the bottom of the organization. These two points alone are significantly different from the performance measurement and budgeting efforts of the 1950s.

JERRY L. MCCAFFERY
DONALD W. WOLFGANG

BIBLIOGRAPHY

Air Combat Command (ACC), 1994. *Government Performance and Results Act Performance Plans Fiscal Year 1995.* HQ, ACC. Washington, D.C.: USGPO.

Army Audit Agency (AAA), 1995. *Annual Performance Plan Fiscal Year 1995.* Department of the Army, Office of the Auditor General. Washington, D.C.: USGPO.

Army Research Laboratory (ARL), 1994. *FY95 Performance Plan.* U.S. Army Research Laboratory. Washington, D.C.: USGPO.

Axelrod, D., 1988. *Budgeting for Modern Government.* New York: St. Martin's Press, Inc.

Defense Commissary Agency (DeCA), 1994. *Annual Performance Plan.* HQ, DeCA. Washington, D.C.: USGPO.

Defense Logistics Agency (DLA), 1994a. *Performance Plan Fiscal Year 1994.* HQ, DLA. Washington, D.C.: USGPO.

———, 1994b. *The DLA Corporate Plan.* HQ, DLA. Washington, D.C.: USGPO.

———, 1994c. *Performance Plan Fiscal Year 1995.* HQ, DLA. Washington, D.C.: USGPO.

Eghtedari, Ali and Frand Sherwood, 1960. "Performance Budgeting in Los Angeles." *Public Administration Review,* vol. 20: 63-85.

Executive Office of the President, Office of Management and Budget (OMB), 1994. *Preparation and Submission of Budget Estimates, Circular A-11.* Director, OMB. Washington, D.C.: USGPO.

Gallo, C. L., 1995. *DLA Planning, Programming, Budgeting, and Execution (PPBE) Schedule.* Executive Director, Strategic Programming & Contingency Operations, HQ, DLA. Washington, D.C.: USGPO.

Hamre, J. J., 1995. *DoD Corporate Level Performance Goals and Measures Under GPRA Action Memorandum.* Under Secretary of Defense, Comptroller. Washington, D.C.: USGPO.

Hoover Commission, 1949. Commission on Organization of the Executive Branch of the Government. New York: McGraw-Hill.

P. L. 103–62, 1993. *Government Performance and Results Act of 1993,* 103d Congress.

Seckler-Hudson, Catheryn, 1953. "Performance Budgeting in Government." *Advanced Management* (March) 5-9, 30-32.

Shycoff, D. B., 1992. *Performance Budgeting Memorandum.* Comptroller of the Department of Defense. Washington, D.C.: USGPO.

U.S. Army Corps of Engineers, 1994. *Performance Plan for Fiscal Year 1995.* U.S. Army Corps of Engineers. Washington, D.C.: USGPO.

PERFORMANCE INDICATOR.

A variable which has the characteristic that changes in its value are associated with changes in the level of success of an organization, an organizational unit, or an individual.

The impetus to develop performance indicators has come from a number of sources. In socialist planning, which began in the Soviet Union in the 1920s and spread from the communist bloc to many socialist countries throughout the world from the 1950s onward, production quotas in terms of physical outputs were a central feature of state manufacturing industries. Interestingly, there was little attention to issues of output measurement in service industries.

In Western economies, parallels have arisen from the need to regulate certain industries, particularly "public" utilities with market power arising from major economies of scale, involving governments in the determination and enforcement of performance criteria. The struggle to find a regulatory framework which is simultaneously economically efficient and politically acceptable has been a persistent feature of economies all over the world. However, the performance indicators (PIs) used are typically rather restricted in range–financial ratios (such as rate of return on investment or percentage of cost recovered) and utilization rates as a proportion of capacity.

Since the 1960s, however, other pressures have driven the public sector in many countries towards increased use of PIs for a wider range of public services. With the increasing influence of systems analysis, and its emphasis on objective setting (particularly in the form of program budgeting), there was an inference that achievement measures should be should be found for the objectives enshrined within each program. Often this exercise was taken to greater levels of quantification, in target setting, with target levels of performance indicators specified to be achieved within given periods of time. The terminology associated with these concepts is, unfortunately, far from standard—for example, Ansoff (1969) uses the term yardstick instead of performance indicator and goal instead of target, although Ansoff does not insist that each goal have a specified time period for its achievement.

In the same period, long-range planning approaches to public services tended to propose service standards (such as number of fire appliances or elementary school places or swimming pools per head of population) which effectively became targets and were used, particularly by special interest lobbies, to judge the performance of public agencies. In the 1960s, too cost-benefit analysis made much of the theoretical possibility that benefits of a service might be measured by "willingness to pay" and costs by "opportunity costs," both of which would therefore attain the status of aggregate PIs; however, in practice there were rather few examples of such analyses outside of academic studies.

Management accounting in the 1970s suggested the need for performance measures related to the value for money categories of economy, efficiency, and effectiveness. When, in the 1980s, the generalized attack on public services in many countries drove governments to impose and publish PIs in order to show their desire to exercise greater control on public expenditure, they generally used this value for money framework (Pollitt 1993). The recent U.S. adoption of Service Efforts and Accomplishments reporting embodies a similar rationale (Harris 1995). Finally, with the move to quality management in the 1990s, there has been a return to the 1960s concept of the publication of service standards, with clearly publicized PIs, and even, in the case of UK Citizens' Charter, redress for non-achievement of the consequent targets.

It has long been recognized that the use of PIs is fraught with a number of serious problems, including difficulties with measurement, collection, aggregation, and interpretation. Each of these will now be considered in turn.

Measurement problems cluster around four areas in particular:

- *Defining the meaning of "performance" and "success" in public organizations:* each of the different disciplinary starting points discussed above suggests different definitions for performance measures;
- *Modeling the influences on organizational performance and success:* provides a distinction between those PIs which measure performance in terms of the results achieved by the organization and those PIs which measure the existence of the critical success factors or key determinants of future performance;
- *Measuring quality rather than just quantity:* usually involves PIs measuring customer satisfaction levels, achievement of service standards, or conformity to externally validated criteria such as ISO 9000;

- *Measuring the value added of the appropriate organizational entity:* this might be the individual, the team, the unit, the department, or the corporate whole: and it necessitates the separation out of the contributions of each of these entities to the overall outcomes experienced by the customers.

Information collection problems revolve mainly around the trade-off between the use of existing or easy-to-collect data, which may, however, be poor proxies for performance, and the collection of bespoke data for a performance management system. The latter may be expensive, particularly if it involves customer-related information, such as data on user satisfaction levels. Where performance indicators are not regarded by staff as useful in the undertaking of their own work, or not relevant in judging its success, then the reliability of recorded information is especially likely to be problematic, however much is spent on data collection and auditing.

Aggregation problems of performance information present the normal dilemma of choosing between compilation of an index, which requires the determination of weights for the different PIs (inevitably involving a degree of arbitrariness), or, on the other hand, presentation of all the PIs, with the attendant danger of information overload and "paralysis by analysis."

Interpretation problems in relation to PIs include the need to understand the context in which the service operates and in which the performance has been measured, the use of comparisons, and the importance of the "image promotion" role of PIs, including their uses in symbolic ways and for political and ideological purposes.

In Figure I the different stages of the input-output-outcome process for a service are shown; conceptually it is possible to determine PIs at each stage. However, it is essential that any given PI is interpreted within the context of this input-output-outcome model and not just as a snapshot of one part of the process. Thus there are great dangers in simply using PIs for levels of programs/activities (such as numbers of curriculum subjects available to matriculation classes in a secondary school, or the numbers of day centers open for elderly citizens), for levels of intermediate outputs (such as the average grades scored by students in a secondary school matriculation class, or the average number of meals served daily by a day center for the elderly), for the level of satisfaction of objectives (such as the percentage of students in matriculation classes who gain admission to full-time employment or to college, or the number of day center attenders who are thereby enabled to remain in their own homes rather than institutional accommodation), or for the level of change in community welfare (such as the increase in competitiveness of a local economy because of the improved educational qualifications of its young people, or the number of elderly residents who express themselves as satisfied with their ability to cope with their everyday lives). In each of these

FIGURE I. AN INPUT-OUTPUT-OUTCOME MODEL FOR ASSESSING PPERFORMANCE

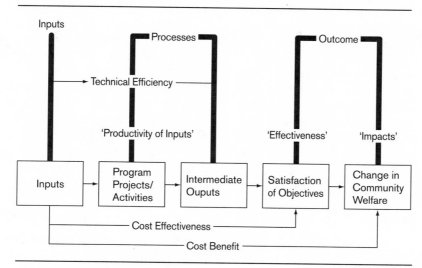

cases, it is generally much more powerful to compute a ratio, comparing these absolute numbers with the level of inputs or the total level of input cost—as demonstrated in Figure I, this would result in PIs which would report productivity per unit of input (or unit costs), cost-effectiveness, or cost-benefit ratios. But more importantly, the value added in the organization at each stage of this value chain needs to be analyzed in order to separate out the differential contribution of different inputs, activities, processes, and outputs.

It is generally agreed that PIs do not mean anything in themselves, but rather only take on meaning when used to compare performances, either over time or between agencies. The argument that analysis of an organization's performance over time is more legitimate than interagency comparisons ignores the difficulties which arise from changes in organizational context over time. In any case, it is a simple fact of life that interagency comparisons do get made by different stakeholders and are often argued to lead to valuable lesson-learning.

How appropriate PIs may be for interagency comparison depends to some degree on their origins. In those organizations where PIs are associated with the sets of objectives agreed to for the organization as a whole and for its subunits, PIs are organization-specific and difficult to compare with other organizations. On the other hand, overall service standards, if they have been established, are usually explicitly designed to expedite interarea and interagency comparisons, although they therefore may not correspond very well to the key objectives of any of the service delivery agencies. Similarly, when PIs are limited to mainly financial measures of economy and efficiency (particularly unit costs and productivity rates of staff), interorganizational comparisons are relatively easy. Finally, organizations which have focused on service quality have often given special prominence to PIs measuring customer response (speed of

answering telephones or initial response to correspondence, number of complaints, etc.) or customer satisfaction levels, as reported in market research, or else they have used as a PI the existence of quality assurance techniques or quality accreditation by some external body. In each of these approaches, comparative analysis is relatively easy.

This highlights the potential of PIs for throwing light upon many dimensions of an organization's performance, some of which are likely to be comparable with other agencies. However, the sensitivity of many stakeholders to the dangers of such comparative analysis may be well-founded, since each one of these dimensions of performance assessment is likely to be very partial in representing the underlying level of success of the organization. Therefore, comparative analysis of performance is more likely to be valid when it focuses upon a portfolio of PIs, rather than a single PI—including both objective quantified PIs and subjective (customer-defined) quality indicators (Bouckaert 1995). Of course, this makes problematic the construction of a single, definitive "league table" of agencies, since it would require a weighting of the different PIs (i.e., the construction of an "index" of performance) and would be unlikely to meet with consensus.

Use and abuse of PIs within an organization is likely to be strongly associated with the perceived purposes of introducing them. There is often a widespread belief within organizations that PIs are being introduced or are being used primarily as a control device. At worst, PI may become perceived as performance criteria imposed from "outside," with no relevance to the performance criteria used internally, interpreted by people ignorant of the subtleties and special factors involved in a particular service or area, and used as an excuse by senior managers to pursue their own agenda at the expense of other stakeholders, or to reduce the standards of service quality. In these circumstances, it is likely that the performance information

1631

reported will be highly misleading, because there is little incentive for staff to report accurately (they do not use the information themselves and feel no professional commitment to the PI system in use) and very strong incentives to ensure that performance reports are unduly favorable. This latter tendency is likely to be exacerbated if it is widely believed that there are some managers in the system who are outrageously abusing the performance reporting system to further the interests of their own budget, staff, or clients. In consequence, performance reporting can be a dysfunctional and highly wasteful activity, if it is conceived essentially as a control mechanism. Indeed, Drucker (1954) insisted from the start on the distinction that performance information should be the tool of the person providing it, not be the means by which that person is judged.

On the other hand, PIs are often justified by those introducing them as serving other purposes—for example, they might serve to indicate more clearly the desired strategic direction of the service, they might enable empowerment of staff lower in the organization hierarchy by allowing more "hands-off" management approaches subject only to satisfactory performance in terms of an agreed set of PIs, or they might encourage organizational learning. Carter, Klein, and Day (1992) label these uses of PIs as, respectively, "dials," "alarm bells," and "tin-openers." Halachmi (1995) has contrasted the use of PIs, in the form of benchmarks and diagnostic information, for control purposes—where they can at best provide an incentive to reduce errors—and for organizational learning purposes—where they can lead staff to search for and reduce potential sources of error, by testing rather than accepting current definitions of needs and constraints, and thereby spawning innovation. This learning process is likely to be more effective if it recognizes, and does not attempt to bury, the varying emphases which different stakeholders put on certain PIs. Organizational learning may also be more dramatic if it can legitimate the setting of PIs and targets in such a way that they "stretch" the organization, opening up a chasm between ambition and resources (Hamel and Prahalad 1994).

Less positively, PIs may be introduced into and used by public agencies for symbolic, political, or ideological purposes (Bovaird 1995). Each of these may be seen as an aspect of the "image promotion" role of PIs. Thus the existence of a performance measurement system may be promoted by an agency as a symbol of increased managerial efficiency, primarily to convince a funding body (such as central government). Again, performance measures may be introduced by government in order to embarrass some of its troublesome satellite agencies or some local authorities controlled by opposition parties, through concentration on PIs expected to show those organizations in a relatively unfavorable light. Finally, a PI system may be devised to support and reproduce an ideological platform, for example the concentration upon PIs related to cost reduction rather than quality of service.

While PIs are often suggested as relatively straightforward instruments, their use clearly needs to be carefully handled. As Pollitt (1993) has suggested, although particular performance indicators may appear to be relatively neutral and essentially technical, to appreciate their full significance one also has to take account of their context and the model of management within which they are deployed. Current approaches to PIs in the public sector may come to be seen as rather primitive, both technically and politically, within a relatively short time period.

TONY BOVAIRD

BIBLIOGRAPHY

Ansoff, H. Igor, 1969. *Business Strategy.* Harmondsworth: Penguin Books.

Bouckaert, Geert, 1995. "Remodelling Quality and Quantity in a Management Context." In Arie Halachmi and Geert Bouckaert, eds., *Public Productivity Through Quality and Strategic Management.* Brussels: International Institute of Administrative Sciences.

Bovaird, Tony, 1995. "Performance Assessment in the UK Public Sector: Pure Symbolism, Limited Learning Systems or the Beginnings of TQM?" In Arie Halachmi and Geert Bouckaert, eds., *Public Productivity through Quality and Strategic Management.* Brussels: International Institute of Administrative Sciences.

Carter, Neil, Rudolf Klein, and Patricia Day, 1992. *How Organizations Measure Success: The Use of Performance Indicators in Government.* London: Routledge.

Drucker, Peter F., 1954. *The Practice of Management.* New York: Harper and Row.

Halachmi, Arie, 1995. "The Pharaoh Syndrome and the Challenge of Public-Sector Productivity." *National Productivity Review* (Winter).

Hamel, Gary and C. K. Prahalad, 1994. *Competing for the Future.* Boston, MA.: Harvard Business School Press.

Harris, Jean, 1995. "Service Efforts and Accomplishments: A Primer of Current Practice and an Agenda for Future Research." *International Journal of Public Administration,* vol. 18, nos. 2-3: 253–276.

Pollitt, Christopher, 1993. *Managerialism and the Public Services.* 2d ed. Oxford: Blackwell.

PERFORMANCE MANAGEMENT.

A process instituted by management, formally or informally, to orient or motivate employees to perform more efficiently and to control employee performance.

Performance management has come in to prominence as a result of the "efficiency movement" (Carr 1994). Motivation and/or control can be manifested in several ways: through developing employee self-control and intrinsic motivation complementary to management objectives; through the authority of management, including rewards and sanctions; or a combination of the two. Historically, performance management has been associated with Frederick Taylor and scientific management. Most performance management systems originated in the private sector, particularly manufacturing and industry, where individual performance, or productivity, is measured in terms of input/output or cost/benefit. Public sector performance management, however, is most often embedded in a climate of service rather than profit, making more difficult the task of measuring individual performance. Performance management for public servants is prevalent in the contemporary environment of public sector reforms, and a performance management system often forms an explicit framework within those reforms.

Background

Over the last two decades there has been a wave of intensive reform in the public sectors of many countries (OECD 1993; Halligan 1994), albeit in diverse cultural and political circumstances. These reforms have been driven by political and economic imperatives for efficiency in terms of personnel and financial performance. As a corollary there has been a shift in social and community expectations about what government, and thus the public sector, should be doing and how they should be doing it. A range of key structural and management strategies are being implemented to bring about the desired changes. Some of these include: cuts to government spending; reducing the size of the work force (downsizing or rightsizing); privatization; competitive tendering and contracting out; user-pays; managing for results; accountability for outcomes; performance management including performance appraisal, and performance-based pay; and training and skills development. These strategies are designed to foster public sector efficiency, effectiveness, accountability, transparency, and value for money—practices and policies previously thought inimical to the public sector and contested in academic and public sector debates. As a result of radical change there is then a need to gauge, evaluate, or measure how well the "new" organization is performing. This has resulted in a performance-focused environment at all levels of the public sector. The difficulty for the public sector is that while public servants may be focusing on efficient performance, there is the constant overlay of political influence which may rapidly change goals, and thus the direction or focus of performance for the organization and the individual.

Performance Management Systems

Performance management systems are used as a way of motivating employees and directing their performance to better achieve organizational goals, objectives, and projected outcomes. Some organizations have systemwide performance management, others are targeted to particular levels or classifications of employees. For example, fixed term contracts with reward/sanction clauses are gaining increasing acceptance as a method of motivating or controlling senior executive performance in the public sector. Contracts may have a renewal clause linked to the achievement of a range of performance objectives reflecting organization goals. Salaried personnel may have to undergo an annual performance review prior to being awarded an increase in pay.

When the approach to enhancing performance goes beyond discrete mechanisms and is structured as an interlinked approach, it is often referred to as a performance management system. Typical features of a performance management system include:

- Organization goals and objectives are defined;
- Agency/department/section goals and objectives are defined which link into the organization goals;
- In some instances, each employee defines personal performance goals which in turn link into those of the department;
- Accountability for decisionmaking is devolved to the site of implementation of the decision;
- People are accountable for their decisions, resultant action, and the effect of that action;
- There is ongoing monitoring of individual, department, and/or organization performance.

It is through this kind of organizational framework that many public sectors have embraced performance management. The ideal is that public sector agencies are endeavoring to provide a good service, more cost-effectively, with fewer employees, by guiding and controlling performance through a range of linked commitment and compliance mechanisms. This may require a major cultural shift for many public sector bureaucracies.

In terms of specific types of approaches to performance management in evidence in the contemporary public sector, by far the most popular are Total Quality Management (TQM) and management by objectives (MBO).

TQM, arguably the most well-known and influential, is "bottom-up" performance management. It is based on the premise that providing a quality product to the customer through individual employees should be the focus of change. TQM focuses on the intrinsic motivation of employees as the key to ongoing quality, yielding big results and continuous improvement: as quality and productivity increase so costs will decline.

MBO, as its name indicates, is objectives-based management involving management and staff. The main features of MBO include the clear statement of organization objectives and a focus on employee performance strengths rather than weaknesses, with supervisors taking a guiding rather than judging role (see Dessler 1980). In MBO all goals must be measurable, and the regular appraisal of individual performance is a key factor.

However, most public sector organizations have a hybrid or mix of approaches, including their own traditional management practices.

Support and Criticisms

How to control or motivate people to continually do a good job, and improve their productivity, has been a problem for managers for centuries. In some respects attempts to solve that problem have not changed either. There are two basic premises from which managers, owners, or employers continue to operate. These are: (1) to try to motivate employees through coercion or discipline—fear of what will happen if effort is not forthcoming; and, (2) to try to foster intrinsic motivation in employees through a reward of some kind. Both of these approaches have problems. What kind of sanction or discipline is appropriate to motivating people to do a good job while at the same time avoiding resentment or disengagement? What kind of reward is appropriate to what kind of performance? Not everyone will be motivated by the same kind of discipline, sanction, or reward (see Schachter 1994; Denhardt 1981). Will either of these strategies be successful over the longer term?

Some argue that performance management in an accountability environment attempts to motivate employees extrinsically through compliance, and that this will actually demotivate employees and foster mediocrity. Sanctions for nonperformance merely foster strict adherence to set objectives. Others maintain that performance goals that are thought unreasonable, or that have been dictated to employees rather than negotiated, will not be "owned" by them. Others maintain that performance management in a collegial or developmental environment fosters commitment, calculated risk taking, problem solving, and intrinsic employee motivation.

Performance management is also a labor union issue. Labor unions are founded on the premise of collective representation. Many performance management systems are founded on the accountability of the individual. Accordingly, labor union views about performance management vary with the type of process in place, the purpose it serves, and its direct and indirect effects on employees (for example, see Somers and Birnbaum 1991; Stronge 1991), and unions often view performance management with skepticism or hostility.

Across the literature, a major criticism of performance management methods is that they are not appropriate for the public or services sector because they have been imported from the private sector, which is market-driven, profit-motivated, and focused on efficiency, the measurement of outputs, and rationalist goals (OECD 1988).

The search for a performance management system that motivates employees over the longer term continues to challenge management. Available research indicates that, whatever the method, the ongoing commitment of management to a collegial, developmental process is fundamental to ongoing success, because it is forward looking and oriented to the future (Halachmi 1992).

JANE COULTER

BIBLIOGRAPHY

Brumback, Gary B., 1988. "Some Ideas, Issues and Predictions About Performance Management." *Public Personnel Management*, 17(4) (Winter) 387–402.

Carr, Adrian, 1994. "The 'Emotional Fallout' of the New Efficiency Movement in Public Administration in Australia: A Case Study." *Administration and Society*, vol. 26, no. 3 (November) 344–358.

Denhardt, Robert, 1981. *In the Shadow of Organization*. Lawrence, KS: The Regents Press.

Dessler, Gary, 1980. *Organization Theory: Integrating Structure and Behavior*. Englewood Cliffs, N. J.: Prentice-Hall Inc.

Halachmi, Arie, 1992. "Performance Targeting and Productivity." *International Review of Administrative Sciences*, vol. 58: 505–518.

Halligan, John, 1994. "Political and Managerial Reform in a Small State: The Relevance of the 1980s." In Ali Farazmand, ed., *Handbook of Bureaucracy*. New York: Marcel Dekker, Inc., pp. 561–576.

Henkel, Mary, 1991. "The New Evaluative State." *Public Administration*, vol. 69 (Spring) 121–136.

Landy, Frank J., 1989. *Psychology of Work Behavior*. California: Brooks/Cole Publishing Company.

Organization for Economic Cooperation and Development (OECD), 1988. *Public Sector Performance Appraisal*. Paris: OECD.

———, 1993. *Public Management Developments: Survey 1993*. Paris: OECD.

Pusey, Michael, 1991. *Economic Rationalism in Canberra: A Nation Building State Changes Its Mind*. Cambridge: Cambridge University Press.

Schachter, Hindy Lauer, 1994. "The Role of Efficiency in Bureaucratic Study." In Ali Farazmand, ed., *Handbook of Bureaucracy*. New York: Marcel Dekker, Inc., pp. 227–240.

Somers, Mark John & Dee Birnbaum, 1991. "Assessing Self-Appraisal of Job Performance as an Evaluation Device: Are the Poor Results a Function of Method or Methodology?" *Human Relations*, 44(10): 1081–1092.

Stronge, James H., 1991. "The Dynamics of Effective Performance Evaluation Systems in Education: Conceptual, Human Relations and Technical Domains." *Journal of Personnel Evaluation in Education*, vol. 5: 77–83.

PERFORMANCE MEASUREMENT. Set of instruments for a regular and systematic collection of performance data within the production process of the politico-administrative system. These data are refined into expressive management data. Performance measurement (PM) can be compared with financial accounting. The emphasis, however, lies on outputs and outcomes rather than inputs of the process.

The history of performance measurement (PM) dates back to experiments in New York City from 1907 to 1912. Using different terms but pursuing a comparable concept, a relatively small group of practitioners and scholars in the

Bureau of Municipal Research led by Director Charles Beard—a historian by education and one of the founders of the discipline of political science—developed and tested a framework of performance-oriented management that was visionary by today's standards (Lynch 1994, p. 11). In 1912, these experiments led to a debate on introducing PM at the federal level in the context of budgeting; however, a long-term implementation failed. In the 1950s, the term was performance budgeting; the measures used then, however, never went beyond relatively simple levels of inputs and—at best—outputs such as tonnages of collected waste or kilometers of constructed roads. In the 1960s, this approach was replaced by the then popular planning, programming, and budgeting system (PPBS). For the first time, the public sector had serious thoughts about effectiveness. Zero-based budgeting (ZBB), a hallmark of the 1970s, was a fascinating concept but was time-consuming and labor-intensive; for these reasons, it was hardly ever implemented in full. Additionally, a lack of unbiased controls caused the expressiveness of the performance measures to vary significantly. Subsequently, PM was removed from the agenda and did not reappear until the fiscal stress of the 1980s and 1990s forced governments to tackle the subject once again.

Current international developments in public management are characterized by a rare unanimity among countries. Tends in public administration, business administration, applied economics, and public law, for example, reveal a stronger emphasis on performance and a weakening of input-oriented analysis and steering. The cornerstone of this development is performance measurement (PM). Nearly all developed countries are facing new challenges as they introduce comprehensive reforms of the public sector. The traditional, centrally controlled and bureaucratic administration of the past is to be replaced by flexible, efficient, and effective "business units" within the administration. Strongly influenced by the ideas of principal agent theory, transaction cost theory, public choice theory, and later trends like Total Quality Management, lean management, and managerialism, a new scientific discipline has evolved in the last few years: the economics of institutions and organizations (Thompson and Jones 1994, pp. 129 ff). Within the management sciences, these approaches find their counterpart in the theories of "New Public Management."

New public management is a comprehensive approach to the reorganization of management in public administration. The overriding principle is a shift of emphasis from inputs to outputs, outcomes, and impacts. Essentially, six basic approaches can be identified:

- *Total Quality/Marketing:* A stronger client orientation is meant to prompt the administration to define its products more deliberately and to bring all its activities into line with these products and their quality.

This quality, in turn, is no longer solely defined by the administration, but also by the clients.

- *Lean Management:* Activities that do not add any value to the end product will no longer be carried out. Contracting out or outsourcing should concentrate the administration's own energies on its genuine strength.

- *Competition:* The creation of external and internal markets is meant to foster a competitive environment for each part of the administration, which should result in an improvement in efficiency and effectiveness virtually automatically. Wherever this is not possible per se, instruments such as benchmarking, competitive testing, or competitive tendering should stimulate competition. The accountability of individual members of staff is to be enhanced by dividing up the parts played by funders, purchasers, and providers, who are then linked within the organization by performance agreements and, for reasons of consistency, lump-sum budgets.

- *Auditing and Evaluation:* The control mechanisms of public administration take their main bearings from inputs. In terms of auditing, the trend is away from purely financial audits towards comprehensive or value-for-money audits. Program evaluation is gaining ground all over the world, and questions affecting limited areas are increasingly subjected to performance evaluations.

- *Organizational Theory:* Today's centralized administration is too vast and unwieldy for efficient and effective production. For this reason, group structures with decentralized autonomous administrative units are formed in order to delegate a higher degree of independence and accountability to the front. However, decentralization always also means a loss of operational control, which reinforces the significance of strategic management.

- *Public Management:* Management instruments are changed in such a way that the yardstick is no longer so much regulation, but the behavior evinced by administrative units and their members of staff. Missions are largely defined in terms of "what," while it is up to the administrative unit as to "how" it will go about supplying the agreed products or reach its objectives.

These six trends have one thing in common: they cannot be translated into practice unless and until an administration is aware of what it produces, in what quantities, of what quality, and what effects this has. Often on the basis of a lack of information-technological facilities, it was not possible before the last few years to establish systematic mechanisms that would have resulted in a substantial improvement in management data. In the late 1970s and early 1980s, it was particularly the U.S. Financial Accounting Standards Board which, with its Service Efforts and Accomplishments Program, laid the foundation for a perfor-

FIGURE I. THE NEW PUBLIC MANAGEMENT FRAMEWORK

mance measurement system. Since the mid-1980s, efforts have been made in various countries—especially at the level of local authorities and states—to set up, on a broad basis, the same systems for performance data which are a matter of course for financial data. In the future, this "performance measurement" will gain considerably in significance.

People tend to want to develop systems and notions that supply equally objective information or have an equally objective significance in each and every case. However, this is only possible on very rare occasions. Just as financial data do not convey any objective truth, the definition of "performance" depends on the observers and their interests. For a social worker, good performance is tantamount to offering as many care hours as possible, while the finance manager would want to keep expenditure on the same product as low as possible, thus aiming to reduce the number of hours on offer. There is no one single truth regarding performance. As a rule, the various stakeholders in administration are not in agreement as to what is good or bad performance. Nonetheless, performance can be measured by means of indicators and/or parameters.

Each and every administrative program undergoes a certain process, which is not always linear and is often muddled but, in principle, invariably runs true to the same pattern. On the strength of requirements displayed by the administration's clients, political objectives are formulated that have to be attained within a certain period of time. This means that the administration must supply certain products, which in turn require certain resources. This is what the ideal planning process would look like, which ultimately results in a definite budget: the resource plan.

During and after actual production, performance is registered and compared with the plan. Even today, we

have a well-developed ability to uncover deviations in the use of resources, and to justify them. Yet the very next step already presents difficulties: we often do not know exactly what we produce because the products have not been defined. And even if they have been, they are frequently not registered in any systematic way. It is therefore vital to apprehend performance in its five dimensions: quality, quantity, timeliness, cost and location, as shown by the example below for education and police service.

Wherever objectives have been set (e.g. the reduction of a city's crime rate by a certain percentage) they are measured quite frequently even today. Regrettably, however,

TABLE I. EXAMPLES OF OUTPUT AND OUTCOME MEASURES

Measures of Service and Products Output	Measures of Outcome and Impact
Elementary and Secondary Education	
Student-days	Test score results
Students graduated	Percentage of graduates employed
Dropout rate	Positions graduates hold after five years
Amount of lessons taught	Graduates' satisfaction with their education
Police	
Hours of patrol	Rates at which cases are cleared
Crimes investigated	Response time
Number of arrests	Residents feeling safe
Number of speed controls	Reduction of crime rate
Number of alarms responded to	Residents' satisfaction with police work

FIGURE II. THE PRODUCTION PROCESS IN THE POLITICO-ADMINISTRATIVE SYSTEM

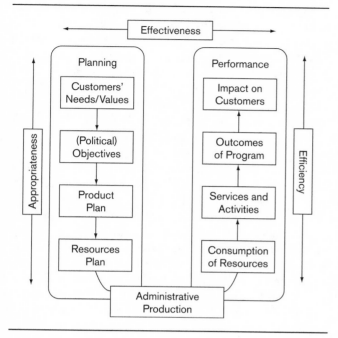

fectiveness, while efficiency is the ratio between outputs and inputs of any process. Some examples of the two types of ratio measures are shown below.

The difference between performance measures and performance indicators lies in the form and value of information given. In general, performance measures are seen as direct and quantitative information which does not create any need for further interpretation. The prerequisite for their use is, of course, the existence of directly measurable objectives such as rates of change, levels of satisfaction, and amount of products delivered. More complex targets may, however, not be easily measurable. It may therefore be necessary to define indicators that give the managers of an administrative entity or the politicians a hint as to what questions need to be asked and what further investigations have to be undertaken. Indicators are never self-explanatory, as they only show part of reality.

Performance measurement is distinguished from program evaluation by its repetitive nature. Program evaluation is almost exclusively used to settle concrete questions regarding a definite project (e.g., the potential effects of a new act). Thus it is basically a one-time procedure although it can, of course, be repeated. In contrast, performance measurement, like financial accounting, is conducted according to the same pattern year after year. This makes it part of the management accounting system, which constantly generates management data. In this way, performance measurement smoothly fits in with a whole number of other instruments of management control in nonprofit organizations.

The instruments of performance measurement include not only measures and indicators, but also methods used to compare performance, such as the analytical part of benchmarking. The main purpose of the analytical part of performance measurement is to ask questions rather than provide answers. In making comparisons, performance

there is often a lack of setting of objectives, which means that their attainment cannot be measured and thus cannot be controlled. Yet the outcome of a program is one of the most important success factors of administration and must be consistently recorded even though it may not always be easy. Here, PM is accorded a great deal of significance. Last but not least, every project raises the question as to whether efforts have really targeted and satisfied client requirements: the impact on clients should largely be identical with their needs. If this is not the case, then the production process can be examined to discover where the mistake was made, and whether it was the result of a lack in performance or of an incorrect planning decision, such as lack of appropriateness.

Pure performance values cannot be ascribed any expressiveness unless they can be related to a reference value. It may be interesting to know that a meals-on-wheels kitchen supplies 20,000 meals a year, but we can only judge its performance if we know, say, what the full costs per meal were, and what a comparable service or product would cost somewhere else. For example, there are such meals-on-wheels kitchens in Switzerland whose full costs exceed the price of a three-course meal in a good restaurant! It is therefore, as a general rule, important to view individual values in certain relations, and to make both historical and interorganizational comparisons.

The two main areas of comparison are effectiveness and efficiency. The ratio between estimates and results—that is, the link between individual levels in the planning and performance processes—is what we may describe as ef-

TABLE II. EXAMPLES OF EFFICIENCY AND EFFECTIVENESS MEASURES/INDICATORS

Effectiveness Measures/Indicators	Efficiency Measures/Indicators
Achievement of quality standards	Cost per service or product
Actual service time compared with a certain standard time	Productivity of employees (amount of products delivered per employee)
Goods/services actually delivered in relation to a planned (contracted) amount and/or range of products and services	Cost of a certain outcome (for example, the reduction of crime rate by 2 percent over three years)
Actual residents' satisfaction with a certain service in relation to a targeted level of satisfaction	Use of resources to produce a certain range of services and products

measures and indicators should act only as catalysts for inquiry and analysis. For this reason, they require a comparative basis, which could either be historical or interorganizational (competitors, other administrative units doing similar things). Of course, a like-with-like comparison is essential and, in the absence of a common base, a performance measure is not only invalid, but worse still, it may be dangerous. If, for instance, a difference has been found in per capita costs, the manager needs to look beneath the performance measure and ask a series of questions, such as:

- Are we comparing like products and services?
- Why are we more expensive?
- How can we pinpoint the differences in per capita costs between the two authorities?

To enable a controller to make comparisons, the prerequisite of performance measurement is a system of full accrual accounting and the existence of generally accepted accounting principles and standards. This does not mean that we have to define values for assets such as monuments or arts, as there is hardly any information available for management that would help run the entity better. It includes, however, valuation of all kinds of assets that the administration actually uses to perform and to produce for its customers. Not only will making this information available create a new sense of managerial handling of assets, but it also will generate real data for real or artificial competition with other administrative units or the private sector.

If an administration decides to implant fully competitive instruments such as competitive testing, competitive tendering, or contracting out, there will be a strong need to take a further step in accounting towards full cost applications, standard costing, and cost-coverage accounting. We can see all over the world that an early introduction of market instruments without an installation of decent performance measurement and costing systems leads to immense problems for the newly formed "competitors" within the administration and thus creates a lot of unnecessary frustration (Buschor and Schedler 1994).

Performance measures must conform to certain rules. Criteria for good performance measures are:

- *Appropriateness:* Measures are well-matched and defined according to a comprehensive and systematic program design avoiding superfluous information (central significance).
- *Adequacy:* Measures permit a satisfactory answer to all the dimensions vital to the administration's activities and programs.
- *Usefulness:* Measures correspond to the needs of the program and the political and managerial needs.
- *Feasibility:* Measures are available at reasonable cost.
- *Timeliness:* Measures are available within the required time frame.
- *Simplicity:* Use of the lowest possible number of measures that are as apt as possible.

Performance measures must be developed and tested over a period of several years. For reasons of comparability, however, it may be expedient to accept a degree of perfection of 80 percent with a constant error rate instead of making annual adjustments that would help to achieve a higher degree of perfection, but prevent the important historical evaluation from being used.

Performance measurement enables administrations to align their planning, budgeting, steering, and controlling activities according to output. Ultimately, this should create a situation in which political decisionmaking bodies will no longer debate itemized budgets but planned and actual performance. This is the crucial change in political culture and in the quality of legislative and government debate. Needless to say, this means that politicians have to learn to focus on outputs and to refrain from meddling in the question of "how." The examples in New Zealand, the Netherlands and—particularly at local levels—in other countries show that this is possible even though it would appear to take longer to get there than one might wish.

It must be emphasised that PM is likely to succeed only if its implementation is accompanied by a fundamental change in the politico-administrative system and its organizational culture. PM is not simply another hat to put on but a highly developed system requiring far-reaching adaptation on the part of its users. Moreover, PM must be adapted to individual information users' requirements, and possibly treated confidentially. This means that pure management information of an internal nature can and must be a great deal more detailed and straightforward than proof of performance provided to external users and observers.

Only when decentralized structures are in place, the administrative culture as a whole has become performance oriented, and decisionmaking bodies are taking their bearings from outputs and outcomes, and performance measurement is capable of supplying policy makers with high-quality data about products—only then can the introduction of performance budgeting be seriously considered. All these prerequisites are necessary to align the highly sensitive instruments of budgeting with performance. Thus, performance measurement may be the first step towards performance budgeting, should that path ever be chosen.

KUNO SCHEDLER
Some parts have been translated from German by
Tony Häflinger & Vivien Blandford

BIBLIOGRAPHY

Anthony, Robert N. and David W. Young, 1988. *Management Control in Nonprofit Organizations.* 4th ed. Homewood, IL: Irwin.

Brace, Paul K., Robert Elkin, Daniel D. Robinson, and Harold I. Steinberg, 1980. *Reporting of Service Efforts and Accomplishments.* New York: Financial Accounting Standards Board.

Buschor, Ernst and Kuno Schedler, eds., 1994. *Perspectives on Performance Measurement and Public Sector Accounting*. Berne, Stuttgart, Vienna: Paul Haupt.

Congressional Budget Office (CBO), July 1993. *Using Performance Measures in the Federal Budget Process*. Washington, D.C.: CBO.

Lynch, Thomas D., 1994. *Public Budgeting in America*. Englewood Cliffs, NJ: Prentice Hall.

Thompson, Fred and L. R. Jones, 1994. *Reinventing the Pentagon: How the New Public Management Can Bring Institutional Renewal*. San Francisco, London: Jossey-Bass.

PERMANENT SECRETARY.

An official responsible to a minister for a central government department whose position is based on a civil service career and permanency.

The term is most closely associated with traditional British usage, but the underlying conception is much more widespread. The concept was transplanted or diffused to British colonies during the nineteenth century, and in countries such as Australia, Canada, India, and New Zealand there emerged a similar office. It may have gone under another name: deputy minister in Canada, permanent head in Australia and New Zealand, and secretary in India, or more generally (and loosely) the department head or secretary, but the underlying principles were similar.

The consideration here will recognize the distinctive contribution of British practice while regarding the term more generically as permanent head in order to encompass the broader applications.

The origins of the two elements of the term require comment. The word secretary has a long history of usage in Britain. It was originally applied to the king's officers who had a seat in one of the houses of Parliament. The burden of parliamentary sittings in conjunction with administrative work eventually led to the separation of the roles. The idea of permanency also predates the nineteenth century but only emerged as a concept with general application after 1830. At the same time the idea of continuity of office holding was enshrined. The term permanent secretary became widely used in Britain during the nineteenth century (even though predecessors existed for some departments in the previous century). For example, a secretary appointed as a permanent official to the Treasury Board in 1805 became a permanent secretary in 1867.

The essence of the permanent secretary concept as it has come to be used internationally is that there should be a single figure of authority at the head of a ministerial department who represents that organization in its relations with the minister and serves as the chief adviser. There have been three basic functions identified with the permanent secretary. The first is the provision of policy advice to ministers. A second function is the implementation of government decisions. The third is responsibility for departmental management. A particular extra function in the British context has been that of financial accountancy; the secretary has had duties as accounting officer of the department involving responsibility for expenditure.

Other features of the permanent secretary can be delineated. Of prime importance is the distinctive relationship with the minister under Westminster-style systems: there is an explicit differentiation between the political and bureaucratic spheres—the secretary is a career public servant; the minister is a member of Parliament—and the two realms are in principle distinct.

The second feature and a source of the secretary's influence is simply the tenure in office, which also provides for continuity and stability in government administration. (This permanency of course may have been more apparent than real in some cases.) The integrity of the office is meant to be ensured by special appointment processes. These have varied considerably among countries, particularly with regard to the directness of the role of the political executive. In Canada, for example, the deputy minister is described as existing "at pleasure."

The permanent secretary is one of several models of departmental management that have existed: there may be a collegial arrangement or a unitary apex; the civil servants may be career professionals or political appointees. The United States relies on senior appointments made by the president which are deemed to be political appointments (although appointees could be professional civil servants). The contrast with France has been even more striking where a permanent secretary has not been interposed between the minister and senior civil servants. A collegial group consisting of the directors of divisions has reported directly to the minister, who has been assisted by a private secretariat, the ministerial cabinet.

The office of permanent secretary has evolved over time as have the characteristics of the occupants (Theakston and Fry 1989). The continuities have been particularly strong in Britain, where their education has continued to be Oxbridge and their gender male.

There have also been major distinctions in the practice as it has evolved in the several branches of the Westminster tradition. The propensity to make lateral appointments has been rare, but this has varied with the time and the country. The distinction between administrative and political careers has not always been so clear as in Britain (although socialization in the latter has reduced the differentiation), with Canada recording a number of civil servants who have transferred to Parliament and high political office.

The heyday of the permanent secretaries occurred earlier this century, although the period for which the permanent secretaries held sway was limited to a few decades in some countries. In the decades succeeding World War II, they were a formidable force during the growth of the administrative state, and this produced the idea of the mandarins who were both revered and derided (e.g., through the Yes Minister television program).

The role of secretaries changed over time as government functions expanded and ministers could no longer maintain direct control over departments; secretaries were more likely to play more independently active roles in policy as well as administering legislation. Public sector reforms of the last 25 years have had profound effects on the permanent secretary, although the impact was registered later in some countries than others. These have struck at the heart of the permanent secretary concept.

Permanency has been abolished in several countries, and the title has consequently changed to departmental secretary or even chief executive officer. Secretaries are now generally on contracts in a number of countries (for example, Australia and New Zealand), and contractualism is growing generally. Their terms may be for five years.

Roles have also changed, becoming more demanding with complexity and changing environments. The management role has become more significant in the last decade or so as managerialism assumed centrality. In some cases the role may have become more focused where policy ministries have been favored. But with the reduced reliance on the department more generally for policy advice, secretaries and their departments have lost policy monopoly. They may have also lost the exclusive status of adviser to the minister. Their relationship to the minister may have been reinforced through the latter's reassertion of authority, while the growth of ministerial advisers in Australia and Canada has added a major new dimension generally to the policy role of departments and their modus operandi.

Secretaries have assumed broader managerial roles where delivery responsibilities have not been separated out organizationally. The relationship to central agencies may have changed with greater delegated authority given to departmental heads.

The world of the permanent secretary has therefore contracted in many respects, and the prospects are not good for retention of the traditional concept. Their descendants are neither permanent nor secretaries in the sense of their predecessors.

JOHN HALLIGAN

BIBLIOGRAPHY

Boston, Jonathan, 1992. "Assessing the Performance of Departmental Chief Executives: Perspectives from New Zealand." *Public Administration*, London, vol. 70 (Autumn) 405–428.

Osbaldeston, Gordon, F., 1989. *Keeping Deputy Ministers Accountable.* Toronto: McGraw-Hill Ryerson.

Spann, R. N., 1976. "Permanent Heads." In Royal Commission on Australian Government Administration, *Appendixes to Report Volume One.* Canberra: Australian Government Publishing Service, pp. 222–275.

Theakston, Kevin and Geoffrey K. Fry, 1989. "Britain's Administrative Elite: Permanent Secretaries 1900–1986." *Public Administration*, London, vol. 67(2) (Summer) 129–147.

PERSIAN/IRANIAN ADMINISTRATIVE TRADITION. The administrative practices and organizational culture of ancient Persia and modern Iran. Iran or Persia has well over 8,000 years of traditions in bureaucracy and public administration on a massive scale. As a bridge land between the eastern and western civilizations of the ancient world, Iran has been one of the oldest centers of world civilization and a pioneer in the development of state, bureaucracy, and public administration in the world, both conceptually and practically. Iranians have in the past gained a global reputation of being excellent administrators, and they were the first people in the world to adopt the concept of "state" and turn that concept into a reality in the ancient time. They were also the first people in the world who by conquest established the first universal "world-state empire" with a realm covering virtually every known corner of the ancient world. However, unlike most other empires, the Achaemenid Persian Empire was based on liberal and just principles of governance and administration.

Iranians have also contributed significantly to the theory and practice of public administration, bureaucracy, and management, and invented a number of managerial and organizational techniques adopted by subsequent empires and civilizations. For millennia political systems and leaders changed in the whole Near/Middle East, but the notoriously efficient and effective bureaucracy of Persia/Iran survived and emerged as a formidable institution of administration and governance. Today, the legacies of the old Iranian administrative system are found in many parts of the modern world, including Western public administration, but more prevalently in the whole region.

This short essay addresses a brief overview of the Iranian public administration and bureaucracy in an historical perspective. This is done in four distinctive periods: (1) the prehistory Susa and the federal Elamite state (6000–650 B.C.E.); (2) the ancient Medean state and the world-state Persian Achaemenid Empire, and the Parthian and Sasanid Empires (720 B.C.E.–651 C.E.); (3) the Medieval and the Islamic periods from 651 to 1926; and (4) the modern Pahlavi and the Islamic Republic periods (1926–present).

Administration of Susa and the Federal Elam (6000–650 B.C.E.)

The earliest experience of state, bureaucracy, and public administration on a massive scale began in Susa (in the present southwest Iran) around 6000 B.C.E. Susa began political life first as a city-state contemporary and rival to Sumer, then as the capital of one of the oldest empires of antiquity, the federated Elamite empire, for 2,500 years. Susa was also a major cosmopolitan and political city in ancient Persia under both the Medes and Achaemenids. Unlike the city-state Sumer, the Elamite empire was formed and administered on a massive scale—it stretched from major parts of Asia in the east to parts of Mesopotamia. Its conquest and occupation of Babylonia and Assyria for 500 years was unattainable by any previous powers. The Elamite Empire was based on a federal system of governance and administration in which five major kingdoms or states were parts, and the Elamite overlordship was well-respected. Combining the strategic advantages of both the highland and lowland civilizations, the Elamites excelled in various developments such as art, architecture, administration, management, agriculture, religion, professions, bureaucracy and administration, and most remarkably the written Elamite language, which became the official language of the bureaucracy for the next millennium in Iran and Mesopotamia.

One of their major administrative achievements was the invention of a gigantic underground canal system, *Qanat*, thousands of miles long and extremely efficient in bringing water from highland areas where rainfall was high to the lowland desert areas. In government and administration, they were perhaps the first in history to adopt and develop a federal political system with well-coordinated intergovernmental relations. Their advanced legal system included the Elamite penal law, civil law, and administrative law, and their use of witnesses and "ordeal trial" was common. Public administration flourished under the Elamites, who made significant contributions to both Iranian and world civilizations. The federal structure of Elam was based on three layers of administrative system: "governors," *Halmenik,* who were under the control of "Viceroy," *Sakanakun,* who was subject to the king of Elam, *Zunkir.* Elamites promoted religion, and the female "Great Goddess" was equal to the male god. Certain kings also adopted the titles "Messenger of God," "Regent," and ruler on earth. Elamite was a great empire, but ancient political history was being drastically reshaped by the emerging Aryans.

Administration under the Medean and Persian Empires: The Achaemenids, Parthians, and Sasanids (650 B.C.E.–651 C.E.)

The Medean Administration (650 B.C.E.–559 B.C.E.)

Around 1000 B.C.E. a group of people of Indo-European origin moved in their second wave of migration to the Iranian plateau and settled there, replacing the natives over a long time (their first migration took place around 2000 B.C.E. but they were assimilated by the native Iranians). These people were divided into two major powers, the Medes and the Persians. The Medes emerged first as a formidable power in war and governance, finding a special place in the Bible. Their rise around 650 B.C.E. ushered a

new political and administrative era in the ancient world. The Medes lived in highland areas, advanced swiftly eastward and westward, and conquered the repressive Assyrian empire in 612 B.C.E., then the federal Elam in 600 B.C.E. and almost all Asia. They were preparing to annex Babylonia, but were subsumed by their Persian cousins under the brilliant military and charismatic leadership of Cyrus the Great, who established the first universal "world-state" empire in the political history.

Thus the first half of the first millennium B.C.E. was a turning point in human history, for the center of the world politics of the age shifted from the watered valleys of the Nile and Mesopotamia to the less climatically favored region of the north and Iran. Obviously, Iranians emerged the most victorious of all.

The Medes also adopted a federal system, used Ecbatana—the place of assembly (present Hamadan in central Iran)—as their capital, had a constitutional assembly of the elite and warriors, and established the most formidable empire known until then. The Aryan Medes developed several cultural characteristics that helped shape the Iranian culture for the next millennia: rise in early dawn, exercise vigorously, play sports, tell truth, avoid lies, and respect divine rule. But the most important Medean achievements were in the areas of state building, bureaucracy, and public administration. They mastered statecraft and established a well-developed centralized state administration second to none in terms of effectiveness and efficiency. They, however, combined religious and secular administration, with the magis playing a powerful role in administration and politics.

Elamite language continued to be used as the official language. The Medes developed a trained, professional bureaucracy with high expertise and prestige, and mastered an administrative system—not the kind that Assyrians practiced uprooting the subject peoples, but a system with high efficiency and effectiveness that maintained respect for local peoples. The bureaucrats also formed a closed association of guild system in which merit-based criteria were used for membership. In short, the Medean administrative system was well-developed as a bureaucratic system.

The Achaemenid Persian Administration (559–330 B.C.E.)

The rise of the Persians in south Iran in the mid-sixth century B.C.E. was a turning point in human history. They had a republican governance system based on the principles of collective decisionmaking, with a king elected by the noble elite. The fall of the Medes to the conquering Cyrus II was also the rise of the mightiest empire in the ancient world. At the age of 40 Cyrus began conquering almost the entire known world, and he was on a new campaign at the age of 71 when he died. Thus Cyrus the Great led the young and vigorous Persians along with their cousin Medes in their turn on the conquest of the world and established the first universal empire based on liberal democratic principles of tolerant governance and administration, freedom of all religions, culture, race, traditions, and professional association.

The Achaemenid World-State Empire founded by Cyrus the Great was the largest and mightiest empire the ancient world had ever known. Their administrative system was the most elaborate and most effective in historical administrative system. Persians took high pride in such a development. At the center of this administration was the Persian bureaucracy, which established itself wherever the army went. The Achaemenids' administrative system left numerous legacies that lasted not only in Iran up to the Present day, but also in the entire region of the modern Near/Middle East, north Africa, and Asia. The empire Cyrus the Great established enjoyed for 200 years a high degree of stability, peace, economic prosperity, trade, commerce, and intellectual development, harboring many foreign-born philosophers such as the Greeks, and promoted all kinds of religions, cultures, languages, and customs among the subject peoples in the far extended corners of the realm.

The multinational and multicultural administrative system under the Achaemenids was unique and innovative in several ways, resembling none of the previous systems nor future empires, including Romans who adopted many of its principles. It was based on three levels of organizational and administrative structure.

First was the central administration in which the Great King held the supreme and sovereign power, then came the royal court with its major bureaucracy, followed by the cabinet or council of ministers or heads of the bureaucracies. This formed the central administration. Second was the satrapy system of governance and administration. The satrapy was a large territory, often including many kingdoms and vassal kingship areas or even empires of the past, and the satrap was actually a mini-king with his own court bureaucracy resembling the central administration. The satrap was chosen by the Great King and replaced by him alone. He was the governor of a vast territory, and responsible for civil and military administration. He was recruited from the Persian nobility, who provided the strategic leadership and administrative elite. Third came the subsatrapy, or provincial governors charged with civil and military administration. This was a more or less decentralized system in which local traditions or customs were allowed to continue in governance and administration, but as far as bureaucracy and administration were concerned centralization prevailed, for the Persian bureaucracy was to remain efficient, effective, and centrally coordinated. It was efficient and effective in tax collection, economic regulation, administration of justice, communications, law and order, and financial management, as well as information gathering for the central administration. Further local administrative organization was allowed under the subsatrapy, al-

lowing ethnic, racial cultural, tribal, and other flexibilities. Therefore, the three-layer administrative system combined the two principles of centralization and decentralization, providing the advantages of both systems. The bureaucracy was large, with a personnel size of an estimated 12–15 million, including full-time, part-time, direct, and indirect. All were paid by the state treasury, which was the most organizationally designed elaborate system of bureaucracy.

The bureaucracy was highly professionalized through training, apprenticeship, colleges and centers of higher education for civil and military careers, and on-the-job experience. The Achaemenid bureaucracy and administration revealed many features found in modern administrative systems. Cyrus the Great founded an administrative system based on merit, which formed the major criterion for organizational and administrative appointment, though political appointment based on patronage was also common, especially in the satrapies. Cyrus's philosophy and commitment to the merit system was based on his liberal democratic principles that a good administration was a meritorious one, and meritorious performance must be rewarded and promoted.

Cyrus was conscious of the settled civilizations of the Mesopotamia and adopted a principle of administration and governance that was democratic, tolerant, and respectful among the subject peoples around the vast realm. He envisioned a "universal state" or empire in which all races, religions, cultures, ethnicities, languages, and so forth would mix and live together peacefully and with prosperity, freely, and justly. Persians never practiced mass slavery, and in many cases the situations and lives of semi-slaves were in fact better than the common citizens of Persia. Indeed, there were many semi-slaves who rose to high position of distinction and gained high esteem in society. Examples include the Jewish eunuchs such as Nehemia, and the priest Ezra, who were granted financial support and military escort to go back to Palestine and rebuild temples in Jerusalem. Cyrus freed the Jews from captivity in Babylon and sent them back to Palestine with money and other possessions.

A hallmark of Cyrus's legacies was his democratic policy of tolerant government and administration, in which all subject peoples would live and prosper regardless of religion, race, culture, language, or political views, as long as they did not challenge the sovereign authority of the king and the Persian state. This respect for subject peoples in satrapal provinces was a major departure from the past practices in government and administration. Cyrus himself was also considered by philosophers and historians as an ideal ruler, an ideal leader, whose policy and personal characteristics set a democratic system of administration that evolved from a republic to an empire, but an empire with a benevolent leadership committed to and in service of the "common good" (see Xenophon's *Education of Cyrus* and the contemporary debates in political science on Cyrus as the "Ideal Ruler for Common Good," especially Nadon 1996).

Was the satrapy system fragile and loosely structured? No. The check and balance system making the satrapy work efficiently and effectively was extremely elaborate, except toward the end of the empire when the system became abused and decayed. Several mechanisms checked the system. First was the independent military commander in the satrapy, who was appointed by the king and functioned autonomously from the satrap. Second was a permanent inspectorate general in the satrapy reporting to the king and central administration. Third was the king's "ears and eyes", high officials with tremendous powers to exercise in their unannounced visits to satrapies. Fourth were the special inspectors of the central administration investigating and auditing the satrapal administrative practices and performances on spot; fifth was the royal judges who, according to Herodotus and other historians, did not discriminate in serving justice, regardless of the social and economic status of the defendants or victims. The law of the Persians was enforced equally and fairly. No one would escape the Persian justice system of administration.

There were other bureaucratic and administrative checks and control systems that helped the central administration with coordination and control. Flexibility was tolerated and encouraged, however.

If Cyrus the Great was a brilliant and charismatic leader and a statesman, his second successor, Darius the Great, was the great administrator in antiquity. Darius expanded the empire even further, but his major legacies were his administrative reforms, which have had long-lasting effects on the administrative systems of Iran and the region even today. Darius was highly interested in micromanagement and believed that no empire state could prosper without a sound economic system. And a sound economy required stable taxation, a dependable government policy with credibility in the market system, a fair justice administration system, and an efficient and effective communication system. He recognized that the vast empire needed to be reorganized, and that he did. He then reformed the whole administrative system. A universal Law of Darius was prepared for the entire realm with judges dispatched all over the empire; a huge network of major highways and road systems was developed, including the Royal Road from Susa to Sardis in Europe with almost 7,000 miles; and an extremely efficient pony express postal system was created and operated. As Herodotus notes, the Persian postal carriers never stopped: "at snow or heat, night or day, rain or sun, flood or drought, nothing stops the Persian communication system." Horse riders delivered messages to the next post in the swiftest way possible, and were rewarded well. Darius also recognized the need for a sound and efficient financial management of the economy. A variable and fixed property tax system was developed; income taxes were levied on individuals and corporations, farmers, and peasants, artisans, professionals, and so forth. Darius gained the reputation of a shopkeeper, while Cyrus was the father and ideal leader.

The administrative reforms of Darius also affected local governments. His innovative approaches to management included strategic management, contracting out practices—examples included the two Jewish and Persian financial institutions in the Babylonian satrapy—to collect fixed property taxes for the state. Under Darius the role of the cabinet and the meritorious, professional bureaucracy in administration was further developed. Unlike the Assyrians before and the Romans later, Persians never practiced a policy of uprooting subject peoples. The equality and fairness that were built into this system of administration also caused some conflicts among some members of the noble elites, who saw too much attention being paid to subject peoples. Darius's administrative system was anti-corruption and anti-waste-based, but expediency was also emphasized in the system as a strategic management principle. The bureaucracy and administration were highly professionalized under the Achaemenid Empire.

Elamite and Aramaic languages played key roles in the bureaucracy, while Old Persian was the court language for political and ceremonial purposes. Susa remained a major cosmopolitan capital city, Ecbatana a major financial treasury center, Babylon a major trade and commercial center, and other cities held similar stature, but the ceremonial and political center of the empire was Persepolis—not under Cyrus but later. Persepolis was the most elaborate cosmopolitan city and a wonder in the ancient world, the richest and most attractive city ever built in the antiquity. Its annual ceremonial New Year festivity, *Now Rooz*, began with all nations and satrapies and peoples from afar bringing tributes and gifts to the king; it brought millions together. The Achaemenid Empire was ended by Alexander who also burned Persepolis, looted its treasury and, after translating its 2,000 books, burned the library as well. Following the victory, Alexander was advised to marry a Persian if he wanted to survive in Persia; that he did. The next hundred years was a dark history for the Persians, for the Macedonians never could adapt to the high level of culture and administrative state traditions that Persians had developed and enjoyed.

The Persians believed in equality and tolerant governance and administration, a cultural belief system based on truth, exercise at dawn, avoidance of sin and of lying and debt, avoidance of polluting water and fire as symbols of cleanliness, and a duality of good and bad in religion, nature, and morality. Good thought, good talk, and good deed or behavior were the principles the Persians left as a major cultural and ethical/moral legacy for their generations to come. These moral, ethical, and cultural values shaped Iranian administrative culture as well as their popular culture.

The Parthian Administration (240 B.C.E.–227 C.E.)

The fall of the Achaemenid world-state empire and the passing dark age of the Macedonian Seleucids were followed by a renewed Iranian greatness under the Parthian Empire (240 B.C.E.–227 C.E.), which lasted long and developed a decentralized administrative system. Its political and military decentralization offered the empire great flexibility in warfare and building strength and creativity, but its lack of centralized coordination caused the empire many constraints. Parthia was a peaceful and defensive empire, but it was a formidable superpower and the first to encounter the rising Romans; these two superpowers divided the ancient world into east and west, and both suffered defeats from each other. Eventually, they cooperated together on some grounds. Yet many peoples and nations including the Jews again looked to Parthian Persia as a protector from the Roman repression. The Parthian administration was generally popular, as opposed to the Romans "who mistreated their subject peoples" (Debevoise 1938, pp. 116–117).

The Sasanid Administration (228–651 C.E.)

The Parthian Empire was followed by the more formidable and highly centralized Sasanid Empire. It was destined to make major changes in the ancient world by dividing the world with the Romans. The Sasanid state was based on a highly centralized, professional administrative system with organizational and bureaucratic rigidities not found under the Achaemenid system. Yet, Sasanids made advanced contributions to organization and administrative theory as well as to governance theory in many profound ways. They mastered statehood and the Iranian traditions of state, culture, and organizational structure reached their height.

Iranian administrators excelled during this period, inventing many managerial techniques including the personal checking account system. In government and administration, several books and treatises were written by professional bureaucrats, experts, and theorists on how to improve administration and political rule. Colleges and universities, including medical colleges and administrative training centers, were established to train prospective doctors and bureaucrats. Merit examinations were a major component of the personnel system, and the large bureaucracy during the 428 years of the empire enjoyed an elevated class position in the stratified society. Centralization also meant a declining power of the landed aristocracy and noble elite, but the bureaucracy toward the end showed signs of bureaucratism and excess in society. Combined with overtaxation, the bureaucracy stretched its limit, and the political system was weakened from within, making it vulnerable to the external Bedouin Islamic Arabs.

The administrative system was reorganized; an elaborate cabinet system was created; a professional bureaucracy was further empowered and expanded in scope and domain of operation and became the most powerful institution of government after the army. Iran became bureaucratized under the Sasanids, whose kings sought to curb the power of the landed aristocracy. During this period, Persian's intellectual contributions to public administration and government reached their high point, gaining Persia/Iran a high reputation for rich culture, state traditions, and administrative advancements/achievements. The office of the prime minister became much more elaborate, and he had to enjoy high respect and recognition from the professional bureaucrats themselves.

Administration Under the Medieval and Islamic Periods: 651–1926

The Sasanid Empire fell to the invading Bedouins in their Islamic conquest. But it took Iran 300 years to accept Islam and when they did, they created Shi'ism as a rival sect of religion to the official Sunni sect of Islam. Iranians chose to support the family of the Prophet Mohammed and his son-in-law, Ali, as the legitimate successor. They provided sanctuaries to the family of the Prophet; they demonstrated another way of Iranian innovation and independent mindset. While the political leadership changed, the bureaucracy remained as the most important institution of governance and administration. Since the Bedouin Arabs had little experience in state and governance administration, they adopted totally the advance Sasanid traditions of state, bureaucracy, and administration.

So, the Iranian bureaucracy survived for generations, and indeed Persianized the Arab/Islamic administration. Arabic language made major changes in Persian language and literary works, but Persians continued to write and practice new ideas, philosophies, and principles of government and administration. The list of Persians' contributions to Islamic civilization and its achievements in science, art, government, and administration is a long one. It includes Razi, who discovered alcohol; Avicenna (Ibn Sina), the scientist and philosopher with many inventions and discoveries in chemistry, dialectic, and theory of knowledge; Farabi the Second Teacher after Aristotle and the First Islamic Teacher with his *The Perfect City;* Khayyam, who invented the Arabic numerals one through ten and algebra and mathematical equations; Ghazzali and his *Theory of Government* and *Counsel of Kings;* Mavardi's *Principles of Government*; and Nezam al-Mulk, who wrote the major book on government, *Seyasatnameh.* There were also many books of advice or *Andarznameh* written by the pre-Islamic and Islamic Iranian theorists.

The Persian/Iranian administrative system flourished even further under the Safavid Empire during 1500–1737, in which a centralized, Shi'a Islamic government was established that renewed Iranian pre-Islamic glory to an extent, and left remarkable legacies in art, culture, architecture, and administration, especially in public enterprise management. The centralized administration of the Safavids was based on a merit system in which examination, training, and professionalization grew significantly. Theirs was an Islamic administration based on the Iranian ancient traditions of bureaucracy and public administration. Public administration was strong and powerful under the Safavids, who paid close attention to public spheres. Religion also flourished with growing independence financially and administratively; the clergy played more important roles in the administration than before. The Safavids reorganized the state and administration and introduced new concepts and ideas into the system.

After the fall of the Safavids, the bureaucracy was the only institution of power and governance that contributed to the survival of Persian governments, despite major turmoil and chaos that characterized Iranian society for the next century. The rise of the Qajar dynasty at the end of the eighteenth century was a new but regressive development for Iran. Europe was out of feudalism and was experiencing the Industrial Revolution, other nations were emerging from nothing, but Iran lagged behind in governance and administration. The despotic and corrupt Qajar kings were resistant to change, feudalistic, decentralizing, and fearful of reform. They needed money and subjected themselves to foreign influence. For the first time Iran became the subject of European and Russian influence and their interferences in Iranian domestic affairs increased, causing major national resentments and protests against foreigners. The British and Russians did the most damage to Iran, which lost several northern provinces to Russia in the two wars of 1818 and 1828. The Qajars' decentralized and corrupt system led to further decline in the once rich Iranian administrative traditions.

After the fall of the Qajars in 1926 due to the Constitutional Revolution of 1905–1911, World War I, the Bolshevik Revolution, and the subsequent revolutionary movements across the country which resulted in the military coup by the army under the British-supported colonel Reza Khan, a new centralized system of government and administration emerged in Iran.

Public Administration in Modern Iran: The Pahlavis and the Islamic Republic (1926–Present)

The Pahlavi Public Administration (1926–1978)

Public administration in modern Iran began in the 1920s when the Pahlavi regime was established by colonel Reza Khan, who abolished the Qajar dynasty, crowned himself

the Shah, adopted the name Iran over Persia, and began a series of administrative reforms to centralize the state. He disregarded the first Constitution of Iran and ruled Iran with absolute dictatorship until 1941 when he abdicated power under Allied pressure.

Reza Shah's administrative reform created a centralized bureaucracy in urban and rural areas—the latter was selective and only reinforced the rural aristocracy, including his own large holdings confiscated from the Qajar landowners. Iranian democracy failed, and public administration and bureaucracy primarily served the new regime interests, just as it did under the Qajars. Capitalism grew, Western concepts of management were adopted, and the bureaucracy took a stronghold in Iranian government and society.

After Reza Shah's abdication, his young and inexperienced son Mohammed Reza Shah was crowned in 1941. The period 1941–1953 was a hallmark of modern Iranian democracy, in which political parties flourished, elections were taken seriously, bureaucracy grew larger, and the scope of and functions of public administration were expanded. Three bases formed the new foundations of Iranian public administration: the ancient traditions of administration, bureaucracy, and management; the Western concepts of organization and management; and the Islamic traditions of administration. During 1951–1953 a popular, national movement led by a nationalist prime minister, Dr. Mosaddegh, challenged the autocracy of the Shah and his foreign supporters. He nationalized the British-controlled Iranian Oil Company, which aroused the British boycott of Iranian oil and the U.S. pressure to topple the Mosaddegh government. This created a crisis in Iran; the Shah fled from the country in August 1953, but was returned by the U.S.–CIA-led military coup d'etat which succeeded in toppling the popular government and restoring the Shah to power. Following this historic event, the Shah devoted much of his energy to consolidating his power; he eliminated all oppositions and challenges and banned all political parties, except the one he created to support the regime.

The Postrevolutionary Islamic Public Administration (1979–present)

The revolution of 1978–1979 was a genuine revolution in which all strata of Iranian population with all ethnicity and political orientations took part. Participation in the revolution was massive. It was led by the religious leadership, *Ulama,* who mobilized the masses against the regime of the Shah. Ayatullah Khomeini, working from exile in Iraq, shattered the regime by sending relentless messages of destruction, and by 1978 the regime was totally shaken, yet brutal enough to crush the opposition. However, what the regime did not anticipate was the mass mobilization phenomenon that flooded the entire country, urban and rural.

The revolution brought about fundamental changes in the political system and public administration of Iran. First, the regime was replaced, monarchy was abolished, and an Islamic Republic was established with a parliament. Elections became important and people became involved in politics. Second, the old elite and its allies were completely uprooted and their properties confiscated and nationalized. This was a revolution by and for the downtrodden (*Mostazafin*) who placed major claims on and expectations from the new government. Third, the administrative orientation changed from repression and regime enhancement to a more public service-oriented and responsive system of administration. Fourth, there was a fundamental change in the bureaucracy and administration. The old bureaucracy became idle because nobody trusted it and bothered with it. Instead, popularly formed organizations as parabureacracies were created alongside the old system and took over the administrative functions. Fifth, red tape was cut down, though not eliminated, and many other changes were introduced in the system. However, institutionalization of the new order has also been accompanied by a degree of rebureaucratization with problems for the people who experience frustration with red tape and other obstacles in the bureaucracy.

In short, a number of changes took place under the new regime in Iran. Perhaps the most important element has been the Islamization of administration and bureaucracy. An entirely different approach has been applied in shaping the new public administration in Iran as a springboard for promotion of Shi'a Islam. Islamic principles and values are being applied to the study and practice of public administration in a holistic way that encompases politics, religion, morality, ethics, and management. Efficiency and effectiveness are balanced by moral and ethical character and conduct and public administrators are being prepared, at least in theory, as humans with concerns for social equity, fairness, and virtuous behaviors as well as for productivity. However, the need for expertise and professionalism is recognized for national development by many factions of the new governing elite. Major challenges have faced the new public administration under the new regime. These include implementation of ambitious developmental projects in industry, commence, art and culture, rural and urban development, and heavy industrialization. Despite the eight-year war with Iraq, Iranian postrevolutionary public administration has achieved some impressive accomplishments in implementing major developmental plans in rural and urban areas, and in social and economic sectors.

Thus, postrevolutionary Iranian public administration underwent three major phases of change: first was a period of some debureaucratization and democratization in 1979; then came a period of radicalization and massive debureaucratization plus reconsolidation of public organizations in 1979–1983; third was the period of stabilization, institutionalization, and gradual rebureaucratization after 1983. The third phase undertook major new functions of reconstruction, infrastructure development, and service delivery. Iranian public administration and bureaucracy are characterized by: the ancient traditions of administration and organization; Islamic principles, however modified; and the Western techniques of organization and management, including computer applications, the Internet, and so forth.

It is important to know that public administration in postrevolutionary Iran is becoming more and more self-sufficient, as the number of colleges and universities preparing a new generation of public administrators and managers is increasing rapidly, a trend which is found in other areas of the economy and society. The new public administration has also been exporting managerial and organizational ideas and practices to some other developing countries in Latin America, Asia, and Africa as well as to the Middle East. In fact, Iran is considered to provide an alternative administrative model for many developing nations. This administrative expertise has received some recognition from such international entities as the UN World Health Organization. However, corruption, red tape, and other bureaucratic pathologies are appearing again in Iranian administrative system. There are many areas for improvement in postrevolutionary public administration of Iran.

ALI FARAZMAND

BIBLIOGRAPHY

Cameron, G. G., 1968. *History of Early Iran.* New York: Greenwood Press.

Debevoise, N. C., 1938. *A Political History of Parthia.* Chicago: University of Chicago Press.

Farazmand, Ali, 1989. *The State, Bureaucracy, and Revolution in Modern Iran: Agrarian Reform and Regime Politics.* New York: Praeger.

———, 1991. "State Tradition and Public Administration in Iran in Ancient and Contemporary Perspectives." In Ali Farazmand, ed., *Handbook of Comparative and Development Public Administration.* New York: Marcel Dekker.

Frye, Richard, 1975. *The Golden Age of Persia.* New York: Harper & Row.

———, 1963. *The Heritage of Persia.* New York: The World Publishing Co.

Halliday, Fred, 1979. *Dictatorship and Development.* New York: Penguin Books.

Lambton, A.K.L., ed., 1980. *Theory and Practice in Medieval Persian Government.* London: Variorum Reprints.

Nadon, Christopher, 1996. "From Republic to Empire: Political Revolution and the Common Good in Xenophon's *Education of Cyrus.*" *American Political Science Review,* vol. 90, no. 2 (June) 361–374.

Olmstead, A. T., 1948. *History of the Persian Empire: The Achaemenid Period.* Chicago: University of Chicago Press.

Xenophon, 1992. *The Education of Cyrus.* New York: Everymans Library.

Zonis, Marvin, 1971. *The Political Elite of Iran.* Princeton, NJ: Princeton University Press.

PERSONAL INTEGRITY.

A descriptive characteristic of individuals who act in accord with their principles or commitments when facing pressures, temptations, or enticements of various sorts to do otherwise. It is commonly used, in addition, to describe one who is ethical, for example, one who is truthful, has convictions, has character, or more generally, someone who is honest. More specifically, though, a person is considered to have integrity who acts in ways consistent with his or her stated commitments, values, or beliefs.

A related definition of integrity is its classical meaning of being undivided or "out of one piece," and is similar to engineering uses of the concept—the structure of the building retains its integrity after many years. This depicts an important notion that to have integrity a public servant's internal commitments "hold together" in some coherent and integrated way. It manifests itself as a well-ordered and integrated set of commitments or beliefs that guide one's actions and show consistency over time. Such integrity takes on a coherence, a fabric of character, woven together in one's character over a lifetime. Rather than a manifestation of separate, isolated beliefs, it is a fabric of several uniquely constituted commitments that creates integrating and unifying connections throughout one's life, resulting in a sense of personal integrity and interrelatedness of one's life choices.

Maintaining Integrity

Integrity is more than merely following rules and regulations, however, more than simple obedience to external controls that prohibit certain kinds of unacceptable public official behavior through law and regulation. Integrity requires an "inner compass," an ongoing set of internal imperatives and commitments, rather than a reliance on external rules and controls, that orients and guides one's actions. Integrity requires the considered, consistent adherence to chosen core values, convictions, or commitments. A person with integrity thus behaves in ways that manifest a set of well-considered, core values or commitments with some degree of constancy over time. In addition, one's sense of personal integrity typically establishes lines over which one will not step—where there are some things that one must do or must not do—lines that are sometimes difficult to define or predict in advance but nevertheless always present in one's character. Maintaining one's integrity, in short, involves doing what is right—according to one's internal set of values and commitments—instead of doing what is easiest.

Lack of Integrity

Failure to act or behave consistently with the commitments one holds or proclaims generates the claim that one lacks integrity. Not following through on agreements, giving false promises, giving in to undue pressure, and exhibiting inconsistencies between what one says and what one does, for example, are considered indicators that an elected or appointed public servant lacks integrity. The self-indulgent behavior of an individual who is unable or unwilling to resist temptation is also characteristic of one who is lacking willpower and integrity. One's lack of integrity can be explained in several ways.

First, one who lacks integrity may not have yet engaged in sufficient deliberation and reflection to develop an integrated, well-ordered set of commitments from which behavior can be guided. To have integrity requires the integration of commitments and interests over time, which takes on a coherence that can orient and enable intentional action by the public servant. John Dewey (Dewey and Tufts 1925) noted that such lack of integrity results from a weak, unstable, vacillating character in which different habits alternate with one another rather than embody one another. Rather than a collection of separate, isolated commitments and beliefs, integrity requires a well-ordered set, or fabric, of commitments developed from continual deliberation, choice, reflection, and then integration into one's habit patterns. Reflection and what Aristotle called "practical reasoning" are personal virtues required to develop such an integrated and ordered set of beliefs and commitments.

Second, lack of integrity can be explained as weakness of will, where the internal strength and resolve to act in accordance with prior commitments or values is weak and dissolves in the face of external pressures or enticements. Historically, scholars have argued that developing and pursuing commitments is the essence of will or willpower. McDougall (1927), for example, said that a strong will displays great energy and steadfastness along certain lines of action. The ability to hold to commitments is at the core of integrity; the person of integrity must have the strength of will to hold true to his or her commitments in the face of conflicts, pressures, and enticements. Moral courage is thus a critical virtue needed by a person of integrity. Hart (1984) suggests that "moral heroism" may even be required for a public servant to maintain commitments and moral convictions, particularly when conflict arises between one's core values and organizational policies, or in more difficult situations when forced to oppose an unjust or immoral policy.

A third explanation for the incongruity between words and actions is deception. In public deception, one's formal statement or proclamation is hollow or deceptive, promising adherence to certain commitments or values while knowing there is no such commitment. Integrity thus requires honesty and a respect for truthfulness. Deception can also involve not being true to oneself; lacking integrity, an individual may engage in personal deception, not reflecting or manifesting in public places what is genuinely in one's heart. Honesty with others as well as with oneself are thus also virtues of a person with integrity.

Integrity Is Fundamental to Public Service

Integrity requires acting consistently with a well-ordered set of commitments and beliefs, and is the foundation upon which public trust and confidence in government rests. Personal integrity is thus fundamental in the public service. However, the recent blurring of the public and private sectors—what scholars label the blending of the polity and the economy in society—creates increasing tensions between the public and private interests in both democratic and reformed communist countries. For example, there is continuing pressure in the U.S., Canada, Australia, and the United Kingdom, as well as newly mounting pressure in the former Soviet-bloc countries, to employ certain managerial strategies more typically used in the private sector. With this movement come efforts to substitute the ethic of public interests with an ethics of private interests, characterized by pressures to adopt short-term business-oriented values and techniques—for example, solely using economic criteria for policymaking to the exclusion of other important criteria such as equity in service delivery and democratic responsiveness.

A Special Moral Obligation

Given these pressures, personal integrity in government becomes increasingly important because central to public service is the ethical precept that there exists a larger public interest that transcends the pursuit of private interests. Individuals working in the public sector incur a special moral obligation, an obligation greater than the responsibilities of the corporate or private sector, an obligation for the welfare of fellow citizens. The role of public servants in most democratic countries is unique and different from those of business executives; it encompasses a "higher purpose" that requires not only a different set of personal characteristics but a higher set of moral responsibilities based on the public servants' (a) fiduciary responsibilities of stewardship and (b) their essential role as catalysts for stimulating action in the public interest. It is directed toward some conception of the public interest rather than individual achievement, thus subordinating particular individual interests to a larger set of communal interests or values. It demands the exercise of power and legitimate public authority without self-aggrandizement.

Public Trust in Governance

The public's trust and confidence in government depends to a large degree on the integrity of elected and appointed officials. The public's trust is an essential element in providing effective public service, and the personal conduct of public officials is continuously scrutinized. The general public in many Western countries has become increasingly skeptical of the integrity of elected officials; since the 1970s, public opinion polls have noted a continuing loss of confidence of the U.S. population in government's ability to carry out its public responsibilities effectively. In 1992, for example, a national survey in the United States found that 71 percent believed that there is no connection between what a politician said and what he or she would do once elected.

There is dissatisfaction, even suspicion, with elected officials who are seen as failing to tell the truth about, or not taking responsibility for, serious local, regional or national problems. This lack of confidence in public leadership requires increased attention to issues surrounding personal integrity. Public confidence in the integrity of government, particularly in Western democracies, can only be restored if citizens are convinced that those in public service—whether elected officials or career public servants—are genuinely concerned about advancing the public interest and not merely the self-advancement of their own individual, private interests.

Interpersonal Trust in Teamwork and Other Collaborative Action

The nature of public service is that not only do public officials act "for us" in pursuing the public interest, they act "with others" in cooperative, collaborative, and collective efforts. Effective action requires contributions from many individuals and institutions in the public service, tied together in multiple webs of interrelationships—as everything from members of teams in organized hierarchical structures to participants in temporary task forces and interorganizational networks. The success of organizational teams, intergovernmental and intersectoral partnerships, and other organized collaborative efforts in complex environments requires a certainty of relationships among people and among groups; the productivity and effectiveness of groups depends upon the interpersonal trust and integrity of the participants. Following through on commitments and agreements is particularly critical in developing interpersonal trust and is the foundation for effective working relationships. Building and maintaining interpersonal trust is thus required for public servants to stimulate and sustain teamwork in the pursuit of the public interest, and personal integrity is the foundation of such trust. In fact, trust and integrity are fundamental to all forms of social interaction.

Unfortunately, there are several psychological tendencies that make public trust and interpersonal trust hard to develop yet easy to destroy. For example, negative or trust-destroying incidents are more noticeable than positive, trust-building incidents; negative, trust-destroying incidents carry much greater weight than positive, trust-building events; sources of trust-destroying news tend to be seen as more credible than sources of good news that confirm trust; and distrust, once initiated, tends to reinforce and perpetuate distrust (Slovic 1993). Interpersonal trust is therefore rather fragile. It is developed rather slowly, but can be easily weakened by a single incident that results in prior agreements being specifically broken or an incident which merely questions one's credibility.

Integrity as Strength of Character

Integrity is a mode of conduct or set of virtues that distinguishes one as having strength of character. Knowing the difference between right and wrong is not enough, however, and does not necessarily characterize one with integrity. Individuals with integrity examine and reflect on the consequences of their actions on prior commitments, and emphasize the collective interests or goals of the group, organization, community, or jurisdiction over self-interests. A person with integrity typically has consistent habits or competencies characterized as strength of character (Luke 1994) including strong core commitments that are "identity-conferring," long-range thinking and future orientation, a strength of conscience, and ego strength.

Identity-Conferring Commitments

At its deepest level, the essence of integrity is developing, pursuing and holding commitments. First, it involves a commitment to moral or virtuous conduct however expressly articulated in the unique culture and history of the region or country. Second, commitments are made toward such things as principles, causes, ideas, and people; and core commitments are those to which they are most faithful and that reflect what is most important to them. Whatever the commitment, the person with integrity is someone who cares deeply. Indifference is incompatible with the possession of core commitments. Core commitments and goals reflect an individual's centrally important values and become identity-conferring commitments (Taylor 1985) that contribute to one's identity, make one what he or she is. Having identity-conferring commitments means not merely having different goals from someone else; it is to be a different person from what one would have been if one had not been as strongly committed (Kupperman 1991). On the other hand, one who lacks identity-conferring commitments generally has only very tentative loyalties to most things—public issues, causes, or even relationships. Commitments may change over time, through action and reflection, but changing fundamental commitments or core values is usually accompanied by a change in the person's identity.

Ego Strength

Integrity requires the individual to have ego strength for "impulse control" and for "moral courage." Ego strength allows a person with integrity to assert a form of self-control that holds in check any immediate impulses and then to examine, reflect on, and consider the consequences of potential actions on prior commitments and on

the public interest. A person of weak ego, or weak character, is likely to be impulsive and yield to temptations quickly. A person who lacks ego strength can be more easily enticed or prompted to act contrary to core or identity-conferring commitments, or can easily allow other people's expectations to overwhelm his or her own shallow commitments. Someone without ego strength can also tend to be an extreme conformist who habitually does what others expect of him or her. Ego strength provides a stronger sense of self that frees one from arbitrary outer pressures, generating an inner strength often necessary to be consistent in pursuing long-term goals and commitments, and to be firm in advancing the public interest in the face of increasing pressures to do otherwise.

Ego strength provides confidence and "moral courage" to face conflict, to disagree publicly on issues integral to one's commitments or values. Acting with integrity can sometimes be disruptive of emerging patterns of others' behavior, and ego strength provides the basis for moral courage or "moral heroism" that may be required. Further, it fosters a personal sense of inner strength that allows for deeper self-reflection and changes in identity-conferring commitments that may slowly evolve from that reflection. Ego strength provides an inner security that allows a public servant to engage in self-reflection and examination of internalized commitments, and to modify core commitments in light of deeper reflection. The moral dilemmas and choices facing an individual in the public service can require considerably more reflection, deliberation, and continual learning than encompassed in any professional code of ethics or set of rules. Blind obedience to such codes and rigid unreflective behavior can actually inhibit the growth of a strong character.

Strength of Conscience

Persons with integrity feel a strength of conscience that exhibits a firm, but not necessarily rigid, internalized set of moral principles (but not rules) which act as a guide to one's behavior and action. Persons with integrity have traversed what are considered four qualitatively different forms of conscience, beginning with the most primitive: a set of crude, basic rules of what not to do ("don'ts"). The next level of conscience is rule conformity, with authority residing outside of oneself; third is a kind of conscience that consists of an organized body of internalized moral rules, influenced by others' rules, yet incapable of being internally questioned or tested. Finally, the fourth level of conscience, the kind exhibited in persons with high integrity, is characterized by a core set of internalized commitments and beliefs, accessible to examination and weighing, which can change and deepen as new commitments are made, new action is tested, and consequences are assessed and reflected back into one's future actions (Peck and Havighurst 1960).

Forward Looking

Being able to resist temptation and immediate pressures for conformity requires one to think and plan beyond the moment, more specifically the ability to think in the long term. Public servants with integrity have a sense of future direction and a concern for the future; they have the ability to scan across the horizon of time and geographical place. The setting of future intentions commits an individual to long-term policies, projects, and people; in addition, it may also provide important guiding constraints on more immediate actions.

This skill to be forward looking is what Dewey and Tufts (1925) called the habit of greater thoughtfulness about the future: a focus on the future gains and impacts of one's actions rather than on the immediate consequences of the act. Focusing on the future, however, does not require a person of integrity to be indifferent to the present; a commitment to attain a future outcome requires appropriate immediate strategies to attain future goals. Such long-term thinking and committing establishes over time a strategic or causal connection that can appear to others as separate and unconnected projects, actions, or behaviors.

Developing One's Integrity

The development of integrity may follow similar processes as the development of strong character; it is learned through repetition and successive trials that vary according to different circumstances and stages of development of the individual. Integrity, and strong character, cannot be developed by following some general principles, rules or code of conduct. Psychological studies indicate that character is shaped by external influences that are most powerful in the first decade of life. Individuals may have actually developed their core character by the time they are morally reflective adults. Nevertheless, like the acquisition of Aristotle's practical reasoning, integrity similarly occurs through a form of habituation (*ethismos*), a refinement of perception, reflection, feeling, and action through repeated efforts. Habit is thus a crucial factor in forming integrity. The strength of habit, or one's integrity, is a result of continual deliberation, choice, reflection and then integration into the self as habit.

JEFFREY S. LUKE

BIBLIOGRAPHY

Bailey, S. K., 1965. "The Relationship Between Ethics and Public Service." In Roscoe Martin, ed., *Public Administration and Democracy: Essays in Honor of Paul Appleby.* Syracuse, NY: Syracuse University Press, pp. 283–298.
Bluestein, J., 1991. *Care and Commitment: Taking the Personal View.* Oxford and New York: Oxford University Press.
Cooper, T. L. and D. W. Wright, 1992. *Exemplary Public Administrators: Character and Leadership in Government.* Oxford and San Francisco: Jossey Bass.
Dewey, J. and J. H. Tufts, 1925. *Ethics.* New York: Holt and Company.
Greiner, G. G. "Moral Integrity of Professions." *Professional Ethics,* vol. 2, nos. 3 and 4: 15–24.
Hardie, W. F. R., 1980. *Aristotle's Ethical Theory.* Oxford: Clarendon Press.
Hart, D. K., 1984. "The Virtuous Citizen, the Honorable Bureaucrat, and 'Public' Administration." *Public Administration Review,* vol. 44 (Special Issue) 111–119.
Kohn, A., 1990. *The Brighter Side of Human Nature: Altruism and Empathy in Everyday Life.* New York: Basic Books.
Kupperman, J. J., 1991. *Character.* New York: Oxford Press.
Lewis, C. W. and B. L. Catron, 1996. "Professional Standards and Ethics." In James Perry, ed., *Handbook of Public Administration.* 2d ed. Oxford and San Francisco: Jossey Bass.
Luke, J., 1994. "Character and Conduct in the Public Service." In T. Cooper, ed., *Handbook of Administrative Ethics.* New York: Marcel Dekker.
McDougall, W., 1927. *Character and the Conduct of Life.* New York: G. P. Putnam's Sons Publishers.
Peck, R. F. and R. J. Havighurst, 1960. *The Psychology of Character Development.* New York: Wiley and Sons.
Sherman, N., 1989. *The Fabric of Character: Aristotle's Theory of Virtue.* Oxford: Clarendon Press.
Slovic, Paul, 1993. "Perceived Risk, Trust, and Democracy." *Risk Analysis,* vol. 13, no. 6: 675–682.
Taylor, G., 1985. *Shame and Guilt.* Oxford: Clarendon Press.

PERT. An acronym for Program (or Project) Evaluation and Review Technique, a planning and management tool.

PERT was first introduced in the late 1950s as a technique for planning and managing large, complex United States government projects. PERT is credited with being a major factor in cutting years from the development of the Polaris ballistic missile program. Subsequently, the PERT method has been successfully applied to an array of government projects, both in the United States and elsewhere, and it is also used extensively as a planning and management tool in the private sector.

A variation of PERT called the Critical Path Method, or CPM, was developed in the same period. While PERT focuses on events and managing the time element, CPM emphasizes activities and the control of project costs. In practical application, the two techniques are nearly identical.

PERT is a planner's and manager's tool for defining and coordinating the various activities that make up a complex project. For the planner, PERT, which depicts the interrelationship of project components and the interdependency of project activities, can guard against incomplete planning. For the manager, PERT provides a means of monitoring progress toward project completion, which alerts the manager to conditions requiring adjustments in project timing and the application of resources.

As a simple example of the use of PERT, consider the construction of a house. The walls of the house cannot be erected until the foundation is in place. Work on the roof trusses cannot begin until weight-bearing walls are positioned. These activities are necessarily sequential, but other aspects of house construction can proceed in parallel. For example, cabinets can be installed while landscaping takes place. The construction of a house consists of series of activities, some sequential and some not; and in order to finish the house in minimum time and least cost, the builder must be aware of the linkages between activities and the amount of time necessary to complete each activity. The builder can employ a PERT diagram to establish a pattern of linkage and time estimates. This diagram and the underlying PERT analysis guide the builder in the day-to-day management decisions of ordering materials and scheduling labor.

The PERT network is a pictorial representation of the logical relationships between events and activities which lead to the completion of a project. An event is the completion of a task or activity. An event does not consume time or resources, but it is indicative of a significant point in the project. Events are shown on the network as a geometric figure, usually a circle. An activity is the actual performance of a job or task. All activity consumes time and nearly always requires the expenditure of resources in the form of manpower and material. Activities are shown in the network by an arrow linking events and designating the logical order of events. A completed network consists of a single beginning event (usually labeled "Project Start"), a number of intermediate events connected by activities, and a single end event (usually labeled "Project Complete").

A planning approach termed backward mapping, greatly facilitates the design of a PERT network. Backward mapping consists of answers to one central question—what must take place before this event can be realized? Beginning with the end event, project completion, the planner steps backward through earlier events by repeatedly asking this central question. Backward mapping turns cause and effect on its head. Instead of reasoning, "if we do A, then B will occur," the planner reasons, "for B to occur, what A will be necessary?"

The first step in applying PERT is to list in reverse order of their expected occurrence all the events that must take place before the project is completed. As PERT stresses events rather than activities, emphasis is placed on the completion of events rather than the performance of tasks. Consequently, careful attention must be given to describing the events. Two basic rules should be followed in labeling events: the word "complete" should appear in the label (the "start" event is an exception) and additional words should descriptive, brief, and unambiguous.

The next step is to make a list of all activities (tasks or jobs) that are necessary for the completion of each listed event. Some events may be preceded by a single activity, but other events may require multiple activities before completion. A skeletal network can now be constructed by placing the events and activities in a logical sequence, uti-

lizing numbered circles to represent events joined by solid arrows to depict activities.

In some situations an event may not take place until one or more predecessor events has taken place, yet no activity links the events. In these situations the logic of the network can be preserved by linking the events with a broken arrow to indicate a "dummy" or "zero-time" activity.

The flow of activities and events is customarily drawn from left to right. A simple PERT network is illustrated in Figure I.

Once the PERT network is drawn, estimates are made of the amount of time necessary to accomplish each activity. Each estimate (labeled t_e in Figure I) is recorded on the diagram over the arrow representing the activity. For each event an earliest expected time (T_E) is calculated by adding all the t_e's along the path leading to that event. T_E's are recorded above the circle representing the event. Frequently there will be more than one path leading to an event. In such cases the T_E is the sum of the t_e's of the path requiring the longest time. This is necessary because an event cannot be considered complete until all activities leading to that event have been completed.

The next step in network construction is to calculate the latest event time (T_L) defined as the latest time by which an event must be completed in order to keep the project on schedule. Calculation of T_L's begins by equating the T_L for the final event, project completion, with the T_E for that event. The planner then moves right to left through the network, beginning with the final event, subtracting the t_e for each activity leading immediately to the event for which the T_L calculation is being made. Should two or more paths lead away from an event, the T_L for that event is the one which has the smallest number, that is, the earliest of the latest completion times (see Figure I). The T_L for an event is recorded below the circle representing that event.

Slack time is defined as the extra time or grace period that might be available to accomplish each activity. The slack time for an activity is calculated by subtracting the T_E from the T_L for the event terminating that activity. In the above illustration event 3 must be completed four weeks into the project ($T_L = 4$) in order not to delay the project,

FIGURE I. A SIMPLE PERT NETWORK

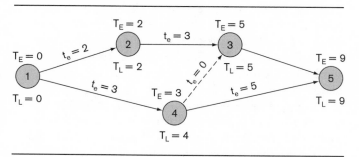

yet the earliest possible time to accomplish this event is three weeks ($T_E = 3$). This makes a one-week period of grace or slack time available to accomplish event 3. By using all or a part of this slack time, activity 1–3 may be extended or its initiation delayed without affecting the project completion time.

On any PERT network one can trace multiple paths from project start to project completion. Within every network is one path composed of activities and events, any one of which if delayed will delay project completion. These are the critical activities and events, and together they make up the critical path for the network. Critical events are those with zero slack time, and all events along the critical path exhibit zero slack. In the above illustration path 1-2-4-5 is the critical path.

Two facts about the critical path illustrate its significance as a project management tool. First, the critical path requires the most time to get from the beginning event to the final event. Second, any event along the critical path that experiences delay will delay the total project completion by the same amount.

PERT serves the manager as well as the planner. The project manager can transfer resources from activities not on the critical path to activities on the critical path in an effort to reduce project completion time. PERT is a dynamic management tool. The manager should continually monitor, update, and revise, if necessary, the PERT network. If estimates for activities are not realized, the critical path may shift. The manager must take notice of such an occurrence and be prepared to redeploy resources as appropriate.

A. ROBERT THOENY

BIBLIOGRAPHY

Barnetson, Paul, 1970. *Critical Path Planning: Present and Future Techniques.* Princeton, NJ: Brandon/Systems Press, Inc.
Evarts, H. F., 1964. *Introduction to PERT.* Boston: Allyn and Bacon.
Wiest, Jerome D. and Ferdinand K. Levy, 1969. *A Management Guide to PERT/CPM.* Englewood Cliffs, NJ: Prentice-Hall, Inc.

PETER PRINCIPLE.

The concept originated by Laurence J. Peter and discussed in his book of the same name (Peter and Hull 1969) that "in a hierarchy, every employee tends to rise to his level of incompetence." Peter's Corollary is "in time, every post tends to be occupied by an employee who is incompetent to carry out its duties."

Based on his observations of schools, government organizations, and businesses, Peter hypothesized that employees are promoted to positions because of their competence in their current position, not because of the competence they might have in a future position. As a result, employees are promoted to positions where they might not have the necessary skills.

While a person might move from a level of competence to a higher level of competence—for example, from a line worker to a lead worker—ultimately, Peter claimed, the final promotion would be to a level of incompetence. As a result, hierarchies are staffed by people operating beyond their level of competence.

There are apparent exceptions to this rule. An incompetent person may be promoted, or a competent one not promoted. Peter argued that these are not exceptions but rather further proof that the Peter Principle is accurate. An already incompetent person who is promoted may be moved in such a way that the new position is outside the hierarchy, as in a promotion to a staff position, for example; or the individual may be "promoted" laterally.

Organizational rules and regulations rather than individual incompetence may seem to cause poor performance. For example, a functionary may refuse to give out information because it is "not in the job description" or may require the completion of multiple forms "because it is required." These bureaucratic behaviors, however, are ruses to mask individual incompetence.

When a super-competent person is dismissed rather than promoted, the principle of incompetence is upheld. Supercompetence disrupts the hierarchy and interferes with the operation of the Peter Principle. Supercompetents who are dismissed from an organization often form their own businesses where their competence can be demonstrated. However, even the brightest supercompetent can fail when he or she moves into an area requiring new competence—for example, when an outstanding computer developer moves into management.

Peter argued that promotion to a level of incompetence not only inflicts damage on the organization, but also harms the physical and psychological health of the individual. Once promoted to a level of incompetence, the individual realizes that he or she is no longer able to meet or exceed expectations. This causes both diminished self-esteem and fear that someone might "find out" about one's incompetence. Thus, the person begins to work harder, and to pay more attention to sometimes inconsequential details. As the Queen in *Through the Looking Glass* (Carroll 1916) notes, "Now *here*, you see, it takes all the running you can do to keep in the same place." Being at one's level of incompetence causes the final placement syndrome, whose symptoms include such things as ulcers, alcoholism, insomnia, chronic fatigue, and even more serious medical problems.

Peter's cure for the Peter Principle was creative incompetence. He argued that it usually is not possible to refuse a promotion, even if one knows that the new position is beyond one's competence. Instead, Peter suggested one should develop strategies to disguise or camouflage competence. You must, Peter said, "create the impression that you have already reached your level of incompetence" but you must do it in such a way that it does not prevent you from carrying out your duties.

The term "Peter Principle" has come to mean any individual or organizational behavior which is irrational and inefficient, yet supported by the hierarchy. The term is widely used and now commonly accepted as a mark that an organization or system is characterized by incompetence and inefficiency.

SUSAN C PADDOCK

BIBLIOGRAPHY

Carroll, Lewis [pseud.], 1916. *Alice's Adventures in Wonderland and Through the Looking Glass.* Chicago, IL: Rand McNally.
Peter, Laurence J. and Raymond Hull, 1969. *The Peter Principle.* New York, NY: William Morrow and Company, Inc.

PHILANTHROPIC ADVISORY SERVICE (PAS).

The division of the Council of Better Business Bureaus, Incorporated (CBBB), that educates donors and promotes ethical practices by charities. The PAS is one of several "watchdog" organizations operating in the United States (see also **National Charities Information Bureau**), all of which seek to educate and inform potential donors and encourage ethical and responsible behavior by charities and other nonprofit organizations.

The PAS was officially founded in 1972, when the Council of Better Business Bureaus formalized a service it had informally provided since its founding in 1912. The CBBB seeks to foster "fair and honest relationships between businesses and consumers, instilling consumer confidence and contributing to an ethical business environment." The work of PAS is an outgrowth of Better Business Bureaus' focus on promoting the highest ethical behavior, since the service considers donors to be consumers of the charities they support.

The primary purpose of PAS, according to CBBB publications, is to educate donors. PAS does not recommend certain charities, but it provides information and reports that enable donors to make informed decisions. The PAS also encourages charities to accept responsibility for self-regulation and ethical practice, and it has developed its own "Standards for Charitable Solicitations" which it applies to assess and report on the performance of individual charities. PAS seeks to contribute to the success of responsible charities by helping them earn the confidence of the donating public. The CBBB believes that both the general public and the soliciting organizations will benefit from the voluntary disclosure of an organization's activities, finances, fund-raising practices, and governance. PAS focuses on charities that are tax-exempt under section 501(c)(3) of the Code of the United States Internal Rev-

enue Service (IRS), but it also prepares reports on a limited number of lobbying, membership, and social welfare organizations (e.g., noncharitable organizations exempt under sections 501(c)(4) and 501(c)(6) of the IRS Code). PAS generally does not report on schools, colleges, and churches soliciting within their own congregations, even though it does encourage them to honor its standards.

The "Standards for Charitable Solicitations" of the PAS were first developed in 1974. The standards were developed by the CBBB with the help of charities, accounting professionals, professional fund-raisers, corporate and foundation funders, member Better Business Bureaus, regulatory officials, and others active in philanthropy, with the specific intent of promoting ethical practices by philanthropic organizations. The current standards, most recently revised in 1982, focus on five key areas of performance: public accountability, use of funds, solicitations and informational materials, fund-raising practices, and organizational governance. The general criteria for each of these categories are as follows:

Public Accountability

1. Soliciting organizations shall provide on request an annual report.
2. Soliciting organizations shall provide on request complete annual financial statements.
3. Soliciting organizations' financial statements shall present adequate information to serve as a basis for informed decisions.
4. Organizations receiving a substantial portion of their income through the fund-raising activities of controlled or affiliated entities shall provide on request an accounting of all income received by and fund-raising costs incurred by such entities.

Use of Funds

1. A reasonable percentage of total income from all sources shall be applied to programs and activities directly related to the purposes for which the organization exists.
2. A reasonable percentage of public contributions shall be applied to the programs and activities described in solicitations, in accordance with donor expectations.
3. Fund-raising costs shall be reasonable.
4. Total fund-raising and administrative costs shall be reasonable. Generally, fund-raising costs should not exceed 35 percent of contributions, and total fund-raising and administrative costs together should not exceed 50 percent of total income.
5. Soliciting organizations shall substantiate on request their application of funds, in accordance with donor expectations, to the programs and activities described in solicitations.

6. Soliciting organizations shall establish and exercise adequate controls over disbursements.

Solicitations and Informational Materials

1. Solicitations and informational materials, distributed by any means, shall be accurate, truthful and not misleading, both in whole and in part.
2. Soliciting organizations shall substantiate on request that solicitations and informational materials, distributed by any means, are accurate, truthful and not misleading, in whole and in part.
3. Solicitations shall include a clear description of the programs and activities for which funds are requested.
4. Direct contact solicitations, including personal and telephone appeals, shall identify the solicitor and his/her relationship to the benefiting organization, the benefiting organization, and the programs and activities for which funds are requested.
5. Solicitations in conjunction with the sale of goods, services, or admissions shall identify at the point of solicitation the benefiting organization, a source from which written information may be obtained, and the portion of the sales or admission price to benefit the charitable organization or cause.

Fund-Raising Practices

1. Soliciting organizations shall establish and exercise controls over fund-raising activities conducted for their benefit by staff, volunteers, consultants, contractors, and controlled or affiliated entities, including commitment to writing of all fund-raising contracts and agreements.
2. Soliciting organizations shall establish and exercise adequate controls over contributions.
3. Soliciting organizations shall honor donor requests for confidentiality and shall not publicize the identity of donors without prior written permission.
4. Fund-raising shall be conducted without excessive pressure.

Governance

1. Soliciting organizations shall have an adequate governing structure, including appropriate governing instruments (e.g., articles of incorporation) that clarify goverance authority over the organization's programs and policies.
2. Soliciting organizations shall have an active governing body that meets regularly.
3. Soliciting organizations shall have an independent governing body, and not more than 20 percent of its

members shall receive direct or indirect compensation for service.

The PAS document, "CBBB Standards for Charitable Solicitations," fully defines these terms and offers more detailed information on many of these standards.

The PAS communicates with the public and potential donors via individual reports on specific organizations, its quarterly publication, "Give, But Give Wisely," and a separately published annual charity index. Over 200 detailed reports on specific organizations were prepared by the PAS in 1994, according to service officials. Detailed reports on single organizations are available free of charge from the CBBB, and a brief summary is available on-line via the CBBB's World-Wide Web site on the Internet. PAS reports and educational materials also are distributed by the local Better Business Bureaus located throughout the nation. The Philanthropic Advisory Service of the Council of Better Business Bureaus may be contacted at: 4200 Wilson Boulevard, Suite 800, Arlington, Virginia 22203-1804, (703) 276-0100, Web Site: http://www.bbb.org/bbb/cbbb. html.

DAVID O. RENZ

BIBLIOGRAPHY

Council of Better Business Bureaus, 1982. "CBBB Standards for Charitable Solicitations." Arlington, VA: Council of Better Business Bureaus.

PHILANTHROPY. Voluntary giving, voluntary serving, and voluntary association to achieve some vision of the public good; includes charity, patronage, and civil society.

Philanthropy is a catchall concept that conflates four ideas: charity, a narrower definition of philanthropy, patronage, and civil society. The usual inclusive contemporary definition of philanthropy is "values, organizations, and practices that entail voluntary action to achieve some vision of the public good" or the "private" production of "public goods." Voluntary action includes voluntary giving, voluntary association, and voluntary service. The Greek roots of philanthropy—love for humankind—and the Latin for agape or unconditional love, *caritas,* which makes its way to English as charity, help readers to understand the origins of the concepts of charity and philanthropy in notions of public virtue and religious worship. Patronage comes from a separate tradition, though public virtue has often been its explained motivation. Civil society is of a more recent origin and will be explained separately.

The first three phenomena—charity, philanthropy, and patronage—are virtually universal in all traditions, varying in incidence, object, and degree over time. The concept of worshipping God through gifts (*dana* in Hinduism and Buddhism) and service (*sewa* in Hinduism and Buddhism) appears in all the god-centered traditions. Enjoinders to followers to divest themselves of worldly attachments or to undertake positive actions that approximate unconditional love on earth can be found in sacred texts and practices associated with daily life and rites of passage in all the great religious traditions. A parable of the "suffering stranger" for whom one has an obligation appears in one form or another in Islam, Judaism, Christianity, Hinduism, and Buddhism. Native American and African expressions of religion contain these same motifs. Charity is required in each, either to be given or to be received as a mendicant. A more state-oriented religious tradition such as Confucianism defines the primacy of the family as the object of generosity, but looks to the good emperor as one who attends his subjects in time of their need.

It is also virtually universal that the institutions that arose from these gifts and which facilitated worship, whether formal worship or ministering to the needy, have been given special treatment in law and practice. Monasteries, pilgrim rest houses, orphanages, these have often, though not always, withstood expropriation by the state and have not been treated as the conventional estate of a citizen or subject. The administration by self-selected directors (i.e., "trustees" of "trusts") is common everywhere. In addition, those who practice certain acts of service were exempt from other requirements of citizenship, such as military duty.

At issue is always what is meant by the notion of "voluntary"–without any gain and anticipation of gain to the giver. It is pointless to argue about the motivation for such behaviors and the persistence of philanthropic institutions. As with all other actions, philanthropic motives are mixed: social respectability, love of God and society, contrition, gratitude, substitutes for other responsibilities, control over others, false consciousness, greed, envy, and so on and on. The effort to find a univariant explanation for philanthropic acts results in either sanctimonious piety or cynicism. Short of finding a "generous gene" or confirmation of a hypothesis out of evolutionary theory, it is sufficient for the purposes here to suggest that philanthropy does not occur because of the coercive force of the state, in anticipation of economic profit, or because it is required by family obligation. Needless to say, there are ways to use aspects of the state, profit motive, and family in ways that diminish the voluntary character of philanthropy.

Tocqueville's "self-interest rightly understood"–that is, a blend of self-interest and a concern for others–seems sufficient. So does the notion of serial reciprocity–individuals tend to give what has been given to them–not usually to those who gave to them, but to others, especially the next generation. Above all, the search for a reductionist motivation is part of a larger social science reductionism–that is, all economic behavior is predicated on a search for profit

maximization; all political behavior is power maximization; all organizational behavior is toward the singular need to survive as an organization. A discussion of philanthropy–voluntary action for some vision of the public good–allows us to realize that motivation is always plural and deeply nested in the values we hold.

As indicated, philanthropy is an umbrella word. Many different subjects seek shelter under it. This might be easily seen in Table I.

Relief, of course, is charity, it is meant directly to alleviate the suffering of others. The narrow definition of philanthropy is that the aim of philanthropy is to affect the root causes of suffering, whether they lie in skills, health, distribution of income or political clout. Here we can also see why patronage has been lumped with philanthropy. Improvement of populations, or their human potential, has historically extended from placing statues of heroes in city squares or victory arches to building Carnegie libraries or supporting John Milton's creative efforts. Although often accomplished by the state, such phenomena we normally associate with individual rulers and elites. As the return to the giver may be more clear in patronage, it is often awkward for those given to the pieties of discussing philanthropy to embrace patronage as philanthropy. The "charity begins at home" critique of philanthropy has this as its origins. That those who support a new production at the Metropolitan Opera also attend its performance is insufficient to lump this form of voluntary action as equivalent to market behavior.

Civil society has come of late to be included as part of philanthropy. The affinity can be easily seen when philanthropic organizations such as private foundations support the creating and strengthening of nonprofit community-based organizations that seek to achieve some public end–philanthropy as empowerment. But the affinity is thought to be more generic. Civil society is the uncoerced space of human association where individuals volunteer their resources to achieve some vision of a better community. It is a dimension of philanthropy.

As a concept, civil society arose in the seventeenth and eighteenth centuries in Britain, Holland, France, and the

TABLE I. PHILANTHROPY AS:

Relief	Improvement	Social Reform	Empowerment
Operates on principle of compassion	Operates on principle of progress	Operates on principle of justice	Operates on principle of participation
Alleviates human suffering	Maximizes human potential	Solves social problems	Builds community

SOURCE: Adapted from Wisely 1995.

North American colonies in relation to quite specific historic forces. In Europe, the call for a nongovernmental sphere that addressed public issues came as a response to the religious wars of the sixteenth and seventeenth centuries. Indeed the first use in English of the phrase "civil society" was in 1596 by Richard Hooker in questioning the establishment of the Church of England. The argument made against the mixing of religion and the state, and the human carnage that was produced as Catholic kingdoms battled Protestant kingdoms for religious hegemony, was that there should be a state-society separation and that religion was to be part of the society, not the state. A second force was the rise of nonstatist commercial society that objected to the state's dominance of economic affairs. The rise of commercial society and its eventual transformation into capitalism viewed civil society as a legitimate sphere of independent activity, free of the state, and largely self-governing. Some of its major theorists—the Physiocrats, Adam Smith, and others—saw commercial society as dampening the destructive heroics of the state, and civil society as a way interests checked interests to achieve improved welfare. The pursuit of interest in terms of the requirements and responsibilities for contracts is also thought to have added to the humanitarian sensibility of the period, a situation where merchants and manufacturers also were in the vanguard of antislavery movements and those aimed at improving public health by improving the conditions of workers.

The U.S. colonial contribution to the tradition of civil society was the insistence on the legitimacy of nonstatist organizations in the conduct of public affairs. Indeed, the Mayflower Compact is the bylaws of a voluntary association. Without going into the Great Awakening, dissent, and congregational government, the religious sources of philanthropy are many and deep in the U.S. experience.

It is interesting to note how civil society was to be implemented in two contrasting incidents. Both countries were seeking to overcome despotism in the same period of history; each brought a different valuation of voluntary action to the enactment of fundamental legislation. In Revolutionary France, seeing "ancient, voluntary institutions" as part of the structure of despotism, the Declaration of the Rights of Man (1789) ordained that no intermediate institution could come between the citizen and the state without the permission of the state. In contrast, the First Amendment to the U.S. Constitution (1791) said that Congress could not pass a law that would come between a citizen and his or her intermediate institution. It is also interesting to note that the Le Chapelier Act, which made voluntary associations illegal, was not repealed by the French government until 1901.

While "civil society" remained a debated concept in the nineteenth century and early twentieth (e.g., Hegel, Marx, and Gramsci), it reappeared full blast in the 1970s in Spain and Latin America and in the 1980s in Eastern Europe and the former Soviet Union when individuals began to question the monopolistic practices of the state regarding what in other polities was accomplished through voluntary associations. The rediscovery there of the importance for individual growth of an uncoerced space for individuals voluntarily to seek for a better society stimulated interest in idea of civil society everywhere. That the advocates of civil society then often became the rulers of the postcommunist regimes presented them with the dilemmas of their commitment to voluntary action and the need for them to use state power to consolidate a new state.

Phrases such as statist and non-statist need a conceptual framework—one that will clarify the public policy implications of philanthropy. See Figure I.

For all the key needs of any group—shelter, education, salvation, nourishment, security, and so forth—there are several modes of providing them: the state, the for-profit sector, the household sector, and the philanthropic sector (nonprofit sector or civil society). What eventually constitutes an aspect of public policy or public practice is which sector is expected to produce what, for whom, and to what degree. This includes how it is paid for—by taxation or coercion, by familial obligation, by voluntary contribution, or as a commodity to be bought and sold. Different sectors are replied upon at different times for different necessities. "Culture" in one state at one time may be the province of the state or shared between the state, civil society, and the household. Likewise with shelter. Public housing, for-profit, household, and nonprofit shelters for the homeless exist side by side, with one sector often dominating at any one time. Security can be provided by a *levee en masse,* a voluntary militia, each household for itself, or mercenaries; goods and services by firms, guilds and coops, states, and households.

If the four sectors are seen for the purposes of later determining public policy, then certain differences and similarities must be noted. Each sector differs by structure and language of authority, dominant resources, and a "bottom line" by which outcomes are evaluated. The state operates under the constraint of dealing with whole categories, the market operates on the constraint of profit, and philanthropy on the principle of no self-inurement. What the sectors do in general and in particular differ over time. The degree of independence differs; there are communities in existence today where the household sector and the state are indistinguishable, the for-profit sector is intermittent and marginal, and the nonprofit sector is an occasional wandering mendicant or a hapless representative from Oxfam. There are other times and places when the sectors are quite distinct and there is considerable contest over their roles. Indeed, the present postcommunist regimes are experimenting with the reemergence of the for-profit and nonprofit sectors and more is dependent on the household sector than was the case in the previous regimes. See Figure II.

FIGURE I

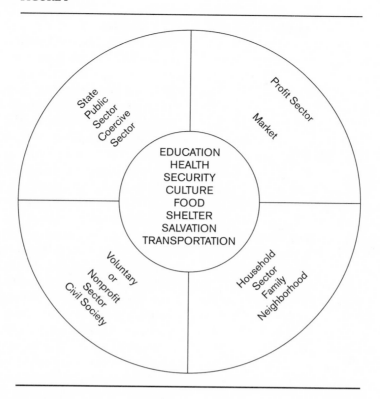

FIGURE II

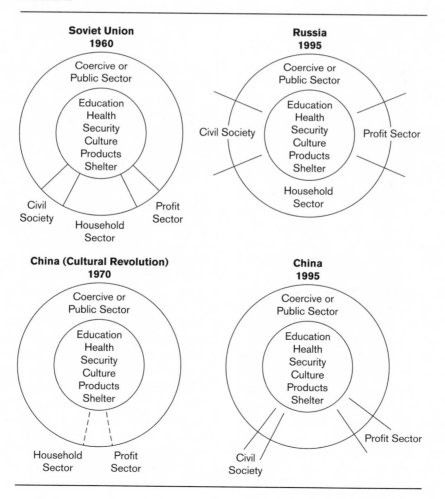

FIGURE III

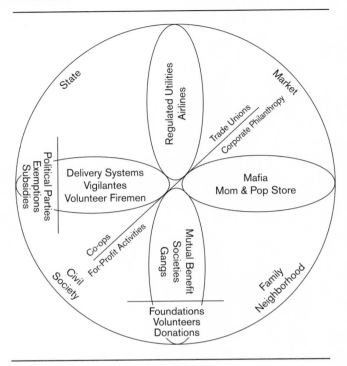

Rather than seeing the sectors as totally distinct, however, Figure III shows the ways the sectors overlap, contribute to each other, and frequently merge.

In other words, the philanthropic sector (or nonprofit sector or civil society) includes foundations, charitable trusts, religious assemblies, private nonprofit organizations (variously called: NPOs, NGOs, INGOs, CBOs, GRSOs, PVOs, QUANGOs), unions, cooperatives, political parties, associations, advocacy groups, and so forth.

The decision of which sector to produce what for whom for any society at any time can be comprehended as an amalgam of the wishes of those who rule, what is tolerated as practice among those who are "minorities," and historical accident. Contemporary economists have explained choice of the nonprofit sector as the result of it undertaking activities where profit maximization would be contrary to the trust that consumers wish to invest in those who provide the service, such as care of the elderly or the very young. Others see choice of the nonprofit sector as a result of governments unable or unwilling to provide what is deemed a necessity by some group for itself or for other groups. That more demand a product than official supply can satisfy or are willing to pay for it, or that the particularity of its implementation exceeds the tendency of the state to allocate by categories—these conditions are said to encourage voluntary associations to accept the responsibility.

It is more persuasive, however, to look at choice of sector as the product of historical chance and values. The experience with most voluntary institutions in U.S. history has

been benign, frequently positive, and much lauded in official prose; likewise with India. Revolutionary France and the recent communist regimes, on the other hand, found most voluntary associations as enemies of equality and social justice and, in the case of the communist regimes, philanthropy in all of its manifestations was seen as a facade for capitalist institutions to maintain their hegemony over the state. Today, however, there is a brief moment where the costs of providing welfare in socialist and conservative regimes alike see increased reliance on the nonprofit sector to be the norm, both for reducing costs and increasing effectiveness. On the other hand, in the United States for example, what had essentially been the province of philanthropy and the state—health care—is now increasingly part of the for-profit sector, and distinctive modes of operation of each sector in health care are being erased.

It is instructive to look at the interrelationship of philanthropy, public policy, and public administration in a particular context and time. Take the United States as an example. Those who refer to the philanthropic sector in the United States (or nonprofit sector or civil society) as a sector *qua* sector are of fairly recent origin. One author describes this as "inventing the nonprofit sector" and places the consciousness of its size, importance, and political relevance to the mid-1970s, roughly corresponding to the dates of the Filer Commission (Hall 1992).

Its growth in the United States, surely, is a factor for special recognition. The last comprehensive count in 1992 identified the "third sector" as including 1,426,000 organizations, 341,000 of which were churches and 689,000 charitable nonprofit organizations. The number of unregistered and informal voluntary organizations defy estimation. In 1994, charitable nonprofits and churches received $568 billion and expended $487. Including volunteers as full-time equivalents, the total employment of nonprofits—paid and volunteered, religious and charitable—represents 10.6 percent of total U.S. employment. It has been estimated that from one nonprofit organization per 4,000 population in 1950, the sector grew to one nonprofit organization per 400 in 1990.

A major public policy issue in the United States is how this sector is and should be regulated. In almost every respect, philanthropy (the nonprofit sector, the independent sector, civil society) is the least regulated of all—far less regulated than government itself, the for-profit sector, and the household sector. The origins of this relative independence are several. While appearing arcane, one major source is the Elizabethan Statutes of Charitable Uses (1601). This act of Parliament guaranteed that for individuals who left "trusts" for purposes of public benefit—religious, charitable, educational, and public convenience—these trusts, if not mismanaged, would be free from expropriation by the state, thus reversing the precedent set by Henry VIII. The enforcement of this was placed in the hands of the Lord Chancellor, a practice that is followed today with the states' attorneys general in courts of law as the protector of the sanctity of trusts and donations. Moreover, the implication of the statute was that taxation of trusts constituted expropriation and hence was illegal, reinforcing the latter-day principle of tax exemption for charitable activities.

Although the Elizabethan Statutes were repealed by many of the states after 1787, the statute was read back into U.S. law through several constitutional cases, chiefly, the *Magill v. Brown* (1833) and *Girard Will* (1844) cases. The special status of endowments and the activity of public benefit was also protected by the contract clause of the Constitution. It is perhaps paradoxical that the major case establishing the character of corporations and hence of industrial capitalism in the United States, the *Dartmouth College Case* (1819), pertains to an "eleemosynary corporation" which was threatened by "state takeover" of its Board of Trustees.

The second major source of the independence of philanthropy, broadly conceived, is the First Amendment as applied to Congress and the Fourteenth Amendment applying the First Amendment to the States. Not only are the restrictive clauses about religion present there, as well as protections of speech and press, but in the right to peaceably assemble and petition government, the Amendment lays the foundation that transforms "assembly" into "association," hence the privileged position in constitutional law of voluntary association, along with voluntary giving and voluntary serving.

The privilege is hardly absolute. What constitutes an association of public benefit has been and is contested at various levels of government. As the prohibition against expropriation finds itself chiefly in the tax code, it may be useful to show how various governments have treated the income of nonprofit organizations. The privilege of tax exemption extends to organizations of public benefit where the nondistributional constraint is accepted (the prohibition against self-inurement on the part of its governance) as well as to those established as trusts. As most nonprofit organizations are exempt from local property and excise taxes, state corporate income and excise taxes, and federal corporate income tax, as well as charitable donations being tax-deductible for donors, it is not surprising that it has been in the tax code where the chief regulation has occurred.

Through efforts by communities, states, and the federal government, what is and what is not of public benefit has been defined and redefined in specific cases, as have specific answers to questions about whether inurement taints the status of particular religious organization and hence its exemption, or whether income from certain types of activities deemed unrelated to philanthropic mission are open to taxation. Moreover the protection against the establishment of religion has sent innumerable rules back to the states seeking through legislation to support prayer or

transportation to parochial schools, while prohibitions of animal slaughter, "nonpublic schooling," conscription, or requirements for various health interventions have been deemed infringements of the free exercise of religion. Whether the benefit is experienced by those who are an appropriate category for charity or whether the benefit assumes a burden government would otherwise have to shoulder are questions that are still being debated in specific cases. These more restrictive formulations of what constitutes philanthropy have become increasingly common as the idea of "tax expenditure" has been accepted in the 1970s, that is, the view that philanthropic activity enjoys a subsidy by the state and its taxpayers and hence must be viewed restrictively.

The landmarks of tax policy in this area at the federal level have been, following on the heels of the Sixteenth Amendment (1913), the 1913 Internal Revenue law that recognized tax exemption and deductibility for purposes of the federal income taxes; the 1934 revenue act which forbade interference in legislation and undertaking "propaganda" by nonprofit organizations; the 1936 act that extended deductibility to gifts by corporations; the 1950 revenue act that established the principle of taxation for unrelated business income of nonprofits; the 1954 revenue code that codified into eventually 25 categories the varieties of tax-exempt organizations; and the 1969 Tax Reform Act that, among many things, reclassified public charities, forced the divestiture by most foundations of stock in parent organizations, and established the principle that private independent foundations would pay an excise cess and thus potentially affect their long-term existence. The cess was dedicated to oversight of "tax-exempt entities" by the Internal Revenue Service.

There remains in 1996 the issue of whether to develop a system of intermediate sanctions, that is, steps between having and losing tax exemption and tax deductibility. The lack of intermediate sanctions, it is argued, makes the Internal Revenue Service timid in its oversight. Moreover, the regulatory role of nonprofits by the taxation system in the U.S. may be sharply attenuated if Congress adopts a flat tax without exemptions for philanthropy.

Various states have tried to regulate how much can be spent on fund-raising by voluntary associations and who can fund-raise. While registration of independent fundraisers remains acceptable, efforts at setting regulations as to amount spent, and the means and sites of solicitation have usually been decided, using the First Amendment, in favor of the nonprofit organizations. In speech issues, the record has also been mostly on the side of nonprofit organizations, except in times of national emergency and more recently in the tangled cases of what speech can be "conditioned" in order to receive federal funds. In 1996 discussion began concerning a more explicit effort to regulate political activity of nonprofits through conditioning eligibility for government grants.

Despite these many incidents circumscribing the edges of civil society, in the main the nonprofit world is virtually unregulated by governments. Only eight states put any energy behind registration and vigilance. The agency charged with overseeing nonprofit organizations in most states is the most Dickensian residue in that particular government—least well supported in personnel and resources, last in computerization, and unreliable for statistics. At the federal level, though much is made of the role of the Internal Revenue Service, the audits are few in number. More convincingly, the nonprofit world is thought so "trustworthy"—unlike government and the for-profit economy—that Congress does not even see fit to appropriate general tax dollars to support nonprofit oversight of the IRS, but relies instead on the excise cess on private foundations.

While the states and the federal government entertain legislation that would curtail or support nonprofit organizations in their work and hence regulate them, the major form of detailed public regulation today in the United States, at least in the health and human service fields, comes through nonprofit organizations contracting with governments to provide services. "Contracting out" permits governments to determine modalities and quality of service. It is argued that this form of regulation reduces the capacity of a nonprofit organization to tailor their services to their beneficiaries and hence mitigates a strength of nonprofit organizations. It is also argued that nonprofit organizations are weakened in their voluntary governance and use of volunteers in delivering services by the conditions imposed by getting and keeping government contracts. With the possibility of block grants to states and local governments in areas where contracting has been common for the federal government, the dimensions of government regulation of nonprofit organizations through grants and contracts may be redefined.

Through laws, constitutional amendments, and policies, governments in the United States have shaped philanthropy. They have given its institutions their modes of governance, its practitioners their boundaries for action. Government resources (i.e., authority, economic goods and services, information, status, and coercion) have defined how civil society operates. In return, it may be said that philanthropy has determined the agendas of governments. By using their resources, voluntary associations, organized philanthropy, or the components of civil society have raised the questions about existing policies—how and on what governments use their resources to secure some level of behavior thought desirable by those who predominate. It has been the role of voluntary associations to use their resources (i.e., legitimacy, economic goods and services, status, information, and violence) to bring about changes in how governments use their resources—getting more or less of a behavior considered relevant to the good life.

The history of public policy in America is the history of individuals with a moral vision of "how things should be," using that vision to persuade others to share the value and their resources to achieve the value in practice, and converting those resources through organization into a force to affect the state's authoritative allocations. Virtually every law and pending question for public discussion had its origin in civil society: creating a republic in the colonial period, forging a stronger central government, relations with Native Americans, abolition of slavery, temperance, common schools, public sanitation, rehabilitation of the mentally distressed and the criminal, capital punishment, abolition of child and sweated labor, woman suffrage, civil rights, gender and sexual identity equality, environment, availability of alcohol and tobacco, nuclear disarmament, alternative energy forms, and so on. To see these organizations primarily as lobbies or pressure groups is to miss the moral component that impels individuals to struggle for the maintenance of the order or to bring about change.

A more specific case in point has been the efforts of philanthropic foundations to affect the public agenda. The history of civil rights, voter registration, and public health requires acknowledgment of the central role played by the Carnegie Corporation, the Ford Foundation, and the Rockefeller Foundation respectively. Indeed, some observers see the nationalizing movement of the twentieth century towards the federal government as chief catalyst for social change to be rooted in the efforts of private foundations (Katz and Karl 1987). Likewise, one cannot analyze the contemporary agenda without referring to the role of conservative foundations and "think tanks."

The relationship between philanthropy and public policy has clearly been two-way. What are some of the major public policy and public administration questions that will arise in the future regarding philanthropy in the United States and elsewhere? These questions are both technical and theoretical. On the technical level, there is the question about the education leaders in philanthropy ought to have in order to strengthen their contributions. The present efforts to adapt business and public management knowledge to the nonprofit setting, especially in the United States, may be misspent. This is so because the presumption of obedience of citizens, the availability of tax dollars for programs, and universalism of public policy (treating individuals in terms of categories) inherent in education for the public service do not obtain for those working in nonprofit organizations. In the latter, beneficiaries need not accept, resources must be found, and the strength of the sector is that it deals with individuals in their greater individuality than the categorical constraint will allow for public laws. A similar dilemma is posed by educating nonprofit managers in programs geared to business: if one of the dangers to civil society is the growing commercialization of nonprofit organizations, would education in a setting that took marketing and profit maximization as goods further that trend?

The more theoretical issues are ones that deal with the health or "illhealth" of philanthropy, civil society, nonprofit organizations, and voluntary associations. For instance, if civil society is repressed (as it was in Spain and Latin America) or suppressed (as it was in the former Soviet Union and in Eastern and Central Europe), can civil society recover? Another pressing question: in those places where considerable development of nonprofit organizations carrying important civil society functions has taken place, and those organizations now face an erosion in membership and suffer from a general public malaise in attitude towards government and achieving public purposes, can philanthropic organizations and governments invest in reversing the erosion? More contemporary is the question: in the forecast realignment of the roles of the sectors regarding welfare in the U.S. and elsewhere, what will be the tension points and cooperative opportunities between public organizations and nonprofit organizations? Likewise in an era when evaluating outcomes is becoming more important than assessing outputs (e.g., what the presence or absence of a youth organization may do to reducing juvenile crime rather than a census of youth served) can a system of public regulation be designed that not only prevents fraud, but also enhances performance?

There are also several questions that have international implications. For instance, can national governments, struggling with global economic competition and adopting low wage or high skill strategies for competitiveness, contain the inequalities thereby created within the polity or within civil society? What role will philanthropic organizations play in negotiating differences in these increasingly divided communities, especially where the state is thought to be compromised? Another question relates to the emerging international dimensions of governments and nonprofit organizations: can the emergence of nonprofit organizations on a worldwide scale, dependent on worldwide and nonnational sources of revenue, develop cooperative relationships within regimes where they work and with international quasi-governmental bodies like the European Community and the United Nations?

In brief, public administration and public policy can be enriched by an understanding of philanthropy. The reverse is also true.

WARREN F. ILCHMAN

BIBLIOGRAPHY

Bowen, William G. *et al.*, 1994. *The Charitable Nonprofits.* San Francisco, CA: Jossey-Bass Publishers.
Gellner, Ernest, 1994. *Conditions of Liberty: Civil Society and Its Rivals.* New York: Allen Lane and The Penguin Press.
Hall, Peter Dobkin, 1992. *Inventing the Nonprofit Sector.* Baltimore, MD: The Johns Hopkins University Press.
Haskell, Thomas L., 1985. "Capitalism and the Origins of the Humanitarian Sensibility." *American Historical Review,* vol. 90, Part 1 (April) 339–360 and Part 2 (May) 547–566.
Hirschman, A. O., 1977. *The Passions and the Interests.* Princeton, NJ: Princeton University Press.
Ilchman, Warren F., Stanley Katz, and Edward W. Queen, II, eds., 1996. *Philanthropy and Culture in Comparative Perspective.* Bloomington: Indiana University Press.
Ilchman, Warren F. and Norman Thomas Uphoff, 1996. *The Political Economy of Change.* Rev. ed. New Brunswick, NJ: Transaction Press.
Independent Sector, 1992. *Nonprofit Almanac 1992–1993.* San Francisco, CA: Jossey-Bass Publishers.
Karl, Barry D. and Stanley N. Katz, 1987. "Foundations and the Ruling Class Elites." *Daedalus,* vol. 116/1 (Winter) 1–40.
Payton, Robert L., 1988. *Philanthropy: Voluntary Action for the Public Good.* New York: Macmillan Publishing Company.
Perez-Diaz, Victor M., 1993. *The Return of Civil Society: The Emergence of Democratic Spain.* Cambridge, MA: Harvard University Press.
Powell, Walter W., ed. 1987. *The Nonprofit Sector: A Research Handbook.* New Haven, CT: Yale University Press.
Putnam, Robert D., 1993. *Making Democracy Work: Civic Traditions in Modern Italy.* Princeton, N. J.: Princeton University Press.
Salamon, Lester M. and Helmut K. Anheier, 1994. *The Emerging Sector: An Overview.* Baltimore, MD: The Johns Hopkins Press.
Schneewind, J. B., ed., 1996. *The Faces of Charity: Philanthropy and Charity in the West.* Bloomington: Indiana University Press.
Smith, Steven R. and Michael Lipsky, 1993. *Nonprofits for Hire: The Welfare State in the Age of Contracting.* Cambridge, MA: Harvard University Press.
Walzer, Michael, 1991. "The Idea of Civil Society: A Path to Reconstruction." *Dissent,* vol. 35 (Spring) 293–304.
Weisbrod, Burton A., 1988. *The Nonprofit Economy.* Cambridge, MA: Harvard University Press.
Wisely, D. Susan, 1995. *A Foundation's Relationship to Its Public.* Indianapolis: Indiana University Center on Philanthropy.
Yamamoto, Tadashi, ed., 1995. *Emerging Civil Society in the Asia Pacific Community.* Tokyo: Japanese Center for International Exchange.

PHILANTHROPY, HISTORICAL AND PHILOSOPHICAL FOUNDATIONS.

The evolution and development of systems of beliefs and related actions that result in benevolence towards others, that serve a public good, and that do not entail expectations of disproportionate reciprocity.

Definitions of Philanthropy

(1) Action or behavior based on a belief system stressing benevolence towards others; (2) the practice of making contribution(s) of monetary value to a humane cause or a common good; (3) sometimes used as a surrogate for "philanthropic sector," or a synonym for independent sector, nonprofit sector, or third sector.

Derived from the Greek "love for mankind," the literal antonym is misanthropy ("hatred of mankind"). However, just as "The tragedy of love is indifference" (William

Somerset Maugham, *Of Human Bondage,* p. 4), not hate, so too the practical opposite of philanthropy is covetousness and apathy, not hatred of mankind.

The first definition, action or behavior based on a belief system stressing benevolence towards others, relates to a system of beliefs that encourage and characterize actions or behaviors of private, public, and corporate individuals aimed at accomplishing some public good. The definition rendered by the *Oxford English Dictionary* (1989), "the disposition or active effort to promote the happiness and well-being of one's fellow-(humans)," best applies here; as does Van Til's (1990) "Philanthropy I (one) . . . the human act of caring magnanimously for others and seeking to bring the good to fruition" (p. 24). This meaning has the closest relationship to altruism and to love (in its platonic and theistic meanings); and is the moral purpose that defines and differentiates philanthropies from institutions comprising the other two sectors (private enterprise and government) (Payton et al., 1988, p. 1). The National Society of Fund-raising Executives defines philanthropy as "The philosophy and practice of giving to nonprofit organizations through financial and other contributions" (National Society of Fund-raising Executives Institute 1986, p. 5). Note that all these definitions establish that philanthropy is both idea and action, not one or the other: thinking philanthropic thoughts without acting upon them is no more philanthropy than is doing something that looks philanthropic for all the wrong reasons. Neither ascetic piety in seclusion nor performing public service because a court sentences someone to do so is philanthropy.

The second definition, the practice of making contribution(s) of monetary value to a humane cause or a common good, applies to a formal economic practice which redistributes resources in a fashion presumed—or calculated—to accomplish some commonly held notion of "good." This is Van Til's (1990) "Philanthropy II" (p. 24), the organized process that seeks to further a philanthropic belief system. This meaning of philanthropy is much more forgiving (and much less philosophically precise) than is the first definition. It is an institutionalized system that operates within the economy of its time and place. The currency of exchange in philanthropy is everything economic (i.e., money, goods, and services).

In general, literature equates this meaning with charity (including volunteerism); some scholars have differentiated it, calling acts of mercy to relieve suffering "charity," acts of community to enhance the quality of life and ensure a better future "philanthropy" (Payton et al. 1988), and support for high culture (i.e., scholarship, art, science, music, and the like) "patronage" (Feingold 1987, p. 156). Governments authorize, influence, and encourage this practice by awarding tax benefits (see **charitable contributions**).

The third definition, a surrogate for "philanthropic sector," or a synonym for independent sector, nonprofit sector, or third sector, describes a sector of relatively discrete laws and management principles; the other sectors are the private or corporate sector and the public or government sector (see **independent sector** for further discussion of this definition).

This article will examine the historical and philosophical roots of philanthropy (per the first definition) and will construct, from this foundation, a functional definition of "a philanthropic belief system."

History of Philanthropy as a Belief System

The meaning of philanthropy is fundamental to any theory of human nature and any discourse on human behavior; it is a system of beliefs and related actions that emerge from the first known writings on religion and social organization.

The *Egyptian Book of the Dead* (around 4000 B.C.E.) praised those who gave bread for the hungry and water for the thirsty (Gurin and Van Til, 1990, p. 4), but the first comprehensive philanthropic belief system appeared in the Old Testament, written some 1500 B.C.E. There, the God of the Jews commanded that all things were His essence and, therefore, the human notion of property ownership was transient and virtual, not literal. This established two fundamental principles for philanthropic behavior: one was that all people, including the poor and hungry, have a right to food and shelter and that the temporal "owners" of these commodities have a responsibility to make them available; the other was the principle of "stewardship" which later formed the foundation of Christian and most modern-day philanthropy (Curti 1973, p. 488). In this fashion, Jews were commanded that philanthropy is a duty, not an option, due to all human beings (to the extent that beneficiaries were prioritized, they were: family first, then coreligionists, then all others).

The Hebrew word *tzedakah*—the closest literal parallel to the word philanthropy—is generally interpreted as meaning an act of kindness entailing both charity and righteous living. In the early thirteenth century, the biblical scholar Maimonides offered Jews a behavioral code of *tzedakah* with eight levels, ranging from the simplest to the most exemplary and worthy. These are, to give: (1) but sadly; (2) less than is fitting but in good humor; (3) only after having been asked; (4) before being asked; (5) in such a manner that the donor does not know who the recipient is; (6) in such a manner that the recipient does not know who the donor is; (7) in such a way that neither donor nor recipient know each other; (8) not alms but help which enables the poor to rehabilitate themselves by lending them money, taking them into partnership, employing them, or giving them work, for in these ways aid is given without any loss of self-respect (ben Maimon 1979, pp. 89–93).

Other pre-Christian organized religions and social systems treated philanthropy differently: some restricted its terms, limited it to the notion of charity (almsgiving) or circumscribed its applicability. Hindu scripture commanded charitable almsgiving in order to support the religion's holy men. Chinese thinkers—including Confucius and the Taoists (of around 500 B.C.E.)—seem to have applied the principles of philanthropy only to extended family, friends and coreligionists up until the early 1800s (Curti 1973, pp. 486–487). The more expansive teachings of India's Buddha (about 450 B.C.E.) created a religion based on temperance, charity for the poor, and the admonition "In five ways should a clansman minister to his friends and familiars—by generosity, courtesy, and benevolence, by treating them as he treats himself, and by being as good as his word" (in Marts, *Man's Concern for His Fellow Man* 1961). And the Moslem Koran commands almsgiving and says, too, that the poor and hungry have a right to such charity.

The ancient Greeks, who gave us *philanthropia* (love for man), assigned its duty to God. Plato defined *philanthropia* as the love of God for humanity, to which Plutarch added that God's love for man is somehow different (and presumably more beneficent) than God's love for other animals (Constantelos 1968, p. 4). The ancient Greeks were given little encouragement or direction regarding the human practice of philanthropy. While individual acts of charity and patronage certainly did occur (anc. King Alexander founded Alexandria University in northern Egypt during the fourth century B.C.E.), on the whole, poverty and deprivation were viewed as necessary and appropriate elements of social order. "Instead of finding means to drive the poor out of poverty (the Byzantines') moral philosophy and religious feelings made poverty easy to endure and to continue" (Constantelos 1968, p. 284).

The ancient Romans' esteem for property and property ownership was such that poverty was considered dishonoring. Debtors could be sold into a slavery to pay off debts, thus subordinating their human value to their property value. And, while there was great patronage for the arts and culture, moral thinkers of the day thought it natural to recoil in horror from a poor man (Seneca) and declared feeding the hungry to be cruelty because it simply prolonged a life of misery (Platus) (Hertz 1964, p. 929).

Christianity, a religion born in poverty, like Judaism focused the notion of public good on the welfare of the individual. Piety, not property, defined Christian virtue. And the pious faithful were drawn, like Christ, to serve and favor the poor and needy while rejecting (or at least fearing) the corrupting influence of property and wealth. This motive for Christian philanthropy is an emulative virtue—acting Christ-like—and is directly related to life after death: "A new commandment I give to you, that you love one another even as I have loved you" (John 13: 34–35). Quoting *Homily* by the fourth century Pseudo-Clementines, "The philanthropist is an imitator of God" (Constantelos 1968, p. 280). There is, as well, in the Christian ethos a certain guilt or danger associated with wealth; note Andrew

Carnegie's quoting of the biblical saying, "It is easier for a camel to enter the eye of a needle than for a rich man to enter the kingdom of heaven," to which he wryly added "the words betoken serious difficulty for the rich" (Carnegie 1962, p. 49).

As the Common Era took shape, moral thinkers secularized the belief system of Christian philanthropy. "If you have not been merciful, . . . you will not receive mercy; if you have not opened your house to the poor, you will be locked out of the Kingdom of Heaven; if you have refused bread to the hungry, you will be deprived of life eternal . . . prayer fails in its goal when it is not accompanied by charity" (Constantelos 1968, interpreting the writings of Basil the Great, p. 21). Pushed to an extreme, this system allowed for a type of redemptive philanthropy in which wealthy people believed they could buy salvation with contributions (and bequests) and sinners believed they could prove repentance by strenuous, even life-threatening, acts of charity. Constantelos (1968) relates the story of a virgin nun in 431 C.E. who felt such guilt after being seduced by a church reader that "(t)o alleviate her moral stigma she devoted her life to the service of the sick and the lepers" (p. 21). By the late seventeenth century, the cynical extension of this logic was spoken of openly: "We often do good, in order that we may do evil with impunity" (Duc de La Rochefoucauld, *Sentences and Moral Maxims*, 1678, quoted in Feingold 1987).

St. Paul elevated the Jewish dictum of stewardship to the center of Christian philanthropy and was given contemporary eloquence, some 1,800 years later, by Andrew Carnegie: "Poor and restricted are our opportunities in this life, narrow our horizon, our best work most imperfect; but rich men should be thankful for one inestimable boon. They have it in their power during their lives to busy themselves in organizing benefactions from which the masses of their fellows will derive lasting advantage, and thus dignify their own lives" (Carnegie 1962, p. 25). Wealth enables philanthropy, and philanthropy justifies wealth: referring to an ancient Roman patron of the arts, Carnegie asserted "Without wealth there can be no Maecenas" (Carnegie 1962, p. 15).

The U.S. Belief System

The United States inherited a belief in philanthropy, predating the arrival of the first European immigrants, from the natives who populated the continent and its islands. Columbus recounted that the gentle Indians of the Bahama Islands who greeted him were "engenuous and free" with all they had, gave away anything that was asked of them, and bestowed each gift "with as much love as if their hearts went with it" (quoted in Bremner 1988, p. 5). Squanto, a Native American once kidnapped by an Englishman and sold into slavery, escaped and returned to

New England where, "during the starving time at Plymouth in the winter of 1620–21," he provided the highest form of philanthropy—he taught the colonists how to become self-sufficient: "How to set their corn, where to take fish, and to procure other commodities, and was also their pilot to bring them to unknown places for their profit, and never left them till he died" (Bremner 1988, pp. 5–6). The existence of documented acts of philanthropy by Native Americans whose form and consistency suggest a belief system paralleling the tenets of Judeo-Christian philanthropy implies that there are many parallel lines to the history and evolution of U.S. philanthropy.

The belief system undergirding contemporary U.S. philanthropy was influenced during the seventeenth and eighteenth centuries by the unique democracy and condition of religious thought that characterized the land. The leadership provided by William Penn was fueled by a devout belief—like most Quakers—in class distinctions as God-ordained social imperatives along with an equally strong commitment to the ideal of stewardship. Cotton Mather (one of the most influential early writers on U.S. philanthropic beliefs) reflected the teachings of the Old Testament when he wrote in 1710 that the performance of good works is an obligation owed to God rather than a means of salvation. His recognition of the need to enlist the support of others in benevolent undertakings (Bremner 1988, pp. 12–13) presaged the approach to organized beneficence and social action observed by de Tocqueville. And, while throughout Europe wealthy people gave large gifts for relief but the idea of charity for prevention was unheard of, visionary leaders like Benjamin Franklin guided the new nation's developing beliefs by insisting "that the purpose of philanthropy is to prevent the distresses of mankind, rather than simply to try to ameliorate them when they had occurred" (Rusk 1961, p. 9).

The following famous account by Alexis de Tocqueville (1862) of how social action and philanthropy occurred in the states during the early 1800s portrays how people responded to the new and experimental democracy which stripped them of class identity and title and established a uniform interdependence based on the relative powerlessness of each citizen (relative to the power held by one aristocrat back in England).

These American are the most peculiar people in the world. You'll not believe it when I tell you how they behave. In a local community in their country a citizen may conceive of some need which is not being met. What does he do? He goes across the street and discusses it with his neighbor. Then what happens? A committee comes into existence and then the committee begins functioning on behalf of that need, and you won't believe this but it's true. All of this is done without reference to any bureaucrat. All of this is done by the private citizens on their own initiative.

Americans of all ages, all conditions, and all dispositions consistently form associations . . . to give entertainments, to found seminaries, to build inns, to construct churches, to diffuse books . . .

The health of a democratic society may be measured by the quality of functions performed by private citizens.

There is no indication that our founding determination to separate church and state was intended to limit or define the government's role relative to philanthropy, though it has been a persistent debate. Our first Catholic president linked philanthropic government to the salvation of wealthy U.S. citizens: "If a free society cannot help the many who are poor, it cannot save the few who are rich" (John F. Kennedy, presidential inaugural speech, January 20, 1961). Political debates surrounding similar quotes from Franklin Roosevelt, Robert Kennedy, Hubert Humphrey, and other less apparently ecumenical quotes from John F. Kennedy are apt to center on the conflicting ideal of humanitarian government and policies favoring rugged and unfettered economic individualism (or "benign neglect").

If "philanthropy . . . is the instrument that societies have used to compensate for the indifference of the marketplace and the incompetence of the state" (Payton 1988, p. 41), then a competent (and compassionate) state would reduce the need for philanthropy. By choosing the extent of its own subsidy, government plays a large role in setting the agenda for organized philanthropy. So, for example, whereas U.S. public libraries generally have been fully supported functions of government, should government choose (as it has with public broadcasting), it could reduce its own expenses and turn these, too, into philanthropic dependencies. The same can be said of public schools, parks, hospitals, prisons, and so forth. (Conversely, it may be argued that the presence of large organized philanthropy releases governments of its fundamental responsibility to meet the basic needs of all its citizens.) This discussion is further complicated by the evolving trend of privatizing public services: while government agencies may themselves solicit and benefit from philanthropic contributions, private for-profit corporations cannot under current law. More importantly, any constituencies for which privatized public agencies bear some responsibility will be seriously threatened on the philanthropic landscape since fewer people may be inclined to contribute charity, time, patronage, or even sympathy to support or collaborate with for-profit corporations. At the same time, there is no U.S. tradition suggesting that the marketplace has any philanthropic responsibility, notwithstanding the 1936 federal law permitting corporations an exemption of up to 5 percent of net income for charity.

A great tradition of U.S. democracy is our recognition, repentance for, and occasional efforts to resolve class inequalities even while we manifestly perpetuate them as we individually strive to move our families from lower to middle to upper class status. So it is that writers have noted the contribution that philanthropy can make to perpetuating class differences even while investing in their dissolution. Andrew Carnegie (1962) led the charge for responsible and organized philanthropy: "one of the serious obstacles to the improvement of our race is indiscriminate charity. . . . Of every thousand dollars spent in so-called charity to-day (sic), it is probable that nine hundred and fifty dollars is unwisely spent—so spent, indeed, as to produce the very evils which it hopes to mitigate or cure" (p. 26).

The U.S. consciousness is conflicted by its bootstrap/ ethos versus its heritage of Judeo-Christian stewardship. As is true of virtually every institution and belief system in America, philanthropy has its detractors, cynics, and manipulators. Often it is attacked through the subtlety of language, when such phrases as "the deserving poor" and "the innocent (presumably versus 'guilty') victims of AIDS" enter the discussion of whom we believe should benefit from philanthropy. Often, more overtly, contemporary organized philanthropy comes under attack from the left— where some view it as imperial, isolated from its truly needy beneficiaries, piloted by the noblesse oblige of the most visible contributors (the elite rich), or exacerbating even deeper problems—and from the right, where some view it as a disruption of the natural laws of economics. The resulting irony is that major donors and administrators of philanthropies are treated with both esteem and cynicism . . . sometimes, even, disdain. The public debate is common: "Newspaper and magazine editors decry the activities of 'do gooders' and 'bleeding hearts'; conservatives denounce 'sentimental humanitarianism'; and radicals sneer at the 'palliatives' offered by 'mere philanthropic reform'" (Bremner 1988, p. 2).

Finally, the belief system that gives rise to philanthropy interacts with the larger societal beliefs and expectations held for those who do philanthropy as a profession. In meeting the public good, there is an expectation that they are somehow doing it on everyone's behalf and that everyone's capital or emotional investment (contributors and noncontributors alike) is somehow tied up in their efforts. Charitable trust laws institutionalize these beliefs and establish stringent fiduciary responsibilities. Even though philanthropy is comprised of actions and behaviors of fault-ridden, error-prone, and ethically-challenged human beings, society holds the belief that the formal practice of philanthropy, insofar as it is related to altruism, is—or ought to be—an unmitigated good; so society as a whole is relatively unaccepting of faults, errors and moral turpitude among organized philanthropy's practitioners. Another common condition of our era is the tendency to be cynical, distrustful, or even disdainful of anyone who self-reports his or her profession as doing selfless public good. (*The Oxford English Dictionary* draws a fine, if not amusing,

point on this distrust by innocently defining "a professional philanthropist, a worker for a charitable or grant-awarding institution" as a "philanthropoid.") In this context, not only do high-profile leaders of philanthropic institutions who are found to criminally abuse their positions fall farther (and more permanently) into disgrace than do private sector crooks; their fall reverberates to the very core of how we might see ourselves as a people, whether or not—and how we might—exercise philanthropy, and perhaps, whether we view the human condition with optimism or defeat.

Defining Philanthropy's Belief System

Van Til (1990) proposes that "philanthropy is, first, an intentional process of voluntary action, voluntary service, and voluntary giving aimed at advancing the public good. Here it is the disposition that is critical, the *intention* of the individual philanthropist and the individual recipient of the philanthropic donation to serve the good of humankind by a particular contribution of time, energy, or money. . . . Among the contributions provided by the donee to the philanthropic venture, therefore, is the linkage of philanthropy to the public good" (pp. 33–34). From Van Til we can lift the two variables of *motive* and *public good* that may enables us to interpret and differentiate belief systems that have compelled or given rise to philanthropic action, and to devise a clear definition of what is meant by a "philanthropic belief system."

Examining the variables of motive and public good opens the door to some of the great philosophical debates concerning philanthropy. And, in the same fashion as the second definition of philanthropy ("The practice of making contribution(s) of monetary value to a humane cause or a common good") entails a formal economic exchange, the debates are compounded by the presumption that philanthropy takes place in a society differentiated by class, with haves and have-nots. So, for example, it was noted that the Byzantines may have purposefully perpetuated poverty through constant almsgiving. In so doing, were they creating a dependent class of laborers? Similarly, organized English philanthropy (supporting hospitals for the poor and building orphanages) grew markedly immediately after a great bubonic plague in London (in 1664–65) in response to concern that the shrinking population would reduce the supply of cheap labor (Wiener 1973, p. 490). Were the motives philanthropic, even if the immediate behaviors appear to be? Is contributing to (and sustaining) class differentials (and dependencies) ever a public good? (A Marxist interpretation of these two examples would contend that the underlying belief systems employed the contrivance of "philanthropy" as a kind of Trojan horse bearing political, economic, and spiritual mechanisms to colonize and mollify a dependent class of working poor.)

In "*The Gospel of Wealth*," Andrew Carnegie (1962) spoke for the first and subsequent generations of wealthy modern-day philanthropists by melding the philosophies of social darwinism and stewardship; the tension thus created is between paternalism, economic self-interest, and egalitarian outcomes. Modern-day debates about shifting ever more welfare and social service costs from government to organized philanthropy might also best be interpreted by asking "What are the motives?" and, "What public good is being served?"

Riley (1992) describes "liberal philanthropy" as a communitarian enterprise, in which "doing good . . . requires a warranted belief that the effects of one's giving will be beneficial to the community" (p. 350). Quoting Benjamin Franklin, "Liberality is not giving much but giving wisely." But whose perspective best suits them to judge the public good . . . and what is wise? The onus is on the value system used to define philanthropy's public good.

Public good must, in the end, be grounded in a value system based on fairness, equity, and respect for the dignity of the individual. If public good is determined either by the will of the majority or as a defense for a minority, it becomes a political construct. Immanuel Kant's categorical imperative—never to treat another human being as a means only but always, too, as an end—is a philosophical construct that provides such a coherent and dynamic belief system. Philanthropy can flourish based on such a belief. Christ's exhortation to "Love thy neighbor as thyself" comes close to this belief system, although (as do all iterations of the Golden Rule) it sets profound limits on the love one may give (or the value one may place on) a neighbor.

Finally, regarding public good, it should be noted that because the human mind is incapable of conceiving of all the ripples or implications of human action, we are constrained from knowing for certain that seemingly beneficent actions do not somehow or sometime cause unintended harm (John F. Kennedy was said to be troubled by this awareness). With this limitation in mind, a definition of public good can be influenced by John D. Rockefeller's admonition that "the best philanthropy . . . does the most good and the least harm" and by the medical profession's Hippocratic Oath, which exhorts its adherents to "never do harm."

The issue of motive is a difficult one. When apparently benevolent actions are motivated by economic, political, or egotistic interests (Alexander's founding of Alexandria University, for example), they are clearly strategies for accomplishing some economic, political, or egotistic goal and fall short of a definition of philanthropy.

The most serious challenge to defining philanthropy's motive is introduced by the seemingly self-evident formulation, "One-way transfers are not all philanthropic, but all philanthropic transfers are one-way" (Payton 1988, p. 47). This raises at least two complications:

1. Good acts intended to buy a place in heaven clearly do not measure up to this standard and are not philanthropic. But what, Payton asks, about good acts that are performed to comply with God's commandment? Can they be viewed as voluntary and, therefore, one-way? (p. 47) The answer must be "yes" since we voluntarily choose to adopt God's commandments. If complying with a deific mandate were to be viewed as entailing a reciprocal transfer of some sort, then, ironically, belief in God would preclude true philanthropy and, arguably only atheists would be capable of philanthropy.

2. Beneficence designed to raise the standards of a whole community, and which results in improving the benefactor's position (safety, health, aesthetics, quality of life, and so forth), is suspect. Arguably, to perform a public good in order to improve one's own quality of life as a member of that public is not philanthropy (not a one-way transfer); rather, it is seeking a return on an investment. However, as alluring as it may sound, this standard would do violence to the definition of philanthropy since only the most extreme ascetics could be expected to view any public action (or private action with public implication) as not ultimately affecting their own condition. It becomes, then, a matter of proportion: two-way transfers involving social and economic reciprocity providing return to the benefactor proportionate to $\frac{1}{n}$ (where n = the entire population of the affected public) is probably philanthropy; whereas two-way transfers providing disproportionately high returns $(>\frac{1}{n})$ may certainly result in important public good, but more aptly may be called social investment.

As you can see, we wobble dangerously close to the edge of concluding that only ascetics and atheists can do the philanthropy of our first definition. Our salvation is the recognition that humans err in trying to attach pure motives to our beliefs and actions. We are, still, of the animal kingdom, driven by the crude instincts of survival, basic comforts, and awe. Our belief systems operate in conjunction with these instincts. In this light, we can describe a philanthropic belief system:

- Charity, volunteerism and patronage can occur both within and without philanthropy. They are actions independent of motive. *The New Palgrave: A Dictionary of Economics* (Eatwell et al. 1987) notes that "altruistic preferences may be unnecessary to explain apparently altruistic behaviour" (p. 86) and their public good may be a temporal matter (what may appear beneficent in the short-term may prove destructive in the long-term, and vice versa).

- True philanthropy must be predicted on (1) the belief that it is "one-way," at least insofar as disproportionate social or economic reciprocity is concerned (Motive), and (2) the measurable certainty that the action will not only improve the condition of its beneficiaries and cause no known harm, but will do so with fairness, equity, and respect for the dignity of each individual (public good).

HANK RUBIN

BIBLIOGRAPHY

ben Maimon, 1979. *The Code of Maimonides, Book 7: The Book of Agriculture.* New Haven, CT: Yale University Press.

Bremner, Robert H., 1994. *Giving: Charity and Philanthropy in History.* New Jersey: Transaction Publishers.

———, 1988. *American Philanthropy.* 2d ed. Chicago, IL: University of Chicago Press.

Carnegie, Andrew, 1962. "The Gospel of Wealth." In Andrew Carnegie, *The Gospel of Wealth and Other Timely Essays.* Massachusetts: The Balknap Press of Harvard University Press.

Constantelos, Demetrios J., 1968. *Byzantine Philanthropy and Social Welfare.* New Jersey: Rutgers University Press.

Curti, Merle, 1973. "Philanthropy." In Philip P. Wiener, ed., *Dictionary of the History of Ideas: Studies of Selected Pivotal Ideas.* New York: Charles Scribner's Sons.

de Tocqueville, Alexis, 1862. *Democracy in America.* London: Longman, Green, Longman & Roberts.

Eatwell, John, MurrayMilgate, and Peter Newman, eds., 1987. *The New Pelgrave: A Dictionary of Economics.* London: McMillan. Vol I.

Feingold, Mordecai, 1987. "Philanthropy, Pomp, and Patronage: Historical Reflections upon the Endowment of Culture." *Daedalus* vol. 116, 1 (Winter) 155–178.

Gurin, Maurice and Jon Van Til, 1990. "Philanthropy in Its Historical Context." In Jon Van Til, ed., *Critical Issues in American Philosophy: Strengthening Theory and Practice.* San Francisco: Jossey-Bass Publishers.

Hertz, J. H., ed., 1964. *The Pentateuch and Haftorahs.* 2d ed. London: Soncino Press.

Marts, Arnaud C., 1953. *Philanthropy's Role in Civilization: Its Contribution to Human Freedom.* New York: Harper & Brothers.

———, 1961. *Man's Concern for His Fellow Man.* Geneva, New York: W.F. Humphrey Press.

Maugham, William Somerset, 1991. *Of Human Bondage.* New York: Bantam.

Miller, Howard S., 1961. *The Legal Foundations of American Philanthropy 1776–1844.* Wisconsin: The State Historical Society of Wisconsin.

National Society of Fund-raising Executives Institute, 1986. *Glossary of Fund-raising Terms.* National Society of Fund-raising Executives Institute.

Oxford University Press, 1989. *Oxford English Dictionary.* New York: Oxford University Press.

Payton, Robert L., 1988. *Philanthropy: Voluntary Action for the Public Good.* New York: MacMillan Publishing Co.

Payton, Robert, Michael Novak, Brian O'Connell, and Peter, Dobkin, 1988. *Philanthropy: Four Views.* New Jersey: Transaction Publishers.

Riley, Jonathan, 1992. "Liberal Philanthropy." In John W. Chapman and William A. Galston, eds. *Virtue.* New York: New York University Press.

Rusk, Dean, 1961. *The Role of the Foundation in American Life.* Claremont, CA: Claremont University College.

Van Til, Jon, ed., 1990. *Critical Issues in American Philanthropy: Strengthening Theory and Practice,* San Francisco, CA: Jossey-Bass Publishers.

Wiener, Philip P. ed., 1973. *Dictionary of the History of Ideas: Studies of Selected Pivotal Ideas.* New York: Charles Scribner's Sons.

PICKETING. A demonstration by one or more employees involving walking in front of a place of employment or other area of symbolic importance with signs, placards, or banners carrying political or collective bargaining messages. The purpose is to bring public attention to a labor dispute, persuade workers to join a union, and/or to discourage employees from entering their place of work. "Organizational picketing" attempts to persuade employees to join the union and accept it as their bargaining agent. "Recognition picketing" aims to obtain the employer's recognition of the union as the bargaining representative of employees. "Common situs" picketing involves both the primary employer and secondary employers that share the same general work space, such as at construction sites or a state office building. The union has a right to picket the primary employer, but the secondary employer has a right to be free from economic pressure from a union with which it has no bargaining relationship. Unions typically argue that employers that occupy the same worksite are in league together, and inherently not neutral in any labor dispute.

In the private sector, picketing may be intended to influence customers to withhold purchases from a business because of a labor dispute. Several instances have involved picketing of items sold in supermarkets, including grapes, lettuce, and apples. Organization of such consumer boycotts is legal, but picketing in support of them is an unfair labor practice under the Taft-Hartley Act.

Picketing is considered a First Amendment right (freedom of assembly and freedom of speech), guaranteed by the U.S. Supreme court in the case of *Thornhill v. Alabama,* 310 U.S. 88 (1940). However, picketing may be halted through a court injunction if it is determined to endanger public health or safety or if it is for an unlawful purpose. Picketing may be considered an unfair labor practice where a union is picketing for recognition but the employer has already recognized a different union as collective bargaining representative, or where another union has already been certified as bargaining agent. Likewise, when informational picketing results in employees of other firms that are doing business with the picketed firm refusing to cross the lines, and the flow of commerce is interrupted, an unfair labor practice may be found by the National Labor Relations Board. Picketing during a strike that becomes violent or that presents physical barriers to individuals attempting to enter the employer's property may also be illegal or constitute an unfair labor practice. Special NLRB provisions apply to "common situs" picketing, where several employers are working at the same site, such as a construction site or a shopping center. The NLRB guidelines are referred to as the Moore Dry Dock standards, named after a 1950 U.S. Supreme Court decision in which the NLRB interpreted applicable provisions of the National Labor Relations Act.

RICHARD C. KEARNEY

BIBLIOGRAPHY

Feldacker, Bruce, 1983. *Labor Guide to Labor Law.* 2d ed. Reston, VA: Reston Publishing Co.

PILLARIZATION.

A broad term referring to a multitude of processes by which compartments arise in pluralist societies. These compartments house either overlapping or mutually exclusive political, philosophical, and ideological elements, and encourage or inhibit the development of separated subcultures in a society.

Pillarization (*verzuiling,* vertical pluralism, segmented pluralism, columnization, compartmentalization) refers to a multitude of processes by which "pillars" emerge within the context of pluralist societies. Pillars (compartments, columns) parallel mutually segregated and polarized networks of organizations, each with a specific philosophical (the *Weltanschauung*) or ideological foundation. Each pillar is somehow related to its own political party. To the degree that memberships in the organization complexes are mutually exclusive and tend not to overlap, the pillars can develop into separated population groups with subcultural characteristics. The networks of organizations are active in spheres that are considered primarily secular (education, health care, labor unions, and so forth), within a society that has recognized in principle the rights of philosophical and ideological pluralism (Billiet 1984).

Anyone familiar with the sociological literature on pillarization will note that this definition, alongside a number of ever-recurring elements, has been significantly altered at five points. First, the mention of "philosophical or ideological foundations" makes the concept applicable to Belgium and avoids tedious discussions on the questions of whether or not there can be a socialist or liberal pillar. Second, spheres that are considered to be primarily secular are mentioned, since the secular or religious nature of the spheres is the object of changing societal definitions. A great deal of controversy has arisen on this point within society. Third, in order to integrate the traditions of sociologists and political scientists, the exclusive relationship with a political party is considered an essential element of pillarization. Fourth, the term "organizational complexes" is replaced by "networks of organizations" since the latter expresses much better the variability in integration and cohesion. Networks are not necessarily vast and monocentric; they can also become loose and polycentric as is more

and more the case since the 1960s in Belgium and in the Netherlands. Fifth, by referring to a multitude of processes, the discussion about the single or main historical causal factor has been avoided (emancipation of religious minorities, mobilization against secularism organized by church leaders, keeping control over the masses by the political elite). Pillars are the outcome of different kinds of interrelated processes: social, political, economical, and religious. After 1945, pillarization was closely related with the development of the "continental" type of the social security system.

Each of the components in this definition should be considered as variables that change according to period and sociopolitical unit. This was already mentioned for the network of organizations. The same argument holds for the philosophical-ideological identity of the pillars, their kind of relationship to political parties, the degree of polarization and separation, and the scope and number of societal functions that the organizations and services fulfill.

Since the middle of the 1950s, pillarization in Belgium and in the Netherlands has attracted the attention of two separate disciplines in the social sciences. On the one hand, there is a sociological tradition that, following J. P. Kruyt (1957), considers pillarization as a structural phenomenon. On the other hand, according to the work of A. Lijphart (1968), there is a political science tradition that focuses attention on conflict regulation in a democratic system characterized by thoroughgoing segmentation. Although the pillarized structures have been considered as providing opportunities and facilitating conditions for the pacification policy of the political elite, and in spite of the fact that the political parties are conceived as the most important pillar organizations, the two traditions developed considerably independently of each other. R. Steininger (1975), for example, points out the strategic role of the political elite in the creation of pillarization. Nevertheless, there are sufficient grounds to relate themes from the two approaches.

Among sociologists, pillarization received a lot of attention from the perspective of sociology of religion. The focus was mainly on the period of religious change. About the Netherlands, prominent works are published by J. Coleman (1978) and J. Thurlings (1971). Organized Catholicism in the Netherlands (pillarization) was considered a facilitating factor that explained the rapid change from the most conservative national church into the most progressive church in a period of ten years (the 1960s). Meanwhile, that period was followed by a process of depillarization. The number of national Catholic organizations in the Netherlands decreased from 161 in 1960 to 61 in 1980. Moreover, the integration between the remaining organizations weakened considerably. With the exception of the Dutch Catholic School Council, nearly all the central core organizations disappeared and only the

Catholic school system remained intact. Such processes of change were studied in a structural way by means of network analysis (Duffhues *et al.* 1985). The structural depillarization in the Netherlands was explained by the crisis in the philosophical-ideological core (Thurlings 1971).

In Flanders (Belgium), Dobbelaere and Billiet (1976, 1983) determined that church involvement had declined drastically but that the pillar commitment had been very stable over the preceding decade. This evolution continued during the second half of the 1970s and was also observed in Wallonia (Voyé 1979). The secularization process, conceived as declining participation in church practices, ethical change, and a rejection of religion as an overarching meaning system, affects by definition the philosophical-ideological foundation of pillarization. How then could these two phenomena, pillarization and secularization, occur simultaneously? The Catholic pillar still embraces the majority of schools, hospitals, health insurance and trade union memberships, youth movements, and cultural associations. The answer was sought in a shift in the meaning system itself in such a way that it remained attractive for both, the churchgoers and the unchurched Catholics. An internal shift from church religiosity to sociocultural Christianity—a secular adaptation in the symbolic universe—was hypothesized. This hypothesis emerged in empirical studies in the domains of education and health care, and it was confirmed in an empirical study dealing with the Christian labor movement (Laermans 1992). In the late 1980s, complementary explanations of the persistence of pillarization dealt with processes of selective organizational control and with the defense of mutual interests. The pillars were no longer conceived primarily as ideological organizations but as political concerns (Huyse 1987).

In the tradition of political science, pillarization received special attention in comparative political studies concerned with conflict regulation in states that are marked by sharp subcultural segmentation. In those studies, the theoretical status of the pillarized structures was ambiguous. On the one hand, emphasis was placed on the aspect of compartmentalization, a structural factor that is extremely threatening for political stability and that consequently elicits a response from the political elite. On the other hand, however, some studies were stressing the supportive functions of pillarization as a stabilizing instrument used by the political elite.

In the consociational democracy tradition, segmented pluralism is considered to be a threat to political stability. The paradoxical situation in which political systems as the Netherlands and Belgium, in spite of far-reaching subcultural segmentation, seemed stable, was attributed to the prudent leadership of the political elite. Consociational democracy has thus been described as the response of the political elite to the challenge of strong subcultural segmentation. Conflict within the fragmented political culture is settled by bargaining among the top leadership of social groups (Lijphart 1968). Agreements were frozen into pacts. This kind of corporatist mediation in the Western democracies is studied in the works of Schmitter (1979).

Without going into the rules and the additional conditions of consociational democracy, it is interesting to see why segmented pluralism was considered to be so dangerous for political stability. The explanation originated from the social psychology of small group memberships, and it reached the consociational democracy tradition through the work of Truman, Bently, Lipset, and Rokkan. Individuals' memberships of groups sharing the same interests would promote polarization and extremism, while their memberships of groups with divergent interests would give rise to moderate positions because of the psychological counterpressure. Traces of this approach can be found in the analyses of A. van den Brande (1967), who stated that the incompleteness of pillarization—that is, the crosscutting of religious, ideological, and linguistic cleavages in Belgium—provides counterpressure and multiple solidarities. Because of that, a permanent mobilization around one line of conflicts was avoided.

The authors who study pillarization in relation to the development of some Western democracies conceive it as a special case of institutionalized cleavages, particularly when the religious cleavage was decisive. Cleavages are institutionalized if the political organizations that resulted from them were capable of satisfactorily articulating, aggregating, and defending the rival interests of their followers within the framework of the legitimate common institutions and political rules (Urwin 1970; Lorwin 1971). This means that the conflicting groups in society are brought by the political and social elite to accent the state as a market within which group objectives can be attained. Pillarization thus implies that the mobilizing energy of social movements is controlled and channeled by the political elite. For S. Rokkan (1977), this formed the core of his general concept of the pillarization process. He distinguishes social mobilization (the corporate channel) and political mobilization (the electoral channel). There is pillarization if the cleavage-specific organizations are active in the two channels and if those channels interlock.

In the 1980s historians continued to study the roots and the development of pillarization, not only on a local level (Blom and Nisset 1985) or on the level of one state (Gerard 1988; Lamberts 1988), but also in comparative studies with Belgium and the Netherlands, and countries such as Austria and Switzerland (Righart 1986). The comparative approach which was so prominent in the political sciences also affected recent studies of sociologists who studied pillarization from the viewpoint of social movements and within the context of the process of modernization (Hellemans 1990).

J. B. BILLIET

BIBLIOGRAPHY

Billiet, J., 1984. "On Belgian Pillarization: Changing Perspectives." In P.P.C.M. Van Schendelen, ed., *Consociationalism, Pillarization and Conflict-management in the Low Countries.* Meppel: Boom, pp. 117–128.

Billiet, J. and K. Dobbelaere, 1976. *Godsdienst in Vlaanderen: van kerks-katholicisme naar sociaal-culturele christenheid.* Leuven: Davidsfonds.

Blom, J. C. H. and C. J. Nisset, 1985. *Broeders sluit U aan. Aspecten van verzuiling in zeven Nederlandse gemeenten.* Amsterdam.

Coleman, J. A., 1978. *The Evolution of Dutch Catholicism, 1958–1974.* Berkeley: University of California Press.

Dobbelaere, K. and J. Billiet, 1983. "Les changements internes au Pillier Catholique en Flandre: d'un Catholicité d'Eglise à une Chrétienté Socioculturelle." *Recherches Sociologiques,* vol. 2: 141–184.

Duffhues, T., A. Felling, and J. Roes, 1985. *Bewegende patronen: Een analyse van het landelijk netwerk van katholieke organisaties en bestuurders 1945–1980.* Baarn: Ambo, Katholiek Documentatiecentrum.

Gerard, E., 1988. "Grondlijnen ven de katholieke verzuiling tussen 1914 en 1945." In J. Billiet, ed., *Tussen bescherming en verovering. Sociologen en historici over zuilvorming.* Leuven: Kadoc, pp. 135–170.

Hellemans, S., 1990. *Strijd om de moderniteit.* Leuven: Universitaire Pers, Kadoc.

Huyse, L., 1987. *De verzuiling voorbij.* Leuven: Kritak.

Kruyt, J. P., 1957. "Sociologische beschouwingen over zuilen en verzuiling." *Socialisme en Democratie,* pp. 11–29.

Laermans, R., 1992. *In de greep van de moderne tijd.* Leuven: Garrant.

Lamberts, E., 1988. "Van Kerk naar zuil: de ontwikkeling van het katholiek organisatiewezen in België in de 19e eeuw." In J. Billiet, ed., *Tussen bescherming en verovering. Sociologen en historici over zuilvorming.* Leuven: Kadoc, pp. 83–134.

Lijphart, A., 1968. *Verzuiling, pacificatie en kentering in de Nederlandse politiek.* Amsterdam: De Bussy.

Lorwin, V., 1971. "Segmented Pluralism: Ideological Cleavages and Political Cohesion in the Smaller European Democracies." *Comparative Politics,* vol. 3-2:141–175.

Righart, H., 1986. *De katholieke zuil in Europa. Het ontstaan van verzuiling onder katholieken in Oostenrijk, Zwitserland, Belgie en Nederland.* Meppel: Boom.

Rokkan, S., 1977. "Towards a Generalized Concept of 'Verzuiling': A Preliminary Note." *Political Studies,* vol. 25: 563–565.

Schmitter, P., 1979. "Modes of Interest Intermediation and Models of Societal Change in Western Europe." In P. Schmitter and G. Lembruch, eds., *Trends Toward Corporatist Intermediation,* London.

Steininger, R., 1975. *Polarisierung und Integration: Eine Vergleichende Untersuchung der strukturellen Versäulung der Gesellschaft in den Niederlanden and Österreich.* Meisenheim a/G: Anton Haim.

Thurlings, J. M. G., 1971. *De wankele zuil. Nederlandse katholieken tussen assimilatie en pluralisme.* Nijmegen: Dekker & Vand de Vegt.

Urwin, D., 1970. "Social Cleavages and Political Parties in Belgium: Problems of Institutionalization." *Political Studies,* vol. 18: 320–340.

van den Brande, A., 1967. "Elements for a Sociological Analysis of the Impact of the Main Conflicts on Belgian Political Life." *Res Publica,* vol. 9: 437–469.

Voyé, L., 1979. "Situation des catholiques en Belgique. De l'adhésion ecclésiale au catholicisme socio-culturel en Wallonie." *Religion et Politique, Actes 15éme Conférence Internationale de Sociologie des Religions,* pp. 293–331.

PLANNING, PROGRAMMING, BUDGETING SYSTEM (PPBS).

A budgeting methodology developed in the 1960s in the federal government that is still employed in the Department of Defense. PPBS provides policy and budget decisionmakers with a long-term perspective on how program demand relates to service requirements and funding.

Introduction

The Department of Defense (DOD) plans, prepares, negotiates, and makes decisions on policy, programs, and resource allocation using the planning, programming, budgeting system (PPBS) implemented by Robert McNamara, Charles Hitch, Robert Anthony, and others during the administrations of Presidents Kennedy and Johnson. Despite criticism that PPBS was a failure in the federal government, the process continues to be used by the DOD and appears to have been modified incrementally so as to operate effectively despite some flaws (Wildavsky 1988, pp. 186–202; Puritano 1981). While the manner in which PPBS operates has varied under different presidents and secretaries of defense, the basic characteristics of the system have remained in place for almost 30 years (Korb 1977).

Perhaps the reason why PPBS has served the policy development and planning needs of DOD resource decisionmaking while it floundered in other federal agencies is that the process was developed specifically for defense, where many program and budget decisions are made on the basis of assessing alternatives and where quantitative data are available and amenable to the application of the tools of economic cost-benefit analysis, systems analysis, operations research, and other sophisticated analytical methodologies exist. Many defense inputs and outcomes may be constrained so as to be measured quantitatively with greater confidence than is the case for domestic programs. On the other hand, PPBS may have survived in the DOD because it is too expensive to change to another systems or for reasons related more to political competition between the Office of the Secretary of Defense (OSD) and the service branches than to analytical utility.

Despite some apparent weaknesses in the application of PPBS in the DOD, the system does produce budget requests for defense on a regular and reliable schedule and provide a highly organized context for policy negotiation and decisionmaking for the service branches and Office of the Secretary of Defense (Joint DOD/GAO Working Group 1983). It also supplies the framework for integrating the views of the Joint Chiefs of Staff (JCS) and a template against which the views and recommendations of other defense and security agencies involved in the resource allocation decision process may be compared, for example, those of the National Security Council, State Department, Central Intelligence Agency, Defense Intelligence Agency, and others. Analysis of the manner in which PPBS operated provides a basis for assessing criticism of defense policy setting and budgeting/resource management as well as policy process reform proposals.

The Policy Development and Planning Phase of PPBS

In assessment of policy planning for defense, it is important to understand that the goals and mission of the DOD are not deliberated and set exclusively within the PPBS system. As noted above, policy direction comes from the President, the State Department, the National Security Council, and other executive branch agencies, as well as from Congress. One set of factors that drives the policy and planning phase of PPBS is the treaties, international commitments, agreements, and understandings of U.S. defense obligations negotiated by policymakers over the twentieth century and particularly since World War II. Also critical to policy development and planning is the assessment of worldwide threats to U.S. and allied interests that are monitored constantly by a variety of intelligence agencies. The second set of factors that drives PPBS is the broad defense policy and programming objectives set by the president and presidential advisors, for example, in the areas of readiness, sustainability, force structure, and modernization.

Department of Defense policy development and planning may be differentiated into three semiautonomous systems, one for macronational security planning, a second for war-fighting planning, and a third for defense resource planning (Korb 1977). In addition, the DOD operates organizationally using two or, arguably, three interdependent management control systems, one for military operations, a second for general administration, and a third for financial management and budgeting. Assessments of threats and commitments, and estimates of resources needed to meet commitments at "acceptable" levels of risk, are defined separately by the Joint Chiefs of Staff in its Joint Strategic Planning Document, by each military service department, and by the OSD. These independent evaluations are then combined by the OSD to produce the Defense Planning Guidance (DPG). The Guidance indicates annually the assets, forces, and other resources needed to satisfy U.S. security obligations. The Defense Planning Guidance covers threats and opportunities, policy, strategy, force planning, resource planning, and fiscal guidance, and includes a summary of major policy issues. The DPG provides the basis for subsequent service branch and OSD programming and budgeting.

Policy and resource planning is accomplished within the framework of the PPBS program structure, comprising 11 programs: support of other nations, strategic forces, general purpose forces, intelligence and communications, airlift and sealift, guard and reserve forces, research and development, central supply and maintenance, training and personnel, administration, and special operations forces. These programs are crosswalked to the appropriations format employed by Congress to budget for the DOD, to warfare planning, to the programming and budgeting control structures of the service branches, and the unified and specified command structure that combines Army, Air Force, Navy, and Marine Corps forces into autonomous, geographically defined area commands. The fact that policy development and planning is continuous suggests that perhaps planning and programming are short-term exercises. In fact, policy and programmatic planning within PPBS takes a long-range perspective of 10 to 20 years and beyond, while programming has a six-year focus, as does budgeting. However, in practice programming tends to focus on a two-year period and much of the budget is decided annually, even though six-year projections are prepared for both programs and budgets.

Much of U.S. defense policy and force structure planning was developed after World War II and codified for the purposes of PPBS in the 1960s and has been changed only marginally since this time. Reductions in force structure were made in the 1970s and are proposed for the 1990s as well. However, even when cuts are made or forces expanded, as in the 1980s, relative force structure composition has been fairly stable. Of course, the mix of capital equipment in the force structure changes constantly, for example, types of ships in the Navy or aircraft in the Air Force.

Because policy planning in PPBS is long-term, some criticisms to the effect that defense policy and planning fail to take into account rapid changes in world conditions may miss the point. Policy and resource planning is often unable to anticipate short-term contingencies and risks of the type that must be accommodated by all types of organizations on a firefighting basis, for example, the Iraqi invasion of Kuwait. Furthermore, many defense contingencies are anticipated with considerable accuracy by DOD analysts, but the knowledge that certain events may occur, even where probabilities may be specified with some confidence, does not resolve the problem of allocating and coordinating resources under circumstances where commitments are extensive and resource demands exceed availability.

Policy development and planning also does not insure that commitments of allies to jointly defend against certain types of threat will be upheld without considerable jawboning by the United States on a short-term basis, as occurred at the beginning of the Persian Gulf sea lane protection operation in 1987 and in the late summer and fall of 1990 at the outset of enforcement of the embargo against Iraq. Given these and other constraints, long-range policy planning will inevitably fail to anticipate some threats, and will be unable to resolve, ex ante, the highly complex problems of coordinating military responsiveness of the type faced in launching the Desert Storm operation against Iraq. This is particularly true where the responsibility for operation is allocated among different services and nations so that mobilization efforts require significant coordination.

In attempting to anticipate the resources needed by the armed services in the future, planning within PPBS is only marginally resource-constrained. For example, planning for defense against all threats to the United States within the context of the Navy's maritime strategy may indicate the need for 16 carrier vessel battle groups (CVBGs) rather than the current fleet size of 11 CVBGs. Planning articulates the amount of resources needed to minimize threat independent of resource constraints so that choices among alternative force structures and threat responses (and intensity levels) may be made knowledgeably during the programming and budgeting phases of PPBS. The PPBS process may be described as the "defense funnel" in which policy and programming choices among alternatives narrow the resource base to fit budgetary feasibility and executability as the decision process moves toward presidential budget preparation, and congressional authorization and appropriation.

Programming in PPBS

The programming phase of PPBS is guided by the Future Year Defense Program (FYDP), which aggregates and translates the program elements (PEs) that are the basic building blocks of projected defense asset requirements into the force program framework of PPBS. Under the two-year budget process mandated by Congress and implemented by the DOD for fiscal years 1988–1989, 1990–1991, and 1992–1993, the FYDP time frame was expanded to six years. The FYDP provides a summary of requirements and alternatives for achieving force structure, readiness, sustainability, and modernization objectives. It is updated three times each year, in January in conformity with the president's budget, in May, and in September. The May FYDP is used to link the most recent changes determined in the Program Objective Memorandum (POM) process to the budget under preparation for the next fiscal year. The September FYDP revision reflects the Secretary of Defense's programmatic decisions and, as such, provides the data base for determining both programming requirements and budgets. The January plan update has been provided to Congress (since 1989) along with the president's budget proposal as required by law.

The task of programming as the second phase of PPBS is to articulate and prioritize six-year defense resource demands into the perspective of a moving two-year cycle. Programming is intended to integrate the capabilities of all the individual components of each service branch into coherent packages, the results of which are summarized in

POMs prepared by the individual military departments. The POMs are merged with views from the JCS on risks and military capability expressed in the Joint Program Assessment Memorandum and analyzed in detail by OSD staff before program decisions for all of defense are made by the Defense Planning Resource Board (DPRB). The DPRB is the final arbitration and decision point of programmatic resource allocation in the OSD and is chaired by the secretary of defense assisted by the deputy secretary, military department secretaries, the chairman of the JCS, and selected other senior defense officials. They represent their positions in DPRB meetings face to face without the assistance of staff and are expected to be knowledgeable and forceful advocates for their programs. Once the DPRB issues its Program Decision Memoranda (PDMs), programming is set and the framework for the next fiscal year's budget is established.

While programming by the military departments is a complex process that differs between service branches, it generally comprises three phases: program planning and appraisal, program development, and program decision and appeals. Programming is considerably more cost-constrained than planning but still places the greatest emphasis on technical capability relative to peacekeeping and war-fighting demands. The process is informed by the input of information and justifications from the Commanders-in-Chief (CINCs) of the unified and specified commands, the military service commands, and Pentagon-based armed service program sponsors. Committees of senior officers deliberate and make recommendations up the chain of command to the military and civilian executive staffs in the department secretariats before final program decisions are made by the secretaries. To illustrate the differences in programming between the services, the Navy system is decentralized to sift program proposals through a gauntlet of separate reviews up to the chief of naval operations and the secretary of the navy. Navy programming, program appraisal, and budgeting are distinct activities performed by separate staffs. On the other hand, programming and budgeting in the Air Force are more centralized, with fewer separate reviews and more overlap in staff functions and responsibilities.

Budgeting in PPBS

Budgeting in PPBS is primarily an effort at rationing resources across and within the military departments in consonance with planning and programming decisions. Budget formulation requires the issuance of preparation guidelines, the amassing of programmatic and cost data, the provision of opportunities for program justification in hearings, the analysis of proposals for adherence to both financial and policy guidelines, and the negotiation of program priorities within the constraints of the budget authority projected to be available in the next two fiscal years and four out-years under the biennial budget process. Budgeting also attempts to respond to short-term contingencies resulting from changes in the international environment and new policy initiatives flowing from Congress, the president, and the secretary of defense.

Budgeting is a highly constrained exercise in pricing the executability of programs within the parameters of affordability and political feasibility. Each service branch prepares its own budget request in response to directives from the president's Office of Management and Budget, the OSD comptroller, and comptrollers in the military department secretariats. Military department budget requests move up the chain of command from field activities, to command-level comptrollers and budget offices, to the central comptrollers' offices in the Pentagon. Military and civilian budget officials analyze input from operational and system commands and the military resource sponsor representatives of programs within each service, conduct budget hearings, issue marks (reductions) internally, and respond to appeals from resource sponsors prior to final service secretary decisionmaking and submission of the formal budget proposals to the OSD.

In overview of PPBS, it is important to reiterate that military department budget staff and comptrollers develop their own estimates of needs, costs, and prices to implement their own priorities and POM decisions while, at the same time, the OSD and the Joint Chiefs of Staff also prepare their positions on the defense-program budget. The OSD comptroller and his or her budget staff compile service budget requests and analyze them in conjunction with the president's OMB defense examiners; the OMB reviews the budget internally with department staff only for the DOD, as distinct from the external manner in which domestic department budgets are analyzed by the OMB. Marks (reductions) are issued by the OSD comptroller to the military departments, another round of appeals is heard at the military department comptroller level, and the adjusted budget requests are returned to the OSD for final decision.

Coordination and reconciliation of the multitudinous budgetary perspectives and demands of the JCS, the separate military departments, and uniformed services (and the unified and specified commands) is the responsibility of the OSD staff who prepare the materials to inform the deliberations of the DPRB. Once DPRB-level policy and program issues have been negotiated and resolved, DPRB recommendations are issued in the form of Program Budget Decisions (PBDs). PBDs provide the basis for preparation of the formal DOD budget once final decisions on high-profile issues have been made by the secretary of defense.

The defense component of the president's budget is issued by the OSD comptroller and the OMB each December and becomes part of the federal budget subsequently transmitted to Congress by the president in January. The PBDs and final secretary of defense (SECDEF) budget decisions also guide the preparation of the National Defense Budget Estimates (green book) issued annually in the spring by the OSD comptroller.

In the process employed by presidential administrations, important input to budget decisions has been provided by the deputy secretary of defense, the bearer of a large part of the responsibility for managing the DOD. The assistant secretary/comptroller, the under-secretary for acquisition (beginning in 1986), and assistant secretaries for other OSD functional areas, including program analysis and evaluation, policy, force management and personnel, legislative affairs, health, and reserve affairs, also provide views and analyses to guide programs and budget decisionmaking.

Budget alternatives and decisions for the acquisition of major capital assets by the DOD, such as missiles, weapon systems, ships, aircraft, tanks, and so forth, are reviewed and analyzed in a budget process that functions semiautonomously from the defense operating budget process. The acquisition budget is integrated with the rest of the DOD budget by the military departments and the OSD under-secretary for acquisition. Congress directed the OSD to centralize and better coordinate the acquisitions process in the 1986 Defense Authorization Act (Goldwater-Nichols Act) and Defense Secretary Dick Cheney made this one of the highest priorities of the new DOD administration in 1989. OSD and the military departments have continued to adjust to the new organizational process for acquisition decisionmaking. Since July 1989, a number of changes in the acquisition budgeting and management process have been implemented. Capital budget proposals are reviewed by the Defense Acquisition Board (DAB), chaired by the under-secretary for defense acquisition and the vice chairman of the JCS, at the OSD level, prior to the integration of capital and operating budget proposals by the DPRB into the president's budget.

The under-secretary for acquisition and the Defense Acquisition Board also are responsible, along with the OSD comptroller, the military department secretariats, and the service comptrollers' offices, for program budget execution and the supervision of weapons and systems procurement by the individual service system commands and program offices. In turn, system command officials and comptrollers are responsible for executing the acquisitions budget, orchestrating the complex and technically difficult tasks of acquisitions program and project management. Given the highly differentiated military department-based nature of program management and the extent of overlapping responsibility for budget execution in the acquisition area, a high degree of organizational complexity is the most impressive characteristic of the defense procurement process.

L. R. JONES

BIBLIOGRAPHY

Adelman, K. and N. Augustine, 1990. *The Defense Revolution*. San Francisco: The Institute for Contemporary Studies.

Art, R., 1985. "Congress and the Defense Budget: Enhancing Policy Oversight." *Political Sciences Quarterly* (Summer 100), 227–248.

Budget of the United States Government, Fiscal Year 1988, Management of the United States Government, vol. 4, Washington, D.C.: U.S. GPO, Dec. 1986, p. 83.

Department of Defense, *Justification of Estimates for Defense Management Report Initiatives*. Jan. 1990.

Fox, R., 1984. "Revamping the Business of National Defense." *Harvard Business Reviews*, vol. 62 (September-October) 63–70.

———, 1988. *The Defense Management Challenge*. Cambridge, MA: Harvard Business School Press.

Gansler, J., 1989. *Affording Defense*. Cambridge, MA: MIT Press.

Joint DOD/GAO Working Group, 1993. *PPBS: Planning, Programming and Budgeting System*. Washington, D.C.: GAO/OACG-84-5, September.

Korb, L., 1977. "Department of Defense Budget Process: 1947–1977," *Public Administration Review* 37 (July-August).

———, 1979. *The Fall and Rise of the Pentagon*. Westport, CT: Greenwood Press.

Lindsay, J., 1987. "Congress and Defense Policy, 1961–1986." *Armed Forces and Society*, vol. 13 (Spring) 371–401.

Luttwak, E., 1982. "Why We Need More Waste, Fraud and Mismanagement in the Pentagon." *Commentary*, vol. 73 (February) 17–30.

Morrison, D., 1986. "Chaos on Capitol Hill." *National Journal* (Sept. 27) 2302–2307.

National Security Planning and Budgeting Report, 1986. Packard Commission Report (June).

Office of the Secretary of Defense, 1989. "White Paper on DOD Congressional Relations." October.

Puritano, V., 1981. "Streamlining PPBS." *Defense* (August) 20–28.

Vann, J., 1987. "The Forgotten Forces." *Military Review* (August) 2–17.

Wildavsky, Aaron, 1988. *The New Politics of the Budgetary Process*. Glenview, IL: Scott Foresman.

PLOWDEN REPORT.

PLOWDEN REPORT. The report published in 1961 on the control of public expenditure which fundamentally changed the nature of planning in British government. Unlike many reports into the conduct of the governance of Britain in the twentieth century, the Plowden Report is notable for the general implementation of its main findings. That this was the case is due, in part, to the opposition by the Treasury to the original plan to have public expenditure matters reviewed by an independent body, with access to cabinet papers. This had been the recommendation of a parliamentary committee daunted by the complexity of administrative practices used by the Treasury in controlling public expenditure. Instead, an internal enquiry was established, chaired by Sir Edwin Plowden, a temporary civil servant with experience with the Ministry of Aircraft Production during the war. He was joined by three businessmen with experience of government and three civil servants, including Treasury representation. Their two main areas of recommendations were of longstanding importance to British public administration; one concerned national economic management, the other internal Treasury structures.

The first reforming set of recommendations concerned the ostensible subject of the inquiry: public expenditure control. Under this heading, the Plowden Committee proposed the establishment of a Public Expenditure Survey Committee (PESC). Such a committee title hides its profound effects. Prior to its establishment, there existed no regularly reliable way in Britain to assess the collective demands of government departments over the short to medium term. The purpose of the new system establishes on an annual basis what the various spending departments are assuming to be necessary for the foreseeable future, defined now as a ten-year period. This would determine the aggregate level of proposed—"hoped for" might be more accurate—public provision. The committee, made up of the principal finance officers of the main spending departments and chaired by a Treasury deputy secretary, considers the total level of bids against the best forecast available on the performance and productivity of the British economy as a whole.

In short, the committee is in a position to provide the Chancellor of the Exchequer with the basic data necessary to present his or her fiscal and monetary plans to Parliament in the form of his or her annual budget. It is at the level of this committee that the essential features of planning the coming British government's economic year are determined: the extent of national wealth to be expected; how much to withdraw from the private sector in the form of taxation for public sector purposes; what shortfall might need to be addressed by taxation and borrowing—or, more latterly, privatization or contractorization. Implicit in this process, therefore, are considerations of budget cuts to various departments' forecasts, depending on the long-run political priorities of the party in power or shorter-run considerations reflecting public opinion.

The second major area of recommendation was in the internal reform of Her Majesty's Treasury itself, a process begun in 1962. A key concept for the Plowden Committee was "management": efficiency, effectiveness, and economy have never been, after all, the conceptual preserve of government reformers of the 1980s and 1990s. For this to be fully realized, the Treasury itself needed substantial internal restructuring. "This was legitimate," suggests Henry Roseveare (1969), "for the reorganization of 1962 mattered less as an elaborate exercise in the efficient reapportionment of functions than as a visible demonstration of the underlying conceptual revolution which had been taking place . . . and which made 'management' the purposeful, creative successor of the old-fashioned, negative 'control'" (p. 301). To that end, the work of the department was organized on functional lines: finance and economic matters were divided from those concerned with pay and management. This division reflected the change from Treasury elements shadowing specific departments in toto (Defense or the Health Service, say) to the arrangement whereby all departmental expenditure issues were the preserve of the one and public employee pay, promotion, and superannuation matters were dealt with by the other, regardless of departmental affiliation.

In Britain, the impact of the Plowden Report was still in evidence in the 1990s. Accurate forecasting is central to all activity. Its acceptance of annual budgeting, that constitutional legacy of the nineteenth century, remains as firm as ever. Treasury oversight is the determining element of decisionmaking. More curiously, the report reflected a now largely rejected Keynesian consensus that government expenditure is the central element in national economic management. Nowhere does it examine neoclassical ideas about the minimalist state; public expenditure running at some 40 percent of national wealth seemingly was a natural, desirable, and continuing condition. How to maximize the effects of that apparently permanent state of affairs was the business of the Plowden Committee.

The Committee's work grew out of an enthusiasm of the late 1950s and early 1960s for changing institutional structures in the context of the economically preeminent nation state. Subsequent institutional interest in Thomas Jefferson's dictum that the government which governs best governs least has placed the Plowden Report intellectually in the sidings of government, even while its main provisions continue to shape British decisionmaking.

PETER FOOT

BIBLIOGRAPHY

Chapman, Richard A. and J. R. Greenaway, 1980. *The Dynamics of Administrative Reform.* London: Croom Helm.
Fry, G. Kingdom, 1969. *Statesmen in Disguise: The Changing Role of the Administrative Class of the British Home Civil Service 1853–1966.* London: Macmillan.
Plowden Group, 1961. *Control of Public Expenditure.* Cmnd 1432. London: HMSO.
Roseveare, Henry, 1969. *The Treasury: The Evolution of a British Institution.* London: Allen Lane.

PLURALISM.

Any system of thought which recognizes more than one essential principle of existence (philosophical pluralism); the idea that within a political system or an institution power is (or should be) shared between a variety of groups (political pluralism); or societies made up a number of identifiable ethnocultural groups, in which social organization is in some way based on distinctions or divisions between these groups (ethnocultural pluralism).

Philosophical Pluralism

Philosophical pluralists believe that being is conditioned by many different factors, rather than one overriding principle. Pluralism is generally seen as the antithesis of structuralism. Philosophical pluralism was first used to denote a critique of the Hegelian theory of the unitary state. Later pluralist theories were developed in conscious opposition to the Marxist philosophical notion that the basic human activity is work, and that the main division in society is therefore based on economic class. A contemporary form of pluralism can be found in postmodern notions of relativism and sociocultural fragmentation. In a wider sense, such principles can be applied to epistemology (methodological pluralism) or religion (religious pluralism).

Political Pluralism

Political pluralism is based on the idea that competing interests and values are inevitable in complex societies and large-scale organizations. Any attempt to impose a consensus is likely to lead to authoritarianism. Democracy requires institutional mechanisms through which differing interests and values can be expressed, to permit peaceful resolution of conflicts. Representative parliaments and political parties are seen as the key mechanism, and thus as the basic characteristic of democracy. Liberal pluralists also claim that free markets have an essential role in avoiding economic conflicts.

The notion of pluralism goes back to the work of the nineteenth-century French political theorist Alexis de Toqueville on democracy in the U.S. Pluralist ideas were also put forward by English guild socialists in the early twentieth century. They argued that the power of the capitalist class and the modern state should be counterbalanced through small decentralized associations. A much weakened state was to serve as the arbiter between conflicting interests. Guild socialism opposed Marxist ideas on the need for a strong state (the "dictatorship of the proletariat") in the transition to socialism.

Pluralism reemerged in U.S. political science from the 1950s (for instance in the work of S. M. Lipset [1963] and R. A. Dahl [1961]) as a critique of functionalism, the then prevailing approach of U.S. social science, which argued that there was an overriding consensus in modern industrial society. Pluralists argued that although there may be some shared values (such as commitment to the Constitution and the basic institutions) there was no general agreement on values and goals. This lead to conflicts between interest groups, which were aggregated by political parties and mediated through the system of representative democracy.

In Europe in the 1960s, political sociologists such as Ralf Dahrendorf (1959) and Raymond Aron argued that conflict was not reducible to a single overriding conflict between labor and capital. Rather, people in industrial societies belonged to many groups and had multiple social roles. A woman might be a nurse, a parent, a homeowner, a mortgage payer, a member of a social club, and so on.

Being powerless in one context (say the labor market) might be alleviated by having prestige or influence in another (say a voluntary association). This was thought to weaken class conflicts: people would not put all their energy into combating the social order as long as they had some roles that provided material or symbolic gratification. Conflicts need not take a destructive form, but could be institutionalized and channeled, to achieve gradual change.

In contemporary pluralist views, elections are just one aspect of democracy, since they only give the opportunity for a general expression of popular will every two to four years. Governments and political parties should set out to secure the participation of as many interest groups as possible in decisions which concern them. This means establishing consultative mechanisms to allow continuous involvement of citizens in planning and decisionmaking. For instance, building a new airport should involve consultations with airlines, trade unions, residents of the area, consumer groups and so on.

Ethnocultural Pluralism

Ethnocultural pluralism may be applied both to colonial societies and to contemporary societies with ethnic minority or immigrant populations. The term "plural society" was first used by J. S. Furnivall (1939) in a study of the Netherlands East Indies (now Indonesia) to refer to a society "comprising two or more elements or social orders which live side by side, yet without mingling, in one political unit." This applied to colonial societies in which the indigenous majority population was ruled by a small white elite. In many cases, other groups took on intermediate or "go-between" roles. These might be people of mixed race or groups specially imported by the colonizers, such as Asians in East Africa. Such societies were based on relations of dominance, protected by racist ideologies and practices.

M. G. Smith (1986) extended the notion of pluralism to apply to tribal divisions within African societies, which were not reducible to the impact of colonialism. He argued that various types of pluralism were to be found in many nations. For instance, the United States had two forms of pluralism: "cultural pluralism" based on ethnic difference within the white population (which did no imply inequality), and "structural pluralism" based on differential (and unequal) modes of incorporation into society of white and nonwhite groups. In the case of Switzerland, Smith described the regional divisions between ethnic groups as "segmental pluralism."

In the United States, notions of pluralism go back to the period of mass immigration prior to World War I. Pluralism implied that ethnic difference and cultural maintenance should be tolerated (though not supported) by the state. The "ethnic revival" of the 1960s revived interest in the notion of ethnocultural pluralism, and this has been sustained by mass immigration and growing diversity since the opening up of the United States to influxes from Asia and Latin America through the 1965 Immigration Act. At the same time the discrimination against and exclusion from power positions of African Americans, Native Americans, and other minorities is seen as a form of structural pluralism that is highly divisive.

Elsewhere, ethnocultural pluralism is a fairly new notion. In Europe, the mass labor immigrations up to the 1970s, and influxes of other types of migrants, including family members, asylum-seekers, and refugees since, have led to debates on ethnocultural diversity. Responses have varied considerably (see **multiculturalism**). In Asia, Africa, and Latin America, the rapid growth of international population mobility since the 1980s has led to increased diversity in many countries. This often complicates existing balances between ethnic groups in postcolonial nations. Many governments reject ideas on pluralism as threats to national identity.

Milton Gordon has linked political and ethnocultural pluralism in what he sees as a clash of values within U.S. society. On the one hand, "liberal pluralism" emphasizes principles of equal treatment and individual meritocracy. On the other, "corporate pluralism" calls for differential treatment and compensation for past injustices. Canadian philosopher Charles Taylor has suggested a similar clash between the "politics of universalism," based on equalization of rights and entitlements of individuals, and the "politics of difference," based on recognition of the unique identity of each ethnic group. This conflict between universalism (based on individual rights) and pluralism (based on recognition of collective identities) is a key issue in most modern societies.

Critiques

Pluralist theories have been frequently criticized on the grounds that they ignore the actual concentration of power in modern societies. The managers of large (often transnational) corporations cannot be controlled by parliaments. Nor are complex government bureaucracies amenable to public supervision. The political parties themselves tend to be controlled by self-appointed elites, and most parliamentary systems are designed in a way that makes it very hard to establish new parties. Ruling elites are generally unwilling to admit members of minority ethnic groups to power positions. Finally, the high level of concentration of ownership of the mass media makes it possible to manipulate public opinion.

Pluralism and representative democracy thus appear as a mere legitimation for the monopolization of power by relatively small groups of people. Some pluralists have responded by acknowledging that power is not equally divided within society, but is rather shared among a number of elites, with differing interests. Others argue that control is exercised by a coalition of elites which base their power on different economic or social sectors, but have closely linked goals—what U.S. President Eisenhower referred to in the 1950s as the "military-industrial complex." This concept is referred to as elite pluralism. In the Marxist view, class is still the salient factor in political and economic power, and continuing class domination is merely masked by representative bodies with little real power. Feminists point to the fact that most power positions are held by men, and that patriarchal ideologies still play a strong part in justifying this. Many recent studies show that race and ethnicity are still major predictors of social status and political participation.

STEPHEN CASTLES

BIBLIOGRAPHY

Dahl, Robert A., 1961. *Who Governs?* New Haven, CT: Yale University Press.

Dahrendorf, Ralph, 1959. *Class and Class Conflict in an Industrial Society.* London: Routledge and Kegan Paul.

Furnivall, J. S., 1939. *Netherlands India: A Study of Plural Economy.* Cambridge: Cambridge University Press.

Gordon, M., 1981. "Models of Pluralism: The New American Dilemma." *Annals of the American Academy of Political and Social Science,* vol. 454:178–88.

Lipset, Seymour M., 1963. *Political Man.* London: Mercury Books.

Smith, M. G., 1986. "Pluralism, Race and Ethnicity in Selected African Countries." In J. Rex and D. Mason, eds., *Theories of Race and Ethnic Relations.* Cambridge: Cambridge University Press, pp. 187–225.

Taylor, C., 1994. "The Politics of Recognition." In A. Gutmann, ed., *Multiculturalism: Examining the Politics of Recognition.* Princeton, NJ: Princeton University Press, pp. 25–74.

POLICE ADMINISTRATION.

The efficient management of a complex organization which has as its primary goals the maintenance of order and the protection of life and property in society. Basic management functions include planning, organizing, staffing, directing, controlling, and integrating the foregoing. The police agency decision process requires insight into the goals and purposes of the agency, its duty under the law and to the people, and the manner and means by which tasks are to be performed and goals achieved. Decisions must be made within the context of democratic norms and values and must be considerate of what is best for the public, the agency, and any individual involved.

Origin and Subsequent History

In the ancient world there had been no police force in the modern sense, primarily because no such force was considered necessary or desirable. Even in antiquity the dangers of the use of military personnel as police forces by autocracies were recognized by enlightened leaders. In 6 C.E., Augustus Caesar devised a system of night patrols, the *vigiles,* for the purpose of detecting and extinguishing fires within Rome. An ancillary responsibility of the *vigiles* was to deal with petty crimes encountered in the course of fire watch duties.

During the last years of his reign, approximately 13 C.E., Augustus instituted a force, termed the urban cohort, specifically to police Rome. Each urban cohort was commanded by a tribune and contained six companies, each under the command of a commissioned officer, referred to as a centurion. Among the specialist personnel were a sergeant in charge of the prison, a sergeant in charge of the city records, and an interrogator. The provinces of the Roman Empire were policed by the Roman army.

When the Western empire was overrun by the barbarians and Roman administration vanished from the former province of Britain, another kind of policing was introduced by the invaders from northern Europe. In this context, the day-to-day business of law enforcement became the responsibility of the local community—a police of the neighborhood, as opposed to a police of the prince.

The English Experience

The modern police department can be traced to the ninth century when Alfred the Great of England structured his kingdom's defenses to prepare for the Danish invasion. To establish internal security, he instituted the system of "mutual pledge." This organized the country, at the lowest level, into groups of ten families. These groups were called tithings. Ten tithings were grouped together into a hundred families called constables. Next, the constables within each geographic area were combined to form administrative units called shires (later called counties). Each shire was governed by a "shire-reeve" (later called sheriff).

In the thirteenth century the night watch was established to protect the safety of pedestrians in urban areas of England during the hours of darkness. From the thirteenth century to the seventeenth century there was little development in the area of policing. During that period of time, each citizen was seen as a police officer since all citizens were charged with the enforcement of laws of the state. Pursuant to the Statute of Winchester (1285), all males were required to maintain weapons in their homes for use in maintaining the public peace.

Highway robbery flourished in England during the sixteenth and seventeenth centuries. To combat this problem, Parliament, in 1693, passed an act providing a reward for the apprehension and conviction of any highwayman or road agent. Those who partook in this practice were known as "thief-takers," precursors to the bounty hunter.

The appointment of novelist Henry Fielding as a magistrate in Westminster, near London, in 1784, proved fortuitous for the evolution of policing. Fielding established a relationship with the local pawnbrokers and requested that they notify him when someone tried to pawn stolen property. He ran advertisements in the local newspapers inviting anyone who was the victim of a property theft to bring to his Bow Street office a description of the property stolen and a description of the criminal. This represented the first formal provision for the reporting of crimes to authorities. Fielding then formed a small group of investigative assistants, known as the "Bow Street runners," who were not salaried and earned their money under the standard thief-taker's reward system. This group is considered the first organized police force used in England.

By the early nineteenth century, the old system of English law enforcement began to collapse. London grew into a large industrial city, with mushrooming problems of poverty, public disorder, and crime. Against this backdrop of chaos, Sir Robert Peel became Home Secretary in 1822. The visionary Peel, acknowledged as the "father" of modern policing, introduced the Metropolitan Police Act of 1829. The act created the Metropolitan Police District, staffed by paid constables. Peel appointed Charles Rowan and Richard Mayne as commissioners to organize and run the new department. The duo set up operation in the back of London's Whitehall Place, which opened onto a courtyard used by the kings of Scotland—Scotland Yard. There Rowan and Mayne fashioned a plan to deploy six divisions of 1,000 men each, with each divided into patrol sectors and beat subdivisions.

The London police introduced three elements. These elements, which remain essential features of modern policing, constituted a new mission, strategy, and organizational structure. The mission was crime prevention, reflecting the utilitarian idea that it was better to prevent crime than to respond after the fact. Crime prevention was to be achieved through a strategy of preventive patrol. Officers would maintain a visible presence in the community by continuously patrolling fixed "beats." Peel borrowed the organizational structure of the London police from the military, including uniforms, rank designations, and the authoritarian system of centralized command and discipline.

Policing Early Cities in the United States

Modern police forces were established in the United States for many of the same reasons that motivated England to create a professional police force. Increasing urbanization, industrialization, and immigration precipitated frequent episodes of large-scale disorder during the 1830s. From the London model, the United States borrowed the mission of crime prevention, the strategy of visible patrol within fixed beats, and a quasi-military organizational structure. By the mid-nineteenth century, metro-

politan police forces, modeled along the lines of Peel's model, were established throughout major cities in the northeastern United States. By the end of the nineteenth century, uniformed police had established an accepted presence in U.S. communities.

While the form of policing practiced in the United States evolved from the British model, it is important to recognize that the countries differed significantly in terms of the nature of the political control over their police departments. In *The Police in America: An Introduction* (1992), Samuel Walker cogently observed that the United States was a far more democratic country than Britain. U.S. voters exercised great control over all government agencies. In London, by contrast, voters had no direct control over the police force. As a result, U.S. police departments were immersed in local politics. This situation led to serious instances of corruption and inefficiency. The commissioners of the London police, freed from political influence, maintained high personnel standards and a sustained level of professionalism.

Underlying Theoretical Framework

During 1988 the Kennedy School of Government of Harvard University convened an assemblage of leading policing practitioners and academicians to discuss the evolving strategy of policing. In the course of discussions the history of U.S. policing was divided into three eras. Each era is distinguished from the others by the dominance of a particular administrative approach to police operations.

The Political Era

The initial period, the political era, dated from the introduction of police into municipalities during the 1840s, continued through the Progressive period, and ended during the early 1900s. Throughout the period U.S. police agencies served the interests of powerful politicians and their cronies. Political machines recruited and maintained police in office, while police helped politicians maintain their political offices.

The Reform Era

The second period, the reform era, began in the 1930s, as practitioners such as August Vollmer, O. W. Wilson, and J. Edgar Hoover vehemently rejected politics as the basis of police legitimacy. Under the stewardship of the reformers, policing became a legal and technical matter left to the discretion of professional police executives under the guidance of law. Civil service status of police officer positions eliminated patronage and ward influences in hiring and firing officers. Focusing on criminal law as a basic source of legitimacy, police in the reform era moved to narrow their functioning to crime control and criminal apprehension. The patrol car became the symbol of policing. When equipped with a two-way radio and later tied in to automated data bases of criminal records, it represented the limits of technology. This technoprofessional model of policing represented mobility, conspicuous presence, control of officers, and "professional" distance from citizens. Activities that drew the police into solving noncriminal community problems and relied on other than "crime-fighting" responses were identified as "social work," and became the object of derision.

The Era of Community Problem Solving

The final era, which began in the 1980s, stresses the service role of the police and envisions a partnership between police agencies and their communities. Research conducted during the 1970s, stimulated in large part by the passage of the Omnibus Crime Control and Safe Streets Act of 1968, suggests that one factor can help police improve their record in dealing with crime: information. If information about crimes and criminals can be obtained from citizens by police and can be properly managed by police departments, investigative and other units may significantly increase their effect on crime. Similarly, research into foot patrol operations suggests that at least part of fear reduction potential is linked to the order maintenance activities of foot patrol officers and that, too, citizens appreciate the interactive opportunities afforded through foot patrols, often providing useful crime reduction information to the officers.

Styles of Policing

The influence of each historical phase identified by the Harvard consortium survives today in what James Q. Wilson terms "policing styles" in his classic writing on the theme, *Varieties of Police Behavior: The Management of Law and Order in Eight Communities* (1968). Wilson further proposed that these styles are matched to the perception of the function of policing and that there are three main functions, or theoretical orientations, in policing: order maintenance, legalistic, and public service.

The Patrol Style (Order Maintenance).   The patrol style is dependent on the perception that the role of the police is one of law and order maintenance, rather than strict enforcement of the law. The practice of such officers would be to ignore certain common violations of the law. The law and the implied threat of action are used more to maintain order than to regulate conduct. The definition of order is constructed in the context of the subculture in which the behavior occurs. This style makes considerable use of discretion and was most characteristic of the political era. It is practiced most often today in lower-class communities where informal police intervention into the lives of residents is employed in the service of keeping the peace.

The Legalistic Style.   This style is marked by a strict concern with enforcing the precise letter of the law. At the same time, however, legalistic departments may assume a "hands-

off" posture to bothersome forms of behavior that do not constitute violations of criminal codes. Adherents to this style believe that there is only one standard of community conduct and that standard is codified law. This was the prominent orientation during the reform era of policing.

The Service Style.   This style emphasizes service to the community. Considerate of both order maintenance and law enforcement prerogatives, the general orientation of this mode is concern with enhancement of the quality of life for all. Service-oriented agencies are more likely to take advantage of community resources, such as drug treatment programs and family counseling, than are other types of departments. This style is commonly found in affluent communities.

Current Practices in the United States

The prevailing contemporary policing strategy is service-oriented and cognizant of the view that many crimes are caused by existing social problems in the community. To control crime, problem-oriented police managers attempt to uncover and effectively address the underlying dynamics of crime "hot spots."

The community policing model attempts to involve the community actively in the identification, prioritization, and resolution of crime problems. Under the community policing model the public and the police are jointly responsible for social order.

Problem-solving and community policing require decentralization of police organizational structures in order to empower patrol officers to effect solutions to problems in concert with citizens. Under community policing the roles of all persons at all levels within the organization change from what they were previously. For example, the patrol officer becomes the beat manager, while the first-line supervisor assumes responsibility for facilitating the problem-solving process. Management's role is to support the process by mobilizing the resources needed to address citizen concerns and problems. Management must also be willing to allow officers to take necessary and reasonable risks in their efforts to resolve neighborhood problems. Community policing is emerging as the most appropriate means of using police resources to improve the quality of life in neighborhoods.

Current International Practices

For purposes of comparison of modern police administration practices internationally, it is instructive to examine the contemporary forms of policing found in England, the original model for professional policing in the industrialized United States. Insights are further obtained by examining Canada, which experienced a westward movement of its population proportionate to that of the United States, and, too, had historical links to the "rugged individualist" notion.

Contemporary Policing in England

Policing in England has been characterized by tolerance of a relatively high level of governmental involvement in the lives of the populace. The preeminent policing style traditionally was the patrol style. As astutely pointed out by Trevor Bennett in Chapter 13 of Dennis Rosenbaum's comprehensive textbook, *The Challenge of Community Policing: Testing the Promises* (1994), since the riots of 1981 in Brixton, London, policing has undergone a substantial program of reform. Investigations into the cause of the riots revealed that the police may have to some extent precipitated the riot because of their unnecessarily "hard" policing in sensitive, multiracial areas and failure to consult the local community over policing matters. A British Crime Survey on the public view of the police reflected that public confidence in the police had declined successively from 1982 through 1988.

A shift toward community policing was subsequently undertaken to restore public confidence. Community contact programs implemented have included police shops (substations) and Neighborhood Watch programs. The contribution of the community to crime prevention and problem solving has been accomplished through consultations in which citizens identify problems and provide the police information that might assist them in their resolution, rather than engaging in joint actions with the police.

The main development toward decentralization, a hallmark of community policing, has been sector policing. While this has resulted in police command units small enough to provide a local police service, restructuring of forces to enhance individual autonomy has been only partially accomplished. The full potential of community policing remains to be realized.

Contemporary Policing in Canada

As previously mentioned, the Canadians share aspects of their evolution with the U.S. Both countries experienced westward movements into frontier regions, and both have a history of rugged individualism. However, there is a core difference between the two countries in their policing heritage. As indicated by Ian McKenzie and Patrick Gallagher in *Behind the Uniform: Policing in Britain and America* (1989), the Canadian perspective in settling its western territories was to send in the police to establish order before the majority of settlers arrived so that freedom and liberty could be enjoyed—in stark contrast to the U.S. notion that freedom and liberty come first, with order following far behind. Creating the ethos for the existence and maintenance of order in a relatively crime-free environment, in which laws are rarely broken because there is no one there to break them, is a different order of things from attempting to do the same thing in an environment which is already crime-ridden and lawless.

In Canada community policing is firmly established as the dominant strategy. The vast majority of Canada's more than 400 police agencies have either officially endorsed or otherwise support community policing as the most appropriate approach for contemporary policing. Barry Leighton correctly pointed out in his essay on community policing, within *The Challenge of Community Policing: Testing the Promises* (1994), that in adopting community policing Canadian police actually returned to their roots. Indeed, the Royal Canadian Mounted Police contend that it has always practiced community policing in serving its scattered rural constituency.

The central components of community policing may be found in a large number of municipal agencies. The Montreal Police Department has established storefront offices as well as a program of residential visitations. The Toronto Police Department features community-based ministations, while the Edmonton Police Service features storefronts strategically located in "hot spots." All three municipal agencies have focused programs of community involvement in problem solving.

MICHAEL K. HOOPER

BIBLIOGRAPHY

McKenzie, Ian K. and G. Patrick Gallagher, 1989. *Behind the Uniform: Policing in Britain and America.* New York: St. Martin's Press.
Moore, Mark H. with others, 1988–1993. *Perspectives on Policing.* Vols. 1–17. Washington, D.C.: National Institute of Justice and John F. Kennedy School of Government, Harvard University.
Roberson, Cliff, 1994. *Introduction to Criminal Justice.* Placerville, CA: Copperhouse Publishing Company.
Rosenbaum, Dennis P., ed., 1994. *The Challenge of Community Policing: Testing the Promises.* Thousand Oaks, CA: Sage.
Schmalleger, Frank, 1993. *Criminal Justice Today: An Introductory Text for the Twenty-First Century.* 3d ed. Englewood Cliffs, NJ: Prentice-Hall.
Sheehan, Robert and Gary W. Cordner, 1989. *Introduction to Police Administration.* Cincinnati, OH: Anderson Publishing Company.
Stead, Philip J., ed., 1977. *Pioneers in Policing.* Montclair, NJ: Patterson Smith Publishing Corporation.
Swanson, Charles R., Leonard Territo, and Robert W. Taylor, 1993. *Police Administration: Structures, Processes, and Behavior.* New York: Macmillan Publishing Company.
Walker, Samuel, 1992. *The Police in America: An Introduction.* 2d ed. New York: McGraw-Hill.
Wilson, James Q., 1968. *Varieties of Police Behavior: The Management of Law and Order in Eight Communities.* Cambridge, MA: Harvard University Press.

POLICE REVIEW BOARD.
Boards empowered to different degrees to receive complaints by citizens regarding misconduct of police officers, to evaluate the charges, and to recommend sanctions. Because civilian

participation is a key feature for some police review boards, they are also called "civilian oversight boards."

Origin and History

Municipal police departments with full-time, paid officers providing around-the-clock services did not evolve in the United States until the late 1800s. During the late 1700s and early 1800s, the predominate law enforcement agency was the office of the sheriff. This law enforcement office was adopted from England. Unlike the British sheriff, who was appointed by the Crown, the U.S. sheriff was elected by the constituency of the county. Early sheriffs were elected to two-year terms, and many counties enacted laws prohibiting a sheriff from succeeding himself in office. It was thought that direct election by the people and a short tenure of office would provide sufficient oversight to prevent abuse of power.

Sir Robert Peel established the London Metropolitan Police department in 1829. This event marked the first time in history that a paid, full-time civilian cadre of officers was responsible for providing law and order. The idea spread to the U.S. and by the turn of the century most major urban cities had police departments. In the United States, early police officers were appointed by patronage by administrators who in turn were appointed by mayors or other municipal politicians who were elected to office. The theory was that this arrangement provided a civilian check on the action of police officers because it was the people who elected the officials who appointed the chief of police. This check and balance system proved to be inadequate in regulating the behavior of municipal police officers because of widespread corruption and injustice. Corrupt politicians appointed corrupt chiefs of police, who in turn appointed corrupt police officers.

The indirect control of the police by the ballot box appeared to be a weak check on police misconduct. In 1894, the Lexow Committee conducted an investigation of the New York Police Department and concluded that corruption was widespread. In 1929, President Herbert Hoover created the National Commission on Law Observance and Enforcement, better known as the Wickersham Commission. The 1931 report of the Wickersham Commission concluded that there was a "lack of effective, efficient, and honest patrol officers. . . . Police [are] inept, inefficient, racist, and brutal and . . . [commit] illegal acts." The 1967 report of the National Advisory Commission on Civil Disorders concluded that the ubiquitous riots of the 1960s were precipitated by police actions. The report accused the police of being insensitive, brutal, hostile, and cynical. It reported that many minority members in the community felt that there was a double standard of justice and protection.

In response to the call by the public to upgrade the professionalism of police departments, in 1967 Congress passed legislation providing for technical and financial as-

sistance to police departments though the newly created office of the Law Enforcement Assistance Administration (LEAA). One of the provisions to be eligible for the generous financial assistance provided in the form of grants by LEAA was that police departments had to have an internal affairs unit to investigate complaints of misconduct. Internal affairs investigation units under the complete control of the police did not appear to provide the necessary check and balance on misconduct. Citizens appeared to be hesitant to participate in a process completely under the control of the police. The reasons for this lack of participation were frequently lack of trust of the police to perform a fair investigation and fear of repercussions. The report of the National Advisory Commission on Criminal Justice Standards and Goals (1973) observed that because of fear of reprisal or harassment, and complex and cumbersome filing procedures many citizens were reluctant to bring complaints against the police. Some departments, for example, had regulations which provided that in the event that a citizen filed a complaint against a police officer and the complaint was not substantiated by the police investigation, the citizen who filed the complaint could be arrested for making a false report. For these reasons many citizens and civil rights leaders called for an independent means of investigating complaints against police officers.

Current Practice in the United States

The purpose of police review boards is to provide a deterrent to the police officer who may violate police procedures, violate criminal law, or use excessive force against citizens. The problem of regulating police conduct is complicated because the United States does not have a centralized, federal police. Without a centralized national police the task appears herculean as there are more than 40,000 municipal, county, state and federal police agencies in the United States with nearly one million employees. Each police department is a semi-autonomous political entity requiring a separate police review board. No one police review board has the authority to oversee the behavior of the police.

Confidence in the Police and Minorities

The desire for police review boards still appears to be related to a lack of confidence in the police by the citizens, especially minority members. In a 1994 Gallup poll 49 percent of the respondents indicated that they had "very little" or "no" confidence in the criminal justice system. When questioned specifically about their confidence in the police, the response differs by the race and income of the respondent. While 90 percent of whites indicated they had "a great deal" or "quite a lot" of confidence in the police, only 69 percent of blacks and 72 percent of nonwhites indicated they had similar confidence in the police. Ninety-five percent of respondents making more than $50,000 annually said they had "a great deal" or "quite a lot" of confidence in the police, whereas only 83 percent of respondents making less than $20,000 annually reported a similar level of confidence in the police. While only 8 percent of whites reported they believed the police had "low" or "very low" honesty and ethical standards, 22 percent of nonwhites and 28 percent of blacks indicated they believed the police had "low" or "very low" honesty and ethical standards.

Perhaps part of the reason for the lack of confidence by minority members in the police is the lack of minorities who are police officers. Minorities and females were effectively barred from police work until the Civil Rights Act of 1964 was amended in 1972 to require that governmental agencies were held to the same standards of equal employment requirements as private business. Until this legislation passed, law enforcement agencies could refuse to hire females and minorities with impunity. Since 1972, the situation has improved but still reflects a bias toward white males in police work.

Another reason that minorities may favor the use of police review boards more than whites is that minorities are more likely to be the victim of police misconduct. Allen Wagner in a 1980 survey in the *Journal of Police Science and Administration* reported that two-thirds of those who filed complaints against the police were blacks. He also reported that blacks were more likely to be arrested and injured than whites. He reported that incidents of police use of force were most likely to occur while the citizen was in police custody out of public view.

Tort Remedy

Rather than depend upon police review boards as an external regulator of behavior, most police personnel favor the use of internal administrative controls and the use of tort remedy. Opponents of civilian review of police conduct argue that citizen review frequently interferes with the crime-fighting abilities of the police as criminals make use of such procedures to harass individual police officers and undermine effective police practices. Opponents argue that police officers must have the right to use force and exercise discretion. If a police officer uses excessive force, violates civil rights, or flagrantly violates administrative rules and regulations, they argue that there are numerous and effective internal (administrative) and external avenues of redress for the citizen. Citizens who are dissatisfied with police administrative response to complaints can file tort and criminal actions against the police in court. While criminal actions are rare and judgments are even rarer, the use of civil suits against the police, and the winning of substantial monetary judgments, is increasing.

Many police officials argue that citizen review boards cause antagonism between the police and the public. They say police officers close ranks in support of accused officers because of the perceived unfairness or bias of civilian police review boards. Civilian members of a police review board may be perceived as naive regarding the use of force and too willing to believe unsubstantiated citizen complaints. Opponents of police review boards tend to believe that police officers who are accused of wrong doing by citizens receive a fairer hearing in the courts.

The courts have addressed the issues of misconduct. Landmark cases by the U.S. Supreme Court include *Weeks v. United States* (1914), *Wolf v. Colorado* (1949), and *Mapp v. Ohio* (1961). While police violation of constitutional rights is prohibited, it was not until the Weeks case that any penalty was attached to such violations. Without any penalty the resulting effect was that municipal, state, and federal police paid little attention to constitutional rights. Throughout the 1800s and early 1900s it was a common practice for police to search without a warrant or probable cause, obtain confessions by the use of force, and in general ignore constitutional rights of suspects. In the Weeks case the U.S. Supreme Court refused to allow the use in federal court of any evidence which had been obtained in violation of the Constitution's protections. This practice was called the "exclusionary rule." Later cases expanded the prohibition not only to evidence directly obtained by illegal means but also to any other evidence indirectly obtained. This practice was called the "fruit of the poisoned tree." The U.S. Supreme Court prohibited the use of such evidence in federal courts but did not prohibit the use of such evidence in state courts. From 1914 to 1949, the U.S. Supreme Court permitted the use of evidence that had been obtained by the police without a search warrant or probable cause in state courts. In the Wolf case the U.S. Supreme Court declared that state courts had to enact procedures to protect the rights of citizens against police abuses of search and seizure, but did not require that state courts use the exclusionary rule adopted by the federal courts. In 1961, in *Mapp v. Ohio* the U.S. Supreme Court reversed itself and required state courts to use the exclusionary rule and disallow evidence that had been obtained by the police without a search warrant or probable cause. Today violations by the police of the constitutional rights of a suspect can result in the evidence obtained being thrown out of court. Furthermore, recent U.S. Supreme Court rulings have allowed criminal charges to be filed against officers who knowingly violate the Fourth Amendment rights of citizens.

Citizens who claim that the police have used excessive force can bring suit against the police in both state and federal court. Federal Section 1984 civil rights actions permit citizens to seek redress for tort claims against law enforcement officers in a federal court rather than a state court. Citizens have prevailed against the police and have received substantial awards.

Police Review Boards

Proponents of police review boards argue that many citizens find seeking redress through the courts time-consuming, financially challenging, and psychologically intimidating. Furthermore, studies tend to suggest that prosecutors are less likely to pursue criminal charges against police officers. Given these objections, proponents argue that civilian oversight boards provide a realistic check and balance of police actions.

A 1991 survey by Samuel Walker and Vic Bumphus reported that 32 of the 50 largest cities had instituted civilian review procedures. It is interesting to note that 17 of the 32 review boards were established after 1986. Some police departments utilizing citizen oversight boards are: Berkeley (CA), District of Columbia, Chicago, Detroit, Kansas City (MO), New York, Oakland, and San Jose.

Wayne Kerstetter in *Police Leadership in America* (1985) classified citizen complaint review boards according to three models: (1) the citizen monitor model, (2) the citizen input model, and (3) the citizen review model. The models represent a continuum from minimum oversight to maximum oversight. The model providing the least oversight is the citizen monitor model. The members who review complaints against police officers are civilian employees of the police department. Boards operating under this model have no power to receive complaints, conduct investigations, or recommend sanctions. They primarily serve as a check over the police department process of internal investigation. Under the citizen input model nonsworn police department personnel have the power to receive and investigate complaints, but do not have the power to recommend sanctions against police officers when complaints are substantiated. The model in which civilian oversight exercises the greatest power is the citizen review model. Under this model members of the police review board are not employees of the police department. A citizen can file a complaint with the police department or directly with the board. The board has the power to investigate the complaint using independent investigators. If the complaint is substantiated, the board has the power to forward to the police administration recommendations for sanctions.

In their 1991 survey, Walker and Bumphus reported that prior to 1985, 80 percent of police oversight boards were staffed by only police personnel. They reported that after 1986, only 36 percent of the oversight boards had no civilian personnel. After 1986, 12 percent of the oversight boards had some civilian involvement, and 52 percent of the oversight boards utilized a civilian review process.

Impact of Police Review Boards

Despite police personnel opposition to civilian oversight boards it appears that their use is increasing. Increasing use, however, does not necessarily mean police review boards are gaining significant oversight power or making a great impact upon police behaviors. Civilian review boards appear to have had little measurable impact. When police review boards are established initially, the number of complaints against the police rises. It is common for complaints

to double when police review boards are established. However, few complaints filed with a police review board are likely to result in disciplinary action. In 1989, of the 482 complaints filed with the Kansas City, Missouri, police department review board only 26 complaints resulted in disciplinary action. In the same year, only 143 of 385 complaints resulted in disciplinary actions for Cincinnati, Ohio, and only 17 of 172 complaints resulted in disciplinary actions for Sacramento, California.

One major obstacle blocking the recommendations of police review boards from resulting in sanctions is the rising power of police unions and bargaining associations. Many large police departments now operate under negotiated union contracts or memorandums of agreement. One of the main provisions of the these contracts or memorandums of agreement is rules and regulations regarding disciplinary procedures and due process rights of the officer. Police unionism can seriously impact the ability of an oversight board to recommend discipline. For example, in a 1995 case in Honolulu, Hawaii, a district court judge blocked the release of the names of disciplined police officers, a release which was permitted under state law. The court ruled that the clause in the memorandum of agreement between the city and the police officers prohibiting the release of the names of disciplined police officers superseded state law. Police review boards must operate within the boundaries of due process to preserve the rights of police officers while attempting to secure the rights of citizens.

During the 1960s police departments were frequently described as "closed societies." Phrases such as "the blue curtain" described the isolation of police from the public and the solidarity of the police against public scrutiny. While the "blue curtain" has not disappeared, it is definitely parted. Both the public and police administrators have taken steps to make the operation of the police more open to the public. The Commission on Accreditation for Law Enforcement Agencies established in 1979 has prorogated accreditation standards which more than 100 police agencies have officially met. The Police Executive Research Forum and the powerful International Association of Chiefs of Police have expressed interest in promoting police review boards. In 1985 the International Association for Civilian Oversight of Law Enforcement was established to promote interaction among individuals involved in civilian oversight.

Federal Law Enforcement

When the U.S. government was founded there were only two federal law enforcement agencies in the United States, the Office of U.S. Marshal and the U.S. Postal Inspector. Oversight was vested in the power of appointment of the administrators who ran these police agencies. The number of federal law enforcement agencies has expanded to more than 50, but the means of oversight has not changed. Federal law enforcement agencies have limited statutory powers, and administrators are appointed by the president with the advice and consent of the Senate. Civilian review boards to evaluate misconduct by federal law enforcement officers do not exit. Complaints of misconduct by federal law enforcement officers are investigated by administrative staff, handled through tort or criminal action, or investigated by Congress. There appears to be no movement to change this procedure and utilize civilians to review complaints of misconduct of federal law enforcement officers.

International

The use of police review boards is not unique to the United States. Their use by other countries depends upon the relationship between the police and citizens of the country. In countries such as Japan and Sweden where the police enjoy strong public support, and police corruption and brutality are rare, there is little or no public demand for the adoption of police review boards. In Sweden, for example, 80 percent of the respondents of a survey indicated that they did not think that the police used excessive force or abused their authority in he performance of their duties.

France has a national police force and they find that it is easier to regulate police misconduct through central administrative rule, the French Code of Criminal Procedures, and the French Penal Code. The Office of Inspector General of police is responsible for investigating all allegations of misconduct by members of the National Police and a similar office exists to investigate misconduct by members of the National Gendarmerie. Given the highly centralized nature of the French police, they find it easier to regular misbehavior without civilian participation than the fragmented U.S. system of law enforcement.

Great Britain has a national but fragmented police system. The Police Act of 1976 established the Police Complaints Boards to handle complaints of police misconduct. The board is composed of citizens and magistrates (lower court judges). Citizens can file complaint with the Police Complaints Board or with the police. The police investigate the complaint regardless with whom the complaint is filed. The board can recommend sanctions, but only the chief constable (similar to the chief of police in the United States) has the power to impose recommended sanctions. There are similar complaints about the Police Complaints Board as there are about U.S. police review boards. The Police Complaints Board is seen as reactive only, limited in its scope of inquiry to individual incidents of misconduct, and conservative in finding officers guilty as charged and imposing sanctions.

JAMES A. FAGIN

BIBLIOGRAPHY

Barker, Thomas and David L. Carter, 1994. *Police Deviance,* 3d ed. Cincinnati, OH: Anderson Publishing Co.

Chang, Dae H. and James A. Fagin, 1985. *Introduction to Criminal Justice.* Lake Geneva, WI: The Farley Court of Publishers.

Kerner Commission, 1968. *Report of the National Advisory Commission on Civil Disorders.* Washington, D.C.: U.S. Government Printing Office.

Kerstetter, Wayne A., 1985. "Who Disciplines the Police? Who Should?" In W. A. Geller, ed., *Police Leadership in America.* Chicago: American Bar Association, pp. 149–182.

Mapp v. Ohio, 367 U.S. 643 (1961).

National Advisory Commission on Criminal Justice Standards and Goals, 1973. *Police.* Washington, D.C.: U.S. GPO.

President's Commission on Law Enforcement and the Administration of Justice. *Task Force Report: The Police.* Washington, D.C.: U.S. GPO.

Standards Relating to the Administration of Criminal Justice, 1974. Chicago: American Bar Association.

Terrill, Richard J., 1992. *World Criminal Justice Systems: A Survey.* Cincinnati, OH: Anderson Publishing Co.

Wagner, Allen E., 1980. "Citizen Complaints Against the Police: The Complainant." *Journal of Police Science and Administration,* vol. 8, no. 3.

Walker, Samuel, 1992. "Answers to 10 Key Questions About Civilian Review." *Law Enforcement News* (March 8), 8.

Walker, Samuel and Vic W. Bumphus, 1991. *Civilian Review of the Police: A National Survey of the 50 largest Cities, 1991.* Omaha: Center for Public Affairs Research.

Weeks v. United States, 232 U.S. 383 (1914).

Wolf v. Colorado, 338 U.S. 25 (1949).

POLICY. A decision or, more usually, a set of interrelated decisions concerning the selection of goals and the means of achieving them. The identification of policy as a set or web of decisions is useful in that it underlines the notion that policy is best seen as a course of action–or inaction–rather than a single, discrete decision or action.

It is tempting, and common, to regard policy and the policy process as somehow ordered and rational. According to rational assumptions, the policy process consists of the identification of a problem demanding a solution or a goal worth achieving, assessment of the alternative means of achieving the desired outcome, the making of a choice between these alternatives, the implementation of the preferred option, and the solution of the problem or the attainment of the objective. However, such a process would imply the involvement of a small number of decisionmakers, a high degree of consensus concerning what constitutes a policy problem or a desirable objective, an ability to calculate and compare the likely consequences of each alternative, smooth implementation of the chosen option, and the absence of obstacles to the achievement of policy goals. It also implies that the process is terminated by the making and implementation of a decision. In the real world, however, policy processes are likely to be less well structured. Multiple decisionmakers, little consensus, incalculable probabilities, imperfect implementation, and unknown or unknowable outcomes might be encountered, and policy can appear messier, less coherent, and less able to achieve the desired outcome than rational models suggest. Policies are in any case distinct from single decisions and incorporate continuity and dynamism.

Sometimes, policy is understood and indeed presented at such a level of generality that notions of implementation or even of decision are barely factors at all. For politicians, policy may on occasion simply reflect a stance or orientation. Policy may be exclusively or primarily declaratory—"to contribute to the creation of a more peaceful world," or "to strive towards a more equal society." Of course it is possible to envisage a kind of hierarchy of policies, whereby subordinate policies—diplomatic support for a specific peace proposal, or progressive taxation—serve to concretize these more abstract aspirations. Such an approach would shift attention away from a focus on policy content and towards a concern with the presence or lack of systematic and ordered attempts at implementation. We would want to know how interrelated and coordinated is the set of decisions which make up the policy as a whole. In other words, an exclusive or excessive emphasis on policy content is unsatisfying. We want to know about the policy process, policy implementation, and policy success.

The policy process is sometimes characterized as a "black box" which converts inputs into outputs. As with the rational approach, this too tends to assume that policymaking only begins after the policy agenda has been set, and that it ends once a decision or set of decisions emerges from the black box. However, it might be useful to regard the policy process as incorporating the determination of what constitutes a policy issue in the first place, and as continuing during the implementation stage. The conceptualization of policy as a set of decisions serves to raise questions relating to which decisions are part of the problem or goal identification stage, which part of the selection of options stage, and which part of the implementation of the policy.

Take implementation. Empirical studies of policies in the real world sometimes cast doubt on the idea that policy can usefully be understood solely as plan or design, and instead draw attention to policy as practice. Decisions which contribute to an overall policy might be made at the implementation stage. Policy is not only what is intended, but also what is done. This suggests a muddier reality in which policy can appear reactive, pragmatic, or adaptive, as well as or instead of proactive, coherent, and purposive. The agents whose formal task it is to implement policy might receive imprecise or ambiguous directives that require them to exercise judgment or discretion. Furthermore, experts in the implementing bureaucracy might not only take the opportunity but be expected to interpret policy and how it should be applied in practice. The presence of complexity will encourage this tendency. In this way, policy might evolve or develop incrementally. In resembling a learning process, policy can become dynamic over time.

What happens inside the black box might also have a bearing on policy. "Policy" has the same linguistic root as "politics"—indeed, in some languages the same word is used—and the notion of politics conjures up the prospect of conflict, power struggles, and clashes of ideas and interests. Given that most policymaking involves large numbers of individuals, groups, and agencies, then we should not be surprised that politics take place. As a result, policy decisions might reflect compromises resulting from debates and bargaining between the various contributors. Compromises such as these might fully satisfy few of the contributors, and might be incoherent or ambiguous in content. Indeed, they might not even address the policy problem at all in any very rational or structured way, and might best be seen as driven by the internal dynamics of the policy process. The definition and determination of the policy problem might itself reflect the interests and power relationships of the various parties engaged in the policy process, and their relative capacity to force a perceived problem or desired objective onto the policy formulation agenda.

We have noted the role agencies as well as individuals might play in policy formulation. The growth of bureaucracy has been a major feature of modern government, and although bureaucracies are formally instruments of government it is a fact that they often play a role in policymaking itself. There are a number of explanations for this phenomenon. Bureaucrats are often experts whose opinions are sought and who expect to be consulted. Furthermore, bureaucracies often have interests of their own to pursue—in maintaining or expanding budgets or missions, for example. They might also develop broad policy goals, preferences, or perspectives of their own—that higher education is good for the economy, that surface navies enhance national security, and so on. Thus bureaucrats might operate both as political participants in the setting of policy as well as incremental decisionmakers in its application.

A policy process can produce an output—for example, a set of decisions resulting in a given allocation of resources—but this does not necessarily mean that the overall objectives of the policy will be achieved. The impact of policy actions might not be what was desired. Unintended consequences and unanticipated effects may stem from the ambiguity or contradictions of policy, from imperfections in implementation, from ill-appreciated complexities in the environment within which a policy is to operate, or from the decision of insufficient or maldistributed resources. Thus economic growth might not correlate very well with, say, reduced taxation or increased expenditure on education. Social inequality might not be greatly affected by the establishment of a social security system. Policies often tacitly incorporate causal theories linking policy actions with policy impacts, but faith in such theories might be misplaced.

Thus, although on first consideration the notion of policy might appear to be a simple and straightforward one, further analysis indicates a much greater complexity. The discipline of policy analysis has grown up around this complexity, containing competing schools of thought and offering differing definitions. A policy must be distinguished from a decision. Policies can be purposive and far-reaching or adaptive and incremental—or even static. Scrutiny of the whole process, from the emergence of a policy issue through to evaluation of a policy outcome, might be necessary if a policy is to be fully comprehended. The policy formulation process might be so intensely political as to render the prospect of coherence improbable. Policies might fail to achieve their objectives, or even have results opposite to those intended. Yet policies are unavoidable, for they are the means by which societies and other social organizations regulate, control, and at least endeavour to advance themselves.

WILLIAM PARK

BIBLIOGRAPHY

Braybrooke, D. and C. E. Lindblom, 1963. *A Strategy of Decision.* New York: The Free Press.

Hill, Michael, ed., 1993. *The Policy Process: A Reader.* New York and London: Harvester Wheatsheaf.

Hogwood, B. W. and L. A. Gunn, 1984. *Policy Analysis for the Real World.* Oxford: Oxford University Press.

Jenkins, W. I., 1978. *Policy Analysis.* London: Martin Robertson.

Lasswell, H. D., 1958. "The Policy Orientation." In D. Lerner and H. D. Lasswell, eds., *The Policy Sciences.* Stanford, CA: Stanford University Press.

Wildavsky, A., 1979. *Speaking Truth to Power: The Art and Craft of Policy Analysis.* Boston: Little Brown.

POLICY ADVICE.

The expert opinion offered to a government executive about a course of action.

The term policy advice combines two words, of which policy is associated with a number of meanings. For the purpose here it is necessary to note that there are different types of policy in the sense of separate fields of government activity, and that different tasks and levels of complexity and difficulty can be distinguished within and between fields which have implications for the nature of advice.

Advice about policy is usually conveyed to the political executive, a top official, or to an organization charged with advising leaders. Conceptions of policy advice vary according to focus and scope. One broad view regards policy advising as covering analysis of problems and the proposing of solutions. It specifies structuring the problem, gathering information, analyzing, formulating options, and communicating the results. In this case policy advising has been equated with the policy formulation process. As an official-centered depiction of policy advising, it is assumed that even if the senior adviser does not undertake all these roles she or he will be responsible for their performance.

Another conception views the process as the open-ended reception of advice: the means by which governments "deliberately acquire, and passively receive . . . advice on decisions and policies which may be broadly called informative, objective or technical" (Peters and Barker 1993, p. 1). This conception points to the broader context of advice in which there are flows of information and influence. Of importance here is whether advice is solicited (and presumably subject to some degree of formal influence) or unsolicited (but has to be taken into account). Advice needs to be differentiated from information. The provision of information alone is not advice; advice adds interpretation and proposals about how to proceed.

Policy advice is offered on a substantive basis for specific fields or sectors (for example, education or health policy, or much finer specializations within these fields), but policy also covers matters of organization, personnel, and politics. Distinctions may be made between strategic (which may be cross-sectoral) and operational advice (which relates to principles of execution), and between political (as electoral and partisan) and policy (as technical and objective) advice. A focus on stages in the policy process yields distinctions between advice about formulation and advice about implementation.

Policy advice in the sense that it is understood today is relatively recent, for it was once believed that the roles of politician and bureaucrat assigned policy to the former and execution to the latter. Rulers have traditionally employed advisers. Only as the complexity of the policy environment increased greatly during the twentieth century was the policy advice function recognized as one upon which political decisionmakers had become increasingly reliant, and one provided by specialists in the art of tendering advice. Such advice may be the product of policy analysts, but this is not necessarily so. Advisers can be laypersons or experts (e.g., scientists), bureaucratic or political, or generalist or specialist. A further complicating factor has been the growing interdependence of policy fields and of policy and administration.

We can make sense of the sources of advice by distinguishing two central dimensions of a policy advisory system. The first is the location of policy advice: whether the sources of advice are internal or external to the governmental system. The internal processes are divided between those which are internal to the civil service—the mainstream departmental advisers—and those which are part of the broader governmental system. This internal to government category covers political units, other branches (e.g., the legislature) and alternative advisory structures which are separate from the formal civil service (e.g., specialized commissions). The external processes take several forms, including government work which has privatized elements, the competing expertise from nongovernmental organizations, public consultation, and the influence of international processes and organizations.

The policy advice system typically comprises several types of bureaucratic and political advisers. The core is the single advice provider (the civil service) for a specific client (the cabinet minister or chief executive). There is generally provision for central advice (both the first minister's unit and central agency) and political advice from special advisers, and some other form of policy instrument is commonly employed (e.g., special administrative unit or task force). Less agreement would be reached on some elements of the advice system: the emphasis on the various components (e.g., the legislature and the role of political appointments); the significance of different organizational options; the role of specialized political units; and the flexibility with regard to strategic processes for managing specific policy issues.

The second dimension is the degree of control exercised by government over policy advice. The advice system is subject to preferences which prevail within a political system. It can be dominated by civil servants with a quasi-monopolistic role or by politicians where there is a reliance on political appointments and the sharing of the spoils of power, particularly under conditions of one- or multiparty government. The type of governmental system is important, the variations in the structure depending on whether formal authority is diffused among branches and levels of government. Under an open pluralist system, there will be more access points for external interests and a tendency to rely more heavily on a broader and more diverse range of contributions. In contrast, the executive-centered system is less directly accessible and susceptible to a range of external influences including advisers. The characteristics of U.S. government–federalism and separation of powers–encourage bargaining and group politics in policymaking, and a greater reliance on external advisers. In contrast, the tradition of other countries is more executive-centered, placing greater emphasis on the professional civil service.

The structure of advice systems also varies between policy fields (e.g., education and transport). Variations in organizations and interests among policy fields have come to be identified as different types of policy networks. Another set of factors center on the personal styles of leaders and how they interpret and apply the principles which operate within their system of government.

The provision of policy advice has been influenced by international developments in managerial and economic theories which have emphasized debureaucratization, evaluation, accountability, decentralization, and performance, and accord prominence to the market and competition. Political ideas have been reaffirmed through the direct challenges mounted by politicians to the strength of the

civil service. Across government policy advice has become more contestable. As a result several trends in the handling of policy advice are worth mentioning.

The first is that the role of the civil servant has been redefined with direct implications for policy advice. The targeting of the civil service monopoly has had several consequences: career civil servants are less prominent in top advisory positions (e.g., the United States), or where they have tended to retain the most senior positions, their experience is broader, their turnover has increased, and more outsiders have been appointed. The nexus between policy specialization and department context was broken in some countries with senior executives more likely to be generalists and managers. Finally there has been a greater willingness to look elsewhere for policy advice, particularly from political advisers.

A second trend is the impact of decentralizing philosophies on operating frameworks. There have been new experiments with separating policy formulation from implementation through policy-focused departments, somewhat along the lines of the traditional Swedish model. The question of what structure works best for policy advice depends on context, but may come down to whether the separation of policy and administration organizationally is best applied across the civil service (as in New Zealand or the United Kingdom) or whether a more pragmatic approach is suitable (Australia and Canada).

Closely related is the increasing reliance on contracting out. This affects not only policy advice, but also the implementation of policy. The use of internal and external markets for the supply of policy advice may be based on competitive tendering for the provision of advice and be conceived in terms of purchaser-provider arrangements based on contracts. Despite the advantages of drawing on independent expertise, there are limits to how far core government functions can be contracted out.

This trend is also linked to the focus on conceiving policy advice within an approach of managing the policy process, which involves consultation, coordination, and process management. At the input end a key question is whether the job can be undertaken in-house or requires the injection of external expertise; there is flexibility with regard to the choice of advisers and appropriate management structures. Close attention must be given to managing partisan settings as the boundaries around the civil service become more permeable and politicians more active. The policy process is subject to strategic management, which draws attention to the need to go beyond policy content: senior executives have to manage networks which incorporate a range of actors and mechanisms and may extend from the local to the international community.

A final area of change, as the market in which advisers work has become more contestable and competitive, is evaluating policy advice. It is argued that all government administration should be subject to some form of evaluation, and that while aspects centered on the political decisionmaker may be off the record, evaluation can still attempt to illuminate the quality and level of policy advising. External review agencies such as legislative committees seek more systematic assessment of policy work and the "value" which is added by agency advice. Departments are expected to relate input data to outcomes, and to develop better performance indicators for measuring the efficiency and effectiveness of policy advice.

JOHN HALLIGAN

BIBLIOGRAPHY

Barker, Anthony and B. Guy Peters, ed., 1993. *The Politics of Expert Advice: Creating, Using and Manipulating Scientific Knowledge for Public Policy.* Edinburgh: Edinburgh University Press.

Boston, Jonathan, 1994. "Purchasing Policy Advice: The Limits to Contracting Out." *Governance* 7 (1) (January) 1–30.

Halligan, John, 1995. "Policy Advice and the Public Service." In B. Guy Peters and Donald Savoie, eds., *Governance in a Changing Environment.* Montreal: McGill University Press.

Hawke, G. R., 1993. *Improving Policy Advice.* Wellington: Institute of Policy Studies.

Meltsner, Arnold J., 1990. *Rules for Rulers: The Politics of Advice.* Philadelphia: Temple University Press.

Peters, B. Guy and Anthony Barker, eds., 1993. *Advising West European Governments: Inquiries, Expertise and Public Policy.* Edinburgh: Edinburgh University Press.

Plowden, William, ed., 1987. *Advising the Rulers.* Oxford: Basil Blackwell.

Smith, Bruce L. R., 1992. *The Advisers: Scientists in the Policy Process.* Washington, D.C.: The Brookings Institution.

POLICY ANALYSIS.

A wide range of intellectual approaches over a number of disciplines in respect of a core activity of government or private organizations. To understand its scope and range requires the separate examination and then synthesis of the two terms.

Policy

"Policy" is a generic term, widely used to point to the means and ends of a deliberative, or decisionmaking, process. Often the two are interchangeable, but the distinction needs to be kept in focus. In a vacuum, and standing alone, the word "policy" means nothing. It needs qualification.

Policy Context

Initially, the term "policy" is normally qualified with the addition of a word or phrase giving it a description and putting it in context. Thus one talks of a foreign, defense, social welfare, agriculture, or monetary policy. Each policy context will have its own distinctive groups of actors, individual decisionmaking processes, preferred methods and agendas, and sets of objectives. A further distinction is that between public and private policy. Most analytical attention is given to the former, since it is there where issues of the proper conduct of those in authority in a democratic society and the scale of the impact of policy decisions are greatest.

The context of policy is fundamental for the understanding of policy analysis. It determines who are the particular participants in the policymaking process; it sets the parameters of the content of policy; it points to where the emphasis on policy lies; and it influences which criteria are appropriate in the analysis of that policy.

Policy as Means

In many fields of public policy, the central issue is to decide on the means by which a given policy objective is to be achieved. This broadly falls into three distinct areas: policy guidelines, strategy, and tactics. Policy guidelines define the manner, style, scope, tone, range, priorities, and degree, according to which those responsible for policy implementation and execution are expected to perform their tasks. Strategy identifies the resources available to policymakers and sets out principles which govern how these are to be used to achieve a given objective. Last, the ways in which these resources are deployed in detail within the framework laid down by strategy are the tactics. The analysis of policy as means can refer to these three elements separately or as a whole, leading to assessment and judgment as to their effectiveness, suitability, implications, and so forth.

Policy as Ends

More frequently, "policy" is used to identify the objectives which decisionmakers wish to achieve. The difficulty is to differentiate those objectives which are long-term, as opposed to short-term; general, as opposed to specific; and teleological–the setting of clearly defined, absolute, and immutable objectives far into the future–as opposed to ontological–the pursuit of objectives that are achievable, given current capabilities, resources, and circumstances. Furthermore there are multiple objectives, operating at various levels with different orders of salience, which tend to blur the distinction between means and ends over time.

A further distinction of analytical importance is that between declaratory policy objectives–essentially statements of good intention issued for political purposes–and developmental policy objectives–namely the initiation of a course of actions which have one clear outcome. As a generalization, the analysis of policy objectives tends to be concerned with choices, alternatives, priorities, and implications.

Policy as Process

Policy choice, both in terms of means and ends, is the product of a decisionmaking process, the composition, manner, style, procedure, and conduct of which is determined in the public sector according to policy context and the prevailing circumstances. No generalization or prescription which points to a better, or worse, decisionmaking process or which makes qualitatively better or worse decisions strictly applies, since each needs to be treated *sui generis*—that is, in its own terms and context.

A further problem is that decisionmaking is a dynamic and continuing process. It is one which constantly adapts according to changes in participants and circumstances. Policy analysis in this respect considers such qualitative facets as the ability of the actors involved; the data available to them; the dynamics of the decisionmaking process; and the importance to society of the outcome.

Analysis

The purpose of public policy analysis, then, is to investigate rigorously the formulation and execution of policies performed in the public's name, by state authorities using public (i.e., the taxpayers') money. The motives for engaging in analysis are varied, depending who is performing the work. They may arise from a concern over the policy objectives themselves; the question of whether or not the means by which they are sought are appropriate; the manner in which decisions were taken; and the management efficiency with which policies are executed.

Policy analyses are primarily conducted by government organizations—such as the UK National Audit Office, the French Cour de Compte, or the U.S. General Accounting Office—by expert consultants or by academics. Whoever undertakes the task, they will bring a specific expertise and their own agenda. Correspondingly, they will focus on one or another of the different aspects of policy noted above. In an open, democratic society, the product of the analysts' work can contribute to the public's requirement for the accountability of government, local authorities, and quasi-nongovernmental organizations.

Analytical Approaches

Ideally, the approach to policy analysis should be holistic, taking each of the policy dimensions and subjecting them to cross-disciplinary analysis. For practical and intellectual reasons, this seldom happens. The practice tends to be more one of the analysts focusing on an aspect of policy. The analysis will likely depend on their intellectual discipline, the policy issue they want to address, and the context in which it is done. Thus, for example, economists by and large focus on issues of the cost effectiveness or public policy choices and opportunity costs; political scientists on decisionmaking processes and, within their areas of specialization, such as foreign affairs or defense, policy content; sociologists also on policy content—welfare, education, health—and on decisionmakers' behavior; lawyers on constitutional and statutory implications of policy; philosophers on the ethical dimension of public policy

choices and the personal conduct of decisionmakers, and so on.

Policy Content Analysis

One of the most valuable contributions that the analyst can make to public policy is to take a public policy decision and the manner of its intended implementation, and explore what its implications will be, not simply in respect of the objectives per se, but more importantly for future options in that and other policy areas. In this, the analyst can become party to the policy debate, both as critic and as contributor. In so doing, the policy analyst quite properly is, or should be, a responsible, authoritative, and accountable contributor to what is the central part of the democratic governmental process—taking policy decisions.

MARTIN EDMONDS

BIBLIOGRAPHY

Bobrow, Davis and John Dryzek, 1987. *Policy Analysis by Design.* Pittsburgh: University of Pittsburgh Press.

MacRae, Duncan and James Wilde, 1985. *Policy Analysis for Public Decisions.* Lanham: University Press of America.

Nagel, S.,1984. *Public Policy: Goals, Means and Methods.* New York: St Martin's Press.

Schultze, Charles, 1977. *The Public Use of Private Interest.* Washington, D.C.: Brookings Institution.

Wildavsky, Aaron, 1979. *Speaking Truth to Power.* Boston: Little Brown.

POLICY LEADERSHIP.

The act of stimulating the formulation and implementation of public policy among multiple, diverse stakeholders and constituencies. Policy leadership is different from the more common notions of organizational leadership; policy leadership mobilizes attention to problematic conditions, and then forges agreement on appropriate policy responses among diverse, often competing groups and constituencies.

Background

Definition of Public Policy

There exists no universally accepted definitions that clearly distinguish policies from non-policies; as a result, there is considerable ambiguity about what constitutes a policy (Polsby 1984). A public policy is generally characterized as a combination of decisions, commitments, and actions directed toward achieving a particular outcome or result which is deemed in the public interest. Public policies can be further distinguished from public programs and projects; a public program is a set of concrete actions and implementation steps directed toward the attainment of a public policy, while a project is typically a single segment or operating activity within a program. A second distinguishing characteristic is that public policies are different from organizational policies; organizational policies are directed at influencing the behavior of employees to achieve an agency's goal or objective.

Public Problems, Policy Discourse, and Policy Leadership

Public policies are developed and implemented as a collective response to address problematic conditions. In pluralist societies, however, public policies are formulated in an environment typically characterized by disbursed authority and shared power among multiple agencies and institutions, and by conflicting goals and values among multiple constituencies and interest groups (Bryson and Crosby 1992). In addition, the social, economic, and environmental problems that public policies increasingly address are most often boundaryless and intertwined with other public problems. As a result, the context of policy leadership is complex and interconnected, and effective policy responses are seldom clear-cut or obvious. No longer is crime "just a police problem," or education "just a school problem," or economic development "just a problem of attracting new industries." Each has multiple interrelated causes, creates ripple effects that spread out over historically separate institutions and jurisdictions, and generates competing and conflicting perspectives on what should be done to improve the situation. One result is that there is seldom a natural consensus on how to approach critical public problems. Policy leadership thus requires a communication and decisionmaking process—a policy discourse—that engages many diverse interests and perspectives in addressing public problems. Effective policy discourse involves individuals, interest groups, stakeholders, and institutions moving through four unique but interrelated phases: converting a problematic situation to a policy problem, setting policy agendas, making decisions, and taking actions.

Policy leadership occurs when an individual or group focuses attention on an issue or problem and raises it to the public agenda; stimulates collaborative and concerted action among diverse stakeholders to address the issue; and ensures sustained action during implementation. A policy leader in an interconnected public policy context is one who can stimulate collective action toward a particular outcome when no one agency or jurisdiction has enough power—resources, influence, or authority—to dictate solutions unilaterally. Policy leadership is essentially interorganizational or transorganizational in nature, and thus follows different steps and requires different skills than contemporary definitions of organizational leadership and small group leadership.

Leadership in Organizational Contexts

Contemporary theories of leadership, however, focus on organizational and intraorganizational contexts and settings. Historically, leadership research has focused on leadership of groups or teams in organizations by people in positions of organizational authority. During World War II, for example, submarine crews and bomber teams were intensively studied to improve their effectiveness, with group leadership identified as significant variable in group productivity and morale. Following World War II, the growing interest in productivity in business and industry sparked continued and expanded research on morale, employee motivation, and small group dynamics. Supervisory or managerial leadership was thus initially defined as a process of influence by one individual who steers or motivates other individuals or group members toward a predetermined goal, typically on matters of organizational relevance.

In the mid-1980s, these earlier small group leadership theories gave way to theories on leading a whole organization. These approaches prescribed a set of skills or steps for effective leadership within U.S. organizations, and aimed to help corporate executives to pursue excellence (Peters and Waterman 1982; Peters and Austin 1985), to take charge (Bennis and Nanus 1985), to stimulate extraordinary performance by employees (Kouzes and Posner 1987) or to change an organizational culture by being transformational (Tichy and Devanna 1986). A clear break with past research and writings on small group leadership, the essence was a focus on leadership of an organization, rather than small group leadership within an organization—a process of influencing the organization as a whole, changing and adapting organizations to better fit and perform in the complex, global environment in which corporations exist. Three of the more common theories of organizational leadership are transformational leadership, visionary leadership, and charismatic leadership.

Transformational Leadership

A wide-ranging and historical analysis of political and social leadership by Burns (1978) identifies two different forms of leadership in society throughout history: transformational and transactional. Transactional leadership involves some form of exchange between the leader and follower, such as wages, gifts, votes, prestige, advancement, or other valued things, in exchange for the individual following the leaders' wishes or meeting the leaders' objectives. The exchange can be economic, political, or even psychological. Other than exchanging things of value, the bargainers have no enduring purpose to hold them together. Transformational leadership, on the other hand, involves a leader drawing followers out of a narrow, parochial interest into a "higher" purpose. Rather than exchanging one thing for another in a process of bargaining, a transformational leader engages followers by tapping their existing and potential motives and aspirations, and then through inspiration, teaching, and modeling transforms them into higher order needs and visions for the purpose of achieving intended change.

It is transforming in that the leader transforms or elevates the followers, interests from self-oriented ends to mission-oriented ends. As a result, leaders and followers experience a shared sense of fates and interdependence of interests, where the higher aspirations of both the leader and follower congeal into one. In an organizational setting, two different descriptions of transformational leadership have emerged, both building on the historical analysis by Burns. The first focuses on leadership that transforms employee performance from the expected to performance beyond expectations, using transformational leadership strategies that engender high performance levels within organizations (Bass 1990). Although there are different transformational leadership styles, they each include four common characteristics that transform followers in this fashion: charisma, inspiration, individualized consideration, and intellectual stimulation. The other transformational approach to leadership highlights strategies to transform organizations in response to the complex and rapidly changing environments that organizations face. Tichy and Devanna (1986) identified three strategies that successful corporate leaders utilize in transforming their organizations to respond to new markets and vastly increase competitiveness: recognize the need for revitalization, create a motivating vision, and create a new organizational architecture that institutionalizes change.

Visionary Leadership

The emphasis on having a compelling vision is a central theme in transformational leadership. Other leadership approaches similarly highlight the importance of visionary leadership, beginning with Berlew (1974), who noted that leadership that "excited" organizational members was one that offered a vision for the organization and which expressed a set of common values and goals. Focus on visionary leadership increased in the mid-1980s and highlighted the need for a compelling, persuasive vision in order to mobilize organizational members to move from where they are to where they have never been but need to go according to the leader's assessment of the situation. Although vision is defined in several different, but related, ways, the central ingredient of visionary leadership is the articulation of a compelling vision that attracts, excites, and animates followers in pursuit of an organizational common goal (Bennis and Nanus 1985).

Charismatic Leadership

The notion of charisma, Greek for "divine gift," captures a third general theory of organizational leadership. Traditionally, a charismatic leader was an individual who had considerable emotional power over followers, particularly in times of crisis that required strong direction. The followers' bond was highly emotional, and the leader relied on this power to influence followers' actions. More recently, charismatic leadership is characterized by a leader-follower bond where the leader grips followers with a specific vision for action or by other means than merely emotional appeals to survive a crisis. A charismatic leader is one who has a strong vision or mission, who produces high levels of personal loyalty and commitment to his or her vision or mission, who is perceived as exceptional and extraordinary, and who therefore enjoys the personal devotion of a large portion of the organizational membership (Bryman 1992).

Common Themes in Contemporary Definitions of Organizational Leadership

Leadership is one of the most studied concepts in the world today. With only a few exceptions, however, the focus is almost entirely on leadership performed by individuals within formal organizations. These three general theories—transformational, visionary, and charismatic—are the most recent perspectives used to analyze and illuminate the types of leadership required for improving organizational performance in a turbulent, unpredictable, and global economy. The three approaches interrelate and overlap, but with only minor differences and emphases: each recognizes that a leader is an instrument of organizational change and prescribes a common set of skills or actions necessary to successfully renew, revitalize, or enliven organizations:

- Having a strong and compelling vision that challenges the status quo, and takes an organization to a new place it has never been;
- Infusing the vision in a way that inspires and motivates employees throughout the organization, dramatically influencing followers to perform in goal-directed ways;
- Empowering others and enlisting followers in the vision to stimulate extra effort to achieve it;
- Developing mutual trust and personal loyalty between the leader and followers.

Leadership in Public Policy Contexts

Leadership outside organizational contexts—policy leadership that targets solving complex, boundaryless public problems in highly interconnected policy arenas—is less well understood and much less researched. Leadership for public policy occurs outside of organizational boundaries—is intergovernmental and intersectoral in nature—and therefore faces constraints and challenges substantially different than those facing contemporary organizational leadership. Richard Neustadt, a noted presidential scholar, pessimistically noted that the constraints and challenges for contemporary presidential leadership are much different than ever before in history and are characterized by at least three interconnected restraints (1990): telecommunications media, particularly television, that encourage leaders to strike poses rather than address real issues; the declining power of political parties and increasing interest group pressure to pursue more narrow agendas; and hardening institutional boundaries between the White House and Congress. Histories and analyses of U.S. presidential and congressional leadership have provided some insights into political leadership at the national level, but are less clear on the steps or tasks needed today for policy leadership.

External Constraints in Providing Policy Leadership

Government executives tend to be driven by the constraints imposed from outside the organization, rather than the unique mission and tasks of the agency (Wilson 1989). First, public problems cross jurisdictional, organizational, and functional boundaries, and are interconnected with other problems. Most public problems are so complex and interconnected, and power to solve the problem is so shared and disbursed (Bryson and Crosby 1992), that no single person, agency, or jurisdiction has sufficient power or authority to develop and implement policy solutions unilaterally.

Second, public policies on any particular issue can affect an increasingly larger number of agencies and constituencies, and perceived adverse effects can evoke widespread resistance. In many Western countries, people's trust and confidence in the ability of government, and of leaders, to solve problems effectively has declined to perhaps the lowest it has ever been. As a result, there is an increasing number and diversity of impassioned activists, special interests, and legitimate agencies and institutions who seek involvement in the development and formulation of public policy, and who can apply considerable resistance to policy change.

Policy leadership is thus provided within a unique interorganizational web of political, economic, environmental, social, and technological concerns; and addressing public problems in such an interconnected policy arena requires many individuals and groups to be involved, decreasing the ability of any one individual, agency, or institution to mobilize a sufficient number of individuals behind any particular policy agenda.

Four Essential Tasks in Policy Leadership

Policy leadership, therefore, is a form of leadership that works in political and interorganizational contexts where authority is shared and power is disbursed in a community, region, and country. In such contexts, policy leadership involves four specific, but interrelated, tasks for developing policy responses aimed at pressing public problems:

1. Raise the issue on the public and policy agendas by focusing attention on the issue or problematic condition;
2. Convene the set of individuals, agencies and interests—stakeholders and knowledgeholders—needed to address the issue;
3. Forge agreements on policy alternatives and viable options for action;
4. Sustain action and maintain momentum during implementation.

Each of these four essential tasks summarizes, in short hand, a more complex set or pattern of activities and processes commonly found in successful policy leadership efforts. However, it must be emphasized that the policy leadership process is not sequential, nor a formal linear model.

Raise the Issue to the Public and Policy Agendas

Effective policy leaders intervene into the policy arena by first directing attention toward an undesirable condition or problem, defining and framing the issue in ways that can mobilize others around the search for responses. The initial step in policy leadership is to act as a "catalyst" focusing the attention of the public, government officials, and members and leaders of many separate organizations and agencies, as well as the broader community of interests. They promote a new issue to higher prominence, or get people to see an old problem in new ways. Because the full list of potential problems requiring public attention is vast, and resources to address each problem are limited, policy leaders fix attention on a particular problem, making the issue more salient, important, and urgent than other issues that may be competing for attention and resources.

Policy Agenda Setting. There exists two types of policy agendas, each encompassing a smaller set of issues (Cobb and Elder 1983). The systemic or public agenda is the larger set of problems or societal concerns that the general public is paying some serious attention to at any given time. There is a smaller, more formal governmental or policy agenda that includes issues being paid serious attention by people in and around government. (A smaller subset of the policy agenda, the decision agenda, includes an even narrower set of issues, alternatives, and policy choices being actively discussed and considered.) Agenda setting is a prelude to policy action. Policy leaders raise an issue in a way that commands increasing attention and increases the likelihood that key stakeholders will either be recruited or attracted to address the issue.

Agenda Setting Is Unpredictable. Policy ideas typically reach a stage of "common currency" and then fade into the background, following a general pattern of appreciation, articulation, debate, adoption, institutionalization, and decay (Schon 1971). However, there is no one single factor which places an issue or problem high on the public, policy, or decision agendas.

Analysis of U.S. federal policy development reveals that agenda setting does not go through a rational, problem-solving process that proceeds neatly in stages, steps, or phases (Kingdon 1984). Rather, there are separate, independent streams of problems, proposed solutions, and politics occurring simultaneously but separately on specific problems, and at some critical point, or succession of points, a catalytic effect occurs, pushing one problem higher on the agenda, and displacing other issues from prominence.

Life Cycle of Issues. Yankelovich (1992) further clarified this life cycle of issues; analyzing the cycle of public opinion and attitudes (expressed in national opinion polls) of two specific issues—AIDS and the "greenhouse effect"—he found that issues reached the public agenda, or what he called the "public consciousness," in widely variable times, from minutes to decades. Although he found that there was a vast variability in the amount of time required for each issue to reach the public agenda, he found some common features: an event that forcefully dramatizes an issue and serves to focus attention, perceived applicability to one's self, the concreteness and clarity to the general public of the issue, the credibility of the sources of information the public receives, and the quantity of publicity the issue generates.

These analyses reveal that issues go through three phases to reach a prominent point on the policy agenda: starting as a condition or latent concern, it rises to the public's attention as a problem when there is sufficient dissatisfaction with the condition. Finally, it becomes an issue that is seen as urgent and pressing, generating political attention and displacing other issues from the policy agenda.

Often, issues move forward on the policy agenda due to the opening of policy windows which are taken advantage of by policy leaders. There are three types of policy windows: those opened by the sudden publicity and emergence of a pressing public problem, those opened by significant political shifts, and windows opened as a result of key decision points being reached (Bryson and Crosby 1992). After the issue has reached the policy agenda, however, attention does not remain sharply focused for a long period of time. It will eventually fade from public attention, even if largely unresolved, and will be replaced by another pressing and urgent issue (Bryson and Crosby 1992; Downs 1972).

Salience, Urgency, and the Use of Stories. Policy leaders focus attention on a condition or problem in such a way that others embrace the issue as a priority. Data is often used to highlight "troubling comparisons"—differing employment rates between regions or states, for example—or to show "worsening trends"—for example, dramatic increases in juvenile crime over the last several years. Data may convince some that an issue is urgent; however, data does not necessarily make a condition or problem salient or tangible. Information is more salient and vivid when it conjures up images, is easy to imagine, is easy to explain or elaborate, and is more likely to be recalled. Vivid information such as stories and anecdotes are thus given greater weight than mere data because it captures one's attention and remains in one's thoughts for longer periods of time—for example when one hears about a neighbor being a victim of juvenile crime—and is particularly salient if the story depicts causal relationships (Nutt 1992)—for example, when a personal story also includes very tangible reasons why juvenile crime is increasing significantly in one's particular neighborhood.

Convening Stakeholders to Address the Issue

Once this issue is on the policy agenda, the second task of policy leadership is to convene the diverse set of people and interests—stakeholders, knowledgeholders, and decisionmakers—needed to stimulate collective action to address the issue. Policy leaders bring people together, different factions with often different perspectives and different sensitivities, to address an undesirable condition, problem area, or urgent issue.

There is a wide variety of ways that collective efforts are successfully mobilized, including, for example, advocacy coalitions, collaborative alliances, issue-oriented networks, political action committees, and stakeholder groups. Some are more formal and permanent, while many are temporary and ad hoc; each, however, attempts to convene major stakeholders, knowledgeholders, and decisionmakers to address an issue they consider problematic in some way. Successful efforts are tailored to the unique local circumstances of that issue (Bryson *et al.* 1990) as well as to the broader environment and national context in which the particular issue is embedded (Gray and Hay 1986).

There are two distinct approaches to convening critical stakeholders around policy issues: one approach is to organize around the problem. Here, policy leaders do not promote solutions; they promote problems. Rather than convening around specific policy alternatives, they mobilize a group around doing something about a problem in a certain direction. This is a policy issue approach where individuals are mobilized around an issue, rather than mobilizing around a particular solution, and they have a passionate stake in getting an issue addressed, but do not necessarily have a strong stake in any particular way to solve the problem (Luke 1997). The second approach is to convene around particular solutions, and is followed by policy entrepreneurs who champion a particular policy response, and mobilize interest and develop coalitions around a particular proposed policy already deemed feasible for addressing the problem (Kingdon 1984; Roberts and King 1989). Mobilizing and coalition-building are common strategies that are used—in addition to political bargaining, trade-offs, and other sorts of compromise strategies—to win support for one's position or preferred solution.

Mobilizing Participation. Whether following the issue approach or the solution approach, policy leaders use their knowledge of the issue domain, their knowledge of stakeholders' interests and interrelationships, personal contacts in related networks, personal charm, and available authority to convince key stakeholders that participation in the effort is worthy of their involvement. One's willingness to respond to the recruitment efforts, and join in a policy development effort, is typically explained in terms of whether stakeholders and knowledgeholders feel they (a) have something to gain by participating, or (b) something to lose if they do not participate. Closer analysis, however, reveals that willingness to participate is more detailed and linked to:

- perceptions of positive benefits relative to personal or organizational interests;
- perceptions of interdependence with other stakeholders or groups in dealing with the issue—it can't be accomplished independently;
- perceptions of convenors' legitimacy and credibility;
- perceptions of other stakeholders' legitimacy, power, and resources.

There are also common reasons for unwillingness or inability to join including potential loss of power, and ideological or cultural differences that create uncompromising conflict in core values.

Convenor Legitimacy. The critical factor in mobilizing participation is convenor legitimacy (Gray and Hay 1986). Without adequate legitimacy by the policy leader, the participation and commitment of stakeholders and knowledgeholders is unlikely to materialize. A convenor can be an individual, an existing group, or agency, and does not necessarily have to be a stakeholder in the particular issue domain; but as a convenor, the policy leader must be perceived as legitimate, having sufficient credibility to elicit the participation of key stakeholders and knowledgeholders. Legitimacy comes from several sources: a perceived expertise and knowledge in the issue area; an ability to be even-handed, characterized by a willingness to consider diverse points of view, but not necessarily unbiased; competence in group facilitation and group processes; a formal or informal position of authority and influence that is recognized by potential participants; and a reputation, history, or track record of successful collaborative efforts that were not merely a vehicle for private gain.

Forge Agreements on Policy Options and Alternatives

Policy leaders convene stakeholders and knowledgeholders and then help convert and transform their concerns for the issue into viable policy responses. This is a critical dimension of policy leadership, and is best characterized as multiparty problem solving among diverse interests that results in the development of multiple strategies to achieve agreed-upon outcomes. The substantial amount of research on collaboration and multiparty problem-solving, however, clearly shows that there is no one theoretical perspective nor single model that guides this direction-setting process among diverse stakeholders.

Forging agreement on policy options and strategies among diverse stakeholders does not follow the textbook notion of a comprehensively rational process—for example, beginning with problem definition to clarify the issue one is trying to change, followed by the generation of a wide variety and comprehensive array of possible strategies for resolving this issue. Finally, following the rational model, an optimal course of action is selected, based on well-defined criterion of preference, from the set of alternatives already identified.

The specific process followed by successful groups is unique and tailored to each situation. The process for generating and selecting appropriate policy responses to public problems seldom, if ever, follows an undisturbed progression through a series of rational, concrete steps which kick in sequentially one after another. Research clearly indicates that there is no single model of policy formulation, no exact order of decisionmaking steps, nor a common set of sequential stages that are followed in designing and selecting strategies for addressing public problems (Wood and Gray 1991; Gersick 1989; Mintzberg *et al.* 1976). Rather, it is more like a stream of individual subdecisions and multiple iterations between information gathering and processing, generating and exploring options, narrowing down, and selecting options.

Essential Routines in the Policy Development Process

Although the process does not progress through a universal sequence of stages or common set of steps, the policy development process is amenable to some conceptual structuring, and revolves around essentially three common or core routines. Communication dominates each of these distinct tasks, yet the core decisionmaking routines are interdependent and occur in a reiterative fashion, and include: direction setting, option generating, and analyzing and selecting policy options.

Direction Setting. Direction setting involves two related tasks: defining and clarifying the issue, and identifying the outcomes or results desired from a policy response. The hardest part of forging agreement on policy options is agreeing on what the problem is; people are unlikely to find or agree on solutions in the absence of an agreed-upon understanding of the problem (Bryson and Crosby 1992). The original issue or problematic condition that mobilized stakeholders is often too ill-defined initially by the group to generate immediate agreement on policy responses. Further, individuals see the problem differently based on their experience, circumstances, and interests. Particularly with complex, interconnected problems–where responsibilities for and causes of problems are indefinite–individuals within a particular "policy system" typically define the problem in a fashion that is optimal to them or their agency (Milward 1982), that ensures one particular solution is considered while obscuring or eliminating other potential solutions, protects an agency's turf, or reflects the way in which a particular agency or stakeholder group collects and analyzes its information (Fischoff 1985).

Disagreements about the definition of the problem are central elements of intense policy debates because different definitions of a problem suggest different strategies for resolving it (Fischoff 1983). In fact, if there is strong conflict around the definition of the problem, with multiple competing definitions, no action will likely be taken (Cobb and Elder 1983). Or, they may turn to the least controversial way to define the problem, which is most likely not the best problem statement for generating innovative and effective alternative strategies (Volkema 1983). Policy leadership thus requires careful defining and framing of the problem in ways that motivate action and mobilize a coalition of stakeholders large enough to secure adoption and implementation of preferred solutions (Bryson and Crosby 1992).

Option Generation. A major barrier to effective option development is inadequate consideration of alternatives. For example, most groups generate only one alternative which receives serious consideration; full and open searches for options are often avoided because of the potential to expand conflict and delay agreement (Nutt 1992). The task of policy leadership is to encourage and stimulate a broader, more systematic search and analysis process that generates multiple options for consideration. Options are generated in two ways: first, by searching for existing ideas, proposals, programs, and strategies that can readily, or with modification, be applied; and second by inventing or designing new strategies, custom-made in order to reach the desired outcome.

Searching. In many cases, policy alternatives already exist in the "policy primeval soup" where solutions to public problems float around, bumping into one another, forming combinations and recombinations (Kingdon 1984). Policy development targeting critical public problems more often resembles this process of "recombination," the coupling and blending of already familiar elements (Kingdon 1984).

Designing and Crafting Policies. Another method for generating potential options is the design of a custom-made policy option. In policy development, this custom-design approach is less frequently used than the recombination approach (Kingdon 1984) due to its time-consuming, and sometimes expensive, nature. In custom design, workgroup members begin with a general notion of a comprehensive strategy to achieve the outcome, engage in a sequence of re-iterative design and search cycles, and build a strategy brick by brick, with the workgroup not really knowing what the strategy will look like until it is nearly completed (Mintzberg *et al.* 1977). This option generation method typically produces only one fully developed strategy because most workgroups are unable to spend enough resources to generate more than one alternative.

Selecting Policy Options. The process of selecting one policy response over other options is not purely rational or analytical; selecting strategies always contains elements of personality, emotions, bargaining, and power. It is essentially a social and political process as well as an intellectual task, which reflects consideration of multiple constituencies, competing values and interests, and specific criteria. Using structured approaches based on problem solving and resolving conflict are more effective in stimulating committed and sustained action than are approaches using coercion or compromise (Bryson *et al.* 1990). The political process in policy development revolves around the persuasion of preferred courses for action; the use of specific criteria in selecting a preferred policy response can reduce dependence on political solutions and can facilitate wider agreement on policy options.

Criteria. Decisionmakers only use a few evaluation criteria to judge and select strategies (Nutt 1992), and typically use four interdependent categories. Conflicting criteria do not necessarily have to be reconciled for agreement, and neither must key stakeholders by equally enthusiastic for each criteria; however, the extent to which all four are discussed and considered enhances the selection process.

Impact criteria seek to assess whether a policy option strategically targets causes rather than symptoms, and impacts change over the long run. Although there are multiple linkages, and multiple causes, not all are equal in influencing the particular public issue. Systemically, there are a few causes that are more impactful and influential in addressing the problem; and some policy responses will more effectively achieve the outcome over the long run because of a more direct causal linkage.

Interest-based criteria seek policy responses based on common or similar interests that will generate sufficient commitment to ensure implementation. Even when interests are not common or similar, they may be complementary and noncompeting. When interests are truly in conflict, there are also strategies where stakeholders can "trade" or bargain things that are valued differently, trading less important items for more important ones (Susskind and Cruikshank 1987).

Resource criteria are used to judge whether there are sufficient resources that can be generated and leveraged to implement the policy. Financial resources are always a primary criterion; seldom is there sufficient funding available to fully fund all potentially effective policy options. The resources necessary to take action, however, is more broadly defined as information, expertise, funding, and competencies.

Policies to address public problems generate varying levels of public acceptance and political support. Public acceptance and *political criteria* therefore evaluate whether the policy option will be acceptable politically and publicly. Public acceptance requires both intellectual and emotional acceptance (Yankelovich 1992), while acceptance by elected officials is facilitated when the policy response satisfies their key constituents, enhances reelection prospects, and appears to be "good public policy" without being too controversial (Kingdon 1984).

Authorization and Adoption. Once sufficient agreement is forged to commit to one policy option, or a set of policy options—a "strategic portfolio"—attention turns to discussions of outsiders' expectations and to the preparing, editing, and packaging of written materials (Gersick 1988). The workgroup must seek and secure authorization in either general or specific terms if individual members do not have the authority to commit critical actors and agencies to the courses of action. Seeking permission or authorization is critical to success and involves such mobilizing strategies as developing sponsors and champions, building networks and coalitions, and gaining access to the formal agenda of the necessary decisionmaking arenas (Bryson and Crosby 1992).

Policy Implementation: Sustaining Action and Maintaining Momentum

Policy adoption is followed by implementation of the policy—either all at once or in stages—and evaluation of the policy changes. Finally, the policies are reviewed by leaders and subsequently maintained, modified, or terminated (Bryson and Crosby 1992). Policy implementation, however, is more complex and difficult than historically assumed, and in most cases, the real task of policy leadership is not in policy adoption or approval but in ensuring its implementation. Solving policy problems requires sustained attention and effort by numerous and diverse policy actors and agencies, most of whom are independent of each other; it is thus easy for the momentum required for successful implementation to fade and for sustained action to fail. The rate of failure of many policies is high—from major policy reform in developing countries and ambitious social welfare mandates in the U.S. to more local efforts of improving community livability.

Unfortunately, the research on implementation focuses predominantly on program and project implementation, rather than policy implementation; nevertheless, general tasks have been derived for the successful implementation of public policy. For example, policy leadership stimulates implementation and sustains action by:

- gaining support and legitimation for the policy;
- building constituents to ensure that supportive coalitions will advocate and champion continued implementation (Sabatier 1988);
- establishing appropriate implementation structures or "action vehicles" (Kanter 1983) to institutionalize the policy;
- accumulating and mobilizing resources;
- managing the interorganizational relationships through rapid information sharing and feedback, producing visible successes and small wins (Weick 1984); and
- maintaining a policy learning approach or adaptive learning posture to monitoring implementation.

Policy Legitimation. Policy implementation will not go forward without policy legitimation. Unless the policy is viewed as legitimate by key decisionmakers, significant movement will not occur. Policy leadership requires an individual or agency to assume the role of policy champion, asserting and persuading that the policy is necessary, vital, and workable. An excellent example is the transition in Eastern European countries from socialist or state-driven economies to more market-oriented economies that occurred in the 1990s. Respected and credible policy leaders with substantial political capital were necessary to initiate the changeover, and policy legitimation confronted a vast array of entrenched interests with much to lose in the economic reform (Crosby 1993). Regardless of the popular sentiments within the countries toward a market economy, without such policy legitimation by credible policy leaders, the reform would not have gone forward.

Building Constituent Support and Advocacy Coalitions. Action cannot be sustained solely on the shoulders of the policy champion. Successful implementation requires that an adequate constituency be developed to support and sustain the policy, and that strong advocacy coalitions be created and maintained. Constituents are typically those who benefit by the new policy; for example, they are the principle clients affected by the policy, or individuals who will have their status or position enhanced by the policy changes, or groups who can bring some sort of resource to its implementation (Crosby 1993). Coalitions are organized around common interests, and can provide a valuable source of energy for implementation. Constituent groups and advocacy coalitions are positive stakeholders which lend force to policy champions, and amplify the legitimation process. Yet their purpose is not merely to gain support and acceptance from the wider environment; rather it is to operationalize the policy through the creation of new beneficiaries and advocates who can sustain the new policy (Crosby 1993).

Implementation Structures. Public policies must be institutionalized if new ways of doing things are to be practiced and expected to become the norm. Mechanisms to institutionalize the new policy are required and become the "action vehicles" (Kanter 1983) to implement and sustain momentum. Ongoing institutional commitment is critical to sustain implementation, and a wide variety of mechanisms are used, from informal networks, partnership agreements (such as joint powers agreements and memoranda of understanding), and formal interorganizational networks to strategic alliances. Solving policy problems requires sustained attention and efforts, often by multiple and independent agencies which transcend a single organizational authority structure, and the more complex policies can further require systemic changes based on shared interests and new levels of interaction. Some sort of institutional structure is thus needed to orchestrate and sustain the ongoing involvement of the multiple agencies, to institutionalize new procedures and communication channels, and to provide new incentives and rewards.

Resource Accumulation and Mobilization. There is always competition for scarce resources in public policy, and successful implementation can easily fail if sufficient human, technical, and financial resources are not allocated or reallocated. The challenge goes beyond securing initial funding, but also requires that the policy has a legitimate and sustained place in agencies' resource allocation process. Even when sufficient resources are accumulated, they must be mobilized in appropriate directions and moved into the right places to implement the policy. Resource mobilization and reallocation often causes the most resistance (Crosby 1993), and may include the elimination of existing programs or functions; realignment of human and material resources to fit the new policy; or the modification or creation of entirely new incentive mechanisms to facilitate action within the new policy framework.

Rapid Information Sharing and Feedback. Successful implementation fundamentally requires information and feedback to assess whether the policy is being implemented as expected, and whether the results produced by the policy are the ones intended. Such information collection is problematic since there is always some time delay between when the change begins and when results can be noticed. Clear milestones for monitoring and reviewing progress, however, must be developed, based on the regular collection and analysis of outcome information, not just activity information. Multiple measures are necessary because no single indicator can provide an accurate picture, and because appropriate measures vary from agency to agency and jurisdiction to jurisdiction. The rapid sharing and feedback of the information is also critical; momentum will not be sustained if real accomplishments are not revealed through data collection. Visible successes and small wins (Weick 1984) maintain focus on the desired outcomes, build confidence, draw attention to new directions resulting from the new policy, and build support and momentum.

Maintaining a Policy Learning Approach. Successful implementation requires not only active guidance to assure and monitor performance, but also adaptation, adjustments, and ongoing learning. In addition, policies should be viewed as experimental attempts to resolve public problems, not the final solution. Effective policy leadership exhibits a "policy-oriented learning" perspective during implementation; as events unfold, and as unanticipated "policy windows" open, policy leaders adapt earlier decisions and actions to the new information generated and take advantage of opportunities that emerge. A policy learning approach to implementation enhances the potential for comparing the results of alternate policy strategies, and learning which policies have bigger impacts on reaching the desired results.

Policy Leadership Skills Are Different

Leadership for pursuing organizational goals is different than leadership in policy arenas that transcend individual organizations—where public problems are defined, addressed, and solved by a multiplicity of diverse and often conflicting stakeholders. In such settings, interorganizational or policy leadership is necessary for bringing an issue or problem to the public agenda, stimulating collaborative and concerted action among diverse stakeholders to address the issue, and ensuring sustained action during implementation. It is a type of leadership that can move diverse, often competing groups toward workable consensus on complex, interconnected problems.

Policy leadership emphasizes stimulating action by diverse groups and interests toward agreed-upon outcomes, and is thus different from organizational leadership, which focuses on influencing organizational members (followers) to achieve organizational improvements. Policy leadership is interorganizational in nature, and at a minimum requires: an ability to think strategically about how public issues can be raised to the policy agenda; an ability to foster dialogue and agreement by multiple agencies on appropriate policy responses; and an ability to sustain policy action over time.

JEFFREY S. LUKE

BIBLIOGRAPHY

Bass, Bernard M., 1990. *Bass and Stogdill's Handbook of Leadership: Theory Research, and Managerial Applications.* 3d ed. New York: Free Press.

Berlew, D. E., 1974. "Leadership and Organizational Excitement." *California Management Review,* 17:21–30.

Bennis, Warren and Burt Nanus, 1985. *Leaders: The Strategies for Taking Charge.* New York: Harper and Row.

Bryman, Alan, 1992. *Charisma and Leadership in Organizations.* Newbury, CA: Sage Publications.

Bryson, John, P. Bromiley and Y. S. Jung, 1990. "Influences of Context and Process on Project Planning Success." *Journal of Planning Education and Research,* 9(3): 183–195.

Bryson, John and Barbara Crosby, 1992. *Leadership for the Common Good.* San Francisco: Jossey Bass.

Burns, James McGregor, 1978. *Leadership.* New York: Harper and Row.

Cobb, R. and C. Elder, 1983. *Participation in American Politics: The Dynamics of Agenda Building.* Baltimore: Johns Hopkins University Press.

Crosby, Benjamin, 1993. "Policy Implementation and Strategic Management: The Challenge of Implementing Policy Change." Washington, D.C.: Implementing Policy Change Project.

Downs, Anthony, 1972. "Up and Down with Ecology–The Issue Attention Cycle." *Public Interest,* vol. 12: 38–50.

Fischoff, Baruch, 1983. "Strategic Policy Preferences: A Behavioral Decision Theory Perspective." *Journal of Social Issues,* vol. 39, no. 1: 133–160.

———, 1985. "Managing Risk Perception." *Issues in Science and Technology,* vol. 2: 83–96.

Gersick, Connie, 1988. "Time and Transition in Work Teams: Toward a New Model of Group Development." *Academy of Management Journal,* 31(1): 9–41.

———, 1989. "Marking Time: Predictable Transitions in Task Groups." *Academy of Management Journal,* 32(2): 274–309.

Gray, B. and T. M. Hay, 1986. "Political Limits to Interorganizational Consensus and Change." *Journal of Applied Behavioral Science,* vol. 22: 95–112.

Kanter, Rosabeth Moss, 1983. *The Change Masters.* New York: Simon & Schuster.

Kingdon, J., 1984. *Agendas, Alternatives and Public Policy.* Boston: Little, Brown.

Kouzes, J.M. and B.Z. Posner, 1987. *The Leadership Challenge.* San Francisco: Jossey-Bass.

Luke, Jeffrey, 1997. *Catalytic Leadership: Strategies for an Interconnected World.* San Francisco: Jossey-Bass

Milward, H. B., 1982. "Interorganizational Policy Systems and Research on Public Organizations." *Administration and Society,* 13(4): 457–478.

Mintzberg, H., D. Raisnghani and A. Theoret, 1976. "The Structure of 'Unstructured' Decision Processes." *Administrative Science Quarterly* vol. 21 (June) 246–275.

Neustadt, R. E., 1991. *Presidential Power and Modern Presidents.* New York: Free Press.

Nutt, Paul, 1989. *Making Tough Decisions.* San Francisco: Jossey Bass.

Pasquero, Jean, 1991. "Superorganizational Collaboration: The Canadian Environmental Experiment." *Journal of Applied Behavioral Science,* vol. 27, no. 2 (June) 38–64.

Peters, Thomas J. and R.H. Waterman, Jr., 1982. *In Search of Excellence.* New York: Harper & Row.

Peters, Thomas J. and Nancy Austin, 1985. "A Passion for Excellence." *Fortune* (May 13) 20-32.

Polsby, N. W., 1984. *Political Innovation in America: The Politics of Policy Initiation.* New Haven, CT: Yale University Press.

Roberts, Nancy and R. T. Bradley, 1991. "Stakeholder Collaboration and Innovation: A Study of Public Policy Initiation at the State Level." *Journal of Applied Behavioral Science,* vol. 27, no. 2 (June) 209–227.

Roberts, N. and P. King, 1989. "Stakeholder Audit Goes Public." *Organizational Dynamics* (Winter) 63–79.

Sabatier, P. A., 1988. "An Advocacy Coalition Framework of Policy Change and the Role of Policy-Oriented Learning Therein." *Policy Sciences,* vol. 21: 129–168.

Schon, Donald, 1971. *Beyond the Stable State.* New York: Norton.

Susskind, L. and J. Cruikshank, 1987. *Breaking the Impasse.* New York: Basic Books.

Tichy, Noel M. and Mary Anne Devanna, 1990. *The Transformational Leader.* New York: John Wiley & Sons.

U.S. Advisory Commission on Intergovernmental Relations, 1992. *Changing Public Attitudes on Governments and Taxes: 1989–1992.* Washington, D.C.: U.S. Government Printing Office.

Volkema, Roger, 1983. "Problem Formulation in Planning and Design." *Management Science* 29(6): 639–652.

Weick, K. E., 1984. "Small Wins: Redefining the Scale of Social Problems." *American Psychologist,* vol. 39, no. 1 (January) 40–49.

Wilson, James Q., 1989. *Bureaucracy: What Government Agencies Do and Why They Do It.* New York: Basic Books.

Wood, Donna and Barbara Gray, 1991. "Toward a Comprehensive Theory of Collaboration." *Journal of Applied Behavioral Science,* vol. 27, no. 2 (June) 139–162.

Yankelovich, D., 1992. "How Public Opinion Really Works." *Fortune* (October 5).

POLICY MONITORING.

An analytical technique derived from agency theory that aids in the understanding of policy implementation by bureaucracies.

Policy monitoring, as a technique used in policy analysis, was developed by B. Dan Wood and Richard W. Waterman (1991). It is both an analytic technique derived from theory and an applied concept. Policy outputs have long been a concern of policy analysts, but have been difficult to assess empirically. Policy monitoring offers a way to study implementation by the bureaucracy in a way that avoids disagreement over what is meant by implementation success and focuses directly on observable, measurable outputs. For example, Waterman and Wood identified changes in a specific type of bureaucratic output: the number of enforcement actions implemented over time of officials in a particular government agency. They used policy monitoring to identify the stimuli that promoted bureaucratic responses and policy change.

As an analytic technique, policy monitoring involves four basic steps: (1) the examination of qualitative evidence (e.g., existing research literature, government documents, historical records, interviews) to ascertain the substantive issues involved in a policy question; (2) the development of a database of outputs related to questions or hypotheses; (3) statistical analysis of agency outputs using quantitative methods; and (4) a reexamination of government records and other qualitative sources to eliminate rival explanations. These factors are iterative; data is continuously collected and analyzed over time, thus providing systematic and continuous oversight. Policy monitoring, thus, has an applied focus.

Policy monitoring is derived from agency theory, which postulates a direct relationship between the activities of the principal (i.e., superordinate) and the agent (i.e., the subordinate). In the principal-agent model, the activities of bureaucratic agents are monitored by policymakers to compensate for the greater amount of information held by agents, compared to principals. Theoretically, such policy monitoring allows policymakers to be well-informed and to mold the behavior of their bureaucratic agents. Without the capacity to monitor agents, principals have difficulty in exerting effective control over their agents, and can be misled by agents who possess more information. Principal-agent theory helps explain why principals require systematic ways to monitor agent behavior. Policy monitoring is both theoretically derived and practical in application. This linkage has long been a key goal of policy analysis.

BEVERLY A. CIGLER

BIBLIOGRAPHY

Waterman, Richard W. and B. Dan Wood, 1993. "Policy Monitoring and Policy Analysis." *Journal of Policy Analysis and Management*, vol. 12, no. 4: 685–699.
Wood, B. Dan and Richard W. Waterman, 1991. "The Dynamics of Bureaucratic Control of the Bureaucracy." *American Political Science Review* 85: 801–828.
———, 1994. *Bureaucratic Dynamics: The Role of Bureaucracy in a Democracy*. Boulder, CO: Westview Press.

POLICY NETWORK.

An assortment of interrelated policy actors interested—for civic, professional, intellectual, or selfish reasons—in pursuing a matter of public policy. The concept policy networks evolved from related notions such as policy subsystems, issue networks, cozy triangles, and iron triangles. All of these phrases depict policymaking processes that reside outside the formal categories of the representative government model. From the vantage point of public administration they are significant because they imply the presence of political administration as opposed to neutral, scientific administration.

Iron Triangles and Economic Interests

Though policy networks are conceptually more sophisticated than notions of iron triangles, it is useful to rehearse the lineage because much of the conceptualization behind iron triangles remains relevant to the meaning of policy networks. Political scientists noted the presence of informal relationships among governmental and nongovernmental agents, an awareness that followed on the heels of an increased awareness of the roles of lobbyists and special interest groups in the governing process. The attempts of journalists writing in newspaper columns to popularize awareness of this pattern of informal relationships led to metaphorical terms such as iron triangles or cozy triangles. Iron triangles referred to not quite legitimate policy processes wherein (1) lobbyists representing special interest groups, (2) staff from a government agency, and (3) members/staff of congressional committees and subcommittees collaborate in ways mutually beneficial to them, but not to the citizenry as a whole. At each point in the triangle, actors are presumed to be motivated by material self-interest or by the economic interests of the organizations they represent. Specifically, congressional representatives are presumed to seek campaign contributions, agency representatives seek budgetary approvals, and interest groups seek favorable legislation leading to government outlays or agreeable regulations. These triangles are sometimes termed cozy because in the process of mutual influence, services are performed, information is exchanged, and relationships are built. They were iron triangles because the relationships were perceived to be so strong and durable that legitimate policymaking processes—whereby legislators are beholden only to voters and to the public interest—are effectively preempted. These images of cozy, iron triangles connote the presence of fragmented yet dominant elite groups who manipulate public policy on behalf of private interests.

All players are presumed to be utility maximizers (that is, rational and self-interested). The governmental agency—along with the legislature and lobbyists—is also conceptualized as a utility-maximizing, self-interested player seeking aggrandizement and expansion of turf in the cozy/iron triangle framework.

Looking at the informal interactions through the lens of issue networks, the above connotations are not self-evident. Again, the underlying assumption of iron triangles is that policy actors wish to maximize self-interest. Iron triangles are arenas for economic exchange. This sort of exchange theory differs markedly from an alternative conception of issue networks as places where intellect, emotion, and values are engaged. By describing these informal interactions as an issue network rather than an iron triangle, Hugh Heclo, in his classic 1978 essay "Issue Networks and the Executive Establishment," introduced a less pejorative view of them. By focusing on a few powerful iron triangles, observers had, according to Heclo, overlooked the multitudinous webs of influence that animate public action and modify the exercise of power. Issue networks are comprised of a large number of participants with varying levels of commitment to the group project and varying degrees of dependence on others in the network. Further, participation is not necessarily based on narrow economic interests. Issue networks have vague boundaries, which for researchers makes them a difficult subject of inquiry. But in practice the ill-defined boundaries make entry into these networks of policy discourse accessible. Participants come and go and may not have coalesced around any particular ideological predisposition. And compared to more structured social systems such as bureaus or corporations, networks appear out of anyone's control. Whether or not any coalition dominates the processes and content of the network is something to be investigated rather than deduced from some arguable theory of human nature. It may be that the glue that holds the network together is a combination of intellectual fascination, emotional commitment, and engagement of one's value system.

Nonetheless, the notion that agencies seek to expand their power and domain represents a feasible hypothesis in explaining agency participation in networks. This assumption—that agencies will maximize self-interests—may be applied when investigating the motives of other participants in the networks as well. Some corporations may rely on governmental agencies and legislative bodies for ensuring a deliberate, paced process free of erratic regulatory demands. The attraction of the policy network may be stable procedure or it may be the possibility of economic gains. For others, the attraction may be the passage of some policy that will enhance their profits or interests. The motivator may be prevention of policy that will detract from their profits or interests. Legislators participate in networks because (from the exchange theory point of view) they need the help of friendly groups who will commit campaign contributions necessary for funding the next electoral campaign. Obviously then, whether the influence of these informal policy subsystems is benign or malignant is a matter of intense debate. The malignant view is usually arrived at by thinking of policy networks as a system of economic exchange. Political scientists were able to offer explanations for why policy turned out the way it did (and why there often was lack of action on proposed legislation) by assuming that all actors were motivated by self-interest to achieve particular ends.

Whether benign or malignant, this network policy process was not the one citizens of the U.S. were brought up to expect: Voters, armed with policy preferences and votes, exercised sovereignty by selecting political candidates who then represented these preferences in the formal legislative arena where policy was formulated and enacted into law. Civil servants were then hired to implement the law. These same civil servants were organized into hierarchical organizations controlled by elected officials, who were in turn controlled by voters. Hence, public administrators were accountable to elected legislators, who were themselves accountable to the voters. The role of public administrators in this democratic accountability model was to implement the legislature's policy pronouncements in a neutrally competent manner. But in policy networks one finds political administration, not neutral administration.

The extent to which issue networks accurately describe the process of policy making is indicative of the extent to which the politics-administration dichotomy lacks viability. To understand policy networks is to uncover a distinctly po-

litical relation between democratic-pluralistic politics and the executive establishment. All these network/triangle models challenge traditional notions of how representative government is supposed to work. The strength of these models is that, to some extent at least, they do offer an explanatory description of public policy outcomes and process.

Improved understanding of policy processes may be useful, but many observers have lamented the way political decisionmaking has moved into these informal arenas. The implications of policy networks for democratic theory are weighty.

Theft of Sovereignty

Whether they are called policy issue networks, iron networks, iron triangles, or cozy triangles, their troubling feature is that they presuppose politics, and are therefore regarded by some as a theft from the people of their sovereignty. Theodore Lowi in his influential book *The End of Liberalism* (1969) lamented the interest group liberalism that was the result of the positive government that grew out of the economic hard times of the 1930s, a government whose sphere seemed to be expanding. What had once been liberal programs designed to restore and maintain, say, the economic vitality of farmers whose livelihoods were at risk, had over the years become a series of mechanisms useful only for maintaining the status quo, a conservative function. Farm price supports remain in place thanks to the iron triangle of agricultural agencies, agribusiness lobbies, and legislators from rural farming districts. Rather than continuing to abide informal policy subsystems, Lowi urged that respect for formal institutions of representative democracy be restored. Informal bargaining weakens democracy, according to this view, and gives rise to cynicism and distrust of government. Spreading access to government by informal means was not, for Lowi, an acceptable democratic alternative. Democratic accountability would be problematic under informal government as exemplified by policy networks.

But not everyone saw it that way. There were certain integrative functions that only these loosely organized networks of policy activists could perform.

Policy Networks as Coherent Political-Administrative Process

Informal issue networks have continued to propagate, despite the protestations of governmental formalists, and one explanation for this is that they perform integrative functions necessary to policy formulation and successful implementation. The yearning for a return to the days of formal democracy seemed nostalgic in the face of ever-increasing presence of organized groups seeking some say-so in public policy debates. The ubiquity of private lobbying organizations as well as a growing intergovernmental web of associations was an increasingly apparent actuality of the public policy process. Throughout the policymaking apparatus of government there were collections of issue-conscious groups influencing events in a complex system of interrelationships. Participants did not necessarily represent monied interests or economic interests, but often brought technical, specialist understanding to questions of policy. Meanwhile, the demand by groups for a place in the policy process did not subside.

Policy networks came to be perceived as more than triumvirates of lobbyists, legislative committees, and executive agencies; more than a raid on the public treasury by privileged networks of venal policy actors. Observers detected crucial integration tasks being performed in policy networks. Policy networks operated as functional subsystems linking program professionals through all levels of government. The presumed autonomy of iron triangles was not in evidence in the functional subsystem conception of policy networks; to the contrary, they were pragmatically indispensable for the coordinative and communicative tasks performed there. Policy networks may be simply a necessary outgrowth of a fragmented polity. Without them policy implementation would be more snarled and jumbled than it is.

The functional utility of policy networks is both political and administrative. They are political in the sense that funds, or regulations, or other policy collateral are extracted from the larger political system. They are administrative in that managerial functions such as coordination, communication, and integration are provided through them. Interorganizational networks link policy actors located at different levels of government, not in a hierarchical way but by virtue of interest, be it economic, professional, or intellectual. The network metaphor directs attention to the relationships between and among political administrators and reconceptualizes the simplistic and reductionist iron triangle metaphor.

Proactive Public Administrators in Political Arenas

Amid the complex of interrelationships, the neat boundaries once presumed to exist between administration and politics break down. The image of public administrators as neutrally competent and possessing a passion for anonymity is difficult to sustain if the policy network model has any credibility. Public administrators who participate in policy networks may be conversant in various networks and knowledgeable about substantive issues, even if they are not conspicuously identifiable with one political position or another.

The price of buying into one or another issue network is watching, reading, talking about, and trying to act on

particular policy problems. Powerful interest groups can be found represented in networks but so too can individuals in or out of government who have a reputation for being knowledgeable. Particular professions may be prominent, but the true experts in the networks are those who are issue-skilled (that is, well-informed about the ins and outs of a particular policy debate) regardless of formal professional training. More than mere technical experts, network people are policy activists who know each other through the issues (Heclo 1978, pp. 102–103).

Though not the sole source of knowledge and ability in a policy network, public administrators are, from the policy network perspective, political administrators. They are activists in their own right. Some writers argue explicitly for an activist posture, as when Michael M. Harmon in 1981 extolled the proactive administrator. Some have urged activism on behalf of social justice, as the new public administration movement did; others have argued for an "entrepreneurial government." Charles J. Fox and Hugh T. Miller (1995) proposed that public administrators be actively involved in policy networks, but conditioned their proposal by offering standards of authentic discourse against which actual policy discourse may be judged democratic or not. Still others contemplate a public conversation involving direct interaction of citizens with agency officials.

Thus public administrators are engaged in "what to do" questions, not only "how" questions. They mobilize key actors and help make policy an actuality. With knowledge as their key asset, uncertainty over the "what to do" question leads others to value their expertise and comprehension of the important dimensions of the problem. Knowledgeable people, along with those who need answers, interact in policy networks. It is here where issues become articulated, evidence debated, and alternative approaches explored.

The network model makes it clear that political interaction is endemic to the craft of public administration. Political administrators frequently find themselves interacting among members of the public, struggling to sort out meanings and values, trying to establish or adjust institutional arrangements, working to route public resources in desired directions. The mutual understandings that stem from the conflict inherent in such undertakings shape subsequent action.

Policy Networks as a Form of Social Organization

Some observers contend that the network form is a third type of social structure, distinct from either markets or hierarchies, two forms of social structure that, rightly or wrongly, dominate theoretical formulations among students of public policy and administration. The nature of the interaction between people is presumed in markets to be driven by rational self-interest. In hierarchies, relations are premised on superior-subordinate obedience. But in networks, the interaction is indeterminate. This indeterminacy possesses some coherence, however. Fox and Miller used the term energy field to allude to a situation which has captivated the intentionalities of policy actors. These policy actors are drawn to some robust, substantive event, and engage in social interaction for the purpose of sensemaking and, possibly, policy action. The meaning that persons in the network ascribe to their relationships and activities is not known in advance, but is worked out in situ. Decisions, actions, group conflict, and policy change take place as a consequence of network interactions. As they interact, network participants socially construct meaning and thereby reinforce one another's sense of the importance of the set of issues at hand. Participants may eventually articulate their political demands in ways that can be acted upon. Or, the network may lose its attraction as events and issues lose their salience. With loose boundaries, people can leave. If they stay, there must be some attraction. The policy network model directs attention to the meaning-making taking place among participants, and is less focused than iron triangles on the idealized form of interaction known as rational self-interest.

CHARLES J. FOX
HUGH T. MILLER

BIBLIOGRAPHY

Fox, Charles J. and Hugh T. Miller, 1995. *Postmodern Public Administration: Toward Discourse*. Thousand Oaks, CA: Sage Publications.

Harmon, Michael M., 1981. *Action Theory for Public Administration*. New York: Longman.

Heclo, Hugh, 1978. "Issue Networks and the Executive Establishment." In Anthony King, ed., *The American Political System*. Washington, D.C.: American Enterprise Institute for Public Policy Research, Ch. 3, pp. 87–124.

Kaufmann, Franz-Xaver, 1991. "The Relationship Between Guidance, Control, and Evaluation." In Franz-Xaver Kaufmann, ed., *The Public Sector: Challenge for Coordination and Learning*. Berlin: Walter de Gruyter.

Lowi, Theodore, 1969. *The End of Liberalism*. New York: Norton.

Miller, Hugh T., 1994. "Post-progressive Public Administration: Lessons from Policy Networks." *Public Administration Review*, 54(4).

Milward, H. Brinton, and Gary L. Wamsley, 1984. "Policy Subsystems, Networks and the Tools of Public Management." In Robert Eyestone, ed., *Public Policy Formation*. Greenwich, CT: JAI Press, pp. 3–25.

Powell, Walter W., 1990. "Neither Market nor Hierarchy: Network Forms of Organization." *Research in Organizational Behavior*. Greenwich, CT: JAI Press, pp. 295–336.

Smith, Martin J., 1991. "From Policy Communication to Issue Networks: Salmonella in Eggs and the New Politics of Food." *Public Administration*, 69 (Summer) 234–55.

POLICY STUDIES.

The study of the nature, causes, and effects of alternative public policies for dealing with specific social problems. Some people in the field, such as Duncan MacRae and Yehezkel Dror, prefer to emphasize policy effects and the evaluation or optimization of these effects; others, such as Thomas Dye and Charles Jones, prefer to emphasize causal determinants and processes. Those who emphasize prescription, however, recognize that one cannot prescribe policies without an awareness of what policies are likely to be adopted and effectively implemented. Likewise, those who emphasize causes recognize that the effects of policies are often an important causal factor in shaping policies.

Policy studies is a field in itself and also an approach that is applicable to all fields of political science and all social science disciplines. Policy studies differs from what political scientists generally do in that most political scientists traditionally have not been concerned with specific policy problems such as environment, poverty, crime, and so on, although many now are. Policy studies also differs in its emphasis on the relations between policies and effects, whereas most political scientists have been concerned almost exclusively with government structures, processes, and behavior. Policy studies draws on the classical political science concern for controversial policy issues and normative evaluation. It also draws on the behavioral political science concern for using quantitative methods, although applied to policy problems. As such, policy studies tends to provide a kind of synthesis between classical and behavioral political science.

Although political science has played an important part in the development of policy studies, the field is truly interdisciplinary. Political science contributes a concern for the political and administrative feasibility aspects of alternative public policies. Economics contributes a concern for benefits and costs, and maximizing benefits minus costs, with an emphasis on deducing prescriptive conclusions from given goals and intuitively or empirically accepted relations. Psychology emphasizes the relevance of rewards and punishments in motivating people, and it provides a research paradigm emphasizing pretests and posttests of experimental and control groups. Sociology is concerned with social problems, social classes, and social statistics. Anthropology, geography, and history provide broadening perspectives across places and times. Natural science contributes a concern for the physical and biological factors that are often important in such policy problems as energy and health. Mathematics provides quantitative tools for measuring, analyzing, and evaluating the effects of alternative public policies. Philosophy shows a special concern for the values toward which public policies are directed and the ultimate logic of policy analysis.

The field of policy studies and its orientation have changed tremendously since 1970, as indicated by the rapidly expanding list of relevant journals, organizations, articles, books, book series, convention papers, conference themes, courses, schools, grants, and academic and government job openings. What has caused these changes? One early stimulus was the general public's concern for civil rights, the war on poverty, peace, women's liberation, environmental protection, and other social problems of the late 1960s and early 1970s. The scholarly implementation of those concerns among academics was facilitated by the development of new statistical and mathematical methods, the spread of computer software, and the development of relevant interdisciplinary relations. The relative attractiveness of the government as employer and research sponsor also increased, as the role of universities in employment and research funding decreased. A more recent stimulus has been the concern for obtaining more government output from reduced tax dollars. In that regard, government retrenchment has decreased government prosperity, but it has increased the prosperity of policy analysts.

Institutions of Policy Studies

The basic institutions of an academic field include training programs, research centers, funding sources, publishing outlets, associations, and placement opportunities. Training programs associated with policy studies can be classified in various categories, but it is quite possible to put programs in more than one category. The categories include whether the program is emphasizing (1) graduate or undergraduate work, (2) training for government teaching, (3) multiple disciplines or one discipline, (4) methodology or substance, (5) classroom or field experience, (6) university budget money or grants and contracts, (7) policy processes or evaluation of policy alternatives, (8) federal or state and local, (9) cross-national or national, and (10) questioning general societal goals or accepting them. Perhaps the most distinguishing characteristic of various programs relevant to the interests of political scientists is whether they emphasize a political science approach, as in the Berkeley Graduate School of Public Affairs; an economics approach, as in the Harvard Kennedy School; or a social-psychology approach as in Northwestern's Evaluation Research Program. Those diverse orientations are increasingly coming together in recognition that each has a unique and valuable contribution to make. Political science emphasizes process and feasibility; economics emphasizes deduction and optimizing; and social psychology emphasizes experimentation and attitudes.

Many political science departments or universities could develop interdisciplinary training programs by simply cross-listing courses, faculty, and students. Benefits from developing a policy studies program include increased job opportunities, grants, program funding, intellectual stimulation, policy relevance, publishing opportunities, enrollment, faculty recruitment, and the oppor-

tunity to build on relevant departments and people. The incremental costs of a policy studies program are quite low given the existing people and facilities at nearly all universities. What may be especially needed is to get university administrators to show more recognition of the opportunities that exist if they can pull together some of their existing resources in a coherent policy studies training program.

Nongovernmental research centers in the policy studies field can be divided into those at universities (such as the Yale Institution for Social and Policy Studies or the UCLA Institute for Social Science Research) and those not at universities (such as Brookings, Abt Associates, Urban Institute, Mitre, and The American Enterprise Institute). As with training programs, research centers can also be classified in terms of quality, but that is much more difficult to do. These does seem to be some consensus that university research centers are good on general principles and creativity, but nonuniversity centers are generally better on following detailed specifications and meeting time constraints. What may be needed are more research centers that can draw upon academic creativity while still being effective in responding to government requests for proposals.

Funding sources in the policy studies field include both government agencies and private funding sources. Leading government sources with a broad orientation include the National Science Foundation (especially the Division of Applied Research and the Division of Policy Analysis) and the National Institutes of Mental Health. Virtually every government agency has the authority to issue a purchase order to buy research products relevant to the interests of the agency, including Defense, Energy, Housing and Urban Development (HUD), Health and Human Service (HHS), Justice, Agriculture, Transportation, Commerce, Labor, and Education. Leading private sources with broad orientation include the Ford Foundation (especially the National Affairs Division and the Committee on Public Policy), Rockefeller, and Russell Sage. Numerous private foundations have specialized interests in various policy problems, as indicated by the *Foundation Directory*.

On the matter of publishing outlets, there are a number of new journals in the field, including *Policy Analysis, Policy Sciences, Public Policy, Public Interest,* and the *Policy Studies Journal.* Although there is substantial overlap among those journals, each has a somewhat separate focus as reflected in their titles. *Policy Analysis* is concerned especially with the methodology of policy studies, with an emphasis on economic reasoning in program evaluation. *Policy Sciences* is also concerned especially with methodology, but with more emphasis on operations research, management science, and cross-national authors. *Public Policy* has focused more on substance than method, but its former political emphasis is moving toward economics. *Public Interest* is concerned mainly with substance and values, particularly from the perspective of nonmathematical sociology. The *Policy Studies Journal* tries to combine substance and method, although mainly with a political science or political orientation and a symposium format.

Other general policy-oriented scholarly journals include *Evaluation Quarterly*, the *Journal of the American Institute of Planners*, the *Journal of Legal Studies*, the *Journal of Political Economy*, the *Journal of Public Economics*, the *Journal of Social Issues*, the *Journal of Urban Analysis*, *Law and Contemporary Problems*, *Law and Society Review*, *Policy and Politics*, *Public Administration Review*, *Public Choice*, *Social Indicators Research*, *Social Policy*, *Social Problems*, *Society*, *Socio-Economic Planning Sciences*, and *Urban Affairs Quarterly*. Disciplinary social science journals such as the *American Political Science Review* are increasingly publishing articles with a policy orientation. A number of scholarly publishers have established a book series or a set of books that deals with policy studies. These include Lexington, Sage, Ballinger, Duxbury, Elsevier, Goodyear, Marcel Dekker, Pergamon, Praeger, St. Martin's, and Academic Press. Some of the better-known series include the Sage Yearbooks in Politics and Public Policy, the Sage Policy Studies Review Annual, the Lexington-PSO series, and the Elsevier Policy Sciences Book Series.

There are now a number of new associations in the policy studies field. As with training programs and journals, they can be partly classified in terms of whether they are associated with political science, economics, or sociology-psychology. The Policy Studies Organization (founded in 1972) is associated especially with political science. The Association for Policy Analysis and Management (founded in 1979) is associated especially with economics, although so is the more mathematical Public Choice Society. The Evaluation Research Society (founded in 1977) represents especially psychology and sociology, and it is in the process of merging with the Evaluation Network and the Council for Applied Social Research. Psychologists and sociologists are also represented by units within the APA and ASA, namely the Society for the Psychological Study of Social Issues and the Society for the Study of Social Problems. There may be a need for more interaction and coordination among these associations in order to promote more interdisciplinary projects such as joint symposia, publications, research, convention panels, legislative testimony, and other activities.

Placement opportunities include the training programs and research centers mentioned previously. For many academic fields, placement opportunities include private business. The counterpart in policy studies is mainly government agencies. They represent the heart of policy studies, since there would be no government policies without government agencies. In other words, they represent not only an outlet for placing students and placing ideas, but also a reciprocal source of ideas relevant to improving the work of the training programs and research centers. Some government agencies, however, are more actively involved in planning and evaluating alternative policies than are other agencies. Federal agencies are especially active, but state and local agencies are becoming more so with the passage of legislation requiring more evaluation and the need to stretch tighter budgets. Among federal agencies, the planning and evaluation units at HUD, HHS, Labor, and Defense are generally well regarded, along with the executive office agencies such as the office of management and Budget (OMB) and the Domestic Council. In doing policy evaluation, Congress has the help of the General Accounting Office, the Congressional Budget Office, the Office of Technology Assessment, and the Congressional Reference Service. A survey of political scientists in government mentioned the need for more policy research by academic political scientists, more exchange of information between academics and practitioners, and more training on how government agencies actually function.

Substance, Process, and Methods of Policy Studies

Core courses in policy studies programs generally cover substance, process, and methods. A key issue in discussing policy studies substance is determining the social problems that are important to policy studies training and research. The answer is generally those social problems to which governments devote a substantial amount of resources. That is a descriptive approach to clarifying policy studies substance. A prescriptive approach points to the social problems on which governments should devote a substantial amount of resources, regardless of whether they do or not. For example, is family policy a subject for active government involvement with regard to husband-wife relations and parent-child relations? Is religious policy such a subject, with regard to facilitating parochial schools, contributions to religious institutions, and some forms of religious behavior? Closely related is the question of the relative importance of different policy problems in a policy studies program. Another key issue in the realm of policy studies substance is how to classify substantive policy problems. One approach classifies problems in terms of the disciplines with which they are most often associated, including problems especially related to political science (e.g., civil liberties or defense), economics (e.g., economic regulation or taxing-spending), sociology-psychology (e.g., race relations or population), and planning (e.g., energy or health).

Key issues in discussing the policy process include the following:

1. Do policies get made more by rational analysis of the relations between alternative policies and goals, or by incremental trial and error?

2. In studying policy adoption and implementation, how much emphasis should be placed on process analysis, as contrasted to the determinants and effects of policy variation?

3. In policy studies training, how much emphasis should be placed on process, as contrasted to methods and substance?

4. To what extent does the process change when we talk about different substantive issues such as crime policy versus environmental policy?

5. How does the policy adoption and implementation process differ across levels of government, branches of government, and across nations?

6. To what extent should the process be an evaluative goal in itself with regard to such matters as public participation, fair procedure, openness, and predictability?

7. To what extent should policy analysts consider political and administrative feasibility in evaluating alternative policies?

8. What is a good policy process in terms of effectiveness, efficiency, and equity on such dimensions as federalism, separation of powers, judicial review, the two-party system, and majority rule with minority rights?

Some issues in discussing policy analysis methods include:

1. How is policy analysis similar to and different from business analysis?

2. How can policy analysts become more sensitive to social values and more questioning of goals when evaluating alternative policies?

3. How can one predict the effects of alternative policies, as contrasted to reacting to policies that have already been adopted?

4. How can one accept goals as given and attempt to determine what policies will maximize them, rather than accepting policies as given and merely attempting to determine what their effects are?

5. How may analysts be given a good grounding in social science research methods, including a concern for meaningful measurement, sampling, determination of relations, and causal analysis?

6. How may analysts be given a good grounding in both finite math and calculus-oriented marginal analysis?

7. How can we keep analysts from going overboard in seeking precision methods when less precise techniques give the same results, or from suffering the opportunity cost of not taking advantage of precision techniques given the same results, or from suffering the opportunity cost of not taking advantage of precision that might be easily available?

8. How can we get analysts to be more sensitive to the subject matter with which they are working, as contrasted to using mechanical quantification without thinking through the implications?

9. How can we get analysts to analyze questions that have relatively broad significance, rather than unduly narrowly focused questions?

The Future of Policy Studies

The future direction of policy studies is likely to be toward more growth, or a stabilizing at a high level of academic and government activity. Growth is likely to continue, since the causal forces responsible are still continuing. Those causal forces include the public concern for important policy problems, although the nature of the problem keeps changing. In the late 1960s and early 1970s, the problems related to civil rights, poverty, Vietnam, women's liberation, and environmental protection. In the early 1980s they related to more inflation, energy, and the Middle East. The causal forces also include improved quantitative methods, increased attractiveness of government as a social science employer and research sponsor, and increased government concern for stretching scarce resources.

Deeper causal forces relate to factors that explain increased government involvement and growth over the last 80 years. Those factors are of three kinds. First there are socioeconomic forces such as (1) the increased severity of world conflicts, (2) the growing importance of public education, (3) the growth of large interstate and multinational business, (4) the growth of big labor and other pressure groups that seek aid and require regulations, (5) increased urbanization and the resulting loss of self-sufficiency, (6) increased severity of periods of inflation and recession, (7) competition with foreign ideologies, and (8) the fact that regulation and government activity generate more regulation and activity. Second, there are certain enabling factors, such as (1) expanded sources of government revenue necessary for carrying on increased government programs, (2) improved managerial techniques for handling large-scale government operations, and (3) changing constitutional interpretations. Third is the ideological shift from the prevailing attitude favoring minimal government toward an attitude that government has many positive responsibilities.

Within the field of policy studies, one might predict more specific increases in the following:

- Training programs (undergraduate and graduate, disciplinary and interdisciplinary, and academic-oriented and practitioner-oriented);
- Policy research centers (university, governmental, and nonuniversity private);
- Funding sources (government line agencies such as HHS, government research agencies such as the National Science Foundation, and private foundations such as the Ford Foundation);
- Publishing outlets (both journals and book publishers);

- Policy-oriented scholarly associations (disciplinary, interdisciplinary, professional, and problem-focused).

Within the social sciences, one might predict increases in the following:

- The percentage of social scientists who identify with policy studies;
- Emphasis on policy evaluation and implementation rather than just explaining variation across decisions;
- Use of microeconomic reasoning, rather than just statistical data processing;
- Concern for a wider variety of policy problems;
- The concern across subfields within each social science discipline for the nature, causes, and effects of relevant public policies;
- Synthesis between the traditional philosophical concern for normative evaluation and the scientific or behavioral concern for quantitative analysis;
- Interaction between social science academics and practitioners in training programs and in government;
- Reaching out to other disciplines in view of the interdisciplinary nature of policy problems.

In general, policy studies seems to be a boom industry as a subdiscipline, an interdiscipline, and a developing new discipline. Policy studies also seems to be providing some new vitality to political and social science, while political and social science provide the foundation for policy studies.

STUART S. NAGEL

POLITICAL COMMISSAR.

The Western term used to refer to personnel concerned with political control and indoctrination in the armed forces of the former USSR on behalf of the Soviet Communist Party (CPSU). More generally, the term is used unflatteringly to denote someone appointed from outside directly to supervise the activities of an organization on behalf of higher authority. The direct translation of the Russian term for such personnel (*Voyenny Kommissar*) is military commissar. The post of military commissar was eventually succeeded by that of assistant commander for political affairs (*Zampolit*), referred to in the West as political officer. They were directed by political administrations parallel to the various levels of the professional military establishment.

Military commissars were first introduced in the Soviet Union during spring 1918 to ensure political control over the many former Tsarist officers employed in the Red Army during the Civil War and foreign military intervention following the Bolshevik Revolution. Military commissars had to countersign all orders and were responsible for political indoctrination of the troops and direction of Communist Party "cells" in military units. With sufficient numbers of trained Communist military commanders and

the army's subsequent transition to a peacetime footing, the principle of unity of command (*edinonachaliye*) was gradually introduced from 1925. The commander gained professional autonomy over operational and administrative matters, while the post of military commissar was replaced by that of assistant commander for political affairs (*Zampolit*), in charge of party political work in the unit and responsible for its morale and political condition. Military commissars were reintroduced in May 1937 as Stalin's purge of the officer corps in 1937–38 promoted many politically inexperienced officers. They were abolished in August 1940, only to reappear with the mass mobilization of reserve officers after the German invasion in June 1941. As the Soviet military position improved, full unity of command was established in October 1942 and military commissars were again replaced by the political officers, whose work became less ideological in tone and more supportive of the professional commander.

By the late 1960s the formal structure of political organs in the Soviet armed forces involved: the main political administration of the Soviet Army and Navy (MPA); the political administrations of the five services (the Ground Forces, Air Force, Air Defense Forces, Navy, and Strategic Rocket Forces); political departments in military districts, groups of forces abroad, fleets, and military institutes; political sections in formations (divisions) and units (regiments); and the political officers themselves at unit (regimental) and subunit (company) level. Political officers were subordinate to their immediate military commander and also to their own equivalent at the next higher level. They worked closely with the Communist Party and Komsomol (Young Communist League) organizations in the armed forces, where very high levels of party or Komsomol membership were achieved, especially among officers.

The Khrushchev period (1955–64) saw considerable debate about the utility and purpose of political workers in the military. Technological modernization demanded more intense specialized technical training of military personnel, yet the military was still expected to serve as a "school for Communism," finding time for political indoctrination of conscripts and for officers' political studies. Professional officers criticized the poor military expertise of many political officers and called for political work to be more directly related to combat training. One of the reasons given for the removal of the charismatic Minister of Defense, Marshal Zhukov, in 1957 was that he had worked to reduce the status of political work in the military.

From 1967 political officers were trained at higher military-political schools directly linked to the various services and service branches, with greater emphasis on acquisition of professional military skills. While continuing with troop indoctrination, they were now also in theory expected to be as technically proficient as any other officer. They were depicted as playing a key role in strengthening troop discipline and care for equipment and in improving subunit efficiency. The CPSU stressed through Soviet military doctrine the increasing significance of the morale-political factor in warfare and the development of "scientific troop control," an area in which political administrations and political officers could make their own distinctive contribution to combat effectiveness.

The tension between the demands of political control, indoctrination, and professional military effectiveness was to some extent resolved to the satisfaction of both the CPSU and the Soviet military leadership in the evolution of the political officer's role. The political control function of the military commissars was gradually superseded by a party apparatus in the armed forces more supportive of the operational needs of the professional military establishment which came to identify with the latter's values and outlook. The main political administration of the Soviet Army and Navy increasingly served as a spokesman for the interests of the professional military establishment in policy debates within the CPSU. On relations with the West, for example, the MPA stressed imperialism's aggressive nature, the need for Soviet military superiority, and the primacy of investment in defense-related heavy industry.

The removal of Article Six of the Soviet Constitution in March 1990 ended the Communist Party's formal right to control all state and social institutions, thereby placing a question mark over the continuation of CPSU political work in the armed forces. Junior officers tended to support a ban on all CPSU organizations in the military and the elimination or radical reform of the MPA. The senior military leadership and the MPA were largely united in opposing such changes and the increasing non-CPSU political activities of many junior officers. In early 1991, the MPA lost its de facto status as a department of the CPSU Central Committee, and was transferred to the Defense Ministry and renamed the Military-Political Administration of the Ministry of Defense. A new CPSU organization was to be created in the armed forces, freeing the MPA for its educational, research and morale-building work. In July, Russian President Boris Yeltsin urged the abolition of all CPSU organs in the military. After the attempted coup against Gorbachev in August 1991, the MPA was finally abolished and its remaining officers were assigned to personnel or combat-training duties. Party-political activity in the armed forces was officially banned some three months before the USSR itself disappeared.

DAVID SCRIVENER

BIBLIOGRAPHY

Lepingwell, John W. R., 1992. "Soviet Civil-Military Relations and the August Coup." *World Politics*, vol. 44 (July) 539–572.

Scott, Harriet Fast, 1984. *The Armed Forces of the USSR*. 3d ed. Boulder, CO: Westview Press.

POLITICAL ECONOMY.

The name given in the eighteenth and nineteenth centuries to that part of the general Enlightenment project which focused on the study of economic activity in a social and political context. More recently, "political economy" may be read either in a general sense to encompass the whole of economics, with particular emphasis on the history of thought and alternative schools of thought, or in a specific sense to indicate the discussion of economic policy. A major theme of political economy has always been the nature of the relationship between the economic sphere and the political sphere.

The period which might be roughly defined as from the birth of Adam Smith (1723–1790) to the death of John Stuart Mill (1806–1873) is regarded as the period of "classical political economy," which may be thought of as both a particular stage in the developing history of economic thought and as a particular school of economic thought. Many of the great questions concerning the organization of production, the benefits of trade, the operation of the market, the role of the state relative to the market, the principles of taxation, and so on, were raised and addressed at this time in a way which marked a clear departure from the narrower and more mercantile considerations of the earlier period, and which redrew the agenda for economic analysis and policy debate. The classical analysis placed economic life at the center of civil society for the first time, thereby stressing the importance of the economy relative to the polity.

Classical political economy gave rise to two rather different offspring. Karl Marx's economic analysis is clearly derived from classical political economy (a term Marx is credited with coining), but the Marxian political economy carries a very different message than that associated with the classical school. By the late nineteenth century, "political economy" was being replaced by "economics" as the general title of the academic discipline and this coincided with a shift from the classical to the neoclassical school. The watershed might be taken as the publication of Alfred Marshall's *Principles of Economics* in 1890. The neoclassical school retains its central role as the end of the twentieth century approaches, but other schools of thought are of considerable significance both academically and in terms of their impact on economic policy making. The most obvious example is provided by the Keynesian school of political economy, which dominated much of the intellectual and policy debate for several decades in mid-century.

In attempting both to sketch some of the central and continuing themes of political economy and to hint at the variety of more detailed positions within political economy, this entry offers a brief discussion of some of the key features of the classical, Marxian, neoclassical, and Keynesian approaches. A more recent attempt to draw on both economics and politics to produce a political economy of a more interdisciplinary kind which might be argued to hark back to the eighteenth century origins of the term is also noted briefly.

Classical Political Economy

The major theme of economic analysis and debate since Adam Smith has been the vision of the market as a self-regulating institution within which autonomous individuals interact. The detailed analysis of the operation of markets has preoccupied economists to the present day, but two central features were established by Smith as the cornerstones of classical political economy. First, on the production side, the operation of markets allowed and encouraged specialization and the social division of labor, which transformed society from a subsistence culture to a productive and growing economy. In this way the extent of the market—the range of possibilities for trade, both domestic and international—was seen as a crucial aspect of the engine for generating the wealth of nations; any artificial obstacles to trade were seen as barriers to progress and prosperity.

The second crucial idea is captured in the famous notion of the invisible hand—the idea being that the institution of the market could transform and coordinate the privately motivated actions of many individuals into mutually beneficial outcomes without the need for central control or planning. This idea, more than any other, underpins the classical economists' faith in the market as the centerpiece of civil society, and provides the key link between classical political economy and classical liberalism. The market is seen as an arena in which free individuals pursue their own ends without interference, constrained only by nature and the consent of others.

Classical political economy is often associated with a laissez-faire stance on economic policy, and the link is clear enough even if it is sometimes overstated. While classical economists from Adam Smith onwards have always seen a role for government intervention in a range of settings (above and beyond the removal of impediments to the operation of free markets), this intervention is to be seen against the background of a general presumption in favor of the market. Although it is agreed that there may be specific market failures which may require government policy solutions, there is a deeper claim to the effect that there will be no general failure of the market process. This doctrine is sometimes labeled Say's law (although, in fact, this "law" has always been hotly contested) and expressed in the phrase "supply creates its own demand," which is intended to convey the idea that, for the economy as a whole, demand and supply are tied together by the fact that the supply of one good is the source of demand for another. This is clearly true in a simple barter economy. However, in a monetary economy the link between supply and demand is not quite so direct, so that the classical faith in

some variant of Say's law and in the impossibility of general gluts or slumps in a free market economy turns on the analysis of money and, in particular the classical assumption that the hoarding of money is irrational. As we shall see, this is one point of departure for later views of the market process.

Marxian Political Economy

Two further aspects of classical analysis provide an entry into Marxian political economy; these concern the theory of value and the determination of prices and wages. The labor theory of value holds (roughly) that the value of any produced item is accounted for by the labor embodied in that item during the process of production. The classical theory of price and wage determination operates first by distinguishing between the natural price and the market price—where a natural price is a price which just covers the full cost of production or reproduction, while the market price reflects short-run considerations of demand and supply—and then by arguing that in the longer run market prices converge to natural prices. Applied to wage determination this idea yields the result that wages tend to subsistence levels—where subsistence is taken to mean the level at which the labor force reproduces itself. The combination of the development of the labor theory of value and the subsistence theory of wage determination provided the basis for the important Marxian idea of exploitation—the idea being that workers are exploited whenever they do not receive the full value of their product.

While Marx's economics were almost entirely consistent with the classical writers, his use of these ideas in the construction of a political economy were very different, so that the contrast between classical political economy and Marxian political economy is not so much a contrast between alternative technical economic analysis of capitalism or of the market, but rather a contrast between alternative approaches to embedding that technical analysis into a broader social theory. While the classical political economists stressed individual autonomy, agency, and rationality in the context of the relatively neutral or impersonal structure of market institutions, Marx stressed the opposite idea: that it is the structural nature of the relationships induced under market arrangements—the relations of production—which are the primary determinants of economic outcomes under capitalism. Thus, for example, the operation of the market necessarily forces the specialization of labor and the exploitation of workers, while at the same time the "choices" offered to individual consumers are more apparent than real as individuals' interests and preferences are manipulated. Only class interests are truly objective on this account—where classes are defined by reference to the relations of production—and so class consciousness becomes the necessary condition for social progress.

While much of the specific analysis of the labor theory of value and the subsistence theory of wages has been abandoned in some modern Marxian political economy, the emphasis on the logic of the relations of production rather than the choices of individuals, and on the ideas of exploitation and class, continue as the hallmarks of Marxian political economy.

Neoclassical Political Economy

The transition from the classical to the still dominant neoclassical approach to political economy began in the 1870s. In some ways the change is not dramatic; much of the analysis familiar to Smith or Mill would still pass muster under the neoclassical banner, but there was an important shift in emphasis as well as several key theoretical changes.

While the focus of analysis in the neoclassical approach is still very much the market, the mode of analysis builds much more directly on the idea of the analysis of explicitly rational choice in the presence of constraints, and the equilibrium that derives from the interaction of such rational choices. This focus on individually rational choice is coupled with a subjective theory of value—a theory couched in terms of individual utility—to provide a theory of prices and wages determined as market equilibria which stands at the center of the neoclassical enterprise, and is in sharp contrast with earlier labor theories of value. The efficiency of market equilibria then stands in place of Smith's invisible hand as the basis of the claim for the reliance on markets. The basic paradigm for economic policy in the neoclassical view is again market failure—as it was for classical theorists—but the view of market failure is certainly both more expansive and more detailed than was the classical view.

In the early years of the neoclassical period a considerable portion of economists' effort was devoted to the discussion of policy options and the normative appraisal of political alternatives (most usually from a broadly utilitarian standpoint). However, neoclassical economics became heavily influenced by the logical positivist movement and there was a concerted attempt to turn economics into a positive, value-free science. In this phase of development, neoclassical economics effectively lost its normative wing. Postpositivist neoclassical economics has seen a resurgence of welfare economics and an attempt to reconnect technical economic analysis with applied ethics.

The relationship between the economy and the polity in the neoclassical approach has been subject to debate. The positivist tradition in neoclassical economics tends to view the state as the ultimate source of social values and the economy as a means which may be harnessed towards the achievement of those values. Thus the economist in this tradition often casts himself or herself in the role of a technician advising political superiors on the appropriate means to achieve politically determined ends. This view is in considerable tension with the individualist ethical position typically espoused within welfare economics, where normative primacy is granted to the voluntary individual choice in the market in a style much more reminiscent of classical political economy and classical liberalism. In this tradition, government is assigned a limited normative role of correcting market failures and, possibly, redistributing income and wealth to alleviate poverty and inequality, rather than allowed to set the normative agenda.

Keynesian Political Economy

The Keynesian critique of classical and neoclassical orthodoxy strikes at the basic proposition concerned with the self-regulating nature of markets. But the critique is aimed not at the identification of specific market failure in particular markets, but at general or systemic market failures in the sense identified with Say's law above. It is the Keynesian analysis of the operation of a monetary economy, and particularly of capital markets, which is intended to demonstrate the potential instability of the market system as a whole—indicated for example by the possibility of general slumps, or the inability for an economy to reach and maintain full employment.

Keynesian political economy shifted the debate in two distinct ways. On the one hand it shifted attention from the operation of specific markets to the operation of the market system as a whole—from microeconomics to macroeconomics. On the other hand it shifted attention from the role of government as being essentially limited to the correction of micromarket failures to the role of government as being overall manager of the economic system charged with directing and stabilizing the course of the macroeconomy. In short, the Keynesian approach to political economy reassesses the relationship between the economy and the polity and places the polity firmly in the dominant role—particularly as regards macroeconomic policy.

Economics and Politics

This is all to suggest that the central theme of political economy has been the relationship between economics and politics in society. In recent years this theme has been taken up in a way that attempts an integrated approach to the economy and polity. By extending the idea of analyzing individually rational choices from the market place to the political arena, the public choice theorists have attempted to provide the basis for an analysis of the political process on all fours with the analysis of the market process, so that the impact of assigning this or that issue to the market, or to the political arena, can be modeled directly.

This approach focuses attention on the institutions of political life which constrain and direct political action in the same general manner as the institutions of the market constrain and direct economic action. All public choices, whether economic or political in nature, are seen as resulting from the interaction of individual choices—but these individual choices are mediated through institutional and constitutional structures. In this way the distinction between the economy and the polity is dissolved to shift attention to more general comparative institutional analysis.

In its various historical periods and in its various schools of thought, political economy explores the relationships between individuals, the economic institutions of production and exchange, and the political domain. The details of economic policy—at either the microeconomic or macroeconomic level—flow from the more fundamental analysis of these relationships. It is fair to say that the broad mainstream of political economy has argued that the institutions of the market are generally self-regulating and can be relied upon to promote the interests of the individuals operating within the economy, with state intervention limited to the correction of market failures and, possibly, the limited redistribution of income and wealth. However, there is a substantial undercurrent of argument pointing to the possibility that the structure of markets may be less benign and more in need of political control. The tension between these two general lines of argument is the background against which specific economic policy debates should be seen.

ALAN HAMLIN

BIBLIOGRAPHY

Blaug, Mark, 1968. *Economic Theory in Retrospect*. 2d ed. Homewood, IL: Richard D. Irwin.
Bose, Arun, 1975. *Marxian and Post-Marxian Political Economy*. Harmondsworth: Penguin.
Buchanan, James M. and Gordon Tullock, 1962. *The Calculus of Consent*. Ann Arbor: University of Michigan Press.
Dasgupta, Amiya K., 1985. *Epochs of Economic Theory*. Oxford: Basil Blackwell.
Keynes, John M., 1936. *The General Theory of Employment, Interest and Money*. London: Macmillan.
Marshall, Alfred, 1920 (originally published 1890). *Principles of Economics*. 8th ed. London: Macmillan.
Mill, John S., 1848. *Principles of Political Economy*. London: John W. Parker.

POLITICAL MACHINE. An informal political party organization, typically operating at the city or county level, that controls official government decisionmaking through its manipulation of the electoral process, corruption, patronage, and provision of services to businesses and citizens. In the contemporary context, the phrase "political machine" is occasionally also used to describe especially efficient and well-run political campaign organizations.

The origins of the term can be traced back to the U.S. Industrial Revolution of the middle to late nineteenth century, where political observers found close parallels between the corrupt, highly disciplined, almost militia-like parties found in certain cities during that period and the factory machine, operating automatically without regard for matters of conscience.

As a form of party organization, political machines are distinguished by the hierarchical structure of internal control and their inducements for activism. The archetypical political machine has a "boss" at the head of the chain of command, with various levels of the organization staffed by "henchmen"—precinct and ward leaders capable of delivering support and votes. The organizational incentive for machine unity is typically some form of political patronage which creates incentives for party operatives to mobilize voters in order to gain control of formal governmental power, thus providing an opportunity to reward the faithful with various forms of government-sponsored largesse, from jobs to lucrative government contracts to favorable treatment through the tax laws. The political machine is often portrayed as an urban phenomenon, usually a local Democratic Party organization dominated by a political boss and his or her close associates, thriving with the support of impoverished lower classes of ethnic origins, especially those of Irish descent.

There are few, if any, topics in U.S. politics more shrouded in myth, legend, and stereotype than urban political machines and their colorful bosses. The stereotype of the political machine that even today dominates thinking about the subject comes largely from the influence of a long list of crusading journalists and political reformers, beginning with such writers as Lincoln Steffens, Gustavus Myers, and Moisei Ostrogski in the last decades of the nineteenth century. Such commentators were outraged by the outright corruption, favoritism, dictatorial tactics, and inefficiency of machine politics. Through manipulation of the nomination and electoral processes, the machine was seen as subverting the popular will and using the acquired government power for selfish aims.

In practice, the political machine has been a far more complex phenomenon than has typically been depicted. Generalization must be done with caution. Machines characterized by a single city boss with tight control existed for a time in a number of U.S. cities, such as New York's Tammany Hall under the leadership of Richard Croker in the late nineteenth century, and Kansas City under Tom Pendergast in the late 1920s through the very early 1940s. Far more common were machines that resembled what political scientist Gerald Pomper in *Passions & Interests* (1992) refers to as "opportunistic feudalism" (p. 73). In cities such as Boston, Philadelphia, and Chicago, machines were controlled largely by coalitions of ward or aldermanic district party officials. Many of the bosses of legend—Tweed of Tammany Hall, James Curley in Boston, Pat Nash and Ed Kelly in Chicago, and the O'Connell brothers in Albany, New York—gained and retained power through their ability to maintain alliances among ward chieftains, rather than because of their dictatorial powers.

Nor were all political machines Democratic and/or urban. Cities such as Cincinnati and San Francisco were controlled by Republican machines for long stretches of their history, and, in Philadelphia, a Republican political machine dominated city politics from the Civil War through the late 1940s. Republican machines, unlike their Democratic counterparts, relied far less on a lower-class, ethnic base, drawing electoral strength instead from Yankee middle-class voters desirous of lower taxes. There have been famous rural and suburban bosses as well as urban bosses, perhaps Sheriff Birch Biggs of Polk County, Tennessee, being among the more notorious. On rare occasions, political machines and bosses have gained nearly total control of state politics. The old Long machine in Louisiana prior to and during the New Deal and the Byrd machine in Virginia in the first decades of the twentieth century approached nearly hegemonic control over state government decisionmaking. But the difficulty of any kind of political control extending beyond the city or county level and the threat of outside scrutiny have largely confined the political machine, as an organizational form, to lower levels of government.

A Context for Machine Development

In rudimentary form, attempts by individuals and small groups of their supporters to rig the electoral process and gain control of formal governmental power for personal gain has a long history in U.S. politics, extending even back to colonial days when local politicians attempted to fill the benches with supporters at New England town meetings. The first political machine, Tammany Hall in New York City, was originally established as a masonic society in 1789. A decade later it had been transformed into a political organization that mobilized voters in precincts and wards in support of Thomas Jefferson's presidential efforts. But it was not until the middle of the nineteenth century that the machine style of party organization came to dominate the politics of U.S. cities.

Party machines experienced their apex in influence upon urban political life from about 1850 to World War I, though a number of powerful machines thrived until well after World War II. The midpoint of the nineteenth century roughly corresponds to the eve of the U.S. Industrial Revolution. At that time the nation had only one city, New York, with a million in population. By the last decade of the century a major transformation in the character of the country had taken place. According to the 1890 census, eleven cities had over a quarter of a million residents, while three topped the one million mark. The rural-urban shift was of gigantic proportions, with city populations growing at three times the rural rate by century's end. It was within

this context that machine politics came to so dominate U.S. cites that political party historians have estimated that three-quarters of major U.S. cities were governed most of the time by political machines between 1890 and 1910.

The machines' rise in such a setting was hardly an accident, nor was it exclusively negative in its impact. Migrants from the hinterland and immigrants from abroad flooded U.S. cities during the last half of the nineteenth century. With the influx, cities found themselves under great pressure to make infrastructure improvements, such as building new streets and sewers, and to provide basic city services such as fire protection and hospital access. The social and welfare needs of the assimilating populations were great as well. Many of the newcomers were indigent, in need of basic shelter and jobs to provide for their families. The plight of immigrant populations was particularly desperate, as they faced a foreign culture in the impersonal setting of a large city, with the added disadvantage of being unable to speak the English language (the Irish were the exception).

In an age when the demand for government action was growing rapidly, existing governmental structures proved to be inadequate. City and county governments in the post–Civil War era epitomized the pervasive influence of a set of core U.S. values hostile to centralized governmental authority. Reflecting the supposed virtues of Jacksonian direct democracy and the long ballot tradition, all manner of public officials were elected from separate constituencies, typically annually, to sit on boards and councils, often unwieldy in their size. Reflecting the Madisonian notion of checks and balances, power tended to be either shared and overlapping or sharply divided among the various boards and councils. City mayors typically had little formal power. In an era when the pressures to plan, coordinate, and develop a unified approach to addressing pressing problems were increasing, local governments lacked the capacity to act.

The moral climate of the times also contributed to a context that was ripe for a machine style of politics. The dominant social ethic was social Darwinism, which made a virtue of rugged individualism and frowned on using government to solve social problems like poverty or the lack of employment. A generally permissive environment also characterized the era. The period from the election of Ulysses S. Grant in 1868 through the 1890s is sometimes referred to as the Gilded Age, noted for exploitive business conduct and a rather lax attitude toward corruption in all sectors of society. The nation became enthralled with industrial capitalism. The end of the Civil War witnessed a decline in the idealistic impulses of the old Radical Republicans, and a withdrawal from politics by the public-regarding, Yankee Protestant political aristocracy took place. Citizen apathy toward local government affairs was common. It was not until well into the late 1880s that the media started devoting attention to local government affairs.

In a very real sense there existed both a leadership and moral vacuum in city and county government. The vacuum, unable to be filled in a formal way by existing government structures, was filled in an extralegal way by the political machine. The social upheaval provided an opportunity for creative political leaders who had gained power to circumvent the formal political process to get things done, unencumbered by the kinds of moral constraints that later contributed to the machine's demise.

How the Machine Operated

Bossism and machine politics can be viewed as representing a form of political entrepreneurialism. Personal profit was the goal. The boss and members of the machine first gained control of the nomination process for public office, a relatively easy task since during the mid- to late nineteenth century parties had total control of the caucus or convention nominating systems. Once the nomination was secured for its candidates, the machine then worked to guarantee that its choices should be chosen in the general election. The influence of the machine over officeholders was such that the machine became the de facto government. Power, financial gain, and jobs for those in the machine were the benefits sought by machine activists. Many of the city bosses became extraordinarily wealthy individuals.

In essence, the machine offered services for a price. The price was votes and support. Although the specific tactics to ensure electoral support for machines and their candidates varied by city and era, often it involved outright vote fraud such as herding repeat voters to the polls in support of machine candidates, altering ballots, and buying votes. Such vote fraud was possible throughout most of the nineteenth century because there were no registration requirements and no secret ballot. Merely getting their supporters to the polls was not enough for a number of early machines, such as Tammany Hall, which devoted just as much effort to physically intimidating opponents by sending party thugs out on election day to "discourage" opponents from going to the polls. Richard Coker, later the boss of Tammany, actually started his political career as an intimidator for the machine. In 1874 he was accused of murdering a Republican opponent at the polls, though charges were dropped because of insufficient evidence.

Later machines were a little more sophisticated. In Kansas City during the heyday of boss Tom Pendergast in the 1930s, machine operatives, accompanied by the city police, would search on election day for opposition workers seeking to get voters to the polls or working in precincts to challenge illegal voters. When found, such workers would be arrested and held in jail until the polls closed.

Control of city and county government by the machine gave it other, more formal weapons against the opposition at the polls. Control of the tax machinery was cru-

cial. Community members who were known to oppose the machine typically had their home and/or business property taxes raised. Party registration was a prerequisite to lower taxes. City building codes could be enforced strictly against those in opposition. Party-controlled courts could be used against machine opponents. Most often opposition soon ceased or left the community altogether.

Viewing the machine only from the perspective of how it dealt with opposition is only a small part of the story. In many if not most cases, machines had genuine, broad-based support from members of the community. Sociologist Robert Merton in his *Social Theory and Social Structure* (1968) has pointed out the importance of distinguishing between the recognized, intended "manifest" functions of the machine (i.e., graft, electoral fraud, intimidation of opponents), and its "latent" functions (providing services to business and help to citizens), largely unintended and unrecognized. What the machine offered were substantial services for the price of votes and support. Those who focus only on the unseemly tactics and ethical violations of machine politics may fail to understand some of the fundamental reasons machines thrived for so long in U.S. politics.

For example, elements of the business community dependent upon government support often welcomed machine politics, despite the additional costs in terms of campaign contributions and kickbacks to the machine. Business owners and citizens found it much easier to deal with a boss and a few machine leaders than with the huge array of public officials, all with their own constituencies and agendas. The machine could circumvent the red tape, inertia, overlapping jurisdictions, and time-consuming delay that characterized local governments. City infrastructures were built, and commerce was enhanced for many in the business community, although largely incidental to the machine's selfish purposes of public plunder.

Acting as the head of the party organization and/or from a base as an elected official, city bosses had the power to bestow substantial benefits upon cooperative and supportive businesses. Building contractors, businesses that needed to be granted a franchise in order to operate in the city such as utilities and public transit companies, those that needed various licenses to operate such as drinking establishments, all sought the "permission" of city government. Illegal businesses, such as prostitution and gambling, needed protection from prosecution. Bribery, extortion, and graft were quite common. Many in the business community were quite willing to pay for favorable considerations or for authorities to look the other way.

At base, however, it was patronage, the system of filling government jobs and positions on the basis of partisan considerations, that was at the core of machine politics. City machines in the post–Civil War era were the equivalent of employment agencies, not just with the ability to provide jobs for party workers, but having the capacity to

offer or aid in the employment of a vast number of other city dwellers. In New York in the 1870s, it was estimated by the reform-minded Citizens League that Tammany Hall controlled over 65,000 jobs. In Chicago as late as the 1970s, despite civil service reform, the party organization still controlled roughly 30,000 jobs, the bulk with city-owned utilities. Additional state government jobs were under the control of the Daley organization. Machine-controlled patronage often extended well beyond government employment per se. Businesses franchised by the city, such as utilities, quickly learned that it was expected that their employees, especially for manual labor tasks, be chosen by party officials.

It was patronage that helped cement the bonds between the machine and lower-class ethnics in U.S. cities. Between 1850 and World War I, more than 25 million immigrants were assimilated into U.S. society, the bulk in urban areas. For the immigrant, shunned by Yankee-dominated private enterprise and the business world, little possibility existed for work other than in an unskilled labor job. The classic, urban political machine of the nineteenth century, through its control of the various city departments or its influence in the hiring by utilities franchised by the city, became the employer of only and last resort.

Sociologists, in particular, have recognized the unique, though largely unintended, contribution of the political machine to the immigrant. Besides helping with employment, precinct and ward leaders in the machine provided a whole range of social services to the newly arrived residents of the cities, from welfare activities like giving food (including the proverbial holiday turkey), coal for fuel, free clothes, and help with rent payments, to assistance with legal counsel, burial of the dead, and organization of neighborhood social activities. The machine is also credited with responding to the aspiration needs of immigrant populations, yielding a measure of recognition and status, when other avenues were closed, to those who became part of the party organization.

The Irish, as part of the first wave of immigrants to the U.S. during the industrial revolution, were the ethnic group that most benefited from machine politics. By the 1890s, the Irish had captured Democratic Party organizations in most Midwestern and Northeastern cities. In many of the cities it was virtually impossible to distinguish between the party and other organizational manifestations of the Irish communities: the churches, neighborhood saloons, volunteer fire departments, and the like. Party workers met the needy as neighbors, spoke their language, and, like those they served, were fully integrated into the ethnic community. Loyalty at the polls to their party "friends" became automatic for many immigrants like the Irish.

Bosses and ward leaders were often community heroes, a source of ethnic pride for the stature they had achieved. Some of the earliest bosses were Irish, including such legendary figures as William Sheehan in Buffalo, "Lit-tle Bob" Davis in Jersey City, and John Kelly and Croker in New York City. The list of Irish bosses in the twentieth century is impressive as well: Ed Kelly, Pat Nash, and Richard Daley in Chicago; David L. Lawrence in Pittsburgh; Frank Hague in Jersey City; the O'Connell brothers in Albany; and the Pendergast brothers in Kansas City, to name but a few of the most prominent.

Other ethnic groups benefited as well, but not nearly as much as the Irish. Almost all later ethnic groups could point to their own famous machine bosses, such as Czech Tony Cermak in Chicago during the 1930s or Italian Carmine De Sapio, leader of Tammany Hall in the late 1940s and 1950s. But the newer waves of immigrants from Southern and Eastern Europe, Italians, Poles, and Jews, were often excluded from many city party organizations and the rewards of machine politics. The entrenched Irish machines of the nineteenth century simply did not need the support of newer ethnic arrivals and saw little need to extend patronage benefits or other forms of government booty to them.

The Demise of the Urban Political Machine

Although there still remain U.S. cities where one-party domination remains strong and control is vested in small numbers of politicians, the classic urban political machine with a political boss probably no longer exists in U.S. politics. The Chicago Democratic machine, closely controlled by Cook County Democratic chairman and Chicago mayor Richard Daley from the mid-1950s to 1976, was the last genuine political machine to dominate a large U.S. city.

The excesses of machine politics, from subverting and making a mockery of the election process to the outright corruption and abuse of governmental power and funds, eventually led to a series of reform movements, beginning near the turn of the century, dedicated to eliminating or diminishing the impact of political party organizations in both the electoral process and in government. At the municipal level, local civil service reform, which removed many government positions from direct party control; increased use of nonpartisan elections and the short ballot; and established council-manager government with at-large rather than ward elections, along with the introduction of the direct primary system of nomination, all diminished the resources that enabled bosses and machines to dominate city politics. Electoral fraud became more difficult as more and more states and localities used formal voter registration systems and introduced the secret ballot. The growth of the national civil service reduced the number of patronage positions local organizations could distribute.

Voter interest in many of the beneficial services and functions performed by machine operatives declined as well. With the coming of Franklin Roosevelt's New Deal, the federal government became concerned with responding to the social and welfare needs of its most needy citizens.

Government-sponsored relief and welfare programs undercut party-provided, ad hoc services of a similar nature.

Even in the face of such challenges, in a number of cities the urban political machine did not die easily. Despite a direct primary system designed to give voters the power to nominate candidates, machines in some locales continued to dictate candidate selection because of their ability to mobilize enough supporters to vote the party slate in usually low-turnout primary elections. Personal registration systems could be circumvented by "ghost" voting, that is, not removing voters from the registration lists who had died or moved away and casting a ballot in their names in subsequent elections. Machine politicians proved very adept at circumventing local reform measures dealing with patronage as well. Since "temporary" and "provisional" jobs were exempted from civil service requirements, a large proportion of city positions were simply reclassified to these categories, enabling the hiring of partisans to continue.

Nor did New Deal social programs destroy some machines. In places like Pittsburgh, Kansas City, and Chicago, skillful organizational leaders developed strong ties with the Roosevelt administration through their abilities to muster Democratic support for the national ticket. As a consequence, some local Democratic organizations actually gained resources and were able to use federal money and patronage from such programs as the Works Progress Administration (WPA) to create highly centralized organizations able to control access to public offices and virtually to dictate local government policy. The power of ethnic appeals, a motivating and unifying force for partisan solidarity, helped sustain machine control in a number of cities well after many of the material benefits offered to supporters were eliminated or diminished.

Overall, a variety of social forces, over time, were too strong for the urban political machine to overcome. As the nation moved to more advanced forms of industrialism with huge, impersonal factories and often sordid working conditions, the machine proved of little use in helping workers deal with social and economic problems. The rise of the union movement, which attempted to mobilize workers on the basis of shared class interests regardless of ethnic differences, proved to be a significant challenge to the political machine. Indeed, in a number of cities it was the political machine rather than the industrialists that attempted to suppress union organizing efforts, alienating many of their former supporters in the process.

The context so favorable to the development of political machines changed as well. While the local parties no doubt contributed to the rising economic standards of underprivileged groups, these persons and their children eventually grew skeptical of the predatory and unethical behavior of bosses and their machines. As urban populations became more educated and assimilated middle-class values, the heavy-handed, crass partisanship of the political machine became increasingly intolerable.

Finally, as the nation moved from an industrial to a postindustrial society, the role of parties in the electoral process diminished. New campaign technologies, the use of television, direct mail, pollsters, and campaign consultants, all have meant that neither candidates nor voters are dependent on local party organizations. The political and moral vacuum that existed during the era in which strong city machines arose is no longer there.

ALLAN J. CIGLER

BIBLIOGRAPHY

Boulay, Harvey and Alan DiGaetano, 1985. "Why Did Political Machines Disappear." *Journal of Urban History*, vol. 12 (November) 25–50.

Cornwell, Elmer E., 1960. "Party Absorption of Ethnic Groups." *Social Forces*, vol. 38 (March) 205–210.

Flynn, Edward, 1962. *You're the Boss.* New York: Collier Books.

Gosnell, Harold F., 1937. *Machine Politics: Chicago Model.* 2d ed. Chicago: University of Chicago Press.

Greenstein, Fred I., 1963. *The American Party System and the American People.* Englewood Cliffs, NJ: Prentice-Hall Inc.

Erie, Steven P., 1988. *Rainbow's End.* Berkeley, CA: University of California Press.

Mayhew, David R., 1986. *Placing Parties in American Politics.* Princeton, NJ: Princeton University Press.

Merton, Robert K., 1968. *Social Theory and Social Structure.* New York: The Free Press.

Mladenka, Kenneth, 1980. "The Urban Bureaucracy and the Chicago Political Machine." *American Political Science Review*, vol. 74 (December) 991–998.

Pomper, Gerald M., 1992. *Passions & Interests.* Lawrence: University Press of Kansas.

Riordan, William L., 1963. *Plunkitt of Tammany Hall.* New York: E. P. Dutton.

Shefter, Martin, 1976. "The Emergence of the Political Machine: An Alternative View." In Willis D. Hawley, *et al., Theoretical Perspectives on Urban Politics.* Englewood Cliffs, NJ: Prentice-Hall Inc.

Steinberg, Alfred, 1972. *The Bosses.* New York: Macmillan Publishing Company.

Wolfinger, Raymond E., 1972. "Why Political Machines Have Not Withered Away and Other Revisionist Thoughts." *Journal of Politics*, vol. 34 (May) 365–398.

POLITICAL NEUTRALITY.

A political value holding that civil servants hired through selection systems based on merit should remain nonpartisan in the way they perform their governmental duties. Such civil servants are to be willingly responsive to the legitimate political leaders of the day and not be swayed in the performance of their duty based on partisan political loyalties.

This value has been one of the fundamental principles on which the U.S. civil service is based. Its origins in the United States can be traced back to the presidency of Thomas Jefferson, but presidents William H. Harrison and John Tyler also took steps to limit the partisan activity of federal employees. U.S. ideas in this regard have been modeled loosely on the English civil service and given legal status in the Pendleton Act of 1883. The new merit system created under this act was to allow the selection of individuals in the classified service based on nonpartisan criteria; therefore, there would be little reason for partisan dismissals. Specific provisions of the Pendleton Act prohibited officials from coercing the political action of any classified employee and from laying political financial assessments on merit system employees.

In order to ensure the responsiveness of civil servants to the party in power and to ensure political neutrality, job tenure was given to merit system employees regardless of changes in the political leadership at the top. Unlike the elected official or the politically appointed official within the bureaucracy, the career merit system employee has an enduring and institutional responsibility, not simply a responsibility lasting the length of an electoral term of office. This responsibility is in doing the business of day-to-day governance—not the business of electioneering.

This concept of neutrality was also carried forward in the organizational structure of the Civil Service Commission created in the Pendleton Act. Like the career civil servant, the Commission was to be organizationally as nonpartisan as possible. Structurally it was removed from the traditional administrative hierarchy so filled with partisan battles between the president and congress. There was a further attempt to minimize partisan considerations in the affairs of the commission by specifying that not more than two of the three commission members could be members of the same political party.

From a larger theoretical basis there was an attempt to separate politics, the making of policy, from administration, the neutral implementation of policy arrived at in the larger political arena. Though the Pendleton Act's principal of the politically neutral merit-based civil servant, this new system could theoretically implement the separation of politics and administration. Politics was handled by the elected official working together with the politically appointed civil servant. Administration was to be handled largely by the career civil servant hired through merit-based selection criteria.

Since the Pendleton Act, subsequent presidents have issued executive orders further restricting the partisan political rights of members of the classified service. Specifically, President Theodore Roosevelt prohibited merit system employees from taking any active part in political management or in political campaigns. This executive order, often referred to as Rule I, was effectively enforced until the administration of Franklin D. Roosevelt. Roosevelt raised increasing concerns over the nonpartisanship of government servants in appointments to some of his emergency agencies created as a part of his New Deal.

Largely in response to Republican fears that Roosevelt was gaining a partisan advantage, the Hatch Act passed Congress in 1939. This act prohibited partisan political activities by all non-politically appointed federal employees.

This prohibition was later expanded to cover federal employees working at the state and local levels, and many states subsequently passed their own equivalent acts aimed at restricting the partisan political activities of state and local employees.

In a democracy any restriction of the political participation rights of a group of citizens is always going to be controversial, and the Hatch Act is no exception. The constitutionality of its restrictions has been upheld twice by the United States Supreme Court in the cases of *United Public Workers v. Mitchell* in 1947, and the *U.S. Civil Service Commission v. National Association of Letter Carriers* in 1973.

By the 1990s a large number of states had changed their Hatch Acts, making them somewhat less restrictive, and the national Congress followed suit. While most of the former restrictions were kept in place, the Hatch Act reforms of 1993 did allow federal employees to engage in a wider range of partisan activities.

ROBERT H. ELLIOTT

BIBLIOGRAPHY

Heclo, Hugh, 1977. *A Government of Strangers: Executive Politics in Washington.* Washington, D.C.: The Brookings Institution.
Rosenbloom, David H. and James D. Carroll, 1995. "Public Personnel Administration and the Law." In Jack Rabin *et al.*, *Handbook of Public Personnel Administration.* New York: Marcel Dekker, Inc.
U.S. Civil Service Commission v. National Association of Letter Carriers, 1973. 413 U.S. 548.
United Public Workers v. Mitchell, 1947. 330 U.S. 75.

POLITICS-ADMINISTRATION DICHOTOMY.

An enduring debate in public administration about whether or not one can have a public administration free from the whims and interference of politics.

The source of the dichotomy is the 1887 article "The Study of Administration" by Woodrow Wilson, published in *Political Science Quarterly.* In a wide-ranging discussion, Wilson asked whether or not there can be an administrative practice in this democratic context which is free from the divisive and capricious impulses of the body politic. The beginnings of the reform movement is the context in which the article was written. The federal Civil Service Reform Act had been passed in 1883. There were continuing and growing calls for substituting merit for the patronage system which had dominated government for half a century. The city manager movement was in its infancy. Efficiency in government was becoming the cry. By staffing public agencies with persons who would apply modern administrative techniques, reformers hoped to improve government. Wilson's comment during the 1912 presidential election is illustrative: "[W]henever government is disentangled from its connection with special interests and made responsive to genuine public opinion, throughout the length and breadth of the great country, it at once gets new ideals and responds to new impulses. It then becomes an instrument of civilization and of humanity."

The public administration literature widely assumes that Wilson was the founder of the academic study of public administration in the United States. There were, however, robust antecedents in Great Britain and in Germany, where bureaucracies had been in place for many decades. Another difficulty in the familiar view of Wilson's role was that his 1887 article is not cited in any of the administrative literature until the 1930s, and it was not until after World War II that his article gained prominence.

In 1887 Wilson clearly acknowledged the existence not only of administrative structures but of thoughtful writing about them in England and Europe. He compared the extensive writing on constitutions, about "the greatest meanings lying at the heart of government, and the high ends set before the purpose of government by man's nature and man's aims" (p. 198). But now the great press of social needs was outweighing the need to discuss principle. In his trenchant phrase," It is getting to be harder to *run* a constitution than to frame one" (p. 200). However, the science of administration was "finding its doctors in Europe . . . a foreign science . . . [employing] only foreign tongues" (p. 202). In Wilson's view, that science had to be "Americanized," conforming it to the democratic tradition of this continent.

Here Wilson employed a conception that reflected his rich use of the language. Since the principles of democracy are inimical to continental monarchies, we need only examine their administrative practices:

> If I see a murderous fellow sharpening a knife cleverly, I can borrow his way of sharpening the knife without borrowing his probable intention to commit murder with it; and so, if I see a monarchist dyed in the wool managing a public bureau well, I can learn his business method without changing one of my republican spots. . . . We can thus scrutinize the anatomy of foreign governments without fear of getting any of their diseases into our veins; dissect alien systems without apprehension of blood-poisoning" (1887, p. 220).

This, then, was the context of the politics-administrative dichotomy, which Wilson put forward as a means of addressing the objections brought by diehard democrats in his own country, that bureaucratic reform would bring a latent monarchism by way of a ruling elite. He addressed their concerns directly. "Liberty cannot live apart from constitutional principle; and no administration, however perfect and liberal its methods, can give men more than a poor counterfeit of liberty if it rest upon illiberal principles of government" (1887, p. 212).

His answer to the objections was: Keep politics and administration separate. The provinces of constitutional law and administrative function are distinctly different. The general laws which direct certain public functions are "above" administration. On the other hand, public administration is "detailed and systematic execution of public law. . . . The broad plans of governmental action are not administrative; the detailed execution of such plans is administrative" (1887, p. 212).

Wilson's motives, however, were not quite so simple. Two other concerns were addressed in his article: the impulsive nature of the electorate and its elected representatives, and the principles of efficiency.

Wilson did not have a high view of the people and their behavior at the ballot box. He decried "that besetting error of ours, the error of trying to do too much by vote" (1887, p. 214). Having enthroned public opinion, the people could agree on nothing simple. Advance was made "through compromise, by a compounding of differences, by a trimming of plans and a suppression of too straightforward principles. . . . [the people] are selfish, ignorant, timid, stubborn, or foolish. . . . The bulk of mankind is rigidly unphilosophical, and nowadays the bulk of mankind votes" (1887, pp. 208–209). The result was not only confusion in political leadership but also the dominance of special interests, which used the disorder and discord to their advantage.

The second concern, that of efficiency, lay close to the heart of a man who saw business and the entrepreneurial spirit as positive goods in U.S. democracy. Echoing the "reinventing government" movement of the late twentieth century, Wilson believed that allowing public managers to act with large powers and unhampered discretion would lead to efficient, and thereby effective, government. Inefficiency always brings confusion, because citizens cannot depend on their government, at whatever level, to operate consistently. For Wilson, efficiency was the simplest arrangement of government by which responsibility could be fixed upon an authoritative official. This clarity of role and purpose would lead to a high level of trust on the part of the people, thereby reinforcing effectiveness, diligence, and competence (1887, p. 213). In 1912, Wilson said: "[T]hose who exercise its [the government's] authority must 'keep house' for the whole people" (1912/1984, p. 194). They would do so by borrowing expertise from the philanthropist, the engineer, the forest expert, students of soils and agricultural methods, masters of technical and vocational education, financiers, lawyers, manufacturers, merchants (1912). Merit would breed trust which would lead to efficiency. Government freed from the confusion of the ballot box used too much, and disentangled from special interests, could then "establish and maintain every condition which will assist the people to a sound and wholesome and successful life" (1912/1984, p. 195). He called this "the new meaning of government."

The element in Wilson's thought that often goes unnoticed is the combination of administrative entrepreneurial freedom and administrative responsibility. Although he did not say so directly, it is clear that elected representatives were to some extent to be displaced by administrative expertise. Wilson saw administrators operating with large powers and unhampered discretion, which he termed "openness and vigor" (1887, p. 222). This was to be balanced by a "ready docility to all serious, well-sustained public criticism." That is, administrators should determine what appraisal of their work is worthwhile, and then suffer appropriate reproach for any wrongdoing or error. Inherent in this view is Wilson's hope that expertise and trust would lead to an administrative practice characterized by a sense of care and guardianship. If responsibility was to be clearly fixed upon an administrative office then accountability should surely follow. It is at this latter point that commentators hesitate, as experience has been a dear teacher in showing us that official discretion too often leads to human indiscretion.

The politics-administration dichotomy remains a perplexing issue for modern public administration. The issues that faced Wilson are similar to those of modern administrative scholarship and practice. The question of how to balance administrative action with political direction is a problem yet to be solved. Wilson's original goals continue to be held by many, that within U.S. democracy we can somehow find an equilibrium between management efficiency, personal integrity, entrepreneurial energy, and innovative program development. The skepticism that persists in academic public administration is simply a contemporary expression of the dilemmas that have faced us since the founding over two hundred years ago. Wilson was right: It *is* harder to run a constitution than to frame one.

PETER J. VAN HOOK

BIBLIOGRAPHY

Simmons, Robert H., and Eugene P. Dvorin, 1977. "Philosophical Perspectives: Weber and Wilson." In R.H. Simmons and E. P. Dvorin, eds., *Public Administration: Values, Policy, and Change.* Port Washington, NY: Alfred Publishing Co.

Waldo, Dwight, 1984. *The Administrative State: A Study of the Political Theory of American Public Administration.* New York: Holmes & Meier.

Wilson, Woodrow, 1885a. "The Modern Democratic State." In Arthur S. Link, ed., *Papers of Woodrow Wilson,* vol. 5. Princeton: Princeton University Press.

———, 1885b. "The Art of Governing." In Arthur S. Link, ed., *Papers of Woodrow Wilson,* vol. 5. Princeton: Princeton University Press.

———, 1887. "The Study of Administration." *Political Science Quarterly,* II(2) (June)197–222.

———, 1912. "The New Meaning of Government." *Woman's Home Companion,* 39(11). (Reprinted in *Public Administration Review* 44(3):193–195, May-June 1984.)

POSITION CLASSIFICATION.

The personnel process of organizing job duties and responsibilities into standard units, called positions, and then grouping positions into "classes" of positions. These classes are used administratively to justify the same treatment with respect to recruitment procedures, selection procedures, compensation, and other aspects of personnel management.

Position classification in government is somewhat different than in most business organizations. Because public accountability has always been a major consideration, and because neutrality, efficiency, and objectivity have been commonly espoused public sector values, laws have closely regulated the process of position classification. To maximize efficiency and to minimize political favoritism, fundamental premises of position classification in U.S. government have been that it is the position, not the individual, which is classified, and that the individual characteristics of an employee occupying a position should not determine the classification of the position.

Under most public sector classification systems, job analysis information leads to decisions establishing positions. Positions are grouped into classes, classes into a class series, and class series into very broad categories called occupational groups. For instance, a position might be called an "Air Pollution Engineer." There may be a number of positions labeled this in a city's Department of Public Health. There may also be engineers dealing with hazardous waste working under a classification called "Hazardous Waste Engineer." These classifications may be grouped together with similar positions dealing with solid waste and water pollution and the classification given a more general label, "Public Health Engineer." This classification may then be divided into a series of levels with each denoting differing gradations of authority and responsibility such as Public Health Engineer I, II, III, and IV. Finally, there may be an even more general occupational grouping of these classifications with others having similar scientific backgrounds such as biologists, chemists, and physicists and labeled the "Environmental Occupational Group" because they all have environmental control responsibilities.

Position classification has been criticized as being overly rigid and unrealistic, and has been accused of making a manager's job more difficult rather than making it more efficient. Recently, there have been efforts to alter the existing classification structure radically and replace it with more flexible alternatives offering "broadbanding" options in two demonstration projects conducted by the federal government. In demonstration projects made possible by the Civil Service Reform Act of 1978, experiments designed to make classifications more flexible have been tried at the Naval Weapons Center in China Lake, California, and the Naval Ocean Systems Center in San Diego, California. Given the increasing demands being made by elected officials for more flexibility and innovation in the personnel processes in government, it is likely that current highly specialized and inflexible position classification systems will undergo considerable change in the next decade.

ROBERT H. ELLIOTT

BIBLIOGRAPHY

Gilbert, R. G. and A. Nelson, 1989. "The Pacer Share Demonstration Project: Implications for Organizational Management and Performance Evaluation." *Public Personnel Management,* vol. 18 (Summer) 209–225.

Shafritz, Jay M., 1973. *Position Classification: A Behavioral Analysis for the Public Sector.* New York: Praeger.

Shafritz, Jay M., Norma M. Riccucci, David H. Rosenbloom, and Albert C. Hyde, 1992. *Personnel Management in Government.* 4th ed. New York: Marcel Dekker, Inc.

U.S. Merit Systems Protection Board, 1992. *Federal Personnel Research Programs and Demonstration Projects, Catalysts for Change.* Washington, D.C.: U.S. Government Printing Office.

POSITIVISM. Views based on the virtues and fecundity of scientific explanation of phenomena. Positivism is a generalized reference to research approaches that employ empirical methods, make extensive use of quantitative analysis, or develop logical calculi to build formal explanatory theory. The term positivism historically accompanies other modernist tendencies such as industrialization, technological advances, the mastery of nature, cause-and-effect determinism, precisely calibrated measurement, atomistic physics, and instrumental rationality.

Early Positivism

The term positivism was coined by French philosopher Henri Comte de Saint-Simon (1760–1825), who pejoratively contrasted the worth of aristocrats with the worth of people with skill, ability, and knowledge—scientists, artists, business owners, musicians, sailors, and various artisans, all of whom had positive ability. Saint-Simon insisted that prosperity and progress depends on those with productive skills, not on the privileged aristocracy. Early positivism had three main interrelated themes: (1) a faith in science, not unlike the faith in a supreme being that it began to supersede; (2) a conception of progress driven by scientific advances; and (3) a political social vision thought to be consistent with the first two orientations. The early positivist aspiration was based on a faith that there is an objective reality, and a belief that it can be completely described using denotative terms that correspond to facts. This faith was, of course, consistent with the spirit of the Enlightenment and was especially triumphant in the post-revolutionary France of the First and Second Republics.

Second, as one might expect by definition, positivism is positive. That is to say, positivists are united by a belief in social and human progress driven by the advances of science toward perfect knowledge. In the thought of Saint-Simon's protégé Auguste Comte (1798–1857), positivism represented the final of three stages in human progress. In Comte's scheme, humankind has transcended first, the theological, or fictitious, stage where supernatural agents were understood to be constitutive of reality. Second was the metaphysical stage where abstract forces, the idea in history, were thought to produce phenomena. Finally, humankind had arrived at the positive stage. Here observation and reason would enable scientific observers to predict and control nature to the benefit of humankind. This notion of unilinear, continuous, and progressive evolution remains vital today, although validity of this proposition has been nowhere demonstrated.

Third, early positivism entailed a utopian political vision. Positivism embraced a syndicalism whereby society and the polity would be organized along functional production domains (mining, transportation, manufacturing, and so on). Within and between these syndicates, conflict would be eliminated by the application of scientific rationality. A meritocracy of ability would replace an aristocracy of birth. Comte, in *Philosophy of Mathematics* (1851) turned positivism into a religion whose motto was "order and progress." In Comte's religion scientists were the high priests; the spiritual reorganization of society within a positivist framework was the principal purpose of this religion. Not God, but humanity itself was the focus of Comte's sociological creed.

In this latter political and ideological manifestation, positivism represents one of the most extreme calls for technocracy, the rule of experts. This strain of thought informs modern organization theory. Because of the technical complexity of many of the tasks taken on by the government—water pollution, space exploration, public health, military operations, or highway design to mention a few—professionals in government have become de facto policy makers. The functions they perform are often incomprehensible to elected politicians or to the citizenry in general. These professionals, who possess knowledge, skills, and abilities essential to accomplishing the practical goals of government and society, have the "positive ability" that so impressed Saint-Simon. Although explicit recommendations for technocracy are unpopular in more democratic eras, it should be remembered that it was against aristocracy and oligarchy that it was originally proposed. Functional positivism remains a compelling logical alternative whenever the legitimacy of entrenched rule of the merely privileged is thought to prevail—conditions that, arguably, preceded the Progressive Era when the spoils system became intolerable. And, the claims of expertise in any modern policy process remain powerful ones and can be regarded as a legacy of early positivism.

In the field of law, positivism is associated with the views of John Austin (1790–1859) and Hans Kelsen (1881–1973). They held that actual legal systems are the appropriate subject of jurisprudential philosophy. Whereas natural

law advocates search for justifications for law independent of the existing legal system, legal positivism sees law as rationalized convention, which is then systematized as a set of rules backed by coercion.

By the time John Stuart Mill wrote *Principles of Political Economy* (1848), movement toward what would eventually be called logical positivism was in evidence. Mill, who is mostly identified with utilitarianism, contributed to positivist thought by moving it away from Comte's religious absolutism and toward freedom and the development of the individual. He argued for limits on governmental intervention in economic affairs. As a harbinger of logical positivism, Mill also posed the notion that humans were in principle as predictable as physical events. Given enough knowledge about a person's motivations and character, that person's next movements could be predicted.

Indeed, the most influential form of positivism in social science (and by extension to public policy and administration) is not Saint-Simon's "positive ability" version of positivism, but logical positivism.

Logical Positivism

History

Logical positivism may be traced to the Vienna Circle, the spiritual founder of which was the great physicist and philosopher Ernst Mach (1838–1916). The Circle was what today might be called a think tank encompassing a group of talented and distinguished or distinguished-to-be philosophers, mathematicians, physicists, and logicians, centered in Vienna in the 1920s. They shared an interest in reforming philosophy and science along strict logical principles. Among the most influential members, all born in the crucial period of nascent modernist hegemony from 1880 to 1905, were Moritz Schlick, Rudolph Carnap, Otto Neurath, Philipp Frank, Herbert Feigl, and Kurt Gödel. Although not members, Alfred Tarski, Ludwig Wittgenstein, and Karl Popper also attended Circle events, conferences, and discussions. Formal events, of course, led to untotaled numbers of late-night discussions within this social constellation of knowledge located in the then-vibrant Vienna. An allied group of the same generation, the Society for Scientific Philosophy, formed in 1929 in Berlin. Organized by Hans Reichenbach and Richard von Mises, it included the subsequently influential Carl Hempel.

By the mid-1930s, after the Circle sponsored international conferences and began spreading their views in a journal and a book series, the shadow of Nazism caused a diaspora of its (mostly assimilated Jewish) members. The majority achieved faculty positions in elite U.S. universities. In the United States, and to a lesser extent in Britain, the philosophers among them went on to found and articulate a new specialty: the philosophy of science. From this high ground they and their students had tremendous in-

fluence on (especially U.S.) social sciences. The so-called behaviorist revolution in political science, for instance, relied authoritatively on the work begun by the logical positivists. Many of the uncritically held assumptions, protocols of research, and productivity reward structures in academic social science may still be traced back to logical positivism. Harold Lasswell's accentuation of quantification and the methods of physical science resounded a positivist tone in public policy studies that reverberates to this day. In public administration Herbert Simon may be seen as operating very much in the spirit of logical positivism. His distinction between fact and value, only the former term important for the study of administration, is informed by that school. From the above listed group of Vienna Circle participants the most often authoritatively cited by behaviorists were Carl Hempel and Hans Reichenbach. Also influential were Herbert Feigl and his student May Brodbeck.

Logical positivism as a strict set of principles, somewhat imperiously imposed, gradually softened as their categories were attacked and modified in response to these attacks. By the 1950s a strictly logical positivist school in the philosophy of science itself could no longer be identified apart from logical empiricism or plain empiricism and various branches of analytical philosophy. Indeed, former members and fellow travelers of the original Vienna Circle produced important work that undermined confidence in the original stances. Gödel's incompleteness theorem, for instance, held that however consistent and powerful a logical system might be internally, it could not validate itself. Accepting any system, therefore, involves a leap of faith. Faith, of course, is one of those metaphysical entities the logical positivists had so hoped to purge. Popper, for another instance, carefully and meticulously eroded the positivists' hopes for scientific certainty.

Theoretical Framework

Logical positivism had as its main goals to eliminate metaphysics from science and to develop a unified language/calculus for making truth claims. Working toward these twin goals, logical positivists worked out a set of common definitions, distinctions, and presuppositions.

In the lexicon of logical positivists, metaphysics is not so much a technical philosophical term as a somewhat pejorative catchall term under which a number of, to them, merely speculative or emotive pretenders to knowledge were subsumed. Theology, ethics, myths, psychoanalysis, phrenology, alchemy, intuition, astrology, and value statements and preferences are members of the class. Following eighteenth-century empiricist David Hume, logical positivists held that knowledge regarding transcendent reality cannot be justified by speculation, intuition, dialectics, nor matters of fact established by pure *a priori* reason alone.

A three-compartment epistemology or theory of knowledge was devised to isolate metaphysics as non-science: (1) analytical/logical truth, (2) factual or empirical knowledge, and (3) nonsense or meaningless utterances.

First, *a priori* knowledge may be acceptable if it is the kind of truth that pure mathematics provides, that is, if it is composed of analytical statements. Analytical statements are true because they are logically consistent and imply each of the components by definition. They are tautologically true in the same way that $2 + 2 = 4$. The articulation of these kinds of truths is now the main task of formal, positive, or rational choice theory in political science. Importantly, analytical truths by themselves can make no claim to be symmetrical with empirical reality.

The second cell of knowledge contains those statements which can be empirically verified. The logical positivists differed, argued, and continually shifted their positions on just how verification might be accomplished. Indeed, this was the weakest redoubt in the system. Statements about facts, such as predictions or theories, may be justified as knowledge when some postulate is deduced from them; in turn, the postulate must be translated into an operational definition and then verified by observation. Consistent with the positivist dedication to empirical facts, all statements—to be scientifically useful—must be definable in terms of observables. But the prescriptive standards of verification were exceedingly difficult to establish. Because logical positivists were unable to persuade themselves that verification was an achievable standard, this second compartment, how one might validate factual or empirical knowledge, remains an important problematic in the philosophy of science.

Outside these two epistemological compartments (analytical logic and observable facts) was the third one. It contained everything nonscientific, noncognitive, nonsensical, and meaningless. Nothing is to prevent humans from delving into these realms, or into poetry or theology, but these statements are incapable of proof. Only two senses of proof deserve the name "science": logical proof and empirical proof.

Habits, Assumptions, and Mental Models

Such an epistemology, based on the pursuit of logic and facts, is congruent with the logical positivists' aspiration to find a universal language of all science which would unify its disparate branches. They originally believed that a universal logic of scientific explanation could be developed. Indeed, that had been the aspiration of Bertrand Russell (1872–1970) and Alfred North Whitehead (1861–1947) as codified in *Principia Mathematica* (1903). Russell was enormously influential to logical positivist thought. In a truncated sense of the word, positivists were rationalists. This is to say, there is an unstated and unprovable assumption that the human mind can articulate systems of logic and mathematics in some way symmetrical to the structure of the universe at least as humans can know it. To aspire to a unified science based in logic and mathematics is to affirm

as worthwhile the search for fundamental and unchanging patterns. Mundane and particular explanations can be fitted to more generalized patterns. Moreover, the nomothetic, abstract, general pattern is privileged over the ideographic, concrete particularities. Such a faith reflects positivism in the original sense described above. The growth of scientific explanation, prediction, and control is the goal. Logic is the means.

This search for regularities and patterns in scientific explanation was confined to what logical positivists referred to as the realm of justification, as opposed to the realm of discovery. How a scientist came to perceive a fact or law was of no concern. To be accepted by others, however, the findings had to be stated in terms of the logic of explanation so that facts and laws might be confirmed and verified by replication.

However, these philosophers eventually realized that many scientifically useful terms were not verifiable as observable fact. And so, they adjusted their argument by retreating one step toward abstraction: all truth claims must be expressed using terms that can be logically linked to observables. But even that looser regimen failed to save the argument. The operationalism of logical positivism—that true statements must be defined in terms of identifiable facts and replicable empirical operations—was compromised. Indeed, in scientific practice, terms are frequently defined relative to one another, and often without reference to observable facts. This realization was profound because these philosophers had set out to demonstrate that terms not verifiable by scientific observation were meaningless. They had wished for science to become a universal language against which all truth claims could be judged. Logical positivism thus undermined its aspirations when its proponents, carefully examining and reexamining their own reasoning, managed to argue their way out of all possible avenues to empirical truth. Indeed, other familiar aspects of this universal-science approach to knowledge have also been subject to critique.

The subjective-objective dichotomy follows from the lines of demarcation between both sense (two kinds, analytical and factual) and nonsense (everything else). This subjective-objective dichotomy reiterates itself between the realm of discovery (subjective) and realm of justification (objective). Next, the fact-value dichotomy follows from the same lines of demarcation. One cannot derive an "ought" statement (values) from factual statements of what is. And finally, the so-called building block theory of knowledge assumes that knowledge is developed linearly, progressively, and cumulatively. This is the familiar optimistic belief in progress toward the formal articulation of the structures of explanation, which, along with the subjective-objective dichotomy and the fact-value dichotomy, rounds out the basic epistemological position of logical positivism. Normative prescriptions about the conduct of inquiry followed from this epistemology. In particular, additional prescriptive themes followed from the attempts to connect theoretical constructs with their possible empirical verification. The prescription has to do with verifying that connection—between theoretical constructs and empirical reality. The two themes of this prescription are the nomothetic model and sense data atomism.

First, the nomothetic (also called covering-law and hypothetico-deductive) model proposes that justifications of any particular research finding begin with some more general law or lawlike proposition. Properly conducted, research will then confirm or disconfirm such hypothetical propositions. Thus a political scientist might wish to establish that people are self-interested (a law) and hypothesize that they will therefore express their self-interest by making certain electoral choices in the voting booth. The researcher would use an indicator or operational definition to test statements such as, "Working class voters will vote for the Democratic Party or the Labor Party." The researchers might offer as explanation, were this proposition verified, that members of the working class vote this way because it is historically more likely that these parties will represent their self-interests. The behavior, actually voting, then confirms or disconfirms logically related progressive levels of generalization back up to the law (about self-interest in this instance). If all researchers could be so disciplined to follow this format, real progress in the understanding of the laws of human behavior might be achieved. The nomothetic model, as manifest in hypothesis-testing protocols, underpins much of what is considered normal social science.

The second prescriptive theme, sense data atomism, is also known as methodological individualism, or more derisively the myth of the given. The original logical positivist position was that hypotheses developed on the analytical side of the bifurcation between mind and matter could be confirmed by uncomplicated observation of matter. Our senses were perfectly adequate to the task of receiving sensations from the objective world. Moreover, it was felt that these sensa impinged on human perceptual apparatus in distinct, uncomplicated, incorrigible microunits of meaning invariance. "Here, brown, spherical, now" might confirm an hypothesis regarding the presence of a basketball. As foreshadowed above, however, the gap between analytical truths and empirical data was the Achilles heel of the original logical positivists' system. Sense data atomism became known as the myth of given because such perceptions were, on closer examination, not as incorrigible as the logical positivists had naively supposed. How could human perception, for instance, know that the object was spherical when one saw only one snapshot face of a round thing at the confirming moment? Worse, "here" implies elsewhere, "brown" requires human knowledge of color schemes, "now" requires a context of then and soon. In other words, humans had to be preprogrammed to report even the most elementary observing event. And if preprogramming were required, how could the observation be the incorrigible confirmation? Metaphysical concepts that logical positivists had so assiduously tried to cordon off, like space, time, and extension, came creeping back, right at the point of perception.

From this exposed flank the entire army of positivist assumptions could be rolled up. Without solid confirmation, the nomothetic model could not be grounded. Without the nomothetic model cumulative knowledge becomes problematic. Questionable now is the notion that empirical facts can perform the reality check on nomothetic propositions that is supposed. Empirical facts and nomothetic propositions interact with one another at the point of perception to form a self-referential system, a tight interaction of found facts and reaffirmed propositional statements. Positivist epistemology leads to self-fulfilling validation: Propositions seek out facts, and facts find propositions to which they may become attached. In other words, the mental state of the researcher is not independent of the facts chosen for evaluation. In the social sciences the relationship between supposed facts and the terms that denote those facts is problematic. Are "mother," "husband," or "teacher" more like facts or more like role prescriptions? If our access to the objective world is problematic how can objectivity be affirmed over subjectivity, or facts distinguished from values?

Positive Theory in the Social Sciences

Though logical positivism is philosophically at a dead end, the term positivism continues to posses currency, but under more modest aspirations—falsifiability and description rather than verifiability and prediction. Contemporary research in the positivist tradition is a process of disproving or falsifying a proposition's antithesis—the null hypotheses—rather than verifying a proposition. Ironically, the efforts of logical positivism have left a lasting residual critique of the positivist project. It is that the generalizability of empirical facts is not philosophically defensible, and, further, that prediction is not achievable because of the inadequacy of the deductive process in verifying universal statements. In the wake of logical positivism, post facto description was left as science's best empirical method, severely limiting the range of claims that researchers can philosophically or empirically defend.

But logical positivism has left innumerable footprints, one of which is the rational choice school of thought, also known as formal theory and positive theory. The aspirations of this school are similar to those of the original logical positivists. These theorists prefer to distinguish their project from "normative theory" or other kinds of political philosophy. They like their research to be value-free, mathematical, logical-deductive in its postulates, and, some also claim, empirical. Using utility maximizing assumptions about human motivations, borrowed from microeconomics, most rational choice work relies on the atomistic, self-interested individual as bedrock truism. Rational choice research is associated with mathematical tools such as difference equations, queuing models, and probability estimation–tools intended to inform and assist policy analysis. Many rational choice theorists study game theory, composed of logic exercises incorporated into computer simulations of interlocking, conflicting interests. Gains and losses among various opposing players are calculated, and rational choices for these players are postulated. This embrace of abstract postulates and the associated games of logic has led critics to charge that rational choice has more to do with mathematics and mental exercise than with policy.

This sort of controversy was paramount in the public administration debate about research methodology that began in the early 1980s–doctoral student research was the salient topic. On one side, Howard E. McCurdy and Robert E. Cleary (1984) wanted to see students develop research designs aimed at reaching objective conclusions about the relationship between two or more substantively interesting variables. This hardscience agenda, aligned nomothetically with rational choice theory and often referred to as positivism (or neopositivism), seeks to apply scientific processes to the evaluation of public administration and policy. Empirical evidence is asserted as a key requirement for any claims that might be made in a public policy arena. Policy outcomes must be measurable, and indeed counted, to be believable. But here the familiar deficiencies already explicated by logical positivist philosophers provide grist for contemporary critics of the hard-science approach. Outcomes measurement is achievable only to the extent that statements (that is, categories, variables, theories, or hypotheses) get their meanings from observed facts. However, philosophers now recognize that words merely "stand in" for things and are not the things themselves. To the extent that variables are metaphors and are not themselves referents, the hard-science approach suffers the very language problems that vexed logical positivism, as described in the previous section.

On the other side, Jay White (1986) objected to the apparent abandonment by McCurdy and Clearly of political philosophy and social critique as suitable dissertation subjects. White sought to carve out some legitimate space for interpretivist and critical theory contenders, asserting that the scientific process itself involves communal interpretation and criticism, as does all knowledge. White also noted that the prescriptions of McCurdy and Cleary allowed little room for, even disparaged the legitimacy of, descriptive science as presented in case studies, histories, descriptions of administrators' experiences, or reports of action research. Yet it was the logical positivists of the 1930s who concluded that the generalizability of empirical facts is not philosophically defensible and that prediction is not achievable. This left description, of the sort advocated by White, as the best that science can aspire to. Contemporary positivists in the social sciences have not transcended the philosophical and logical limitations that the Vienna Circle logical positivists ruefully yet responsibly accepted as inherent in their system.

Undeterred, positivist social science proceeds apace, albeit with aspirations more modest than prediction and verification (naive protocols of social science notwithstanding). Falsifiability and description are, indeed, philosophically defensible. Again, the tedious process of falsifying a proposition's antithesis, the null hypotheses, is used to confirm or disconfirm the truth of propositions indirectly. Hence, even though the logical positivists abandoned, and in effect repudiated, the notion of scientific verification, the project of discovering truth based on scientific explanation of phenomena continues, and along with it the promise and pitfalls of cause-and-effect determinism, outcomes measurement, utility-maximizing individuals, and instrumental rationality. Positivism continues to influence the contemporary debate over proper scientific conduct. The debate, a lively one, is about justifying, confirming, or in some way making scientifically credible claims offered in policy arenas.

CHARLES J. FOX
HUGH T. MILLER

BIBLIOGRAPHY

Abbagnano, Nicola, 1967. "Positivism." Trans. by Nino Langiulli. In Paul Edwards, ed., *The Encyclopedia of Philosophy*, vol. 6, pp. 414–419. NY: Macmillan.

Ayer, A. J., 1959. "Editor's Introduction." In A. J. Ayer, ed., *Logical Positivism*. Westport, CT: Greenwood Press, pp. 3–28.

Brodbeck, May, 1968. *Readings in the Philosophy of the Social Sciences*, New York: Macmillan.

Clark, David L., 1985. "Emerging Paradigms in Organizational Theory and Research." In Yvonna S. Lincoln, ed., *Organizational Theory and Inquiry: The Paradigm Revolution*. Newbury Park, CA: Sage, pp. 43–78.

Comte, Auguste, 1851. *Philosophy of Mathematics*. New York: Harper Bros.

Curtis, Michael, 1962. *The Great Political Theories*. Vol. 2, expanded edition. New York: Avon Books.

Feigl, Herbert, 1968. "The Wiener Kreis in America." In Donald Fleming and Bernard Bailyn, eds., *The Intellectual Migration*. Cambridge, MA: Harvard University Press.

Guba, Egon G., 1985. "The Context of Emergent Paradigm Shift." In Yvonna S. Lincoln, ed., *Organizational Theory and Inquiry: The Paradigm Revolution*. Newbury Park, CA: Sage, pp. 79–104.

Lasswell, Harold D., 1951. "The Policy Orientation." In Daniel Lerner and Harold D. Lasswell, eds., *The Policy Sciences: Recent Developments in Scope and Method*. Stanford, CA: Stanford University Press.

McCurdy, Howard T. and Robert E. Cleary, 1984. "Why Can't We Resolve the Research Issue in Public Administration?" *Public Administration Review*, 44:49–55.

Mill, John Stuart, ([1848] 1986). *Principles of Political Economy*. New York: Viking.

Nagel, Ernest, 1961. *The Structure of Science*. New York: Harcourt, Brace and World.

Popper, Karl R., 1959. *The Logic of Scientific Discovery.* New York: Basic Books.

Russell, Bertrand and Alfred North Whitehead, ([1903] 1962). *Principia Mathematica.* Cambridge: Cambridge Universtiy Press.

White, Jay D., 1986. "On the Growth of Knowledge in Public Administration." *Public Administration Review,* 46:15–24.

POST-COMMUNIST BUDGETING.

The changes taking place in the countries of Central and Eastern Europe and the former Soviet Union where command economies are now being transformed into democratic, market-based political economies. In the past, resource allocation was based on the basic structures of central control and central planning. Although the countries differed in some of the details, the basic pattern consisted of a multiyear plan that included economic and social objectives, production targets, and the allocation of resources. Goals were developed at the highest level of the ruling Communist Party. Prices for selected consumer goods and services were kept artificially low through central government subsidies. Profitable enterprises subsidized unprofitable ones, thereby creating artificially high employment levels. This, in essence, was the command economy of the former Communist countries.

The state budget in the former Communist regimes was far different from the budget in most Western democracies. While negotiations took place between the spending agencies and the ministry of finance (like the budgetary processes of Western democracies), the central planning agency–and ultimately, the ruling body of the Communist Party–determined the outcome of budgetary deliberations. In short, planning dictated budgets, not the other way around. The typical structure of the budget under the former Communist regimes included spending on the large bureaucracy (larger than the comparable administrative structure in Western capitalist countries), spending for the military, state investment, the subsidies for state-owned firms, consumer subsidies, and the financing of free (or nearly free) government services. Revenues came from state-owned firms and cooperatives, turnover taxes (which was a fixed amount included in the retail price of goods whose value was unknown to the consumer), taxes paid by individuals (generally a smaller percentage than in capitalist countries), and government loans (Kornai 1992, pp. 134–138).

One outcome of the regime changes that took place between 1989 and 1991 in the former socialist countries of Central and Eastern Europe, and the former Soviet Union, has been a strengthening of the role of the ministry of finance. The strengthening comes from two sources. First, there is a gradual evolution toward pluralistic political processes that give rise to the types of negotiations among spending agencies and controllers that characterize budgeting in Western democracies. Second, because of their precarious fiscal condition and pressure from international lending agencies (such as the World Bank and the International Monetary Fund) to control spending, the ministries of finance are taking an increasingly vigorous role in managing fiscal decisions. Similarly, parliaments, once completely dominated by the Communist Party, now provide the forum for debate about policy priorities as reflected in the governments' annual budgets.

Budget Processes

Budget processes in post-Communist countries are developing the rudimentary structural characteristics found in budget systems in developed democracies (Caiden 1993). These include proper classification of spending, monitoring of spending, and the cost-benefit evaluation of resource allocation (Andic 1994). In addition, revenue sources have been diversified and broadly reflect the revenue alternatives available in Western democratic countries. These include individual and corporate income taxes, broad-based consumption taxes (principally the value-added tax), social security taxes, and various fees and charges. Reform of revenues is crucial to have a tax system that responds to the conventional criteria of adequacy, equity, impact on economic activity, and collectability. The process of reform is dependent on a sequencing that does not necessarily unfold in a "textbook" fashion. For instance, sustainable economic growth is necessary to provide incomes that will support a robust income tax without having adverse effects on economic activity. This has not been achievable in most post-Communist countries. Tax collection has lagged the imposition of new taxes that are theoretically adequate, though less so in practice. Tax evasion through a large second economy is a major problem in post-Communist countries and has a long history in the region. The causes of the large second economy include low wages, vague property rights, and a philosophical aversion to state control despite official ideology to the contrary. The symptoms highlight two aspects of fiscal reform that are critical for post-Communist transition. First, tax compliance is dependent on a level of political trust and acceptance of the regime–a condition that is still part of the broad political transition in the post-Communist countries. Second, on a more technical level, compliance requires improved tax administration procedures. The two dimensions are interrelated. Technical advice is being offered by the International Monetary Fund, the World Bank, and tax collection agencies from various Western countries in areas such as tax auditing, taxpayer services, enforcement mechanisms, data collection and analysis, and staff training (Andic 1994, p. 58).

Budget Composition

The composition of the budget in post-Communist countries has been changing dramatically since 1989. Two areas stand out: intergovernmental fiscal relations and social policy. In many of the former socialist countries subnational governments have been given considerable service delivery responsibilities. The fiscal framework to accompany this development includes greater discretion to impose local taxes and intergovernmental transfers through various grant mechanisms and/or a share in the national income tax. Hungary is a leading example.

Local governments receive approximately 80 percent of their revenues from the central government in three broad categories: (1) normative formula-based grants for a range of locally provided services (e.g., health care, education, social services) that are based on per capita calculations; (2) special purpose grants provided on a project basis; and (3) a share of the personal income tax (30 percent in 1994). Grants provide approximately 50 percent of local government revenues. The remaining percentage of local government revenues comes from local taxes and charges such as taxes on land and property, communal taxes, taxes on tourism, taxes on business activity, and fees and charges.

In the area of social policy the overall trend has been a reduction in safety net programs, more targeting of benefits, the gradual elimination of subsidies for housing and food, unemployment benefits that are related to work history, and a shift toward financing and delivery at the subnational level. Once again, Hungary is an instructive example. In 1995 family allowances were ended as a matter of right, social assistance benefit and maternity benefits were reduced, and tuition was introduced in higher education. Throughout the former socialist countries of Eastern Europe and the former Soviet Union pension systems are being restructured. In several countries budgetary burdens have been eased by raising the retirement age for men and women to 65 years and 60 years respectively. Countries in the region are developing self-financing systems that are actuarially sound.

To summarize: post-Communist budgeting shows gradual evolution to democratic budgetary processes. This includes the provision of more accountability of the spending agencies through budget office and parliamentary review, and greater emphasis on analytic rigor through justifications that accompany agency submissions and their substantiation. Training in public finance and budgeting for fiscal personnel is aimed at achieving these dual objectives. Meanwhile, the budgets will reflect a reduced public sector (certainly compared with the fiscal systems of the Communist regimes), increased fiscal decentralization, and restructuring of social benefits to individuals.

JEFFREY D. STRAUSSMAN

BIBLIOGRAPHY

Andic, Suphan, 1994. "Organizational Dimensions of Public Finance in Transition Economies: An Assessment of the Recent Literature." In *Institutional Change and the Public Sector in Transitional Economies.* Salvatore Schiavo-Campo, ed. Washington, D.C.: The World Bank, pp. 53–96.

Caiden, Naomi, 1993. "The Roads to Transformation: Budgeting Issues in the Czech and Slovak Federal Republic." *Public Budgeting & Finance* 13 (Winter) 57–71.

Kornai, Janos, 1992. *The Socialist System.* Princeton, NJ: Princeton University Press.

Tanzi, Vito, ed., 1993. *Transition To Market.* Washington, D.C.: International Monetary Fund.

POSTMODERN ORGANIZATION. Newly evolving organizational forms. Although the concept of "postmodern organization" does not yet have clear definition—and may never have clear definition given the turbulence of the period we are now entering—it is usually considered to be a combination of premodern and modern organizational forms, but with certain distinctive features.

A postmodern world is in the midst of being born in public sectors throughout the world. New organizational forms are being constructed in response to the profound social, economic, and political changes that the public sector now faces.

In essence, the "postmodern organization" is a hybrid of large and small organizational forms, complex and simple structures, and collaborative interinstitutional relationships. The successful postmodern organization operates with a clear mission, in large part because its boundaries are inevitably unclear. Leadership in the postmodern organization is situation-specific. Verbal and written modes of communication interact in highly turbulent interpersonal work environments. An emphasis is placed in the postmodern organization on knowledge as the new form of capital, and on the meaning of work and high level involvement with regard to those working in these organization.

Unfortunately, as we move beyond this superficial analysis, many points of contention and ambiguity appear. The lack of clarity in defining the concept of "postmodern organization" in part resides in the lack of clarity regarding the term "postmodern" itself. The only thing that everyone can agree on is that postmodern originates in, yet is somehow different from, the modern era—hence the name "postmodern." The term is still defined with reference to its predecessor, "modernism," rather than having broken off as a free and independent movement or set of ideas and images with its own distinctive name. In many ways, "postmodernism" is a fad and is at the same time about fads. Even though postmodernism is filled with superficial, facile, and often internally contradictory analyses, it must not be dismissed, for these analyses offer insightful and valuable (even essential) perspectives and critiques regarding an emerging era (for example, Anderson 1990; Jameson 1991).

The inconsistency and fragmentation of our contemporary world makes it even more difficult to define the term "postmodern organization." At the same time, this inconsistency and fragmentation makes it very difficult to build a coherent theory regarding public policy and administration. Each of the major themes of postmodernism (constructivism, language as reality, globalism, and segmentalism) contributes to an even more basic theme that often makes the very analysis of the postmodern condition particularly difficult. In essence, it is virtually impossible to make a definitive statement about our contemporary world because this world is filled with contradictions and discrepancies. We are living in a world that is simultaneously premodern, modern, and postmodern. For every phenomenon that can be identified as postmodern, we can find another phenomenon that is clearly modern or even premodern, and yet another that is a mixture of premodern, modern, and postmodern.

Ironically, all of these diverse phenomena provide evidence of the universal presence of a postmodern world. The inconsistencies of the hypothesized postmodern era allows the postmodern analyst never to be proven wrong. Any evidence (other than absolute uniformity, which will never be the case) fits into the postmodern model, for the more discrepant the evidence, the more confirming it is of the postmodern hypothesis. The world picture that is being conveyed by the postmodernists can't be disproved, for contradictory evidence is itself part of the postmodern premise.

The postulation of a fragmented and inconsistent postmodern world, however, seems to be more than just a semantic or intellectual ploy to avoid any disproof of the postmodern perspective. There is ample evidence to suggest that fragmentation and inconsistency is a central (if not the central) ingredient of our contemporary era. Our postmodern world—and, in particular, the public sector—is filled with fragmented and incoherent images of the future, as well as fragmented images of our current and desired states of public affairs. One cannot help but wonder if this fragmentation and inconsistency—and the accompanying edginess—are permanent. Does postmodernism suggest that we are in a major transition between a modern society and some new society that has not yet become clear or at least been properly named? Is the postmodern world in which we now live instead a rather long-lasting phenomenon? We may be moving into a fragmented world that will not readily change. We may never (at least in our lifetime) be able to return to a world of greater simplicity and regional or national coherence and consistency.

Dimensions of Postmodern Organizational Life

The nature of organizational life in public institutions is often examined in terms of five dimensions: (1) size and complexity, (2) mission and boundaries, (3) leadership, (4) communication, and (5) capital and institutional values. Major shifts occurred in each of these dimensions as our public institutions moved during the nineteenth century (in

the Western world) or even twentieth century (in many developing countries) from support for premodern (primarily agricultural and trade-based) communities to a modern era in which they supported industry-based cities. Shifts of a similar magnitude are now occurring throughout the world as we move into a postmodern era that requires our public institutions to serve ill-defined and changing communities that are information-based and turbulent.

Size and Complexity

We find in the premodern era the dominance of small and simple public administrative structures, many human services being provided by the family, church, or (informally and spontaneously) by the community. Emphasis was placed on stability and gradual growth. By contrast, emphasis was placed during the modern era not on the process of growth itself nor on the gradual expansion in public services, but rather on the outcome of growth, that is, large size and an accompanying increase in organizational efficiency and breadth of service to the community. Organizational structures were no longer simple in the modern era. However, these structures were usually uniform within and between organizations (being bureaucratic in nature). Furthermore, these structures were compatible with hierarchically based forms of leadership and authority, and with the highly energy-intensive and technology-driven processes of mass production.

In moving to a postmodern era, emphasis tends to be placed in the public (and private) sector not on growth and large size, but instead on keeping things small or moderate in size. Structures are neither simple nor uniform—despite the emphasis on smallness. Rather, the postmodern public institution is typified by fragmentation, inconsistency, and a mixture of differing organizational structures, policies, and procedures. While many people view this state of public institutions as transitional in nature—between the modern era and some new, as yet undetermined, era—there is reason to believe that this will be a much longer-term state for these institutions.

Postmodernists often emphasize a basic principle concerning the interplay between order and chaos—namely that order and chaos are to be found (or more accurately, are to be conceptually constructed) in any system (Gleick 1987; Prigogine and Stengers 1984). Sometimes public institutions seem to make sense. The policies and procedures look right (at least in public records) and things seem to be moving along in a predictable manner. At other times, everything seems to be fragmented and chaotic. Nothing makes any sense in the institution and one wonders if "the center can hold." Chaos theorists suggest that these seemingly contradictory observations are actually a result of examining the organization at different levels. Organizations (like virtually all other systems) contain layers of chaos and order. When confronted with a seemingly chaotic and unpredictable public institution, we have only to move up one level (to greater abstraction), or down one level (to greater specificity), if we wish to find order.

The behavior of a specific public administrator, for instance, may begin to make some sense once we begin to examine overall dynamics in his or her department rather than just look at his or her individual behavior. Organizational theorists now tell us about ways in which competent managers become incompetent (or "deskilled") as a result of the dysfunctional organizational dynamics that are operating in public (and private) institutions and the ways in which this deskilling contributes in some manner to the maintenance of stability in this institution. Similarly, the operation of a mayor's or city manager's office may appear to be orderly from the rather distant perspective of the general public (as witnessed in planning documents, press releases, and public appearances) or it may appear as very chaotic, given the diverse perspectives being taken by the press and by opposition parties regarding this office. At a different level, however, an "orderly" office may look quite chaotic (inadequate funding, bad timing, recalcitrant constituency). Alternatively, a "chaotic" office might look very orderly (given the very skillful political strategies being used to arrive at a compromise on some specific issue). At any level, we might find confusion, rivalry, and other forms of "nonrational" and chaotic behavior; however, we might find the same behavior to be quite "understandable" given the complex forces facing this public institution.

Mission and Boundaries

The premodern public institution typically had unclear boundaries (particularly with regard to public and private life and allegiances) and an unclear mission. There was little need for a clear definition of institutional purposes since most services were provided by family members, members of the church, and so forth. Public agencies were chartered primarily to confront emergencies and meet a few community needs (parks, utilities, certain forms of transportation). Education, health, and family assistance were either not provided or were financed by the family or church. A system of bartering and exchange of goods and services (for example, the farmer's market) eliminated the need for any substantial monetary system, hence there were few funds available to support extensive public services.

During the modern era, boundaries became quite clear—in particular, the boundaries between private and public institutions. Mission statements for public institutions, on the other hand, tended to remain rather unclear or inconsistent. In modern societies, clear distinctions were made between public and private responsibilities, with public institutions being assigned responsibility for safety, sanitation, public health, education, and so forth. Furthermore, public institutions became clearly segregated from places where employees worked and where they lived and worshipped. We knew when we were entering and leaving a public institution and often defined this institution with reference to its sheer existence rather than with regard to any specific mission or purpose.

Postmodern conditions have precipitated a crisis with regard to both the mission and boundaries of public institutions. In order to survive, most public institutions during the postmodern era have been moved to clarify their mission statement, in part because they usually no longer have clear boundaries (Boulding 1973). Given that public institutions can't do everything, while being asked to do more with fewer funds, these institutions repeatedly must reexamine their purposes and values. Without a clear sense of purpose and values, these institutions soon collapse, splinter, or become aimless tax-consuming scavengers that feed destructively on other sectors of our society. In the modern world, boundaries (and identities defined by roles and rules) served as "containers" of anxiety. In the postmodern world, we must look to an inner sense of self and to an outer structure of support and community for shelter, stability, and insight in an edgy and turbulent world (Gergen 1991). Our public institutions must define their mission in such a way as to assist this process.

Leadership

Public leaders in the premodern era tended to be "great people," who were selected for their character and education. The great people not only led their society, they also influenced history and established societal values. Leaders were either born to greatness or provided with an elitist program of study and mentorship. They tended to exert authority through a paternalistic concern for the welfare and proper education of those who depended on them.

By contrast, the more democratically and rationally oriented modern era tended to emphasize structures, processes, and procedures, that ensured an appropriate (and circumscribed) expression of leadership and influence. Events—not great people—determined the course of modern history, and values were identified as products of the system and bureaucracy rather than as products of any specific individual(s). Modern authority was expressed through the autonomy of rules, regulations, roles, and organizational structures.

The postmodern world has called both the premodern and modern notions of leadership into question. The postmodern leader is neither inherently great nor merely a product of a system or bureaucracy. Individual leadership can be effectively exerted and will be influential if applied at the right time, in the right place, in the right manner, with regard to the right problem or goal. This contingent or situational model of leadership requires careful consideration of both individual and organizational character and style (Hershey and Blanchard 1977). It requires a tolerance for ambiguity, a recognition of the need for one to learn from his or her mistakes, and a clear sense of personal mission and purpose.

Public leaders of the postmodern world must navigate a treacherous "white-water" environment, which is filled with unpredictability (Vail 1989). Much as in the case of white-water rapids, there are eddies and swirls as well as quiet but powerful flows of water. Those who work in the public sector must navigate these white-water conditions as leaders, inventors, visionaries, and colleagues. What are the skills needed to navigate the white water? Some postmodernists identify the need for short-term survival tactics as well as long-term strategies and note that these should be based on broad visions and deeply embedded institutional values, as well as clearly defined personal aspirations and an accompanying commitment to service (Greenleaf 1970). Other postmodernists suggest that leadership requires a spiritual center—an internal coherence—for one to navigate the white water (Vail 1989). Still others suggest that leaders must be able to reflect on their own practices and learn from their past mistakes rather than repeatedly making the same mistakes (Argyris and Schön 1978; Senge 1990).

Communication

Oral forms of communication were dominant in the premodern world. Small, simple communities allowed men and women to communicate freely with one another. A strong sense of interdependence and homogeneity of interests and values minimized the need for written documents. With the emergence of industrialized and highly complex urban environments during the modern era came an increasing need for written communication (contracts, letters of agreement, legal recordings of transactions, and so forth) as a substitute for direct interpersonal contact. Rather than seeing and listening to another person, one read his or her memorandum or written proposal.

The postmodern community, by contrast to the modern, tends once again to be more orally based. We call each other and leave voice messages, rather than writing letters. Community is constructed through computerized networks rather than around geographic proximity. We eliminate our secretaries and clerks, and seek to reduce paperwork. Short face to face meetings, adhocracy, task forces, and temporary systems have replaced longstanding bureaucratic structures that were dependent on written rules and the documentation of policies, procedures, and program ideas. In this orally based world, gossip and story telling take on new relevance and appreciation. People must learn how to bond together in temporary groups. They also must learn how to detach from one another in order to move on to other groups or projects.

Communication is considered in a unique and provocative manner by various postmodern theorists (for example, Bateson 1979). They suggest that organizations are to be distinguished from many other systems because of their primary reliance on the flow of information. Information flow, in turn, is embedded in a complex network of relationships and conversations. Some postmodernists (especially those who identify themselves as "deconstructionists") are likely to consider organizations as nothing other than relationships and extended conversations.

From this perspective, structures and products are secondary in most contemporary public institutions to the conversations that occur inside these institutions regarding these structures and products—or (even more often) regarding the intricate relationships that exist among people working within the institution. Storytelling and narration becomes an effective change strategy in the postmodern era. If organizations are extended conversations, then stories can be conceived as the life blood and source of system maintenance in an organization. The construction and reconstruction of stories about life inside public institutions may be critical to processes of personal and organizational transformation that occur within them.

Capital and Institutional Values

Land was one of the dominant and most tangible forms of capital in the premodern era. Ancestry and reputations were two less tangible, but equally important, forms of capital. The divine right of kings (or other community leaders) prevailed in premodern communities. In the Western world, the Catholic Church emphasized property and prohibited the use of money to make money (it was a capital sin to charge interest on a loan). Emphasis was placed on property rather than money. Members of the community, in turn, tended to focus on security and conformity. They looked toward their own family, church, and employer (as surrogate parent) for support and asked for little from public institutions.

The modern forms of capital, by contrast, were money and buildings. Reputation and ancestry became less important. Wealth was more liquid—and volatile. This new form of capitalism, supported by Calvinist doctrine and the Protestant church, became dominant and highly influential (at least in middle and upper classes of the Western world) during the modern era (Weber 1958). One's worldly success (as manifest in the nonconspicuous accumulation of monetary wealth) was a sign of one's worth. Poverty was considered sinful in some very basic sense and a sign of one's inadequacy or laziness. In the public sector, Protestantism led away from an emphasis on charity and good works (a Catholic perspective) to an emphasis on adequate (though never generous) public support (education, health, and so forth) for those less fortunate.

The new capital of the postmodern era is information and expertise (Drucker 1989). Values of the postmodern worker complement this new capital. Emphasis is placed on motivational rather than security factors. Increasing attention is given to the meaning of work and recognition derived from colleagues and one's boss(es) regarding the quality of one's work. High-involvement programs dramatically increase the participation of all constituencies in the design of new public sector services and delivery systems (Lawler 1986). The new values of the postmodern "knowledge worker" center on the ownership of one's work and the meaning and purpose of one's affiliation with public institutions.

Postmodern Change and Turbulence

The premodern world seems (at least from our postmodern vantage point) to have moved at a leisurely and considered pace. Change tended either to be gradual or nonexistent. By contrast, the modern era was commonly described as one in which change occurred at an ever accelerating pace (Toffler 1980). The future was closing in upon the present at breathtaking speed and we braced ourselves for this shock. Preparation for accelerated change in public institutions primarily took place through effective planning and anticipation of impending events and shifting political, economic, and social conditions. Analyses of trends and cause-and-effect relationships enabled modern day public administrators to lead by preparing for any of a number of contingencies.

What then of the postmodern world? Change in our newly emerging era will continue to accelerate—sometimes. At other times, change is likely to be gradual or nonexistent. Furthermore, we will be unable to predict with any accuracy what the rate of change will be at any one point in time. Thus, we must learn to cope not just with accelerated change, but also with reduced rates of change and, more importantly, with uncertainty. Cause and effect is no longer linear in nature. Rather everything seems to impact on everything else at the same time.

"Living on the edge" is exciting and addicting. It is a "threshold" experience—a "flow" experience (Csikszentmihalyi 1990)—that brings us into a special realm that resides between boredom and anxiety. The edge is a boundary— the intersect between different systems and different cultures. It is at the edge or boundary of any system that we find maximum information and maximum unpredictability, for the edge is the point where a system is conducting transactions with the outside world.

Many organizations that would be labeled "postmodern" are poised on the edge of chaos—not chaos as it is usually defined in terms of anarchy or complete disorganization, but rather as this term was originally used and is now being used again, as a state of unpredictability and complexity. Furthermore, it now appears that in most instances (especially in public institutions) we are talking about systems that hover on the edge of or move back and forth between states of order and chaos. Kauffman (1991) has described this interplay between chaos and order in terms of three different categories or states in which all systems (including organizations) can be placed. One of these states is highly ordered and structured. Kauffman draws an analogy between this state and the solid state that water takes when

it is frozen. A second state is highly chaotic. Kauffman equates this state to the gaseous form which water takes when it is evaporating. The third (most interesting) state is one of transition between order and chaos, which Kauffman equates with the liquid state of water. The differentiation between solid, gaseous, and liquid networks can be of significant value in setting the context for any discussion of postmodernism.

We must look not only at ordered networks—the so-called solid state—and at chaotic networks—the so-called gaseous state—but also at liquid networks that hover on the brink of chaos, if we are to understand and influence our unique postmodern institutions. The third (liquid) state holds particularly great potential when we examine and seek to understand confusing and often elusive organizational phenomena such as mission, leadership, and communication. Turbulent rivers, avalanches, and shifting weather patterns typify the liquid state. Liquid systems contain both chaotic elements and elements of stability (quiet pools of water and eddies; solid snowpacks; stable weather patterns) that interplay with the more chaotic elements of the system.

Most public institutions today live on the edge, in the liquid state, poised on the edge of chaos. The theory of self-organizing criticality, first formulated by Bak and Chen (1991), suggests that small events such as a change in leadership will usually produce only minor alterations in the structure and dynamics of the organization (an organizational snowpack will get a bit wider or a bit higher). However, sometimes, the change in leadership will create a major alteration (an organizational avalanche). Furthermore, while the outcomes are dramatically different, the same processes are involved in the initiation of both minor and major changes, and onset of the major event can not be predicted—in part because the same process brings about both outcomes (Waldrop 1992).

The liquid state and the edge are places of leadership and innovation ("the leading edge"). They are settings where things get done—yet often in the context of a very challenging and exhausting "white-water" environment. Edges have no substance. They come to a point and then disappear. Public administrators must learn how to live and work in this new world of edges. The postmodern prophets may provide some valuable clues as to how this world might best be faced, as well as encouraging us to revise our modern day assumptions about the nature, purpose, and dynamics of public institutions in which we work and postmodern communities in which we live.

WILLIAM H. BERGQUIST

BIBLIOGRAPHY

Anderson, Walter T., 1990. *Reality Isn't What It Used to Be.* New York: Harper and Row.

Argyris, Chris and Donald Schön, 1978. *Organizational Learning: A Theory of Action Perspective*. Reading, MA: Addison-Wesley.

Bak, Per and Kan Chen, 1991. "Self-Organized Criticality." *Scientific American* (January) 46–53.

Bateson, Gregory, 1979. *Mind and Nature: A Necessary Unity*. New York: Dutton.

Boulding, Kenneth, 1973. "Intersects: The Peculiar Organizations." In Kenneth Bursk/The Conference Board, eds., *Challenge to Leadership: Managing in a Changing World*. New York: Free Press.

Csikszentmihalyi, Mihaly, 1990. *Flow: The Psychology of Optimal Experience*. New York: Harper and Row.

Drucker, Peter, 1989. *The New Realities*. New York: Harper and Row.

Gergen, Kenneth, 1991. *The Saturated Self: Dilemmas of Identity in Contemporary Life*. New York: HarperCollins.

Gleick, James, 1987. *Chaos: Making a New Science*. New York: Viking-Penguin.

Greenleaf, Robert, 1970. *The Servant as Leader*. Peterborough, NH: Windy Row Press.

Hershey, Paul and Kenneth Blanchard, 1977. *The Management of Organizational Behavior*. 3d ed. Englewood Cliffs, NJ: Prentice-Hall.

Jameson, Frederick, 1991. *Postmodernism or the Cultural Logic of Late Capitalism*. Durham, NC: Duke University Press.

Kauffman, Stuart, 1991. "Antichaos and Adaptation." *Scientific American* (August) 78–84.

Lawler, Edward, 1986. *High Involvement Management*. San Francisco: Jossey-Bass.

Prigogine, Ilya and Isabel Stengers, 1984. *Order Out of Chaos*. New York: Bantam.

Senge, Peter, 1990. *The Fifth Discipline*. New York: Doubleday Currency.

Toffler, Alvin, 1980. *The Third Wave*. New York: William Morrow.

Vail, Peter, 1989. *Managing as a Performing Art*. San Francisco: Jossey-Bass.

Waldrop, M. Mitchell, 1992. *Complexity: The Emerging Science at the Edge of Order and Chaos*. New York: Simon and Schuster.

Weber, Max, 1958. *The Protestant Ethic and the Spirit of Capitalism*. New York: Scribner.

POVERTY. Lack of resources required to meet basic needs. For much of human history, poverty has been considered a natural condition about which little could be done. In the modern era poverty has been a focus of public policy attention with many governments taking an active, although often unsettled, role in reducing poverty. Yet, from highly industrialized to largely agrarian societies, poverty remains a worldwide phenomenon.

A key theme in discussion of the topic in the United States is the so-called "paradox of poverty amid affluence." Why is poverty a major feature of society in the world's wealthiest nation? A variation of this theme brought new attention to poverty in the early 1960s with the publication of *The Other America* by Michael Harrington (1962). The "paradox" helps keep alive the two views of the causes of poverty: structural and individual. Structural explanations place blame on the social, economic, and political systems; individual explanations focus on the failure of individuals to pursue available opportunities.

The extent of poverty, the cause of poverty, and the proper response to it remain controversial topics. In the United States, efforts to ameliorate conditions of poverty have been the subject of continuing disagreement. "Welfare reform," with varying objectives, has been on the agenda of every U.S. president since John F. Kennedy. Debates about the proper governmental role regarding the poor go back much further.

After reviewing approaches to defining poverty, this article summarizes information about the composition of the population in poverty, policy responses to poverty, and finally a sense of the controversy regarding the poverty problem.

Definitions of Poverty

While there may be agreement that poverty means lack of adequate command over the goods and services necessary to meet basic needs, it is more difficult to give the concept specific and operational meaning. Any definition has political and moral overtones, making the development of a definition much more than a technical task. Most definitions of poverty, however, can be clustered into either "relative poverty" or "absolute poverty."

Relative poverty assumes that those with access to significantly fewer resources than most others in society are poor. For example, persons with incomes in the bottom one-fifth of the population or those with incomes less than half of the national median income might be included in a definition of relative poverty. Definitions of this type emphasize distribution of resources more than their presence, absence, or scarcity. With a relative definition, short of complete equality, there always will be some who are defined as living in poverty and some who are defined as living in prosperity.

Absolute poverty, the approach more commonly used as a policy or program guide, is based on the assumption that some minimum level of goods and services is required to meet the needs of an individual or family. Usually this minimum is converted into monetary terms and a "poverty line" is established. Those below the line are considered in a condition of poverty and those above are not. The most common means for establishing a poverty line, both by international organizations and individual countries, is to determine the cost of a nutritionally adequate diet and then multiply that amount by some factor, such as 2.5 or 3.0, to account for nonfood needs such as housing and clothing. The amount is either calculated per capita or adjusted for family size. An absolute definition gives the appearance of objectivity, but it too is fundamentally subjective. Any number of specific formulae based on any number of assumptions can be proposed as the line below which a person or family is considered to be living in poverty.

The official poverty standard in the United States, used for all government statistics on poverty, is determined annually by the Social Security Administration. The basic definition established in 1964 has remained essentially unchanged with only annual adjustments to reflect changes in the Consumer Price Index, the cost of a standard set of goods. The base figure is the cost of the "economy food plan" of the Department of Agriculture, which is multiplied by 3 for a family of four and by somewhat different multipliers for other family sizes. In 1991, the poverty line was $15,911 for a family of four; $8,163 for an individual, and $31,548 for a family of nine or more.

The U.S. poverty standard is criticized both for over- and underestimating the extent of poverty. It is said to overestimate the extent of poverty because it does not take into account in-kind government transfers such as food stamps, housing subsidies, and medical care; it is said to underestimate poverty because the official poverty line is set so low that it is inadequate for keeping an individual or family above a realistic poverty threshold. Also, the poverty count is based on a survey of households and this excludes many, such as the homeless, who are destitute.

Despite its problems, establishing an operational measure of poverty serves several purposes. For one, it provides a basis for an eligibility standard for various targeted policies intended to provide assistance to those who are poor. Second, it allows an aggregate measure of poverty as a means to assess the extent of the poverty problem and to monitor the problem over time and across jurisdictions.

Extent of Poverty

Trends in the extent of poverty in the United States have alternatively been the basis for optimism and disappointment. Based on census poverty figures, there was a substantial reduction in the percentage of Americans in poverty in the late 1960s and early 1970s. In 1960, 22.2 percent of the population had incomes below the poverty line, but by 1973, the percentage had dropped to 11.1 percent, the lowest figure yet achieved. The percentage of the population considered to be living in poverty leveled off and remained steady through the 1970s, and was then followed by a modest upward trend during the 1980s and early 1990s. The official poverty rate stood at 15.1 percent in 1993, not as high as the 1960 figure, but well above the 1973 low.

The United States appears to have proportionately more poverty than many other Western nations. In a study of industrialized nations summarized in Sawhill's *Challenge to Leadership* (1988), the United States has a higher percentage of its population in poverty, using an absolute poverty measure, than all but one of eight nations (p. 217). Australia has a somewhat higher rate, but Britain, Canada, Norway, Sweden, Switzerland, and West Germany are lower. At least a partial explanation is the more fully developed welfare systems in European nations.

Expanding the view to Third World countries increases the complexity of efforts to measure the extent of poverty and demonstrates the inherently subjective character of poverty. Economic and social conditions vary widely, making comparisons difficult. Some have argued that "poverty American style" would be a luxury for millions of people in less developed countries around the world. Worldwide, with the standard set at US $370 per capita per year, studies indicate that over 1 billion persons are below the poverty line. In addition to incomes that are low, many persons in less developed countries live without access to clean drinking water and other infrastructure features taken for granted even among those below the poverty line in industrialized nations.

Composition of the Population in Poverty

Poverty is not evenly distributed in the population. A majority of the poor in the United States are white, but a higher percentage of racial and ethnic minorities are poor. The percentage of minorities in the poverty population is higher than their percentage in the population as a whole. After the decline in the percentage of blacks who were poor in the 1960s, the percentage has remained at a relatively stable level, somewhat above 30 percent.

Women, particularly single women with children, are a larger portion of the poverty population than in earlier decades. Female-headed households increased from approximately 18 percent of the poor population in 1960 to more than 37 percent in 1990, a trend some writers have labeled the "feminization of poverty."

Poverty is not evenly distributed by age. In the United States, the elderly are much less likely to be poor than they were a few decades ago. The development of Social Security, supported by a strong political lobby, has been a significant factor in reducing the percentage of the elderly population who are poor. Conversely, children are more likely to live in conditions of poverty; nearly 20 percent of children in the United States are poor, a number that has grown the past two decades.

The rural-urban distribution of poverty is shifting. In the United States and other industrialized countries, the poor are increasingly likely to live in urban areas, although rural poverty is still a major problem and policy concern. In less developed countries, the direction of change is toward an increase in urban poverty, but in Africa and Asia, and less so in Latin America poverty is still predominantly rural.

Concepts advanced to understand the character of poverty include the "culture of poverty" and the "urban underclass." The culture of poverty refers to adaptation to continuing conditions of poverty in the form of fatalism, present time orientation, low aspirations, and other attitudes and behaviors. The urban underclass is a related term that focuses attention to geographic pockets of poverty with attendant economic, social, and cultural conditions, including labor force detachment and single parenthood.

Policy Responses

Responses to poverty in the United States might be thought of in three phases. First, the New Deal during the Depression legitimized the role of government in social welfare policy and established several major social programs. Second, the 1960s represented the "rediscovery" of poverty and the initiation of the Great Society and the War on Poverty. The third phase, from the 1970s to the present, has seen a variety of efforts to reform welfare and social policy.

Social welfare policy in the United States has grown incrementally and is marked by a hodgepodge of programs. These programs can be grouped into three broad categories: cash assistance, in-kind support, and direct services. Cash assistance programs include Aid to Families with Dependent Children (AFDC; what is often meant by the term "welfare"). AFDC is a joint federal-state program with wide variations in benefits from state to state. Food stamps, vouchers redeemable for food products, is an example of an in-kind program and is the largest in-kind program in the U.S. Medicaid, a program of medical care for the poor, is an example of a direct service.

In 1995, welfare reform again rose to a central place on the federal and many state policy decision agendas. Approximately half of the 50 states had received waivers to experiment with AFDC and related programs in the past few years. The federal government was considering time limits on the receipt of welfare, job programs, and other changes. The rhetoric was to "end welfare as we know it." These efforts have culminated, at least temporarily, in the Personal Responsibility and Work Opportunity Reconciliation Act of 1996 and reform legislation in a number of states.

Controversial Issues in Poverty

The fundamental controversy regarding poverty in the United States has to do with the causes of poverty and the appropriate responses to it. While there are many variations and nuances, the liberal and conservative labels are typically used to capture the two primary viewpoints. The liberal position places the principal blame for poverty on the structure of society and the economy. Government is looked to for the necessary corrective action through redistributive policy and assistance programs. The conservative viewpoint stresses the lack of initiative of those who are poor, arguing that opportunities are available but are not pursued. On this perspective, a vibrant market combined with minimal governmental assistance is the vehicle to reduce poverty.

Whether and to what extent government support programs (welfare) provide a perverse incentive is a continuing

issue. This position has been most visibly portrayed in Charles Murray's 1984 publication of *Losing Ground*, which argues that the perverse incentives in U.S. social programs have caused poverty to increase. While the argument in *Losing Ground* is widely disputed, there is agreement that welfare programs individually and in combination have an incentive structure that runs counter to self-sufficiency. However, there is much less certainty about the extent to which recipients in fact behave in conformity with that incentive structure. There are many conflicting economic and cultural incentives at work in society.

Poverty continues to be an intractable social problem. The increasing complexity of society, the increasing automation in the workplace and the subsequent decline in unskilled jobs that pay a wage capable of supporting a family above the poverty level, the lack of consensus about welfare, health, and other policy areas, all make the future of the poverty problem an uncertain one. Whether the recent reform in the United States will produce fundamental change, and whether that change will ultimately be judged positively or negatively, only time will tell.

RALPH S. HAMBRICK, JR.
DEBRA J. ROG

BIBLIOGRAPHY

Chelf, Carl P., 1992. *Controversial Issues in Social Welfare Policy: Government and the Pursuit of Happiness.* Newbury Park, CA: Sage.

Danziger, Sheldon H., Gary D. Sandefur, and Daniel H. Weinberg, 1994. *Confronting Poverty: Prescriptions for Change.* Cambridge, MA: Harvard University Press.

Harrington, Michael, 1962. *The Other America: Poverty in the United States.* New York: Macmillan.

Jencks, Christopher and Paul E. Peterson, eds., 1991. *The Urban Underclass.* Washington, D.C.: The Brookings Institution.

Moynihan, Daniel P., ed. 1969. *On Understanding Poverty: Perspectives from the Social Sciences.* New York: Basic Books.

Murray, Charles, 1984. *Losing Ground: American Social Policy, 1950–1980.* New York: Basic Books.

Piven, Frances Fox and Richard A. Cloward, 1993. *Regulating the Poor: The Functions of Public Welfare,* updated ed. New York: Random House.

Sawhill, Isabel V., 1988. "Poverty and the Underclass." In Isabel V. Sawhill, ed., *Challenge to Leadership: Economic and Social Issues for the Next Decade.* Washington, D.C.: The Urban Institute Press, pp. 215–252.

Schiller, Bradley R., 1989. *The Economics of Poverty and Discrimination.* 5th ed. Englewood Cliffs, NJ: Prentice-Hall.

U.S. Bureau of the Census, Current Population Reports, 1992. *Poverty in the United States: 1991.* Washington, D.C.: U.S. Government Printing Office.

van der Hoeven, Rolph and Richard Anker, eds., 1994. *Poverty Monitoring: An International Concern.* New York: St. Martin's Press.

Wilson, William Julius, 1987. *The Truly Disadvantaged: The Inner City, the Underclass, and Public Policy.* Chicago: The University of Chicago Press.

PRACTICE OF PUBLIC ADMINISTRATION.

The formation and implementation of public policy carried out by nonelected paid personnel through interaction with elected officials, political appointees, the judiciary, organized interests, and the citizenry.

The Historical Emergence of Public Administration

Administrative practice has been an essential component of government since ancient times. Kings, emperors, and tyrants, as well as the political leaders of modern constitutional states, have all required the skills and talents of persons whose careers were devoted to assisting with the formation of public policies and translating them into actions such as regulation, service delivery, and the provision of subsidies.

However, the practice of public administration emerged into particular prominence during the latter part of the nineteenth century as a concomitant of urbanization, industrialization, and technological development. With the shift of population to the cities, the accelerated growth of industry in urban areas, and the expanding use of technology throughout society, the need for specialization in government also increased. Government grew in size and complexity to deal with problems associated with dense and culturally diverse urban populations, large scale industrial development, and technology. These factors were transforming traditional modes of transportation, communication, production, habitation, public sanitation, education, health care, entertainment, and almost every aspect of life.

Specialists and specialized organizations were established by government at all levels to address these problems. Functions such as sanitation, law enforcement, firefighting, public health, recreation, and education that had been carried out largely by volunteers, or on a very small scale by a few paid public employees whose efforts were augmented by volunteers, had to be provided on larger scales with more full-time paid specialists. This growth in public administrative personnel was accelerated during the early twentieth century by the expansion of the federal government during World Wars I and II, and the New Deal of President Franklin Delano Roosevelt during the Great Depression of the 1930s. In the 1960s, president Lyndon Johnson's War on Poverty programs also contributed to the expansion of the practice of public administration.

Normative Theories of Administrative Practice

The first normative theory of the practice of public administration of this era reflected the U.S. Progressive reform movement of the late nineteenth and early twentieth centuries. Typically associated with an essay written by Woodrow Wilson in 1887 for the *Political Science Quarterly* entitled "The Study of Administration," this theoretical perspective asserted that it was necessary to separate politics from the practice of public administration. Arguing against public administration dominated by machine politics and the spoils system, which were prevalent during the late nineteenth century, Wilson and other Progressives called for separation in order to attain more efficient administration of government. They maintained that efficiency could be achieved only by developing a science of administration founded on generic principles that were as universal as those of any branch of scientific endeavor.

This "politics-administration dichotomy" was hardened into the accepted doctrine for the practice of administration by those who came after Wilson. Frank Goodnow's *Politics and Administration* (1900) was the first text after Wilson's essay that moved in this direction. In the decades that followed, William F. Willoughby's *The Principles of Public Administration* (1927) and Leonard D. White's *Introduction to the Study of Public Administration* (1948) carried this normative theoretical perspective forward.

The practice of public administration from this viewpoint was essentially the efficient carrying out of the decisions of political decisionmakers using what were assumed to be scientific principles of administration. Administrative practice focused on functional rationality about efficient means of implementing policy decisions, while substantive reasoning about the ends or goals of public policy remained under the purview of politicians.

By the late 1930s the difficulties in this "classical" view of administrative practice were becoming evident. In *The Frontiers of Public Administration* (1936), John Gaus, Leonard White, and Marshall Dimock expressed concern about carrying the separation of politics from administration too far and noted that cultural, historical, and geographical contexts were important influences on the practice of public administration. This kind of thinking amounted to backing away from the notion of "one best way" for administering a given function of government wherever it occurred and, thereby, called into question the possibility of truly scientific administration. Gaus, White, and Dimock also observed that administrators do, after all, exercise considerable discretion, thus they are not simple instruments of their political masters.

The challenges to the classical normative formulation of the practice of public administration continued and accelerated through the next three decades. Scholars such as Paul Appleby and John Gaus flatly and forcefully rejected the notion that administration could be separated from politics. A key attack on the scientific status of administrative principles dominant during 1900–40 came from Herbert Simon in his *Administrative Behavior* (1976). Simon critically analyzed the accepted principles of administration formulated by theorists such as Luther Gulick, finding them contradictory and without scientific universality. Principles concerning such organizational attributes as span of control, homogeneity of function, and unity of command were found to be only "proverbs" or general diagnostic rules of thumb rather than lawlike scientific generalizations.

By the early 1970s a movement called the "New Public Administration" called for the abandonment of the old paradigm. These scholars advocated a frank acknowledgment that public administrators are unavoidably involved in political relationships and transactions, inescapably confronted with the need to exercise discretion, and, therefore, bound to be influenced by values of some kind. While administrators may have technical expertise, its application to administrative problems and decisions is conditioned by values—acknowledged or otherwise.

Given these assumptions, proponents of the New Public Administration argued it is better that administrative practice be oriented around consciously chosen values and principles rooted in a professional ethic than left to the vagaries of personal ethics. Their preference tended to be for social equity as the central ethical principle for administrative practice.

Also, the New Public Administration, released from the constraints of neutrality and science, viewed the relationship of the administrator to the citizenry differently. In the classical normative formulation of their practice, administrators had no direct and formal relationship to the people; their bond was to elected officials elected by the voters. However, if administration is admitted to be political to some extent and shaped by values, citizens and administrators together should sort out the appropriate values to guide administrative practice. Citizens should be included in the administrative process through explicit systematic planned opportunities for participation. Thus, for the New Public Administration, administrators were no longer viewed as neutral instruments of elected officials, but as agents of change, open to citizens, in pursuit of social equity in the operation of government.

The New Public Administration did not become a sustained reform movement to which one can assign credit for redefining administrative practice, but it clearly signaled the demise of the classical paradigm. Since that time it has not been possible to think seriously of the public administrator as a practitioner of scientific principles removed from the influence of politics. Empirical research such as that conducted by Aberbach, Putnam, and Rockman (1981) has demonstrated decisively that public administrators are necessarily involved in politics and policy making, especially in the United States, but also in Western European democracies.

The Current State of Theories of Administrative Practice

No single normative theory of public administrative practice has achieved dominance since the classical perspective was called into question and found wanting. However, conceptualizations of administration which have continued to unfold since the 1970s include public administrators as: (1) bureaucratic politicians, (2) manager/leaders, (3) moral agents, and (4) fiduciary or representative citizens.

As Kettl (1993) points out in his recent report on "Public Administration: The State of the Field," the view of administrative practice as political bargaining and negotiating has its roots in Graham Allison's work in the late 1960s. It has been continued by political scientists such as James Q. Wilson, who focus on public bureaucracy as a network of political forces and the administrator as a political actor. This work tends to be based on descriptive theory about how administration actually functions rather than on normative theoretical views about how it ought to work. It is noteworthy that, having recognized the political nature of administration, there is a relative absence of normative political theory for the administrative role in this literature. This reluctance to engage in the development of normative theory may reflect the vestiges of positivism remaining among public administration scholars—a certain uneasiness with moving beyond observable description to a treatment of values.

The second current perspective depicts the administrator as a manager/leader. As Kettl observes, this view has emerged from Simon's (1976) assertion that decisionmaking is the central administrative function. Although there are varying emphases on the exercise of power, in some forms this loose collection of theoretical perspectives begins to resemble classical public administration in its quest for rational principles and specific technical expertise. Kettl suggests that the main difference from traditional public administration is its emphasis on top level managers as leaders rather than simply subservient instruments of political leadership.

The view of the public administrator as moral agent has grown out of the rise of administrative ethics as a field of study since the mid-1970s. This literature tends to view the fact of administrative discretion as requiring a central focus on the professional ethics of the administrator as a guide for discretionary action. Both the personal ethics of the administrator and the norms of bureaucratic politics are generally rejected as adequate bases for decisions and conduct.

However, beyond this central common concern there is little agreement about the normative ethical foundations for administrative practice. The competing perspectives include constitutional values and principles, the values and norms of the ethical tradition of citizenship in the United States, founding thought, social equity, the public interest, and democratic values. A somewhat different viewpoint emphasizes the priority of character or virtue as the primary guide for conduct over any particular set of values and principles.

The view of public administrators as fiduciary or representative citizens is reflected in an ongoing stream of literature that first emerged in the "National Conference on Citizenship and Public Service" in 1983. The proceedings of this conference were published in a special issue of *Public Administration Review* in March 1984. Common to this general line of thought is the notion that professional public administrators have taken over functions and responsibilities formerly borne by citizens in simpler times. It understands public administrative practice as derived from the role of the citizen.

This citizenship perspective embodies two slightly different nuances of emphasis on administrative practice as: (1) holding the office of citizen in trust for the citizenry, or (2) somehow representing the citizens in the course of administrative work. The former stresses the importance of administrative practice as subordinate to the activity of citizens and oriented toward encouraging active participation by the citizenry in policymaking, policy implementation, and service delivery. The latter is concerned more with acting on behalf of the citizenry in the process of administration—attempting to reflect the views of the people rather than allowing technical and organizational concerns to dominate.

Conclusion

It remains to be seen whether anything like the consensus supporting the classical formulation of administrative practice will ever again be achieved. The four views summarized above have different emphases, but are not necessarily irreconcilable in their basic assumptions. They all assume that public administrators play far more significant and substantive roles in governance than was the case in the classical view. All four acknowledge the unavoidably value-laden nature of administrative practice, and while all recognize that administrators use science to varying degrees, none assumes that administration can be defined as a science in itself. They all also admit the political nature of administration and the role of administrators in the policy making process. The next step may be a normative theory of administrative practice which brings the key elements of these four streams of thought into some kind of integration.

TERRY L. COOPER

BIBLIOGRAPHY

Aberbach, Joel D., Robert D. Putnam, and Bert A. Rockman, 1981. *Bureaucrats and Politicians in Western Democracies.* Cambridge, MA: Harvard University Press.
Cooper, Terry L., 1994. "The Emergence of Administrative Ethics as a Field of Study." In Terry L. Cooper, ed., *Handbook on Administrative Ethics.* New York: Marcel Dekker, pp. 3–30.
Frederickson, H. George and Ralph Clark Chandler, eds., 1984. "Citizenship and Public Administration." *Public Administration Review,* special issue (March).
Gaus, John M., Leonard D. White, and Marshall E. Dimock, 1936. *The Frontiers of Public Administration.* Chicago: University of Chicago Press.
Goodnow, Frank, 1900. *Politics and Administration: A Study in Government.* New York: Russell & Russell.
Kettl, Donald F., 1993. "Public Administration: The State of the Field." In Ada W. Finifter, ed., *Political Science: The State of the Discipline II.* Washington, D.C.: The American Political Science Association, pp. 407–428.
Marini, Frank, ed., 1971. *Toward a New Public Administration: The Minnowbrook Perspective.* Scranton, PA: Chandler Publishing Company.
Simon, Herbert A., 1976. *Administrative Behavior: A Study of Decision-Making Processes in Administrative Organization.* 3d ed. New York: The Free Press.
White, Leonard D., 1948. *Introduction to the Study of Public Administration.* 3d ed. New York: Macmillan.
Willoughby, William F., 1927. *The Principles of Public Administration: With Special Reference to the National and State Governments of the United States.* Washington, D.C.: The Brookings Institution.
Wilson, Woodrow, 1887. "The Study of Administration." *Political Science Quarterly,* vol. 2: 197–220.

PRAGMATISM. A philosophy without foundations, one that does not resort to premises or absolutes beyond the realm of experience to ground its statements—hence, any statement is subject to experimentation and verification.

Pragmatism was developed in the United States at the beginning of the twentieth century. It was a philosophy inspired by dissatisfaction with traditional European philosophy and by the necessity to develop philosophical principles that fit the U.S. situation. Hence, pragmatic philosophers rejected the premise that there were metaphysical certainties that constrained truth and judgement. For the pragmatist, the primary element of any philosophy was experience. For the pragmatist, if reality existed, it must surely be experience. It must also be experienceable. Consequently, pragmatists dismissed any reality that could not be experienced as frivolous or mythical.

The initial outlines of pragmatic philosophy emerged as pragmatic philosophers demonstrated that formal logic depended upon experience. Charles S. Pierce argued that statements were true because they could be proven by experience, and because they had meaning within the realm of individual experience. Pierce demonstrated that meaning could, in many instances, only be established by acting upon or applying symbols to test their consequences. William James approached pragmatism from the discipline of psychology; and understood experience from a psychological standpoint, William James convincingly argued in *Principles of Psychology* (1890) that reality was fundamentally shaped by the psychological mindset of individuals. James extended this argument in *A Pluralistic Universe* (1920) by showing that individuals could experience multiple realities. He argued that the monists and idealists were wrong to contend that a single standard for rationality and logic could settle contradictory experiences. Multiple, competing truths could be pursued and perpetuated by individuals in a universe that could best be described as pluralistic, not monolithic. Hence, no single standard of rationality could apply throughout this complex universe that was constantly in flux, and under development. However, it was John Dewey (1929) who demonstrated that the pluralistic principles of pragmatic logic and psychology had social implications.

Dewey converted pragmatism to a social philosophy by arguing that human institutions must be founded upon an experimental as opposed to a fixed set of principles. Enamored with administrative organizations, Dewey found that these institutions could function without any fixed, monolithic, or transcendental principles upon which to ground their authority. Such institutions, Dewey argued, were the epitome of the democratic spirit. On one hand they could function according to prevailing, majority standards for truth and rationality. On the other, they were constantly searching for improved institutional standards that could meet new and unique challenges.

Dewey effectively crafted a philosophical argument for progressive administrative institutions that fit well into the reform spirit of the Progressive Era. He argued that capitalists had developed administrative organizations that efficiently functioned to enhance the interests of the wealthy few. The experts in such organizations served narrow, not public interests. To reform industrial society, Dewey argued that administrative bodies must be organized so as to use their power in the public interest. One way to do this was to use administered organizations to develop laws and policies that would regulate capitalism and enhance the general good.

Dewey also intended these administrative bodies to reform U.S. society by other methods than simply developing regulations, laws, and policies. They would reform by socializing less rational individuals into scientific discourse. Dewey was an inveterate social reformer who believed that once a confused nineteenth-century citizenry learned how to use the scientific method they could improve their situation. Hence, the rigorous language used by experts within the organization could serve to aid the common citizen in solving problems. Conversely, once the masses of people learned to participate in organizations, their values would inform the organizational experts who might otherwise remain isolated from commoners. Dewey repeatedly argued that administrative organizations could function as new communities where scientific experts collaborated with the citizenry in identifying and solving their common problems.

Dewey proposed pragmatic organizations as a corrective to the nineteenth-century liberal state. Whereas the liberal state relied upon constitutional law and inalienable human rights, leaders of the pragmatic organization regarded all institutional principles as subject to experimentation and scientific testing. Dewey carried this argument so far as to claim that, through experimentation, the administrative organization could create improved moral norms by which individuals could function. Dewey provided philosophic justification to other Progressives who believed that the individualistic norms of the nineteenth century no longer applied to the interdependency inherent in an industrialized, urban society. Pragmatists came to regard the nineteenth-century state, with its emphasis on inalienable, constitutionally protected rights, as a barrier to Progressive reform.

Under pragmatic thought, institutions were viewed as instruments for accomplishing human purposes. Institutions were legitimate because of their effectiveness. This led pragmatic philosophers and organizational theorists into conflict with nineteenth-century constitutionalists who defended the legitimacy of U.S. state institutions on abstract legal grounds. Consequently, when pragmatic reformers examined U.S. institutions, they were not so much interested in whether these institutions were congruent with the established constitutional principles, but whether they served the present needs of the U.S. population. Pragmatists manifested a willingness to change institutional principles and structure with a zealousness that shocked liberals who were accustomed to changing institutions only after they were sure that such changes were constitutionally permissible.

In addition to providing philosophical arguments to zealous reformers in the Progressive movement, pragmatism served as a continuing philosophic frame for post Progressive organizational theory. The pragmatic mindset surfaced in the thought of Elton Mayo (1945) and Chester Barnard. The human relations school of organizational theory, in stressing the social nature of organizations, incorporated vestiges of pragmatic theory. The contingency approach to organizational theory acknowledges a truth first identified by pragmatic philosophy; i.e., that there are no foundational truths upon which any organizational philosophy can be developed.

Pragmatically inspired organizational theory emphasized an active, effective organization, one that changed its structure to accomplish the goals of the organization. Acting in this tradition, the human relations or "Theory Y" tradition argued that the organization must take responsibility for enhancing the experience of its employees. The human relations school viewed organizations as institutions which could enrich the life of workers in the organization. Elton Mayo (1945) conceived an argument subsequently developed by Herbert Simon: that organizations could influence, even define the nature of rationality for both employees and clients of the organization.

JAMES STEVER

BIBLIOGRAPHY

Dewey, John, 1929. *The Quest for Certainty.* New York: Minton Balch & Co.
Diggins, John P., 1994. *The Promise of Pragmatism: Modernism and the Crisis of Knowledge and Authority.* Chicago: University of Chicago Press.
James, William, 1890. *Principles of Psychology.* New York: Dover.
James, William, 1920. *A Pluralistic Universe.* Cambridge, MA: Harvard University Press.
Mayo, Elton, 1945. *The Social Problems of an Industrial Civilization.* Boston: Harvard University.
Sleeper, Ralph W., 1986. *The Necessity of Pragmatism.* New Haven, CT: Yale University Press.
Westbrook, Robert B., 1991. *John Dewey and American Democracy.* New York: Cornell University Press.

PRICES AND INCOMES POLICY.

A direct government instrument which seeks to reduce the rate of change of the price of labor and capital and of final goods and services by altering the behavior of those groups involved in pricing decisions. A direct instrument has an unmediated influence on the target variable and is thus distinguished from other economic policy weapons, for example, monetary and fiscal policy, which rely on an intermediate variable such as consumer expenditure or interest rates.

Although the term incomes policy is of post–World War II origin, the direct control of wages and prices has a 4,000-year history which stretches back to the legal canon of Hammurabi in ancient Babylon. More recently such policies were an integral part of economic planning in the Soviet Union, and after World War II in its East European satellites, China, and other centrally planned states. During World War II, price and wage controls were a key part of wartime economic organization. Most OEEC/OECD market economies and other mixed capitalist economies, particularly in the 35 years after 1945, introduced such policies at some time, in some form, and for different periods. The aims of such policies have been to address, first, the problems of the equity of income distribution; second, the issue of economic incentives, which are necessary for the efficient allocation of resources; and third, the question of domestic economic imbalance, and in particular the control of inflation. These aims may conflict and the authorities will then be forced to decide on the balance of priorities. In the postwar period the emergence of inflation as an endemic problem led many capitalist countries to view the counterinflationary aspects of incomes policy with particular favor.

The use of incomes policy itself depended on the acceptance of a model of economic behavior and the infla-tionary process. Some advocates of incomes policy argued that cost increases, caused by more powerful and more aggressive labor unions, had become the prime source of inflationary developments, and that the unions' push for higher money wages was largely independent of the level of economic activity and of market forces.

However, in 1958, Professor A. W. Phillips, of the London School of Economics, identified the seminal relationship which queried this view and focused attention on a trade-off between the ratio of change of money wage rates and the level of unemployment: at higher levels of aggregate demand, wage inflation would rise and unemployment would fall. This implied a menu of policy choice. A reduction in the rate of inflation could be achieved by reducing the level of aggregate economic activity by fiscal or monetary policy. However, the social, political, and economic costs of this lay in the consequent rise in the level of unemployment. Other proponents of prices and incomes policy recommended it as a way of avoiding these costs. The purpose was to lower the money wage rate change for any given level of unemployment. Finally, adherents of prices and incomes policy argued that such instruments could contribute to the lowering of inflationary expectations and thus cut into the wage-price or price-price spiral.

The administration of incomes policy over the postwar period led to the identification of various styles. A fundamental distinction was drawn between those policies which were voluntary and those which relied on sanctions. The former depended on the educational impact of public pronouncements such as the U.S. wage-price guideposts, 1962–1967, or the wider discussion and publication of the alleged consequences of irresponsible inflationary settlements, for example in the UK the Council for Productivity, Prices, and Incomes (1958). These methods left the authorities to identify inappropriate levels of wage and price increases, but did not involve them as energetic actors in forcing down the agreed price or wage increase. More aggressive methods were adopted when failures to cooperate resulted in "ear stroking" or "ear bashing." Here politicians, with varying degrees of assertiveness, made public pronouncements to persuade or cajole recalcitrant groups, often in the anticipation of creating a public opinion backlash against those groups. Government statements concerning the wage claim of the UK National Union of Mineworkers 1974 illustrate this. More formal agreements to voluntary compliance were often attempted in bilateral or trilateral corporatist style incomes policies with labor unions' and employers' organizations, as in the Netherlands 1945–1950, and the UK Social Contract (1974).

Sanctions, or the threat of such, were employed by governments in the form of using their discretionary power as direct purchasers, employers of labor, and price setters in public utilities. Thus in the period 1970–1974 nationalized industries in the UK were subject to stricter price controls than private enterprises. This tactic was reinforced at times with government threats to use fiscal or other policy instruments to put pressure on the decisionmakers, such as warnings of limits on government spending in the UK in 1979 and President John F. Kennedy's threat of discriminatory purchasing in a bid to enforce U.S. steel price controls in 1962. Most significantly the sanctions were, at times, built into a statutory framework with powers to prevent, limit, or postpone increases, or to demand early notification of the intentions to raise wages or prices. The UK Prices and Incomes Act of 1966 and the Counter Inflation Act of 1972 exemplify such legislation. An evolutionary feature of incomes policy was the widening of control from wages to other forms of income, to prices, and to productivity considerations in increasingly complex attempts to balance the competing aims of incomes policy and to take account of exceptional cases.

A large number of empirical econometric studies were completed in the three postwar decades, mainly in the United States and the United Kingdom. These were designed to test the impact of prices and incomes policies by comparing wage and/or price inflation during periods of application of the policy with estimates of what would have happened in the absence of such application. The extent to which success depended on the profile of publicity given to the policy, and the size and nature of the change in the wage or price inflation for any given level of unemployment, was the basis of many of these studies. The overall summary of the research is that the impact of the policies on wage determination and the rate of wage and price inflation was modest, partly because any impact in the early stages of application was frequently dissipated in a post–incomes policy restoration of income levels.

Critics of the policies rely heavily in this evidence, and the break down in the Phillips trade-off, in drawing the conclusion that the policies are not effective. They argue that inflation is created by demand or money supply, and not induced by union aggressiveness, and can only be successfully tackled by fiscal, monetary, and supply side policies. They further emphasize that the policies create distortions in the economy which weaken allocative efficiency and create resentment, disillusionment, and political confrontation.

Relics of incomes policy techniques survive, such as the control of public sector wage increases. Also, the rapid inflation in post-Soviet Russia in the early 1990s led some to debate the place of incomes policy in squeezing costs and prices there. But a major shift in policy attitudes in the 1980s led Western governments to retreat from the use of direct policy instruments themselves and to recommend that ex-socialist economies rely on the market to allocate resources, and on a tight monetary and fiscal stance to control wages and prices.

RICHARD M. ALEXANDER

BIBLIOGRAPHY

Bilson, Beth, ed., 1986. *Wage Restraint and the Control of Inflation: An International Survey.* New York: St. Martin's Press.

Danziger, Sheldon H., Gary D. Sandefur, and Daniel H. Weinberg, 1994. *Confronting Poverty: Prescriptions for Change.* Cambridge, MA: Harvard University Press.

Fishbein, Warren H., 1984. *Wage Restraint by Consensus: Britain's Search for an Incomes Policy Agreement 1965–1979.* London: Routledge and Kegan Paul.

Marresse, Michael, 1994. "An Incomes Policy for Russia?" *Economic Systems,* vol. 18, no. 1 (March).

Smith, D. C., 1966. *Incomes Policies: Some Foreign Experiences and Their Relevance for Canada.* Ottawa: Queen's Printer.

United Nations, Secretariat for the Economic Commission for Europe, 1967. *Incomes Policies in Postwar Europe: A Study of Policies, Growth and Distribution.* Geneva: United Nations.

PRIMARY JURISDICTION. In administrative law, having initial jurisdiction in resolving a dispute. A rather simple way for courts to avoid reviewing an administrative controversy is to invoke the doctrine of primary jurisdiction. Bernard Schwartz (1993) pronounced this doctrine "one of the foundations of modern administrative law" (p. 269). The primary jurisdiction doctrine serves to allow administrative agencies primary or initial jurisdiction without court intrusion in resolving disputes involving administrative agencies. When Congress has failed to define jurisdiction for a particular matter, the court is confronted with the problem of deciding whether it has primary or initial jurisdiction in the particular question brought to its attention. The court is brought into the controversy initially when an aggrieved party tries to bring legal action against another party in court. In giving consideration to the suit, the court may elect to apply the doctrine of primary jurisdiction; it usually does this, thus dismissing the case. The court will inform the interested parties that a particular administrative agency should have primary or initial jurisdiction in the case. That is, the administrative agency should have first crack at resolving the dispute before the court voices its opinion on the matter. However, a court will occasionally inform the parties that the decision reached by the agency should be considered final, thereby giving the agency both primary and exclusive jurisdiction. The primary jurisdiction doctrine acknowledges that public agencies should normally be permitted to settle disputes affecting their agencies first unless: (1) the agency has ruled previously on a similar question; (2) the regulation or issue in the dispute is patently unreasonable; or (3) the issue poses a question which is clearly within the jurisdiction and competence of the judiciary.

A few cases serve to illustrate how the courts have applied the doctrine in practice. In *Texas and Pacific R. R. Co. v. Abilene Cotton Oil Co.,* 204 U.S. 426 (1907), the Abilene Cotton Oil Company sued the Texas and Pacific Railroad

Company because of a perceived rate overcharge. The Supreme Court ruled in essence that the ICC should be given primary jurisdiction in the overcharge dispute. In effect, the Court said that shippers with complaints about rate charges should first take their case to the ICC and then, if necessary, file suit in the district court.

What specific reasons have the courts given for using the primary jurisdiction doctrine? In *Far East Conference v. United States,* 342 U.S. 570, 674–575 (1952), the Court asserted that administrative matters are best handled by administrators, not judges. This is the intent of Congress when it creates agencies. The courts should not ignore this reality. Agencies are best equipped to promote unified regulatory policies through informed opinion and flexible procedures: "Uniformity and consistency in the regulation of business entrusted to a particular agency are secured, and the limited functions of review by the judiciary are more rationality exercised, by preliminary resort for ascertaining and interpreting the circumstances underlying legal issues to agencies that are better equipped than the courts by specialization, by insight gained through experience, and by more flexible procedure." In *Burlington Northern, Inc. v. United States,* 103 S.Ct. 514 (1982), the Supreme Court ruled that the Interstate Commerce Commission has primary jurisdiction in determining the rates railroads charge shippers. In reversing the D.C. Circuit Court of Appeals, the high court scolded the lower court for interfering with the rate-setting authority of the ICC by vacating an ICC rate order. Speaking for the Court, Chief Justice Burger noted that, "the more appropriate course would have been to remand to the Commission for explanation rather than to undertake itself to construe the order, and in so doing to interfere with the Commission's primary jurisdiction contrary to important congressional policies" (p. 522).

But courts do not always find it appropriate to employ the primary jurisdiction doctrine to dismiss cases involving agencies. In *Nader v. Allegheny Airlines,* 426 U.S. 290 (1976), Ralph Nader sued Allegheny Airlines in federal district court for compensatory and punitive damages after he was bumped from an Allegheny flight for which he had confirmed reservations. Nader specifically charged that Allegheny Airlines' secret overbooking practices were deceptive, thus inconveniencing travelers who believed they in fact had confirmed reservations. Therefore, his suit claimed that Allegheny Airlines was guilty of fraudulent misrepresentation. Should CAB be given primary jurisdiction to settle the claim? While the lower courts said yes and employed the primary jurisdiction doctrine, the Supreme Court said no. It argued: "Referral of the misrepresentation issue to the Board cannot be justified by the interest in informing the court's ultimate decision with 'the expert and specialized knowledge' . . . of the Board. The action brought by petitioner does not turn on a determination of the reasonableness of a challenged practice—a

determination that could be facilitated by an informed evaluation of the economics or technology of the regulated industry. The standards to be applied in action for fraudulent misrepresentation are within the conventional competence of the courts, and the judgment of a technically expert body is not likely to be helpful in the application of these standards to the facts of this case" (p. 305).

In *Farmers Ins. Exchange v. Superior Court,* 826 P2d 730 (Cal. 1992) the California Supreme Court agreed with the U.S. Supreme Court's decision in Nader, contending that the primary jurisdiction doctrine applies when practical concerns compel courts to allow administrative agencies the initial opportunity to resolve technical regulatory questions, but not when nonregulatory issues arise such as fraudulent misrepresentation that cannot be resolved appropriately by agency experts (p. 737–738). This court stressed that primary jurisdiction is a mutually beneficial and practical doctrine, concluding that it " evolved for the benefit of courts and administrative agencies, and unless precluded by the Legislature, it may be invoked whenever a court concludes there is a 'paramount need for specialized agency fact-finding expertise' " (p. 746).

KENNETH F. WARREN

BIBLIOGRAPHY

Schwartz, Bernard, 1993. "Administrative Law Cases During 1992." *Administrative Law Review,* vol. 45 (Summer).
Warren, Kenneth F., 1996. *Administrative Law in the Political System.* 3d ed. Upper Saddle River, NJ: Prentice Hall.

PRIME MINISTER'S OFFICE (PMO).

In Canada, the partisan political staff that advises, schedules, briefs, represents, and runs errands for the prime minister (PM) of Canada. This executive support agency protects and promotes the personal and professional interests of the prime minister. For this reason, the prime minister has appointed the most loyal and trusted advisers to this executive body. On the personal level these officials boost the prime minister's ego, and shield the PM from political enemies or from the intrusion of the media.

As it has evolved, the PMO consists of the key executive assistants and personal advisors of the prime minister who counsel and recommend on matters having to do with general public relations, the mass media, and relations with Parliament, executive bureaucratic organizations such as the Privy Council Office (PCO), and with party organizations in the provinces and territories.

Duties

The PMO provides the prime minister with the staff support he or she needs to do what the public expects of a political leader. People who work in the PMO fill a variety of functions that are essential to the prime minister's political success in domestic as well as in foreign affairs.

It is not easy to generalize about the duties of the officials in the PMO, because they reflect the personal style and political priorities of the prime minister. Some act as gatekeepers and guardians of the prime minister's time. Others deal exclusively with government backbenchers and other members of Parliament. Still others serve as links with the federal bureaucracy and executive agencies of government. Some advise the prime minister on political matters, partronage appointments, and the political mood of the country. Others may write speeches, organize the prime minister's schedule, and boost the PM's morale. The PMO includes English and French translators, a correspondence unit, and a special project unit to assist the prime minister in all matters related to Canada. Correspondence to the prime minister can reach as much as 300,000 pieces per week. The correspondence unit of the PMO receives, answers, and files mail.

In the PMO, a legislative advisor prepares the briefing book for the prime minister. This is the document the prime minister has on his or her desk when rising in the House of Commons to respond to questions from the opposition or from elected party members. The legislative adviser keeps the prime minister informed about the parliamentary calendar, the public's mood, and the flow of legislation through the House of Commons and the Senate.

Staff members review every speech the prime minister delivers, every official announcement, and everything that might have legal bearing on what the prime minister does outside of Parliament. The communications staff manages the prime minister's relations with the Ottawa press gallery and media establishment. It organizes press conferences, supervises photo opportunities and public exposure during prime ministerial trips, and generally keeps in touch with the media. Some prime ministers find it expedient to designate staff people to link the PMO to certain groups—premiers, political party leaders, mayors, women, and aboriginal leaders.

Political Roles

The PMO comprises the people who owe almost total loyalty to the prime minister and to whom he or she turns for advice on everything from the mundane to the most serious matters of governance and matters of political party leadership. Good staff people in the PMO are usually self-effacing, working only for their boss and hiding from the limelight. The people in the PMO have become increasingly important as the prime minister's connections with the public have grown closer and as the position of prime minister has taken on an institutional life of its own.

On matters involving the prime minister's professional role the PMO assists in everything from drafting the Speech from the Throne and other speeches to guiding the prime minister through the maze of political and bureaucratic hurdles confronting executive leaders in Canada.

Policy Coordination

The PMO collaborates with the Privy Council Office to develop a national policy framework, including a public relations strategy for the government. The PMO is therefore a practical policy think tank charged with an advisory capacity on the political fortunes of the prime minister and his cabinet.

At root the position of the prime minister rests on the exercise of powers in three interrelated areas handled by the PMO. The first involves recommending the appointment of individuals to key positions that enhance the reputation and credibility of the government. The second involves the organization of the cabinet itself so that it is capable of governing efficiently and is representative of the complex network of interests in the country. The third is that the prime minister be always in a position to provide leadership and direction to the government.

Accordingly, the PMO supports the prime minister in carrying out the role demanded of a head of the vast bureaucracy of government, of a leader of a political party, and of a member of parliament.

The highly trusted political staff in the PMO provides advice on the impact of government policies on public support for the prime minister's party. But it is also the PMO that keeps relations with the federal bureaucracy in good standing. With its help the prime minister is able to command the loyalty of the federal bureaucracy in the implementation of government policy.

The PMO establishes a solid and stable center of power in the political executive, which enables the prime minister to establish the whole country as a constituency of support for the government. The extremely high level of visibility for the prime minister thus makes the PMO a powerful political resource.

JAMES J. GUY

BIBLIOGRAPHY

Axworthy, Thomas, 1988. "Of Secretaries to Princes." *Canadian Public Administration* vol. 31, no. 2 (Summer) 247–264.

Guy, James J., 1995. *How We Are Governed: The Basics of Canadian Politics and Government.* Toronto: Harcourt, Brace Publishers.

Hockin, Thomas A. ed., 1977. *Apex of Power.* Scarborough: Prentice-Hall Canada.

Lalonde, Marc, 1971. "The Changing Role of the Prime Minister's Office." *Canadian Public Administration* (Winter) 509–537.

PRIVATE FOUNDATION.

A charity that fails to qualify as a public charity. This usually occurs if the charity receives contributions from only one family or business or if its primary source of revenue is investment income. A private foundation is subject to special excise taxes that public charities are exempt from. Most private foundations are grant-making organizations.

The United States

A private foundation is an IRS Code Section 501(c)(3) charity that fails to qualify as a public charity. A public charity generally receives contributions and other revenue (e.g., ticket sales by a symphony) from many unrelated individuals. There is a mathematical test, known as "the public support test," which measures the amount of contributions and revenue received from unrelated donors. Although there are a few types of charities that achieve public charity status without having to pass the test (e.g., churches, hospitals, and schools), most charities achieve their public charity status by meeting the public support test.

A charity will be a private foundation if it cannot pass the public support test. This usually occurs if the charity receives contributions from only one family or business (e.g., the Ewing Marion Kauffman Foundation) or it receives substantially all of its revenue from investment income and very few contributions from the public (e.g., the Pew Charitable Trusts). There are over 33,000 private foundations in the United States.

There are two categories of private foundations: private nonoperating foundations and private operating foundations. Private nonoperating foundations are the most common. Usually their sole activity is to make awards for charitable purposes, either by making grants to other charitable organizations or directly to worthy beneficiaries (e.g., the Ford Foundation). By comparison, a private operating foundation engages in a hands-on charitable enterprise but is classified as a private foundation because there is an insufficient number of unrelated donors to the charity for it to pass the public support test (e.g., the Getty Art Museum).

There are two disadvantages to private foundation status. The first is that donors to a private foundation receive fewer income tax benefits for their contributions. However, the tax treatment of a contribution to a private operating foundation is generally as favorable as that for a contribution to a public charity. The second disadvantage is that private foundations are subject to a series of excise taxes. Public charities, by comparison, are exempt from these taxes.

Reduced Tax Benefits for Charitable Contributions

A donor's income tax deduction for a charitable contribution to a private nonoperating foundation is reduced in two ways. The first reduction occurs if a donor contributes appreciated property (for example, stock with a value greater than its purchase price). Whereas the donor can usually claim an income tax deduction for the value of the property contributed to a public charity, the donor can only deduct the cost if it is given to a private nonoperating foundation.

The second disadvantage occurs with respect to the annual deduction limitation for individuals (but not corporations). This law limits an individual's charitable income tax deduction to a percentage of his or her income each year. Whereas an individual can deduct 50 percent of his or her adjusted gross income for cash gifts to public charities, the threshold is reduced to 30 percent for cash gifts to private foundations. For gifts of appreciated property, the thresholds are 30 percent and 20 percent, respectively. These rules are explained in greater detail in this publication under the heading "**charitable contributions**."

Congress exempted private operating foundations from both of these reductions. A contribution to a private operating foundation generally qualifies for the same income tax benefits as a contribution to a public charity.

Excise Taxes Imposed on Private Foundations

Reasons for the Taxes. Private foundations, but not public charities, are subject to a series of technical excise taxes. Congress enacted these taxes as part of the Tax Reform Act of 1969 after it discovered abuses with several private foundations. The taxes punish the types of activities that were found at that time.

The reason Congress imposed excise taxes on private foundations but exempted public charities was because it assumed that each public charity would be sufficiently scrutinized by its numerous contributors so that added enforcement by the IRS was unnecessary. It assumed that if a scandal occurred at a public charity, the negative publicity would hurt the organization and its ability to solicit contributions. By comparison, a scandal at a family foundation is not likely to be publicized. Even if it were publicized, the organization might not suffer since it is not dependent on charitable contributions from the public. Consequently, the only way to police such an organization is to access penalty taxes for inappropriate conduct.

The excise taxes have accomplished their principal objective. They have eliminated most of the abusive situations that may have existed in 1969. The amount of revenue that the federal government collects from these excise taxes is extremely small, which indicates that private foundations are substantially complying with the laws.

Types of Excise Taxes. Although all of the private foundation taxes are usually referred to as excise taxes, one of the taxes is essentially an income tax (the 2 percent tax on net investment income). The other taxes are penalty taxes that are designed to eliminate abusive situations that might otherwise arise when there is a conflict of interest between the charitable purposes of the foundation and a donor who might control the foundation.

The penalty taxes are generally assessed in two tiers: the first tier is a penalty tax that is assessed when a prohibited transaction occurs. The private foundation and the affected parties are then required to remedy the situation to bring all parties into compliance with the law. If the situation is not corrected, there is a second tier penalty tax that is so large that it is virtually a confiscatory tax. The consequences of paying the second tier tax are so detrimental that most parties will go out of their way to avoid it, thereby assuring compliance with the private foundation laws.

For example, if a donor sells land to a private foundation for $100,000, there is a 5 percent self-dealing penalty tax ($5,000) assessed against the donor. The transaction should then be reversed: the property should be returned to the donor and the payments should be returned to the private foundation, with interest. If the transaction is not reversed within a year, the second tier tax will be imposed against the donor: a confiscatory tax equal to 200 percent of the amount of the self-dealing transaction (i.e., 200 percent of the $100,000 purchase price of the property, or $200,000). Given the choice between returning $100,000 to the private foundation or paying $200,000 to the government, the donor is extremely likely to reverse the transaction and return the money to the private foundation.

The private foundation excise taxes and the associated IRS code section are:

1. *The 2 percent excise tax on net investment income, Section 4940.* To help pay for audits of private foundations, there is a 2 percent income tax assessed against the net investment income of private foundations.

2. *Prohibitions on self-dealing between a private foundation and "disqualified persons," Section 4941.* Most sales, loans and payments between a private foundation and a disqualified person (such as a donor, the donor's family, and the trustee of the private foundation) are prohibited. If such a transaction occurs, the transaction must be reversed to restore the private foundation to its prior status.

3. *The excise tax for failure to distribute income, Section 4942.* Private foundations are required to make annual "qualifying distributions" of their "minimum investment return" (generally, 5 percent of the foundation's net investment assets).

4. *The excise tax on excess business holdings, Section 4943.* A private foundation must dispose of stock in a business within five years if it (or if it in combination with "disqualified persons," such as family members) holds more than 20 percent of the stock of the business. This prevents a private foundation from holding stock in many closely held businesses. If the private founda-

tion acquires the stock through a charitable bequest, the private foundation may hold the stock for up to five years before it must be disposed.

5. *The excise tax on investments that may jeopardize charitable purposes, Section 4944.* Jeopardizing investments generally include those that show lack of business prudence, such as trading in uncovered puts and calls.

6. *The excise tax for some of the "taxable expenditures" and the failure to meet "expenditure responsibility" requirements, Section 4945.* A payment for any noncharitable purpose is a taxable expenditure. In addition, a taxable expenditure includes a grant to any person or organization (other than a public charity) unless the private foundation exercises "expenditure responsibility" to follow up on the outcome of the grant. Consequently, private foundations usually incur greater administrative costs to make grants to individuals (e.g., scholarship grants or research travel grants) because they must maintain close scrutiny over how the funds are expended. Grants to public charities are generally exempt from the expenditure responsibility requirements, so that smaller private foundations often restrict grants to public charities in order to reduce administrative costs.

International

The number of private foundations depends to a great extent on the culture of a nation and its laws. For example, there are 33,000 private foundations in the United States, 6,000 in Germany, but only 500 in France. Perhaps the difference between France and Germany is partially attributable to a French law that requires a foundation to have a minimum asset balance of 5 million francs and to have a French government official serve as a member of the governing body.

CHRISTOPHER HOYT

PRIVATIZATION. The transfer of government functions and responsibilities in the areas of financing, service delivery, and regulation to other sectors in society. The primary forms of privatization are: (1) divestiture, and sale of state-owned enterprises and assets; (2) contracting out of services, previously delivered by government agencies, to the private and nongovernment organization (NGO) sectors; and (3) deregulation, through the removal of statutory controls on the behavior of organizations, and individuals.

Privatization manifestly produces changes in the role of government, but it need not necessarily follow that governments will absent themselves altogether from the field of activity where privatization occurs. The privatization of public utilities, and the use of purchase-of-service contracting, for example, usually require governments to exchange one set of functions (service delivery) for another (regulation). And in many instances of privatization, governments are likely to retain some degree of financing responsibility, particularly in regard to the provision of subsidies, vouchers, or grants to low-income users of services.

Origin and Development

The U.S. management theorist Peter Drucker has been credited with first introducing the term in his book *The Age of Discontinuity* (1969), where he argued for reprivatization as an antidote for what he described as "the sickness of government." However, it was not until the 1980s that the "privatization idea" attracted widespread interest and support amongst public policymakers in the United States and internationally.

Chronologically, the first major program of privatization was initiated in 1974 by General Augusto Pinochet in Chile, under unusual political and economic circumstances (he staged a military coup in 1973, overthrowing the elected socialist government and violently repressing all subsequent political opposition). But the most influential—and to date the most comprehensive—expression of a democratic privatization policy worldwide has occurred in Britain, particularly during the successive governments of Margaret Thatcher (1979–1990). The widespread influence of the British model of privatization might be attributed to three factors: (1) its scale—where in excess of US $80 billion worth of state-owned enterprises has been sold since 1979; (2) its scope—most notably in the politically sensitive and technically complex public utility and network industries; and (3) its symbolism—involving the transformation of an archetypal postwar *dirigiste* (interventionist) state.

By the mid-1990s, privatization bore all the hallmarks of being an international movement, with most governments—in developed, and developing countries alike—embracing the policy prescriptions of privatization to a greater or lesser extent. International organizations and agencies such as the Organization for Economic Cooperation and Development (OECD), the World Bank, and the International Monetary Fund have played an important role in the global promulgation of privatization policy.

The Theory of Privatization

The theoretical foundation of privatization is built around the three strands of neoliberal political ideology, the public choice school of political science, and neoclassical economics. Yet the intellectual roots of privatization go back much further than this. The key themes of limited government, contractualism, the functionality of private property

rights, and the superiority of the market mechanism over conscious human agency were enunciated in their seminal form by the English political philosopher John Locke (*The Second Treatise on Government,* 1690), and the Scottish founder of classical economics, Adam Smith (*Wealth of Nations,* 1776). Indeed, the basic question which underlies privatization—namely where and how should the boundary between the state, the market, and the individual most appropriately be set?—is as old as political philosophy itself.

The neoliberal case for privatization is founded on a vigorous critique of the Keynesian postwar interventionist state. The interventionist state, it is argued, imposes an enormous cost on individual freedom, the incentive structure, and private property rights; yet it has failed in its own terms as a competent manager of the economy, and planner and provider of physical and social infrastructure. The failings of the state as planner, manager, and guardian of individual freedom are usually juxtaposed with the self-regulating, unobtrusive efficiency of the free market. Government is seen to represent an inferior alternative to the market and voluntary exchange in almost all areas of planning, production, and service delivery (exceptions include the production of public goods, such as defense), and thus the overriding goal is less and smaller government. The neoliberal position is best represented in the writings of Friedrich Hayek (*The Road to Serfdom,* 1994; *The Constitution of Liberty,* 1978), Robert Nozick (*Anarchy, State, and Utopia,* 1974), and Milton Friedman (*Capitalism and Freedom,* 1962).

The largely a priori and ideological position of the neoliberals is lent important quasi-scientific and empirical support by the public choice school of political science. Public choice theorists such as James Buchanan and Gordon Tulloch (*The Calculus of Consent,* 1962), and William A. Niskanen (*Bureaucracy and Representative Government,* 1971) have sought to explain the growth of government budgets, and the seemingly insatiable demand for more government services. The explanation lies, it is argued, in the self-interested behavior of elected politicians, senior bureaucrats, and interest groups, each of whom benefit directly from the growth in expenditure on public services. The way to break the ever spiraling escalation in demand is to alter the incentive structure in government, and to break the nexus between politics and production, policy and administration through divestiture and contracting out.

Neoclassical economics provides the substantive economic logic in the theory of privatization. The competitive framework and incentive structure of the market generally produce superior technical and allocative efficiency outcomes compared to centralized planning and production. The market is also held to be the guarantor of consumer sovereignty. But to operate optimally, the market environment requires the existence of effective competition and consumer choice, as well as the elimination of supply and demand distortions resulting *inter alia* from government social policy measures. Consequently, many economists of the neoclassical school would argue that effecting a change in ownership or service delivery from public to private hands represents in itself a necessary but not sufficient condition for optimizing efficiency, and consumerist outcomes. In order for this to be achieved, privatization needs to be accompanied by organizational restructuring (most notably in the case of monopolies), and the creation of a functioning market environment.

In addition to the above arguments based in political and economic theory, privatization has gained support for a number of other, generally more pragmatic, reasons. The primary attraction of privatization for many governments appears to lie in the financial, and fiscal management benefits that are seen to accrue from privatization. Revenue gained from asset sales helps governments to manage public sector debt, and purchase-of-service contracting reduces public expenditure and budget deficits due to lower-cost private sector, or nongovernment organization, provision. In addition, in areas of public infrastructure development, where substantial project financing is required, privatization opens up important new sources of private investment capital, and ensures that development can proceed without having any discernible impact on public borrowing.

The ability of privatization to contribute to a widening of share ownership (often described as "popular capitalism") has been a significant factor in a number of countries, most particularly in Britain, Chile, Eastern Europe, and Russia. Privatization reduces the strength of public sector trade unions, through effectively transferring public employees to the private sector, and removing public sector unions from involvement in strategic industries. In some instances, privatization has been used explicitly as a means of reducing the power and pace-setting function (in terms of improved salaries and conditions) of the public sector trade union movement.

Privatization in the United States

The U.S. practice of state intervention in the economy and in society has traditionally differed in a number of important respects from European traditions of government. Historically, U.S. legislators have favored regulation over direct government ownership of industries as a vehicle for economic and social policy.

The pattern of public ownership in the United States, which by international standards is relatively small, has meant that divestiture has not occupied the same prominent position in national privatization policy as elsewhere. Rather, the focus of privatization policy in the United States from the mid-1980s has been directed at substantially extending the contracting out of government functions, and at releasing much of the regulatory pressure, built up over decades, on the private sector.

The President's Commission on Privatization, set up under the Reagan administration in 1987, produced a set of wide-ranging recommendations aimed at giving impetus to U.S. privatization policy. Among its recommendations were proposals to sell Amtrak, to contract out urban mass transport, prisons, airports, and postal services, and to use federal aid programs to support privatization initiatives in developing countries. More recently, the Clinton administration has been influenced by the popular treatise on contemporary government, *Reinventing Government,* by David Osborne and Ted Gaebler (1993), the basic thesis of which is that governments should devolve responsibility for service provision to private sector and nongovernment organizations, in order to concentrate on policy development and policy direction.

Purchase-of-service contracting is now common practice among municipal governments across the United States; the United States has been a world leader in the complex area of privatization of prisons and correctional facilities; and there has been a significant attenuation of economic and social regulatory measures at the federal and state levels into the late 1990s.

Privatization Across the Globe

The British privatization program has been the most significant to date, and it has had a formative influence on governments throughout the world. By the mid-1990s, the face of the British economy was completely different from the way it looked 15 years earlier. The British government has relinquished ownership and operational control in almost every industry sector in which it was previously engaged, including transport, heavy manufacturing, banking, energy, and public utilities; and public sector employment has been halved. The only significant setbacks in the privatization policies of successive Conservative governments in Britain have been the withdrawal of nuclear power stations from the sale of the electricity supply industry in 1990–91, and the aborted sale of the postal service in 1994.

While the British experience of divestiture has captured most attention, the British government has initiated a number of interesting public administration measures, directed at reducing public sector monopolies and at introducing competition into public service provision. These measures include the compulsory competitive tendering of selected local government services, and an attempt to establish "internal markets" in the National Health Service. The direction of regulatory policy, though, has not only been toward deregulation. Along with the removal of regulatory constraints in some areas of the economy, new public administration structures have been developed to regulate the activities of the privatized public utilities.

By the early 1990s, most of the other member countries of the OECD had instituted their own privatization policies, with Germany (most notably, in former East Germany under the privatization agency, the *Treuhand*), France, Italy, Japan, New Zealand, and Canada in particular having undertaken major sales of public enterprises and assets. Although initially more hesitant than some other OECD states, the Australian government has deregulated telecommunications, and sold, in whole or in part, its airline, shipping, and banking interests. The Victorian state government leads the way among subnational governments in Australia, with the sale of public utilities and the introduction of compulsory competitive tendering in local government.

Eastern European countries and countries of the former Soviet Union have embarked on massive privatization programs, as an integral part of moving from command to market economies, and in return for Western financial aid. But these privatization programs have been complicated by, first, the scale of the sales involved (50,000 enterprises in the former Soviet Union alone); second, the poor financial health and commercial viability of many of the enterprises to be sold; and third, the virtual absence of domestic capital markets in these countries. Attempts to create local equity markets by distributing free privatization vouchers to the general population have not been particularly successful.

The structural adjustment programs of the World Bank have been used as an instrument to encourage governments in the Third World to pursue active divestiture, and public sector reform programs. Among developing economies, those nations most dependent on World Bank loans—countries in Latin America, the Caribbean, and sub-Saharan Africa—were the most active in privatizing state-owned enterprises over the period 1980–91.

The Impact of Privatization

The vigor with which privatization is being pursued across the globe belies both the controversy that at times attends its implementation, and the contested nature of its impact.

Privatization can change fundamental property relations in society, and it may challenge established public expectations and habits about service auspice and service levels; hence privatization policy almost invariably contains a residual capacity for political controversy. But in addition to this, international experience shows that privatization policy will engender particular controversy if (1) public assets are seen to be sold for markedly less than their true value, or alternatively when purchase-of-service contracts are awarded without due care, or due process; (2) when foreign capital or foreign corporations are allowed to become dominant participants; and (3) where the application of privatization policy to a particular domain lacks legitimacy, either because the economic case is weak, or because it has failed to win key stakeholder support.

The impact of privatization has attracted increasing interest, although in many instances it is still far too early to evaluate anything other than the immediate, post-change impact of privatization.

The evidence on the economic impact of privatization is equivocal, with some researchers finding that privatization raises efficiency and productivity substantially, and others concluding that it appears to make little difference. The performance gains appear to be less in those instances where enterprises or services have been subjected to a process of reform and restructuring prior to being sold or contracted out. There is unanimity, however, in the view that the market conditions in which the enterprise or service operates are critical to its economic performance. The more competitive the environment, the better the outcomes, not just for the business concerned but for its customers as well. The inability to create an appropriate set of market conditions for privatized businesses and services has been a common failing in privatization programs worldwide.

Public regulation is often an important corollary of privatization, although there is considerable debate about the form and scope of the regulatory task. Regulation provides an important mechanism for governments to ensure that an active market environment is created and maintained, that the behavior of monopolists is controlled, and that the interests of different classes of consumers are protected. Privatization can have adverse distributional and equity impacts—on low-paid workers, on low-income consumers, on minorities, on rural areas. As a consequence, governments have been required to make policy adjustments aimed at ameliorating these negative impacts, including introducing stronger social regulation and financing subsidy programs.

In the late twentieth century, privatization has become a dominant response to the problems of contemporary governance. It is unlikely, however, to prove the most appropriate response in all cases. Ironically, much of the core rationale for privatization is similar to that used at an earlier period to justify large-scale nationalization, with the current problem of "government failure" displacing the earlier problem of "market failure." In the future, governments may well revise their approach to the central issues of ownership and service provision, if managing the interface between public accountability and private control becomes too complex or difficult.

JOHN ERNST

BIBLIOGRAPHY

Buchanan, James and Gordon Tulloch, 1962. *The Calculus of Consent.* Ann Arbor, MI: University of Michigan Press.
Donahue, John D., 1989. *The Privatization Decision: Public Ends, Private Means.* New York: Basic Books.
Drucker, Peter, 1969. *The Age of Discontinuity.* New York: Harper & Row.

Ernst, John, 1994. *Whose Utility? The Social Impact of Public Utility Privatization and Regulation in Britain.* Buckingham: Open University Press.

Foster, C. D., 1992. *Privatization, Public Ownership and the Regulation of Natural Monopoly.* Oxford: Blackwell.

Friedman, Milton, 1962. *Capitalism and Freedom.* Chicago: University of Chicago Press.

Gayle, Dennis J. and Jonathan N. Goodrich, eds., 1990. *Privatization and Deregulation in Global Perspective.* New York: Quorum Books.

Hayek, Friedrich, 1944. *The Road to Serfdom.* London: Routledge and Kegan Paul.

———, 1978. *The Constitution of Liberty.* Chicago: University of Chicago Press.

Kamerman, Sheila B. and Alfred J. Kahn, eds., 1989. *Privatization and the Welfare State.* Princeton, NJ: Princeton University Press.

Locke, John, ([1690] 1952). *The Second Treatise on Government.* Englewood Cliffs, NJ: Prentice-Hall.

Marsh, David, 1991. "Privatization Under Mrs. Thatcher: A Review of the Literature." *Public Administration,* vol. 69 (Winter) 459–480.

Niskanen, William A., 1971. *Bureaucracy and Representative Government.* Chicago: Aldine-Atherton.

Nozick, Robert, 1974. *Anarchy, State and Utopia.* New York: Basic Books.

Organization for Economic Cooperation and Development, 1992. *Regulatory Reform, Privatization and Competition Policy.* Paris: OECD.

Osborne, David and Ted Gaebler, 1993. *Reinventing Government: How the Entrepreneurial Spirit Is Transforming the Public Sector.* New York: Plume.

Ramanadham, V. V., ed., 1993. *Privatization: A Global Perspective.* London: Routledge.

Report of the President's Commission on Privatization, 1988. *Privatization: Toward More Effective Government.* Urbana, IL: University of Illinois Press.

Smith, Adam, ([1776] 1937). *The Wealth of Nations.* New York: Modern Library.

Vickers, John and G. Yarrow, 1988. *Privatization: An Economic Analysis.* Cambridge, MA: The MIT Press.

PRIVY COUNCIL. The body on the advice of which the British sovereign exercises his or her statutory and some prerogative powers. The Privy Council also has some functions independent of the reigning monarch, such as general supervisory responsibilities in some spheres such as medicine, the universities, and other professional associations. It issues charters and appoints high sheriffs for the counties of England and Wales. Its prerogative responsibilities include the approval of legislation of the Channel Islands and the Isle of Man. It has some significance outside the United Kingdom, as its Judicial Committee is a point of referral for a number of Commonwealth countries who retain the right of legal appeal to the sovereign under their constitutions, should their own civil or criminal courts of law be unable to resolve matters nationally. Most members of the Commonwealth, therefore, have a Privy Council Office.

It has been described as "one of the more genteel engine rooms of the executive state" (Dynes and Walker 1995, p. 36). It arranges formal matters such as royal proclamations and orders in council (the latter are made, for example, when announcing alterations in ministerial positions). The council is only ever called into full session on the death of the sovereign or when he or she announces the intention to marry. For the most part, not less than four privy counsellors are summoned to attend meetings; three privy counsellors constitute a quorum. There are usually about 450 privy counsellors worldwide. For some time, membership has been regarded as an honorific accorded to members of the British Cabinet, senior backbenchers (political party affiliation being no bar to membership) and senior judges. Curiously, the nonpartisan traditions of the Privy Council are in no way threatened by the fact that its political head is usually the leader of the House of Commons and member of the Cabinet, a government appointee, who also oversees the government's legislative business. This apparently impossible mixture of the political and the constitutional is achieved by ensuring that most of the work rests upon the Clerk of the Privy Council, an appointment that is made from the ranks of the senior British civil service.

Historically, the Privy Council has its origins in the public administration system that characterized England and Wales after the Norman Conquest. By the fourteenth century, the Council was clearly differentiated from the courts of law, on the one hand, and Parliament on the other. One might legitimately wonder whether this "separation of powers" was what Montesquieu was, otherwise erroneously, considering when analyzing the British constitution and system of government. Certainly, after about 1300, the members of the Council (between 12 and 20) intermittently controlled all the business of the administration: "Its meetings, held almost daily, were occupied with the Sovereign's finances, foreign relations, regulations of aliens and trade, Church government, defense, preservation of order and redress of grievances" (Privy Council 1995, p.1). Strong monarchs used the Privy Council to their own ends. Queen Elizabeth I, for example, employed offshoots of the Council—the Council of the North and the Council for Wales—as what political scientists might describe as nation-building paradigms, using the power of patronage to keep regional barons from invoking civil war or raising (in this case) a challenge to Tudor legitimacy. Over a long period, the increase in the volume of government business led to specialization, real expertise, and the growth of committees. Much of this activity was gradually transferred to government departments. The Privy Council is now concerned principally with the residue of what was once, at least in theory, the executive governance of England and Wales in its entirety.

Discussion of the role of the Privy Council today has centered on two areas, one British, the other international. The British dimension concerns the accountability of the intelligence services (now more usually referred to as the security services). Following developments in the United States since the 1970s regarding legislative oversight of the U.S. Central Intelligence Agency and its sister services, certain arguments have been made regarding the desirability or otherwise of submitting the British security services to some further degree of accountability beyond those that have operated since World War I. The most natural suggestion, to some, has been that of putting the security services under the supervision of selected members of the Privy Council. This line of argument rests on the constitutional position that the purposes, functions, and activities of the British security services fall within the purview of the royal prerogative.

The second controversy concerns the international dimension of the Judicial Committee of the Privy Council. This body derives its appellate jurisdiction from the right of subjects of the Crown to appeal for redress to the sovereign in Council if they believe that their courts of law have failed to do them justice. This right of appeal sits, it is alleged, uncomfortably with the status of national independence. Consequently, the political and constitutional arguments in such places as Australia and Canada have tended to focus on the apparent illogicality and supposed awkwardness of celebrating national integrity with the less-than-independent fact of legal life that the last court of appeal is to the British Privy Council. It needs to be said that, despite this difficulty, a number of Commonwealth states that are republics (i.e., do not regard the British Sovereign as their head of state) sustain this access to the Privy Council.

PETER FOOT

BIBLIOGRAPHY

Baldwin, J. F., 1965. *The King's Council in England During the Middle Ages.* London: Smith Peter.
Dicey, A. V., 1979. *The Privy Council.* London: Hyperion Press.
Dynes, Michael and David Walker, 1995. *The New British State.* London: Times Books.
Privy Council, 1995. "The Privy Council." London: Privy Council.

PRIVY COUNCIL OFFICE (PCO).

In Canada, an executive administrative body that advises the Canadian cabinet and its committees. The PCO is a "central agency" which is defined as any part of the Canadian government bureaucracy, the main function or only purpose of which is to support the decisionmaking activities of the cabinet.

Under Canada's Constitution Act of 1867 the PCO was assigned the limited task of preparing and registering orders in council, which are laws and decrees passed by the cabinet without reference to the House of Commons or the Senate. Over the years by convention, the PCO greatly expanded its functions to serve the government in power as a nonpartisan advisory and administrative agency. It was formally established in 1940 as a secretariat to the cabinet.

The title of the PCO should be distinguished from the Queen's Privy Council (an institution that evolved directly from the private council of the British monarch), which is the formal name used in Canada for the cabinet. Technically, the Queen's Privy Council consists of all previous and present cabinet ministers in addition to some others on whom the title and its honors have been bestowed.

By comparison with other government departments, the PCO is a small organization. Its restricted size is an advantage for providing direct support to the prime minister and the cabinet because it avoids the duplication of expertise and activities found in other departments of government that support ministers in carrying out their portfolio responsibilities.

Administrative Support to the Political Executive

As a distinguished administrative institution, the PCO is an executive department of government that provides public service support to the prime minister and other ministers in the Cabinet. Under the direction of the most senior federal public servant, who is called the clerk of the privy council and the secretary to the cabinet, the PCO supports the prime minister and the cabinet to facilitate the effective operation of the government of Canada. The clerk of the privy council and the secretary to the cabinet provides direct support to the cabinet from the perspective of the values, traditions, procedures, and expertise of the public service. As the head of the public service department of the cabinet, the clerk of the privy council and the secretary to the cabinet serves as the principal link between the prime minister and the public service and is responsible to the prime minister for its overall effectiveness.

The Privy Council Office provides public service support to the prime minister across the entire spectrum of policy questions and operational issues facing the government. These are people who are usually recruited from other government departments and serve in the PCO for a limited period, after which they leave for positions in other departments. This rotational administrative policy brings new expertise into the PCO on a regular basis and enables its staff of over 300 to brief the prime minister, the plenary cabinet, and its subcommittees on the activities of the government and matters of national policy.

The prime minister looks to the PCO for advice the support in appointing senior office holders and organizing the government and in operating the cabinet decisionmaking system, in setting overall policy directions, in advising on particular initiatives, and in managing specific issues that are of special concerns to the government.

The PCO assists the prime minister in leading and directing the government and supports the prime minister's power to recommend appointments by providing substantive policy and management advice on senior appointments, including the appointment of deputy ministers and heads of agencies.

Advisory Role

The PCO provides advice to the prime minister on the relations of the government with Parliament and the Crown, on the roles and responsibilities of cabinet ministers, and on the organization of government.

The PCO also gives advice to the PM on the overall conduct of government business. This includes handling major issues and subjects that are important to the prime minister. The PCO tries to cover all ground so that every important group is consulted and so that a full range of alternatives are known prior to the decisions—that the prime minister and the cabinet have all the information they need to made decisions. In this context, the PCO works closely with the PMO, the department of finance, the treasury board, and other agencies of government to give ministers comprehensive briefings on the most central issues before the cabinet.

Administering the Flow of Government Business

The PCO manages the flow of government business to ensure that the decisionmaking process functions smoothly according to the standards, design, and instructions of the prime minister. A key role of the PCO is to support the prime minister in providing administrative leadership and direction to the government. In this regard the PCO sets cabinet agendas, takes minutes at cabinet meetings, and transmits cabinet decisions to the federal bureaucracy.

The PCO ensures administrative continuity when governments change. This can involve advice on many matters, such as to departing prime ministers on winding down their governments, to incoming prime ministers on establishing their government administrations, to new ministers for briefings, and can involve providing other administrative supports in periods of government transition. The objective is to safeguard that Canada is constitutionally governed by elected representatives at all times.

As a secretariat to the cabinet the professional civil servants in the PCO assist ministers when they must deal formally with their cabinet colleagues. The content of a minister's proposal is normally not a concern of the secretariat. However, the proper administrative process for presenting a minister's proposal needs the coordination of the PCO.

The PCO also ensures that orders in council (government regulations issued directly by the cabinet in the name of the governor-general) and other cabinet instruments are promulgated in order to give effect to government decisions requiring the approval of the governor-general and to keep the government informed about its own laws and regulations. In effect, the PCO ensures the efficient organiza-

tion and flow of information in a complex governmental system.

In all parliamentary democracies government is based on the responsibilities of ministers and their relationship to the crown (state) and to Parliament. In their constitutional capacity as advisors to the crown, ministers need an special administrative body to assist them in the conduct of government. The PCO is the general public service department to the cabinet.

JAMES J. GUY

BIBLIOGRAPHY

Campbell, Colin and George Szablowski, 1979. *The Super-Bureaucrats: Structure and Behavior in Central Agencies.* Toronto: Macmillan.
Doerr, Audrey, 1981. *The Machinery of Government in Canada.* Toronto: Metheun.
Privy Council, 1995. *The Privy Council Office.* Ottawa: PCO.
Robertson, Gordon, 1971. "The Changing Role of the Privy Council Office." *Canadian Public Administration* (Winter) 487–508.

PROCUREMENT. The acquisition of goods and services needed by government and private organizations to accomplish their goals. There is considerable disagreement regarding the scope and content of this concept and the activities it encompasses. B. J. Reed and John W. Swain (1990) see procurement as but one of three purchasing concerns, the first being the decision of what to buy, the second the specific processes and procedure for purchasing these goods and services, and the third, finding the goods or services the agency requires at the lowest possible cost. Purchasing encompasses all three concerns, while procurement is the narrower application of the specific processes and procedures for buying the goods and services (p. 180). Stephen B. Gordon (1991) also construes procurement as the narrower concept. Purchasing "encompasses the total process of supplying goods and services to user agencies.... (It) includes acquisition as well as the procurement of equipment and supplies" (p. 340). Donald W. Dobler, David N. Burt, and Lamer Lee, Jr. (1990), however, turn the concept around. To them "the procurement concept encompasses a wider range of supply activities than does the purchasing concept," for instance, participation in development of requirements and specifications; administering purchase contracts; and a number of other roles (p. 21). Similarly, Michiel R. Leenders and Harold E. Fearon (1993) conclude that it is purchasing that describes the process of buying and that procurement is a "somewhat broader term (that) includes purchasing" (p. 4).

The broadest conceptualization, however, was by the U.S. Commission of Government Procurement, whose reports in 1967–72 saw procurement as methods of contracting; legal remedies; planning; budgeting; drafting procurement legislation; and many other processes that many observers would construe as purchasing, perhaps, but not procurement. It may be observed that the broader, more encompassing definition of procurement comes from the private sector and the narrower definition comes from the public sector. This may have explanatory value but this correlation is not tested beyond the literature offered here. So where do we stand? What is procurement?

If we are compelled to try to arrive at a conclusive definition where we can say that these processes and procedures are exclusively procurement and those are not, we probably cannot do so. Within the context of this essay, however, the narrow definition of procurement will prevail. This is not an arbitrary conclusion. It simply reflects the observation that the literature that holds for the narrow perspective is directed at the public sector, the perspective of this endeavor, while the broader perspective is generally held by those observing from the perspective of the private sector. And in the end, we might also consider with Leenders and Fearon that the terms are "almost interchangeable" (p. 4). What remains is an attempt to extend and refine our understanding of procurement through examination of selected issues that reflect upon procurement processes and procedures.

Procurement Principles

One guiding principle for procurement is the requirement that government purchases be made by competitive bids, first enacted for the U.S. federal government in the Procurement Act of 1809. The Armed Services Act of 1947 and Public Law 152 of the same year instituted "negotiated procurement." In 1984 the Competition in Contracting Act reinforced the principle of fair and open competition in procurement. These and other principles are expressed and implemented today in purchase of goods and services at both federal and other government levels. Most common, especially at lower levels of government, is the competitive sealed bid in which intention to buy is announced and the bidder wins who bids lowest and meets stipulated specifications for the goods or services. If the principles imbedded within the competitive sealed bid are not attainable, the buyer may choose to use a "competitive sealed proposal," "a negotiated bid," or "noncompetitive negotiation" (Reed and Swain 1990, pp. 188–189). These alternatives might be considered if there is one or just a few bidders or if some specification is not attainable, for instance if the federal government wished to purchase a nuclear submarine.

Principles and Ethics

Adoption of these and other procurement principles is at least in part a response to unethical manipulation of pro-

curement policies and procedures. The media constantly reminds us of abuses at all levels of government, but especially enjoys procurement of preposterously high-priced military equipment such as toilet seats and screwdrivers. Other unethical behavior, not all related to procurement, includes bribes, promise of future employment, privileged "insider" information, and manipulation of bidding procedures and specification criteria, all prohibited through Public Law 100–679, enacted in 1988 and incorporated within the Federal Acquisition Regulation. There are endless other lists of ethical do's and don'ts embodied within codes, legislation, guidelines, and other documents. These include the Model Procurement Code for State and Local Government, 1986 edition, created by the American Bar Association to, among other things, stipulate what is legal and what is ethical in intergovernmental procurement. Most of the codes have common admonishments, but there are differences according to perspectives. A government employee, according to Department of Defense Directive 5500.7, May 6, 1987, besides the restrictions mentioned above on relationships with vendors, is encouraged to uphold the Constitution, to be loyal to government and agency, to expose corruption, and to avoid conflict of interest. From the perspective of the businessowner vending to government, there should be a code of business ethics (overseen and enforced) that would include rotation of buyers to break up overly cozy buyer-vendor relationships and to protect the integrity of the procurement system. Contractors, of course, should not encourage the behavior forbidden elsewhere, that is, they should not offer gifts (bribes), privileged information, or future jobs.

Procurement Constraints

Although not necessarily problems of ethical procurement, there are many other considerations that may influence procurement decisions. Procurement officers, for instance, are urged to "buy American," or to buy products manufactured in prisons. Most federal agencies except the Department of Defense and the National Aeronautics and Space Administration are encouraged to buy from the General Services Administration, which sets standards for purchases and which buys and stores in volume, presumably at lower costs than agencies making procurements individually (Leenders and Fearon 1993, p. 459). At the lower levels of government agencies are often restricted by commitments they have made to purchase certain items or services jointly with other local governments, for instance liability insurance pools. Small businesses also enter into such purchasing agreements. And it is all too common that legislators and their private and public interest group clientele are continuously engaged in pork barrel politics as they pursue procurement decisions favorable to their interests.

Centralized Decisionmaking

Another issue is the location of procurement authority in agencies and governments. Generally the choice is between central and decentralized decisionmaking. Decentralized procurement is conducted by lower ranking managers in the private sector or public program administrators in the public sector. It is argued that decentralized actors are closer to programs and projects and, therefore, know better what is needed, what specifications are required, what quantity, and at what time, with the organization able to rely upon the judgment and competence of the decisionmaker to answer these questions. It is also feared, however, that the decentralized officeholder might be more likely to distort his or her judgment to the benefit of the vendor, there being considerable distance from organization control levels and the program decisionmaker. According to Leenders and Fearon (1993), however, writing from a private sector perspective, "the advantages of centralized purchasing are so great in comparison with decentralized that almost all but the smallest firms are centralized" (p. 35). Among these advantages include standardization through a common supervisor, reduction of duplication, economies of scale, and most of all, the development of expertise that will accrue to a department head or other procurement official. There is very little difference between the public and private sectors. Local governments also strongly prefer centralization, with special emphasis on accountability placed in one person who is guided by detailed regulations and formal procurement methods.

As indicated above, the principles of procurement do not vary much from private to public sectors, although there are differences in emphasis from one perspective to another. It was interesting to note, for instance, that the definition of procurement, described tentatively at the beginning of this paper, was narrow for the public sector authors (Reed and Swain, Gordon) and broad and inclusive for the private sector authors. The primary consequence for public sector officeholders is that occasionally, processes and procedures perceived by the public official as procurement might be perceived as purchasing by the business purchasing manager. This aberration in concepts might be, for the most part, abrogated by the observation by most of this set of authors that the activities of purchasing and procurement are essentially interchangeable.

State and Local Intergovernmental Relations

In 1979 the American Bar Association developed the Model Procurement Code for State and Local Governments and they condensed it in 1982 for use by smaller units of local government (Leenders and Fearon 1993, pp. 556–557), including intergovernmental relations (Article 10) and the issues thus far examined. It is not possible for state, local, and federal governments to avoid interactions with each other. One of the major themes embodied in these relationships is the interventionist thesis. Simply put, through grants, mandates, loans, and other transfer mechanisms, the federal government attaches conditions that require state and local governments to adopt certain procedures and policies in exchange for the transfers. Receipt of grant money, for instance, may be conditional upon the recipient office adhering to affirmative action or federal accounting procedures. State governments have similar relationships with local governments. A considerable amount of literature exists describing the conflictual and cooperative aspect of these relationships. Conflict arises inasmuch as one government entity does not appreciate being directed by another. Federal actors, for instance, feel that if state and local government agencies and private enterprises are going to be in the procuring business, they should adhere to federally approved procuring principles. This was the rationale offered by the American Bar Association subsequent to creation of the Model Procurement Code (Leenders and Fearon 1993, p. 556).

The trend now, however, is toward progressively more local cooperation, particularly in procurement. Gordon (1991) offers four ways local governments cooperate in procurement: "intergovernmental cooperative purchasing; joint administrative (consolidated) purchasing; joint use of facilities; and the interchange of personnel, information, and technical services with other local governments" (p. 351). The crux of these four cooperative procedures is that the governments use the greater strength of their increased numbers, joining forces to obtain lower prices and lower costs. In intergovernmental cooperative procurement two or more governments decide what they want in common, jointly offer bids, and follow other procurement procedures to buy. In shared administrative purchasing, the governmental units share an administrative agency that provides procuring services. Finally, governments can share facilities, information, and staff, possession of which further benefits the procuring processes.

Conclusions

This paper began with a consideration of the scope and content of procurement. The issues selected for discussion should have provided some insight resulting from this endeavor. Procurement is buying. How much more than that may simply be a matter of institutional and personal preferences. Ultimately the activities included in procurement will be executed whether we refer to them as acquisition, procurement, or purchasing. Some observers find no substantive difference, only a matter of semantics. However, it is difficult to ignore the difference in scope between the private and public sectors.

Some final thoughts that may direct the future evolution of procurement are suggested in the literature. Is it the function of procurement actors to attempt to affect public policy? Certainly efficient and effective procurement will produce more efficient and effective policy. But should it be the burden of the procural process to promote social goals such as more energy efficient products and services or to develop the capabilities of minority-owned businesses (Gordon 1991, p. 353)? Should we give our procuring offices and officers more discretion in selecting and applying procuring processes and procedures? What is the appropriate trade-off between control, rules, regulations, and accountability on the one hand, and flexibility, judgment, and innovation on the other? Stephen Kelman in *Procurement and Public Management* (1990) leans strongly toward the latter, arguing that benefits will far outweigh costs of any administrative abuses, and that a little discretion will yield significant improvement in vendor relations and other measures of procurement performance (p. 90). These and other questions are left for the contemplation of the reader.

KENT HIBBELIN

BIBLIOGRAPHY

Dobler, Donald W., David N. Burt and Lamar Lee, Jr., 1990. *Purchasing and Materials Management.* New York: McGraw-Hill.
Gordon, Stephen B., 1991. "Purchasing." In John E. Petersen and Dennis R. Strachota, eds., *Local Government Finance.* Chicago, IL: Government Finance Officers Association, pp. 339–354.
Held, Gilbert, 1991. *The Equipment Acquisition Book: What, When, Where and How to Buy.* New York: Van Nostrand Reinhold.
Kelman, Stephen, 1990. *Procurement and Public Management.* Washington, D.C.: AEI Press.
Leenders, Michiel R. and Harold E. Fearon, 1993. *Purchasing and Materials Management.* 10th ed. Homewood, IL: Irwin.
Reed, B. J. and John W. Swain, 1990. *Public Finance Administration.* Englewood Cliffs, NJ: Prentice Hall.
Stewart, Rodney D. and Ann L. Stewart, 1988. *Managing Millions.* New York: John Wiley & Sons.

PRODUCTIVITY.

The ratio of outputs (work done, products distributed, services rendered) and outcomes (impact achieved) to inputs (labor, capital, materials, space, energy, time, etc.). Productivity improvement represents favorable changes in that ratio. Thus, it is important to recognize the differences between various ratios of improvement.

- *Inputs decline, outputs/outcomes remain constant.* This ratio represents a cutback management situation in which management is forced to respond productively. For example, faced with a cutback in staff, a state mental health facility may reorganize, allowing for the same level of services with more efficient use of remaining staff.

- *Inputs remain constant, outputs/outcomes improve.* Many critics advocate this case. They often expect "quick fixes" based on limited perspectives or critiques by groups external to the agency. For example, they might propose that each social services worker increase applications processed by 25 percent. This might be a reasonable goal, but only in the long run as better management of inputs improves outputs. But still, without the capacity to invest in better management, and to provide adequate services to more applicants, this case is less reasonable than the next.

- *Inputs decline substantially, outputs/outcomes improve substantially.* Some elected officials and private sector critics advocate this scenario. It is, however, almost always based upon unreasonable and naive assumptions, for example that waste is of enormous proportions.

- *Inputs increase moderately, outputs/outcomes improve substantially.* This is a more likely case, as it allows for continued modest investments in improved productive capacity. But in the short run, a true productivity program is more likely to experience temporarily decreasing productivity—constant outputs while inputs increase modestly to allow for improved internal capacities, which will then increase outputs at a later stage. For example, in a state correctional facility investments in training, buildings and equipment may be necessary in year 1 prior to improved correctional services in year 2.

- *Inputs decline substantially, outputs/outcomes decline less rapidly.* Although the output to input ratio is apparently increasing, drastic cutbacks in resources often result in cutbacks in services which fall most heavily on those citizens least likely to have alternatives. In a situation of deep cutbacks a municipal college, for example, may be forced to cut psychological counseling services to students—most of whom are unlikely to be able to purchase such services privately and will therefore be less likely to graduate.

Producing Public Services

Productive management, public and private, has evolved from simple "common sense" in the late nineteenth cen-

FIGURE I. HOW IS PRODUCTIVITY IMPROVED?

1. Same output/outcomes
   - Less input
2. More output/outcomes
   - Same input
3. Much more output/outcomes
   - Much less input
4. Much more output/outcomes
   - More input
5. Less output
   - Much less input

FIGURE II. PRODUCTIVITY IMPROVEMENT: A MULTIFACETED APPROACH

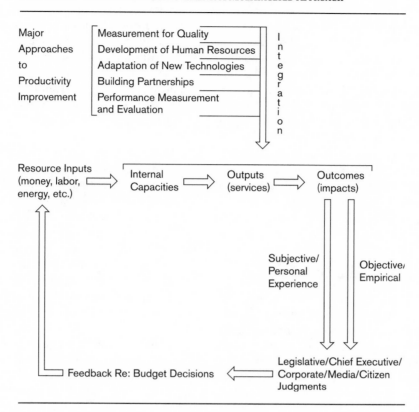

tury to complex systems in the late twentieth century (Holzer 1992). Today, to produce public services, the best public organizations have developed multiple, reinforcing capacities, as summarized in "An Overview of Productivity and Performance" (in Holzer and Gabrielian 1995). Government agencies which have been formally recognized as high achievers, as state-of-the-art:

- apply quality management principles;
- use measurement as a decisionmaking tool;
- work hard to motivate employees;
- adapt new technologies; and
- develop public-private partnerships.

Management for Quality

In government, management improvement programs operate under many labels. The program's name, however, is less important than its substance: comprehensive, quality-oriented productivity improvement in an environment of increasing demands and reduced resources (Poister 1988). Such programs improve performance systematically. Typically, they follow multiple steps:

- Clarifying goals with, and obtaining support from, top management and elected officials;
- Locating models as successful blueprints to modify, and as warnings of potential mistakes;

- Identifying promising areas, such as those functions faced with large backlogs, slipping deadlines, high turnover, or many complaints;
- Building a team through which all interested parties—particularly management, labor and clients—can identify obstacles and suggest improvements;
- Planning a well-managed project, including objectives, tasks, responsibilities, and time frames;
- Measuring progress against financial and service data;
- Modifying project plans based upon continuing discussion of problems, opportunities, and priorities;
- Addressing potential and actual problems, such as misunderstandings, misconceptions, resistance, and slippages;
- Implementing improvement actions on a routine basis, without unnecessarily raising expectations;
- Evaluating and publicizing results.

Although enhanced quality has always been a productive concern, one contemporary approach to public productivity improvement is Total Quality Management, or TQM. The opportunities and problems which we can identify through this lens are not necessarily confined to TQM-type projects, but suggest the subtleties of systemic problem solving in any ambitious management capacity-building project. It is important to recognize that TQM is not a new invention. Rather, it is an innovative repackaging of several decades of public sector productivity improvement, as is evidenced by the *Public Productivity and Management Review* (seventeen volumes and more than five hundred articles from 1975 to 1994), the *Productivity Improvement Handbook for State and Local Government* (Washnis 1980, 1,492 pp.) and the *Public Productivity Handbook* (Holzer 1992, 705 pp.). The TQM movement in government also draws heavily on decades of industrial quality improvement work in the private sector, such as that of Deming and Juran. Although neither "TQM" nor "quality improvement" were terms generally found in the public sector literature as late as 1988, the past several years have witnessed an accelerated improvement and publication movement under this terminology. In many cases, what were formerly "productivity" projects are now redescribed as "quality" efforts.

Performance Measurement and Evaluation

Productivity measurement is not new. Concerns with public sector productivity measurement have been as constant as concerns with high taxes, corruption, or incompetence. Measurement is implicit in questions from all parts of the political spectrum, in discussions among business people and union people, in analyses by reporters and academicians: "Is crime up?" "Are the streets cleaner?" "What benefits will a new building produce?" "Is the air quality better?" "How well are our children doing in school?"

Productivity measurement is continually evolving. A century ago efficient production of outputs was paramount; in the public sector such outputs are normally services. But we have since added concerns as to outcomes or impact–public sector performance–to our measurement agendas.

Managers who are responsible for day-to-day management (Hatry and Fisk 1992) now often have access to information with which to implement public policy, and often use that data to:

■ Make more productive resource allocation decisions, tying spending to problem solving;
■ Hold programs accountable;
■ Match results with plans;
■ Compare agencies or subunits to similar entities or to past levels of achievement;
■ Question the causes for apparent progress or lack thereof;
■ Predict periods of work overload or underload;
■ Evaluate benefit-cost linkages.

Data about inputs, outputs, and outcomes can help defend or expand a program, rather than let it suffer from relatively subjective, political decisions. Measures help answer such questions as: Is an organization doing its job? Is it creating unintended side effects or producing unantici-

pated impacts? Is it responsive to the public? Is it fair to all, or does it favor certain groups, inadvertently or deliberately? Does it keep within its proper bounds of authorized activity? In short, is it productive?

Although multiple measures of public sector services cannot usually be aggregated as productivity "indexes" (analogous to the bottom line of profit in the private sector), it is possible to measure public sector performance given certain guidelines:

1. If service quality is to be maintained or improved, a measurement program must be oriented to effectiveness, rather than just quantity or efficiency.
2. Management's uses of productivity measures are often in the budgeting and fiscal area: estimating resource requirements, justifying budgets, reducing costs, reallocating resources, investing increased resources, and improving benefit-cost linkages.
3. A measurement program, which requires substantial expertise and careful planning, should ask and begin to answer the following questions:

■ In terms of program performance: How much of a service is provided? How efficiently are resources used? How effectively is a service provided?
■ In terms of effectiveness indicators for performance: What is the intended purpose of the service? What are the unintended impacts of the service? How effective is the service in prevention of problems before they arise? Is the service adequate? Is the service accessible? Are clients satisfied with services? Are services distributed equitably? Is a product durable? To what extent is a service provided to clients with dignity?
■ In terms of desirable characteristics of performance measures: Is a service significant? Is the service appropriate to the problem being addressed? Is performance quantifiable? Are services readily available? Are services delivered in a timely manner? Are services delivered in a relatively straightforward manner? Is a measure of performance valid? Is a measure acceptable? Is performance measured completely? Are measures accurate? Are measures reliable?
■ In terms of management's uses of productivity measures, are measures used to help: Set goals? Estimate resource requirements? Develop budget justifications? Reduce costs? Develop organization improvement strategies? Control operations? Reallocate resources? Hold individuals or organizational units accountable? Motivate employees to improve performance? Compare agencies or subunits to similar entities or to past levels of achievement? Predict periods of work overload or underload? Link increased resources to policy outcomes

or to systemwide problems? Improve benefit-cost linkages? Develop more sophisticated capacities for measurement?

- In terms of data collection: Are existing records analyzed? Are clients surveyed? Are taxpayers surveyed? Are services rated by professional or trained observers? Are special data collection techniques utilized?
- In terms of the analysis of productivity data: Are before versus after comparisons made? Are measures displayed in a time series? Are comparisons made with other areas, jurisdictions, or client groups? Are comparisons made with targets?

Development of Human Resources: Motivating Employees

Turn-of-the century scientific management assumed that in exchange for a fair day's pay someone competent could always be found to fill any vacant slot in the organization, to complete any task. Money would be a sufficient motivator; personality, individuality, and social interests were irrelevant to job performance.

But research in private firms and public agencies made it clear that such assumptions were not valid: People remained individuals, even in the workplace, and were affected and moved by many forces, of which money was only one. As individuals, they could be "turned on" or "turned off" by their organizational roles, depending on what the situation offered them psychologically, and whether the organization treated them as mature, vibrant adults or as lazy, dependent drones. Managers began to realize that people tend to join social groups on the job, and these groups develop production-oriented norms of their own to which the individual is expected to adhere. Human behavior, therefore, reflects not only organizational, but personal and group, pressures. A productive organization is humane, structured around not only the task but its members and their human needs. The art of leadership inheres in getting people to work well for the organization by understanding and responding to their needs—by motivating them. Guy (1992), for example, points out that many interdependent factors contribute to creating a productive work environment: organizational culture, team-building that maximizes the strengths of employees while compensating for their weaknesses, open communication channels, flexibility in the midst of predictability, and balancing of the needs of the organization with the needs of employees.

Government's most extensive and expensive investments are people—most public organizations devote from 50 to 85 percent of their budgets to employee salaries and benefits. Because those "human resources" have complicated needs, the most progressive public organizations have adopted enlightened human resource practices, rejecting an authoritarian, bureaucratic style. Typically, they:

- Recognize that motivation requires management of many, interrelated elements. Ban, Faerman, and Riccucci (1992) hold that to achieve their goals, public organizations need to take an integrated approach to personnel management, linking workforce planning, recruitment, hiring, training, and other personnel policies. Building and maintaining a productive work force includes: (1) developing a formal work force plan; (2) actively recruiting job applicants; (3) redesigning tests or developing creative alternatives to written tests; (4) linking training and development activities to organizational mission; and (5) revising personnel policies to meet the needs of employees.
- Understand that money can be an important motivator, but is not the only motivational option. A sense of being able to make a difference in the organization is more important to the job satisfaction of public sector managers than to that of private managers (Balfour and Wechsler 1991).
- Carefully apply performance appraisal systems. Daly (1992) points out that productivity is a function of motivation, and motivation—extrinsic or intrinsic—is itself a function of the recognition of an individual's work effort. Such recognition can come from a well-conceived and well-managed system of performance appraisal.

Adaptation of New Technologies

Advanced technologies are as important to the public as to the private sectors, and the public sector has often pioneered new systems. Government employees have invented lasers, solid state technology, the basic design of most commercial and military aircraft, instrument landing systems, the first modern computer, titanium (and other stronger and lighter materials), the CAT scan, plastic corneas, advanced fishing nets, nuclear power, Teflon, wash and wear fabric, resuscitation devices and plastic wrap (Public Employees Roundtable, 1990). Public Technology, Inc. is devoted to the development and diffusion of productive technologies for the public sector. NASA has a continuing program to help the private sector exploit innovations resulting from the space program.

Technology is not limited to computer applications. In as mundane an area as refuse collection, for example, departments of sanitation in New York City, Scottsdale, Arizona, and other localities have developed and applied technological changes:

- Trucks designed specifically for operation by two people, rather than the traditional three-person team.
- Remote-control arms which allow the driver to lift and empty large containers of refuse.
- Robotic truck painters, which a management-labor team approached the private sector to design.

- Tire-changing machines designed specifically to the agency's standards and intended to alleviate the high degree of manual work in the operation.
- Purchase of "high dump" street cleaning brooms, which are faster, safer and can dump refuse into another vehicle.
- Comparison testing of refuse collection equipment from different manufacturers.
- Redesign of the equipment used to transport refuse from barges to landfills.

Partnerships: Multiple Tenets of Cooperation

Privatization has gained momentum. Touted regularly by politicians and emphasized by the media, it may now be the most popular argument for public sector productivity improvement. Their logic is that contracting out or turning over services to the private sector produces large savings with virtually no loss of quality or reduction in service levels (Savas 1992). Thus, advocates hold that outsourcing or privatization can deliver a much greater portion of services which are now public. But skeptics hold that many services are necessarily government's responsibility, and that a public to private shift will not automatically enhance productivity in a jurisdiction or department (Barnekov and Raffel 1992). A recurring theme in the privatization literature is that what makes a difference is competition, not the fact of privatization by itself, and that private monopolies are no better than the public ones. Thus, privatization is productive as long as it assumes competition.

While competition is certainly important, cooperation is also an essential productivity enhancement strategy that is very often overlooked. Cooperative arrangements of service provision today may be a more accurate characterization of emerging day-to-day relationships. Joint public-private initiatives are options to which innovative public officials often turn. Rather than privatizing, raising taxes, or soliciting donations for visible projects (i.e., tax supplements), these new relationships are joint problem-solving efforts which may be initiated by either "side." Cooperation between labor and management, different public agencies, neighboring local governments, government and voluntary organizations, executive and legislative branch, or governmental entities of different levels have proven to be effective arrangements aimed at improving government service and cutting costs. The ability to think and act outside the rigid but familiar "bureaucratic box" can be essential for pooling resources and improving productivity in an increasingly resource-scarce atmosphere.

Different forms of partnerships may enhance productivity improvements in public organizations. In the New York City Transit Authority an independent labor-management consulting institute facilitated solutions to problems that government agencies and labor unions faced. The case

of the Small Business Administration and the Service Corps of Retired Executives demonstrates a coproduction model that has proven effective in the link between a federal agency and a group of citizen-volunteers. Cooperation between the Delaware Public Administration Institute and the state legislature showed how all sides benefited from such cooperation; for public administrators it resulted in vastly improved knowledge of the legislative environment, and for the legislature it resulted in greater professionalism of their work.

Conclusion

The most innovative and productive public agencies do not simply execute one good program. Rather, they integrate advanced management techniques into a comprehensive approach to productivity improvement. They institutionalize productivity improvements by identifying, implementing, measuring, and rewarding major cost savings and performance enhancements in their agency. They benchmark their efforts against similar organizations across the nation. They have a client orientation. Perhaps most important, productive programs are built on the dedication, imagination, teamwork, and diligence of public servants.

MARC HOLZER

BIBLIOGRAPHY

Balfour, Danny L. and Barton Wechsler, 1991. "Commitment, Performance, and Productivity in Public Organizations." *Public Productivity and Management Review*, 15 (1): 355–368.

Ban, Carolyn, Sue R. Faerman and Norma M. Riccucci, 1992. "Productivity and the Personnel Process." In Marc Holzer, ed., *Public Productivity Handbook*. New York: Marcel Dekker, Inc., pp. 401–423.

Barnecov, Timothy K. and Jeffrey A. Raffel, 1992. "Public Management of Privatization." In Marc Holzer, ed., *Public Productivity Handbook*. New York: Marcel Dekker, Inc., pp. 99–115.

Daly, Dennis M., 1992. "Pay for Performance, Performance Appraisal, and Total Quality Management." *Public Productivity and Management Review*, 16:2 (Fall) 39–52.

Epstein, Paul and Alan Leidner, 1990. "Productivity Forum for Computer Technology." *Public Productivity and Management Review*, 14:2 (Winter) 211–220.

Guy, Mary E., 1992. "Productive Work Environment." In Marc Holzer, ed., *Public Productivity Handbook*. New York: Marcel Dekker, Inc., pp. 321–335.

Hatry, Harry P. and Donald M. Fisk, 1992. "Measuring Productivity in the Public Sector." In Marc Holzer, ed., *Public Productivity Handbook*. New York: Marcel Dekker, Inc., pp. 139–160.

Holzer, Marc, ed., 1992. *Public Productivity Handbook*. New York: Marcel Dekker, Inc.

Holzer, Marc and Vatche Gabrielian, eds., 1995. *Case Studies in Productive Public Management: Capacity Building in Government*. Burke, VA: Chatelain Press.

Hyde, Albert C., 1992. "Implications of Total Quality Management for the Public Sector." *Public Productivity and Management Review*, 16:1 (Fall) 23–24. Also see Hyde,

"The Proverbs of Total Quality Management,"
pp. 25–38.

Keehley, Pat and Steve Medlin, 1991. "Productivity Enhancements Through Quality Innovations." *Public Productivity and Management Review,* 15(2): 217–228.

LOGIN (Local Government Information Network). St. Paul, Minnesota: The Norris Institute.

Milakovich, Michael E., 1996. "Total Quality Management for Public Service Productivity Improvement." In Marc Holzer, ed., *Public Productivity Handbook.* New York: Marcel Dekker, Inc., pp. 577–602.

Mizaur, Donald, 1992. Unpublished paper presented to the Fifth National Conference on Public Sector Productivity in Newark, New Jersey. Charlottesville, Virginia, Federal Quality Institute.

Poister, Theodore H., ed., 1988. "Success Stories in Revitalizing Public Agencies." *Public Productivity Review,* 11:3 (Spring) 27–104.

Public Employees Roundtable, 1990. "Unsung Heroes" (newsletter 1987–1990) and brochures. Washington, D.C.

Public Productivity and Management Review. Thousand Oaks, CA: Sage Publications, Inc. Quarterly.

Savas, E. S., 1992. "Privatization and Productivity." In Marc Holzer, ed., *Public Productivity Handbook.* New York: Marcel Dekker, Inc., pp. 79–98.

Taylor, Paul W., 1991. "Working with Quality at the New York State Department of Transportation." *Public Productivity and Management Review,* 15:2 (Winter) 205–212.

Washnis, George J., ed., 1980. *Productivity Improvement Handbook for State and Local Government.* New York: John Wiley and Sons.

PRODUCTIVITY POLITICS. The political constraints that shape productivity program options and choices.

State and local governments must operate today in an environment of scarcity. The scarcity may be real or only perceived. But even the perception is very real in its political consequence—a "cutback" environment. This environment is marked by an inadequacy of resources, whether due to revenue scarcity or shortfalls precipitated by indecision between conflicting public policies. Clearly, it is related to the nature of our economy today: inflation, recession, unemployment, fluctuating credit markets, and general economic uncertainty. All these produce problems with which governments must deal. Yet at the same time they reduce government revenues as well as erode the value of each available dollar. Fiscal constraints often prevent investments that are needed to make real productivity gains. The same constraints aggravate the very conditions for which investment was needed in the first place. Thus, capital expenditures are delayed; infrastructures deteriorate as maintenance is deferred; facilities and equipment cannot be repaired but must be replaced; new facilities to meet changed conditions cannot be purchased or even planned for; and workforce strains mount as greater demands are made upon employees who are denied the means to meet those demands more efficiently and with greater effectiveness.

In addition to the problems listed above, the environment of scarcity leads to the public's diminishing belief in their government's efficacy. This is especially so in those states and cities suffering from the heaviest fiscal constraint burdens, and where geographic location, aging characteristics, and demographic conditions place the heaviest demands. The negative attitudes reveal grave doubts about the instrumental value of government in solving society's problems and delivering those services traditionally associated with our state and local governments. Here we face the terrifying prospect of a democratic polity losing its faith in government as a means of serving society's needs and contributing to the achievement of its highest aspirations.

Just as resource scarcity makes it increasingly difficult for governments to be perceived as productive, lack of confidence may contribute to the fiscal constraints we now experience. Doubts of efficacy can translate into taxpayer resistance, which makes it harder to obtain political support for the long-term commitments needed for improvement. The perceived failures of governments to deliver adequate services and effectively achieve program goals are lightly ascribed to an inefficient, lazy, and uncaring workforce. Whether or not such perceptions are well founded, the blame heaped upon the workforce results in a loss of dignity, contributes to the development of uncaring attitudes, makes for lowered morale, and is generally destructive of the quality of working life.

Lack of confidence, however, has not led the public to conclude that governments should withdraw from attempts at problem solving or stop delivering the services expected of them. Rather, as one British observer has aptly remarked, "Americans are asking more and more of a government they trust less and less." While we may be in the midst of changes that will result in modified assignments for our various units of government (and while there may be a reapportioning of responsibilities among public, private, and third sector agencies), the basic problems will not go away. The services contributing to the maintenance of our society will remain pertinent to the missions and activities of state and local governments.

Productivity issues are at the eye of this storm. The viability of the democratic political system and the rebuilding of faith in the worth of "public service" are at stake—without the latter, the former is indeed at peril! The value and utility of government seems genuine, but the need for what governments do and the demands for what they should do remain. We have to do more, then, with less. It is necessary that there be an economy of program choices. Once selected for implementation, programs must be demonstrably and understandably effective. The means of overcoming the difficulties caused by scarcity and negative attitude might very well be the productivity enhancement route. Going this way, however, requires an understanding that the efforts demand a long-term commitment, the overcoming of political constraints, and changes in the political behavior of various actors. The challenge is to restore the integrity of public service in the eyes and minds of public servants and those they serve. This is tantamount to rebuilding faith in political action as a means of seeking redress. Our nation's history is replete with instances of remarkable responses by the political system to severe crises. Indeed, it sometimes seems that only under crisis are issues and needs sharply defined.

At this moment it is clear that state and local governments must acquire the capabilities to accomplish more with less. A shift in responsibilities among the several governmental levels with regard to various programs is occurring or will occur, and this might well entail some hard political decisions about resource reallocations or total elimination of some programs. There must be an intensified concern for managerial competence at the state and local levels. Just as important is the necessity to broaden participation by the workforce in productivity decisions.

Conceptual Framework

To pursue these goals, certain political constraints will have to be recognized and overcome. The framework that follows will indicate what the political climate needs to be and will examine a critical set of factors that affect and are affected by this political context. This conceptual framework is erected on four major elements. Their interrelationships constitute the forces that mold and determine the politics of productivity. These are: key assumption factors, reward factors, external factors, and structural factors.

Key Assumption Factors

Key assumptions seem to dominate the political atmosphere and to color the premises or expectations surrounding productivity programs. These include the following: productivity improvement is simply a matter of "jacking up the workforce," that is, low productivity is mainly a matter of an elevated workforce input; there are private sector models for productivity improvements that have only to be transferred to the public sector; if governments were more businesslike, the private sector "successes" would automatically reveal themselves in the conduct of the government's business; because organizational change is merely a matter of rationality, policy decision or directive will automatically elicit desired behaviors.

Reward Factors

Rewards involve a mix of elements. In order for public sector productivity improvement to occur, cooperation must be obtained from an array of "actors"–legislators, elected and appointed officials, managers, technical experts, workers, and often client and other interest groups as well. That cooperation does not arise spontaneously. Quite the contrary, the improvement of bureaucratic efficiency and effectiveness inevitably imposes some kind of organizational change. Work routines, organizational structure, task technology, labor agreements, managerial styles–these and any number of other organizational characteristics become possible targets for modification. While change may be essential, it is also true that resistance to change is inevitable. Whether viewed as inertia or homeostasis, such resistance appears built-in and natural. As various theorists have argued, change will actually take place only when the forces operating in favor of it are stronger than the forces opposing it. To stimulate the necessary initiatives and to overcome the inevitable resistance to productivity improvement efforts, it is necessary that there be provided quid pro quo–some reward.

Reward factors involve, then, the difficult matter of incentives. Given the prevalent assumptions about productivity gains through increased worker inputs and the prevailing climate of citizen alienation vis-à-vis their governments, incentive rewards (whether monetary or through other forms of recognition) are often viewed as sheer cost items to be avoided. Yet, incentive rewards are key elements if productivity improvement programs are to be successful.

The vital role of public sector unions in the design and implementation of these efforts is crucial. To ensure the viability and continuity of such cooperation, the costs to the unions and their leadership for the risks assumed must be offset–though the reward may be nothing more than a moratorium on officials blaming the workforce for lack of productivity gains. For unions to be effective role participants in a public administration system marked by bilateralism, they must be able to convince their followership that there are visible and real payoffs for them. Investments in new promotion and career lines, job protection, security against giveback demands, and other such items are the kind of rewards a union must win if its followership is to be maintained. Contracting out may appear attractive as a money-saving approach and may also be politically supportable, but eschewing a contracting-out option in given situations may bring greater returns over the long haul. Unions may cooperate in gaining membership support for work rule changes or in designing and operating more meaningful performance appraisal systems.

External Factors

External factors refer to those forces and events that lie outside the formal political system but impinge upon it by thrusting issues and problems into the political arena. They alter the priorities of a system's agenda. The dynamics that flow from them force consideration of system (structural factor) changes. This usually happens where built-in system inertia offers resistance to the changes the external factors demand. The forces generated by economic conditions, demography, and energy scarcities are all examples.

Structural Factors

Structural factors are those system or process features that stand as constraints or obstacles to the launching and long-term support of productivity improvement programs. Examples of these are: the high turnover rate among elected officials; budgetary processes that emphasize short-term appropriations over the multiyear budgeting that is essential to plan and implement productivity projects; and the impact of single-issue interest groups on the party system and policy formulation processes.

The Impingements of Constituency Pressures

One of the key problems to be faced is how to resist political pressures to do everything at once, in all agencies, across all functional areas. This is particularly so now because of the special nature of the political environment. These pressures illustrate the way in which external factors interact with internal elements to produce a perverse effect. They undermine politically desired structures while destroying the potential for long-term political successes.

The nature of the system makes it extremely difficult for legislators and other elected officials to eliminate or severely reduce programs that should, by objective criteria, be the logical candidates for such actions. While overall confidence in government's efficacy may have waned, the decline in program and service demands is not necessarily proportional. At the least, it is not in "sync" with such a curve. The very nature of special interest concerns, the kinds of resources that back them up, the needs of state governments' subjurisdictions, and the relationship of these to the tactics of getting reelected serve to make such decisions difficult.

When resource constraints must be faced, the cry for elimination of waste and the search for efficiency in managerial capacity escalates. Support for productivity programs becomes popular, and the rush is on to ensure that more is done with less. Productivity programs are mounted in every agency, at the same time and with the same degree of expectation attached to each. If we have learned anything, however, it is that this approach is the prescription for failure. Rather, a pilot operation with testing for transferability represents a sounder approach. Within such pilots, measurement systems and instrumentalities must be devised. Participative management—a requirement for a successful effort—must be built slowly, one step at a time. An accompanying decentralization approach requires organizational restructuring, which includes participative roles for both labor and management.

The security and tenure of elected officials is in large measure dependent upon their abilities and styles to satisfy the interests of various constituencies. Given the political climate, such officials are keenly threatened by the confidence crisis. They seek to demonstrate to their different publics that they are exerting every effort to ensure that programs and services of special concern will not be reduced severely or eliminated. They urge large-scale productivity programs and force heavy demands on public managers to show short-term efficiency gains in their respective functional or agency areas. While in some degree such results might be obtained, more often than not these efficiencies will be achieved at an effectiveness cost to the very programs the public officials wanted to protect. This is self-defeating. Reduced or distorted effectiveness serves to exacerbate citizen alienation toward government and their elected representatives; it aggravates their negative attitudes with regard to governmental efficacy. Thus, political dynamics result in pressures to attempt too much at one time, an overcommitment to productivity efforts, and a sacrifice of the long-term gains that might have been possible otherwise. The likely result is to strain rather than structurally reinforce state and local government political systems.

Implementation Process Problems

The process of implementing a productivity improvement project involves, among other things, the emergence of a leader, the acquisition of resources, the performance of systematic analyses, the identification of targets and goals, and the identification of the means (e.g., technology change, work operations redesign, and change in labor-management relations). For the public sector organization, these elements take shape within parameters laid down by the structure and function of the political system.

Concerning the question of leadership, the relationship between the rewards system and the political system is clear. The leader/initiator role involves the risks of entrepreneurship. It will be undertaken only when the risks appear reasonably manageable and when the expected rewards make the effort and the gamble worthwhile. Given today's environment in which productivity is becoming a significant value, the person who leads a productivity project to success should be (other things being equal) in line for advancement and other forms of recognition.

Most productivity improvement efforts take considerable time to reach fruition and to yield visible benefits. Even the introduction of dramatic new technology, such as the computer, requires time-consuming groundwork with budget providers, line and staff workers, managers, and users, as well as time for easing the system in and awaiting the results. Other productivity measures take even longer; many take years and years. Compared to such time frames, the political term appears short. Elected officials who sponsor such efforts, or the appointed bureaucrats who lead them, are likely to find that tension has been generated but that relief is not provided in time to serve the re-election or reappointment candidacy. There is no reward.

The acquisition of monetary and other resources is subject to the same difficulties. Legislators are understandably disinclined to be held accountable for expenditures when the benefits of the spending will accrue to their successors. Elected officials dependent upon electoral support for survival are less attracted to program promises that constituents will see fulfilled in the distant future. They are not inclined to support productivity improvement decisions involving any serious program cuts when those decisions thwart immediate constituent satisfactions. These considerations may negate all but short-range solutions and superficial improvements.

Productivity improvement requires the services of staff analysts. Most bureaucrats lack training in sampling, measurement, data analysis, and judgment of the strengths and limitations of the conclusions drawn from data. Systematic analysis of organizational operations provides baseline productivity information, against which subsequent improvement can be measured. It provides insight into potentials for productivity improvement by identifying bottlenecks, idle time, error rates, and other indicators of wasteful or ineffective operations. Analytical staff may be attached to an executive office, or analysts may be deployed throughout the various agencies of a jurisdiction. In any case, their work will have meaning only if they are supported by people with clout. Like staff workers everywhere, they have only their expertise with which to exert influence. Practicing analysts quickly learn which agencies or departments are "protected" and therefore not to be evaluated. They are constantly faced with the problem that others will put their findings to use in inappropriate ways—perhaps punitively or perhaps by extending them beyond the limitations within which they are valid. Treading the line between professionalism and practical relevance is a continuous challenge. In public sector organizations, the number and variety of interested parties is often effectively inhibited and neutralized. Accordingly, the impact of productivity programs suffers to the extent that the findings are partial or trivial.

Bilateralism and the Roles of Labor and Management

The role of labor, especially a unionized workforce, is significant in attaining productivity goals. This is particularly so in those jurisdictions where: labor-management relations proceed under comprehensive legislation guaranteeing the right of workers to be represented by unions of their own choosing; the parties have achieved experience and maturity in collective bargaining; and the unions have developed the organizational capacity for effective representation in all phases of contract administration and implementation. The last category includes the unusual communications network that provides a constant inflow of information regarding day-to-day functioning of substantive programs and service activities from all worksite locations. This communications capability is system comprehensive; inherent in its mix of formal and informal elements is the capacity for easy adjustment as organizational ecology changes.

It is this apparatus, plus the loyalty that a competent, service-oriented union gets from its members and the influence it can then exert over their behavior, that allows it to be influential throughout the whole sphere of government operations. Public sector unions that have developed to this extent are significant in a system exhibiting bilateral characteristics. The union becomes the repository of a vast and significant amount of information. This operational information storehouse, when drawn upon through formal sets of relations or informal information exchanges (functioning at the chief executive, agency head, and all managerial levels down to first-line supervisors) can substantially contribute to organizational conflict resolution, generate productivity ideas, and enhance managerial efficacy. It is a process that works best when competent union leadership and professional staff are matched with strong and competent managerial personnel.

Bilateralism connotes system change through structured means. It recognizes the mutual benefits to be gained by management and organized labor through regular information exchange. It is key to achieving planned organization change that productivity objectives in most instances require. The unique knowledgeability garnered by the union should be tapped on a regular basis in a systematic fashion. If it is, then it must be recognized that the workforce, as personified by its unions, is sharing in decisionmaking.

When labor relations in a unionized environment have reached this developmental stage, another vital element emerges. For at this point the unions represent continuity in a system that, in other parts, is marred by substantial discontinuities. Their collective knowledgeability and influence over the workforce is sustained over time and through the parade of incoming and outgoing administrations. The unions constitute an element of stability that can be a counterforce to the instability resulting from high turnover rates of commissioners and department heads.

The maintenance of equilibrium as policy shifts and organizational changes occur depends on knowing how workers will be affected by or will react to the proposed changes. It also depends on knowing before the change is put into motion whether or not it is feasible or desirable. Unions have real needs to be consulted in advance before programs are added or changed by legislative mandate, or before major organizational modifications are ordered by administrators. If the union as an organizational entity is properly viewed as an integral part of the political and administrative system, then it, too, is affected by a system change. Thus, concern for maintaining its organizational equilibrium has to be taken into account if overall stability is not to be seriously undermined.

Consultation and genuine participation with the unions in making decisions that involve system change is a necessity. This has to be recognized and understood by the elected public officials in all categories of public management. Union-management cooperation is at the heart of productivity improvement activities, and is a crucial aspect of what we know today as participative management. The opportunity for participation is, of course, one of the reward factors that must be built into productivity programs. That there is a growing recognition of the need for labor involvement is seen by the increasing prominence of joint labor-management productivity committees in many state and local government jurisdictions. These committees have comprehensive projects under way already.

This presentation does not review in depth the many ways such joint labor-management productivity committees are functioning in the productivity arena. Suffice it to say that despite some unanswered questions as to their genesis, accomplishments, and viability, there is growing support for them as the desirable means of securing labor-management cooperation in productivity endeavors. They are increasingly the vehicle for energizing and catalyzing productivity improvement programs. Our contention is that such institutionalized forms of cooperative participation (through negotiated collective bargaining agreements within the context of a mature labor relations environment) augur well for a greater chance of success.

This change in the labor relations environment can affect our previously held notions about so-called productivity bargaining. What can best come out of collective bargaining are not the presumable productivity gains that might flow from so-called "givebacks" or particular changes in work rules, work designs, and job descriptions; rather, what can be achieved is a *process* through which productivity improvement efforts can be developed and effective methods for their implementation achieved. While it is not the whole of the productivity process, a collective bargaining agreement to establish joint labor-management productivity committees (including provisions for financial and staffing resources to support their activities) can result in a firm foundation on which to build such a process.

In addition to establishing a productivity process, joint labor-management committees also modify the traditional view of labor relations as being essentially adversarial. This does not mean that their posture as adversaries will or should disappear totally. A committee can add, however, to the conduct of labor-management relations; new agreed-upon rules of the game can be initiated as to how the parties will relate to each other in a mutually beneficial, cooperative venture. New forums can be instituted where continuing negotiations over a specific problem-solving effort will occur. These joint committees cannot and should not sit as authoritative bodies for modifying or overriding previously negotiated contracts. They can, however, bring about agreements that will supplement or provide feedback into the labor-management relations process. This kind of input will influence the character and tone of the negotiations at the next round of bargaining.

The outcome of productivity improvement efforts will contribute to a next-stage maturation of labor-management relations. Such a maturation must occur if the unions are to continue as viable service-rendering agencies for those they represent—especially in view of other external factors that loom in their future. Role and behavior modifications must also occur for the managers, legislators, and other elected political influentials who are actors in the process. This is so because of the impact that these same external factors will present.

Demographic and Value Changes in the Workforce

The external factors just alluded to are already discernible from available data. They have to do with changes in individual or societal values and the projected sociodemographic profile of the public workforce. They are influential in regard to the quality of worklife issues that are intimately related to productivity improvement endeavors. They require responsible political and managerial leadership to reconsider perceptions about the desires and expectations of the public workforce. Furthermore, they introduce elements of instability into public sector labor organizations that will intensify demands on the unions to win additional work environment and work purpose decisions. At the same time the unions will feel public pressure to act more sensitively with respect to the prevalent productivity improvement forces.

The sociodemographic profile of the public workforce in the decades ahead is already visible. From blue collar through white collar occupational categories, it will be a more educated, though not necessarily more experienced, labor population. It will contain even more women than at present; more of the working women will be co-heads of households with children; more of the women will be moving into more technically demanding jobs and into the upper level of managerial and executive positions. At the same time that the 25–45 age group (the most productive and demanding years of the baby boom generation) predominates in the workforce, there will be an older group remaining beyond the traditional retirement age. The younger people who gain entry into the public workforce will reflect even more profound attitudes with respect to "opportunity and power" values. And minorities will continue in their demands for larger shares of public service employment opportunities.

The implications of these projections are of dynamic import. Substantive segments of the workforce are more restless, more demanding of rights and opportunities, and increasingly alienated from the public services of which they are a part. This stems from perceptions that their education and training are inadequately valued, that their talents are not used as they could be, that older and less qualified personnel stand in their way of advancement and recognition, and that existing managerial styles are at odds with their aspirations for participation and recognition. The increasing number and the future composition of women in the workforce will require greater attention to alternative work weeks, flex-time, part-time work, work-sharing opportunities, and on-site child care facilities.

The unions will also have to respond more intensively to the kinds of representation this changed constituency of theirs will demand—both in internal organization and position postures. It is important that they seize the opportunities being offered by the productivity improvement environment and the emergence of joint labor-management committees. These give unions a chance to gain a greater slice of the opportunity and power pies while making a real contribution to productivity improvement.

Management will have to recognize the reality of these developments and adjust to the same external environment factors. Elected public executives and top-level career managers must learn to be fully appreciative of the need for participative management styles. They will have to adjust quickly to the new labor-management relations climate. Greater attentions will have to be paid to career advancement lines and expanded training opportunities. They will also have to develop a better honed capacity for communicating needs and the change processes to political actors—especially executives and managers, who hold the keys to fashioning reward systems that allow for adequate managerial responses to the changing values and nature of the workforce.

Conclusion

If enhancement of public sector productivity improvement is to become a reality, all the political actors must participate and share in the learning process that must inevitably occur. That the learning curve will not respond easily is apparent from the kinds of structural constraints and inertias already discussed. What can be hoped for is that the existing crisis, with the threats to political office security it stimulates, and impacts from astute managers, knowledgeable labor leaders, and an aroused public, will generate dialogue and focus attention on the matter. Perhaps, then, an exponential boost of the learning curve will result.

Though we have proclaimed productivity of critical importance on our public agenda, it is not a new issue. It has been and will remain central to the continued advancement of the art and science of public administration. If the current focus on public sector productivity has taught us anything, it is how far that advancement must yet travel: how little we know of managing people so as to stimulate a heightened awareness of their individual and collective efforts for the well-being of a democratic polity. This observation further emphasizes the intimacy of the relationship between public administration and the study of politics and political life. It indicates what public administration can contribute to the quality of life in a democratic society.

SEYMOUR Z. MANN

PRODUCTIVITY SAVINGS. The direct and indirect benefits derived from implementing a productivity improvement plan.

Within a framework of scarce resources and the desire for smaller, more efficient governments, the productivity of public sector agencies and programs has taken on greater political, economic, and social significance. Government is expected to do more with less and make optimal use of diminishing public resources. The public expects government to provide quality services, while at the same time they want to pay less for these services. Successfully designed and implemented productivity improvement programs will enable governments to make the best use of scarce human and material resources, which will ultimately result in productivity savings.

Productivity improvement programs focus on both the efficient use of government resources and the effectiveness of the programs and policies implemented by government. Public sector productivity efforts that are well designed and effectively administered will result in win-win relationships. Employees will benefit through a more equitable distribution of workloads, greater input, better informed decisions, more challenging work, and a better understanding of expectancies. Executives and managers will benefit from a more motivated, informed, and focused workforce. Elected officials will benefit from a more efficient and effective workforce, which is what the public expects and is what gets elected officials reelected. Clients will benefit from improved services, less "red tape," and fewer frustrations associated with dealing with government. And, ultimately, the public will benefit from a more efficient use of tax dollars (Holzer 1992, p. 11).

Productivity Measurement

The effective measurement of the relationship of service delivery outputs and outcomes to inputs, such as time, labor, and capital, is necessary in order to assess and identify productivity savings. The traditional definition of productivity is the ratio amount of output to the ratio amount of input. The Bureau of Labor Statistics, recognizing the broader impact of public sector services, defines productivity measurement as those measures that relate inputs to final products, not just outputs. Within this framework, productivity savings, in the most basic sense, would be a reduction in the ratio amount of inputs as compared to the ratio amount of outputs and final products.

However, calculating productivity savings is more complex than that. Productivity is more than efficiency (the ratio of outputs to inputs); it also encompasses effectiveness—how does the output satisfy agency or program objectives? According to the Office of Personnel Management, productivity is not only "doing things right," it is also "doing the right things." Productivity not only encompasses what level of service is provided at what cost, but also quality, timeliness, and responsiveness. For example, processing 20 percent more driver license applications per clerk is not productive if the number of errors doubles, or if the computer system cannot handle the increased demand.

In recognition of the effectiveness factor, OPM defines productivity as: (a) increasing efficiency, (b) increasing the usefulness and effectiveness of governmental services or products, (c) increasing the responsiveness of services to public need, (d) decreasing the cost of services, and (e) decreasing the time required to provide the services.

Direct Benefits

The benefits of a well-implemented productivity improvement program can result in monetary savings. Operating costs will decrease, and productivity savings will be realized, as employees learn to work smarter, or more efficiently. Outputs can be increased without adding any new staff. Operating costs will also decrease as the number of employees required to perform a specific function is reduced. A reduction in the equipment or overhead necessary to complete a job will also result in monetary savings. For example, if one sanitation work crew of four men and one truck can collect the same amount of trash as two work crews utilizing two sanitation trucks to collect refuse, a municipality will save a substantial amount of money. Not only are personnel costs reduced, but, in addition to needing fewer trucks, the costs associated with gas, oil, insurance, and maintenance of a second truck are eliminated.

Monetary savings can often be achieved through the use of technology. The up front costs can be high, but the long-term savings provide a substantial return on the initial investment. The savings are often realized through a reduction in the number of employees. Since personnel costs, on average, consume 80 percent of an agency's budget, most monetary savings achieved are usually the result

of a decrease in personnel expenditures. Increased efficiency, created through technological advances, also increases productivity savings.

The Oregon Vendor Information Program (VIP), the first automated bid access system in the country, is a successful example of technology-related productivity savings. VIP replaced 50 years of public purchasing protocol, encumbered with a labor-intensive, cost-prohibitive paper bid distribution system. A productivity savings of $144,000 was realized in the first year through the elimination of postage costs. Vendors now use modem-equipped personal computers, or those in libraries, community colleges, and local chambers of commerce, to call the state's Vendor Information System computer. They can register on-line, download the appropriate RFPs, and have access to historical information, such as who won the bid the last time, who lost, and what the amount was of the winning and losing bids.

The entire system cost less than $400,000, mostly for the computer and public relations effort to sell this new way of doing business to the vendor community. In the first 16 months of operation, state officials in Oregon said they realized more than $17 million in savings on the same products that had been purchased under the old system. Increased competition among vendors, reduction in printing and postage costs, and a reduction in staff were cited as the major sources of savings. Not only are more vendors bidding for state business—instant access to RFPs has increased the number of bidding vendors by one-third—but the historical information available to them on similar previous contracts has improved the quality of the bids.

Likewise, the city of St. Louis Park, Minnesota, used technology to increase residential compliance with recycling regulations, which ultimately saved the municipality 30 percent in "tipping" fees (i.e., dumping). In order to increase compliance with curbside recycling, the municipality instituted a system of rewards for residents who recycled. In order to keep track of homeowners who recycled, and enable the municipality to credit the refuse bill of residents who participated in the program, bar code technology was incorporated into their recycling program. Residents were given bar code stickers to place on their recycling bins. As their recyclables are collected, the collectors scan the bar codes on their bins with a hand held scanner. Records from the scanners are uploaded daily to a personal computer at the recycling operations office, thus eliminating the time-consuming manual process.

St. Louis Park was rewarded with productivity savings for their efforts. Compliance increased from 45 percent to 90 percent. The cost of implementing the program, $30,000, was realized in ten months. St. Louis Park residents pay 30 percent less for refuse collection than residents in surrounding communities because less garbage is going to the landfill and more refuse is being recycled.

Shared Savings Program

An innovative approach to reaping the savings of productivity improvement programs exists in the public works department in Pittsburg, California. Feeling the impact of the tax-cutting initiative Proposition 13, and the ever-present pressure to contain the costs of municipal services such as the maintenance of roads, sewers, water lines, and parks, the director of the department implemented some radical changes. To attain the full potential of the best employees, and to have them work hard to lower operating costs, the department of public works provided financial bonuses to the employees who participated in a formal program to improve productivity. The creativity and effort of the employees to reduce and contain costs is rewarded, on a quarterly basis, with a check. A full 60 percent of whatever money was saved is divided equally among the participants.

This productivity savings program was met with opposition on the part of employees who were not selected to participate and ultimately lost their jobs. Opposition on the part of taxpayers was based on the belief that public employees should not receive bonuses for doing their jobs efficiently and any savings incurred should benefit the municipality, in the form of lower taxes. In spite of the opposition, the program was successfully implemented, with modifications such as a cap on the bonuses individual employees could earn. The Shared Savings Program went on to win two prestigious awards for their efforts: the Innovation Award from Harvard University and the Exemplary State and Local Award (EXSL) from Rutgers University.

Gain Sharing

The type of savings described above, in the Shared Savings Program, is a form of gain sharing. Private industry sometimes uses profit-sharing plans as an incentive for employees to control, and ultimately lower, the percentage of labor costs in total product costs. As the percentage decreases, the dollar value of the savings is shared with the employee. In the public sector, this method of sharing productivity savings with employees is known as gain sharing. Group sharing plans are more common in the private sector, where a profit motive and more stable production conditions exist. They are, however, gaining popularity in the public sector as governments strive to increase productivity and benefit from the savings derived from a more efficient program.

A solid waste program in Flint, Michigan, illustrates the use of the economic incentives. A gain sharing plan was established that rewarded employees, as a group, for decreases in overtime, an increase in the amount of garbage collected, and a decrease in the cost per ton of waste collected. The Urban Institute reports that in a two-year period, controllable overtime expenditures were practically eliminated and personnel costs decreased by 3.3 percent (Balk 1980).

Indirect Benefits

Productivity improvement efforts cost money. Not only must employees invest their time, but investments may also include additional staff, training, consultants, and capital equipment. Often, the value of the productivity improvement, or productivity savings, is not easily measured or calculated. Therefore, it is sometimes argued that the cost of implementing productivity improvement programs exceeds the savings derived from the initiative. It is often difficult or misleading to put a dollar value on services which are extremely valuable to a community. How much are safe streets worth? What about healthy children or quality education?

Epstein (1982) writes of the "asphalt paradox." This paradox results when a productivity improvement effort is so efficient it actually costs the municipality more money. Improved performance enabled work crews to resurface roads at a far greater pace than previously performed. While personnel costs were held constant, the improved program cost the municipality more than the original program. Work crews were able to resurface more roads, so more money was spent on asphalt. Their increased efficiency, within a short-term perspective, cost the municipality money. The long-term perspective, however, illustrate the savings. Under the original program it would have cost the municipality 25 percent more on personnel to resurface all the roads under the improved program. Examples such as this are very common in the public sector, where short-term expenditures hide the long-term benefits.

Another type of indirect savings is cost avoidance. This occurs when a productivity improvement plan is implemented, the quality of services improves, and future expenditures are avoided. For example, Modesto, California, implemented a program to systematically prune and care for their shade trees. While this program cost the city some additional expense in annual operating costs, it is estimated that through proper maintenance the community avoided other costs incurred through property damage caused by falling limbs and through tree replacements. By properly maintaining their urban forest, the costs of replacing damaged or diseased trees were avoided.

Likewise, improving public safety, particularly police and fire services, will result in cost avoidance or cost suppression. It is very difficult to measure the value of preventive measures. Implementing a community policing program costs a community money, as does a program to ensure homes are equipped with smoke detectors. These preventive measures will ultimately save the community resources, but it is difficult to prove that the fires prevented or crimes not committed are a direct result of the productivity initiatives.

Another example of a productivity initiative that resulted in indirect savings is the Electronic Benefits System program of Ramsey County, Minnesota. The county undertook an effort to improve the system of providing benefits to welfare recipients. While this program did not save the county a substantial amount of money, it greatly enhanced the quality of service provided to their clients by providing easy access to welfare benefits and at the same time reducing fraud. The county reduced the paper, printing, and postage costs associated with printing and mailing welfare checks to clients, but incurred equivalent expenses through the costs associated with electronic transfers of cash.

Ultimately, savings will result from productivity improvement efforts, some more direct, and measurable, than others.

KATHE CALLAHAN

BIBLIOGRAPHY

Balk, Walter, 1980. "Organizational and Human Behavior." In George J. Washnis, ed., *Productivity Improvement Handbook for State and Local Government.* New York: John Wiley & Sons, pp. 477–502.

Epstein, Paul, 1982. "Measuring Productivity in Government: Federal, State and Local." *Public Productivity Review* (September) pp. 65–72.

Hatry, Harry and Donald M. Fisk, 1992. "Measuring Productivity in the Public Sector." In Marc Holzer, ed., *Public Productivity Handbook.* New York: Marcel Dekker, Inc., pp. 139–160.

Holzer, Marc, 1988. "Focus: Productivity Improvement in New York State–The Science and Art of Capacity Building." In Catherine Gerard, ed., *Managing New York State.* New York: Governor's Office of Employee Relations, Number 1.

———, ed., 1992. *Public Productivity Handbook.* New York: Marcel Dekker, Inc.

U.S. Office of Personnel Management, (October 1980). "Manager's Guide for Improving Productivity."

The programs provided as examples of productivity savings are all winners of the Exemplary State and Local Award. For further information contact: National Center for Public Productivity, Rutgers University, Graduate Department of Public Administration, 360 King Blvd., Newark, New Jersey, 07102 (201) 648-5504.

PROFESSION.

Generally, an occupation requiring specialized knowledge that can only be gained after intensive preparation. This is a term with many connotations and nuances and subject to much controversy when applied to U.S. public administration.

Early definitions emphasized the ideas of calling and vocation to which one publicly professed devotion. The calling typically came from God or another supreme authority, or from a great mentor or institution (such as a university). The term was originally applied to religious orders, law, medicine, and the military, these being considered the most noble and learned vocations. Professional education and training were based in liberal arts, and therefore stressed broad philosophical, ethical, political, and cultural competencies. Training in the vocation meant training in the order and ways of life of societies as well as specific vocational functions. The intent was to cultivate profound understanding of the vocation's place and contributions to the broader society.

Early professionals often dabbled in several vocations, contributing significantly to each. Most were members of an aristocratic class, or of a protective order which afforded them the leisure to serve in these pursuits independent of economic demands. As T. H. Marshall indicated (1939), "The professional man does not work in order to be paid, he is paid in order that he may work" (p. 325). Furthermore, professionals were expected to avoid attention to entrepreneurial activities such as competition, advertising, and profit. This was especially true for those entering politics and government. As Philip Elliot (1972) described, "the ideology called on them to keep their distance from business" (p. 53).

Nineteenth- and twentieth-century versions of profession have departed significantly from this early conception. A comparative, sociologically derived model is now common, though subject to increasing criticism. This model centers on the development of a specialized body of esoteric theory and method-based empirical knowledge which requires a significant period of training to master for purposes of application. This type of knowledge is often contrasted with more mechanical, nontheoretical knowledge employed by trades and other occupations. It is also commonly treated as ethically and politically neutral–that is, derivable only from the rigors of objective, value-free methods.

Other characteristics of this model emerge from attempts of those seeking professional identity to control the development and application of the specialized knowledge in society. Darrell Pugh (1989) summarized several of them for public administrators in one of the field's leading professional publications, *Public Administration Review.* They involve: (1) a cast of mind (i.e., a self-awareness); (2) a corpus of theory and knowledge; (3) a social ideal; (4) ethical standards; (5) formal organization to promote its interests; and (6) a "hall of fame" to recognize outstanding leaders (p. 1).

Attempts by emerging professions to monopolize a body of knowledge stem in part from the desire to ensure that it is cultivated and applied with the highest standards. In a narrow, instrumental sense this embodies ethical standards (i.e., preserving the integrity of knowledge-producing methods) and a social ideal (i.e., achieving knowledge unbiased by extramethodological influences). However, sociological study tends increasingly to focus on self-serving aspects, such as a profession's restrictions on entrance for the sake of raising salaries and benefits as well as prestige, and for crowding out or regulating away rival forms of knowledge in related occupations. The medical profession's suffocating control over lay midwifery and folk medicine exemplify the point.

Today, established professions also typically acquire policing power over themselves through legislation, and then often display great reticence in meting out sanctions for infractions by its members. Most of a profession's legal, political, and economic resources are devoted to enhancing rather than policing professional careers. In short, as Magali S. Larson (1977) argues, modern, specialized professions have turned their knowledge into a powerful, self-serving, and often condescending form of property. They have become a new form of elite—an elite of experts.

Frederick C. Mosher (1968) assembled substantial evidence to show that by the late 1960s a "professional state" had emerged that exists in tension with the norms of democratic governance. Many government agencies (especially in the United States) are heavily populated and dominated by professions, so much so that the civil service system has in many places been transformed into a professional career system. Mosher highlighted the elitism and careerism of this professional state for students of government, and his work represents a major hub of criticism for those who object to professionalizing the field of public administration.

Beginning in the 1920s and 1930s, a number of prominent public administration academics and practitioners established some key features of the sociological model of profession for the field. It has a recognizable curriculum, now institutionalized in university degree programs. Most prominent among these is the Master of Public Administration degree. The field has an accreditation body, the National Association of Schools of Public Affairs and Administration (NASPAA), its development beginning slowly in the late 1950s. It boasts several long-standing professional associations, the more prominent being the American Society for Public Administration (ASPA) (formed in 1939) and the International City Managers Association (ICMA) (formed around 1914; now the International City/County Managers Association). They also created (mid-1960s) the National Academy of Public Administration (NAPA) to recognize its leading academics and practitioners, and have more recently (early 1980s) adopted a code of ethics.

Critics challenge professionalization of public administration on several grounds. First, it is believed that professionalizing under the sociological model will make administrators less responsive to the public's wishes. They will act for their own professional interests, in league with allied special interests, and thereby pervert their foremost obligations as guardians of the public interest.

Second, attempts by such a profession to protect its specialized knowledge are an inherently elitist activity that has no place in democratically administered government. Knowledge of governance must be shared openly for the sake of bolstering legitimate democratic dissent and participation. Widespread knowledge of governance is also essential for effectively limiting governing powers and protecting individual rights.

Third, many scholarly critics have challenged the status of the field's corpus of knowledge. A most common and serious argument is that the field is necessarily interdisciplinary, and therefore has no scientific or disciplinary foundation. Another is that its central principles and theories have been seriously discredited at various points since the 1940s, and that continuing attempts to build the field on scientific bases are misguided at best. Attempts to refound the field on normative rather than scientific grounds have burgeoned since the 1960s, resulting in a great deal of insightful theorizing and debate. No solid consensus has developed, however, around any normative basis for professionalization.

Fourth, it is often pointed out that despite the trappings of professionalism under the sociological model, public administration remains very weak as a profession. Only a tiny percentage of public administrators actually belong to its associations. Most university programs are not yet accredited by NASPAA, and degree programs in the field vary widely in scope and subjects. NASPAA curricular standards are as yet unsettled and subject to major revisions, the most recent coming in 1993–94. Furthermore, entrance into government administrative positions remains open at all levels, and still subject to more traditional appointment methods such as partisan patronage.

The most common method of achieving administrative office is through previous success in another profession. Most administrators identify with another profession (law, medicine, engineering, military, forestry, social work, etc.), and often see their administrative work as merely an extension of their primary profession. Indeed, some professions, such as education, have tailored administrative curricula specifically to their professional degree programs.

Finally, even within sociology itself the sociological model of profession has come under fire on both normative and empirical grounds. This parallels a general decline in public attitudes about professions. Their insularity, self-interestedness, and attendant abuses have eroded their reputations. The public has become rather jaded about professional experts. In this light, some public administration scholars understandably question efforts to emulate them.

These objections, as Darrell Pugh notes, are weighty and compelling (1989, p. 6). Yet, despite these objections, attempts at further professionalization continue in public administration, and not without some support from influential critics. Many detractors are not averse to promoting self-awareness among public administrators for their involvement in distinctive and essential governing roles. Such awareness can enhance their knowledge, skill, and accountability in agency decisions. Many see professional associations as helpful to such endeavors. It may be within this context that Dwight Waldo (1968) made his now famous statement that while public administration "perhaps should not become a profession in the strict sense, nevertheless an appropriate attitude and strategy . . . is to act as though public administration is, or might become a profession" (pp. 9–11). Philip Cooper developed this point further in a 1982 article in *The Bureaucrat* by suggesting that:

> . . . the purpose [of professionalism] is to improve performance and not to acquire status. In such an effort, professionalism is a means related to the achievement of certain ends. Public administration professionalism might be thought of as an aspect of responsibility. One might suggest that professionalism is one of the internal or subjective checks that guide public administrators in the manner advocated by Carl Friedrich (p. 50).

As Cooper subsequently notes, this approach treats professionalism "as an aspect of responsibility defined by the nature of the public administrator's task and environment" (p. 51). This involves much more than technical competency. It includes political responsibilities long associated with the idea of statecraft. This normative orientation shares more in common with early conceptions of profession as a vocation or calling than with the modern sociological model.

Many articles and books on professionalization, by public administration scholars such as John Rohr, David K. Hart, Terry Cooper, Ralph Chandler, Brian Cook, James Bowman, Darrell Pugh, Guy Adams, Larry Terry, Gary Wamsley, Lawrence Keller, and Curtis Ventriss, express views similar to Cooper's and take them in varying directions. All of them call attention to the need for administrators to balance technical competency with the broader political responsibilities of governance. Such responsibilities include cultivating leadership, citizen formation, and citizen participation roles; confronting abusive or irresponsible authorities; resisting public opinion when it seeks to trample the rights of minorities; internalizing and applying a variety of regime values; and building and sustaining vital institutional capacities.

Aspects of status attained through professional organization and other means may also contribute to effectiveness and accountability. For example, senior executive status, as provided in the creation of the Senior Executive Service of the federal government (1978), may provide additional motivation and much-deserved recognition among colleagues for exemplary service and ability. At the same time, the structure of the SES makes them more responsive to elected and politically appointed officials. Lower-level administrators need such exemplars to emulate, and for help in "learning the ropes" as they acquire increased responsibility.

The controversy over professionalism in public administration will continue for many important reasons. Much of the dissatisfaction, however, stems from attempts to emulate the normatively impoverished sociological model. Self-awareness and association among public administrators can be very beneficial for society if they emerge from publicly fulfilling and accountable purpose. Advocates, as well as constructive critics, share the task of shaping and implementing a model of professional administration that is more politically and ethically appropriate to liberal democratic regimes such as that found in the United States.

RICHARD T. GREEN

BIBLIOGRAPHY

On the history and development of professions generally, see:

Elliot, Philip, 1972. *The Sociology of the Professions.* New York: Herder & Herder.

Friedson, E., ed., 1971. *The Professions and Their Prospects.* Beverly Hills, CA: Sage Publications.

Geison, Gerald L., 1983. *Professions and Professional Ideologies in America.* Chapel Hill: University of North Carolina Press.

Hargrove, Erwin C., 1972. *Professional Roles in Society and Government: The English Case.* Sage Professional Papers in Comparative Politics. Beverly Hills, CA: Sage Publications.

Holmes, Geoffrey S., 1982. *Augustan England: Professions, State and Society, 1680–1730.* London: George Allen & Unwin.

Howe, Elizabeth, 1980. "Public Professions and the Private Model of Professionalism." *Social Work,* vol. 25 (May) 179–191.

Larson, Magali Sarfatti, 1977. *The Rise of Professionalism: A Sociological Analysis.* Berkeley: University of California Press.

Marshall, T. H., 1939. "The Recent History of Professionalism in Relation to Social Structure and Policy." *Canadian Journal of Economics and Political Science,* vol. 5.

Reader, W. J., 1966. *Professional Men: The Rise of the Professional Classes in Nineteenth-Century England.* New York: Basic Books.

Vollmer, Howard M. and Donald J. Mills, 1966. *Professionalization.* Englewood Cliffs, NJ: Prentice-Hall.

On professionalism in U.S. public administration, see:

Adams, Guy B., 1993. "Ethics and the Chimera of Professionalism: The Historical Context of an Oxymoronic Relationship." *American Review of Public Administration,* vol. 23 (June) 117–139.

Bowman, James S., 1982. "A Professional Perspective for PA." *The Bureaucrat,* vol. 11, no. 4 (Winter) 49–53.

Chandler, Ralph C., 1984. "The Public Administrator as Representative Citizen: A New Role for the New Century." *Public Administration Review,* vol. 48:196–206.

Cook, Brian J., 1992. "Administration in Constitutive Perspective." *Administration & Society,* vol. 23, no. 4:403–429.

Cooper, Phillip J., 1982. "Defining PA Professionalism." *The Bureaucrat,* vol. 11, no. 1 (Spring) 49–52.

Cooper, Terry L., 1987. "Hierarchy, Virtue, and the Practice of Public Administration: A Perspective for Normative Ethics." *Public Administration Review,* vol. 47 (July-August) 320–328.

———, 1991. *An Ethic of Citizenship for Public Administration.* Englewood Cliffs, NJ: Prentice-Hall.

Gazell, James J. and Darrell Pugh, eds., 1993. "Symposium: Professionalization and Professionalism in Public Administration." *International Journal of Public Administration,* vol. 16.

Green, Richard T., Lawrence F. Keller, and Gary L. Wamsley, 1993. "Reconstituting a Profession for American Public Administration." *Public Administration Review*, vol. 53, no. 6 (November-December) 516–524.

Hart, David K., 1984. "The Virtuous Citizen, The Honorable Bureaucrat, and 'Public' Administration." *Public Administration Review*, vol. 44 (March-April) 111–119.

Mosher, Frederick C., 1968. *Democracy and the Public Service.* New York: Oxford University Press.

Pugh, Darrell L., 1989. "Professionalism in Public Administration: Problems, Perspectives, and the Role of ASPA." *Public Administration Review*, vol. 49, no. 1 (January-February) 1–8.

Rohr, John A., 1989. *Ethics for Bureaucrats: An Essay on Law and Values.* New York: Marcel Dekker.

———, 1986. *To Run a Constitution: The Legitimacy of the Administrative State.* Lawrence: University Press of Kansas.

Terry, Larry D., 1990. "Leadership in the Administrative State: The Concept of Administrative Conservator." *Administration & Society*, vol. 21, no. 4:395–412.

Ventriss, Curtis, 1993. "The Ideology of Professionalism in Public Administration: Implications for Education." *International Journal of Public Administration*, vol. 16, no. 12:1911–1932.

Waldo, Dwight, 1968. "Scope of Theory of Public Administration." In James C. Charlesworth, ed., *Theory and Practice of Public Administration: Scope, Objectives, Methods.* Philadelphia: American Academy of Political and Social Science, pp. 9–11.

Wamsley, Gary L., Robert N. Bacher, Charles T. Goodsell, Philip S. Kronenberg, John A. Rohr, Camilla Stivers, Orion F. White, and James F. Wolf, 1990. *Refounding Public Administration.* Newbury Park, CA: Sage Publications.

Willbern, York, 1954. "Professionalization in the Public Service: Too Little or Too Much." *Public Administration Review*, vol. 14 (Winter) 13–21.

PROFESSIONALISM.

Behaving in accord with the knowledge, ethics, thinking processes, and culture of a particular group of people who claim to practice according to a specialized collection of knowledge and beliefs, and whose status is recognized within a community.

Traditionally, there were three recognized professions: law, medicine, and divinity with, sometimes, the addition of the military. According to this view, all other working life pursuits were simply occupations, vocations, or trades. In recent years, the concept of a profession has been more widely defined, enabling the term to encompass many other callings and careers. However, as the term is more widely applied, there is a risk that the status of the professional person may be reduced as larger and therefore less elite groups come to be represented. The distinctive competencies of a small group are usually the key element that separates a professional group from other members of a society.

According to some theories, a profession may come to be recognized as such in a number of ways. These include an attitude model, an exclusivity model, and a developmental (or process) model. The attribute model suggests that if a group of people are recognized as members of a particular group because they possess unique attributes, then they will be accorded recognition as a profession. The exclusivity model suggests that professions exist because members act to limit or prevent access to their professional group. In contrast, the developmental (or process) model suggests that a group of people representing a particular specialization come to be gradually accorded professional status by following a particular strategy that eventually leads to their recognition.

The attribute model suggests that a professional group will possess the following group of characteristics that distinguishes group members from others in society. According to this model, a profession and its members will have:

- A well-defined body of knowledge, nurtured by members;
- A sense of service to the community and clients;
- A code of ethical behavior;
- A strong sense of group identity;
- An organization to manage the group, its knowledge, and members' behavior;
- A recognized image, preferably reinforced by the status of an outstanding individual.

This model might be applied by the members of the public sector who seek to establish themselves as professionals. Within the public sector there is a body of knowledge that can probably be regarded as being nurtured and controlled by members. Because of a government's social, financial and, hopefully, fiduciary relationship with its electorate, the process of government calls for a specialized understanding of the machinery of government and an ability to manage in a risk-averse, highly publicized, and politicized environment that is often not understood or appreciated by those outside the sector. Perhaps they see government behavior as bound by many rules and procedures without appreciating the accountability requirements that make the business of government quite different to the demands of business.

The social and fiduciary relationship between government and the people tends to help foster a culture of service to the community among members of public sector organizations. Although this commitment may vary between individuals and over time, there is a tradition of service fostered by most public sector organizations and transmitted to management and staff as part of the organization's culture. The existence of a code of ethics is usually seen as a typical foundation of a professional group. Such a code defines the behaviors of members in a very public way, implying to the public that sanctions exist for breaches to these ethical rules. Although the existence of a code of ethics demonstrates to the public that the professional body takes responsibility for the self-regulation of members on behalf of those who deal with professionals, its application in the public sector appears to be limited, perhaps because, as with groups such as teachers and nurses, public servants are employed persons rather than self-employed and their self-regulation is affected by the control of employers.

A professional group with a well-established organization, and an active membership, that is well-supported by organizations who employ the skills of recognized professionals provides a significant foundation for a professional organization. This can be enhanced by the professional organization fostering an active research program to strengthen the knowledge base of the profession, an active personal development program for suitably qualified members as the basis of entry, and the maintenance of professional status on a continuing basis. Related to this knowledge base is often the existence of a strong technical jargon.

George Bernard Shaw once described professions as "conspiracies against the laity." His view probably reflects an important reality about professions and their use of language. A rich, complex, technical language is very helpful for groups wishing to establish a distinctive professional culture for members, relevant to their status. This semantic structure ensures that those who are not part of the professional group are excluded by their lack of access to the language and culture of the group and is a very important feature of a profession. While the jargon might be necessary to ensure technical accuracy, it also acts as a significant and effective barrier to access. In the public sector, this jargon is often found in a language based on acronyms, which is also a very effective barrier to those outside the public sector.

Finally, the professional image of a group is highly significant. A sense of elitism and recognition of significant individuals is another way in which a profession determines its status. A founding figure or a current, high-profile patron can be significant advantage. The accounting profession may look to Pacioli as the founder of the accounting profession, other groups may look to sponsorship from a key figure such as the president. The status of the individual concerned, whether historical or contemporary, seems to be critical to the recognition accorded a professional group.

The attribute model may help members of the public sector think about their status as a professional. While it could be said they administer a body of knowledge, there would be many who would attempted to challenge the public sector control of this knowledge. In most countries it seems that many other aspects of the attribute model are well satisfied. The sense of public service, a strong emphasis on ethical behavior, a well-developed group identity, and well-established professional bodies that support the ideals of public service all provide part of the professional identity of the public sector practitioner. Perhaps the most difficult aspect relates to image. Are members of the public sector regarded as professionals within the community they are working? Who acts as their patron? What professional recognition is afforded members by members of the

government and by the wider public? The answers to these questions will help define public sector members as professionals within the context of the attribute model.

A second way of examining professions and professionalization is to examine the way in which a group of people exclude others from the practice of a particular group of activities by some type of gatekeeping behaviors. This gatekeeping approach enables professionals, having acquired a group of skills, to rely on the profession to which they belong to help them practice as professionals by ensuring their services can only be offered by registered members of the professional body. One of the typical activities of a profession is the setting and maintenance of educational and other entry standards. This is readily apparent in a traditional profession such as medicine where the need for a high level of technical expertise is well understood. Some professional groups manage to gain legislative professional standards that both ensures that members of a profession meet the technical and knowledge standards of that group and acts as a barrier to broader entry to the profession. In this situation the line between a professional and an occupation is quite clear as the well-defined barriers, especially those defined by law, ensure there is no ambiguity about professional status. Legislation provides definition and protects status. For the public sector practitioner, it is clear that access to the profession is not strictly defined in law, although the qualifications and experience attaching to particular positions do provide effective barriers to access. It would be quite difficult for the public sector to define its professional status by overt gatekeeping, as described by the exclusivity model, however, informal barriers to entry may be used to limit access to positions within the sector.

The third model, the process or developmental model of professionalism, may provide public sector practitioners with a means of establishing themselves as a profession without necessarily meeting all the requirements of the attribute model. This model suggests that a group of people, whether or not they possess all the attributes listed earlier, can become recognized as professionals because they act in a particular way, have particular skills in demand, and possess qualifications that are recognized and respected within the community. It is the strategies and processes employed by the group to meet the general educational expectations of a professional that seem to position their group in a way that affords professional recognition within the public sector and the broader community and seems to be the key to this model. This path to professionalism is slow and subject to high levels of negotiation between different groups likely to assist the recognition of the new professional group. An enhancement of education levels, new gatekeeping in terms of educational attainment and work experience to determine membership, and the formation of a widely recognized and supported representative group will be required before professional recognition is likely. While this path is open to public sector practitioners, it represents a slow and complex route to professional status.

Professional status is a worthwhile goal for public sector practitioners. It provides a source of identity and mutual reinforcement of the goals and values of public sector organizations and enhances the status of individuals performing the full range of public sector activities. Such recognition also enhances the status of public sector organizations and their role in society, a vital outcome if the public sector is to preserve its relevance in the complex relationship between government, the community, and the private and not-for-profit sectors.

GUY CALLENDER

BIBLIOGRAPHY

Blair, R. D. and J. Rubin, 1980. *Regulating the Professions: A Public Policy Symposium.* Lexington, MA: Lexington Books.
Brown, R. G. and K. Johnston, 1984. *Pacioli on Accounting.* New York: Garland Publishing.
deLeon, L., 1994. "The Professional Values of Public Managers, Policy Analysts and Politicians." *Public Personnel Management,* vol. 23, no. 1 (Spring) 135–152.
Freidson, E., ed., 1973. *The Professions and their Prospects.* Beverley Hills, CA: Sage.
Jackson, J. A., 1970. *Professionals and Professionalization.* Cambridge, MA: University Press.
Kalbers, L. P. and T. J. Fogarty, 1995. "Professionalism and Its Consequences: A Study of Internal Auditors." *Auditing, A Journal of Practice and Theory,* vol. 14, no. 1 (Spring) 64–86.
Solomon, H. L., 1991. *The Professional Contribution to the 'Clever Country' Concept.* Canberra: AGPS.

PROGRAM BUDGETING. The collection of information into program packages so that reviewers can understand what general objectives are being supported by budget resources.

In 1949, the first Hoover Commission report called for making budget outcomes more intelligible by bringing more program data into the budget process. This data was to concentrate on performance outcomes. Congress specifically included a call for such performance information in the National Security Act Amendments of 1949 as it reorganized and created the new Department of Defense (DOD) from the old separate military departments. The Budgeting and Accounting Procedures Act of 1950 essentially required performance budgeting for all federal agencies. Program budgeting was an intermediate step in this process. The Department of the Army had commissioned a series of studies of army organizational and budget patterns. In 1948 and 1949, a report by a private firm on army organization and budgeting cited the lack of coordination between planning and budgeting; the lack of a general staff control over large portions of the budget; the absence of systematic machinery and responsibility for planning and

follow-up on execution of those plans; the lack of coordination among plans; and the failure to evaluate programs and policies in terms of cost.

In response to this study and other internal studies, the Army proceeded to develop and install a formalized programming system for the Department of the Army. All the army's efforts were divided into 14 primary programs and each of these was subdivided into program segments. Each of these programs reported to one director; that director supervised the heads of the program sectors in the program. Later a taxonomy would be developed for units in successive steps down the chain of command. In the beginning, there were primary programs for Troop, Training, Intelligence, Procurement, Civilian Personnel, Command and Management, and so on. Each of these primary programs had a mission statement and an objective. Frederick Mosher, who wrote the classic reference on program budgeting (1954), provides a hypothetical example of these:

Army Mission: to provide ground forces for defense of strategic areas.
Army Objective: two divisions to be ready to defend a tropical area.
Program Objectives:
1. Troop Program to provide for X divisions.
2. Training Program to provide for jungle training.
3. Major Procurement Program to provide jungle equipment.

In terms of process, program creation came between the planning and budgeting cycles. Planning discovered what the threat was, or how it had changed from the previous cycle. Programming created the packages of forces needed to meet the threat or changes in the threat. Budgeting priced out those packages in terms of what and how much should be purchased in any one fiscal year (see the entries on **budgeting**; **performance budget**; **planning, programming, budgeting**; and **budget reform**).

Then, as now, this was a complex process. The planning stage began with the requirements of the Joint Chiefs of Staff and was focused on the fiscal year that would occur almost three years later. The programming phase was scheduled to last six months. Most commands had interests in more than one program. Mosher (1954) notes that all the technical commands had interests in at least 13 of the army's primary programs (p. 68), and had to operate under a system of multiple responsibility for both program development and execution. Interestingly, Mosher notes that often the programming phase was not finished in time to lead in to the budget phase, a criticism also true in recent years. When this happens, the programming and budgeting phases are coordinated in the end game of the budget process.

The planning process and the program guidance systems made this program budget process a centralized, top-down process, where the vision of a relatively few planners and programmers could be resourced through the budget process. Although program packages were still enthusiastically discussed in the early 1960s (Massey 1963), the system that DOD went on to create under Robert McNamara focused more on technical evaluation of alternatives through cost-benefit analysis than it did in budgeting by program. Robert Lee (1989) observes that in the early 1960s PPB stood for "Program Package Budgeting" because budgets were presented in terms of program packages and their outputs (p. 82). This was changed to give more emphasis to "Planning" later in the 1960s, in particular planning done in the Office of the Secretary of Defense. At state and local levels, reform-minded governments tended to go directly to performance budgeting or program budgets supported with performance statistics.

Program budgeting was a step forward for DOD since it helped create and control what had been three separate military departments. As an organizing concept, it also helped make the mass of detail in defense budgets intelligible. However, program budgeting alone was not enough, in either the defense sector or in nondefense governmental units. As soon as programs were defined, program reviewers wanted to know what it was that the program was buying; often they wanted to know how much they could reduce the program and still operate without causing undue hardship. Program budget frameworks did not answer questions like this any more than providing the information grouped in terms of number of personnel and the costs of supporting supplies did. In some jurisdictions, program budgeting was even counterproductive. A unit could define all its activities as a program (e.g., the sales tax program), and describe its activities at a level which masked the usual budget controls on personnel and supporting expenses but did not provide enough information on the outputs of the program to be useful, and still claim to be using a modern, reformed budget system. As a budget reform, program budgeting must be seen as a transitional form, from line item budgeting to forms such as performance or zero-based budgeting where some measure of output or activity affect was linked to the budget form.

JERRY L. MCCAFFERY

BIBLIOGRAPHY

Lee, Jr., Robert D. 1989. *Public Budgeting Systems*. 4th ed. Rockville, MD: Aspen Publications.

Massey, Robert J, 1963. "Program Packages and the Program Budget in the Department of Defense." *Public Administration Review* 23:30–34.

Mosher, Frederick C, 1954. *Program Budgeting: Theory and Practice*. New York: Stratford Press.

PROGRESSIVE MOVEMENT.
A late nineteenth- and early twentieth-century cultural and political movement, centered in the United States, and intent upon reforming industrializing, urban societies so as to enable them to achieve modernist goals.

Rapid nineteenth-century industrialization and urbanization created unprecedented problems both for the United States and the nations of Western Europe: rapid urban population growth, economic cycles that periodically created high unemployment, urban sanitation problems, and political exploitation of a dependent urban citizenry. Though each country struggled with these challenges, the response of the United States came to be known as the Progressive Movement. Hence, "progressivism" consists of those political principles that guided the Progressive Movement.

The Progressives were responding to rapid development of the United States in the latter decades of the twentieth century—development that changed the U.S. landscape. By mid-nineteenth century, the wilderness and frontier were settled. By the end of the century, large cities had eclipsed the cultural and political role of the small community. These new urban areas provided jobs and shelter to immigrant populations who migrated to the United States for a new start. However, neither the rugged individual ethic of the frontier nor the self-sufficient lifestyle idealized by the rural experience could serve as a guide to these new urban citizens. Instead, dependent immigrant populations fueled the growth of political machines where political bosses gained the loyalty of the immigrant by providing a meager array of services. These machines were notoriously corrupt and inefficient. They became the target for reformers who sought to displace the machines with more efficient governments.

The first wave of reform consisted of individuals known as "muckrakers," a term denoting those who raked the muck of corruption and scandal. They were largely journalists who used popular magazines and newspapers to expose the corruption of the political bosses. The second wave consisted of individuals who argued that it was not enough to expose corruption. Their more permanent solution was to replace the inefficient political machines with efficient administrative institutions. Included in this latter wave were intellectuals such as Walter Lippmann, Herbert Croly, and Walter Weyl. Lippmann, for example, began his career as a muckraker for *McClure's* magazine, but eventually recognized the limitations of continual journalistic diatribes against corruption. He promoted the development of public sector administrative institutions that served the broad public interest. Collectively, both types of reformers came to be known as "Progressives." The term came from their argument that only innovative political institutions could assure the continued progress of industrialized societies toward modernist goals.

At first glance, those who constituted the Progressive Movement comprised a set of reactions to industrialization with no common ideology. At the zenith of the movement, populists, philosophical idealists, investigative journalists, and educated professionals called themselves Progressives. To call all of these groups Progressives is to define the term loosely. However, as the movement developed, those who subscribed to the tenets of pragmatic philosophy gave the movement a more durable, coherent philosophical base and reform agenda. The pragmatists argued that to be truly progressive the United States must embrace new institutions and new cultural values. This pragmatic reform agenda, which used science and experimentation to create new U.S. governmental institutions, diverged from that of the Populists. This latter group favored loosely organized collective action, often directed against banks and railroads and other powerful interests that the Populists regarded as oppressive to the common people. However, beyond opposition to these enemies, the Populists did not maintain a comprehensive reform vision. They harbored instead a preference for the traditional social order.

These conflicting interests within the Progressive Movement were never reconciled. The energy of the reform effort was diverted by World War I. After the war, the coalition of forces that gave Progressivism its energy did not reassemble. The Great Depression, economic recovery, and the exigency of survival moved the concerns of the Progressives to the margins.

JAMES STEVER

BIBLIOGRAPHY

Hofstadter, Richard, 1955. *The Age of Reform.* New York: Random House.
Lippmann, Walter, 1914. *Drift and Mastery.* New York: Mitchell Kennerley.
Stever, James A., 1988. *The End of Public Administration: Problems of the Profession in the Post-Progressive Era.* New York: Transnational Publishers.
Wiebe, Robert H., 1967. *The Search for Order, 1877–1920.* New York: Hill & Wang.

PROJECT CONTROL.

The planning, scheduling, and controlling of project activities so that the goal is achieved in a specified period of time. A project is a set of discrete but interrelated activities involving the conceptualizing of the goal, its definition, design, development, application, and evaluation (Lewis 1993a). Projects can be simple (for example, an award dinner for an organization) or extremely complex (the construction of a modern jet aircraft). The most salient feature of a project is that it has an end point, a moment at which it ceases to exist.

The critical element of project control is determining the sequencing of priorities for project elements, and the timelines within which elements should be accomplished. The three best known control tools are Gantt milestone charts, PERT (Project Evaluation and Review Technique), and CPM (Critical Path Method). Each focuses on managing time within a project so that the most efficient use of resources is achieved, and the project is completed on schedule.

Henry L. Gantt, a contemporary of Frederick W. Taylor and a champion of the early scientific management movement, was an early proponent of project control. Gantt created a series of horizontal bars, called a Gantt milestone chart, each of which indicates by its length the amount of time a particular activity is planned to take. A Gantt chart does not clearly indicate sequential relationships between activities, a significant deficit in complex industrial projects.

During World War II, the Allied command used a variety of techniques to plan and coordinate invasions, and to monitor the overall progress of war efforts. These were the precursors of a project control technique developed for the Polaris submarine project by the U.S. Navy, called PERT, shorthand for Project Evaluation and Review Technique. Using PERT, the Navy brought the first Polaris submarine to completion two years ahead of its forecasted schedule. At about the same time, the DuPont Corpora-

FIGURE I

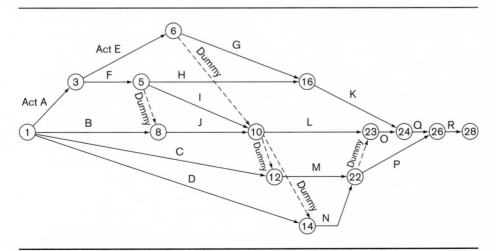

tion was developing a similar technique, which they called CPM, for Critical Path Method.

Both PERT and CPM allow for estimating and controlling time, and for highlighting the interdependence among activities and events which move the project toward its desired ends. With PERT and CPM particularly important activities can be identified, and appropriate resources can be applied to ensure that they do not become bottlenecks. PERT applies statistical analysis (probabilities) to its planning networks, whereas CPM does not.

Although CPM and PERT technically are not identical, in normal usage the terms are often used interchangeably. CPM is used more often in projects where the activities are known, and when some history can be applied to the estimates of time for each activity. PERT is more useful when such a history does not exist, or when there is a high level of uncertainty in estimates. Both techniques utilize arrow network diagrams to illustrate the interrelationships among tasks and events in a project graphically. There are now a number of computer programs available which make CPM and PERT networks easy to produce and to monitor (Spinner 1992). (see Figure I.)

A few of the more important terms used in CPM and PERT are: An *event* is the starting point or ending point of an activity. A *leader event* denotes the beginning moment of an activity. A *milestone* is an outstanding moment in the complex of activities; for example, the completion of a major phase of a complex project. An arrow diagram pulls these elements together with lines and arrows indicating direction. Each line has a time estimate attached to it, so that the total time of a path can be calculated.

In PERT, each activity has three different estimates of time: optimistic, most likely, and pessimistic. Estimates of time are stated in formulas. Slack time is the excess time available to complete an activity. Slack can be expressed as a positive or a negative number, indicating the amount of freedom a manager has.

The critical path is the route through the network with the longest estimated time from the first leader event through the last ending event in the project. The total of the time estimates in the critical path provides an indicator of how likely it is that a project will be completed within the time allotted. In PERT this probability of meeting completion date is usually stated in a formula.

Backward chaining is the technique by which a project manager calculates backwards chronologically from project completion through the activities and events. When all activities and events have been identified and laid out in proper sequence, they are displayed in an arrow diagram which indicates the direction of the activities, precedence (sequence), and the amount of time (usually in days) that each activity and the total project will require from first to last event.

While every project should involve a final evaluation, it is crucial that there be points of evaluation as the project progresses. In its simplest form, a project control system can be described as a feedback loop, in which information is regularly fed back into the system so that it can monitor its own performance, and difficulties can be identified and addressed.

Project control in modern public administration has become very complex. There is a variety of training and educational programs available, including workshops (from one day to one week in length) to graduate courses at colleges and universities. Project control has become a sub-specialty within public administration and industrial management.

PETER J. VAN HOOK

BIBLIOGRAPHY

Busch, Dennis H., 1991. *The New Critical Path Method: CPM–The State-of-the-Art in Project Modeling and Time Reserve Management.* Chicago: Probus.

Harrison, F. L., 1992. *Advanced Project Management: A Structured Approach.* 3d ed. New York: Halsted.

Lewis, James P., 1993a. *The Project Manager's Desk Reference: A Comprehensive Guide to Project Planning, Scheduling, Evaluation, Control, and Systems.* Chicago: Probus.

———, 1993b. *How to Build and Manage a Winning Project Team.* New York: AMACOM.

Lockyer, Keith, 1984. *Critical Path Analysis and Other Project Network Techniques.* 4th ed. London: Pitman.

Spinner, M. Pete, 1992. *Elements of Project Management: Plan, Schedule, and Control.* 2d ed. Englewood Cliffs, NJ: Prentice-Hall.

Wiest, Jerome D., 1977. *A Management Guide to PERT/CPM: with GERT/PDM/DCPM and Other Networks.* 2d ed. Englewood Cliffs, NJ: Prentice-Hall.

PROJECT MANAGEMENT.

The process of managing, allocating, and timing resources to achieve a specific goal in an efficient and expedient manner; also, the combination of people and techniques required to coordinate the resources necessary to complete projects within established goals.

The Project Management Institute (Drexel Hill, PA) defines project management as the art of directing and coordinating human and material resources throughout the life of a project by using modern management techniques to achieve predetermined objectives of scope, cost, time, quality, and participant satisfaction. The Project Management Institute (PMI) views the management of projects as consisting of eight areas of expertise: scope, time, money (cost), quality, communications, human resources, contracts and supply, and risk management.

Integration of various components of project management is a vital concern of company project managers. In the context of integration, project management is defined as the systematic integration of technical, human, and financial resources to achieve goals and objectives.

The origins and history of project management can be traced back as early as the Egyptian pyramids, the Great Wall of China, the Panama Canal, Roman buildings and roads, and shipbuilding. Project management in modern times can be traced to the management of large-scale ad hoc endeavors, such as the Manhattan Project, and on a smaller scale to the practical models provided by project engineering. Although no one can claim credit for project management's invention, its actual formal beginnings often are cited in the United States ballistic missile program or the space program.

Writing in the *Harvard Business Review* in 1961, Gerald Fisch spoke of the obsolescence of the line-staff concept and a growing trend toward "functioning teamwork" approaches to organization. Also in 1961, IBM established systems managers with overall responsibility for various computer models across functional division lines, which is a component of modern project management. In the 1960s and 1970s, a wide variety of organizations experimented with the use of alternative project management organizational forms. At present, project management has reached a high degree of maturity and is used widely in industrial, educational, governmental, and military circles. As a result, a distinctive field of literature has emerged dealing with project management endeavors in contemporary organizations.

The evolution of project management is reflected in the development of the project management-related literature. By 1962 a substantial amount of literature had developed, principally prepared by practitioners who were immersed in ongoing projects and anxious to tell their stories about the new concept of project management, which seemed to contradict many of the established ways of managing activities. Since the early 1960s, over 100 books have been published on the various aspects of project management. Hundreds of articles have appeared in management and technical publications. Professional associations such as the Project Management Institute (PMI) hold seminars and symposia each year where members present papers about their special areas of interest in project management.

One of the first comprehensive articles that caught the attention of the project management community was published by Paul O. Gaddis in the *Harvard Business Review* (1959). This article, titled "The Project Manager," described the role of that individual in an advanced technology industry, the prerequisites for performing the project management job, and the type of training recommended to prepare an individual to manage projects. Several basic notions put forth by Gaddis contributed to a conceptual framework for the management of projects that hold true today. These basic notions were:

- A project is an organizational unit dedicated to delivering a development product on time, within budget, and within predetermined technical performance specifications.
- The project team consists of specialists representing the disciplines needed to bring the project to a successful conclusion.
- Projects are organized by tasks, requiring an integration across the traditional functional structure of the organization.
- The project manager manages a high proportion of professionals organized on a team basis.
- The superior-subordinate relationship is modified, resulting in a unique set of authority, responsibility, and accountability relationships.
- The project is finite in duration.
- A clear delineation of authority and responsibility is essential.
- The project manager is a "(person) of action, a (person) of thought, and a front (person)."
- Project planning is vital to project success.
- The project manager is the person between management and the technologist.
- The subject of communication deserves a great deal of attention in project management.
- Project teams will begin to break up when the members sense the project has started to end its course.
- The integrative function of the project manager should be emphasized.
- Status reporting is appropriate and valuable to project management.
- The role played by project management in the years ahead will be challenging, exciting, and crucial.

Gaddis's prediction of project management's future was accurate. Project management is an idea whose time has come in the strategic management of organizations. In the 1960s, companies with complex tasks operating within a dynamic environment began to search for new management techniques and organizational structures that could be quickly adapted to a changing environment. However, other than the aerospace, defense, and construction industries, the majority of companies in the 1960s maintained an informal policy of project managing. It was not until the 1970s, in response to the increased size and complexity of their activities, that a growing number of companies resorted to a formal project management process.

On all but the smallest projects, a systems approach became a necessary prerequisite to steer projects to completion within budget, time, and quality parameters. Whether manual, mechanical, or computerized, the systems approach provides procedural and organizational bases for managing daily activities. These systems support project personnel in planning, integrating, and monitoring project fundamentals such as money (using cost control systems or cash flow forecasting), time (using Gantt or PERT/CPM planning and scheduling techniques) and quality (using follow-up, control, and assurance procedures). The systems approach is most effective provided there is adequate involvement of the people doing the work.

Getting things done through people is project management's major goal. For a project to be successful, people must work together. Team-building, conflict management, and communication skills are people-related abilities needed to make project activities work. Everything on a project starts with people. And a project progresses as a result of human interaction.

A project's life cycle has four distinct phases: (1) conceptual, (2) planning, (3) execution, and (4) termination. Project activity varies sharply over the course of the project's life cycle. In an industrial manufacturing project, each phase is typified by the following activities:

- *The conceptual phase.* Includes identifying needs, establishing feasibility, searching for alternatives, preparing proposals, developing basic budgets and schedules, and naming the starting project team.
- *The planning phase.* Involves implementing schedules, conducting studies and analyses, designing systems, building and testing prototypes, analyzing results, and obtaining approval for production.
- *The execution phase.* Encompasses procuring and implementing systems, verifying performance, and modifying systems as required.
- *The termination phase.* Includes training operational personnel, transferring materials, transferring responsibility, releasing resources, and reassigning project team members.

Terminology in project life cycle planning can vary considerably. For instance, these same four phases can be called (1) initiation, (2) growth, (3) operations, and (4) shutdown.

Important to all projects and to the management of projects are time and scheduling. Generally, in project management there are two approaches to scheduling: a series schedule, in which each stage is completed before the next one begins, and a phased schedule in which stages overlap. If the use of time must be optimized, a phased schedule is called for. Phased scheduling is also called fast-track scheduling. In this approach, parts of the design phase are initiated before conceptual planning is finished, materials procurement is kicked off before the design phase is completed, and implementation begins before all materials have been procured or manufactured. Phased programming saves time, and a project is completed earlier using a fast-track program than it would be with a sequential schedule.

The fast-track approach is such an integral part of project management that some people consider the terms synonymous. Whether or not the terms mean precisely the same thing, fast-track scheduling has brought project management of age. Phased programs require expertise in management interfacing, whereas the traditional series schedules do not. Projects laced with interfaces and overlapped activities call for artful application of project management tools and practices. Because cost, schedule, and performance are normally at odds with one another, fast-tracking project management teams must weave their way through both technical and managerial obstacle courses in order to reach project completion.

A wide variety of undertakings exists within the public and private sectors where project management concepts are applicable and have been successfully implemented. Many forms of project management have merged, but the basic concepts and techniques apply to all. The matrix structure has been the most widely accepted form of project management, and will likely continue to be so in situations involving complex interdisciplinary efforts. Other forms of project management include the use of temporary task forces and team building for multifunctional efforts.

Some justification is necessary to determine if a particular endeavor is better served by the use of a project management approach rather than through the regular functional organization. Although no specific formula or simple rule can determine when it is best to use project management, several criteria can identify when project management is beneficial, namely:

- In an ad hoc undertaking concerned with a single definable end product.
- In an undertaking which is of greater complexity of scope than normal.
- In an undertaking with stringent time, cost, and technical performance requirements.
- In an undertaking which requires significant contribution by more than two functional organizations.
- In an undertaking requiring a quick response to change and value of time.
- In an undertaking which is unique or infrequent to present organization.
- In an undertaking with a high degree of interdependence among the tasks.
- In an undertaking where a company's reputation is at stake or where rewards of success or penalties for failure are particularly high.

In sum, the project management approach and use of various project management techniques optimize ways in which the goals of comprehensive, complex public and privately funded projects are accomplished. Technological advances in the use of computers and software will only increase dependence on the efficiencies of project management techniques, which are well adapted to computerization.

Ross Prizzia

BIBLIOGRAPHY

Badiru, Adedeji, 1993. *Quantitative Models for Project Planning, Scheduling and Control.* Westport, CT: Quorum Books.

Barkley, Bruce T., 1994. *Customer-Driven Project Management: A New Paradigm in Total Quality Implementation.* New York: McGraw-Hill, Inc.

Cleland, David I., 1990. *Project Management: Strategic Design and Implementation.* Blue Ridge Summit, PA: TAB Books, Inc.

Cleland, David I. and William R. Kind, eds., 1988. *Project Management Handbook.* 2d ed. New York: Van Nostrand Reinhold.

Gaddis, Paul O., 1959. "The Project Manager." *Harvard Business Review* (May-June).

Kerzner, Harold, 1984. *Project Management: A Systems Approach to Planning, Scheduling and Controlling.* New York: Van Nostrand Reinhold.

Kimmons, Robert L. and James H. Loweree, eds., 1989. *Project Management: A Reference for Professionals.* New York: Marcel Dekker, Inc.

Randolph, W. Alan and Barry Z. Posner, 1992. *Getting the Job Done! Managing Project Teams and Task Forces for Success.* Englewood Cliffs, NJ: Prentice-Hall.

PROPERTY TAX.

A tax which has a jurisdictions stock of property as its base.

Introduction

The property tax is one of the oldest taxes utilized by society. It was in effect during the Middle Ages when the serfs would pay taxes to the lord of the manor, and has been a mainstay of local United States finance since colonial times. Originally intended to be a tax on all wealth, it has become a relatively narrow-based tax, usually taxing only tangible real estate. It has been estimated that the ratio of the revenue raised by the property tax to total wealth has remained at about 1 percent over the last century (Musgrave and Musgrave 1980). Overall, the property tax is the mainstay of most local finance, although there is a tremendous amount of variability in how it is administered among jurisdictions in the various states. Table I illustrates the importance of this tax for some specific local jurisdictions. It should be noted that for many jurisdictions and in the aggregate, its importance is slowly falling over time.

The property tax can be justified on at least three equity grounds. It is based on ability to pay, and thus holders of more property will pay more in taxes than holders of less property. It also helps to decrease the concentration of wealth in the United States, which most feel is a benefit. And, finally, it can be argued that taxes on the stock of wealth are payments for benefits that accrue to the holders of wealth.

The principal source of revenue for most school districts is the property tax. This has led to a good deal of litigation, in which some state courts have held that to finance education based on wealth is not equitable and adjustments must be made. These adjustments range from "power equalization," in which some property tax revenues raised in wealthy school districts are transferred to poorer school districts, to a more extensive role of the state in school finance. Perhaps the most extreme case is in California when, after the Proposition 13 tax revolt and in the context of the *Serrano v. Priest* court decision, the state assumed the predominant role in school finance, which led for a time to school districts receiving about 70 percent of their revenues from the state. Current litigation in other states seems to be leading to similar results.

Definition of the Property Tax

Equation 1 defines the property tax in term of its three component parts, with R = revenues collected, t = the tax rate, and B = the tax base:

$$R = tB \qquad \text{(Equation 1)}$$

Algebraically, the revenues collected, often referred to as the property tax levy, are equal to the product of the tax rate and the tax base. In many jurisdictions, however, the needed revenues are first determined, and then the right-hand variables in the equation are calculated. The jurisdiction may determine the total expenditures it deems necessary, then subtract the amount of non-property tax revenues that it will collect and the residual expenditures will be initially set equal to the revenues that the property tax must raise. With a given base (see below), the rate is then calculated. If this rate is too high for political reasons, either expenditures must be cut or other non-property tax revenues must be increased. The principal exceptions to this process are in states or localities in which the rate is capped, and thus the revenues raised are also capped. In this case, other revenues must be increased and/or expenditures must be cut.

The base is often the crucial variable. In particular, there are two issues concerned with the base that are often addressed. The first is the determination of whether all property should be taxed at the same rate or whether different types of property should be taxed at different rates—for example, whether residential property should face the same tax rate as commercial property. Those states that tax all property at the same rate are utilizing a single-roll system, while those that divide property into more than one classification are utilizing a split-roll or classified system. In most states, the mechanistic determination of the property tax bill is done through adjustment of assessment ratios (see below).

The second issue relates to the calculation of the dollar value of the individual properties that sum to the aggregate base. This sum is usually called the assessed value of the base. There are generally two standards for this calculation (Mikesell 1995). The first is market value—that is,

TABLE I. THE IMPORTANCE OF THE PROPERTY TAX

	1964–65	1970–71	1980–81	1990–91
Total Taxes as a Percent of General Fund				
County	47.1	42.9	34.2	36.7
Municipality	30.5	49.3	41.0	34.3
Township	68.4	69.7	56.0	56.5
Special District	21.7	20.9	12.9	11.9
School Districts	51.1	45.6	35.9	38.0
Total	39.9	45.9	36.0	34.4
Property Tax as a Percent of Total Taxes				
County	91.8	87.4	76.3	73.9
Municipality	69.9	66.2	53.7	52.2
Township	92.3	91.3	94.1	92.9
Special District	100	100	80.8	70.1
School Districts	97.8	90.1	96.0	97.6
Total	86.1	81.4	75.9	75.4
Property Tax as a Percent of General Fund				
County	43.3	37.4	26.1	27.2
Municipality	21.3	32.7	22.0	17.9
Township	63.2	63.6	52.7	52.5
Special District	21.7	20.9	10.4	8.4
School Districts	50.0	41.1	34.4	37.1
Total	34.4	37.4	27.4	25.9

SOURCE: *Government Finances,* selected years.

how much the property would sell for in a competitive market. This reflects the property's highest and best use. The crucial term in this definition is competitive, which includes the accumulation of adequate knowledge by both buyers and sellers concerning market conditions, adequate time for the transaction to occur, no coercion of either buyers or sellers, and all transactions occurring at arms length. Usually, selling prices are considered accurate reflections of market values, although if the above conditions are not met, any assessment based on these prices may be challenged.

There is often a particular exception in this assessment category—agricultural land. In order to forestall the hurried conversion of rural property to urban property, this property can be assessed at its value in use, not what its market price would be. Value in use assumes that the owner will continue to use the property in the same manner, not necessarily its highest and best use. This exception is important in areas in which there is rapid urban growth and leads to an underevaluation of the true worth of the property.

In two states—California and Florida—acquisition value is the standard utilized for property assessment. In this system (which has been nicknamed the "welcome stranger" system), property is reassessed when it is sold. By definition, the sale price would equal the market value (again assuming a competitive market). However, unlike under the market value standard the property would not be entirely reassessed until it was resold. Rather, automatic formulas would slowly boost the assessment until that time. This results in a stable and predictable tax bill for the existing owner, but at the cost of very similar properties facing very different tax bills because of different sales dates, and apparently a significant reduction in mobility (O'Sullivan, Sexton, and Sheffren 1995).

The ratio of assessed value to market value is sometimes called the assessment ratio. The closer to one, the more accurate the assessment. Assessment ratios tend to be much higher under the market value system than under the acquisition value system. In some states, assessed values for tax purposes are set at a fixed percentage of market values, which merely forces the tax rate to be correspondingly higher.

Several other policy decisions must be made after the assessment standard is chosen. In particular, both process and timing decisions need to be reached under the market value system. Process decisions relate to how the market value is ascertained, whereas timing decisions relate to how often this discovery is made. These questions are automatically answered under the acquisition value system, because value is determined at the time of sale.

There are three principal methods for determining market value. The first is the use of a market data approach.

In this case, sales of comparable property are examined and then adjustments are made to ensure an even closer comparability. For example, if a three-bedroom home has recently sold, the assessor can use that data, with adjustments, to determine the value of a two-bedroom house in the same neighborhood. Often econometric regression analysis is utilized to help the assessor determine values. However, for unique residential properties or business or industrial properties, this method may not produce accurate results, and there is also the possibility of error when adjustments are made.

A second method for determining market value can be used for properties that generate a stream of income. In this income method, the present value of the net income stream is calculated and used as a surrogate for the cash value. The principal problems of this method are the determination of the true costs of earning that income so that the net stream is used (creative accounting is the anathema here) and the choice of appropriate discount rate for calculation purposes.

A third method, sometimes called the cost approach, estimates value by first calculating the depreciated value of the improvements on a site and then adding that total to the value of the land, which has been determined by either the market data or income approach techniques. The original costs can be calculated by either using reproduction or replacement costs and then these estimates are depreciated, taking into account physical, functional, or economic wear and obsolescence. Typically, this method is used for unique properties which cannot be assessed in any other manner.

Assessment timing must also be chosen. There are three basic alternatives. The first is that all property can be reassessed each year. Typically, this would be very expensive and so often ad hoc adjustments are made to the value of the property based on its description discovered in one of the above methods. However, if there has been a decline in property values, because of, for example, fires, floods, or the encroachment of blight, or a dramatic increase in property value, because of a new park, new roads, or new schools, this method would most accurately reflect the market value. Under this method, most property owners would see marginal adjustments to their property tax bill each year.

A second method is based on reassessing a particular portion of the base on a fixed schedule. For example, a fixed third of the properties in an area would be reassessed once every three years. This would be administratively easier than the first method, although it could lead to large changes in the property tax bill after the reassessment has occurred as well as some intertemporal short-run inequities.

The final method reassesses all of the properties in the jurisdiction at set intervals. For example, in Minnesota, reassessment occurs every four years. This method would likely lead to large increases in property tax bills, but fewer inequities.

In most property tax systems, there are a variety of exemptions that are available to specific types of property owners. For example, in some states, the elderly can take advantage of deferring their tax payments (but not liability) until they die and the estate is settled, at which point the accumulated tax and interest is paid. In many other cases, homeowners (as distinct from business or industrial property owners) receive a homeowner reduction in the assessment of their base. In all states, government-owned property is exempt from the tax, and in all states, property belonging to legitimate nonprofit organizations is not taxed. Finally, in many states, circuit breakers are in place, which allow tax reductions if the owners of the property meet certain characteristics, for example, having low income. All of these exemptions lead to a lower tax base, and with the revenue demands remaining constant, lead to a higher tax rate on other owners. Thus, exemptions must be carefully thought through because of their equity implications.

The final part of equation 1 is the determination of the property tax rate. In localities without rate limitations, the rate is determined by dividing the revenues to be raised by the base. In those with rate limitations, the rate is fixed by law. Typically, the rate is expressed in dollars per assessed value. It should be noted that if the assessment process is not carefully done, the statutory rate that all the property owners face will not equal the effective rate that different property owners may face. For example, if one person's property is accidentally underassessed, that person will face a lower effective rate than a person whose property is accurately assessed.

Incidence and Efficiency Concerns

The calculation of the incidence of the property tax is not particularly straightforward and without controversy. In particular there are three different views which have to be applied to a multiple number of types of property (Rosen 1995).

The Traditional View

In this view, the property tax is best examined as an excise sale tax on land and structures. Here, the incidence depends upon the elasticities of the supply and demand schedules for land and buildings. Since the amount of land is fixed in the short run, the supply schedule for land is perfectly vertical, and thus there is nothing that the owner of land can do to evade the tax. The full burden of the tax is on the landowner. If the owner of the land that is being taxed wishes to sell the land, any buyer would recognize that there is a tax liability associated with the land. The buyer would thus offer a lower price. Note that even

though the successful buyer would be paying taxes in the future, because the land sold at a reduced price, the new owner will not be bearing the tax. The old owner will bear it through the mechanism of the price reduction (technically called tax capitalization). Technically, then, to determine the true incidence of the tax, the owners of the land when the tax was initially imposed must be determined—they are the ones who are forced to pay the tax. To the extent that the supply of land is not fixed in the long run (because of zoning law changes), then some of the tax may be shifted to buyers depending upon the relevant elasticities.

To analyze the traditional view of the tax on land improvements, it is necessary to begin by considering a national market for capital, which can be used for a variety of purposes, some of which may not be structures. The price of capital behaves like any other price—as a rationing device among alternative uses. The classic view is that in the long run, builders can get all the capital they want at the market price and thus the supply curve of structures is perfectly flat. In this case, the tax burden is fully shifted to the occupants of the structures, or tenants, who bear the tax in proportion to the amount of housing they consume.

To the extent that wealthier individuals tend to own proportionally more land than poor individuals, the part of the property tax that is on land is probably progressive. Further, if the proportion of income devoted to housing falls as income increases, then the structures part of the tax is likely to be regressive. Most evidence seems to indicate that land ownership does increase with income and so the land tax is progressive. However, there is a good deal of disagreement concerning the changing proportion of income devoted to housing as income increases. Some argue that housing decisions are long-run and therefore a concept of permanent income is necessary. If this is empirically true, it seems as if the percentage of permanent income applied to housing is fairly constant, and thus the tax is proportional. If, however, annual income is considered, then the percentage does fall as income increases and the tax is regressive.

The New View

The new view of the property tax adopts a general equilibrium framework (Mieszkowski 1972). In this view, the property tax is thought of as a general wealth tax, with some wealth being taxed below the average rate and some taxed above the rate. In this case, both the average level of the tax and the differences from that average must be analyzed, both from a general tax effect perspective and the excise sales tax perspective.

First assume that the property tax can be seen as a uniform tax on all capital (whose supply to the economy is fixed, in the short run). The incidence is the same as that discussed in the traditional view: the tax falls on the owners of the factor that is in fixed supply—the owners of capital. Since wealthier people own more capital than poor

people, in this first approximation, the tax is unambiguously progressive.

However, the property tax is not a uniform tax. Effective rates may vary by type of property, assessment procedure, and jurisdiction. By definition, some rates are above the average and some below. According to the new view, the property tax can be thought of as a set of excise taxes on capital. In this case, capital leaves the high-tax-rate areas and migrates to low-tax-rate areas. As it moves to the low-rate areas, its before-tax rate of return is lowered (under the usual assumptions of diminishing productivity) while the rate of return increases in the high-tax areas. Ultimately, the after-tax rates of return are equal throughout the economy. Further, as capital moves, returns to other factors also change, with the final impact depending upon the mobility of factors. The least mobile types of capital are more likely to bear the tax. In this short or intermediate run, the incidence depends on capital-labor ratios, factor mobility, and demand. In the longer run, with a variable supply of capital, it may partially depend on the property tax rate. If the property tax decreases the supply of capital, labor productivity may fall and the real wage may fall.

In general, the effect of the tax is to lower the return to capital, but this may be offset by specific excise tax and long run effects.

The Property Tax as a User Fee

Because the property tax is a tax used by local jurisdictions, there is some argument that it is merely the price of locating in that jurisdiction. What the resident buys with this price is the bundle of services that the jurisdiction provides. In this Tiebout-like model, the property tax is a user fee that the resident voluntarily pays for locating in this community. In this case, there are no excess burden effects (Hamilton 1975). It should also be noted that to the extent that the property tax is deductible, the federal income tax lowers the price of public services to those who itemize and thus probably results in a higher demand for public services by itemizers. If this third view is accurate, it strongly implies that looking at the property tax in isolation is incorrect—government services and property values must also be examined.

Is There a Correct View?

These three views are not mutually exclusive, and each might be valid in different contexts. For example, if the question is the total elimination of the property tax and its replacement with a national sales tax, the new view is most appropriate because this change affects all communities and requires the new view's general equilibrium framework. But if one community is thinking about lowering its property tax and substituting a sales tax, the classic view is more insightful, because for a single community, the supply of capital is probably perfectly elastic. Or, if taxes and benefits are changed at the same time and there are enough opportunities for individuals to pick and choose among communities and these individuals are mobile, then the user fee view might be best utilized. As can be seen, incidence and efficiency effects are often difficult to ascertain with property taxes.

Current Policy Issues

There are at least three basic public policy issues that are relevant to the current property tax in the United States: the continued unpopularity of the property tax, the difficulty of accurate administration, and the effects of tax limits on the use of the tax.

The property tax is often an unpopular tax, although its popularity is closely related to eras of property tax reform. Between 1972 and 1991, it was the least popular tax in eight of those years, with a 20-year average of 30 percent of the respondents thinking it was the least fair tax (ACIR 1991; for the period 1979 through 1988, the federal income tax was considered least fair).

There are several reasons that make this dislike a rational response by the taxpayer. The tax is based on estimated value and many property owners believe that they are being unfairly assessed. The tax is highly visible, and for many paid in one or two large installments, often due at difficult times of the year (in California, the installments are due two weeks before Christmas and one week before the federal income tax deadline). Most of the other homeowner taxpayers have their property tax withheld by the mortgage company in an impound account so that the taxpayer is still writing a check every month that noticeably includes the tax payment. Closely related to this is the accurate perception of the taxpayer of the "localness" of the tax. Since it is the tax most carefully controlled by local units of government, the taxpayer feels that it is more controllable. The element of controllability added to its visibility again makes it unpopular. Finally, the tax is often considered to be regressive, which while potentially true in a few cases under the old view, is not accepted under the new view or the user tax view. The ultimate policy issue in this case is how to make the tax more acceptable to the taxpayer. A potential solution is to demonstrate the clear linkage between the local benefits the tax provides and the taxes being paid.

The remaining policy issues are closely connected to the first. Poor property tax administration can lead to increased dislike of the tax, because the assessed value may be wrong. Being wrong can lead to two distinct problems. The first is at the individual level. An incorrect assessment would lead to an incorrect tax bill. Obviously, if the assessment is too low, there will be few complaints. However, if the assessment is incorrectly high, the taxpayer will object. Unfortunately, there appears to be a high degree of variation of assessments, which leads to a high level of distrust (Mikesell 1995). The second problem is a result of poor individual assessments. If the aggregate base is wrong, then,

for a given revenue, the tax rate set is also wrong. Wrong rates could lead to misallocation of resources and efficiency consequences. Continued training and allocation of additional resources to the tax collection agencies could help to ameliorate this problem, although typically when jurisdictions face fiscal stress, this is an area in which cutbacks often occur.

The final policy issue is the increasing use of tax limits to ensure that the property tax does not become excessively high. Unfortunately, excessively high is a debatable term—1991 rates ranged from 4.4 percent in Detroit to .37 percent in Honolulu (Bureau of the Census 1993). What does seem to occur when property tax limits are imposed, such as Proposition 13 in California in 1978 (Stocker 1991) is a centralization of finance and movement away from local fiscal control to state fiscal control. Tax limits are likely to remain in place for the foreseeable future.

Conclusions

The property tax will always be part of the tax system of the United States. It still provides local government with some fiscal autonomy, it is a relatively stable source of revenue for government, and while its growth may not always be dramatic, it is predictable. With the policy issues identified above reconciled, the tax will become even more important in the future.

JEFFERY I. CHAPMAN

BIBLIOGRAPHY

Advisory Commission on Intergovernmental Relations, 1991. *Changing Public Attitudes on Governments and Taxes, 1991.* Washington, D.C.: ACIR.

Bureau of the Census, 1993. *Statistical Abstract of the United States, 1993.* Washington, D.C.: U.S. Department of Commerce, Bureau of the Census.

Hamilton, Bruce, 1975. "Zoning and Property Taxation in a System of Local Governments." *Urban Studies* 12 (June) 205–211.

Mikesell, John, 1995. *Fiscal Administration.* 4th ed. San Francisco: Wadsworth.

Mieszkowski, Peter M., 1972. "The Property Tax: An Excise Tax or a Profits Tax?" *Journal of Public Economics* 1:73–96.

Musgrave, Richard A. and Peggy B. Musgrave, 1980. *Public Finance in Theory and Practice.* 3d ed. San Francisco: McGraw Hill.

O'Sullivan, Arthur, Terri A. Sexton, and Steven M. Sheffren, 1995. *Property Taxes and Tax Revolts: The Legacy of Proposition 13.* Cambridge: Cambridge University Press.

Rosen, Harvey S., 1995. *Public Finance.* Chicago: Irwin.

Stocker, Frederick D., 1991. *Proposition 13: A Ten-Year Retrospective.* Cambridge: Lincoln Institute of Land Policy.

PROSTITUTION POLICY. Law and administrative policy governing the sale of sexual services, including, but not limited to, sexual intercourse.

Origin and History

Prostitution has existed in most societies and at most times, although its form has varied. The vast majority of purchasers of sexual services are men, while most prostitutes are women. Male and transsexual prostitutes usually sell sex to male clients. In Western countries today women work as prostitutes from the street, in brothels, and from saunas, "massage parlors," and escort agencies. Prostitution, including sex tours from industrialized to Third World countries, is a multibillion-dollar industry. It has been estimated that up to 500,000 women may work as prostitutes in the United States.

Until the nineteenth century most Western countries did not criminalize prostitution, although prostitution was often informally regulated by selective enforcement of public order or vagrancy offenses. However by the early nineteenth century in the United States, and the early twentieth century in many other Western countries, laws imposing criminal penalties for prostitution-related activities such as street soliciting, brothel-keeping, and pimping were gradually enacted. The move towards criminalization coincided with increasing middle-class concern about threats to social order and public manifestations of deviant behavior such as street soliciting. Concerns about exploitation of women and girls and moral panic over allegations of forced prostitution of white women resulted in the making of international agreements for the "Suppression of the White Slave Traffic" in the first three decades of the twentieth century, thus contributing to the policy of prohibiting prostitution. The scapegoating of prostitutes as vectors for the spread of venereal disease strengthened the case of those who sought the imposition of criminal sanctions.

Policy Approaches

The three main public policy approaches which have been taken to prostitution are:

- Criminalization (often described as prohibition);
- Decriminalization (abolition of criminal penalties for prostitution and related activities); and
- Regulation (sometimes called legalization).

By the end of the nineteenth century the policy of criminalizing the "social evil" of prostitution had become widespread. It continues to apply in many Western countries. Prostitution laws in countries which have followed the English model, such as Australia, New Zealand, and Canada, generally follow the approach of the 1957 report of the English Wolfenden Committee, which recommended against criminalization of the act of prostitution itself, but supported retention of offenses designed to discourage exploitation of women, such as living on the earnings of prostitution, and to prevent public nuisance, such as laws prohibiting soliciting in public places. In these jurisdictions some forms of prostitution (for example use of premises by a single prostitute in England and escort agency prostitution in some parts of Australia) are not criminal offenses.

United States prostitution laws are more draconian. At a federal level the 1910 Mann Act prohibits the transportation interstate or overseas of women or girls for sexual purposes. In the majority of states the act of prostitution is a misdemeanor and all states criminalize activities such as brothel-keeping and pimping. Pimping is usually a felony. Most states follow the Model Penal Code under which buying sex is an offense, but penalties are usually less severe for clients than for prostitutes.

Few, if any, countries have completely decriminalized prostitution, although some jurisdictions have repealed some offenses applicable to prostitutes, while retaining provisions covering pimping and brothel-keeping. This policy was supported in a 1983 Report to the United Nations by Special Rapporteur Monsieur J. Fernand-Laurent, which suggested that the most effective policy for elimination of prostitution required eradicating sex discrimination and "not treating prostitutes as criminals," while punishing pimps and all forms of procuring. Prostitutes are rarely prosecuted in Denmark and Sweden, where greater emphasis is placed on social programs designed to reduce demand for prostitution and the need for women to support themselves by selling sex. Prostitution has been partially decriminalized by some states in Australia.

The argument for decriminalization was historically based on the libertarian principles of nineteenth-century philosopher John Stuart Mill. Criminologists such as Norval Morris and Gordon Hawkins, in their 1970 book *The Honest Politician's Guide to Crime Control*, also suggested that the cost of laws punishing "victimless crimes" such as prostitution and gambling outweighed the benefits. They argued that criminal offenses are expensive to enforce, drive up the price of sexual services, thus encouraging participation of organized crime networks, and are inevitably associated with police corruption. In the nineteenth century English feminist leaders such as Josephine Butler opposed repressive prostitution laws. Since the 1970s most feminists have supported repeal of laws punishing prostitutes.

Prostitution was regulated in France and several other Western European countries until well into the twentieth century. Typical provisions required women to register with police, live in brothels licensed by local authorities, and attend regular medical examinations. In 1949 the General Assembly of the United Nations adopted the Convention for the Suppression of the Traffic in Persons and the Exploitation of the Prostitution of Others, which promoted an end to the policy of regulation and the punishing of those who exploited prostitutes. The Netherlands, Switzerland and some cities in (formerly West) Germany retain some aspects of regulation today, but regulation continues to be opposed by the United Nations and by many feminist groups, which regard it as a form of legalized slavery.

Nevada is the only American state which permits and regulates prostitution. State law retains penalties for procuring, pimping, and keeping or advertising a house of prostitution, but counties with a population of less than 250,000 can license brothels and other places of prostitution. Seven counties license brothels by ordinance, five prohibit them, and four permit them in rural areas. In 1987 there were 43 legal brothels. Ordinances require prostitutes to obtain a work permit and be fingerprinted and medically examined. Some counties restrict the movement of prostitutes, although constitutionality of these provisions is questionable.

In some Australian states there are more limited systems of regulation (these are often described as decriminalization with controls), which have removed some offenses applicable to prostitutes, controlled location of brothels (as in Victoria and the Australian Capital Territory), or prohibited street soliciting in specified areas (as in New South Wales). A similar approach was recommended in Canada in 1985 by the Report of the Special Committee on Pornography and Prostitution.

Current Trends

In the past 20 years support for criminalization has mainly come from business and property owners concerned about the effects of street soliciting or concentrations of brothels on property values. Over the same period prostitutes' organizations in Europe, the United States, and Australia have sought an improvement in their working conditions and an end to police harassment. Feminists have argued that prostitution is a symptom of women's sexual and economic inequality, although they disagree on whether laws directed at those profiting from prostitution should be retained. The AIDS epidemic has prompted arguments that criminalizing prostitution discourages prostitutes and their clients from seeking treatment or cooperating with public health authorities. Despite these changes in the debate about prostitution policy, few jurisdictions have reformed their prostitution laws.

MARCIA NEAVE

BIBLIOGRAPHY

Reports for Government and International Bodies:

■ *Australia*

Neave, Marcia A., 1984. *Inquiry into Prostitution: Options Paper.* Melbourne: Victorian Government Printer.
———, 1985. *Inquiry into Prostitution: Final Report.* Melbourne: Victorian Government Printer.
Select Committee of the Legislative Assembly upon Prostitution, 1986. *Report.* Sydney: Parliament of New South Wales.

Select Committee on HIV, Illegal Drugs and Prostitution ACT Legislative Assembly, 1991. *Interim Report.* Australian Capital Territory.

■ *Canada*

Kiedrowski, John S. and Jan M. Dijk, 1984. *Pornography and Prostitution in Denmark, France, West Germany, The Netherlands and Sweden.* Working Papers on Pornography and Prostitution, No. 1, Department of Justice, Canada.
Sansfacon, Daniel, 1984. *Pornography and Prostitution in the United States.* Working Papers on Pornography and Prostitution, No. 2, Department of Justice, Canada.
Special Committee on Pornography and Prostitution, 1985. *Pornography and Prostitution in Canada* (Fraser Report). Ottawa: Canadian Government Publishing Centre.

■ *England*

Great Britain Home Office and Scottish Home Department Committee on Homosexual Offences and Prostitution, 1957. *Report* (Wolfenden Report). Cmnd. 247, London, H.M.S.O.

■ *United Nations*

United Nations, Economic and Social Council, Activities for the Advancement of Women: Equality Development and Peace, March 17, 1983. Report of Mr. Jean Fernand-Laurent, Special Rapporteur on the Suppression of the Traffic in Persons and the Exploitation of the Prostitution of Others, E/1983/7.
United Nations, 1984. *Report of Mr. Benjamin Whitaker, Special Rapporteur of the Sub-Commission on Prevention of Discrimination and Protection of Minorities* (updating the *Report on Slavery,* submitted to the Sub-Commission in 1996). New York.

Books:

Bullough, Vern L. and Bonnie Bullough, 1964. *The History of Prostitution.* New York: University Books.
Daniels, Kay, ed., 1984. *So Much Hard Work: Women and Prostitution in Australian History.* Sydney: Fontana-Collins.
Decker, J. F., 1979. *Prostitution: Regulation and Control.* Littleton, Colorado: Rothman.
Hobson, Barbara M., 1987. *Uneasy Virtue: The Politics of Prostitution and the American Reform Tradition.* New York: Basic Books, Inc.
Millet, Kate, 1973. *The Prostitution Papers.* New York: Ballantine Books.
Morris, Norval and Gordon Hawkins, 1970. *The Honest Politician's Guide to Crime Control.* Chicago: University of Chicago Press.
Perkins, Roberta and Garry Bennett, 1985. *Being a Prostitute: Prostitute Women and Prostitute Men.* Sydney: Allen & Unwin.
Walkowitz, Judith R., 1980. *Prostitution and Victorian Society: Women, Class and the State.* Cambridge: Cambridge University Press.

Articles:

Cheney, Belinda M., 1988. "Prostitution: A Feminist Jurisprudential Perspective." *Victoria University of Wellington Law Journal,* vol. 18:239–257.
Freeman, Jody, 1989. "The Feminist Debate Over Prostitution Reform: Prostitutes' Rights Groups, Radical Feminists, and the (Im)possibility of Consent." *Berkeley Women's Law Journal,* vol. 5:75–109.

Kadish, Sanford H., 1968–69. "The Crisis of Overcriminalization." *American Criminal Law Quarterly*, vol. 7:17–34.

Milman, Barbara, 1980. "New Rules for the Oldest Profession: Should We Change Our Prostitution Laws?" *Harvard Women's Law Journal*, vol. 3 (Spring) 1–82.

Reanda, Linda, 1991. "Prostitution as a Human Rights Problem: Problems and Prospects of United Nations Action." *Human Rights Quarterly*, vol. 13 (2):202–228.

Scibelli, Pasqua, 1987. "Empowering Prostitutes: A Proposal for International Legal Reform." *Harvard Women's Law Journal*, vol. 10 (Spring) 117–157.

PROVINCE. The intermediate unit of government between central government and the basic units of local government in multitiered systems of government. The province corresponds to the level of the U.S. county, although in the Anglo-American tradition the county generally is exclusively regarded as local government. Provinces are intermediate local authorities, and they are also territorial divisions for performing national functions.

The term province as such is currently in use in several Western European countries, namely Belgium, Italy, the Netherlands and Spain. In other countries a different terminology refers to intermediate government, such as the *départements* in France, the *amtskommmuner* in Denmark, the *landsting* in Sweden, and the *fylkes* in Norway.

This article will be limited to the countries mentioned here; in the general discussion some country-specific elements will be brought forward.

Common Denominators

The province is an example of territorial decentralization: It embodies the concept of self-government and administration by the inhabitants of the province (Norton, 1994, p. xix). An elected council with an executive body assumes the political responsibility. The province is a general purpose authority which is to act in all matters in the provincial interest. Generally, the provincial autonomy is established in the constitution.

Provinces occupy an ambivalent position towards central government. Provincial autonomy is on the brink between provincial self-government and central authority. The position and the actual influence of the province in regard to central government are a product of the functions of provincial government, the discretion of the provincial government, and their access to central government (Page and Goldsmith, 1987, p. 4).

Provincial Organization

The province has a tripartite institutional structure: the council and an executive body which is presided over by a governor.

The council is chosen on the basis of direct elections, except for Spain, where the council is elected indirectly. In most countries the provincial elections are special elections at regular intervals. Sometimes, the elections are tied to other elections because of a relatively high number of elections or because the provincial elections contribute to the composition of Parliament. Although the provincial councilors in the Netherlands constitute the first chamber of Parliament, provincial elections have always been organized independently.

The executive body of the province is appointed by the council from its members. The members of the executive board act as a collegial body.

The governor's position may take different forms. In Belgium and the Netherlands the governor is a central government representative, appointed by central government, with specific personal competences. In other countries the governor is chosen by the council or the executive body. In France *le président du conseil* has considerable powers and is in charge of the administration. In other countries the governor has a vote in the executive body.

Provincial Competences

When discussing provincial competences, traditionally a distinction is made between autonomous competences, mandated competences, and joint administration.

The autonomous competences allow the province to act according to its own insights in all matters in the provincial interest. Yet this may be circumscribed differently in the different countries. In the Scandinavian countries the provinces cannot act in matters that by law should be carried out by other organizations. In Belgium, Italy, and the Netherlands provinces can act as long as they do not enter the sphere of competences of other authorities.

In some matters provinces are required to act according to the guidelines set out by central government, although possibly some discretion remains. The so-called mandated competences may be compulsory, or may apply only if the province aims for central grants.

The last category is joint administration. In these matters, provinces act as executive agents of central government.

Recent years have witnessed in almost all countries a reduction of provincial autonomy to the benefit of increased mandated functions. On the whole, provinces provide services that benefit from operating on a larger scale than the municipal level or they are responsible for planning activities. Examples of functional areas in which provinces are most likely to act are urban planning, environment, infrastructures, education, public utilities, and health care. On the whole, provincial functions are more extensive in the Scandinavian countries. However, in all countries mentioned here, the provincial level is less important than the local level in terms of service provision.

Central Supervision Versus Provincial Discretion

Usually a representative of central government is present internal or external to the provincial structures. In Belgium and the Netherlands the governor is a central government representative.

Before the 1982 reforms in France the central government representative, the prefect, who was appointed by and responsible to the minister of the interior, had the executive control of the department. After the reforms this was transferred to the governor, but the prefect continues to coordinate central policies in the department. In Italy and Spain a representative of the central government played a similar role to the French prefect. Now, due to the regionalization process, the control is exercised by a regional control council rather than the prefect, but substantially nothing changed.

In Sweden, the territories of regional boards of central government largely coincide with the provinces. The regional board is a hybrid structure which consists of members of the county council, but is presided over by a government appointee, who is responsible for the provision of central services.

Another way of exercising central control is by means of administrative tutelage. In Norway important financial decisions have to be approved by central government. In Denmark, the budgets and the general legality of decisions are supervised by central government. Additionally in most policy fields specific forms of supervision exist. In the Netherlands the legality of provincial decisions is checked; in Belgium also the opportunity of decisions is checked.

In the process of regionalization the actual control may be transferred to the regions, as is the case for Spain, Italy and Belgium.

In countries experiencing processes of regionalization or federalization the position of the provinces is increasingly put under pressure. In Belgium, Italy, and Spain the actual control over provinces has been transferred to the newly created member states or regions. But the creation of a new layer of government in those countries has also resulted in a centralist movement at the regional level, undermining the position of the provinces.

Financial Position

In most countries provinces can levy taxes, although the degrees to which they are allowed to do so may vary. Sometimes these taxes are collected centrally, such as in France or Norway. However, except for Sweden, taxes are not the most important source of revenue, but rather government grants. Global grants are allocated on the basis of general criteria with no strings attached. They may be used partially to redistribute income between provinces. Specific grants are tied to the provision of specific services or the execution of central policies.

The amount of public spending by the provinces is highest in the Scandinavian countries; but on the other hand, the largest share of provincial spending there is compulsory, such as on health care and social services. Provincial spending decreases as one goes to the south of Europe.

In most countries, provinces have become increasingly dependent upon direct financial support by the government and their own resources have declined in importance. Specific grants are on the whole more important than global grants. The financially dependent position of provinces equally qualifies provincial discretion. In financial terms provincial government is also less important than the basic units of local government.

LINDA WOUTERS AND
RUDOLF MAES

BIBLIOGRAPHY

Batley, R. and G. Stoker, eds., 1991. *Local Government in Europe: Trends and Developments.* London: Macmillan.

Norton, A. L., 1994. *International Handbook of Local and Regional Government: A Comparative Analysis of Advanced Democracies.* Hants: Edward Elgar.

Page, E. C. and M. J. Goldsmith, eds., 1987. *Central and Local Government Relations: A Comparative Analysis of Western European Unitary States.* London: Sage.

PUBLIC ADMINISTRATION.

1. The occupational sector, enterprises, and activities having to do with the formulation and implementation of policy of governmental and other public programs and the management of organizations and activities involved. 2. The academic field concerned with the study of, improvement of, and training for the activities mentioned in 1.

Public administration refers to two distinguishable but closely related activities: (1) a professional practice (vocation, occupation, field of activity), and (2) an academic field which seeks to understand, develop, criticize, and improve that professional practice as well as to train individuals for that practice. The simple meaning of the term is quite direct: it refers on the one hand to the administration or management of matters which have principally to do with the society, polity, and its subparts which are not essentially private, familial, commercial, or individualistic, and on the other hand to the disciplined study of such matters. In this simplest meaning, public administration has to do with managing the realm of governmental and other public activities. This simple definition conveys the essence of public administration and probably covers the vast majority of activities and concerns of contemporary public administration.

Such a simple view, though, needs modification to account for at least two important considerations: First, it must be recognized that professional management of the public's affairs involves not only management in the narrowest sense (keeping the books, handling personnel decisions, implementing decisions which have been made elsewhere in the politico-socio-economic systems, etc.), but also significantly involves the planning, formulating, modifying, and urging of goals and purposes of much of public affairs. Second, it must be recognized that some matters of public administration are handled in ways which are not purely private but are also not precisely governmental.

The first consideration—that public administration is involved in the substance of policy as well as in the implementation of policy decisions—is frequently alluded to with terms such as the demise of the politics-administration dichotomy, the impossibility of value-free public administration, and the need for proactivity by public administrators. These terms reflect the widespread, though not universal, belief or allegation that it is no longer, if ever it was, defensible to interpret public administration as solely involved in technically objective solutions or in the neutral implementation of decisions made by nonadministrative parts of the political system (e.g., partisan leadership; electoral processes; party processes; partisan bargaining; and parliamentary, legislative, and judicial institutions). This belief and related understandings have led to significant public administration attention to policy and policy process. Some have felt a need for a rubric which emphasizes such a policy focus and which might also encompass or indicate receptivity to areas of studies which are closely related (e.g., planning, urban affairs, economic analysis, public policy analysis), and terms such as public affairs are sometimes used for this purpose. In general, though, public administration still functions as the umbrella term throughout the world, though it must be realized that the term implies a broader range of concerns and activities than the narrow meaning of management or administration may convey.

The second consideration—that not all public administration occurs in and through governmental organizations—also has led to a broadening of the meaning of public administration. At various times in the past of public administration it has seemed that its essence and activities could be identified by referring to nonmarket approaches to social purposes, but this perspective has been mitigated by the recognition that public programs and benefits could be developed through and provided with some market characteristics. Thus there have been developments such as governmental or quasi-governmental activities which compete with private sector activities or provide benefits through use of a price mechanism; sometimes water, utilities, sewers, health care, education, and other benefits are provided in this way. There are also devices such as public corporations, quasi-public corporations, public-private cooperative enterprises, and government contractual arrangements with nongovernmental organizations to provide certain benefits or perform certain functions. Indeed, even for large parts of the world where the private-public distinction has not been as prevalent or obvious as other places (for example, where the economy is essentially directed or nonmarket), the movement toward market or marketlike mechanisms for the provision of public goods is increasingly a matter or rhetoric, planning, or action.

When these considerations are taken into account, public administration is probably best defined as the practice and study of the professional formulation and influence of public policy and the implementation of such policy on a regular and organized basis on behalf of the public interest of a society, its civic subparts, and its citizenry.

Development of the Field

As first defined above, public administration has existed virtually since human beings first cooperated on behalf of their society for common purposes. Clear and explicit discussion both of the task of formulating decisions and of carrying out the details of those decisions may be found among the most ancient documents of various civilizations. Attention to the proper education and training of individuals for the various tasks involved is also clear and explicit in many such documents. The systematic study and codification of the technical aspects of such endeavors in a style reflecting the contemporary field of public administration may be variously dated.

It is usual, for example, to date the contemporary social scientific awareness of bureaucracy (a term which can include both private, or "business," administration and public administration) with the work of the German social scientist Max Weber (1864–1920). Such dating, though, is more a matter of convenience or recognition of important scholarly influence than of historical accuracy. For example, the German and French writer Baron de Grimm (1723–1807), the German philosopher Georg W. F. Hegel (1770–1831), and other philosophers and social commentators explicitly discussed bureaucracy; and the English economist and social philosopher John Stuart Mill (1806–1873)—especially in his 1861 *Considerations on Representative Government*—offered profound insights into public bureaucracy and its possible relationship to representative government. Similarly, in many European countries—especially those which see public administration as essentially a subfocus of public law—understandings of systematic modern public administration may be traced to ancient Roman law and its heritage, to the eighteenth-century German and Austrian Cameralists and Prussian government, to the nineteenth-century Napoleonic Code and its influences, and to the general heritage of positive law.

In the United States, it is usual to credit the reformism of the Populist and Progressive era of politics (about 1880–1920) and especially Woodrow Wilson's academic article "The Study of Administration" (in the *Political Science Quarterly* in 1887) for the systematic and self-conscious development of the field of public administration. It is usual also to identify the early years of U.S. public administration with scientific management, a school of thought largely attributed to Frederick Winslow Taylor (1856–1915) which emphasized a task analysis and efficiency approach to management; and with the subsequent human relations movement, which emphasized the human and social aspects of work environments and motivations somewhat in contradistinction to the scientific management movement. Both of these latter movements had their orgins in industrial and business management, but were very influential on public administration in the United States and around the world. The period of U.S. history between the Great Depression and the World War II (about 1929–1945) is commonly held to represent U.S. public administration in a self-confident–though some also say naive–phase; this period is frequently referred to in the United States and elsewhere as the period of classical public administration or orthodox public administration. The period between the end of World War II and the 1960s is usually interpreted as a period of the growth of a behavioral, empirical approach to the social sciences and to public administration and its concerns. Not only in the United States, but in the industrialized and industrializing world generally, this period has been characterized as bringing scientific and technological advances to public administration. The dynamics of the Cold War competition between the United States and Western allies and the USSR and its allies, and the manifestation of this competition in various forms of technical assistance, aid in economic development, and administrative assistance had an impact upon public administration. In the 1960s and 1970s, much of the world of science and technology came under attack. In the United States, these decades and their challenges have come to be interpreted against the backdrop of the civil rights movement (and related movements such as feminism), Vietnam War activism, the "new left," anti-institutionalism, and particular manifestations of youth rebellion. Other parts of the world also experienced similar movements, frequently exacerbated by issues of neocolonialism, nationalism, anti-institutionalism, environmentalism, anti-technologism, and general critiques of scientific and technological perspectives and, indeed, the entirety of "modernity." All of these matters had effects upon politics, the social sciences, and public administration. In the United States and elsewhere, many of these developments were accompanied by significant critiques of public administration. One manifestation of this was a dialogue about the need for fundamental rethinking in public administration (and, for some, the need for a "new public administration"). In the last couple of decades, this had been augmented by tremendous technological developments (e.g., in computer applications and in communications developments) on the one hand, and ever more sophisticated philosophical and methodological interpretations asserting that we are transcending "modernity" in ways which call much of our contemporary understanding and technological approaches into question on the other hand. At the present time, public administration worldwide is in creative tension and undergoing rapid change and attempts at reconceptualization. What the effects of all this will be over time, or what the next developmental stage will be, is unclear but generally appears to have an energizing effect upon the field.

Configuration of the Field

Public administration is sometimes treated as though it is one of the social sciences, a discipline in some sense. As the number of programs offering doctoral degrees in the field has increased, this interpretation has gained strength. In some countries, public administration is a formal, degree-granting field at both the baccalaureate and postbaccalaureate levels. In some countries, public administration is not a degree-granting field, and education for the public administration academic and practitioner is pursued through undergraduate and graduate degree programs in economics, political science, law, and other such fields. In some other countries, public administration is a degree program at the post-baccalaureate but nondoctoral level (i.e., degrees or certificates exist at the master's level, but undergraduate study and doctoral study are pursued under the disciplinary auspices of other disciplines such as law, economics, history, sociology, political science, etc.). In some countries, those who aspire to public administration careers at the highest levels of the professional civil service compete for admission to special academies and schools which serve this specific purpose. And, of course, some of these types of educational programs exist in mixed forms in many places.

In the United States, it is relatively unusual for public administration to be a free-standing degree program at the baccalaureate level (though there are some well-established and prestigious programs of this sort–especially in schools of public affairs, schools of management, or schools of public administration–and this approach may be on the increase). The more traditional and still usual pattern is for baccalaureate education in public administration to be a major or minor specialization within a political science degree program. Master-level degrees are increasingly emphasized as desirable or expected credentials for full commitment to professional careers in many fields (e.g., not only in business administration and public administration, but also in fields such as education, social work, nursing, and education where the appropriate degree for professional entry was once the baccalaureate), and the master's degree—usually, but not always, the master of public administration (MPA)—is becoming the recognized degree for those who aspire to careers in public administration. It should be remembered, though, that public organizations and activities cover virtually the whole spectrum of contemporary specialties and that the educational background and specialties of public administrators therefore reflect this diversity. Many individuals who spend their working lives in public administration (as well as business administration) organizations and enterprises will have come from educational backgrounds such as police, justice, firefighting, engineering, health services, liberal arts and sciences education, and technical training of a broad range. Increasingly, though, the expectation is for postbaccalaureate (degree or nondegree, and frequently "in-service" or "on the job") education for those who spend a career in the public service regardless of what the preservice education or training may have been.

Education for the academic part of the field of public administration—especially at the doctoral level—continues to rely heavily upon the social science disciplines. Even when doctoral degree education is in public administration (or public affairs, public policy, urban affairs, or other labels), the program of studies is interdisciplinary with heavy reliance upon the social science disciplines. Doctoral education for public administration—as for business administration and the social science disciplines—also involves significant attention to statistics, information systems, computer-assisted modeling, and other technical areas.

As modern and contemporary public administration evolved, it tended to develop a more or less regular set of subfields, approaches, and topical interests. These generally have to do either with the functional and technical specializations of public administration, with specific methods and approaches, or with the phenomena of specific locales and issue areas of public administration.

Thus, public administration has some subfields which deal with concerns which, in one form or another, have been part of the field since its earliest days. Budget and finance (how to provide, handle, and account for material resources), personnel (the policies and management of human resources), planning, operations management, organizational design and management, communications and communications systems, record-keeping, accounting of various kinds, reporting of various kinds and for a variety of purposes land clientele, internal and external public relations, and a host of similar concerns constitute some of the technical and functional foci of the field. In addition to these, there are various concerns dealing with the environment and context of administration: the constitutional and legal context; the context of the political, economic, and societal structure, requirements, and processes; the values, history, traditions, and habits of the society and its components; the values, history, requirements, and processes of the organizations, programs, and components of specific relevance at any given time; and many other such factors (as well as their interrelationships).

Specific approaches, methods, or procedural preferences sometimes also have aspects of subfield about them. Specializations such as program and organizational evaluation, organizational development, operations research, quantitative aids to management, and the like are partly defined by methodological affinity or choice, but tend also to become subfields of research, education, and training. Similarly, participative management, participative policy processes, focus group approaches, some approaches to leadership, some aspects of strategic planning, and the like are partly defined by conclusions about organizational and administrative dynamics; partly by epistemological and methodological preferences; and partly by political or civic values and theories—and they, too, tend to become something like subfields in research, education, and training. The general dialogue in the social sciences and humanities—and even in some aspects of the physical and life sciences—concerning methodologies and epistemologies which are sometimes referred to with terms such as positivism and postpositivism, while not manifesting itself as subfield concentrations or subfields, manifests itself as something of a watershed in public administration as it has in other fields.

There are also specializations and foci having to do with the specific form and level at which administration occurs: international administration; national administration; federal/confederal administration, state/province administration, district/department/sector administration; city, county, and local administration; intergovernmental and interorganizational administration; "not for profit" administration; and so forth. Issue areas present other topics and specializations: police, fire, schools, military, medical, environmental, technology and technology transfer, science and scientific applications, government-business-industry cooperation, and a host of other specific issue concerns spawn specializations of knowledge, application, training, and experience.

When one realizes that all these (and many more) can be viewed as components of a huge matrix where any one (or more) can be related to any other one (or more), the complexity and variety of the field of public administration is suggested. A good sense of the present configuration of the field can be gained by consulting the considerable set of general public administration textbooks in use around the world. Perusal of these will give a good sense of the functional, topical, methodological, and curricular definition of the field. Comparison of current textbooks with earlier ones can provide a good sense of the changes and development of the field, and comparison of textbooks from one country to another can provide a sense of how approaches may vary internationally. There are also many professional and academic journals of the field worldwide; these journals can provide a good sense of the current state and interests of the field, as well as some sense of the different emphases from one setting to another.

Public Administration as a Cultural and Social Phenomenon

The phenomena of public administration are also objects of study for purposes other than the development of public administration. That is, public administration can be the focus of study of other disciplines or concerns, much as religion can be a topic of investigation for a sociologist who is not religious and has no interest in improving religious experience for the godly. Thus, complex organizations, bureaucracy, and a variety of organizational, administrative, and policy phenomena constitute topics of interest to scholars from a variety of disciplines, fields, and perspectives. Economists, sociologists, political scientists, philosophers, historians, students of literature and of communications and rhetoric, and a host of other academic specialists find public administration and its phenomena worthwhile objects of investigation. The field of public administration, for its part, contributes to, profits from, and incorporates such studies.

Concern for Identity and Legitimacy

A characteristic of public administration in recent decades has been a concern for the identity or legitimacy of the field. This may, in fact, be several separable concerns, which are frequently subsumed under the idea of "identity crisis." There are at least six aspects of this concern: (1) questioning and clarification which is typical of the formation of disciplines and fields; (2) concern over whether public administration is, properly speaking, a profession; (3) unease about theoretical unification, (4) puzzling effects of the applied nature of the field or the fact that the field has a professional or occupational concern as well as a scholarly or academic concern; (5) ambivalence about bureaucracy, hierarchy, and instrumental relationships; and (6) concern about the political legitimacy of public administration.

A concern for disciplinary identity is a typical concern in the general configuration and reconfiguration of disciplined understanding of the world. As public administration worries about its own identity, and especially as it does so against the backdrop of the social sciences and related fields of practice, it sometimes does so without clear memory or full appreciation of the recency of the present configuration and identities of disciplinary identities. Political science and sociology—to take two examples close to public administration dialogue—have only within the last century and a half invented themselves in their present identity. The history of such fields has been one of dialogue, tension, and uncertainty about epistemology, methodology, identity, and even chief phenomena of study. Indeed, this state of affairs is characteristic not only of the history but also of the present state of such fields. Thus, it is not surprising that identity questioning and insecurity has been characteristic of public administration from the inception of its self-conscious awareness as a field. The Wilson essay frequently cited as an example of the birth of a self-aware field of public administration in the United States was concerned precisely and explicitly with the question of the identity of a field of study and practice. The development of the field as a focus for study and training, concerning as it did an emphasis upon a new field or an interdisciplinary field, obviously had to focus on the continual definition of itself and on the distinguishing of itself from other foci and fields; this would seem true of all such developments, though it is sometimes not remembered in discussions of the development of fields which have been long established.

Though questions about the autonomy of the field may be less seriously raised than they have been in the past, they are still encountered from time to time and from several directions. For example, while a generic approach (i.e., the idea that administration or management is essentially the same field regardless of whether it is applied to business, education, health institutions, social work or social services, and so on) may not be as strongly asserted as it once was, the basic idea is still encountered in various forms. Sometimes institutions of higher education organize in ways which reflect this notion (e.g., a public administration department in a college or school of business or management), though there are many reasons other than the epistemological, intellectual, professional, or pedagogical why an institution might choose a particular organizational arrangement. There are professional and academic conferences, associations, and journals which project public administration as a subunit in a somewhat generic field of management.

On the other hand, countervailing interpretations are indicated by professional and organizational conferences, associations, and journals which project public administration as a subfield in the discipline of political science. As indicated earlier, such dynamics seem to be a normal part of configuration and reconfiguration of intellectual enterprises generally. It is likely that public administration has as much integrity and clarity about its enterprise as most other fields have at a comparable stage of development; it seems unlikely that worry over precise disciplinary status should be more of a hindrance to public administration than it has been or is to other fields.

Sometimes worry over the issue of professional status is part of the perceived identity crisis. Thus, it is sometimes asked whether public administration is or can aspire to be a profession, and frequently this is framed with specific reference to traditional professions. Though such a question may have interesting implications, there seems to be a developing consensus that it is important to articulate appropriate professional standards, expectations, and ethics without worrying unduly about whether the field is a profession in all the senses of the traditional professions (e.g., law, medicine, and religious ministry). Still, questions about professional status have contributed to the sense some have of identity crisis.

A related aspect of this identity insecurity is concern over unifying theory: it is frequently said that public administration lacks a unifying theory such as some other fields or disciplines are alleged to have. It is true that public administration may tend to draw from a more multidisciplinary pool of knowledge than some fields, though even this is more often than not exaggerated (as reflection upon the developing edges of even hard sciences would suggest). It may be true that the practitioner connection gives public administration a somewhat more eclectic appearance than some fields; but, again, this eclecticism and its related complexities and nuances may be more usual in the development of fields than is sometimes recognized (as reflection upon the diversity of investigations and applications in most of the social or human sciences may suggest). As to theoretical unity or clear dominant paradigms, it is likely that the presence of such in many fields, as well as its absence in public administration, may be regularly overstated.

The fact that the field of public administration is both an academic endeavor and a professional field is sometimes thought to limit the field's disciplinary possibilities. Thus some suggest that public administration should be thought of as an applied field of practice and training, while basic research and education should be recognized as taking place in other fields which are thought to be more clearly disciplines or sciences. Sometimes the suggestion is made—most notably identified with Dwight Waldo—that public administration may be a field, discipline, or science in the way that medicine is; and that like medicine, it may be both a scientific and practitioner concern which draws on such other fields of learning as it finds fruitful to its own purposes and activities. The roles of basic research and applied purpose are likely to be the focus of dialogue in public administration (as well as in many other fields) for the foreseeable future. Public administration is likely to continue to have research, education, training, and practice concerns for the foreseeable future also. In this regard, the field may resemble established fields such as medicine or

engineering and new fields such as genetic science, polymer science, or cognitive science; and it is as unlikely that the field of public administration will be limited by practical and applied concerns as it is that these other fields will.

An interesting aspect of public administration as a field of academic study and as a field of training for professional practice is its seeming ambivalence about itself. For example, a few years ago, Aaron Wildavsky, a friendly critic, wondered in print why, since public administration seemed so essentially involved with hierarchy and bureaucracy, public administration scholars seemed so unwilling to embrace or defend these characteristics. Thus it may seem from some perspectives that scholars of public administration seem to deplore so much of which seems characteristic of, indeed definitional of, their field. Even within the field itself there have been arguments and dialogue which seem to interpret large parts of the academic field of public administration as essentially opposed to public administration. From a somewhat different perspective, though, the "critics from within" frequently feel they are not attacking the essence of public administration, but rather arguing that some characteristics which have seemed essential to others are in fact not essential but could be changed, eroded, reduced, or removed to the improvement of the field. From this perspective, then, characteristics such as bureaucracy and hierarchy may not be unavoidable and definitional characteristics of public administration, but rather may be unfortunate aspects which an improved public administration would mitigate or avoid.

Perhaps the most important aspect of the concern about legitimacy and identity of the field has to do explicitly with the question of political legitimacy. Long ago, most debate about whether a specific government was legitimate or not would have rested upon questions of the line of succession or mystical or religious indication of the identity of the legitimate ruler. For much of the present-day world—and certainly most of the world in which public administration would have conscious identity—the question of governmental legitimacy turns on the public good (in many cases expressed in terms of the interest of the citizenry or even the will of the people). Under this understanding of legitimacy, questions of the legitimacy of public administration (essentially nonelected skill-based participants in rule) are difficult. A traditional answer to the problem posed has been that the public administrators bring their skills, training, and job experience to serve the purposes and directions indicated by the peoples' representatives (who frequently, and especially within representative governments, have been selected through some devices, such as elections, in which the citizens have had a voice). This is sometimes referred to as administrative neutrality: the idea that civil servants will bring their knowledge and skills to the service of whichever party or set of individuals is chosen to govern from time to time. This answer is still the largely unquestioned theory of public administration legitimacy in many parts of the world. Where public administration has been interpreted more frequently as having large aspects of discretion, policy formulation responsibilities, and relatively autonomous leadership roles, though, the possibility or appropriateness of neutrality has been increasingly called into question. This has left the field of public administration with the need to understand and explicate precisely how public administrators are or can be legitimate with reference to the citizenry and duly established political orders. Working out the important ramifications of such questions leads to dialogue and debate about the foundations of public administration legitimacy, and this leads some to articulate a sense that the field is in search of its role, identity, and purpose.

When these and other aspects—the mix, priority, and relative weight of specific aspects varies from context to context and polity to polity—of public administration identity are given serious and continuous deliberation and debate, it is understandable that fundamental questions about the status of public administration take on critical importance. The issues and the dialogue are not presently at rest, and they are not likely to be in the foreseeable future.

Future of the Field

Though the field of public administration is perennially concerned about the identity and security of the field, the future and identity seem secure even if the exact intellectual configuration cannot be precisely predicted.

The "practice" of public administration is affected everywhere by political and resource changes. Visible aspects of such changes at the present time are concerns over the resources devoted to governmental and public activities (taxes, the portion of the economy devoted to governmental or public sector activities, etc.); increased interest in many places in introducing greater aspects of market factors into heretofore nonmarket public sector activities; continued interest in countering hierarchical and impersonal ("red tape," etc.) aspects; and continued concern about responsibility and accountability to the citizenry and its interests. The practice of public administration also experiences today, as it always has, the challenges of technological developments. Such concerns and interests bespeak possible changes in public administration, but they probably do not threaten the existence or identity of the practice, occupations, or vocations of public administration.

The "academic" part of public administration has continually undergone change, and in recent history it has continually interpreted such change as fundamental or as a matter of identity and essence. Intellectual history and the sociology of knowledge would suggest that we should expect the study of public administration to be buffeted by the winds of intellectual change, growth, and challenge (as all active fields of thought will be). Thus, public administration will participate in, and be influenced by, developments in virtually all areas of human thought. Presently, the field is visibly influenced not only by incremental developments of preexisting themes and directions, but also by the host of intellectual, philosophical, methodological, epistemological, and esthetic developments which are loosely grouped under labels such as postmodernism. The field has always been influenced by, and participated in, the intellectual climate and dialogue of its times. It will continue to do so. And this will be a sign, not particularly of crises of identity or future, but rather of vitality and engagement.

FRANK MARINI

BIBLIOGRAPHY

Gladden, E. N., 1972. *A History of Public Administration.* 2 vols. London and Portland, OR: Frank Cass and Co., Ltd.

Lynn, Naomi B. and Aaron Wildavksy, eds., 1990. *Public Administration: The State of the Discipline.* Chatham, NJ: Chatham House.

Mill, John Stuart, ([1861] 1991). *Considerations on Representative Government.* Buffalo, NY: Prometheus Books.

Mosher, Frederick C., ed., 1975. *American Public Administration: Past, Present, Future.* University: University of Alabama Press.

Perry, James L., ed., 1989. *Handbook of Public Administration.* 2nd ed. 1996 San Francisco: Jossey-Bass, Inc..

Shafritz, Jay M. and Albert C. Hyde, eds., 1992. *Classics of Public Administration.* 3d ed. Pacific Grove, CA: Brooks/Cole.

Wilson, Woodrow, 1887. "The Study of Administration." *Political Science Quarterly*, vol. 2 (June).

PUBLIC ADMINISTRATION COMMITTEE (PAC). A standing committee of the United Kingdom Joint University Council (JUC).

It originates from the Joint University Council for Social Studies, an organization of member universities formally established in 1918 as part of the United Kingdom's reconstruction program at the end of World War I. In 1936 the JUC became the Joint University Council for Social Studies and Public Administration with T. S. (later Lord) Simey as the first chairman of its Public Administration Subcommittee. From its early days the subcommittee acted as a pressure group on government as well as a body to coordinate and develop the study of public administration in its member institutions. In the period immediately after World War II, it was mainly concerned with the standards and syllabuses for various courses leading to diplomas in public administration, and the relationship of those courses to the examinations introduced by the Local Government Examinations Board. In the 1950s one of its initiatives led to the two volumes of case studies, *Administrators in Action* (Willson 1961 and Rhodes 1965), published by Allen and Unwin for the Royal Institute of Public Administration. In the 1960s it contributed to pressure on the UK government to provide more funds for research, which led to the appointment of the Heyworth Committee, one of whose recommendations led to the setting up of the Social Science Research Council 1965.

Beginning in the 1970s, the PAC built a distinguished record of achievements which include the publication of a refereed international scholarly journal, now called *Public Policy and Administration,* numerous books originating from PAC-sponsored research workshops, evidence to royal commissions and other government inquiries, cosponsored seminars with both the Civil Service College and the Local Government Management Board, and the sponsorship of an annual conference for practitioners and academics. Its focus on teaching public administration led it to sponsor a research project into public administration teaching and research in Britain *Teaching Public Administration* (1973) and, later, to sponsor a periodical also called *Teaching Public Administration,* which specializes in publishing articles on concepts and practices in public administration teaching and training. In the mid-1990s the PAC represented nearly one hundred member universities. Following the demise of the Royal Institute of Public Administration in 1992, the PAC was invited by the UK government to assume responsibility for the UK's National Section membership of the International Institute of Administrative Sciences.

RICHARD A. CHAPMAN

BIBLIOGRAPHY

Beith, A. J., 1971. "The Origins and Development of the Public Administration Committee," *PAC Bulletin,* vol. 10:18–28.
Chapman, Richard A., 1973. *Teaching Public Administration.* London: JUC.
———, 1980. "The PAC and Teaching Public Administration in the 1970s," *Public Administration Bulletin,* vol. 34:9–20.
Rhodes, Gerald, 1965. *Administrators in Action.* Vol. II. London: George Allen and Unwin.
Willson, F. M. G., 1961. *Administrators in Action.* Vol I. London: George Allen and Unwin.

PUBLIC ADMINISTRATION EDUCATION.
The system of formal education for those in government service.

Introduction

Public administration education ensues from the interdependent relationship between a nation's public service and its institutions of higher learning. The specific nature and dimensions of that relationship differ between nations according to how each answers the following key questions: Who should have access to public administration educa-

tion? And, what should be taught in public administration curriculums?

How a nation answers these questions will determine whether public employment, especially at the higher levels, is more or less open to and representative of various segments of society, the range of administrative competence and technical expertise in the public service, and the extent to which governmental services are directed toward the entirety or to special segments of society. Changes in the degree of democratization of the public service or desired qualifications for civil servants cannot fully occur without prior change in the educational system, which, in turn, is heavily influenced by public policy and the actions of the public service. Thus public administration education is about more than just the skills and competencies of civil servants as it exerts a profound and enduring effect on the relationship between a government and its citizenry.

Who Should Be Educated?

In the modern era, public administration education has been driven primarily by the growing demand to train officials to occupy expert or specialized positions within the bureaucratic structure of government. Universities and postgraduate schools of administration have been the primary conduit for providing such trained officials. Hence the question of who should be educated for public administration is closely linked to what portion of a nation's population has access to higher education.

Historically, most systems of education for public administration have been elitist in nature, reflecting the social and economic stratification of society. That is, access to the educational institutions that trained higher civil servants and bureaucratic officials was limited to the upper classes of society, thus limiting the lower classes to government positions that did not require higher education. The class structure of education and the public service assured that the upper classes dominated the higher administrative and policy making levels of government.

Three European systems—the French, British, and Continental—that developed during the nineteenth century have provided the basic pattern or structure for most of the world's systems of public administration education. While each of these systems has been subjected to democratizing pressures, they still retain the basic character of educating an administrative elite to lead the public service.

On the basis of the Napoleonic reforms the French created a highly rationalized and centralized structure for administrative education, centering on the Ecole Nationale d'Administration (ENA), a postgraduate school that provides three years of pre-entry training for the nation's top civil servants. Nearly all the ENA's students were drawn from the top graduates of the Ecole Libres des Sciences Politiques, an exclusive school only affordable to the upper classes. The result of this system is a highly cohesive and homogeneous class of higher civil servants.

The British reformed what was widely perceived as a corrupt administrative system in the mid-nineteenth century by focusing on drawing their top civil servants from graduates of their two most exclusive private universities, Oxford and Cambridge. The system aimed to create a "pure" class of administrative generalists, educated in the classics and humanities, which would populate the top permanent posts in the civil service. Like the French system, this approach produced an unrepresentative, homogeneous class of higher civil servants, but one based on an ideal of government leadership by cultured gentlemen in contrast to the French ideal of the rational, expert administrator.

On the Continent (mainly Prussia and Austria), education for public administration came to center on the profession of law. Following a period of "cameralism" during the seventeenth and eighteenth century when civil servants received a university education in public finance, police science, and economics, a shift occurred towards drawing civil servants from the legal profession as the public bureaucracy focused more on the application of law and due process (legal codes, regulations, rules, and precedence). While the substantive focus differed from the French and British systems, the end result of education for administration was the same: an unrepresentative class of government administrators, symbolizing control of public organizations and employment by an expert and/or cultural elite drawn from a relatively narrow segment of society.

The United States lagged behind European nations in the development of public administration education and the creation of an administrative class. The growth of the "spoils" system in the nineteenth century reflected a strong egalitarian spirit in the nation and a resistance to links between higher education and public service. U.S. citizens feared and despised European systems of officialdom dominated by university trained elites. Even as the nation began to move away from the spoils system towards a merit system of public employment with the passage of the Pendleton Act in 1883, care was taken to link public employment to the practical requirements of the job (rather than general education) and to allow lateral entry to higher level positions (to prevent the development of a closed class of administrators).

Over time, however, the United States has increasingly embraced a professionlized public service based on the growth of specialized, professional education in public and private universities. The trend away from higher education as a privilege based on prior social status and towards higher education as a right for all who are intellectually capable has helped to open higher education and top levels of the public service to a greater segment of society. But the growing reliance on professionalism and expert knowledge in education and the administration of public policies and organizations has contributed to the creation of an intellectual elite whose professions dominate the personnel policies and practices of many public agencies.

What Should Be Taught?

Despite the clear trend towards greater specialization and professional training for public administrators, the question of the appropriate aims and content of public administration education has been a vital issue for the field throughout its history. In the first issue of the *Public Administration Review* Robert M. Hutchins and William E. Mosher exchanged contrasting views on what constitutes a proper education for public administrators. Hutchins argued that future public administrators need not, and should not, be taught specific administrative skills. Instead, the best preparation for their careers can be found in a solid, liberal education.

Mosher, on the other hand, defended professional training for public administrators, particularly at the graduate level. In contrast to Hutchins, who did not view public administration as academic subject matter but as an arena of practical knowledge which can only be gained through experience, Mosher saw the need to provide public administrators with a professional education in the practices and methods of administration (i.e., public law, organization theory, budgeting and finance, personnel) in much the same manner as established professions such as law and engineering. While not a substitute for experience and on-the-job learning, professional education would provide the basis for a more informed and effective corps of public servants, and for the development and dissemination of a common body of administrative knowledge and values.

Contemporary education in public administration in the United States and a number of other countries clearly has followed the general model outlined by Mosher. The master's of public administration (MPA) has become the most recognized professional degree for government administrators and increasingly for those employed in nonprofit agencies. In the U.S., the MPA is accredited by the National Association for Schools of Public Affairs and Administration (NASPAA) and supported by professional associations such as the American Society for Public Administration (ASPA) and the American Political Science Association (APSA). Most MPA curricula center on the core functions, skills, or techniques deemed to be required of public administrators, in addition to a variety of substantive and methodological specializations.

This apparent consensus on the degree of choice for the field does not mean that the debate has ended as to what constitutes the best approach and content for public administration education. Some have pointed out the shortcomings of an excessively rational and technical education for the public service that risks producing unreflective, professional functionaries who have little or no appreciation of their role and importance in the broader issues of governance in a complex society.

Thus there has been a continuing and growing concern for teaching new models of leadership, citizenship, judgment, and ethics; for issues of diversity and empowerment; and for careerlong learning and professional growth. Public administration programs continue to make adjustments in their curricula, professional literature, and educational opportunities to meet many of these concerns in addition to the teaching of administrative skills and techniques. Many educators in the field are addressing the need to approach public administration education in a manner that takes account of the public administrator as a lifelong learner and as a whole person rather than as a one-dimensional technician.

Conclusion

The design of education for public administration takes place increasingly in a context that reflects an awareness of the interdependence between education and the public service. While the class-based, elitist models of the past have largely given way to pressures for greater opportunity, diversity, and representation in both higher education and the public service, the professional orientation of public administration education has created new tensions and questions about who sets the educational agenda, what criteria determine access to public sector employment, and the skill, values, and perspectives of public servants. Thus the questions of who has access to higher education and what is taught in public administration programs remain as key issues for defining and building an effective and representative public service.

DANNY L. BALFOUR

BIBLIOGRAPHY

Balfour, Danny L. and Frank Marini, 1991. "Child and Adult, X and Y: Reflections on the Process of Public Administration Education." *Public Administration Review,* vol. 51, no. 6 (November-December) 478–485.

Hutchins, Robert M., 1938. "Shall We Train for Public Administration? Impossible." In Waldo, Dwight, ed., 1953, *Ideas and Issues in Public Administration: A Book of Readings.* New York: McGraw-Hill, pp. 227–229.

Mosher, Frederick C., 1982. *Democracy and the Public Service.* New York: Oxford University Press.

Mosher, William E., 1938. "Schools Can Do Much." In Waldo, Dwight, ed., 1953. *Ideas and Issues in Public Administration: A Book of Readings.* New York: McGraw-Hill, pp. 229–233.

Ventriss, Curtis, 1991. "Contemporary Issues in American Public Administration: The Search for an Educational Focus." *Public Administration Review,* vol. 51, no. 1 (January-February) 4–14.

Weber, Max, 1994. *Political Writings.* Lassman, Peter, and Ronald Speirs, eds. Cambridge, UK: Cambridge University Press.

PUBLIC ADMINISTRATION JOURNALS.

Journals, refereed and nonrefereed, that publish articles directly impacting the thought and practice of public administration.

Origin and Subsequent History

Public administration journals collectively function as a forum for intellectual discussion and debate among both scholars and practitioners (Forrester and Watson 1994; Legge and Devore 1987; Vocino and Elliott 1982). Publication of articles ranging in content from theory building to the application of hands-on techniques afford public administrators an extensive and eclectic knowledge base. Moreover, journals focusing on public administration research reflect the goals and concerns expressed by society during different time periods. For instance, a host of journals focusing on urban affairs and policy issues appeared in the late 1960s and 1970s, commensurate with a greater social consciousness expressed not only by the United States but countries throughout the world. When viewed from a broad perspective, public administration journals provide a history of thought and practice in the field, and illuminate the development of specialized areas of scholarly interest.

The historical development of public administration journals may be traced back to the turn of the century with the publication of *Political Science Quarterly* (1886), *Annals of the American Academy of Political and Social Science* (1890), and the *American Political Science Review* (1906), as shown in Table I. These journals indicate the deep roots of public administration in the discipline of political science. Primarily focusing on theoretical concerns relating to public administration, these journals were the first to address arguments surrounding the politics-administration dichotomy. Issues pertaining to the separation of public administration from politics were of great interest to practitioners and legislators around the turn of the century, given the advent of merit systems and other efforts to abolish patronage. However, within a scant ten-year time frame, the field began slowly to expand beyond these initial concerns, developing a broader base by exploring a variety of management science research questions. A more unique and even specialized literature began appearing in journals such as the *National Civic Review* (1912) and the *Federal Reserve Bulletin* (1915), both of which emphasized practitioner aspects of public administration.

The scope of public administration literature continued to rapidly expand during the 1920s with the establishment of *Military Review* (1921), *Foreign Services Journal*

TABLE I PUBLIC ADMINISTRATION JOURNALS

Journal	Inception Date	Published/Financially Supported by:
Administration & Society	1969	originally titled *Journal of Comparative Administration,* published by Sage; 1974: edited by Syracuse & UHouston; 1976: edited by UMKC & U Kansas; 1977: edited by UMKC & VPISU; 1980: edited by VPISU (quarterly)
Administrative Science Quarterly	1956	published by the School of Business & Public Administration, Cornell U; 1983: published by Graduate School of Business, Cornell U (quarterly)
American Behavioral Scientist	1959	originally titled *PROD (Political Research: Organization & Design): An Informal Newsletter of Research Ideas,* published by Princeton; 1960: retitled *The American Behavioral Scientist;* 1966: published by Sage (monthly) became more formal in late 1960s and early 1970s
American Journal of Economics & Sociology	1941	American Journal of Economics & Sociology, Inc. (quarterly)
American Journal of Political Science	1957	The Midwest Political Science Assn., Wayne State U. Press; 1978: dropped Wayne State U, added U Texas Press (quarterly)
American Political Science Review	1906	published under the auspices of the American Political Science Association (quarterly)
American Politics Quarterly	1973	published by Sage (quarterly)
American Review of Public Administration	1967	originally titled *Midwest Review of Public Administration,* published semiannually by Midwest Review of P.A., Inc. in cooperation with Greater Kansas City Chapter of ASPA and Park College; 1981: retitled to *American Review of Public Administration;*1987: now published by the University of Missouri (St. Louis, Columbia, Kansas City) (quarterly)
Annals of the American Academy of Political & Social Science	1890	American Academy of Political & Social Science
Arms Control Today	1971	originally entitled the *ACA Newsletter;* published by the Arms Control Assn (monthly, except January/February, July-August)
Australian Journal of Public Administration	1942	originally titled *Public Administration,* The Journal of the Australian Regional Groups of the Royal Institute of Public Administration; 1976: retitled the *Australian Journal of Public Administration;* 1980: renamed The Australian Institute of Public Administration; 1983: renamed The Royal Australian Institute of Public Administration
British Journal of Political Science	1971	U Essex (quarterly)
Business & Society	1972	originally titled *Business & Society Review Innovation,* published by Warren, Borham & Lamont, Inc; 1975: retitled *Business & Society Review;* 1987: published by Management Reports, Inc.; role of business in a free society (quarterly)
Cambridge Journal of Economics	1977	Cambridge Political Economy Society, by Academic Press (bimonthly)
Canadian Journal of Economics	1968	sponsored by the Canadian Economics Assn (quarterly)
Canadian Journal of Political Science	1968	addresses political science; overlaps with public administration in the area of federalism (quarterly)
Canadian Public Administration	1958	The Institute of Public Administration of Canada (quarterly)
The CATO Journal: An Interdisciplinary Journal of Public Policy Analysis	1981	The Cato Institute, Washington, D.C.; publishes a variety of articles (triannually)
CATO Policy Report	1979	The Cato Institute; a newsletter (bimonthly)
Cities: The International Journal of Urban Policy & Planning	1984	Butterworth-Heinemann Ltd., Oxford, England (bimonthly)
Civic Affairs: Monthly Journal of City Government in India	1954	unknown
Civil Service Journal	1960	U.S. Civil Service Commission; 1979: U.S. Office of Personnel Management
Community Development Journal: An International Forum	1966	published by Oxford U Press, England; an independent journal (quarterly)
Comparative Political Studies	1968	published by Sage; an interdisciplinary journal (quarterly)
Comparative Strategy: An International Journal	1978	The Strategic Studies Center, SRI International, published in England; 1986: no longer sponsored by SRI
Conflict	1978	The Institute for Conflict of Policy Studies; 1979: became an independent publication

TABLE I (Continued)

Journal	Inception Date	Published/Financially Supported by:
Contemporary Economic Policy	1982	originally titled *Contemporary Policy Issues,* published jointly by the Western Economic Assn, Int'l & California State U-Long Beach; 1994: retitled *Contemporary Economic Policy* (quarterly)
CUPA Journal	1949	College & University Personnel Assn (quarterly)
Current Municipal Problems	1959	published by Callaghan & Co. Chicago; a compilation of articles (quarterly)
Development & Change	1969	The Institute of Social Studies, the Hague
Development Policy Review	1983	published by Sage for the Overseas Development Institute, London (quarterly)
Documentation in Public Administration	1973	Indian Institute of Public Administration; an index of articles (quarterly)
Economic Development & Cultural Change	1952	University of Chicago (quarterly)
Economic Development Review: The Journal for the Economic Development Practitioner	1983	The American Economic Development Council (quarterly)
Economic Inquiry	1966	originally titled *Western Economic Journal,* published by the Western Economic Assn; 1982: renamed the Western Economic Assn International
Economic Quarterly [or Review], of various		
Educational Evaluation & Policy Analysis	1979	The American Educational Research Assn (quarterly)
Environment & Planning A: International Journal of Urban & Regional Science	1969	published by Pion, London
Environment & Planning C: Government & Policy	1983	published by Pion, London; edited at London School of Economics & Political Science and Wayne State U
Evaluation Review	1977	originally titled *Evaluation Quarterly,* 1980: retitled *Evaluation Review*
Environment & Behavior	1969	published by Sage; an interdisciplinary journal
Federal Reserve Bulletin	1915	Board of Governors of the Federal Reserve System
Financial Accountability & Management: In Government, Public Services & Charities	1985	published by Basil Blackwell Publishers, England; independent (quarterly)
Foreign Service Journal: The Magazine for Foreign Affairs Professionals	1924	American Foreign Service Assn, originally titled the *American Foreign Service Journal;* 1951: retitled the *Foreign Service Journal*
Forum for Applied Research & Public Policy	1986	U of Tennessee in cooperation with the Tennessee Valley Authority (TVA) & Oak Ridge Associated Universities; 1989: dropped TVA [energy, science & technology, environment & economic development]
GAO Review	1966	U.S. GAO
Governance: An International Journal of Policy & Administration	1988	published by Blackwell Publishers (quarterly)
Governing	1987	Congressional Quarterly, Inc. (monthly)
The Government Accountants Journal	1950	originally titled *The Federal Accountant,* published by the Federal Government Accountants Assn; 1957: cosponsored also by Graduate School of Business at Cornell U; 1961: dropped Cornell & added George Washington U; 1967: dropped George Washington U; 1975: renamed the Assn of Government Accountants; 1977: retitled *The Government Accountants Journal*
Government Finance Review	1972	originally titled *Government Finance,* official publication of the Municipal Finance Officers Assn of the U.S. and Canada; 1984: renamed the Government Finance Officers Assn of U.S. and Canada; 1985: retitled *Government Finance Review*
Government Information Quarterly: An International Journal of Policies, Resources, Services and Practices	1984	JAI Press (quarterly)
Government Publications Review: An International Journal of Issues & Information Sources	1973	Pergamon Press; governing the field of documents at all levels of government, the U.N. & international (quarterly)
Harvard Business Review	1922	published by the Graduate School of Business Administration at Harvard University
Harvard Journal of Law & Public Policy	1978	Harvard Society for Law and Public Policy
History of Political Economy	1965	Duke University

(Continued)

TABLE I (Continued)

Journal	Inception Date	Published/Financially Supported by:
Hospital & Health Services Administration: Quarterly Journal of the American College of Hospital Administrators	1956	American College of Hospital Administrators
Human Ecology: An Interdisciplinary Journal	1973	published by Plenum Publishing, London; overlaps with urban planning (an international journal)
Human Relations	1947	Tavistock Institute of Human Relations, London & The Research Center for Group Dynamics, Ann Arbor, MI, published by Tavistock Publications; 1965: no longer directly affiliated with The Research Center; 1967: published by Plenum
Human Rights Quarterly: Comparative & International Journal of the Social Sciences, Philosophy, and Law	1979	U Cincinnati (quarterly)
Indian Journal of Public Administration	1955	Indian Institute of Public Administration (quarterly)
Intergovernmental Perspective	1975	U.S. Advisory Commission on Intergovernmental Relations
International Journal of Government Auditing	1971	The International Organization of Supreme Audit Institutions (INTOSAI) (quarterly)
International Journal of Public Administration	1978	published by Marcel Dekker; 1992: official journal of the Barnard Society
International Journal of Urban & Regional Research	1977	published by Edward Arnold, London; 1991: published by Blackwell Publishers, London (quarterly)
International Review of Administrative Sciences	1928	published in Brussels under the auspices of the International Committee of the Congress of the Administrative Sciences; 1931: published under the auspices of the International Institute of the Administrative Sciences
Journal of Accounting & Public Policy	1982	published by Elsevier Science Publishing Co. and sponsored by University of Maryland at College Park
Journal of Administration Overseas	1962	originally titled *Journal of Local Administration Overseas*, published for the Dept of Technical Cooperation, England; 1966: published for the Ministry of Overseas Development; 1967: retitled *Journal of Administration Overseas*
Journal of Conflict Resolution	1957	U Michigan; 1973: published by Sage (quarterly)
Journal of Developing Areas	1966	published by Western Illinois University
Journal of Government Information: An International Review of Policy, Issues & Resources	1982	formerly *Government Publications Review*
Journal of Health & Human Resources Administration	1978	Southern Public Administration Education Foundation
Journal of Management Science & Policy Analysis	1983	originally titled *Management Science & Policy Analysis*, published by ASPA's section on Management Science & Policy Analysis by Sangamon State U; 1988: retitled the *Journal of Management Science & Policy Analysis*, published by Marist College
Journal of Park & Recreation Administration	1983	American Academy for Parks & Recreation Administration, Indiana U and Illinois U; a scholarly journal
Journal of Policy Analysis & Management	1940	originally designed as a Yearbook of the Graduate School of Public Administration, Harvard U; 1969: began to publish academic articles & became a quarterly; 1981: retitled *Journal of Policy Analysis & Management*, published by Wiley for the Association for Public Policy & Analysis
Journal of Politics	1939	Southern Political Science Assn (SPSA) & U Florida; 1972: SPSA & U Alabama; 1975: SPSA & VPISU; 1978: SPSA & Vanderbilt U; 1979: SPSA, U Florida & VPISU; 1981: VPISU, U Florida, Georgia State U, & SPSA; 1985: SPSA & Emory U; 1988: SPSA & U Texas (quarterly)
Journal of Public Administration Research & Theory	1991	affiliated with ASPA's Section on Public Administration Research, cosponsored by U Kansas, U Pittsburgh, Syracuse U, and U Southern California
Journal of Public Economics	1972	published by North-Holland Publishing Co.
Journal of Public Policy	1981	published by Cambridge University Press out of University of Strathclyde, Center for the Study of Public Policy
Journal of Public Policy & Marketing	1982	U Michigan (Grad School of Business Admin) (semiannual since 1991)

TABLE I (Continued)

Journal	Inception Date	Published/Financially Supported by:
Journal of Regional Science	1958	Regional Science Research Institute, in cooperation with the U Pennsylvania (Wharton School)
Journal of State Government	1926	originally titled *The Legislator;* 1929: volume 2 published; 1930: retitled *State Government,* published for the American Legislators Assn (founded 1925); 1930s: renamed The Council of State Governments; 1986: retitled *The Journal of State Government*
Journal of the Community Development Society	1970	Community Development Society
Journal of Urban Affairs	1979	originally titled *Urban Affairs Papers,* published by the Urban Affairs Association and VPISU
Journal of Urban History	1974	published by Sage and supported by Florida Atlantic University and University of Alabama-Birmingham; 1975: new cosupporter is University of New Hampshire; 1977: cosupported by UAB and VPISU; 1979: supported by UAB; 1990: supported by UNC-Charlotte
Knowledge: Creation, Diffusion, Utilization: An Interdisciplinary Social Science Journal	1979	published by Sage in cooperation with Princeton U (Wilson School); 1982: moved to Carnegie-Mellon U; 1985: moved to U Pittsburgh; 1988: moved to U Illinois; 1991: moved to George Washington U
Law & Policy	1979	originally titled *Law & Policy Quarterly: An Interdisciplinary Journal,* published by Sage; 1984: retitled *Law & Policy,* published by Basil Blackwell for SUNY Buffalo
Law & Society Review	1966	published by Sage for the Law & Society Assn, USA
Legislative Studies Quarterly	1976	U Iowa (Comparative Legislative Research Center), an international journal
The Long-Term View: A Journal of Informed Opinion	1992	U Massachusetts School of Law-Andover; a public policy journal where each issue is devoted to a single topic (e.g., "Congressional Term Limits")
Military Review: The Professional Journal of the United States Army	1921	U.S. Army
Minerva: A Review of Science, Learning & Policy	1963	International Assn for Cultural Freedom, published by Eastern Press Ltd, London; 1978: published by the International Council on the Future of the University; reflects on university policies and the roles of universities in society (quarterly)
Municipal Finance Journal	1980	published by Panel Publishers, edited at LSU; 1994: edited at Wichita State U
Nagarlok: Urban Affairs Quarterly	1969	The Indian Institute of Public Administration
National Civic Review	1912	originally titled *National Municipal Review,* published for the National Municipal League; 1959: retitled the *National Civic Review* (monthly)
National Tax Journal	1948	National Tax Assn; 1974: also copublished by Tax Institute of America and the Fund for Public Policy Research; 1976: dropped Fund for Public Policy Research
Nonprofit & Voluntary Sector Quarterly	1972	published by Transaction for the Association of Voluntary Action Scholars; now published by Jossey-Bass (quarterly)
Organization Development Journal	1983	Organization Development Institute (quarterly)
Organization Science: A Journal of the Institute of Management Science	1990	published by the Institute of Management Science, Rhode Island; a multidisciplinary Journal studying organizations
Organization Studies	1980	The European Group of Organizational Studies & the Maison des Sciences de l'Homme, Paris; 1992: dropped Maison (an international quarterly)
Philosophy & Public Affairs	1971	sponsored & published by Princeton U (quarterly)
Policy Analysis	1975–1981	U California-Berkeley
Policy & Politics	1972	MacMillan Journals, Ltd., London; 1976: published by Sage (England); 1979: published by School for Advanced Urban Studies, U Bristol
Policy Sciences	1970	Elsevier Publishing Co.; 1986: Martinus Nijhoff Publishers; 1987: Klumer Academic Publishers
Policy Studies Journal	1972	published by the Policy Studies Organization and supported by the University of Illinois; 1984: supported by Florida State University; 1985: supported by Syracuse University and University of Kansas; 1988: supported by Syracuse University and CUNY; 1992: supported by SIU Carbondale and Iowa State University

(Continued)

TABLE I (Continued)

Journal	Inception Date	Published/Financially Supported by:
Policy Studies Review	1981	Policy Studies Organization; 1982: cosponsored by U Kansas; 1983: dropped U Kansas & added Arizona State U (Morrison Institute for Public Policy); 1987: (now at School of Justice Studies) at ASU
The Political Quarterly	1930	published by MacMillan, London; 1946: published by Turnstile Press, London; 1957: published by Stevens & Sons, Ltd.; now published by Political Quarterly Publishing Co
Political Science Quarterly	1886	published by Columbia University; 1909: also edited by the Academy of Political Science
Political Studies	1953	published by Clarenden Press for the Political Studies Assn of the United Kingdom; 1983: published by Butterworths; 1989: published by Basil Blackwell
Polity	1968	Journal of the Northeastern Political Science Assn (quarterly)
Presidential Studies Quarterly	1970	Center for the Study of the Presidency
Professional Ethics: A Multidisciplinary Journal	1992	U Florida
Public Administration: An International Quarterly	1923	the Institute of Public Administration, London, originally titled *Journal of Public Administration*, 1926: retitled *Public Administration;* 1953: renamed the Royal Institute of Public Administration
Public Administration & Development: An International Journal of Training, Research, & Practice	1981	the Royal Institute of Public Administration, London (number of issues varies yearly)
Public Administration Quarterly	1977	originally titled *Southern Review of Public Administration*, sponsored by ASPA Region 5; 1983: retitled *Public Administration Quarterly*, sponsored by Rider College and Auburn University at Montgomery; 1983-1989: various issue sponsors; 1989: reaffiliated with Region 5 (SECOPA) as well as with the Alabama Chapter of ASPA; 1990: affiliated with ASPA Section for Professional and Organizational Development and sponsored by SECOPA
Public Administration Review	1940	quarterly; 1967 had 5 issues; 1968 had 6 issues; ASPA
Public Budgeting & Finance	1981	Public Financial Publications, Inc., and cosponsored by ASPA's Section on Budgeting & Financial Management, the American Assn for Budgeting & Program Analysis, and George Mason U; 1985: dropped George Mason U and added Syracuse U; 1987: added George Washington U; 1989: dropped Syracuse U; 1990: dropped George Washington U and added VPISU
Public Budgeting & Financial Management	1989	Marcel Dekker and Penn State U-Harrisburg (triannually); 1994: Florida Atlantic University (quarterly)
Public Choice	1960	VPISU
Public Finance	1946	published in Holland (quarterly)
Public Finance (not referred)	1974	originally titled *Public Finance & Accountancy*, Journal of The Chartered Institute of Public Finance & Accountancy, London; 1993: retitled *Public Finance*
Public Finance Quarterly	1973	Sage; 1978: edited at U Florida; 1981: W Washington U; 1983: U South Alabama; 1990: UNO (Davis has always edited the journal)
Public Manager	1971	originally titled *The Bureaucrat*, Nat'l Capital Area Chapter of ASPA (NCAC); 1978: NCAC & Fed Exec Institut Alumni Assn & Mississippi State U; 1981: Florida In'tl U & FEIAA; 1994: retitled *The Public Manager*, published by The Bureaucrat, Inc.
Public Opinion Quarterly	1937	Princeton U (School of Public Affairs), The Public Opinion Quarterly, Inc; 1952: became the journal of the American Assn for Public Opinion Research; 1968: moved to Columbia U; 1985: not affiliated with Columbia U; 1978: published by Elsevier Press
Public Personnel Management	1938	originally titled *Personnel Administration*, Society for Personnel Administration; 1972: renamed *Personnel Administration & Public Personnel Review*, Society for Personnel Administration & the Public Personnel Assn.; 1973: retitled *Public Personnel Management*, Int'l Personnel Mgt Assn.
Public Productivity & Management Review	1975	originally titled *Public Productivity Review*, Center for Productive Public Mgt @ John Jay College, CUNY; 1982: also cosponsored by ASPA Section on Mgt Science; 1989: moved from CUNY to Rutgers University; 1990: added a new cosponsor–The International Productivity Network

TABLE I (Continued)

Journal	Inception Date	Published/Financially Supported by:
Publius	1971	Temple U; 1983: Temple U & U North Texas (quarterly)
Quarterly Journal of Local Self Government Institute	1930	Local Self Gov't Institute (Bombay) in cooperation with The All-India Institute of Local Self-Gov't (quarterly)
Review of Politics	1939	U Notre Dame
Review of Public Personnel Administration	1980	Univ of South Carolina, Bureau of Gov'tal Research & Services (USC); 1983: USC & ASPA Section on Personnel & Labor Relations (SPACR)
Sage Public Administration Abstracts	1974	Sage Publications (quarterly)
Sage Urban Studies Abstracts	1973	Sage Publications (quarterly)
Social Science Quarterly	1920	originally titled *Southwestern Political & Social Science Quarterly,* Southwestern Political Science Assn & U Texas (narrowly targeted journal); 1931: retitled *Southern Social Science Quarterly;* 1933: renamed the southwestern Social Science Assn, added U Oklahoma; 1939: dropped U Oklahoma; 1954: added U Texas; 1968: retitled *Social Science Quarterly*
State and Local Government Review	1969	University of Georgia (triannually)
State Legislatures	1975	National Conference of State Legislatures (10 issues/yr)
Town Planning Review	1930	Liverpool U Press (triannually)
Urban Geography	1980	published by Winston & Sons, USA
Urban Affairs Quarterly	1965	published by Sage and sponsored by CUNY; 1971: sponsored by University of Michigan; 1974: sponsored by Northwestern University; 1986: sponsored by UMSL (quarterly)
Urban Studies	1964	published by Oliver & Boyd, Ltd, London; 1970: published for U Glasgow; 1971: published by Longman Group, Ltd; 1990: published by Carfax (quarterly)
Western Political Quarterly	1948	published by the Institute of Government at the University of Utah for the Western Political Science Association and the Pacific Northwest Political Science Association; 1956: also sponsored by the Southern California Political Science Association; 1978: also sponsored by the Northern California Political Science Association (quarterly)
World Bank Economic Review	1987	World Bank; disseminates World Bank sponsored research (quarterly & refereed articles)

(1924), and *Journal of State Government* (1926), all of which concentrated on government administration at the state and federal levels. Other journals, such as *Harvard Business Review* (1922), *Social Science Quarterly* (1920), and the *International Review of Administrative Sciences* (1928), each delved into public administration research even though their initial mission was related to other disciplines, notably business. The early 1920s also witnessed the first professional journal in the field, entitled *Public Administration: An International Quarterly,* published in 1923 by the Institute of Public Administration in London, England.

The following decade continued to show an expansion of public administration journals, albeit at a somewhat slower pace. Possibly the political and economic turmoil of the 1930s in both the United States and in other nations affected the number of journals established during this time. Many of the journals during the 1930s continued to have a political science orientation, as evidenced by titles such as the *Political Quarterly,* published in London (1930), *Public Opinion Quarterly* (1937), the *Journal of Politics* (1939),

and the *Review of Politics* (1939). Three journals were more closely tied to the art and practice of public administration: the *Quarterly Journal of Local Self Government* (1930) and *Town Planning Review* (1930), published in India and England, respectively, while *Public Personnel Management* (1938) was published in the United States by the Society for Personnel Administration (renamed the International Personnel Management Association in 1973).

Over the next 55 years a tremendous expansion took place regarding the creation of public administration journals. Moreover, the development of an interdisciplinary approach became apparent within the field, as evidenced by journals covering general public administration, public policy, urban studies, budgeting and finance, and organization studies. International journals and those journals with solely a practitioner emphasis also continued to grow in number. Most especially, however, journals established in the 1940s provided the first real opportunities for public administration to develop its own identity, apart from the discipline of political science.

Public Administration Review (PAR), historically well respected for its dissemination of theoretical and practical knowledge, and the *Journal of Policy Analysis and Management (JPAM)*, which began as a nonacademic *Yearbook of the Graduate School of Public Administration*, both began publication in 1940. *JPAM* eventually narrowed from a public administration focus to a policy focus and is currently published by the Association for Public Policy Analysis and Management (APPAM). Two other journals first published during this time include the *Australian Journal of Public Administration* (1942) and the *CUPA Journal* (1949). The 1940s also gave birth to three important economic journals, the *American Journal of Economics and Sociology* (1941), *Public Finance* (1946), and the *National Tax Journal* (1948). These journals, in addition to the *Western Political Quarterly* (1948) and the Tavistock Institute's *Human Relations Journal* (1947), all included relevant research in the field of public administration. The 1940s not only gave rise to a wide variety of journals serving to house public administration literature, but also witnessed an ultimate steady state between theoretical and practitioner outlets.

The 1950s generated several new journals which expanded the field of public administration to include the area of urban and municipal affairs. The new urban and municipal journals include *Economic Development and Cultural Change* (1952), *Civic Affairs* (1954), *Journal of Regional Science* (1958), *Current Municipal Problems* (1959), *Government Accountants Journal* (1950), and *Hospital and Health Services Administration* (1959). The arrival of these journals perhaps coincides with scholarly interest, particularly in U.S. society, in post–World War II suburbanization problems (Wright 1978). Changes in the federal system to accommodate funding of deferred wartime needs (e.g., schools, water treatment facilities, libraries, infrastructure improvements, public health care) and the growth and development of intergovernmental relations spawned a multitude of specialized urban studies. The era also gave rise to political science journals that, like their predecessors, addressed topics of concern to mainstream public administrators, such as the *American Journal of Political Science* (1957) and *Political Studies* (1953, England). A surge of interest in the behavioral and organizational sciences also took place during this time. Two of these science journals include the *American Behavioral Scientist* (1959) and *The Journal of Conflict Resolution* (which began publication by the University of Michigan in 1957). *Administrative Science Quarterly*, also of this genre, began publication in 1956. Two new international journals originating in the 1950s include the *Indian Journal of Public Administration* (1955) and *Canadian Public Administration* (1958).

The number of professional journals exploded in the latter half of the 1960s. Twenty-three of these journals are found in Table I. Seven journals—*Civil Service Journal* (1960), *Journal of Administration Overseas* (1962), *Minerva: A Review of Science, Learning and Policy* (1963), *GAO Review*

(1966), *American Review of Public Administration* (1967), *Administration and Society* (1969), and *State and Local Government Review* (1969)—are directly related to public administration. An additional six journals—*Urban Studies* (1964, England), *Urban Affairs Quarterly* (1965), *Community Development Journal* (1966, England), *Journal of Developing Areas* (1966), *Environment and Planning A: International Journal of Urban and Regional Science* (1969, England), and *Nagarlok: Urban Affairs Quarterly* (1969, India)—reveal the ongoing interest in urban and municipal affairs stemming from the previous decade. Four other journals disseminate economic studies, three are directly linked to political science, and three journals are not necessarily bound to any one discipline.

The proliferation of professional journals in the 1960s was complemented by an equally impressive introduction of outlets in the 1970s. Table I identifies 42 of the journals established in the 1970s. The journals introduced during this decade are for the most part based in the United States and cover an extremely wide range of disciplines and topics. The massive number of journals that came forth in the 1960s and especially in the 1970s mirror the intense social consciousness expressed by politicians and administrators during this time, as well as their debates over public policy problems. Not surprisingly, most of the new journals in the 1970s are directly concerned with public policy issues across several fields of study. Among these journals are *Policy Sciences* (1970), *Publius: The Journal of Federalism* (1971), *Policy and Politics* (1972), *Policy Studies Journal* (1972), *Intergovernmental Perspective* (1975), *Policy Analysis* (1975), *Public Productivity and Management Review* (1975), *Evaluation Review* (1977), *Comparative Strategy* (1978), *Conflict* (1978), *Harvard Journal of Law and Public Policy* (1978), *Journal of Health and Human Resources Administration* (1978), *Human Rights Quarterly* (1979), *Knowledge* (1979), *Educational Evaluation and Policy Analysis* (1979), *CATO Policy Report* (1979), and *Law and Policy* (1979).

In particular, the journals focusing on evaluation and policy analysis during the 1970s reveal that at the time there was a fast-growing interest in the application of computers, statistics, social science data, and research methodology in the investigation of public administration issues. Especially throughout the Kennedy (1960–1963) and Johnson (1963–1968) presidential administrations, a vast number of far-reaching and very expensive social programs were implemented. Many of these programs aimed toward reducing poverty and eliminating urban blight, caused in part by an increase in suburbanization during the 1950s, and subsequent decline in the central city tax base. Scholars, politicians, and practitioners alike were interested in assessing the cost and effectiveness of social welfare and urban renewal projects begun in the 1960s. This interest, coupled with an increasing methodological sophistication on the part of social researchers, very possibly resulted in the onslaught of policy-and evaluation-focused journals.

The same policy interests stimulating publications in the field of program evaluation similarly served to increase the number of budgeting and finance publications, including the origin of *International Journal of Government Auditing* (1971), *Government Finance Review* (1972), *Journal of Public Economics* (1972), *Public Finance Quarterly* (1973), *Public Finance* (1974, London), and the *Cambridge Journal of Economics* (1977).

The decade of the 1970s, continuing the trend since 1940, gave rise to several general public administration and urban journals. *Public Administration Quarterly* (1977), the *International Journal of Public Administration* (1978), and *The Public Manager* (1971) address public administration from a more general framework while five outlets—the *Journal of Community Development Society* (1970), *Human Ecology* (1973), *Journal of Urban History* (1974), the *International Journal of Urban and Regional Research* (1977), and the *Journal of Urban Affairs* (1979)—continue the trend toward exploring urban affairs. Additionally, there was the creation of *Nonprofit and Voluntary Sector Quarterly* (1972) along with four reference journals—*Documentation in Public Administration* (1973), *Government Publications Review* (1973), *Sage Urban Studies Abstracts* (1973), and *Sage Public Administration Abstracts* (1974).

The growth rate of new journals slowed significantly during the 1980s and declined to a mere trickle of new publications in the 1990s. Universities and other nonprofit organizations limited their publication activities due to extensive budget cutbacks beginning in the early 1980s. The slowed pace of development may also be due to the saturation of the "publication" market that occurred from the onslaught of new journals over the preceding 25 years. Thus, since 1984 the growth rate of new journals has been about one per year. Yet, despite financial limitations and market saturation, 26 journals appeared for the first time in the 1980s, most of which addressed public policy, budgeting and economics (often overlapping with policy), and practitioner needs. The new nonbudgeting journals include: *Journal of Public Policy* (1981), *CATO Journal* (1981), *Policy Studies Review* (1981), *Journal of Public Policy and Marketing* (1982), *Development Policy Review* (1983), *Environment and Planning C: Government and Policy* (1983), *Journal of Management Science and Policy Analysis* (1983), *Forum for Applied Research and Public Policy* (1986), and *Governance: International Journal of Policy and Administration* (1988).

The new budgeting and economic journals, all quite diverse, include *Municipal Finance Journal* (1980), *Contemporary Economic Policy* (1982), *Journal of Accounting and Public Policy* (1982), *Financial Accountability and Management* (1985), *World Bank Economic Review* (1987), and *Public Budgeting and Financial Management* (1989). A few new general public administration journals also began—*Review of Public Personnel Administration* (1980), *Public Administration and Development* (1981), and *Governing* (1987). There were also two new organization journals, those of *Organization Stud-*

ies (1980) and *Organization Development Journal* (1983), and three new urban-related outlets, those of *Urban Geography* (1980), *Economic Development Review* (1983), and *Cities* (1984). So far, in the decade of the 1990s, only four new publications have been established—those of *Organization Science* (1990), *Journal of Public Administration and Research Theory* (1991), *The Long-Term View* (a policy journal—1992), and *Professional Ethics* (1992). The appearance of *Professional Ethics* (1992) indicates the current and growing interest of scholars in ethical issues relating to the workplace and the inclusion of ethics as an area of study in academic programs.

Since the turn of the century, the number of journals including refereed and nonrefereed, practitioner and academic, domestic and international, has grown to represent a vast collection of wide-ranging knowledge. The journals previously discussed are viewed by public administrators as outlets through which they publish their research or from which they extract critical sources of information. Some journals function to serve both the practitioner and academician. While the list of journals is very extensive, it may not be completely exhaustive because of the manner in which the phrase "public administration journals" has been defined. Even so, when more refined definitions are employed, we still considered the list to be fairly complete. Core public administration journals are those that mention key terms or phrases such as public administration, public management, or other similar words in their mission statements, and whose articles are "blind refereed" (the manuscript reviewers are unaware of the author(s)' identity). Examples of such journals include *Public Administration Review* and the *Journal of Public Administration Research and Theory*. Specific public administration journals, also blind refereed, use key words relating to the field in their mission statements but are intended to address more narrow areas of interest. Examples of such journals include the *Journal of Policy Analysis and Management*, *Review of Public Personnel Administration*, *Public Budgeting and Finance*, and *Urban Affairs Quarterly*. Nearly all of the core and specific journals contributing to the field of public administration have been included in our historical analysis.

While boundary-spanning journals are also refereed (as defined above), these journals are designed to overlap with other disciplinary areas—to name just two, *Publius: The Journal of Federalism* overlaps with the discipline of political science while *Public Finance Quarterly* overlaps with the discipline of economics. These journals are intended to explore public administration theory and practice pertaining to specific disciplines. Boundary-spanning nonpublic administration journals are also refereed and publish critical research that addresses public administration problems, but their primary mission is not directly linked to the field. These journals, such as *Journal of Politics* and *Journal of Urban History, Law and Policy*, are not necessarily related to any one unique discipline, field, or specific area of study. These are journals where public administrators are least likely to publish on any regular basis. Nevertheless, these journals are a repository of literature that considers and analyzes key theories upon which public administrators, and particularly scholars in the field, can build research. In most cases the readership has been confined to the academic community.

There are also a number of nonrefereed journals, which may fall in any of the above mentioned categories. Articles in outlets such as *Civil Service Journal, GAO Review,* and *Public Finance* (London) do not undergo an extensive review process, and are more likely to deal with current issues as opposed to theoretical questions. While academics and practitioners do publish in these journals, the readership seems to be largely restricted to the practicing bureaucrat. Finally, there are reference journals, such as *Sage Public Administration Abstracts,* whose primary intent is to gather and distribute information about books, articles, abstracts, and monographs representing the field of public administration. There are relatively few of these sources but those in existence serve a valuable role in helping students, professors, and administrative professionals find needed information. Very recently these journals have come to be supplemented with a variety of serial and computer on-line services, including: *Vance Public Administration Bibliographies, Index to U.S. Government Periodicals, Monthly Catalog of U.S. Government Publications, Public Affairs Information Service, Social Science Citations Index, American Statistical Index, County and City Data Book, Book of the States, Statistical Abstract of the United States, ABI/Inform, Business Periodicals Index, Newsbank,* CARL, and Lexus/Nexus.

Niche and Mission of Journals as Practiced in the United States

The mission of journals is in part dictated by the niche they are attempting to fill. Journals today exhibit a variety of missions, from very specific to quite general in nature. The mission of any one journal, however, is likely to vary significantly over time as the niche becomes more tightly or more broadly defined. In 1921, for instance, the *Social Science Quarterly* began publishing articles pertaining only to political science and social science issues in a limited number of Southwestern states. Over time, the journal expanded its horizons to include social science research stemming from all regions of the country and from a broad collection of disciplines and fields. To date, *Social Science Quarterly* is considered to have perhaps the broadest scope of the professional journals. Another example of how changes in niche result in a different mission for a journal is the case of the *Yearbook of the Graduate School of Public Administration.* First published in 1940 by Harvard University,

the publication began as a collection of nonrefereed essays. Retitled in 1981 as the *Journal of Policy Analysis and Management,* and under the ownership of APPAM, the journal has become a highly regarded policy journal. Certainly not all journals go through such extreme changes, but most show evidence of refining their publication focus at one time or another.

The niche a journal fills is also evidenced by the organization which publishes the outlet. Not all journals are successful in filling their selected niche and thereby cease publication, such as *Policy Analysis,* which began publication in 1975 out of the University of California-Berkeley and issued its last volume shortly thereafter in 1981. On the other hand, some publications find it necessary to change their niche and host in order to survive. Many journals try to fill the needs of members in a professional association and are thus published by the representative organization, as in the situation of *Public Administration Review,* published by the American Society for Public Administration.

Other journals striving to fill a broader transorganizational niche have no professional or institutional affiliation and thus are considered independent. Some journals classified as independent are in essence "owned" by a single individual. Consequently, details involving the location and process of publication for these journals are exclusively determined by the individual—for example, *Municipal Finance Journal.* Other publications are property of a university or group of universities, such as the *American Review of Public Administration,* owned by the University of Missouri. Privately owned journals, such as *Governance,* are not uncommon in public administration, nor is it uncommon to find that a journal once owned privately would later became affiliated with a professional organization. Where a journal is housed most likely affects the types of articles published, the dynamics of its circulation, and its very ability to flourish.

In their quest to fill a particular niche, journals will change titles, publishers, editors, and even editorial board members. A name change alone may signify that the journal's editorial board has come to better understand their audience's needs and preferences. Examples include the *Journal of Urban Affairs,* which began as the *Urban Affairs Papers,* and the *National Civic Review,* initially titled more narrowly as the *National Municipal Review.* Switching publishing houses is also very common, either within or between public and private sectors (several public administration journals are now published by either Sage or Blackwell Publishers, both private companies). Among universities, there is seemingly no clear publication trend, although as editors leave one university for another, so too, at times, does the journal. However, editors who in essence carry their journal with them from one university to the next often do so to the consternation of university and department officials.

Public Administration Journals in Other Nations

Public administration journals are not the sole invention of the United States but are widely published in several other nations, most notably in England and India. Indeed, perhaps the oldest public administration journal, entitled *Public Administration: An International Quarterly*, is published in London, England. As in the United States, these journals encompass diverse disciplinary areas, including political science, economics, organization studies, urban affairs, and general public administration. Indicative of the interest in these disciplinary areas are the *Political Quarterly* (London), the *Cambridge Journal of Economics, Organization Studies* (Paris), *Human Ecology* (London), *Nagarlok* (India), and the *Indian Journal of Public Administration* (India), respectively. Moreover, practitioner interests are represented by journals such as *Public Administration and Development* (London) and *Public Finance* (London), among others. These journals, as in the United States, are either owned by professional organizations such as *Comparative Strategy* in England, or have an independent status (e.g., *Financial Accountability and Management*, published in England). Several publications have a domestic focus, but unlike journals in the United States, many have a strong international concern, as evidenced by the *Community Development Journal* (England).

Canada is also extensively involved in publishing journals of interest to the public administration audience. *Canadian Public Administration*, published by the Institute of Public Administration of Canada, is the most widely known, central journal in the field. Other important journals deserving mention include the *Canadian Journal of Economics* and the *Canadian Journal of Political Science*. Canadian authors publish regularly in these journals and in the English-based outlets. To date, however, far less is known about the theory and practice of public administration in countries beyond Canada, England, and India, particularly in Eastern European nations and countries in Africa, Asia, and South America. Currently there is a paucity of widely circulating journals devoted to the examination of administrative practices in developing nation-states. Unfortunately, this means that a limited amount of knowledge about international administration never gets incorporated into the U.S. literature base. Thus, a potential growth area for journals in the field, now and for some time in the future, will be in the realm of international policy and administration.

Journals will continue to serve as a critical forum for disseminating examinations of public administration. In the early twentieth century, the journals reflected both the pursuits of scholars to try to understand political science and sociology and the attempts by practitioners to professionalize the administration of government at all levels. Since the 1940s, journals have come to mirror the expansiveness and complexities of government administration, along with the social changes of the day. Many of the journals are general public administration journals while others are highly specialized or boundary-spanning, all of which are needed in dealing with an involute field. As we learn more about administrative practices in those parts of the world still relatively unexplored, we can expect the creation of even more journals, reflecting the expansion and evolution of public administration.

JOHN P. FORRESTER AND
SHEILAH S. WATSON

BIBLIOGRAPHY

Forrester, John P. and Sheilah S. Watson, 1994. "An Assessment of Public Administration Journals: The Perspective of Editors and Editorial Board Members." *Public Administration Review* 54(5):474–482.

Legge, Jr. Jerome S. and James Devore, 1987. "Measuring Productivity in U.S. Public Administration and Public Affairs Programs 1981–1985." *Administration and Society* 19(2):147–156.

Vocino, Thomas and Robert H. Elliott, 1982. "Journal Prestige in Public Administration: A Research Note." *Administration and Society* 14(1):5–14.

Wright, Deil S., 1978. *Understanding Intergovernmental Relations: Public and Participants' Perspectives in Local, State, and National Governments.* North Scituate: Duxbury Press.

PUBLIC ADMINISTRATION, NEW.

A movement or redirection of the field toward more equitable and humanistic theory and practice.

The Origins and History of New Public Administration

There occurred on December 28 and 29, 1967, in Philadelphia, Pennsylvania, a conference on "The Theory and Practice of Public Administration: Scope, Objectives and Methods," organized by the American Academy of Political and Social Science. This conference included 18 of the best known "scholars and public officials" in the field of public administration. Several essays prepared for that conference, the written commentaries on those essays, and the conference discussion were later published by the American Academy of Political and Social Science under the conference title (Charlesworth 1968). Only one of the conferees was, at the time of the conference, less than 50 years of age, and most of them have been well-known in the field for at least 20 years.

Shortly after that conference, one of those in attendance (Dwight Waldo) wondered aloud if public administration held much interest for younger persons and if younger persons held a different set of perspectives on the subject than did their seniors. He subsequently asked three of his junior colleagues (H. George Frederickson, Henry Lambright, and Frank Marini) to organize a conference consisting primarily of persons under 35 years of age. In September, 1968, a meeting was held in the Adirondack Mountains at the Minnowbrook Conference Center of Syracuse University that involved about 35 young practitioners and academics in public administration.

The Minnowbrook Meeting, as it came to be known, was the starting point of the new public administration. The papers prepared for that meeting appeared in *Toward a New Public Administration: The Minnowbrook Perspective* (Marini 1971).

Initial Results

Probably the chief outcome of the Minnowbrook meeting for the participants and the field—other than the fact that it rather suddenly added visibility to a constituency which had been relatively invisible and unheard—was the extent to which it ameliorated "pluralistic ignorance": the condition where many individuals hold similar positions but each individual believes he or she is idiosyncratic or alone in his or her position. Though there was no unanimity on this (or much else) at Minnowbrook, most of the participants discovered that some of the doubts, concerns, and hopes which they had theretofore considered their own views were widespread among the other participants. In some movements this has been (and is) referred to as a "raising of consciousness"—it explains some of the subsequent momentum of the new public administration.

A second important facet of the Minnowbrook conference was the rather determined effort not to "institutionalize" the conference participants or follow the usual norms of interaction at professional meetings. The participants demanded of themselves that they communicate authentically and noncompetitively. They attempted, with partial success, to act out a new type of academic professionalism. And although there were efforts at Minnowbrook to adopt a resolution, form an organization, or in some other way give permanence to the group and deliver a manifesto to the public administration community, the decision was to "stay loose." The product of the conference was not a "position" but rather a dialogue and discussion—and a commitment on the part of some participants to continue the dialogue. This determination not to organize and institutionalize probably explains what many perceive to be a lack of momentum associated with new public administration.

The subsequent meetings were not Minnowbrook reunions, but other meetings designed to bring new voices into the discussions. A meeting held in the summer of 1969 in Sonoma County, California, was arranged by two Minnowbrook alumni (and they invited two other Min-

nowbrook alumni), but the majority of the participants were new. The general topics at Sonoma were much more consciously concerned with reform of the establishment of public administration and the discussion of trends worth starting or accelerating. Other important aspects of the Sonoma meeting were a tentative discussion and exploration of some experiential learning exercise and the serious discussion of creating a more complete learning-living community, at least on a temporary basis. Again the participants sought new norms of professional interaction, this time by making the meeting almost totally self-organizing and with an "emergent" program. One aspect of the program was an examination through an experiential learning exercise of the nature of professional communication. There were other later meetings involving Minnowbrook participants and others in Austin, Texas, and Los Angeles, California.

Almost exactly one year after the Minnowbrook meeting, Dwight Waldo, who through Syracuse University had provided the initiative and financial support for the Minnowbrook conference, arranged a series of panels for the annual conference of the American Political Science Association on the general theme of "Public Administration in a Time of Turbulence" (Waldo 1971). In connection with these panels, a meeting was held which incorporated as many of the panel participants (late twenties, thirties, and early forties were ages requested), alumni of past meetings, and "new blood" as could conveniently get together.

New Public Administration and ASPA

By this time, these activities were being widely noticed. They were also generally misunderstood. The activities and the misunderstandings seemed to come to a head at the national conference of the American Society for Public Administration (ASPA) at Philadelphia in the spring of 1970. The activity at Philadelphia was very different from earlier activity of the so-called "new PA," and was in important respects quite unrelated to the earlier activity. Yet in the minds of many, the events at Philadelphia were an integral part of the earlier activity and were the inevitable climax which had been prematurely rumored at the previous annual conference of ASPA.

By the time of the Philadelphia meetings, a structure of some sort perhaps had begun taking shape around some subgroups of the "new PA" people. At least the idea of a mailing list (a "network" as it was described) had been discussed and some personalities had emerged who were not averse to filling leadership roles in a more organized "new PA movement." As a result of the activity of the previous year and a half, a certain curiosity had also grown up in broader public administration circle which made a more concrete definition of the "movement" at once more possible and more a matter of concern.

Quite coincidentally, some problems of ASPA also came to a head at Philadelphia. The Philadelphia meeting was a landmark in ASPA's history: the slate of candidates nominated by ASPA's nominating committee (and such nomination was virtual election up to this point) was defeated, the executive director of ASPA made public his intention to resign, and in other ways ASPA probably changed forever. Not infrequently, the interpretation is that new PA came in from Los Angeles, Syracuse, Minnowbrook, and Sonoma and "took over ASPA" or "toppled the establishment." Such an interpretation is probably misleading. The defeat of the "official" slate and the resignation of the executive director were events quite independent of new PA.

There were aspects of the Philadelphia meeting which were related to the movement referred to as new PA, and these aspects may, in the long run, be more significant than the dramatic shift of officers. Largely as a result of the rigidity of those responsible for giving final approval to program content at Philadelphia, a number of young people who were identified with the meetings and dialogue of the previous year and a half were rebuffed when they sought a slate of panels to pursue their concerns. A creative response to such rebuff led to the organization of an "unconvention" (designed to be more creative and fruitful than a frequently proposed "counterconvention"). Though the leadership of ASPA saw the light and allocated some snatches of program time and resources at the last minute, the unconvention was organized largely through the entrepreneurial skills and hard work of a few of those identified with new PA.

The distinctive characteristics of the unconvention were: extraordinary steps to include and recruit young, "unknown," and minority group ASPA members to the meeting; a self-organizing program (topics of concern were nominated from the floor in a large open meeting, suites were made available to conveners, each convener agreed to take one of the topics to a suite, and an informal discussion of the topic ensued among those who showed up at the time and place); and topics of concern which were strikingly different from the official ASPA convention. The unconvention topics were a mixture of advocacy or activist public administration and the kinds of intellectual themes which are treated in other sections of this essay. Two examples: One panel was titled, "How To Be a Radical Administrator and Keep Your Job; or How To Be a Radical Administrator and Lose Your Job Creatively." Another was "Phenomenology in the Radical Reconstruction of Public Administration." By the end of the conference more participants were attending unconvention panels than the formally organized conference panels.

In the years since the Philadelphia ASPA conference and the unconvention, several persons associated with the new public administration were elected to positions of leadership in ASPA. ASPA, in part because of the uncon-

vention and the new public administration, is a highly democratic professional association. Few such organizations have a better record of electing women, minorities, and younger persons to positions of leadership.

Later Development

Almost directly from this meeting, some participants proceeded to a meeting arranged by one of the organizers of the Minnowbrook meeting on the theme of neighborhood control and citizen participation in administrative policy formulation (Frederickson 1973). This meeting—held in Boulder, Colorado, and sponsored by the Center for Government Research—was consciously designed to include participants from various age groups, various minority groups, and a sizeable contingent of practitioners.

Since that time there have been both formal and informal meetings and conferences which have carried on essentially a new public administration agenda. The best known of these is the Public Administration Theory Network, which meets annually and publishes *Administrative Theory and Praxis: A Journal of Dialogue in Public Administration Theory*. This journal is published twice yearly and is administered at the California State University at Hayward.

Finally, in 1988 the original Minnowbrook participants, now in their fifties, organized Minnowbrook II. It was held at the same site as the original conference and followed a similar format. In all there were 68 scholars and practitioners who participated. They were equally divided between those who entered the field of public administration in the 1960s, including most of the original "minnows" as well as several others who have had a significant impact on the field, and those who started in the 1980s. The purpose was to see if there were generational differences between the two groups. The March-April 1989 issue of *Public Administration Review* (Volume 49, number 2) is entirely dedicated to the papers and dialogue of Minnowbrook II.

The 1968 Minnowbrook themes were relevance, antipositivism, dissatisfaction with the state of the field, change and innovation, improved human relations, reconciling public administration and democracy, client-centered bureaucracy, and social equity. The 1988 conference included many of the same themes, particularly ethics, social equity, human relations, and the reconciliation of public administration and democracy. However, there were several new themes in 1988, notably leadership, constitutional and legal perspectives, technology policy, and economic or market logic. The 1988 conference was less hostile toward positivism and more open to social and policy science applications. The 1988 conference could be best described as emphasizing amelioration, theory refinement, and problem solving as compared to the radical tone of a wholesale redefinition of the field which characterized the 1968 meeting (*Public Administration Review* 1989).

In Retrospect

There was considerable opposition to the new public administration. First, it was suggested that there was nothing particularly new in the new public administration (Wilcox 1971). The reply to this claim was:

> Parts of new public administration would be recognized by Plato, Hobbs, Machieavelli, Hamilton and Jefferson as well as many modern behavioral theorists. The newness is in the way the fabric is woven, not necessarily in the threads that are used, and in arguments as to the proper use of the fabric—however threadbare (Frederickson 1980, p. 5).

It was also claimed that the new public administration was, and is, too idealistic. It is, of course, true that humanistic and equitable perspectives in public administration are idealistic. The primary response on the part of persons associated with new public administration has been that one cannot be too idealistic.

It was claimed, with considerable evidence, that new public administration was more rhetoric than substance. That was certainly true in the early stages of the development of new public administration. Gradually, over the years, the substantive base of humanistic and social equity perspective in the field has grown and become a generally accepted part of our literature and theory.

It was Victor Thompson (1975) who developed the strongest argument against the new public administration. In *Without Sympathy or Enthusiasm* he contends that the new public administration is a radical left-leaning movement that would "steal the popular sovereignty." He called for a restrained, neutral public administration which limited itself to carrying out the will of elected officials.

In 1968, at the time Minnowbrook I was held, Dwight Waldo was editor-in-chief of the *Public Administration Review*, Frank Marini was the managing editor, and George Frederickson was the research and reports editor. Because of their connections to Minnowbrook and the new public administration, it was decided that it would be inappropriate to use *PAR* to promulgate, push, or sponsor a new public administration agenda. As a result of this decision there is little evidence of the phrase "new public administration" in *PAR*, with the exception of letters to the editor (Henderson 1969; p. 1969; Bjur 1970; Elden 1970). Inevitably there were articles and symposia on themes such as social equity, neighborhood control and citizen participation, and humanistic bureaucracy, which are a prominent part of new public administration.

What Is the New Public Administration?

The themes associated with new public administration that were initially developed at Minnowbrook and have had some enduring effect are as follows.

1. The field has shifted focus in significant measure from the management of agencies to policy issues. The quality of schooling, the effects of law enforcement, and the quality of the environment have become "units of analysis" or policy issues at least as important as managerial practices in the schools and in the policy and public works departments. The public policy approach to public administration has flourished, and it has had a significant effect on the quality of government.

2. Social equity has been added to efficiency and economy as the rationale or justification for policy positions. Equal protection of the law has come to be considered as important to those charged with carrying out the law (public administrators) as it is to those elected to make the law (Frederickson 1974).

3. The notion of administrative neutrality is rejected. The question is what public administrators stand for, believe in, or are committed to.

4. Ethics, honesty, and responsibility in government have returned again to the lexicon of public administration. Career service bureaucrats are no longer considered to be merely implementors of fixed decisions as they were in the dominant theory of the late 1950s and early 1960s; they are now understood to hold a public trust to provide the best possible public service with the costs and benefits being fairly distributed among the people (Rohr 1978).

5. The Minnowbrook perspective argues that, as public needs change, government agencies often outlive their purposes. Increments of growth and decrements of decline have come to have more equal weight in the lexicon of the public administrator. To terminate an unneeded or ineffective organization or program is now accepted as an especially honorable administrative responsibility. An extensive literature on cutback management has developed (Levine 1980).

6. Change, not growth, has come to be understood as the more critical theoretical issue. As responsive government both grows (when new needs are clear) and declines (where agencies' services are no longer critical), managing change, not just growth, should be a standard for effectiveness in public administration.

7. Effective public administration has come to be defined in the context of an active and participative citizenry (Frederickson 1972).

8. Studies of decisionmaking were dominant in the 1950s and 1960s but in the 1970s it came to be better understood that the more difficult challenge is to carry

out decisions. Theories of implementation and action theory were developed.

9. The correctness of the rational model and the usefulness of the strict concept of hierarchy have been severely challenged (Harmon and Mayer 1986).
10. While pluralism continues to be widely accepted as a useful device for explaining the exercise of public power, it has ceased to be the standard for the practice of public administration (Fleishman 1981).

The definitive work on the substance of new public administration is *New Public Administration,* by H. George Frederickson, published by the University of Alabama Press in 1980.

The phrase "new public administration" is still found in the lexicon of public administration. But, in the 25 years that have passed since Minnowbrook I, the vision of a new public administration has been challenged by an era of bureaucrat bashing, cutback administration, privatization, and a sharp decline in public confidence in government. In the practical world of government, particularly the federal government, the effects of new public administration have been impressive, particularly associated with the values of social equity. Affirmative action programs and minority setasides would be examples. The record may be even better at state and local levels of government.

By the mid-1990s the dominant theory was taken from economics and the market was the most powerful metaphor. The public choice perspective, while sharing some value with new public administration, has proved more influential in theory, but less so in practice.

The values espoused by those associated with the new public administration, particularly social equity and humanistic administration, are very much a part of the dominant literature and theory, but not under the banner of new public administration. The decisions not to organize, not to "use" *PAR,* and to emphasize the issues and values of new public administration rather than the phrase, certainly resulted in fewer of the symbols of a movement which has endured. Yet much of the substance of the new public administration is now part of the field's received wisdom.

H. GEORGE FREDERICKSON AND FRANK MARINI

BIBLIOGRAPHY

Charlesworth, James C., ed., 1968. *Theory and Practice of Public Administration: Scope, Objectives and Methods.* Monograph 8, October. Philadelphia: American Academy of Political and Social Science.
Fleishman, Joel L., 1981. "Self-Interest and Political Integration." In Joel L. Fleishman, Lance Liebman, and Mark H. Moore, eds. *Public Duties: The Moral Obligations of Government Officials.* Cambridge, MA: Harvard University Press, 52–92.
Frederickson, H. George, ed., 1972. "Citizenship, Politics and Administration in Urban Neighborhoods." *Public Administration Review,* special issue, vol. 32 (October) 565–738.
———, 1973. Neighborhood Control in the 1970s: Politics, Administration and Citizen Participation. New York: Chandler.
———, 1974. "Social Equity and Public Administration: Symposium." *Public Administration Review,* vol. 34 (January/February) 1–51.
———, 1980. *New Public Administration.* University: University of Alabama Press.
———, 1981. "Toward a New Public Administration." In Frank Marini, ed., *Toward a New Public Administration: The Minnowbrook Perspective.* Scranton, PA: Chandler, p. 309.
Harmon, Michael M. and Richard T. Mayer, 1986. *Organization Theory for Public Administration.* Boston, MA: Little, Brown.
Levine, Charles, 1980. *Managing Fiscal Stress: The Crisis in the Public Sector.* Chatham, NJ: Chatham House.
Marini, Frank, ed., 1971. *Toward a New Public Administration: The Minnowbrook Perspective.* San Francisco: Chandler.
Public Administration Review, 1969a. Keith M. Henderson, "Letter to the Editor" (January-February) 108.
Public Administration Review, 1969b. Richard S. Page, "A New Public Administration?" (May-June) 303.
Public Administration Review, 1970b. Wesley Bjur, "Letter to the Editor" (March-April) 201.
Public Administration Review, 1970b. James Elden, *et al.,* "Letter to the Editor" (July-August) 466.
Public Administration Review, 1989, vol. 49 (March-April) 218–227. See especially the summarizing pieces by Richard T. Mayer, Mary Ellen Guy, Marc Holzer, David Porter, Mary Timney Bailey, and Robert Cleary.
Rohr, John A., 1978. *Ethics for Bureaucrats.* New York: Marcel Dekker.
Thompson, Victor, 1975. *Without Sympathy or Enthusiasm.* University, AL: University of Alabama Press.
Waldo, Dwight, ed., 1971. *Public Administration in a Time of Turbulence.* Scranton, PA: Chandler .
White, Jr. Orion F., 1969. "The Dialectical Organization: An Alternative to Bureaucracy." *Public Administration Review,* vol. 29 (January-February) 32–63.
Wilcox, Robert, 1971. "The New Public Administration: Have Things Really Changed That Much?" *Public Management,* vol. 53, no. 5 (May) 25–28.

PUBLIC AFFAIRS.

Essentially, those elements of public life that relate to, or affect, the people of a nation or state. As such, public affairs is a term that is almost limitless in its definition based upon one's perspective or context, ranging from all areas of international domestic and foreign policy, civil affairs, and corporate social performance. In fact, this entire encyclopedia is designed to be an information source in the area of public affairs. In a sense, it is ironic that there would even be an entry for public affairs in an encyclopedia of public affairs.

Although used in a general context to define all those elements that relate to the people of a nation or state, the term "public affairs" takes on additional meanings in the area of public policy and administration. Currently in the United States, public affairs and public administration are sometimes used interchangeably; public affairs and public administration both address the administration of governmental affairs. On the other hand, public affairs and public administration are sometimes seen as separate and unequal; one is subsumed under the other. Some see public administration as the broad or umbrella term; public affairs is subsumed under public administration. Others see public affairs as the broader term; public administration is subsumed under public affairs. Regardless, the important distinctions between the two terms seem not to be in the administration of public affairs, but in the theory, disciplinary identity, and educational agenda of the fields of public policy and administration. In other words, the distinctions seem less crucial in the practice of governmental (or public) administration and more crucial to the basic theoretical definitions and perspectives of the field, and the paradigms of politics and governmental administration.

Dwight Waldo, one of the founders of modern public administration, described the distinctions in his 1955 text *The Study of Public Administration:* "a fertile source of confusion and error, closely related to the science-art controversy, is the fact that the words 'public administration' have two usages. They are used to designate and delineate both (1) and area of intellectual inquiry, a discipline or study and (2) a process of activity—that of administering public affairs. While the two meanings are of course closely related, they are nevertheless different; it is a difference similar to that between biology and the study of organisms and the organisms themselves" (p. 3).

To understand the perceived differences between public affairs and administration it is necessary to examine the historical context in which these distinctions have come to pass. Traditional perspectives of public administration have their roots in the classical, or generic, approach to public administration, which reached its fullest development in the United States during the 1930s and became the standard of doctrine in many countries. The classical approach rested upon the premise that administration was simply the implementation of public policies determined by others. The focus of administration was upon efficiency, effectiveness, and the neutrality of the administrative agent.

At the core of the classical perspective was the definition of public administration as a discipline which derived its definition from the "politics-administration" dichotomy as first discussed by Woodrow Wilson (1887) in his classic article, "The Study of Administration," and broadly discussed in Frank Goodnow's classic public administration text, *Politics and Administrative.* The politics-administration dichotomy defined politics and administration as two separate entities. Politics, which were value-laden and "[having] to do with policies or expressions of the state will" (Goodnow 1900, p. 10) were seen as

the purvey of elected officials of the state. Administration, on the other hand, "has to do with the execution of the policies" (p. 11) and was seen as the purvey of civil servants or public administrators. Administration was believed to be objective, value-free, and impartial/apolitical. This belief was strengthened by the rise of the scientific management movement at the beginning of this century and the definition of the scientific principles of administration.

The Great Depression and ensuing New Deal in the United States presented realities that challenged the classical perspective. These events brought to light the essential interrelationships between politics and administration. Administrators were not detached agents implementing public policies. Rather, administrators had both to interpret and implement the policies. The old adage that there is no Republican way to build a road was found to be untrue for it was seen that there is indeed a Republican way to interpret how to build the road. Administrators do more than simply and objectively implement public policy. Instead, they administer public affairs.

The demise of the politics-administration dichotomy in the late 1940s and early 1950s in the United States led to a widening of the definition of public administration to include, or be subsumed under, public affairs. As James Fesler stated in his 1975 article "Public Administration and the Social Sciences," "administration is inseparable from the total process of government; indeed public administration is nothing more (but also nothing less) than a way of looking at government. He [Appleby] invited a reorientation away from universal principles and mere efficiency and toward the more exciting policy-formation processes operative amid the American democracy's pluralistic forces" (p. 106).

The recognition that administration is political led to the call to bring together political theory and public administration and to a restructuring of educational institutions and theoretical paradigms. Prior to this time, although political science is considered by many to be the "mother" discipline of public administration, administration was often seen as separate from, and sometimes less than, the field of political science. Political science had always vied with the generic administration approach for dominion over the field of public administration. The 1960s brought this competition to a crest. At this time in U.S. universities, those programs that embraced the political approach to public administration gravitated toward organizing administration and policy programs into schools or programs of public affairs and policy studies which were separate from departments of political science. As Allan Schick stated in his 1975 article "The Trauma of Politics: Public Administration in the Sixties," "the [reorganization] trend began in the late 1960s under the same impulse that [earlier in history] spurred the establishment of generic schools: dissatisfaction with the core curriculum as an aid to public policymaking. Both the generic and policy-oriented schools concentrate on statistical analysis and the use of information technologies, though the policy schools seem to be more enraptured by economic analysis. The key differences between the two schools is the place of politics [which] is often concealed by similar terminologies and methods" (p. 167).

Today, there are probably few differences between how public administration is conceived within schools of public affairs, departments of political science, and departments or programs of public administration. If the place of politics is key, then this place is definitely concealed by similar terminologies, methods, and theoretical perspectives. However, the organizational distinctions still remain as a vestige of the restructuring of the field of public administration in the 1960s to include politics and political theory.

A comparison of data published in the National Association of Schools of Public Affairs and Administration's 1994 *Directory of Programs* indicates that how programs of public affairs and administration are organized within universities has changed somewhat over time. In 1973, there were 101 programs of public affairs and administration in the United States. In 1993, there were 223 such programs. In 1973, 25 percent of the programs were in separate schools of public affairs or administration; 11 percent were in combined professional schools; 23 percent were in separate departments of public affairs or administration; and 36 percent were in programs within departments of political science (6 percent were in other arrangements). In 1993, 15 percent were in separate schools of public affairs or administration; 2 percent were in combined professional schools; 37 percent were in separate departments of public affairs or administration; and 32 percent were in programs within departments of political science (13 percent were in other arrangements). Over time, the proportion of schools of public affairs or administration has declined while the proportion of separate departments has increased (as have other arrangements). The proportion of programs in departments of political science has remained fairly stable. If academic organizing in the United States is an appropriate symbolic variable for understanding the distinctions between public affairs and administration, then it appears that these distinctions may have become less salient over time.

To summarize, public affairs is a broad, global term that encompasses any and all of business, or affairs, of a nation or state. Public affairs and public administration are probably synonymous terms with regard to the application of skills and techniques to the management and understanding of governmental affairs. Public affairs and public administration are sometimes seen as different in theoretical and educational contexts because of the movement in the 1960s to bring together political theory and public administration, which resulted in different organization models of programs of public administration and public affairs within university settings. Some of these organizational vestiges remain with us today.

CHERYL SIMRELL KING

BIBLIOGRAPHY

Fesler, James, 1975. "Public Administration and the Social Sciences: 1946–1960." In F. Mosher, ed., *American Public Administration: Past, Present, Future.* University: University of Alabama Press.

Goodnow, Frank, 1900. *Politics and Administration.* New York: Macmillan.

National Association of Schools of Public Affairs and Administration, 1994. *Directory of Programs.* Washington, D.C.: NASPAA.

Schick, Allan, 1975. "The Trauma of Politics: Public Administration in the Sixties." In F. Mosher, ed., *American Public Administration: Past, Present, Future.* University: University of Alabama Press.

Waldo, Dwight, 1955. *The Study of Public Administration.* New York: Random House.

Wilson, Woodrow, 1887. "The Study of Administration." Reprinted in J. M. Shafritz and A. C. Hyde, eds., 1987. *Classics of Public Administration.* Chicago: The Dorsey Press.

PUBLIC ASSISTANCE.

Cash payments based on need to allow individuals and families without other sources of income to acquire food, shelter, and other basic necessities.

Public assistance consists of a subset of economic security programs that are described more completely in the entry on **public welfare**. The major cash grant public assistance programs in the United States are Temporary Assistance to Needy Families (TANF), Supplemental Security Income (SSI), and general assistance. Temporary Assistance to Needy Families was created by the Personal Responsibility and Work Opportunity Reconciliation Act of 1996 in an attempt to transform the public assistance system. TANF replaces AFDC, which was created under the Social Security Act of 1934. AFDC originally provided grants to children in households where the mother was raising the child or children alone. In that early incarnation, Aid to Dependent Children, as it was called then, was viewed as a way of helping widows take care of their children without going to work. Programs of cash assistance to the elderly, blind, and permanently and totally disabled were added to public assistance over the years. Supplemental Security Income was created by amendments to the Social Security Act in 1972, replacing the Old Age Assistance (OAA), Aid to the Blind (AB), and Aid to the Permanently and Totally Disabled (APTD) programs. General assistance is a residual program that operates in many states to provide assistance to adults without children who are not eligible for SSI.

History and Characteristics of the Programs

When the Social Security Act was adopted, it was generally believed that social insurance eventually would meet the needs of all of America's elderly citizens. As other components were added over the years, many assumed that eventually it would meet the income security needs of the entire population. Thus, programs like Aid to Dependent Children and Old Age Assistance were viewed as stopgap measures that would eventually be replaced by social insurance programs. Clearly there was little expectation that ADC would be transformed into the kind of AFDC program that existed in the early 1990s.

AFDC grew by accretion and amendment over the years. First, mothers became eligible for assistance. Then, in the 1960s, states were allowed to extend eligibility to both parents through the Unemployed Parent (UP) program. Only a limited number of states opted to do that, but the Family Support Act of 1988 required all states to adopt the UP component if they were to continue to participate in the AFDC program. The Family Support Act of 1988 brought about other major changes in AFDC. The Act included various elements intended to reduce dependency on welfare by (1) providing recipients with education, skills, and support services that would allow them to enter the workforce and requiring that participants participate in these programs, (2) stepping up child support enforcement, (3) and providing sanctions that permit states to withhold benefits from recipients who refuse to participate in workforce readiness programs and pursue employment.

AFDC was supported by a mixture of federal, state, and local funds. The federal government provided matching grants for AFDC that ranged from 50 percent to 83 percent of the total grant amount. The individual states picked up the remaining 17 percent to 50 percent, with the level of the state contribution dependent on the state's wealth as measured by per capita income. Some states required local governments, primarily counties, to help fund the state share of the costs.

The national government set the basic parameters of the program with the states determining eligibility and benefit levels within the framework of federal law. The states administer the program and are held accountable for meeting particular administrative standards. There are no minimum payment levels required under federal law, and state definitions of need and maximum benefit levels vary considerably.

Politicians and citizens alike grew increasingly dissatisfied with AFDC and other public assistance programs in the 1980s and 1990s. They complained that AFDC fostered dependency, undermined the work ethic, and subverted family values. They criticized its entitlement status, lack of time limits on receipt of benefits, and failure to require work of recipients. One of the critics' most important complaints was that AFDC households were increasingly headed by unwed mothers, many of whom were in their teenage years.

Although President Clinton pledged in his 1992 election campaign to end welfare as we knew it, it was a new Republican majority in Congress that finally forced action. The election of that conservative majority in 1994 led to far more dramatic changes than many had expected. The Personal Responsibility and Work Opportunity Reconciliation Act of 1996 replaced AFDC with the Temporary Assistance for Needy Families block grant. That block grant frees states from many of the requirements that they faced under AFDC, creating new opportunities and constraints in their place. The program is no longer an entitlement, and the amount of funds available to the states each year is limited. The legislation emphasizes work and personal responsibility. Recipients must be placed in a job or a work program within two years after they start receiving benefits. Unless otherwise exempt, they must be placed in community service work activities within sixty days after entering the program, if they are not working. Each recipient has a lifetime limit of five years of benefits. States are free to set benefit levels for recipients.

Supplemental Security Income, on the other hand, is a national program which guarantees minimum benefits for all participants. A federal benefit level is established. This is supplemented by some states, particularly those that were operating OAA, APTD, or AB programs with higher benefit levels when SSI was implemented. SSI is administered by the Social Security Administration, thus assuring similar treatment of recipients no matter where they live. Because its recipients are generally considered to be incapable of working, SSI has not been subject to the kinds of political attacks that have been made on AFDC. However, questions have arisen about whether some adult recipients are, in fact, disabled, and there is some pressure to reduce the number of disabled children receiving benefits. That pressure comes from politicians who believe the families of those children should assume greater responsibility for their care and who believe that inappropriate standards were established to determine the eligibility of children. The Personal Responsibility and Work Opportunity Reconciliation Act of 1996 changes eligibility rules for children, making it more difficult for them to qualify.

Extent of Use

Participation in public assistance programs varies over time and among states. Use is related to economic conditions, but is also subject to the benefits levels and qualifying criteria used by the various states. Use of AFDC, which many had expected to decline as work related social insurance programs grew in importance, escalated in recent years. Particularly rapid growth occurred in the late 1960s and early 1970s; there was another spurt fueled by the recession of the early 1990s.

The number of families receiving AFDC benefits increased from 259,000 in 1945 to 1.0 million in 1965. By 1975, it had exploded to 3.5 million. After remaining fairly stable for some time, the AFDC rolls grew rapidly from 3.8 million in 1989 to 4.9 million in 1993, and then declined slightly to 4.8 million in 1995. The total number of recipients was 13.9 million in 1993 compared to 4.3 million in 1965 and 907,000 in 1945. By 1995, it had declined slightly to 13.4 million. These changes were brought about by several factors. The population in need grew and the program expanded to fill this need. Explicit efforts were made to mobilize the poor to apply for benefits. The courts removed some restrictions on the receipt of benefits and eligibility rules were loosened by Congress, state legislatures, and program administrators. Eligibility expanded to encompass previously excluded individuals and families. In addition, the number of single-parent families increased steadily and dramatically, leaving more mothers and their children vulnerable to poverty and need. Dramatic declines have been reported by the states since 1995, brought about apparently by an expanding economy and welfare reforms emphasizing work that states were initiating even before PRWORA was adopted in 1996.

The average monthly payment, which was $48 per family in 1945, grew to $133 in 1965, $219 in 1975, $342 in 1985, and $373 in 1992. In inflation adjusted dollars, however, there was a considerable drop in the value of monthly benefits from 1965 to 1992. Expressed in 1980 dollars, the average monthly payment was $422 in 1965; it had fallen to $373 in 1992. This decline in value was brought about by at least two factors. First, other sources of help began to displace AFDC, particularly the food stamp program and Medicaid. Second, AFDC became increasingly unpopular among voters and elected officials. As a result, payments did not keep up with inflation.

The number of recipients and benefit levels varies considerably among the states. The number of recipient families ranged from 819,000 in California to 6,700 in Wyoming in 1992. As a percentage of population, the recipients ran from 1.9 percent in Idaho to 7.1 percent in Michigan. The average was 4.7 percent of a state's population. The maximum benefit for a family of three in 1993 ranged from $120 in Mississippi to $924 in Alaska. The average maximum benefit for a family of three was $394.

In January 1974, shortly after the SSI program was initiated, 3.2 million individuals received federally administered benefits. By December 1993, this number had grown to 6.1 million. The number of recipients of SSI for the aged declined from 1.9 million to 1.5 million during that

period as an increasing share of the elderly became eligible for social security retirement benefits. The number of blind people receiving benefits increased gradually from 73.8 thousand to 86.2 thousand. The number of disabled recipients exploded, increasing from 1.3 million in 1974 to 4.5 million in 1993. Much of this increase in disability recipients was the result of a court case that significantly expanded opportunities for children to receive benefits. It was also a product of the more receptive treatment of disabled adults and children under federal administration of the program.

General assistance is a residual category of support offered in most states to assist those not eligible for one of the other programs. It often aids adults who are unable to meet their own needs. Data on numbers of general assistance recipients are less consistent and reliable. The available data suggest that the states have not allowed general assistance to grow in the same manner that AFDC has grown over the years. The average monthly number of recipients reported by the states was 1.1 million in 1960 and stood at 1.2 million in 1992. In 1980, the last year for which the data are available, the average benefits per case was $127 per month.

Issues

In recent years, three issues dominated debate over AFDC and, to some extent, other public assistance programs. Did the structure of the program undermine families? Did the program reduce the will to work and thus encourage dependency among a particular segment of the population? Did benefit levels affect interstate migration of the poor? These issues were a product of developments in the programs and changing social practices and attitudes. For example, the belief that welfare mothers should work grew as increasing numbers of women entered the labor force. If working-class moms could work, why not the mothers of the poor?

For many years, it was argued that AFDC caused fathers to abandon their families to make them eligible for AFDC, since two-parent families were excluded from program benefits. Legislation in the 1960s began to address this situation as states were allowed to change their programs to include two-parent families. The Family Support Act of 1988 changed things even more by requiring all states to make two parent families eligible for participation.

All welfare programs provide some disincentive to work. Conservative critics have argued that welfare programs in the United States foster the growth of out of wedlock births. Although these effects can be quite negligible and the empirical evidence is very mixed, these critics emphasize arguments that the welfare state fosters dependency in a population that could otherwise care for itself. Such criticism always carries considerable weight in the

United States with its culture that emphasizes individual responsibility and opportunity.

Beginning in 1981 with the conservative Reagan administration, states were encouraged to apply for waivers to federal AFDC rules so that they could operate welfare-to-work (workfare) experiments. These experiments were intended to find ways to help move welfare recipients into the workforce. Experiments carried out in a small number of states (e.g., California and Massachusetts) led to the Family Support Act of 1988, a major revision to the AFDC legislation. This revision required all states to (1) initiate Job Opportunities and Basic Skills (JOBS) programs, which provide support services to help move AFDC recipients into the labor force, (2) require participation in work related activities by certain welfare recipients, (3) offer AFDC benefits to two-parent families, and (4) undertake vigorous programs to obtain child support payments from absent fathers. State initiated JOBS programs have followed various strategies in the attempt to foster self-sufficiency. Despite these changes, political discontent with public assistance continued to mount, leading to the welfare reform legislation of 1996.

Analysts and politicians speculate about whether variations in public assistance benefit levels encourage the poor to migrate from one state to another. It is argued that high benefit levels encourage interstate migration of recipients. Political leaders in several states have made this argument quite strongly in recent years. Research on this topic has produced conflicting findings. Whether the poor migrate in search of improved benefits or not, the fact that political leaders believe that they do has been sufficient for several states to seek changes in federal policy that would allow them to exclude recent migrants from the welfare rolls. Under waivers approved by the Department of Health and Human Services, a small number of states already restrict for twelve months the benefits of new clients migrating from lower benefit states to the benefit levels available in their former states. The reform proposals adopted by Congress prohibit benefits to both legal and illegal aliens.

EDWARD T. JENNINGS, JR.

BIBLIOGRAPHY

Bane, Mary Jo and David T. Ellwood, 1994. *Welfare Realities: From Rhetoric to Reform.* Cambridge: Harvard University Press.

Berkowitz, Edward D. 1991. *America's Welfare State: From Roosevelt to Reagan.* Baltimore: Johns Hopkins University Press.

Ellwood, David T., 1988. *Poor Support: Poverty in the American Family.* New York: Basic Books.

Grimaldi, Paul L. 1980. *Supplemental Security Income: The New Federal Program for the Aged, Blind, and Disabled.* Washington, D.C.: American Enterprise Institute for Public Policy Research.

Gueron, Judith M. and Edward Pauly, 1991. *From Welfare to Work.* New York: Russell Sage Foundation.

Jennings, Edward T. Jr. and Neal S. Zank, eds. *Welfare System Reform: Coordinating Federal, State, and Local Public Assistance Programs.* Greenwood, CT: Greenwood Press, 1993.

Marmor, Theodore R., Jerry L. Mashaw, and Philip L. Harvey, 1992. *America's Misunderstood Welfare State: Persistent Myths, Enduring Realities.* New York: Basic Books.

Mead, Lawrence M. 1992. *The New Politics of Poverty: The Nonworking Poor in America.* New York: Basic Books.

Murray, Charles, 1984. *Losing Ground: American Social Policy, 1950-1980.* New York: Basic Books.

Nathan, Richard, 1993. *Turning Promises into Performance: The Management Challenge of Implementing Workfare.* New York: Columbia University Press.

Trattner, Walter I., 1979. *From Poor Law to Welfare State: A History of Social Welfare in America.* New York: The Free Press.

PUBLIC AUTHORITIES.

Governmental entities which, though chartered by state or local governments to carry out public purposes, have a distinct legal identity and independent corporate status, and operate outside the conventional structure of the executive branch. Authorities embody characteristics of both public and private sector organizations, for while they are wholly governmental in powers and functions, they retain a corporate form and accountability mechanisms more akin to those of private business corporations.

Authorities offer a flexible public response to a specific perceived need. As a consequence, authorities' charters are unique and individually crafted through the political process. This, along with the fact that not all authorities use the term "authority" in their names, has resulted in a degree of confusion as to which organizations are to be identified as public authorities, with Annmarie Walsh noting as recently as 1978 that the literature still lacked a clear definition of the term. Fortunately, a consensus has emerged in recent years, reflecting the view that in addition to providing public services under a government charter, identifying features of public authorities are that they are governed by independent, appointed boards of directors and lack power to levy taxes directly. Special districts, which are not distinguished from authorities in the U.S. Census Bureau's Census of Governments, typically are granted powers of taxation, and are sometimes overseen by popularly elected governing boards.

While often wielding potent governmental powers, such as the power of eminent domain, authorities are: exempt from all or most of the requirements of a merit-based civil service; exempt from standard government procurement and contracting practices; "off-budget," in that they raise revenues in the private, tax-exempt bond market as well as through other means; and freed from adherence to sunshine laws and other reporting requirements to which conventional executive branch agencies are bound. Despite notable exceptions such as the Tennessee Valley

Authority, in the United States the term government corporation is more often used to refer to national level entities, while the term public authorities is most often used to refer to state and local level organizations of this form.

Origins and History

The first public authority so named dates back to 1908 with the creation of the Port of London Authority. The term "public authority" derives from the enabling statute's language, which opened nearly every paragraph with the phrase "Authority is hereby given." While the Port of London Authority provoked some interest in the authority concept, the rapid expansion in use of public authorities in the United States and abroad came more than two decades later, triggered in part by the creation and astounding initial successes of the Port Authority of New York, now one of the best known and most powerful public authorities in the world.

New York state business leader Julius Henry Cohen is credited with bringing the authority model to the United States as a means of securing cooperative action between the state governments of New York and New Jersey with respect to development of New York City's port. Cohen returned from a visit to London in 1916 convinced that the government boundary-spanning capacities of public authorities could be helpful here. Established in 1921, the Port Authority of New York quickly earned a reputation for its professionalism, capable management, and extraordinary project success. As word of the Port Authority's accomplishments spread, it came to serve both as a catalyst and as a prototype for the "public authorities movement," which through the second quarter of this century stretched throughout the United States and abroad.

Public authorities proliferated during the 1930s and early 1940s in the United States, virtually all to carry out public purposes related to transportation, public utilities, and other infrastructure needs. While the New York Port Authority's successes provided an important model, two other major forces played a key role in advancing authority creation. The first was the governmental reform movement of the early twentieth century, which favored authorities as a means to advance reformers' aims of injecting "more efficient, more businesslike, more professional" qualities into government operations. The second major force impacting authority growth came in the form of the leadership role taken on by the U.S. national government, especially during the presidency of Franklin D. Roosevelt.

As New York state governor, Roosevelt's dealings with the New York Port Authority had led him to a belief in what the authority model offered as an alternative to conventional government form. Roosevelt brought his advocacy to Washington, D.C., as president, where his faith in their capacities for rapid and effective action led him to incorporate them as a part of the New Deal. Perhaps one of the best-known public authorities in the world, the Tennessee Valley Authority (TVA), was created in 1933 by President Roosevelt as a national level authority responsible for the agricultural and industrial development of the Tennessee Valley region. Its ambitious regional development program, carried out initially under the leadership of David Lilienthal, has led it to serve even today as a model for action in countries throughout the developing world.

Roosevelt also believed in the potential of public authorities to help severely financially strapped state and local governments undertake job-creating public works initiatives even in the face of the economic ravages of the Great Depression. In 1934 he wrote each of the 48 U.S. state governors, urging that their states adopt legislation facilitating creation of public authorities. Within three years, 29 states had such enabling legislation on the books.

Beyond Roosevelt's personal advocacy, however, the U.S. national government assumed an even more direct and powerful role in promoting public authority expansion through the provisions of national policy. In 1937, U.S. national housing policy mandated that all federal dollars for construction and operation of low-cost public housing be channeled through local housing authorities, spawning immediate state chartering of hundreds of such bodies. Similarly, the act establishing the federal Urban Renewal Program in 1949 contained provisions requiring that all national grants for slum clearance and urban renewal be awarded not to general purpose local governments but to independent local redevelopment authorities created to assume these tasks.

The number of authorities operating in the United States continued to grow slowly but steadily in the post–World War II period, still used primarily for infrastructure and transportation functions. But the 1960s and 1970s brought a new wave of authority expansion in the United States, triggered this time by more "homegrown" forces—the result of experimentation linked to the emergence of new capacities and activism on the part of U.S. states.

Events of this period were shaped by a handful of key state governors who sought to reestablish the states' role as laboratories for domestic policy innovation. Finding their efforts thwarted by public referenda defeats, resistant legislators, and inflexible state administrative agencies, they turned to public authorities as mechanisms for implementing new initiatives. Foremost among them was Governor Nelson A. Rockefeller of New York State. Authorities such as the State University Construction Fund, the Urban Development Corporation, and more than a dozen other state authorities were brought into existence by Rockefeller to mount an ambitious capital development agenda for the state. And Rockefeller pioneered expansion of authorities beyond their traditional roles and functions, creating new bodies (such as the New York State Housing Finance Agency) which operated not as conventional builders and managers, but instead as lending institutions for a variety of public and private projects deemed to be in the public interest of the state. Rockefeller's lead efforts helped to expand the authority concept beyond the traditional roles and policy arenas to which it had been confined, and his efforts were quickly replicated across the country.

The trend toward continued growth in the use of public authorities in the United States has extended into the 1980s and 1990s, fed both by ongoing state and local fiscal strains and by the new "reinventing government" movement. Today, state and local public authorities are estimated to number close to 7,000, are responsible for some of the most essential governmental services (transportation, water and sewer, electric power), and wield exceptional economic power as actors in the U.S. federal system.

Underlying Theoretical Framework

Exploring the logic underlying the creation and flourishing of public authorities leads to exploration of some of the most fundamental and complex theoretical questions facing students of public administration and policy. The conceptual underpinnings of public authorities are in many ways markedly different from those of most general purpose governments. In fact, authorities are frequently advanced as a means for correcting for some of the weaknesses and constraints inherent in conventional state and municipal government form. Moreover, as hybrid institutions grafted onto an existing and already crowded governance landscape, authorities also foster some rather thorny management problems with deep roots in administrative theory.

Expertise and the Politics-Administration Dichotomy

From their origin, public authorities represented one of the institutions epitomizing faith in Woodrow Wilson's (1887) politics-administration dichotomy, whose underlying premise held that in order to ensure policy is carried out in the most economical and efficient manner possible, administration must be separated from politics. Like proponents of the city manager movement, another administrative innovation of the reform era, champions of the public authority movement weighed what Herbert Kaufman (1956) termed the core public administration value of "neutral competence" far more heavily than the countervailing core values of executive leadership (dominant for example, in strong-mayor city charters) and representativeness. In the public authority model, nonpartisan "experts" under the management of a professional executive director carry out the purportedly "technical" mission of the organization in a "businesslike" manner, thereby enhancing

economy and efficiency in the achievement of government's aims.

While the politics-administration dichotomy has long since been discounted by most scholars, proposals to create new public authorities often continue even today to be marketed to the public as the means for separating administration from politics in those public endeavors deemed to be of critical long-term importance to the public. Indeed, the contemporary "reinventing government" movement of the 1990s holds up public authorities as one of the pragmatic and flexible "reengineered" governmental forms, capable of implementing policy more effectively by shifting administration into the hands of competent experts. However, the fact that authorities are influential in determining "who gets what (services and facilities), when, and how" (Harold Lasswell's classic definition of politics), should leave little doubt that they remain far more than mere administrative instrumentalities.

Coordination and Accountability

Any analysis of public authorities inevitably evokes discussion of two additional enduring issues central to theories of policy and public administration: the search to secure coordination and coherence among related public policies and programs, and the ever-present requirement for democratic accountability.

Jameson Doig (1983) observed that public authorities are among the best examples of public organizations exercising the kind of "large powers and unhampered discretion" advocated by Woodrow Wilson (1887). According to Wilson, grants of independence and broad discretion, accompanied by the clear assignment of managerial responsibility, would encourage entrepreneurial behavior that facilitates swift and effective action. A valid concern, however, is that as a consequence of this granting of independent "large powers," those authority efforts that logically call for coordination with the functional programs of other conventional executive branch agencies are left free to operate in a fragmented manner or perhaps even at cross purposes with the programs of general purpose government.

The dilemma for those seeking enhancement of public sector efficacy is that the public authority may well be a double-edged sword. While able to carve through the barriers to rapid change and innovation, it is also capable to adversely impacting government efforts aimed at securing some coherence among the operations of various public programs.

With respect to public authorities, the issues surrounding accountability continue to be the most vexing ones. Scholars writing about public authorities in recent years have expressed concerns about how it is to be ensured in a democratic setting that authorities are held politically accountable. Though boards of directors (appointed with varying degrees of direct governmental ties) hold formal responsibility for overseeing authority activities, questions have been raised about the manner of their appointment and how their representation of particular interests within a state or community affects the board's capacity to serve as the conduit for expression of the public interest.

Other concerns regarding accountability emanate from a very different direction. It has been argued that boards have been prone to assume a largely passive role in the governance of authorities, tending not to be heavily involved in operational decisionmaking or even in the formulation of new directions for authority policy and action, deferring instead to the leadership and competence of the executive director. The weaknesses in political accountability inherent in governmental organizations in which "experts oversee experts" is of enduring theoretical as well as pragmatic concern.

Current Practice in the United States

Today public authorities have assumed a place as important institutional actors participating in the complex web of intergovernmental relations and public-private sector partnerships that shape and implement policies at the state and local level in the United States. Their ranks are likely to continue to swell, an increase directly connected to the variety of useful roles they can play in contemporary governance.

Financially, their off-budget status as separate legal entities offers distinct fiscal advantages. Authorities serve as convenient vehicles for skirting borrowing and spending restrictions imposed on general purpose subnational governments by the 50 state constitutions. Over the past three decades, capital expenditures have continued to account for a smaller and smaller share of state and local government budgets. At the same time, public authorities have increasingly become the favored vehicle for funding capital initiatives at the subnational level.

Annmarie Walsh (1990) observed that the complex and creative financial activities of authorities largely escape the eye of citizens and scholars because they represent an "insider's game." It is not difficult to imagine why this trait would be valued by some political leaders and private interests who promote the creation of authorities and staff their governing boards. For instance, pro-growth interests advocating goals of metropolitan expansion and economic development recognize the need for significant and sometimes controversial infrastructure investment in order to advance these objectives. Authorities are not only a vehicle for circumventing the bond issue referenda mandated by state constitutions, but also seem to deflect the attention of the media, which often appears not to comprehend fully the place of authorities in the contemporary policy and administrative mileau.

Authorities can also, some would contend, serve as a means for enhancing the public sector's capacity to act more innovatively and expeditiously. Circumstances may exist where responsibility for a key governmental function falls to a traditional executive agency that is not duly attentive to the need to adopt alternative ways of carrying out its mission or to the need to "fast-track" certain projects. This agency may also be incapable of changing and adapting in response to new conditions. It is clear why the creation of a new public authority unencumbered by the existing personnel, standard operating procedures, and organizational culture of its predecessor would have appeal as an alternative avenue for program development and administration.

Finally, a number of the problems and issues facing subnational governments today are multijurisdictional in nature. While creation of regional governments offers one dramatic way for dealing with these problems, this approach has been advanced as a solution to metropolitan fragmentation and has failed to receive widespread acceptance in the United States. Public authorities provide an alternative route for dealing with multijurisdictional needs. They offer a limited, de facto form of areawide governance, often centered on a single issue (frequently transportation-related) about which there is regional political consensus on the need to act. However, even under these circumstances, Dennis Muniak (1990) has shown that efforts to use public authorities to solve multijurisdictional problems can be fraught with controversy and delay because of the not always readily apparent realignment of power among various governments that often results.

Recent Trends and Emerging Issues

Historically, one argument often advanced for the establishment of public authorities concerned their ability to be financially self-sustaining. Today, however, total fiscal self-sufficiency is less and less common. General purpose governments now frequently capitalize authorities' initial endeavors, and while they are purportedly expected to repay these funds once in operation, this often fails to occur. Further, a tendency for state and local government to underwrite, to some extent, the annual operating expenses of public authorities has been evident in recent years. While the national government has long provided annual operating grants to some local authorities (e.g., public housing authorities, mass transit authorities, etc.), states and localities are now often found to dedicate or earmark certain tax revenues or lottery receipts to fund authority operations or pay off authority bonds. And despite the fact that authorities remain legally responsible for their own indebtedness, states bound by only "moral obligation" rather than full faith and credit bond guarantees have nonetheless been prompted out of concern over adverse impacts on state bond ratings to pay authority bond holders. Authorities today are not nearly as financially self-supporting as was true a few decades ago.

Mayoral and gubernatorial efforts to expand their control over authority resources and actions have also been evident in recent years. While skillful political actors have undoubtedly always influenced authorities, public executives increasingly cognizant of the potential financial ramifications of authority behavior, the rising economic and political might wielded by these independent bodies, and the potentially important implications for existing government initiatives of their widening range of activities have moved to enhance their capacity to oversee and coordinate authority actions.

Finally, though authorities have sometimes been touted as a kind of institutional elixir for solving complex public policy problems, some glaring examples of weaknesses in their abilities to perform that role has surfaced in recent years. An example can be seen in the case of public housing authorities where corruption, poor judgment, and managerial deficiencies have marred their capacity to provide decent living accommodations for some of the nation's most needy. That the federal government has identified 92 public housing authorities as "troubled" and has recently found it necessary to take over the housing authorities of Philadelphia and Chicago, much as court-appointed receivers have done with those in Boston, Kansas City, and Washington, D.C., should serve as a vivid reminder that authorities do not automatically provide a quick organizational fix for resolving major public sector policy quandaries.

Variations in Practice in Other Nations

With the exception of a few studies such as Jerry Mitchell's work (1993), there has been little systematic analysis of state and local public authorities in the United States. Likewise, there is a paucity of substantial research on subnational authorities as they function elsewhere in the world. While authorities are found in both developed and developing nations (including Great Britain, India, Thailand, Israel, Australia, Canada, Japan, and Germany) we know relatively little about how they function or the uses to which they are put. The fact that they go by different names in other countries (as in Australia, for instance, where they are known as "statutory corporations") impedes the undertaking of comparative study.

The limited anecdotal material available makes clear, though, that while authority functions may be similar around the globe, there are known differences in terms of structure and oversight. For example, authorities in Britain and Germany are quite different in the manner in which they blend into the policy and administrative arenas. While in recent years U.S. mayors and governors have begun to move to hold authorities more accountable, in Europe they have always been more closely linked with the general purpose governments that created them and that exercise greater control over project priorities and over the use of surplus revenues than in the United States.

DENNIS C. MUNIAK

BIBLIOGRAPHY

Axelrod, D., 1992. *Shadow Government: The Hidden World of Public Authorities and How They Control Over $1 Trillion of Your Money.* New York: Wiley.
Doig, J. W., 1983. "'If I See a Murderous Fellow Sharpening a Knife Cleverly . . .': The Wilson Dichotomy and the Public Authority Tradition." *Public Administration Review,* vol. 43, no. 4: 292–304.
Henriques, D., 1986. *The Machinery of Greed: Public Authority Abuse and What to do About It.* Lexington, MA: Lexington Books.
Kaufman, H., 1956. "Emerging Conflicts in the Doctrines of Public Administration." *American Political Science Review,* vol. 50 (December) 1059–1073.
Mitchell, J., 1992. *Public Authorities and Public Policy: The Business of Government.* Westport, CT: Greenwood Press.
———, 1993. "Accountability and the Management of Public Authorities in the United States." *International Review of Administrative Sciences,* vol. 59: 477–492.
Muniak, D. C., 1990. "Federal Divestiture, Regional Growth and the Political Economy of Public Authority Creation: The Emergence of the Metropolitan Washington Airports Authority." *Policy Studies Journal,* vol. 18 (Summer) 943–960.
Smith, R. G., 1969. *Public Authorities in Urban Areas.* Washington, D.C.: National Association of Counties.
Walsh, A. H., 1978. *The Public's Business: The Politics and Practices of Government Corporations.* Cambridge, MA: MIT Press.
———, 1990. "Public Authorities and the Shape of Decision-making." In J. Bellush and D. Netzer, eds., *Urban Politics, New York Style.* Armonk, NY: M. E. Sharpe.
Wilson, Woodrow W., 1887. "The Study of Administration." *Political Science Quarterly,* vol. 2 (June) 197–222.

PUBLIC BROADCASTING. Radio and television stations operated by public sector authorities and funded to a significant degree by budget appropriation, statutory levies, or charges. Where privately or cooperatively owned, public broadcasters are identified by a financial dependency on audience subscription, grants from philanthropic bodies, reception license fees, or allocations from government and other public sector sources. A general philosophy of placing the public good before profit maximization distinguishes public broadcasters from commercial radio and television stations.

Public broadcasters function on a not-for-profit basis, unlike commercial broadcasters, whose principal activity involves selling airtime for advertising. Some operate commercial stations to finance, or cross-subsidize, their nonprofit broadcasting activity. Public broadcasters transmit on frequencies accessed by broad populations (e.g., AM, FM radio bands, shortwave radio frequencies, or VHF and UHF television bands) and where communications infrastructure is advanced, they may also have access to cable or satellite services.

Origin and History

Public broadcasting originated in Europe after World War I, when radio developed as a popular mass communications medium. Radio was made possible by U.S. inventor, Lee de Forest, whose invention of an electrical component, the "Audion" vacuum tube (triode valve), in 1906 facilitated the broadcast transmission of the human voice and music. This marked a major advance on Guglielmo Marconi's wireless telegraphy, or the radio transmission of Morse code signals, which he first accomplished in 1895. A demonstration in 1906 by the U.S. Army's General Dunwoodie laid the groundwork for the development of early radio's most popular form of receiver, the crystal set.

World War I put a stop to experimental radio broadcasters, as military forces took over licenses issued to amateurs, electrical component manufacturers, and educational institutions. By the war's end, Germany had established an extensive, fairly reliable radio network linking its Western Front command. The potential for radio to communicate effectively with large numbers of people across widely dispersed locations was not lost on the defeated German troops, or the Allied military leadership. In the chaotic period following the cessation of hostilities, Bolshevik and anarchist forces in the German armed forces took over the radio network and used it to recruit troops and civilians to their cause.

Alarmed Allied commanders saw civilian radio as a dangerous technology, a potential tool for subversion. They were successful in delaying the reintroduction of broadcast radio in Germany until 1923, and lobbied in the United States and Great Britain for a significant public sector role in the planning, regulation, and operation of broadcasting.

Europe

In Great Britain, a heavily regulated, private broadcasting monopoly was established in 1922, with John Reith appointed manager of the British Broadcasting Company. This was nationalized in 1927 and the British model of public service broadcasting was born. Reith remained at the helm of the British Broadcasting Corporation (BBC), which operated under Royal Charter, initially with little effective independence from government. Commercial advertising was prohibited and revenue was generated from a listeners' license fee. Commercial broadcasters were excluded from the airwaves and Reith developed a broadcasting philosophy for the BBC that was elitist and didac-

tic, often confusing the notion of the public good with his estimation of what was good for the public. Listeners were left with little choice and their views were not a priority for at least the first ten years, after which audience research was begun.

By 1933, when the Nazis nationalized an oligopoly of ten private broadcasting companies in Germany, the exclusion of the private sector from radio broadcasting had became the norm across Europe.

Public broadcasting monopolized the airwaves until the 1960s, when it was challenged by radio stations operating illegally across international borders. A number of these stations were based on ships at sea and "pirate radio" was the term coined to describe this challenge to what many listeners considered boring, stodgy programming offered by entrenched public broadcasters.

Great Britain chose a public/private mix of operators, sharing a common broadcast infrastructure, when television was introduced in 1955. Other European nations allowed restrictive forms of commercial advertising on their public television networks.

A trickle of private commercial radio broadcasters began in Europe during the 1970s as governments loosened regulatory restrictions. By the late 1980s, this turned into a flood, as European nations further deregulated the broadcast media in response to pressure from the private sector, challenges from illegal broadcasters (particularly in Italy and France), and the introduction of cable television. A third tier of subscription based, nonprofit broadcasters emerged at the same time, declaring themselves the vehicle for genuine community access to the media.

The United States

Public broadcasting in the United States developed from educational, college-based radio stations, some of which were established after Congress passed the first broadcast licensing law in 1912.

The Navy took control of all broadcasting licenses when the United States entered the European conflict in 1917, lobbying for the continuation of a Navy-sponsored monopoly after the war. This was defeated in Congress and private broadcasting stations proliferated, with authorities overwhelmed by the demand for broadcast licenses. By the late 1920s a regulatory regime was introduced and enforced, leading to the development of national commercial networks. Nonprofit radio stations based at university and college campuses and funded by states were reestablished after World War I. Some local authorities, such as New York City Council, also set up their own stations. Station closures were common during the 1930s Depression and those granted FM licences after 1940 were restricted to a band with few listeners.

Educational television emerged in the 1950s and the 1965 Carnegie Commission Inquiry into educational media led Congress to pass the Public Broadcasting Act two years later. The Act established the Corporation for Public Broadcasting as a conduit for federal funds to nonprofit broadcasters, via the Public Broadcasting Service (for television) and National Public Radio. These were both established in 1970 and funding from them supplemented listener subscriptions, donations, corporate underwriting, and commercial sponsorship (a softer, less intrusive form of advertising) as the noncommercial stations' main sources of revenue.

The first fully listener-funded station not connected to a religious or educational body was established in Berkeley, California, in 1949 by the nonprofit Pacifica Foundation. After a shaky start, a small Pacifica network was developed around the nation. During the 1960s, community stations, which were listener owned and operated, were licensed, and in 1975 a National Federation of Community Broadcasters was established. With the development of cable television, many local governments imposed requirements on cable operators to reserve channels for community or local authority use.

Canada and Australia

The British Public broadcasting radio model was adopted across its empire, with a number of less dependent former colonies, such as Australia and Canada, developing hybrid systems. These combined elements of the British and U.S. models with a mix of public and private stations, which proved both enduring and popular. Australia's public broadcaster, the commercial-free Australian Broadcasting Corporation (ABC), is seen as one of the most important positive influences on national life. Advertiser access to Canadian public broadcaster radio stations was removed in 1976, although commercials have remained a feature of television, contributing nearly a quarter of the Canadian Broadcasting Corporation's revenue. In both countries, nonprofit, volunteer-run, subscriber-funded and controlled stations have grown in number since the 1970s, adopting the mantle of community radio and targeting minority groups. Community television followed radio's footsteps in the 1980s and 1990s.

International

Public broadcasting across international borders played a significant part in the battle for hearts and minds during the Cold War. While funding for domestic public broadcasters in the United States remained insignificant, overseas broadcasting services, such as the Voice of America and the covert Radio Free Europe/Liberty, Free Asia, and Swan (broadcasting to Cuba) were well supported by federal departments and agencies as they broadcast deep into enemy territory, using high powered transmitters on short wave frequencies. Like their counterparts in the socialist bloc (Radio Moscow or Radio Beijing), the credibility of these broadcasters as accurate and dispassionate news and comment sources suffered from their financial, ideological, and policy proximity to government.

Other international public broadcasters, such as Deutsche Welle, Radio Nederland Wereldomroep, the BBC Word Service and Radio Australia, have developed reputations as more reliable news sources, particularly for those living under authoritarian governments. Even some of the world's poorest nations maintain an official international radio network, broadcast on shortwave frequencies. More developed nations fund international television networks. These services are designed to keep expatriates in touch with the homeland and to promote the national interest at a global level.

Underlying Theoretical Framework

Public broadcasters generally express a commitment to popular audience appeal, tempered by adherence to broad notions of public good, cultural development, identity with the national interest, the right of individuals to be informed, and in many nations, the commitment to publish without fear or favor.

The public broadcaster's brief generally details a desire to inform, educate, and entertain its audience. Where they operate alongside private commercial stations, public broadcasters generally commit to providing viewers and listeners with at least some programming considered by commercial stations to be too narrowly focused, controversial, or innovative for their advertisers or audiences.

Independence from government varies, although there tends to be a direct correlation between an autonomous public broadcaster and the degree to which freely elected or democratic institutions of government exist.

Community broadcasters promote public access and participation in the ownership and operation of their stations. Staff are largely volunteers, audience subscription funding is emphasized, and notions of the passive media consumer are challenged.

Current Practice in the United States

Noncommercial, public, and community stations account for just over 10 percent of the 8,500 radio and television broadcasters in the United States. Approximately one thousand radio and television stations could be described as public, or community, stations and are eligible to receive federal funding. Eight-eight percent of the U.S. population is able to tune into, or watch, a public station.

In the mid- to late 1990s, with Republicans in the ascendancy in Congress, a federal funding squeeze on public broadcasting continued. Conservatives argue that with the growth of cable outlets catering for minorities, publicly funded broadcasting is no longer necessary. Federal funding directed through the Corporation for Public

Broadcasting amounted to $285 million in 1995, the equivalent of a dollar per citizen for the year. This is significantly less than most major nations' funding of public broadcasters. The Canadian Broadcasting Corporation, for example, receives $US 750 million per year from government, while each Australian contributes the equivalent of $US 22 annual federal income tax to support the Australian Broadcasting Corporation. A typical public station in the United States may derive a quarter of its operating costs from federal funding and rely on annual audience subscriptions of approximately $25 per individual, in addition to on-air sponsorship announcements from local business. Annual station operating budgets can range up to $4 million.

U.S. public and community broadcasters provide a depth to news, current affairs, and documentary programs unmatched in the commercial media. They remain a source of innovative, challenging programs, in addition to spawning commercial successes, such as "Sesame Street." However, the severe financial restraints on U.S. public stations force leading networked news programs to seek sponsorship from major corporations, while quiz shows, reruns of failed dramas produced for commercial networks, appeals, prizes, and giveaway competitions are common features of public broadcaster formats on television and radio.

As new communications technology facilitates the emergence of global media and markets for programs, the U.S. public television sector is developing links overseas. A consortium of U.S. public television stations is linking with stations in Europe, Latin America, and the Pacific Rim, to develop coproduction ventures.

Variations of Practice in Other States, Regions, and Regimes

A reduction in the size and scope of the public sector spending has been a feature of most developed nations' economies in the 1980s and 1990s. As a result, public broadcasters in these countries have been forced to reevaluate their roles and performance, particularly in Europe, where deregulation of media industries and international satellite delivery of services has seen large-scale entry of commercial competitors into the mass media.

The reappraisal of the role of the public broadcaster is particularly rigorous in nations emerging from decades of totalitarian rule. This extends beyond the former Soviet bloc to countries such as South Africa, where the South African Broadcasting Corporation is undergoing a transformation from state propaganda instrument to an independent public broadcaster in a racially and culturally diverse democracy. This is occurring in conjunction with growth in commercial and community broadcast media.

In other developing countries, public broadcasting programming continues to be heavily influenced by government. Where democracy is emerging, so too is community and commercial radio. In Mali, for example, they are presenting a challenge to the state public broadcaster, which broadcasts in French, the official language, but one understood by only 10 percent of the population. As a public education vehicle, public broadcasters are at their most effective in nations where illiteracy and poor infrastructure hamper development. International development aid is focusing on broadcasting in Indochina, the Pacific, the Americas, and Africa. Such innovations as cheap wind-up clockwork radio receivers may also enhance access to radio and the effectiveness of public broadcasters in these regions.

In totalitarian countries such as China, global media entrepreneurs are competing to secure contracts to supply programming, advertising, and subscription services to the state run, controlled, and censored public broadcasting services. The huge media audiences of nations like China are now accessible by satellite and cable-delivered services. Some major world media players are prepared to sanitize their programming to gain entry to these increasingly affluent markets.

DAVE LANE

BIBLIOGRAPHY

Barnett, Steven and Andrew Curry, 1994. *The Battle for the BBC: A British Broadcasting Conspiracy?* London: Aurum Press.
Corporation for Public Broadcasting (CPB). Internet Web Site.
Etzioni-Halevy, Eva, 1987. *National Broadcasting Under Siege.* New York: St. Martin's Press.
Hilliard, Robert L. and Michael C. Keith, 1992. *The Broadcast Century: A Biography of American Broadcasting.* Stoneham, MA: Butterworth-Heinemann.
Lewis, Peter M. and Jerry Booth, 1990. *The Invisible Medium: Public, Commercial and Community Radio.* Washington, D.C.: Howard University Press.
The Media Report, 1994–95. Weekly radio program on Radio National. The Australian Broadcasting Corporation, Melbourne, Australia.
National Federation of Community Broadcasters (NFCB). Internet Web Site.
Sennitt, Andrew G., ed., 1995. *World Radio TV Handbook.* vol. 49. Amsterdam: Billboard Books.
Willis, Edgar E. and Henry B. Aldridge, 1992. *Television, Cable and Radio: A Communications Approach.* Englewood Cliffs, NJ: Prentice Hall.
Wood, James, 1992. *History of International Broadcasting.* London: Peter Peregrinus in Association with the Science Museum.

PUBLIC CHOICE.

The application of economic logic–methodological individualism and rational, self-interested decisionmaking–to questions and issues that have traditionally been the concern of political scientists and public administrators.

Public choice theory, like the older normative theory of public finance from which it evolved, starts with the demand for and the supply of collectively provided goods and services. With two exceptions, the theory of demand for a collectively provided good is identical to the theory of consumer demand for a private good. In both instances, demand reflects individual willingness and ability to pay to consume a good or service. Total demand for the service is, therefore, assumed to be a decreasing function of the price of the good, an increasing function of consumer income, and the size of the market for the good. The two differences between the theory of demand for a collectively provided good and the theory of consumer demand for a private good are that the quantity of service provided within a jurisdiction is determined by a political process, usually assumed to be some form of majority rule, and is necessarily uniform throughout the jurisdiction. This fact justifies the conclusion that, if efficiency is the sole object of public policy, public provision should be restricted to pure public or collective goods, owing to their basic characteristics: impossibility of exclusion and jointness of supply, that is, free riders cannot be excluded from their enjoyment, and one person's enjoyment of the good is not diminished by someone else's.

If demand reflects willingness and ability to pay, the quantity demanded of a collectively provided service will depend upon its price (P), the permanent income of the citizenry (Y), and population size (C):

$$Di = f[P^\epsilon, Y^\alpha, C^\beta,]$$

where:

ϵ = the price elasticity of demand for good i;
α = the income elasticity of demand for good i; and
β = a value from 0 to 1, representing the degree of publicness of good i.

(Borcherding 1977; Bergstrom and Goodman 1972). The functional relationship that would obtain in any particular case would, of course, reflect existing political institutions as well as culturally mediated tastes and preferences. There is a fair amount of evidence that this model of voter demand for collectively provided goods works reasonably well in practice. Literally hundreds of studies have demonstrated that family/per capita income, tax price, community size, and population served better explain cross-sectional variations in collectively supplied service levels that any other set of "determinants" (Oates 1994). Of course these variables work best where service levels are determined by direct referenda (Holcombe 1977). The one bug in the ointment is the "flypaper effect," so called because intergovernmental transfers tend to stick where they land. That is, intergovernmental grants appear to produce far larger increases in the output of government services than predicted by the income and price elasticities of the basic demand model—although this finding could easily be an artifact of the use of expenditure data as a proxy for the consumption of collec-tively provided services. Larkey (1979), for example, found little or no evidence of the flypaper effect in his study of general revenue sharing. Most municipalities used GRS funds to reduce taxes, either immediately, or, by investing them in plant, equipment, maintenance, or training, in the future.

The Median Voter and Bowen Equilibrium

In democracy, D_i should reflect the tastes and elasticities of the median voter (Bowen 1943) and, based on Holcombe (1977), would be in equilibrium where:

$$Vm = Tm$$

where:
Vm = the marginal benefit of good or service i to the median voter m
Tm = the marginal cost of good or service i to the median voter m

Then, where the cost of the good is equally shared by all voters (n), it follows that the marginal cost of the good to all voters is:

$$MC = \sum_{j=1}^{n} T_i$$

Since the Samuelsonian efficiency condition (1954, 1955), where the sum of the marginal costs of providing the collective good equals the sum of marginal benefits to all contributors, is:

$$\sum_{j=1}^{n} V_j = \sum_{j=1}^{n} T_j$$

It follows, that, for a Bowen equilibrium to be efficient, the marginal cost-to-benefit to the average voter would have to be equal to the marginal benefit-to-cost to the median voter, that is, the following condition would have to be satisfied:

$$V_m \bigg/ \sum_{j=1}^{n} V_j = T_m \bigg/ \sum_{j=1}^{n} T_j$$

Consequently a Bowen equilibrium will be efficient if and only if marginal net benefits sum to zero at the output or supply level preferred by the median voter. This is of course something of a "knife-edged condition," except where the tastes, willingness, and ability to pay of all the voters in a jurisdiction are practically identical. One mechanism that might lead to the satisfaction of this condition is Tiebout sorting (named after the late Charles M. Tiebout, 1956) in which voters move to the communities whose governments best satisfy their preferences for collectively provided goods and services. While most economists grant that Tiebout sorting takes place, there is little consensus as to its significance. William Fishel (1992), for example, claims that the evidence from zoning and voting demonstrates that it is fairly complete; John Yinger, Howard S. Bloom, Axel Borsch-Supan, and Helen F. Ladd (1988), however, claim that the evidence from tax capitalization is equivocal.

This is a significant claim, because at the local level, to the extent that service and tax levels are capitalized in real property values, reliance on the property tax reduces differences between the mean and the median voter even in the absence of Tiebout sorting. Reliance on proportional or progressive income taxes probably has a similar effect at state and, perhaps, federal levels of government. The key point to be stressed here is, as Bowen explained (his conclusion was later popularized by Downs 1959–60), the average voter's demand for collectively provided goods will normally exceed the preferred consumption level of the median voter. This means that in a democracy, where costs are equally shared or, perhaps, even where taxes are proportional to income, collectively provided goods will tend to be undersupplied.

Downs further argued that collectively provided services are underproduced because their benefits are less visible to the median voter than their costs. However, it is by no means self-evident that government services are really worth more than they cost at the margin. If anything, the opposite assumption–that the benefits of government services are palpable and appear to be free–seems more plausible. Pure public goods are the only exception to this generalization that I know of. These goods are often undersupplied, almost by definition. There aren't many of them, though. Government waste reduction seems like one, and so does careful and honest evaluation of government programs, which could be one explanation for their short supply (Stanbury and Thompson 1995).

There is strong evidence of Bowen/Downs undersupply. For, example, Fabio Silva and Jon Sonstelie (1995) recently tested William Fischel's (1989) hypothesis that, by requiring equal spending per pupil across all school districts in the state, and thereby reducing Tiebout sorting and widening the gap between the preferences of the average and the median voter, the California Supreme Court in *Serrano v. Priest* caused a reduction in public spending to support elementary and secondary education. Before Serrano, California ranked eleventh among states in public school spending per pupil, 13 percent above the average of all other states. By 1990, California had fallen to thirtieth, 10 percent below the average. The mechanism that produced this outcome was, of course, a popular initiative, Proposition 13, which limited property tax rates, rolled back assessed valuations, and, by curtailing the main source of local revenue for public schools, shifted decisions about education spending levels to the state. Before *Serrano* similar initiatives had been consistently rejected by California voters. Silva and Sonstelie found that about

one-half of the decline in public spending to support elementary and secondary education could be attributed to Serrano. They attributed the remainder to rapid enrollment growth in California during the 1980s.

Lindahl Equilibrium

There is a second condition whereby the knife-edged condition described earlier might obtain, at least in theory: where decisions about collective provision are made unanimously. Unanimity can be satisfied under Lindahl equilibrium (Feldman 1980), a special case of the Samuelsonian efficiency condition. Formally, Lindahl equilibrium is defined as a vector of expenditure shares $[S_1, S_2, \ldots, S_n]$ and a level of provision $[D^*]$ such that for all i, where i's expenditure share is S_i, the quantity of the good desired is D^* [i.e. because i's expenditure or T_i is $S_i D^*$, $\sum S_i = 1$]. Furthermore:

$$Vi\,[D] = Si$$

$$V\,i\,[D^*] = Si, \text{ for all } i$$

$$\sum Vi\,[D^*] = \sum Si = 1$$

Under this formulation, demand for all i is presumed to be normal, that is, the higher i's share S_i, the lower the Di will want. Hence, if the Lindahl equilibrium were D_1 and one i reduced their contribution to the provision of the good, the share of all other i would increase and $D_1 > D_2$.

This voting rule is seldom used, however, because of the transactions costs associated with finding Lindahl equilibrium–search, bargaining, and monitoring costs (Heckathorn and Maser 1990). Because of this fact, James Buchanan and Gordon Tullock (1962) suggest that an optimal constitution would minimize the sum of the costs imposed upon dissatisfied minorities, a decreasing function of the size of required majorities, and transactions costs, an increasing of function. Indeed, the U.S. founders tried to design a constitutional order with this goal, albeit not this formulation, in mind. The founders designed the federal Constitution to protect lives, liberties, and property from the overweening ambition of a reckless and extravagant executive, the passions of minorities, and the interests of narrow or temporary majorities. This structure was intended to insure that the United States would have a government of law and that the law would change slowly and incrementally and only when the direction of change was endorsed by a large majority of the citizenry. The founders relied upon partisanship, jealousy between the two chambers of Congress, and the particularities of committee interests to make the federal government an agent of negotiation and compromise that would reach its decisions through the discovery of a lowest common denominator (Thompson 1979).

Legislative Decisionmaking

Representation promotes efficiency in two other ways. First of all it minimizes the transactions costs of political participation (economists see participation as a cost, not a benefit). Second, it transforms some public goods, where each individual voter's preferences are known only to himself or herself and costs are shared, into private goods, where benefits and costs are denominated in dollars and knowledge of the net benefit schedule of each voter/legislator is equally available to all (Shepsle and Weingast 1984). Once the public goods problem is laid to rest, efficiency should be easy to arrive at. According to the Coase Theorem (Coase 1960), where we are dealing with private goods and decisions are made one good at a time, any decision rule will produce an efficient outcome–except where prevented by restrictions on side payments, transactions costs, or just plain ignorance (Dahlman 1979).

Explaining Oversupply

The basic model for a collectively provided good implies the likelihood of undersupply. To many public choice theorists this likelihood appears to fly in the face of reality. What they want to do is explain what they observe: an excess of government. Two serious attempts to explain government excess have been mounted and, while neither entirely succeeds, both have taught us something about government. These are the interest group theory of politics and William Niskanen's theory of spending coalitions, which introduced the notions of structurally induced equilibrium and agency theory to the study of politics and bureaucracy.

The economic theory of interest group politics is largely the creation of the "Chicago school" of regulatory theorists: George Stigler (1971), Richard Posner (1971, 1974), and Sam Peltzman (1976). They argued that a variety of government programs (agricultural subsidies, military procurement, tariffs and import quotas, most regulation of business, and the structure of the tax system) are the product of an exchange between elected officials, who receive votes and campaign contributions, and members of groups, who reap higher incomes from their political investment. The theory predicts that politicians will use their power to transfer income from those with less political power to those with more: from the rich and the poor to the middle class and from disorganized, diffuse interests to well-organized concentrated interests–for example, geographically targeted benefits and predominantly federally financed costs (Ferejohn 1974; Shepsle and Weingast 1981; Hird 1991). Who gets what depends upon the costs and benefits to individual group members of participating in political processes and the ability of groups to influence policymakers.

Of course, political scientists have known about interest groups for generations. What was new about the economic theory of interest group politics? First, economists better understood the costs and benefits of government actions and their distributional consequences, which focused attention on the size of individual payoffs rather than the wealth of the player. Second, economists brought Mancur Olson's theory of collective action to bear upon the question of interest group influence on the public policy process. Olson demonstrated (Olson 1965; Olson and Zeckhauser 1966) that political participation (interest group activity, voting, etc.) imposed private costs upon the participant but tended to create benefits that were nonexclusive, which in turn led to free riding and the "exploitation of great by the small." This focused attention on public policies that could deny benefits to nonparticipants, the concentration of benefits produced by those policies, and the support thresholds required to claim those benefits. Third, economists based their theory on an assumption that is often wrong, but still might be of considerable utility in partial equilibrium analysis, that elected officials are exclusively concerned with maximizing the probability of their reelection, which is an increasing function of interest group support (since voters won't attend to issues or even vote unless they are persuaded to do so by campaign advertising and election workers).

The biggest problem with the economic theory of interest group politics is that, while it often tells a plausible story about existing public policies, empirical tests of its basic assumptions and predictions seldom work very well, compared, say, to the presumption that legislators pursue their own notions of the common good (Peltzman 1984, 1990; Kalt and Zupan 1990). And, of course, one should be mindful that the economic theory of interest group politics was created primarily to explain government regulation of prices and entry in industries such as trucking and airlines–both of which have been subsequently deregulated.

The one central claim of the economic theory of interest group politics that has gone unchallenged is that many of the benefits of government action–tariffs, agricultural marketing orders, import quotas, various types of price and entry control regulation, tariffs, pork barrel spending, and the like–do not accrue to their nominal recipients (Buchanan, Tollison, and Tullock, 1980). These types of policies create rents. Rents involve payments to the owners of factors of production (land, labor, capital, technology) that exceed their minimum supply prices. It is, therefore, usually wasteful for government to create rents. (The only exception to this generalization occurs where rent creation contributes to a more equal income distribution and where it also involves fewer leaks than alternative redistributive mechanisms.) The Davis-Bacon Act of 1931 is a good example of government rent creation. It requires that contractors on federal projects pay union wages. If the law did not cause wages to be above their minimum supply price, the Davis-Bacon Act would have no point, since contractors would be unable to get the work done, were they unwilling to pay prevailing wages. However, these rents do not accrue to their nominal recipients. Potential employees tend to compete them away. In other cases, where the rents created by government action are not competed away, they are usually capitalized in asset prices, especially real property values.

Gordon Tullock (1967) was probably the first scholar to think systematically about the consequences of rent seeking. He argued that, if everyone could freely participate in the rush for the spoils, each rent seeker would expend the full amount of the potential transfer in its pursuit, in which case the rents created by government would be dissipated by the directly unproductive activities incurred to capture them. Indeed, in an implicit analogy to the effect of product differentiation in the economics of imperfect competition, Tullock hypothesized that the waste involved in capturing rents could actually exceed the rent to be captured. In a related vein, Mancur Olson (1982) argued that, if rents are extensive and efforts to retain them pervasive, the inevitable result is a kind of policy gridlock, which devours ever more resources in defense of the economic status quo, stultifies change, and, by diverting investment away from productive activities and inhibiting the process of creative destruction, reduces the rate of economic growth.

Indeed, an outsider cannot help but notice the amounts of money spent on campaigns for public office in this country or the resources employed to influence the outcomes of legislative, administrative, and judicial processes. What seems remarkable about the U.S. political system is not that it produces more rents than in other countries—that doesn't seem to be the case (see Krueger 1974)—but that the creation, maintenance, and distribution of rents attracts (or the gestation and implementation of any policy initiative, for that matter) requires so much more effort here than elsewhere.

William Niskanen and the Budget-Maximizing Bureaucrat

In a second attempt to explain government excess, William Niskanen, Chairman of the Cato Institute and former head of the President's Council of Economic Advisors (1971; Blais and Dion 1991), showed that a revenue-maximizing, single-product bureau with absolute monopoly and agenda-setting powers would be technically efficient but produce up to two times the optimal quantity of output. While there are, perhaps, too many monopoly bureaus, their agenda-setting powers are often limited, most

use a variety of technologies to provide an array of services, and technical inefficiency is widespread. Hence, anyone who leaps from the presumed monopoly power of bureaus to the allocative efficiency of government is undoubtedly overreaching.

Having said that, one must still recognize the remarkable scientific contribution made by Niskanen. First of all he, more than anyone else, demonstrated that the behavior of government officials, like corporate bureaucrats, could be deduced from their tastes and opportunities and that this approach is more effective than assuming that they are merely well-trained robots. Second, Niskanen showed how the ability to control agendas presented to median voters could shift outcomes from their preferred positions—that is, how structure could induce a political equilibrium. For example, confronted with a choice between nothing and a higher than preferred spending level (i.e. $Vm < Tm$), the median voter should prefer the higher spending level as long as total benefits exceeded total costs ($|V_m > Tm$). Of course, this same mechanism in the hands of a different agenda setter could lead to undersupply, but Niskanen argued that in the U.S. congressional system, committees and subcommittees, the effective legislative and budget agenda setters, are likely to be dominated by program advocates (see Munger 1984). Finally, Niskanen adapted the structure-conduct-performance paradigm—according to which structure (the number of competitors, the degree of product differentiation, technology, the degree of vertical integration with suppliers, and so on) determines conduct (price and output, investment, and so forth), and conduct yields performance (efficiency, product variety, etc.) (see Duncombe 1992)—from industrial organization theory to the behavior of government bureaus. As a consequence, he demonstrated that monopoly supply is a necessary condition for allocative inefficiency. Niskanen's strictures against bureaucratic monopoly have probably had more influence on the theory and practice of public administration than any other idea drawn from the public choice literature.

Political scientists have embraced Niskanen's notion of structurally induced equilibrium, primarily perhaps because it appeals to their concern with political institutions and their fascination with games of strategy. There is now an extensive literature on structurally induced equilibrium (see Bendor 1990). One conclusion that can be drawn from this literature is that, if referenda are not carefully restricted to a single issue dimension, the drafter can manipulate them to produce almost any outcome desired. Another widely accepted conclusion is that an inability on the part of the legislature to achieve a stable collective choice could be a source of considerable bureaucratic discretion—even were there no problems measuring bureaucratic performance or designing incentive mechanisms (Bendor 1990). Of course, "could" is not the same as "is" (McCubbins and Schwartz 1984; McFadden 1977).

There is a second reason for the popularity of structurally induced equilibrium with political scientists: it explains why voting cycles seldom occur in U.S. legislatures. Rational choice theory tells us that if preferences are not single-peaked—that is, if they involve choice among points in a zero-beta, n-dimensional space—for example, the issue is purely a question of distribution of income or wealth, voter preferences will not produce a stable majority, that is, an undominated Nash equilibrium (McKelvey 1976). Under the rules governing legislative decisionmaking in the United States, however, the status quo is always included in the last pairwise comparison made. This means that if it is included in the cycle, its supporters will never let it come up against an option that would beat it. Hence, once a cycle starts it can never end; in the mean time the status quo remains in effect. Legislators seem intuitively to understand this point and they studiously avoid issues that produce cycles. In any case Keith Poole and Howard Rosenthal (1991) have demonstrated that zero-beta, n-dimensioned issues rarely appear in congressional roll-call votes—either all issues voted upon are single-dimensioned or individual preferences on all relevant dimensions are highly correlated. Evidently legislators have better outlets for their energies than chasing their tails.

Both economists and political scientists have also recognized the decisive role played by individually motivated agents in the determination of bureaucratic outcomes. Most, however, question Niskanen's assumption that bureaucrats are revenue maximizers (Blais and Dion 1991). In the meantime new theories have been developed that rely on more imaginative descriptions of bureaucratic tastes and opportunities. Contemporary models of bureaucracy stress the informational endowments of bureaucrats, the implicit and explicit contracts that link their actions to rewards, and their discretionary powers. The presumption that individuals within the state's administrative apparatus are singlemindedly driven to expand and protect existing programs and develop new programs of intervention has given way to the presumption that their utility functions might include some or more of the following arguments: effort and risk aversion, perquisite consumption, control benefits and other nonpecuniary benefits, and reputation. Moreover, the dichotomy between competitors and monopolists proposed by the structure-conduct-performance paradigm—price takers versus price setters—has been largely superseded in the industrial organization literature by a new technology of games under incomplete information.

The newer models of bureaucratic behavior often seem inherently plausible. But like the economic theory of interest group politics, they generally fail to yield successful empirical predictions beyond the ones for which they were custom tailored (see Conybeare 1984). For example, a while back L. R. Jones and F. Thompson (Thompson and Jones 1986) proposed a bilateral monopoly model of the budget process, with the central control office on one side

and agencies on the other. The assumption was that budgeteers were primarily interested in cutting budgets—that is after all what they are paid to do—and that agency officials were motivated by a variety of considerations—task accomplishment, perquisite consumption, control benefits and other nonpecuniary benefits, and reputation. The typical outcomes of this model were less than optimal budgets and outputs and higher than minimum unit costs. If this model were valid, however, and other things were equal, both budgeteers and agency heads would consistently oppose competition whenever it raised its ugly head. That does not seem to be the case. In many instances, officials in central control agencies have recently taken the lead in promoting competition within government.

Another example is due to Terry M. Moe (1990), who argues that political authorities, especially legislators, favor administrative controls that are ineffective by design. He claims that legislators shun serious policy control and, instead, seek "particularized" control because they "want to be able to intervene quickly, inexpensively, and in ad hoc ways to protect or advance the interest of particular clients in particular matters" (p. 140). Detailed rules that impose rigid limits on an agency's discretion and its procedures help to satisfy this appetite. Consequently, detailed object-of-expenditure budgets are the norm, for example, not for historical reasons, but because they are suited to the needs of temporary governing coalitions, which are likely to be far more concerned with who gets public monies and where it goes than with what it buys for the public at large. Furthermore, Moe argues that the rigidity characteristic of the U.S. administrative process is largely the product of the efforts of temporary ruling coalitions to prevent future majorities from interfering with their handiwork.

While Moe's specific conclusions may not be particularly compelling to some, he has nevertheless made an important intellectual contribution. Most public choice scholars have formulated the agency problem in terms of legislator or bureaucrat as agent and median voter as principal. Moe raises the possibility of temporal cycles, with agents responding to successive majorities, thereby reformulating the agency problem in terms of multiple principals. So far, it is not clear whether multiple principals reduce an agent's discretion, as suggested by Moe, or whether they increase it, as implied by Bendor. On this issue, however, the smart money seems to be on Moe.

Summing Up

Public choice theorists are often cynical about politics and pessimistic about the workings of government. Most would disallow any role for what Steve Kelman (1987) calls "public" or "civic" spirit, except to the extent that self interest is defined to include an interest in the welfare of others (a tactic which has the effect of denying to public choice any Popperian bite whatsoever).

Moreover, as Michael Trebilcock (1994) explains, public choice theorists implicitly reject the notion that ideas have power (which, if true, would render public choice an exercise in futility), although the recent trend to privatization, deregulation, and tax reform can hardly be explained any other way. As Trebilcock puts it, these policies show that ideas have force and that "politics, to an important extent, is partly about what are thought to be good ideas as well as what are thought to be politically salient interests."

FRED THOMPSON

BIBLIOGRAPHY

Bendor, J., 1990. "Formal Models of Bureaucracy: A Review." In Naomi B. Lynn and Aaron Wildavsky, eds., *Public Administration: The State of the Discipline.* Chatham, NJ: Chatham House Publishers, pp. 373–417.

Bergstrom, T. and R. Goodman, 1972. "Private Demands for Public Goods." *American Economic Review* 63(3):280–296.

Blais, André and Stéphane Dion, eds., 1991. *The Budget-Maximizing Bureaucrat: The Empirical Evidence.* Pittsburgh: University of Pittsburgh Press.

Borcherding, T. E., 1977. "The Sources of Growth of Public Expenditures in the United States, 1902–1970." In Borcherding, ed., *Budgets and Bureaucrats: The Sources of Government Growth.* Durham, NC: Duke University Press, pp. 46–70.

Bowen, H. R., 1943. "The Interpretation of Voting in the Allocation of Resources." *Quarterly Journal of Economics* 58(1):27–48.

Buchanan, James M. and G. Tullock, 1962. *The Calculus of Consent: Logical Foundations of Constitutional Democracy.* Ann Arbor: University of Michigan Press.

Buchanan, J. M., R. D. Tollison, and G. Tullock, eds., 1980. *Toward a Theory of the Rent-Seeking Society.* Ann Arbor: University of Michigan Press.

Coase, R., 1960. "The Problem of Social Cost." *Journal of Law and Economics* 3(1):1–44.

Conybeare, John A. C., 1984. "Bureaucracy, Monopoly and Competition: A Critical Analysis of the Budget-Maximizing Model of Bureaucracy." *American Journal of Political Science* 28(3) (August) 479–502.

Dahlman, C., 1979. "The Problem of Externality." *Journal of Law and Economics* 23(2):140–62.

Downs, A., 1957. *An Economic Theory of Democracy.* New York: Harper and Row.

———, 1959–60. "Why the Government Budget Is Too Small in a Democracy." *World Politics* 12(4) (Winter) 541–563.

Duncombe, William D., 1992. "Costs and Factor Substitution in the Provision of Local Fire Services." *Review of Economics & Statistics* 74(1) (February) 180–184.

Feldman, A. M., 1980. *Welfare Economics and Social Choice Theory.* Boston: Martinus Nijhoff.

Ferejohn, John A., 1974. *Pork Barrel Politics: Rivers and Harbors Legislation. 1947–1968.* Stanford, CA: Stanford University Press.

Fischel, William A., 1989. "Did Serrano Cause Proposition 13?" *National Tax Journal* 42(4) (December) 465–473.

———, 1992. "Property Taxation and the Tiebout Model: Evidence for the Benefit View from Zoning and Voting." *Journal of Economic Literature* 30(1) (March) 171–177.

Heckathorn, D. and S. M. Maser, 1990. "The Contractual Architecture of Public Policy: A Critical Reconstruction of Lowi's Typology." *Journal of Politics* (November).

Hird, J. A., 1991. "The Political Economy of Pork: Project Selection in the U.S. Army Corps of Engineers." *American Political Science Review* 85(2):429–456.

Holcombe, R. G., 1977. "The Florida System: A Bowen Equilibrium Referendum Process." *National Tax Journal* 30(1) (March) 77–84.

Kalt, J. and M. Zupan, 1990. "The Apparent Ideological Behavior of Legislators." *Journal of Law and Economics* 33(1): 103–132.

Kelman, S., 1987. *Making Public Policy: A Hopeful View of American Government.* New York: Basic Books.

Krueger, A. O., 1974. "The Political Economy of the Rent-Seeking Society." *American Economic Review* 64(2) (June) 291–303; reprinted in Buchanan, Tollison, and Tullock, 1980, 51–70.

Larkey, Patrick D., 1979. *Evaluating Public Programs; The Impact of General Revenue Sharing on Municipal Government.* Princeton, NJ: Princeton University Press.

McCubbins, Matthew and Thomas Schwartz, 1984. "Congressional Oversight Overlooked: Police Patrols Versus Fire Alarms." *American Journal of Political Science* 28(2): 165–179.

McFadden, D., 1977. "Revealed Preferences of a Government Bureaucracy, Parts I and II." *Bell Journal of Economics* 6(2) (Autumn) 401–416; 7(2) (Spring) 52–72.

McKelvey, Richard, 1976. "Intransitivities in Multidimensional Voting Models and Some Implications for Agenda Control." *Journal of Economic Theory* 12:427–482.

Moe, T. M., 1990. "The Politics of Structural Choice: Toward a Theory of Public Bureaucracy." In Oliver E. Williamson, ed., *Organization Theory: From Chester Barnard to the Present and Beyond.* New York: Oxford University Press.

Monissen, H. G., 1991. "Rent-Seeking in General Equilibrium: A Didactic Illustration." *Public Choice* 72 (December) 111–130.

Mueller, D. C., 1989. *Public Choice II.* Cambridge, UK: Cambridge University Press.

Munger, Michael, 1984. "On the Mutuality of Interests between Bureaus and High Demand Review Committees." *Public Choice* 43:211–215.

Niskanen, W. A., 1971. *Bureaucracy and Representative Government.* Chicago: Aldine-Atherton.

Oates, Wallace E., 1994. "Federalism and Government Finance." In John M. Quigley and Eugene Smolensky, eds. *Modern Public Finance.* Cambridge, MA: Harvard University Press, pp. 126–151.

Olson, M., 1965. *The Logic of Collective Action: Public Goods and the Theory of Groups.* Cambridge, MA: Harvard University Press.

———, 1982. *The Rise and Decline of Nations: Economic Growth, Stagflation, and Social Rigidities.* New Haven, CT: Yale University Press.

Olson, M. and R. Zeckhauser, 1966. "An Economic Theory of Alliances." *Review of Economics & Statistics* 48(3) (August) 266–279.

Peltzman, S., 1976. "Toward a More General Theory of Regulation." *Journal of Law and Economics* 14(2):109–148.

———, 1984. "Constituent Interest and Congressional Voting." *Journal of Law and Economics* 27(1):181–210.

———, 1990. "How Efficient is the Voting Market?" *Journal of Law and Economics* 33(1):27–63.

Poole, Keith T. and H. Rosenthal, 1991. "Patterns of Congressional Voting." *American Journal of Political Science* 35(1) (February) 228–278.

Posner, R. A., 1971. "Taxation by Regulation." *Bell Journal of Economics and Management Science* 2(1):22–50.

———, 1974. "Theories of Economic Regulation." *Bell Journal of Economics and Management Science* 5(2):335–358.

Romer, Thomas and Howard Rosenthal, 1992. "Economic Incentives and Political Institutions: Spending and Voting in School Budget Referenda." *Journal of Public Economics* 49(1) (October) 1–33.

Samuelson, P. A., 1954. "The Pure Theory of Public Expenditure." *Review of Economics and Statistics* 36 (November) 387–389.

———, 1955. "A Diagrammatic Exposition of a Theory of Public Expenditure." *Review of Economics and Statistics* 37 (November) 350–356.

Shepsle, K. A. and B. R. Weingast, 1981. "Political Preferences for the Pork Barrel: A Generalization." *American Journal of Political Science* 25(1):96–111.

———, 1984. "Political Solutions to Market Problems." *American Political Science Review* 78 (June) 417–434.

Silva, Fabio and Jon Sonstelie, 1995. "Did Serrano Cause a Decline in School Spending?" *National Tax Journal* 48(2) (June) 199–215.

Stanbury, W. T. and F. Thompson, 1995. "Toward a Political Economy of Government Waste." *Public Administration Review* 55(5) (September-October) 418–427.

Stigler, G., 1971. "The Theory of Economic Regulation." *Bell Journal of Economics and Management Science* 2(1):3–21.

Thompson, F., 1979. "American Legislative Decisionmaking and the Size Principle." *American Political Science Review* 73(4):1100–1108.

Thompson, F. and L. R. Jones, 1986. "Controllership in the Public Sector." *Journal of Policy Analysis and Management* 5(3):547–571.

Tiebout, Charles M., 1956. "A Pure Theory of Local Expenditures." *Journal of Political Economy* 64(4) (October) 416–424.

Trebilcock, Michael J., 1994. *The Prospects for Reinventing Government?* Toronto: C. D. Howe Institute.

Tullock, G., 1967. "The Welfare Costs of Tariffs, Monopolies and Theft." *Western Economic Journal* 5(2) (June) 224–232: reprinted in Buchanan, Tollison, and Tullock, 1980, pp. 39–50.

Wittman, Donald, 1989. "Why Democracies Produce Efficient Results." *Journal of Political Economy* 9(6) (December) 1395–1424.

Yinger, J., Howard S. Bloom, A. Borsch-Supan, and Helen F. Ladd, 1988. *Property Taxes and House Values: The Theory and Estimation of Intrajurisdictional Property Tax Capitalization.* Boston: Academic Press.

PUBLIC ENTERPRISE.

A business owned and operated by government.

For some, the whole process of development–of creating, fostering, and guiding the necessary social and economic forces for development, for which usually only the state has adequate resources and power–may be regarded as public enterprise. Mostly, however, the term is used within the discipline of public administration with a rather more precise meaning. A. H. Hanson (1959) was codifying from an already long tradition of scholarship, and from a series of significant United Nations documents in the early post–World War II period, when he offered this definition: "in a more restricted and more familiar sense . . . (public enterprise means) state ownership and operation of industrial, agricultural, financial and commercial undertakings" (p. 115).

Although the idea of public enterprise has taken a battering in recent years, the practice is as old as civilization itself. In the more general sense, it was responsible for the planning and construction of vast schemes of flood control and irrigation along the major waterways around which the early civilizations developed; it built the Great Pyramids of Egypt and the Great Wall of China. In the more limited sense, it stored and distributed the grain, salt, and other staple foods on which those civilizations depended. Such enterprise was associated with systems of "hydraulic agriculture," or agriculture involving the control of water on a large scale: those were systems which both permitted and demanded intensive cultivation, clear division of labor and social coordination on a massive scale. The works already indicated were often accompanied by the development of major highway and canal networks, and they were integral to the development not only of civilized society but also of organized government.

Later, when the new technologies spawned by the Industrial Revolution and associated developments in law and commerce made large-scale private enterprise possible, a major question for society became that of charting the appropriate roles of public ownership and public regulation. Early attempts to promote the public interest through unregulated private competition were generally unsuccessful, leaving governments, parliaments, political parties, and ideologies to contest whether the public interest was better protected from the greed of profit-seeking private entrepreneurs by public ownership and operation of basic services (which we would now call infrastructure services) or by public regulation of services owned and operated privately. In developing countries, however (and this category long included smaller European countries such as Norway and Sweden and "New World" countries like Australia, Canada, and New Zealand, as well as countries emerging from mid-twentieth century decolonizations), this choice was often simply not available: in the virtually total absence of a private market (not its failure, as many modern would-be rewriters of history would have it), the only capacity for the initiation, development, and operation of services rested in the institutions of the state.

One of the most surprising elements of late twentieth century ideology-making is the strength of the view that neither public ownership nor public regulation is necessary, that "the market" will provide the level playing field needed to ensure that public (consumer?) interests are protected. But there are also numerous critics of this ideology who are convinced that the market alone cannot do this, and some grounds for believing that most societies will return before long to the more traditional liberal stance that either public ownership or public regulation is necessary to ensure a tolerable degree of concern for public interest issues. In such societies, it is likely that a significant public sector will be maintained, with public enterprises functioning alongside private enterprises in the "mixed economy" style familiar through most of the non-Communist world for much of the twentieth century. Indeed, one of the rather spectacular results of the commercializing, corporatizing and privatizing drives that have affected so many public sectors in the closing decades of the twentieth century is that new organizational forms are emerging which are neither fully private nor fully public. While these forms of public-private mix present a new fascination for public administration scholarship, they provide a very clear indication that the mixed economy is alive and well.

Roughly since the advent of the Thatcher government in Britain in 1979 and the enthusiasm of international financial agencies such as the World Bank and the IMF thereafter in pushing Thatcherite ideology in other countries, aided and abetted by the now-strident "public choice" school of economics, public policymaking in the area of public enterprise has divided into two strands. One, associated with all the rhetoric of smaller government and the beauty of market solutions, has aimed at shifting publicly owned enterprises to the private sector, or simply abandoning them. The other, accepting realistically that public sectors will remain even if somewhat reduced in size, has seen the introduction in a great many countries of reform programs designed to increase the efficiency of enterprises remaining in public ownership. Privatization is dealt with elsewhere in this encyclopedia; the remainder of this article is concerned with ongoing public enterprise systems, and the reform drives of the recent period.

Understanding Public Enterprise Systems

The study of public enterprise has focused almost exclusively on developments of the post–Industrial Revolution period, and has been concerned with exploring several main themes. These relate particularly to the reasons for establishing public enterprises, the functions they perform, how they are organized, how they obtain staffing and financial resources, how profits and losses are handled, and the patterns of relationships operating between them, their supervising ministers, the creating legislatures, and other "stakeholders" such as clients, employee groups, auditors, and (where relevant) official regulators. The degree of managerial autonomy they exercise is another important theme: it flows out of a consideration of these relationship patterns, and it leads to the further important issue of the extent to which they are subject to "community service obligations" which may be in conflict with primary commercial objectives.

Why Public Enterprise?

In addressing this question, we are, of course, concerned with the activity—why governments go into business—rather than forms of organization. Decisions about structures come later, after activities have been determined. While triggers for the activity have been extremely varied, a classification suggested in a study of the Swedish experience is nevertheless very useful in providing a framework for understanding the process at work. Thus Verney (1959) contrasted the "natural growth" character of Sweden's public enterprises with the "nationalization" character of Britain's (p. 7).

In the first, the enterprises grew from their birth under public ownership in a relatively sparsely populated country with an undeveloped capital market. This is a classic situation repeated so often in "young" economies, where public enterprise is necessarily the primary engine of development. While there is no known count of public enterprises so established, the number is very considerable; it is clear that in many developing countries (including earlier developers such as Australia, Canada, and the United States) most public enterprises fall into this category. Even where strong capital markets exist, projects may be simply too big or (in federations) too constitutionally complicated for any but governments to undertake them. Often intersector accommodations have emerged whereby it is tacitly agreed that it is appropriate for the public sector to provide the infrastructure services needed to enable the private sector to establish and operate production industries.

In the second, enterprises are already operating under private ownership, but for one reason or another they are then brought into public ownership through acts of nationalization. The reasons for such acts may be political or ideological, ranging from the fairly moderate belief that, if there has to be monopoly, accountability is better served if it is to a public ownership rather than left in private hands, to the more radical Marxist conviction about the virtue of socializing "the means of production, distribution, and exchange." Alternatively, they may be economic or strategic, ranging from a belief that "commanding heights" industries should remain in public hands to a need to "rescue" industries self-destructing in private hands. Around the world, many public enterprises have had this "ambulance for sick industry" guise, and in some a period in public ownership has revived them sufficiently to allow governments to contemplate next-stage privatizing action. Again, enterprises shift to public ownership for nationalistic and foreign-policy reasons, as in the desire of newly independent countries to substitute domestic for foreign control of major industries, and in the punitive confiscations of properties of enemy countries or their nationals, of collaborators of former occupying forces, and of unpopular racial or ethnic groups.

All these reasons, and more, explain why public sectors have grown to the proportions familiar in the 1960s and 1970s, before the small government movement got under way. And, even in the late twentieth century as many acts of privatization are taking place, some new public enterprises are appearing for reasons consistent with those summarized above, and others are emerging as part of the late twentieth-century administrative reform movement itself. The commercializing drives that are an important part of that movement are, in many countries, moving what have long been budget-funded activities into self-funding off-budget units operating on user-pays principles, and so new public "businesses" arise. As has been argued elsewhere, while the boundaries of the public sector are always changing and we are certainly experiencing contractions in many countries today, we are a long way from witnessing the death of public enterprise (Wettenhall 1983, 1993).

The Functions of Public Enterprise

Within the group of "industrial, agricultural, financial, and commercial undertakings" identified by Hanson in the definition of public enterprise given at the beginning of this article, enterprise managements will normally be seen organizing and operating ongoing public business concerns. Often also, notably where the enterprises are of the "natural growth" kind, they will be involved in the planning and construction work that goes on before business operations can be commenced.

In most mixed-economy countries, public utility industries such as water supply, sewerage, power (electricity and gas), communications (posts, telephones, broadcasting) and transport (rail, bus, shipping, ports, airlines, airports) have long been candidates for public ownership, either as monopolies or (as the United States) in some kind of competition with private operators. Often—and particularly in developing countries—extractive and manufacturing industries such as oil, minerals, forest products, fertilizers, pharmaceuticals, automobiles, and farm machinery will also be, all or in part, in public ownership. As a rough measure of their economic contribution we are told that, for many such countries, these enterprises take up about 20 percent of capital investment. In the centrally planned economies the proportion of public to private enterprise will be very high: in Romania in the 1960s, for example, 96 percent of industrial output came from public enterprises (Hanson et al. 1968, p. 2).

Some writers separate the large group of commodity marketing undertakings, which are found in many countries, from the generality of public enterprise. But for our purposes this is scarcely necessary. It may be that mostly they do not actually produce the relevant commodities, but they acquire these commodities from the producers and thereafter have commercial responsibility for their sale and for distribution of proceeds to the producers. Some of them are indeed big businesses, and they share many of the characteristics of other public enterprises. Similarly the public financial institutions—insurers, banks, and other lending agencies—cannot be said to produce in the industrial sense; rather they are facilitators of the productive

work of others, but in doing this they are commercial enterprises in the fullest sense.

A bigger complication occurs when a public enterprise management engaged in producing a good or service for sale is required by its sponsoring government to regulate the work of others engaged in productive activity in the same industry. Though not uncommon, this functional duality has often proved troublesome, and it certainly offends late twentieth-century notions of establishing competitive "level playing fields." A significant item in the modern reform agenda therefore seeks the clear organizational separation of productive and regulatory functions.

How Public Enterprises Are Organized

What public enterprises do and how they are organized are questions which are both conceptually and practically distinct. Experience shows that there is no single way of organizing such enterprise, and discourse that seeks to establish an identity between one such way and the activity of public enterprise (such discourse is fairly common) is less than helpful.

The theory of the evolution of public enterprise organization formulated by leading U.S. scholar Harold Seidman (1954, pp. 183–185) postulates that, in a first stage, advocates and designers of public enterprise systems believed that the ordinary machinery of the state was all that was required. Thus public enterprises would be vested in departments of the central government or, where the scale was appropriate, established local governments. It was only after considerable experience was acquired in running public enterprises in this way—here the Australian state railway systems in the period 1850–1880 provided an important laboratory (see Wettenhall 1990, pp. 3–5)—that it came generally to be appreciated that special administrative arrangements were needed for government-in-business. In their study of the German railways, Macmahon and Dittmar (1939) spoke of "a vast amount of spontaneous experimentation" going on to discover a suitable managerial instrument. Most countries entered Seidman's second stage when they "hived off" public enterprise activity from the central departments to specially incorporated bodies (usually termed boards, commissions, or authorities) with commercial and managerial autonomy to conduct the enterprises according to the standards of the commercial world. Later, some discovered that they had conferred too much autonomy; some of their public (or statutory) corporations had defied properly constituted governments on policy questions, and it was felt that accountability to those governments had to be restored. At this point, many countries moved to Seidman's third stage, involving a deliberate search for a formula that would allow entrepreneurial commercially oriented management and at the same time ensure ultimate accountability of those managements to government.

This is of course a global theory, digesting from the experience of many countries. Across countries, movement happened at different times and at different paces. Thus Canada and Australia were leaders in the widespread use of the device of the public corporation (usually termed crown corporation in the first, statutory corporation in the second; see Dawson 1992, Musolf 1959, Eggleston 1932, Wettenhall 1990); perhaps surprisingly, Australia's near neighbor, New Zealand, mostly remained faithful to departmental organization of public enterprises (Mascarenhas 1982). Even within single countries there can be inconsistency; in many, public enterprises can still be found within departments, within municipal structures (local government), and hived off to autonomous corporations. Almost everywhere, the post office was late to fall into line: the conversions from first-stage postmaster general departments to third-stage corporations did not occur until well into the second half of the twentieth century.

A variant form of public sector corporation has long been known, and has become increasingly popular in the recent reform period. This is the government-owned (or state-owned) company, formed when a government opts to use the standard companies act registration procedure to bring a new managing organization into being instead of enacting special legislation, which is the method traditionally used to create public, statutory, or crown corporations. Only in the company form is the capital organized in the form of shareholdings. This form thus facilitates joint ownership arrangements whereby government participates with private interests in the formation and/or management of an enterprise; where the government shareholding is greater than 50 percent, the enterprise is normally considered to be public.

The internal organization of public enterprises arranged departmentally or municipally is normally assimilated into the regular structures of the relevant public/civil or local government service. However, in the corporate public sector—whether statutory corporation or government-owned company—the organization is usually marked by the existence of a governing board as the top organ of the enterprise, with the enterprise's executive management answering to that board.

Staffing and Financial Resources

Where the enterprises are arranged departmentally or municipally, staffing and financial regimes again usually follow those of the relevant central or local government service. Minor adaptations may be made, such as the use of trust funds to provide greater financial flexibility than is possible through full subjection to regular central budget processes.

Enterprises in the corporate public sector are characterized by their separation from these central processes. While exceptions can be found, the general rule is that they have their own employment services and budgetary systems separate from those of their sponsoring governments. Thus they will recruit their own staffs independently of the central staffing system, and these staffs will not be civil/public servants in the generally accepted sense. Also they will draw most or all of their funds from charges for the goods and services they provide rather than from taxation revenues, they will often undertake their own borrowing, and they will be noted in central budgets only in so far as it is necessary to register transactions between them and government.

Profits and Losses

The transactions referred to in the last paragraph above are of several kinds. Since there are many profitable public enterprises, dividends and interest payments on loans from government flow back into central consolidated revenue funds. Conversely, there are also loss-making public enterprises—it is sometimes necessary for governments to make transfers to fund these losses, and monies then flow out of consolidated funds to the accounts of corporate managements. Outflows occur also where governments have commitments to fund the costs of noncommercial community service obligations imposed on corporate managements, and—usually in establishment phases—where governments advance funds for the development of corporate enterprises; such funds may be by way of investment (to acquire equity, on which dividends are payable) or loan (on which interest is repayable, together with eventual repayment of capital). Last but by no means least, a great many corporate public enterprises are subject to taxation as are private enterprises, and so the taxes they pay also take the form of transfers into consolidated revenue.

The earnings of public enterprises go first to covering their operating expenses, and then to payment of essential outgoings such as interest on loans and taxation. Surpluses are then applied variously to payment of dividends, to building up financial reserves, and to reinvestment in the enterprise itself, such as acquisition of new technology or enlargement of facilities.

Relationships and Autonomy

Where public enterprises have been vested in corporate bodies, a complex pattern of relationships exists. These relationships are often discussed in terms of accountability, and it is now customary to acknowledge the existence of a network of stakeholders. The sponsoring government is clearly the preeminent stakeholder (and, in the companies, the sole or majority shareholder). Maintenance of a positive, constructive link with the relevant portfolio minister must therefore be high on the corporate agenda: this minister will have certain formal powers in relation to the corporation laid down in the creating statute or in the articles of association registered under the companies act. Maintaining such a link also means maintaining good relations with senior officials in the minister's department and, in some countries, in special "focal points" established to coordinate the activities of a range of ministries in relation to their constituent public enterprises. Others within the government system with formal power or influence in relation to the corporation are likely to be the minister for finance, the auditor-general, and regulatory agencies such as planning, monopolies, and price surveillance commissions. Where strong parliamentary systems exist, there will also be a strong link to the legislature and to relevant investigating committees that it may have established—the corporations may sometimes find the requirements of accountability to the legislature and to the executive government to be in conflict. The list of stakeholders includes also customers, employee unions, special interest groups (who may on occasions have representation on the corporation board), suppliers of essential materials, and other operators in the industry with whom a degree of cooperation is necessary. The corporate management needs to cultivate good relationships with all these groups.

Recent research has indicated also that "corporate management" is something less than a unit. There are often tensions between governing boards and executives, who may be developing separate linkages with various stakeholders; the role of the board in particular is in need of clarification (Corkery *et al.* 1994).

Traditional scholarship has seen the enjoyment of a considerable measure of corporate autonomy as a sine qua non for successful public enterprise operation, and there can be little doubt that capricious political interventions in matters of managerial detail (e.g., staff appointments) have been ruinous for many public enterprises. The modern approach tends to be more sophisticated: it certainly wants to protect enterprises from interventions in matters that are properly the prerogative of corporate managements, but it also asserts that ultimate, strategic, broad policy responsibility must remain with governments.

Community Service Obligations

It has long been recognized that there will be tension between two expectations that governments and parliaments have about public enterprises. The first is that they should behave commercially, seeking to earn sufficient revenues at least to cover all expenses, and more recently, with the decline of socialist ideology, to earn surpluses to be applied to the purposes indicated under "Profits and Losses" above. The second is that, since they are part of the public sector, they should be available for use as required as instruments of social policy. In furtherance of the second, they have been required from time to time, usually by ministerial direction, to do things (like keeping unproductive coal mines open in order to provide continued employment in depressed regions) which would never be tolerated by commercially driven private enterprise. In consequence, their profitability suffers and often disappears, and their managements are unjustly accused of gross inefficiency.

At least since 1896 in the Australian state of Victoria (Wettenhall 1987, ch. 7), the need has been seen for a mechanism to allow governments to direct public enterprise managements in such ways but to ensure that, at the same time, their accounts and their business reputation do not suffer. This has involved transfer payments from the treasury (or other relevant ministry) to the corporate account, or other form of adjustment, commensurate with the degree of financial loss caused by the need to discharge the relevant community service obligation (CSO).

The Reform Movement of the Later Twentieth Century

This movement has been virtually universal in its effects, and several beginning "models" have been suggested. They mostly have it in common that they seek to substitute new "strategic" forms of accountability and control for the trivial, destructive forms of political control that so often damaged older public enterprises, and to recreate conditions for bold entrepreneurial action by enterprise managements. The reform agenda includes clarification of corporate objectives and removal of noncommercial tasks from enterprise corporations, regular corporate planning, better reporting and accounting systems, precise performance indicators and setting of corporate performance targets, identification and separate funding of CSOs, and executive salaries and benefits closer to those of private enterprise.

One of the earliest expressions of this reform agenda was contained in the 1968 report of France's Nora Commission, and it led to wide acceptance of a system of contracts binding governments and the corporate bodies managing public enterprises as their agents: the corporations are bound to achieve stated goals and objectives, and governments to keep faith with enterprise managements in providing facilitative operating environments, making adjustments for those CSOs, and so on. Agreements of this sort have appeared in many countries, called variously performance contracts (in France and Francophone countries), memoranda of understanding (India), statements of corporate intent (New Zealand), and the like. Others have added the notion of a "signaling system," among other things locating signals in the performance data coming forward that point to significant departures from plan, and so trigger quick remedial action. And the economic rationalists who have been particularly active through the 1980s and early 1990s in Britain, New Zealand, Australia and some other countries and in the big lending agencies, which are themselves mostly multinational public enterprises, have pushed massively for market solutions and level playing field competition—often leading toward privatization and, where that is not wanted or not feasible, almost always moving public enterprises closer to commercial, market-oriented styles of behavior.

There has been a tendency in the modern reform period for (some) reformers to coin new terms like state-owned enterprise, government business enterprise, and government trading enterprise, and then to deny any connection between their creations and reconstructions and the much longer public enterprise tradition. To the extent that they do this, they also deny themselves the ability to profit from the many useful lessons contained in past public enterprise experience.

Cross references: **government corporation, privatization, stautory corporation**.

ROGER WETTENHALL

BIBLIOGRAPHY

Aharoni, Yair, 1986. *The Evolution and Management of State-Owned Enterprises*. Cambridge, MA: Ballinger.

Corkery, Joan, Colm O Nuallain and Roger Wettenhall, eds., 1994. *Public Enterprise Boards: What They Are and What They Do*. Hong Kong: Asian Journal of Public Administration for International Association of Schools and Institutes of Administration.

Dawson, R. MacG., 1992. *The Principle of Official Independence*. London & Toronto: King.

Eggleston, F. W., 1932. *State Socialism in Victoria*. London: King.

Einaudi, M., M. Bye and E. Rossi, 1955. *Nationalization in France and Italy*. Ithaca: Cornell University Press.

Fernandes, Praxi and Pavle Sicherl, eds., 1981. *Seeking the Personality of Public Enterprise*. Ljubljana: International Center for Public Enterprises in Developing Countries.

Floyd, Robert H., Clive S. Gray and R.P. Short, 1984. *Public Enterprise in Mixed Economies: Some Macroeconomic Aspects*. Washington: International Monetary Fund.

Friedmann, W. and J. F. Garner, eds., 1970. *Government Enterprise: A Comparative Study*. London: Stevens.

Glaeser, Martin G., 1957. *Public Utilities in American Capitalism*. New York: Macmillan.

Goodman, Edward, 1951. *Forms of Public Ownership and Control*. London: Christophers.

Hanson, A. H., 1956. *The Management of Public Utilities by Local Authorities*. The Hague: Nijhoff for International Union of Local Authorities.

———, 1959. *Public Enterprise and Economic Development*. London: Routledge and Kegan Paul.

Hanson, A. H. *et al.*, 1968. *Organization and Administration of Public Enterprises: Selected Papers*. New York: United Nations.

Jones, Leroy P., ed., 1982. *Public Enterprise in Less Developed Countries*. Cambridge: Cambridge University Press.

Kaul, Mohan *et al.*, 1991. *Public Enterprise Management: Strategies for Success*. 2 vols. London: Commonwealth Secretariat.

Khera, S. S., 1963. *Government in Business*. Bombay: Asia Publishing House.

Lilienthal, David E., 1944. *TVA: Democracy on the March*. Harmondsworth: Penguin.

Macmahon, A. W. and W. R. Dittmar, 1939. "Autonomous Public Enterprise: The German Railways." *Political Science Quarterly*, vol. 54 (December) 481–513.

Mascarenhas, R. C., 1982. *Public Enterprise in New Zealand*. Wellington: Institute of Public Administration.

Mishra, R. K. and S. Ravishankar, eds. 1986. *Public Enterprises in the World*. Bombay: Himalaya.

Mitchell, Jerry, ed., 1992. *Public Authorities and Public Policy: The Business of Government*. New York: Praeger.

Musolf, Lloyd D., 1959. *Public Ownership and Accountability: The Canadian Experience*. Cambridge, MA: Harvard University Press.

Powell, Victor, 1987. *Improving Public Enterprise Performance: Concepts and Techniques*. Geneva: International Labour Office.

Ramamurti, Ravi and Raymond Vernon, eds., 1991. *Privatization and Control of State-Owned Enterprises*. Washington: World Bank.

Ramanadham, V. V., 1984. *The Nature of Public Enterprise*. London: Croom Helm.

———, ed., 1986. *Public Enterprise: Studies in Organizational Structure*. London: Cass.

Robson, W. A., 1962. *Nationalized Industry and Public Ownership*. 2d ed. London: Allen & Unwin.

Sadique, Abu Sharaf H. K., ed., 1976. *Public Enterprise in Asia: Studies on Coordination and Control*. Kuala Lumpur: Asian Centre for Development Administration.

Seidman, Harold, 1954. "The Government Corporation: Organization and Controls." *Public Administration Review*, vol. 14 (Summer) 183–192.

———, 1983. "Public Enterprise Autonomy: Need for a New Theory." *International Review of Administrative Sciences*, vol. 49: 65–72.

———, 1988. "The Quasi World of the Federal Government." *The Brookings Review*, vol. 6 (Summer) 23–27.

Sharkansky, Ira, 1979. *Wither the State: Politics and Public Enterprise in Three Countries*. Chatham, NJ: Chatham.

Shirley, Mary and John Nellis, 1991. *Public Enterprise Reform: The Lessons of Experience*. Washington: World Bank.

Suarez, Ricardo Acosta, ed., 1985. *The Management of Interlinkages*. Ljubljana: International Center for Public Enterprises in Developing Countries.

Thurston, John, 1937. *Government Proprietary Corporations in the English-Speaking Countries*. Cambridge, MA: Harvard University Press.

UN Development Administration Division, 1986. *The Role of the Public Sector in the Mobilization of Domestic Financial Resources in Developing Countries*. New York: United Nations.

UN Technical Assistance Administration, 1954. *Some Problems in the Organization and Administration of Public Enterprises in the Industrial Field*. New York: United Nations.

Verney, D. V., 1959. *Public Enterprise in Sweden*. Liverpool: Liverpool University Press.

Vintera, Jan *et al.*, 1967. *The Role of Public Enterprises in the Formulation and Implementation of Development Plans in Centrally Planned Economies*. New York: United Nations.

Vratusa, Anton *et al.*, 1985. *Essays on Relations Between Governments and Public Enterprises*. Ljubljana: International Center for Public Enterprises in Developing Countries.

Walsh, Annmarie Hauck, 1978. *The Public's Business: The Politics and Practice of Government Corporations*. Cambridge, MA: MIT Press.

Wettenhall, Roger, 1983. "Privatization: A Shifting Frontier Between Private and Public Sectors." *Current Affairs Bulletin* (Sydney), vol. 60 (November) 14–22.

———, 1987. *Public Enterprise and National Development: Selected Essays.* Canberra: Royal Australian Institute of Public Administration, Australian Capital Territory Division.

———, 1990. "Australia's Daring Experiment with Public Enterprise.'" In Alexander Kouzmin and Nicholas Scott, eds., *Dynamics in Australian Public Management: Selected Essays.* Melbourne: Macmillan.

———, 1993. "Public Enterprise in an Age of Privatization." *Current Affairs Bulletin* (Sydney), vol. 69 (February) 4–12.

Wettenhall, Roger and O Nuallain, Colm, eds., 1990. *Public Enterprise Performance Evaluation: Seven Country Studies.* Brussels: International Institute of Administrative Studies.

PUBLIC GOODS.　Goods that are provided by government based on their nonmarketability (nonrival consumption and nonexcludability); also known as collective goods.

To offer explanations of the goals and purposes of political action requires one to cite the importance of public goods and the role, if any, of government in providing (financing) and producing (delivering) public goods. Public goods have long been the subject matter of political debates and controversy as to what is or is not in the public interest, the proper scope of government, and the very legitimacy of government. Increasingly there has also been debate as to whether or not government is always the best source of their production or delivery. Given the controversy involving public goods and government's role in their provision and production, it is not surprising to find debate as to which goods are truly public goods.

What Is a Public Good?

Most social sciences have little trouble in defining their subject matter. Political science is the major exception. There are many connotations of the political or what some refer to as the collective life individuals share in common with one another. Differing points of view as to the proper boundaries of that shared life give rise to conflicting ideological positions as to what goods are public and what goods are private.

For political scientists and most citizens, public goods and services are those provided by governments, paid for through taxation, and produced or delivered by government agencies or their agents. National defense, social security benefits, and local public services such as police, fire and public works come to mind.

Normative political theorists and moral philosophers describe public (or social) goods as those that define or are the hallmark of a just or good society. They are goods that all citizens should enjoy based on their basic equality as citizens. The "good society" is one that provides public goods that are truly good for all. The ends of a policy are

public (or political) goods such as protection, liberty, equality, community, and so forth. Or, to cite John Rawls (1971), a just society is one based on the assumption that certain social primary goods such as self-respect will be provided for all so that they can ensure their own private needs and wants.

There is a third approach to describing the essential characteristics of public goods. Based on their methodological individualism, economists have a rather unique way of conceptualizing public goods. Their connotation is one that is central to public choice theory (which seeks to apply the logic of rational self-interest to the explanation of political behavior and institutions). Their connotation helps explain the whys of governmental intervention when it comes to providing some public goods, but also why government may not always be the most effective or efficient producer of public goods and service.

Within the social sciences' division of labor, economists have long assumed responsibility for explaining private goods or those that we as consumers individually buy and consume for ourselves, such as food, shelter, and leisure. The economist's interest in public goods stems largely from her or his need to account for the presence of market failure or a situation where there are not private suppliers for certain goods and services because of their essential nonmarketability. The existence of public goods, for economists, signifies a role for government and the need for political explanations of why the problem of collective action can be solved.

There are many reasons for market failure. Consumers and producers may lack information of one another in order to do business. In some cases private producers are unable to finance the production of a certain good (a canal system in Adam Smith's day or a natural gas pipeline from Canada to the United States today). Two of the other prominent explanations are central to the economist's definition of public goods. They are the presence of nonrival consumption and nonexcludability of "free riders" or nonpaying consumers. The presence of a true or pure public good requires both conditions to be present. In that many times both are not present together, many public goods are held to be impure or quasi-public goods.

Nonrival consumption is present whenever the consumption of a good does not limit the ability of another consumer to consume that same good. All citizens enjoy protection from national defense efforts. Their consumption is mutual, not rival. In the case of a private good, the purchase of a car or hamburger, for example, brings with it property rights and usually the ability to prevent others from sharing in the benefits of the private good.

Nonexcludability is present where producers or suppliers of a good cannot prevent nonpaying consumers from enjoying the benefits of its consumption. Public goods, it can be said, cannot be rejected. Once supplied, all can use them. In the case of national defense, a government cannot prevent foreigners, even enemies within their borders, from enjoying the benefits of its national defense efforts. Roads, parks, lighthouses, even outdoor rock concerts, are often times available for all whenever the costs to the producer of excluding nonpayers are prohibitive. To the degree that the four are also examples of nonrival consumption, many consumers enjoy them to the point where the producers incur increased costs as a result of the added consumption resulting from zero-cost pricing. Nonexclusion can, in theory, increase social efficiency whenever all are made better off, in that the many may get by with a "little help from their friends" or from the providers of the nonexcludable good.

Consumers reveal their preferences for a particular private good by purchasing it at a certain price and in certain amounts. Each consumer's demand curve is different. The consumers of a pure public good may also have individual demand curves, but since the public good will be provided to all, the consumers of public goods have good reason not to reveal it or to strategically hide their preferences when it comes to paying for the public good. In a "prisoner dilemma" situation, the consumer with a preference for a public good will wait to see if others will be willing to pay for it. If all hide their preferences, the provision of the good will not occur–that is, unless the self-interests of consumers of public goods can be changed or redirected to be supportive of any collective efforts to provide a certain public good. Government coercion is one, but only one, solution to the problem of providing nonmarketable or public goods.

In reality, there are few, if any, pure public goods. Economists acknowledge that there are mixed or quasi-public goods that have properties of being both public and private. (Noneconomists often take the view that private and public goods cannot be clearly separated.) Of the two standards that define a public good, nonrival consumption is the one economists often take to be the more pragmatic test of a public good. Excludability makes for "privateness" and presents a limit to greater social efficiency theoretically guaranteed when nonrival consumption is present.

Many goods that could be deemed to be examples of public goods fit somewhere on the continuums between rival and nonrival and between excludability and nonexcludability. Thus, besides the examples of pure private and pure public goods, there are the hybrid types of mixed or quasi-public goods that are illustrative of goods high in nonrivalness but where excludability is possible and high in nonexcludability but have the property of showing rivalness when it comes to their consumption.

Television signals are goods that show nonrival consumption but can be marketed as a result of the provider being able to exclude those who do not pay. (In reality some can be free riders or can enjoy cable TV programs after spending their money for the technology that will allow them to bypass paying the cable company. Perfect exclusion is difficult.)

Consumers may individually decide to provide and consume a good which is often public in nature. Club goods, as in the case of a private park, are those that are more likely to be provided only if there is a demonstrated ability exclude other individuals, especially nonpayers. When club goods are status goods, as in the case of country clubs, for example, their purchase price may be increased because of a higher price being possible thanks to the exclusivity or status attached to the good. Clubs and status goods demonstrate how some quasi-public goods come to substitute for more public or nonexcludable goods such as parks and recreation.

Lighthouses have long been cited as examples of a public good. Many ships can use the services of a lighthouse and no one ship, in theory, can be excluded from using its services. As Ronald Coase ("The Lighthouse in Economics," 1974) points out, in the case of England, ships can voluntarily pay for the lighthouse's services and ask government to help collect the service fees for the lighthouse's construction and management. Nonexcludability does not have to limit the availability of lighthouse services. Voluntary agreements to pay many substitute for the need of a government to coerce ships into paying for the lighthouses' services. They also help save public revenue that would be required in order to monitor the consumers of governmental lighthouses. However, it could be argued that some threat of coercion may be still needed in order to secure some quasi-voluntary compliance on the part of the users.

Roads and parks illustrate goods that have usually the property of nonexcludability, but will show, at times, a high degree of rival consumption. All cars, theoretically speaking, can potentially use a road and many people can use a park without interfering with one another. However, if too many people use them, crowding sets in and the road or park begins to show rival consumption as to space and time demands. The introduction of a toll road will make a road less public for reasons of excludability and a willingness to pay. Toll roads, however, ease the problem of rival consumption through reducing crowding. The presence of excludability, in the forms of the toll road, makes the road less public at the same time it increases it through adding to its nonrival consumption features.

The existence of many of these and other mixed or quasi-public goods is a result of governmental intervention to provide, even produce them. Their being both partially private and public raise questions as to whether governments should provide them in the first place and for whom. The connotation of a collective good is invoked to capture the perspective that those mixed or quasi-public goods with positive social or public externalities are more worthy of public support than those which have fewer. Economists, in this context, have also coined the concept of a merit good to describe those goods that have communal or political benefits for all. Being in the public interest, they should be and are often times publicly provided though not always publicly produced.

What constitutes a public good is a matter of degree and a result of the different standards invoked to judge its "publicness." At a minimum, public goods are those that are publicly provided. However, it can be argued that governments provide many private or selective goods which benefit the few and not the many. For this reason, it may be better to note public goods as those that have positive externalities for a society or for those not formally designated to benefit from their provision. At a minimum, a private or selective good can be thought of as a quasi-public good that is usually governmentally provided because of its positive externalities or potential for reducing negative externalities or social costs. At a maximum, a quasi-public good is a good that benefits the many collectively. It has many positive externalities so as to be inclusive rather than exclusive. In that there are many politically expressed rhetorical claims for the "true" benefits of a quasi-public good, there is a lot of confusion, debate, and conflict as to what quasi-public goods governments should help provide. The direct and indirect benefits of "welfare" are a primary example.

How Governments Provide Public Goods

Economists and public choice theorists present a more restrictive connotation of what is truly a public good than many political scientists who define governmental provision as the chief defining characteristic of public goods. Based on their methodological individualism, the former find few pure public goods and acknowledge government's role and the importance of politics in the provision of mixed or quasi-public goods. Their attention to the importance of rational self-interest allows them to also argue that government, by its nature, may be limited in its own efforts to provide truly public goods. Economists and public choice theorists help to provide some of the criticism of government when it comes to governmental spending and decisions about who receives the public goods that governments provide.

There have been many explanations as to why governmental spending is as high as it is or as low as it is in a given country. Some of these efforts focus on why citizens prefer private as to public goods (least restrictive definition). Individuals preferring private to public goods do so because they see mostly the benefits of private goods and as a consequence they minimize their costs. The opposite is more

the case when it comes to public goods. Citizens, as taxpayers, see primarily the costs of the public goods, thereby minimizing their benefits. Other explanations of a preference for private goods to public goods focus on cultural values (such as American individualism) or, as in the case of John Kenneth Galbraith (1958), the role of advertising: inducing individuals to consume more private goods, thereby increasing their unwillingness to purchase public goods.

Theories as to when and why citizens show a preference for public goods help to explain why their elected and nonelected representatives (public bureaucrats) are able to increase the supply of public goods despite a preference on the part of citizens for private goods. Elected politicians are viewed as selectively providing public goods that are mainly for their constituents and in their own political or budgetary self-interest. Democracy, in that it is ruled by the majority, increases the preference for public goods when a minority can be enlisted to help purchase them for the majority. Indirect taxation, deficit financing, and fiscal illusions (created by the indirect linkage between consuming and financing of public goods) are additional explanations of how individuals come to support increased governmental spending for public goods.

Political, as opposed to economic, explanations of how and why governments provide certain public and quasi-public goods and not others center on legislative behavior and the presence of interest group liberalism (the ability of political interests to organize effectively in order to secure their political self-interests). To this, the economist and public choice theorist add their own explanations of political behavior to the political theorists' accounts of why collective political action may be difficult, but also why some interest groups are more successful than others in pressing their political demands.

Based on the presumption of rational self-interest, voters are found to have valid reasons for not voting. The benefits of voting are not self-evident. In part, this is a result of political parties appealing to the majority, which leads to voters lacking clear political choices. Politicians are portrayed as self-interested politicians seeking to provide public goods in return for electoral support. Public bureaucrats are held to be budget maximizers who personally benefit from increasing the size of their organizations and the increased supervision responsibilities that go with size. The political world described by economists and public choice theorists is one where governmental spending is a result of political self-interest, rather than a pursuit of the public interest(s).

From many political theorists' observations of legislative politics, successful collective action is always problematic. The obvious explanation is the presence of conflicting views of what constitutes the public's interests(s). In their methodological individualism, economists and public

choice theorists find reason for collective political action being a rather elusive instrumental public good. Individuals, being rational, will not always equally contribute to the collective effort to secure the interest(s) they share in common with others. Public good theory emphasizes the strong possibility of free riders (those who enjoy but do not pay or contribute to the acquisition of a public good that they consume) which, in turn, motivates others not to contribute or cooperate in common effort or action.

From historical evidence, political theorists realize that many political interests and even some larger public interests are realized. A variety of explanations have been offered in order to explain why these occur. Some are in accord with the assumptions of methodological individualism. Others are not.

Mancur Olson (1965) suggests that efforts in collective action are facilitated through the provision of selective incentives to the members of the collective effort in order to solicit their support for it. Olson's byproduct theory is based on the assumption that individuals come to value the marginal benefits of collective action to be received as selective benefits are provided. This byproduct theory is consistent with the tenets of methodological individualism.

In theory, some individual may feel so strongly about an issue that he or she will contribute more to the collective effort than others and even if others do not themselves contribute. Intensity of concern does not require an alternative explanation of individual altruism. There is a possibility of sociability or individuals enjoying their participation with others. As evidenced in the writings of normative democratic theorists, participation may be extolled for both its social and psychological benefits as well as its political accomplishments. And if the individual members believe that others are contributing equally (more likely in small groups where monitoring is available for verification), then the added trust between members may help expedite successful collective political efforts.

Public goods have been defined as those being in the public interest. They have also been described as occurring wherever there is the elimination of public "bads" (graffiti, pollution, and so forth). Collective action to prevent public bads is extremely difficult, for while a single individual creates only the smallest of harm, collectively many individuals may create a lot of harm. Preventing collectively induced harm has often been left to governmental intervention and regulation of those who produce the negative externalities and social costs for society. However, supportive regulation of environment quality is often compromised as a result of the political power and influence of concerned political interests. Logging interests want to cut more trees and cattle ranchers want to graze more cattle. For those interested in preventing overuse of natural resources, governmental regulation is not always seen as the only viable alternative for dealing with the "tragedy of the commons."

Individual logging or grazing interests, it has been argued, can preempt the need for governmentally coerced moratoriums in their efforts to increase prices by limiting cutting or grazing. Voluntary agreements are held up as solutions to the problem of government failure (nonmarket failure). Individual logging or grazing interests, in theory, could agree to ration their use of the natural resources. As a theoretical solution to a public good problem, such action is often viewed as not always forthcoming.—that is, unless the concerned individuals have a common perception of the crises to be adverted or have an underlying sense of community that facilitates their collective commitment or the trust necessary for successful collective efforts and provision of public goods, such as conservation.

The examples of collective political action being possible without governmental regulation and coercion illustrate the growing theme that government may not always be the primary choice when it comes to the production (delivery) of public goods and service.

Who Should Produce Public Goods?

Criticism of governmental spending has centered on how public goods should be funded, what those goods should be, and to whom they should be provided. Governmental production of certain public goods such as postal service has long been criticized on the basis of perceived poor performance, poor customer relations, and the problems with a bureaucratic delivery of the services. Economic downturns and budget crises of the 1980s and 1990s have prompted reexamination of governmental bureaucracies' abilities to produce effective and efficient public goods and services. A lengthy history of governmental contracting with other governments or the private sector serves as a reminder that governmental production is not the only service delivery alternative. Efforts to "reinvent government" (Osborne and Gaebler, 1992) are centered on finding new and better ways of delivering certain public goods and services.

In many cases, governments provide both the resources (revenue) and the actual production of those goods and services they choose to provide or finance. In the case of police, fire, and public works, it is usually a governmental bureaucracy that delivers the public goods or services to citizens as customers. As an alternative to private provision and private production, the public bureaucracy is held superior both in terms or provision (financing), but also in the greater assurance that all may receive a particular public good or service. Public bureaucracies are both commended and criticized for their efforts in redistribution. Public fire departments, unlike private, for example, do not discriminate as to whose fires they put out, for the fire's negative externalities are a public problem. (Private contracting for a public service such as fire suppression in the 1800s was limited to those buildings with private insurance.) Public delivery of fire suppression and many other services guarantees that a larger public concern is properly met.

Public as well as private bureaucracies, however, have been criticized for being highly inefficient as a result of their budgetary maximization strategies, less responsiveness to citizens and customers' wants, and slowness to adopt needed innovations. The case for private production (with public provision) of certain public goods has been made in terms of the greater efficiency of private production, thanks in large part to the presumed competition between private sector producers and their ability to lower the costs of providing public services through lower salaries and fringe benefit packages, a smaller workforce, and better deployment of service crews. Any absence of competition (numbers of producers) limits the willingness of private producers to be as efficient as they could be.

However, increased competition between different public bureaucracies to deliver certain public services, such as police services, increases service efficiency. And, in theory, so does the presence of different communities offering a variety of packages of public goods and services to their citizens and the presence of citizens willing to move in search of a more desirable place to live (Tiebout, 1956).

Contracting with private or other governmental producers is not always the best of policy options when it comes to the production or delivery of certain public goods and services. An inability to measure successfully the quality of the output or performance of a contracted public service (such as social services or prisons) limits the ability of governments to write effective contracts ensuring service accountability. The costs of monitoring contracts may be prohibitive or even impossible due to the lack of availability of funds for adequate contract compliance. The inability to have meaningful competitive bidding, the high start-up costs incurred by switching contractors, and the possibility of long-term costs increasing for service contractors (as a result of underestimated costs or the lack of competition over time) raise questions about the promise of private delivery of public goods and services through contracting.

Private provision but with public production or delivery of public goods and services is a fourth theoretical possibility. Private individuals and organizations can purchase, for a user fee, a particular good or service from a governmental agency. Fees charged for using governmental facilities, obtaining public documents, or "renting" police officers for special events and tasks are examples. Unlike the case of public provisions, the citizen's financing of public goods in this case is more voluntary than coercive (an issue

of taxation). The public goods in question are selective so as to be basically private goods and services that just happen to be produced or performed by governmental personnel. Governments may give all people the public documents they need for a price, but in doing so they may also give some people more or fewer public goods and services given their pricing structure, people's ability to pay, and any "side payments" made by those wanting to purchase selective or "quasi-private" goods such as extra police protection. Unfair competition, possible social inequities in receiving some public goods, and even corruption of the service delivery process are criticisms of this public service delivery model.

The four possible combinations of public and private provision and production do not exhaust the possibilities for production and delivery of public goods and services. The rise of tax limitation movements and increased budgetary constraints starting in the 1980s have led to proposals for greater coprovision and coproduction of public goods and services. As a coprovider, a citizen helps to finance a public good or service through either making voluntary donations (for example, to her or his child's school or educational foundation) or by volunteering her or his time, labor, and effort to help the school in some capacity such as fund raising, mentoring other's children, painting classrooms, and so forth. Helping with her or his child's own education would also constitute coprovision. In some cases, the parent, as coprovider, is also a coproducer, or one who helps to perform some services that contribute to the delivery of education as a public good. In parenting and mentoring, for example, the parent and volunteer may complement or even substitute for the classroom teacher's efforts.

In the case of coprovision, the citizen role in helping to finance, in part, public goods and services is viewed as compatible with efforts of governments and nonprofit organizations to help provide a particular public good or service. In the case of a coproduction of public goods and services, the assumption is usually that the citizens, as volunteers, work with governmental service agents to help produce or deliver public goods such as education, crime prevention, or the removal of graffiti from walls. Not all citizen volunteerism, when it comes to public goods and services, is necessarily always in conjunction with governmental service agents. If citizens can finance their children's private education on their own, then some may, individually or collectively, produce or deliver public goods and services without governmental assistance.

Citizens in rural America have long provided and produced many of their own public goods and services without much in the way of formal governmental assistance. Volunteer fire suppression and emergency rescue or ambulance service are primary examples of this. Citizens in some of America's inner cities have engaged in collective self-help or volunteerism efforts when governmental production or delivery of certain public goods or services has been inadequate or missing altogether. Where crime prevention is a serious problem and personal safety always in doubt, citizen volunteerism becomes a de facto policy option.

Before there were paid and professional public service delivery agents, there were only volunteers and voluntary or collective self-help efforts. The role for volunteers in the delivery of public goods and services has increased as limits to effective governmental production and delivery of some of them have become evident. The important role of volunteers in providing new public goods and services such as recycling, neighborhood conservation (the aesthetics and upkeep of homes and yards), and neighborhood mediation, to name a few, illustrate the role of volunteerism as an alternative policy option to paid and professionally produced public goods and services. Volunteerism, either directly or indirectly—as in the case of the upsurge in governmental contracting with nonprofit organizations that depend heavily on volunteers—plays an increasing public role in providing and producing public goods and services. They help to extend the number and scope of the public and quasi-public goods and services that citizens can consume.

Coprovision, as a policy option, is without criticism when it comes to public goods and services. Donations and volunteer time and labor help a society and its governments provide added public and quasi-public goods. On the other hand, coproduction and citizen volunteerism, in general, are more controversial, for they are often perceived as ways of substituting volunteers for paid professional personnel, thereby threatening the jobs of the latter. Critics within the halls of government point to the volunteer's lack of training and the hidden costs of supervision as reasons why citizen volunteerism is not always the best of ways to help governments produce public goods and services.

Public Goods Theory as Political Theory

To engage in theorizing about the nature of public goods is to engage in political theorizing. The nature of public goods goes to the very essence or purposes of government and the public sector. They are the subject matter of both political rhetoric and policy arguments. The right to public goods is often put forth as one of the basic rights of citizenship. Increasingly in the 1990s, the alleged civic responsibilities of citizens are discussed in terms of who shares the responsibility to help provide and produce public goods and resources, given a growing desire on the part of some citizens for less governmental spending. Public goods define the presence of market failure. They may also help define the presence of the very real limits to government and governmental spending, the outer boundaries of the political or public life individuals share a common re-

sponsibility for as citizens. In the end, the study of public goods is not easily separated from normative political theory and what constitutes the good society.

GEORGE FREDERICK GOERL

BIBLIOGRAPHY

Benjamin, Roger, 1980. *The Limits of Politics: Collective Goods and Political Change in Industrial Societies.* Chicago: University of Chicago Press.

Buchanan, James, 1980. "What Governments Try to Do: 'Public Goods and Public Bads.'" In John Crecine, ed., *Financing the Metropolis.* Beverly Hills, CA: Sage Publications.

Coase, Ronald, 1974. "The Lighthouse in Economics." *Journal of Law and Economics,* vol. 17 (October), 357–376.

Galbraith, John Kenneth, 1958. *The Affluent Society.* Boston: Houghton Mifflin.

Lowi, Theodore, 1979. *The End of Liberalism,* 2nd ed. New York: Norton.

Malkin, Jesse and Aaron Wildavsky, 1991. "Why the Traditional Distinction between Public and Private Goods Should Be Abandoned." *Journal of Theoretical Politics,* vol. 3 (July), 355–378.

Musgrave, Richard and Peggy Musgrave, 1984. *Public Finance in Theory and Practice.* 4th ed. New York: McGraw Hill.

Moe, Terry M., 1980. *The Organization of Interests.* Chicago: University of Chicago Press.

Olson, Mancur, 1965. *The Logic of Collective Action.* Cambridge, MA: Harvard University Press.

Osborne, David and Ted Gaebler, 1992. *Reinventing Government.* Reading, MA: Addison Westley.

Ostrom, Elinore, 1990. *Governing the Commons.* Cambridge, England: Cambridge University Press.

Ostrom, Vincent and Elinor Ostrom, 1977. "Public Goods and Public Choices." In E. S. Savas, ed., *Alternatives for Delivering Public Services.* Boulder, CO: Westview Press.

Pennock, J. Ronald, 1966. "Political Development, Political Systems, and Political Goods." *World Politics,* vol. 18 (April), 415–434.

Rawls, John, 1971. *A Theory of Justice,* Cambridge: Harvard University Press.

Tiebout, Charles, 1956. "A Pure Theory of Local Expenditures." *Journal of Political Economy,* vol. 64: 416–424.

PUBLIC HEARING. Based upon the concept that if one's rights are affected by a governmental action one should receive notice of the action and have the opportunity to be heard; more formally defined as "the right to appear and give evidence and also the right to hear and examine witnesses whose testimony is presented by opposing parties" (*Farmers Elevator Company v. Railroad Company,* 266 Illinois 573). The term "public hearing" is linked to our democratic ideals and the concept of due process.

Specific rights to public hearings are normally established by legislation. They are often called for in situations in which public interest is important to the action to be taken. Public hearings are usually held in relation to issues before legislative bodies, land use boards, and administrative agencies which influence and regulate actions. A frequent example is in zoning and the applications of the zoning laws in our communities. Few matters excite people as much as the affairs of their local community, particularly those actions that take place in their personal sphere of influence.

Public hearings often are held to promote the public interest so that the view of all is not overshadowed by the opinion of the few who are the decisionmakers. The hearing provides an opportunity for various competing interests, both public and private, to make their viewpoints known. Accordingly, in order to ensure that there is an opportunity for the presentation of all views and to question government actions, many governmental bodies have established the requirement of a public hearing.

Notice is necessary in the procedural process. Local knowledge is at the core of the public hearing process. The type of notice which has been approved by the courts varies. In some instances, publication in newspapers of limited circulation in a particular area has been approved as a sufficient form of notice to the public. In some instances, publications in legal newspapers which are typically seen by real estate interests and banking interests are sufficient to satisfy the procedural requirements. On the other hand, some states and municipalities have gone out of their way to make sure that hearing notices are put in the local newspapers and, in land use situations, posted on the premises to be affected. Often actual notice is given to those who can clearly be identified as having a special interest or to those who clearly may be affected by the action being considered.

A public hearing has a concept of "fairness." To be fair, everyone should be given the opportunity to be heard. However, in order to have the process carried out in an organized fashion, there may be time limitations on speakers and some formality to the process.

The federal government has established the Administrative Procedure Act and Section 554 describes how a hearing should be conducted. It requires the agency to:

1. Provide appropriate persons proper notice regarding the time, place, and nature of the hearing, the legal authority and jurisdiction under which the hearing is to be held, and the matters of fact and law to be involved;
2. Take into consideration the needs of the parties or their representatives in scheduling the time and the place of the hearing;
3. Afford all concerned parties the opportunity to submit and consider all relevant facts, arguments, and proposed settlements as time and public interest permits;
4. Forbid agency employees who have acted as investigators or prosecutors in a case to participate in a hearing decision, except as counsel or witnesses.

Subsequent sections of the federal act also show how matters have evolved so that agencies take further steps such as allowing persons to be represented by counsel, to conclude business in a "reasonable time," to arrive at decisions in light of the "whole record" or based on "substantial evidence," and require that they keep a complete transcript of the hearing proceedings (Warren 1996, p. 324).

A public hearing is not a trial but it can be viewed similarly. Although it provides the opportunity to present viewpoints, it involves presentation of facts as well. It is not a formal process, so normally the body that is hearing the matter allows a great deal of latitude. This is particularly appropriate since the presentation by members of the public at large is frequently unorganized and it may be the first time that a citizen has ever spoken before a public body.

Public agencies are given some latitude in decisionmaking because of the opportunity that they have to hear from the public. However, the matters which are presented at the public hearing may also form the basis of future litigation. Therefore, separating fact from emotion and opinion is an important part of the decisionmaking process as well. Many, although not all, of the actions undertaken by legislative bodies or by agencies of government are subject to judicial review. There have been many lawsuits on the meaning of terms which are inherently vague such as "proper notice" and "reasonable time" because they are the basis for allowing court review. Often the courts must decide the citizen's right to challenge agency decisions and determine whether decisions have been made on the basis of full and informed information, a determination made on facts.

It should be noted that a public hearing is distinctly different from the right to attend meetings. Attendance and the opportunity to hear what is going on are generally covered under Sunshine Laws or open meetings laws. However, there is no requirement under Sunshine Laws or open meetings laws for participation. The idea formulated behind a public hearing is for individuals to have an opportunity to present information, that is, to participate.

MARY R. DOMAHIDY AND
DOUGLAS R. BEACH

BIBLIOGRAPHY

Kelly, Eric Damian, 1988. "Zoning." In Frank S. So and Judith Getzels, eds., *The Practice of Local Government Planning.* Washington, D.C.: International City Management Association, pp. 251–286.
Pope's Legal Definitions, 1920. Chicago: Callaghan.
Warren, Kenneth, 1996. *Administrative Law in the Political System.* 3d ed. Englewood Cliffs, NJ: Prentice Hall.

PUBLIC MANAGEMENT. The application of the craft, art, and science of management to a context where political values govern the evaluation of success and

where the rule of law dictates constraints on administrative discretion. Because political preferences bring policy shifts, the ability to navigate in politicized waters is a skill that is as essential to the public manager as the ability to plan, organize, staff, direct, budget, and perform other standard managerial duties. Public management means "doing" government. And, because politics is a key dimension to government, public management requires mastery of political as well as administrative skills.

Public managers work in city, county, state, and federal government, as well as special districts. They work in executive, judicial, and legislative agencies in roles as varied as the missions of those agencies. For example, missions range from wastewater treatment plants to foster care for children; from highway engineers to agricultural extension agents; from welfare services to weather forecasting; from public health services to law enforcement; from public education to firefighting; from national defense to economic development; from environmental protection to emergency preparedness; from tax collection to neighborhood zoning; from parks and recreation facilities to court administration; from public libraries to highway safety; from national research and development laboratories to regulatory commissions. Managing each of these enterprises requires substantive knowledge of the policy arena pertaining to the mission, mastery of generic managerial skills, a keen ability to maximize political values to advance the work of the agency, and an abiding respect for democratic policies and procedures.

Evolution of the Term

As the 1900s progressed, a bifurcation developed among those who wrote about the work of government (Ott, Hyde, and Shafritz 1991). While some wrote about the administrative side of the enterprise, others wrote about the policy side. Graduate programs developed that emphasized either the public policy aspects or the administrative aspects. In the meantime, those who were actively engaged in the work of government were wrestling with both sides of the coin: policy *plus* administration. As a corollary event, business administration programs made a transition from the word "administration" to the word "management," as public administration programs began to replace the term "administration" with "management." At the least, the term "public management" merely reflects the transition in popularity from the word "administration" to the word "management." At most, it reflects the appreciation that public managers must juggle both policy and administration to be effective.

By this time, the term "public management" is widely accepted and connotes an action orientation to the coordination and interconnectedness that is inherent in the operation of public programs. Its precedent "public adminis-

tration" has not so much changed as it has fallen from favor as the more contemporary term "management" has risen in popularity. Some argue that "administration" reflects too much of a policy emphasis and too little of the management emphasis. Others argue that the term "administration" fails to reflect the convergence of policy and administration that marks the work of today's public manager. Still others view the focus of public "administration" as being too near the apex of public agencies and thus not cognizant enough of the many layers of managers in specialized units within public agencies.

While the focus of public management is on the efficient delivery of services, it is refined through the lens of public policy. Thus, subfields of public management include generic managerial components: budgeting and financial management, human resources, and information technology. Yet these are inextricably embedded in a democratic political context that radically alters the work of public management as contrasted to management in for-profit concerns.

Public Management vis-à-vis Partisan Politics

Public management requires balancing responsibility and action with political sensitivity and public service values. As a term, "public management" denotes the convergence of public policy analysis with administration and acknowledges that management and politics walk side by side in public management endeavors. While elected officials may want an agency to aggressively pursue the implementation of a given policy, the experience of career public managers may speak to the wisdom of maintaining a steady course between extreme interpretations of the policy. Since elected officials come and go and career managers remain, they function as conservers who straddle the extremes that are reflected in elected officials' priorities.

While some refer to "public management" as an inclusive term for all elected as well as appointed and career civil service posts, others reserve the term for only nonelected posts. In its most inclusive usage, public managers may include those who are elected, such as the president, governors, mayors, and some elected municipal and county executives; those who are political appointees, such as agency directors and city managers; plus those who rise to office through competitive civil service procedures, such as bureau chiefs and department heads. More often, the term "public management" is reserved for the activities conducted by career managers who gain their appointments through competitive civil service procedures. To the extent possible, these managers refrain from becoming actively involved in partisan campaigns and elections in order to remain as neutral as possible as they interpret and implement public policy.

Public Management vis-à-vis Public Policy

Public management is that aspect of public administration that is concerned with efficiency, accountability, goal achievement, and other managerial and technical questions (Graham and Hays 1993). The relationship between public management and the policy process is intertwined. Public management goes beyond simplistic mechanics of administration. It is about a dynamic multidisciplinary field that borrows from finance, human resources, planning, policy analysis, politics, and organization development. The public manager maintains a delicate balance:

- Between helping to make policy and to implement it;
- By facilitating the governing body's decisionmaking regarding policy initiatives;
- By resolving conflicts and building coalitions among groups with conflicting interests;
- By maintaining a steady course while managing change; and
- By enabling citizens to participate in government.

Contemporary public management as a field of endeavor reflects the changing emphasis from administrators who hold policy advocacy at arm's length to managers who, charged with responsibility for managing public programs, use policy advocacy to facilitate their program operations. This action orientation reflects the necessity for incorporating an appreciation of democratic theory and practice with efficient management (Waldo 1984). It merges a focus on policy with a focus on administration and reflects the interorganizational linkages, economic context, and partisan considerations that converge in the process of governance (Newland 1994).

Public management is an enterprise in pursuit of significance (Denhardt 1993). As a craft, it is reflective of the postmodernist age, where boundaries are fuzzy, the environment is turbulent, and the line between facts and values is often indistinguishable. Denhardt (1993) finds that contemporary public managers pursue their work through five means: a commitment to values, a concern for serving the public, empowerment and shared leadership, pragmatic incrementalism, and a dedication to public service.

Public managers report that they spend their time directing, organizing, coordinating, planning, managing people, managing money, and managing information. They describe themselves as leaders, administrators, implementors, coaches, and mediators (Bozeman 1993; Ingraham and Romzek 1994; Perry 1989; Rainey 1991). To succeed at public management, one must be a master of a number of topics, as the list in Table I shows.

Public management reflects a marriage between the policy process and policy implementation. The marriage commingles analytic fact, intuitive judgment, democratic values, and political reality to produce programs that fulfill legislative intent and satisfy citizen demands. Knowing how and when to intervene in the policy process is a required skill for public managers. In the early years of the twentieth century, it was generally assumed that public managers should follow behind the policy process, and refrain from exerting influence at any stage. Their purpose was thought to be the implementation of policy after it had been decided by elected officials. As the twentieth century draws to a close, contemporary thinking has changed. In order to do their job effectively, public managers are expected to know if, when, and how to affect the policy process. When managers have a hand in sculpting the policies that drive their programs, they increase their capacity to design programs that fulfill legislative mandates.

From a functional perspective, public organizations convert resources in the form of tax revenues and political capital into programmatic outputs. A review of the scholarship on public management reveals an evolution from a focus on economy in terms of eliminating waste and cutting cost (1880–1932) to improving efficiency through good management (1933–1960) to improving effectiveness through planning and policymaking to improving efficiency through improved management (1961–present) (Swiss 1991).

The bottom line for public management is that it must always carry out legislative intent, whether that intent is decreed by city councils, county commissions, state legislatures, or the U.S. Congress. Beyond the letter of the law, public managers seek to operate their programs so as to fill in the chinks left by policies that contradict one another, that leave gaps between services, or that fail to address public needs. The scope of a public manager's tasks depends on that person's position in an agency. At the lowest level, public management begins when a public employee has responsibility and authority that extends beyond discrete professional tasks to the supervision of others, and/or to the coordination of tasks.

Public Management Versus Business Management

It has been said that government and business are alike in all unimportant respects. To a degree this is true. Public management differs from private management primarily

TABLE I. Public Management Involves

Providing Leadership
Shaping Policy
Planning Programs
Designing Organizational Environments
Communicating with Constituencies
Budgeting Resources
Staffing
Directing Work Flow

because the public sector is political. For this reason, management systems that work well behind the closed doors of business establishments are illegal through the open windows of government organizations. The following differences are significant in the impact they have:

Public agencies usually have a larger number of competing goals;
Public agencies operate under public scrutiny;
Public managers operate under fragmented authority structures;
Public organizations have more legal restrictions on their actions; and
Public organizations have more restrictions on their staffing–they cannot hire, fire, or promote as flexibly (Ott, Hyde, and Shafritz 1991, Swiss 1991).

Organizational leadership in public organizations differs from that in private organizations and thus causes the work of the public manager to differ from that of the private manager. In public organizations, leadership is shared between elected or appointed officials and career executives. Political executives are elected or appointed by elected officials and serve as change agents in the most fundamental sense: to make the work of government reflect the partisan ideology of the administration currently elected to office. The career executives are also change agents but are advocates for change that is in accord with their understanding of the need for, and the potential levers of, change initiatives. The typical appointed executive holds office for a relatively short time, usually around two years, thus causing their time horizon to be near term. Career executives, on the other hand, may hold office for many years and thus, their time horizon is substantially extended (Ingraham and Romzek 1994). This affects program planning as well as evaluation. It also creates a tension between appointed executives who want to make swift changes and career officials who have experienced the arrival and departure of numerous appointed officials.

Accountability structures also differ for those in public management. Public sector stakeholders are comprised of elected officials, agency superiors, professional peers, clientele groups, special interest groups, and citizens. The courts also play a significant role in holding public agencies accountable for performance and for adherence to law. Managerial discretion and authority is more limited in public management than in private business. The ability to hire, fire, and promote is constrained by job protections that are in place to free employees from partisan favoritism. The budgetary process is often complicated by real cracks in the theoretical connection between programmatic needs, constituent demands, and resource flow. Demands for government accountability inhibit flexibility and make reporting requirements onerous. These facts of life attenuate the ability to operate from what would otherwise be viewed as a sound managerial base (Ingraham and Romzek 1994).

Current thinking in public management is moving from earlier notions of neutral competence to current notions of the value of the public service as an instrument for advancing the public good. This requires a widespread commitment to competent and effective management on the part of both career and political executives in order to manage in the public interest (Ingraham and Ban 1986). This also requires an interdependence between the public and private sectors and an ability to build interorganizational and intersectoral linkages (Starling 1993).

Public management must respond to a number of constituents, including elected officials, taxpayers, and agency clientele, as well as subordinates, superiors, and peers within their agencies. The demands of these constituencies are often mutually exclusive and to satisfy one is to create another. Thus, the balancing act that is required in public management is never ending and rarely easy. The character of the polity affects the work of public managers, just as market mechanisms affect the work of business managers. As the market determines success or failure of business ventures, political values as well as market values determine the success or failure of public ventures.

The public interest model of public management requires a connection between professional concerns and social needs while avoiding partisan conflicts. Public managers are charged with the legitimate direction of society. Given the complexities of interorganizational linkages, rapid change, and economic restructuring, public managers must implement policies that are effective and legitimate and that are representative of society as well as fair (Uveges and Keller 1989).

Summary

Public management is the enterprise of doing the business of government. Public management cannot be properly understood without being placed in its political, economic, and constitutional context. Everything that government does must first pass through a sieve that blends connections between levels and branches of government, partisan politics with substantive mission, economic efficiency with constitutional freedoms, and a tacit agreement between business and government and nonprofit enterprises about the boundaries which surround them. Public management is complex and requires a sophisticated appreciation for the interconnections that exist between all segments of society.

MARY E. GUY

BIBLIOGRAPHY

Bozeman, Barry, ed., 1993. *Public Management: The State of the Art.* San Francisco, CA: Jossey Bass.
Denhardt, Robert B., 1993. *The Pursuit of Significance: Strategies for Managerial Success in Public Organizations.* Belmont, CA: Wadsworth.

Graham, Cole Blease, and Stephen W. Hays, 1993. *Managing the Public Organization.* Washington, D.C.: CQ Press.

Ingraham, Patricia W. and Carolyn R. Ban, 1986. "Models of Public Management: Are They Useful to Federal Managers in the 1980s?" *Public Administration Review* 46(2):152–160.

Ingraham, Patricia W. and Barbara S. Romzek, 1994. *New Paradigms for Government: Issues for the Changing Public Service.* San Francisco, CA: Jossey Bass.

Newland, Chester A., 1994. "A Field of Strangers in Search of a Discipline: Separatism of Public Management Research from Public Administration." *Public Administration Review,* 54(5):486–488.

Ott, J. Steven, Albert C. Hyde, and Jay M. Shafritz, eds., 1991. *Public Management: The Essential Readings.* Chicago, IL: Nelson-Hall.

Perry, James L., ed., 1989. *Handbook of Public Administration.* San Francisco, CA: Jossey Bass.

Rainey, Hal G., 1991. *Understanding and Managing Public Organizations.* San Francisco, CA: Jossey Bass.

Starling, Grover, 1993. *Managing the Public Sector.* Belmont, CA: Wadsworth.

Swiss, James E., 1991. *Public Management Systems: Monitoring and Managing Government Performance.* Englewood Cliffs, NJ: Prentice Hall.

Uveges, Jr., J. A. and L. F. Keller, 1989. "The First One Hundred Years of American Public Administration: The Study and Practice of Public Management in American Life." In J. Rabin, W. B. Hildreth, and G. J. Miller, eds., *Handbook of Public Administration.* Volume 35. New York: Marcel Dekker, pp. 1–42.

Waldo, Dwight, 1984. *The Administrative State: A Study of the Political Theory of American Public Administration.* 2d ed. New York: Holmes & Meier.

PUBLIC PENSIONS (RETIREMENT).

Income support payments paid to those who have retired from the workforce, usually in the age range 60 to 65 years.

Definition and Scope

Public pensions generally refer to income support payments paid to those who have retired from the workforce, usually in the age range 60 to 65 years in most OECD countries. The payments may be in the form of a basic flat-rate entitlement where the only qualification is that the recipient has reached a defined retirement age; or, payments may be based on contributions made throughout the recipient's working life and paid at a level related either to former earnings or contributions level. In some countries the term public pension may also refer to income support payments for those unlikely to work again due to disability or other contingency. In this discussion, the term public pensions will refer only to retirement provisions and the focus is on the types of provision commonly found in the OECD nations.

Public pensions are a central feature of the social security systems in all of the OECD countries. In recent times public pension provision has grown in the newly industrialized countries of East Asia and the developing nations of Central and Southern America. In the former Soviet bloc countries, public pensions are being reconstituted along the lines of the types of systems common to the OECD nations, and with the assistance of the World Bank, rudimentary schemes have been introduced to the poorer nations of Asia and Africa (World Bank 1994).

Public pensions have the highest share of expenditures of all social programs in the OECD countries: on average, they accounted for just over 10 percent of GDP and around 25 percent of government expenditure in 1995. In many countries these pensions account for more than health and education, which together dominate other public social programs in size and growth (OECD 1985).

Historical Development

The development of the modern welfare state is strongly linked to the growth in provision of public pensions. This is because public pensions, as the first major programs of income transfers, provided a legitimate and popular cornerstone around which subsequent social policy programs were built. When examining the different forms of social security systems which have developed among the OECD countries, it is often the case that the original form of public pension provision has strongly influenced the character and nature of the entire range of welfare state programs.

The historical development of public pensions in the advanced industrial nations can be roughly divided into three phases, observable in most countries. The first stage covers the period 1880 to World War II when the rudiments of the pension systems were initially established and then consolidated in the interwar period. The second stage, the postwar era to around the mid-1970s, saw a rapid expansion and enrichment of these original programs when entitlement rules were entrenched and the pension system became a "fact of life" for workers in most of the industrial economies. The third stage (post–1975), represents the maturation of these pension programs and a substantial increase in expenditure on these programs as the population ages. In the industrial economies, tightened economic circumstances and changing demographics have provoked public discussion and policy debates over the need to restructure public pension systems.

Types of Pension Systems

Pension provision across the OECD area has three components: state provision, provision linked to employment, and private savings. The decades of the 1950s to the 1970s saw a growth in the national resources going to each of these three components. State provision was extended to new groups and increased with the maturing of existing provisions. Occupational provision became more widespread, and with gradual improvements in coverage, indexation of payments, and portability of benefits between jobs, the benefits from occupational pensions were enriched over time. Finally, the effects of general economic growth since 1945 also means that a greater proportion of the retired population have resources of their own, whether through savings or in forms such as private home ownership.

Two models of public pensions can be differentiated historically: flat-rate benefit systems and earnings-related benefit systems. This distinction has been gradually blurred over time by the topping up of flat-rate systems with earnings-related elements, and by the introduction of minimum standards within the earnings-related systems. The OECD (1988a) has identified three broad systems of entitlement in member countries:

- Basic flat-rate systems;
- Mixed systems that provide a basic pension plus an earnings-related component;
- Insurance systems that comprise an earnings-related pension above some minimum standard.

Table I sets out the administrative and financing characteristics generally associated with each of these system types and locates each of the OECD nations within each type of system.

Current Trends and Issues

Since 1975 the OECD economies have experienced a significant slowdown in economic growth and the problems of financing public pension programs have become increasingly apparent. Despite the immediate economic constraints, public expectations about entitlement to retirement benefits have changed slowly—if at all—and the real value of pensions has continued to rise.

The growing pressure on public pension schemes has various origins. The main concerns expressed in the social policy literature are the increasing resources that are already being transferred from the working population to the retired population, and the fear that these resources will further increase in the future because of an aging population and the maturation of existing schemes. Contributing to these problems is the fall in birthrates observed over the past 30 years, which will reduce the size of the future working population and will further exacerbate the actuarial

TABLE I. CLASSIFICATION OF OECD COUNTRIES BY PUBLIC PENSION TYPE

	Basic	Mixed	Insurance
Form of benefits	Flat-rate	Flat-rate & Employment-related	Employment related
Financing	General revenues	General revenues/ contributions	Mainly contributions
Administration	Public	Public, semipublic, private	Semipublic
Countries	New Zealand 1 + 2	Australia 1 + 4	Austria 3
	Iceland 1	Canada 1 + 3	Belgium 3
		Denmark 1 + 2 + 4	France 3 + 4
		Finland 1 + 2 + 3	Germany 3
		Ireland 2 + 3	Greece 3
		Norway 1 + 3	Italy 3
		Sweden 1 + 3 + 4	Luxembourg 3
		United Kingdom 2 + 3 + 5	Japan 3 + 5
			Netherlands 3 + 4
			Portugal 3
			Spain 3
			Switzerland 3 + 4
			Turkey 3
			United States 3

1. Universal:	Available to all who meet age, residency requirements.
2. Social Assistance:	Minimum flat-rate public assistance.
3. Social Insurance:	Earnings-related benefits to eligible contributors.
4. Mandatory Occupational Pensions:	Government-mandated contributory schemes.
5. Contracting-out possibilities:	Allows contributors to opt out of mandatory schemes to private schemes.

SOURCE: Adapted from OECD (1988a, p. 17).

DIAGRAM I. DEMOGRAPHIC STRUCTURES AND INCOME TRANSFERS

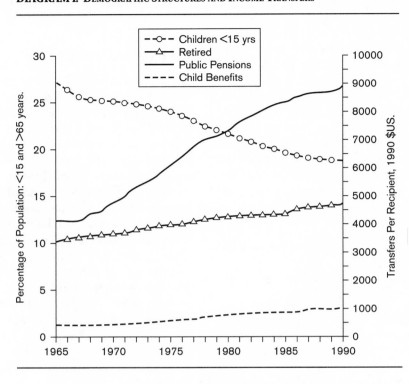

problems of existing schemes. Diagram I illustrates several key aspects of this problem. Looking across 18 of the major OECD nations, we see the significant fall in birthrates, the growth in the retired population—which is projected to rise sharply after 2010, due to the baby boom generation—and the doubling of the per capita real value of public pensions.

The severity of these problems varies between countries depending on specific institutional, economic, and demographic structures; however, it is possible to give a general account of the dynamics of the pension problem. Public pension schemes in OECD countries generally operate on a pay-as-you-go basis: the revenue collected from general taxation or earmarked contributions from the working generation are immediately used to finance the benefits of the currently retired generation. Thus, changes in the number of retirees relative to the working population have an immediate effect on the actuarial situation of these schemes. The most common way in which the ratio of retirees to the working population is altered arises from changes in the demographic structure and aging of the population.

As noted above, the OECD countries have experienced a substantial increase in the proportion of elderly people in the population, with a considerable impact on the share of public pension in national resources; this development will become more important in the future as the aging trend is accentuated. Aging will take place from the "bottom," as the fertility rate in most countries has

been well below the replacement level since the end of the 1960s (see Diagram I); even if the fertility rate were to return to higher levels in the future, the aging of the baby boomer generation will be felt for several decades after the turn of the century. Taken together, both effects substantially decrease the number of active workers per retiree in the decades to come, leading to the necessity for most of the OECD countries to adjust their present pension schemes in several possible ways (either singly or in combination): reducing the current level of benefits; increasing the contributions paid by the working generation; or reducing the number of people eligible for benefit.

As a result, public pension schemes in OECD countries are increasingly the subject of proposed or actual reform. Despite differences in the types of schemes in various nations, the need to restructure public retirement programs seems common to all systems. Fears of an evolving crisis, especially in the more generous social insurance systems, and a growing conflict between the needs of the young and the old (compare the growth of the real value of retirement pensions and child benefits in Diagram I) are becoming a more prominent part of public policy debates across the OECD nations (Smeeding et al. 1988). These debates are not the outcome of any system specific problems, but a general response to changing economic, social, and demographic environments.

DEBORAH MITCHELL

BIBLIOGRAPHY

Heidenheimer, A., H. Heclo and C. Adams, 1990. *Comparative Public Policy.* New York: St. Martin's Press.

OECD, 1985. *Social Expenditure 1960–1990: Problems of Growth and Control.* Paris: OECD.

———, 1988a. *Reforming Public Pensions.* Paris: OECD.

———, 1988b. *The Future of Social Protection.* Paris: OECD.

Smeeding, T., B. Torrey and M. Rein, 1988. "Patterns of Income and Poverty: The Economic Status of Children and the Elderly in Eight Countries." In J. Palmer, T. Smeeding and B. Torrey, eds., *The Vulnerable.* Washington, D. C.: Urban Institute Press, pp. 89–119.

World Bank, 1994. *Averting the Old Age Crisis.* Oxford: Oxford University Press.

PUBLIC PERSONNEL ADMINISTRATION.

The management of a system whereby public agencies recruit, compensate, and discipline their employees. The system is normally characterized by a watchdog differentiation between the structures that perform personnel tasks and structures that protect employee rights and insulate the process from politics.

Wallace Sayre, an expert in public administration, is widely cited as the source of the comment: public and private management systems are fundamentally alike in all unimportant ways (Henry 1995). Public personnel administration is illustrative of this truism because agencies must seek to sustain the highest levels of professionalism in their operations and yet be responsive to the desires of the elected officials whom they serve. Furthermore, the U.S. business culture produces ongoing pressures for government to be more efficient and effective according to the management trends of a particular era. Finally, government agencies must be more responsive than their private sector counterparts in removing any barriers to equality of opportunity because, like the majority, minority citizens are entitled to reasonable access to positions in government. These three themes of balancing merit and accountability, efficiency, and equity have shaped public personnel administration in the United States.

Professionalism Versus Politics

The German sociologist Max Weber (1946) noted in his writing on bureaucracy that a professionally trained administrative corps selected on the basis of individual merit is highly preferable to more traditional systems in which officials gain and retain their positions by virtue of birth or political sponsorship. Western nations began the conversion to professionalism during the nineteenth century. Great Britain undertook its administrative reforms in the 1850s. United States reform efforts in the 1880s were modeled on the British example. France embraced professionalism beginning with the rule of Napoleon. Ferrel Heady

noted, in his work on comparative administration (1991), that the career civil service in France has sustained the nation through multiple political and social upheavals. German professionalism was set in place during the Bismarck period in the nineteenth century. German career professionals have served each successive regime regardless of the morality of its guiding ideology.

Patronage and Merit Systems

Because the United States lacked a nobility whose members assumed hereditary positions, the principal obstacle to professionalization was the patronage system of rewarding faithful party members with jobs in government with little regard to their qualifications. Once in place, these patronage appointees engaged in widespread fraud, waste, and abuse. At the extremes, they would authorize payments for equipment and supplies that were never delivered. Another common practice was to pay inflated prices for shoddy work from contractors with whom they were politically affiliated. At the very least, the system often led to the appointment of unqualified persons who would collect government salaries for work that was done poorly or not at all.

To overcome the evils of patronage government adopted merit systems of selection. Under merit, administrative agencies recruit, screen, and appoint employees on the basis of their abilities and training. Merit systems explicitly prohibit the use of political affiliation in the selection of career employees. In Europe, especially France and Germany, this has led to an administrative corps recruited into the lowest professional echelons of the bureaucracy; they then spend their entire careers in government service. France has professional schools which train many of its professional bureaucrats. In both France and Germany, career officials enjoy exceptional levels of authority. In France, bureaucrats are even considered members of the ruling elite and often seek elected office upon retirement.

By contrast, the U.S. civil service was influenced by the Jacksonian notion that any person of normal intelligence was capable of successfully running the government. U.S. civil service systems, therefore, were characterized early on by provisions for persons to enter the bureaucracy laterally at the middle or upper echelons rather than serving their entire careers in government. As a practical matter, however, most current U.S. bureaucracies recruit at the entry level and then promote from within. Generally speaking, the only career professionals in the United States who have sought national elective office upon retirement have come from the military bureaucracy.

Civil Service Systems

U.S. bureaucracies at all levels of government are characterized by the existence of independent citizen commissions that are created to insulate the recruitment process from political interference. Frequently, these commissions oversee personnel bureaucracies that are responsible for all phases of the human resource management. Beginning in the 1970s, however, the merit system protection function frequently was separated from the administration of other personnel functions better to police the process.

The federal government created the United States Civil Service Commission in 1883 to insulate federal recruitment from political interference. The three members of the commission served overlapping terms and no more than two of them could be from a single political party. The object was to replace partisanship with merit in the recruiting process. Soon after, however, the reformers realized that satisfactory employees needed protection from arbitrary discharge if there was to truly be a merit system of government employment. Otherwise, a merit-protected employee could be removed for any reason other than politics and replaced with a partisan of the manager's choosing. This led Congress to adopt the principle of discharge only for cause in 1897 and strict due process protection in 1912 (Sylvia 1994).

The Second Civil Service Act of 1897 defined discharge for cause as removal only for misfeasance (doing the job incorrectly), malfeasance (violations of law or agency policy), or nonfeasance (not performing the duties of the job). Of course, any employee can be terminated if the agency must engage in layoffs to balance its budget. During layoffs, however, agencies must strictly adhere to the principle of seniority. Thus, a more senior satisfactory employee may not be laid off to preserve the employment of a less senior person. The rule is popularly known as "last hired first fired."

Due Process

The Fifth Amendment of the Constitution of the United States specifies that the government of the United States may not deprive citizens of life, liberty, or property without due process of law. Government employees who work under merit systems have been granted a property interest in their jobs by civil service legislation. Federal employees were granted due process protection in 1912 with the Lloyd-LaFollette Act. State and local governments have also adopted rigorous due process standards which have been upheld by the courts. When a supervisor is so dissatisfied with an employee that discharge is believed to be warranted, the supervisor must adhere to the agency's discharge procedures, which must meet certain legal standards prescribed by the courts. This protection is extended to state and local government employees by the Fourteenth Amendment. Because public agencies are also the government, their due process procedures must meet a much higher standard than any private employer.

The due process to which public employees are entitled covers agency actions before as well as after discharge.

Before a tenured civil servant can be removed, he or she must receive notice of the impending discharge, an explanation of the reasons for it, and the opportunity to respond to the charges. Thus, a state's civil service rules might specify that an employee must be given a written notice of an impending discharge ten days in advance of a meeting with the supervisor at which time the employee would be given a chance to explain why the discharge should not take place. These predischarge procedures are a check against making a mistake on the part of the supervisor who is acting for the agency. Post-discharge due process protections are even more elaborate.

Tenured employees are generally entitled to post-discharge hearings by an independent hearing examiner when they believe that the discharge was for a reason other than cause or that they did not receive appropriate pre-discharge protections. Some jurisdictions allow for an external review for suspensions and demotions as well as discharge.

Public employees paid a price for these elaborate protections from partisan political manipulations. Under the provisions of the Hatch Act of 1939, federal employees are prohibited from seeking partisan political office while employed by the government. They were prohibited from holding office in a political party and from giving funds to partisan political candidates. These so called Hatch prohibitions were subsequently adopted by state and local governments. Such insulation from partisan concerns was, in some cases, the result of the states own desires to root out the spoils system from program administration. Others passed legislation modeled on the federal Hatch prohibitions to comply with federal requirements that state agencies expend federal funds must use operate under merit systems. More recently, a number of states and the federal government have modified their Hatch rules to enhance the opportunities of public employees to participate in the political process.

Efficiency and Effectiveness

Governments reflect the values of the cultures that produce them. The founders, for example, believed strongly in representative democracy and limited government. The emergence of the industrial U.S. in the second half of the nineteenth and the early twentieth century led to the institutionalization of efficiency and effectiveness as the twin values against which U.S. bureaucracy would thenceforth be judged.

Merit systems have as their goal the selection of the best possible civil service corps (effectiveness). To achieve this, elaborate selection processes that include pencil and paper tests and extensive reference checks were developed that are to screen out the unworthy while searching for the one best person to do the job. These selection systems parallel industry's wholesale adoption of the methods of

Frederick Taylor, who believed there was one best way to perform every task. In merit systems, by extension, there must be one best person, if we can only develop systems to find him or her.

The efficiency value was reflected in the development of government classification systems that determine the value of an employee according to the duties, qualifications, and responsibilities prescribed for the position he or she occupies. Duties and responsibilities can be shifted, reassigned, or deleted as necessary to obtain the most efficient configuration to perform a given government function. The federal government undertook uniform classification of employees in 1923.

The selection and classification systems of the federal government were the responsibilities of the Civil Service commission until the government had grown so complex as to render a centralized classification system no longer efficient. The classification act of 1949 delegated the function to the agencies, although the commission retained oversight authority. The commission retained hegemony over the selection process until the Civil Service Reform Act of 1978, when selection too was delegated to the agencies.

Equal Employment Opportunity

The quest for social justice for African Americans, other minorities, and women led to fundamental legislative changes that impact on all phases of public intercourse including political participation and representation, housing, education, and employment. In addition to race, the 1964 Civil Rights Act prohibited discrimination on the basis of religion, ethnicity, color, and gender. Title VII of the Act specifically prohibits discrimination in any phase of employment. Title VII combined with various presidential orders to profoundly alter civil service systems in the United States.

In 1961, newly elected President John Kennedy issued an executive order instructing agencies to engage in self-examination to identify any artificial or fundamentally unfair barriers to minority employment in government. Agencies were also instructed to engage in affirmative action to remove barriers and to reach out to minority communities through such activities as offering the civil service entrance examination on the campuses of predominantly black colleges. President Johnson issued an executive order in 1965 that required government contractors to give assurances that they were equal employment opportunity employers as a condition in the contracting process. The Office of Contract Compliance was created within the Department of Labor to enforce the order.

Oversight of federal agency compliance was assigned to the Civil Service Commission in 1965 even though the Equal Employment Opportunity Commission (EEOC) existed to enforce laws against employment discrimination

in the rest of society. The Commission accepted the responsibility reluctantly to keep it out of the hands of the EEOC.

Responsibility for equal employment opportunity and affirmative action provided a built-in contradiction for the commission, which defined its mission as preservation of merit. While the commission struggled with its dilemma, line agencies moved more aggressively to enhance minority employment opportunities. In 1972, the commission reluctantly approved the first use of goals and timetables by the United States Army to increase minority employment. All in all the commission was never comfortable with its role in affirmative action, which in many ways conflicted with its more traditional role as protector of merit. Ultimately, equal employment opportunity enforcement was transferred to the Equal Employment Opportunity Commission under the provisions of the 1978 Civil Service Reform Act.

Affirmative action was for the commission another responsibility that asked it to police itself. Previously, responsibility for recruitment and merit protection had been identified as problematic for the Civil Service Commission by various blue ribbon groups as early as 1936. When it was revealed that commission staff had colluded with officials of the Nixon administration to circumvent the merit selection process, policymakers undertook the most sweeping reforms in almost one hundred years.

The 1978 Civil Service Reform Act

First and foremost, the act expanded the definition of merit. Originally, merit meant selection on the basis of qualifications and prohibited politics as a criterion for selection or discharge. In 1978, the definition was expanded to include equal employment opportunity, equal pay for equal work, efficiency and effectiveness in the use of the federal workforce, and whistleblower protection for those who report fraud, waste, abuse, or gross mismanagement. The act specified a number of structural reforms as well.

The Civil Service Commission was abolished. In its place, the act created an Office of Personnel Management that was directly accountable to the president. This office oversees the personnel process government wide. The act created a Merit System Protection Board to hear complaints of merit violations and employee appeals from adverse personnel actions. An Office of Special Counsel was created to investigate whistleblower charges of fraud waste and abuse or gross mismanagement. The act also created a federal Labor Relations Authority to oversee union management relations in the federal government. Significantly, enforcement authority for equal employment opportunity in federal agencies was transferred to the Equal Employment Opportunity Commission, which had enforced the various civil rights acts in the private sector since 1964. The goal of these changes was to create a government employment system that reflected modern U.S. values in employment fairness and government efficiency. In the latter regard, Congress sought to reassert authority over the bureaucracy by making top career officials directly accountable to the elected administrations for whom they work.

Senior Executive Service

The creation of the Senior Executive Service in 1978 may be the most significant alteration of relationships between career civil service employees and their politically appointed overseers in this century. Previously, the top three career grades were divided into ten steps much like lower level grades. Each year, satisfactory employees would advance a step within their grade.

Political appointees of an incoming administration would find themselves in what Hugh Heclo called "a government of strangers." Prior to 1978, new administrations would appoint secretaries and undersecretaries who were eager to put forward the administration's agenda. Their goals, however, could be frustrated by career officials at the top of the bureaucracy who did not agree with the administration. Career officers could frustrate political administrators, not by refusing to perform, but by doing so with an excruciating attention to detail and adherence to bureaucratic rules and procedures. Minimally sufficient compliance was protected by a myriad of civil service regulations that made it virtually impossible to remove them or to withhold merit pay increases.

Since the 1978 reforms, senior executives are collapsed into a single class in which pay is based upon performance and exceptional performers may receive one-time bonuses amounting to many thousands of dollars. To be eligible for these rewards, senior executives must distinguish themselves as program administrators and innovators of extraordinary abilities. Those who do not perform satisfactorily are subject to transfer or demotion back into the lower grades. This ability to remove substandard performers enables policymakers to carry out the mandates that brought their administration to power.

Maintaining one's place in the Senior Executive Service requires career officials to come up with policy initiatives and creative ways for achieving administration goals. When an administration's policies differ dramatically from the values of senior career executives, wholesale turnover in senior positions may occur. Such was the case, for example, when the Reagan administration attempted to depart dramatically from long established policies in the Department of Agriculture.

The blending of professionalization and policy accountability is not unique to the federal government. States such as California adopted systems to make senior career officials accountable to elected leaders years before the federal government. State level systems, moreover, make it easier to remove an uncooperative career official than the federal system. In California, for example, ten days' notice is all that is necessary to reassign a policymaking career official to a lesser position. Federal administrators, by contrast, cannot remove recalcitrant bureaucrats for the first 180 days of the administration.

Recent Events

For 12 years from 1976 to 1988 Presidents Carter and Reagan consistently criticized the federal government, and by extension federal employees, for bureaucratic waste and inefficiency. The 1978 reforms of the civil service system were, in part, a reflection of President Carter's cynicism about government. The Reagan presidency made broad-based attacks on domestic programs with which it disagreed. These resulted in accelerated retirements among senior career employees. And the Office of Personnel Management dramatically reduced federal retirement benefits, making the public service much less appealing than it had been previously.

President George Bush, a long-time public servant, recognized the need to reinvigorate the public service. To this end, he appointed a blue ribbon commission to address the problem. The Volker Commission on the Status of the Public Service reported in 1989 that morale was low and retirements were high. The best and the brightest were leaving government service and recruiting talented young people would prove problematic in the existing negative climate. The Volker Commission was particularly concerned about the ability of agencies to recruit Senior Executives from the ranks of midlevel career officials. The commission noted that continued shortages may cause a reconsideration of the program because, under current rules, 90 percent of an agency's senior executives must be recruited from the career service. Subsequent reforms undertaken by the Clinton administration sought to empower rank and file federal employees.

Reinventing Government

The U.S. fixation with efficiency and effectiveness again manifested itself in the Clinton administration's efforts to reinvent government. In 1993, President Clinton announced that Vice President Al Gore would personally lead a task force that would undertake a "National Performance Review." Among its goals were to hold public employees responsible for program outcomes. The administration also sought ways to cut cumbersome regulations and procedures that serve only to impede efficient program administration. The review also recommended the adoption of customer service orientations by agencies and, wherever practicable, the utilization of market dynamics to enhance agency performance.

An early and logical target for the review team was the cumbersome personnel policy and procedure manual of the federal service. During a hundred-odd years of civil service, the Civil Service Commission and the Office of Personnel Management created volumes of rules regulating every phase of personnel management. The result was thousands of pages of regulation that challenged the patience of administrators seeking to recruit, train, manage, and discipline career employees.

The Gore report proposed to replace the detailed regulations with broad standards that would allow agencies to develop their own procedures. The report recommended that OPM assist agencies as they seek to develop their own examinations and selection processes. The report further recommended that agency classification systems be streamlined. Finally, the report recommended that the rules whereby unsatisfactory employees are removed also be streamlined.

Delegation of selection procedures to the agencies was intended by the 1978 act. The adoption of standards that would allow agencies to develop their own policies and procedures could be accomplished by a presidential order. Altering the classification system or significantly changing the due process protections due federal employees both would require actions by Congress, which have not occurred at this writing.

Reforms of personnel systems have not been unique to the federal government. Many states have also taken the step of separating the personnel administration function from merit protection. Much of the movement to enhance managerial discretion and flexibility through a reduction in rules and regulations was initiated at the local level.

Future Trends

Public personnel systems have been periodically reexamined since their inception. In the future we can anticipate further modifications as professionalism continues to grow as a value regarding government. As the threat of patronage style corruption declines, administrators at all levels of government will be given additional flexibility in how they manage all segments of the peoples business including how career employees are recruited.

The decline of patronage, moreover, has led to a reenfranchisement of federal employees who may take a much more active role in politics than was possible under traditional civil service systems. In 1993, President Clinton signed into law legislation which greatly enhances the opportunities for federal employees to participate in the political process short of seeking partisan political office. While they must resign their positions before seeking partisan office, federal employees may contribute to candidates and participate in political campaigns. Much the same phenomenon has transpired at the state and local level, where career employees take an active part in the public lives of their communities.

We also can anticipate continuing pressure from those who seek further modification and expansion of equal employment protections for various groups who will organize and pressure legislatures at various levels to include their members under equal employment opportunity laws. Persons with disabilities, for example gained such protections under the 1991 Americans with Disabilities Act. Also in the 1990s, gay and lesbian groups gained state-level employment protections under California's equal employment statute. The public debate of the 1990s will doubtlessly continue to focus on affirmative action as those interests who oppose its additional expansion mobilize politically. In short, public personnel systems will continue to evolve along with the values of the culture in which the systems operate.

RONALD D. SYLVIA

BIBLIOGRAPHY

Ban, Carolyn and Norma M. Riccucci, eds., 1991. *Public Personnel Management.* New York: Longman Publishing.

Executive Office of the President, National Performance Review, 1993. *From Red Tape to Results: Creating Government That Works Better and Costs Less.* Washington, D.C.: U.S. Government Printing Office.

Heady, Ferrel, 1991. *Public Administration: A Comparative Perspective.* 4th ed. New York: Marcel Dekker, Inc.

Heclo, Hugh, 1977. *A Government of Strangers.* Washington, D.C.: The Brookings Institution.

Henry, Nicholas, 1995. *Public Administration and Public Affairs.* 6th ed. Englewood Cliffs, NJ: Prentice Hall.

Ingraham, Patricia W. and David H. Rosenbloom, eds., 1992. *The Promise and Paradox of Civil Service Reform.* Pittsburgh, PA: University of Pittsburgh Press.

Klingner, Donald E. and John Nalbandian, 1993. *Public Personnel Management: Contexts and Strategies.* 3d ed. Englewood Cliffs, NJ: Prentice Hall.

National Commission on the Public Service Task Force, 1989. *Rebuilding the Public Service.* Washington, D.C.: National Commission on the Public Service.

Sylvia, Ronald D., 1994. *Public Personnel Administration.* Belmont, CA: Wadsworth.

Taylor, Frederick W., 1967. *The Principles of Scientific Management.* New York: Norton.

Thompson, Frank J., ed., 1979. *Classics of Public Personnel Administration.* Oak Park, IL: Moore Publishing.

Weber, Max, 1946. *Essays in Sociology.* Trans. by H. H. Gerth and C. Wright Mills. New York.: Oxford University Press.

PUBLIC POLICY ANALYSIS. A methodology that "uses multiple methods of inquiry and argument to produce and transform policy-relevant information that may be utilized in political settings to resolve public problems" (Dunn 1991). During the past three decades, policy analysis has been one of the fastest growing specializations in the social sciences in the United States. It has also become a small-scale industry. Millions of dollars are spent each year on the analytical evaluation of domestic and foreign policies–from welfare reform and environmental protection to international aid and military defense. In the process, policy analysts conduct evaluations for a diverse set of groups: the executive office of the presidency, legislative committees staffs, cabinet agencies, political interest groups, policy think tanks, academic social scientists, and private consulting forms, among others. Whether the intent is to document the accomplishments of government or to criticize its failures, there is today almost always a study available that addresses the issue to make the case. Policy analysis has emerged as an important component of the policymaking process in American government.

Specifically, policy analysis is designed to supply information about complex social and economic problems and to assess the processes through which their resolution is pursued. It can focus on policy program outcomes ("outcome" or "impact" analysis) or on the processes by which a policy program is formulated and implemented ("process" analysis). Moreover, such analysis can either focus on the outcome expected to result from a policy (ex ante analysis), or on the actual results from its introduction (ex post analysis). As such, public policies can be evaluated at all phases of the policymaking process: in the identification and articulation of policy problems, in the formulation of alternative policy options, the discussion of the feasibility of policy adoption, the implementation of particular policy choices, or at the termination of a policy to determine its final impact. Ideally, policy analysis provides politicians and citizens with an intelligent basis for discussing and judging conflicting ideas, proposals, and outcomes.

The use of social science methods to analyze public policies is a relatively recent phenomenon. Until the late 1950s, the systematic investigation of policy issues was carried out on a small scale and was seldom a formal part of the policy process. Since then various intellectual developments have combined with political developments to give rise to the field of policy analysis, which in a very short period of time became a major focus of the social sciences (deLeon 1989). Although it is difficult to pinpoint a single stimulus behind the intellectual origins of the discipline or field, the publication of *The Policy Orientation* in 1951 by Harold Lasswell and Daniel Lerner is generally acknowledged to constitute the formal academic beginning of the policy research movement. The goal of the new endeavor was ambitious: it was to be nothing less than the "policy science of democracy," a discipline "directed toward the knowledge needed to improve the practice of democracy" (Lasswell and Lerner, 1951). Lasswell envisioned the creation of a broadly interdisciplinary approach that would include a diverse range of scientific inputs, from anthropological research to the application of methods from the physical sciences, mathematics and statistics in particular. He further envisioned a discipline focused as much on the

analysis of the policymaking process as on the analysis of policy outcomes.

In spite of these lofty intellectual beginnings, policy analysis today is more typically identified with more pragmatic political and academic developments of the 1960s. Specifically, it is closely associated with President Lyndon Johnson's Great Society and the War on Poverty program. During the Johnson years, social-scientific policy analysis was widely celebrated as the proper basis for decisionmaking in public policy. As one leading policy writer put it, "research was touted as a determinant in and of itself of new policy directions, or at least as an input with a presumed special claim and higher standing than others in the policymaking process."

During this period, policy analysis developed as a rigorous empirical methodology designed to support the "rational model" of policy decisionmaking. The rational model of decisionmaking and the empirical approach to policy analysis closely mirror one another. The model is typically outlined in five methodological steps: (1) decisionmakers first empirically identify the existence of a problem; (2) they formulate the goals and objectives that would lead to an optimal solution; (3) they determine the relevant consequences and probabilities of alternative means to the solution; (4) they assign a value, that is, a numerical cost or benefit to each consequence; (5) finally, they combine the information about consequences, probabilities, and costs and benefits, and select the most efficient and effective alternative.

Built around concepts and methods adapted from the natural and physical sciences, policy analysis emerged as a commitment to develop empirical knowledge about specific social and economic problems, as well as the processes of governmental intervention. As scientific findings, such knowledge could be generally applied to a wide range of social problem-solving contexts. For example, if policy scientists were to command a body of empirically tested propositions about the concepts and variables related to family planning, they could use such findings to help either promote or restrict such activities in the population as a whole. For policy analysts, as applied scientists, the decision to promote or hinder family planning is a value question (concerned with what "ought" to be the case) that falls beyond the realm of empirical social science (concerned with what "is" the case). Deciding such "ought" questions is a task that belongs to politically elected officials. Policy analysis, so defined, concerns itself only with questions concerning how to carry out politically established goals efficiently and effectively.

The field's empirical orientation is quickly gleaned from any standard policy analysis textbook. The topics include empirical research designs, the measurement of outcomes, the use of sampling techniques, data gathering procedures, and the development of causal models with predictive power (Putt and Spring 1989). Such concerns are manifested in a collection of empirical-analytical techniques: cost-benefit analysis, quasi-experimental research designs, multiple regression analyses, survey research, mathematical simulation models, and systems analysis (Sylva *et al.* 1991).

The two most standard methodologies are experimental evaluation research and cost-benefit analysis. The methodology of experimental evaluation research constitutes the ideal logic of rigorous scientific assessment. Sometimes referred to as "evaluation research" in the policy literature, experimental research represents the formal application of the scientific method to the social action context of public programs. Pioneered in large part by applied psychologists, especially those concerned with the evaluation of educational programs, experimental research focuses on the identification of the basic policy objectives, and the relevant consequences that result from following them. Often termed "impact" evaluation or analysis, such research emphasizes those aspects of the problem situation or target situation that are to be changed by the program, the measurement of their state before the introduction of a program, and their measurement again after completion of the program.

Typically, evaluation research involves four basic steps. First, it requires the specification of one or more programmatic objectives as the criteria for analysis. For example, a job training program with a goal of preparing unemployed people for new work careers might have instruction for jobs in word processing as one of its specific objectives. Second, once one or more objectives have been identified, it is necessary to find or develop quantitative indicators that appropriately measure them. For instance, an empirical indicator of academic success for a skills enhancement program might be the percentage of students who obtain a C average or higher at the end of a reporting period. Third, after the indicators have been selected the next task is to determine the appropriate target population and the corresponding sample for evaluation. The target population is defined in terms of the program under consideration; the sample is chosen to represent the population. In the final step of the research the task is to analyze the data collected after the experiment has been carried out. In the language of research methodology, a hypothesis is tested to determine whether the program has an effect on various conditions and factors which are constitutive of the program in question. If a program is effective, the statistical presentation of experimental data should show a positive correlation between the program and the experimental group's responses. Statistical procedures are used to analyze the variance between control and experimental groups.

Once an outcome of a program has been empirically established—by experimental or nonexperimental methods—policy analysis can further measure it in terms of cost-benefit analysis. That is, the program's inputs can be measured against the "costs" accrued in achieving it. Whereas evaluation research focuses on the calculation of program consequences, cost-benefit analysis assigns numerical costs and benefits to the inputs and outputs and calculates in monetary terms the most efficient of the alternative programs. The basic objective is to determine whether an investment of funds in a program is economically advantageous. In more sophisticated analyses, the method is also used to identify the policy goal that benefits the largest number of people in the society as a whole.

The idea of cost-benefit analysis is conceptually simple. The analyst first identifies the monetary costs of the input factors needed to accomplish a particular program, then assigns monetary values to the estimated or actual outcomes associated with the programs, and finally calculates the efficiency of the program as a ratio of costs accrued to benefits produced. An efficient program is one in which the benefits outweigh the cost. In using cost-benefit analysis to formulate public policy the decisionmaker relies on a specific type of ethical decision rule based on the theory of "utilitarianism," often referred to as the principle of the "greatest good for the greatest number."

Cost-benefit analysis can also be delineated in four steps. The first step involves defining who pays for and benefits from a program. The payees and beneficiaries of a program may be a social group, neighborhood, city, state, or society as a whole. In most cases, this is determined by the type of policy under consideration. Most typically, the beneficiaries of a policy are limited to those with some direct involvement in the program, for example, those who have completed a job training program. After the target groups have been identified, step two deals with assigning monetary values to the inputs and outputs. The costs tend to be easier to monetarize than the benefits. The latter often involves assigning values to such things as scenic beauty and human life, for which there are neither readily available indicators or moral agreement. Step three involves discounting the costs and benefits to account for the fact that things like equipment and buildings tend to lose value as they grow older, while other items may become more valuable. Step four, the final step of the cost-benefit analysis is the calculation of a cost-benefit ratio. The cost-benefit ratio provides a single numeric value that summarizes the relationship between costs and benefits. Ratios of less than 1.0 mean that costs exceed benefits and ratios above 1.0 mean that benefits exceed costs.

Policy analysis has not been without its critics. The primary concern stems from the fact that the field has often been unable to provide the kinds of useful findings that it has largely promised. Numerous studies have shown that much of the policy analysis that has been generated has not been used in any direct way in the policy decision-making process. It is a concern that has led scholars to ask what constitutes usable knowledge. Some of these scholars have focused on how better to coordinate policy research with the needs of decisionmakers. Others, however, have located the problem deeper in the empirical methods of policy analysis. For these writers the problem lies in policy analysis's technocratic understanding of the policymaking process. Policy analysts, they argue, have generally privileged technical analysis over political modes of thought and inquiry, a point reflected in the field's separation of empirical and normative inquiry. They have, as such, failed to appreciate the extent to which political reason reflects a different kind of knowledge with its own logic and purposes. In doing so, policy analysts are seen to rule out much of what is important to political decisionmakers. All too often they have provided information relevant mainly to the questions of lesser importance. The major political questions of the day are frequently beyond the purview of the endeavor. A growing number of scholars are rethinking the methodological foundations of the field. For them new ways must be found to bring the normative dimensions of policy more squarely into the research process itself. This question remains one of the important epistemological challenges for the future of the discipline.

FRANK FISCHER

BIBLIOGRAPHY

deLeon, Peter, 1989. *Advice and Consent: The Development of the Policy Sciences.* New York: Russell Sage Foundation.

Dunn, William N., 1991. *Introduction to Policy Analysis.* Englewood Cliffs, NJ: Prentice-Hall.

Fischer, Frank, 1995. *Evaluating Public Policy.* Chicago: Nelson-Hall.

Gramlich, Edward M., 1990. *A Guide to Cost-Benefit Analysis.* Englewood Cliffs, NJ: Prentice-Hall.

Lassell, Harold D. and Daniel Lerner, eds., 1951. *The Policy Sciences: Recent Developments in Scope and Methods.* Stanford, CA: Stanford University Press.

Putt, Allen D. and Springer, J. Fred, 1989. *Policy Research: Concepts, Methods, and Applications.* Englewood Cliffs, NJ: Prentice-Hall.

Silva, Ronald D., Kenneth J. Meier, and Elizabeth Gunn, 1991. *Program Planning and Evaluation for Public Managers.* Prospect Heights, IL: Waveland Press.

PUBLIC POLICY ENTREPRENEUR.

One who is innovative and imaginative in altering stated policy goals, procedures, and objectives in ways that enhance the efficiency and effectiveness of public programs.

The public policy entrepreneur has been referred to as a "role type." Derived from the term "role theory," a role type characterizes certain generalized behavior (or roles) associated with particular individuals in organizational settings. The role of public policy entrepreneur may be acted out by individuals in positions to influence government policy whether they be administrators, elected politicians, street level bureaucrats, political executives such as cabinet secretaries and city managers, or even individuals with positions outside government.

In other words, the role of public policy entrepreneur may transcend other role types individuals choose to portray which are more or less restricted to the position one holds. This is why Palumbo and Maynard-Moody (1991) define a role as "a particular set of exceptions and behaviors associated with an office or position" (pp. 107–108).

In private sector management, the term "entrepreneur" refers to one who manages or assumes the risk of running a business where success or failure is tied to one's financial security. Public servants, on the other hand, do not assume such monetary risks or reap such monetary rewards when successful. Instead, their rewards are primarily intrinsic.

When successful, the public policy entrepreneur receives acclaim and recognition from certain segments of government and from the public for his or her insight and innovative ability to get things done. This is especially true when that change brings about undisputed positive results. On the other hand, when the public policy entrepreneur experience failure, the opposite is true and he or she must carry the burden for an unsuccessful, if not misguided, policy agenda. This burden may be exacerbated if the public policy entrepreneur's campaign came at an exorbitant monetary cost to the taxpayer and/or a political cost to those in government who supported the campaign for change.

If the public policy entrepreneur is a middle manager or street level bureaucrat, for example, the risk of failure may be more severe. This is because in the U.S. system of government, middle managers and street level bureaucrats are expected to implement policy and leave the formulation of public policy to elected politicians, and on some occasions to political executives. As a result, the middle manger or street level bureaucrat who chooses to step outside of his or her traditional role and take on the added role of public policy entrepreneur may suffer greater career setbacks, including retaliation by his or her superiors if those superiors were not in agreement with the campaign for change which proved to be unsuccessful.

The term public policy entrepreneur may at first appear to be a contradiction in the context of the many public sector obstacles that serve to impede innovative change and preserve the status quo. This is especially true in presidential regimes, such as in the United States, where an intricate system of separation of powers and checks and balances provides, if not encourages, numerous veto opportunities.

Even in parliamentary systems such as Great Britain, where the U.S. system of separation of powers does not exist and the executive derives its power from the legislature, the public policy entrepreneur still must cultivate public opinion, which in both regimes plays a significant role in determining policy outcomes. The public policy entrepreneur works within the political system, oftentimes galvanizing support from the grassroots, and from there building coalitions of support to convince lawmakers and the courts that the public either demands, or desperately needs, the type of change he or she is proposing.

Paula J. King and Nancy C. Roberts (1987) conclude that public policy entrepreneurs must also be conceptual leaders, strategists, and political activists. The function of conceptual leader is where new ideas are generated. The strategist is able to orchestrate successful plans to put ideas into action. The function of political activist involves a manipulation of the political system to bring about the ideal situation to push forward with one's plan of action.

Theodore Marmor and Phillip Fellman (1986) contend that public policy entrepreneurs must be both strongly committed to policy ideals and equally strong managers in order to be successful in achieving their objectives. It is this trait that separates the public policy entrepreneur from the "political zealot" who may be strongly committed to a policy ideal but lacks the patience and political skill to turn ideas into reality. One reason is that many public policy entrepreneurs spend their entire careers in one policy area and therefore develop a higher level of expertise and influence within that particular arena.

Although some public policy experts might disagree, Dennis Palumbo, Michael Musheno, and Steven Maynard-Moody (1986) claim that public policy entrepreneurs are shakers and doers who "must go beyond the narrow rules" or confines of government to be successfully creative (pp. 69–82). The authors also recognize that, if true, such conditions present situations where public policy entrepreneurs may produce as much harm as good.

An example of a positive policy outcome brought about by going beyond the "limits of government" is the success of United States President Franklin Delano Roosevelt (1882–1945) in bringing the nation out of the Great Depression in the 1930s. This was done with the help of what the authors refer to as "several unconstitutional programs" as well as Roosevelt's unsuccessful attempt to pack the Supreme Court with justices more favorable to his policy agenda. This "court-packing scheme" caused those on the court to become more accommodating and cease declaring the programs unconstitutional.

On the negative flip side is the "Iran-Contra Affair" in 1986 where Colonel Oliver North and other officials in the National Security Council, in their zeal to support the anti-Communist Contra rebel forces in Nicaragua, violated the United States' constitutional provision of "separation of powers" by selling military arms to the Iranians and then illegally funneling the funds from the sale of the arms to the Contra rebels. The United States Congress had decided against providing aid to the Contras due to reported human rights violations. U.S. public opinion at the time was also against United States involvement.

In light of the activities of the National Security Council, efforts to tighten restrictions on government officials surfaced. As a result, the Tower Commission (1987) concluded that "It is not possible to make a system immune from error without paralyzing its capacity to act" (p. 4). In other words, the commission realized that implementing measures to hold public officials more accountable would, in the process, restrict their ability to act imaginatively, and that imagination, innovation, and creativity are essential for government to work effectively.

It is clear that numerous public policy entrepreneurs are successful in their efforts to bring about policy innovation and substantive change without violating the rules of government. On the other hand, there may be tragic situations where government resistance to positive change may demand stretching those rules. Such was the case with President Franklin Delano Roosevelt, who through his "fireside chats" utilized public opinion to help convince Congress and eventually the Supreme Court to approve his New Deal policies and help bring the nation out of the Great Depression.

JAMES D. WARD

BIBLIOGRAPHY

King, Paula J. and Nancy C. Roberts, 1987. "Policy Entrepreneurs: Catalysts for Policy Innovation." *Journal of State Government,* vol. 60:172–178.

Marmor, Theodore and Phillip Fellman, 1986. "Policy Entrepreneurship in Government: An American Study." *Journal of Public Policy,* vol. 6, no. 3; 225–253.

Palumbo, Dennis, Michael Musheno, and Steven Maynard-Moody, 1986. "Public Sector Entrepreneurs: The Shakers and Doers of Program Innovation." In Joseph W. Wholey, Mark A. Abramson, and Christopher Bellavita, eds., *Performance and Credibility: Developing Excellence in Public and Nonprofit Organizations.* Lexington, MA: Lexington Books, pp. 69–82.

Palumbo, Dennis and Steven Maynard-Moody, 1991. *Contemporary Public Administration.* White Plains, NY: Longman Publishing Group.

Tower, John, Edmund Muskie, and Brent Scowcroft, 1987. *The Tower Commission Report.* New York: Times Books.

PUBLIC SECTOR ADMINISTRATIVE RE-FORMS.   The efforts to improve the quality of public management and the creation of a New Public Management (NPM).

Recent Public Sector Administrative Reforms

The wide use of this term, which has taken place since the late 1970s, indicates not only conformity on the symbolic level, but also an actual convergence of the recent bureaucracy reform agendas in most of the OECD countries. Terms such as "search for excellence," "quality management," "public sector productivity," and "organizational well-performing," which are used alongside the dominating label (NPM), do not mark different types of reform, but suggest that NPM embraces a variety of very similar reform strategies and concepts (Aucin 1990; Hood 1990; Pollitt 1990; Reichard 1993). The attempt at improving the availability and quality of public services can be found as a common denominator at the center of all these developments. This goal is to be attained by shifting from bureaucratic to managerial structures and methods with an emphasis on entrepreneurial behavior.

The Rise of NPM as a "New Paradigm" of Public Administration

Since the mid-1980s there has been a common trend to redefine the understanding of the role of the state and public administration in society in many of the industrialized countries. The following predominant subjects are the main points on the reform agenda (Caiden 1991; Marcou and Verebelyi 1993; OECD 1990–1993; Reichard 1993):

- *A state cutback*: A reflection on the core tasks of public administration, a critical check and abandonment of responsibilities, privatization, functioning more as a provider or enabler and less as the producer of services.
- *Continued democratization efforts*: Improved possibilities of citizens' participation, more orientation towards the needs of clients and citizens.
- *Deregulation and decentralization*: Cutback of rules and central supervision, more freedom to act on the community level, debureaucratization, orientation towards market-type mechanisms and competition, contracting out, public-private partnership, invitation of tenders.
- *Reorganization of the public sector also internally*: Independence of organizational units and new (businesslike) management concepts, responsibility for results, controlling.
- *Improvement of financial and personnel management*: Result-orientated and flexible budgeting, global budgets, internal cost accounting, a more performance-oriented personnel policy and pay, personnel development.

When combined, these subjects of administrative reform indicate a serious gap in modernization and performance in the public sector as an international problem. Thus the discussion led to the conclusion that a "new paradigm" in public administration was necessary (Banner 1993; Reinermann 1993). This renewal of public service means a general change in the culture of public organizations from bureaucracy to a management oriented toward efficiency and effectiveness.

To speak of a new paradigm in public administration means that there is a fundamentally new concept in all the countries approaching an administrative modernization. All approaches at an administrative reform of tasks, organization, personnel, and financial matters have a great deal

in common, but there are nevertheless specific differences in approaching solutions depending on national administrative cultures, levels, and types of administration (OECD 1990–1993).

To understand the overall concept and general goal of the NPM paradigm of administration as well as the national and structural variations of different NPM approaches, it is helpful first to have a look at the causes of the reform movement before turning to the specifics.

Driving Forces and Theoretical Background

With a striking uniformity two main driving forces can be traced behind the current public sector modernization. The main problem the public sector of all highly developed industrial nations has to cope with is an economic crisis that causes a chronic shortage of finance (OECD 1993b) and a thorough societal value change aiming at self-actualization, which leads citizens to be more critical and demanding with regard to public services. Because of these two different influences which force the public sector of all developed nations to modernize, the NPM can be said to be money-driven as well as value-driven. Considering this fact, it is obvious that the NPM's typical aim is reconciling and combining the perhaps conflicting goals to create cheaper (or "leaner") services that are nevertheless more customer- and/or citizen-oriented.

Concerning the economic crisis, a heightened awareness of the expansion of public bureaucracies combined with increasing costs of public services and of massive public deficits has brought the role of the state up for discussion. This discussion has been concentrated on the questions of whether services should be delivered by the public or the private sector, and whether the state should act as a provider or as an enabler only. As a consequence of a growing social and civic sensitivity, governmental and administrative behavior and decisionmaking, particularly on a local level, are more keenly evaluated by the citizens based on personal quality and utility assessments. Therefore public administration has to be more responsive to the citizens' demands by supplying more value for money, freedom of choice, flexibility, and transparency. Since the societal value change has also affected the personnel of the public sector, there is an increased requirement for devolving and delegating responsibilities for decisionmaking on the utilization of resources in order to ensure work motivation. Therefore new requirements for guaranteeing the consistency of policies and organizational cohesiveness by soft but efficacious coordinating mechanisms have been evolved.

Following the twofold nature of its subject and of the driving forces behind it, the theoretical background of NPM can be considered to have two main roots. Most of the NPM doctrines can be traced back on the one hand to the ideas of New Institutional Economics (NIE)–that is, the theory of public choice (see Mascarenas 1993)–and on the other hand to the business-type Managerial Movement (see Aucin 1990).

The new Institutional Economics delivered the ideas of contest, user choice, transparency, and of focusing attention upon incentive structures. Many NPM doctrines are built upon these ideas. In particular, the intention to achieve a smooth relationship between public organizations and external actors and to offer incentives to the employees bears the influence of the NIE. On the other hand, the impact of "New Managerialism," focused on professional proficiency, can be discovered behind the NPM doctrines. New Managerialism means that leaders should be free to manage in order to achieve provable results, guided by the insight that the improvement of organizational performance can only be achieved through a development of organizational culture.

Consequently the theoretical background of the NPM can be seen as a movement towards a more economical rationality in public administration. Market forces and monetary incentives should spread out their stimulating and directing powers. Public services should be understood as service industries with an entrepreneurial resource and result management.

So the theoretical backroun of the NPM is based upon ideas of a neoconservative or liberal economic policy (Thatcher, Reagan, etc.), particularly the NIE. Thus it can also be understood as a political-ideological movement (Reichard 1993). This seems to be true especially in the British case. But on the other hand it is not only conservative governments who promote NPM approaches. For example, in Australia and New Zealand Labor governments forced the NPM reform (Damkowski and Precht 1995). Thus the intention to overcome the performance deficits in public services, and not a modification of the allocation of power, in society seems to be at the top of the list.

Main Characteristics of Recent Administrative Reforms

Considering the characteristics of the NPM, it has to be observed that recent administrative reforms are consequently concentrated on the introduction of internal markets, charges, vouchers, franchising and contracting-out practices. The immediate rationale for such measures is the desire to foster competition and choice in the public services, as well as to provide for a response to the more restricted economic conditions, and to cope with the need to control public expenditure.

The prevalence of managerial and economic premises is clearly demonstrated by the general principles of administrative reforms, summarized by Christopher Hood (1991). The seven characteristics discerned by Hood are newly structured into the following five elements in order to avoid overlaps:

More responsibility. There has to be more accountability in public organizations through the clear assignment of action. Professional management tries to (re)establish control to leadership, which needs to be accountable for its decisions.

Flexibility in human resource and financial management. Proven private sector management tools and techniques have to be imported. In consequence, this means a shift from beaureaucratic administration to more flexibility in hiring and rewarding, as well as to more public relations in government.

To limit or cut (direct) cost and to raise labor discipline, resource demands must be checked continuously, because in general there is a constraint to do more with less.

Performance-based culture and quality measurement. To foster accountability, clear statements of goals are needed. Likewise, the enhancement of efficiency necessitates a consistent observation of objectives. Instead of heading toward rather abstract rules, there has to be a greater emphasis on goals, targets, contracts, incentives, or indicators, which can serve as explicit standards and measures of performance, and should be, if possible, expressed in quantitative terms.

Consequently there should be an intensified focus on output controls, because the allocation of rewards and resources has to be linked to measured success or results and not only to input requests or requirements.

Decentralization. Another remarkable trend is the disaggregation of units. The intention is to divide large organizations that are difficult to survey into manageable units—possibly by privatization or quasi-privatization—that are able to develop individual strategies and courses of action to a grater extent. These units are to be structured around their products; they should operate on decentralized budgets, and they should be allowed to make contracts with other public or private organizations.

Deregulation and reregulation. Competition is used more and more in the public sector as a tool to lower costs and improve performance standards, which can be compared to those achieved in a market-economy system. A movement to term contracts and to develop public tendering procedures takes place. This is a shift from the direct regulation of decisions to a regulation of the conditions of decisionmaking.

The differentiated subject matters and targets listed above reflect the complicated situation the public sector faces today, as well as the giant task of impending administrative reforms and the difficulties that have to be solved.

Administrative reform appears to be an ongoing movement for the foreseeable future. Most of the countries approaching administrative reform reported to the OECD that they have not yet attained their reform goals and objectives (OECD 1993b). Many countries are lingering between the feeling of suffering from insufficient progress and the danger of hectic overwork, without knowing what will happen afterwards.

Evaluation, Monitoring, and the Relation to the Political Arena as Common Difficulties

Since NPM emphasizes the quality of performance and consequently increasing result assessment, the absence of an adequate systematic monitoring and evaluation of public sector management reforms, in particular of the extent of management improvements, appears to be a major problem (OECD 1993b).

This statement is valid for the outcomes and results of broader political reform programs and also for the implementation of more specific programs. Even if the monitoring of programs is carried out more often, as often happens in the English-speaking countries, the controlling of policymaking by program evaluation and cost-benefit analysis is the exception to the rule. Most attempts at comprehensive performance measurement and monitoring on a program level are based upon the budgeting process and concentrated upon comparing the achieved results with invested financial resources, thereby accomplishing input measurement only. The main obstacles for improvements of evaluating concepts and procedures are presently deficiencies of political decisionmaking, the absence of clear specifications or goals of reform programs, and the lack of management of change.

Thus, the prevailing problems in the field of applied measurement are to be found in the difficulty of setting clear objectives and identifying measurable outputs without causing unreasonable costs. One particular problem of evaluation is the lack of quantifiable measures which are easy to apply. Many difficulties exist in measuring productivity, efficiency and service delivery. Additionally there are problems in determining the gap between aims and results by collecting and analysing comparable data.

Difficulties also arise in connection with the attempt at estimating or measuring the impact of reform programs. In every institution there is some sort of "natural" resistance against organizational change. This includes the fact that the groups involved in the institution have different priorities. This problem is particularly serious in the political arena, where the different interests and demands of organized groups have to be balanced. As a result, there often exists a preponderance of fragmented individual projects instead of an orientation toward a broad reform.

The implementation of reform programs is frequently restrained because of the absence of a political consensus. The allocation of responsibilities between managers and politicians concerning reform issues is also sometimes unclear. Moreover, there are a lot of reasons for a conflict between short-term payoffs and long-term objectives that are not obtainable within the intervals between the elections.

A lack of incentives is another source of problems on the operational level. For instance, ground-floor agencies, which are pressed to achieve a reduction of spending anyway, cannot easily be convinced that additional efforts to save resources will serve their own interests. A lack of incentives will also be experienced where reform results are mainly attributed to the central units in charge, thereby neglecting the initiatives of the performing divisions.

Another widely recognized problem is the changing or even intensifying workload of the public sector staff that is bound up to administrative reforms. There is a lot of demoralization and uncertainty because of the change of individual skills and personal relationships which NPM administrative reforms imply. New demands in management skills are required from civil servants and senior officials, whereas their traditionally important and prestige-bearing skills are devaluated.

Moreover, serious problems arise where private sector working conditions are to be transferred into the public sphere. There are lots of agreed salary scales and constraints imposed by law in the somehow overprotected public sector. Very often there is not enough flexibility to reward exceptional performance by granting additional payments, so that symbolic rewards may be a last resort.

In view of the serious problems that are bound up with current administrative reforms, one has to ask the question why NPM could nevertheless become such a sweeping success.

Trying to answer this question, one has to go back to the main driving forces of the NPM movement. Considering the desperate financial situation of most of the public organizations and in view of the growing frustration of people inside and outside the public sector, everyone involved in public affairs had to agree that "something had to happen." In other words, there was a broad and general need for change. The success of NPM is due to the fact that it offered a framework of general applicability which can claim to suit the needs of every kind and level of administration.

The second reason for the success of NPM is that it can claim to be politically neutral. It has been presented as an apolitical framework that can serve to pursue different values and functions within multiple political priorities. The new management system has been offered as an universally applicable tool that can be used to strive at various political goals and can be accommodated to various settings (Hood 1991).

Variations of the NPM Pattern Caused by Practical Application

The shift from bureaucratic administration to businesslike professional management was promoted as a strategy fitting for all levels, and branches of the public sector, local as well as central governments, and every kind of administrative culture in any country whatever. NPM has been presented as a remedy to cure management ills in various organizational contexts, as well as in various areas of policymaking, from education to health care, from helping the poor to pleasing the rich.

According to its general applicability in various settings, the style of NPM obviously differs depending on the political and historical conditions of administrative cultures under which it has to operate.

Therefore, it should be obvious that NPM is not a monolithic administrative reform doctrine that appears similar in all countries, governmental levels, and agencies. According to specific (political) goals or national administrative cultures, NPM approaches differ in two main respects. First, there are substantial differences in the role the state takes on in the process of reform and second, there are essential differences in the orientation of reform: the targeted subject matters with which to improve efficiency and goal attainment in public services. In both respects (dimensions of reform) three variations of typical NPM reform approaches can be observed (Reichard 1993).

The role of the state can be classified depending on the engagement or the involvement of central government authority:

A.1: *An autocratic top-down approach with a mandatory implementation strategy and supervision by central government.* Reform action has its origin at the central government level and pressure is exerted on subordinated authorities to join the reform approach.

A.2: *A participative approach with support from the central government level for subsequent levels.* Reforms are fostered by central governments through the creation of basic conditions. Authorities are allowed to conduct experiments, which are now permissible in law, and have more independence due to decentralization, giving more responsibilities and duties to local authorities or communities.

A.3: *An isolated bottom-up approach mainly on the community level.* Reforms occur without (notable) support from higher authorities and with fewer reform efforts on the central level or none at all.

The orientation of NPM reform subject matters is mainly different in the way the public sector (the state) tries to benefit from the private sector. The following typical patterns of learning from the private sector can be observed:

B.1: *Inner authority use of business management tools.* Some NPM approaches are concentrated on the adoption and use of private sector business practices to improve the performance of public organizations. Public management is to be developed by the use of techniques such as controlling, budgeting, human resource development, and the development of public accountancy (introduction of a businesslike accountancy).

B.2: *Adoption of private enterprise structures and market-type mechanisms in the public sector.* This means a focus of reform efforts on a renewal of the relations between different public sector units (offices), authorities, levels, and politics and administration. Public organizations (e.g., communi-

ties) are transformed into combines (companylike groups) with entrepreneurial service structures. Authorities become partially independent agencies (sometimes as limited companies), responsible for their resources and results. Tasks and performance quality and quantity of agencies are defined by (temporal) contracts.

Internal public sector units function providers or purchasers. Goods and services are exchanged by offering and ordering them (internally of public services) and performances are credited or debited on cost based prices. Competition should be encouraged, for example through benchmarking.

B.3: *Orientation of public services toward their (market) environment.* Introducing competition by giving authorities or departments with demands the choice to purchase performances either from internal public or private providers ("make or buy decisions"); contracting out of tasks and services which are cheaper or better delivered by private enterprises; calling out public orders for tender; state cutbacks by transferring tasks to the private sector through privatization; more participation of citizens through client or citizen surveys, direct forms of democracy (propositions), mediation, and so forth.

This differentiation of reform approaches into two reform dimensions (role of the state, reform orientation) with three distinct patterns in each dimension has an analytical character. An analytical approach towards systematization has been chosen in the present context, first to draw attention to typical, characteristic, important, or interesting reform attempts, and second because not all of the existing single approaches could be mentioned, nor was it possible to deal with all of their details.

Actual approaches (in reality) have many facets. They comprise aspects of both dimensions and most contain elements from at least two of the dimension patterns. This problem is particularly relevant in the case of organizationally independent bodies such as agencies or limited liability companies.

The transformation of administrative bodies into agencies or similar institutions makes them widely independent institutions. Agencies are mostly equipped with global budgets and thus responsible for the employment of their resources (funds, personnel, material). Because of this, a renewal of the internal structures and external relations of the organizations becomes possible. Internally there is the opportunity to use business practices, such as business accountancy systems and entrepreneurial financial and personnel management. Relations with clients/customers might be defined on a more commercial basis. Supervision of higher authorities could be exercised less by detailed decisions and handicaps and more by the control of results and the measurement of goal attainment.

Additionally, there is the opportunity to open the "market" of such independent institutions (agencies) to private enterprises. Through the forces of competition, pressure is to be exerted upon public managers in order to improve the performance of organizations or to reduce production. Thereby, a lowering of public expenditures and/or an improvement of service quality is to be achieved.

However, the formation of independent administrative bodies as such and the introduction of free-market conditions (with private and public competitors) are two distinct approaches, even if both approaches are often, especially in English-speaking countries, carried out in conjunction with each other. As long as only the establishment of independent organization is concerned, approaches have the character of the type B.2 (internal adoption of enterprise and market-type features). For example, in Germany public agency-like organizations (*Eigenbetriebe*) and public enterprises are only rarely forced to compete with private rivals. Above all they were established to enhance flexibility in management. In New Zealand the creation of market economical conditions is one of the core issues of the NPM. But no pure competition conditions are introduced where enterprises and sectors that are of importance for the economic or welfare politics of the government are concerned (Damkowski and Precht 1995).

By the establishment of market conditions with competition between private and public organizational bodies, a type B.3 element (orientation towards the market environment) is added. Therefore, attempts to transform authorities into independent organizations are partly treated in parts B.2 and B.3.

The example of the voucher system (see B.2) also makes it perfectly clear that it is often difficult to draw a sharp distinction between the three patterns of reform orientation. If private suppliers are integrated in the competitive aspect of a voucher system as in the United States and increasingly in Sweden too, the voucher reform approach contains elements from at least two of the analytical reform patterns, B.2 and B.3.

The *National Performance Review* report *Creating a Government That Works Better and Costs Less* (Gore 1993) in particular, which presents the intended reform measures of the Clinton administration, shows that actual (national) reform approaches have a varied character. It comprises a multitude of steps and measures which can be found in all three typical patterns of the dimension of reform orientations (Table I).

The Different Roles of the State in the Process of Reform
A.1

The most striking example for an autocratic top-down approach is Great Britain. All reform programs of the Thatcher and Major era were launched on the highest government level with definite prescriptions of reform subjects and under governmental supervision of reform development. The prime minister's office and a specific department in the ministry of finance were the organizational

TABLE I PUBLIC SECTOR REFORM MEASURES

Chapter 1:   Cutting Red Tape
Step 1: Streamlining the budgeting process
Step 2: Decentralizing personnel policy
Step 3: Streamlining procurement
Step 4: Reorienting the inspectors general
Step 5: Eliminating regulatory overkill
Step 6: Empower state and local government

Chapter 2:   Putting Customers First
Step 1: Giving customers a voice and a choice
Step 2: Making service organizations compete
Step 3: Creating market dynamics
Step 4: Using market mechanism to solve problems

Chapter 3:   Empowering Employees to Get Results
Step 1: Decentralizing decisionmaking power
Step 2: Holding all federal employees accountable for results
Step 3: Giving federal workers the tools they need to do their job
Step 4: Enhancing the quality of worklife
Step 5: Forming a labor-management partnership
Step 6: Exerting leadership

Chapter 4:   Cutting Back to Basics
Step 1: Eliminate what we don't need
Step 2: Collecting more
Step 3: Investing in greater productivity
Step 4: Reengineering programs to cut costs

SOURCE: Damkowski and Precht 1995, p. 88.

and intellectual starting points, both led by private managers accountable for most reform initiatives (Reichard 1993; Damkowski and Precht 1995):

- In 1979 the Rayner Scrutinies began, a special efficiency unit with the task of checking the government authorities' spending, which led mainly to cutting of personnel (OECD 1993b).
- The Financial Management Initiative (FMI) (since 1982) was directly led by the chancellor of the exchequer.
- The Next Steps Initiative, beginning in 1988, intensified the transformation of government authorities into agencies (e.g., the social and labor offices, the British Museum, and the British Patent Office). Up till now, 90 such agencies have been established with 60 percent of British civil servants working in them and even more expected to do so in the future.
- The intention of the Citizens' Charter published in 1991 is to improve the quality of public services. The Citizens' Charter is a nationwide framework of rules which define minimal performance standards. Every public institution has to build up its own charter,

which comprises quality standards, principles of performance, and so on. Citizens are understood as the clients of public services and their expectations and assessments of public performances are part of the definition of standards. The accountability for the quality of performances is delegated to the civil servants on site and they are responsible for the keeping of the published standards. Citizens (clients) have the right to insist on this.

As a consequence of the vast influence government and politics exerted on the British reform approach, there was a rather critical discussion of the (political) intentions and effects in British administrative science (see Pollitt 1990). Many authors deny that the intention of the government was mainly to improve efficiency and effectiveness in civil services, but suggest rather that the intention was to get more influence and control in this area and try to reduce the influence of unions and local Labor governments. The governmental policy mainly resulted in reduction in the number of civil servants and their privileges and a cutback of performances provided by public institutions, in favor of the private sector. Consequently this led to a partial destruction of British local government (Reichard 1993).

In New Zealand the Labor government started public sector reforms in 1984 with an uncompromising top-down modernization strategy, very similar to the UK reform approaches launched by Conservative governments. Senior civil servants of the Treasury, an elite ministry, had the main responsibility for the creation of the reform conception(s) and the realization(s) of reform programs.

Labor governments (1984–1990) and the Liberal-Conservative government (since 1990) enforced public service reforms in the fields of state-owned enterprises (SOEs), government management of the central state sector and public finance, and local government (districts, towns and cities).

The public management reforms in Canada and the United States are high-profile approaches as well, launched at the highest and most central level of the political and administrative system. The topics of reform initiatives also appear to be very similar; NPM-type initiatives in the early 1980s included cutback policies by contracting out and privatization, especially during "Reagonomics" in the United States (Damkowski and Precht 1995). One the other hand, some specific differences in the shape of reforms occured, according to the different structures and types of the states.

Because of the independence of authorities on all three levels of government in the United States. (central state, federal states, and communities) many of the management improvement programs appear to be uncoordinated and without a common direction (apart from the considerably increasing number of agencies). Thus the scope of central government programs was limited. The

measures taken during the Reagan administration to increase the direct influence of the president on actions and performances of subordinated authorities was restricted to the federal level. Pressure on communities to carry out reforms could only be exerted by the cutting of financial assignments. Communities reacted to the loss of incomes either with contracting out measures or by the imposition of new or increased charges. Thus no unified reform approach could be pushed through by central government or the president (Reichard 1993; Damkowski and Precht 1995).

The Canadian NPM reform approach shows a more unified and coordinated character than the U.S. one. It seems that a fundamental change of the structure of the whole Canadian public sector took place from 1984, when the NPM reforms started (Damkowski and Precht 1995). An explanation for this homogeneous appearance of the Canadian public management reform (it seems to be designed in every detail) is the concentration of the responsibility for the tasks of implementation, monitoring, and evaluation of the reform in a few institutions (agencies)— the Privy Council office (PCO), the Public Service Commission (PSC), the Treasury Board Secretariat (TBS), and the Canadian Centre for Management Development (CCMD), directly under the control of the prime minister or the cabinet.

Despite the above mentioned differences in the scope and concepts, both North American reform approaches underwent a very similar significant change in the main emphasis of reform almost at the same time. In Canada the main focus of reform efforts turned in 1989 with the Public Service 2000 program of prime minister Brian Mulroney from a rather strict orientation towards economy and efficiency to the improvement of services and a orientation towards people. This development was mainly influenced by the CCMD. Reform measures now place more emphasis upon a more client-oriented culture of service and the quality of service delivery. In the United States the reform climate changed with the beginning of the Bush era. As in Canada, reform measures were less cutback oriented but more reform- and administration-friendly. Under the Clinton administration this development was enlarged.

A.2

The characteristic of participative reform approaches is the involvement of parties and/or institutions affected by reform measures in the reform process. The participation of institutions can mean that subordinated authorities or agencies are free to carry out reform measures by themselves, restricted only by basic political or juridical conditions and sometimes with support from higher administrative bodies. For example, Finland, Japan, the Netherlands, and Norway have tried to achieve a successful reform process by central reform departments such as advisory boards, committees, agencies, research institutions, and provisional councils, without preventing local bodies from taking initiatives.

Participation also stands for consultation and negotiation, organized with all parties involved. Communicative procedures of this kind can be found particularly in Australia, Italy, Ireland, and Spain; they ensure a heightened probability of the acceptance of the ongoing change by involving everybody in the reform process in a responsible way (OECD 1993a, 1993b).

Two outstanding examples of participative reform approaches are the Scandinavian free commune experiments and the Australian approach. The free commune experiments show how central governments can successfully provide conditions for subsequent independent reform measures. The Australian way of NPM shows how communicative procedures are able to foster a frictionless translation of reform measures into action.

The role of the public government in the public sector of Scandinavian countries is rather important. For example, in Denmark, Norway, and Sweden more than 50 percent of public sector staff are community employees (the corresponding figure for France is 10 percent). Thus, the free commune experiments are of great significance for Scandinavian public administrations (Damkowski and Precht 1995).

The free communes in Scandinavia can independently decide which (specific) public services to produce or deliver and which not to. A change of the legal base of communities was necessary to give public managers this freedom to manage. First a new local government act passed Parliament in Sweden in 1984, which made the free commune experiments (pilot projects in the beginning) possible. Then similar acts in Norway, Denmark, Finland, and Iceland followed. The former legislation placed communities under obligations to provide specific services. Thus the new free commune policies, with concepts such as service management, debureaucratization, motivation without manipulation, and reduction of political administration, meant not only a new shape of public management, but a new orientation of the welfare policies in the Scandinavian countries towards more economy and efficiency (Damkowski and Precht 1995).

The main difference from the autocratic top-down approaches was that central government gave subordinated authorities the opportunity to take reform measures, but they were not forced to do so, nor were they told how to do so. Free communes were released to fulfill most of the former central political and legal tasks and handicaps. They were allowed to take measures such as the contracting out of public services and the introduction of a goal- and result-oriented management. Consequently district and community councils had less influence upon the daily business of administration. The responsibility of management decisions is consequently delegated to the front line.

The Commonwealth of Australia has developed a socially and politically very special NPM approach, which considers the requirements of a welfare state and the particular significance of the public sector in the economy and in society. Public sector labor unions and employees had been integrated in the process of development to a very high degree. Thus, the preparation of the approach needed a rather long time, but after that it could be put into action without much resistance (see Kouzmin 1993).

The goals and measures of goal attainment of the Australian approach do not go far from the frame of the NPM mainstream (OECD 1993a, 1993b; Reichard 1993; Damkowski and Precht 1995):

■ *Increased performance orientation (effectiveness).* A preferred reliance on outputs and outcomes rather than on inputs and regulations and a more strategic management through clearly defined general and program goals; made possible by more flexibility of public management through the reduction of central administrative and financial handicaps and supervision.

■ *Increased efficiency (economy) and client orientation.* A heightened awareness of costs and customer needs by accountability of managers and market economical pressure by competition.

■ *Better human resource management.* Development of multiprofessional and multiskilled personnel; the improvement of career chances, for example by cutting down discriminatory structures; and a better work climate with participative leadership and decisionmaking.

In 1992 the first evaluation of results of reform measures took place. Assessments of the success of the reform varied to some extent. Judgments about the development of accountability and responsibility in the public sector were different. While the House of Representatives Standing Committee of Finance and Public Administration claimed that the main difficulties of the reform appeared in the public management field, the Ministry of Finance reported major progress in this area.

The fault which critics of NPM reform approaches very often find with the NPM, not only in Australia but especially in the UK, is that the concentration on the improvement of efficiency affects the aspect of effectiveness, in particular the quality of services.

No matter how successful the reform goal attainment is estimated to be so far, the participative implementation strategy seems to be quite appropriate for a successful change in public sector management. The Management Advisory Board discovered that authorities supported the reform broadly, and took many initiatives to enhance their concentration on clients.

Consequently the Management Advisory Board concluded that the participative element of reform should be intensified to foster the further development of the reform.

A.3

The approaches in other countries, for instance Germany and Greece, are characterized by a rather broad and decentralized approach, which may cover the whole public administration, without being necessarily planned, steered, and regulated by agencies on the level of the central government (OECD 1993a, 1993b).

Particularly in Germany, public sector reform is mainly a bottom-up movement. Public management modernization is on the way in many local authorities, but one of its foremost problems is the unique character of its various individual approaches. Coordination and supervision is missing to some extent, even if the communities in Germany are quite independent.

Typical Orientations of the Subject Matter Themes of Reform

B.1

A first specific subject matter theme of reform is the field of accountancy and bookkeeping. In Austria and Switzerland, for instance, reform measures are mainly concentrated on the adoption of businesslike management techniques inside authorities or other public institutions. In both countries experiments with business-type accountancy and bookkeeping systems (in Austria on all governmental levels and in Switzerland mainly on the state level—cantons) have taken place. Controlling, budgeting, and personnel development are additional businesslike measures to improve internal management, especially in the Austrian public administration sector. In Belgian local government, business-type accountancy and subsequent types of program budgeting are the dominating reform measures (OECD 1993a, 1993b; Reichard 1993).

In Australia the Financial Management Improvement Program (FMIP) and the Program Management and Budgeting (PMB) framework are to enhance the efficiency and effectiveness of the internal management of public authorities and to encourage them to state provable outcome-oriented goals. Apart from other budgetary and legal reforms, the introduction of the running cost system (1987–88) led to more responsibility and awareness of costs through more flexibility in the use of resources (e.g., global budgeting, factual and annual transferability of budgetary funds, more freedom in financial management, partial right of disposal of savings). Managers generally received more freedom to manage, but on the other hand were obliged to check results and to evaluate the success of programs.

The British FMI approach shows very similar features: the strengthening of responsibility through a reorganization of the public service (building of result and cost centers), the introduction of a result-oriented management with a special emphasis on performance measurement, and the development of program budgets, as well as the improvement of human resource management (performance-related pay) (Damkowski and Precht 1995).

Approaches with measures similar to those of the British and Australian financial management programs can be found in the Netherlands, France (*Centres de Responibilité*) and on the community level in Germany (Neues Steuerungsmodell).

The use of management techniques such as zero-based-budgeting is widespread in local governments of the United States. Larger municipalities are doing strategic planning in an entrepreneurial way. Goal attainments and outputs, for instance, are evaluated and monitored by the use of feedback mechanisms, for example by the measurement of customer satisfaction and the quality of results.

The tradition of budgetary reform approaches—operating budgets, program budgets, and the like—was continued in the United States and in Canada as attempts to optimize the allocation of resources by decentralizing budget responsibility (Reichard 1993; Damkowski and Precht 1995).

B.2

In the United States the adoption of business-type structures and market-type mechanisms has a rather long tradition. Unlike most of the European countries, entrepreneurship and competition, for example via benchmarking, were well-known features in the U.S. public sector before the recent NPM movement came into existence. For example, the community of Phoenix, Arizona, uses benchmarking with various private corporations (e.g., American Express, Rank Xerox).

The British Chartermark system is intensive used as an instrument for strict result control. The keeping of performance goals is evaluated in terms of economy and orientation towards the needs of clients. Only services which are able to prove the keeping of their postulated performance standards get a stamp of quality, a so-called Chartermark. If institutions fail to get a Chartermark for certain performances they are obliged to reduce or stop their activities in these subject matters (Damkowski and Precht 1995).

The Swedish concept of planned markets with types of internal competition (public competition) represents the reform orientation of an adoption of private enterprise structures and market-type mechanisms to a very great extent. Within this concept one can find many of the elements and strategies of the NPM, for example MBO or contract management, bureaucratic competition, output and client orientation, and responsibility for results.

The public hospitals of the provincial regions (*landsting*), for instance, are equipped with global budgets and they have to compete for patients (clients) to increase their budgets. Goal and result attainment is measured by performance indicators (reference numbers). Only hospitals who can approve a high use of their capacity, a high number of potential consumers, and the keeping of performance standards achieve increased budget assignments or a higher dividend from profit.

Another approach of the Swedish public management by competition is the concept of a provider or mixed market: Independent public agencies conclude contracts about the materials they need with the central procuring office (*beställarnamnd*). The contracts define services which agencies have to deliver (to clients) in order to get the agreed materials. Thus agencies compete for the fixed amount of available materials, because those who provide good services and service quality to the public get more material resources. Procurement contracting systems as in Sweden can also be found in Belgium (public procurement) and in the United States (procurement management) (Damkowski and Precht 1995).

A very interesting feature of the Canadian Public Service 2000 program to create basic conditions for competition is the use of information systems, for example, ACCORD (Administration and Control of Contracts and Regional Data) or CADEX (Customs Automated Data Exchange). The ACCORD system gives services the ability to get information about performance standards, as requested by internal clients, and performance qualities, as offered by internal competitors. The CADEX system supports TQM approaches. It allows data to be obtained via the "electronic highway" about quality requirements from external clients to build up quality definitions and achieve quality improvements (Damkowski and Precht 1995).

Another means to initiate competition is a voucher system. In the United States and Sweden, for instance, vouchers (e.g., housing vouchers and child care certificates) to be redeemed against the use of public social facilities or social services—in the United States mostly organized as agencies—are distributed to citizens. Citizens thus are free to choose, for example between different kindergartens or welfare institutions for the elderly. In Sweden the next period's budget depends partially on the vouchers an institution received in the previous period.

In the United States consumers have not only the freedom of choice between different public suppliers, but also between public and private suppliers. The Swedish voucher system was at first limited to public organizations; however, private suppliers are increasingly being included in the system (Damkowski and Precht 1995).

Since in Canada and the United States the emphasis of reforms shifted away from privatization and cutback policies, the agency concept became—as in many other countries—of great importance. In 1989 an increasing transformation of federal offices into Special Operating Agencies (SOAs) started in Canada.

These SOAs are independent organizations, released from most of the traditional handicaps and obliged courses of action. SOAs should focus on results and apply more business-type approaches to provide the best service to clients. In 1988 the internal adoption of business-type structures and market-type mechanisms became more and more the dominating approach to improving the administration on governmental level in the United States as well. The main question of reform was no longer, "how much government do we need?" but "what kind of government?" with a "renewed focus on improving quality of government services and products" (OECD 1993a). In 1988 most of the new federal agencies in the United States had been established to bring inefficient service delivery to an end (Damkowski and Precht 1995).

British agencies are decentralized subordinated governmental institutions with an independent management. The relations between agencies and ministries are laid down by framework agreements, which define the subject matters, financing, and performance standards. The goal attainment of agencies is frequently scrutinized by a large number of performance indicators. These examinations of agency performance serve as a basis for negotiations about payments, competences, equipment, and sometimes the existence of agencies (workplace and enterprise bargaining) (Reichard 1993; Damkowski and Precht 1995).

The restructuring of administrative bodies into independent organizations is also an important feature of the reform approaches in New Zealand and Australia. In New Zealand many state-owned enterprises and parts of ministries or other authorities are transformed into limited liability companies; government business enterprises (GBEs) in Australia play an eminent role in the national economy (e.g., electricity and water supply, marketing of agricultural goods, public transport). If it does not seem appropriate to run public institutions as companies of private law, in New Zealand it is prefered to establish executive agencies, very much like the British agencies, with a combination of features from public and private institutions. The agencies of Australia (Australian Public Service, APS) are working on a quasi-commercial basis as well.

Both the limited liability companies and the executive agencies, for instance in New Zealand, are independent in the use of their personnel and financial resources. Within the limits of result-oriented contracts between ministers and company or agency managers, the latter are responsible for the performance of services. Hierarchical administrative control mechanisms (input-oriented control) are reduced and replaced by modes of output and outcome control (principal-agency approach). The results in public services are checked in terms of goal attainment (performance standards) and outputs are measured by performance indicators. Similar to the principal-agency approach in New Zealand is the Swedish goal or final steering concept (*mal-styrning*) on the community level. This means that political leaders should not be engaged in operating matters and thus get improved abilities for strategic planning. Thereby, a strict division of labor between managers, who are accountable for the operating activities, and political leaders, who have the responsibility of policymaking, has to take place.

Politicians should concentrate on the setting of goals and basic conditions and the controlling of results (Damkowski and Precht 1995).

B.3

In the 1980s, most NPM approaches—above all in the English-speaking countries, but also in Scandinavia—started predominantly with a cutback of governmental and administrative activities. Because of the overwhelming costs of more and more welfare state expenditures, the growth of public deficits got out of hand. Thus measures of deregulation and privatization dominated the NPM agenda. For example, in Canada, 14 Crown corporations were wound up and 23 central state-owned enterprises were privatized after 1985 (OECD 1993b).

The government of New Zealand dissolved many public monopolies to exercise control over public services through market competition. Expensive performances or services low in quality were no longer accepted.

In Australia some of the public services which had to compete with the private sector for orders from central government turned out to be quite competitive. In some cases public organizations competed successfully with private enterprises in economic branches which formerly belonged to the private sector only. On the other hand, many public managers criticized the commercialization policies of the government because the specific conditions of the public sector (payment conditions, legal, political, and financial handicaps, etc.) prevented public enterprises and agencies from competing with the private sector (Damkowski and Precht 1995).

In Canada, Sweden, and the United States, private market conditions should also encourage those public enterprises and agencies which remain under public control to behave in an entrepreneurial manner. Management by contract systems and an increased reliance on competition are introduced in a lot of public sectors. Goods or services considered necessary by governments are invited for tenders. Thus, public suppliers have to compete with private ones to get orders and the so-called make or buy decisions become possible. If public organizations or departments are not able to offer appropriate performances, services are contracted out (outsourcing). In Great Britain, nondepartmental bodies (NDPB), which are institutions almost resembling the next-steps agencies of the Thatcher era, but mostly more independent in management affairs, operate like private enterprises in the market. They are only partly funded by public budgets and thus have to have economical success as well.

Competition for quality is another instrument of the British cutback policy. Through market-type competition and competition surrogates a reduction of unnecessary and useless public services are to be achieved. On the community level, a comparison of performance standards of-

fered by different service providers is taking place, just as the National Audi Commission does nationwide. It is possible for private and public suppliers to compete for orders. In this way orders are invited for tender in Great Britain concerning those services which in other countries clearly belong to the sovereign area of the state, for example, prison administration, driving license agency, passport office, tax office data processing.

Nearly all ministerial operations and activities of subordinated bodies in Great Britain are invited for tenders. With this market testing the performances of private service providers are checked and agencies are to make increasing efforts to improve public service quality. Public agencies, departments, or civil servants have to compete with private rivals for orders and contract. If public competitors fail to get tenders or contracts because of high costs or less quality or competence, this results in negative consequences for civil servants, such as pay decrease and demotion. Many institutions of the formerly monopolistic British public sector—with and without business character—are exposed to this compulsory competitive tendering.

The British NPM approach goes far beyond a partial removal of services away from the public sector and the contracting out of some services. Like some municipalities in the United States, Great Britain draws near to the contracting state, which produces performances not by itself, but makes performances possible by a plentitude of contracts with private providers. This enabling state facilitates contractors that operate independently under competitive conditions and thus creates opportunities for service delivery, but it does not administrate much and produces even less (Damkowski and Precht 1995).

Another nonmarket way in which local governments particularly orient themselves towards their environment is through the participation of citizens. In many countries for instance there are demands for propositions when questions of public importance, such as ecological problems, are to be decided. It is difficult for public administrations to make good decisions when different pressure groups with different interests are involved, for example in matters of traffic engineering. In the United States and increasingly in European countries, the technique of mediation is used to solve such problems. Mediation means that negotiations with all the parties involved take place in order to reach broadly accepted solutions.

Citizens in New Zealand are included in local and municipal planning and decision processes to a great extent. Citizens get information about public affairs and matters in a variety of ways; for example, in the town of Christchurch this information sharing takes place through the distribution of pamphlets; in meetings, where spending and project affairs are discussed; and by comprehensible reports, about such matters as the budget and planning affairs.

Moreover, annual surveys are carried out to investigate citizens' satisfaction with public services.

Citizens in Sweden who are consumers of local services are included in the decisionmaking of public institutions. Consumers of such services as schools, kindergartens, and homes for the elderly are formally integrated in the administration as committee members (Damkowski and Precht 1995).

A rather unconventional way of outsourcing in the United States is to hand over responsibility of public services to citizens. The combating of crime, the care of green areas, and so forth are to be done by citizens, organized in "neighborhood service departments," on a voluntary basis (Damkowski and Precht 1995).

KAI MASSER

BIBLIOGRAPHY

Aucin, P., 1990. "Administrative Reforms in Public Management: Paradigms, Principle, Paradoxes and Pendulums." *Governance,* vol. 3:115–137.

Banner, G., 1993. "Der Carl Bertelsmann Preis 1993: Anregungen für die kommunale Verwaltungsreform in Deutschland." In Bertelsmann Stiftung, ed., *Demokratie und Effizienz in der Kommunalverwaltung.* Vol. 1. Gütersloh: Verlag Bertelsmann Stiftung, pp.147–171.

Bouckaert, G. and Chr. Pollitt, eds., 1995. *Quality Improvement in European Public Services: Concepts, Cases and Commentary.* London: Sage.

Caiden, G., 1991. *Administrative Reforms Comes of Age.* Berlin and New York: De Gruyter Walter.

Damkowski, W. and C. Precht, 1995. *Public Management: Neue Steuerungskonzepte für den öffentlichen Sektor.* Stuttgart: W. Kohlhammer.

Gore, A., 1993. *From Red Tape to Results: Creating a Government That Works Better and Costs Less.* Report of the National Performance Review. Washington; D.C.: Times Books.

Hill, H. and H. Klages, eds., 1995. *New Trends in Public Sector Renewal.* Frankfurt: Peter Lang Publishing House.

Hood, C. C., 1990. "A Public Management for All Seasons." *Public Administration,* vol. 69 (Spring) 3–17.

Klages, H. and O. Haubner, 1995. "Strategies of Public Sector Modernization: Three Alternative Perspectives." In G. Bouckaert and A. Halachmi, eds., *Challenge of Management in a Changing World.* San Francisco: Jossey Bass.

Kouzmin, A., 1993. "The Dimensions of Quality in Public Management: Australian Perspectives and Experiences. In H. Hill and H. Klages, eds., *Qualitäts: und erfolgsorientiertes Verwaltungsmanagement.* Aktuelle Tendenzen und Entwürfe, Berlin: Duncker & Humblot, pp. 211–251.

Marcou, G. and I. Verebelyi, eds., 1993. *New Trends in Local Government in Western and Eastern Europe.* Brussels: International Institute of Administrative Science.

Mascarenas, R. C., 1993. "Building an Enterprise Culture in the Public Sector: Reform of the Public Sector in Australia, Britain and New Zealand. *Public Administration Review,* 319–328. July/August 1993, vol. 53, no. 4.

Organization for Economic Cooperation and Development, 1990. *Public Management Developments.* Survey. Paris: OECD.

———, 1991. *Public Management Developments.* Update. Paris: OECD.

———, 1992a. *Draft Policy Conclusions on the Use of Market-Type Mechanisms.* Paris: OECD.

———, 1992b. *Public Management Developments.* Update. Paris: OECD.

———, 1993a. *OECD Country Profiles.* Paris: OECD.

——— 1993b. *Public Management Developments.* Survey. Paris: OECD.

Pollitt, C., 1990. *Managerialism and the Public Services: The Anglo-Saxon Experience.* Oxford: Blackwell.

Reichard, Ch., 1993. "Internationale Trends im kommunalen Management." In G. Banner and Ch. Reichard, *Kommunale Managementkonzepte in Europa.* Cologne: W. Kohlhammer.

Reinermann, H., 1993. *Ein neues Paradigma für die öffentliche Verwaltung.* Speyerer Arbeitshefte 97. Speyer: Post-Graduate School of Administrative Sciences.

Stiftung, Bertelsmann, ed., 1993. *Carl Bertelsmann Preis 1993.* Vols. 1 and 2, Gütersloh: Verlag Bertelsmann Stiftung.

Strehl, F., 1995, "Public Administration Reforms: Actual Characteristics and Trends." In H. Hill and H. Klages, eds., *New Trends in Public Sector Renewal.* Frankfurt: Peter Lang Publishing House.

PUBLIC SECTOR ENGINEERING.

The application of scientific principles for the benefit of the community via public infrastructure and technology provided through government.

Public sector engineering has generally involved the provision of public goods. Although there is no recognized branch of engineering named "public sector engineering" it exists as a phenomenon. The breadth and impact of this phenomenon is extremely large. It entails the contribution made by the traditional engineering disciplines of civil, military, electrical, and systems engineering as well as the more recent fields of aerospace, telecommunications, environmental, and computer systems engineering. Visible contributions from these fields include first the vast public physical infrastructures of today: transport systems, water supply, sewerage, energy provision (through mainly gas, electricity, and oil), as well as the provision of buildings and facilities for public activities and services. Achievements ranging from the space program to the water supply systems of Zambia are the results of public sector engineering.

Engineering work has had a pervasive influence throughout the world. This work has played an important part through the operation of public bodies, following the global trend earlier this century for the public (and often monopoly) supply of services. This was often due to the inefficient and patchy coverage of essential services by multiple private corporations. Robert Moses' period of office in New York City, for example, saw a period of some four decades in which that city was shaped through engineering infrastructure development. Moses oversaw 14 new expressways, 416 miles of parkways, and seven bridges linking New York to the mainland. His power brokering—and subsequent engineering work—provided 658 more playgrounds, reshaped numerous parks and many other community facilities such as sports fields, and reclaimed marshes as public land.

The "urban renewal" in New York provided vast physical results, and not surprisingly some negative impacts as well. Two hundred and fifty thousand people were thrown out of their homes, replacing the housing of the poor with more upmarket facilities for the rich. New housing for the poor was sterile and cheap. The "Triborough" created by Moses to complete much of this work lacked the traditional public accountability, since the authority was judged by the courts to be a private corporation, closed to scrutiny by interested citizens and community. Nonetheless, whether such enormous infrastructure building would have been possible without Moses is debatable.

The development and operation of the Tennessee Valley Authority is another example of the profound influence of public sector engineering in our history. The TVA represented a new model of economic and social development through public enterprise and engineering, inspiring renewed social confidence in hard economic times.

The massive infrastructure investment in the U.S. had an interesting parallel in Australia. Sir John Monash, perhaps Australia's greatest public sector engineer, similarly demonstrated the powerful and creative contribution of public enterprise and public engineering through the creation in 1919 of the State Electricity Commission of Victoria. The initiation of this organization enabled the development of brown coal (with a high water content by world standards) to be dried and used to fire steam turbine generators for the production of electricity to some three million people in the state. Monash's vision and leadership oversaw the development of an efficient, vertically integrated electricity operation well before "vertical integration" entered the academic textbooks, and he succeeded where private enterprise and privately sponsored engineers had failed.

The role of public sector engineering has also been significant in the development of public sector management systems. Recently, performance measurement concepts have risen to become a priority. These performance measurement methods follow Frederick Taylor's seminal ideas of scientific management, although such ideas are now being applied with more recognition of organizations as social systems. In measuring and improving performance, the systems engineering framework has made a major contribution to understanding and articulating the analysis of public sector issues. The systems approach—where inputs, process(es), outputs, and outcomes may be then compared to the objectives originally sought in a public program—has proven to be a simple method of reviewing public sector performance.

Advances in the application of welfare economics have also seen contributions from public sector engineering. Following the application of welfare economics to assess motorway options in the United Kingdom in the early

1960s, much development work and extensive application has occurred. This work has been further developed through the U.S. Corps of Engineers. Water resources projects as well as other applications have seen these techniques applied and now widely practiced.

In developing countries, major engineering contributions have also been made through the public sector, often as a tangible means of delivering the objectives of unilateral or bilateral aid. Engineering projects have been valuable in this context. A new bridge or highway is a defined project making a contribution to the economic development of a country and one in which the scope for leakage of aid monies through corruption can be contained.

Public sector engineering has profoundly changed for the better the conditions of life for most of the world's people. Today, when the task is often to balance what is commercially and technically possible with what may be socially or environmentally desirable, public sector engineering continues to assist through its techniques of assessment and analysis of benefits and costs.

GRAEME A. HODGE

BIBLIOGRAPHY

Caro, Robert A., 1974. *The Power Broker: Robert Moses and the Fall of New York.* New York: Alfred A. Knopf Inc.

Hodge, Graeme A., 1993. *Minding Everybody's Business: Performance Management in Public Sector Agencies.* Melbourne: Montech Pty. Ltd.

Serle, Geoffrey, 1982. *John Monash: A Biography.* Melbourne: Melbourne University Press in Association with Monash University.

PUBLIC SERVICE.

A collective term referring to employees who work at the local, state, and national levels of government. This is in contrast to employees working for private sector business organizations. Employees working in the public service are normally compensated using moneys raised through a government's taxing powers and are thus truly "servants to the tax-paying public."

The public service is a comprehensive term that includes elected officials, appointed officials, and members of the career civil service. In a democratic regime, elected officials work with both appointed and career employees to implement public programs. The public service thus stands as a crucial actor enabling elected officials to convert public policies discussed during the political campaign into concrete programs at the grassroots level. In more totalitarian regimes, the public service serves a similar function, although there is usually considerably more centralized control of the implementation process, and public servants have far less latitude when making implementation decisions.

The nature of the public service in countries throughout the world is a legacy of numerous cultural shaping forces over the centuries. For European nations, the social stratification of the feudal era still finds its counterparts in the subdivision of the civil service into broad categories similar to the major classes in society. Countries formerly under colonial rule developed services mirroring the principal features of their dominant colonial rulers. Given the close historical ties between the United States, Canada, and Great Britain, it is not surprising that many features of the American and Canadian civil service systems can be traced back to their English origins. For the Japanese, the American influence in the years after World War II was combined with features of Confucian, Buddhist, British, French, and German thought. In the former Soviet Union, centuries of centralized control created a vast bureaucratic structure that was traditionally tightly monitored by those with political power. Opinions vary greatly regarding the degree to which this monitoring served to exercise true control over the public services bureaucracy.

Although there are, inevitably, differences in approach and in implementation, merit systems based on competitive examination for selection into the public service are common internationally. Other common features of civil service systems throughout the world are the elitist character of the upper strata of the service, the strong guarantees of tenure of civil servants, the efforts to prevent the political manipulation of the civil service, the strong reliance on seniority in determining advancement, high expectations of conduct, low monetary rewards, and widespread unionization of public servants.

The public service systems in developing and transitional societies still face multiple problems caused by the effects of religion, race, tribe, or caste. They also face problem caused by limited educational opportunities for civil servants and the compounding problem of the "brain drain"–the loss of their best brainpower to more attractive opportunities outside their own borders.

Some governmental systems require entry at bottom rungs of this service, with advancement completely from within, such as the English model. Other systems, such as that of the United States, allow "lateral entry," that is, entry from outside the system at different levels, based on the amount of merit a candidate brings to the position.

In the United States, since the passage of the Pendleton Act in 1883, career public service positions at the national level have been selected based on "merit" criteria, using competitive written examinations. Today, approximately 90 percent of federal government employees work in some sort of merit system. Merit systems are also very common at the state and local levels for the public service.

In the United States, employees in the public services who are not hired through merit system procedures at the national level are usually working in positions exempt from these procedures for some specific reasons. Exempt employees may be in upper-level policy making positions, such as cabinet officers and some of their immediate subordinates; or they may be members of the executive office of the President, containing staff aids, presidential advisers, legal counsel, economic advisers, budget advisers, and so forth. A small number of public servants work in advisory or staff relationships with members of Congress or members of the United States Supreme Court. These public servants were chosen based on more political selection criteria rather than chosen on criteria founded on, merit procedures. To mention just three examples, common political criteria include: political party service, service during the election campaign, or past reputation in governing circles. These people are the functionaries charged with formulating legislation and helping steer that legislation through Congress, or developing policy and helping a president implement that policy through the bureaucracy.

Public servants, both merit appointees and political appointees, often are treated differently than private sector employees in such areas as constitutional rights, ethical obligations, rights to participate in partisan political activities, and financial disclosure obligations. Public servants lives are much more open to scrutiny by the press and other interested groups. These employees often describe themselves as living in a "goldfish bowl" atmosphere.

ROBERT H. ELLIOTT

BIBLIOGRAPHY

Hays, Steven W., and T. Zane Reeves, 1984. *Personnel Management in the Public Sector.* Boston: Allyn and Bacon.

Shafritz, Jay, Norma M. Riccucci, David H. Rosenbloom, and Albert C. Hyde, 1992. *Personnel Management in Government.* 4th ed. New York: Marcel Dekker.

Stahl, O. Glenn, 1983. *Public Personnel Administration.* 8th ed. New York: Harper & Row.

PUBLIC TRUST. The collective willingness by citizenry to risk placing confidence in a given government and/or political system, with only a limited potential for making that government or system accountable to any form of popular will.

The modern concept of the public trust is necessitated by the changes in the basic conceptualization of the state, which took place in the seventeenth century. During this period the *raison d'être* of the state changed from that of a purposive association to a civil association. The classic view of the state, dating from the Greeks, was seen as a socially and economically tight-knit group of civic friends who jointly sought a common vision of the good life. The civil association, by contrast, was viewed as a collection of autonomous individuals who chose to cooperate with one another as a matter of convenience and mutual benefit in

order to pursue their own interests, especially that of full self-realization.

The civil association, then, is seen as the creation of free persons, who entrust the government of the association to equally free agents, with the understanding that the government's primary task is to use the common wealth to enhance the welfare and security of each constituent member. Moreover, it is also understood as part of this arrangement that should any given government fail in executing its agential trust, it may be dismissed by popular will and replaced with a new government chosen by a majority of individuals who constitute the civil association. In this way, the extension and withdrawal of the public trust or confidence in government becomes the main engine that drives the rise and fall of governments, and ultimately the civil association itself.

The nature of the civil association poses two main problems in establishing public confidence in governments. The first of these issues is rooted in the concepts of the public, which prevail in the civil association, and the second is based on the difficulties associated with what is called "socially secured autonomy," which the civil association has been established to achieve for its members.

As indicated, the civil association is composed of autonomous, basically self-interested, agents. Consequently, it is difficult to speak of "the public" or the "public interest" in unitary terms. For purposes of constituting the government, a majority of individuals is formed in an electoral process. However, between elections this majority soon divides into numerous shifting coalitions based upon interests.

As a result, it is often extremely difficult for the agents constituting the government to identify the public whose confidence they seek to win. In fact, winning the trust of those with one set of interests frequently guarantees the loss of confidence by others. This is particularly true when government seeks to implement redistribute policies that enhance one group's interests at the expense of another, or when it faces single-interest groups who judge the entire actions of a government by its record on one policy, such as abortion or environmental protection.

Equally challenging to the task of building confidence in the government of a civil association is the popular demand for, what might be called, "socially secured autonomy." Their term refers to the requirement that government not only free the individual to pursue his or her own interests but also provide extensive social support for this pursuit. The concept of socially secured autonomy is well illustrated by the notion of individual rights in a modern liberal democracy. These rights normally encompass the freedom to express oneself, move about freely, and use one's property (consonant with the rights of others), as well as entitlements to Social Security, full employment, education, health care, and even support for one's economic enterprises.

The pursuit of socially secured autonomy sets up a political society marked at once by the instrumental pursuit of self-interest and by high levels of interdependence between individuals and collectives. This tendency is reinforced by a technologically based economy with high levels of specialized labor and organizational function.

As a consequence of these developments, individuals pursuing their own notions of self-realization must continually employ a wide variety of equally self-interested agents, who, in fact, will exercise great discretion and authority in the conduct of the individual's affairs and, ultimately that person's destiny.

Moreover, because, like oneself, these agents are, presumably, self-interested, one risks possible exploitation by the agents when their interest diverges from one's own. Potentially, then, life in a civil association rather than being a triumphal march toward personal autonomy and self-realization can become a nightmare of vulnerability to the indifference, and even rapaciousness, of one's fellows.

Nowhere are these risks more serious than with the government of the civil association. Despite a civil association's traditional reluctance to give great powers to the agents and agencies of government, the quest for socially secured autonomy has led modern liberal democracies to entrust government with great discretion and authority so that it can act positively as a support mechanism for the massive project of individual self-realization.

With great power has come corresponding temptations for self-interested agents and self-perpetuating agencies to misuse this power when it is to their advantage to do so. As John Locke (1632–1704), the political philosopher, put it in *The Second Treatise on Civil Government:* "For he that thinks absolute power purifies man's blood and corrects the baseness of human nature, need read but the history of this or any other age, to be convinced of the contrary" ([1690] 1986). To make matters more serious, the very requirements of governance frequently demand that agents and agencies give up both short- and long-range interests for the general welfare of the civil association.

Uncorrected, the unalloyed pursuit of self-interest by those who govern the civil association can place its members in the most undesirable of positions, that of granting power over one's life and fortunes to those in whom one has no confidence. In such a situation, what pretends to be an arrangement to make the pursuit of one's self-realization more successful threatens to become the instrument of one's exploitation. Consequently, it is unlikely that the civil association can remain viable unless some means can be found to build confidence in the government that rests in either leveraging or counterbalancing the self-interests of its agents. It is to this issue that the rest of this discussion is devoted.

If we are to examine the role confidence plays in government, it is useful first to review the role reliance with confidence plays in society in general. To rely with confidence is to believe in a relationship in which others will act in a predictably benign way toward us when we are required to depend on them.

Reliance with confidence is basically a reciprocal relationship. It is extended to a person or collective, it is usually returned in kind. If it is denied or given sparingly to others, the, in turn, withhold or limit their extension of confidence. This both granting and withholding confidence tends to establish self-reinforcing cycles, unless broken by one or more striking events.

In the lived world, confidence is normally extended widely, freely, and without much in the way of reflection. In fact, unreflective extension of confidence in others might be called the social state of grace in which most of us live most of the time. The reason for this situation lies in the great social advantage that reliance with confidence gives us in life.

Any cooperative action or venture depends heavily upon reliance with confidence. Cooperation with others makes us dependent and interdependent upon them. As a result, we become, to a great or lesser extent, vulnerable to them and their actions. The more secure we are in our reliance upon others, the more easily and free we can enter into cooperative relationship with them. The less we can rely in confidence, the more circumscribed and closely monitored our cooperative endeavors must become.

Accordingly, if one has a high general level of reliance with confidence in others this not only multiplies the opportunities for cooperative activity but also makes such opportunities much easier and more efficient for one to utilize. By the same token, cooperative action firmly rooted in reliance with confidence enables a far more open, richer, and honest sharing of information among those involved. Therefore, to the extent that the success or failure of a cooperative activity depends upon an effective and accurate collective definition and appreciation of the situation, those actors who are able to rely upon one another with complete confidence possess an immense advantage over those who to not.

The social values of reliance with confidence are easily translated into significant advantages for the citizens of a civil association. As we have seen, the citizens of the civil association want the benefits of socially secured autonomy, but they are often fearful of the large, complex, and vigorous governments that can most easily achieve this goal. To make matters more complex, the pursuit of individual self-realization that underlies the civil association makes citizens less willing to sacrifice their private lives for their public lives. As a result, they are less willing to expend the effort necessary to participate extensively in and monitor a potentially powerful and exploitative government.

The ability for one to rely with confidence upon the public agents and agencies of the civil association resolves many of the dilemmas surrounding this situation. In essence, it allows the public to delegate the immense power and direction necessary to create a vigorous and competent modern administrative state with a minimum of effort and a maximum of security.

Despite its obvious advantages, however, there are a number of reasons either to withhold one's confidence in government or to grant it only on a limited, probationary, and tentative basis. The powers of the state are normally the most considerable of any social institution. As Locke's words suggest, this very concentration of power is so tempting to the ambitious and unscrupulous that it inevitably raises the real and present danger of abuse.

The existence of careerism, self-serving bureaucracies, and exploitative public agents are all facts of life in any modern government; moreover, despite the actuality of popular control over government, this is as true of a civil association as any other political arrangement. Indeed, the dominant theme of self-realization often leads to the acceptance of much self-serving behavior among public agents as part of human nature, and a necessary, even useful, byproduct of a social and economic climate that encourages acquisitiveness and personal growth.

The use of large centralized administrative establishments to conduct the business of most modern states raises further blocks to the easy extension of citizen confidence in government.

Any large government presents immense problems involving action and information that are hidden from the public. Some of these issues relate to the secretive nature of bureaucracies and to the protective drive of politicians, but even more problems can be traced to the sheer inability or unwillingness of most citizens to monitor or understand what a modern government does. As a result of these factors, the credibility of government and its openness can easily become suspect by the citizen, further eroding his or her confidence in government.

Finally, in a civil association, the public itself is often the source of much of its own lack of confidence in the government. The citizens of a civil association often seek to benefit from a vigorous government while remaining as free as possible from its power, authority, and restrictions. To the degree the government and its administrative arm cannot satisfy these frequently conflicting demands for freedom and socially secured autonomy, it becomes viewed by turns as overbearing and incompetent; in sum, not worthy of public confidence.

The degree to which the government of a civil association is able to overcome these sources of distrust depends heavily upon three closely related factors: the collective capacity of citizens to

- place confidence in social systems nearly as easily as the place confidence in persons;

- rest confidence upon a basis that is neither naively overconfident nor needlessly restrictive of opportunities; and
- rely with confidence upon the stewardship of government.

In order to extend confidence in most modern governments, citizens must have the capacity to place confidence in social systems as well as persons. The reason for this is that, from a citizen's perspective, large administrative states are composed of individuals who are strangers to the citizen, working in social systems called bureaucracies that are easily interpreted as arcane and opaque. If the citizen can only extend confidence interpersonally, then government can warrant confidence only if that trust can be conducted on a real or simulated interpersonal basis; and this requires the civil associations to either remain a compact and intimate social unit or to develop a number of pseudo-personal relationships between the mass of governed and their governors.

The first strategy creates a political association that is so small that it risks being externally vulnerable to aggression and being internally inadequate to provide the economic basis for material self-realization. The second strategy, as will be seen, risks being inauthentic and, ultimately, disillusioning to citizens.

Fortunately, under the right conditions, citizens are willing to place confidence in social systems, including the institutions of government; because of the social development of individuals. Although most individuals learn to rely upon others with confidence on an interpersonal basis in the nurturing family unit, their reliance with confidence ultimately becomes a generalized worldview—the sociological state of grace referred to previously. The worldview can be extended to both individuals and social systems (including governments), unless the individual's experience and education teach him or her otherwise.

The potential for a social system's confidence in a civil association is shown by that association's very existence as a set of intentionally established political institutions. It must be admitted, however, that a system's confidence is often both more limited and problematic in a civil association than in other political arrangements because of the highly individualistic basis of the civil association, which often causes people to resent social, particularly political, institutions as artificial and unnecessary constraints upon individual liberty and the expression of human potential.

The second factor that underlies the establishment of effective public confidence in government is the conditions under which the public is asked to believe in the "predictably benign intentions" of the government. If the public is asked to extend confidence in government without reservation, it risks betrayal. If it is required to place its confidence in public agents and agencies under only the most circumscribed conditions, it risks forming a government so limited as to be impotent.

Public confidence in government lies between two polar points, which could be called "unreflective" and "reflective" confidence. Unreflective confidence is based upon the public's familiarity or faith, which gives rise to their worldview of the government's predictable benign intentionality, described earlier. The public's faith is extended freely and unconsciously as an expectation; hence, the term "unreflective confidence." Its major weakness from a political standpoint is the public's potential naiveté in a situation in which the government's temptations of authoritative power may lead to the betrayal.

By contrast, reflective confidence is rooted in people's skepticism about the confidant's reliability. It gives rise to the public's suspicion and thus to their desire to control the relationship with those upon whom they are forced to rely. Reflective confidence is extended by people contingently, usually based upon rationally calculated, intentionally constructed a priori agreements—thus the name "reflective confidence." The major political liability for people, then, is their need for extensive and minute control of elected and appointed officials. This sort of control has two liabilities. First, it robs public officials of the discretion to conduct a government vigorous and effective enough to contribute to an environment for individual self-development. Second, it overtaxes the limited willingness of the members of the civil association to expend their energies on public life.

Certainly, there are numerous situations in which the contingencies of hidden information and action and the limitations on popular interest in government require de facto unreflective confidence in government. By the same reasoning, there are situations in which no reasonable government would expect the citizen to extend other than reflective confidence to public agents and agencies. In order to be *both* responsible and effective, however, the government of a civil association must nurture a form of confidence in government that lies between these two poles, requiring of its citizens neither abject faith nor fundamental distrust; and it is argued that this mode of confidence is trust.

Trust represents conditions upon which people's confidence can be built that are midway between the poles of unreflective and reflective confidence. As such having trust allows people to have confidence that is neither naive nor unnecessarily circumspect. Citizen's trust governments because they allow themselves to extend this confidence freely, but with caution. Thus we can, first, view trust as a general social phenomenon and, then, examine the role it plays in building public confidence in government.

On one hand, as Niklas Luhmann (1979) has observed in *Trust and Power*, having trust allows us to risk extending confidence freely in situations in which it is not warranted from a strictly empirical and rational viewpoint. When people trust, we are encouraged to overdraw on what we actually know or feel about an individual or collective, as we might overdraw on our checking account at a relatively lenient bank. On the other hand, those who trust hedge their bets with a modicum of *distrust* in order to limit the possibility of a betrayal of their confidence. If one has unreflective confidence, one does not contemplate the possibility of betrayal at all. Those having reflective confidence, by contrast, are often obsessed with betrayal. Those with trust entertain it only as a possibility, nothing more.

Yet, because people with trust do account for the potential of betrayal, they require the trustworthiness of those in whom confidence is to be placed. Stated differently, those who trust occasionally require those in whom trust is placed to show outward signs of the inward (or collective) resolve to be reliable and caring.

The uniqueness of this position becomes clearer when it is contrasted with the extremes of unreflective and reflective confidence. Those with unreflective confidence simply assume the reliability and concern of the confidant and, therefore, see no need to test it. In fact, raising the very question of the confidant's reliability ends, or at least suspends, a person's state of unreflective confidence itself. Alternately, those with reflective confidence assume a high potential for unreliability and seek to use externally enforced agreements and accountability systems as the basis for their extending provisional and limited confidence in the other.

Those who trust find a middle way. They extend confidence based upon the belief in the confidant's trustworthiness, a belief based as much upon social hunch as careful reasoning. Thus they are neither as naive nor as thoughtless as those with unreflective confidence nor are they as risk-obsessed and calculating as those with reflective confidence.

It is now possible to see why trust plays such an important role in establishing the basic conditions necessary to build confidence in the government of a civil association. If one recalls the earlier discussion of the problems that confront the public when building such confidence one can see that a public that trusts seems to deal with these problems quite directly, because having trust enables the public to cope effectively with the civil association's need to delegate great authority to government and its reluctance to do so, and it allows for limited citizen willingness to participate in controlling and monitoring public agents and agencies.

To begin with, a public with trust encourages the government to delegate power based upon the general impression, rather than the detailed knowledge, of that government's stewardship. This view is particularly useful when the government is large and difficult for citizens to know

intimately. It is also useful when citizens are not willing to take the time to pursue the information they are able to obtain.

Because those who trust treat betrayal as only one possibility among many, they do not require that governance be built around mistrust, as do those with reflective confidence. Instead, for these people distrust can play a necessary fail-safe role, while their trust takes center stage. As a result, their distrust becomes a check on, *not the essence of,* the public agent's role. Accordingly, government need not be immobilized by a public fear that can only be satisfied (if at all) by a government made safe at the risk of its own impotence.

In addition, trust is both economic and convenient when compared to reflective confidence. By one taking a risk in trusting another, one need not rationally calculate all the contingencies in which betrayal could occur and provide for them in some way. This feature of trust is particularly appealing in a civil association in which public life normally plays a subordinate role to private life and in which the time the average citizen is willing to expend on monitoring the conduct of public agents is limited, at best.

A significant question must be addressed. If trust is based upon risk, why should anyone, let alone the citizens of a powerful and potentially exploitative government, take this risk? Unless a plausible answer can be given, trust loses its attractiveness as a potential basis for placing confidence in the government of a civil association. To answer this question it is useful for a moment to return to the discussion of trust as a social phenomenon. Annette Baier (1994) has observed that we trust those who care about our cares. By this she means not only those who share and further our interests but also those who hold the same values as intrinsically dear as we do. If we are lucky, we learn to risk trust on this basis, first, in our families and, then, with our close associates. At length, based upon these relationships, we build a general reservoir of social trust that has frequently been called "trust in trust." Once this reservoir is established, we are able to risk trusting strangers and, eventually, abstractions such as firms, bureaucracies, and states. In short, we learn to trust social systems as well as persons.

It does not take much imagination to see that the more trust in trust is present in a society, the easier it will be to develop trust in trusting government. Even though social trust is a necessary condition for building trust in government, it is rarely sufficient. The public must have other reasons to account government as trustworthy than that its members have found that social trust generally works in the familiar lived world. These other reasons are to be found in the third factor upon which confidence in government was said to rest, public stewardship.

Put succinctly, the public finds government worthy of risking trust to the degree that its members judge government to be exercising effective public stewardship. In its broadest sense, stewardship means the government's dedication and ability to realize the fundamental regime values that justify the continued existence of a political society to those who compose it.

In a civil association these regime values can be stated variously as liberty, equality, the rights of property, and individual self-realization or socially secured autonomy. Operationally, however, stewardship is judged by the degree to which citizens can reasonably assume that government (1) intends their general welfare, (2) is responsive to their will, (3) is responsible for the conduct of its agents and agencies, (4) is competent to act upon their behalf (5) is vigorous enough to pursue the welfare of the public, and (6) is enough constrained by respect for basic and statutory law not to abuse the considerable power it has been given by the people.

Admittedly, these judgments will often be made by the public in a less-than-rational manner, based upon fragmentary information and shaped more by the media than by extensive experience with public life. Nonetheless, the more the public perceives government as exercising stewardship in these terms, the more likely they will take the risk of trusting it.

That the citizens of a civil association will actually make the assumptions just discussed is scarcely a foregone conclusion. As seen, reoccurring abuse of governmental power, the complexity and remoteness of the modern administrative state, and the conflicting demands inherent in socially secured autonomy all work to assure this.

Consequently, those who seek to have citizens trust the government have their work cut out for them. In this regard, for broad approaches seem to dominate current political efforts to build trust in government: public choice, personalization, localization, and institutionalization.

These strategies are arrayed along a continuum. At one end of the continuum are strategies based upon the assumption that trust in government is most easily built upon the idea of citizens having some direct, personal, and immediate control over those who govern them. At the other end of the continuum are strategies that presume trust can be built upon one or another form of communal social affiliation.

Public choice strategy seeks to build trust in government by tying public policy and its implementation as closely as possible to rational, individual choices made in terms of votes, investment of tax dollars, or choices made among competing governmental services. The object is to place government under the control of market forces that are capable of transforming the rational self-interested choices of individuals into benefits that serve both individuals and the commonwealth equally.

What the citizen trusts in this model is his or her own rational self-interest, aggregated by the hidden hand of the market into a general good. What the citizen distrusts, and the model supposedly eliminates, is the contamination of public will when it is translated by a political and bureaucratic elite in the political process.

This strategy is appealing to the self-interested individualism that underlies the civil associations, but its critics say that it not only ignores the values and interests that are held in common by the political community but also disadvantages those citizens who do not have the economic means or political sophistication to vote with their dollars or their ballots.

Personalization is based upon the assumption that real trust can only grow out of the full psychological intimacy of a truly intersubjective relationship with another human being; therefore, those employing this strategy to build trust in government try to transform the impersonal associations that characterize an administrative state into something resembling interpersonal relationships. States are personalized in living monarchs; elected officials use media to develop personalized relations with constituents they will never meet; and government bureaucracies use customer-service improvement programs to personalize routine functions by making them more responsive to individual citizen needs. Here, the citizen trusts the validity of his or her judgment of a public official's trustworthiness based upon an intersubjective relationship with the official. What the citizen does not trust are faceless, impersonal bureaucrats and bureaucracies.

Again, this strategy has undoubted appeal in a society oriented to individuals. Here, many see larger social structures as blunting and perverting rather than facilitating genuine human relationships and the interpersonal trust that can flow from them. Moreover, personalization can actually be a highly effective means of rebuilding trust in government when political institutions are under the most serve sorts of challenges. This is clearly shown by Franklin Delano Roosevelt's (1933–1945) fireside chats to the American public during the darkest days of the American Depression and World War II. Yet, personalization of fundamentally impersonal relationships can also backfire easily, simply because it is hard to reproduce the rich and intimate character of a genuine intersubjective relationship with another human being in an impersonal setting. Such relationships are frequently inauthentic and ultimately disappointing as a result. For example, the serious and concerned young couple in the 30-second commercial who warn us against the dire consequences of a public policy turn out to be actors reading a script full of half-truths; the "down home" politician in the television advertisement is revealed by the press as an urban sophisticate with feet of clay; the smiling agency customer service representative winds up to be as constrained by rules and policies as the faceless bureaucrat.

In each case, the inauthentic personalized relationship ultimately disillusions the citizen. Worse yet, it casts further doubt upon the credibility of political actors and the political system itself. Without credibility, trust as a mode of instilling confidence has little chance of success.

Localism as a strategy seeks to build trust in government by placing as much governance as possible at the level of the local jurisdiction or neighborhood, where it can be directly controlled by the citizens acting as a community. The assumption is that trust can best grow in a human association with a clearly defined common purpose, based upon close personal relationships, for it is here that all clearly share our cares. Thus, localism combines the belief that trust roots best in intersubjective relationships, with the classical political contention that trust flourishes in a purposive community of civic friends seeking a common vision of the good life.

Localism assumes that the citizen trusts the civic friends who share his or her cares and, as important, the social institutions of the community they and their forebears have developed. Correspondingly, it is held that citizens do not trust the anomic world of modern society nor the large-scale, legislated institutions that characterize that society.

Localism is clearly attractive as a trust-building mechanism, since it roots governmental trust in a considerable amount of direct citizen control, as well as strong interpersonal ties forged within the context of a community of civic friends. When viewed from the strongly individualist perspective of the civil association, however, it has two severe problems. First, close-knit purposive communities can be as restrictive of individual freedoms and liberties as any oppressive centralized national bureaucracy. Second, the demand for socially secured autonomy requires both capitalization and bureaucratization on a scale that is far beyond the scope of most local communities. Therefore, the extent localism can be achieved without undermining a vigorous and effective national government, capable of providing adequate social and military security, is always problematical.

The final trust-building strategy, institutionalism, seeks to develop trust in government by using political institutions that direct public agents and agencies to honor and promote the fundamental regime values that justify the continued existence of the civil association. The assumption is that citizens can trust bureaucrats who are, essentially, strangers and bureaucracies that are impersonal abstractions if both are governed by institutionally defined and enforced duties and obligations. In the case of the civil association, these duties and obligations encourage and constrain public agents and agencies to observe and promote the regime values that underwrite socially secured autonomy, liberty, equal treatment, reasonable use of property, and the publicly financed assistance necessary to achieve self-realization.

Institutionalization would seem an effective strategy to win public trust in a civil association that depends upon a large, relatively centralized administrative state. The very nature of the civil association often militates against its success, however. As will be recalled, civil associations are often seen as political societies composed of anomic individuals who cooperate with one another for mutual convenience and benefit. In such a society, institutions are often seen as necessary evils that are potential threats to the exercise of individual liberty. To the degree that this is so, they are often viewed with suspicion, no matter how socially or politically useful they may be.

Even a cursory review of these trust-building strategies indicates that they appear to conflict with one another, so that trust based upon one strategy could easily have the affect of diminishing trust based upon the others. For example, trust resting on public choice may seem like thinly disguised, socially destructive self-interest to those who prefer to trust government on a communitarian or institutional basis.

Yet, if one looks at what all these strategies are attempting to do, one finds a common, if paradoxical, project underpinning them. It is the project that energizes and justifies the modern state as a civil association: the employment of one's life, property, and most of all, liberty to pursue happiness, viewed as self-realization. The paradox inherent in this project is that one requires liberty to control one's own destiny, but the most vigorous sort of social cooperation to achieve it. Thus, those who would govern the civil association find themselves dealing with two themes that can exist in either creative or destructive tension with one another: individual opportunism and nurturing social support—the themes of socially secured autonomy.

Therefore, public agents who would build trust in the government of a civil association quickly become preoccupied with the paradox of individual opportunism and social cooperation that lies at the heart of individual self-realization as a collective project. To warrant public trust, then, the government of a civil association must continually demonstrate that it cannot only manage but also make creative use of the tension between individual pursuits and the social cooperation essential to accomplishing them.

Despite their seeming disparities, all of the strategies outlined previously represent attempts to manage the paradox of socially secured autonomy in ways that will make government more credible, thus, more trustworthy. For example, public choice tells us that market and quasi-market forces allow us to make individual, self-interested choices, which when politically aggregated, will automatically provide the social support and nurture we need. Personalization promises to put large-scale remote and impersonal political relationships on an intersubjective basis, where we can most easily exercise personal control over them and obtain a maximum of concerned support from the public agents involved. Localism seeks to provide both greater direct individual control over government and a nurturing social environment supplied by a community of civic friends. Institutionalization holds forth the hope of establishing a government limited to and bound by regime values, which not only protect individual liberty, equality, and use of property but also encourage the overall support required to achieve individual self-realization.

Each of these strategies seems to wax and wane in popularity. As important, each is also consistently rejected by a portion of the populace who cannot abide the premises and values upon which it rests. Therefore, it is likely that the search for ways to deal with the paradox of socially secured autonomy will continue unabated, as will the corresponding quest for the warrants that cause the public to deem a government trustworthy.

It is not unrealistic to think public administrators will play a significant role in facilitating this quest for warrants of governmental trustworthiness. It may be that their role will be less to advocate any one of these flawed strategies than to ensure that the quest continues creatively and earnestly by those who govern. This role will require that administrators continually remind those that they serve of four things: First, the paradox of socially secured autonomy is unlikely to be eliminated in the foreseeable future. It will continue as long as the civil association continues to spread and be emulated as a highly desirable political system.

Second, eliminating the inherent tensions in the paradox of socially secured autonomy is not a particularly wise course of action. Trading freedom for security, or security for freedom, rarely makes sense. The former frequently leads to forms of totalitarianism that are better at denying human freedom than achieving social security. The latter denies human development the social support it requires and thereby defeats its own vaunted goal of individual self-actualization.

Third, the very fact that the civil association not only lives with but also virtually in the paradox of socially secured autonomy suggests that the citizens who compose it are highly complex human beings with equally complex natures. In view of this, trust-building efforts based upon simplistic models of human nature as entirely self-interested or benignly social are unlikely to be very effective in accomplishing this task.

Fourth, the most viable efforts to build public trust by public agents and agencies, in all likelihood, will be those that cause the public to face and use creatively the paradox inherent in socially secured autonomy: the relationship between one's autonomy and one's inevitable independence upon others.

HENRY D. KASS

BIBLIOGRAPHY

Baier, Annette, 1994. *Moral Prejudices: Essays on Ethics*. Cambridge: Harvard University Press.
Bailey, Fredrick George, 1988. *Humbuggery and Manipulation: The Art of Leadership*. Ithaca: Cornell University Press.
Berry, Jeffery, Kent Portney, and Ken Thompson, 1993. *Rebirth of Urban Democracy*. Washington, D.C.: Brookings Institution.
Carnevale, David, 1995. *Trustworthy Government*. San Francisco: Jossey Bass.
Craig, Stephen C., 1993. *The Malevolent Leaders: Popular Discontent in America*. Boulder, CO: Westview Press.
Gambetta, Diego, 1988. *Trust: Making and Breaking Cooperative Relations*. New York: Basil Blackwell.
Golembiewski, Robert, and Mark McConkie, 1975. "The Centrality of Interpersonal Trust in Group Processes." In Cary L. Cooper, ed., *Theories of Group Processes*. New York: John Wiley and Sons.
Lewis, J. David, and Andrew Weigert, 1985. "Trust as Social Reality." *Social Forces*, vol. 63 (June): 967–985.
Locke, John, [1690] 1986. *The Second Treatise on Civil Government*. Reprint. Buffalo: Prometheus Books.
Luhmann, Niklas, 1979. *Trust and Power. Chichester:* John Wiley and Sons.
Oakshott, Michael, 1975. *On Human Conduct*. Oxford: Clarendon Press.
Ostrom, Vincent, 1973. *The Intellectual Crisis in American Public Administration*. Tuscaloosa: University of Alabama Press.
Selznick, Philip, 1992. *The Moral Commonwealth*. Berkeley: University of California.
Silver, A., 1985. "Trust in Social and Political Theory." In G. D. Suttles and M. N. Zold, eds., *The Challenge of Social Control*. Norwood, NJ: Ablex.

PUBLIC WELFARE. A set of programs to provide economic security to those unable to meet their own needs and social services for those unable to function effectively in contemporary society.

In the United States, the public welfare system has its origins in the poor laws of an earlier era, but owes its current form and shape to bursts of social policy activity during the New Deal of President Franklin Roosevelt, the New Society ambitions of the Lyndon Johnson presidency, and efforts to transform the welfare system in the 1990s. It is a system in the sense that it encompasses a set of programs that are related to each other, although it was not designed to function as an integrated whole. In fact, it is an amalgam of programs that frequently overlap, duplicate, and contradict each other. In 1991, for example, the national government administered seventy-five programs to help the economically disadvantaged.

Although there are many programs of the welfare state that make benefits and services available to the middle class and poor alike, the United States, more than other nations, has set up programs that separate out the poor and unemployed for special treatment. Thus, although many nations have national health insurance plans that cover the entire population, the United States has no national health insurance program. Instead, it has Medicare to provide health insurance for the elderly and Medicaid to provide health insurance for the poor. While other nations have family allowances, the United States does not, opting instead for public assistance to the needy.

The public welfare system in the United States is intergovernmental in nature. Although individual states and localities initiate a number of their own programs to address specific problems, most welfare activity in the United States takes place though programs that originate in national legislation, have joint federal/state funding, and are largely administered by state and local units of government.

Components of the Welfare System

What kinds of programs make up the public welfare system? The system includes cash assistance programs, voucher and in-kind programs, and social services. The cash assistance components of the welfare system are: Temporary Assistance for Needy Families (TANF); Supplementary Security Income (SSI) for the elderly, blind, and disabled; and general assistance programs operated by the states for individuals who do not qualify for one of the federally subsidized categorical programs. The Earned Income Tax Credit of the national income tax is another form of cash assistance to low-income families. The voucher and in-kind programs include food stamps, Medicaid health insurance, school lunch and school breakfast programs, public housing, and subsidized housing. Social services include a variety of family service, mental health, and age group and gender specific programs.

The public assistance programs are described under the **public assistance** heading in this encyclopedia.

Separate from this system of public welfare is a social insurance system whose beneficiaries are eligible because of contributions by themselves or their employers to the funding of those programs. These include the Old Age, Survivors, and Disability Insurance Program of the Social Security Act, the related Medicare health insurance program, and the Unemployment Insurance program.

Much of the American welfare system is a product of the Social Security Act of 1934. That act created a program of Old-Age and Survivors Insurance, commonly called Social Security, to provide pensions for much of the workforce. While the coverage of that program was originally limited, it has expanded over the years to cover almost the entire work force, except teachers in public schools and a small group of other workers. It has also grown to include a disability insurance program and a health insurance program for the elderly known as Medicare.

In addition to creating the Social Security program, the Social Security Act provided for creation of a program of public assistance for mothers with children that was called Aid to Dependent Children. It was later renamed Aid to Families with Dependent Children and is usually referred to as AFDC. AFDC was replaced by Temporary Assistance for Needy Famlies (TANF) in 1996. Over time, programs of Aid to the Blind (AB), Aid to the Permanently and Totally Disabled (APTD), and Old Age Assistance (OAA) were added to the public assistance programs supported under the Social Security Act. These programs were replaced by the Supplemental Security Income Act of 1972 which created a new system of national assistance for the elderly, blind, and disabled who were not eligible for coverage under the provisions of the Social Security program.

Unemployment Insurance is another component of the American welfare system. The Unemployment Insurance program operates under provisions of the Social Security Act and is administered by state governments. It provides weekly cash payments to covered unemployed workers. These payments cover only a portion of the worker's lost income and continue for a limited period of time, generally twenty-six weeks. Unemployed workers are eligible only if they had been employed for a specified period of time and had sufficient earnings in covered employment.

Congress added significantly to this general range of economic security programs in the 1960s when it adopted the food stamp program, an array of employment and training activities, low-income housing subsidies, and various social services, such as day care for eligible populations.

Issues

The public welfare system is confronted by a number of issues. Does it provide adequately for those in need? Does it undermine the work ethic and foster dependency? Does it undermine the family? Does it treat people fairly and equitably?

Liberals maintain that shortcomings of a market economy, unequally dispersed power, and racial discrimination create conditions under which some citizens are unable to participate fully in social and economic systems. To address these inadequacies, liberals have promoted support systems and services to insure that all citizens' basic needs are met and opportunities for economic opportunity are equalized. Supporters of the welfare state have spent years trying to extend its reach, enhance the adequacy of its support mechanisms, and make the welfare system more equitable and fair. This has meant a long search for ways to expand programs or to create new programs to fill gaps in existing arrangements. It has also meant trying to nationalize public welfare. The creation of the Supplemental Security program, for example, was heralded as a significant move because it increased benefits levels for recipients in low benefit states by providing a national minimum benefit. When cash benefits of welfare proved insufficient to meet the needs of recipients, support was forthcoming for in-kind benefit programs such as food stamps.

Conservative critics have come to prominence in recent years as their political fortunes improved. They have sought to restrict the welfare state, reduce the generosity of programs, and promote local control. Thus, they have favored efforts to impose work requirements on welfare recipients, place time-limits on benefits, reduce benefit levels, eliminate programs, and transfer program authority to state governments. Liberals, who long considered work requirements for welfare recipients to be undesirable, have come to promote their own versions of how to link welfare to work, primarily by increasing opportunities, expanding services to remove barriers to work, and using the tax code to reward work.

Although the question is not asked often these days, it is still reasonable to ask whether welfare benefits are adequate to address basic human needs for food, shelter, health, and development. Some argue that the tools are there to meet the needs of the poor, if resources could only be more effectively coordinated. Others maintain that a system that provides only $120 a month in cash support for a family of three in Mississippi has along way to go before it makes adequate provision for the population. Cash benefits have declined in value over the past twenty-five years, but in-kind support was expanded and increased. Many of the poor, particularly the working poor, are ineligible for income or in-kind assistance.

There is general recognition that there are gaps in certain components of the current welfare system. For example, although the United States Congress failed to act on health care reform in 1994, most members of Congress recognized that there were large numbers of individuals who were without adequate health insurance because it was unavailable to them or too expensive for them to afford. When the quest for comprehensive reform which would have addressed issues of cost, availability and adequacy of coverage, and quality of care was defeated, the chance to expand coverage for vulnerable groups was missed.

Despite these shortcomings of the current system, conservative critics maintain that it is too large in scope and generous in its benefits. Touting the virtue of individual responsibility, they assert that the programs of the welfare state foster dependency, encourage unwed mothers to have children, and promote the disintegration of the family. They argue that it is unfair for those who work to have to pay taxes to support those who do not.

Conservative critics and some liberals say that programs like AFDC did too little to encourage work. Only by moving people from welfare to work will the corrosive effects of the system on the human spirit be eliminated. Liberals tend to believe that there are many barriers to moving people from welfare to work; they favor eliminating those barriers by providing education and training that would allow welfare recipients to compete in the job market and providing support services that would allow them to function as effective, productive workers. Conservatives maintain that the mere existence of the welfare system provides substantial disincentives to work and family stability. By providing economic security, it allows people to reject personal responsibility for their own well-being. The most radical of these critics would simply do away with all public welfare programs. Those with more modest criticisms would eliminate some services, restrict access to others, and impose substantial work requirements on welfare recipients who are able to work. Liberal and conservatives alike came to speak of mutual obligations of welfare recipients in recent years, asserting a belief that just as the state has an obligation to help the poor, so also do welfare recipients have an obligation to take steps to help themselves.

Republican majorities elected to the U.S. Congress in 1994 and reelected in 1996 have been committed to major changes in, even the elimination of, major components of the American welfare system. Most prominent among the changes are proposals to limit and reduce funding, consolidate programs, set stringent limits on who would be eligible and how long they could receive benefits, and largely transfer many programs to the states in a variety of block grants. Many of these changes were realized with the adoption of the Personal Responsibility and Work Opportunity Reconciliation Act of 1996, provisions of which are discussed under the entry for **public assistance.**

EDWARD T. JENNINGS, JR.

BIBLIOGRAPHY

Bane, Mary Jo and David T. Ellwood, 1994. *Welfare Realities: From Rhetoric to Reform.* Cambridge: Harvard University Press.

Berkowitz, Edward D. 1991. *America's Welfare State: From Roosevelt to Reagan.* Baltimore: Johns Hopkins University Press.

Ellwood, David T., 1988. *Poor Support: Poverty in the American Family.* New York: Basic Books.

Grimaldi, Paul L. 1980. *Supplemental Security Income: The New Federal Program for the Aged, Blind, and Disabled.* Washington, D.C.: American Enterprise Institute for Public Policy Research.

Gueron, Judith M. and Edward Pauly, 1991. *From Welfare to Work*. New York: Russell Sage Foundation.

Jennings, Jr., Edward T. and Neal S. Zank, eds., 1993. *Welfare System Reform: Coordinating Federal, State, and Local Public Assistance Programs*. Greenwood, CT: Greenwood Press.

Marmor, Theodore R., Jerry L. Mashaw, and Philip L. Harvey. 1992. *America's Misunderstood Welfare State: Persistent Myths, Enduring Realities*. New York: Basic Books.

Mead, Lawrence M. 1992. *The New Politics of Poverty: The Nonworking Poor in America*. New York: Basic Books.

Murray, Charles, 1984. *Losing Ground: American Social Policy, 1950–1980*. New York: Basic Books.

Trattner, Walter I. 1979. *From Poor Law to Welfare State: A History of Social Welfare in America*. New York: The Free Press.

Q

QUALIFIED IMMUNITY.

QUALIFIED IMMUNITY. An exemption from being sued, subject to specific restrictions. It is contrasted to absolute immunity, which is unconditional and without exception (see **absolute immunity**; **sovereign immunity**; and **official immunity**). It must be noted that the conditions applied under the qualified immunity doctrine may be more or less extensive. Some qualified immunity privileges still provide far-reaching protection. There is now a trend toward curtailing immunity to increase accountability and provide remedies against abuses committed by government agencies and their officials. All types of immunity may be qualified in one way or another, whether applying to states, governments, or public officials, domestic or foreign.

Qualified Immunity of Domestic Origin

Under common law, government and state agencies enjoyed absolute immunity; state officials were as liable as any private citizen, but gradually they were given absolute immunity by statute and court decision. Absolute immunity, it was then believed, permitted expeditious and effective administration, sheltered from the threat of liability. The dark side of this doctrine was that the parties harmed by public officials were left without redress even when bureaucrats acted in bad faith and with malicious intent. As Kenneth Warren (1996) has observed, government agencies and public officials were thus placed above the law (p. 465). The danger of injustice increased as the influence of governmental institutions became more pervasive.

Eventually, limits began to be imposed on immunity privileges, although this process evolved slowly and unevenly. The Tucker Act of 1855 conferred jurisdiction on United States district courts to hear claims against the United States involving contracts. In 1882, the Supreme Court in *U.S. v. Lee* questioned the logic of the sovereign immunity doctrine: "Courts of justice are established, not only to decide upon controverted rights of the citizens as against each other, but also upon rights in controversy between them and the government" (106 U.S. 196). Qualified immunity would eventually permit it.

In 1946, Congress passed the Federal Tort Claims Act, allowing suits against the United States government, under certain circumstances, for tortious acts committed by its officials. This act forced the federal government to assume some responsibility for the damage caused by its agents; but it severely limited the tort action suits that could be initiated. The Supreme Court itself was restrictive in its interpretation of the act, making it even more difficult to win tort suits against the federal government. In 1976, Congress amended sections 702 and 703 of the Administrative Procedure Act, thus allowing the U.S. government to be sued for relief, other than money damages.

Reform proved easier at the state level, although another half century elapsed before it could happen on a large scale. Over the past 30 years, however, most states have, either by statute or court decision, eliminated or greatly restricted the doctrine of sovereign immunity. Statutes have been enacted providing for waivers of sovereign immunity: some fairly cautious and limited, as in Utah and California, others comprehensive, as in Washington and New York.

Even more extensive is the retreat from sovereign immunity in judicial practice during the same period. In *Muskopf v. Corning Hospital District,* a landmark case in this evolution, the California court held that "the rule of governmental immunity from tort liability . . . must be discarded as mistaken and unjust." Sovereign immunity in tort "is an anachronism, without rational basis, and has existed only by the force of inertia" (359 P. 2d 457, 458, 460, Cal. 1961). Increasing numbers of state courts have rejected, to varying extents, the doctrine of sovereign immunity from tort liability.

In 1978, the Supreme Court, in *Monell v. Department of Social Services of New York,* reversed its earlier stand and ruled that local governing bodies can be sued under Section 1983 of the Civil Rights Act of 1871 when the action falls under certain categories (which it specified), if the governing bodies' policies deprive plaintiffs of their constitutional rights. In *Owen v. City of Independence, Missouri* (1980), the Supreme Court noted that

> Section 1983 was intended not only to provide compensation to the victims of past abuses but to serve as a deterrent against future constitutional deprivations as well. . . . The knowledge that a municipality will be liable for all of its injurious conduct, whether committed in good faith or not, should create an incentive for officials who may harbor doubts about the lawfulness of their intended actions to err on the side of protecting citizens' constitutional rights. Furthermore, the threat that damages might be levied against the city may encourage those in policy-making positions to institute internal rules and programs designed to minimize the likelihood of unintentional infringements on constitutional rights (445 U.S. 651–652).

This was a clear enunciation of the profound merit of curbing sovereign immunity.

In the meantime, government officials, once totally liable under common law, had progressively been granted absolute immunity from tort action (see **official immunity**), and the vast expansion of officials immunity prevented too many private individuals from obtaining damages in court even when maliciously victimized by public administrators. Growing concern about injustice led to the application of qualified immunity to government officials.

The Civil Rights Act of 1871, Section 1983, provided a foundation for a host of damage actions against state (but not federal) officials. For example, in *Scheuer v. Rhodes* (1974), the Supreme Court, reversing two lower court rulings, held that state public officials were not entitled to absolute immunity, but to a "qualified immunity" of "varying scope." It must vary according to "the scope of discretion and responsibility of the office and all circumstances as they reasonably appeared at the time of the action on which liability is sought to be based" (416 U.S. 232, 247). The Court concluded that granting immunity to administrative officials depended upon whether they could show that they acted reasonably under the circumstances and in good faith.

As Stephen Breyer and Richard Stewart (1992) noted, in 1971, the U.S. Supreme Court qualified the immunity of federal public servants, without the help of a federal statute (p. 1001). In *Bivens v. Six Unknown Federal Narcotics Agents* (1971), the Court ruled that federal officials could be sued for damages resulting from their violations of plaintiff's constitutional rights. The Supreme Court justified its position with the rationale enunciated in the classic case of *Marbury v. Madison* (1803), "The very essence of civil liberty certainly consists in the right of every individual to claim the protection of the laws, whenever he receives an injury" (403 U.S. 396). One wonders why it took so long to remember this fundamental principle of justice. And the Court emphasized that "federal courts may use any available remedy to make good the wrong done" (p. 396). The Supreme Court ruled, therefore, that the damage suit was appropriate and that federal courts could provide relief by ordering money damages to be paid to the plaintiff. The case was remanded to the Second Circuit Court of Appeals, which decided that although governmental officials should be protected by the official immunity doctrine (see official immunity), they are not entitled to immunity from tort action in all situations, particularly when their actions violate constitutional rights.

Breyer and Stewart (1992) also noted that the courts have made the Bivens type of action an effective way of initiating against federal public servants the same kind of constitutionally based damage action made possible by Section 1983 of the Civil Rights Act against state officers (p. 1002). In *Wood v. Strickland* (1975), the Supreme Court made public officials more vulnerable to tort action by ruling that they could not be immune from damage suits if "they reasonably should have known" that the action they took in carrying out their official responsibilities violated the constitutional rights of the persons concerned (Warren

1996, pp. 492–494). This constitutes an extra incentive for public servants to pay attention to the rights of the people they deal with, and to avoid rash decisions.

In Britain and many of the countries influenced by the English law tradition, government and officials liability is the rule (see **sovereign immunity** and **official immunity**). Public authorities enjoy no immunity from the ordinary law of tort, except insofar as statutes specify such exemptions. Some immunity is given to persons executing the orders of courts, such as sheriffs and prison wardens. Police officers have a narrow statutory immunity in executing arrest warrants. But administrative authorities have virtually no immunity. A few statutes exempt local officials from personal liability for what they have done in good faith (in those cases, however, the public agency itself can be made liable), and judges enjoy special immunity from tort suits, but they may be liable in damages if they exceed their authority while acting in "bad faith."

In France, and in many of the countries following its administrative law system, public institutions are normally liable for harm done, in some situations, even without any wrong having been committed, where harm has been caused to an individual for the public good—a system of state responsibility far beyond anything developed in the common law world. Public officials are not liable for their service-related faults, but the state is. They are liable for their personal faults (see **official immunity**).

Qualified Foreign Immunity

Foreign immunity has also been affected by the trend away from absolute protection from tort action, although to a lesser extent. The sovereign state, long absolutely immune, saw an erosion of its privileges when it began engaging in large-scale business activity—state merchant vessels or state-owned commercial enterprises competing on the open market with their private counterparts. It was, of course, unfair to shelter state enterprises from tort actions in situations in which their private competitors were totally liable.

Their immunity began to be qualified after World War I. In 1926, the Brussels Conference unanimously accepted that there should be no immunity for state-owned ships engaged in commerce. This was eventually extended to other state business activities, as in *Dralle v. Republic of Czechoslovakia* (Supreme Court of Austria, 1950), involving the nationalized branch of a cosmetics firm. Other state instrumentalities or property remain protected by absolute immunity. The United States Foreign Sovereign Immunity Act of 1976 denies jurisdictional immunity in the case of property taken by the state in violation of international law.

Foreign armed forces, in the absence of any international agreement regulating their status in given situations, remain entitled to absolute immunity. However, as military units came to be deployed abroad for the purpose of collective defense, for example, under North Atlantic Treaty Organization (NATO) arrangements, special agreements were negotiated between the states concerned, qualifying the traditional immunity of these foreign forces.

Diplomatic personnel have enjoyed absolute immunity dating back to classical antiquity, but the vast expansion of diplomatic representation has led to some restrictions. Various conventions negotiated under the auspices of the United Nations now identify diverse categories of persons serving on diplomatic missions and specify the level of immunity accorded to each group. Diplomatic agents in the classic role of representatives in foreign embassies retain very extensive immunity, but a few exceptions are now specified, for example, professional business activity outside the agents' official functions. Other categories of diplomatic personnel, such as diplomats representing states at the UN, or high UN officials, such as the Secretary-General, enjoy an immunity somewhat comparable to what is granted to officials in the preceding category, but with a small number of additional restrictions. The foundation of all immunity privileges is now explicitly functional; but it must be acknowledged that diplomats could be equally effective in their mission with more extensively qualified immunity.

The trend in the area of foreign immunity is toward greater qualification and restriction. However, most nation states retain their fixation on sovereignty and remain extremely reluctant to accept limitations in the enjoyment of their privileges. Foreign immunity is therefore significantly less qualified than its domestic counterpart.

JEAN-ROBERT LEGUEY-FEILLEUX

BIBLIOGRAPHY

Blum, K. M., 1993. "Qualified Immunity: A User's Manual." *Indiana Law Review*, vol. 26: 187–226.

Breyer, Stephen G., and Richard B. Stewart, 1992. *Administrative Law and Regulatory Policy*. 3d ed. Boston: Little, Brown.

Brown, L. Neville, and John S. Bell, 1993. *French Administrative Law*. 4th ed. Oxford: Clarendon Press.

Davis, Kenneth Culp, and Richard J. Pierce, Jr., 1994. *Administrative Law Treatise*. 3d ed. (3 vols. with 1994 supplement). Boston: Little, Brown.

Engle, S., 1992. "Choosing Law for Attributing Liability Under the Foreign Sovereign Immunities Act: A Proposal for Uniformity." *Fordham International Law Journal*, vol. 15: 1060–1098.

Henkin, Louis, Richard Crawford Pugh, Oscar Schachter, and Hans Smit, 1993. *International Law*. 3d ed. St. Paul, MN: West.

Pierce, C. J., 1994. "The Misapplication of Qualified Immunity: Unfair Procedural Burdens for Constitutional Damage Claims Requiring Proof of the Defendant's Intent." *Fordham Law Review*, vol. 62 (April): 1769–1793.

Schwartz, Bernard, 1994. *Administrative Law*. 4th ed. Boston: Little, Brown.

Thomas, C. W., 1992. "Resolving the Problem of Qualified Immunity for Private Defendants in Section 1983 and Bivens [Bivens v. Six Unknown Named Agents of the Federal Bureau of Narcotics, 91 S. Ct. 1999 (1971)]." *Louisiana Law Review*, vol. 53 (November): 449–493.

Wade, Sir William, and Christopher Forsyth, 1994. *Administrative Law*. Oxford: Clarendon Press.

Warren, Kenneth F., 1996. *Administrative Law in the Political System*. 3d ed. Upper Saddle River, NJ: Prentice-Hall.

QUALITY AWARDS IN EUROPE.

A performance measurement instrument that fosters innovation and quality in the public sector by identifying excellent public organizations through independent panels, with the active participation of public agencies. The aim of quality awards is to make the success factors of excellent administrative practices visible and public. This definition excludes awards that are given to organizations for outstanding past achievements without using performance indicators and without submitting to a competitive selection process. For example, the grant of the Distinguished Service Cross to public organizations in Germany does not fall into the quality award category because the selection is not by competitive process. Nevertheless, the previous definition is broad enough to include innovation awards in the public sector. As Sandford Borins (1995) has pointed out, the difference between specific and general quality awards is gradual rather than fundamental: Given the elusive nature of innovation in the public sector, judges of specific innovation awards will always have to include the organization's effectiveness in their overall judgment.

Quality awards are an important benchmarking instrument and are closely related to other benchmarking instruments, such as the ISO 9000 series and citizen's charters. The ISO 9000 series is an internationally recognized standard for quality assurance. (ISO is the International Organization for Standardization, which is a federation of national standards bodies.) This international standard gives indications on how to set up quality systems in organizations where a contract between seller and buyer requires the demonstration of a supplier's capability to supply to mutually agreed requirements. Thus, the ISO 9000 series, in its present form, only requires an organization to build a quality system, such that its products comply to stated specifications. It does not require, albeit it does not prevent, an organization from aiming for full customer satisfaction, or even customer delight (Ware 1993).

Charters are important official documents expressing committment to the modernization of the public services. "The potential of charters is to express a consensus on a societal model on the behaviour and responsibilities, rights and duties, expectations and trust, of politicians in government, civil servants in public services and citizens" (Bouckaert 1995, p. 194). The essential idea behind charters is to increase the quality of life in society and to pay more attention to the needs of citizens. The ultimate purpose is to renew citizen trust not only in public services but also in the state.

Figure I visualizes the position of quality awards in this benchmark family: Certification according to the ISO 9000 series checks whether a certain (minimum) level of quality management has been attained by an organization. The standard that has to be reached is conformity of product quality. This standard approach also underlies the British Charter Mark Award. It is attributed to public organizations that have fulfilled certain criteria of quality service delivery. Nevertheless, in contrast the static approach of ISO 9000, the evaluation scheme of the Charter Mark Award puts emphasis on built-in mechanisms of improved service delivery over time. Quality awards, however, do not look for the "good" public organizations, but for the "best of the class." In other words, quality awards look for the maximum level of quality in public services; thus they not only have to express themselves in the high quality of service they deliver but also in regard to working relations.

The Origin of Quality Awards

Quality awards have their origin in the total quality management (TQM) movement. Whereas the standardization approach, such as ISO 9000–9004, helps organizations to reach a minimum level of quality, the intention of TQM is to make organizations work out their own specific quality

FIGURE I. BENCHMARK INSTRUMENTS AND PERFORMANCE-LEVEL TARGETS

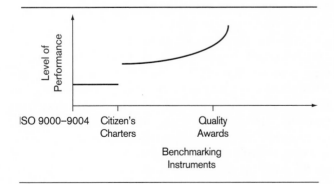

SOURCE: E. Loeffler, (1996), *The Modernization of the Public Sector in an International Comparative Perspective: Concepts and Methods of Awarding Quality in the Public Sector in OECD Countries*, Speyerer Forschungsberichte No. 151, second edition. Research Institute for Public Administration: Speyer, p. 35.

improvement system (Antilla 1993, p. 19). Yet, the two schools are not as contradictory to each other as different quality movements may suggest: Standards give organizations an idea of the different aspects of quality and enable them to obtain a minimum standard of quality, which can be the starting point for total quality management. The German experience with awards is that the participation of an organization in an award program only makes sense if the organization has already reached a certain level of quality management, thereby, standards can be a useful instrument.

As already pointed out, quality awards competitions stem from the private sector and have been transferred to the public sector as a result of a paradigmatic shift taking place in public administration in postindustrial countries (Reinermann 1993).

Quality awards are introduced as surrogates of competition in the public sector where a market does not exist. The competition among the participants of an awards program is intended to motivate members of public organizations to take an active role in their organization's quality management. If they win the award, they then may act as a model for other organizations; if they do not win the award, they then learn that they need to do better in the future. Public sector quality awards have another important function. Whereas with private goods there is a price reflecting a complex measure of all the quality characteristics economic actors attribute to a good, there is no such indicator with public goods. There results a complicated problem in the assessment of quality in the public sector. Here, quality awards can be an instrument to measure quality by using multidimensional indicators.

This technical function is closely related to the third function of public quality award programs, which is to help public organizations improve their quality assurance systems by learning from each other. Quality awards identify excellent public organizations, and their success factors are made visible to other public organizations (Haubner et al. 1993, p. 46). This means that there is also a cooperative element in quality competition awards, which is perhaps the most important function of such quality awards if they claim to be an instrument in fostering innovations and quality in the public sector.

It is obvious that there is a tension between the competitive and cooperative elements of public quality award competitions. On one hand, participants of award programs want to know what are their strong and weak points and how good they are compared to other organizations. On the other hand, nobody wants to "lose," so organizers of quality awards have to stress the cooperative element of the award and that "every participant wins" (Information Sheet of the Second Speyer Quality Award 1994) by learning from others. They must also emphasize

FIGURE II. CLASSIFICATION OF QUALITY AWARDS

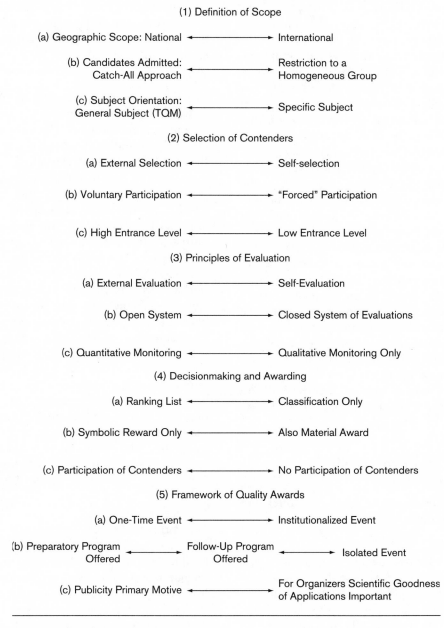

(1) Definition of Scope

(a) Geographic Scope: National ←————→ International

(b) Candidates Admitted:
Catch-All Approach ————→ Restriction to a
Homogeneous Group

(c) Subject Orientation:
General Subject (TQM) ————→ Specific Subject

(2) Selection of Contenders

(a) External Selection ←————→ Self-selection

(b) Voluntary Participation ←————→ "Forced" Participation

(c) High Entrance Level ←————→ Low Entrance Level

(3) Principles of Evaluation

(a) External Evaluation ←————→ Self-Evaluation

(b) Open System ←————→ Closed System of Evaluations

(c) Quantitative Monitoring ←————→ Qualitative Monitoring Only

(4) Decisionmaking and Awarding

(a) Ranking List ←————→ Classification Only

(b) Symbolic Reward Only ←————→ Also Material Award

(c) Participation of Contenders ←————→ No Participation of Contenders

(5) Framework of Quality Awards

(a) One-Time Event ←————→ Institutionalized Event

(b) Preparatory Program
Offered ←————→ Follow-Up Program
Offered ←————→ Isolated Event

(c) Publicity Primary Motive ←————→ For Organizers Scientific Goodness
of Applications Important

© SOURCE: Klages 1995, modified by the author

that winning the award itself is not so important. This trade-off that has to be made by the organizers reveals the inherent problem of award programs. If the learning aspect is central, it might be more functional for the program if they avoided the term "competition" and looked for another term. Alternately, if their aim is to introduce competition where there is no market competition, then winning the award becomes the crucial element of the program.

Categories of Quality Awards

There are many different kinds of quality awards. Figure II summarizes the classification of quality awards, providing an idea of the different ways a public quality award program can be organized.

Determining the scope of a quality award is a rather pragmatic decision, but it has serious methodological implications. The workload and difficulties of the evaluation process for award organizers of all kinds of public agencies will be greatest after they have decided to vie for an international award, with no specific subject. When it comes to the selection of contenders, self-selection is the most common approach of award organizers. The information campaign does not necessarily reach all potential candidates, but it helps to foster the sense of competition in the public sector. External selection can ensure that only superior organizations participate in the award.

There is common agreement among organizers that participation in quality awards has to be voluntary if motivation among the candidates is to be maintained. A similar decision—whether the selection of participants is external or internal—has to be made in the evaluation process. In the first case, objectivity and coherence are more easily obtained; in the second case, there is the opportunity for organizational learning about strengths and weaknesses. Since self-evaluations have to be supplemented by external evaluations, most quality awards organizers prefer internal evaluation. The other important choice in the evaluation process concerns the "openness of the reference model": Does the award winner have to correspond to a normative model of an ideally shaped organization, or is the award open to different concepts of "modernizing"? Finally, is the evaluation based on verbal descriptions of the candidates or is it based on standardized indicators of quantitative measurement? Most developers of quality awards do not establish a ranking list because of tricky methodological problems.

Important Quality Awards for Public Agencies in Western Europe

Awards for excellent administrative practices are offered in several European countries.

Scandinavian Countries

In all Scandinavian countries, quality awards were originally organized for the private sector only but now they have been extended to the public sector. In Finland, the Finnish Quality Award (Suomen Laatupalkinto) was made open to public agencies in 1994. It is administered by the Finnish Society for Quality and the Public Sector Reform Unit in the Ministry of Finance in Helsinki. The assessment model and scoring system of the Finnish Quality Award is based mainly on the Malcolm Baldrige Quality Award. Ideas and experiences have also been adopted from the Swedish Quality Award and the Quality Award of the European Foundation for Quality Management. In contrast to the Malcolm Baldrige Quality Award, the Finnish Quality Award has one additional category, environmental issues and public responsibility. The scoring system of the Finnish Quality Award 1995 is rather similar to the 1995 version of the Malcolm

Baldrige Quality Award. Also, in Sweden and Denmark private quality organizations have proclaimed their intention to run quality awards both for the private and the public sector. In Norway, the minister of administrative affairs launched a one-time event, "Excellence in Government" (Berg 1995).

Italy

In Italy, a new generation of laws, issued between 1990 and 1993, laid the cornerstone for innovations in the Italian public administration. The most important law of this new administrative legislation (for more details, see Brunelli 1995) is law 241/90, which introduces the principle of transparency in administrative procedures: For each procedure, the public agency must define the maximum allowed response time and specifiy the organizational unit that is responsible for the final result. Also, the user must have free access to any administrative document he or she needs. This law is also at the center of the Innovation Award for Relations Between the Public Administration and the Public (Premio Innovazione nella Pubblica Amministrazione) that was run in 1993 by Sistemi Pubblica Amministrazione (SPA), a private institution in Milano, aimed at improving the managerial capacity of the Italian public administration. The application process was based on self-nomination of all kinds of public administrations and the assessment of the applicants was founded on the degree of implementation of Law 241/90. SPA also organized extensive site visits for public organizations excelling in the award's questionnaire. As a result, 20 excellent public administrations were identified as a model for innovative communication patterns with clients (SPA 1993).

Portugal

The Portuguese public administration, largely based on a Weberian model (Secretariat for Administrative Modernization 1991, p. 1) has been working intensively on the Programme of Administrative Modernization since 1986. It is a comprehensive quality awards program that also includes the Portuguese Public Service Quality Contest, and it is an important building block of the new reforms launched in 1992 (OECD 1993, p. 147). The Quality Contest is open to all public administration central services in Portugal and has taken place every year since 1992. The objective is to stimulate self-assessment of public services and to encourage public agencies to develop their own standards of quality. The questionnaire puts emphasis on the existance of specific quality programs in public agencies. The assessment model of the Portuguese Public Service Quality Contest clearly is based on improvements by incremental administrative reforms rather than on productivity and responsiveness by the application of TQM. Award winners obtain the right to distinguish themselves from other public agencies by using the award mark.

Great Britain

The Charter Mark Award can be interpreted as a special kind of quality award, lying on the lower end of the spectrum between ISO 9000–9004 and quality awards. It recognizes and rewards superior performance in the delivery of services. The Charter Mark scheme is an integral part of the British Citizen's Charter (Prime Minister 1991), a panel of advisers in the British Cabinet Office. All public organizations that serve the public sector directly are eligible to apply for the Charter Mark. In a written application, they have to demonstrate the extent to which they have adopted the principles set out in the Citizen's Charter. The panel of judges will then make visits to short-listed organizations. The principles of the Citizen's Charter serve as an assessment model of the Charter Mark Award. These principles are the setting, monitoring, and publication of standards by public organizations, information and openness, choice and consultation, courtesy and helpfulness, putting things right, value for money, customer satisfaction, measurable improvements in the quality of service over the past two years, and plans to introduce or have in hand at least one innovative enhancement to services without any extra cost to the taxpayer or consumer (Citizen Charter Unit 1993, pp.14–22).

In contrast to other European quality awards, the scoring system only differentiates between pass and fail. The first 36 Charter Marks were awarded in September 1992. In 1993, the number of award winners rose to 93 public organizations. Charter Marks are awarded for three years only. Afterwards, Charter Mark holders may reapply.

Outlook

There is a multitude of quality competition awards arising in (and within) the Organization for Economic Cooperation and Development (OECD) countries, and there is also the danger that there will be competition among the award organizers. One is inclined to think that such competition would help to sweep away low-quality awards that are not useful to the participants. This would also give potential contenders more of an opportunity to win. However, there are good reasons to assume that this competition would be highly dysfunctional for the participants and the award organizers. First of all, there is no competition for quality but only for the quantity of public organizations taking part in the awards program. This means that there will be an incentive to lower the entrance barrier for publicity reasons. As a result, there will be a selection of good organizations from mediocre organizations instead of a selection of the best organizations from outstanding participants. Besides, in theory, a public organization wish-

ing to participate in an award competition will have a choice of which contests to enter, but there is still the question of will there be enough market transparency to evaluate the different alternatives.

The outcome of a complex award program is difficult to evaluate ex ante, and participants might feel attracted to awards that they think they have good chances to win, regardless of the learning outcome. Finally, if there is an inflation in the number of award programs, the prestige associated with winning a particular award declines. Therefore, there should be consensus in the political and scientific community that organizers should concentrate their resources and know-how on doing their best with one award.

In order to insure a high functional contribution of quality awards to the management process, the organizers of award programs should practice self-assessment continually. Only by seeking the feedback of the members and by intensive research into the sources of negative effects can these effects be wiped out. Another valuable tool for quality award organizers is intensive cross-boundary cooperation in which organizers are able to exchange their different approaches and findings and the reactions of public organizations.

ELKE LOEFFLER

BIBLIOGRAPHY

Antilla, Juan, 1993. "Quality Award Criteria Signpost the Way to Excellence in Quality Performance." *Laatuviesti*, vol. 19 (February): 19–21.

Berg, Anne Marie, 1995. "Excellence in Government–Performance Evaluation of Government Agencies." In Hermann Hill and Helmut Klages, eds. *New Trends in Public Sector Renewal: Recent Trends and Developments in Awarding Excellence*, pp. 161–174. Frankfurt: Peter Lang Verlag.

Borins, Sandford, 1995. "Public Management Innovation Awards in the U.S. and Canada." In Hermann Hill and Helmut Klages, eds. *New Trends in Public Sector Renewal: Recent Trends and Developments in Awarding Excellence*, pp. 213–240. Frankfurt: Peter Lang Verlag.

Bouckaert, Geert, 1995. "Charters as Frameworks for Awarding Quality: The Belgian, British and French Experience." In Hermann Hill and Helmut Klages, eds. *New Trends in Public Sector Renewal: Recent Trends and Developments in Awarding Excellence*, pp. 185–200. Frankfurt: Peter Lang Verlag.

Brunelli, Alberto Bonetti, 1995. "The Italian Innovation Award for Relations Between the Public Administration and the Public." In Hermann Hill, and Helmut Klages, eds. *New Trends in Public Sector Renewal: Recent Trends and Developments in Awarding Excellence*, pp. 241–278. Frankfurt: Peter Lang Verlag.

Citizen Charter Unit, ed., 1993. *The Citizen's Charter: Charter Mark Scheme 1993–Guide for Applicants*. London: Cabinet Office and Central Office of Information.

Halachmi, Arie, 1995. "Potential Dysfunctions of Quality Award Competitions." In Hermann Hill and Helmut Klages, eds.

New Trends in Public Sector Renewal: Recent Trends and Developments in Awarding Excellence, pp. 293–314. Frankfurt: Peter Lang Verlag.

Haubner, Oliver, Hermann Hill, and Helmut Klages, 1993. Speyerer Qualitätswettbewerb 1992. "Auf der Suche nach Spitzenverwaltungen." *VOP* (January): 46–50.

Hill, Hermann, and Helmut Klages, eds., 1993. *Spitzenverwaltungen im Wettbewerb. Eine Dokumentation des 1. Speyerer Qualitätswettbewerbs 1992.* Baden-Baden: Nomos-Verlag.

Klages, Helmut, 1995. "Strategic Choices in the Process of Planning and Pursuing a Quality Award." In Hermann Hill and Helmut Klages, eds. *New Trends in Public Sector Renewal: Recent Trends and Developments in Awarding Excellence,* pp. 279–292. Frankfurt: Peter Lang Verlag.

Office of the Auditor General, 1989. *Attributes of Well-Performing Organizations.* Ottawa: Canada. Minister of Supply and Services.

Operation for Economic Cooperation and Development (OECD), ed., 1993. *Public Management Developments. Survey 1993,* Paris: OECD.

Prime Minister (England), 1991. *The Citizen's Charter. Raising the Standard.* CM 1599, London: HMSO, July.

Reinermann, Heinrich, 1993. "Ein neues Paradigma für die öffentliche Verwaltung–Was uns Max Weber heute empfehlen dürfte." *Speyerer Arbeitshefte,* vol. 97.

Secretariat for Administrative Modernization, ed, 1991. "Quality Public Services: Reflections on the Portuguese Experience." Unpublished paper, Lisbon.

Sistemi Pubblica Amministrazione (SPA) Ricerche, ed., 1993, *Premio Innovazione nella Pubblica Amministrazione,* Milano: D'Anselmi Editore.

Ware, J. E. 1993, ISO 9000–The World Trend, *Proceedings of the EOQ '93 World Quality Congress in Helsinki,* Finland, vol. 3: 5–13.

QUALITY CIRCLES.

QUALITY CIRCLES. Problem-solving tools to improve productivity and job performance in business, industry, and government work settings. Quality Circle (QC) experiments enjoy a rich history, dating back more than 30 years. Conceived for Japanese industry, QCs are now common in business, government, and nonprofit organizations throughout the industrialized world. Circles have been used in South Africa, Colombia, Singapore, the United Kingdom, and the United States. Although QCs were originally designed as a stand-alone innovation, most current approaches to improve worker productivity have assimilated circles as major elements in more inclusive Total Quality Management (TQM) strategies.

In their most common form, many circles convene within an organization, each group charged with addressing problems in similar jobs or related work. Circle members may range from three to twelve employees, although, typically, groups include six to twelve people. These employees voluntarily join teams, which regularly address problems in individual job performance as well as whether jobs mesh in a given process (for example, personnel staffing). Primary activities involve revisiting job design and work flow continually and comparing these methods and approaches with eventual outcomes.

By virtue of their assignment to find new problems and long-term solutions, teams possess comparatively sweeping authority. QC advocates reason that day-to-day job experience promotes unique insight into how jobs and the work environment can be improved and how job tasks and the overall work process can be redesigned. Because job knowledge is valued over hierarchical status, in theory, QCs illustrate bottom-up innovations in productivity improvement. Communication and problem solving is directed from the lowest rungs of the organizational ladder to the top. This implicit trust in workers as authors of change means that, in principle, QCs challenge most traditional or classical approaches to organization in which control over such issues was concentrated at the top. Even though hierarchical authority appears undermined by this philosophy, extensive research has found that successful QCs rely heavily upon executive support. Effective implementation of quality circles, accordingly, begins and ends at the top.

The Quality Movement and Japan's Economic Transformation

Quality Circles trace their origin to postwar Japan's industrial recovery, through systematic efforts to build quality into goods manufactured for world trade. The Japanese Union of Scientists and Engineers was charged with finding a method to bridge the gap between job design and how work was actually produced. An American named W. E. Deming assisted the Japanese Union's efforts. Deming had long promoted the use of statistical tools in solving quality problems but met with enthusiastic audiences only in Japan (Fitzgerald and Murphy 1982). Although quality improvement strategies in general owe much to Deming's lessons about objective-setting and measurement, QC philosophy and practices were also subtly and powerfully shaped by Japanese cultural characteristics.

In one sense, the foundation for Quality Circles was set centuries ago in the strong Japanese work ethic and related values of collectivism and collaboration. Unlike American society, in which individuals compete to distinguish themselves from the group, the Japanese worker is expected to collaborate for the betterment of the larger community. Though French, Italian, and Spanish organizations have been described as highly centralized and marked by status distinctions, Japanese companies often are less concerned with rigid lines of authority (Lammers and Hickson 1979). Japanese workers are more respected for their expertise than their status or official position alone. Accomplishment for their team is frequently met with company approval via social recognition; development and educational opportunities; frequently, lifetime employment; and, not to be downplayed, economic rewards (Watanabe 1991). With a company's focus often fixed on long-term results rather than short-term profits, a circle's constant fine-tuning of a work process (known as *keisen*) is tolerated, even encouraged, if ultimately it means a better product.

By 1982, Quality Circles had become so embedded in Japanese corporations that five of every six Japanese workers were said to belong. Roughly two million QCs are now estimated to be active, representing substantial worker influence and involvement in the work-improvement process. Each circle member contributes an average 55 recommendations per year, which boosted Japanese productivity and quality steadily and substantially throughout the 1980s (Fitzgerald and Murphy 1982).

By the end of the decade, these achievements catapulted Japan into a new role as a leader in world trade. According to one perspective, Japan's "overnight success" can be explained by its singular focus on quality. Good pricing and other factors are clearly secondary. Product quality and the Japanese economic miracle, consequently, owes more to the "continuous improvement" doctrine than other contributing factors, such as technological innovation in the workplace (for example, industrial robotization). As such, the Japanese experience serves as testimony to the vigor of Quality Circles—at least as employed in Japan—to transform not just the workplace but an entire economy.

Quality Circle Accomplishments: What Research Tells Us

As word of QC accomplishments spread beyond Japan, work institutions elsewhere in Asia and in the West asked how they could adopt Quality Circles. In many cases, the manner of implementation was irrelevant, as long as it was timely: Executives and leaders wanted quick returns on QC's extraordinary promise. Researchers asked different questions. Some inquired as to the transferability of QCs to non-Japanese settings; others considered the factors and conditions behind circle effectiveness.

In comparisons of effective circles in Japan, the United States, and Singapore, size emerged as a critical factor. Groups should be limited to six to ten members. To a lesser extent, successful QCs are more likely voluntary and highly participative. They tended to enjoy a "people-building philosophy," top management commitment, union support, and a climate conducive to creativity and a continuous study process (Gosh and Song 1991).

With regard to outcomes, even though QCs have been cited as good examples of worker empowerment, some studies of Western industrial QCs indicated that they may not improve worker attitudes. Circles may, however, help to improve product quality, efficiency, cost savings, and work conditions (Adam 1991). But in other studies,

QC members enjoyed higher performance ratings and were promoted more often than other employees. Presumably, QCs were a major factor insofar as they offered development opportunities and increased individual visibility and positive regard for their members (Buch and Spangler 1990).

Elsewhere, a comparison of QC members with non-members revealed that QC members submitted more suggestions but showed little difference from other employees on key organizational outcomes such as productivity (Steel et al. 1990). In a wide variety of organizations, QC employees registered reduced turnover and at least stabilized absenteeism. In addition, QCs appear to bond members to the overall organization (Buch 1992), a finding that on its face contradicts earlier speculation (by Adam 1991) that QCs fail to change worker attitudes or integrate employees.

Most QC writers agree, however, that to a great extent a circle's effectiveness rests on the quality of members' participation and commitment to its purposes. Often, the nature and quality of employee involvement depends upon whether their observations and suggestions are respected and acted upon by higher-ups. Where superiors are threatened by sharing information, decisionmaking authority, and job responsibility with circle members, QCs have generally been short-lived (Brennan 1992). Even high-performing workers reject QCs if adequate training in problem solving and group dynamics has not been provided or first-line supervisors and other hierarchical superiors fail to act on QC solutions. As QCs have been tried and refined in many settings across many cultures, one general rule appears consistently: Those that have produced the greatest successes have tended to be part of a planned, systemwide change effort (Heath 1990).

For these and other reasons, QCs have gradually become incorporated into system- or organization-wide quality improvement efforts, generally known in the U.S. as Total Quality Management (TQM). In many accounts of TQM, Quality Circles have largely evolved into self-directed work groups, which target tactical issues in getting the work done. Worker empowerment, formerly a critical implementation issue in QCs, has become part of an overall program to promote employee development and training and to encourage participation in decisionmaking.

Quality Improvement Efforts in the Public Sector: U.S. Governmental Bodies as Case Studies

Governmental institutions have been particularly receptive to quality and productivity improvement strategies inasmuch as they promise remedies for bureaucratic inefficiency and waste, and customer dissatisfaction, as well as help for shrinking budgets. The U.S. federal government reportedly loses an estimated US $400 billion annually to quality problems (McKenna 1993). TQM and Quality Circles have been adopted in U.S. federal agencies, including the Forest Service, the National Aeronautics and Space Administration, and the Air Force Systems Command.

Leading this assault on waste and inefficiency is the U.S. Federal Quality Institute, founded in 1988 and comprising a revolving group of 35 representatives from federal agencies. It has assisted the federal quality effort through training and technical assistance and has organized model TQM projects. Successful ventures reported reduced cost in airplane repairs for the Navy, lower labor cost at the Johnson Space Center, and greater accuracy in processing income tax returns at the Internal Revenue Service (Reynolds 1992).

Thirty-six out of the 50 states report some type of quality improvement activity, including Arizona, Arkansas, Pennsylvania, and Ohio. Cities from Portland, Oregon, and Austin, Texas (U.S.), to Ottawa-Carleton (Ontario, Canada) have turned to TQM to cope with fiscal stress, improve the delivery of services, and improve efficiency. These experiments report not only financial savings but also improved morale, faster service, and improved customer communication and service satisfaction (Kline 1992).

In some respects, quality innovations are the latest catchword or trend in business and government: Quality Circle managers like to say that they are contributing to a popular movement. However, systematic research suggests that Quality Circles are better understood as an umbrella label, tying together a vast array of approaches differing not only in design but also in execution and results. Researchers have yet to agree as to what works and why, and whether a particular tool such as QCs will produce the same results across work and national cultures.

Quality Circles: Form and Functions

Though Quality Circles vary in form across work institutions as well as cultures, some fundamental shared characteristics can describe a typical QC's organization and roles. The map of a QC's structure in many cases mimics a traditional organizational pyramid. At the top is the steering or executive committee, composed of representatives of upper management, human resource staff, and the individual(s) in charge of the QC program. This group generally serves as the policymaking body, overseeing and coordinating the QC effort. Committee members may be permanent or serve a fixed term. The steering committee typically meets at least monthly.

The QC administrator usually represents the single point of authority for the QC program. In this capacity, he or she maintains records of circle activities and works to ensure good communication within and between circles. The administrator also serves as a linchpin or liaison between circles and the executive committee. Typical additional functions include training, budgeting, public relations, and coordination.

The next role in the chain of command is the QC facilitator, who monitors circle progress on a routine basis. The facilitator provides direction in the appropriate use of QC tools and techniques and, like the administrator, also attends to communication between and among QC parties. More so than the administrator, a facilitator tends to focus on QC *process,* or how each circle accomplishes goals and solves problems. In larger companies, the facilitator may be independent of the administrator and this position tends to be filled by many individuals who facilitate a large number of circles; in smaller systems, one individual may wear both hats. In either case, this individual serves to link both the day-to-day work of the circles with policymakers by facilitating communication.

QC leaders are supervisors or workers trained in the QC process who help to coordinate a circle's work. They keep meetings on task and monitor their progress often, depending on a recorder who maintains the circle's written records. They may also consult with the facilitator, attend to feedback about prior suggestions, schedule special consultations, and arrange for presentations by outside experts.

Circle members are instrumental to its effectiveness. They must regularly attend, contribute ideas to, and "own" the circle's work. At a minimum, the following conditions appear necessary for QC effectiveness (for extensive coverage on circle implementation, see Fitzgerald and Murphy 1982). At a minimum members must:

- voluntarily join QCs;
- agree to basic QC ground rules and norms;
- accept and assist the circle leader;
- complete training in the QC process, group dynamics, and problem solving; and
- learn and apply QC tools and techniques to measure and track quality defects and sticking points.

QC tools include flowcharts, control charts and cause-and-effect diagrams. Flowcharts help to determine quality costs, which are divided into prevention, inspection and appraisal, and internal failure and external failure costs. Control charts can determine random or particular variation in processes, and cause-and-effect diagrams present how a work process assumes its shape (Kline 1993).

Quality: A New Direction for Governments?

The cornerstone of both Quality Circle and TQM philosophy is continual improvement, building quality into a service process or manufacture so that "zero defects" mark the outcome. The aim is to provide the customer, client, or public with an ever-higher quality of service, however the citizen-consumer defines it. By and large, a quality improvement agenda represents a new direction for government organizations. Circles and other tools depart from traditional ways of conducting the public's business, in which evaluating an organization's performance meant reliance on efficiency criteria–abandoned long ago by most business and industry–and greater embracement of outcome-based measures. Whether citizens will see great changes from these innovations or will support the use of such tools on a grand or national scale is an unanswered question. Whether legislatures and other elected officials will continue this experiment long enough for adequate testing of quality improvement techniques also remains to be seen (see also **Total Quality Management**, **productivity and quality improvement**.)

ANN-MARIE RIZZO

BIBLIOGRAPHY

Adam, Everett E., Jr., 1991. "Quality Circle Performance." *Journal of Management,* vol. 1, no. 1 (March): 25–40.

Brennan, Maire, 1992. "Mismanagement and Quality Circles: How Middle Managers Influence Direct Participation." *Management Decision,* vol. 30, no. 6 (November): 35–46.

Buch, Kimberly, 1992. "Quality Circles and Employee Withdrawal Behaviors: A Cross-Organizational Study." *Journal of Applied Behavioral Science,* vol. 28, no. 1 (March): 62–74.

Buch, Kimberly, and Raymond Spangler, 1990. "The Effects of Quality Circles on Performance and Promotions." *Human Relations,* vol. 43, no. 6 (June): 573–583.

Fitzgerald, Laurie, and Joseph Murphy, 1982. *Quality Circles: A Strategic Approach.* San Diego: University Associates.

Gosh, B. C., and Lim Kia Song, 1991. "Structures and Processes of Company Quality Control Circles (QCCs): An Explanatory Study of Japan, the USA and Singapore." *Management Decision,* vol. 29, no. 7 (December): 45–54.

Heath, Phillip M., 1990. "Quality–And How to Achieve It." *Management Decison,* vol. 28, no. 8: 42–47.

Kline James J., 1992. "Total Quality Management in Local Government." *Government Finance Review,* vol. 8, no. 4 (August): 7–12.

———, 1993. "Quality Tools Are Applicable to Local Government." *Government Finance Review,* vol. 9, no. 4 (August): 15–20.

Lammers, Cornelis J., and David J. Hickson, 1979. "A Cross-National and Cross-Institutional Typology of Organizations." In Cornelis J. Lammers and David J. Hickson, eds. *Organizations Alike and Unlike: International and Interinstitutional Studies in the Sociology of Organizations.* London: Routledge and Kegan Paul.

McKenna, Joseph P., 1993. "Total Quality Government: More than Political Fashion." *Industry Week,* vol. 242, no. 12 (June 21): 44–46.

Reynolds, Larry, 1992. "The Feds Join the Quality Movement." *Management Review,* vol. 81, no. 4 (April): 39–41.

Steel Robert P., Kenneth R. Jennings, and James I. Lindsey, 1990. "Quality Circle Problem Solving and Common Cents: Evaluation Study Findings from a United States Mint." *Journal of Applied Behavior Science,* vol. 26, no. 3 (August): 365–382.

Watanabe, Susumu, 1991. "The Japanese Quality Control Circle: Why It Works." *International Labour Review,* vol. 130, no. 1 (January-February): 57–81.

QUALITY CONTROL. The managerial activity that aims to insure that planned standards of performance in the quality and delivery of services, the completion of a process, or the production of goods is maintained at a particular, predetermined level. It also aims to assist an organization to improve its level of performance to meet the continuing demands of users. In the public sector, the establishment of quality assurance standards has been given considerable attention, although the performance levels achieved are often difficult to substantiate, especially to the satisfaction of stakeholders such as politicians and taxpayers.

Techniques of quality control vary considerably. The traditional approach to quality control adopted a regulatory function that was often independent of the area of the workplace from which work originated. Images of quality control inspectors, searching for errors and flaws in the way in which a process had been completed and adopting a narrow, error-focused audit approach were not unusual. The resistance to this approach that also emerged was not surprising. Staffs performing the work resented the policing approach to the review of their work. Where quality control staff reported to another department of the organization's management, a sense of powerlessness and remoteness from the quality control process was often experienced.

In this environment, quality control failed to gain support from staffs, except in insuring their conformity to minimum standards of performance. The mass production techniques that proved so successful in the early twentieth century also lead to significant deskilling of work and undoubtedly encouraged the development of a control approach to quality. This approach was often standard practice in manufacturing organizations, which, of course, needed to maintain consistent quality of work performance if their mass-produced products were going to succeed in the market and provide consumers with a reliable product. In this case, quality control usually amounted to a thorough check of the product at the end, rather than during, the production process, further distancing the employee from the quality process.

However, the approach to quality control pioneered by the Volvo car company in the 1970s provided an international breakthrough in the automotive industry. In essence, Volvo moved away from the deskilling of its workforce and gave groups responsibility for manufacturing entire vehicles, including responsibility for the standard of quality of the vehicle. This approach provided the employees that were responsible for production with autonomy for the way in which the teams arranged the performance of their work and for the standard of their group's output.

Although this devolution of quality control responsibilities appeared radical at the time, much of the existing and subsequent theory of motivation in workplaces supports such an approach to quality control. Devolved responsibility for quality control requires that quality standards be defined in ways that staffs understand and are possible of performing, and that provide regular–preferably immediate–feedback on performance. If quality control can be developed in this way, individuals and groups can accept responsibility for monitoring the quality of their work. Group performance also appears to be enhanced where quality control and quality enhancement are linked. In other words, staffs are given responsibility not only for maintaining certain standards of performance but also for improving performance. This responsibility enhances the sense of empowerment granted to employees and can motivate them to search for further methods of improving quality in their workplaces.

The technique of using Quality Circles, or work teams, to explore quality problems and propose realistic solutions is now well established in many organizations and provides a formalized, proactive approach to quality control. There are many examples, not just in manufacturing, where this approach to quality improvement has yielded higher work standards. For example, one national, government-owned and -operated postal service trains people in quality and work-flow analysis so that they are able not only to better identify areas of work that would benefit from quality improvement but are also equipped to design the changes required, report to management, and, given management approval, proceed to implement their changes. This approach uses the people who understand their own work to identify the key areas of performance improvement. It is a quality control system that could be replicated in many public sector organizations. Its strength lies in its empowerment of staff to suggest the most efficient ways of implementing change and management's transfer of responsibility to those who best understand the work to be done and the situations most likely to yield quality improvements.

When managing the quality control process in this way, management should not consider the quality process delegated. Managers have a responsibility for overall quality and need to develop quality assurance measures that both empower staffs and provide managers with some feedback on how quality control is working. This feedback can be provided by the same feedback system that is used by employees to monitor the performance of their own teams. Some methods can be simple but effective: periodic surveys of client satisfaction (both internal and external), monitoring of client complaints, sample testing of work standards, and reporting of quality improvements initiated by staffs, and their impact on work standards. Observation of the way in which a quality improvement contributes to work performance is also a possible way of validating the improved processes.

An important consideration in this area is deciding how workers are to be rewarded for their involvement in the quality improvement process. Traditionally, some organizations have used a cash bonus approach to encourage staff involvement. Many of the companies using these schemes have experienced difficulties with them, perhaps because there is some variation in the perceptions of the staff and management as to the worth of the proposed quality improvement and the financial reward that should be granted, or whether a reward should be given at all. More successful approaches to quality improvement seem to use symbolic rewards, such as certificates, honor rolls, and other intrinsic rewards that demonstrate a recognition of the value of the individual or team involved in the quality control project. This again fits motivation theory in terms of recognition of the contribution of individuals and their worth to the organization; it also recognizes the worth of a team effort. Another reason for moving away from individual cash awards may lie in the need to move the focus of quality control from being a backward or retrospective activity–fixing things up after they have gone wrong–to a proactive approach. The latter approach means that quality standards can be defined and established as goals of performance, attainable levels of performance that are respected by those involved and those who have the responsibility to complete the job. For example, this means that a worker's energy goes into insuring that service consistently meets the needs of clients and that clients are satisfied with their treatment, rather than simply focusing on service problems and their causes.

The main quality control challenges for public sector managers appear to arise from the ambiguity that often exists in public organizations, the lack of funding for adequate training, the difficulties of developing sophisticated standards of quality and dealing with the issue of accountability for quality standards and quality concepts. There is no doubt that in much of the work of public sector organizations, defining quality standards in administrative functions provides a significant challenge. However, more clearly defining the goals of an organization and its individual work units may provide a means of establishing goals that can be incorporated into quality standards and related quality control measures. Insuring that the staff is aware of the standards, accepts their nature and content of the standards, and feels responsible for their implementation in the workplace, may yield substantial improvements in the standard of work performance and a diminished need for a control approach to quality management.

GUY CALLENDER

QUALITY IMPROVEMENT. Continuous incremental enhancements to work practices. Two basic premises of quality improvement are a focus on the customer, resulting in quality service and program provision; and staff participation, empowerment, recognition, and reward.

The idea of quality improvement is derived, predominantly, from concepts of quality management. W. E. Deming (1986), P. Crosby (1988), and J. Juran (1988) are names commonly associated with the development of a management approach referred to as Total Quality Management (TQM). In practice, quality improvement initiatives, as part of a broader quality management framework, were first applied to the production lines of large manufacturing companies, such as the motor vehicle manufacturing sector, especially in Japan.

Employee participation in the decisionmaking processes relating to quality improvement and a focus on customers were critical aspects of the quality management approach. Quality Circles, comprising production line employees, were created to solve production problems, to recommend viable solutions to senior management, and to be responsible for implementation of the proposed solutions. Staffs were also empowered to stop the assembly line when things went wrong and to fix them.

The application of quality improvement principles to the manufacturing sector in Japan initially involved a long-term strategic commitment—up to 10 years—to quality improvement. The long-term nature of the implementation process of quality management was seen to fit well with the management culture of organizations in Japan. So, in the early years, the concept of quality management was not applied for some time in Western democracies; for instance, in the United States, which supported a shorter time frame for implementing strategic changes. As a consequence, the Western world lagged behind Japan in the application of quality management and improvement approaches.

As a way of achieving competitive advantage by reducing unit costs, quality improvement practices are meant to diminish the number of production faults and to improve the quality of the final output or product. Thus the need to go into recovery mode by, in the quality idiom, "getting things right the first time," is obviated. Quality improvement in this context often involves the application of complex statistical and analytical tools that chart the flow of production and the ratio of inputs to outputs.

Quality improvement principles are also applied to service industries, such as hotels, airlines, and tourism operations. Such writers as T. Peters and R. Waterman (1982), K. Albrecht and R. Zemke (1985), and J. Carlzon (1987) are typically associated with quality service management. Similar principles of quality improvement apply. Unlike the manufacturing sector, however, service industries do not always have a standard product, nor do they tend to use complex statistical analysis to the same degree. Therefore, it is sometimes more difficult to define in precise terms the determinants of quality services. In this area, quality improvement involves enhancing the tangible aspects, as well as the intangible dimensions, of service.

For example, in-cabin service of an airline may involve the serving of a meal. The quality of service may well be determined by considering the actual meal—Was it appealing? Did it taste good?—as well as the demeanor of the flight attendant who served it. If the flight attendant was happy and humorous and the meal was appetizing and well presented, a passenger might perceive that the airline had in fact exceeded expectations of quality service. If, however, the meal was good but the flight attendant was exceedingly unpleasant, a passenger may perceive the quality of the meal to be only average. Because perceptions of a service interaction will vary from individual to individual, perceptions about what quality service really is will also differ accordingly. This situation has obvious implications for the application of quality improvement principles as part of a management enhancement initiative.

Notions of quality management and service, and thus the idea of quality improvement, have been embraced by public sectors globally in recent years for two primary reasons. First, fiscal imperatives have required governments to reduce their operating costs for the public sector and to find better and more productive ways of delivering programs and services. Second, there has been a pressure for governments to consider more comprehensively the needs of their constituents, or "customers," at a time of fiscal constraint, so that appropriate services and programs are better targeted to those who require, or are compelled, to receive a service.

Fundamental to quality improvement is the involvement and empowerment of employees in the decisionmaking and implementation processes and a focus on the public sector "customer" in determining a standard of service. Quality improvement can have both an internal and an external application, particularly involving staffs who interface directly with customers or clients. Workers in this role may be empowered to make decisions when things go wrong, particularly when issues are not necessarily covered by standard practice.

Quality principles also indicate that the role of the executive manager requires change. As far as quality is concerned, the executives are there to serve those who are serving the customer; so, instead of operating exclusively on a top-down basis, quality programs involve bottom-up as well as top-down decisionmaking. The focal point of quality improvement revolves around the needs of customers.

Internally, quality improvement initiatives may apply to the systems, legislation, and processes that will support the enhanced delivery of programs, services, or products to the public in a way that is consistent with the agency mission or vision statement. Some examples of quality improvement may involve such things as cutting down on "red tape"; opening a "one-stop shop" in a convenient location; or setting up a toll free number for inquiries. Executive management also benefits from quality improvement initiatives through an increase in knowledge of the operational side of the organization.

As existing systems and processes are reviewed from the employee's perspectives, so management can be exposed to and begin to appreciate another view. In our increasingly complex world and working environments this factor is an important aspect of quality improvement programs because individual managers rarely know all there is to know about the organization.

An incentive program to reward staffs who commit to the quality improvement ethos is also a vital part of a quality management approach. In the public sector, it is not always possible to provide a monetary reward, but other incentives may be offered. For example, use of an organizational parking spot or the posting of a photograph in the reception area of an "employee of the month" can be reasonable substitutes for monetary gain. These measures are significant where "public service" is regarded as a main motivating force for public sector employees.

The concept of customers is not always easy to understand in the public sector, where there may be diverse stakeholder groups. For instance, in a prison system, who is the customer?—the prisoner or the community? Maybe both are customers, but, obviously, if this is the case, each customer group will have different wants, needs, and expectations in terms of service. Quality improvement, then, may involve multidimensional improvement initiatives. Nevertheless, it is expected that customers' needs and expectations will be considered in developing a quality improvement program.

There are many different ways to ascertain what customers expect. The first and most obvious is for public servants to make assumptions about what customers want. In the present approach to quality improvement, making decisions on the basis of assumptions without consulting the customers is not acceptable. Therefore, the assumptions need to be tested through more direct contact with customer groups. Conducting interviews, sending out questionnaires, running focus groups, and appointing customers to consultative groups are just some of the ways of testing basic assumptions about customer expectations.

It is important, however, to consult with customers honestly because they expect their ideas to be reflected in the process of quality improvement. Nevertheless, in the public sector it is not always possible to be responsive to the customers' needs. Political priorities, lack of resources, and existing legislative frameworks may all limit the ability of public servants to address customers' expectations truly. These limitations do not have to restrict the idea of a customer driven quality improvement program, however. Public sector managers can be sensitive to the political agenda and still serve the government as a primary customer. At the same time, managers can also be aware of the needs of program beneficiaries and users as customers. This obviously requires a balance between political imperatives and meeting the needs of other customer groups.

The principle of quality improvement is also based on public sector organization managers' and staffs' willingness and ability to evaluate performance. This aspect of quality improvement requires a high degree of trust between executive management and line staff so that the implementation of quality improvement initiatives does not result in a net loss of jobs—or, if this is a likely outcome, how such a result would be managed also needs to be made explicit. This issue of trust is important, particularly at a time when governments are tending to look at savings through reducing the number of labor units across public sectors. In fact, productivity improvement through the identification of inefficient work practices and the implementation of initiatives, such as quality improvement, may offer governments far greater benefits than the financial cost achieved through radical downsizing and a reduction in labor unit numbers.

Some public sector organizations have developed innovative approaches to quality improvement, such as the organization that implemented a "most useless thing I do competition"; or the organization that initiated an imaginative project management approach to crisis management. Whatever the approach, staff involvement, empowerment, recognition, reward, and celebration are essential elements of the quality improvement program. (Celebration can be a sensitive issue in the public sector, however, at a time of constraint, and may attract unwelcome media attention. The form of celebration, therefore, needs to be discreet.) Use of the quality improvement jargon also should be matched to the actions of executive staffs so that espoused values and the real values of the program are obviously in accord.

Any quality improvement program also requires some type of formal and informal monitoring process so that progress can be monitored over time. Therefore, quality improvement is linked to the concept of managing for results, in which some kind of output and outcome performance indicators are institutionalized and monitored, usually in accordance with predetermined goals. How these goals are stated and how realistic they are in practice are important in supporting the concept of quality improvement.

Quality improvement standards may also be achieved by modeling excellence, that is, by taking after another business, organization, or unit in the same organization or country, that the staff considers to be a leader in the field, for whatever reason. The next step is then to determine, in a tangible form, the aspects of excellence that are to be modeled.

The idea of "best practice" can also be useful. Statements of best practice may be produced by the organization itself or by a central agency of government that has the task of improving performance standards across the sector. Benchmarking, or standard setting, is another approach. For example, the customers of an organization may assist the organization in setting a standard, or benchmark, which meets or exceeds customers' expectations of a program or service.

Other methods, such as program evaluation and customer feedback, can provide information about performance. Formal standards may be developed through a professional body and may involve accreditation processes in terms of professional associations or bodies, such as with hospitals or prison systems. These organizations are accredited in terms of national standards. Therefore, quality improvement relates to improvements in terms of established standards.

For improving the quality of internal systems and processes, public sector organizations may also seek accreditation from the national body on quality management in terms of formal quality standards, some of which have universal force. Furthermore, these public sector organizations require service providers, such as consultants or contractors, to be similarly accredited as part of a competitive tendering process for services.

From a sectorwide perspective, there also has to be some incentive for chief executive officers (CEOs) of public sector organizations to be rewarded for their quality improvement initiatives. CEOs need to be confident that if they manage within the spirit of a quality improvement program there will be recognition of this and that they will not be penalized by additional across-the-board cuts. Otherwise, the organizational incentive is removed, and reducing performance, rather than providing quality improvement, becomes a critical part of political maneuvering within the sector. With this possible scenario, there may be more value in maintaining a fat organization rather than a lean one.

The concept of quality improvement, which involves continuous incremental enhancements to management practice and service delivery, sometimes competes with newer fads or fashions from the private sector that the public sector tends to mimic. For instance, reengineering processes that support more radical change is popular in the public sector. Though it is certainly acknowledged that some change processes probably justify a more rapid approach, organizations also need to consider the longer-term benefits, or disadvantages, of incremental versus radical change.

Quality improvement, therefore, is a strategy for organizational enhancement that involves all key constituent groups in the decisionmaking process—staffs, customers (even if they are diverse), and executive managers. Improvement occurs over time with all the relevant players contributing to the results. Quality improvement initia-

tives also place a special emphasis on the value of people as our richest resource.

JUDY JOHNSTON

BIBLIOGRAPHY

Albrecht, K., 1988. *At America's Service*. Homewood, IL: Dow Jones-Irwin.
———, 1990. *Service Within*. Homewood, IL: Dow Jones-Irwin.
Albrecht, K. and R. Zemke, 1985. *Service America*. New York: Warner Books.
———, 1991. *Delivering Knock Your Socks Off Service*. New York: Amacom.
Carlzon, J., 1987. *Moments of Truth*. New York: Harper & Row.
Carr, D., and I. Littman, 1990. *Excellence in Government*. Arlington, VA.: Coopers and Lybrand.
Cohen, S., and R. Brand, 1993. *Total Quality Management in Government*. San Francisco: Jossey-Bass.
Crosby, P., 1988. *The Eternally Successful Organization*. New York: Mentor.
Deming, W. E., 1986. *Out of the Crisis*. Cambridge, MA: MIT Center for Advanced Engineering Study.
Juran, J., 1988. *Juran on Planning for Quality*. New York: Free Press.
McDavid, J. and D. B. Marson, 1991. *The Well-Performing Government Organization*. The Institute of Public Administration of Canada.
Morgan, C., and S. Murgatroyd, 1994. *Total Quality Management in the Public Sector*. Buckingham: Open University Press.
Osborne, D., and T. Gaebler, 1992. *Reinventing Government*. Reading, MA: Addison-Wesley.
Peters, T., and N. Austin, 1985. *A Passion for Excellence*. London: Collins.
Peters, T., and R. Waterman, Jr., 1982. *In Search of Excellence*. New York: Warner.
Zemke, R., and D. Schaaf, 1989. *The Service Edge*. New York: Plume.

QUALITY OF WORK LIFE (QWL).

An amorphous mix of organizational conditions or practices. The general goals of QWL are the creation of a satisfying and productive workplace that provides workers and managers with a safe and comfortable place in which each wants to work toward producing quality goods and services. The QWL view of workers stresses that the employee is not only a performer of mindless tasks but also an employee with a brain; and the work environment should encourage, not discourage, its use. If the work environment is structured to do that, everyone wins: the worker, the manager, the customer, and the client.

Quality in the American Experience

In the United States, the 1930s and 1940s were marked by emphasis on quantity. The ability of U.S. shipbuilders to turn sheet steel into Liberty ships to ferry armed forces and equipment to Europe speeded the end of World War II.

After the war, quantity and size dominated the thinking of producer and customer. "Bigger and better" was the catchy advertising phrase, and, with this emphasis on size and quantity, attention to quality waned.

Continuing into the 1950s and 1960s, the competitive advantage of the United States was its ability to mass-produce consumer products at a price that the workers could afford. The production of superior quality items was also within the purview of Europe; but, at this time, Japan produced low-quality and low-cost products.

In the 1970s, the sharp jump in oil prices, the increase in wage rates, and a more-discerning consumer forced a shift in thinking from quantity to quality and from big to small. On one hand, German and Japanese cars were smaller, more fuel efficient, and were delivered with fewer defects. On the other hand, American cars of the early 1970s were not only bigger and more expensive but were also built to last only as long as did the owner's payments for it. "Built-in obsolescence" characterized the quality of U.S. cars, and it also described the overall American view of quality. Quality was an optional attribute of a product.

In the 1980s, global competition characterized the business environment, and other countries began to catch up with the United States in their ability to mass-produce large quantities of high-quality goods at a reasonable cost. The international market had now become a more level playing field for other nations as they competed with the United States. U.S. business was forced, in turn, to address the poor quality of some of its products.

Now, in the late 1990s, producing quality products and delivering quality service have become paramount in the strategic planning of American business.

Seventy-five years ago, capital and raw materials were the expensive components of the production process, and geography mattered. Today, technology has rendered geography unimportant in business decisionmaking since businesses can locate wherever a skilled workforce is available. Human resources are expensive, however, and therefore the cost-sensitive organization treats its human resources well.

The movement to increase the quality of work life for employees surfaced at the same time that product quality emerged as the dominant organizational concern. The QWL proponents link the quality of the product or service produced and the positive perceptions of workers toward their work environment.

Goals of Good Quality of Work Life

Those who write about improving the QWL do not agree upon a single set of goals that this will accomplish. Some goals of the QWL movement are to

- raise productive efficiency (Galenson 1991);
- improve the physical and mental conditions of work (Galenson 1991);

- improve people's relationship with work and their fellow workers (Nirenberg 1993);
- transform organizations into communities that will become an important focus of one's life experience (Nirenberg 1993);
- increase employee satisfaction (Bruce and Blackburn 1992);
- enhance employee's individual growth potential (Nadler and Lawler 1983);
- increase work motivation (Bruce and Blackburn 1992); and
- facilitate the perception of physical and mental well-being among employees.

The QWL movement thus links improvements in the work life of the employees with increases in organizational productivity. Hence, investment in employees should reap rewards for the agency or business unit.

QWL Techniques

QWL techniques run the gamut from minor changes in the work structure to major realignments of the authority structure. Some of the components of a positive QWL focus on changes in the work environment that are clear and tangible, and others are less precise and more open to debate about the meaning of the QWL goal.

Although some aspects of a QWL environment are within organizational control and can be provided as company policy, some of these organization-based QWL components are ambiguous. Organizational specifications that promote a positive QWL environment include:

- fair and adequate compensation;
- the opportunity to use and develop human capacities;
- social integration, including the ability to interact with fellow employees;
- the possibility of personal growth and security; and
- the recognition that employees need to balance demands of home and work (Walton 1973; Nirenberg 1993; Bruce and Blackburn 1992).

Governments have been involved in regulating the workplace since the industrial revolution, and, increasingly, government rules and regulations have embraced a positive QWL orientation. The components of QWL that may be codified by law include: (1) fair treatment, which includes the absence of discrimination on the basis of race, gender, age, national origin, sexual preference, and disability; (2) personal safety, including healthy working conditions without environmental hazards present, and freedom from harassment, including sexual harassment; (3) the availability of family leave for both children and elderly parents; (4) limitations on the number of hours that can be worked in a week; and (5) requiring businesses to provide health coverage to their workers.

Other components of the QWL that may be part of a total compensation package available to the employee include flex-time, provisions for telecommuting or use of a home office, child or elderly care, dental insurance, flexible benefit packages, job sharing, time off, and promotion-from-within policies.

Some QWL techniques engender controversy because they involve sharing power and authority between line-level workers and supervisors or management. These controversial QWL techniques are Quality Circles, labor-management problem-solving teams, job restructuring and redesign, and gain sharing.

The components of a positive quality of work life environment include issues that (1) are within an organizations' policymaking domain, (2) are legitimized by government law or regulation, (3) are part of a total compensation package, and, finally, (4) change the way power and authority are distributed within the organization.

Union Reaction to the QWL

The activities associated with QWL techniques overlap with concerns usually associated with employee unions; and some unions see the QWL agenda as a threat to their long-term strength in dealing with management. Unions are apprehensive that if labor-management cooperation results in improved working conditions through QWL initiatives, then the unions may become superfluous and workers will lose a significant avenue of protection. Union objections to QWL techniques are reflections of their lack of trust in management. And although it is clear to unions that management gains from improvements in the work processes, it is not at all clear that the employees will also be advantaged by participating in these improvements. Some unions believe that employee participation will be only symbolic and that management will continue to make decisions according to their own agendas. Other labor organizations are convinced that cost savings will accrue only to management and that employees will not share in the savings that they themselves have generated (Parker 1985). Unions are also concerned that the QWL techniques are simply another way for management to increase productivity without paying for it (Galenson 1991). Unions find QWL practices most acceptable when the emphasis is on making the work more comfortable and safe for the employees. The QWL emphasis on increased productivity is less attractive to union leadership. Although successful implementation of QWL techniques can result in improved labor-management relations, the strongly adversarial union-management relationship in the United States complicates the future of QWL initiatives.

The Future of QWL Initiatives

It is easy for a firm to be generous when resources are plentiful; however, the pressure of increasing competition and shrinking budgets makes its good intentions another disposable aspect of organizational life. The components of a positive QWL environment would be safer from budget cuts if the executives in business and government felt an obligation to the organization's employees, in addition to their obligation to stockholders and citizens. Also, QWL techniques would be safer from the budget ax if business and government leaders adopted a long-term perspective that would allow the benefits of QWL practices to become obvious, instead of opting for the quick fix.

Quick fixes to save money in the short-run include layoffs, sharing the cost of benefits, eliminating employee benefits that appear to be perquisites, cutting salaries, reducing flexibility, and eliminating training. One month of quick-fix strategies can destroy ten years of building morale and commitment through QWL techniques.

Nothing remains secure in the business and political environment, so even if the individuals at the helm are well intentioned, threats to the survival of the organization may turn QWL strategies into gestures that can be just as easily taken away. The challenge facing those who work in large organizations is to incorporate, as part of the conventional wisdom, the link between a high quality of work life and a healthy, productive organization. If QWL initiatives can be woven into the fabric of organizational life, they will be less likely to be eliminated.

DOROTHY OLSHFSKI AND ROBERT B. CUNNINGHAM

BIBLIOGRAPHY

Bruce, W., and W. Blackburn, 1992. *Balancing Job Satisfaction and Performance*. Westport, CT: Quorum.

Galenson, W., 1991. *New Trends in Employment Practices*. New York: Greenwood.

Nadler, D. E., and E. E. Lawler, 1983. "Quality of Work Life: Perspectives and Directions." *Organization Dynamics* (Winter): 24–37.

Nirenberg, J., 1993. *The Living Organization*. Homewood, IL: Business one–Irwin.

Parker, M., 1985. *Inside the Circle: A Union Guide to QWL*. Boston: South End Press.

Walton, R. E, 1973. "Quality of Working Life: What Is It?" *Sloan Management Review* (Fall): 11–21.

QUANGOs (QUASI-AUTONOMOUS, NON-GOVERNMENTAL ORGANIZATIONS).

A popular portmanteau expression used in the United Kingdom to describe a public body, created by government and composed of appointed members, fulfilling functions otherwise performed by either central or local authorities accountable to Parliament. In the arcane world of the modernized Whitehall, QUANGOs include nonministerial government departments and nondepartmental public bodies.

By the mid-1970s, Whitehall and Westminster had noticed the proliferation of QUANGOs and the emergence of a secondary bureaucracy. This tier of government was generally made up of what the British often refer to as "the Great and the Good"—people with a track record of public service: prominent peers, academics, senior judges, and retired civil servants and their equivalants from the private sector. The range of subjects covered was very wide. Bird sanctuaries in Royal Parks, wine purchases for government hospitality, pornography for psychiatric purposes, and pesticides in agriculture were just some of the 2,000 areas covered by QUANGOs by the end of the decade (Dynes and Walker 1995).

Margaret Thatcher was elected prime minister in May 1979 on a radical platform that included the commitment to sweep away, where possible, unelected, insufficiently accountable bodies, especially those with powers to spend public moneys and, thereby, apparently, to impact inflation levels. Large-scale cuts in the number of QUANGOs were imposed, even where replacement organizations seemed to have many similar features.

QUANGOs became a feature of British political debate again in the early 1990s. Following Prime Minister Thatcher's political demise, the growth of new QUANGOs under her successor, John Major, was held by some to be politically startling and constitutionally unsettling.

It is here that a distinction needs to be made between types of QUANGOs. First, there are traditional QUANGOs that carry out work instead of government departments, referred to as nondepartmental public bodies (NDPBs). It is these that are vulnerable to the charge of being unaccountable. Second, there are new kinds of quasi-autonomous, nongovernmental organizations that are the product of deregulation, devolution, privatization, and the creation of private monopolies out of public monopolies (water, gas and electricity supplies being obvious examples). These bodies are referred to as nonministerial government departments (NMGDs). They include the regulating authorities for the pricing of energy and other utilities. Although such organizations are somewhat distant from direct ministerial oversight, in practice their activities can be seen to be part of the relevant department's area of responsibilities. Categorization is difficult, however, because of definition: what some call QUANGOs are defined by government as "Next Steps Executive Agencies."

The challenge to the 1990s versions of QUANGOs centered on political accountability and the type of appointee. The Labour government versions of QUANGOs in the 1970s traded on the traditional British ethos of public service, choosing individuals of widely known probity, experience, and judgment, but the 1990s Tory version of these organizations was frequently held to look too much like jobs for party supporters and well-wishers to command widespread public support (Jenkins 1995). The birth and rebirth of British QUANGOs in the past quarter-century reflects the cross-party reluctance to abandon bureaucratic centralism. At best, their existence reflects the flexibility inherent in the United Kingdom's unwritten constitution. At worst, they represent a substantial challenge to accountability and the plural democratic context that gives accountability its meaning and purpose.

PETER FOOT

BIBLIOGRAPHY

Dynes, Michael, and David Walker, 1995. *The Times Guide to the New British State: The Government Machine in the 1990s.* London: Times Books.
Jenkins, Simon, 1995. *Accountable to None: The Tory Nationalisation of Britain.* London: Hamish Hamilton.
Plowden, William, 1994. *Ministers and Mandarins.* London: Institute for Public Policy Research.

QUASI-GOVERNMENTAL.
Almost or virtually government; resembling or simulating, but not really the same as, government.

The years since the end of World War II have been monumental in political history. Most prominent has been the creation of several score of new countries. Perhaps equally important is that the concept of "government" has changed radically, with the multiplication of formats that carry a variety of labels. For purposes of generalization, it is possible to put these forms under the heading of "quasi-governmental." The catalog of quasi-governmental organizations includes public enterprises, parastatal and paragovernmental bodies, government corporations, statutory authorities, special authorities, private organizations that do work for government under contract, QUANGOs (quasi-autonomous nongovernmental organizations), and "government-oriented" bodies (private corporations that do much of their work for government). Yet other bodies that are labeled boards, commissions, or authorities (which may be governmental or quasi-governmental) are charged with regulating the activities of corporations and other entities that are ostensibly private. A growing concern with not-for-profit organizations (the "third sector" between public and private) also belongs in this discussion, insofar as many such organizations work for government agencies under contract. None of these terms has a precise definition that is accepted universally. What is called a government corporation or statutory authority in one place may be virtually indistinguishable from what is called a QUANGO, parastatal, or a not-for-profit organization elsewhere.

There are several explanations for the spread of quasi-governmental entities, depending on the place, historical era, and the kind of entity at issue. Some quasi-governmental entities developed with the spread of service demands from one place to another. What one government offered, the population of another jurisdiction also demanded. Political parties, labor unions, citizens' movements, and the mass media criticized the services that were offered and demanded something new. As government grew, so did problems of management. Some elected officials and high-level administrators claimed to be overburdened and suggested that organizations be cast loose from their control. The result was quasi-governmental organizations.

Numerous organizations are rendered quasi-governmental by virtue of extensive governmental regulations. A typical provider of electricity, gas, and telephone service in the United States is a corporation owned by shareholders but thoroughly penetrated by explicit government regulations that define the services to be provided—which customers must and must not be served, the quality of the product, the prices that may be charged, and the level of profit that will be permitted. Other issues may be affected implicitly or indirectly by government regulators. The spending of public utilities for such items as executive salaries and public relations may be limited by what regulators will tolerate when the utility is seeking permission for rate increases.

Expectations and Disappointments

In many new and poor countries, quasi-governmental public enterprises were fashionable vehicles for rapid economic development. The label "public enterprise" symbolizes the attractions and the problems of a major category of quasi-governmental entities. It is said that public enterprises combine the features of two worlds: the *public* of government and the *enterprise* of the private sector. Government-owned companies would combine the best of the private and public sectors. Government leverage and investments would be used by public sector entrepreneurs freed from the constraints normally associated with the government bureaucracy. They could pay themselves and their employees what they were worth in the market, develop product- and service-lines rapidly in order to exploit market opportunities, and set their prices according to the efficient rules of supply and demand. If it was politically necessary to invest heavily in the development of a particular region or social sector, or to subsidize certain activities, then the government would know the costs of these investments or subsidies and could compensate the corporation accordingly.

The expectation was that public enterprise could be held more accountable than governmental ministries and departments. Some financiers would lend only to a public enterprise or some other quasi-governmental entity that enjoyed at least the semblance of being legally distinct from the government.

The reality of quasi-governmental public enterprises was more complex and less attractive than these expectations. All too often, the format of the public enterprise combined the worst, not the best, of traditional public and private sectors. It was easier to loot the public treasury or to allow mismanagement to run wild when a corporation enjoyed access to governmental resources but was freed from conventional bureaucratic controls applied to units of the government, per se. Often, central government did not deliver on promises to compensate their corporations for social or developmental projects. The flood of money that spilled into international banks as a result of the leap in oil prices during the mid-1970s added fuel to the dangers. Government corporations borrowed heavily and unwisely. They put together much of what came to be described as the debt bomb of the Third World.

In some American jurisdictions there are pragmatic reasons for creating quasi-governmental bodies. Constitutional and statutory limitations on "government" debt encourage state and local officials to establish special authorities. These authorities raise money on their own credit, typically pledging to the purchasers of their bonds the income to be derived from their hospitals, college dormitories, parks, or toll roads.

Contracting-out is a variety of quasi-governmental practice that has become a popular device for government entities to pay for services that are provided by companies, nonprofit organizations, the administrative units of some other governmental jurisdiction, or a joint venture between one or more governmental or nongovernmental entity. Federal, state, and local agencies in the United States have contracted out many activities that formerly were performed by government employees: solid waste management, firefighting, ambulance services, security services, management of incarceration, the administration of health insurance for public employees, plus health, counseling, and educational services for recipients of public assistance.

Implications

Quasi-governmental bodies have implications for classic issues of public administration. They confuse the assignment of accountability or the maintaining of the chain of control and responsibility from voter to elected officials and then to administrators answerable to elected officials. The lack of clarity as to what is government affects the equality of opportunities for employment in the public service (i.e., including quasi-governmental entities) and contracting opportunities as well as the receipt of public service. It is not clear what is within the organizational framework of government or how much finance is under governmental control. Many activities of quasi-governmental organizations do not appear in government budgets or in the records of governmental revenues and expenditures. Quasi-governmental bodies confuse those who would usually know what governmental bodies they can call upon for program implementation, what governmental bodies they should control in the name of democratic accountability, and what magnitude of finance is subject to governmental control.

There are advantages in the varieties of quasi-governmental bodies. Policymakers and clients have expanded options. Policymakers can choose just the kind of body they want to use in implementing a program. They can mix governmental, private, and quasi-governmental personnel, funding, and management. Clients may be in a position to choose similar services from a variety of providers.

The most obvious problem of quasi-governmental formats lies in the sheer number of bodies on the organizational landscape and the confusion of political accountability. The growth of many activities outside the core departments of government taxes the capacity of elected officials to know what is happening within the realm of their responsibility. The reputed autonomy of quasi-governmental bodies provides a reason for government officials not to meddle in their administration. It also provides the environment in which disasters develop outside the notice of key officials.

The autonomy of contractors and other quasi-governmental entities can frustrate policymakers who want to change things, or clients who want to complain. Just to know where to turn is a problem when services are designed, financed, implemented, and supervised by different units that are governmental, quasi-governmental, and what may appear to be nongovernmental but actually may be quasi-governmental.

At least some of the motives for creating new organizations are devious and seek to obscure the fact that government is doing more by creating the impression that some other body is actually doing the work. The complex structures of quasi-governmental institutions provide opportunities to hide or distort reports of activities and their financial condition. In many countries quasi-governmental entities are a favorite haunt of politically connected scoundrels who enrich themselves at the public's expense.

So many kinds of bodies do the work of government that public officials and academics cannot define "government" or clearly distinguish governmental from nongovernmental entities. The lack of clear definition for gov-

ernment confuses the reckoning of governmental finance and handicaps policymakers who wish to use government finance as a lever of economic policy or to realize social goals. It is said that a lever might move the world if there were only a place to anchor it. One must also know the size of that lever in order to use it well. For governmental expenditures and revenues, the size of the lever is confused by much ambiguity and some deception. Confusion or deception about what is government produces some indications that government is getting smaller, but other indicators show that it continues to grow larger. Americans can point to stable or even shrinking numbers of federal government employees, even though federal budgets grew many times from the late 1940s.

There are also special issues one must deal with concerning joint ventures. These are partnerships between two or more governmental authorities, or one or more governmental authorities with one or more private organizations. A joint venture can benefit from the resources and expertise of all of the partners; however, it can be even more confusing as to responsibility and accountability than a simpler entity like a government company or a contract between a single government department and a private firm.

Quasi-governmental entities and joint ventures may be especially prolific in a federal system like that of the United States, with a long history of intergovernmental relations. A rich stew of more than 86,000 governmental units and untold numbers of intergovernmental programs have produced countless variations of programs imbued with governmental finance and governmental standards that are not administered by civil servants, per se.

A Counter Movement: Privatization

"Privatization" emerged as a stylish mode of organization partly as a counter to the quasi-governmental organization. International consultants and lenders now insist on some kind of privatization just as they once insisted on the creation of quasi-governmental entities. Like "quasi-governmental" organizations, however, privatization is marked by numerous and confusing conceptions. One notion of privatization is the simple transference of ownership and management of activities from government departments or government-owned enterprises to the private sector. However, other conceptions involve the distancing of government from the management of activities via contracting-out or vouchers or the selling of part but not all of governmental shares in an enterprise to the private sector. In this way, privatization is used as a currently fashionable label for a quasi-governmental practice. In some settings, the term "privatization" has been used for the transfer of functions from governmental departments or local authorities to companies wholly owned by those bodies. In these formulations, privatization is most clearly a case of putting a currently fashionable label on what used to be fashionable under the heading of "public enterprise." As a result, some kinds of privatization are creating the same varieties of public enterprise that gave rise to the development of privatization as a cure for the problems caused by public enterprises.

It is tempting to accept the widespread support for privatization as involving greater creativity and efficiency; however, its dangers, like the dangers of the support for quasi-governmental bodies, seem most likely to appear in poor countries with great demands for policy benefits and weak traditions of administration. Among the symptoms of poorly conceived privatization have been sales of governmental assets to favored individuals, sometimes financed by loans from government or international agencies, where there appears little prospect of repaying the debt.

IRA SHARKANSKY

BIBLIOGRAPHY

Doig, Jameson W., 1983. "'If I See a Murderous Fellow Sharpening a Knife Cleverly. . .' The Wilsonian Dichotomy and the Public Authority Tradition." *Public Administration Review*, vol. 43, no. 2 (March-April): 292–304.

Hood, Christopher, 1984. *The Hidden Public Sector: The World of Para-Government Organizations*. Glasgow: Centre for the Study of Public Policy, University of Strathclyde.

MacAvoy, Paul W., W. T. Stanbury, George Yarrow, and Richard J. Zeckhauser, eds., 1969. *Privatization and State-Owned Enterprises: Lessons from the United States, Great Britain and Canada*. Boston: Kluwer.

Savas, Emanuel S., 1967. *Privatization: The Key to Better Government*. Chatham, NJ: Chatham House Publishers.

Sharkansky, Ira, 1979. *Wither the State? Politics and Public Enterprise in Three Countries*. Chatham, NJ: Chatham House Publishers.

Smith, Bruce L. R., and D. C. Hague, eds., 1971. *The Dilemma of Accountability in Modern Government: Independence Versus Control*. New York: St. Martin's Press.

QUASI-JUDICIAL POWER.

The authority conferred upon a person or group by law or regulation that grants or empowers that person or group to receive evidence and render a determination that is binding upon the parties to the proceeding. It refers to the fact-finding power of an administrative agency. The exercise of this authority almost always occurs when a public body, possessing regulatory jurisdiction, resolves disputes, engages in fact-finding based upon evidence received, or interprets its rules or prior decisions and applies those findings to a particular factual situation. The disputes can be between the agency and a party subject to its jurisdiction or between nonagency parties subject to the jurisdiction of the agency.

Quasi-judicial power is not "true" judicial power because the power is not the same as the original power conferred upon the judicial branch of government; it is power delegated by a governmental authority. That is, on the national level, the source of actual judicial power comes from the U.S. Constitution, Article 3, and quasi-judicial power has no direct constitutional sanctioning. Quasi-judicial power is power conferred by the executive or legislative branch of government to agencies or individuals implementing policy or regulations prescribed by the executive or legislative branches or by others so as to assist these agencies or individuals in the implementation, monitoring, or regulation of the delegated power. For example, local election boards are charged by the legislative arm of government with conducting elections. That charge confers upon the election board the power to regulate elections, determine qualifications of candidates for office, and resolve disputes either between candidates and the election board or among the candidates themselves. A typical function that requires an election board to exercise its quasi-judicial power encompasses, for example, hearing a complaint by a candidate for office that one (or more) of his or her opponents is not properly qualified to participate as a candidate for that office and rendering a decision as to that candidate's eligibility. In the exercise of the authority delegated to it, the election board could conduct hearings and investigate and receive evidence as to relevant facts (e.g., age qualification, proof of residency, or proof that the candidate had performed or was eligible under other criteria that may apply) and, after conducting that inquiry, render a decision as to the eligibility of the candidate based upon the fact-finding or evidentiary process engaged in by the board. The final ruling would then be binding upon the parties to the proceeding, unless appealed in the manner prescribed by rule or law.

Administrative agencies possessing quasi-judicial power normally are required to adopt rules and regulations for the conduct of their proceedings or are subjected to laws or statutes that prescribe the rules and regulations under which their administrative bodies can exercise their powers. Many times, the administrative agencies have the power to establish rules and regulations for the conduct of their own affairs, and the orders issued by the agencies establish precedents. These precedents, in turn, are used by those regulated by that body when measuring their own conduct.

THOMAS A. CONNELLY

BIBLIOGRAPHY

Carp, Robert A., and Ronald Stidham, 1996. *Judicial Process in America*. 3d ed. Washington, DC: Congressional Quarterly Press.

Warren, Kenneth F., 1996. *Administrative Law in the Political System.* 3d ed. (especially chaps. 2,7, and 9) Upper Saddle River, NJ: Prentice-Hall.

QUIET EXPENDITURES.

QUIET EXPENDITURES. The disbursement or consumption of public resources by a governmental agency that (1) occurs without a formal budgetary or other appropriations process, or (2) occurs in such a way that the accountability of a governmental unit to its citizens is directly or indirectly weakened.

Background

The primary theoretician of quiet expenditures is Herman Leonard (1986), who defines quiet spending as the "unappropriated disbursements of public resources" (p. 6). Quiet spending can be practiced by any level of government and many other types of public organizations, such as special districts and public authorities. Quiet expenditures in government occur in a variety of different formats that include local property and sales tax abatements; the deferred maintenance and depreciation of local, state, and federal capital assets; the unfunded liabilities reflected in retirement programs at all levels of government; the use of state and local public debt to finance construction of industrial and commercial facilities for use by private firms; and public facilities that are leased to private businesses.

There are essentially two ways to define the existence of quiet expenditures. The basic method of determining whether quiet spending has occurred is to ask whether such spending was accompanied by a formal appropriation of funds by the governmental unit spending or consuming the funds. Quiet spending happens without formal appropriation of the necessary funds by legislators or without voter approval through referenda, as is the case, for example, in granting a local property tax abatement. A secondary method is to examine what impact a spending decision has on the accountability of a governmental unit to citizens and others responsible for monitoring the performance of government. If direct accountability is weakened by the fundamental structure of a spending decision—as when a multiyear lease that requires no voter referendum is substituted for the issuance of bonds that traditionally requires a referendum—quiet spending may be at work. When used extensively, quiet expenditures create a fundamental accountability problem for governments.

Characteristics of Quiet Spending

Quiet spending by government occurs in four basic ways: direct and indirect unbudgeted outlays; the creation of payment obligations and liabilities in current budget years for future payments, but without careful planning by public officials for how future payments will be made; foregoing future revenue streams; and consuming physical assets without a regular means of funding depreciation. All forms of quiet spending share several common characteristics.

First, systematic information about such spending is frequently unavailable to citizens and public managers or, at best, extremely difficult to obtain. By its very nature, quiet spending occurs without careful or precise reports about its magnitude, incidence, and life span. This is what makes it "quiet" spending—citizens and managers are often unaware that it is occurring. For example, many governments keep no formal record of the depreciation of their physical assets, so tracking capital disinvestment may be difficult for concerned citizens or managers. Similarly, tax abatements for business development are not usually recognized in comprehensive annual financial reports or in annual budgets.

Second, it is hard to forecast accurately the benefits and costs of many forms of quiet spending because quiet expenditures are often quite complex and because such expenditures exhibit sometimes subtle impacts on public fiscal conditions. Public loan guarantees only invoke direct expenditures when loan defaults occur. Tax abatements are based on the estimated value of property over a multiyear time frame, and it is often difficult to determine the exact effects of tax abatements on the fiscal health of the jurisdiction. Public pension fund balances must rely on the connection between current recipients of retirement fund benefits and current workers contributing to the retirement fund, with increasingly risky assurances that current workers will even receive the benefits of the program. Failure to maintain public infrastructure is common because citizens prefer the quicker and more visible benefits of new public works construction to the slower and less visible benefits of gradual maintenance expenditures for existing facilities.

Third, quiet spending programs are rarely reviewed once they are established. Instead, they are implemented and left in place with little periodic scrutiny. The absence of regular reports about the magnitude of quiet spending makes it difficult to mount systematic monitoring efforts. In addition, quiet expenditures are frequently generated by public agency decisions that do not require widespread public discussion, public hearings, or voter referenda. Tax abatements are often decided in private negotiation with business firms, then implemented via routine administrative channels; changes in pension spending are typically decided in administrative rather than public hearings; and other tax expenditures are seldom reviewed with the same attentiveness as annual budget appropriations.

Fourth, the beneficiaries of quiet spending are often separate from those paying the costs. The reasons for this separation can be spatial or temporal. For instance, tax abatements directly benefit business firms in a specific geographical location, but the remaining citizens of the jurisdiction, as well as successive generations of urban taxpayers, must bear the costs reflected in foregone tax revenues. Similarly, the last generation of current retirees may require Social Security funding from the current generation of those now working.

Fifth, quiet spending appears to be costless. The reason is that, in standard accounting terms, quiet expenditures reflect the traditional credits but no debits. That is, quiet expenditures typically result in the purchase of services, the transfer of public resources, and the provision of benefits to someone, but without the usual recognition of costs or allowance for future disbursements. Thus, a tax abatement is granted and a firm locates within the jurisdiction; the cost of the abatement occurs through time as tax revenues are not collected for the abated property. Likewise, the deterioration of public assets such as highways and parks occurs quite slowly, without creating the perception that substantial costs are building. In large part, this helps explain the popularity of quiet spending: It occurs outside the regular appropriations process, and there is little systematic accounting for its magnitude.

Examples of Quiet Expenditures

Leonard (1986) identified four major types of quiet spending that commonly affect government finances and operations: (1) public employee retirement systems (including Social Security); (2) tax expenditures in federal, state, and local governments; (3) public asset disinvestment; and (4) public leasing. Each of these forms of quiet spending has unique dynamics that create fiscal stress outside the normal budgetary appropriations cycle.

Unfunded Public Pension Liabilities

The fundamental quiet expenditure created by public employee retirement systems is known as unfunded liability. Unfunded liabilities are likely to emerge in public retirement systems that rely on a "pay-as-you-go" method of financing retirement programs, in which the governmental unit only raises sufficient revenues to pay for retirement expenses in the current year. The problem with a pay-as-you-go public employee retirement system is that "it allows for the accumulation of debt, that is, *persons in the future will be owed benefits, and taxpayers at that time will be forced to meet those costs*" (Lee and Johnson 1994, p. 336, emphasis supplied).

The primary source of unfunded pension liabilities is the widespread use by public agencies of "defined benefit plans" (Reed and Swain 1990). Such plans generally guarantee a predefined level of benefits to retirees that is not specifically connected to the amount the employee con-

tributed to the retirement fund. As a result, unfunded liabilities equal to the difference between the employees' contributions and the total level of promised benefits accrue to the retirement fund.

Federal, State, and Local Tax Expenditures

Tax expenditures are one of the most common forms of quiet spending, partly because they occur at all levels of government. At the federal level, tax expenditures are defined as "revenue losses attributable to provisions of the federal tax laws which allow a special exclusion, exemption, or deduction from gross income" that reduce the level of revenues that would otherwise be collected (Mikesell 1991, p. 338). Typical federal tax expenditures are embodied in home mortgage deductions, accelerated depreciation, child care credits, capital consumption allowances, and medical deductions. In 1994, the estimated value of federal tax expenditures in 14 functional categories was more than US$478 billion (U.S. Department of Commerce 1993).

Another form of tax expenditure is generated by private-use tax-exempt state and local bonds, such as the bonds issued by public authorities to finance construction of industrial facilities that are then leased to private firms. Quiet expenditures occur here in different ways. In the first place, the interest paid to individuals who purchase tax exempt bonds is not subject to income taxation, which creates one form of quiet spending because revenues are foregone. Second, private firms benefit from the use of tax-exempt industrial bonds because of lower interest expense that is actually a government subsidy. The difference between the interest costs of private corporate bonds compared to public industrial bonds is the approximate amount of quiet expenditures, in this case. This creates an indirect subsidy to the business that is not recognized in any form of public budgetary hearing or appropriations process.

The process by which private firms are able to obtain the use of tax-exempt public debt creates an accountability problem for governments. In this sense, the absence of accountability for tax-exempt private-use bonds is reflected in the absence of voter approval: Contrary to other forms of general obligation debt, industrial revenue bonds typically require no voter approval. This is a critical problem because governmental agencies usually scrutinize closely their decisions to borrow large sums of money. In particular, public referenda are often used to allow citizens to express their opinion about governmental assumption of long-term debt. This process is frequently missing when state and local governments issue public bonds that are ultimately used for private purposes.

Quiet expenditures also take the form of state and local tax incentives granted to business firms engaged in interstate and interurban location competition. State and local governments frequently grant tax abatements to business firms in order to convince firms to locate within certain political boundaries (Eisenger 1988). In such cases, the governmental units sacrifice a stream of future revenues, especially in cases where the business firm might have located within a jurisdiction even without the award of a tax abatement.

Infrastructure Underinvestment and Unfunded Public Asset Depreciation

Public asset disinvestment is perhaps the most subtle form of quiet spending. It takes a variety of forms. One form involves the idea that a society may underinvest in or undersupply public infrastructure, thereby lowering the overall productivity of the economy and harming the quality of life enjoyed by citizens. Another form involves the failure of public agencies to maintain the condition of the infrastructure facilities for which they are responsible.

The capacity of publicly supplied infrastructure to stimulate or sustain regional and national economic growth has long been a component of federal, state, and local development strategies. Both D. A. Aschauer (1990) and R. W. Eberts (1990) found that the level of per capita nonagricultural output is strongly related to core infrastructure investment. In this context, the undersupply of public infrastructure that has been identified in the United States in the late 1980s and early 1990s is a form of quiet spending because it undermines the economy's ability to create jobs and to sustain economic growth (Peterson 1990).

A more direct form of quiet spending is the tendency of governmental agencies to defer maintenance of public capital facilities. Failure to maintain existing facilities has two primary fiscal impacts on government. First, the productivity of infrastructure is harmed when, for example, frequent watermain breaks or deteriorated streets hinder economic growth. Indirectly, this retards growth in public revenues associated with economic growth, and more directly results in a lowered quality of public services for all citizens. Second, fixed capital maintenance cannot be postponed indefinitely; eventually, future generations of citizens and their governments will have to correct years of deferred maintenance by increasing expenditures for capital improvements, renovation, and rehabilitation. This forces future citizens to pay the costs rendered by current citizens.

A key reason many governmental bodies do not invest the proper level of resources into infrastructure maintenance is the failure to account properly for annual depreciation within accepted financial and budgetary reporting systems. One result is the consequent failure to fund adequate annual depreciation through the retained earnings or current revenues of the public agency. Moreover, even if public agencies recognize the need to set funds aside to counteract the depreciation of infrastructure, this problem of insufficient funds can be more serious if there are major differences between the original historical cost of capital assets and the current replacement costs of those assets. This situation creates another side to quiet expenditures because fund set-asides based on historical cost will fall short of the actual replacement cost of assets.

Leasing Arrangements

Leonard (1986) has argued that tax and expenditure limitations and changing economic conditions have forced public managers, administrators, and elected officials to search for other ways of acquiring capital assets, such as vehicles or communications equipment, without issuing state or local bonds. One way of avoiding or circumventing these limitations, for example, limits on debt issuance, is the use of leasing arrangements to acquire capital assets. Thus, rather than trying to purchase a fleet of vehicles by issuing general obligation bonds, which would require voter approval, many public agencies have resorted to leasing that same vehicular fleet by means of a multiyear lease with periodic annual payments. In one sense, this decision can increase the efficiency of the public organization if the annual lease expense is less than the amount of annual debt service that would have been required if equivalent assets had been purchased. In another sense, though leasing ostensibly emerges as a topic of consideration in annual appropriations hearings, it nonetheless causes problems of quiet spending.

Public leasing strategies are considered quiet expenditures for several reasons. First, because multiyear commitments to paying for capital assets are typically involved when leases are used, one generation of citizens and public administrators ends up forcing future generations to pay for today's consumption. This parallels one of the problems created by public capital disinvestment. Second, Leonard (1986) views public leasing as simply another form of borrowing, accompanied by the use of an asset. It is not treated formally as borrowing, however—which would require closer scrutiny by citizens, as in most cases of multiyear loans. It is thus seen as simply an annual expenditure, instead of the multiyear obligation that it actually represents.

Remedies and Responses to Quiet Spending

Quiet expenditures remain a seductive way in which governmental agencies and jurisdictions can spend public resources without appearing to do so. However, there are a variety of approaches for public administrators and public managers who desire closer knowledge of and control over quiet spending. Conceptually, two different approaches deserve attention: direct responses to particular kinds of quiet spending and indirect responses to improve overall public accountability when quiet expenditures are used.

Techniques for Different Forms of Quiet Spending

A variety of specific techniques can be utilized by public managers to control quiet spending. In terms of public pension systems, government units can rely more on defined *contribution* plans (in which withdrawals are limited by contributions), which reduce the level of unfunded liability created by defined *benefit* plans (in which withdrawals must meet a minimum benefit standard) (Reed and Swain 1990). Federal tax expenditures might be addressed through the recision of selected groups of deductions, exemptions, and credits. With respect to state and local tax expenditures, more stringent guidelines for their use and a more open process of governmental approval are two ways to make such spending less quiet. Alternatively, the quiet spending embodied in tax expenditures might be nudged firmly toward a formal appropriations process. For example, tax abatements could be abandoned in favor of outright cash grants, which could be considered during appropriations hearings; the amount of the grant might be equal to the present discounted value of the anticipated stream of abated taxes. Public asset disinvestment could be addressed with much more systematic and formal accounting for the economic value of public infrastructure; and this examination should recognize the contribution to private economic growth and the depreciation of public assets on a replacement-cost basis.

Enhancing Public Accountability for Quiet Spending

Perhaps most seriously, frequent use of quiet spending tactics by public agencies weakens governmental accountability. In this sense, quiet spending violates two cornerstones of accountability in public administration: comprehensive financial reporting and some prescribed form of public consent or authorization. Realistically, though, quiet spending is unlikely to disappear. Therefore, perhaps the most rational objective becomes outlining ways to strengthen the underlying accountability embedded in quiet spending programs. There are several ways in which enhanced accountability can be introduced (Leonard 1986).

First, public managers should improve traditional public fund accounting practices, which have evolved largely to control direct expenditures, not indirect costs or foregone opportunities. Most forms of quiet spending– public leasing being the notable exception–occur largely outside the realm of standard accounting practices. Fixed asset accounting, for example, is hindered by the accounting profession's insistence that historical cost be used. Tracking the replacement needs of public infrastructure is difficult in the absence of data on the replacement cost of fixed assets. Consequently, accounting standards may need to change to recognize explicitly the sizable financial liabilities created by many quiet spending programs. Overall, this will require the alteration of accounting standards and the culture of public accounting so as to recognize the nature and mechanics of quiet spending.

A second means of introducing more accountability to quiet spending is the continued imposition of "mechanical limits on governmental spending" (Leonard 1986, p. 222). Leonard calls these tax and expenditure limitations (TELs). TELs have sometimes been successful, but public officials should distinguish whether TELs have improved accountability or simply made it more difficult for governments to deliver public services. TELs may have increased accountability by making legislators sensitive to tax-increase proposals, and perhaps more willing to debate quiet spending programs publicly.

Finally, increased public awareness of the magnitude of quiet spending is needed. One way of doing this is to improve the quiet spending reporting responsibilities of public managers. For example, the federal government regularly reports the estimated revenue loss associated with income tax expenditures, and several states and localities have also begun to report regularly the volume and estimated costs of revenues foregone due to tax incentives and tax abatements. An example is the Minnesota Tax Expenditure Budget (Mikesell 1991, pp. 343–347).

SAMUEL NUNN

BIBLIOGRAPHY

Aschauer, D. A., 1990. "Why is Infrastructure Important?" In A. H. Munnell, ed., Conference Series No. 34, *Is There a Shortfall in Public Capital Investment?* pp. 21–50. Boston, MA: Federal Reserve Bank.

Eberts, R. W., 1990. "Public Infrastructure and Regional Economic Development." *Economic Review* 26 (1):15–27.

Eisenger, P. K., 1988. *The Rise of the Entrepreneurial State: State and Local Economic Development Policy in the United States.* Madison: University of Wisconsin Press.

Lee, Jr., R. D., and R. W. Johnson, 1994. *Public Budgeting Systems.* 5th ed. Gaithersburg, MD: Aspen Publishers.

Leonard, H. B., 1986. *Checks Unbalanced: The Quiet Side of Public Spending.* New York: Basic Books.

Mikesell, J. L., 1991. *Fiscal Administration: Analysis and Applications for the Public Sector.* 3d ed. Pacific Grove, CA: Brooks-Cole.

Peterson, G. E., 1990. "Is Public Infrastructure Undersupplied?" In A. H. Munnell, ed., Conference Series No. 34, *Is There a Shortfall in Public Capital Investment?* pp. 113–130. Boston, MA: Federal Reserve Bank.

Reed, B. J., and J. W. Swain, 1990. *Public Finance Administration.* Englewood Cliffs, N. J.: Prentice-Hall.

U.S. Department of Commerce. 1993. *Statistical Abstract of the United States,* 1993. Washington, D.C.: U.S. GPO.